Africa 68-69

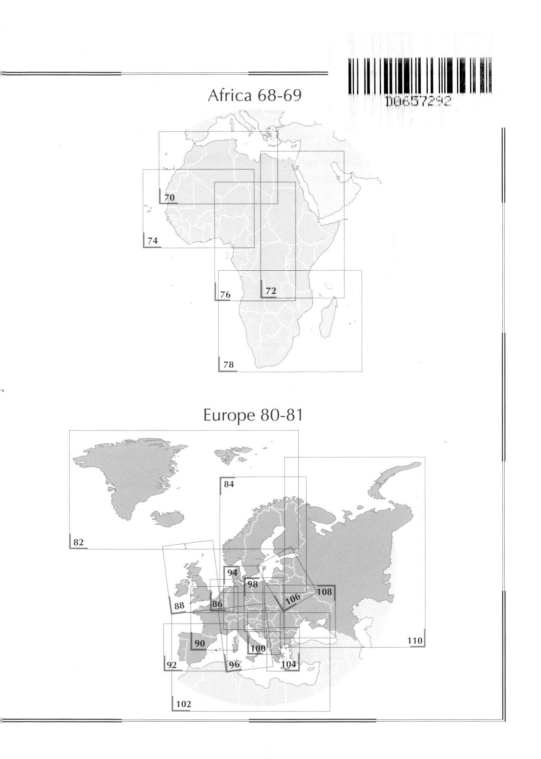

Europe 80-81

WORLD ATLAS

ESSENTIAL

LONDON, NEW YORK, MELBOURNE, MUNICH, DELHI

LONDON, NEW YORK, MELBOURNE, MUNICH, DELHI

FOR THE SEVENTH EDITION
SENIOR CARTOGRAPHIC MANAGER David Roberts
SENIOR CARTOGRAPHIC EDITOR Simon Mumford
CARTOGRAPHY Encompass Graphics Ltd., Brighton, UK
PRODUCTION CONTROLLER Danielle Smith   PRODUCTION EDITOR Joanna Byrne
PUBLISHER Jonathan Metcalf   ART DIRECTOR Philip Ormerod
ASSOCIATE PUBLISHER Liz Wheeler

DORLING KINDERSLEY CARTOGRAPHY
PROJECT CARTOGRAPHY AND DESIGN
Julia Lunn, Julie Turner

CARTOGRAPHERS
James Anderson, Roger Bullen, Martin Darlison,
Simon Mumford, John Plumer, Peter Winfield

DESIGN
Katy Wall

INDEX-GAZETTEER
Natalie Clarkson, Ruth Duxbury, Margaret Hynes, Margaret Stevenson

PRODUCTION
Hilary Stephens, David Proffit

EDITORIAL DIRECTION
Andrew Heritage

ART DIRECTION
Chez Picthall

First published in Great Britain in 1997 by
Dorling Kindersley Limited,
80 Strand, London WC2R 0RL
Penguin Group (UK)

2 4 6 8 10 9 7 5 3 1

001 - 180686 - Apr/2011

Second Edition 1998, Third Edition 2001, Fourth Edition 2003,
Fifth Edition 2005, Sixth Edition 2008, Seventh Edition 2011.

Previously published as the Concise World Atlas

A CIP catalogue record for this book is available from the British Library.

ISBN: 978-1-4053-6314-3

Printed and bound by Tien Wah Press, Singapore.

Discover more at **www.dk.com**

Key to map symbols

Physical features

Elevation

6000m/19,686ft
4000m/13,124ft
3000m/9843ft
2000m/6562ft
1000m/3281ft
500m/1640ft
250m/820ft
0
Below sea level

△ Mountain

▽ Depression

△ Volcano

)(Pass/tunnel

Sandy desert

Drainage features

———— Major perennial river

——— Minor perennial river

– – – Seasonal river

———— Canal

| Waterfall

Perennial lake

Seasonal lake

Wetland

Ice features

Permanent ice cap/ice shelf

Winter limit of pack ice

Summer limit of pack ice

Borders

▬▬▬ Full international border

▬ ▬ ▬ Disputed de facto border

• • • • Territorial claim border

x—x—x Cease-fire line

▬ ▬ ▬ Undefined boundary

———— Internal administrative boundary

Communications

———— Major road

——— Minor road

———— Railway

✈ International airport

Settlements

◉ Above 500,000

◉ 100,000 to 500,000

○ 50,000 to 100,000

○ Below 50,000

● National capital

● Internal administrative capital

Miscellaneous features

+ Site of interest

〰〰 Ancient wall

Graticule features

———— Line of latitude/longitude/ Equator

– – – Tropic/Polar circle

25° Degrees of latitude/ longitude

Names

Physical features

Andes
Suhuru   Landscape features
Ardennes

Land's End   Headland

Mont Blanc
4,807m   Elevation/volcano/pass

Blue Nile   River/canal/waterfall

Ross Ice Shelf   Ice feature

PACIFIC OCEAN
Sulu Sea   Sea features
Palk Strait

Chile Rise   Undersea feature

Regions

FRANCE   Country

JERSEY
(to UK)   Dependent territory

KANSAS   Administrative region

Dordogne   Cultural region

Settlements

PARIS   Capital city

SAN JUAN   Dependent territory capital city

Chicago
Kettering   Other settlements
Burke

Inset map symbols

Urban area

City

Park

▪ Place of interest

▫ Suburb/district

Contents

The World Today

Flags of the World.........................6-7
The Political World........................8-9
The Physical World......................10-11
Time Zones................................12-13
Geology & Structure......................14-15
World Climate.............................16-17
Ocean Currents...........................18-19
Life Zones................................20-21
Population................................22-23
Languages.................................24-25
Religion..................................26-27
The Global Economy.......................28-29
Politics and Conflict....................30-31

The World's Regions

North & Central America

North & Central America..................34-35
Western Canada & Alaska..................36-37
Eastern Canada...........................38-39
USA: The Northeast.......................40-41
USA: The Southeast.......................42-43
  Bermuda
USA: Central States......................44-45
USA: The West............................46-47
  Los Angeles & Hawaii

USA: The Southwest.......................48-49
Mexico...................................50-51
Central America..........................52-53
The Caribbean............................54-55
  Jamaica, St. Lucia, & Barbados

South America

South America............................56-57
Northern South America...................58-59
Western South America....................60-61
  Galapagos Islands
Brazil...................................62-63
Southern South America...................64-65
The Atlantic Ocean.......................66-67

Africa

Africa...................................68-69
Northwest Africa.........................70-71
Northeast Africa.........................72-73
West Africa..............................74-75
Central Africa...........................76-77
  Sao Tome & Principe
Southern Africa..........................78-79

Europe

Europe...................................80-81
The North Atlantic.......................82-83
Scandinavia & Finland....................84-85
The Low Countries........................86-87
The British Isles........................88-89
  London

continued....

Europe continued

France, Andorra, & Monaco.................90-91
  Paris, Andorra, & Monaco
Spain & Portugal...............................92-93
  Azores & Gibraltar
Germany & the Alpine States..............94-95
  Liechtenstein
Italy...96-97
  San Marino & Vatican City
Central Europe.................................98-99
Southeast Europe..........................100-101
  Bosnia & Herzegovina
The Mediterranean.........................102-103
  Malta & Cyprus
Bulgaria & Greece..........................104-105
The Baltic States & Belarus..............106-107
Ukraine, Moldova,
  & Romania.................................108-109
European Russia.............................110-111

North & West Asia

North & West Asia..........................112-113
Russia & Kazakhstan.......................114-115
Turkey & the Caucasus....................116-117
The Near East................................118-119
  West Bank
The Middle East.............................120-121
Central Asia..................................122-123

South & East Asia

South & East Asia...........................124-125
Western China & Mongolia...............126-127

Eastern China & Korea   128-129
  Hong Kong (Xianggang)
Japan..130-131
  Tokyo & Nansei-Shoto
South India & Sri Lanka...................132-133
North India, Pakistan,
  & Bangladesh.............................134-135
Mainland Southeast Asia.................136-137
Maritime Southeast Asia.................138-139
  Singapore
The Indian Ocean...........................140-141

Australasia & Oceania

Australasia & Oceania.....................142-143
The Southwest Pacific.....................144-145
Western Australia...........................146-147
Eastern Australia............................148-149
  Sydney
New Zealand.................................150-151
The Pacific Ocean...........................152-153
Antarctica.....................................154
The Arctic Ocean............................155

Index– Gazetteer

Overseas Territories
  & Dependencies...........................156-159
Glossary of Geographical
  Terms.......................................160-161
Continental Factfiles.......................162-163
Geographical Comparisons...............164-166
Index-Gazetteer of Places
  & Countries...............................167-256

Flags of the World

NORTH & CENTRAL AMERICA

CANADA
PAGES 36-39

UNITED STATES
OF AMERICA
PAGES 40-49

MEXICO
PAGES 50-51

BELIZE
PAGES 52-53

COSTA RICA
PAGES 52-53

EL SALVADOR
PAGES 52-53

GUATEMALA
PAGES 52-53

HONDURAS
PAGES 52-53

SOUTH AMERIC.

GRENADA
PAGES 54-55

HAITI
PAGES 54-55

JAMAICA
PAGES 54-55

ST KITTS & NEVIS
PAGES 54-55

ST LUCIA
PAGES 54-55

ST VINCENT &
THE GRENADINES
PAGES 54-55

TRINIDAD &
TOBAGO
PAGES 54-55

COLOMBIA
PAGES 58-59

URUGUAY
PAGES 64-65

CHILE
PAGES 64-65

PARAGUAY
PAGES 64-65

ALGERIA
PAGES 70-71

LIBYA
PAGES 70-71

MOROCCO
PAGES 70-71

TUNISIA
PAGES 70-71

BURUNDI
PAGES 72-73

AFRICA

TANZANIA
PAGES 72-73

UGANDA
PAGES 72-73

BENIN
PAGES 74-75

BURKINA FASO
PAGES 74-75

CAPE VERDE
PAGES 74-75

CÔTE D'IVOIRE
(IVORY COAST)
PAGES 74-75

GAMBIA
PAGES 74-75

GHANA
PAGES 74-75

SIERRA
LEONE
PAGES 74-75

TOGO
PAGES 74-75

CAMEROON
PAGES 76-77

CENTRAL AFRICAN
REPUBLIC
PAGES 76-77

CHAD
PAGES 76-77

CONGO
PAGES 76-77

DEM. REP.
CONGO
PAGES 76-77

EQUATORIAL
GUINEA
PAGES 76-77

MAURITIUS
PAGES 78-79

MOZAMBIQUE
PAGES 78-79

NAMIBIA
PAGES 78-79

SEYCHELLES
PAGES 78-79

SOUTH
AFRICA
PAGES 78-79

SWAZILAND
PAGES 78-79

ZAMBIA
PAGES 78-79

ZIMBABWE
PAGES 78-79

UNITED
KINGDOM
PAGES 88-89

FRANCE
PAGES 90-91

MONACO
PAGES 90-91

ANDORRA
PAGES 90-91

PORTUGAL
PAGES 92-93

SPAIN
PAGES 92-93

AUSTRIA
PAGES 94-95

GERMANY
PAGES 94-95

POLAND
PAGES 98-99

SLOVAKIA
PAGES 98-99

ALBANIA
PAGES 100-101

BOSNIA &
HERZEGOVINA
PAGES 100-101

CROATIA
PAGES 100-101

KOSOVO
PAGES 100-101

MACEDONIA
PAGES 100-101

MONTENEGRO
PAGES 100-101

ASIA

MOLDOVA
PAGES 108-109

ROMANIA
PAGES 108-109

UKRAINE
PAGES 108-109

RUSSIAN
FEDERATION
PAGES 110-115

KAZAKHSTAN
PAGES 114-115

ARMENIA
PAGES 116-117

AZERBAIJAN
PAGES 116-117

GEORGIA
PAGES 116-117

KUWAIT
PAGES 120-121

OMAN
PAGES 120-121

QATAR
PAGES 120-121

SAUDI ARABIA
PAGES 120-121

UNITED ARAB
EMIRATES
PAGES 120-121

YEMEN
PAGES 120-121

AFGHANISTAN
PAGES 122-123

KYRGYZSTAN
PAGES 122-123

JAPAN
PAGES 130-131

INDIA
PAGES 132-135

SRI LANKA
PAGES 132-133

MALDIVES
PAGES 132-133

PAKISTAN
PAGES 134-135

BANGLADESH
PAGES 134-135

BHUTAN
PAGES 134-135

NEPAL
PAGES 134-135

CAMBODIA
PAGES 136-137

AUSTRALASIA & OCEANIA

PHILIPPINES
PAGES 138-139

SINGAPORE
PAGES 138-139

FIJI
PAGES 144-145

KIRIBATI
PAGES 144-145

MARSHALL
ISLANDS
PAGES 144-145

MICRONESIA
PAGES 144-145

NAURU
PAGES 144-145

PALAU
PAGES 144-145

NICARAGUA
PAGES 52-53

PANAMA
PAGES 52-53

ANTIGUA & BARBUDA
PAGES 54-55

BAHAMAS
PAGES 54-55

BARBADOS
PAGES 54-55

CUBA
PAGES 54-55

DOMINICA
PAGES 54-55

DOMINICAN REPUBLIC
PAGES 54-55

GUYANA
PAGES 58-59

SURINAME
PAGES 58-59

VENEZUELA
PAGES 58-59

BOLIVIA
PAGES 60-61

ECUADOR
PAGES 60-61

PERU
PAGES 60-61

BRAZIL
PAGES 62-63

ARGENTINA
PAGES 64-65

DJIBOUTI
PAGES 72-73

EGYPT
PAGES 72-73

ERITREA
PAGES 72-73

ETHIOPIA
PAGES 72-73

KENYA
PAGES 72-73

RWANDA
PAGES 72-73

SOMALIA
PAGES 72-73

SUDAN
PAGES 72-73

GUINEA
PAGES 74-75

GUINEA–BISSAU
PAGES 74-75

LIBERIA
PAGES 74-75

MALI
PAGES 74-75

MAURITANIA
PAGES 74-75

NIGER
PAGES 74-75

NIGERIA
PAGES 74-75

SENEGAL
PAGES 74-75

GABON
PAGES 76-77

SAO TOME & PRINCIPE
PAGES 76-77

ANGOLA
PAGES 78-79

BOTSWANA
PAGES 78-79

COMOROS
PAGES 78-79

LESOTHO
PAGES 78-79

MADAGASCAR
PAGES 78-79

MALAWI
PAGES 78-79

EUROPE

ICELAND
PAGES 82-83

DENMARK
PAGES 84-85

FINLAND
PAGES 84-85

NORWAY
PAGES 84-85

SWEDEN
PAGES 84-85

BELGIUM
PAGES 86-87

LUXEMBOURG
PAGES 86-87

NETHERLANDS
PAGES 86-87

IRELAND
PAGES 88-89

LIECHTENSTEIN
PAGES 94-95

SLOVENIA
PAGES 94-95

SWITZERLAND
PAGES 94-95

ITALY
PAGES 96-97

MALTA
PAGES 96-97

SAN MARINO
PAGES 96-97

VATICAN CITY
PAGES 96-97

CZECH REPUBLIC
PAGES 98-99

HUNGARY
PAGES 98-99

SERBIA
PAGES 100-101

CYPRUS
PAGES 102-103

BULGARIA
PAGES 104-105

GREECE
PAGES 104-105

BELARUS
PAGES 106-107

ESTONIA
PAGES 106-107

LATVIA
PAGES 106-107

LITHUANIA
PAGES 106-107

TURKEY
PAGES 116-117

ISRAEL
PAGES 118-119

JORDAN
PAGES 118-119

LEBANON
PAGES 118-119

SYRIA
PAGES 118-119

BAHRAIN
PAGES 120-121

IRAN
PAGES 120-121

IRAQ
PAGES 120-121

TAJIKISTAN
PAGES 122-123

TURKMENISTAN
PAGES 122-123

UZBEKISTAN
PAGES 122-123

CHINA
PAGES 126-129

MONGOLIA
PAGES 126-127

NORTH KOREA
PAGES 128-129

SOUTH KOREA
PAGES 128-129

TAIWAN
PAGES 128-129

LAOS
PAGES 136-137

MYANMAR (BURMA)
PAGES 136-137

THAILAND
PAGES 136-137

VIETNAM
PAGES 136-137

BRUNEI
PAGES 138-139

EAST TIMOR
PAGES 138-139

INDONESIA
PAGES 138-139

MALAYSIA
PAGES 138-139

PAPUA NEW GUINEA
PAGES 144-145

SAMOA
PAGES 144-145

SOLOMON ISLANDS
PAGES 144-145

TONGA
PAGES 144-145

TUVALU
PAGES 144-145

VANUATU
PAGES 144-145

AUSTRALIA
PAGES 146-149

NEW ZEALAND
PAGES 150-151

The Political World

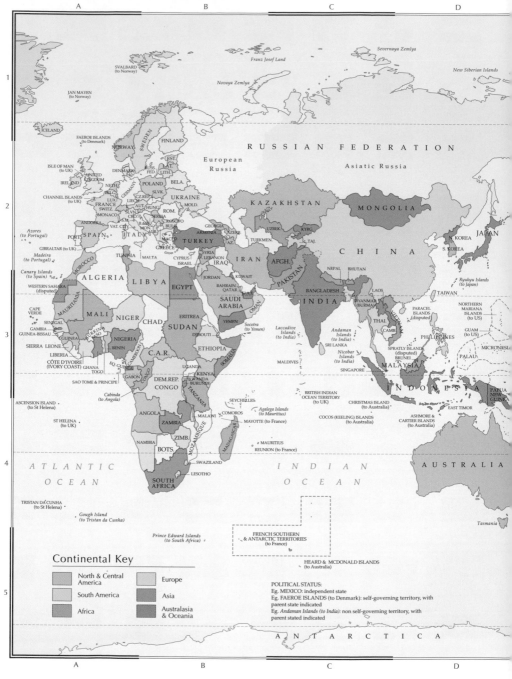

Severnaya Zemlya

Franz Josef Land

New Siberian Islands

SVALBARD
(to Norway)

Novaya Zemlya

JAN MAYEN
(to Norway)

ICELAND

FAEROE ISLANDS
(to Denmark)

NORWAY

SWEDEN

FINLAND

R U S S I A N   F E D E R A T I O N

European
Russia

Asiatic Russia

ISLE OF MAN
(to UK)

DENMARK

EST.
LAT.
LITH.

UNITED
KINGDOM

RUSS.
FED.

IRELAND

NETH.

GERMANY

POLAND

BELA.

CHANNEL ISLANDS
(to UK)

LUX.
FRANCE

CZ.REP.
SLVK.

UKRAINE

KAZAKHSTAN

MONGOLIA

SWITZ.

LIECH.
AUT.
HUNG.

MOLD.

Azores
(to Portugal)

ANDORRA

MONACO

SLVN.
CRO.

SER&MON.

ROM.

PORT.

SPAIN

VAT.CITY

ITALY

BOS.
MAC.

BULG.

GEORGIA

UZBEK.

KYRG.

JAPAN

ARMENIA

AZERB.

GIBRALTAR (to UK)

GREECE

ALB.

TURKEY

AZ.

TURKMEN.

TAJ.

C H I N A

KOREA

S. KOREA

Madeira
(to Portugal)

TUNISIA

MALTA

CYPRUS

SYRIA

LEBANON

ISRAEL

IRAN

AFGH.

NEPAL

BHUTAN

Ryukyu Islands
(to Japan)

Canary Islands
(to Spain)

MOROCCO

ALGERIA

LIBYA

EGYPT

IRAQ

JORDAN

KUWAIT

PAKISTAN

BANGLADESH

LAOS

TAIWAN

WESTERN SAHARA
(disputed)

BAHRAIN
QATAR

I.A.E.

SAUDI
ARABIA

OMAN

I N D I A

MYANMAR
(BURMA)

THAI.

PARACEL
ISLANDS
(disputed)

NORTHERN
MARIANA
ISLANDS
(to US)

CAPE
VERDE

MAURITANIA

MALI

NIGER

CHAD

SUDAN

ERITREA

YEMEN

Socotra
(to Yemen)

Laccadive
Islands
(to India)

Andaman
Islands
(to India)

CAMB.

GUAM
(to US)

SENEGAL

GAMBIA

BURKINA

DJIBOUTI

SRI LANKA

Nicobar
Islands
(to India)

SPRATLY ISLANDS
(disputed)

PHILIPPINES

MICRONESIA

GUINEA-BISSAU

GUINEA

NIGERIA

BENIN

C.A.R.

ETHIOPIA

SOMALIA

MALDIVES

SINGAPORE

BRUNEI

MALAYSIA

PALAU

SIERRA LEONE

LIBERIA

CÔTE D'IVOIRE
(IVORY COAST)

GHANA

TOGO

EQ. GUINEA

CAMEROON

GABON

CONGO

UGANDA

KENYA

RWANDA

BURUNDI

I N D O N E S I A

SAO TOME & PRINCIPE

DEM.REP.
CONGO

TANZANIA

SEYCHELLES

Agalega Islands
(to Mauritius)

BRITISH INDIAN
OCEAN TERRITORY
(to UK)

CHRISTMAS ISLAND
(to Australia)

EAST TIMOR

PAPUA
NEW
GUINEA

Cabinda
(to Angola)

ASCENSION ISLAND
(to St Helena)

ANGOLA

MALAWI

COMOROS

MAYOTTE (to France)

COCOS (KEELING) ISLANDS
(to Australia)

ASHMORE &
CARTIER ISLANDS
(to Australia)

ST HELENA
(to UK)

ZAMBIA

MOZAMBIQUE

MADAGASCAR

MAURITIUS

REUNION (to France)

NAMIBIA

ZIMB.

BOTS.

A T L A N T I C

O C E A N

SWAZILAND

I N D I A N

O C E A N

A U S T R A L I A

TRISTAN DA CUNHA
(to St Helena)

SOUTH
AFRICA

LESOTHO

Gough Island
(to Tristan da Cunha)

Tasmania

Prince Edward Islands
(to South Africa)

FRENCH SOUTHERN
& ANTARCTIC TERRITORIES
(to France)

HEARD & MCDONALD ISLANDS
(to Australia)

Continental Key

North & Central America	Europe
South America	Asia
Africa	Australasia & Oceania

POLITICAL STATUS:
Eg. MEXICO: independent state
Eg. FAEROE ISLANDS (to Denmark): self-governing territory, with
parent state indicated
Eg. Andaman Islands (to India): non self-governing territory, with
parent stated indicated

A N T A R C T I C A

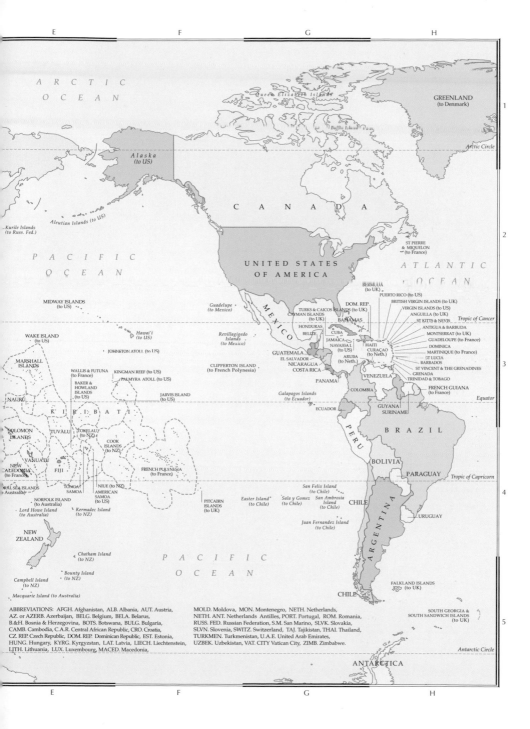

ABBREVIATIONS: AFGH. Afghanistan, ALB. Albania, AUT. Austria, AZ. or AZERB. Azerbaijan, BELG. Belgium, BELA. Belarus, B.&H. Bosnia & Herzegovina, BOTS. Botswana, BULG. Bulgaria, CAMB. Cambodia, C.A.R. Central African Republic, CRO. Croatia, CZ. REP Czech Republic, DOM. REP. Dominican Republic, EST. Estonia, HUNG. Hungary, KYRG. Kyrgyzstan, LAT. Latvia, LIECH. Liechtenstein, LITH. Lithuania, LUX. Luxemburg, MACED. Macedonia,

MOLD. Moldova, MON. Montenegro, NETH. Netherlands, NETH. ANT. Netherlands Antilles, PORT. Portugal, ROM. Romania, RUSS. FED. Russian Federation, S.M. San Marino, SLVK. Slovakia, SLVN. Slovenia, SWITZ. Switzerland, TAJ. Tajikistan, THAI. Thailand, TURKMEN. Turkmenistan, U.A.E. United Arab Emirates, UZBEK. Uzbekistan, VAT. CITY Vatican City, ZIMB. Zimbabwe.

The Physical World

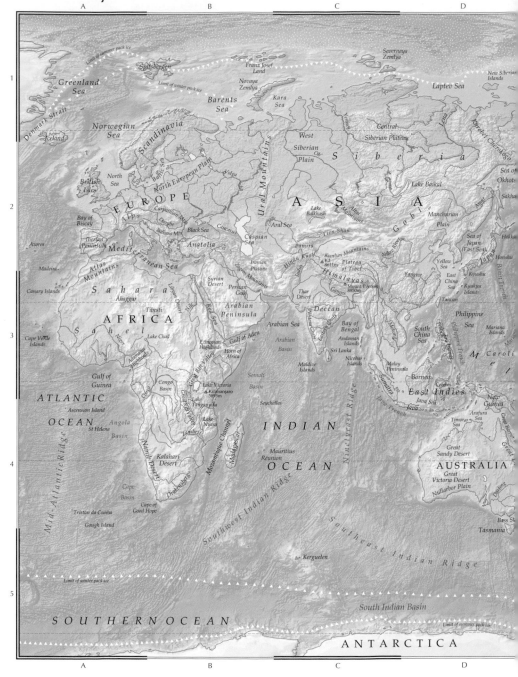

A   B   C   D

Limit of summer pack ice

1

Greenland Sea

Spitsbergen

Franz Josef Land

Severnaya Zemlya

New Siberian Islands

Limit of winter pack ice

Novaya Zemlya

Laptev Sea

Denmark Strait

Barents Sea

Kara Sea

Iceland

Norwegian Sea

Scandinavia

West Siberian Plain

Central Siberian Plateau

Ob

Lena

Yenisey

Khrebet Cherskogo

North Sea

Baltic Sea

Volga

Ural Mountains

S i b e r i a

Sea of Okhotsk

British Isles

North European Plain

Lake Baikal

Amur

Sakhalin

2

E U R O P E

A S I A

Bay of Biscay

Alps

Carpathian Mts

Danube

Aral Sea

Altai Mountains

Gobi

Manchurian Plain

Azores

Balkans Mts

Black Sea

Caucasus

Caspian Sea

Tien Shan

Sea of Japan (East Sea)

Hokkaido

Iberian Peninsula

Anatolia

Pamirs

Kunlun Mountains

Plateau of Tibet

Yellow River

Yellow Sea

Honshu

Kyushu

Madeira

Atlas Mountains

Mediterranean Sea

Iranian Plateau

Hindu Kush

K2 8611m

Yangtze

East China Sea

Ryukyu Islands

Canary Islands

Zagros Mountains

Syrian Desert

Himalayas

Mount Everest 8850m

Taiwan

S a h a r a

Tibesti

Libyan Desert

Nile

Red Sea

Persian Gulf

Thar Desert

Deccan

Philippine Sea

Mariana Islands

Ahaggar

Arabian Peninsula

Ganges

Caroli

3

Cape Verde Islands

S a h e l

A F R I C A

Niger

Lake Chad

Arabian Sea

Bay of Bengal

Andaman Islands

South China Sea

M

ATLANTIC

Gulf of Guinea

Ethiopian Highlands

Gulf of Aden

Arabian Basin

Sri Lanka

Nicobar Islands

Malay Peninsula

Philippine Trench

Adamawa Highlands

Horn of Africa

Maldive Islands

Borneo

Ascension Island

Congo Basin

Congo

Lake Victoria

Kilimanjaro 5895m

Somali Basin

Seychelles

Sumatra

Java Trench

East Indies

New Guinea

OCEAN

St Helena

Angola Basin

Lake Tanganyika

Great Rift Valley

I N D I A N

Java Sea

Celebes

Java

Arafura Sea

Timor Sea

Great Barrier

4

Mid-Atlantic Ridge

Zambezi

Lake Nyasa

Madagascar

Mozambique Channel

Mauritius

Réunion

O C E A N

Ninetyeast Ridge

AUSTRALIA

Great Sandy Desert

Great Victoria Desert

Nullarbor Plain

Darling

Kalahari Desert

Namib Desert

Drakensberg

Cape Basin

Cape of Good Hope

Southwest Indian Ridge

Southeast Indian Ridge

Bass St

Tasmania

Tristan da Cunha

Gough Island

Kerguelen

5

Limit of winter pack ice

South Indian Basin

Limit of summer pack ice

S O U T H E R N O C E A N

A N T A R C T I C A

A   B   C   D

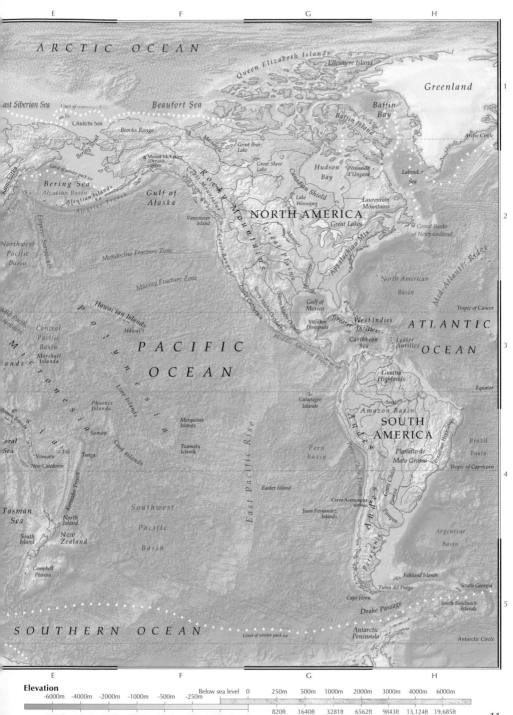

E F G H

ARCTIC OCEAN

Queen Elizabeth Islands
Ellesmere Island
Greenland   1

East Siberian Sea   Limit of winter pack ice   Beaufort Sea
Baffin
Bay

Chukchi Sea
Baffin Island   Arctic Circle

Bering Strait
Brooks Range
Mackenzie
Great Bear
Lake   Labrador
Sea

Mount McKinley
(Denali)
6194m
Limit of winter pack ice
Great Slave
Lake   Hudson
Bay   Péninsule
d'Ungava

Bering Sea
Aleutian Basin
Aleutian Islands
Rocky Mountains
Canadian Shield
Laurentian
Mountains

Aleutian Trench
Gulf of
Alaska
Vancouver
Island
Coast Ranges
Lake
Winnipeg
NORTH AMERICA
Great Lakes
Grand Banks
of Newfoundland   2

Emperor Seamounts
Northwest
Pacific
Basin
Mendocino Fracture Zone
Great Plains
Missouri
Mississippi
Appalachian Mts
North American
Basin
Mid-Atlantic Ridge

Murray Fracture Zone
Sierra Madre Occidental
Gulf of
Mexico   Tropic of Cancer

Hawaiian Islands
Sierra Madre Oriental
Yucatán
Peninsula
Greater
Antilles
West Indies
Antilles
ATLANTIC

Central
Pacific
Basin
Hawai'i
Middle America Trench
Caribbean
Sea   Lesser
Antilles
OCEAN   3

Mid-Pacific
Seamounts
Marshall
Islands
PACIFIC
Polynesia
OCEAN
Guiana
Highlands

Mariana Islands
Micronesia
Phoenix
Islands
Line Islands
Galápagos
Islands
Amazon
Equator

Marquesas
Islands
Amazon Basin
SOUTH
AMERICA

Coral
Sea
Samoa
Cook Islands
Tuamotu
Islands
Peru
Basin
Andes
Planalto de
Mato Grosso
Brazilian Highlands
Brazil
Basin

Vanuatu   Fiji
Tonga
East Pacific Rise
Gran Chaco
Pantanal
Tropic of Capricorn

New Caledonia
Easter Island
Cerro Aconcagua
6959m
Juan Fernández
Islands
Pampas   4

Tasman
Sea
North
Island
Southwest
Pacific
Basin
Patagonia
Argentine
Basin

South
Island
New
Zealand

Campbell
Plateau
Kermadec Trench
Falkland Islands
Tierra del Fuego
South Georgia

Cape Horn
Drake Passage
South Sandwich
Islands   5

SOUTHERN   OCEAN
Limit of winter pack ice
Antarctic
Peninsula
Antarctic Circle

E F G H

Elevation

-6000m	-4000m	-2000m	-1000m	-500m	-250m	Below sea level 0	250m	500m	1000m	2000m	3000m	4000m	6000m

| -19,658ft | -13,124ft | -6562ft | -3281ft | -1640ft | -820ft | -328ft/-100m | 0 | 820ft | 1640ft | 3281ft | 6562ft | 9843ft | 13,124ft | 19,685ft |

Time Zones

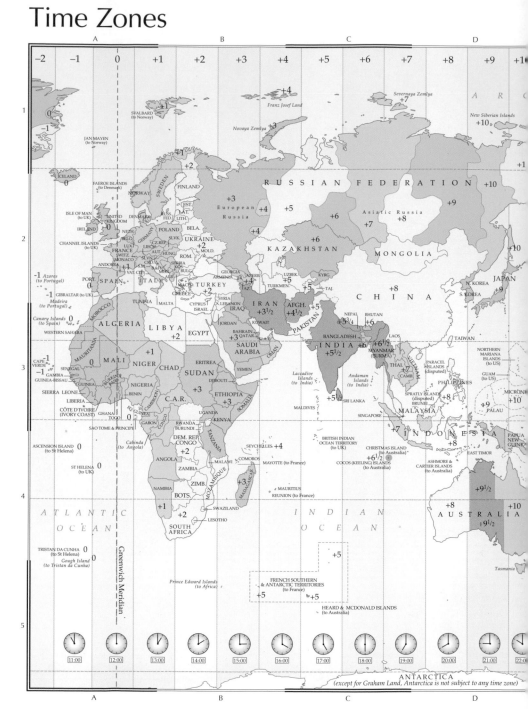

The numbers represented thus; +2/-2, indicate the number of hours each time zone is ahead or behind UCT (Coordinated Universal Time)

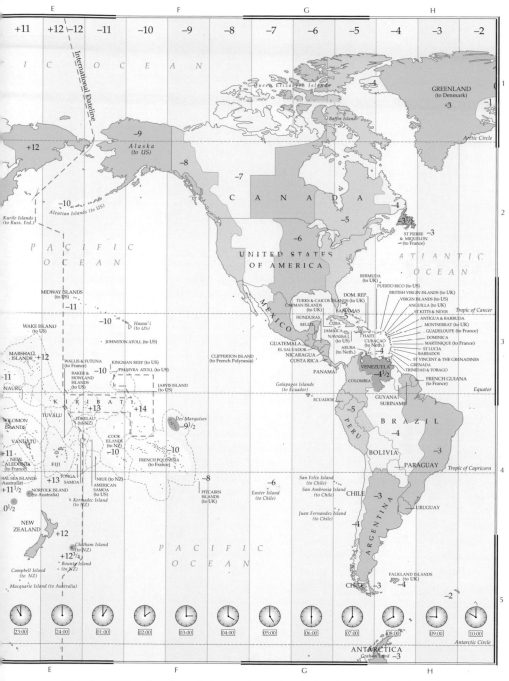

The clocks and 24-hour times given at the bottom of the map show time in each time zone when it is 12.00 hours noon UCT

Geology & Structure

Ural Mountains

EURASIAN PLATE

Alps

ANATOLIAN PLATE

IRANIAN PLATE

Himalayas

ARABIAN PLATE

PHILIPPINE PLATE

AFRICAN PLATE

INDO-AUSTRALIAN PLATE

ANTARCTIC PLATE

Geological Regions		Mountain Ranges	
Continental shield	Igneous rock types	Alpine (5 to 23 Ma)	Caledonian (386 to 439 Ma)
Sedimentary rocks	Coral formation	Hercynian (290 to 362 Ma)	Ma= millions of years ago

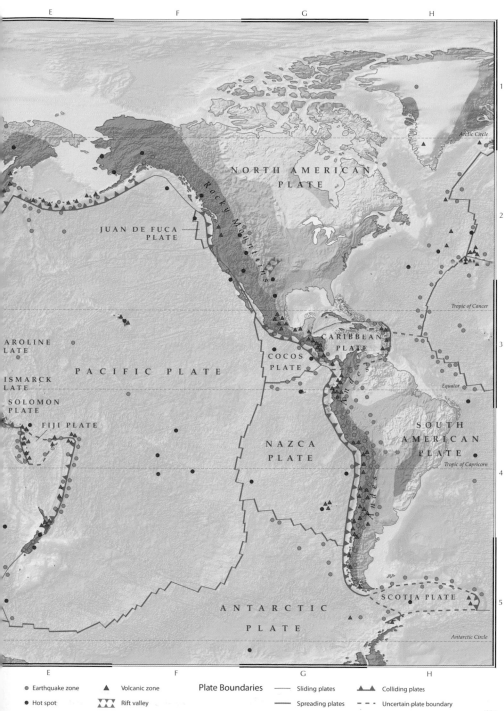

E   F   G   H

NORTH AMERICAN PLATE

Rocky Mountains

Arctic Circle

JUAN DE FUCA PLATE

CARIBBEAN PLATE

COCOS PLATE

PACIFIC PLATE

CAROLINE PLATE

BISMARCK PLATE

SOLOMON PLATE

FIJI PLATE

Andes

Tropic of Cancer

Equator

NAZCA PLATE

SOUTH AMERICAN PLATE

Tropic of Capricorn

Andes

SCOTIA PLATE

ANTARCTIC PLATE

Antarctic Circle

● Earthquake zone	▲ Volcanic zone	**Plate Boundaries**	—— Sliding plates	▲▲ Colliding plates
● Hot spot	◇◇◇ Rift valley		—— Spreading plates	‑ ‑ ‑ Uncertain plate boundary

World Climate

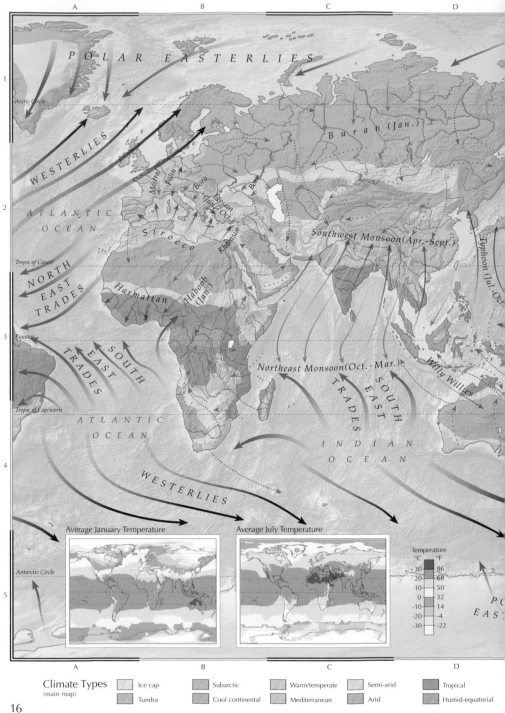

POLAR EASTERLIES

Arctic Circle

WESTERLIES

ATLANTIC
OCEAN

Tropic of Cancer

NORTH
EAST
TRADES

Equator

SOUTH
EAST
TRADES

Tropic of Capricorn

ATLANTIC
OCEAN

WESTERLIES

Antarctic Circle

Mistral

Bora

Etesian (Jun.-Oct.)

Pöun

Bora

Sirocco

Harmattan

Haboob (Jan.)

Khamsin

Buran (Jan.)

Southwest Monsoon (Apr.-Sept.)

Northeast Monsoon (Oct.-Mar.)

SOUTH
EAST
TRADES

Willy Willies

Typhoon (Jul.-Oct.)

INDIAN
OCEAN

PO
EAS

Average January Temperature

Average July Temperature

Temperature	
°C	°F
30	86
20	68
10	50
0	32
-10	14
-20	-4
-30	-22

Climate Types
(main map)

Ice cap	Subarctic	Warm/temperate	Semi-arid	Tropical
Tundra	Cool continental	Mediterranean	Arid	Humid-equatorial

16

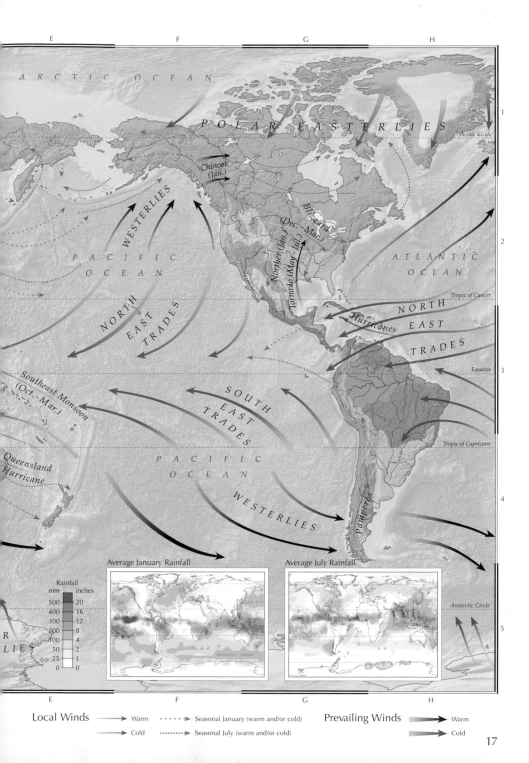

E F G H

A R C T I C O C E A N

P O L A R E A S T E R L I E S

Arctic Circle

Chinook
(Jan.)

Blizzard
(Dec. - Mar.)

Norther (Jan.)

Tornado (May - Jul.)

WESTERLIES

P A C I F I C
O C E A N

A T L A N T I C
O C E A N

N O R T H

E A S T

T R A D E S

Tropic of Cancer

N O R T H

Hurricanes

E A S T

T R A D E S

Equator

Southeast Monsoon
(Oct. - Mar.)

S O U T H
E A S T
T R A D E S

Tropic of Capricorn

Queensland
Hurricane

P A C I F I C
O C E A N

W E S T E R L I E S

Pamperos

L I E S

Average January Rainfall

Average July Rainfall

Rainfall	
mm	inches
500	20
400	16
300	12
200	8
100	4
50	2
25	1
0	0

Antarctic Circle

E F G H

Local Winds ——➤ Warm · · · · ·➤ Seasonal January (warm and/or cold) Prevailing Winds ——➤ Warm

  ——➤ Cold · · · · · ·➤ Seasonal July (warm and/or cold)   ——➤ Cold

1

2

3

4

5

Ocean Currents

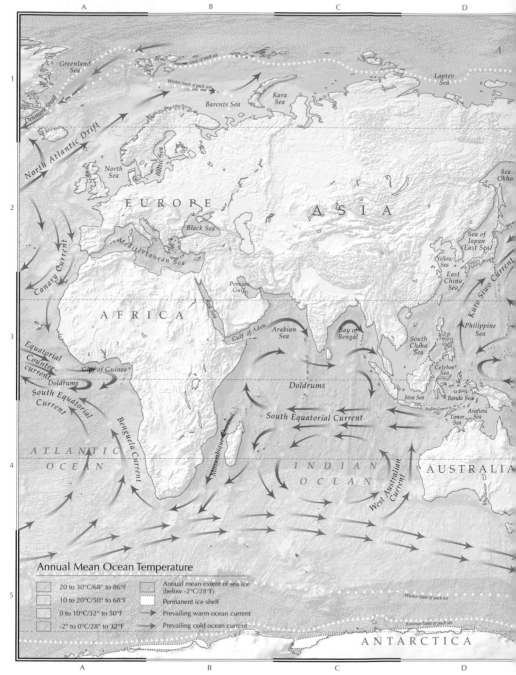

Annual Mean Ocean Temperature

- 20 to 30°C/68° to 86°F
- 10 to 20°C/50° to 68°F
- 0 to 10°C/32° to 50°F
- -2° to 0°C/28° to 32°F

- Annual mean extent of sea ice (below -2°C/28°F)
- Permanent ice shelf
- → Prevailing warm ocean current
- → Prevailing cold ocean current

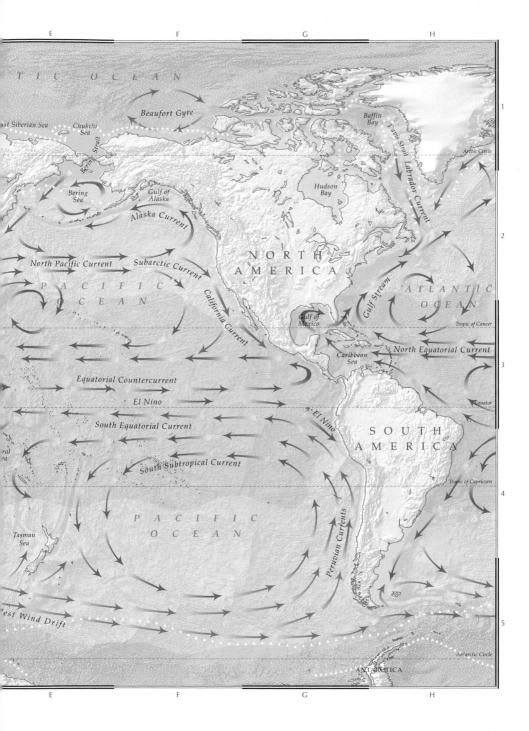

Beaufort Gyre

st Siberian Sea

Chukchi
Sea

Bering
Strait

Bering
Sea

Gulf of
Alaska

Alaska Current

North Pacific Current

Subarctic Current

P A C I F I C
O C E A N

California Current

Baffin
Bay

Davis Strait

Labrador Current

Arctic Circle

Hudson
Bay

N O R T H
A M E R I C A

Gulf of
Mexico

Gulf Stream

A T L A N T I C
O C E A N

Tropic of Cancer

Caribbean
Sea

North Equatorial Current

Equatorial Countercurrent

El Nino

South Equatorial Current

South Subtropical Current

El Nino

Equator

S O U T H
A M E R I C A

Tropic of Capricorn

P A C I F I C
O C E A N

Tasman
Sea

ral
ea

Peruvian Currents

est Wind Drift

Antarctic Circle

ANTARCTICA

Life Zones

ARCTIC

Greenland
Sea

Spitsbergen

Franz Josef
Land

Novaya
Zemlya

Severnaya
Zemlya

New Siberia
Islands

Denmark Strait

Iceland

Barents
Sea

Kara
Sea

Laptev Sea

Khrebet Cherskiy

Norwegian
Sea

Scandinavia

West
Siberian
Plain

Ob

Central
Siberian Plateau

Siberia

Sea of
Okhot

Ural Mountains

Lena

British
Isles

North
Sea

Baltic Sea

North European Plain

EUROPE

Alps

Carpathian Mts

Danube

Volga

Aral Sea

A S I A

Altai
Mountains

Lake Baikal

Sakha

Manchurian
Plain

Bay of
Biscay

Iberian
Peninsula

Balkans Mts

Black Sea

Caspian
Sea

Anatolia

Caucasus

Tien Shan

Gobi

Yellow
River

Sea of
Japan
(East Sea)

Hokka

Honshū

Mediterranean Sea

Atlas Mts

Iranian
Plateau

Pamirs

Hindu Kush

Kunlun Mountains

Plateau
of Tibet

Yangtze

East
China
Sea

Kyūshū

Ryukyu
Islands

Sahara

Ahaggar

Zagros Mountains

Persian
Gulf

Himalayas

Yellow
Sea

Taiwan

Tibesti

Libyan Desert

Nile

Arabian
Peninsula

Thar
Desert

Ganges

Deccan

Mekong

South
China
Sea

Mariana
Islands

AFRICA

Sahel

Niger

Lake Chad

Gulf of Aden

Arabian Sea

Bay of
Bengal

M. Caroli

Ethiopian
Highlands

Horn of
Africa

Sri Lanka

Malay
Peninsula

Adamawa
Highlands

Gulf of
Guinea

Congo

Great Rift Valley

Lake Victoria

Borneo

East Indies

New
Guinea

Coral Barrie

Congo
Basin

Lake
Tanganyika

Sumatra

Java Sea

Java

INDIAN

ATLANTIC

Lake
Nyasa

Zambezi

Madagascar

Mozambique Channel

Timor
Sea

Arafura
Sea

OCEAN

OCEAN

Great
Sandy Desert

AUSTRALIA

Namib Desert

Kalahari
Desert!

Great
Victoria Desert

Nullarbor Plain

Darling

Drakensberg

Cape of
Good Hope

Bas. Str

Tasmania

△◦ Kerguelen

ANTARCTICA

Life Zones

| | Polar | | Mountain | | Broadleaf forest | | Temperate forest |

| | Tundra | | Needleleaf forest | | Temperate grassland | | Mediterranean |

20

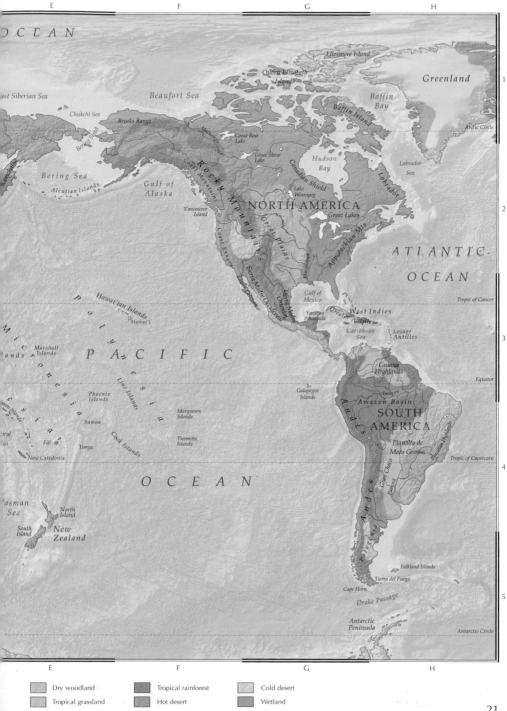

E   F   G   H

OCEAN

East Siberian Sea

Chukchi Sea

Beaufort Sea

Ellesmere Island

Queen Elizabeth Islands

Greenland   1

Baffin Bay

Baffin Island

Brooks Range

Mackenzie

Great Bear Lake

Arctic Circle

Labrador Sea

Bering Strait

Bering Sea

Gulf of Alaska

Aleutian Islands

Kamchatka

Great Slave Lake

Hudson Bay

Canadian Shield

Labrador

Rocky Mountains

Coast Mountains

Lake Winnipeg

NORTH AMERICA

Great Plains

Great Lakes

Appalachian Mts

ATLANTIC-OCEAN   2

Vancouver Island

Coast Range

Sierra Madre Occidental

Sierra Madre Oriental

Mississippi

Gulf of Mexico

Tropic of Cancer

Hawaiian Islands

Hawai'i

Yucatán Peninsula

Greater Antilles

West Indies

Lesser Antilles

Caribbean Sea

P   o   l   y   n   e   s   i   a

P A C I F I C   3

Marshall Islands

Micronesia

Islands

Guiana Highlands

Galápagos Islands

Amazon

Equator

Phoenix Islands

Line Islands

Marquesas Islands

Amazon Basin

SOUTH AMERICA

Samoa

Andes

Fiji

Tonga

Cook Islands

Tuamotu Islands

Planalto de Mato Grosso

Brazilian Highlands

Tropic of Capricorn   4

New Caledonia

O C E A N

Gran Chaco

Paraná

Tasman Sea

North Island

New Zealand

South Island

Andes

Patagonia

Falkland Islands

Tierra del Fuego

Cape Horn

Drake Passage   5

Antarctic Peninsula

Antarctic Circle

E   F   G   H

Dry woodland	Tropical rainforest	Cold desert	
Tropical grassland	Hot desert	Wetland	

Population

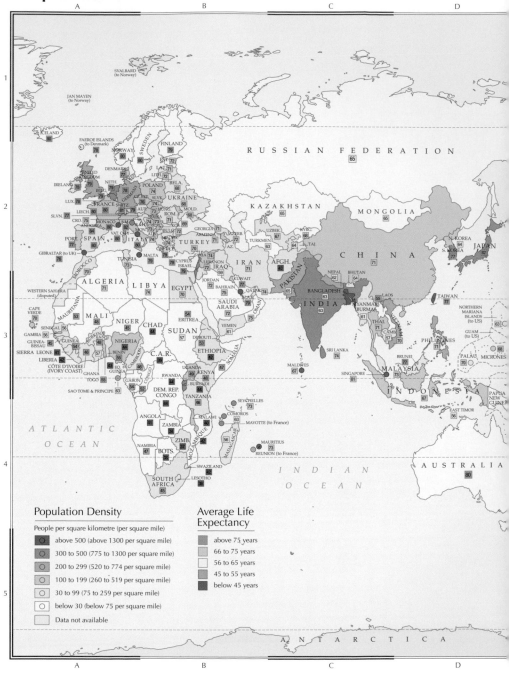

Population Density

People per square kilometre (per square mile)

- above 500 (above 1300 per square mile)
- 300 to 500 (775 to 1300 per square mile)
- 200 to 299 (520 to 774 per square mile)
- 100 to 199 (260 to 519 per square mile)
- 30 to 99 (75 to 259 per square mile)
- below 30 (below 75 per square mile)
- Data not available

Average Life Expectancy

- above 75 years
- 66 to 75 years
- 56 to 65 years
- 45 to 55 years
- below 45 years

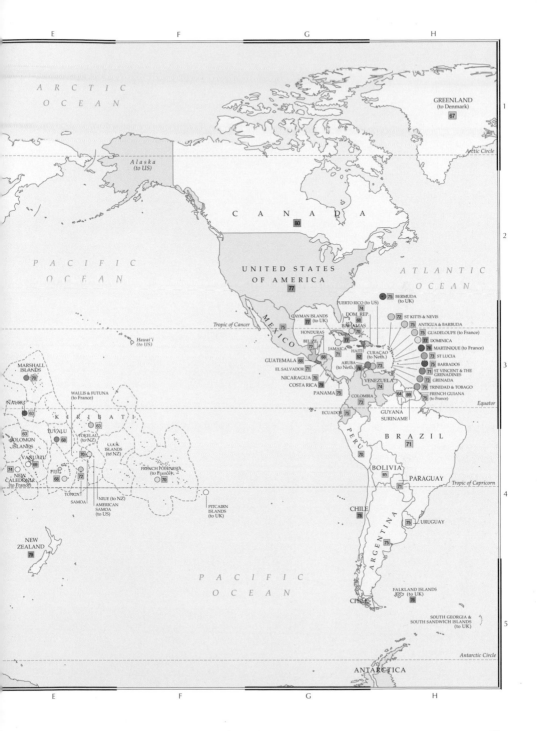

ARCTIC
OCEAN

GREENLAND
(to Denmark)
67

Arctic Circle

Alaska
(to US)

PACIFIC
OCEAN

C A N A D A
80

UNITED STATES
OF AMERICA
77

ATLANTIC
OCEAN

BERMUDA
(to UK) 75

PUERTO RICO (to US) 74
CAYMAN ISLANDS 77
(to UK)
DOM. REP. 68
BAHAMAS 70

MEXICO 75

Tropic of Cancer

Hawai'i
(to US)

MARSHALL
ISLANDS
70

HONDURAS
77
BELIZE 72
JAMAICA 71
GUATEMALA 68
EL SALVADOR 71
NICARAGUA 70
COSTA RICA 78
PANAMA 75

ST KITTS & NEVIS 72
ANTIGUA & BARBUDA 75
GUADELOUPE (to France) 75
DOMINICA 77
MARTINIQUE (to France) 76
ST LUCIA 73
BARBADOS 75
ST VINCENT & THE 71
GRENADINES
GRENADA 73
TRINIDAD & TOBAGO 70
FRENCH GUIANA 75
(to France)

HAITI 52
ARUBA 76
(to Neth.)
CURAÇAO 73
(to Neth.)
VENEZUELA 74
COLOMBIA 73
64 69

WALLIS & FUTUNA
(to France)

NAURU
63

KIRIBATI

TOKELAU
(to NZ)
63

TUVALU
68

COOK
ISLANDS
(td NZ)
70

SOLOMON
ISLANDS
69

VANUATU
69

NEW
CALEDONIA
(to France)
71

FIJI
66

72

ECUADOR 75

GUYANA
SURINAME

PERU
70

B R A Z I L
71

Equator

FRENCH POLYNESIA
(to France)
70

TONGA
SAMOA

NIUE (to NZ)
AMERICAN
SAMOA
(to US)

PITCAIRN
ISLANDS
(to UK)

BOLIVIA
65

PARAGUAY
71

Tropic of Capricorn

NEW
ZEALAND
79

CHILE
78

ARGENTINA
75

URUGUAY 75

PACIFIC
OCEAN

CHILE

FALKLAND ISLANDS
(to UK)
78

SOUTH GEORGIA &
SOUTH SANDWICH ISLANDS
(to UK)

Antarctic Circle

ANTARCTICA

Languages

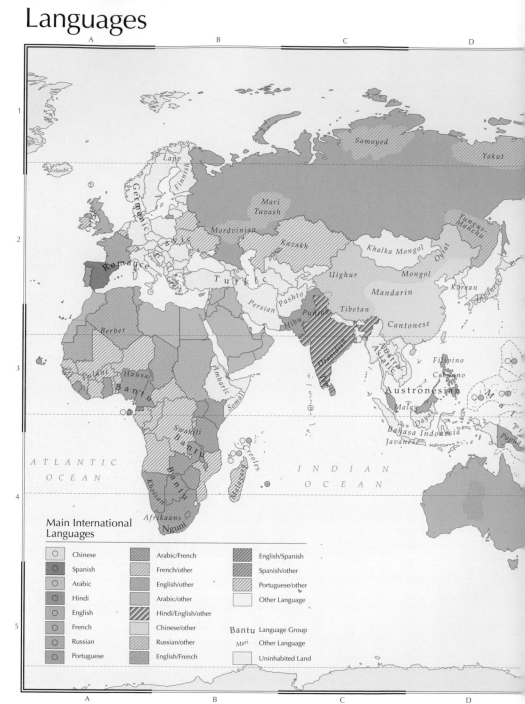

Main International Languages

○ Chinese	Arabic/French	English/Spanish
○ Spanish	French/other	Spanish/other
○ Arabic	English/other	Portuguese/other
○ Hindi	Arabic/other	Other Language
○ English	Hindi/English/other	
○ French	Chinese/other	**Bantu** Language Group
○ Russian	Russian/other	Mari Other Language
○ Portuguese	English/French	Uninhabited Land

E　　　　　　　F　　　　　　　G　　　　　　　H

ARCTIC
OCEAN

Greenlandic

Danish　Arctic Circle

Aleut

Eskimo-Aleut

American Indian

Athabascan

Algonquin

PACIFIC
OCEAN

Tropic of Cancer

Nahuatl

Maya

Arawak

Carib

Equator

Quechua

Aymara

Polynesian

Tropic of Capricorn

Maori

PACIFIC
OCEAN

Antarctic Circle

E　　　　　　　F　　　　　　　G　　　　　　　H

Religion

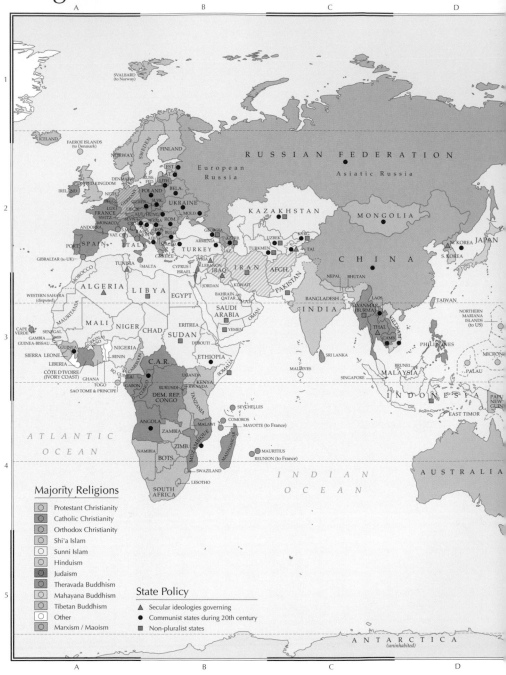

Majority Religions

◉	Protestant Christianity
◉	Catholic Christianity
◉	Orthodox Christianity
◉	Shi'a Islam
◉	Sunni Islam
◉	Hinduism
◉	Judaism
◉	Theravada Buddhism
◉	Mahayana Buddhism
◉	Tibetan Buddhism
○	Other
◉	Marxism / Maoism

State Policy

▲	Secular ideologies governing
●	Communist states during 20th century
■	Non-pluralist states

Map labels:

SVALBARD (to Norway)

ICELAND
FAEROE ISLANDS (to Denmark)
NORWAY
SWEDEN
FINLAND

RUSSIAN FEDERATION

European Russia   Asiatic Russia

DENMARK
UNITED KINGDOM
IRELAND
NETH.
BELG.
LUX.
FRANCE
SWITZ.
MONACO
ANDORRA
PORT.
SPAIN
GIBRALTAR (to UK)

RUSS. FED.
EST.
LAT.
LITH.
POLAND
BELA.
GERMANY
CZECH
SVK.
UKRAINE
AUT.
HUNG.
SLO.
CRO.
ROM.
MOLD.
S.M.
ITALY
BOS.
SER.
KOS.
BULG.
MON.
ALB.
MAC.
GREECE
VAT. CITY
MALTA

KAZAKHSTAN
MONGOLIA

GEORGIA
ARMENIA
AZERB.
UZBEK.
KYRG.
TURKMEN.
TAJ.

CHINA

N. KOREA   JAPAN
S. KOREA

TURKEY
CYPRUS
SYRIA
LEBANON
ISRAEL
IRAQ
IRAN
AFGH.
JORDAN
KUWAIT
PAKISTAN
NEPAL   BHUTAN

MOROCCO
TUNISIA

WESTERN SAHARA (disputed)
ALGERIA
LIBYA
EGYPT

MAURITANIA
MALI
NIGER
CHAD
SUDAN
ERITREA
DJIBOUTI
SAUDI ARABIA
BAHRAIN
QATAR
U.A.E.
OMAN
YEMEN

BANGLADESH
INDIA
MYANMAR (BURMA)
LAOS
THAI.
CAMB.
VIET.

TAIWAN

NORTHERN MARIANA ISLANDS (to US)

PHILIPPINES

MICRON.

CAPE VERDE
SENEGAL
GAMBIA
GUINEA-BISSAU
GUINEA
SIERRA LEONE
LIBERIA
CÔTE D'IVOIRE (IVORY COAST)
GHANA
TOGO
BENIN
BURKINA FASO
NIGERIA
EQ. GUINEA
SAO TOME & PRINCIPE
CAMEROON
GABON
CONGO
C.A.R.
ETHIOPIA
SOMALIA
UGANDA
KENYA
RWANDA
BURUNDI
DEM. REP. CONGO
TANZANIA

SRI LANKA
MALDIVES

BRUNEI
SINGAPORE
MALAYSIA

PALAU

INDONESIA

EAST TIMOR

PAPUA NEW GUINEA

SEYCHELLES
COMOROS
MAYOTTE (to France)

ANGOLA
ZAMBIA
MALAWI
MOZAMBIQUE
MADAGASCAR
NAMIBIA
ZIMB.
BOTS.
SWAZILAND
LESOTHO
SOUTH AFRICA

MAURITIUS
REUNION (to France)

ATLANTIC OCEAN

INDIAN OCEAN

AUSTRALIA

ANTARCTICA (uninhabited)

The Global Economy

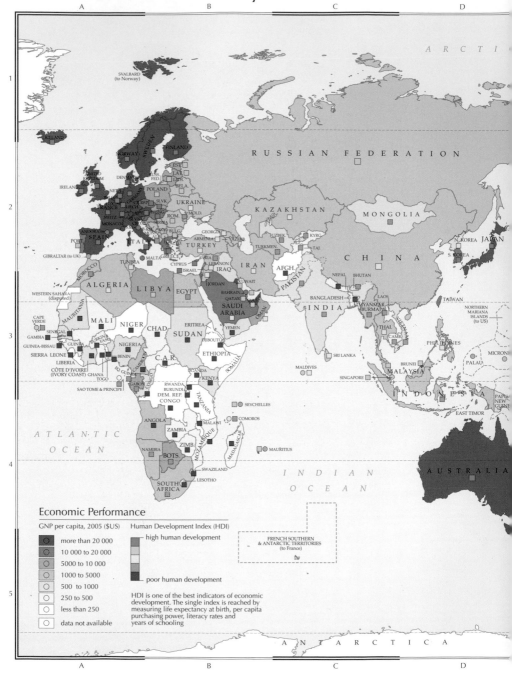

Economic Performance

GNP per capita, 2005 ($US)

- more than 20 000
- 10 000 to 20 000
- 5000 to 10 000
- 1000 to 5000
- 500 to 1000
- 250 to 500
- less than 250
- data not available

Human Development Index (HDI)

- high human development
- poor human development

HDI is one of the best indicators of economic development. The single index is reached by measuring life expectancy at birth, per capita purchasing power, literacy rates and years of schooling

GREENLAND
(to Denmark)

Arctic Circle

Alaska
(to US)

C A N A D A

P A C I F I C
O C E A N

UNITED STATES
OF AMERICA

A T L A N T I C
O C E A N

M E X I C O

Hawai'i
(to US)

BERMUDA
(to UK)

TURKS & CAICOS ISLANDS (to UK)
DOM. REP
PUERTO RICO
(to US)
ST KITTS & NEVIS
CAYMAN ISLANDS
(to UK)
BAHAMAS
ANTIGUA & BAR.
Tropic of Cancer
HONDURAS
CUBA
BELIZE
GUADELOUPE (to France)
JAMAICA
DOMINICA
MARTINIQUE (to France)
HAITI
GUATEMALA
CURAÇAO
(to Neth.)
ST LUCIA
EL SALVADOR
ARUBA
BARBADOS
NICARAGUA
(to Neth.)
ST VINCENT &
THE GRENADINES
COSTA RICA
GRENADA
PANAMA
VENEZUELA
TRINIDAD & TOBAGO
FRENCH GUIANA
COLOMBIA
(to France)
Equator
MARSHALL
ISLANDS
ECUADOR
GUYANA
SURINAME

NAURU

K I R I B A T I

P E R U
B R A Z I L
TUVALU
TOKELAU
(to NZ)
SOLOMON
ISLANDS
SAMOA
COOK
ISLANDS
(to NZ)
VANUATU
BOLIVIA
NEW
CALEDONIA
(to France)
TONGA
PARAGUAY
FIJI
FRENCH POLYNESIA
(to France)
Tropic of Capricorn

PITCAIRN
ISLANDS
(to UK)
CHILE

NEW
ZEALAND

ARGENTINA
URUGUAY

P A C I F I C
O C E A N

CHILE

FALKLAND ISLANDS
(to UK)

CHILE

Antarctic Circle

A N T A R C T I C A

29

Politics and Conflict

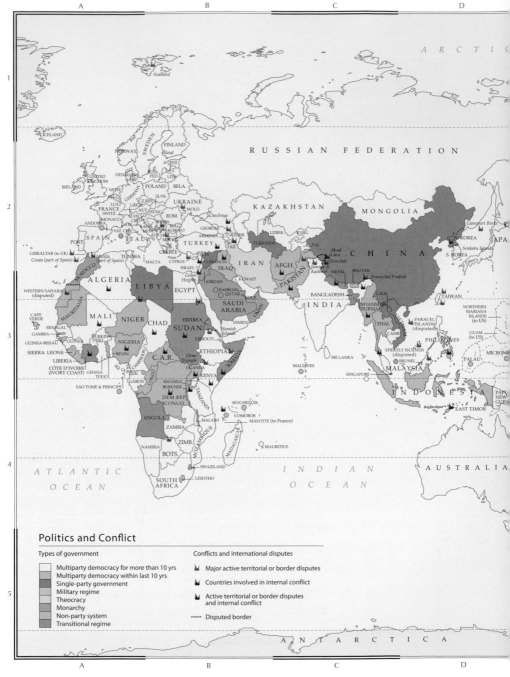

Politics and Conflict

Types of government

- Multiparty democracy for more than 10 yrs
- Multiparty democracy within last 10 yrs
- Single-party government
- Military regime
- Theocracy
- Monarchy
- Non-party system
- Transitional regime

Conflicts and international disputes

- ⚔ Major active territorial or border disputes
- ⚔ Countries involved in internal conflict
- ⚔ Active territorial or border disputes and internal conflict
- ⋯⋯ Disputed border

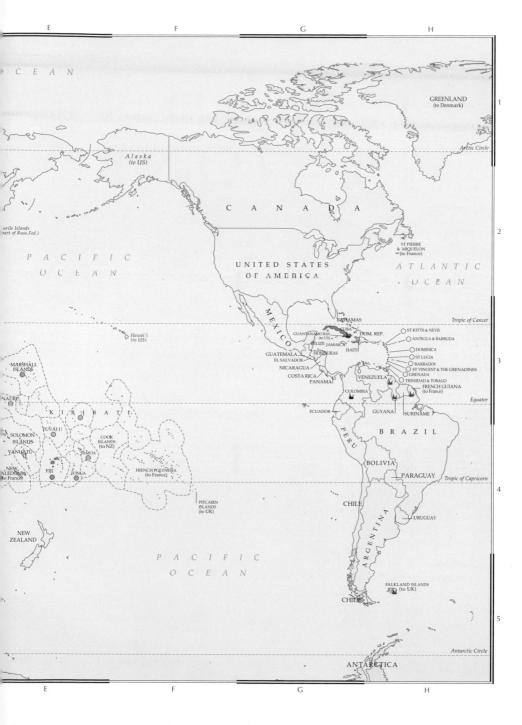

E   F   G   H

GREENLAND
(to Denmark)

1

Arctic Circle

Alaska
(to US)

C A N A D A

urile Islands
part of Russ.Fed.)

ST PIERRE
& MIQUELON
(to France)

2

P A C I F I C
O C E A N

UNITED STATES
OF AMERICA

A T L A N T I C
O C E A N

Tropic of Cancer

Hawai'i
(to US)

BAHAMAS

GUANTANAMO BAY CUBA
(to US)   DOM. REP.

ST KITTS & NEVIS

ANTIGUA & BARBUDA

BELIZE JAMAICA HAITI

DOMINICA

MARSHALL
ISLANDS

GUATEMALA HONDURAS
EL SALVADOR

ST LUCIA

BARBADOS

ST VINCENT & THE GRENADINES

NICARAGUA

GRENADA

3

NAURU

COSTA RICA
PANAMA

VENEZUELA

TRINIDAD & TOBAGO

FRENCH GUIANA
(to France)

K I R I B A T I

COLOMBIA

Equator

SOLOMON
ISLANDS

TUVALU

ECUADOR

GUYANA

SURINAME

VANUATU

COOK
ISLANDS
(to NZ)

P E R U

B R A Z I L

NEW
CALEDONIA
(to France)

SAMOA

FIJI TONGA

FRENCH POLYNESIA
(to France)

BOLIVIA

PARAGUAY

Tropic of Capricorn

4

PITCAIRN
ISLANDS
(to UK)

CHILE

A
R
G
E
N
T
I
N
A

URUGUAY

NEW
ZEALAND

P A C I F I C

O C E A N

FALKLAND ISLANDS
(to UK)

CHILE

5

Antarctic Circle

ANTARCTICA

E   F   G   H

31

The
WORLD'S
REGIONS

North & Central America

EUROPE

Barents Sea

SVALBARD
(to Norway)

Mohns Ridge

Greenland Sea

JAN MAYEN
(to Norway)

Denmark Strait

Iceland

Reykjanes Basin

Newfoundland

St. John's

Nansen Basin

Nansen Cordillera

North Pole

Kap Morris Jesup

Christian X Land

Kong Christian IX Land

Kong Frederik VI Kyst

North Atlantic Mid-Ocean Canyon

Lomonosov Ridge

Makarov Basin

Alpha Cordillera

Mendeleyev Ridge

Kong Frederik VIII Land

Ellesmere Island

Lincoln Sea

GREENLAND
(to Denmark)

NUUK

Davis Strait

Labrador Sea

Labrador Basin

Labrador

Torngat Mountains

Smallwood Reservoir

Laptev Sea

ARCTIC OCEAN

Wandel Sea

Chukchi Plateau

Canada Basin

Queen Elizabeth Islands

Baffin Bay

Baffin Island

Hudson Strait

Ungava Peninsula

Ungava Bay

James Bay

Lake Nipigon

East Siberian Sea

Wrangel Island

Chukchi Sea

Beaufort Sea

Banks Island

Victoria Island

Foxe Basin

Southampton Island

Gulf of Boothia

Hudson Bay

Belcher Islands

Lancaster Sound

Great Bear Lake

Great Slave Lake

Lake Athabasca

Reindeer Lake

Lake Winnipeg

CANADA

Saskatoon

Regina

Limit of summer pack ice

Arctic Circle

Mackenzie

Mackenzie Mountains

Athabasca

Calgary

Edmonton

ASIA

Bering Strait

Saint Lawrence Island

Nunivak Island

Brooks Range

Alaska
(to US)

Mount McKinley
(Denali) 6194m

Alaska Range

Mount Logan
5959m

Juneau

Rocky Mountains

Coast Mountains

Vancouver

Rocky Mou

Nelson Forks

Nechako

Aleutian Basin

Bering Sea

Norton Sound

Yukon

Anchorage

Bristol Bay

Aleutian Range

Alaska Peninsula

Kodiak Island

Gulf of Alaska

Alexander Archipelago

Queen Charlotte Islands

Vancouver Island

Victoria

Seattle

Cascadia Basin

Mount Rainier
4392m

Eugene

Cascade Range

Boise

Aleutian Islands

Aleutian Trench

PACIFIC OCEAN

80

112

113

153

0 km _____ 1000

0 miles _____ 1000

Population

● National capital

○ below 50,000

○ 50,000 to 100,000

◉ 100,000 to 500,000

◼ above 500,000

ATLANTIC
OCEAN

Sargasso Sea

Neres Plain

Hatteras Plain

BERMUDA (to UK)

Bermuda Rise

Halifax
Georges Bank
Montréal
OTTAWA
Lake Ontario
Albany
Boston
Cape Cod
New York
Toronto
Niagara Falls
Philadelphia
Lake Erie
Baltimore
WASHINGTON D.C.
Richmond
Raleigh

Appalachian Mountains

Lake Huron
Lake Michigan
Milwaukee
Detroit
Cleveland
Columbus
Lansing
Chicago
Indianapolis
Springfield
Ohio
Madison
Saint Paul
Des Moines
Lincoln
Kansas City
Columbia

Nashville
Atlanta
Montgomery
Memphis
Jackson
Little Rock
Arkansas
Red River
Oklahoma City

Jacksonville
Blake Plateau
Columbia

BAHAMAS
NASSAU

Straits of Florida

TURKS & CAICOS ISLANDS (to UK)
Miami
HAVANA
CUBA
Tampa
CAYMAN ISLANDS (to UK)
Guantánamo Bay (to US)

VIRGIN ISLANDS (to US)
BRITISH VIRGIN ISLANDS (to UK)
PUERTO RICO (to US)
ANTIGUA & BARBUDA
ANGUILLA (to UK)
ST KITTS & NEVIS
MONTSERRAT (to UK)
GUADELOUPE (to France)
Lesser Antilles
DOMINICA
MARTINIQUE (to France)
ST LUCIA
ST VINCENT & THE GRENADINES
BARBADOS
GRENADA

Greater Antilles

DOMINICAN REPUBLIC
SANTO DOMINGO
HAITI
PORT-AU-PRINCE
JAMAICA KINGSTON

Caribbean Sea

ARUBA (to Neth.)

CURAÇAO (to Neth.)
BONAIRE (to Neth.)

PORT-OF-SPAIN
TRINIDAD & TOBAGO

66

56

Equator

SOUTH
AMERICA

Andes

Colombian Basin

Panama Basin

Cocos Ridge

Colón Ridge

PANAMA
PANAMA CITY

COSTA RICA
SAN JOSÉ

NICARAGUA
MANAGUA
Lake Nicaragua

HONDURAS
TEGUCIGALPA

EL SALVADOR
SAN SALVADOR

GUATEMALA
GUATEMALA CITY

BELIZE
BELMOPAN

Yucatan Peninsula

Gulf of Mexico

Mississippi Delta
New Orleans
Baton Rouge
Houston

MEXICO
MEXICO CITY
Popocatepetl
Pico de Orizaba 5700m

Sierra Madre Oriental

Monterrey
Rio Grande
Dallas
Austin
San Antonio
El Paso

Sierra Madre Occidental

Guadalajara
Acapulco

Galápagos Islands (to Ecuador)

Guatemala Basin

Middle America Trench

Cocos Ridge

East Pacific Rise

PACIFIC
OCEAN

Revillagigedo Islands (to Mexico)

CLIPPERTON ISLAND (to French Polynesia)

Clarion Fracture Zone

Gallego Rise

Lower California
Gulf of California

San Diego
Los Angeles

Grand Canyon
Colorado
Phoenix

Death Valley -86m
Mount Whitney 4418m
Salt Lake City

Great Basin

San Francisco
San Jose

...Fracture Zone

UNITED STATES
OF AMERICA

P l a i n s

Missouri

Denver

Sierra

153

153

153

Tropic of Cancer

Equator

N

35

Western Canada & Alaska

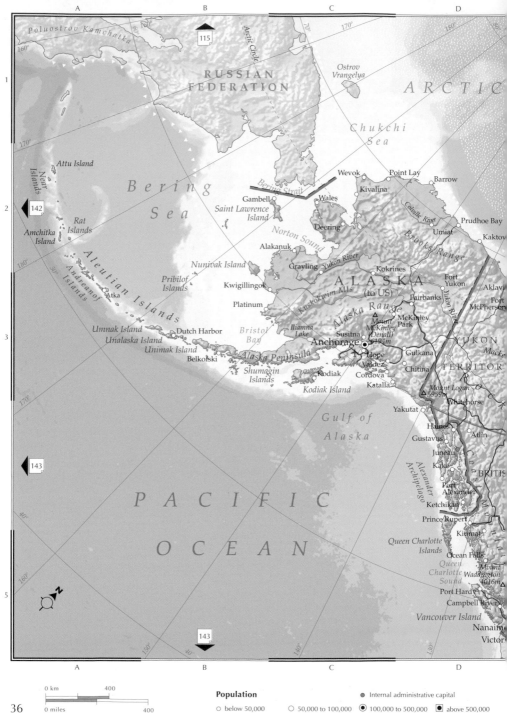

Poluostrov Kamchatka

RUSSIAN
FEDERATION

Arctic Circle

115

Ostrov
Vrangelya

ARCTIC

Chukchi
Sea

Bering Strait

Wevok   Point Lay
Kivalina   Barrow

142

Near
Islands

Attu Island

Bering

Sea

Gambell
Saint Lawrence
Island

Wales

Deering

Colville River

Umiat   Prudhoe Bay

Kaktov

Brooks Range

Rat
Islands

Amchitka
Island

Norton Sound

Alakanuk

Aleutian Islands

Andreanof
Islands

Atka

Pribilof
Islands

Nunivak Island

Kwigillingok

Platinum

Grayling   Yukon River

Kuskokwim Mts

Kokrines

ALASKA
(to US)

Fort
Yukon

Fairbanks

Aklavi

Fort
McPherson

Yukon River

Umnak Island
Unalaska Island
Unimak Island

Dutch Harbor

Belkofski

Bristol
Bay

Iliamna
Lake

Alaska Range

Mount
McKinley
(Denali)
6194m

Susitna

McKinley
Park

YUKON

Alaska Peninsula

Shumagin
Islands

Anchorage

Hope
Valdez

Gulkana

Chitina

Kodiak

Cordova

TERRITORY

Mackē

Kodiak Island

Katalla

Mount Logan
5959m

Whitehorse

Gulf of
Alaska

Yakutat

Haines

Gustavus

Atlin

PACIFIC

Juneau

Kake

BRITIS

Alexander
Archipelago

Port
Alexander

Ketchikan

Prince Rupert

Kitimat

OCEAN

Queen Charlotte
Islands

Ocean Falls

Queen
Charlotte
Sound

Mount
Waddington
4016m

Port Hardy
Campbell River

Vancouver Island

Nanaim

Victor

143

143

0 km   400

0 miles   400

Population

○ below 50,000   ○ 50,000 to 100,000   ◉ 100,000 to 500,000   ■ above 500,000

● Internal administrative capital

OCEAN

Alert

155

Knud Rasmussen Land

GREENLAND
(to Denmark)

Ellesmere Island

Queen Elizabeth Islands

Axel
Heiberg
Island

Ellef Ringnes
Island
Isachsen

Amund
Ringnes
Island

Prince Patrick
Island

Mould Bay

Bathurst
Island

Cornwallis
Island

Devon Island

Baffin
Bay

Arctic Circle

82

Davis Strait

Beaufort
Sea

Banks
Island

Melville
Island

Resolute
(Qausuittuq)

Lancaster Sound

Somerset
Island

Boothia
Peninsula

Baffin Island

achs Harbour
(Ikaahuk)

iktoyaktuk

Amundsen
Gulf

Holman

Viscount Melville
Sound

Prince of
Wales Island

Gulf of Boothia

Cumberland Sound

vik

Paulatuk

Victoria
Island

McClintock Channel

King William
Island

Boothia
Peninsula

Igloolik

Melville
Peninsula

Nettilling
Lake

Fort
Good Hope

Kugluktuk
(Coppermine)

Cambridge Bay
(Ikaluktutiak)

Gjoa Haven
(Uqsuqtuuq)

Kugaaruk
(Pelly Bay)

Foxe
Basin

Amadjuak
Lake

Iqaluit
(Frobisher Bay)

Great
Bear
Lake

Echo Bay

Burnside

Back

NUNAVUT

Repulse Bay

Southampton
Island

Hudson Strait

NORTHWEST
TERRITORIES

Mackenzie

Garry Lake

Baker Lake

Coral
Harbour

Péninsule
d'Ungava

ngsten

Edzo

Yellowknife

Reliance

Dubawnt

Rankin Inlet

Coats
Island

Mansel
Island

QUÉBEC

Fort Simpson

Great Slave
Lake

Lutselk'e
(Snowdrift)

Whale Cove

Fort Providence

Fort Liard

Hay River

Fort Smith

Lake Athabasca

Arviat

Hudson

Bay

Fort Nelson

OLUMBIA

Churchill

Belcher
Islands

38

are

Fort Vermilion

Wollaston Lake

Reindeer Lake

Southern
Indian Lake

Nelson

James
Bay

C

A

N

A

D

A

Prince George

Fort St. John

ALBERTA

Grande Prairie

Athabasca

Fort
McMurray

Athabasca

SASKATCHEWAN

Buffalo
Narrows

Lynn Lake

Thompson

Flin Flon

The Pas

Lake
Winnipeg

MANITOBA

ONTARIO

Edmonton

Mount Robson
3954m

Leduc

North Saskatchewan

Saskatchewan

Prince Albert

Red Deer

Kamloops

Calgary

Kindersley

Yorkton

Saskatoon

Regina

Lake
Manitoba

Winnipeg

Lake of the
Woods

Kelowna

Cranbrook

Medicine Hat

Qu'Appelle

Brandon

Weyburn

Estevan

Lake Superior

Lake Huron

ncouver

Lethbridge

Milk River

Melita

Lake
Michigan

45

U N I T E D   S T A T E S   O F   A M E R I C A

Elevation

| -6000m | -4000m | -2000m | -1000m | -500m | -250m | Below sea level | 0 | 250m | 500m | 1000m | 2000m | 3000m | 4000m | 6000m |

| -19,658ft | -13,124ft | -6562ft | -3281ft | -1640ft | -820ft | -328ft/-100m | 0 | 820ft | 1640ft | 3281ft | 6562ft | 9843ft | 13,124ft | 19,685ft |

Eastern Canada

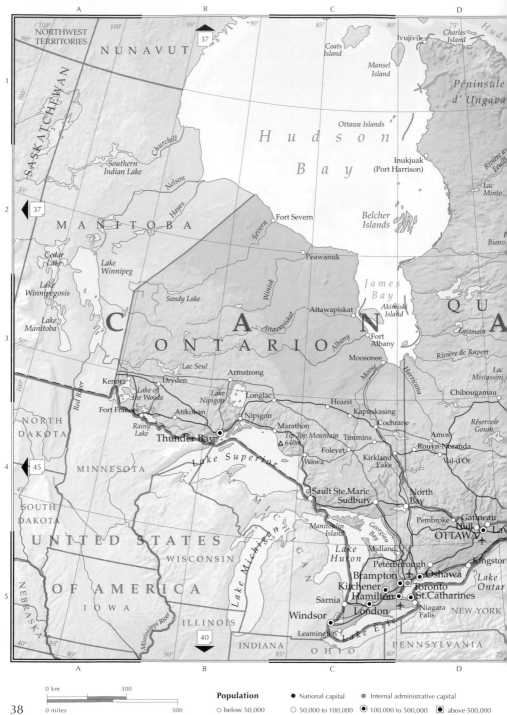

NORTHWEST TERRITORIES

NUNAVUT

SASKATCHEWAN

Churchill

Southern
Indian Lake

Nelson

Hayes

MANITOBA

Severn

Cedar
Lake

Lake
Winnipeg

Lake
Winnipegosis

Sandy Lake

Lake
Manitoba

Winisk

Lac Seul

Armstrong

Kenora

Dryden

NORTH
DAKOTA

Red River

Lake of
the Woods

Lake
Nipigon

Longlac

Fort Frances

Atikokan

Rainy
Lake

Nipigon

Thunder Bay

MINNESOTA

Lake Superior

Coats
Island

Mansel
Island

Ivujivik

Charles
Island

Péninsule
d' Ungava

Hudson

Ottawa Islands

Hudson
Bay

Inukjuak
(Port Harrison)

Rivière de Feuill

Lac
Minto

Fort Severn

Belcher
Islands

Bienv

Peawanuk

CANADA

ONTARIO

James
Bay

Attawapiskat

Akimiski
Island

QU

Eastman

Attawapiskat

Albany

Fort
Albany

Moosonee

Rivière de Rupert

Lac
Mistassini

Moose

Harricana

Chibougamau

Réservoir
Gouin

Hearst

Kapuskasing

Cochrane

Amos

Marathon

Tip Top Mountain
△ 640m

Timmins

Rouyn-Noranda

Val-d'Or

Foleyet

Wawa

Kirkland
Lake

Sault Ste.Marie

Sudbury

North
Bay

Pembroke

Gatineau
Hull

La

SOUTH
DAKOTA

UNITED STATES

NEBRASKA

OF AMERICA

IOWA

WISCONSIN

Lake Michigan

Manitoulin
Island

Lake
Huron

Georgian
Bay

Midland

Peterborough

Brampton

Kitchener

Sarnia

Hamilton

London

Windsor

Leamington

OTTAWA

Kingston

Lake
Ontar

Oshawa

Toronto

St.Catharines

Niagara
Falls

NEW YORK

INDIANA

OHIO

PENNSYLVANIA

ILLINOIS

Lake Erie

MICHIGAN

0 km   300

0 miles   300

Population   ● National capital   ● Internal administrative capital

○ below 50,000   ○ 50,000 to 100,000   ◉ 100,000 to 500,000   ◼ above 500,000

Baffin Island
65°
Strait
Resolution Island
60°
55°
Button Islands
Akpatok Island
Ungava Bay
Kuujjuaq
soak
Rivière à la Baleine
Caniapiscau
Nain
Hopedale
Makkovik
Cape Harrison
Labrador Sea
55°
40°
1
50°
Cartwright
NEWFOUNDLAND
Schefferville
Smallwood Reservoir
Lake Melville
66
2
50°
Churchill
St.Anthony
E C D
Réservoir de Caniapiscau
Gagnon
Réservoir Manicouagan
A
& LABRADOR
Strait of Belle Isl.
Gander
Grand Falls
St.John's
3
Havre-St-Pierre
Île d'Anticosti
Corner Brook
Newfoundland
45°
Sept-Îles
aurentian Mountains
Baie-Comeau
St. Lawrence
Gaspé
Gulf of St. Lawrence
Cape Race
Lac St-Jean
Chicoutimi
Péninsule de Gaspé
Matane
Îles de la Madeleine
Channel-Port aux Basques
50°
Cabot Strait
ST PIERRE & MIQUELON (to France)
quière
Rimouski
Rivière-du-Loup
Edmundston
PRINCE EDWARD ISLAND
66
4
La Tuque
Charlesbourg
NEW BRUNSWICK
Glace Bay
Sydney
Charlottetown
Cape Breton Island
Quebec
Moncton
Trois-Rivières
St-Georges
Oromocto
New Glasgow
Drummondville
Fredericton
Amherst
Truro
ontréal
MAINE
Saint John
NOVA SCOTIA
Sherbrooke
Bay of Fundy
Dartmouth
Halifax
Sable Island
VERMONT
Liverpool
NEW HAMPSHIRE
Yarmouth
ATLANTIC
40°
MASSACHUSETTS
5
Cape Cod
OCEAN
CONNECTICUT
RHODE ISLAND
70°
65°
40°
60°
55°
66

Elevation

-6000m	-4000m	-2000m	-1000m	-500m	-250m	Below sea level	0	250m	500m	1000m	2000m	3000m	4000m	6000m
-19,658ft	-13,124ft	-6562ft	-3281ft	-1640ft	-820ft	-328ft/-100m	0	820ft	1640ft	3281ft	6562ft	9843ft	13,124ft	19,685ft

USA: The Northeast

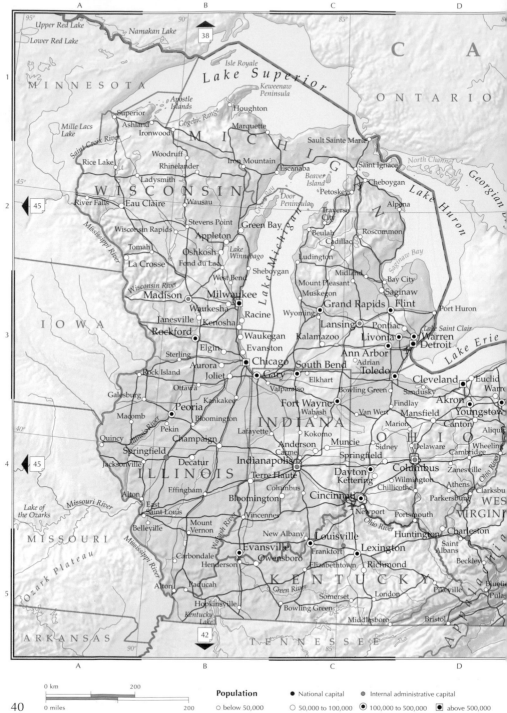

Population

○ below 50,000

○ 50,000 to 100,000

● National capital

◉ 100,000 to 500,000

○ Internal administrative capital

◼ above 500,000

0 km 200

0 miles 200

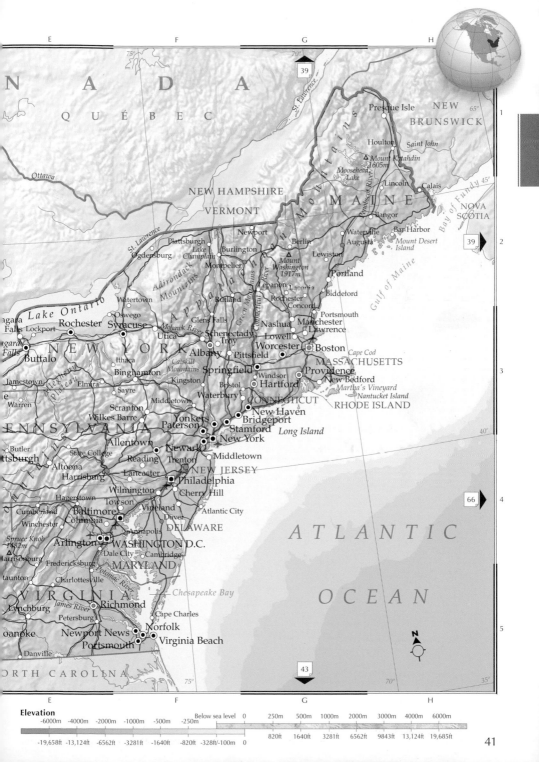

C A N A D A

QUÉBEC

NEW
BRUNSWICK

Presque Isle

Ottawa

Houlton   Saint John

△ Mount Katahdin
1605m

Moosehead
Lake

Lincoln   Calais

NOVA
SCOTIA

NEW HAMPSHIRE
VERMONT

St. Lawrence

Plattsburgh
Lake
Champlain
Ogdensburg   Burlington

Newport   Berlin

M A I N E

Waterville
Augusta

Bar Harbor

Bay of Fundy

Montpelier

Lewiston

Mount Desert
Island

Mount
Washington
1917m

Lebanon

Portland

Gulf of Maine

Rutland

Laconia

Watertown   Rochester
Concord   Biddeford

Lake Ontario

Oswego

Glens Falls
Mohawk River
Utica   Schenectady
Syracuse   Troy   Lowell
Albany   Nashua
Manchester
Lawrence
Portsmouth

agara
Falls   Lockport   Rochester

Niagara
Falls   Buffalo

N E W   Y O R K

Ithaca

Binghamton

Pittsfield   Worcester   Boston

Cape Cod

MASSACHUSETTS
Springfield   Providence
Windsor   New Bedford
Hartford   Martha's Vineyard
Nantucket Island
RHODE ISLAND

Jamestown   Elmira

Warren

Sayre

Catskill
Mountains

Kingston
Bristol
Waterbury

CONNECTICUT

e

Allegheny Plateau

Middletown

Scranton
Wilkes Barre
Yonkers
Paterson

New Haven
Bridgeport
Stamford

Long Island

Butler

State College

Allentown   Newark   New York

P E N N S Y L V A N I A

ttsburgh

Altoona

Reading   Middletown
Trenton

Harrisburg   Lancaster   NEW JERSEY

Wilmington   Philadelphia

Hagerstown   Cherry Hill

Cumberland   Towson   Vineland
Baltimore   Atlantic City

Winchester   Columbia   Dover

Spruce Knob   Annapolis   DELAWARE
1482m

△   Arlington   WASHINGTON D.C.

arrisonburg   Dale City   Cambridge

Fredericksburg   MARYLAND

A T L A N T I C

taunton

Charlottesville   Potomac River

V I R G I N I A   Chesapeake Bay

O C E A N

Lynchburg   James River   Richmond

Petersburg   Cape Charles

oanoke   Newport News   Norfolk
Portsmouth   Virginia Beach

Danville

N

RTH CAROLINA

Elevation

| -6000m | -4000m | -2000m | -1000m | -500m | -250m | Below sea level 0 | 250m | 500m | 1000m | 2000m | 3000m | 4000m | 6000m |

| -19,658ft | -13,124ft | -6562ft | -3281ft | -1640ft | -820ft | -328ft/-100m | 0 | 820ft | 1640ft | 3281ft | 6562ft | 9843ft | 13,124ft | 19,685ft |

41

USA: The Southeast

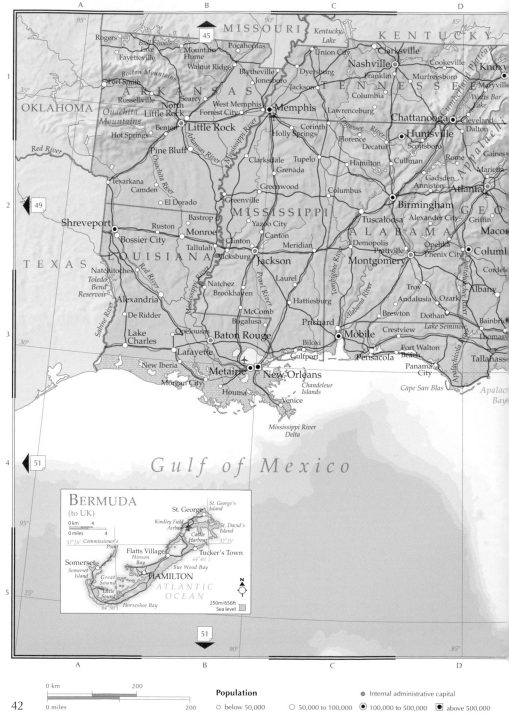

45

49

51

MISSOURI

Rogers
Bull Shoals
Lake
Fayetteville
Mountain
Home
Walnut Ridge
Pocahontas
Blytheville
Jonesboro
Jackson
Union City
Dyersburg
Clarksville
Nashville
Cookeville
Franklin
Murfreesboro
Knoxv
Maryville
Watts Bar
Lake
Kentucky
Lake
KENTUCKY

TENNESSEE

Boston Mountains
Fort Smith
Russellville
North
Little Rock
Searcy
West Memphis
Forrest City
Memphis
Columbia
Lawrenceburg
Chattanooga
Cleveland
Dalton

OKLAHOMA

ARKANSAS

Ouachita
Mountains
Benton
Little Rock
Holly Springs
Corinth
Florence
Decatur
Scottsboro
Huntsville
Rome
Gaines
Marietta

Hot Springs
Pine Bluff
Clarksdale
Tupelo
Grenada
Hamilton
Cullman
Gadsden
Anniston
Atlanta

Red River
Ouachita River
Arkansas River
Mississippi River
Tennessee River

Texarkana
Camden
El Dorado
Greenwood
Columbus
Birmingham
Griffin
GEO
Macon

MISSISSIPPI
Greenville
Shreveport
Ruston
Bastrop
Yazoo City
Tuscaloosa
Alexander City
Opelika
Phenix City
Columb

Bossier City
Monroe
Clinton
Canton
Meridian
Demopolis
Prattville
Montgomery
Cordele

TEXAS
LOUISIANA
Tallulah
Vicksburg
Jackson
Troy
Andalusia
Ozark
Albany

Natchitoches
Toledo
Bend
Reservoir
Natchez
Brookhaven
Laurel
Brewton
Dothan
Bainbridge

Alexandria
De Ridder
McComb
Bogalusa
Hattiesburg
Crestview
Thomas

Lake
Charles
Opelousas
Baton Rouge
Biloxi
Prishard
Mobile
Fort Walton
Beach
Lake Seminole
Tallahass

Lafayette
Gulfport
Pensacola
Apalac

New Iberia
Metairie
New Orleans
Panama
City
Cape San Blas
Bay

Morgan City
Houma
Venice
Chandeleur
Islands

Mississippi River
Delta

Red River
Sabine River
Pearl River
Tombigbee River
Alabama River
Apalachicola
Chattahoochee River

Gulf of Mexico

BERMUDA
(to UK)

0 km   4
0 miles   4

Commissioner's
Point
Somerset
Somerset
Island
Great
Sound
Little
Sound
Horseshoe Bay

Kindley Field
Airbase
Castle
Harbour
Flatts Village
Hinson
Bay
Sue Wood Bay
HAMILTON

St. George
St. George's
Island
St. David's
Island
Tucker's Town

*ATLANTIC
OCEAN*

250m/656ft
Sea level

N

0 km   200
0 miles   200

Population

○ below 50,000
○ 50,000 to 100,000
◉ 100,000 to 500,000
■ above 500,000

● Internal administrative capital

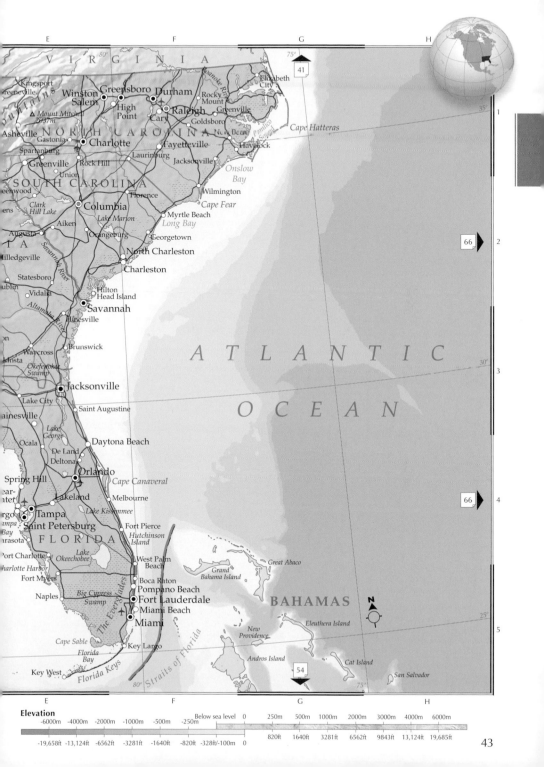

VIRGINIA

Kingsport
reeneville
Winston
Salem
Greensboro
Durham
Elizabeth
City
High
Point
Raleigh
Cary
Greenville
Rocky
Mount
Goldsboro
Asheville
NORTH CAROLINA
New Bern
△ Mount Mitchell
2037m
Charlotte
Fayetteville
Havelock
Cape Hatteras
Gastonia
Spartanburg
Laurinburg
Jacksonville
Greenville
Rock Hill
Union
SOUTH CAROLINA
eenwood
Clark
Hill Lake
Columbia
Lake Marion
Florence
Wilmington
Cape Fear
Myrtle Beach
Onslow
Bay
Aiken
Orangeburg
Long Bay
Augusta
Georgetown
illedgeville
North Charleston
TA
Charleston
Statesboro
Hilton
Head Island
Vidalia
ublin
Altamaha River
Savannah
inesville
Brunswick
on
Waycross
Okefenokee
Swamp
osta
Jacksonville
Lake City
Saint Augustine
ainesville
Lake
George
Ocala
Daytona Beach
De Land
Deltona
Orlando
Cape Canaveral
Spring Hill
ear
ater
Lakeland
Melbourne
argo
ampa
Bay
Lake Kissimmee
Tampa
arasota
Saint Petersburg
Fort Pierce
FLORIDA
Hutchinson
Island
ort Charlotte
Lake
Okeechobee
West Palm
Beach
harlotte Harbor
Fort Myers
Boca Raton
Naples
Big Cypress
Swamp
Pompano Beach
Fort Lauderdale
The Everglades
Miami Beach
Miami
Cape Sable
Key Largo
Florida
Bay
Key West
Florida Keys
Straits of Florida

ATLANTIC

OCEAN

BAHAMAS

Great Abaco
Grand
Bahama Island
New
Providence
Eleuthera Island
Andros Island
Cat Island
San Salvador

N

41
66
66
54

1
2
3
4
5

E   F   G   H

Elevation

| -6000m | -4000m | -2000m | -1000m | -500m | -250m | Below sea level | 0 | 250m | 500m | 1000m | 2000m | 3000m | 4000m | 6000m |

-19,658ft -13,124ft -6562ft -3281ft -1640ft -820ft -328ft/-100m 0   820ft 1640ft 3281ft 6562ft 9843ft 13,124ft 19,685ft

43

USA: Central States

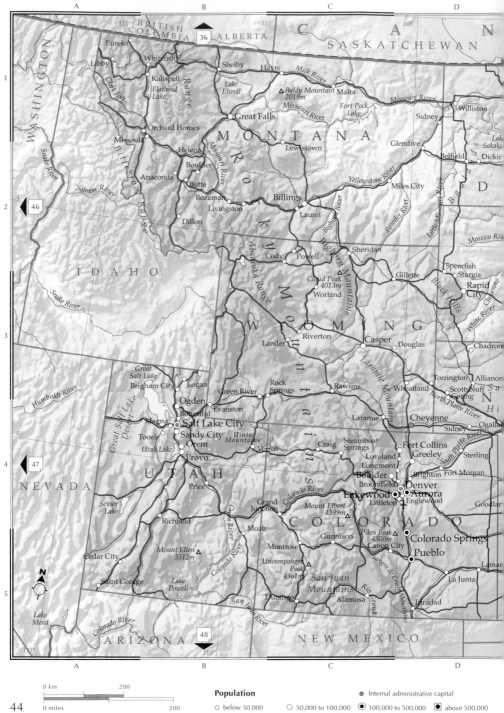

Population

○ below 50,000 ○ 50,000 to 100,000 ◉ 100,000 to 500,000 ▪ above 500,000

● Internal administrative capital

0 km 200

0 miles 200

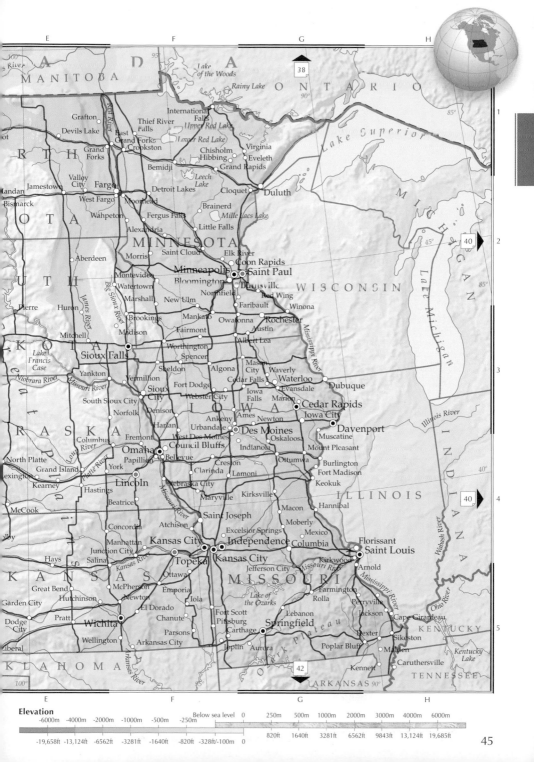

Elevation

-6000m	-4000m	-2000m	-1000m	-500m	-250m	Below sea level	0	250m	500m	1000m	2000m	3000m	4000m	6000m
-19,658ft	-13,124ft	-6562ft	-3281ft	-1640ft	-820ft	-328ft/-100m	0	820ft	1640ft	3281ft	6562ft	9843ft	13,124ft	19,685ft

45

USA: The West

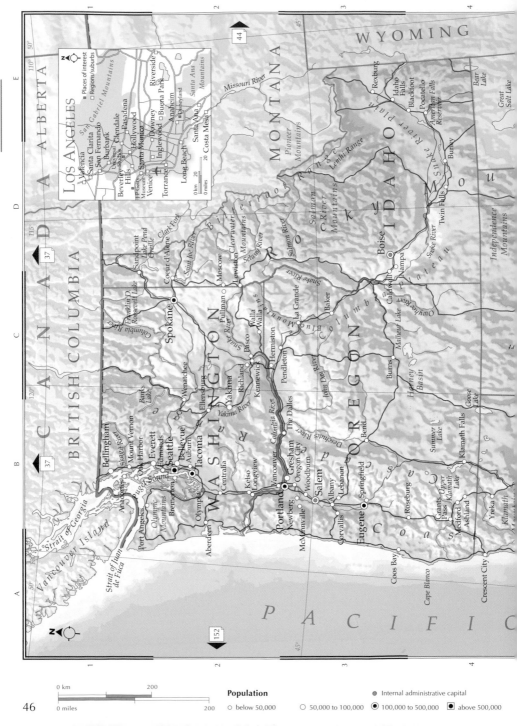

LOS ANGELES

Places of interest
Regions/suburbs

Valencia
Santa Clarita
San Fernando
Burbank
Glendale
Pasadena
Hollywood
Beverly Hills
Universal Studios
Santa Monica
Venice
Inglewood
Downey
Buena Park
Disneyland
Anaheim
Riverside
Santa Ana
Long Beach
Torrance
Costa Mesa

0 km 20
0 miles 20

WYOMING

Missouri River

MONTANA

Rexburg
Idaho Falls
Blackfoot
Pocatello
American Falls Reservoir
Burley
Twin Falls
Snake River

Bear Lake
Great Salt Lake

ALBERTA

CANADA

BRITISH COLUMBIA

Sandpoint
Lake Pend Oreille
Coeur d'Alene
Moscow
Lewiston
Pullman

IDAHO

Boise
Caldwell
Nampa

Independence Mountains

Franklin D. Roosevelt Lake
Columbia River
Spokane

Clark Fork
Saint Joe River

Clearwater Mountains
Selway River
Salmon River

Bitterroot Mountains

Salmon River Mountains

Snake River

Pioneer Mountains
Lemhi Range

Onyhee River
Malheur Lake

ROCKY

Wenatchee
Ellensburg
Yakima

WASHINGTON

Banks Lake

Walla Walla
Pasco
Richland
Kennewick
Hermiston
Pendleton

La Grande
Baker

Blue Mountains

Columbia Plateau

Burns
Harney Basin

Bellingham
Mount Vernon
Oak Harbor
Everett
Edmonds
Seattle
Bellevue
Auburn
Tacoma

Skagit River

Puget Sound

Vancouver Island

Strait of Georgia

Anacortes

Centralia

Kelso
Longview

Vancouver
Gresham
Oregon City
Woodburn
Salem
Albany
Lebanon
Springfield
Eugene

The Dalles
Bend

Deschutes River

OREGON

Summer Lake
Klamath Falls
Goose Lake

Olympic Mountains
Port Angeles
Bremerton
Olympia
Aberdeen

Strait of Juan de Fuca

Newberg
McMinnville
Corvallis

Portland
Columbia River

Yakima River

John Day River

Roseburg
Grants Pass
Upper Klamath Lake
Medford
Ashland
Yreka

Coast

Klamath

Coos Bay

Cape Blanco

Crescent City

PACIFIC

Population

○ below 50,000
○ 50,000 to 100,000
◉ 100,000 to 500,000
■ above 500,000

● Internal administrative capital

0 km 200
0 miles 200

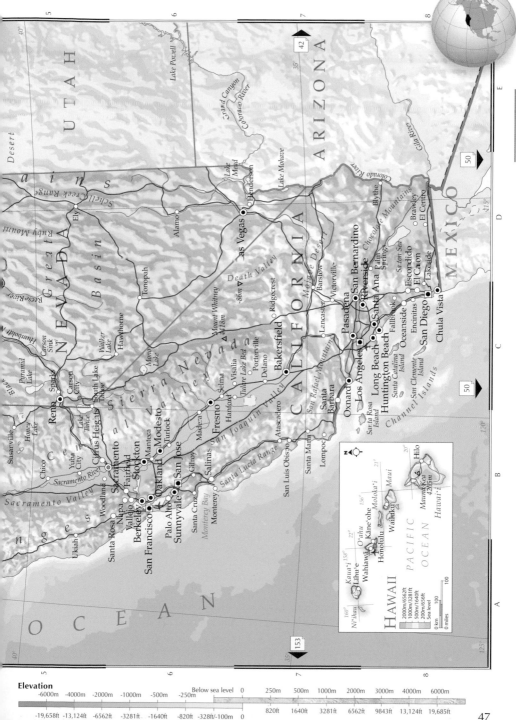

Elevation

-6000m	-4000m	-2000m	-1000m	-500m	-250m	Below sea level	0	250m	500m	1000m	2000m	3000m	4000m	6000m
-19,658ft	-13,124ft	-6562ft	-3281ft	-1640ft	-820ft	-328ft/-100m	0	820ft	1640ft	3281ft	6562ft	9843ft	13,124ft	19,685ft

47

USA: The Southwest

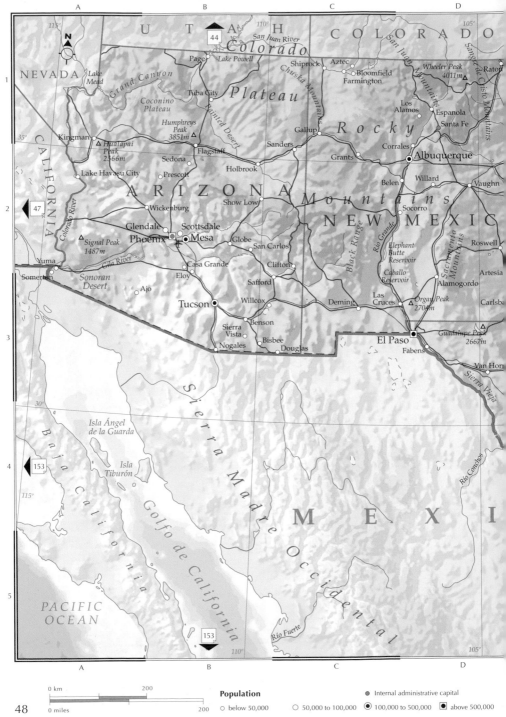

UTAH
COLORADO
NEVADA
San Juan River
44
Colorado
Page Lake Powell
Shiprock Aztec
Lake Mead
Bloomfield
Farmington
Grand Canyon
Tuba City
Plateau
Wheeler Peak 4011m
Raton
Coconino Plateau
Chuska Mountains
Los Alamos
Espanola
Santa Fe
Humphreys Peak 3851m
Gallup
Rocky
Kingman
Hualapai Peak 2566m
Sanders
Corrales
Albuquerque
Flagstaff
CALIFORNIA
Sedona
Holbrook
Grants
Lake Havasu City
Prescott
Belen
Willard
Vaughn
ARIZONA
Mountains
47
Show Low
NEW MEXICO
Wickenburg
Socorro
Colorado River
Roswell
Glendale
Scottsdale
Signal Peak 1487m
Phoenix
Mesa
Globe
San Carlos
Black Range
Rio Grande
Elephant Butte Reservoir
Sacramento Mountains
Yuma
Gila River
Casa Grande
Clifton
Caballo Reservoir
Alamogordo
Artesia
Somerton
Sonoran Desert
Eloy
Safford
Ajo
Willcox
Deming
Las Cruces
Organ Peak 2704m
Carlsbad
Tucson
Benson
Guadalupe Peak 2667m
Sierra Vista
Bisbee
El Paso
Nogales
Douglas
Fabens
Van Horn
Isla Ángel de la Guarda
Sierra Vieja
Isla Tiburón
153
Baja California
Sierra Madre Occidental
Rio Conchos
MEXICO
PACIFIC OCEAN
Golfo de California
153
Rio Fuerte

Population

○ below 50,000
○ 50,000 to 100,000
◉ 100,000 to 500,000
◼ above 500,000

● Internal administrative capital

0 km 200
0 miles 200

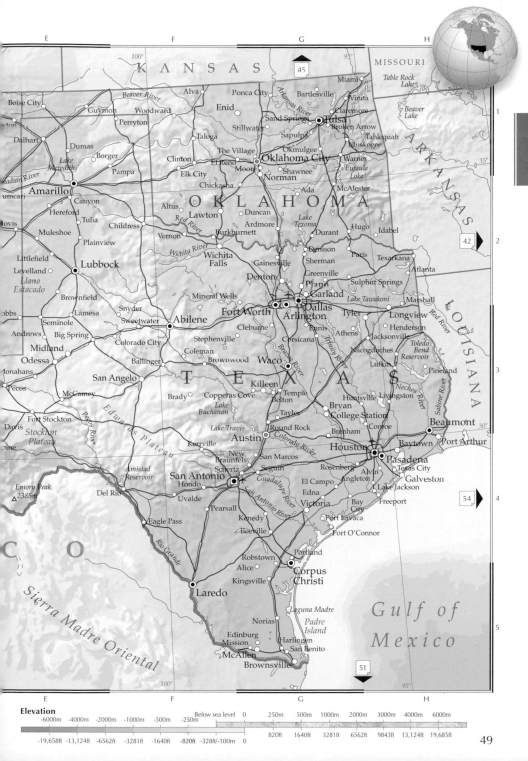

Elevation

-6000m	-4000m	-2000m	-1000m	-500m	-250m	Below sea level	0	250m	500m	1000m	2000m	3000m	4000m	6000m
-19,658ft	-13,124ft	-6562ft	-3281ft	-1640ft	-820ft	-328ft/-100m	0	820ft	1640ft	3281ft	6562ft	9843ft	13,124ft	19,685ft

Mexico

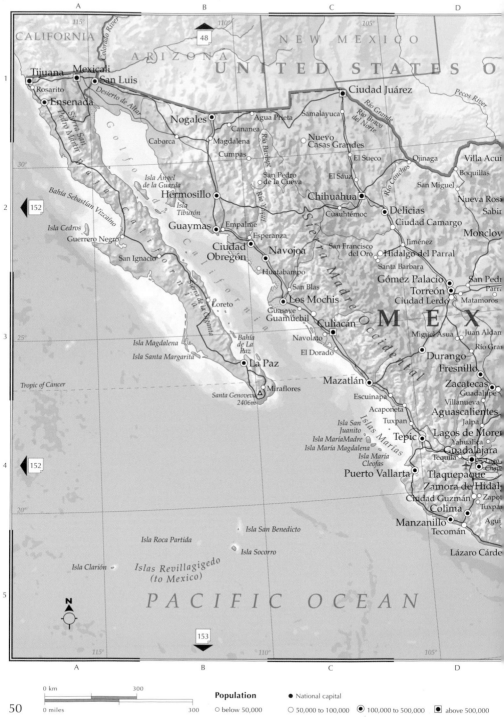

48

Tijuana Mexicali
Rosarito San Luis
Ensenada

Desierto de Altar

Colorado River

115°

110°

105°

Ciudad Juárez

Pecos River

Río Grande
Río Bravo
del Norte

Nogales Agua Prieta Samalayuca
Cananea
Caborca Magdalena Nuevo
Cumpas Casas Grandes

El Sueco Ojinaga Villa Acuñ
El Sáuz Boquillas
San Miguel Nueva Rosi

30°

Sierra San Pedro Mártir

Golfo de California

Isla Ángel
de la Guarda
Isla
Tiburón

San Pedro
de la Cueva

Bahía Sebastián Vizcaíno

152

Isla Cedros
Guerrero Negro

San Ignacio

Hermosillo

Guaymas Empalme
Esperanza
Ciudad
Obregón Navojoá
Huatabampo
San Blas

Cuauhtémoc

Chihuahua
Delicias
Ciudad Camargo

San Francisco
del Oro
Jiménez
Hidalgo del Parral
Santa Barbara

Sabin
Monclov

Río Yaqui
Río Bavispe

Río Conchos

Sierra Madre Occidental

Gómez Palacio San Pedr
Torreón Parra
Ciudad Lerdo Matamoros

M E X

Loreto

Guasave
Guamúchil Culiacán
Navolato
El Dorado

Los Mochis

Miguel Asua Juan Aldan

25°

Isla Magdalena
Isla Santa Margarita

Bahía
de La
Paz

Durango Río Gran
Fresnillo
Zacatecas
Guadalupe
Villanueva
Aguascalientes
Jalpa

Santa Genoveva
2406m

La Paz

Tropic of Cancer

Miraflores

Mazatlán
Escuinapa
Acaponeta
Tuxpan
Tepíc

Sierra de la Giganta

Baja California Sur

152

Isla San
Juanito
Isla MaríaMadre
Isla María Magdalena
Isla María
Cleofas

Islas Marías

Lagos de Morer
Yahualica
Guadalajara
Tequila Lago
Tlaquepaque Chap
Zamora de Hidal
Ciudad Guzmán Zapot
Colima Tuxpa
Manzanillo Agui
Tecomán

Puerto Vallarta

20°

Isla San Benedicto

Isla Roca Partida

Isla Socorro

Lázaro Cárde

Islas Revillagigedo
(to Mexico)

Isla Clarión

N

5 PACIFIC OCEAN

115° 110° 105°

153

0 km 300

0 miles 300

Population ● National capital

○ below 50,000 ○ 50,000 to 100,000 ◉ 100,000 to 500,000 ▣ above 500,000

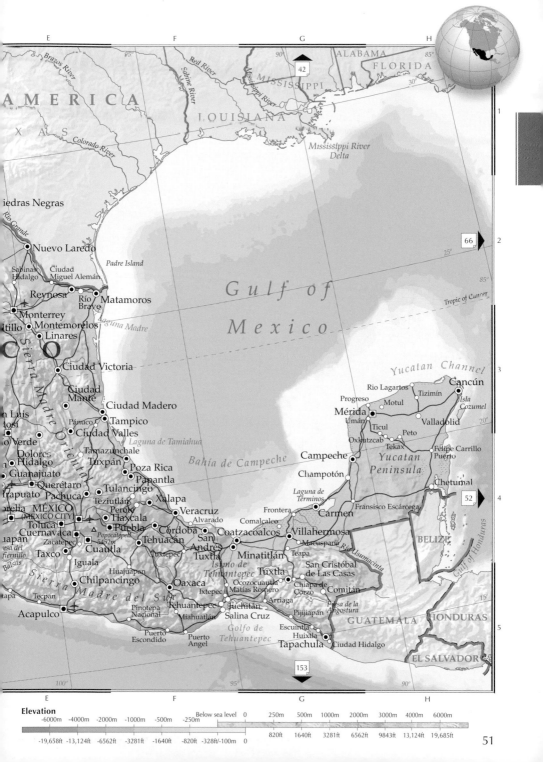

E   F   G   H

Brazos River

Red River

Sabine River

95°

90°

42

ALABAMA

FLORIDA

85°

MEXICO

MISSISSIPPI

Mississippi River

30°

LOUISIANA

1

A M E R I C A

X A S

Colorado River

Mississippi River Delta

Piedras Negras

Río Grande

66

2

Nuevo Laredo

Padre Island

25°

85°

Sabinas Hidalgo

Ciudad Miguel Alemán

Gulf of

Reynosa

Río Bravo

Matamoros

Tropic of Cancer

Monterrey

Mexico

Saltillo

Montemorelos

Laguna Madre

Linares

3

C O

Ciudad Victoria

Yucatan Channel

Cancún

Ciudad Mante

Río Lagartos

Progreso

Tizimín

Isla Cozumel

San Luis

Pánuco

Ciudad Madero

Mérida

Motul

20°

Tampico

Umán

Valladolid

go Verde

Ciudad Valles

Ticul

Peto

Dolores

Tamazunchale

Laguna de Tamiahua

Oxkutzcab

Tekax

Felipe Carrillo

no Hidalgo

Tuxpán

Bahía de Campeche

Campeche

Yucatan

Puerto

Guanajuato

Poza Rica

Champotón

Peninsula

Querétaro

Papantla

Chetumal

rapuato

Pachuca

Tulancingo

Laguna de Términos

52

4

arelia

MÉXICO

Teziutlán

Xalapa

Frontera

Fransisco Escárcega

(MEXICO CITY)

Perote

Veracruz

Comalcalco

Carmen

Toluca

Tlaxcala

Alvarado

Villahermosa

BELIZE

uapan

Popocatépetl

Puebla

Córdoba

Coatzacoalcos

Macuspana

Gulf of Honduras

esa del fiernillo

5452m

Tehuacán

San

Minatitlán

Teapa

Balsas

Cuernavaca

Zacatepec

Cuautla

Andrés

Tuxtla

San Cristóbal

Taxco

Juxtepec

Tuxtla

de Las Casas

Iguala

Istmo de

Comitán

Sierra

Huajuapan

Tehuantepec

Ocozocuautla

Chiapa de

Chilpancingo

Oaxaca

Ixtepec

Matías Romero

Corzo

Madre del Sur

Tehuantepec

Juchitán

Arriaga

Presa de la Angostura

15°

apa

Tecpán

Pinotepa

Miahuatlán

Salina Cruz

Pijijiapán

Acapulco

Nacional

Golfo de

Escuintla

GUATEMALA

HONDURAS

Puerto Escondido

Puerto Angel

Tehuantepec

Huixtla

Tapachula

Ciudad Hidalgo

EL SALVADOR

5

153

100°

95°

90°

E   F   G   H

Elevation

| -6000m | -4000m | -2000m | -1000m | -500m | -250m | Below sea level | 0 | 250m | 500m | 1000m | 2000m | 3000m | 4000m | 6000m |

| -19,658ft | -13,124ft | -6562ft | -3281ft | -1640ft | -820ft | -328ft/-100m | 0 | | 820ft | 1640ft | 3281ft | 6562ft | 9843ft | 13,124ft | 19,685ft |

51

Central America

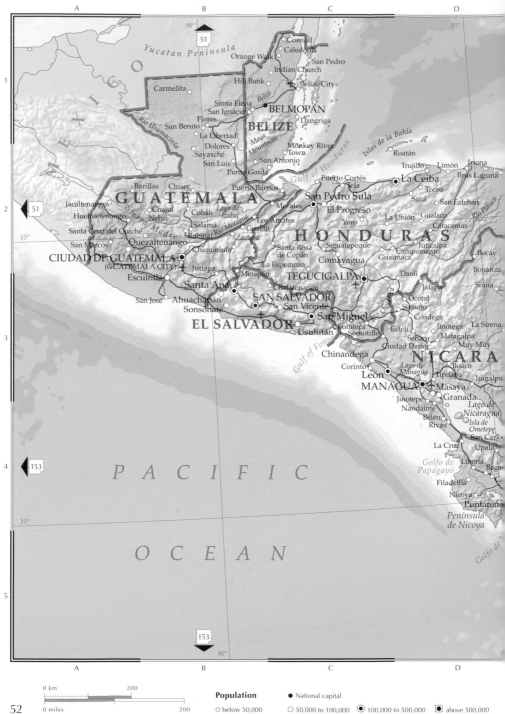

90°

51

Yucatan Peninsula

85°

1

Carmelita

Corozal
Caledonia
Orange Walk
San Pedro
Indian Church
Hill Bank
Belize City

Santa Elena
San Ignacio
Flores
BELMOPAN
San Benito
Dangriga
La Libertad
BELIZE
Dolores
Maya
Sayaxché
Monkey River
Town
San Luis
San Antonio
Punta Gorda
Roatán
Islas de la Bahía
Limón
Iriona
Barillas
Chisec
Puerto Barrios
Puerto Cortés
Trujillo
La Ceiba
Brus Laguna
Tela
Tocoa

GUATEMALA
51

Jacaltenango
Chajul
Cobán
Lago de
Izabal
Morales
San Pedro Sula
Savá
San Esteban
Huehuetenango
Nebaj
Salamá
Los Amates
El Progreso
La Unión
Gualaco
Río Patuca
Santa Cruz del Quiché
Rabinal
Río Motagua
Gralán
Yoro
HONDURAS
Catacamas
San Marcos
Chiquimula
Zacapa
Santa Rosa
de Copán
Siguatepeque
Juticalpa
Bocay
Quezaltenango
La Esperanza
Comayagua
Guaimaca
Campamento
Bonanza
CIUDAD DE GUATEMALA
Metapán
Guaimaca
(GUATEMALA CITY)
Jutiapa
Danlí
Jalapa
Siuna
Escuintla
Santa Ana
Chalatenango
TEGUCIGALPA
San José
Ahuachapán
SAN SALVADOR
Ocotal
Somoto
Condega
Sonsonate
San Vicente
San Miguel
Estelí
Jinotega
La Sirena
EL SALVADOR
Usulután
Cholúteca
Somotillo
Sébaco
Matagalpa
Muy Muy
Ciudad Darío
Chinandega
Boaco
NICARA
Corinto
Lago de
Managua
Tipitapa
Juigalpa
León
MANAGUA
Masaya
Jinotepe
Granada
Nandaime
Lago de
Nicaragua
Belén
Isla de
Rivas
Ometepe
San Carlo
La Cruz
Upala
Golfo de
Liberia
Papagayo
Baga
Filadelfia
Nicoya
Puntarena
Península
de Nicoya

Gulf of Honduras
Gulf of Fonse
Río Choluteca
Golfo de

2

15°

PACIFIC

153

3

OCEAN

10°

153

4

5

90°

A   B   C   D

0 km   200
0 miles   200

Population   ● National capital

○ below 50,000   ○ 50,000 to 100,000   ◉ 100,000 to 500,000   ◼ above 500,000

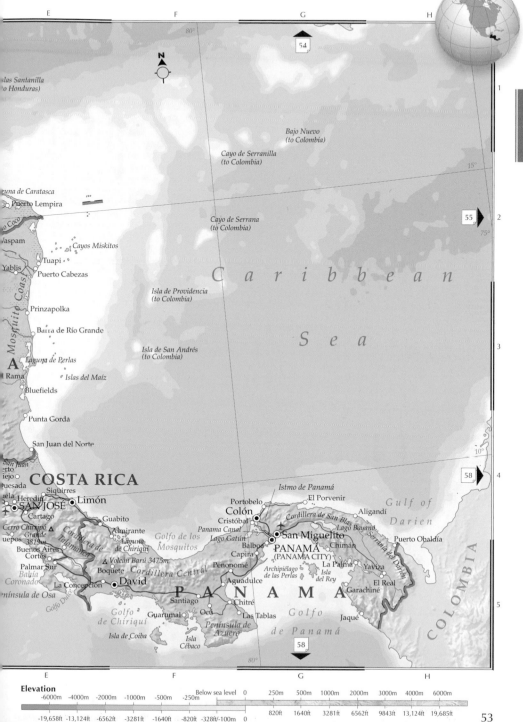

Islas Santanilla
(to Honduras)

Laguna de Caratasca

Puerto Lempira

Río Coco

Waspam

Yablis

Tuapi

Puerto Cabezas

Cayos Miskitos

Prinzapolka

Barra de Río Grande

Laguna de Perlas

Rama

Bluefields

Punta Gorda

San Juan del Norte

Mosquito Coast

NICARAGUA

Bajo Nuevo
(to Colombia)

Cayo de Serranilla
(to Colombia)

Cayo de Serrana
(to Colombia)

Isla de Providencia
(to Colombia)

Isla de San Andrés
(to Colombia)

Islas del Maíz

C a r i b b e a n

S e a

54

55

58

80°

15°

75°

10°

80°

N

1

2

3

4

5

E   F   G   H

COSTA RICA

San Juan
Puerto
Viejo

Quesada

Siquirres

Heredia

SAN JOSÉ

Cartago

Limón

Guabito

Almirante

Laguna
de Chiriquí

Golfo de los
Mosquitos

Cerro Chirripó
Grande
3819m

Buenos Aires

Cortés

Palmar Sur

Bahía
Coronado

Península de Osa

Golfo Dulce

La Concepción

David

Boquete

Volcán Barú 3475m

Cordillera de Talamanca

Cordillera Central

Istmo de Panamá

Portobelo

Colón

Cristóbal

Panama Canal

Lago Gatún

Balboa

Capira

Penonomé

Aguadulce

Chitré

Santiago

Guarumal

Ocú

Las Tablas

El Porvenir

Aligandí

Cordillera de San Blas

Lago Bayano

San Miguelito

PANAMÁ
(PANAMA CITY)

Chimán

La Palma

Isla
del Rey

Archipiélago
de las Perlas

Garachiné

El Real

Yaviza

Puerto Obaldía

Serranía del Darién

Gulf of
Darien

Puerto
Obaldía

Jaqué

Golfo
de Panamá

Golfo
de Chiriquí

Isla de Coiba

Isla
Cébaco

Península de
Azuero

P A N A M A

C O L O M B I A

53

Elevation

-6000m -4000m -2000m -1000m -500m -250m   Below sea level 0   250m 500m 1000m 2000m 3000m 4000m 6000m

-19,658ft -13,124ft -6562ft -3281ft -1640ft -820ft -328ft/-100m 0   820ft 1640ft 3281ft 6562ft 9843ft 13,124ft 19,685ft

The Caribbean

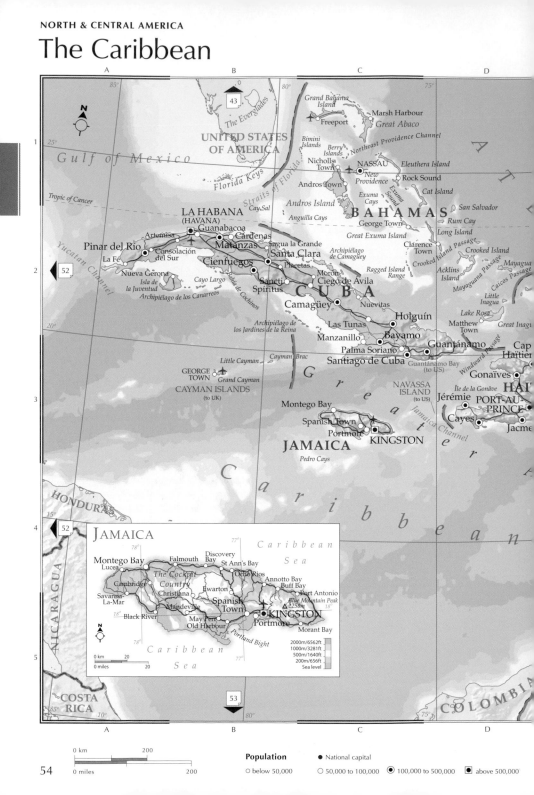

Population

National capital
○ below 50,000
○ 50,000 to 100,000
◉ 100,000 to 500,000
■ above 500,000

54

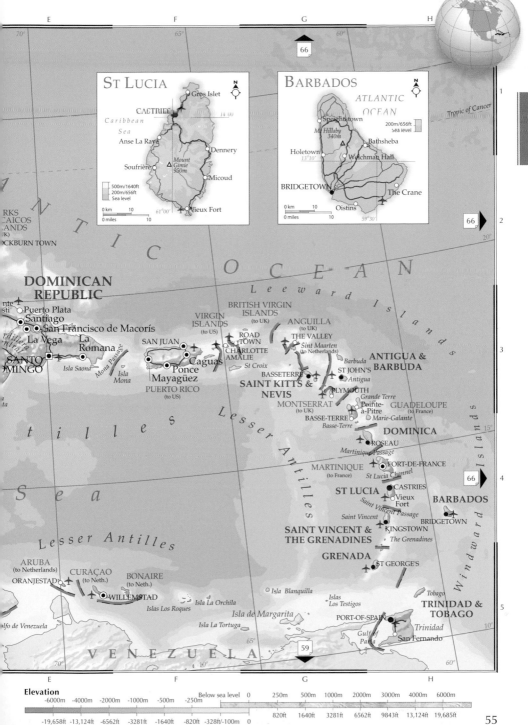

St Lucia

Caribbean Sea

Gros Islet
CASTRIES
14°00
Anse La Raye
Dennery
Soufrière
Mount Gimie 950m
Micoud
61°00
Vieux Fort

500m/1640ft
200m/656ft
Sea level

0 km   10
0 miles   10

Barbados

ATLANTIC OCEAN

Speightstown
Mt Hillaby 340m
Bathsheba
Holetown
13°10
Weichman Hall
BRIDGETOWN
Oistins
The Crane
59°30

200m/656ft
sea level

0 km   10
0 miles   10

66

66

66

Tropic of Cancer

20°

ATLANTIC OCEAN

TURKS & CAICOS ISLANDS (UK)
COCKBURN TOWN

DOMINICAN REPUBLIC
nte
sti
Puerto Plata
Santiago
San Francisco de Macorís
La Vega
La Romana
SANTO DOMINGO
Isla Saona
Isla Mona
Mona Passage

SAN JUAN
Caguas
Ponce
Mayagüez
PUERTO RICO (to US)

VIRGIN ISLANDS (to US)
BRITISH VIRGIN ISLANDS (to UK)
ROAD TOWN
CHARLOTTE AMALIE
St Croix

ANGUILLA (to UK)
THE VALLEY
Sint Maarten (to Netherlands)
Barbuda

ANTIGUA & BARBUDA
ST JOHN'S
Antigua

SAINT KITTS & NEVIS
BASSETERRE
PLYMOUTH
MONTSERRAT (to UK)
BASSE-TERRE
Basse-Terre

Grande Terre
Pointe-à-Pitre
GUADELOUPE (to France)
Marie-Galante

DOMINICA
ROSEAU
Martinique Passage

MARTINIQUE (to France)
FORT-DE-FRANCE
St Lucia Channel

ST LUCIA
CASTRIES
Vieux Fort
Saint Vincent Passage

BARBADOS
BRIDGETOWN

SAINT VINCENT & THE GRENADINES
Saint Vincent
KINGSTOWN
The Grenadines

GRENADA
ST GEORGE'S

Leeward Islands
Lesser Antilles
Antilles
Sea
Windward Islands

15°

ARUBA (to Netherlands)
ORANJESTAD
CURAÇAO (to Neth.)
WILLEMSTAD
BONAIRE (to Neth.)
Isla Blanquilla
Islas Los Roques
Isla La Orchila
Islas Los Testigos
Tobago
Isla de Margarita
Isla La Tortuga

TRINIDAD & TOBAGO
PORT-OF-SPAIN
Trinidad
San Fernando
Gulf of Paria

olfo de Venezuela
Golfo de Venezuela
VENEZUELA

10°

59

70°   65°   60°

Elevation

-6000m	-4000m	-2000m	-1000m	-500m	-250m	Below sea level 0	250m	500m	1000m	2000m	3000m	4000m	6000m
-19,658ft	-13,124ft	-6562ft	-3281ft	-1640ft	-820ft	-328ft/-100m 0	820ft	1640ft	3281ft	6562ft	9843ft	13,124ft	19,685ft

South America

ATLANTIC OCEAN

Mid-Atlantic Ridge

Equator

Ceará Plain

Amazon Fan

Demerara Plain

Puerto Rico Trench

Lesser Antilles

Greater Antilles

Caribbean Sea

Venezuelan Basin

Colombian Basin

Panama Basin

Peru Basin

Peru-Chile Trench

Hispaniola

Jamaica

Trinidad

Puerto Rico

Santa Marta
Barranquilla
Cartagena
Montería

COLOMBIA
BOGOTÁ
Cúcuta
Bucaramanga
Medellín
Manizales
Pereira
Cali
Ibagué
Pasto

VENEZUELA
CARACAS
Valencia
Maracay
Maracaibo
Barquisimeto
Barinas
San Cristóbal
Cumaná

Orinoco

GUYANA
GEORGETOWN
Linden

(claimed by
Venezuela)

SURINAME
PARAMARIBO

FRENCH GUIANA
(to France)
CAYENNE

(claimed by
Suriname)

Guiana Highlands

Manaus

Branco

Rio Negro

Amazon Basin

Santarém

Belém

São Luís

Teresina

Fortaleza
Mossoró
Natal
João Pessoa
Recife
Maceió
Aracaju

Planalto da Borborena

São Francisco

Salvador

Represa de Sobradinho

Abrolhos Bank

BRAZIL

BRASÍLIA

Goiânia

Brazilian Highlands

Mato Grosso

Planalto de Mato Grosso

Serra Formosa

Serra do Cachimbo

Chapada dos Parecis

Cuiabá

Porto Velho

Xingu

Tocantins

Araguaia

Madeira

Tapajós

Purus

Juruá

Içá

Japurá

Putumayo

Napo

Marañón

Ucayali

ECUADOR
QUITO
Esmeraldas
Portoviejo
Manta
Guayaquil
Machala
Riobamba
Cuenca
Chimborazo
6310m

Gulf of Guayaquil

Piura
Chiclayo
Trujillo
Callao
LIMA

PERU

Andes

Cusco
Arequipa
Tacna
Arica

Lake Titicaca

BOLIVIA
LA PAZ
SUCRE
Cochabamba
Oruro
Santa Cruz

Altiplano

Beni

Rio Branco

67
66
35
35

0 km 500
0 miles 500

Population   • National capital

o below 50,000   o 50,000 to 100,000   ◉ 100,000 to 500,000   ▣ above 500,000

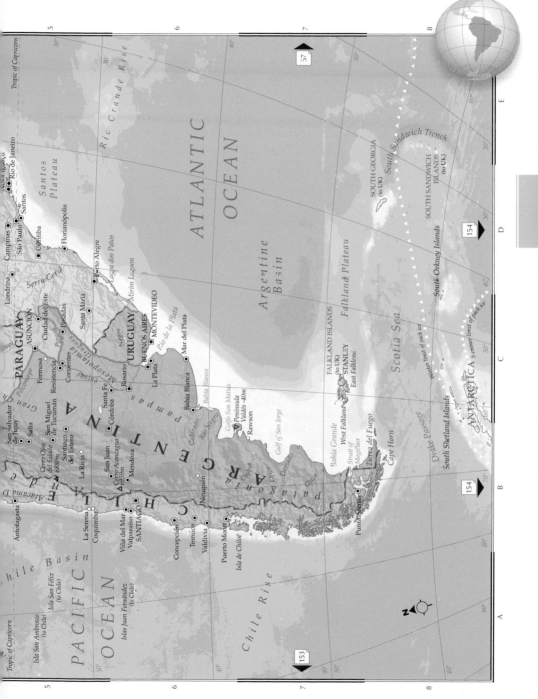

ATLANTIC

OCEAN

PACIFIC

OCEAN

ARGENTINA

CHILE

PARAGUAY

URUGUAY

ASUNCIÓN

BUENOS AIRES

MONTEVIDEO

SANTIAGO

Rio de Janeiro

São Paulo

Santos

Curitiba

Florianópolis

Pôrto Alegre

Santa Maria

Ciudad del Este

Posadas

Campinas

Londrina

Serra Geral

Santos Plateau

Rio Grande Rise

Tropic of Capricorn

Argentine Basin

Falkland Plateau

FALKLAND ISLANDS (to UK)

STANLEY

East Falkland

West Falkland

Scotia Sea

South Orkney Islands

SOUTH GEORGIA (to UK)

SOUTH SANDWICH ISLANDS (to UK)

South Sandwich Trench

South Shetland Islands

Summer limit of pack ice

Winter limit of pack ice

ANTARCTICA

Drake Passage

Cape Horn

Tierra del Fuego

Strait of Magellan

Punta Arenas

Bahía Grande

Río Gallegos

Desado

Chico

Chubut

Golfo San Jorge

Rawson

Peninsula Valdés -40m

Golfo San Matías

Bahía Blanca

Bahía Blanca

Mar del Plata

La Plata

Río de la Plata

Río de la Plata

Rosario

Santa Fe

Córdoba

Paraná

Paraná

Negro

Mesopotamia

Gran Chaco

Pilcomayo

Pilcomayo

Bermejo

Corrientes

Resistencia

Formosa

Salta

San Miguel de Tucumán

Santiago del Estero

La Rioja

San Salvador de Jujuy

Cerro Ojos del Salado 6880m

Cerro Aconcagua 6959m

San Juan

Mendoza

Neuquén

Río Negro

Colorado

Pampas

Patagonia

Limay

Isla de Chiloé

Puerto Montt

Valdivia

Temuco

Concepción

SANTIAGO

Valparaíso

Viña del Mar

Coquimbo

La Serena

Antofagasta

Desierto de Atacama

Chile Basin

Chile Rise

Isla San Félix (to Chile)

Isla San Ambrosio (to Chile)

Islas Juan Fernández (to Chile)

Tropic of Capricorn

Laguna dos Patos

Mirim Lagoon

57

154

154

153

N

Caribbean Sea

Lesser Ant

ARUBA (to Netherlands)
CURAÇAO (to Neth.)
BONAIRE (to Neth.)

Península de la Guajira

Golfo de Venezuela

Islas Los Roques
Isla
La Or

Santa Marta
Ríohacha
Makao
Puerto López
Punto Fijo
Coro
Puerto Cumarebo
Dabajuro
Sabaneta
Puerto Cabello
CARACA

Barranquilla
Ciénaga
Pico Cristóbal Colón 5775m
La Concepción
Maracaibo
San Felipe
Valencia
Maracay

Soledad
Sabanalarga
Cabimas
San Juan de los Mor

Cartagena
Valledupar
Machiques
Ciudad Ojeda
Caroa
Barquisimeto

El Carmen de Bolívar
San Carlos del Zulia
Valera
Acarigua
Valle de la Pascu

Sinceleio
Magangué
El Vigía
Mérida
Guanare
Calabozo

Montería
Cereté
Ocaña
Pico Bolívar 5001m
Barinas
Río Guanare

Planeta Rica
Aguachica
Pamplona
San Fernando

Aguachica
Caucasia
Cúcuta
San Cristóbal
Río Apure
Río Arauca
V E N

Dabeiba
Yarumal
Bucaramanga
Arauca

Bello
Barrancabermeja
Río Meta

Medellín
Puerto Berrío
Puerto Carreñ

Itagüí
Sogamoso
Puerto Ayacuc

Nuquí
Quibdó
Tunja
Yopal
Río Orinoco

Manizales
Zipaquira

Pereira
BOGOTÁ

Armenia
Girardot
Villavicencio

Buenaventura
Tuluá
Ibagué
Espinal
Río Meta
Río Guaviare
Puerto Inírida

Buga
Palmira

Cali
Neiva

Popayán
Garzón
San José del Guaviare
Río Vaupés
Mitú

Tumaco
Pitalito
Florencia

Nevado de Cumbal 4764m
Pasto
Mocoa
Río Apaporis

Ipiales
Orito

C O L O M B I A

Orinoquía-Amazonía

Equator

E C U A D O R
Río Putumayo
Río Caquetá
Río Japurá

Río Napo

P E R U
Amazon
Río Içá

PANAMA
Gulf of Darien
Golfo de Panamá

PACIFIC OCEAN

0 km   200
0 miles   200

Population
○ National capital
○ below 50,000
○ 50,000 to 100,000
◉ 100,000 to 500,000
▣ above 500,000

ATLANTIC

OCEAN

SAINT VINCENT &
THE GRENADINES

BARBADOS

GRENADA

Isla Blanquilla
Isla de
Margarita
Portuga
La Asunción
Islas Los Testigos
Tobago
Porlamar
maná
Carúpano
TRINIDAD &
TOBAGO
Cariaco
Güira
Gulf of
Paria
Trinidad
Puerto La Cruz
Barcelona
San Mateo
Serpent's Mouth
Maturín
Anaco
Cantaura
raza
El Tigre
Tucupita

Río Orinoco

Ciudad Guayana
Upata
Ciudad
Bolívar
Embalse de Guri
Matthews
Ridge
Charity
U E L A
El Callao
El Dorado
Spring Garden
Aurora
Parika
GEORGETOWN
New
Amsterdam
Totness
PARAMARIBO
Nieuw Amsterdam
St-Laurent-du-Maroni
Sinnamary
Kourou
Peters Mine
Bartica
Rockstone
Linden
Nieuw
Nickerie
Salto
Angel
Kamarang
GUYANA
Orealla
Apoera
Kaaimanston
CAYENNE
Mount Roraima
2810m
SURINAME
W. J. van
Blommesteinmeer
Grand-
Santi
Ouanary
Pakaraima Mountains
Kurupukari
Juliana Top
1230m
FRENCH
GUIANA
(to France)
St-Georges
(Venezuela claims all
of Guyana west of
Essequibo River)
Lethem
Camopi
Tumuc-Humac Mountains
(claimed by
Suriname)
Acarai Mountains
(claimed by
Suriname)
Rio Negro
Equator
B R A Z I L
z o n   B a s i n
Amazon
Amazon
Amazon
Rio Purús
Rio Tapajós

Río Paragua
Rio Caroní
Rio Caura
Guiana
Rio Orinoco
Guiana   Highlands
Cuyuni River
Essequibo River
Courantyne River
Maroni River
Montagnes
de la Trinité
Montagne
Tortue

55
67
62
62

60°
55°
10°
5°

E   F   G   H

Elevation

-6000m	-4000m	-2000m	-1000m	-500m	-250m		Below sea level	0	250m	500m	1000m	2000m	3000m	4000m	6000m

-19,658ft -13,124ft -6562ft -3281ft -1640ft -820ft -328ft/-100m 0   820ft 1640ft 3281ft 6562ft 9843ft 13,124ft 19,685ft

Western South America

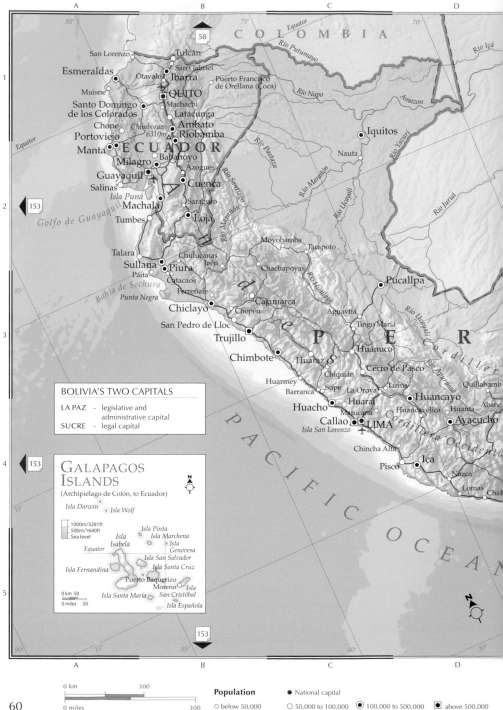

BOLIVIA'S TWO CAPITALS

LA PAZ - legislative and administrative capital
SUCRE - legal capital

GALAPAGOS ISLANDS
(Archipiélago de Colón, to Ecuador)

1000m/3281ft
500m/1640ft
Sea level

Isla Darwin   Isla Wolf

Isla Pinta
Isla Marchena
Isla
Isabela   Isla
Genovesa
Isla San Salvador
Equator   Isla Santa Cruz
Isla Fernandina

Puerto Baquerizo
Moreno   Isla
Isla Santa María   San Cristóbal
Isla Española

0 km   50
0 miles   50

Population
○ below 50,000
○ 50,000 to 100,000
◉ 100,000 to 500,000
◼ above 500,000

● National capital

0 km   300
0 miles   300

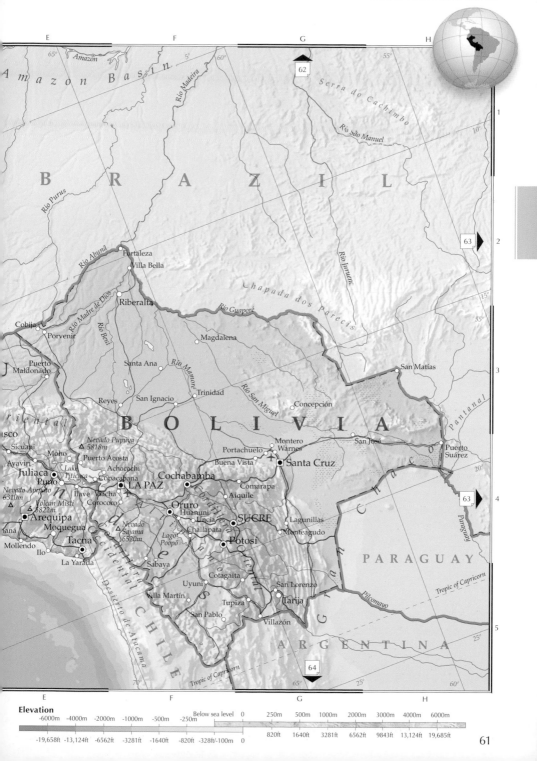

65°   Amazon   5°   60°   55°

Amazon Basin

Rio Madeira

Serra do Cachimbo

62

Rio São Manuel

10°   1

B R A Z I L

Rio Purus

Rio Abuná   Rio Jauru   63   2

Fortaleza
Villa Bella

Rio Madre de Dios   Chapada dos Parecis   15°

Riberalta   Rio Guaporé   55°

Rio Beni

Cobija
Porvenir   Magdalena

Puerto   Santa Ana   Rio Mamoré   San Matías
Maldonado   J   3
    Reyes   San Ignacio   Trinidad   Rio San Miguel
    Concepción
Sicuani   B O L I V I A   Pantanal
ISCO   Nevado Pupuya   San José
    △ 5818m   Montero   Puerto
Moho   Puerto Acosta   Portachuelo   Warnes   Suárez
Ayaviri   Achacachi   Buena Vista   Santa Cruz   20°
Juliaca   Lago   Copacabana   Cochabamba   63   4
Puno   Titicaca   Comarapa
Nevado Ampato   Ilave   Viacha   LA PAZ   Aiquile
6310m   Corocoro   Oruro   Lagunillas
△   Volcán Misti   Huanuni   SUCRE
Arequipa   5822m   Uncía   Monteagudo
Moquegua   Nevado   Challapata   Potosí
Tacna   Sajama   Lago   P A R A G U A Y
Mollendo   6520m   Poopó
Ilo   Sabaya   Cotagaita
La Yarada   Uyuni   San Lorenzo   Tropic of Capricorn
    Villa Martín   Tupiza   Tarija
    San Pablo   Villazón   Paraguay
    Pilcomayo   25°   5
    A R G E N T I N A
70°   64
    Tropic of Capricorn   65°   60°

Elevation

-6000m	-4000m	-2000m	-1000m	-500m	-250m	Below sea level 0	250m	500m	1000m	2000m	3000m	4000m	6000m

-19,658ft -13,124ft -6562ft -3281ft -1640ft -820ft -328ft/-100m 0   820ft 1640ft 3281ft 6562ft 9843ft 13,124ft 19,685ft

Brazil

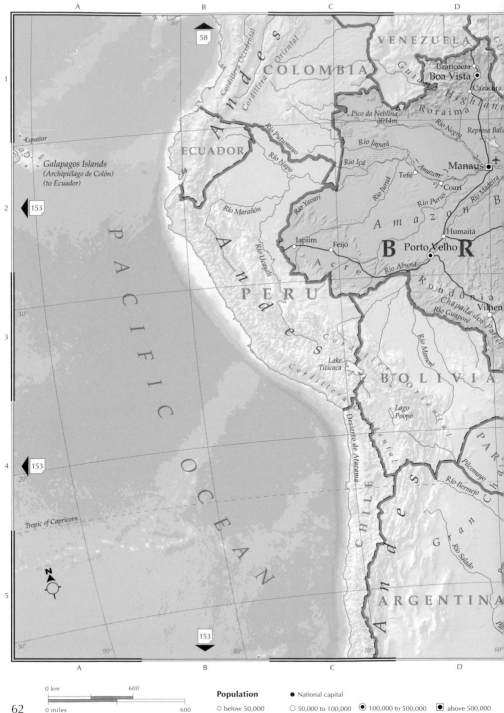

58

153

153

153

Equator

Galapagos Islands
(Archipiélago de Colón)
(to Ecuador)

VENEZUELA

COLOMBIA

ECUADOR

Boa Vista

Uraricoera

Caracora

Guiana Highlands

Roraima

Pico da Neblina
3014m

Río Negro

Represa Bal

PACIFIC OCEAN

Cordillera Occidental

Cordillera Oriental

Río Putumayo

Río Napo

Río Japurá

Río Içá

Río Marañón

Río Yavari

Río Juruá

Río Purus

Río Madeira

Manaus

Tefé

Coari

Amazon

Amazon

Japiim

Feijó

B

Porto Velho

R

Humaitá

PERU

Acre

Río Abunã

Rondonia

Chapada dos Parec

Vilhen

Río Guaporé

Lake
Titicaca

Cordillera

Cordillera Oriental

Río Mamoré

BOLIVIA

Lago
Poopó

Desierto de Atacama

PARA

Pilcomayo

Río Bermejo

CHILE

Andes

Río Salado

Gran

C

Tropic of Capricorn

ARGENTINA

N

62

Population		● National capital

0 km 600

0 miles 600

○ below 50,000   ○ 50,000 to 100,000   ◉ 100,000 to 500,000   ■ above 500,000

BRAZIL

ATLANTIC OCEAN

Equator

Tropic of Capricorn

Elevation

					Below sea level	0	250m	500m	1000m	2000m	3000m	4000m	6000m
-6000m	-4000m	-2000m	-1000m	-500m	-250m								
-19,658ft	-13,124ft	-6562ft	-3281ft	-1640ft	-820ft	-328ft/-100m	0	820ft	1640ft	3281ft	6562ft	9843ft	13,124ft	19,685ft

Southern South America

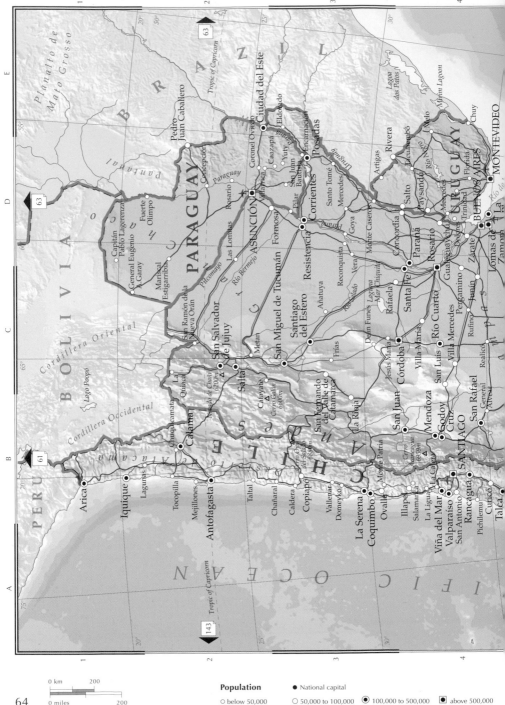

Population

- ● National capital
- ○ below 50,000
- ○ 50,000 to 100,000
- ◉ 100,000 to 500,000
- ◼ above 500,000

0 km   200

0 miles   200

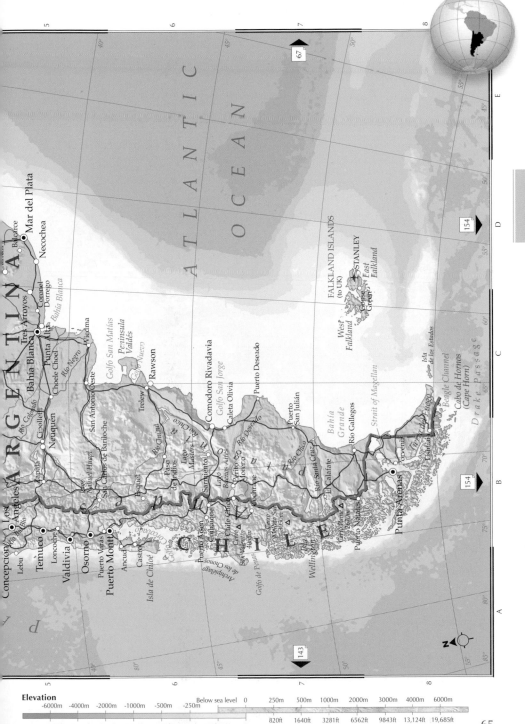

ATLANTIC

OCEAN

ARGENTINA

Mar del Plata
Balcarce
Necochea
Coronel
Dorrego
Tres Arroyos
Bahía Blanca
Punta Alta
Choele Choel
Coronel
Viedma
Río Negro
Golfo San Matías
Península
Valdés
Golfo Nuevo
Rawson
Trelew

Neuquén
San Antonio Oeste
San Carlos de Bariloche
Lago
Nahuel Huapi
Paso
de Indios
Esquel
Lago
Musters
Sarmiento
Río Chico
Lago
Buenos
Aires
Comodoro Rivadavia
Golfo San Jorge
Caleta Olivia
Puerto Deseado

Río Colorado
Colorado
Zapala
Río Negro

Puerto
San Julián
Bahía
Grande
Río Gallegos
Río Santa Cruz
El Calafate

FALKLAND ISLANDS
(to UK)
West
Falkland
East
Falkland
STANLEY
Goose
Green

Isla
de los Estados
Strait of Magellan
Beagle Channel
Cabo de Hornos
(Cape Horn)
Drake Passage

Tierra del Fuego
Porvenir
Ushuaia
Punta Arenas
Puerto Natales

CHILE

Concepción
Los
Angeles
Lebu
Temuco
Loncoche
Valdivia
Osorno
Loncoche
Puerto Varas
Ancud
Castro
Puerto Montt
Isla de Chiloé
Archipiélago
de los Chonos
Golfo de Penas
Golfo
Corcovado
Puerto Aísén
Coihaique
Chile Chico
Cochrane
Isla
Wellington

Río Bío Bío

Perito
Moreno

Monte San
Valentín
4058m
Monte Fitz Roy
3405m
Monte San
3050m

154
154
143

z

Elevation

-6000m	-4000m	-2000m	-1000m	-500m	-250m	Below sea level	0	250m	500m	1000m	2000m	3000m	4000m	6000m
-19,658ft	-13,124ft	-6562ft	-3281ft	-1640ft	-820ft	-328ft/-100m	0	820ft	1640ft	3281ft	6562ft	9843ft	13,124ft	19,685ft

The Atlantic Ocean

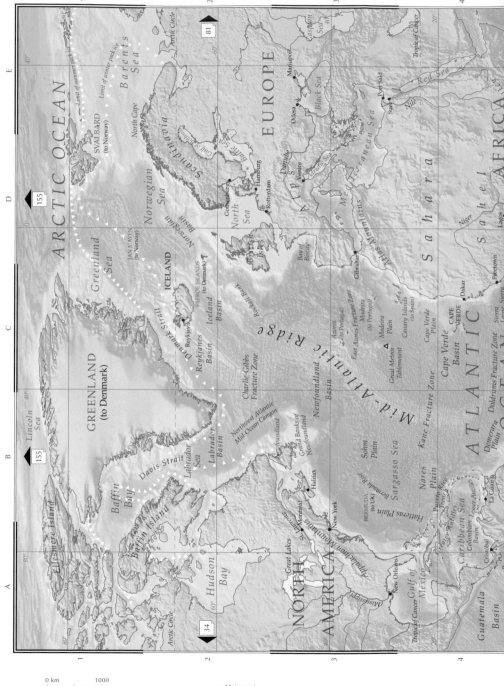

ARCTIC OCEAN

EUROPE

AFRICA

NORTH AMERICA

ATLANTIC OCEAN

Ellesmere Island

Lincoln Sea

Baffin Bay

Baffin Island

GREENLAND (to Denmark)

Davis Strait

Labrador Sea

Labrador Basin

Denmark Strait

Greenland Sea

JAN MAYEN (to Norway)

SVALBARD (to Norway)

Barents Sea

North Cape

Scandinavia

Gulf of Bothnia

Norwegian Sea

Norwegian Basin

ICELAND

Reykjavík

Reykjanes Basin

Iceland Basin

FAEROE ISLANDS (to Denmark)

Rockall Bank

Charlie-Gibbs Fracture Zone

Mid-Atlantic Ridge

Arctic Circle

Limit of summer pack ice

Limit of winter pack ice

Hudson Bay

Great Lakes

St Lawrence

Montreal

Appalachian Mountains

Halifax

New York

Gulf of Mexico

New Orleans

Mississippi

Tropic of Cancer

Newfoundland

Grand Banks of Newfoundland

Northwest Atlantic Mid-Ocean Canyon

Sohm Plain

Sargasso Sea

Bermuda Rise

BERMUDA (to UK)

Hatteras Plain

Nares Plain

Kane Fracture Zone

Newfoundland Basin

Demerara Plain

Caribbean Sea

Colombian Basin

Lesser Antilles

Puerto Rico Trench

Greater Antilles

Cristóbal

La Guaira

Guatemala Basin

North Sea

Baltic Sea

British Isles

Gothenburg

Hamburg

Rotterdam

Danube

Alps

Venice

Mediterranean Sea

Bay of Biscay

Gibraltar

Atlas Mountains

Azores (to Portugal)

East Azores Fracture Zone

Madeira (to Portugal)

Madeira Plain

Canary Islands (to Spain)

Great Meteor Tablemount

Cape Verde Plain

Cape Verde Basin

CAPE VERDE

Kane Fracture Zone

Doldrums Fracture Zone

Demerara Plain

Sahara

Sahel

Niger

Lagos

Dakar

Freetown

Sierra Leone

Caspian Sea

Black Sea

Mariupol

Odesa

Red Sea

Port Said

Suez

Nile

Tropic of Cancer

Arctic Circle

0 km 1000
0 miles 1000

• Major port

INDIAN OCEAN

Tropic of Capricorn

Madagascar

Mozambique Channel

Lake Victoria
Lake Tanganyika
Lake Nyasa
Zambezi
Great
Congo

Southwest Indian Ridge

Mozambique Plateau

Cape Town
Cape of Good Hope

Agulhas Plateau
Agulhas Basin

Enderby Plain

Limit of winter pack ice
Antarctic Circle

Orange Fan

Angola Basin
Zone Guinea Basin
Ascension Fracture Zone
ASCENSION ISLAND (to UK)
ST HELENA (to UK)

Zubov Seamount
Walvis Ridge

Cape Basin

Atlantic-Indian Ridge

BOUVET ISLAND (to Norway)

Atlantic-Indian Basin

Lazarev Sea

Limit of summer pack ice

ANTARCTICA

Pernambuco Plain
Fernando de Noronha (to Brazil)
Brazil Basin
Recife
Paraná Plain

Mid - Atlantic Ridge

Ilha da Trindade (to Brazil)

TRISTAN DA CUNHA (to St Helena)
Gough Island (to Tristan da Cunha)

S-tess Seamount

Gough Fracture Zone

SOUTH OCEAN

Vitória Seamount
Rio Grande Rise

Santos Plateau
Rio de Janeiro

Argentine Basin

Zapiola Ridge

SOUTH GEORGIA (to UK)
SOUTH SANDWICH ISLANDS (to UK)
South Sandwich Trench
East Scotia Basin
America-Antarctica Ridge

Weddell Plain

SOUTH AMERICA

Andes

Paraná
Buenos Aires

Gulf of San Matías
Gulf of San Jorge

FALKLAND ISLANDS (to UK)
Falkland Plateau

Scotia Sea

South Orkney Islands

Weddell Sea

Yaghan Basin
Cape Horn
South Shetland Islands

Drake Passage

Peru-Chile Trench

Chile Basin

PACIFIC OCEAN

Peru Basin

Galápagos Islands (to Ecuador)

Tropic of Capricorn

Chile Rise

Mornington Abyssal Plain

Bellinghausen Plain

Antarctic Circle

Bellingshausen Sea

N

Elevation

-6000m	-4000m	-2000m	-1000m	-250m	0
-19,658ft	-13,124ft	-6562ft	-3281ft	-820ft	0

141

154

154

153

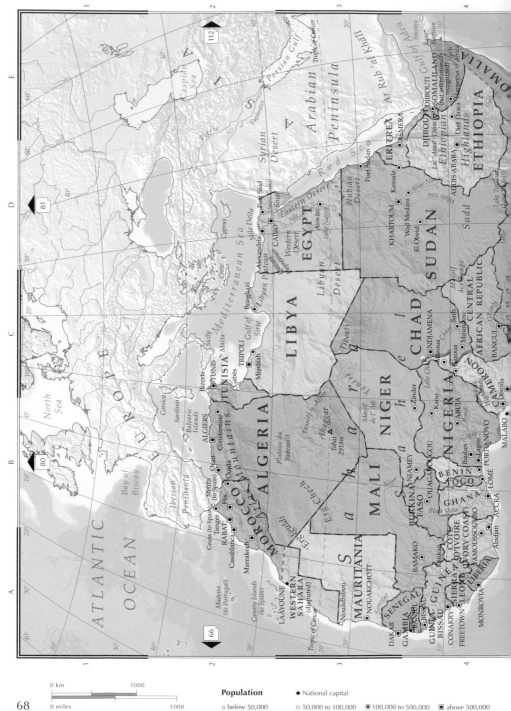

Population   ● National capital

○ below 50,000   ○ 50,000 to 100,000   ◉ 100,000 to 500,000   ▣ above 500,000

AFRICA

INDIAN OCEAN

141

154

154

67

ATLANTIC OCEAN

Mid-Atlantic Ridge

Atlantic-Indian Ridge

Southwest Indian Ridge

Walvis Ridge

Angola Basin

Cape Basin

Orange Fan

Agulhas Plateau

Agulhas Basin

Madagascar Basin

Madagascar Plateau

Somali Basin

Guinea Basin

Ascension Fracture Zone

ASCENSION ISLAND
(to Saint Helena)

SAINT HELENA
(to UK)

TRISTAN DA CUNHA
(to Saint Helena)

Gough Island
(to Tristan da Cunha)

Prince Edward Islands
(to South Africa)

Crozet Plateau

Winter limit of pack ice

Tropic of Capricorn

Tropic of Capricorn

MADAGASCAR

ANTANANARIVO

Toliara

Fianarantsoe

Mahajanga

COMOROS
MORONI

MAYOTTE
(to France)

Aldabra Group

Mozambique Channel

MOZAMBIQUE

Nacala
Nampula
Pemba

Dar es Salaam
Zanzibar

Mombasa

NAIROBI
Kilimanjaro
5895m

KIGALI
RWANDA
BUJUMBURA
BURUNDI
DODOMA
TANZANIA

Lake Victoria
Lake Rukwa
Lake Tanganyika
Masai Steppe

Lake Nyasa
MALAWI
LILONGWE
Blantyre
Beira

DEM. REP. CONGO

KINSHASA
BRAZZAVILLE
CONGO
GABON
SÃO TOMÉ

Cabinda
(to Angola)

LUANDA
ANGOLA
Bié Plateau
Huambo
Lubango
Namibe
Môco 2619m

Kananga
Mbuji-Mayi
Ilebo
Matadi
Cuango
Cuanza
Kwango
Kasai

Kolwezi
ZAMBIA
LUSAKA
Lake Kariba
Kabwe
Lake Kabwe

Great Rift Valley

Zambezi

Luangwa

Cuito

Cuanco

Cubango

ZIMBABWE
HARARE
Bulawayo
Victoria Falls
Francistown
Gweru

BOTSWANA
GABORONE
Okavango Delta
Kalahari Desert
Nossob

NAMIBIA
WINDHOEK
Etosha Pan
Namib Desert
Orange

SOUTH AFRICA
PRETORIA/TSHWANE
Johannesburg
MAPUTO
MBABANE
SWAZILAND
MASERU
LESOTHO
BLOEMFONTEIN
Durban
East London
Port Elizabeth
Great Karoo
Drakensberg
CAPE TOWN
Cape of Good Hope

Limpopo
Orange

69

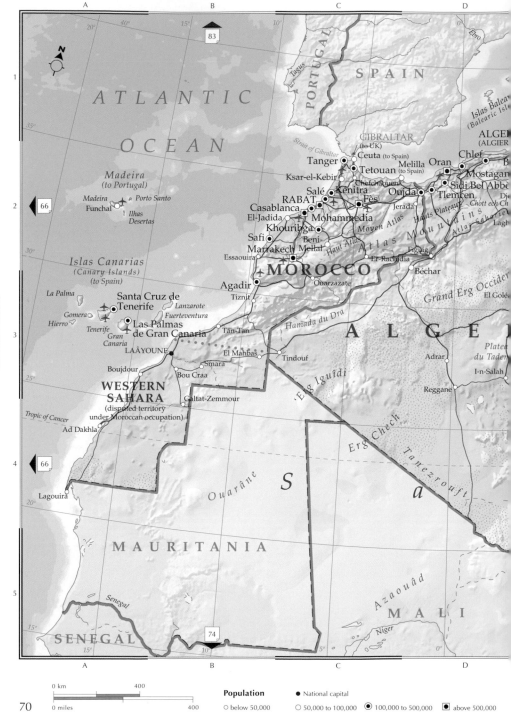

ATLANTIC

OCEAN

SPAIN

PORTUGAL

GIBRALTAR
(to UK)

Tagus

Strait of Gibraltar

Tanger
Ceuta (to Spain)
Tetouan
Melilla
(to Spain)
Ksar-el-Kebir
Chefchaouen
Salé
Kenitra
Fes
Oujda
RABAT
Casablanca
Mohammedia
El-Jadida
Jerada
Khouribga
Moyen Atlas
Safi
Beni-
Marrakech
Mellal
Haut Atlas
Atlas
Essaouira
Er-Rachidia

MOROCCO
Ouarzazate
Béchar
Agadir
Tiznit

Madeira
(to Portugal)
Madeira
Porto Santo
Funchal
Ilhas
Desertas

Islas Canarias
(Canary Islands)
(to Spain)
La Palma
Santa Cruz de
Lanzarote
Tenerife
Fuerteventura
Gomera
Hierro
Tenerife
Las Palmas
Gran
de Gran Canaria
Canaria
LAÀYOUNE

Tan-Tan
Hamada du Dra

El Mahbas
Tindouf

Smara
Boujdour
Bou Craa

WESTERN
SAHARA
(disputed territory
under Moroccan occupation)
Galtat-Zemmour

Tropic of Cancer

Ad Dakhla

Lagouira

Ouarâne

S

MAURITANIA

Senegal

SENEGAL

ALGE
(ALGIER)
Chlef
Oran
Mostaga
Sidi Bel Abbè
Tlemcen
Chott ech Ch
Hauts Plateaux
Lagh
Figuig
Atlas Saharie
Mountains
Grand Erg Occide
El Goléa

ALGER

Platea
du Tader
Adrar
I-n-Salah

Reggane

Erg Iguîdi

Erg Chech

Tanezrouft

a

Azouâd

MALI

Niger

Islas Balear
(Balearic Is.)

Ebro

83

66

66

74

0 km   400
0 miles   400

Population   ● National capital

○ below 50,000   ○ 50,000 to 100,000   ◉ 100,000 to 500,000   ◼ above 500,000

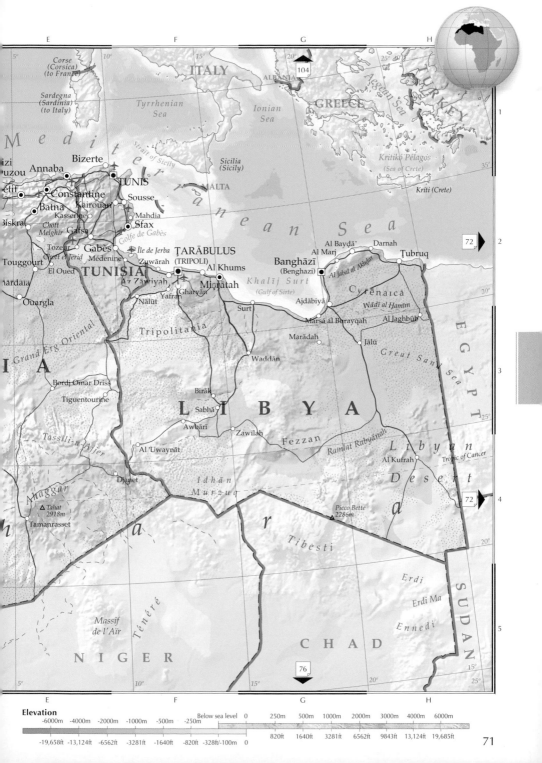

E   F   G   H

Corse
(Corsica)
(to France)

Sardegna
(Sardinia)
(to Italy)

ITALY

104

GREECE

Tyrrhenian
Sea

Ionian
Sea

*Kritikó Pélagos
(Sea of Crete)*

Aegean Sea

TURKEY

Kriti (Crete)

Strait of Sicily

Sicilia
(Sicily)

MALTA

M e d i t e r r a n e a n   S e a

izi
uzou
etif

Annaba
Bizerte
TUNIS
Constantine
Sousse
Kairouan
Mahdia
Batna
Kasserine
Biskra
Gafsa
Chott Melrhir
Sfax

72

Al Baydā'
Al Marj
Darnah
Ṭubruq

Tozeur
Chott el Jerid
El Oued
Gabès
Île de Jerba
Médenine
ṬARĀBULUS
(TRIPOLI)
Zuwārah
Al Khums
Banghāzī
(Benghazi)
Al Jabal al Akhḍar
Cyrenaica

TUNISIA
Az Zāwiyah
Miṣrātah
Yafran
Gharyān
Surt
Ajdābiyā
*Khalīj Surt
(Gulf of Sirte)*
Marsá al Burayqah
Wādī al Ḥamīm
Al Jaghbūb

Ouargla
Nālūt
Waddān
Marādah
Jālū

EGYPT

ardaia

Tripolitania

Great Sand Sea

Grand Erg Oriental

Bordj Omar Driss
Tiguentourine
Bīrāk
Sabhā
L I B Y A

Tassili-n-Ajjer
Awbārī
Zawīlah
Fezzan
Ramlat Rabyānah
Libyan

Al 'Uwaynāt
Al Kufrah
Tropic of Cancer

Djanet
Idhān Murzuq
Desert

Ahaggar
△ Tahat
2918m
Tamanrasset
*Picco Bette
2286m* △
Tibesti

72

Massif
de l'Aïr
Ténéré
Erdi
Erdi Ma
Ennedi

SUDAN

N I G E R
C H A D

76

E   F   G   H

Elevation

-6000m	-4000m	-2000m	-1000m	-500m	-250m	Below sea level	0	250m	500m	1000m	2000m	3000m	4000m	6000m
-19,658ft	-13,124ft	-6562ft	-3281ft	-1640ft	-820ft	-328ft/-100m	0	820ft	1640ft	3281ft	6562ft	9843ft	13,124ft	19,685ft

Northeast Africa

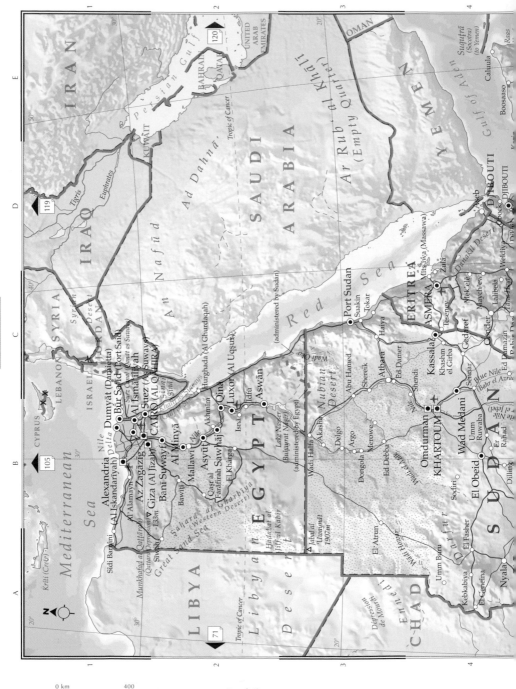

IRAN

Persian Gulf

BAHRAIN

QATAR

UNITED
ARAB
EMIRATES

120

OMAN

Suqutrā
(Socotra)
(to Yemen)

Ras

Caluula

KUWAIT

Tropic of Cancer

Ar Rub al Khālī
(Empty Quarter)

Boosaaso

Gulf of Aden

DJIBOUTI
DJIBOUTI

119

IRAQ

Tigris
Euphrates

Syrian
Desert

SAUDI

ARABIA

Ad Dahnā'

JORDAN

An Nafūd

Red Sea

Port Sudan
Suakin
Tokar

(administered by Sudan)

Danakil Desert

Mits'iwa (Massawa)
Zula

ERITREA
ASMERA
Tesseney
Gedaref

Weldiya

Mek'ele

Maych'ew

Lalibela
Dese
Bahir
Dar Debre Tabor

SYRIA

LEBANON

ISRAEL

CYPRUS

105

Mediterranean
Sea

Kriti (Crete)

Al Iskandariyah Dumyāt (Damietta)
Bûr Said (Port Said)
Alexandria
Az Zaqāzīg
Al Ismā'īlīyah
Suez (As Suways)
CAIRO (AL QĀHIRA)
Giza (Al Jīzah)
Banī Suwayf
Al Minyā
Mallawi
Asyūt
Akhmīm
Sawhāj
Qasr al Gharbīya
Faráfirah
El Khārga

Sinai

Suez Canal (Qanāt as Suways)

Bawiti

Sīwah

Al Ghardaqah)
Hurghada (Al Ghurdaqah)

Qina

Luxor (Al Uqsur)
Isna
Idfu
Aswān

Lake Nasser
Buhayrat Nāsir

(administered by Egypt)

Wadi Oko

Nubian
Desert

Wadi Halfa

Akasha
Delgo
Argo
Dongola
Ed Debba
Merowe

Haiya

Atbara
Shereik
Ed Damer
Abu Hamed
Shendi

Kassala
Khashm
el Girba

Blue Nile (Bahr el Azraq)

Sennar

Gedaref

Gonder

Al Qadarif

Qattara Depression
(Munkhafad al Qattārah)
-133m

Al Alamayn

Sidi Barāni

Great
Sand Sea

Sahara al Gharbīya
(Western Desert)

Jabal al
Uwaynāt
1907m

El'Atrun

Er Rahad

EGYPT

LIBYAN

DESERT

LIBYA

Tropic of Cancer

71

CHAD

Dépression
de Mourdi

Ennedi

Wadi Howar

Darfur

Umm Buru

Kebkabiya

El Fasher
El Geneina

Nyala

Wadi el Milk

Ed Dueim

Omdurman
KHARTOUM
Wad Medani
Umm
Ruwaba

El Obeid

Dilling

Sodiri

Er Rahad

SUDAN

White Nile (Bahr el Jebel)

0 km   400

0 miles   400

Population   ● National capital

○ below 50,000   ○ 50,000 to 100,000   ◉ 100,000 to 500,000   ▣ above 500,000

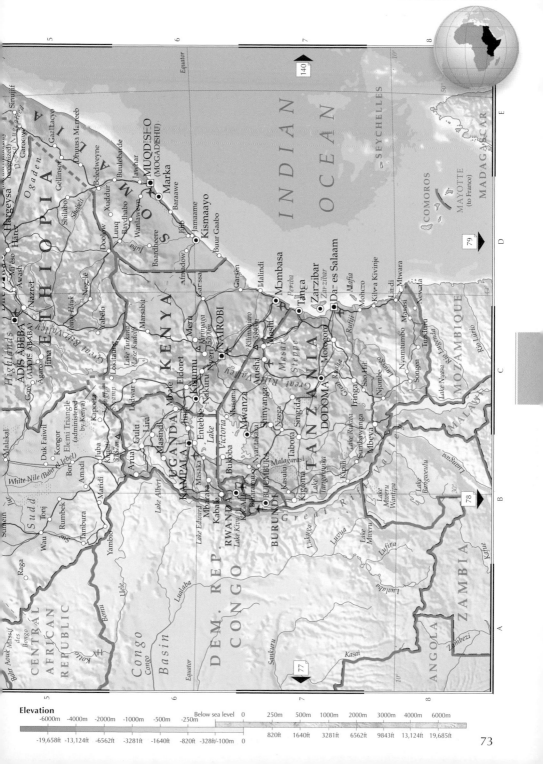

5   6   7   8

Equator

140

INDIAN OCEAN

SEYCHELLES

MADAGASCAR

COMOROS

MAYOTTE (to France)

79

SUDAN

ETHIOPIA

Highlands

Great Rift Valley

ADIS ABEBA (ADDIS ABABA)

Nazret

Ogaden

Hargeysa

Hārer

SOMALIA

Sinuuji

Gaalkacyo

Garoowe

Obbia

Ohyusa Mareeb

Beledweyne

Buulobarde

Jawhar

MUQDISHO (MOGADISHU)

Marka

Baraawe

Jamaame

Kismaayo

Buur Gaabo

Baardheere

Doolow

Luuq

Wanlaweyn

Baydhabo

Xuddur

Gellinsor

Shilabo

Buuloburde

KENYA

Malindi

Mombasa

Zanzibar

Zan zibar

Dar es Salaam

Pemba

Tanga

Mafia

Mohoro

Kilwa Kivinje

Mtwara

Newala

Masasi

Gar issa

Lamu

Moshi

Kilimanjaro 5895m

Meru

Nyeri

Kenya 5199m

Nanyuki

NAIROBI

Kirinyaga 5200m

Eldoret

Kisumu

Nakuru

Lake Turkana (Lake Rudolf)

Lodwar

Lokitaung

Marsabit

Wajir

Kabelo

Negele

Jima

Goge

Asayta

Āwasa

Dasē

Mī'eso

Āwash

Ayatu

Gidole

Mēga

Doba La Cega

recognized by Ethiopia

Elemi Triangle (administered by Kenya)

TANZANIA

DODOMA

Morogoro

Iringa

Mbeya

Songea

Njombe

Sao Hill

Sumbawanga

Mbarali

Rufiji

Great Ruaha

Masai Steppe

Arusha

Shinyanga

Singida

Nzega

Tabora

Kigoma

Kasulu

Ujiji

Nyamtumbo

Tunduru

Lindi

Great Rift Valley

Lake Nyasa (Lake Malawi)

MALAWI

MOZAMBIQUE

Rio Lúrio

78

UGANDA

KAMPALA

Entebbe

Jinja

Masaka

Mbale

Gulu

Lira

Masindi

Arua

Moyo

Juba

Nimule 3187m

Kitgum

Mount Elgon

Lake Kyoga

Lake Albert

Lake Edward

RWANDA

KIGALI

BURUNDI

BUJUMBURA

Lake Kivu

Lake Victoria

Bukoba

Mwanza

Musoma

Kabale

Kaliro

Great Rift Valley

Lake Rukwa

Lake Tanganyika

Malagarasi

Lukuga

Lugua

Lake Mweru

Lake Mweru Wantipa

Lake Bangweulu

ZAMBIA

ANGOLA

Zambezi

Kafue

DEM. REP. CONGO

Congo Basin

Congo

Luvua

Lualaba

Luapula

Lomami

Aruwimi

Kasai

Sankuru

Malakal

Duk Faiwil

Kongor

Bor

Amadi

Maridi

Yambio

Tambura

Rumbek

Tonj

Wau

Raga

CENTRAL AFRICAN REPUBLIC

Bahr Aouk Massif des Bongo

Kotto

Bomu

Uele

White Nile (Bahr el Jebel)

Sudd

Sobat

Sue

Equator

77

Elevation

						Below sea level	0							
-6000m	-4000m	-2000m	-1000m	-500m	-250m			250m	500m	1000m	2000m	3000m	4000m	6000m
-19,658ft	-13,124ft	-6562ft	-3281ft	-1640ft	-820ft	-328ft/-100m	0	820ft	1640ft	3281ft	6562ft	9843ft	13,124ft	19,685ft

West Africa

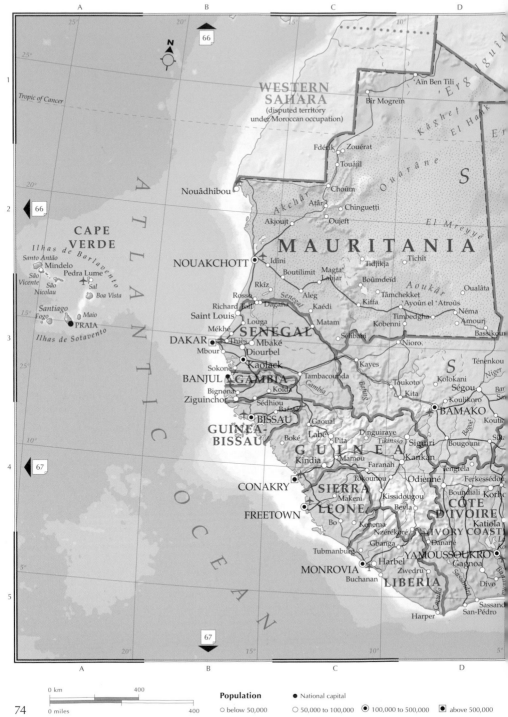

A   25°   **B**   20°   15°   **C**   10°   **D**

66

N

25°   Tropic of Cancer

WESTERN SAHARA
(disputed territory
under Moroccan occupation)

Aïn Ben Tili

Bir Mogreïn

66

Fdérik   Zouérat

Touâjil

20°

Nouâdhibou

CAPE VERDE

Ilhas de Barlavento

Santo Antão   Mindelo
São   Pedra Lume
Vicente   São   Sal
Nicolau   Boa Vista

15°   Santiago   Maio
Fogo

PRAIA

Ilhas de Sotavento

Choûm

Atâr   Chinguetti

Akchâr

Idîni   Akjoujt   Oujeft

Atlântic Ocean

NOUAKCHOTT

Boutilimit   Magta   Lahjar

Rkîz

Rosso   Aleg

Senegal

Dagana   Kaédi

Richard Toll

Saint Louis   Louga   Matam

Mékhé   Sélibabi

SENEGAL

DAKAR   Thiès   Mbaké

Mbour   Diourbel

Sokone   **Kaolack**

BANJUL **GAMBIA**

Bignona   Kolda

Ziguinchor   Sédhiou

Bafatá

BISSAU

GUINEA-BISSAU

Gaoual

Boké   Labé   Pita

Kindia   Mamou

CONAKRY

SIERRA LEONE

Makeni   Kissidougou

FREETOWN

Bo   Konema

Tubmanburg

Gbanga

MONROVIA   Harbel

Buchanan   Zwedru

LIBERIA

Harper

MAURITANIA

Tidjikja   Tîchît

Boûmdeïd

Aoukâr

Tâmchekket   Oualâta

Kiffa   Ayoûn el 'Atroûs   Néma

Kobenni   Amourj

Nioro   Bassikou

Kayes   Ténékou

Niger

Toukoto   Kolokani   Ségou

Kita   Koulikoro

BAMAKO

Tambacounda

Gambia

Baoulé

Bani

Dinguiraye   Siguiri   Bougouni

Tikinsso

GUINEA

Faranah   Kankan

Tokounou   Odienné   Ferkessédou

Beyla   Boundiali   Korho

Nzérékoré   **CÔTE D'IVOIRE**

Danané   Katiola

YAMOUSSOUKRO   Gagnoa

Divo

Sassand   San-Pédro

A   **B**   **C**   **D**

67

67

20°   15°   10°   5°

0 km   400

0 miles   400

Population   ● National capital

○ below 50,000   ○ 50,000 to 100,000   ◉ 100,000 to 500,000   ▣ above 500,000

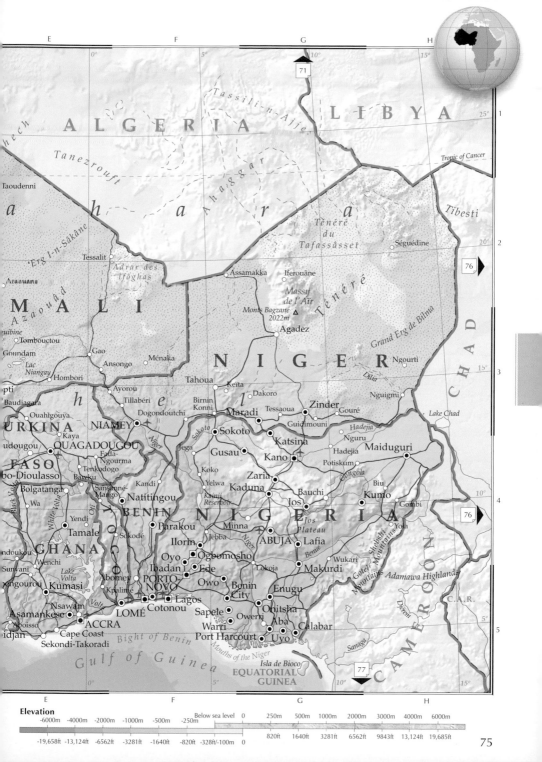

E   F   G   H

0°   5°   10°   15°

71

A L G E R I A   L I B Y A   25° 1

Tanezrouft   Tropic of Cancer

Tassili-n-Ajjer

Taoudenni

a   h   a   r   a   Tibesti

Ténéré
du
Tafassâsset

Séguédine   20° 2

Tessalit   Assamakka   Iferouâne   76

Adrar des
Ifôghas

Araouane   Massif
de l'Aïr   Ténéré

M A L I   Monts Bagzané
2022m   Agadez   Grand Erg de Bilma

Azaouâd

ouibine

Tombouctou   N I G E R   Ngourti

Goundam   C H A D

Lac
Niangay   Gao   Ansongo   Ménaka   Tahoua   Keita   Dakoro   Dilia   Nguigmi   15° 3

pti   Hombori   Ayorou   Tillabéri   e   l   Tessaoua   Zinder   Gouré

Baudiagara   h   Dogondoutchi   Birnin
Konni   Maradi   Guidimouni   Lake Chad

Ouahigouya   Sokoto   Hadejia

URKINA   NIAMEY   Jega   Sokoto   Katsina   Nguru   Maiduguri   10°

udougou   Kaya   Fada-   Gusau   Kano   Hadejia
QUAGADOUGOU   Ngourma   Koko   Potiskum   Zongola

FASO   Tenkodogo   Yelwa   Zaria   Biu
bo-Dioulasso   Banfora   Kandi   Kaduna   Bauchi   Kumo

Bolgatanga   Sansanné-   Kainji   Jos   Gombi

Wa   Mango   Natitingou   Reservoir   Jos
Plateau   76   4

Yendi   BENIN   N I G E R I A   Yola

ndoukou   Tamale   Sokodé   Parakou   Minna   ABUJA   Lafia

GHANA   Ilorin   Jebba   Wukari

Sunyani   Wenchi   Oyo   Ogbomosho   Lokoja   Makurdi

ngourou   Kumasi   Lake   Ede   Benue   Adamawa Highlands
Volta   Abomey   Ibadan
PORTO-   Owo
Kpalimé   NOVO   Benin   Enugu   C.A.R.

Nsawam   LOMÉ   City   5°
Asamankese   Cotonou   Lagos   Sapele   Onitsha

Aboisso   Cape Coast   Warri   Owerri   Aba   Calabar
idjan   Sekondi-Takoradi   Port Harcourt   Uyo

Bight of Benin   Mouths of the Niger

Gulf of Guinea   Isla de Bioco   77   5
EQUATORIAL
GUINEA   C A M E R O O N

0°   5°   10°   15°

E   F   G   H

Elevation

| -6000m | -4000m | -2000m | -1000m | -500m | -250m | Below sea level 0 | 250m | 500m | 1000m | 2000m | 3000m | 4000m | 6000m |

-19,658ft -13,124ft -6562ft -3281ft -1640ft -820ft -328ft/-100m 0   820ft 1640ft 3281ft 6562ft 9843ft 13,124ft 19,685ft

Central Africa

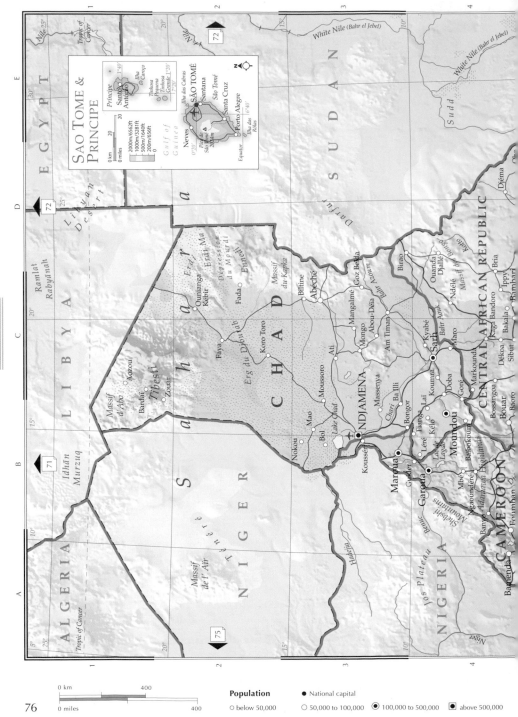

SÃO TOMÉ & PRINCIPE

Principe
Santo
António
Ilha das Cabras
SÃO TOMÉ
Santana
Tinhosa
Pequena
Tinhosa
Grande
São Tomé
Santa Cruz
Porto Alegre
Gulf of
Guinea
Neves
Pico de
São Tomé
Ilha das
Rôlas
Equator

0 km   20
0 miles   20

2000m/6562ft
1000m/3281ft
500m/1640ft
200m/656ft

White Nile (Bahr el Jebel)

EGYPT

Libyan Desert

Ramlat Rabyānah

LIBYA

Idhan Murzuq

ALGERIA

Tropic of Cancer

Massif de l'Aïr

NIGER

Ténéré

Hadejia

Massif d'Abo
Bardaï
Aozou
Tibesti
Zouar

Sahara

Erg du Djourab

Faya
Koro Toro

Ennedi
Fada
Erdi Ma
Dépression du Mourdi
Ounianga
Kébir

Bîltine
Abéché
Goz Beïda
Mangalmé
Mongo
Abou-Déïa
Am Timan
Massif du Kapka

Ati
Moussoro
Mao
Massenya
Bol
Lake Chad
Nokou

N'DJAMENA
Kousséri
Chari Baguirmi
Bongor
Fianga
Léré
Laï
Kélo
Lagdo
Kyabé
Sarh
Maro
Kyabé
Moundou
Doba
Goré
Koumra
Bébédjia
Kounoungou
Markounda
Dékoa
Kaga Bandoro
Bakala
Sibut
Bozoum
Bossangoa
Bouar
Baoro
Bouca

CHAD

Darfur

SUDAN

White Nile (Bahr el Jebel)

Sudd

Djéma
Obo
Bria
Ouanda
Djallé
Ndélé
Massif des Bongo
Bamingui
Ippy
Bambari
Kaga Bandoro

CENTRAL AFRICAN REPUBLIC

Maroua
Guider
Garoua
Mbé
Ngaoundéré
Shébshi
Mountains
Banyo
Adamawa Highlands

CAMEROON

Foumban
Bamenda

NIGERIA

Jos Plateau

Benue

Niger

0 km   400
0 miles   400

Population

● National capital

○ below 50,000   ○ 50,000 to 100,000   ◉ 100,000 to 500,000   ▣ above 500,000

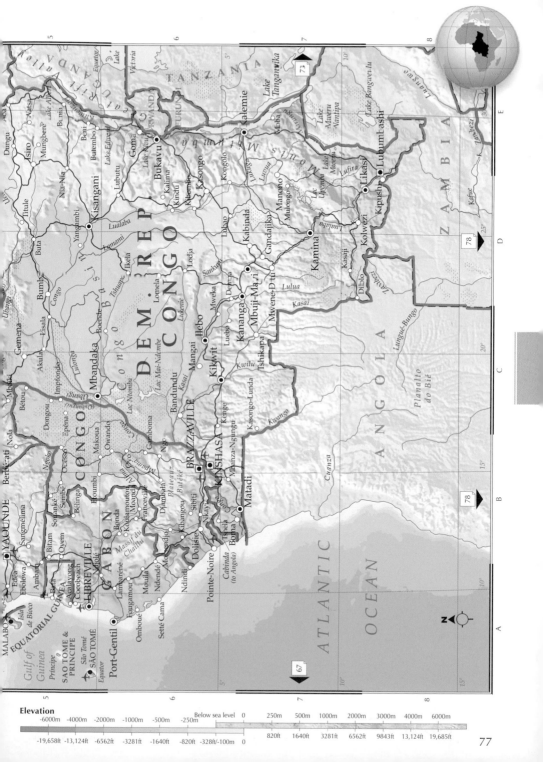

Elevation

-6000m	-4000m	-2000m	-1000m	-500m	-250m	Below sea level	0	250m	500m	1000m	2000m	3000m	4000m	6000m

-19,658ft	-13,124ft	-6562ft	-3281ft	-1640ft	-820ft	-328ft/-100m	0	820ft	1640ft	3281ft	6562ft	9843ft	13,124ft	19,685ft

Southern Africa

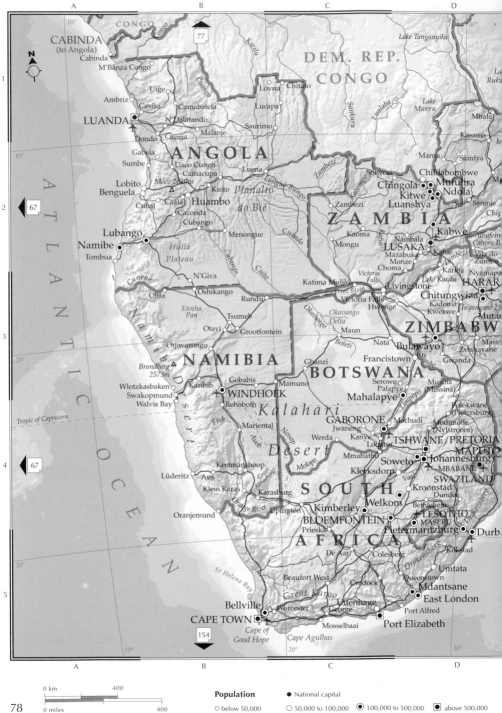

10°

CONGO

CABINDA
(to Angola)
Cabinda

77

M'Banza Congo

N

Uíge
Ambriz
Caxito
LUANDA
Dondo
Camabatela
N'Dalatando
Malanje
Cuanza
Gabela
Sumbe

Lovua
Chitato
Lucapa
Saurimo

**DEM. REP.
CONGO**

Lake Tanganyika

Sankuru

Lualaba

Lake
Mweru

Mbala

Kasama

10°

ANGOLA

Uaco Cungo
Camacupa
Luena
Planalto
do Bié

Lobito
Benguela
Cubal
Môco 2620m
Kuito
Caála
Huambo
Caconda
Cubango

67

2

Lubango
Namibe
Tombua

Huíla
Plateau

Menongue

Cunene

N'Giva

Olifa
Oshikango
Rundu

Etosha
Pan

Tsumeb

Otavi
Grootfontein

Zambezi

Longué-Bungo

Cuando

Cuito

Katima Mulilo
Caprivi Strip

Okavango
Delta

Maun

Boteti

Kaoma
Mongu

Zambezi

ZAMBIA

Solwezi
Zambezi

Chililabombwe
Chingola   Mufulira
Kitwe   Ndola
Luanshya

Mansa
Samfya

Serenje
Chip

Kabwe

Nambala
LUSAKA
Mazabuka
Monze
Choma

Kafue
Zumbo

Albufeira
Cahora B.
Vila do
Zumbo

Karība
Nyamapa
HARAR

Victoria
Falls
Livingstone
Victoria Falls
Hwange

Lake Kariba
Kadoma
Kwekwe

Chitungwiza
Inyangani 25
Mutar

20°

NAMIBIA

Brandberg
2573m

Otjiwarongo

Ghanzi

Nata
Bulawayo

Francistown

ZIMBABW

Masv
Zvishavane
Gwanda

3

Karibib
Wlotzkasbaken
Swakopmund
Walvis Bay

Gobabis
Mamuno

BOTSWANA

Serowe
Palapye
Mahalapye

Musina
(Messina)

Tropic of Capricorn

Rehoboth
WINDHOEK

Mariental

Kalahari

Fish

Nosep

Jwaneng
GABORONE
Werda
Kanye
Lobatse

Mochudi

Polokwane
(Pietersburg)

Modimolle
(Nylstroom)

TSHWANE / PRETORIA

MAPUTO

67

4

Lüderitz
Aus
Klein Karas

Keetmanshoop

Desert

Auob

Molopo

Mmabatho
Klerksdorp

Soweto
Johannesburg

MBABANE
SWAZILAND

Oranjemund

Karasburg

Upington

SOUTH

Kimberley

Prieska

BLOEMFONTEIN

Vaal

Kroonstad
Dundee

Welkom
Bethlehem

MASERU
LESOTHO

Pietermaritzburg

Durb

30°

Beaufort West

Cradock

De Aar
Colesberg

Umtata
Queenstown
Mdantsane
East London

Kokstad

Drakensberg

5

AFRICA

St Helena Bay

Great Karoo

George

Worcester
Bellville
CAPE TOWN
Cape of
Good Hope

Oudtshoorn

Uitenhage
Mosselbaai

Port Alfred
Port Elizabeth

Cape Agulhas

154

ATLANTIC OCEAN

Namib Desert

0 km   400

0 miles   400

Population

○ below 50,000
○ 50,000 to 100,000
◉ 100,000 to 500,000

● National capital

■ above 500,000

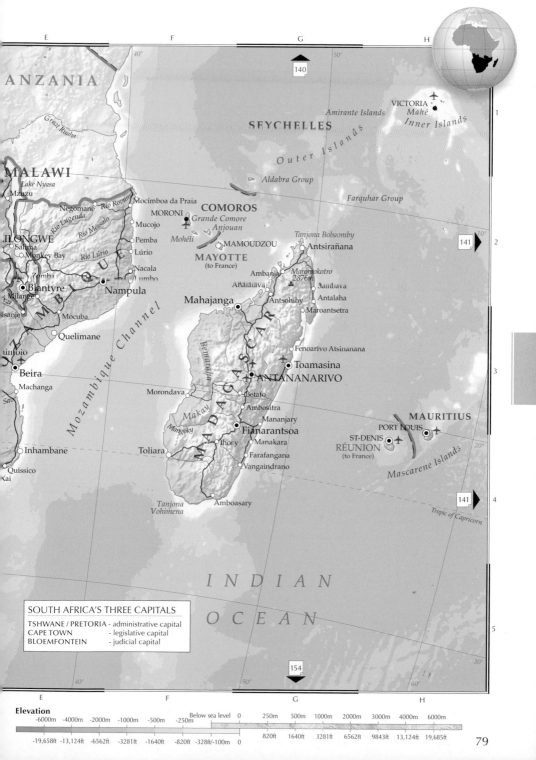

E   F   G   H

140

ANZANIA

MALAWI
Lake Nyasa
Mzuzu

ILONGWE
Salima
Monkey Bay
Zomba
Blantyre
Milange
isanje

Negomane
Rio Rovuma
Rio Lugenda
Rio Messalo
Rio Lúrio

Mocímboa da Praia
Mucojo
Pemba
Lúrio
Nacala
Lumbo

COMOROS
MORONI
Grande Comore
Anjouan
Mohéli
MAMOUDZOU
MAYOTTE
(to France)

SEYCHELLES
Amirante Islands
VICTORIA
Mahé
Inner Islands

Outer Islands

Aldabra Group

Farquhar Group

141

Mocuba
Quelimane

Nampula

Beira
Machanga

Inhambane
Quissico
Xai

Ambanja
Maromokotro
Ahalalava
Antsohihy
2876m
Sambava
Antalaha
Maroantsetra

Mahajanga
Antsohihy

Tanjona Bobaomby
Antsirañana

Fenoarivo Atsinanana

Toamasina

Morondava
Betafo
ANTANANARIVO
Ambositra
Mananjary
Manakara
Farafangana
Vangaindrano

Makay
Mangoky
Betsiboka
Fianarantsoa
Ihosy

Toliara

MAURITIUS
PORT LOUIS
ST-DENIS
RÉUNION
(to France)
Mascarene Islands

Amboasary
Tanjona Vohimena

Tropic of Capricorn

141

I N D I A N

O C E A N

SOUTH AFRICA'S THREE CAPITALS
TSHWANE / PRETORIA - administrative capital
CAPE TOWN - legislative capital
BLOEMFONTEIN - judicial capital

154

E   F   G   H

Elevation

-6000m	-4000m	-2000m	-1000m	-500m	-250m	Below sea level 0	250m	500m	1000m	2000m	3000m	4000m	6000m
-19,658ft	-13,124ft	-6562ft	-3281ft	-1640ft	-820ft	-328ft/-100m 0	820ft	1640ft	3281ft	6562ft	9843ft	13,124ft	19,685ft

79

Europe

A   B   C   D

155

50°   30°   20°   70°   10°   0°

Limit of winter pack ice

1

Charlie - Gibbs Fracture Zone

Reykjanes Ridge   REYKJAVÍK   **ICELAND**   *Arctic Circle*   *Vatnajökull*

Norwegian Basin

Iceland Basin   *Faeroe-Iceland Ridge*

Norwegian Sea

FAEROE ISLANDS
(to Denmark)

Trondheim

Hatton Ridge   *Faeroe-Shetland Trough*

66   *Mid - Atlantic Ridge*   **2**

Rockall Bank   *Shetland Islands*   Bergen   OSLO

Rockall Trough   *Outer Hebrides*   *Orkney Islands*   Stavanger

British Isles   Glasgow   *North Sea*   Gothenburg   Jönköp
Belfast   Edinburgh   Aalborg

Ireland   **UNITED**   DENMARK   COPENHA
IRELAND   ISLE OF MAN   **KINGDOM**   Odense   Malm
DUBLIN   (to UK)
Liverpool   Manchester
Britain

Celtic Sea   Birmingham   Hamburg   **3**
Cardiff   LONDON   **NETHERLANDS**   Hannover

Celtic Shelf   THE   Rotterdam   BERLIN
HAGUE   **BELGIUM**   Bonn   Woc
English Channel   BRUSSELS   PRA
CHANNEL IS.   Liège   **GERMANY**   CZE
(to UK)   le Havre   LUXEMBOURG   Frankfurt   REPU
Rennes   *Seine*   LUXEMBOURG   am Main   BRA
PARIS   Strasbourg   VIENNA
Nantes   Orléans   Stuttgart   AUST
Loire   Munich
FRANCE   Zürich   Salzburg
SWITZERLAND   Innsbruck   AUSTRIA
66   Lyon   BERN   Milan   LJUBLJANA   **4**
A Coruña   Bordeaux   *Massif Central*   Mont Blanc   Turin   Venice   Trieste
Galicia Bank   4807m   SLOVEN
Porto   *Duero*   Toulouse   Nice   Bologna   CRO
PORTUGAL   *Iberian*   Zaragoza   Marseille   MONACO   SAN   Adriatic
Tagus Plain   MADRID   ANDORRA   Pisa   MARINO
LISBON   *Ebro*   **ITALY**   VATICAN CITY   SAR
SPAIN   Barcelona   *Corsica*   ROME
Horseshoe Seamounts   *Peninsula*
Seville   *Guadalquivir*   Valencia   *Sardinia*   Naples   Bari
Madeira   Málaga   Palma   *Algerian Basin*   *Tyrrhenian Sea*
(to Portugal)   GIBRALTAR   *Balearic Islands*   Cagliari   Cosenza
(to UK)   *Strait of Gibraltar*   Ceuta   *Mediterranean*   Palermo
(to Spain)   Mount Etna   Catania
Melilla   3340m   **5**
(to Spain)   MALTA   *Sic*
Canary Islands   VALLETTA
(to Spain)   *Atlas Mountains*   **AFRICA**   68

A   B   C   D

0 km   500

0 miles   500

Population   ● National capital

○ below 50,000   ◎ 50,000 to 100,000   ◉ 100,000 to 500,000   ▣ above 500,000

Barents Sea
North Cape
Ostrov Kolguyev
155
Arctic Circle
70°
80°
Murmansk
Kola
Peninsula
Ob'
Irtysh
White
Sea
Archangel
Ural Mountains
Northern Dvina
FINLAND
R U S S I A N
112
2
Lake Onega
Perm'
F E D E R A T I O N
70°
50°
Tampere
Saint Petersburg
Vologda
Ufa
Lake Ladoga
Turku HELSINKI
Yaroslavl'
Kazan'
Alang
Uppsala
TALLINN
50°
STOCKHOLM
ESTONIA
Nizhniy
Ul'yanovsk
Novgorod
MOSCOW
Samara
Orenburg
LATVIA
Ural
RĪGA
Volga Uplands
3
LITHUANIA
Vitsyebsk
Aral Sea
ingrad
Kaunas
Central
Syr Darya
sk
VILNIUS
Russian
KALININGRAD
MINSK
Upland
(to Russ.Fed.)
Babruysk
Ural
oszcz
Homyel'
WARSAW
BELARUS
Voronezh
Volga
WARSAW
Brest
Pripet
Marshes
Don
Kraków
Dnieper Lowlands
KIEV
Kharkiv
Amu Darya
60°
L'viv
Volgograd
Dnieper
Astrakhan
VAKIA
UKRAINE
Dnipropetrovs'k
Volga Delta
Chernivtsi
Donets'k
-28m
40°
APEST
MOLDOVA
Rostov-na-Donu
112
4
NGARY
Cluj-Napoca
CHIŞINĂU
Stavropol'
ROMANIA
Odesa
Sea of
BELGRADE
Braşov
Azov
Caucasus
Caspian Sea
RBIA
BUCHAREST
Crimea
El'brus 5642m
Constanţa
Simferopol
OSOVO
BULGARIA
Varna
Black Sea
T. PRISTINA
Balkan Mountains
GORA
SOFIA
Burgas
MACED
SKOPJE
TURKEY
ANIA
Aegean
Anatolia
Zagros Mountains
30°
GREECE
Sea
ATHENS
Piraeus
5
Peloponnese
Tigris
50°
Irákleio
Cyprus
Euphrates
ea
Crete
30°
40°
118

The North Atlantic

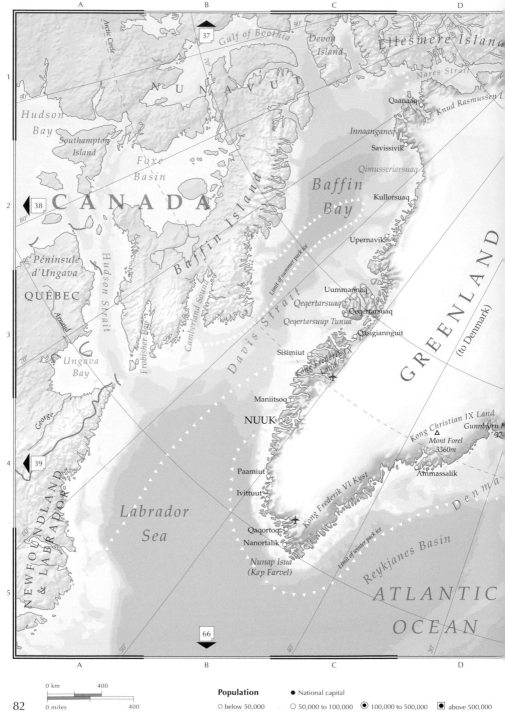

ARCTIC OCEAN

Lincoln Sea

Kap Morris Jesup

Wandel Sea

Independence Fjord

Nord

Zemlya Frantsa-Iosifa

Kvitøya

Novaya Zemlya

SVALBARD
(to Norway)

Nordaustlandet

Kong Karls Land

Kong Frederik VIII Land

Spitsbergen

Barentsøya

Edgeøya

Barents Sea

LONGYEARBYEN
Barentsburg

Storfjorden

Limit of winter pack ice

Greenland Sea

Kong Christian X Land

Daneborg

Limit of summer pack ice

Bjørnøya
(to Norway)

Petermann Bjerg
2940m

Nordkapp
(North Cape)

FINLAND

Kong Oscar Fjord

Ittoqqortoormiit

Kangertittivaq

Kangikajik

Mohns Ridge

JAN MAYEN
(to Norway)

Norwegian Sea

Vestfjorden

Arctic Circle

trait

Norwegian Basin

ICELAND

Bolungarvík

Siglufjördhur

Raufarhöfn

fjördhur

Húsavík

Akureyri

Stykkishólmur

Seydhisfjördhur

REYKJAVÍK

Neskaupstadhur

Selfoss

Djúpivogur

Vatnajökull

SWEDEN

Gulf
of
Bothnia

horlákshöfn

Hvannadalshnúkur
2119m

Surtsey

Vestmannaeyjar

N

FAEROE ISLANDS
(to Denmark)

NORWAY

TÓRSHAVN

Shetland
Islands

Elevation

-6000m	-4000m	-2000m	-1000m	-500m	-250m	Below sea level	0	250m	500m	1000m	2000m	3000m	4000m	6000m

-19,658ft -13,124ft -6562ft -3281ft -1640ft -820ft -328ft/-100m 0

820ft 1640ft 3281ft 6562ft 9843ft 13,124ft 19,685ft

83

Scandinavia & Finland

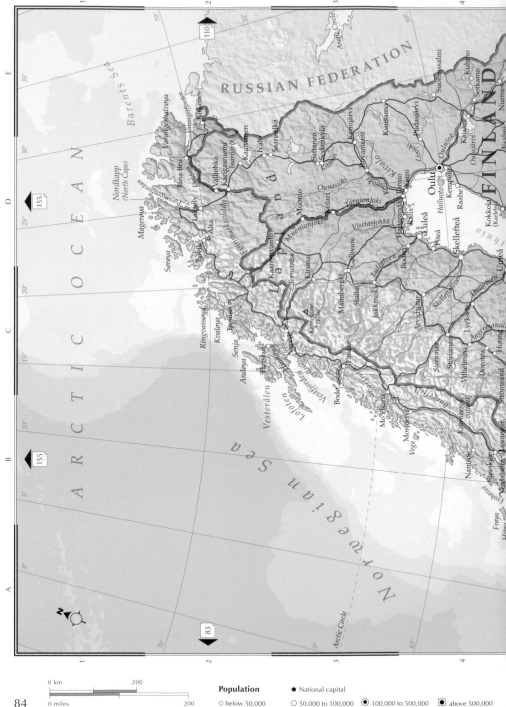

RUSSIAN FEDERATION

FINLAND

Barents Sea

ARCTIC OCEAN

Norwegian Sea

Nordkapp (North Cape)

Arctic Circle

Oulu

Luleå

Kebnekaise 2117 m

Population

● National capital

○ below 50,000

○ 50,000 to 100,000

◉ 100,000 to 500,000

■ above 500,000

0 km   200

0 miles   200

84

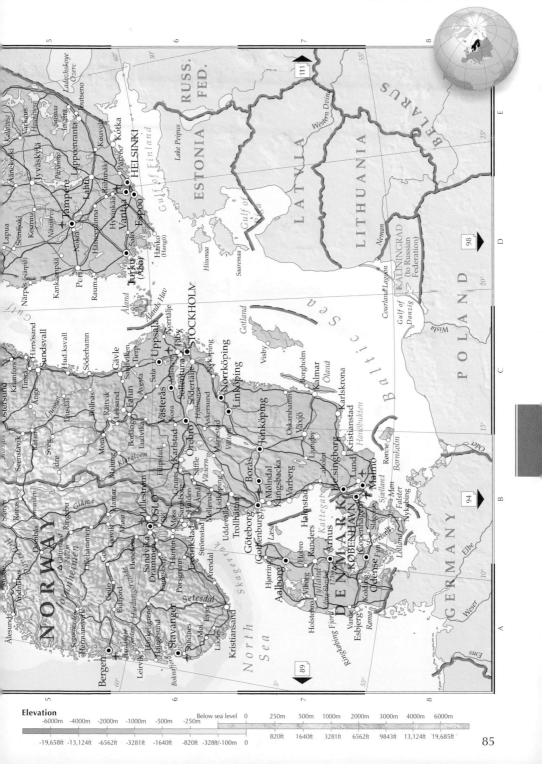

Elevation

-6000m	-4000m	-2000m	-1000m	-500m	-250m	Below sea level	0	250m	500m	1000m	2000m	3000m	4000m	6000m
-19,658ft	-13,124ft	-6562ft	-3281ft	-1640ft	-820ft	-328ft/-100m	0	820ft	1640ft	3281ft	6562ft	9843ft	13,124ft	19,685ft

The Low Countries

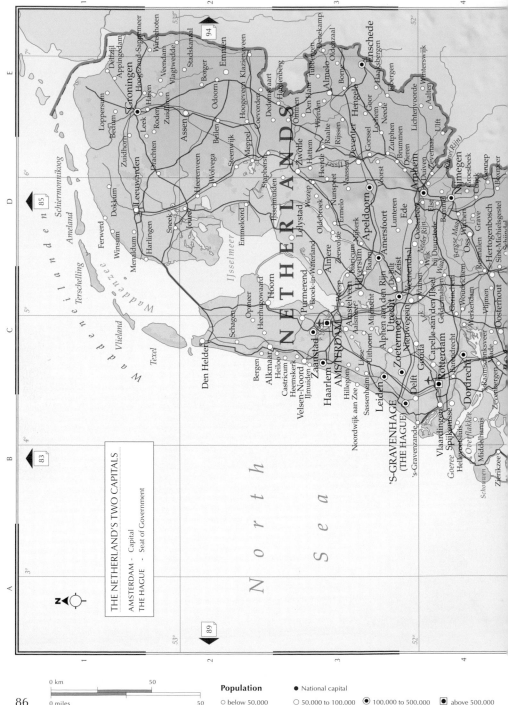

THE NETHERLAND'S TWO CAPITALS

AMSTERDAM - Capital
THE HAGUE - Seat of Government

Population
- National capital
○ below 50,000
○ 50,000 to 100,000
◎ 100,000 to 500,000
▣ above 500,000

0 km — 50
0 miles — 50

GERMANY

Rhine (Rhein)

LUXEMBOURG

BELGIUM

FRANCE

Lorraine

Ardenne

Botrange 694m

Venlo
Eindhoven
's-Hertog
Veldhoven
Someren
Eersel
Bladel
Reusel
Bergeyk
Valkenswaard
Nederweert
Weert
Budel
Neerpelt
Lommel
Bree
Maaseik
Kinrooi
Roermond
Beesel
Tegelen
Posterholt
Echt
Sittard
Geleen
Heerlen
Kerkrade
Vaals
Simpelveld
Geleen
Stein
Maastricht
Eijsden
Visé
Herstal
Liège
Seraing
Verviers
Eupen
Malmédy
Hautes Fagnes

Lotharingen / Zuid-Brabant
Westerschelde
Vlissingen
Zeebrugge
Knokke-Heist
Blankenberge
Oostende (Ostend)
Middelkerke
Koksijde
Veurne
Nieuwpoort
De Panne
Poperinge
Ieper
Roeselare
Torhout
Diksmuide

Antwerpen (Antwerp)
Brugge (Bruges)
Gent (Ghent)
BRUSSEL/BRUXELLES (BRUSSELS)
Schaerbeek
Charleroi
Namur
Mons
Tournai
Dinant
Rochefort
Bastogne
Arlon

LUXEMBOURG
Grevenmacher
Ettelbrück
Diekirch
Wiltz
Vianden
Echternach
Esch-sur-Alzette
Differdange
Pétange
Rumelange
Dudelange

Meuse
Somme
Oise
Sambre

Elevation

						Below sea level	0	250m	500m	1000m	2000m	3000m	4000m	6000m
-6000m	-4000m	-2000m	-1000m	-500m	-250m									
-19,658ft	-13,124ft	-6562ft	-3281ft	-1640ft	-820ft	-328ft/-100m	0	820ft	1640ft	3281ft	6562ft	9843ft	13,124ft	19,685ft

North Sea

ATLANTIC OCEAN

Shetland Islands
Unst
Yell
Fetlar
Mainland
Lerwick

Fair Isle

Orkney Islands
Sanday
Kirkwall
Mainland
Hoy
John o'Groats
Thurso

Ben Hope
927m △

Ullapool

The Minch

Isle of Lewis
Stornoway
Harris

North Uist
South Uist
Barra

St Kilda

Outer Hebrides

The Little Minch

Isle of Skye
Stromeferry
Mallaig

Rhum
Eigg
Coll
Tiree
Isle of Mull
Firth of Lorn
Jura
Islay

Inner Hebrides

North West Highlands
Inverness
Loch Ness
Aviemore

Fraserburgh
Peterhead
● Aberdeen

Montrose
Arbroath
St Andrews
Forfar

● Dundee
Perth

Moray Firth
Elgin
Spey
Dee
Tay

SCOTLAND

Grampian Mountains

Ben Nevis
1347m △
Fort William
Oban

Firth of Forth
Dunfermline
Stirling
Forth
Firth of Forth
● Edinburgh

Glasgow
Hamilton
Clyde

Greenock
Paisley
East Kilbride
Kilmarnock
Prestwick
Ayr

Isle of Arran
Kintyre

Coleraine

Berwick-upon-Tweed

Galashiels
Hawick
Cheviot Hills

SOUTHERN

NORTHERN

Newcastle upon Tyne
South Shields

Tyne

0 km   100
0 miles   100

Population

● National capital ● Internal administrative capital

○ below 50,000 ○ 50,000 to 100,000 ◉ 100,000 to 500,000 ■ above 500,000

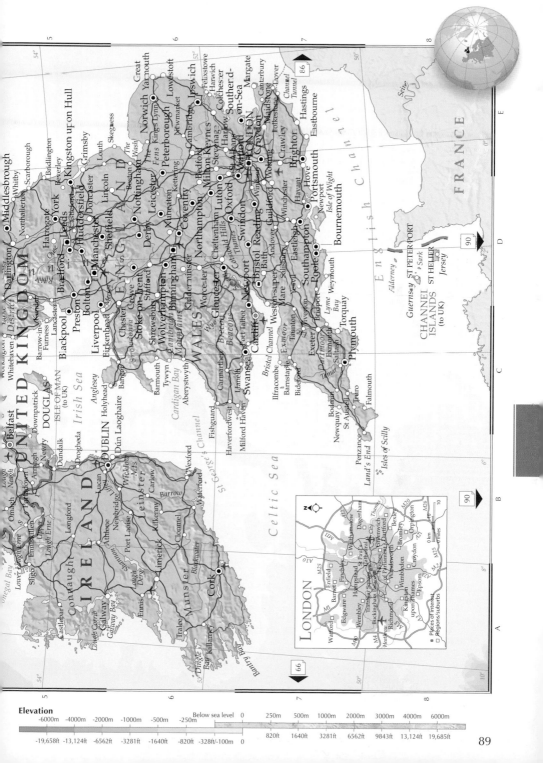

Elevation

-6000m	-4000m	-2000m	-1000m	-500m	-250m	Below sea level	0	250m	500m	1000m	2000m	3000m	4000m	6000m
-19,658ft	-13,124ft	-6562ft	-3281ft	-1640ft	-820ft	-328ft/-100m	0	820ft	1640ft	3281ft	6562ft	9843ft	13,124ft	19,685ft

France, Andorra & Monaco

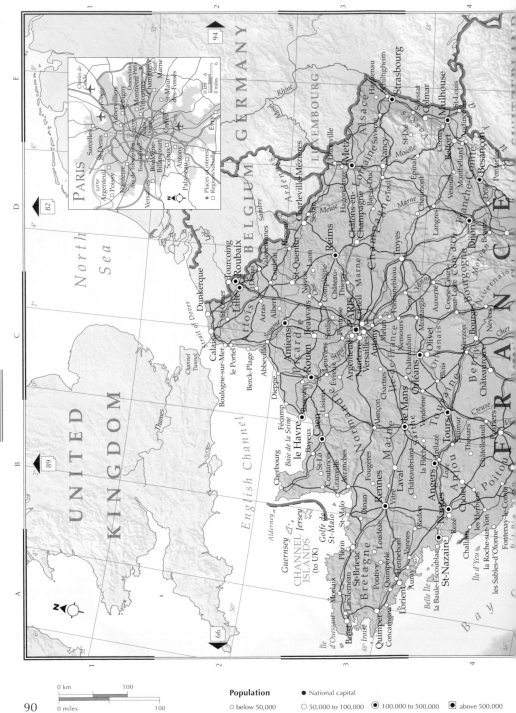

Population

● National capital

○ below 50,000　○ 50,000 to 100,000　◉ 100,000 to 500,000　▣ above 500,000

0 km 　　100

0 miles 　　100

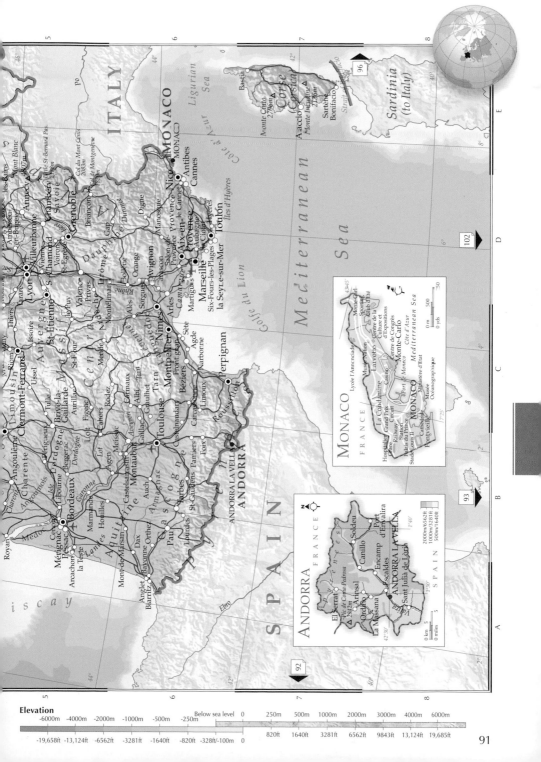

ITALY

MONACO

Po

Mont Blanc

Mont Cenis
Col du Mont Cenis
2083m

Col de Montgenèvre
1850m

les-Bains

Ambérieu-
en-Bugey

Annecy

Chambéry

Savoie

Villeurbanne

Voiron

Lyon

Chamond

St-Etienne

St-Egrève

Grenoble

Briançon

Vienne

Gap

Dauphiné

Isère

Ligurian
Sea

Bastia

Corse
(Corsica)

Monte Cinto
2706m

Ajaccio
Monte Incudine
2136m

Sartène
Bonifacio

Strait of Bonifacio

Sardinia
(to Italy)

Tarare

Thiers

Rhône

Drôme

Digne

Manosque

Haute-
Provence

Côte d'Azur

Nice
Antibes
Cannes

MONACO

Issoire

Ussel

St-Flour

Auvergne

Le Puy

Aurillac

Privas

Montélimar

Valence

Die

Durance

Aix-en-
Provence

Provence

Hyères
Toulon

les d'Hyères

la Seyne-sur-Mer

Six-Fours-les-Plages

Marseille

Orange

Avignon

Alès

Sorgues

Salon-de-
Provence

Arles

Martigues

Durance

Nîmes

Camargue

Languedoc

Montpellier

Sète

Agde

Béziers

Narbonne

Mediterranean
Sea

Golfe du Lion

Limousin

Clermont-Ferrand

Riom

Tulle

Brive-la-
Gaillarde

Périgueux

Dordogne

Figeac

Rodez

Cévennes

Tarn

Albi

Carmaux

Gaillac

Montauban

Castres

Castelnaudary

Carcassonne

Limoux

Perpignan

Roussillon

SPAIN

Angoulême

Charente

Cognac

Limousin

Isle

Libourne

Bergerac

Lot

Agen

Garonne

Marmande

Cahors

Meissac

Villeneuve

Toulouse

Auch

Armagnac

Tarbes

St-Gaudens

Foix

Pamiers

ANDORRA

ANDORRA LA VELLA

Royan

Médoc

Arcachon

la Teste

Mérignac

Pessac

Bordeaux

Cenon

Gascogne

Landes

Mont-de-Marsan

Dax

Orthez

Pau

Lourdes

Aquitaine

Anglet

Biarritz

Bayonne

Pyrénées

Ebro

iscay

MONACO

FRANCE

Lycée l'Annonciade

Musée National

Monte-Carlo

Sporting
Club d'Été

Larvotto

Centre de la
Culture et
d'Expositions

Monte-Carlo

Casino

Centre de Congrès

La Condamine

Grand Prix
Railway
Circuit

Stadium

Stade Louis II

Musée Naval

Monaco

Port de Monaco

FRANCE

Cathédrale

Monastère d'État

Fontvieille

Musée
Océanographique

Côte d'Azur

Mediterranean Sea

0 m   500
0 yds   550

ANDORRA

FRANCE

Soldeu

Port
d'Envalira

Pyrénées

El Serrat

Ordino

Arinsal

La Massana

Pic de Coma Pedrosa
2942m

Canillo

Encamp

Escaldes

ANDORRA LA VELLA

Sant Julià de Lòria

SPAIN

2000m/6562ft
1000m/3281ft
500m/1640ft

0 km   5
0 miles   5

Elevation

					Below sea level								
-6000m	-4000m	-2000m	-1000m	-500m	-250m	0	250m	500m	1000m	2000m	3000m	4000m	6000m
-19,658ft	-13,124ft	-6562ft	-3281ft	-1640ft	-820ft	-328ft/-100m	0	820ft	1640ft	3281ft	6562ft	9843ft	13,124ft	19,685ft

Spain & Portugal

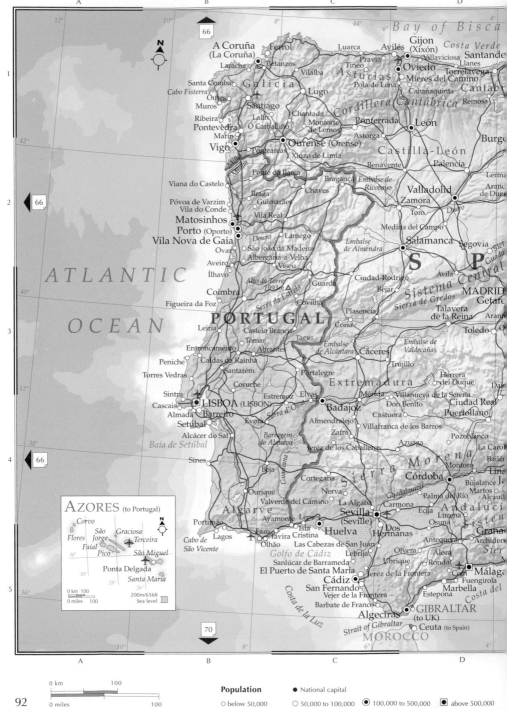

EUROPE

Spain & Portugal

Population

○ below 50,000 ○ 50,000 to 100,000 ◉ 100,000 to 500,000 ■ above 500,000

● National capital

Germany & the Alpine States

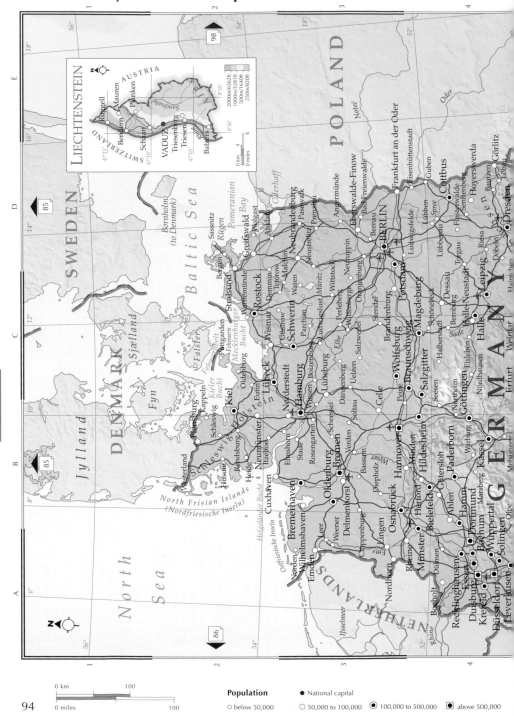

LIECHTENSTEIN

AUSTRIA

SWITZERLAND

Ruggell
Mauren
Planken
Schellenberg
Bendern
Eschen
Gamprin
Schaan
VADUZ
Triesenberg
Triesen
Balzers

2000m/6562ft
1000m/3281ft
500m/1640ft
250m/820ft

0 km   4
0 miles 4

SWEDEN

DENMARK

POLAND

GERMANY

NETHERLANDS

Baltic Sea

North Sea

Pomeranian Bay

Greifswald Bay

Oder

Oderhaff

Bornholm
(to Denmark)

Sjælland

Fyn

Jylland

North Frisian Islands
(Nordfriesische Inseln)

Ostfriesische Inseln

Mecklenburger Bucht

Kieler Bucht

Helgoländer Bucht

Ijsselmeer

Berlin
Potsdam
Frankfurt an der Oder
Eisenhüttenstadt
Guben
Cottbus
Forst
Hoyerswerda
Görlitz
Löbau
Bautzen
Dresden
Döbeln
Riesa
Meißen
Torgau
Leipzig
Halle
Halle-Neustadt
Eisleben
Dessau
Bernburg
Magdeburg
Schönebeck
Halberstadt
Stendal
Brandenburg
Wolfsburg
Braunschweig
Salzgitter
Hildesheim
Hannover
Göttingen
Northeim
Nordhausen
Mühlhausen
Erfurt
Kassel
Warburg
Paderborn
Gütersloh
Bielefeld
Herford
Minden
Hameln
Detmold
Lippstadt
Hamm
Dortmund
Bochum
Essen
Duisburg
Krefeld
Mönchengladbach
Düsseldorf
Solingen
Wuppertal
Remscheid
Köln
Recklinghausen
Gelsenkirchen
Bottrop
Bocholt
Münster
Dülmen
Coesfeld
Ahlen
Osnabrück
Rheine
Nordhorn
Lingen
Cloppenburg
Oldenburg
Delmenhorst
Bremen
Bremerhaven
Wilhelmshaven
Emden
Leer
Norden
Bassum
Diepholz
Vechta
Weener
Cuxhaven
Stade
Buxtehude
Rosengarten
Verden
Hamburg
Neumünster
Norderstedt
Itzehoe
Heide
Husum
Flensburg
Schleswig
Rendsburg
Kiel
Eutin
Oldenburg
Lübeck
Wismar
Schwerin
Rostock
Warnemünde
Stralsund
Bergen
Sassnitz
Greifswald
Wolgast
Anklam
Pasewalk
Prenzlau
Neubrandenburg
Neustrelitz
Waren
Güstrow
Parchim
Ludwigslust
Boizenburg
Lüneburg
Celle
Uelzen
Soltau
Scheeßel
Rotenburg
Lauenburg
Danneberg
Salzwedel
Wittenberge
Perleberg
Wittstock
Pritzwalk
Kyritz
Rathenow
Oranienburg
Bernau
Eberswalde-Finow
Bad Freienwalde
Angermünde
Templin
Lübben
Luckenwalde
Jüterbog
Lübbenau
Senftenberg
Finsterwalde
Elsterwerda
Wittenberg
Bitterfeld

Rügen
Fehmarn
Falster

Eider
Elbe
Weser
Ems
Rhine
Saale
Spree
Noteć
Oder
Havel
Müritz

0 km   100
0 miles 100

Population   ● National capital

○ below 50,000   ○ 50,000 to 100,000   ◉ 100,000 to 500,000   ■ above 500,000

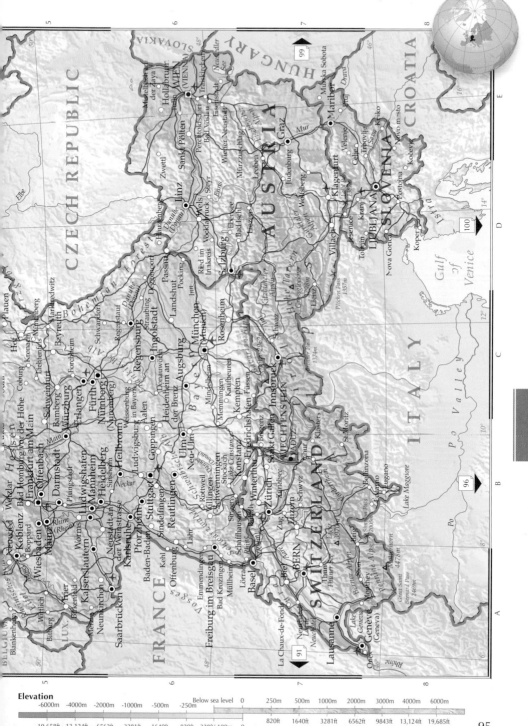

Elevation

						Below sea level	0	250m	500m	1000m	2000m	3000m	4000m	6000m
-6000m	-4000m	-2000m	-1000m	-500m	-250m									

						820ft	1640ft	3281ft	6562ft	9843ft	13,124ft	19,685ft
-19,658ft	-13,124ft	-6562ft	-3281ft	-1640ft	-820ft	-328ft/-100m	0					

SLOVAKIA
HUNGARY
100
Drava
Sava
BOSNIA &
HERZEGOVINA
CROATIA
Adriatic Sea
95
Dalmatia
Dogana
Serravalle
Fiorina
Gualdicciolo
Borgo Maggiore
SAN MARINO
Chiesanuova
Faetano
Monte Titano
739m
Murata
Montegiardino
Calungo
ITALY
ITALY
SAN MARINO

SLOVENIA
Istria

GERMANY
AUSTRIA
Brenner Pass
1374m
Inn
Brunico
Bressanone
Alpi
Dolomitiche
Trieste
Tarvisio
Cortina d'Ampezzo
Udine
Gemona del Friuli
Portogruaro
Gulf of
Venice
Foci del Po

Merano
Bolzano
Trento
Edolo
Bergamo
Lombardia
Sesto San Giovanni
Brescia
Monza
Como
Lago di Como
Lago di Garda
Arco
Bassano del Grappa
Vicenza
Verona
Mantova
Cremona
Padova
Mestre
Treviso
Pordenone
Venezia
(Venice)
Chioggia
Rovigo
Adige
Po

SWITZERLAND
Lake
Constance
Rhine
Lugano
Varese
Lago Maggiore
Milano
(Milan)
Pavia
Novara
Vercelli
Rhône
Lake Geneva

LIECHTENSTEIN

Great Saint
Bernard Pass
2469m
Aosta
Gran Paradiso
4061m
Mont Blanc
4807m
Little St-Bernard
Pass 2188m

FRANCE

Susa
Moncalieri
Rivoli
Torino
(Turin)
Asti
Castagnole
Alessandria
Appennino
Monovi
Savigliano
Cuneo
Piemonte
Mondovi
Finale Ligure
San Remo
Imperia
Ventimiglia
MONACO

Piacenza
Reggio nell'Emilia
Parma
Genova
(Genoa)
Ligure
Golfo di Genova
Savona
La Spezia
Massa
Carrara
Viareggio
Pisa
Livorno
Cecina

Modena
Carpi
Bologna
Ferrara
Comacchio
Imola
Faenza
Forlì
Cesena
Ravenna
Rimini
SAN
MARINO
Fano
Pesaro
Sansepolcro
Arezzo
Firenze
(Florence)
Prato
Pistoia
Lucca
Pistoia
Chianti
Siena
Toscana
Grosseto
Orbetello
Portoferraio
Isola
d'Elba
Piombino
Archipelago Toscano

Ligurian
Sea

Corse
(Corsica)
(to France)

Strait of Bonifacio

Falconara Marittima
Civitanova Marche
Ancona
Fermo
Ascoli Piceno
Giulianova
Teramo
Pescara
Ortona
Chieti
L'Aquila
Avezzano
Tivoli
VATICAN CITY
Civitavecchia
Viterbo
Terni
Foligno
Nodi
Perugia
Lago Trasimeno
Marche
Umbria Marchigiano
Appennino
ITALIA

0 km   100
0 miles   100

Population   ● National capital

○ below 50,000   ○ 50,000 to 100,000   ◉ 100,000 to 500,000   ◼ above 500,000

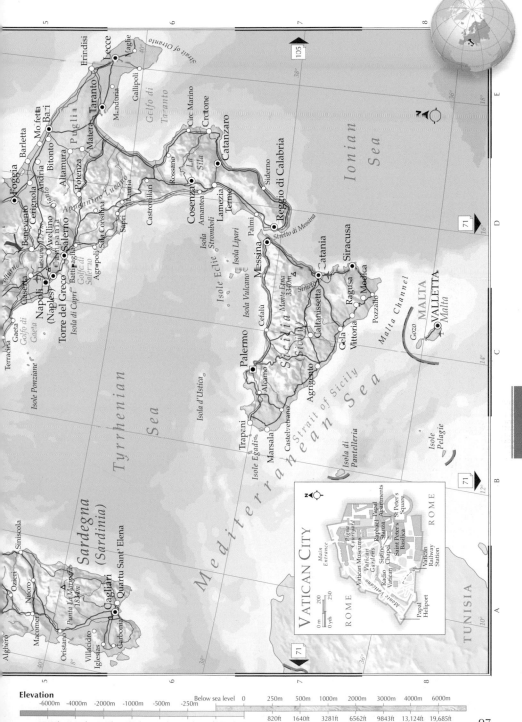

Elevation

-6000m	-4000m	-2000m	-1000m	-500m	-250m	Below sea level	0	250m	500m	1000m	2000m	3000m	4000m	6000m
-19,658ft	-13,124ft	-6562ft	-3281ft	-1640ft	-820ft	-328ft/-100m	0	820ft	1640ft	3281ft	6562ft	9843ft	13,124ft	19,685ft

Central Europe

Population   ● National capital

○ below 50,000   ○ 50,000 to 100,000   ◎ 100,000 to 500,000   ◼ above 500,000

0 km 100
0 miles 100

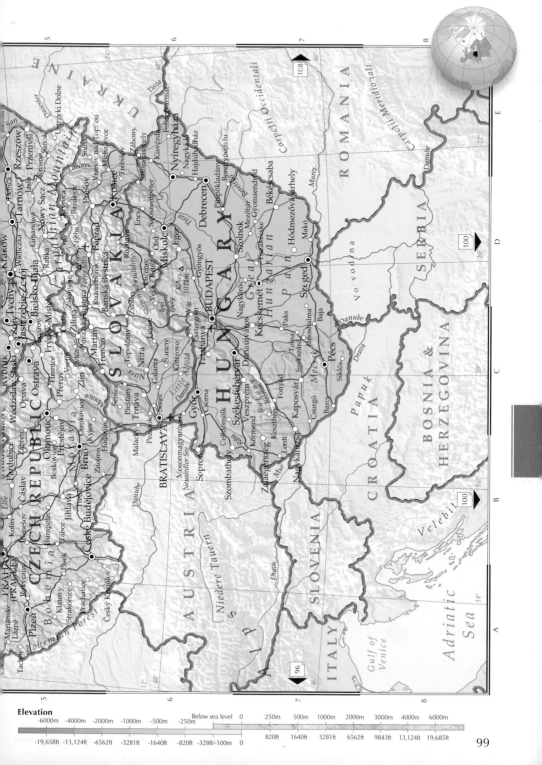

Elevation

-6000m	-4000m	-2000m	-1000m	-500m	-250m	Below sea level	0	250m	500m	1000m	2000m	3000m	4000m	6000m

| -19,658ft | -13,124ft | -6562ft | -3281ft | -1640ft | -820ft | -328ft/-100m | 0 | 820ft | 1640ft | 3281ft | 6562ft | 9843ft | 13,124ft | 19,685ft |

Southeast Europe

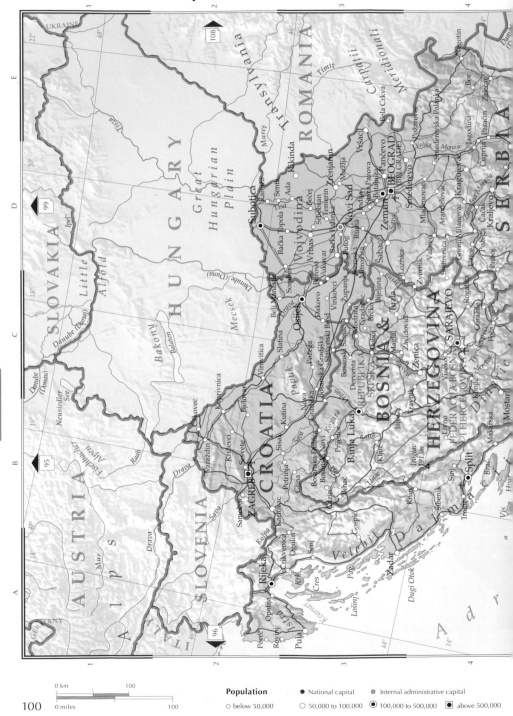

Population
○ below 50,000
○ 50,000 to 100,000
◉ 100,000 to 500,000
● National capital
○ Internal administrative capital
■ above 500,000

100

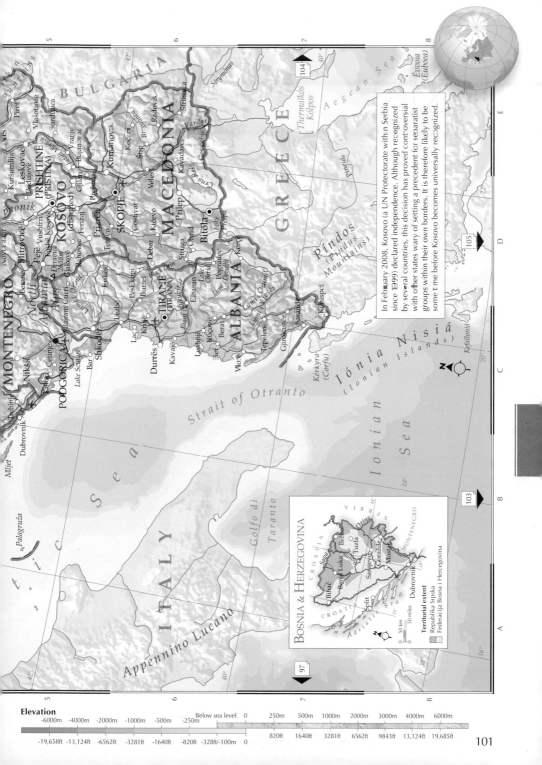

In February 2008, Kosovo (a UN Protectorate with n Serbia since 1999) declared independence. Although recognized by several countries, this decision has proved controversial with other states wary of setting a precedent for separatist groups within their own borders. It is therefore likely to be some t me before Kosovo becomes universally recognized.

Elevation

-6000m	-4000m	-2000m	-1000m	-500m	-250m	Below sea level	0	250m	500m	1000m	2000m	3000m	4000m	6000m
-19,658ft	-13,124ft	-6562ft	-3281ft	-1640ft	-820ft	-328ft/-100m	0	820ft	1640ft	3281ft	6562ft	9843ft	13,124ft	19,685ft

The Mediterranean

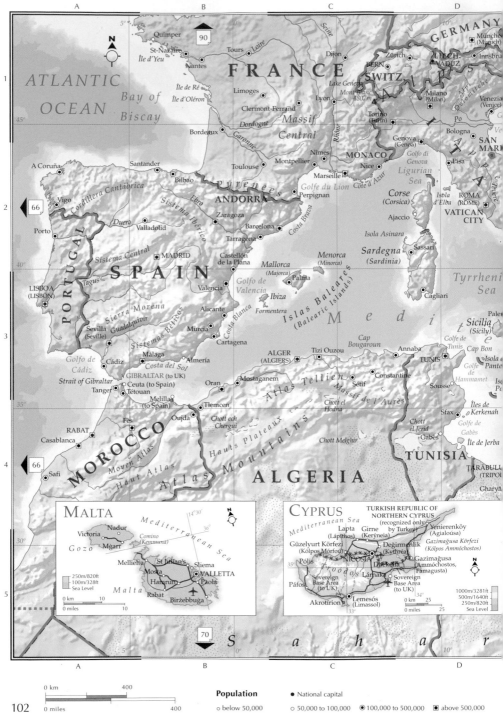

ATLANTIC OCEAN

Bay of Biscay

Quimper
St-Nazaire
Île d'Yeu
Nantes
Île de Ré
Île d'Oléron

FRANCE

Tours
Loire
Limoges
Clermont-Ferrand
Dordogne
Bordeaux
Garonne
Toulouse

Dijon
Lyon
Seine
Mont Blanc
4807m
Rhône
Massif Central

Zürich
BERN
SWITZ.
Lake Geneva

GERMANY
München
(Munich)
Innsbru
LIECH.
VADUZ

Milano
(Milan)
Torino
(Turin)
Po

Venezia
(Venice)

66

PORTUGAL

A Coruña
Vigo
Porto
Duero
Santander
Cordillera Cantábrica
Bilbao
Sistema Ibérica
Ebro
Zaragoza
ANDORRA
Barcelona
Tarragona

SPAIN

Valladolid
Sistema Central
MADRID
Tagus
LISBOA
(LISBON)
Castellón de la Plana
Valencia
Golfo de Valencia
Ibiza
Formentera

Pyrenees
Nîmes
Montpellier
Perpignan
Golfe du Lion
Marseille
Côte d'Azur
MONACO
Nice

Genova
(Genoa)
Golfo di Genova
Ligurian Sea
Corse
(Corsica)
Ajaccio
Isola d'Elba
Isola Asinara

Bologna
Pisa
ROMA
(ROME)
SAN MARI
VATICAN CITY

Mallorca
(Majorca)
Palma
Menorca
(Minorca)
Islas Baleares
(Balearic Islands)

Sardegna
(Sardinia)
Sassari
Cagliari

Tyrrheni Sea

Sierra Morena
Guadalquivir
Sistema Béticos
Alicante
Costa Blanca
Murcia
Cartagena

Golfo de Cádiz
Cádiz
Málaga
Almería
Costa del Sol
GIBRALTAR
(to UK)
Ceuta (to Spain)
Strait of Gibraltar
Tanger
Tétouan
Melilla
(to Spain)

Sevilla
(Seville)

Ibiza

Medi

ALGER
(ALGIERS)
Tizi Ouzou
Oran
Mostaganem
Tlemcen

Cap Bougaroun
Annaba
Constantine
Sétif
Atlas Tellien
Massif de l'Aurès

Golfe de Tunis
Cap Bon
TUNIS
Golfe de Hammamet
Sousse

Sicilia
(Sicily)
Pale
Isola d
Pante
Ise
Pe

Fès
Oujda
Chott ech Chergui
Moyen Atlas
Haut Atlas
Atlas Mountains
Hauts Plateaux
Chott el Hodna
Chott Melghir
Chott el Jerid

Îles de Kerkenah
Sfax
Golfe de Gabès
Gabès
Île de Jerba

RABAT
Casablanca
Safi
MOROCCO

66

ALGERIA

TUNISIA
TARABULUS
(TRIPOLI)
Gharya

MALTA

Mediterranean Sea

Victoria
Nadur
Mġarr
Gozo
Comino
(Kemmuna)
Mellieha
Mosta
Hamrun
Rabat
St Julian's
Sliema
VALLETTA
Paola
Birżebbuġa
Malta

250m/820ft
100m/328ft
Sea Level
0 km   10
0 miles   10

S
a
h
a
r

CYPRUS

TURKISH REPUBLIC OF NORTHERN CYPRUS
(recognized only by Turkey)

Mediterranean Sea

Lapta
(Lápithos)
Girne
(Kerýneia)
Güzelyurt Körfezi
(Kólpos Mórfou)
Pólis
Páfos
Pródos
Sovereign Base Area
(to UK)
Akrotírion
Lemesós
(Limassol)

Yenierenköy
(Agialoúsa)
Değirmenlik
(Kythréa)
NICOSIA
Dikélia
Lárnaka
Sovereign Base Area
(to UK)

Gazimağusa Körfezi
(Kólpos Ammóchostos)
Gazimağusa
(Ammóchostos,
Famagusta)

1000m/3281ft
500m/1640ft
250m/820ft
Sea Level
0 km   25
0 miles   25

---

0 km   400
0 miles   400

Population   ● National capital

○ below 50,000   ○ 50,000 to 100,000   ◉ 100,000 to 500,000   ◼ above 500,000

Elevation

-6000m	-4000m	-2000m	-1000m	-500m	-250m	Below sea level	0	250m	500m	1000m	2000m	3000m	4000m	6000m
-19,658ft	-13,124ft	-6562ft	-3281ft	-1640ft	-820ft	-328ft/-100m	0	820ft	1640ft	3281ft	6562ft	9843ft	13,124ft	19,685ft

Bulgaria & Greece

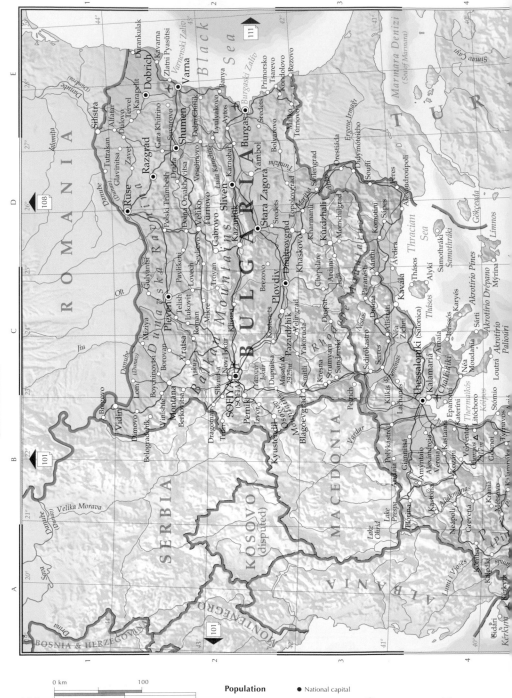

0 km   100

0 miles   100

Population
    ● National capital

○ below 50,000   ○ 50,000 to 100,000   ◉ 100,000 to 500,000   ◼ above 500,000

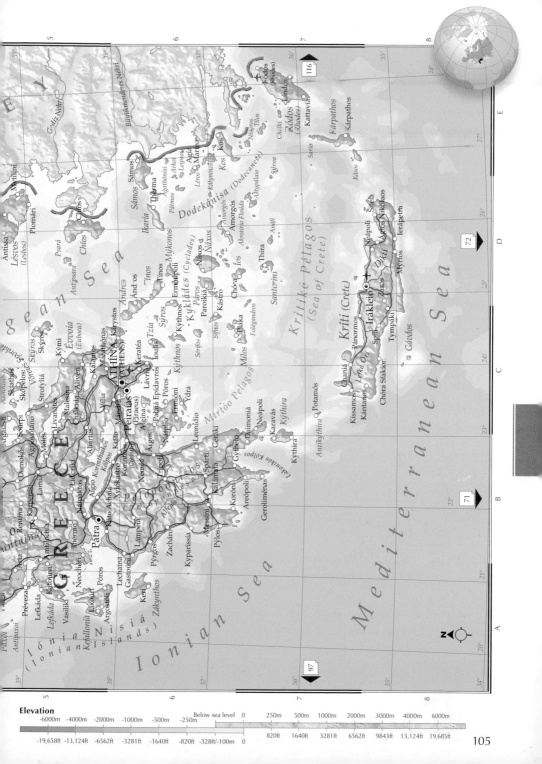

Pátroi
Antíppaxoi
Préveza
Lefkáda
Lefkáda
Vasilikí
Meganísi
Argostóli
Póros
Keri
Neochóri
Kástonia
Amfilochía
Thermo
Agrínio
Neápoli
Astakós
Mesolóngi
Lampéia
Gastoúni
Lecháina
Zacharo
Pýrgos
Kyparissía
Pýlos
Koróni
Messíni
Kalamáta
Areópoli
Gýtheio
Gerolíménas
Leonídio
Neápoli
Karavás
Kýthira
Kythira
Kýthira
Antikýthira
Potamós
Kissamos
Kántanos
Chóra Sfakíon
Chaniá
Lefká Óri
Gávdos
Spíli
Tympáki
Pánormos
Iráklefo
Moíres
Kríti (Crete)
Díkti
Ierápetra
Myrtos
Ágios Nikólaos
Neápoli
Sitía
Kattaviá
Kásos
Kárpathos
Fárpathos
Ródos (Rhodes)
Chálki
Líndos
Tílos
Nísyros
Sými
Kos
Astypálaia
Agathónisi
Léros
Kálymnos
Pátmos
Arkói
Amorgós
Akrotírio Floúda
Amorgós (Dodecaneses)
Dodekánisa (Dodecanese)
Anáfi
Thíra
Íos
Folégandros
Sikínos
Santoríni
Páros
Náxos
Paroikiá
Chóra
Kými
Sérifos
Sífnos
Mílos
Kímolos
Kástro
Sýros
Ermoúpoli
Tínos
Mýkonos
Kyklades (Cyclades)
Kýthnos
Tzía
Ioúlis
Tinos
And·os
Ándros
Psará
Chíos
Plomári
Antíssa
Mytilíni
Lésvos
(Lesbos)
Sámos
Sámos
Ikaría
Thíma
Fourni

Aegean Sea

Kritikó Pélagos
(Sea of Crete)

Mediterranean Sea

Mirtóo Pélagos

Ionian Sea

Iónia Nisiá
(Ionian Islands)
Kefallonía
Zákynthos

Lakonikós Kólpos

G R E E C E

Pátra
Kórinthos
Kórinthos
Korinthiakós Kólpos
Ydra
Sýroi
Athína
Pátroi
Spárti

ATHÍNA
(ATHENS)
Peiraías
(Piraeus)

Elevation

Below sea level						0	250m	500m	1000m	2000m	3000m	4000m	6000m
-6000m	-4000m	-2000m	-1000m	-500m	-250m								
-19,658ft	-13,124ft	-6562ft	-3281ft	-1640ft	-820ft	-328ft/-100m	0	820ft	1640ft	3281ft	6562ft	9843ft	13,124ft 19,685ft

The Baltic States & Belarus

SWEDEN

FINLAND

RUSSIAN FEDERATION

ESTONIA

LATVIA

LITHUANIA

KALININGRAD
(to Russian Federation)

Gulf of Finland

Baltic Sea

Gulf of Riga

Gotland

Öland

TALLINN

Tartu

Narva

RIGA

Šiauliai

Panevėžys

Klaipėda

Kaliningrad

Daugavpils

Population

● National capital

○ below 50,000   ○ 50,000 to 100,000   ◉ 100,000 to 500,000   ◼ above 500,000

0 km   100

0 miles   100

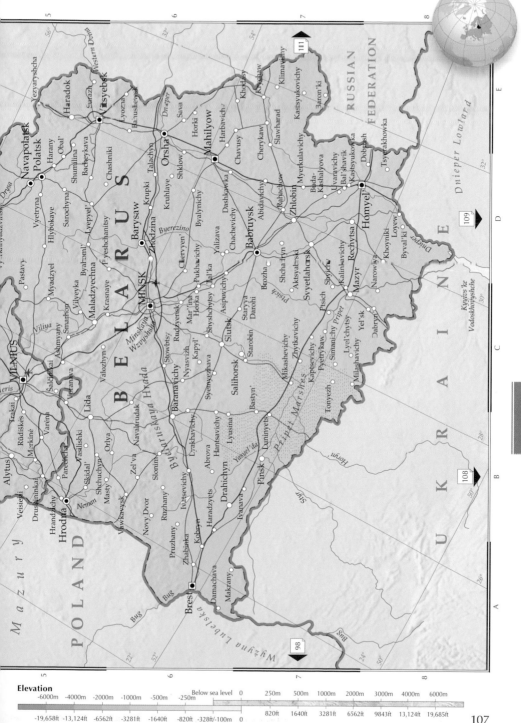

Elevation

						Below sea level	0						
-6000m	-4000m	-2000m	-1000m	-500m	-250m			250m	500m	1000m	2000m	3000m	4000m	6000m

| -19,658ft | -13,124ft | -6562ft | -3281ft | -1640ft | -820ft | -328ft/-100m | 0 | 820ft | 1640ft | 3281ft | 6562ft | 9843ft | 13,124ft | 19,685ft |

Ukraine, Moldova & Romania

Population

○ below 50,000

○ 50,000 to 100,000

◉ 100,000 to 500,000

◼ above 500,000

● National capital

0 km   100

0 miles   100

E   F   G   H

30°   32°   34°   36°   38°   52°

110

Dnieper
(Dnipro)
Horodnya
Shchors
Shostka
Hlukhiv

1

Chernihiv
Konotop
40°

Nizhyn
Bakhmach
yivs'ke
skhovyshche
Oster
Romny
Sumy

RUSSIAN

Nosivka

XIV
VV
Brovary
Pryluky
Yahotyn
Pyryatyn
Lebedyn
Okhtyrka
Zolochiv
Derhachi
Lyubotyn

FEDERATION

yarka
Vasyl'kiv
Istiv
Bila Tserkva
Bohuslav
Kaniv
Hrebinka
Lubny
Myrhorod
Kharkiv
50°

Kanis'ke
Vodoskhovyshche
Kharkiv

110

Merefa

Znatob"sk

Zolotonosha
Cherkasy
Hlobyne
Poltava
Izyum
Oskil
Kup"yans'k

venyhorodka
Smila
Chyhyryn
Kremenchuts'ke
Vodoskhovyshche
Kreminna
Rubizhne
Syeverodonets'k

Tal'ne
Shpola
Svitlovods'k
Kremenchuk
Slov"yans'k
Lysychans'k

Oleksandrivka
Dniprodzerzhyns'ke
Vodoskhovyshche
Kramators'k
Zolote
Luhans'k

an
Mala Vyska
Znam"yanka
Oleksandriya
Novomoskovs'k
Kostyantynivka
Stakhanov

Holovanivs'k
Kirovohrad
Dniprodzerzhyns'k
Pavlohrad
Horlivka
Krasnodon

Ulyanivka
Zhovti Vody
P"yatykhatky
Dnipropetrovs'k
Synel'nykove
Yenakiyeve
Krasnyy Luch

Vil'shanka
Dolyns'ka
Makiyivka
Torez

Pervomays'k
Bobrynets'
Pokrovs'ke
Donets'k

Kryve Ozero
Arbuzynka
Inhulets'
Kryvyy Rih
Zaporizhzhya
Amvrosiyivka
48°

Novyy Buh
Ordzhonikidze
Marhanets'
Orikhiv
Dokuchayevs'k

Voznesens'k
Kam"yanka-Dniprovs'ka
Nikopol'
Dniprorudne
Volnovakha
Polohy
Novoazovs'k

Pivdennyy Buh
Kakhovs'ka
Vodoskhovyshche
Tokmak
Molochans'k
Mariupol'
Don

B l a c k
Mykolayiv
Dnieper
(Dnipro)
Kakhovka
Melitopol'
Gulf of Taganrog
Yeya

Zhovtneve
Yakymivka
Prymors'k

Ochakiv
Kherson
Novotroyits'ke
Berdyans'k

Odesa
Hola Prystan'
Tsyurupyns'k
Heniches'k
Sea of Azov

Illichivs'k
Chaplynka
46°

Kalanchak
Armyans'k
RUSSIAN

Krasnoperekops'k

Rozdol'ne
Dzhankoy
Kerch Strait
FEDERATION

Chornomors'ke
Krasnohvardiys'ke
Zatoka
Syvash
Kerch

Nyzhn'ohirs'kyy
Lenine
Kuban'

Yevpatoriya
Kryms'kyy
Pivostriv
Feodosiya

Saky
Simferopol'
Bakhchysaray
Alushta
44°

Sevastopol'
Krymski Hory

Yalta
Alupka

B l a c k   S e a

116

32°   34°   36°   38°   40°

E   F   G   H

Elevation

| -6000m | -4000m | -2000m | -1000m | -500m | -250m | Below sea level | 0 | 250m | 500m | 1000m | 2000m | 3000m | 4000m | 6000m |

-19,658ft | -13,124ft | -6562ft | -3281ft | -1640ft | -820ft | -328ft/-100m | 0 | 820ft | 1640ft | 3281ft | 6562ft | 9843ft | 13,124ft | 19,685ft

European Russia

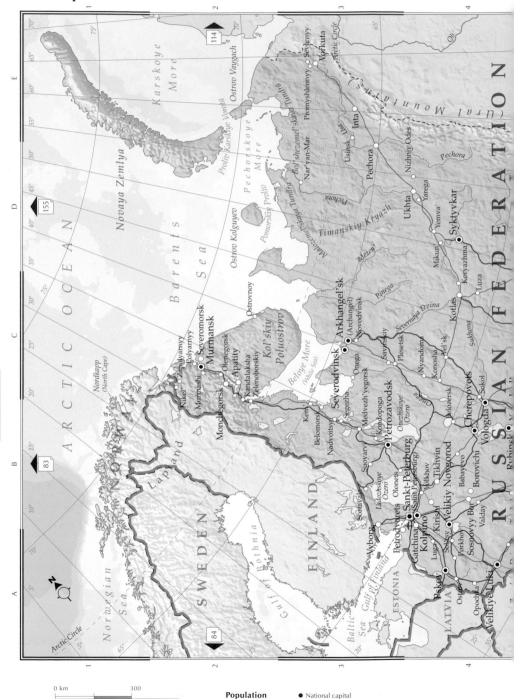

Population

○ below 50,000

○ 50,000 to 100,000

◉ 100,000 to 500,000

■ above 500,000

● National capital

0 km 300

0 miles 300

Elevation

-6000m	-4000m	-2000m	-1000m	-500m	-250m	Below sea level	0	250m	500m	1000m	2000m	3000m	4000m	6000m
-19,658ft	-13,124ft	-6562ft	-3281ft	-1640ft	-820ft	-328ft/-100m	0	820ft	1640ft	3281ft	6562ft	9843ft	13,124ft	19,685ft

North & West Asia

Franz Josef Land

Norwegian Sea

North Cape

Barents Sea

Murmansk

Kola Peninsula

Archangel

Summer limit of pack ice

Winter limit of pack ice

Ostrov Kolguyev

A R C T I C

Ostrov Komsomolets

Ostrov Oktyabr'skoy Revolyutsii

Ostrov Bol'shevik

Severnaya Zen

Kara Sea

East Nobaya Zemlya Trench

Novaya Zemlya

Poluostrov Yamal

Poluostrov Taymyr

Kheta

North Siber

Central Siberian Plateau

Noril'sk

Arctic Circle

81

White Sea

Northern Dvina

Lake Onega

Lake Ladoga

Saint Petersburg

MOSCOW

Kaliningrad

KALININGRAD
(to Russ. Fed.)

Gulf of Bothnia

Baltic Sea

Vologda

Yaroslavl'

Nizhniy Novgorod

Central Russian Upland

Ul'yanovsk

Voronezh

R U S S I A N   F

West Siberian Plain

Ural Mountains

Perm'

Yekaterinburg

Ob'

Kazan'

Ufa

Samara

Saratov

Orenburg

Ural'sk

Chelyabinsk

Ishim

Omsk

Irtysh

Novosibirsk

Ob

Tomsk

Chulym

Novokuznetsk

Krasnoyarsk

Yenisey

Stony Tunguska

Lower Tunguska

Angara

Irkut

Sayanskiy Khrebet

S i

G

E U R O P E

Don

Volgograd

Rostov-na-Donu

Stavropol'

El'brus 5642m

Danube

Black Sea

Astrakhan

Volga

Ural

Caspian Sea

Aral'sk

Aktau

Aral Sea

Sur Darya

Ustyurt Plateau

Kyzyl Kum

K A Z A K H S T A N

Kirghiz Steppe

ASTANA

Karaganda

Kazakh Uplands

Lake Balkhash

Ozero Zaysan

Altai Mountains

Semipalatinsk

A

S

Kyzylorda

Taraz

Almaty

Ili

Istanbul

Mediterranean Sea

Adana

CYPRUS

Caucasus

Kitle Dağları

GEORGIA

TBILISI

ANKARA

ARMENIA

YEREVAN

AZERB.

BAKU

TURKEY

Lake Van

Tabriz

Aleppo

Mosul

SYRIA

IRAQ

DAMASCUS

BAGHDAD

BEIRUT

LEBANON

ISRAEL

JERUSALEM

AMMAN

JORDAN

Dead Sea -392m

Gaziantep

UZBEKISTAN

Dasoguz

TURKMENISTAN

Garagum

Amu Darya

ASGABAT

TASHKENT

BISHKEK

Tien Shan

Pik Pobedy 7443m

KYRGYZSTAN

DUSHANBE

TAJIKISTAN

Hindu Kush

KABUL

Jalalabad

Kunlun Mountains

TEHRAN

Qom

Isfahan

IRAN

Iranian Plateau

Herat

AFGHANISTAN

Khyber Pass

Himalayas

Thar Desert

Indus

Ganges

Zagros Mountains

Euphrates

Tigris

Basra

KUWAIT

KUWAIT

Shiraz

Zahedan

Bandar-e 'Abbas

Murray Ridge

Indus Fan

Ganges Fan

Syrian Desert

An Nafud

SAUDI ARABIA

RIYADH

MANAMA

BAHRAIN

QATAR

DOHA

Dubai

Persian Gulf

U.A.E.

Gulf of Oman

ABU DHABI

MUSCAT

Sur

OMAN

Jedda

Red Sea

Nile

At Ta'if

Arabian Peninsula

Ar Rub' al Khali

AFRICA

Tropic of Cancer

SANA

YEMEN

Ta'izz

Aden

Gulf of Aden

Socotra
(to Yemen)

Arabian Sea

Bay of Bengal

103

69

112

Population	
• National capital	
○ below 50,000	◉ 100,000 to 500,000
○ 50,000 to 100,000	◼ above 500,000

0 km   800

0 miles   800

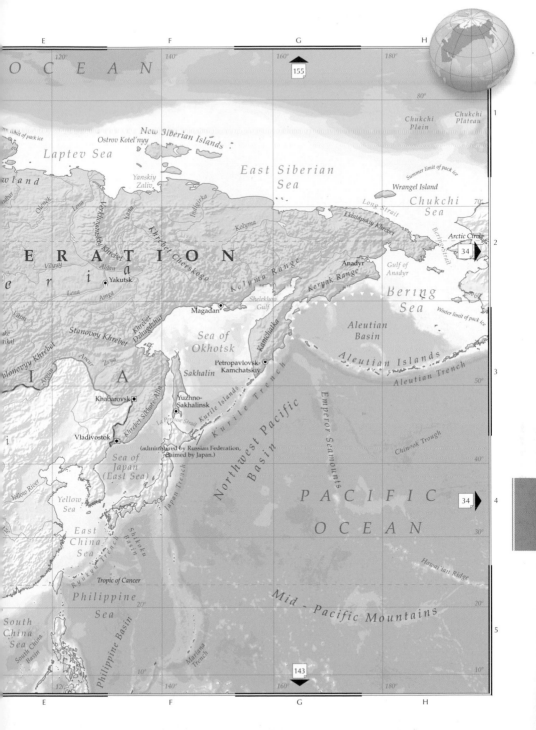

E   F   G   H

120°   140°   160°   180°

155

O C E A N

80°

Chukchi Plain

Chukchi Plateau

1

limit of pack ice

New Siberian Islands

Ostrov Kotel'nyy

Laptev Sea

East Siberian Sea

Summer limit of pack ice

Wrangel Island

Yanskiy Zaliv

Long Strait

Chukchi Sea

70°

Olenëk

Lena

Anabar

Khrebet Cherskogo

Indigirka

Kolyma

Ekiatapskiy Khrebet

Bering Strait

Arctic Circle

Vilyuy

Aldan

Koryak Range

Anadyr

Gulf of Anadyr

60°

34

2

E R A T I O N

a

Yakutsk

Kolyma Range

Shelekhov Gulf

Bering Sea

Aldan

Amga

Magadan

Kamchatka

Aleutian Basin

Lena

Stanovoy Khrebet

Khrebet Dzhugdzhur

Sea of Okhotsk

Aleutian Islands

50°

blonovyy Khrebet

Amur

Zeya

Petropavlovsk-Kamchatskiy

Sakhalin

Aleutian Trench

3

baikal

Arguñ

Khabarovsk

Khrebet Sikhote-Alin'

Yuzhno-Sakhalinsk

Kurile Islands

Kurile Trench

Northwest Pacific Basin

Emperor Seamounts

Chinook Trough

i

Vladivostok

La Pérouse Strait

(administered by Russian Federation, claimed by Japan.)

40°

Yellow River

Sea of Japan (East Sea)

Japan Trench

P A C I F I C

34

4

A

Yellow Sea

East China Sea

Shikoku Basin

O C E A N

30°

Ryukyu Trench

Hawaiian Ridge

Tropic of Cancer

Philippine Sea

20°

Mid - Pacific Mountains

20°

South China Sea

South China Basin

Philippine Basin

Mariana Trench

10°

5

120°   140°   160°   180°

143

E   F   G   H

Russia & Kazakhstan

Population

- ● National capital
- ○ below 50,000
- ○ 50,000 to 100,000
- ◉ 100,000 to 500,000
- ▣ above 500,000

0 km | 600
0 miles | 600

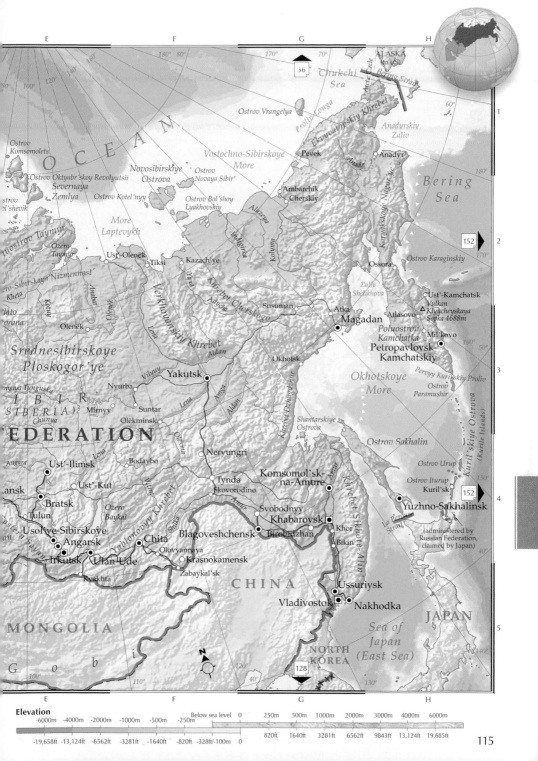

Elevation

						Below sea level	0	250m	500m	1000m	2000m	3000m	4000m	6000m
-6000m	-4000m	-2000m	-1000m	-500m	-250m									
-19,658ft	-13,124ft	-6562ft	-3281ft	-1640ft	-820ft	-328ft/-100m	0	820ft	1640ft	3281ft	6562ft	9843ft	13,124ft	19,685ft

Turkey & the Caucasus

Population

- ○ below 50,000
- ○ 50,000 to 100,000
- ◉ 100,000 to 500,000
- ◼ above 500,000

● National capital

0 km   200

0 miles   200

E   40°   45°   45°   50°   H

111

RUSSIAN

FEDERATION

Caspian

Sea

Caucasus

Gagra
Gudaut'a
Sokhumi   *Apkhazet'i*   Mestia   *Kazbek*
Och'amch'ire   *5047m*   *Caucasus*

K'ut'aisi   South
Samtredia   Ossetia   **GEORGIA**   Zaqatala   Xaçmaz

P'ot'i   Gori   Tsalka   **T'BILISI**   Quba   Siyäzän
K'obulet'i   *Lesser Cau.*   Rust'avi   Säki
Bat'umi   *Achara*   Akhalts'ikhe   *Greater Caucasus*   Sumqayıt
Hopa   *Kura*   Märäzä   **BAKI**
Pazar   Artvin   Mingäçevir   (BAKU)
Trabzon   Of.   **Vanadzor**   **Gäncä**
Giresun   *Doğu Karadeniz Dağları*   Gyumri   Sevan   Qazımämmäd
Gümüşhane   Kars   Artvi   **ARMENIA**   *Sevana Lich*   Nagorno-   Imişli   Äli-Bayramı
                Sarıkamış   **YEREVAN**   Karabakh
ahiye   İspir   Pasinler   Horasan   *Aras*   Artashat   Xankändi   Biläsuvar
Erzincan   Tercan   Erzurum   Ağrı   *Büyükağrı Dağı*   Goris
Kemah   Doğubayazıt   *(Mount Ararat)*   Länkäran
Keban   Bingöl   Patnos   Erciş   *5137m*   **AZERBAIJAN**   *Aras*
Baraji   Elazığ   Muradiye
Malatya   Muş   Tatvan   *Van*   Van
        Bitlis   *Gölü*   Naxçıvan
Atatürk   Silvan   Siirt   Gevaş
Baraji   *Daryācheh-ye*
Adıyaman   Diyarbakır   Batman   *Orūmīyeh*
Silverek   Şırnak
Viranşehir   Mardin
Şanlıurfa   Ceylanpınar   Nusaybin   **IRAN**
            Kurdistan
uhayrat
l Asad   *Al Jazīrah*   *Tigris*
        Euphrates
Jabal Bishrī
RIA   **IRAQ**   *Reshteh-ye Kühhā-ye Alborz*
                        (Elburz Mountains)
        Buhayrat
        ath   *Kühhā-ye Zāgros*
        Tharthār   120   *(Zagros Mountains)*

1

2   122

3   40°
    50°

4   120

35°

5

E   40°   45°   F   45°   G   H

Elevation

-6000m -4000m -2000m -1000m -500m -250m   Below sea level 0   250m 500m 1000m 2000m 3000m 4000m 6000m

-19,658ft -13,124ft -6562ft -3281ft -1640ft -820ft -328ft/-100m 0   820ft 1640ft 3281ft 6562ft 9843ft 13,124ft 19,685ft

The Near East

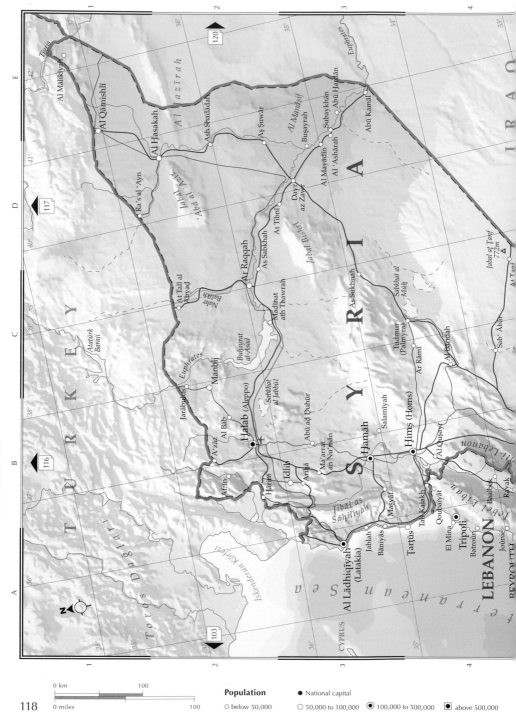

Population

● National capital

○ below 50,000   ○ 50,000 to 100,000   ◉ 100,000 to 500,000   ◼ above 500,000

0 km   100

0 miles   100

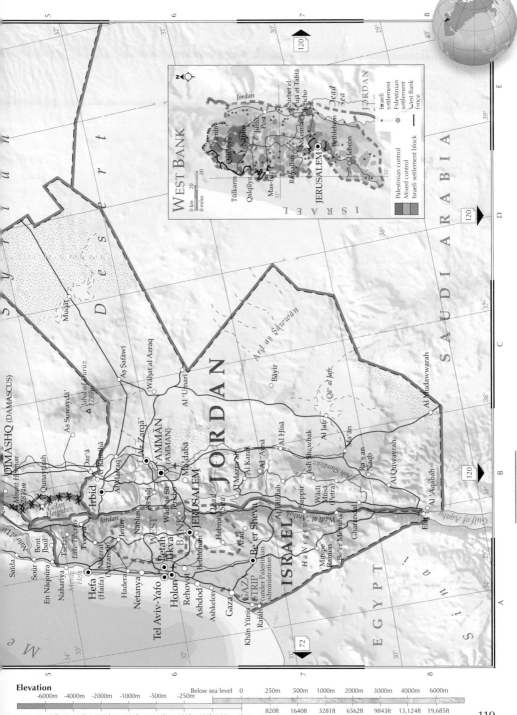

The Middle East

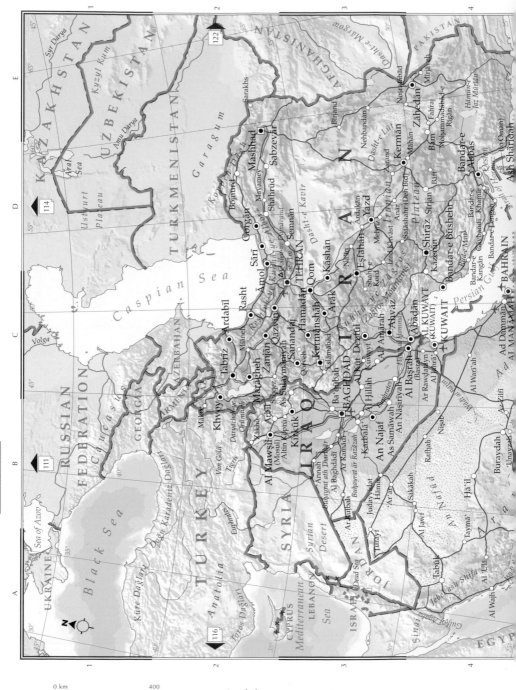

Population

- National capital

○ below 50,000	● 100,000 to 500,000
○ 50,000 to 100,000	■ above 500,000

0 km 400

0 miles 400

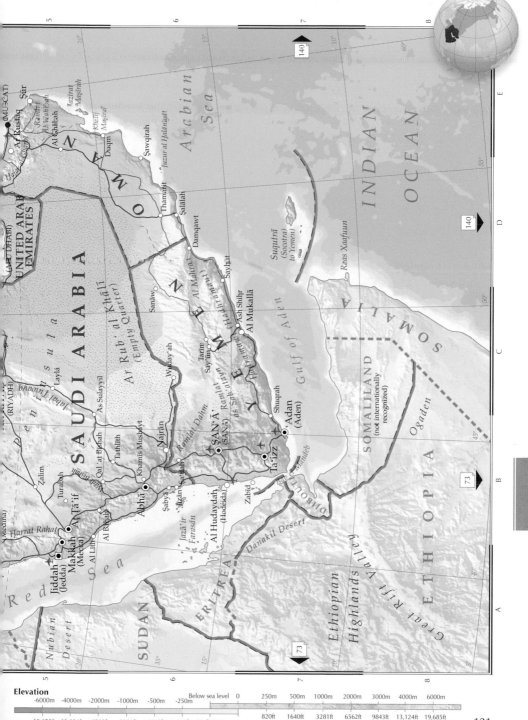

Elevation

-6000m	-4000m	-2000m	-1000m	-500m	-250m		Below sea level 0	250m	500m	1000m	2000m	3000m	4000m	6000m
-19,658ft	-13,124ft	-6562ft	-3281ft	-1640ft	-820ft	-328ft/-100m	0		820ft	1640ft	3281ft	6562ft	9843ft	13,124ft	19,685ft

Central Asia

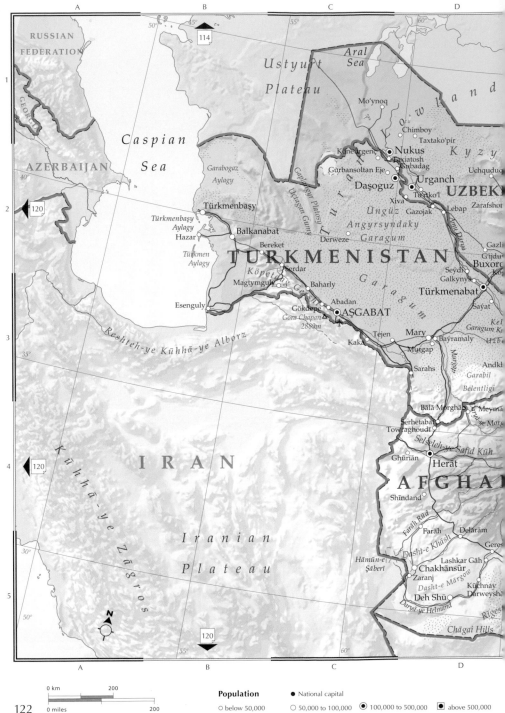

RUSSIAN FEDERATION

GEORGIA

AZERBAIJAN

Caspian Sea

Ustyurt Plateau

Aral Sea

Mo'ynoq

Chimboy

Taxtako'pir

Küneürgenç
Taxiatosh
Qubadag
Nukus
Nukus

Gürbansoltan Eje

Garabogaz Aylagy

Türkmenbaşy

Türkmenbaşy Aylagy
Hazar

Daşoguz

Xiva
Tórtko'l

Üngüz Angyrsyndaky Garagum

Gazojak
Lebap
Zarafshon

Uchquduq

Urganch

UZBEK

Gazl

Ústyurt Platosy

Uñ̄guz Garagum Gumy

Balkanabat

Bereket

Derweze

Serdar

Magtymguly

Köpet Dag Gerşi

Esenguly

Türkmen Aylagy

Baharly

Gökdepe
Gora Chapan
2889m

Abadan

AŞGABAT

TURKMENISTAN

Garagum

G'ijdu

Buxoro

Seydi
Galkynyş

Ko

Türkmenabat

Sayat

Kel

Garagum Ka

Reşteh-ye Kühhā-ye Alborz

Kaka

Tejen

Mary

Bayramaly

Muẗgap

Sarahs

Andkt
Garabil

Belentligi

Balā Morghāb
Meymaneh

Serhetabat
Towraghoudī

Selseleh-ye Safīd Kūh

Ghūriān

Herāt

AFGHAN

Shīndand

IRAN

Kühhā-ye Zāgros

Iranian Plateau

Farāh Rūd

Farāh

Delārām

Geres

Hāmūn-e Şāberī

Chakhānsūr

Zaranj

Dasht-e Mārgow

Lashkar Gāh

Küchnay
Darweysha

Deh Shū

Daryā-ye Helmand

Riges

Chāgai Hills

N

0 km   200

0 miles   200

Population   ● National capital

○ below 50,000   ○ 50,000 to 100,000   ◉ 100,000 to 500,000   ▣ above 500,000

KAZAKHSTAN

Ozero Balkhash

Peski Saryyesik-Atyrau

Peski Taukum

Peski Moyynkum

115

Ili

Borohoro Shan

Sur Darya

Gora Manas 4482m

BISHKEK
Kara-Balta — Tokmak
Talas Kemin
Ivanimpol

TOSHKENT
(TASHKENT)
Yangiyo'l Chirchiq
Angren
Nurota
Langar

KYRGYZSTAN

Chatkal Range

Kirgiz Range

Tash-Kumyr
Khrebet Moldo-Too

Dzhalal-Abad

Namangan

Ozero Issyk-Kul'
Balykchy
Karakol
Kyzyl-Suu
Kadzhi-Say
Kara-Say

Naryn
Karakol
Kokshaal-Tau

Pik Pobedy
7443m

126

Gulistan
Jizzax
Olmaliq
Bekobod

Qo'qon
Andijon

Osh
Fergʻona

Chatyr-Tash

Navoiy
Samarqand Uroteppa
Khujand

Kitob
Qarshi

Zeravshan
DUSHANBE
Denov
TAJIKISTAN
Norak
Nurek

Khovdarkan
Sulyukta
Kek-Art
Sary-Tash
Daroot-Korgon
Qarokul

Surkhob
△ Qullai Ismoili Somoni
7495m

XINJIANG
UYGUR
ZIZHIQU

Taklimakan
Shamo

Boysun
Qürghonteppa
Danghara
Jarqoʻrgʻon
Kulob
Moskva
Qakhkhum
Ghudara
Murghob

C
H
I
N
A

Balkh
Termiz
Dusti
Farkhor
Khorugh
Feyzabad
Ishkoshim
Dzhelandy
Qizilrobot

Mazar-e
Sharif
Kholm
Kondoz
Talaqan
Khanabad
Baghlan
Pol-e Khomri

Baroghil Pass 3777m
(claimed by India)

AKSAI CHIN
(administered by China,
claimed by India)

Hindu Kush
Karakoram Range

Pamir Range

Indus

Aksai
Chin

DEMCHOK/
DEMQOG
(administered by China,
claimed by India)

Barikowt
Mahmud-e Raqi
Charikar
KABOL
(KABUL)
Maydan Shahr
Mehtar Lam
Asadabad
Jalalabad

Khyber Pass 1080m
(A 'line of control'
was agreed between
India and Pakistan
in 1972)

Gardiz
Ghazni
Khowst

126

XIZANG
ZIZHIQU
(Tibet)
(administered by China,
claimed by India)

AFGHANISTAN

Zarghun
Shahr
Qalat

Indus
Raji

Himalayas

PAKISTAN

Sulaiman Range

INDIA

134

NEPAL

Toba Kakar Range
Spin Buldak
ndahar

Elevation
-6000m -4000m -2000m -1000m -500m -250m   Below sea level 0   250m 500m 1000m 2000m 3000m 4000m 6000m

-19,658ft -13,124ft -6562ft -3281ft -1640ft -820ft -328ft/-100m 0   820ft 1640ft 3281ft 6562ft 9843ft 13,124ft 19,685ft

123

South & East Asia

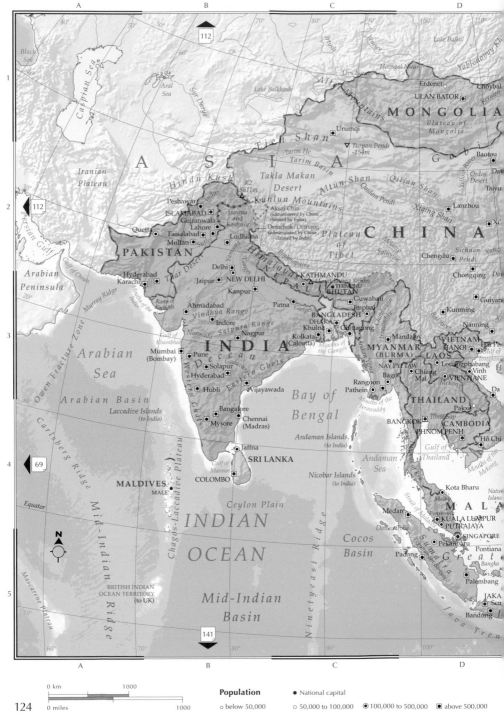

	A	B	C	D

112

Black Sea

Caspian Sea

Aral Sea

Syr Darya

Lake Balkhash

Irtysh

Yenisey

Lake Baikal

Hövsgöl Nuur

Erdenet

Choybalsan

ULAN BATOR

Keruten

Yablonovyy Kh.

1

Iranian Plateau

A S I A

Tien Shan

Altai Mountains

Urumqi

M O N G O L I A

Plateau of Mongolia

G o b i

Ordos Desert

Baotou

Yellow River

Taiyu

Hindu Kush

Takla Makan Desert

Tarim He

Tarim Basin

Turpan Pendi -154m

Altun Shan

Qilian Shan

Xiqing Shan

Lanzhou

Xi'

2

112

Persian Gulf

Gulf of Oman

Peshawar

Indus

K2 8611m

Kunlun Mountains

Aksai Chin (administered by China, claimed by India)

C H I N A

Sichuan Pendi

112

ISLAMABAD

Jammu and Kashmir

Demchok/Demqog (administered by China, claimed by India)

Plateau of Tibet

Chengdu

Gujranwala

Lahore

Quetta

Faisalabad

Mullan

Sutlej

Ludhiana

Mekong

Salween

Chongqing

Do

PAKISTAN

Himalayas

Brahmaputra

Delhi

Yamuna

Ganges

Mount Everest 8650m

KATHMANDU

NEPAL

THIMPHU

BHUTAN

Guwahati

Kunming

Guiyan

Arabian Peninsula

Hyderabad

Karachi

Mouths of the Indus

Rann of Kachchh

Jaipur

NEW DELHI

Kanpur

Patna

Ganges

Imphal

BANGLADESH

DHAKA

Nanning

3

Arabian Sea

Murray Ridge

Gulf of Khambhat

Ahmadabad

Vindhya Range

Narmada

Satpura Range

Indore

Nagpur

I N D I A

Kolkata (Calcutta)

Khulna

Chittagong

Mouths of the Ganges

Mandalay

Irrawaddy

MYANMAR (BURMA)

VIETNAM

HANOI

Hai Ph

Gulf of Tonking

Owen Fracture Zone

Mumbai (Bombay)

Pune

Deccan

Godavari

Solapur

Hyderabad

Eastern Ghats

Western Ghats

Vijayawada

LAOS

NAY PYI TAW

Bago

Louangphabang

Chiang Mai

Vinh

VIENTIANE

Da

Arabian Basin

Laccadive Islands (to India)

Hubli

Bangalore

Bay of Bengal

Rangoon

Pathein

Mouths of the Irrawaddy

THAILAND

Pakxé

Mekong

Carlsberg Ridge

Mysore

Chennai (Madras)

BANGKOK

Tonlé Sap

CAMBODIA

PHNOM PENH

Hô Chi

4

69

Jaffna

Gulf of Mannar

SRI LANKA

Andaman Islands (to India)

Andaman Sea

Gulf of Thailand

Mouths of the Mekong

MALDIVES

MALE

Chagos-Laccadive Plateau

COLOMBO

Nicobar Islands (to India)

Kota Bharu

Natu

Mascarene Plateau

Mid-Indian Ridge

Equator

Ceylon Plain

INDIAN OCEAN

Ninetyeast Ridge

Cocos Basin

Malay Peninsula

M A L A

Medan

Strait of Malacca

KUALA LUMPUR

PUTRAJAYA

SINGAPORE

Pekanbaru

Pontiana

Dumai

Sumatra

Bangka

5

BRITISH INDIAN OCEAN TERRITORY (to UK)

Mid-Indian Basin

Padang

Sunda Strait

Great

JAKA

Sen

Bandung

Java Tren

Palembang

N

141

	A	B	C	D

0 km	1000	**Population**	● National capital
0 miles	1000	○ below 50,000 ○ 50,000 to 100,000 ◉ 100,000 to 500,000 ◼ above 500,000	

E   F   50°   150°   G   170°   180°   H

113

Northwest Pacific Basin

Emperor Seamounts

Qiqihar
Manchurian Plain Harbin *Lake Khanka*   Sakhalin   *Kurile Islands*   *Kurile Trench*

Shatskiy Rise

Mapmaker Seamounts

Changchun
Liao He
Shenyang
Dandong   **NORTH KOREA**
BEIJING **PYONGYANG**
Tianjin Dalian
Bo Hai   **SOUTH KOREA**
SEOUL

JAPAN
Sea of Japan (East Sea)

Hokkaido

Tsugaru

Honshu   Sendai   *Japan Trench*

Qingdao
Jinan
N Plain
anjing

Yellow Sea

Korea Strait

Nagoya   **TOKYO**
Kyoto   Yokohama
Osaka   *Fuji-san 3776m*
Hiroshima
Kitakyushu   *Shikoku*
Kyushu

152

Mid - Pacific Mountains

Changhai
East China Sea

uhan
Hangzhou
Nanchang
ngsha

Shikoku Basin

Ryukyu Islands

Ryukyu Trench

PACIFIC OCEAN

Fuzhou
Taiwan Strait
ntou   **TAIPEI**
ngzhou   **TAIWAN**
Hong Kong (Xianggang)   Kaohsiung
men)

Philippine Sea

Philippine Basin

Kyushu-Palau Ridge

West Mariana Basin   East Mariana Basin

Melanesian Basin

Luzon Strait

CEL
NDS
sted)   Baguio   *Luzon*

Mariana Trench

M i c r o n e s i a

uth China
Sea   *Mindoro*

MANILA
PHILIPPINES   *Samar*

RATLY ISLANDS
(disputed)   *Panay*   *Yap Trench*
Bacolod   CEBU
Negros
Palawan   *Sulu Sea*

Eauripik Rise

Equator

152

Zamboanga   Mindanao
Davao

Ontong Java Rise

BANDAR
NEI SERI BEGAWAN   *Celebes Sea*

M e l a n e s i a

Manado   *Halmahera*
Bismarck Archipelago

Solomon Islands

orneo
alikpapan
I N D O N E S I A
nda Islands

Makassar Strait

Moluccas

Jayapura

Solomon Sea

Banjarmasin   *Celebes*
Makassar   *Buru*
Flores   *Banda Sea*
rabaya   *Seram*
Ambon
Bali   *Lesser Sunda Islands*
ralang   *Flores*
Sumba   *Timor*   DILI   **EAST TIMOR**
Arafura Sea

Pegunungan Maoke

New Guinea

Timor Sea   *Timor Trough*   **A U S T R A L I A**

Coral Sea

142

E   F   140°   G   150°   H   160°

Western China & Mongolia

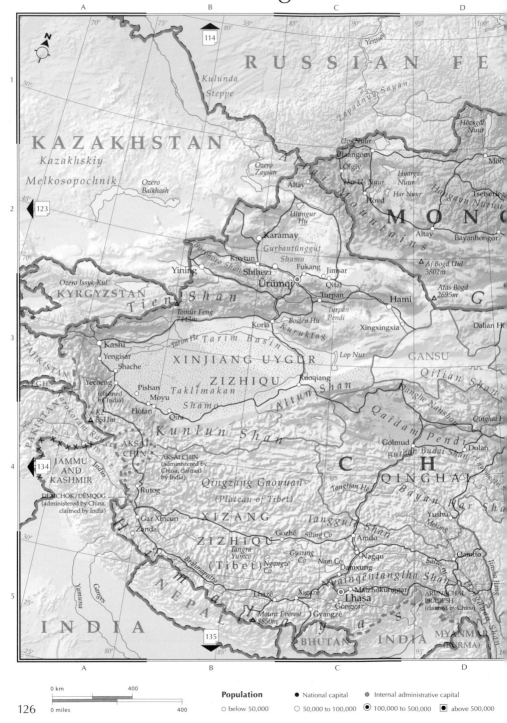

Population

○ below 50,000
○ 50,000 to 100,000
◉ 100,000 to 500,000
■ above 500,000

● National capital
● Internal administrative capital

0 km 400
0 miles 400

Ozero Baykal
55°
RATION
Selenge
Sühbaatar
Darhan
Erdenet
gan
Dzuunmod
ULAANBAATAR
(ULAN BATOR)
OLIA
Onon
Onon Gol
Kerulen
Ondörhaan
Baruun-Urt
Saynshand
Dalandzadgad
yn Nuruu
b i
Tengger
Shamo
ning
Wuhai
(Halbowan)
Ich Lang Shan
NINGXIA
N
GANSU
SHAANXI
Han Shui
ICHUAN

110°
115°
120°
Shilka
Onon
Choybalsan
Menenglyn
Tal
Mu Us
Shadi
Ulan Qab (Jining)
Great Wall of China
SHANXI
HENAN
HUBEI
CHONGQING
HUNAN
GUIZHOU
105°
110°

Ergun (Ergun He)
Ergun
Hulun Buir
(Hailar)
Manzhouli
Hulun
Nur
Hulingol
Xilinhot
Erenhot
Chifeng
(Ulanhad)
Hohhot
Baotou
Huang He
(Yellow River)
BEIJING
TIANJIN
HEBEI
SHANDONG
Huang He (Yellow River)
JIANGSU
ANHUI
JIANGXI
FUJIAN
25°
115°

Jagdaqi
Amur (Heilong Jiang)
RUSS. FED.
HEILONGJIANG
JILIN
Tongliao
Liao He
LIAONING
Liaodong Wan
Korea
Bay
Bo Hai
Lake
Khanka
NORTH
KOREA
SOUTH
KOREA
JAPAN
Sea of
Japan
(East Sea)
Yellow
Sea
SHANGHAI SHI
ZHEJIANG
East
China
Sea
Nansei-shotō
(to Japan)
Tropic of Cancer
TAIWAN
120°

50°
130°
135°
45°
135°
40°
130°
35°
30°
25°
125°

Da Hinggan Ling
MONGOLIZIZHIQU
(Inner Mongolia)

115
128
129
129

Elevation

-6000m	-4000m	-2000m	-1000m	-500m	-250m	Below sea level	0	250m	500m	1000m	2000m	3000m	4000m	6000m
-19,658ft	-13,124ft	-6562ft	-3281ft	-1640ft	-820ft	-328ft/-100m		820ft	1640ft	3281ft	6562ft	9843ft	13,124ft	19,685ft

Eastern China & Korea

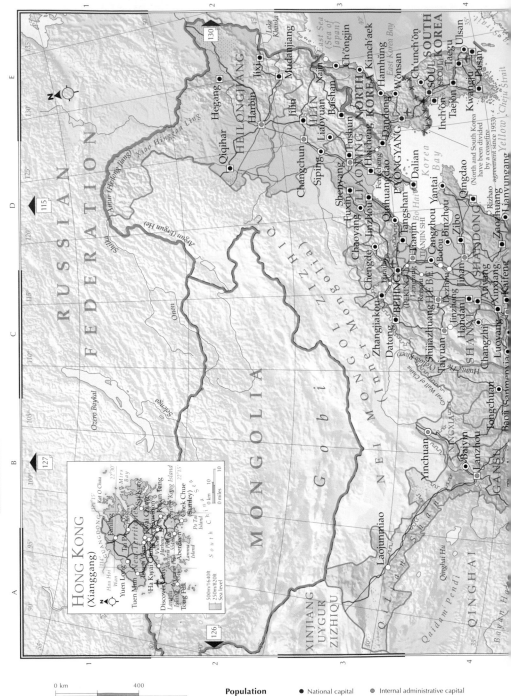

Population
○ below 50,000 ○ 50,000 to 100,000 ◉ 100,000 to 500,000 ■ above 500,000
● National capital ● Internal administrative capital

0 km   400
0 miles   400

152

139

136

136

Elevation

						Below sea level	0	250m	500m	1000m	2000m	3000m	4000m	6000m
-6000m	-4000m	-2000m	-1000m	-500m	-250m									
-19,658ft	-13,124ft	-6562ft	-3281ft	-1640ft	-820ft	-328ft/-100m	0	820ft	1640ft	3281ft	6562ft	9843ft	13,124ft	19,685ft

129

Japan

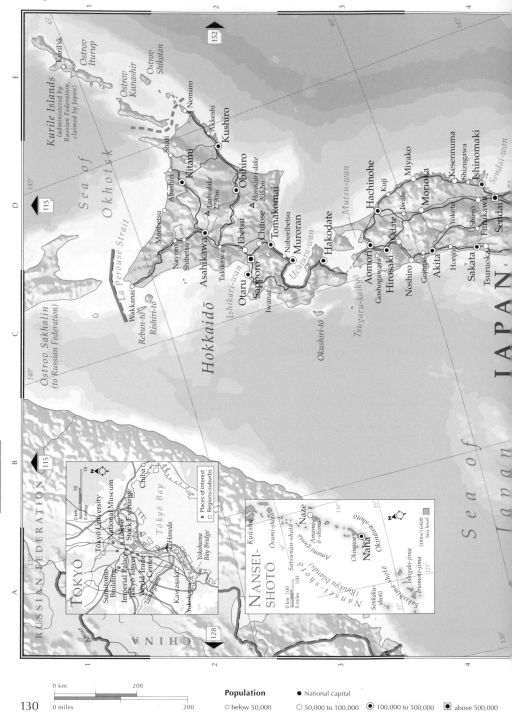

Population

● National capital

○ below 50,000   ◑ 50,000 to 100,000   ◉ 100,000 to 500,000   ◼ above 500,000

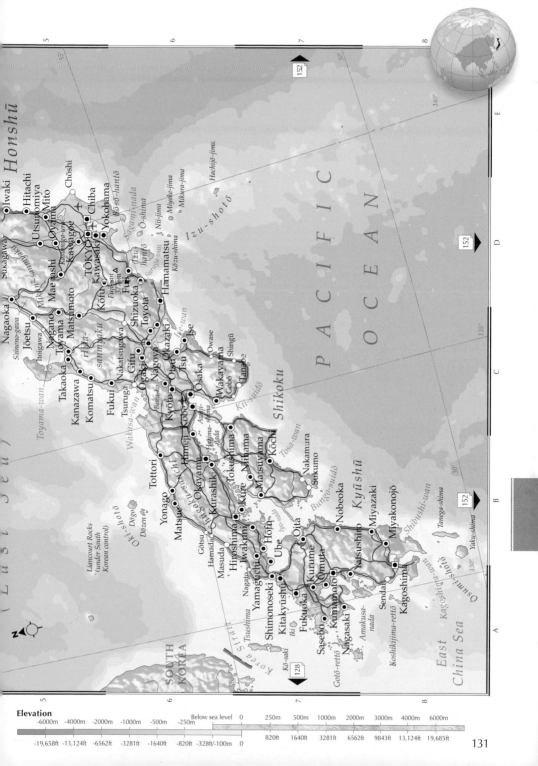

Southern India & Sri Lanka

0 km   300

0 miles   300

Population

● National capital

○ below 50,000   ○ 50,000 to 100,000   ◎ 100,000 to 500,000   ■ above 500,000

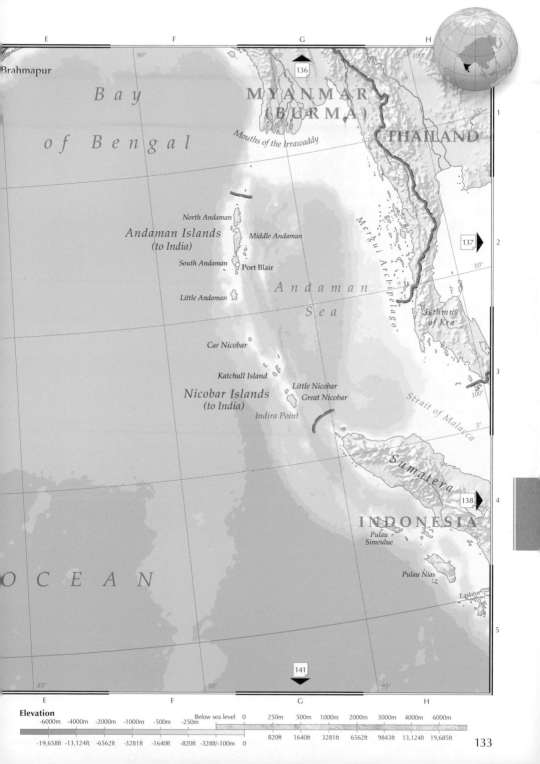

Brahmapur

Bay

of Bengal

MYANMAR
(BURMA)

136

THAILAND

Mouths of the Irrawaddy

North Andaman

Andaman Islands
(to India)

Middle Andaman

South Andaman

Port Blair

Andaman

Sea

137

Little Andaman

Mergui Archipelago

Isthmus
of Kra

Car Nicobar

Katchall Island

Little Nicobar

Great Nicobar

Nicobar Islands
(to India)

Indira Point

Strait of Malacca

138

Sumatera

OCEAN

INDONESIA

Pulau
Simeulue

Pulau Nias

Equator

141

Elevation

					Below sea level	0	250m	500m	1000m	2000m	3000m	4000m	6000m
-6000m	-4000m	-2000m	-1000m	-500m	-250m								
-19,658ft	-13,124ft	-6562ft	-3281ft	-1640ft	-820ft -328ft/-100m	0	820ft	1640ft	3281ft	6562ft	9843ft	13,124ft	19,685ft

Northern India, Pakistan & Bangladesh

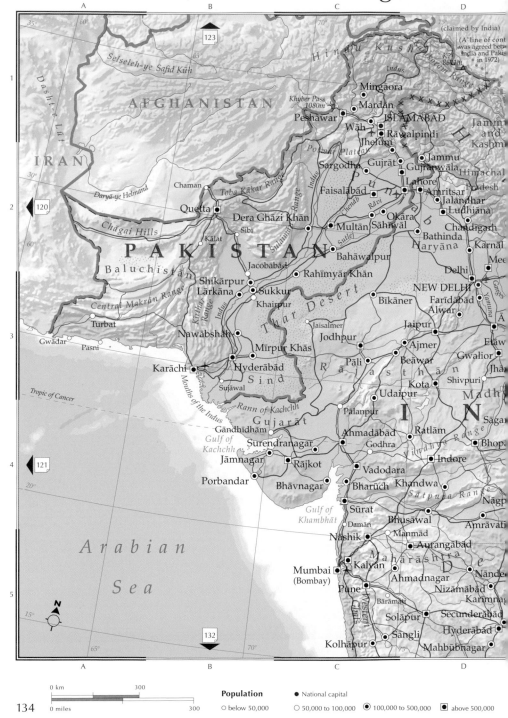

(claimed by India)

(A "line of cont
was agreed betw
India and Pakis
in 1972)

Selseleh-ye Safīd Kūh

Hindu Kush

Karakoram Range

123

Dasht-e Lūt

K2
8611m

AFGHANISTAN

Indus

Mingaora

Khyber Pass
1080m

Mardān

**Jammu
and
Kashmir**

Peshāwar

Wāh

ISLĀMĀBĀD

IRAN

Rāwalpindi

Jhelum

Jammu

**Himachal
Pradesh**

Potwar Plateau

Sargodha

Gujrāt

Gujrānwāla

120

Indus

Faisalābād

Lahore

Amritsar

Jalandhar

Chaman

Ludhiāna

Toba Kākar Range

Chenab

Ravi

Okāra

Chandīgarh

Daryā-ye Helmand

Quetta

Dera Ghāzi Khān

Multān

Sāhīwāl

Haryāna

Bathinda

Karnāl

Chāgai Hills

Sibi

Sutlej

Bahāwalpur

Mee

Baluchistān

Kālat

Jacobābād

Rahīmyār Khān

Delhi

P A K I S T A N

Shikārpur

Sukkur

NEW DELHI

Lārkāna

Khairpur

Bīkāner

Farīdābād

Alwar

Central Makrān Range

Turbat

Thar Desert

Jaisalmer

Jaipur

Ā

Gwādar

Pasni

Nawābshāh

Mīrpur Khās

Jodhpur

Ajmer

Etaw

Gwalior

Jha

Kirthar Range

Indus

Pāli

Beāwar

Karāchi

Hyderābād

Sind

R a j a s t h ā n

Kota

Shivpuri

Madh

Tropic of Cancer

Sujāwal

Udaipur

I

N

Mouths of the Indus

Rann of Kachchh

Pālanpur

Sāga

Gāndhīdhām

Gujarāt

Ahmadābād

Ratlām

Vindhya Range

**Gulf of
Kachchh**

Surendranagar

Godhra

Bhopa

121

Jāmnagar

Rājkot

Vadodara

Indore

Porbandar

Bhāvnagar

Bharūch

Khandwa

Satpura Range

Nāgp

Sūrat

**Gulf of
Khambhāt**

Daman

Bhusāwal

Amrāvati

A r a b i a n

Nāshik

Manmād

Aurangābād

Mahārāshtra

Nānde

D e

S e a

Mumbai
(Bombay)

Kalyān

Ahmadnagar

Nizāmābād

Pune

Karīmna

Secunderābād

N

Bārāmati

Solāpur

Western Ghats

Hyderābād

132

Kolhāpur

Sāngli

Mahbūbnagar

0 km	300
0 miles	300

Population

● National capital

○ below 50,000

○ 50,000 to 100,000

◉ 100,000 to 500,000

■ above 500,000

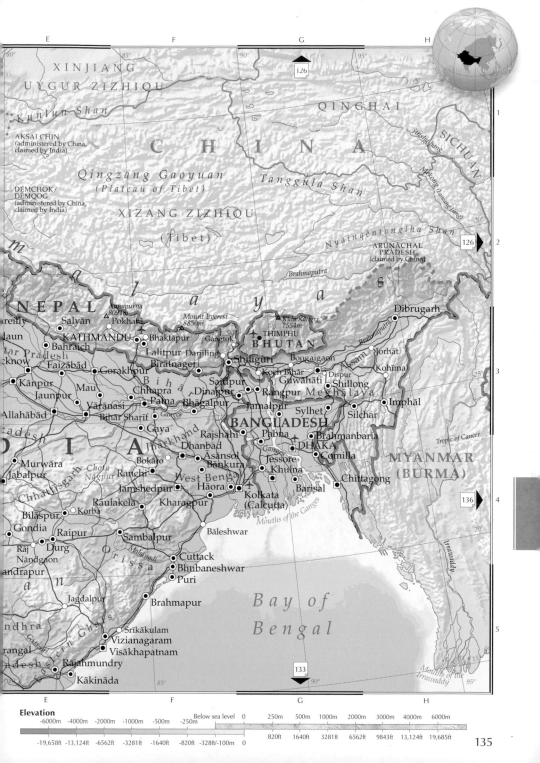

XINJIANG
UYGUR ZIZHIQU
Kunlun Shan

QINGHAI

SICHUAN

C H I N A

AKSAI CHIN
(administered by China,
claimed by India)

Qingzang Gaoyuan
(Plateau of Tibet)

Tanggula Shan

DEMCHOK/
DÊMQOG
(administered by China,
claimed by India)

XIZANG ZIZHIQU

(Tibet)

Nyainqêntanglha Shan

ARUNACHAL
PRADESH
(claimed by China)

Brahmaputra

126

Brahmaputra

Dibrugarh

NEPAL
reilly   Salyān   Pokhara
laun   Bahrāich   KATHMANDU   Bhaktapur   Gangtok
cknow   Faizābād   Lalitpur   Darjiling
Kānpur   Mau   Gorakhpur   Biratnagar Shiliguri
Jaunpur   Chhapra   Dinajpur   Koch Bihar
Varanasi   Patna   Bhagalpur
Allahābād   Bihar Sharif Ganges   Jamalpur
            Gaya

Annapurna
8091m
Mount Everest
8850m
Kula Kangri
7554m

THIMPHU
BHUTAN

Bongaigaon
Guwahati
Rangpur   Meghalaya
Sylhet

Assam

Jorhat
Kohima
Dispur
Shillong   Imphal

Silchar

Jabalpur   Murwāra
Bilāspur   Korba
Gondia
Rāj   Durg
Nāndgaon
andrapur

Dhanbad
Bokaro
Ranchi
Jamshedpur
Raulakela
Kharagpur

Chota
Nagpur

Rajshahi
BANGLADESH
Pabna
Āsānsol   DHAKA
Bānkura   Jessore   Comilla
           Khulna
West Bengal
Hāora
Kolkata
(Calcutta)   Barisal

Brahmanbaria

Tropic of Cancer

MYANMAR
(BURMA)

Chittagong

136

Sambalpur
Raipur
Cuttack
Bhubaneshwar
Puri

Bāleshwar

Mouths of the Ganges

Jagdalpur   Brahmapur

Srikākulam
Vizianagaram
Visākhapatnam
rangal
Rājahmundry
Kākināda

Bay of
Bengal

Mouths of the
Irrawaddy

133

ndhra

Elevation

-6000m	-4000m	-2000m	-1000m	-500m	-250m	Below sea level	0	250m	500m	1000m	2000m	3000m	4000m	6000m
-19,658ft	-13,124ft	-6562ft	-3281ft	-1640ft	-820ft	-328ft/-100m	0	820ft	1640ft	3281ft	6562ft	9843ft	13,124ft	19,685ft

Mainland Southeast Asia

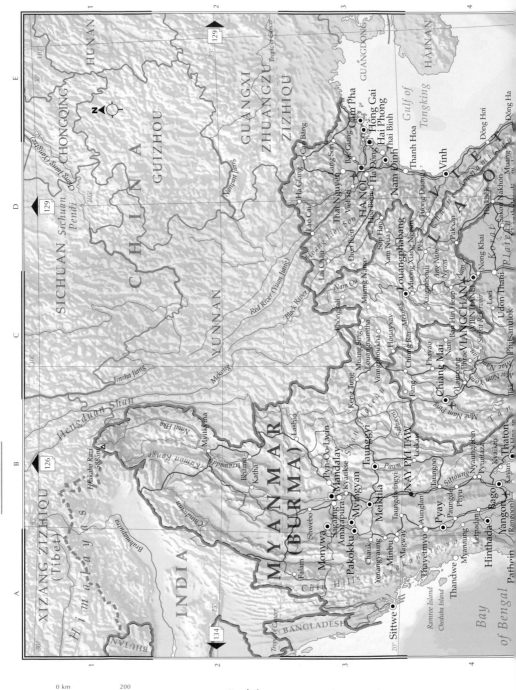

Population   ● National capital

○ below 50,000   ○ 50,000 to 100,000   ◉ 100,000 to 500,000   ▣ above 500,000

0 km   200
0 miles   200

139

138

138

133

Elevation

-6000m	-4000m	-2000m	-1000m	-500m	-250m	Below sea level	0	250m	500m	1000m	2000m	3000m	4000m	6000m

-19,658ft	-13,124ft	-6562ft	-3281ft	-1640ft	-820ft	-328ft/-100m	0	820ft	1640ft	3281ft	6562ft	9843ft	13,124ft	19,685ft

Maritime Southeast Asia

SINGAPORE

MALAYSIA

Johore Strait

Causeway

Lim Chu
Kang
Choa Chu
Kang
Jurong
Industrial
Estate
Selat Pandan
Pulau Sudong
Pulau Pawai

Bukit Panjang
Bukit Timah 176m
Queenstown
Telok Blangah

Hougang
New Town
City
Sentosa

New Town
Bedok

Pulau
Ubin
Pulau
Tekong

Changi

New Town

103°50'
103°40'

104°

1°20'

Strait of Singapore

Urban areas
Open areas
Nature reserves

MYANMAR
(BURMA)

LAOS

VIETNAM

Gulf of
Tongking

Hainan Dao
(to China)

PARACEL ISLANDS
(disputed by China, Taiwan
and Vietnam)

THAILAND

Mekong

CAMBODIA

South China

Sea

SPRATLY ISLANDS
(disputed by China, Malaysia,
Philippines, Taiwan and Vietnam)

Andaman
Sea

Gulf of
Thailand

Mouths of
the Mekong

Nicobar Islands
(to India)

Isthmus of Kra

Banda Aceh Sigli
Langsa
Meulaboh
Medan
Tebingtinggi
Pematangsiantar
Pulau Simeulue
Kepulauan
Banyak
Danau
Toba
Sibolga
Pulau Nias

George
Town
Pulau
Pinang

Butterworth
Taiping
Ipoh

Kota Bharu

Kuala Terengganu
Dungun

Cukai

Kuala Lumpur

PUTRAJAYA
Melaka
Muar
Batu Pahat

Klang
KUALA LUMPUR

M A L A Y S I A

Kuantan

Kepulauan
Natuna

Gunung Kinabalu
Kota Kinabalu
BANDAR SERI
BEGAWAN
BRUNEI
Miri

Balabac

Keluang
Johor Bahru
SINGAPORE

Selat Serasan

Bintulu

Sibu

Batang Rajang

Sarawak

Sungai Kaya

Sri Aman

Kuching

B o r n e o

Equator

Padang
Pulau Siberut
Kepulauan
Mentawai
Sungaipenuh

Pekanbaru
Singkawang
Singapore

Solok
Rengat

Kepulauan
Lingga
Kualatungkal

Pontianak

Sidas

Sungai Kapuas

Pegunungan Müller

Sungai Kaya

Batang Hari
Jambi

Selat Karimata

K a l i m a n t a n

Sampit

Sungai Barito

Samarinda
Balikpapan

Amuntai
Kandang

Pangkalpinang
Palembang
Bengkulu
Lahat

Bangka

Pulau
Belitung

I N D

Banjarmasin

Pulau
Laut

S u m a t e r a
(Sumatra)

Kotabumi

Cirebon
Tegal

Bandar Lampung

Serang

Bogor
Sukabumi
Bandung

JAKARTA
Pekalongan
Semarang
Kudus

Java Sea

Maka

Pulau
Madura

I N D I A N

O C E A N

Selat Sunda

Tasikmalaya
Cilacap
Magelang
Yogyakarta
Surakarta

J a w a
(Java)

Surabaya
Probolinggo
Jember Mata

Malang
Kediri
Madiun

Denpas

Bali
Lombok

A

B

C

D

MALAYSIA'S TWO CAPITALS

KUALA LUMPUR   - Capital
PUTRAJAYA   - Administrative capital

0 km   200
0 miles   200

Population

○ below 50,000
○ 50,000 to 100,000

● National capital

◉ 100,000 to 500,000
■ above 500,000

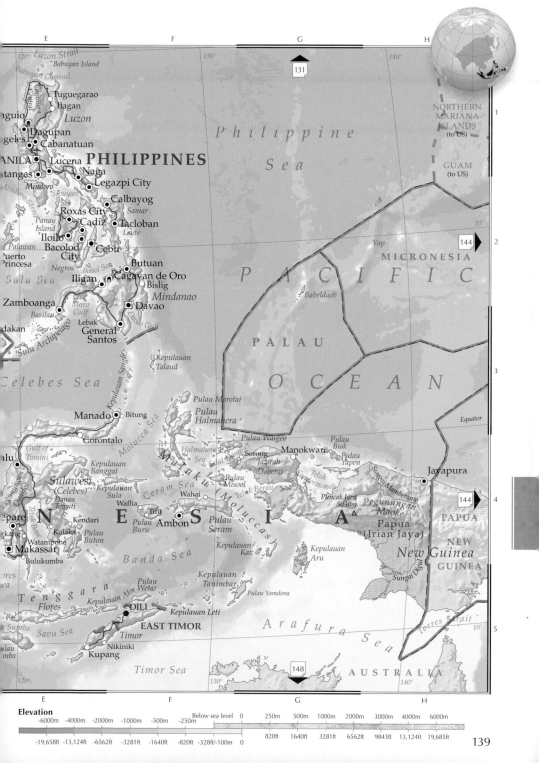

Luzon Strait
120°
Babuyan Island
Babuyan Channel
Cordillera Central
Tuguegarao
Ilagan
Luzon
guio
Dagupan
eles
Cabanatuan
ANILA
Lucena
PHILIPPINES
tangas
Naga
Mindoro
Mindoro Strait
Legazpi City
Sibuyan
Calbayog
Roxas City
Samar
Panay Island
Cadiz
Tacloban
Iloilo
Leyte
Palawan
Bacolod City
Cebu
Puerto Princesa
Butuan
Negros
Bohol Sea
Cagayan de Oro
Sulu Sea
Iligan
Bislig
Mindanao
Zamboanga
Moro Gulf
Davao
Basilan
Lebak
Davao Gulf
dakan
General Santos
Sulu Archipelago

Kepulauan Talaud

Celebes Sea

Kepulauan Sangir

Philippine Sea

P A C I F I C

Yap
MICRONESIA
144

Babeldaob

P A L A U

O C E A N

Equator

130°
140°

1

144
2

NORTHERN MARIANA ISLANDS
(to US)

GUAM
(to US)

10°

3

Manado
Bitung
Gorontalo
Molucca Sea
Pulau Morotai
Pulau Halmahera
Pulau Waigeo
Pulau Biak
Manokwari
Pulau Yapen
Jayapura
alu
Gulf of Tomini
Kepulauan Banggai
Halmahera Sea
Maluku
Sorong
Jazirah Doberai
Teluk Cenderawasih
Sungai Mamberamo
Kepulauan Sula
Ceram Sea
Wahai
Pulau Misool
Teluk Berau
Pulau
Danau Towuti
Sulawesi (Celebes)
N
E
S
Waflia
Tifu
Pulau Buru
Ambon
Maluku (Moluccas)
Pulau Seram
I
Puncak Jaya 5030m
Pegunungan Maoke
Papua (Irian Jaya)
A
PAPUA
epare
Kendari
Teluk Bone
Kolaka
Pulau Buton
Pulau
Kepulauan Kai
Sungai Digul
New Guinea
NEW GUINEA
kang
Watampone
Makassar
Banda Sea
Kepulauan Aru
Bulukumba
Kepulauan Tanimbar
Pulau Yamdena

4

Flores
ores ea
Pulau Wetar
Kepulauan Alor
Pulau Wetar
Kepulauan Leti
DILI
EAST TIMOR
A r a f u r a   S e a
Torres Strait
10°
Sumba
mba
Savu Sea
Timor
Nikiniki
Kupang
Timor Sea
lau
AUSTRALIA
120°
130°
140°

148
5

E
F
G
H

Elevation

-6000m -4000m -2000m -1000m -500m -250m
Below sea level 0 250m 500m 1000m 2000m 3000m 4000m 6000m

-19,658ft -13,124ft -6562ft -3281ft -1640ft -820ft -328ft/-100m 0
820ft 1640ft 3281ft 6562ft 9843ft 13,124ft 19,685ft

The Indian Ocean

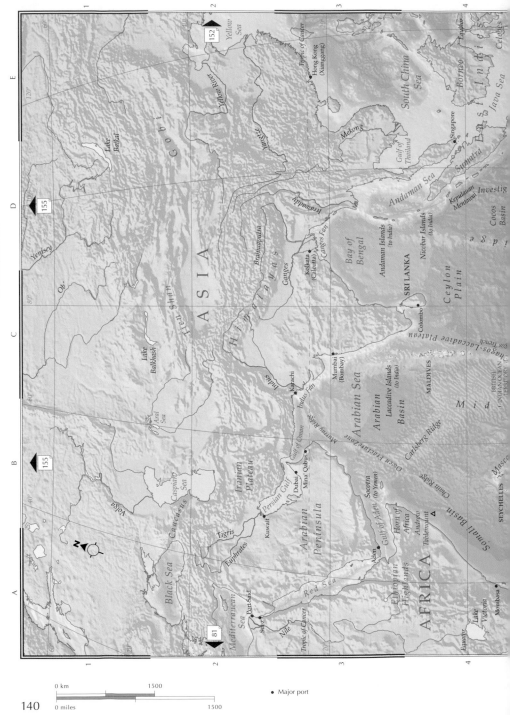

ASIA

AFRICA

East Indies

South China Sea

Borneo

Java Sea

Celebes

Equator

Gobi

Lake Baikal

Yellow Sea

Yellow River

Tropic of Cancer

Hong Kong (Xianggang)

Yangtze

Mekong

Gulf of Thailand

Singapore

Sumatra

Andaman Sea

Kepulauan Mentawai

Investig

Cocos Basin

Yenisey

Ob'

Irrawaddy

Brahmaputra

Ganges Fan

Kolkata (Calcutta)

Bay of Bengal

Andaman Islands (to India)

Nicobar Islands (to India)

Ceylon Plain

C a s p i

Tien Shan

Himalayas

Ganges

SRI LANKA

Colombo

Lake Balkhash

Indus

Karachi

Indus Fan

Mumbai (Bombay)

Arabian Sea

Laccadive Islands (to India)

MALDIVES

Chagos-Laccadive Plateau

BRITISH INDIAN OCEAN TERRITORY

Chagos Trench

Aral Sea

Arabian Basin

Carlsberg Ridge

M i d

Volga

Caspian Sea

Caucasus

Iranian Plateau

Persian Gulf

Dubai

Mina Qabus

Gulf of Oman

Murray Ridge

Owen Fracture Zone

Socotra (to Yemen)

Chain Ridge

Museo

SEYCHELLES

Kuwait

Tigris

Euphrates

Arabian Peninsula

Gulf of Aden

Aden

Horn of Africa

Andréta

Tablemount

Somali Basin

Black Sea

Mediterranean Sea

Port Said

Suez

Nile

Red Sea

Tropic of Cancer

Ethiopian Highlands

AFRICA

Equator

Lake Victoria

Mombasa

0 km   1500

0 miles   1500

• Major port

AUSTRALIA

Freemantle

Tropic of Capricorn

North Australian Basin

Exmouth Plateau

Cuvier Plateau

Perth Basin

Naturaliste Plateau

Diamantina Fracture Zone

Wharton Basin

COCOS ISLANDS (to Australia)

East Indiman Ridge

Broken Ridge

Osborn Plateau

Ninetyeast Ridge

South-east Indian Ridge

South Indian Basin

Limit of winter pack ice

Limit of summer pack ice

Antarctic Circle

I N D I A N   O C E A N

Argo Fracture Zone

Vityaz Fracture Zone

Exeter Fracture Zone

Central Indian Ridge

Amsterdam Island

St-Paul Island

FRENCH SOUTHERN & ANTARCTIC TERRITORIES (to France)

Kerguelen Plateau

Kerguelen

Crozet Basin

Banzare Seamounts

S O U T H E R N   O C E A N

A N T A R C T I C A

Mascarene Basin

MAURITIUS

REUNION (to France)

Madagascar Basin

Mascarene Plain

Tananarive

Indian Ridge

HEARD & McDONALD ISLANDS (to Australia)

Crozet Plateau

Crozet Islands

Lena Tablemount

Ob' Tablemount

MADAGASCAR

MAYOTTE (to France)

Davie Ridge

Madagascar Plateau

Indomed Fracture Zone

South-west

Enderby Plain

Mozambique Channel

Mozambique Plateau

Natal Basin

Prince Edward Islands (to South Africa)

Atlantic-Indian Basin

Zambezi

Limpopo

Tropic of Capricorn

Durban

Africana Seamount

Agulhas

Agulhas Plateau

Agulhas Basin

Antarctic Circle

152

154

154

67

Elevation

-6000m	-4000m	-2000m	-1000m	-250m	0
-19,658ft	-13,124ft	-6562ft	-3281ft	-820ft	0

141

Australasia & Oceania

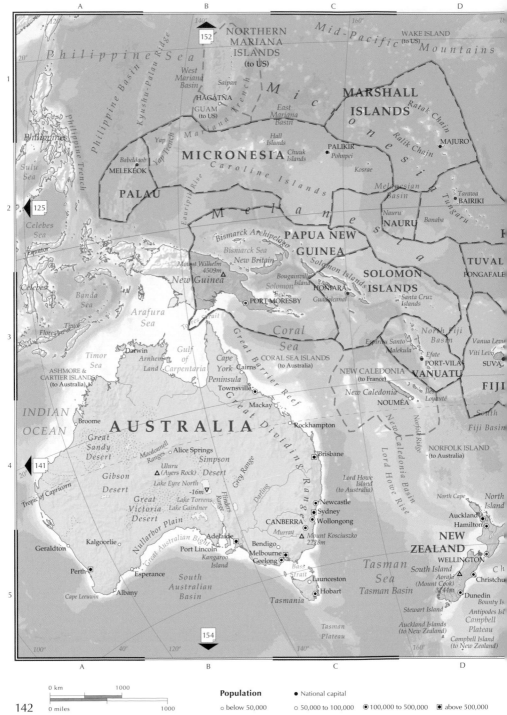

Population
- ● National capital
- ○ below 50,000
- ○ 50,000 to 100,000
- ◉ 100,000 to 500,000
- ◼ above 500,000

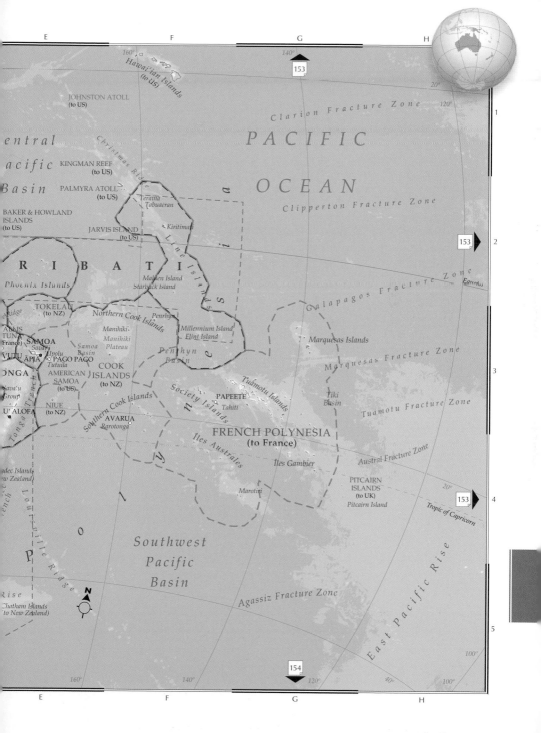

E   F   G   H

160°   140°

153

JOHNSTON ATOLL
(to US)

Hawaiian Islands
(to US)

Clarion Fracture Zone   120°   1

PACIFIC   20°

entral

acific   KINGMAN REEF
                (to US)

Basin   PALMYRA ATOLL
                (to US)

OCEAN

Christmas Ridge

Clipperton Fracture Zone

Teraina
Tabuaeran

BAKER & HOWLAND
ISLANDS
(to US)

JARVIS ISLAND
(to US)

Kiritimati

Line Islands

153   2

R   I   B   A   T   I

Malden Island
Starbuck Island

Galapagos Fracture Zone   Equator

Phoenix Islands

Ridge   TOKELAU
                (to NZ)   Northern Cook Islands

ALIS
TUNA
France)   Savai'i
                Upolu   Samoa
VITU   Basin
APIA

Penrhyn

Manihiki·
Manihiki
Plateau

Marquesas Islands

Marquesas Fracture Zone

Millennium Island
Flint Island

3

TONGA   PAGO PAGO
                Tutuila

COOK
ISLANDS
(to NZ)

AMERICAN
SAMOA
(to US)

Penrhyn
Basin

Tiki
Basin

Tuamotu Fracture Zone

Sava'u
Group

Tuamotu Islands

Society Islands

Tonga Trench

U'ALOFA   NIUE
                (to NZ)

Southern Cook Islands

AVARUA
Rarotonga

PAPEETE
Tahiti

FRENCH POLYNESIA
(to France)

Austral Fracture Zone

Lyra

Iles Australes

adec Islands
w Zealand)

Iles Gambier

PITCAIRN
ISLANDS
(to UK)
Pitcairn Island

20°

153   4

Tropic of Capricorn

Kermadec

Marotiri

O

Southwest
Pacific
Basin

East Pacific Rise

Rise

Chatham Islands
(to New Zealand)

N

Agassiz Fracture Zone

40°   100°

100°   5

160°   140°   120°

154

E   F   G   H

143

The Southwest Pacific

NORTHERN
MARIANA
ISLANDS

Saipan
Tinian
Rota
GUAM
(to US)   HAGATÑA   (to US)

MARSHALL
ISLANDS

Enewetak
Atoll   Bikini Atoll   Rongelap
Atoll   Ailuk Ato.

Ujelang Atoll   Wotje Ato.
Kwajalein   Maloela
Atoll   Atoll
Namu Atoll   Maju
Ailinglaplap Atoll

Yap

MICRONESIA

Babeldaob

MELEKEOK

Chuuk
Islands   PALIKIR   Pohnpei   Jaluit Atoll   Mili Atoll

Caroline   Islands   Kosrae   Ebon Atoll   Mak.

PALAU

139

Mal.
Tara.
BAIRIKI

NAURU   Nonot.

Abema.

Equator   Banaba

Admiralty
Islands   St.Matthias Group

Bismarck Archipelago
Bismarck Sea   New Ireland

New Guinea

INDONESIA

Madang   PAPUA NEW GUINEA
Central Range   Mount Wilhelm   New
4509m   Britain   Bougainville
Lae   Island

New Guinea
Highlands Range   Solomon Sea   Choiseul

Gulf of
Papua   Santa Isabel   SOLOMON

PORT MORESBY   New Georgia   Malaita   ISLANDS

Arafura Sea   D'Entrecasteaux   HONIARA
Islands   Guadalcanal

Torres Strait   San Cristobal   Santa Cruz
Islands

Louisiade
Archipelago   Rennell

Arnhem
Land   Groote
Eylandt   Coral   Sea   Banks Islands

Gulf of
Carpentaria   Cape
York
Peninsula   CORAL SEA ISLANDS
(to Australia)   Espiritu Santo   Maéwo
Pentecost
Malekula   Ambrym
Epi

146

Barkly Tableland   Efate   PORT-VILA

Great Barrier Reef   NEW   VANUATU
CALEDONIA   Erromango
(to France)   Tanna
Aneityum

NORTHERN

TERRITORY   New   Ouvéa   Lifou
Caledonia   Maré
Îles Loyauté

Tropic of Capricorn   QUEENSLAND   NOUMÉA
Macdonnell

Ranges   AUSTRALIA

149

0 km   750
0 miles   750

Population   ● National capital

○ below 50,000   ○ 50,000 to 100,000   ◉ 100,000 to 500,000   ■ above 500,000

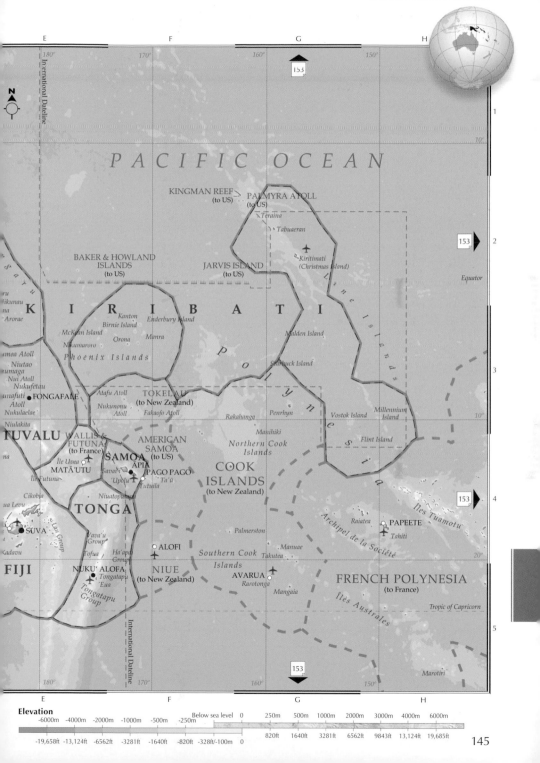

E   F   G   H

180°   170°   160°   150°

153

N

International Dateline

PACIFIC OCEAN

1

10°

KINGMAN REEF
(to US)

PALMYRA ATOLL
(to US)

Teraina

Tabuaeran

BAKER & HOWLAND
ISLANDS
(to US)

JARVIS ISLAND
(to US)

*Kiritimati
(Christmas Island)*

153

2

Equator

oru
Nikunau
na
Arorae

K   **I**   **R**   **I**   **B**   **A**   **T**   **I**

Kanton
Birnie Island

Enderbury Island

Malden Island

Line Islands

McKean Island

Nikumaroro

Orona

Manra

Po

Starbuck Island

moa Atoll
Niutao
numaga
Nui Atoll
Nukufetau

Phoenix Islands

l

3

10°

unafuti ● FONGAFALE
Atoll
Nukulaelae

Atafu Atoll

*Nukunonu
Atoll*

TOKELAU
(to New Zealand)

Fakaofo Atoll

Rakahanga

Penrhyn

Vostok Island

*Millennium
Island*

y

Niulakita

TUVALU

WALLIS &
FUTUNA
(to France)

Île Uvea

Manihiki

*Northern Cook
Islands*

Flint Island

n

na

MATÃ'UTU

SAMOA

Savai'i

ÄPIA

Upolu

Tutuila

**AMERICAN
SAMOA**
(to US)

PAGO PAGO

Ta'ū

**COOK
ISLANDS**
(to New Zealand)

e

153

4

Île Futuna

Cikobia

ua Levu

Kadavu

Lau Group

● SUVA

TONGA

Niuatoputapu

*Vava'u
Group*

Tofua

*Ha'apai
Group*

○ ALOFI

Palmerston

Takutea

Manuae

*Southern Cook
Islands*

Raiatea

Archipel de la Société

○ PAPEETE
Tahiti

Îles Tuamotu

i

20°

FIJI

NUKU'ALOFA

Tongatapu
'Eua

*Tongatapu
Group*

NIUE
(to New Zealand)

AVARUA
Rarotonga

Mangaia

FRENCH POLYNESIA
(to France)

Îles Australes

Tropic of Capricorn

International Dateline

180°   170°   160°   150°

153

Marotiri

5

E   F   G   H

Elevation

-6000m	-4000m	-2000m	-1000m	-500m	-250m	Below sea level	0	250m	500m	1000m	2000m	3000m	4000m	6000m

-19,658ft   -13,124ft   -6562ft   -3281ft   -1640ft   -820ft   -328ft/-100m   0   820ft   1640ft   3281ft   6562ft   9843ft   13,124ft   19,685ft

Western Australia

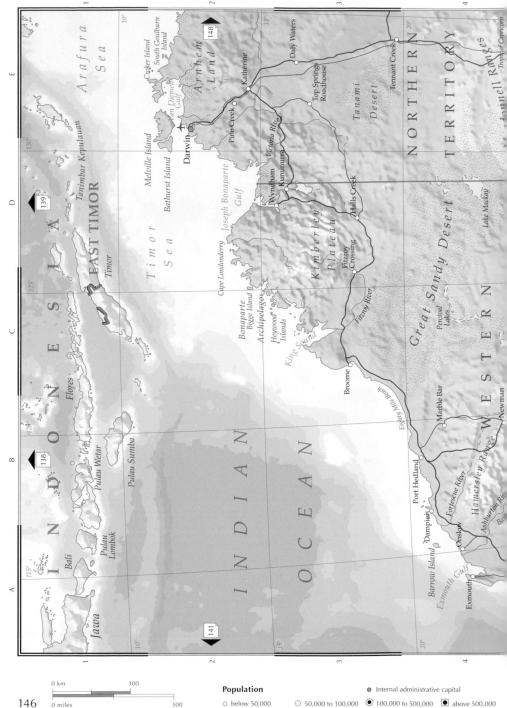

0 km   300

0 miles   300

Population

○ below 50,000   ○ 50,000 to 100,000   ◉ 100,000 to 500,000   ■ above 500,000

● Internal administrative capital

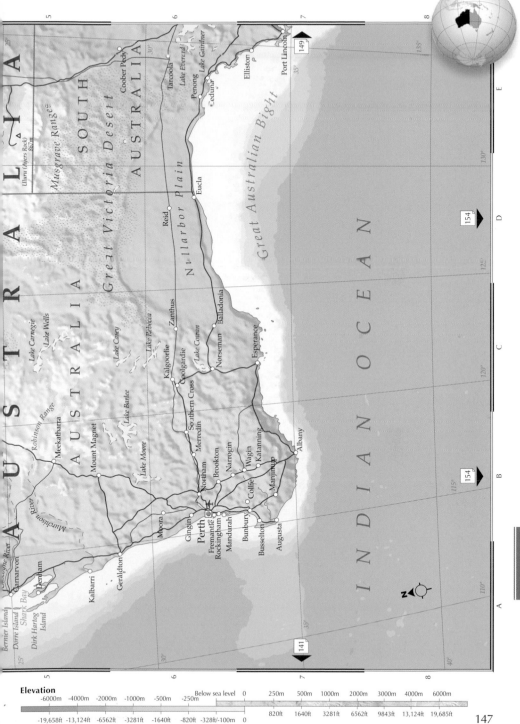

AUSTRALIA

SOUTH AUSTRALIA

Uluru (Ayers Rock)
867m

Musgrave Ranges

Great Victoria Desert

Coober Pedy

Tarcoola

Lake Everard

Penong
Lake Gairdner

Ceduna

Elliston

Port Lincoln

Nullarbor Plain

Eucla

Reid

Great Australian Bight

INDIAN OCEAN

Bernier Island
Dorre Island
Dirk Hartog Island

Shark Bay

Denham

Carnarvon

Gascoyne River

Kalbarri

Murchison River

Robinson Range

Meekatharra

Geraldton

Mount Magnet

Lake Moore

Lake Barlee

Moora

Gingin

Perth
Fremantle
Rockingham
Mandurah

Bunbury
Busselton
Augusta

Northam
Brookton
Collie
Wagin
Katanning
Manjimup

Narrogin

Merredin

Southern Cross

Coolgardie
Kalgoorlie

Lake Cowan

Norseman

Lake Rebecca

Zanthus

Balladonia

Esperance

Albany

Lake Carey

Lake Carnegie
Lake Wells

N

141

149

154

154

Elevation

| -6000m | -4000m | -2000m | -1000m | -500m | -250m | Below sea level | 0 | 250m | 500m | 1000m | 2000m | 3000m | 4000m | 6000m |

-19,658ft -13,124ft -6562ft -3281ft -1640ft -820ft -328ft/-100m 0 820ft 1640ft 3281ft 6562ft 9843ft 13,124ft 19,685ft

Eastern Australia

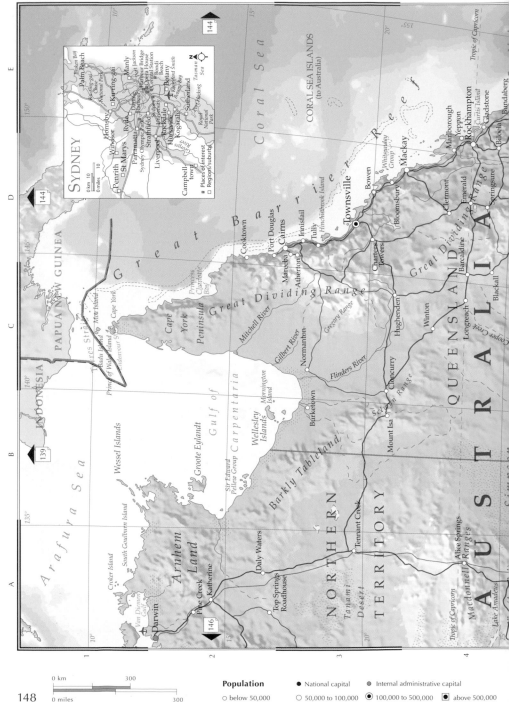

144
144
139
146

SYDNEY

Broken Bay
Palm Beach
Manly
Ku-ring-gai National Park
Ku-ring-gai
Harbour Bridge
Opera House
St Central Station
Hornsby
Ryde
Botany
Windsor
Parramatta
Bondi Beach
Strathfield
Botany Bay
St Marys
University
Sydney Olympic Park
Eastlakes Smith
Penrith
Liverpool
Leumeah
Rockdale
Hurstville
Kogarah
Sutherland
Campbell town
La Perouse
Royal National Park
0 km 10
0 miles 10

■ Places of interest
□ Regions/suburbs

CORAL SEA ISLANDS
(to Australia)

Coral Sea

Tropic of Capricorn

Population

○ below 50,000
○ 50,000 to 100,000
◉ 100,000 to 500,000
■ above 500,000

● National capital
◉ Internal administrative capital

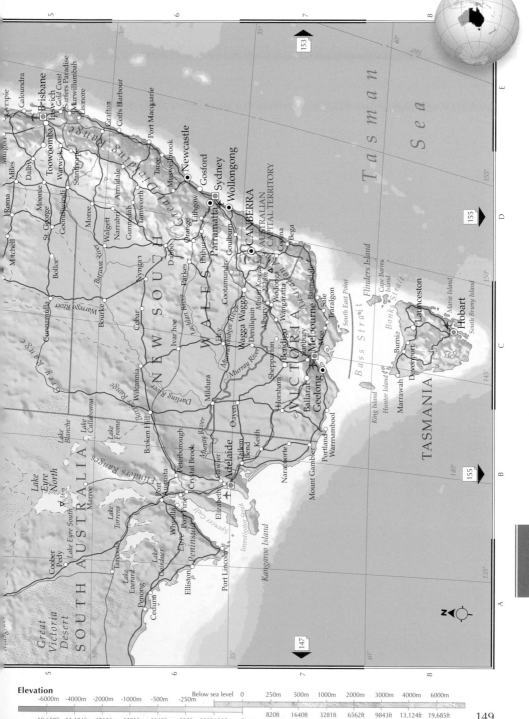

5   6   7   8

153

155

155

147

Nanango
Gympie
Galoundra
Brisbane
Ipswich
Toowoomba
Warwick
Stanthorpe
Gold Coast
Surfers Paradise
Murwillumbah
Lismore
Grafton
Coffs Harbour
Port Macquarie

Roma
Miles
Dalby
Moonie
Goondiwindi
Moree
Narrabri
Gunnedah
Tamworth
Armidale
Taree
Muswellbrook
Newcastle
Gosford
Sydney
Wollongong

Mitchell
St George
Bollon
Walgett
Nyngan
Dubbo
Orange
Bathurst
Lithgow
Parramatta
Goulburn
CANBERRA
AUSTRALIAN
CAPITAL TERRITORY
Cooma
Bega

Cunnamulla
Bourke
Cobar
Ivanhoe
Condobolin
Parkes
Forbes
Cootamundra
Wagga Wagga
Mount Kosciusko
2228m
Wodonga
Wangaratta
Wodonga
Albury

Warrego River
Darling River
Wilcannia
Menindee
Lachlan River
Hay
Deniliquin
Murrumbidgee River
Shepparton
Bendigo
Benalla
Bairnsdale
Sale
Traralgon
South East Point

Broken Hill
Mildura
Murray River
Swan Hill
Horsham
Ballarat
MELBOURNE
Melbourne
Geelong
Morwell
Warrnambool
Portland
Mount Gambier

NEW SOUTH WALES

VICTORIA

SOUTH AUSTRALIA

Great Victoria Desert

Lake Eyre North
Lake Eyre South
Lake Blanche
Lake Callabonna
Lake Frome
Marree
Coober Pedy
Lake Torrens
Lake Gairdner
Lake Everard
Tarcoola
Penong
Ceduna
Elliston
Flinders Ranges
Peterborough
Crystal Brook
Port Augusta
Port Pirie
Whyalla
Wudinna
Port Lincoln
Eyre Peninsula
Spencer Gulf
Kangaroo Island
Investigator Strait
Gawler
Adelaide
Elizabeth
Murray Bridge
Tailem Bend
Keith
Naracoorte
Meningie
Bordertown

Tasman Sea

Bass Strait
Banks Strait
Flinders Island
Cape Barren Island
King Island
Hunter Island
Marrawah
Three Hummock Island
Burnie
Devonport
Launceston
Maria Island
Hobart
South Bruny Island

TASMANIA

N

Elevation

-6000m	-4000m	-2000m	-1000m	-500m	-250m	Below sea level	0	250m	500m	1000m	2000m	3000m	4000m	6000m
-19,658ft	-13,124ft	-6562ft	-3281ft	-1640ft	-820ft	-328ft/-100m	0	820ft	1640ft	3281ft	6562ft	9843ft	13,124ft	19,685ft

New Zealand

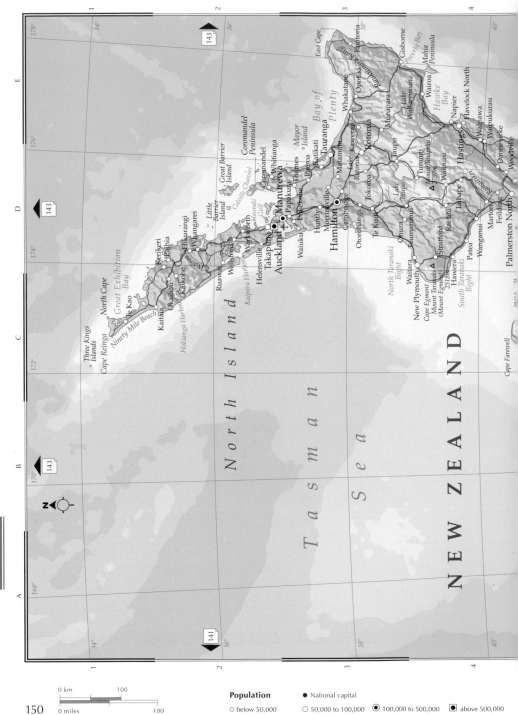

Population

- ○ below 50,000
- ○ 50,000 to 100,000
- ◉ 100,000 to 500,000
- ◼ above 500,000
- ● National capital

0 km   100

0 miles   100

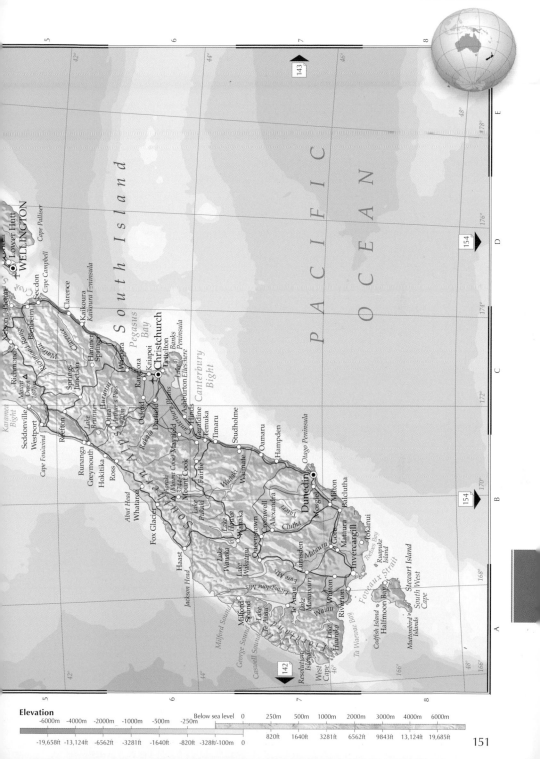

143

154

154

142

South Island

PACIFIC

OCEAN

WELLINGTON
Lower Hutt
Cape Palliser
Cape Campbell
Seddon
Blenheim
Richmond
Nelson
Picton
Hector
Kaikoura
Kaikoura Peninsula
Clarence
Cape Foulwind
Westport
Seddonville
Reefton
Mount Owen
1875m
Springs Junction
Hanmer Springs
Waiau
Rangiora
Kaiapoi
Christchurch
Lyttelton
Banks Peninsula
Pegasus Bay
Lake Ellesmere
Greymouth
Runanga
Hokitika
Ross
Lake Brunner
Otira
Arthur's Pass
920m
Oxford
Darfield
Ashburton
Hinds
Rakaia
Geraldine
Temuka
Canterbury Plains
Canterbury Bight
Whataroa
Abut Head
Fox Glacier
Aoraki/Mount Cook
3744m
Mount Cook
Fairlie
Timaru
Studholme
Oamaru
Hampden
Lake Pukaki
Lake Tekapo
Waitaki
Waimate
Haast
Jackson Head
Lake Wanaka
Lake Hawea
Wanaka
Cromwell
Alexandra
Clutha
Waitaki
Otago Peninsula
Dunedin
Mosgiel
Milton
Balclutha
Milford Sound
George Sound
Caswell Sound
Lake Te Anau
Te Anau
Eyre Mts
Queenstown
Lake Wakatipu
Livingstone Mts
Lumsden
Mataura
Gore
Clinton
Tokanui
Invercargill
Lake Manapouri
Resolution Island
West Cape
46°
Te Anau
Lake Hauroko
Waiau
Riverton
Wyndham
Halfmoon Bay
Ruapuke Island
Foveaux Strait
Codfish Island
Stewart Island
South West Cape
Mutton bird Islands
Te Waewae Bay
Paterson Inlet

Elevation

-6000m	-4000m	-2000m	-1000m	-500m	-250m	Below sea level	0	250m	500m	1000m	2000m	3000m	4000m	6000m
-19,658ft	-13,124ft	-6562ft	-3281ft	-1640ft	-820ft	-328ft/-100m	0	820ft	1640ft	3281ft	6562ft	9843ft	13,124ft	19,685ft

The Pacific Ocean

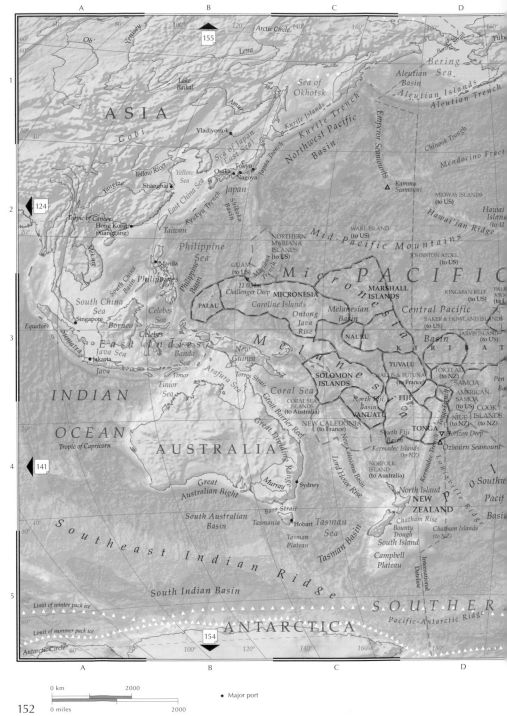

0 km   2000

0 miles   2000

● Major port

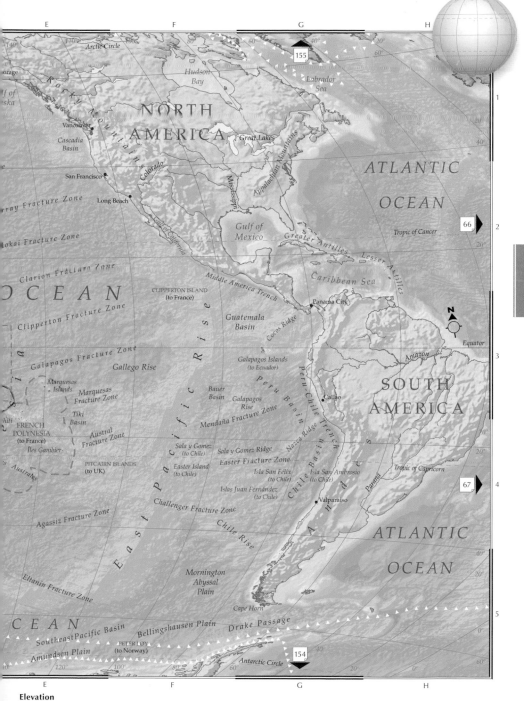

Arctic Circle

orage

Hudson
Bay

Labrador
Sea

NORTH
AMERICA

Vancouver

lf of
ska

Cascadia
Basin

Great Lakes

ATLANTIC

San Francisco

Colorado

Appalachian Mountains

OCEAN

rray Fracture Zone

Long Beach

Gulf of
Mexico

Tropic of Cancer

66

Mokai Fracture Zone

Greater Antilles

Lesser Antilles

OCEAN

Clarion Fracture Zone

Middle America Trench

Caribbean Sea

CLIPPERTON ISLAND
(to France)

Clipperton Fracture Zone

Guatemala
Basin

Panama City

N

Cocos Ridge

Galapagos Fracture Zone

Gallego Rise

Galapagos Islands
(to Ecuador)

Equator

Amazon

SOUTH

Marquesas
Islands

Marquesas
Fracture Zone

Bauer
Basin

Galapagos
Rise

Peru Basin

Callao

AMERICA

hiti

Tiki
Basin

Mendaña Fracture Zone

Peru-Chile Trench

FRENCH
POLYNESIA
(to France)

Austral
Fracture Zone

Iles Gambier

Sala y Gomez
(to Chile)

Sala y Gomez Ridge

Nazca Ridge

Tropic of Capricorn

s Australes

PITCAIRN ISLANDS
(to UK)

Easter Island
(to Chile)

Easter Fracture Zone

Isla San Felix
(to Chile)

Isla San Ambrosio
(to Chile)

Challenger Fracture Zone

Islas Juan Fernández
(to Chile)

Chile Basin

Paraná

67

Agassiz Fracture Zone

Chile Rise

Valparaiso

East Pacific Rise

Andes

ATLANTIC

Eltanin Fracture Zone

Mornington
Abyssal
Plain

OCEAN

Cape Horn

OCEAN

Southeast Pacific Basin

Bellingshausen Plain

Drake Passage

PETER I ØY
(to Norway)

154

Amundsen Plain

Antarctic Circle

Elevation

-6000m -4000m -2000m -1000m -250m 0

-19,658ft -13,124ft -6562ft -3281ft -820ft 0

Antarctica

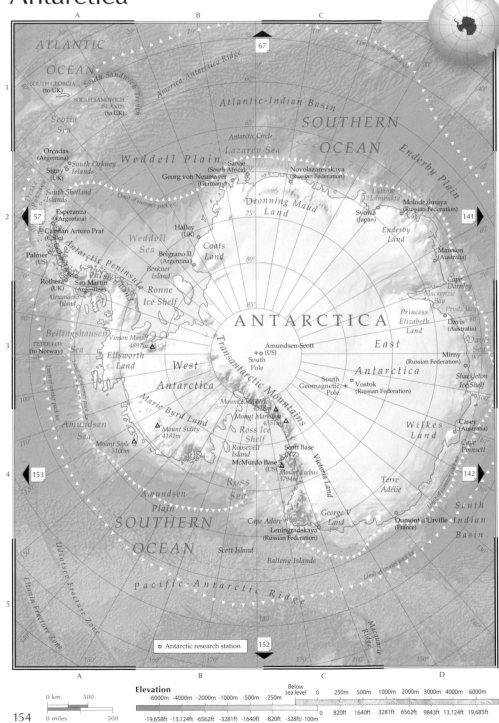

ATLANTIC
OCEAN

SOUTH GEORGIA
(to UK)

SOUTH SANDWICH
ISLANDS
(to UK)

Scotia
Sea

South Sandwich Trench

America-Antarctica Ridge

Atlantic-Indian Basin

SOUTHERN

OCEAN

Limit of winter pack ice

Antarctic Circle

Lazarev Sea

Weddell Plain

Enderby Plain

Orcadas
(Argentina)

South Orkney
Islands

Signy
(UK)

South Shetland
Islands

Drake Passage

Limit of summer pack ice

Esperanza
(Argentina)

Capitán Arturo Prat
(Chile)

Palmer
(US)

Rothera
(UK)

San Martín
(Argentina)

Alexander
Island

Georg von Neumayer
(Germany)

Sanae
(South Africa)

Novolazarevskaya
(Russian Federation)

Lützow-
Holmbukta

Molodezhnaya
(Russian Federation)

Syowa
(Japan)

Enderby
Land

Mawson
(Australia)

Halley
(UK)

Dronning Maud
Land

Weddell
Sea

Coats
Land

Belgrano II
(Argentina)

Berkner
Island

Ronne
Ice Shelf

Antarctic Peninsula

Palmer Land

Cape
Darnley

Mackenzie
Bay

Prydz Bay

Princess
Elizabeth
Land

Davis
(Australia)

Bellingshausen
Sea

PETER I ØY
(to Norway)

Vinson Massif
4897m

Ellsworth
Land

West
Antarctica

ANTARCTICA

East

Antarctica

Amundsen-Scott
+ (US)
South
Pole

South
Geomagnetic
Pole

Vostok
(Russian Federation)

Mirny
(Russian Federation)

Davis
Sea

Shackleton
Ice Shelf

Limit of winter pack ice

Amundsen
Sea

Marie Byrd Land

Mount Sidley
4181m

Mount Siple
3100m

Transantarctic Mountains

Mount Kirkpatrick
4528m

Mount Markham
4351m

Ross Ice
Shelf

Roosevelt
Island

Scott Base
(NZ)

McMurdo Base
(US)

Mount Erebus
3794m

Wilkes
Land

Casey
(Australia)

Cape
Poinsett

Amundsen
Plain

SOUTHERN

OCEAN

Ross
Sea

Cape Adare

Leningradskaya
(Russian Federation)

Victoria Land

George V
Land

Terre
Adélie

Dumont d'Urville
(France)

South
Indian
Basin

Scott Island

Balleny Islands

Macquarie
Ridge

Eltanin Fracture Zone

Udintsev Fracture Zone

Pacific-Antarctic Ridge

⊙ Antarctic research station

Elevation

-6000m -4000m -2000m -1000m -500m -250m | Below sea level | 0 | 250m 500m 1000m 2000m 3000m 4000m 6000m

-19,658ft -13,124ft -6562ft -3281ft -1640ft -820ft | -328ft/-100m | 0 | 820ft 1640ft 3281ft 6562ft 9843ft 13,124ft 19,685ft

0 km   500

0 miles   500

Arctic Ocean

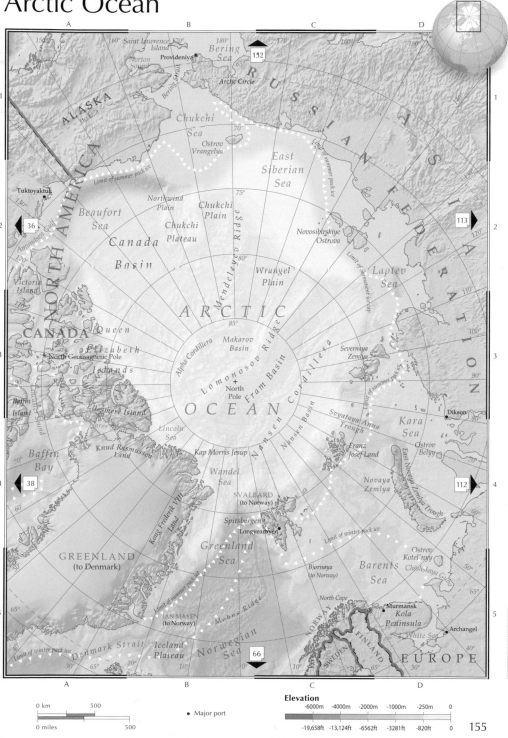

150°   160°   Saint Lawrence   170°   180°   170°   160°   150°

Island

Bering Sea

132

Norton Sound

Providenya

Arctic Circle

Bering Strait

65°

ALASKA
(to US)

Chukchi
Sea

70°

Ostrov
Vrangelya

East
Siberian
Sea

RUSSIAN

1

Limit of summer pack ice

Limit of summer pack ice

140°

Tuktoyaktuk

Limit of summer pack ice

Northwind
Plain

75°

113

130°

NORTH AMERICA

Beaufort
Sea

Chukchi
Plain

Chukchi
Plateau

120°

Amundsen Gulf

Canada

Basin

80°

Novosibirskiye
Ostrova

Limit of permanent ice

Laptev
Sea

110°

120°

F E D E R A T I O N

2

Victoria
Island

Wrangel
Plain

A R C T I C

100°

90°

Queen

85°

Makarov
Basin

Severnaya
Zemlya

Limit of summer pack ice

3

CANADA

Elizabeth

North Geomagnetic Pole

Alpha Cordillera

Lomonosov Ridge

Fram Basin

+
North
Pole

Svyataya Anna
Trough

Kara
Sea

Dikson

80°

Baffin
Island

Islands

O C E A N

Nansen Cordillera

Nansen Basin

Franz
Josef Land

Ostrov
Belyy

East Novaya Zemlya Trough

90°

Ellesmere Island

Lincoln
Sea

Kap Morris Jesup

Knud Rasmussen
Land

Novaya
Zemlya

70°

Baffin
Bay

Wandel
Sea

SVALBARD
(to Norway)

112

4

60°

Kong Frederik VIII
Land

Spitsbergen

Longyearbyen

Limit of winter pack ice

Ostrov
Kotel'nyy

50°

Chëshskaya Guba

GREENLAND
(to Denmark)

Greenland
Sea

Bjørnøya
(to Norway)

Barents
Sea

65°

North Cape

NORWAY

Murmansk
Kola
Peninsula

Archangel

5

65°

JAN MAYEN
(to Norway)

Mohns Ridge

Norwegian
Sea

SWEDEN

FINLAND

White Sea

40°

Limit of winter pack ice

Iceland
Plateau

Denmark Strait

65°

30°

20°

10°

0°

10°

20°

66

30°

E U R O P E

36

38

Elevation

| -6000m | -4000m | -2000m | -1000m | -250m | 0 |

0 km   500

0 miles   500

● Major port

-19,658ft   -13,124ft   -6562ft   -3281ft   -820ft   0

Overseas territories & dependencies

Despite the rapid process of global decolonization since the Second World War, around 8 million people in more than 50 territories around the world continue to live under the protection of France, Australia, the Netherlands, Denmark, Norway, New Zealand, the UK, or the USA. These remnants of former colonial empires may have persisted for economic, strategic or political reasons and are administered in a variety of ways.

AUSTRALIA

Australia's overseas territories have not been an issue since Papua New Guinea became independent in 1975. Consequently there is no overriding policy toward them. Norfolk Island is inhabited by descendants of the H.M.S Bounty mutineers and more recent Australian migrants.

Ashmore & Cartier Islands
Indian Ocean
Status: External territory
Claimed: 1931
Capital: Not applicable
Population: None
Area: 2 sq miles
(5.2 sq km)

Christmas Island
Indian Ocean
Status: External territory
Claimed: 1958
Capital: The Settlement
Population: 1403
Area: 52 sq miles
(135 sq km)

Cocos Islands
Indian Ocean
Status: External territory
Claimed: 1955
Capital: No official capital
Population: 596
Area: 5.5 sq miles
(14 sq km)

Coral Sea Islands
South Pacific
Status: External territory
Claimed: 1969
Capital: None
Population: 8 (meteorologists)
Area: Less than 1.2 sq miles
(3 sq km)

Heard & McDonald Is.
Indian Ocean
Status: External territory
Claimed: 1947
Capital: Not applicable
Population: None
Area: 161 sq miles
(417 sq km)

Norfolk Island
South Pacific
Status: External territory
Claimed: 1774
Capital: Kingston
Population: 2141
Area: 13 sq miles
(34 sq km)

DENMARK

The Faeroe Islands have been under Danish administration since Queen Margreth I of Denmark inherited Norway in 1380. The Home Rule Act of 1948 gave the Faeroese control over all their internal affairs. Greenland first came under Danish rule in 1380. Today, Denmark is responsible for the island's foreign affairs and defense.

Faeroe Islands
North Atlantic
Status: External territory
Claimed: 1380
Capital: Tórshavn
Population: 48,917
Area: 540 sq miles
(1399 sq km)

Greenland
North Atlantic
Status: External territory
Claimed: 1380
Capital: Nuuk
Population: 56,452
Area: 840,000 sq miles
(2,175,516 sq km)

FRANCE

France has developed economic ties with its *Territoires d'Outre-Mer*, thereby stressing interdependence over independence. Overseas *départements*, officially part of France, have their own governments. Territorial *collectivités* and overseas *territoires* have varying degrees of autonomy.

Clipperton Island
East Pacific
Status: Dependency of French Polynesia
Claimed: 1935
Capital: Not applicable
Population: None
Area: 2.7 sq miles
(7 sq km)

French Guiana
South America
Status: Overseas department
Claimed: 1817
Capital: Cayenne
Population: 229,000
Area: 32,253 sq miles
(83,534 sq km)

French Polynesia
South Pacific
Status: Overseas territory
Claimed: 1843
Capital: Papeete
Population: 264,000
Area: 1608 sq miles
(4165 sq km)

Guadeloupe
West Indies
Status: Overseas department
Claimed: 1635
Capital: Basse-Terre
Population: 405,500
Area: 687 sq miles
(1780 sq km)

Martinique
West Indies
Status: Overseas
department
Claimed: 1635
Capital: Fort-de-France
Population: 397,000
Area: 425 sq miles
(1100 sq km)

Mayotte
Indian Ocean
Status: Territorial
collectivity
Claimed: 1843
Capital: Mamoudzou
Population: 194,000
Area: 144 sq miles
(374 sq km)

New Caledonia
South Pacific
Status: Overseas territory
Claimed: 1853
Capital: Nouméa
Population: 249,000
Area: 7374 sq miles
(19,100 sq km)

Réunion
Indian Ocean
Status: Overseas
department
Claimed: 1638
Capital: Saint-Denis
Population: 827,000
Area: 970 sq miles
(2500 sq km)

St. Pierre & Miquelon
North America
Status: Territorial collectivity
Claimed: 1604
Capital: Saint-Pierre
Population: 7063
Area: 93 sq miles
(242 sq km)

Wallis & Futuna
South Pacific
Status: Overseas territory
Claimed: 1842
Capital: Matá'Utu
Population: 15,289
Area: 106 sq miles
(274 sq km)

NETHERLANDS

The country's remaining overseas territories were formerly part of the Dutch West Indies. The Netherlands Antilles dissolved in 2010 leaving the constituent islands with varying degrees of autonomy, but the Netherlands remains responsible for their security.

Aruba
West Indies
Status: Autonomous
part of the Netherlands
Claimed: 1643
Capital: Oranjestad
Population: 103,065
Area: 75 sq miles (194 sq km)

Bonaire
West Indies
Status: Special municipality of
the Netherlands
Claimed: 1816
Capital: Kralendijk
Population: 14,006
Area: 113 sq miles
(294 sq km)

Curaçao
West Indies
Status: Autonomous
part of the Netherlands
Claimed: 1816
Capital: Willemstad
Population: 141,766
Area: 171 sq miles
(444 sq km)

Sint Maarten
West Indies
Status: Autonomous
part of the Netherlands
Claimed: 1816
Capital: Philipsburg
Population: 40,917
Area: 13 sq miles (34 sq km)

NEW ZEALAND

New Zealand's government has no desire to retain any overseas territories. However, the economic weakness of its dependent territory Tokelau and its freely associated states, Niue and the Cook Islands, has forced New Zealand to remain responsible for their foreign policy and defense.

Cook Islands
South Pacific
Status: Associated territory
Claimed: 1901
Capital: Avarua
Population: 19,596
Area: 91 sq miles
(235 sq km)

Niue
South Pacific
Status: Associated territory
Claimed: 1901
Capital: Alofi
Population: 1398
Area: 102 sq miles
(264 sq km)

Tokelau
South Pacific
Status: Dependent territory
Claimed: 1926
Capital: Not applicable
Population: 1416
Area: 4 sq miles (10 sq km)

NORWAY

In 1920, 41 nations signed the Spits-bergen Treaty recognizing Norwegian sovereignty over Svalbard. There is a NATO base on Jan Mayen. Bouvet Island is a nature reserve.

Bouvet Island
South Atlantic
Status: Dependency
Claimed: 1928
Capital: Not applicable
Population: None
Area: 22 sq miles (58 sq km)

Jan Mayen
North Atlantic
Status: Dependency
Claimed: 1929
Capital: Not applicable
Population: None
Area: 147 sq miles
(381 sq km)

Continued on page 158

Overseas territories & dependencies

Peter I. Island
Southern Ocean
Status: Dependency
Claimed: 1931
Capital: Not applicable
Population: None
Area: 69 sq miles (180 sq km)

Svalbard
Arctic Ocean
Status: Dependency
Claimed: 1920
Capital: Longyearbyen
Population: 2572
Area: 24,289 sq miles
(62,906 sq km)

UNITED KINGDOM

The UK still has the largest number
of overseas territories. These are
locally-governed by a mixture
of elected representatives and
appointed officials, and they
all enjoy a large measure of internal
self-government, but certain powers,
such as foreign affairs and defense,
are reserved for Governors
of the British Crown.

Anguilla
West Indies
Status: Dependent
territory
Claimed: 1650
Capital: The Valley
Population: 13,600
Area: 37 sq miles
(96 sq km)

Ascension Island
South Atlantic
Status: Dependency
of St. Helena
Claimed: 1673
Capital: Georgetown
Population: 940
Area: 34 sq miles
(88 sq km)

Bermuda
North Atlantic
Status: Crown colony
Claimed: 1612
Capital: Hamilton
Population: 67,837
Area: 20 sq miles (53 sq km)

British Indian Ocean Territory
Status: Dependent
territory
Claimed: 1814
Capital: Diego Garcia
Population: 4000
Area: 23 sq miles
(60 sq km)

British Virgin Islands
West Indies
Status: Dependent territory
Claimed: 1672
Capital: Road Town
Population: 27,000
Area: 59 sq miles
(153 sq km)

Cayman Islands
West Indies
Status: Dependent territory
Claimed: 1670
Capital: George Town
Population: 60,456
Area: 100 sq miles (259 sq km)

Falkland Islands
South Atlantic
Status: Dependent territory
Claimed: 1832
Capital: Stanley
Population: 3140
Area: 4699 sq miles
(12,173 sq km)

Gibraltar
Southwest Europe
Status: Crown colony
Claimed: 1713
Capital: Gibraltar
Population: 29,286
Area: 2.5 sq miles (6.5 sq km)

Guernsey
Channel Islands
Status: Crown dependency
Claimed: 1066
Capital: St. Peter Port
Population: 65,573
Area: 25 sq miles (65 sq km)

Isle of Man
British Isles
Status: Crown dependency
Claimed: 1765
Capital: Douglas
Population: 80,085
Area: 221 sq miles (572 sq km)

Jersey
Channel Islands
Status: Crown dependency
Claimed: 1066
Capital: St. Helier
Population: 91,626
Area: 45 sq miles (116 sq km)

Montserrat
West Indies
Status: Dependent territory
Claimed: 1632
Capital: Plymouth
(currently uninhabitable)
Population: 4655
Area: 40 sq miles (102 sq km)

Pitcairn Islands
South Pacific
Status: Dependent territory
Claimed: 1887
Capital: Adamstown
Population: 50
Area: 18 sq miles (47 sq km)

St. Helena
South Atlantic
Status: Dependent territory
Claimed: 1673
Capital: Jamestown
Population: 4255
Area: 47 sq miles (122 sq km)

South Georgia & The South Sandwich Islands
South Atlantic
Status: Dependent territory
Claimed: 1775
Capital: Not applicable
Population: No permanent
residents
Area: 1387 sq miles
(3592 sq km)

Tristan da Cunha
South Atlantic
Status: Dependency
of St. Helena
Claimed: 1612
Capital: Edinburgh
Population: 276
Area: 38 sq miles (98 sq km)

Turks & Caicos Islands
West Indies
Status: Dependent territory
Claimed: 1766
Capital: Cockburn Town
Population: 36,605
Area: 166 sq miles
(430 sq km)

UNITED STATES
OF AMERICA

America's overseas territories
have been seen as strategically
useful, if expensive, links with its
"backyards." The US has, in most
cases, given the local population a
say in deciding their own status.
A US Commonwealth territory, such
as Puerto Rico, has a greater level
of independence than that of a US
unincorporated or external territory.

American Samoa
South Pacific
Status: Unincorporated
territory
Claimed: 1900
Capital: Pago Pago
Population: 65,628
Area: 75 sq miles (195 sq km)

Baker &
Howland Islands
South Pacific
Status: Unincorporated
territory
Claimed: 1856
Capital: Not applicable
Population: None
Area: 0.5 sq miles (1.4 sq km)

Guam
West Pacific
Status: Unincorporated
territory
Claimed: 1898
Capital: Hagåtña
Population: 178,000
Area: 212 sq miles
(549 sq km)

Jarvis Island
South Pacific
Status: Unincorporated territory
Claimed: 1856
Capital: Not applicable
Population: None
Area: 1.7 sq miles (4.5 sq km)

Johnston Atoll
Central Pacific
Status: Unincorporated
territory
Claimed: 1858
Capital: Not applicable
Population: Not applicable
Area: 1 sq mile (2.8 sq km)

Kingman Reef
Central Pacific
Status: Administered territory
Claimed: 1856
Capital: Not applicable
Population: None
Area: 0.4 sq mile
(1 sq km)

Midway Islands
Central Pacific
Status: Administered
territory
Claimed: 1867
Capital: Not applicable
Population: None
Area: 2 sq miles
(5.2 sq km)

Navassa Island
West Indies
Status: Unincorporated
territory
Claimed: 1856
Capital: Not applicable
Population: None
Area: 2 sq miles (5.2 sq km)

Northern
Mariana Islands
West Pacific
Status: Commonwealth
territory
Claimed: 1947
Capital: Saipan
Population: 86,616
Area: 177 sq miles (457 sq km)

Palmyra Atoll
Central Pacific
Status: Unincorporated
territory
Claimed: 1898
Capital: Not applicable
Population: None
Area: 5 sq miles (12 sq km)

Puerto Rico
West Indies
Status: Commonwealth
territory
Claimed: 1898
Capital: San Juan
Population: 4.0 million
Area: 3515 sq miles
(9104 sq km)

Virgin Islands
West Indies
Status: Unincorporated
territory
Claimed: 1917
Capital: Charlotte Amalie
Population: 108,448
Area: 137 sq miles
(355 sq km)

Wake Island
Central Pacific
Status: Unincorporated
territory
Claimed: 1898
Capital: Not applicable
Population: 200
Area: 2.5 sq miles
(6.5 sq km)

Glossary of geographical terms

The following glossary lists all geographical terms occuring on the maps and in the main-entry names in the Index–Gazetteer. These terms may precede, follow or be run together with the proper elements of the name; where they precede it the term is reversed for indexing purposes – thus Poluostov Yamal is indexed as Yamal, Poluostrov.

A

Å *Danish, Norwegian*, River
Alpen *German*, Alps
Altiplanicie *Spanish*, Plateau
Älv(en) *Swedish*, River
Anse *French*, Bay
Archipiélago *Spanish*, Archipelago
Arcipelago *Italian*, Archipelago
Arquipiélago *Portuguese*, Archipelago
Aukštuma *Lithuanian*, Upland

B

Bahía *Spanish*, Bay
Baía *Portuguese*, Bay
Baḩr *Arabic*, River
Baie *French*, Bay
Bandao *Chinese*, Peninsula
Banjaran *Malay*, Mountain range
Batang *Malay*, Stream
-berg *Afrikaans, Norwegian*, Mountain
Birket *Arabic*, Lake
Boğazı *Turkish*, Strait
Bucht *German*, Bay
Bugten *Danish*, Bay
Buḩayrat *Arabic*, Lake, reservoir
Buḩeiret *Arabic*, Lake
Bukit *Malay*, Mountain
-bukta *Norwegian*, Bay
bukten *Swedish*, Bay
Burnu *Turkish*, Cape, point
Buuraha *Somali*, Mountains

C

Cabo *Portuguese*, Cape
Cap *French*, Cape
Cascada *Portuguese*, Waterfall
Cerro *Spanish*, Mountain
Chaîne *French*, Mountain range
Chau *Cantonese*, Island
Cháy *Turkish*, Stream
Chhâk *Cambodian*, Bay
Chhu *Tibetan*, River
-chôsuji *Korean*, Reservoir

Chott *Arabic*, Salt lake, depression
Ch'ün-tao *Chinese*, Island group
Cambodian, Mountains
Cordillera *Spanish*, Mountain range
Costa *Spanish*, Coast
Côte *French*, Coast
Cuchilla *Spanish*, Mountains

D

Dağı *Azerbaijani, Turkish*, Mountain
Dağları *Azerbaijani, Turkish*, Mountains
-dake *Japanese*, Peak
Danau *Indonesian*, Lake
Đao *Vietnamese*, Island
Daryá *Persian*, River
Daryácheh *Persian*, Lake
Dasht *Persian*, Plain, desert
Dawḩat *Arabic*, Bay
Dere *Turkish*, Stream
Dili *Azerbaijani*, Spit
-do *Korean*, Island
Dooxo *Somali*, Valley
Düzü *Azerbaijani*, Steppe
-dwíp *Bengali*, Island

E

Embalse *Spanish*, Reservoir
Erg *Arabic*, Dunes
Estany *Catalan*, Lake
Estrecho *Spanish*, Strait
-ey *Icelandic*, Island
Ezero *Bulgarian, Macedonian*, Lake

F

Fjord *Danish*, Fjord
-fjorden *Norwegian*, Fjord
-fjørdhur *Faeroese*, Fjord
Fleuve *French*, River
Fliegu *Maltese*, Channel
-fljór *Icelandic*, River

G

-gang *Korean*, River
Ganga *Nepali, Sinhala*, River
Gaoyuan *Chinese*, Plateau
-gawa *Japanese*, River

Gebel *Arabic*, Mountain
-gebirge *German*, Mountains
Ghubbat *Arabic*, Bay
Gjiri *Albanian*, Bay
Gol *Mongolian*, River
Golfe *French*, Gulf
Golfo *Italian, Spanish*, Gulf
Gora *Russian, Serbian*, Mountain
Gory *Russian*, Mountains
Guba *Russian*, Bay
Gunung *Malay*, Mountain

H

Ḩadd *Arabic*, Spit
-haehyôp *Korean*, Strait
Haff *German*, Lagoon
Hai *Chinese*, Sea, bay
Ḩammádat *Arabic*, Plateau
Hámún *Persian*, Lake
Hawr *Arabic*, Lake
Háyk' *Amharic*, Lake
He *Chinese*, River
Helodrano *Malagasy*, Bay
-hegység *Hungarian*, Mountain range
Hka *Burmese*, River
-ho *Korean*, Lake
Hô *Korean*, Reservoir
/olot *Hebrew*, Dunes
Hora *Belorussian*, Mountain
Hrada *Belorussian*, Mountains, ridge
Hsi *Chinese*, River
Hu *Chinese*, Lake

I

Île(s) *French*, Island(s)
Ilha(s) *Portuguese*, Island(s)
Ilhéu(s) *Portuguese*, Islet(s)
Irmak *Turkish*, River
Isla(s) *Spanish*, Island(s)
Isola (Isole) *Italian*, Island(s)

J

Jabal *Arabic*, Mountain
Jál *Arabic*, Ridge
-järvi *Finnish*, Lake
Jazírat *Arabic*, Island
Jazíreh *Persian*, Island

Jebel *Arabic*, Mountain
Jezero *Serbian/Croatian*, Lake
Jiang *Chinese*, River
-joki *Finnish*, River
-jökull *Icelandic*, Glacier
Juzur *Arabic*, Islands

K

Kaikyó *Japanese*, Strait
-kaise *Lappish*, Mountain
Kali *Nepali*, River
Kalnas *Lithuanian*, Mountain
Kalns *Latvian*, Mountain
Kang *Chinese*, Harbor
Kangri *Tibetan*, Mountain(s)
Kaôh *Cambodian*, Island
Kapp *Norwegian*, Cape
Kavír *Persian*, Desert
K'edi *Georgian*, Mountain range
Kediet *Arabic*, Mountain
Kepulauan *Indonesian, Malay*, Island group
Khalîg, Khalíj *Arabic*, Gulf
Khawr *Arabic*, Inlet
Khola *Nepali*, River
Khrebet *Russian*, Mountain range
Ko *Thai*, Island
Kolpos *Greek*, Bay
-kopf *German*, Peak
Körfäzi *Azerbaijani*, Bay
Körfezi *Turkish*, Bay
Kõrgustik *Estonian*, Upland
Koshi *Nepali*, River
Kowtal *Persian*, Pass
Kúh(há) *Persian*, Mountain(s)
-kundo *Korean*, Island group
-kysten *Norwegian*, Coast
Kyun *Burmese*, Island

L

Laaq *Somali*, Watercourse
Lac *French*, Lake
Lacul *Romanian*, Lake
Lago *Italian, Portuguese, Spanish*, Lake

Laguna *Spanish,* Lagoon, Lake
Laht *Estonian,* Bay
Laut *Indonesian,* Sea
Lembalemba *Malagasy,* Plateau
Lerr *Armenian,* Mountain
Lerrnashght'a *Armenian,* Mountain range
Les *Czech,* Forest
Lich *Armenian,* Lake
Liqeni *Albanian,* Lake
Lumi *Albanian,* River
Lyman *Ukrainian,* Estuary

M

Mae Nam *Thai,* River
-mägi *Estonian,* Hill
Maja *Albanian,* Mountain
-man *Korean,* Bay
Marios *Lithuanian,* Lake
-meer *Dutch,* Lake
Melkosopochnik *Russian,* Plain
-meri *Estonian,* Sea
Mifraz *Hebrew,* Bay
Monkhafad *Arabic,* Depression
Mont(s) *French,* Mountain(s)
Monte *Italian, Portuguese,* Mountain
More *Russian,* Sea
Mörön *Mongolian,* River

N

Nagor'ye *Russian,* Upland
Najal *Hebrew,* River
Nahr *Arabic,* River
Nam *Laotian,* River
Nehri *Turkish,* River
Nevado *Spanish,* Mountain (snow-capped)
Nisoi *Greek,* Islands
Nizmennost' *Russian,* Lowland, plain
Nosy *Malagasy,* Island
Nur *Mongolian,* Lake
Nuruu *Mongolian,* Mountains
Nuur *Mongolian,* Lake
Nyzovyna *Ukrainian,* Lowland, plain

O

Ostrov(a) *Russian,* Island(s)
Oued *Arabic,* Watercourse
-oy *Faeroese,* Island
-øy(a) *Norwegian,* Island
Oya *Sinhala,* River
Ozero *Russian, Ukrainian,* Lake

P

Passo *Italian,* Pass
Pegunungan *Indonesian, Malay,* Mountain range
Pelagos *Greek,* Sea
Penisola *Italian,* Peninsula
Peski *Russian,* Sands
Phanom *Thai,* Mountain
Phou *Laotian,* Mountain
Pic *Catalan,* Peak
Pico *Portuguese, Spanish,* Peak
Pik *Russian,* Peak
Planalto *Portuguese,* Plateau
Planina, Planini *Bulgarian, Macedonian, Serbian, Croatian,* Mountain range
Ploskogor'ye *Russian,* Upland
Poluostrov *Russian,* Peninsula
Potamos *Greek,* River
Proliv *Russian,* Strait
Pulau *Indonesian, Malay,* Island
Pulu *Malay,* Island
Punta *Portuguese, Spanish,* Point

Q

Qá' *Arabic,* Depression
Qolleh *Persian,* Mountain

R

Raas *Somali,* Cape
-rags *Latvian,* Cape
Ramlat *Arabic,* Sands
Ra's *Arabic,* Cape, point, headland
Ravnina *Bulgarian, Russian,* Plain
Récif *French,* Reef
Represa (Rep.) *Spanish, Portuguese,* Reservoir
-rettó *Japanese,* Island chain
Riacho *Spanish,* Stream
Riban' *Malagasy,* Mountains
Rio *Portuguese,* River
Río *Spanish,* River
Riu *Catalan,* River
Rivier *Dutch,* River
Rivière *French,* River
Rowd *Pashtu,* River
Rúd *Persian,* River
Rudohorie *Slovak,* Mountains
Ruisseau *French,* Stream

S

Sabkhat *Arabic,* Salt marsh
Şaḥrá' *Arabic,* Desert
Samudra *Sinhala,* Reservoir
-san *Japanese, Korean,* Mountain
-sanchi *Japanese,* Mountains
-sanmaek *Korean,* Mountains
Sarír *Arabic,* Desert
Sebkha, Sebkhet *Arabic,* Salt marsh, depression
See *German,* Lake
Selat *Indonesian,* Strait
-selkä *Finnish,* Ridge
Selseleh *Persian,* Mountain range
Serra *Portuguese,* Mountain
Serranía *Spanish,* Mountain
Sha'íb *Arabic,* Watercourse
Shamo *Chinese,* Desert
Shan *Chinese,* Mountain(s)
Shan-mo *Chinese,* Mountain range
Shaṭṭ *Arabic,* Distributary
-shima *Japanese,* Island
Shui-tao *Chinese,* Channel
Sierra *Spanish,* Mountains
Sòn *Vietnamese,* Mountain
Sông *Vietnamese,* River
-spitze *German,* Peak
Štít *Slovak,* Peak
Stoeng *Cambodian,* River
Stretto *Italian,* Strait
Su Anbarı *Azerbaijani,* Reservoir
Sungai *Indonesian, Malay,* River
Suu *Turkish,* River

T

Tal *Mongolian,* Plain
Tandavan' *Malagasy,* Mountain range
Tangorombohitr' *Malagasy,* Mountain massif
Tao *Chinese,* Island
Tassili *Berber,* Plateau, mountain
Tau *Russian,* Mountain(s)
Taungdan *Burmese,* Mountain range

Teluk *Indonesian,* Malay, Bay
Terara *Amharic,* Mountain
Tog *Somali,* Valley
Tônlé *Cambodian,* Lake
Top *Dutch,* Peak
-tunturi *Finnish,* Mountain
Tur'at *Arabic,* Channel

V

Väin *Estonian,* Strait
-vatn *Icelandic,* Lake
-vesi *Finnish,* Lake
Vinh *Vietnamese,* Bay
Vodokhranilishche (Vdkhr.) *Russian,* Reservoir
Vodoskhovyshche (Vdskh.) *Ukrainian,* Reservoir
Volcán *Spanish,* Volcano
Vozvyshennost' *Russian,* Upland, plateau
Vrh *Macedonian,* Peak
Vysochyna *Ukrainian,* Upland
Vysočina *Czech,* Upland

W

Waadi *Somali,* Watercourse
Wádí *Arabic,* Watercourse
Wâhat, Wâhat *Arabic,* Oasis
Wald *German,* Forest
Wan *Chinese,* Bay
Wyżyna *Polish,* Upland

X

Xé *Laotian,* River

Y

Yarımadası *Azerbaijani,* Peninsula
Yazovir *Bulgarian,* Reservoir
Yoma *Burmese,* Mountains
Yü *Chinese,* Island

Z

Zaliv *Bulgarian, Russian,* Bay
Zatoka *Ukrainian,* Bay
Zemlya *Russian,* Land

Continental factfile

North & Central America

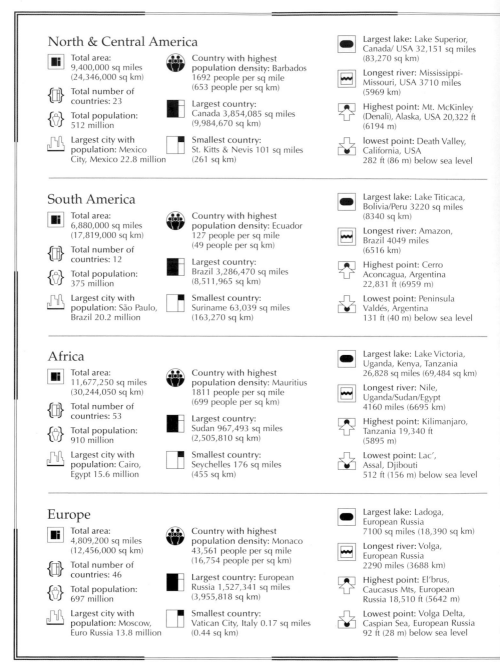

Total area:
9,400,000 sq miles
(24,346,000 sq km)

Total number of
countries: 23

Total population:
512 million

Largest city with
population: Mexico
City, Mexico 22.8 million

Country with highest
population density: Barbados
1692 people per sq mile
(653 people per sq km)

Largest country:
Canada 3,854,085 sq miles
(9,984,670 sq km)

Smallest country:
St. Kitts & Nevis 101 sq miles
(261 sq km)

Largest lake: Lake Superior,
Canada/ USA 32,151 sq miles
(83,270 sq km)

Longest river: Mississippi-
Missouri, USA 3710 miles
(5969 km)

Highest point: Mt. McKinley
(Denali), Alaska, USA 20,322 ft
(6194 m)

lowest point: Death Valley,
California, USA
282 ft (86 m) below sea level

South America

Total area:
6,880,000 sq miles
(17,819,000 sq km)

Total number of
countries: 12

Total population:
375 million

Largest city with
population: São Paulo,
Brazil 20.2 million

Country with highest
population density: Ecuador
127 people per sq mile
(49 people per sq km)

Largest country:
Brazil 3,286,470 sq miles
(8,511,965 sq km)

Smallest country:
Suriname 63,039 sq miles
(163,270 sq km)

Largest lake: Lake Titicaca,
Bolivia/Peru 3220 sq miles
(8340 sq km)

Longest river: Amazon,
Brazil 4049 miles
(6516 km)

Highest point: Cerro
Aconcagua, Argentina
22,831 ft (6959 m)

Lowest point: Peninsula
Valdés, Argentina
131 ft (40 m) below sea level

Africa

Total area:
11,677,250 sq miles
(30,244,050 sq km)

Total number of
countries: 53

Total population:
910 million

Largest city with
population: Cairo,
Egypt 15.6 million

Country with highest
population density: Mauritius
1811 people per sq mile
(699 people per sq km)

Largest country:
Sudan 967,493 sq miles
(2,505,810 sq km)

Smallest country:
Seychelles 176 sq miles
(455 sq km)

Largest lake: Lake Victoria,
Uganda, Kenya, Tanzania
26,828 sq miles (69,484 sq km)

Longest river: Nile,
Uganda/Sudan/Egypt
4160 miles (6695 km)

Highest point: Kilimanjaro,
Tanzania 19,340 ft
(5895 m)

Lowest point: Lac',
Assal, Djibouti
512 ft (156 m) below sea level

Europe

Total area:
4,809,200 sq miles
(12,456,000 sq km)

Total number of
countries: 46

Total population:
697 million

Largest city with
population: Moscow,
Euro Russia 13.8 million

Country with highest
population density: Monaco
43,561 people per sq mile
(16,754 people per sq km)

Largest country: European
Russia 1,527,341 sq miles
(3,955,818 sq km)

Smallest country:
Vatican City, Italy 0.17 sq miles
(0.44 sq km)

Largest lake: Ladoga,
European Russia
7100 sq miles (18,390 sq km)

Longest river: Volga,
European Russia
2290 miles (3688 km)

Highest point: El'brus,
Caucasus Mts, European
Russia 18,510 ft (5642 m)

Lowest point: Volga Delta,
Caspian Sea, European Russia
92 ft (28 m) below sea level

North & West Asia

Total area:
9,585,500 sq miles
(24,826,600 sq km)

Total number of countries: 24

Total population:
398 million

Largest city with population: Tehran, Iran 11.9 million

Country with highest population density: Bahrain 2596 people per sq mile (1004 people per sq km)

Largest country: Asiatic Russia 5,065,471 sq miles (13,119,582 sq km)

Smallest country: Bahrain 239 sq miles (620 sq km)

Largest lake: Caspian Sea 142,243 sq miles (371,000 sq km)

Longest river: Ob'-Irtysh, Asiatic Russia 3461 miles (5570 km)

Highest point: Pik Pobedy, Kyrgyzstan/China 24,408 ft (7439 m)

Lowest point: Dead Sea, Israel/Jordan 1286 ft (392 m) below sea level

South & East Asia

Total area:
7,936,200 sq miles
(20,554,700 sq km)

Total number of countries: 24

Total population:
3979 million

Largest city with population: Tokyo, Japan 34.2 million

Country with highest population density: Singapore 18,644 people per sq mile (7213 people per sq km)

Largest country: China 3,705,386 sq miles (9,596,960 sq km)

Smallest country: Maldives 116 sq miles (300 sq km)

Largest lake: Tonle Sap, Cambodia 1000 sq miles (2850 sq km)

Longest river: Chang Jiang (Yangtze) 3965 miles (6380 km)

Highest point: Mount Everest, Nepal 29,035 ft (8850 m)

Lowest point: Turpan Hami, (Turfan basin), China 505 ft (154 m) below sea level

Australasia & Oceania

Total area:
3,376,700 sq miles
(8,745,750 sq km)

Total number of countries: 14

Total population:
32 million

Largest city with population: Sydney, Australia 4.4 million

Country with highest population density: Nauru 1670 people per sq mile (644 people per sq km)

Largest country: Australia 2,967,893 sq miles (7,686,850 sq km)

Smallest country: Nauru 8 sq miles (21 sq km)

Largest lake: Lake Eyre, Australia 3700 sq miles (9583 sq km)

Longest river: Murray-Darling, Australia 2330 miles (3750 km)

Highest point: Mt. Wilhelm, Papua New Guinea 14,795 ft (4509 m)

Lowest point: Lake Eyre, Australia 52 ft (16 m) below sea level

Antarctica

Total area: 5,450,500 sq miles (14,000,000 sq km) of which approx. 324,300 sq miles (840,000 sq km) is ice-free.

Total number of countries: The Antarctic Treaty has 30 participating nations and 14 with observer status. Claims by Australia, France, New Zealand, Norway, Argentina, Chile, and the UK are not recognized by other member states.

Total Population: No indigenous population. 74 research stations, (42 are staffed all year-round). Population varies between about 1000 (winter) and 4000 (summer).

Total volume of ice:
7,200,000 cu miles (30,000,000 cu km): contains 90% of Earth's fresh water

Sea ice: 1,158,300 sq miles (3,000,000 sq km) in February. 7,722,000 sq miles (20,000,000 sq km) in October

Lowest temperature: Vostok station -89.5°C (-129°F)

Highest point: Vinson Massif 16,072 ft (4897 m)

Lowest Point: Coastline 0ft/m

Geographical comparisons

Largest countries

Russ. Fed.	6,592,735 sq miles	(17,075,200 sq km)
Canada	3,854,085 sq miles	(9,984,670 sq km)
USA	3,717,792 sq miles	(9,629,091 sq km)
China	3,705,386 sq miles	(9,596,960 sq km)
Brazil	3,286,470 sq miles	(8,511,965 sq km)
Australia	2,967,893 sq miles	(7,686,850 sq km)
India	1,269,339 sq miles	(3,287,590 sq km)
Argentina	1,068,296 sq miles	(2,766,890 sq km)
Kazakhstan	1,049,150 sq miles	(2,717,300 sq km)
Sudan	967,493 sq miles	(2,505,810 sq km)

Smallest countries

Vatican City	0.17 sq miles	(0.44 sq km)
Monaco	0.75 sq miles	(1.95 sq km)
Nauru	8 sq miles	(21 sq km)
Tuvalu	10 sq miles	(26 sq km)
San Marino	24 sq miles	(61 sq km)
Liechtenstein	62 sq miles	(160 sq km)
Marshall Islands	70 sq miles	(181 sq km)
St. Kitts & Nevis	101 sq miles	(261 sq km)
Maldives	116 sq miles	(300 sq km)
Malta	122 sq miles	(316 sq km)

Largest islands

Greenland	849,400 sq miles	(2,200,000 sq km)
New Guinea	312,000 sq miles	(808,000 sq km)
Borneo	292,222 sq miles	(757,050 sq km)
Madagascar	229,300 sq miles	(594,000 sq km)
Sumatra	202,300 sq miles	(524,000 sq km)
Baffin Island	183,800 sq miles	(476,000 sq km)
Honshu	88,800 sq miles	(230,000 sq km)
Britain	88,700 sq miles	(229,800 sq km)
Victoria Island	81,900 sq miles	(212,000 sq km)
Ellesmere Island	75,700 sq miles	(196,000 sq km)

Richest countries (GNI per capita, in US$)

Luxembourg	65,630
Norway	59,590
Switzerland	54,930
Liechtenstein	50,000
Denmark	47,390
Iceland	46,320
USA	43,740
Sweden	41,060
Ireland	40,150
Japan	38,980

Poorest countries (GNI per capita, in US$)

Burundi	100
Somalia	120
Congo, Dem. Rep	120
Liberia	130
Malawi	160
Ethiopia	160
Guinea-Bissau	180
Sierra Leone	220
Eritrea	220
Afghanistan	222

Most populous countries

China	1,331,400,000
India	1,135,600,000
USA	303,900,000
Indonesia	228,100,000
Brazil	191,300,000
Pakistan	164,600,000
Bangladesh	147,100,000
Russian Federation	141,900,000
Nigeria	137,200,000
Japan	128,300,000

Least populous countries

Vatican City	821
Tuvalu	11,992
Nauru	13,528
Palau	20,842
San Marino	29,615
Monaco	32,671
Liechtenstein	34,247
St. Kitts & Nevis	39,349
Marshall Islands	61,815
Antigua & Barbuda	69,481

Most densely populated countries

Monaco	43,561 people per sq mile (16,754 per sq km)
Singapore	18,644 people per sq mile (7213 per sq km)
Vatican City	4829 people per sq mile (1866 per sq km)
Malta	3241 people per sq mile (1256 per sq km)
Maldives	3181 people per sq mile (1230 per sq km)
Bangladesh	2845 people per sq mile (1098 per sq km)
Bahrain	2596 people per sq mile (1004 per sq km)
Taiwan	1835 people per sq mile (709 per sq km)
Mauritius	1811 people per sq mile (699 per sq km)
Barbados	1692 people per sq mile (653 per sq km)

Most sparsely populated countries

Mongolia........4 people per sq mile......... (2 per sq km)
Namibia...........7 people per sq mile......... (3 per sq km)
Australia..........7 people per sq mile......... (3 per sq km)
Iceland ....8 people per sq mile......... (3 per sq km)
Suriname........8 people per sq mile......... (3 per sq km)
Botswana........8 people per sq mile......... (3 per sq km)
Mauritania ......8 people per sq mile......... (3 per sq km)
Libya ....9 people per sq mile......... (4 per sq km)
Canada ....9 people per sq mile......... (4 per sq km)
Guyana ....10 people per sq mile......... (4 per sq km)

Most widely spoken languages

1. Chinese (Mandarin)	6. Arabic
2. English	7. Bengali
3. Hindi	8. Portuguese
4. Spanish	9. Malay-Indonesian
5. Russian	10. French

Largest conurbations

Tokyo...34,200,000
Mexico City 22,800,000
Seoul 22,300,000
New York 21,900,000
São Paulo..20,200,000
Mumbai 19,850,000
Delhi...19,700,000
Shanghai..18,150,000
Los Angeles 18,000,000
Osaka 16,800,000
Jakarta..16,550,000
Kolkata...15,650,000
Cairo...15,600,000
Manila...14,950,000
Karachi..14,300,000
Moscow 13,750,000
Buenos Aires 13,450,000
Dacca..13,250,000
Rio de Janeiro..12,150,000
Beijing 12,100,000
London 12,000,000
Tehran...11,850,000
Istanbul 11,500,000
Lagos 11,100,000
Shenzhen 10,700,000

Longest rivers

Nile (NE Africa) .... 4160 miles ...... (6695 km)
Amazon (South America) .... 4049 miles ...... (6516 km)
Yangtze (China)............................ 3915 miles ...... (6299 km)
Mississippi/Missouri (US) .... 3710 miles ......(5969 km)
Ob'-Irtysh (Russ. Fed.) .... 3461 miles ...... (5570 km)
Yellow River (China) .... 3395 miles ...... (5464 km)
Congo (Central Africa) .... 2900 miles ...... (4667 km)
Mekong (Southeast Asia) .... 2749 miles...... (4425 km)
Lena (Russian Federation)........ 2734 miles ...... (4400 km)
Mackenzie (Canada) .... 2640 miles ...... (4250 km)
Yenisey (Russ. Federation) ...... 2541 miles ...... (4090 km)

Highest mountains (Height above sea level)

Everest .... 29,035 ft .... (8850 m)
K2 .... 28,253 ft .... (8611 m)
Kanchenjunga I .... 28,210 ft .... (8598 m)
Makalu I .... 27,767 ft .... (8463 m)
Cho Oyu .... 26,907 ft .... (8201 m)
Dhaulagiri I............................... 26,796 ft .... (8167 m)
Manaslu I .... 26,783 ft .... (8163 m)
Nanga Parbat I......................... 26,661 ft .... (8126 m)
Annapurna I .... 26,547 ft .... (8091 m)
Gasherbrum I............................ 26,471 ft .... (8068 m)

Largest bodies of inland water (Area & depth)

Caspian Sea
    143,243 sq miles (371,000 sq km).......3215 ft (980 m)
Lake Superior
    32,151 sq miles (83,270 sq km).......1289 ft (393 m)
Lake Victoria
    26,560 sq miles (68,880 sq km).........328 ft (100 m)
Lake Huron
    23,436 sq miles (60,700 sq km).........751 ft (229 m)
Lake Michigan
    22,402 sq miles (58,020 sq km).........922 ft (281 m)
Lake Tanganyika
    12,703 sq miles (32,900 sq km).... 4700 ft (1435 m)
Great Bear Lake
    12,274 sq miles (31,790 sq km)...... 1047 ft (319 m)
Lake Baikal
    11,776 sq miles (30,500 sq km).... 5712 ft (1741 m)
Great Slave Lake
    10,981 sq miles (28,440 sq km).........459 ft (140 m)
Lake Erie
    9915 sq miles (25,680 sq km)...........197 ft (60 m)

......continued on page 166

Geographical comparisons continued

Deepest ocean features

Challenger Deep, Mariana Trench (Pacific)
36,201 ft .... (11,034 m)
Vityaz III Depth, Tonga Trench (Pacific)
35,704 ft .... (10,882 m)
Vityaz Depth, Kurile-Kamchatka Trench (Pacific)
34,588 ft .... (10,542 m)
Cape Johnson Deep, Philippine Trench (Pacific)
34,441 ft .... (10,497 m)
Kermadec Trench (Pacific)
32,964 ft .... (10,047 m)
Ramapo Deep, Japan Trench (Pacific)
32,758 ft .... (9984 m)
Milwaukee Deep, Puerto Rico Trench (Atlantic)
30,185 ft .... (9200 m)
Argo Deep, Torres Trench (Pacific)
30,070 ft .... (9165 m)
Meteor Depth, South Sandwich Trench (Atlantic)
30,000 ft .... (9144 m)
Planet Deep, New Britain Trench (Pacific)
29,988 ft .... (9140 m)

Greatest waterfalls　(Mean flow of water)

Boyoma (Congo) ....600,400 cu. ft/sec (17,000 cu.m/sec)
Khône (Laos/Cambodia) ... 410,000 cu. ft/sec (11,600 cu.m/sec)
Niagara (USA/Canada) .... 195,000 cu. ft/sec (5500 cu.m/sec)
Grande (Uruguay) .... 160,000 cu. ft/sec (4500 cu.m/sec)
Paulo Afonso (Brazil) .... 100,000 cu. ft/sec(2800 cu.m/sec)
Urubupunga (Brazil) ....97,000 cu. ft/sec (2750 cu.m/sec)
Iguaçu (Argentina/Brazil).........62,000 cu. ft/sec (1700 cu.m/sec)
Maribondo (Brazil)................53,000 cu. ft/sec (1500 cu.m/sec)
Victoria (Zimbabwe)................39,000 cu. ft/sec (1100 cu.m/sec)
Kabalega (Uganda)................42,000 cu. ft/sec (1200 cu.m/sec)
Churchill (Canada)................35,000 cu. ft/sec (1000 cu.m/sec)
Cauvery (India) ....33,000 cu. ft/sec (900 cu.m/sec)

Highest waterfalls

Angel (Venezuela) ....3212 ft.............(979 m)
Tugela (South Africa) ....3110 ft.............(948 m)
Utigard (Norway) ....2625 ft.............(800 m)
Mongefossen (Norway) ....2539 ft.............(774 m)
Mtarazi (Zimbabwe) ....2500 ft.............(762 m)
Yosemite (USA) ....2425 ft.............(739 m)
Ostre Mardola Foss (Norway) .....2156 ft ....(657 m)
Tyssestrengane (Norway)............2119 ft.............(646 m)
*Cuquenan (Venezuela)...............2001 ft.............(610 m)
Sutherland (New Zealand)...........1903 ft.............(580 m)
*Kjellfossen (Norway) ....1841 ft ....(561 m)

* indicates that the total height is a single leap

Largest deserts

Sahara.............3,450,000 sq miles (9,065,000 sq km)
Gobi.................... 500,000 sq miles (1,295,000 sq km)
Ar Rub al Khali ...... 289,600 sq miles (750,000 sq km)
Great Victorian ..... 249,800 sq miles (647,000 sq km)
Sonoran .... 120,000 sq miles (311,000 sq km)
Kalahari .... 120,000 sq miles (310,800 sq km)
Garagum .... 115,800 sq miles (300,000 sq km)
Takla Makan .... 100,400 sq miles (260,000 sq km)
Namib......................52,100 sq miles (135,000 sq km)
Thar..........................33,670 sq miles (130,000 sq km)

NB – Most of Antarctica is a polar desert, with only
2 inches (50 mm) of precipitation annually

Hottest inhabited places

Djibouti (Djibouti) ....86.0°F .... (30.0°C)
Timbouctou (Mali)......................84.7°F .... (29.3°C)
Tirunelveli (India) ....84.7°F .... (29.3°C)
Tuticorin (India)..........................84.7°F .... (29.3°C)
Nellore (India)............................84.5°F .... (29.2°C)
Santa Marta (Colombia) ....84.5°F .... (29.2°C)
Aden (Yemen)............................84.0°F .... (29.0°C)
Madurai (India)...........................84.0°F .... (29.0°C)
Niamey (Niger).............................84.0°F .... (29.0°C)

Driest inhabited places

Aswân (Egypt)................................0.02 in ....(0.5 mm)
Luxor (Egypt)..................................0.03 in ....(0.7 mm)
Arica (Chile) ....0.04 in ....(1.1 mm)
Ica (Peru).......................................0.10 in ....(2.3 mm)
Antofagasta (Chile)....................0.20 in ....(4.9 mm)
El Minya (Egypt) ....0.20 in ....(5.1 mm)
Asyût (Egypt).................................0.20 in ....(5.2 mm)
Callao (Peru)..................................0.50 in .....(12.0 mm)
Trujillo (Peru)................................0.55 in .....(14.0 mm)
El Faiyûm (Egypt) ....0.80 in .....(19.0 mm)

Wettest inhabited places

Buenaventura (Colombia) .... 265 in ....(6743 mm)
Monrovia (Liberia) .... 202 in ....(5131 mm)
Pago Pago (American Samoa) .... 196 in ....(4990 mm)
Moulmein (Myanmar) .... 191 in ....(4852 mm)
Lae (Papua New Guinea) .... 183 in ....(4645 mm)
Baguio (Luzon I., Philippines)..... 180 in ....(4573 mm)
Sylhet (Bangladesh)...................... 176 in ....(4457 mm)
Padang (Sumatra, Indonesia)...... 166 in ....(4225 mm)
Bogor (Java, Indonesia)..................166 in....(4225 mm)
Conakry (Guinea)..........................171 in......(4341 mm)

GLOSSARY OF ABBREVIATIONS

This Glossary provides a comprehensive guide to the abbreviations used in this Atlas, and in the Index.

A
abbrev. abbreviated
Afr. Afrikaans
Alb. Albanian
Amh. Amharic
anc. ancient
Ar. Arabic
Arm. Armenian
Az. Azerbaijani

B
Basq. Basque
Bel. Belorussian
Ben. Bengali
Bibl. Biblical
Bret. Breton
Bul. Bulgarian
Bur. Burmese

C
Cam. Cambodian
Cant. Cantonese
Cast. Castilian
Cat. Catalan
Chin. Chinese
Cro. Croat
Cz. Czech

D
Dan. Danish
Dut. Dutch

E
Eng. English
Est. Estonian
est. estimated

F
Faer. Faeroese
Fij. Fijian
Fin. Finnish
Flem. Flemish
Fr. French
Fris. Frisian

G
Geor. Georgian
Ger. German
Gk. Greek
Guj. Gujarati

H
Haw. Hawaiian
Heb. Hebrew
Hind. Hindi
hist. historical
Hung. Hungarian

I
Icel. Icelandic
Ind. Indonesian
In. Inuit
Ir. Irish
It. Italian

J
Jap. Japanese

K
Kaz. Kazakh
Kir. Kirghiz
Kor. Korean
Kurd. Kurdish

L
Lao. Laotian
Lapp. Lappish
Lat. Latin
Latv. Latvian

Lith. Lithanian
Lus. Lusatian

M
Mac. Macedonian
Mal. Malay
Malg. Malagasy
Malt. Maltese
Mon. Montenegro
Mong. Mongolian

N
Nepali. Nepali
Nor. Norwegian

O
off. officially

P
Pash. Pashtu
Per. Persian
Pol. Polish
Port. Portuguese
prev. previously

R
Rmsch. Romansch
Roman. Romanian
Rus. Russian

S
SCr. Serbo - Croatian
Serb. Serbian
Slvk. Slovak
Slvn. Slovene
Som. Somali
Sp. Spanish
Swa. Swahili
Swe. Swedish

T
Taj. Tajik
Th. Thai
Tib. Tibetan
Turk. Turkish
Turkm. Turkmenistan

U
Uigh. Uighur
Ukr. Ukrainian
Uzb. Uzbek

V
var. variant
Vtn. Vietnamese

W
Wel. Welsh

X
Xh. Xhosa

Key to country factboxes within the Index:

Formation
Date of independence

Population
Total population / population density - based on total land area .

Calorie consumption
Average number of calories consumed daily per person.

A

Aa *see* Gauja
Aachen *94 A4 Dut.* Aken, *Fr.* Aix-la-Chapelle; *anc.* Aquae Grani, Aquisgranum. Nordrhein-Westfalen, W Germany
Aaiún *see* Laâyoune
Aalborg *85 B7 var.* Ålborg, Ålborg-Nørresundby; *anc.* Alburgum. Nordjylland, N Denmark
Aalen *95 B6* Baden-Württemberg, S Germany
Aalsmeer *86 C3* Noord-Holland, C Netherlands
Aälst *87 B6* Oost-Vlaanderen, C Belgium
Aalten *86 E4* Gelderland, E Netherlands
Aalter *87 B5* Oost-Vlaanderen, NW Belgium
Aanaarjävri *see* Inarijärvi
Äänekoski *85 D5* Länsi-Suomi, W Finland
Aar *see* Aare
Aare *95 A7 var.* Aar. *river* W Switzerland
Aarhus *see* Århus
Aarlen *see* Arlon
Aat *see* Ath
Aba *77 E5* Orientale, NE Dem. Rep. Congo
Aba *75 G5* Abia, S Nigeria
Abā as Su'ūd *see* Najrān
Abaco Island *see* Great Abaco, N Bahamas
Ābādān *120 C4* Khūzestān, SW Iran
Abadan *122 C3 prev.* Bezmein, Büzmeýin, *Rus.* Byuzmeyin. Ahal Welaýaty, C Turkmenistan
Abai *see* Blue Nile
Abakan *114 D4* Respublika Khakasiya, S Russian Federation
Abancay *60 D4* Apurímac, SE Peru
Abariringa *see* Kanton
Abashiri *130 D2 var.* Abasiri. Hokkaidō, NE Japan
Abasiri *see* Abashiri
Abay Wenz *see* Blue Nile
Abbaia *see* Ābaya Hāyk'
Abbatis Villa *see* Abbeville
Abbazia *see* Opatija
Abbeville *90 C2 anc.* Abbatis Villa. Somme, N France
'Abd al 'Azīz, Jabal *118 D2 mountain range* NE Syria
Abéché *76 C3 var.* Abécher, Abeshr. Ouaddaï, SE Chad
Abécher *see* Abéché
Abela *see* Ávila
Abellinum *see* Avellino
Abemama *144 D2 var.* Apamama; *prev* Roger Simpson Island. *atoll* Tungaru, W Kiribati
Abengourou *75 E5* E Côte d'Ivoire
Aberbrothock *see* Arbroath
Abercorn *see* Mbala
Aberdeen *88 D3 anc.* Devana. NE Scotland, United Kingdom
Aberdeen *45 E2* South Dakota, N USA
Aberdeen *46 B2* Washington, NW USA
Abergwaun *see* Fishguard
Abertawe *see* Swansea
Aberystwyth *89 C6* W Wales, United Kingdom
Abeshr *see* Abéché
Abhā *121 B6* 'Asīr, SW Saudi Arabia
Abidavichy *107 D7 Rus.* Obidovichi. Mahilyowskaya Voblasts', E Belarus
Abidjan *75 E5* S Côte d'Ivoire
Abilene *49 F3* Texas, SW USA
Abingdon *see* Pinta, Isla
Åbo *see* Turku
Aboisso *75 E5* SE Côte d'Ivoire
Abo, Massif d' *76 B1 mountain range* NW Chad
Abomey *75 F5* S Benin
Abou-Déïa *76 C3* Salamat, SE Chad
Aboudouhour *see* Abū aḍ Ḑuḩūr
Abou Kémal *see* Abū Kamāl
Abrantes *92 B3 var.* Abrántes. Santarém, C Portugal
Abrashlare *see* Brezovo
Abrolhos Bank *56 E4 undersea bank* W Atlantic Ocean
Abrova *107 B6 Rus.* Obrovo. Brestskaya Voblasts', SW Belarus
Abrud *108 B4 Ger.* Gross-Schlatten, *Hung.* Abrudbánya. Alba, SW Romania

Abrudbánya *see* Abrud
Abruzzese, Appennino *96 C4 mountain range* C Italy
Absaroka Range *44 B2 mountain range* Montana/Wyoming, NW USA
Abū aḍ Ḑuḩūr *118 B3 Fr.* Aboudouhour. Idlib, NW Syria
Abu Dhabi *see* Abū Ẓabī
Abu Hamed *72 C3* River Nile, N Sudan
Abū Ḩardān *118 E3 var.* Hajine. Dayr az Zawr, E Syria
Abuja *75 G4 country capital* (Nigeria) (Nigeria) Federal Capital District, C Nigeria
Abū Kamāl *118 E3 Fr.* Abou Kémal. Dayr az Zawr, E Syria
Abula *see* Ávila
Abunã, Rio *62 C2 var.* Río Abuná. *river* Bolivia/Brazil
Abut Head *151 B6 headland* South Island, New Zealand
Abuye Meda *72 D4 mountain* C Ethiopia
Abū Ẓabī *121 C5 var.* Abū Ẓabī, *Eng.* Abu Dhabi. *country capital* (United Arab Emirates) (United Arab Emirates) Abū Ẓaby, C United Arab Emirates
Abū Ẓaby *see* Abū Ẓabī
Abyaḍ, Al Baḥr al *see* White Nile
Abyla *see* Ávila
Abyssinia *see* Ethiopia
Acalayong *77 A5* SW Equatorial Guinea
Acaponeta *50 D4* Nayarit, C Mexico
Acapulco *51 E5 var.* Acapulco de Juárez. Guerrero, S Mexico
Acapulco de Juárez *see* Acapulco
Acarai Mountains *59 F4 Sp.* Serra Acaraí. *mountain range* Brazil/Guyana
Acaraí, Serra *see* Acarai Mountains
Acarigua *58 D2* Portuguesa, N Venezuela
Accra *75 E5 country capital* (Ghana) (Ghana)SE Ghana
Achacachi *61 E4* La Paz, W Bolivia
Achara *117 F2 var.* Ajaria. *autonomous republic* SW Georgia
Acklins Island *54 C2 island* SE Bahamas
Aconcagua, Cerro *64 B4 mountain* W Argentina
Açores/Açores, Arquipélago dos/ Açores, Ilhas dos *see* Azores
A Coruña *92 B1 Cast.* La Coruña, *Eng.* Corunna; *anc.* Caronium. Galicia, NW Spain
Acre *62 C2 off.* Estado do Acre. *region* W Brazil
Acre *62 C2 off.* Estado do Acre. *state* W Brazil
Açu *63 G2 var.* Assu. Rio Grande do Norte, E Brazil
Acunum Acusio *see* Montélimar
Ada *100 D3* Vojvodina, N Serbia
Ada *49 G2* Oklahoma, C USA
Ada Bazar *see* Adapazarı
Adalia *see* Antalya
Adalia, Gulf of *see* Antalya Körfezi
Adama *see* Nazrēt
'Adan *121 B7 Eng.* Aden. SW Yemen
Adana *116 D4 var.* Seyhan. Adana, S Turkey
Adâncata *see* Horlivka
Adapazarı *116 B2 prev.* Ada Bazar. Sakarya, NW Turkey
Adare, Cape *154 B4 cape* Antarctica
Ad Dahna *120 C4 desert* E Saudi Arabia
Ad Dakhla *70 A4 var.* Dakhla. SW Western Sahara
Ad Dalanj *see* Dilling
Ad Damar *see* Ed Damer
Ad Damazin *see* Ed Damazin
Ad Dāmir *see* Ed Damer
Ad Dammām *120 C4 var.* Dammām. Ash Sharqīyah, NE Saudi Arabia
Ad Dāmūr *see* Damoûr
Ad Dawḩah *120 C4 Eng.* Doha. *country capital* (Qatar) (Qatar) C Qatar
Ad Ḑiffah *see* Libyan Plateau
Addis Ababa *see* Ādīs Ābeba
Addoo Atoll *see* Addu Atoll
Addu Atoll *132 A5 var.* Addoo Atoll, Seenu Atoll. *atoll* S Maldives
Adelaide *149 B6 state capital* South Australia
Adelsberg *see* Postojna
Aden *see* 'Adan
Aden, Gulf of *121 C7 gulf* SW Arabian Sea
Adige *96 C2 Ger.* Etsch. *river* N Italy

Adirondack Mountains *41 F2 mountain range* New York, NE USA
Ādīs Ābeba 73 C5 *Eng.* Addis Ababa. *country capital* (Ethiopia) (Ethiopia) Ādīs Ābeba, C Ethiopia
Adıyaman *117 E4* Adıyaman, SE Turkey
Adjud *108 C4* Vrancea, E Romania
Admiralty Islands *144 B3 island group* N Papua New Guinea
Adra *93 E5* Andalucía, S Spain
Adrar *70 D3* C Algeria
Adrian *40 C3* Michigan, N USA
Adrianople/Adrianopolis *see* Edirne
Adriatico, Mare *see* Adriatic Sea
Adriatic Sea *103 E2 Alb.* Deti Adriatik, *It.* Mare Adriatico, *SCr.* Jadransko More, *Slvn.* Jadransko Morje. *sea* N Mediterranean Sea
Adriatik, Deti *see* Adriatic Sea
Adycha *115 F2 river* NE Russian Federation
Aegean Sea *105 C5 Gk.* Aigaíon Pelagos, Aigaío Pélagos, *Turk.* Ege Denizi. *sea* NE Mediterranean Sea
Aegviidu *106 D2 Ger.* Charlottenhof. Harjumaa, NW Estonia
Aegyptus *see* Egypt
Aelana *see* Al 'Aqabah
Aelok *see* Ailuk Atoll
Aelönlaplap *see* Ailinglaplap Atoll
Aemona *see* Ljubljana
Aeolian Islands *97 C6 var.* Isole Lipari, *Eng.* Aeolian Islands, Lipari Islands. *island group* S Italy
Aeolian Islands *see* Eolie, Isole
Æsernia *see* Isernia
Afar Depression *see* Danakil Desert
Afars et des Issas, Territoire Français des *see* Djibouti
Afghānestān, Dowlat-e Eslāmī-ye *see* Afghanistan
Afghanistan *122 C4 off.* Islamic Republic of Afghanistan, *Per.* Dowlat-e Eslāmī-ye Afghānestān; *prev.* Republic of Afghanistan. *country* C Asia

AFGHANISTAN
Central Asia

Official name The Islamic Republic of Afghanistan
Formation 1919 / 1919
Capital Kabul
Population 32.3 million / 128 people per sq mile (50 people per sq km) / 24%
Total area 250,000 sq. miles (647,500 sq. km)
Languages Pashtu*, Tajik, Dari*, Farsi, Uzbek, Turkmen
Religions Sunni Muslim 84%, Shi'a Muslim 15%, Other 1%
Ethnic mix Pashtun 38%, Tajik 25%, Hazara 19%, Uzbek and Turkmen 15%, Other 3%
Government Presidential system
Currency Afghani = 100 puls
Literacy rate 28%
Calorie consumption 1539 calories

Afmadow *73 D6* Jubbada Hoose, S Somalia
Africa *68 continent*
Africa, Horn of *68 E4 physical region* Ethiopia/Somalia
Africana Seamount *141 A6 seamount* SW Indian Ocean
'Afrīn *118 E3* Ḩalab, N Syria
Afyon *116 B3 prev.* Afyonkarahisar. Afyon, W Turkey
Agadès *see* Agadez
Agadez *75 G3 prev.* Agadès. Agadez, C Niger
Agadir *70 B3* SW Morocco
Agana/Agaña *see* Hagåtña
Āgaro *73 C5* Oromīya, C Ethiopia
Agassiz Fracture Zone *143 G5 fracture zone* S Pacific Ocean
Agatha *see* Agde
Agathónisi *105 D6 island* Dodekánisa, Greece, Aegean Sea
Agde *91 C6 anc.* Agatha. Hérault, S France
Agedabia *see* Ajdābiyā
Agen *91 B5 anc.* Aginnum. Lot-et-Garonne, SW France
Agendicum *see* Sens
Aghri Dagh *see* Büyükağrı Dağı

Agiá *104 B4 var.* Ayiá. Thessalía, C Greece
Agialoúsa *see* Yenierenköy
Agía Marína *105 E6* Léros, Dodekánisa, Greece, Aegean Sea
Aginnum *see* Agen
Ágios Efstrátios *104 D4 var.* Áyios Evstrátios, Hagios Evstrátios. *island* E Greece
Ágios Nikólaos *105 D8 var.* Áyios Nikólaos. Kríti, Greece, E Mediterranean Sea
Āgra *134 D3* Uttar Pradesh, N India
Agra and Oudh, United Provinces of *see* Uttar Pradesh
Agram *see* Zagreb
Ağrı *117 F3 var.* Karaköse; *prev.* Karakılısse. Ağrı, NE Turkey
Agri Dagi *see* Büyükağrı Dağı
Agrigento *97 C7 Gk.* Akragas; *prev.* Girgenti. Sicilia, Italy, C Mediterranean Sea
Agriovótano *105 C5* Évvoia, C Greece
Agropoli *97 D5* Campania, S Italy
Aguachica *58 B2* Cesar, N Colombia
Aguadulce *53 F5* Coclé, S Panama
Agua Prieta *50 B1* Sonora, NW Mexico
Aguascalientes *50 D4* Aguascalientes, C Mexico
Aguaytía *60 C3* Ucayali, C Peru
Aguilas *93 E4* Murcia, SE Spain
Aguililla *50 D4* Michoacán, SW Mexico
Agulhas Basin *69 D8 undersea basin* SW Indian Ocean
Agulhas Plateau *67 D6 undersea plateau* SW Indian Ocean
Ahaggar *75 F2 high plateau region* SE Algeria
Ahlen *94 B4* Nordrhein-Westfalen, W Germany
Ahmadābād *134 C4 var.* Ahmedabad. Gujarāt, W India
Ahmadnagar *134 C5 var.* Ahmednagar. Mahārāshtra, W India
Ahmedabad *see* Ahmadābād
Ahmednagar *see* Ahmadnagar
Ahuachapán *52 B3* Ahuachapán, W El Salvador
Ahvāz *120 C3 var.* Ahwāz; *prev.* Nāsiri. Khūzestān, SW Iran
Ahvenanmaa *see* Åland
Ahwāz *see* Ahvāz
Aigaíon Pelagos/Aigaío Pélagos *see* Aegean Sea
Aígina *105 C6 var.* Aíyina, Egina. Aígina, C Greece
Aígio *105 B5 var.* Egio; *prev.* Aíyion. Dytikí Ellás, S Greece
Aiken *43 E2* South Carolina, SE USA
Ailinglaplap Atoll *144 D2 var.* Aelönlaplap. *atoll* Ralik Chain, S Marshall Islands
Ailuk Atoll *144 D1 var.* Aelok. *atoll* Ratak Chain, NE Marshall Islands
Aináži *106 D3 Est.* Heinaste, *Ger.* Hainasch. Limbaži, N Latvia
'Aïn Ben Tili *74 D1* Tiris Zemmour, N Mauritania
Aintab *see* Gaziantep
Aïoun el Atrouss/Aïoun el Atroûss *see* 'Ayoûn el 'Atroûs
Aiquile *61 F4* Cochabamba, C Bolivia
Aïr *see* Aïr, Massif de l'
Air du Azbine *see* Aïr, Massif de l'
Aïr, Massif de l' *75 G2 var.* Aïr, Air du Azbine, Asben. *mountain range* NC Niger
Aiud *108 B4 Ger.* Strassburg, *Hung.* Nagyenyed; *prev.* Engeten. Alba, SW Romania
Aix *see* Aix-en-Provence
Aix-en-Provence *91 D6 var.* Aix; *anc.* Aquae Sextiae. Bouches-du-Rhône, SE France
Aix-la-Chapelle *see* Aachen
Aíyina *see* Aígina
Aíyion *see* Aígio
Aizkraukle *106 D4* Aizkraukle, S Latvia
Ajaccio *91 E7* Corse, France, C Mediterranean Sea
Ajaria *see* Achara
Ajastan *see* Armenia
Aj Bogd Uul *126 D2 mountain* SW Mongolia
Ajdābiyā *71 G2 var.* Agedabia, Ajdābiyah. NE Libya
Ajdābiyah *see* Ajdābiyā

Ajjinena *see* El Geneina
Ajmer *134 D3 var.* Ajmere. Rājasthān, N India
Ajo *48 A3* Arizona, SW USA
Akaba *see* Al 'Aqabah
Akamagaseki *see* Shimonoseki
Akasha *72 B3* Northern, N Sudan
Akchâr *74 C2 desert* W Mauritania
Aken *see* Aachen
Akermanceaster *see* Bath
Akhalts'ikhe *117 F2* SW Georgia
Akhisar *116 A3* Manisa, W Turkey
Akhmîm *72 B2 var.* Akhmîm; *anc.* Panopolis. C Egypt
Akhtubinsk *111 C7* Astrakhanskaya Oblast', SW Russian Federation
Akhtyrka *see* Okhtyrka
Akimiski Island *38 C3 island* Nunavut, C Canada
Akinovka *109 F4* Zaporiz'ka Oblast', S Ukraine
Akita *130 D4* Akita, Honshū, C Japan
Akjoujt *74 C2 prev.* Fort-Repoux.
Akkeshi *130 E2* Hokkaidō, NE Japan
Aklavik *36 D3* Northwest Territories, NW Canada
Akmola *see* Astana
Akmolinsk *see* Astana
Aknavásár *see* Târgu Ocna
Akpatok Island *39 E1 island* Nunavut, E Canada
Akragas *see* Agrigento
Akron *40 D4* Ohio, N USA
Akrotíri *see* Akrotírion
Akrotírion *102 C5 var.* Akrotiri. *UK air base* S Cyprus
Aksai Chin *124 B2 Chin.* Aksayqin. *disputed region* China/India
Aksaray *116 C4* Aksaray, C Turkey
Aksayqin *see* Aksai Chin
Akşehir *116 B4* Konya, W Turkey
Aktash *see* Oqtosh
Aktau *114 A4 Kaz.* Aqtaū; *prev.* Shevchenko. Mangistau, W Kazakhstan
Aktyubinsk *see* Aktobe
Aktjubinsk/Aktyubinsk *see* Aktobe
Aktobe *114 B4 Kaz.* Aqtöbe; *prev.* Aktjubinsk, Aktyubinsk. Aktyubinsk, NW Kazakhstan
Aktsyabrski *107 C7 Rus.* Oktyabr'skiy; *prev.* Karpilovka. Homyel'skaya Voblasts', SE Belarus
Aktyubinsk *see* Aktobe
Akula *77 C5* Equateur, NW Dem. Rep. Congo
Akureyri *83 E4* Nordhurland Eystra, N Iceland
Akyab *see* Sittwe
Alabama *42 C2 off.* State of Alabama, *also known as* Camellia State, Heart of Dixie, The Cotton State, Yellowhammer State. *state* S USA
Alabama River *42 C3 river* Alabama, S USA
Alaca *116 C3* Çorum, N Turkey
Alacant *see* Alicante
Alagoas *63 G2 off.* Estado de Alagoas. *region* E Brazil
Alagoas *63 G2 off.* Estado de Alagoas. *state* E Brazil
Alais *see* Alès
Alajuela *52 E4* Alajuela, C Costa Rica
Alakanuk *36 C2* Alaska, USA
Al 'Alamayn *72 B1 var.* El 'Alamein. N Egypt
Al 'Amārah *120 C3 var.* Amara. Maysān, E Iraq
Alamo *47 D6* Nevada, W USA
Alamogordo *48 D3* New Mexico, SW USA
Alamosa *44 C5* Colorado, C USA
Aland Islands *85 C6 var.* Åland Islands, *Fin.* Ahvenanmaa. *island group* SW Finland
Åland Islands *see* Åland
Åland Sea *85 C6 var.* Åland Sea. *strait* Baltic Sea/Gulf of Bothnia
Åland Sea *see* Ålands Hav
Alanya *116 C4* Antalya, S Turkey
Alapayevsk *114 C3* Sverdlovskaya Oblast', C Russian Federation
Al 'Aqabah *119 B8 var.* Akaba, Aqaba, 'Aqaba; *anc.* Aelana, Elath. Al 'Aqabah, SW Jordan
'Arabīyah as Su'ūdīyah *see* Saudi Arabia
Alasca, Golfo de *see* Alaska, Gulf of
Alaşehir *116 A4* Manisa, W Turkey

Al 'Ashārah *118 E3 var.* Ashara. Dayr az Zawr, E Syria
Alaska *36 C3 off.* State of Alaska, *also known as* Land of the Midnight Sun, The Last Frontier, Seward's Folly; *prev.* Russian America. *state* NW USA
Alaska, Gulf of *36 C4 var.* Golfo de Alasca. *gulf* Canada/USA
Alaska Peninsula *36 C3 peninsula* Alaska, USA
Alaska Range *34 B2 mountain range* Alaska, USA
Al-Asnam *see* Chlef
Alattio *see* Alta
Al Awaynāt *see* Al 'Uwaynāt
Alaykel'/Alay-Kuu *see* Kēk-Art
Al 'Aynā *119 B7* Al Karak, W Jordan
Alazeya *115 G2 river* NE Russian Federation
Al Bāb *118 B2* Ḩalab, N Syria
Albacete *93 E3* Castilla-La Mancha, C Spain
Al Baghdādī *120 B3 var.* Khān al Baghdādī. Al Anbār, SW Iraq
Al Bāha *see* Al Bāḩah
Al Bāḩah *121 B5 var.* Al Bāha. Al BāḨjah, SW Saudi Arabia
Al Baḩrayn *see* Bahrain
Alba Iulia *108 B4 Ger.* Weissenburg, *Hung.* Gyulafehérvár; *prev.* Bálgrad, Karlsburg, Károly-Fehérvár. Alba, W Romania
Albania *101 C7 off.* Republic of Albania, *Alb.* Republika e Shqipërisë, Shqipëria; *prev.* People's Socialist Republic of Albania. *country* SE Europe

ALBANIA
Southeast Europe

Official name Republic of Albania
Formation 1912 / 1921
Capital Tirana
Population 3.2 million / 302 people per sq mile (117 people per sq km) / 44%
Total area 11,100 sq. miles (28,748 sq. km)
Languages Albanian*, Greek
Religions Sunni Muslim 70%, Orthodox Christian 20%, Roman Catholic 10%
Ethnic mix Albanian 93%, Greek 5%, Other 2%
Government Parliamentary system
Currency Lek = 100 qindarka (qintars)
Literacy rate 99%
Calorie consumption 2848 calories

Albania *see* Aubagne
Albany *147 B7* Western Australia
Albany *42 D3* Georgia, SE USA
Albany *41 F3 state capital* New York, NE USA
Albany *46 B3* Oregon, NW USA
Albany *38 C3 river* Ontario, S Canada
Alba Regia *see* Székesfehérvár
Al Bārīdah *118 C4 var.* Bāridah. Ḩimṣ, C Syria
Al Başrah *120 C3 Eng.* Basra, *hist.* Busra, Bussora. Al Başrah, SE Iraq
Al Batrūn *see* Batroûn
Al Baydā' *71 G2 var.* Beida. NE Libya
Albemarle Island *see* Isabela, Isla
Albemarle Sound *43 G1 inlet* W Atlantic Ocean
Albergaria-a-Velha *92 B2* Aveiro, N Portugal
Albert *90 C3* Somme, N France
Alberta *37 E4 province* SW Canada
Albert Edward Nyanza *see* Edward, Lake
Albert, Lake *73 B6 var.* Albert Nyanza, Lac Mobutu Sese Seko. *lake* Uganda/Dem. Rep. Congo
Albert Lea *45 F3* Minnesota, N USA
Albert Nyanza *see* Albert, Lake
Albertville *see* Kalemie
Albi *91 C6 anc.* Albiga. Tarn, S France
Albiga *see* Albi
Ålborg *see* Aalborg
Ålborg-Nørresundby *see* Aalborg
Albuquerque *48 D2* New Mexico, SW USA
Al Burayqah *see* Marsá al Burayqah
Alburgum *see* Aalborg
Albury *149 C7* New South Wales, SE Australia
Alcácer do Sal *92 B4* Setúbal, W Portugal

Alcalá de Henares 93 E3 *Ar.* Alkal'a; *anc.* Complutum. Madrid, C Spain
Alcamo 97 C7 Sicilia, Italy, C Mediterranean Sea
Alcañiz 93 F2 Aragón, NE Spain
Alcántara, Embalse de 92 C3 *reservoir* W Spain
Alcaudete 92 D4 Andalucía, S Spain
Alcázar *see* Ksar-el-Kebir
Alcazarquivir *see* Ksar-el-Kebir
Alcoi *see* Alcoy
Alcoy 93 F4 *Cat.* Alcoi. País Valenciano, E Spain
Aldabra Group 79 G2 *island group* SW Seychelles
Aldan 115 F3 *river* NE Russian Federation
al Dar al Baida *see* Rabat
Alderney 90 A2 *island* Channel Islands
Aleg 74 C3 Brakna, SW Mauritania
Aleksandriya *see* Oleksandriya
Aleksandropol' *see* Gyumri
Aleksandrovka *see* Oleksandrivka
Aleksandrovsk *see* Zaporizhzhya
Aleksin 111 B5 Tul'skaya Oblast', W Russian Federation
Aleksinac 100 E4 Serbia, SE Serbia
Alençon 90 B3 Orne, N France
Alenquer 63 E2 Pará, NE Brazil
Alep/Aleppo *see* Ḥalab
Alert 37 F1 Ellesmere Island, Nunavut, N Canada
Alès 91 C6 *prev.* Alais. Gard, S France
Aleşd 108 B3 *Hung.* Élesd. Bihor, SW Romania
Alessandria 96 B2 *Fr.* Alexandrie. Piemonte, N Italy
Ålesund 85 A5 Møre og Romsdal, S Norway
Aleutian Basin 113 G3 *undersea basin* Bering Sea
Aleutian Islands 36 A3 *island group* Alaska, USA
Aleutian Range 34 A2 *mountain range* Alaska, USA
Aleutian Trench 113 H3 *trench* S Bering Sea
Alexander Archipelago 36 D4 *island group* Alaska, USA
Alexander City 42 D2 Alabama, S USA
Alexander Island 154 A3 *island* Antarctica
Alexander Range *see* Kirghiz Range
Alexandra 151 B7 Otago, South Island, New Zealand
Alexándreia 104 B4 *var.* Alexándria. Kentrikí Makedonía, N Greece
Alexanderette *see* İskenderun
Alexandretta, Gulf of *see* İskenderun Körfezi
Alexandria 72 B1 *Ar.* Iskandarīyah. N Egypt
Alexandria 108 C5 Teleorman, S Romania
Alexandria 42 B3 Louisiana, S USA
Alexandria 45 F2 Minnesota, N USA
Alexándria *see* Alexándreia
Alexandrie *see* Alessandria
Alexandroúpoli 104 D3 *var.* Alexandroúpolis, *Turk.* Dedeagaç, Dedeagaç. Anatolikí Makedonía kai Thráki, NE Greece
Alexandroúpolis *see* Alexandroúpoli
Al Fâshir *see* El Fasher
Alfatar 104 E1 Silistra, NE Bulgaria
Alfeiós 105 B6 *prev.* Alfiós; *anc.* Alpheius, Alpheus. *river* S Greece
Alfiós *see* Alfeiós
Alföld *see* Great Hungarian Plain
Al-Furāt *see* Euphrates
Alga 114 B4 Kaz. Algha. Aktyubinsk, NW Kazakhstan
Algarve 92 B4 *cultural region* S Portugal
Algeciras 92 C5 Andalucía, SW Spain
Algemesí 93 F3 País Valenciano, E Spain
Al-Genain *see* El Geneina
Alger 71 E1 *var.* Algiers, El Djazaïr, Al Jazair. *country capital* (Algeria) N Algeria
Algeria 70 C3 *off.* Democratic and Popular Republic of Algeria. *country* N Africa

ALGERIA
North Africa

Official name People's Democratic Republic of Algeria
Formation 1962 / 1962
Capital Algiers
Population 33.9 million / 37 people per sq mile (14 people per sq km) / 59%
Total area 919,590 sq. miles (2,381,740 sq. km)
Languages Arabic*, Tamazight (Kabyle, Shawia, Tamashek), French
Religions Sunni Muslim 99%, Christian and Jewish 1%
Ethnic mix Arab 75%, Berber 24%, European and Jewish 1%
Government Presidential system
Currency Algerian dinar = 100 centimes
Literacy rate 70%
Calorie consumption 3022 calories

Algeria, Democratic and Popular Republic of *see* Algeria
Algerian Basin 80 C5 *var.* Balearic Plain. *undersea basin* W Mediterranean Sea
Algha *see* Alga
Al Ghābah 121 E5 *var.* Ghaba. C Oman
Alghero 97 A5 Sardegna, Italy, C Mediterranean Sea
Al Ghurdaqah *see* Hurghada
Algiers *see* Alger
Al Golea *see* El Goléa
Algona 45 F3 Iowa, C USA
Al Hajar al Gharbi 121 D5 *mountain range* N Oman
Al Hamad *see* Syrian Desert
Al Ḥasakah 118 D2 *var.* Al Hasijah, El Haseke, *Fr.* Hassetché. Al Ḥasakah, NE Syria
Al Hasijah *see* Al Ḥasakah
Al Ḥillah 120 B3 *var.* Hilla. Bābil, C Iraq
Al Ḥisā 119 B7 Aţ Ţafīlah, W Jordan
Al Ḥudaydah 121 B6 *Eng.* Hodeida. W Yemen
Al Ḥufūf 120 C4 *var.* Hofuf. Ash Sharqīyah, NE Saudi Arabia
Aliákmon *see* Aliákmonas
Aliákmonas 104 B4 *prev.* Aliákmon; *anc.* Haliacmon. *river* N Greece
Aliártos 105 C5 Stereá Ellás, C Greece
Alicante 93 F4 *Cat.* Alacant, *Lat.* Lucentum. País Valenciano, SE Spain
Alice 49 G5 Texas, SW USA
Alice Springs 148 A4 Northern Territory, C Australia
Alifu Atoll *see* Ari Atoll
Aligandí 53 G4 Kuna Yala, NE Panama
Aliki *see* Alykí
Alima 77 B6 *river* C Congo
Al Imārāt al 'Arabīyah al Muttaḥidah *see* United Arab Emirates
Alindao 76 C4 Basse-Kotto, S Central African Republic
Aliquippa 40 D4 Pennsylvania, NE USA
Al Iskandarīyah *see* Alexandria
Al Ismā'īlīya 72 B1 *var.* Ismailia, Ismā'īlīya. N Egypt
Alistráti 104 C3 Kentrikí Makedonía, NE Greece
Alivéri 105 C5 *var.* Alivérion. Évvoia, C Greece
Alivérion *see* Alivéri
Al Jabal al Akhḍar 71 G2 *mountain range* NE Libya
Al Jafr 119 B7 Ma'ān, S Jordan
Al Jaghbūb 71 H3 NE Libya
Al Jahrā' 120 C4 *var.* Al Jahrah, Jahra. C Kuwait
Al Jahrah *see* Al Jahrā'
Al Jamāhīrīyah al 'Arabīyah al Lībīyah ash Sha'bīyah al Ishtirākīy *see* Libya
Al Jawf 120 B4 *off.* Jauf. Al Jawf, NW Saudi Arabia
Al Jawlān *see* Golan Heights
Al Jazair *see* Alger
Al Jazirah 118 E2 *physical region* Iraq/Syria
Al Jīzah *see* Gîza
Al Junaynah *see* El Geneina
Alkal'a *see* Alcalá de Henares
Al Karak 119 B7 *var.* El Kerak, Karak, Kerak; *anc.* Kir Moab, Kir of Moab. Al Karak, W Jordan
Al-Kasr-el-Kebir *see* Ksar-el-Kebir
Al Khalīl *see* Hebron

Al Khārijah 72 B2 *var.* El Khârga. C Egypt
Al Khums 71 F2 *var.* Homs, Khoms, Khums. NW Libya
Alkmaar 86 C2 Noord-Holland, NW Netherlands
Al Kufrah 71 H4 SE Libya
Al Kūt 120 C3 *var.* Kūt al 'Amārah, Kut al Imara. Wāsiţ, E Iraq
Al-Kuwait *see* Al Kuwayt
Al Kuwayt 120 C4 *var.* Al-Kuwait, *Eng.* Kuwait, Kuwait City; *prev.* Qurein. *country capital* (Kuwait) (Kuwait) E Kuwait
Al Lādhiqīyah 118 A3 *Eng.* Latakia, *Fr.* Lattaquié; *anc.* Laodicea, Laodicea ad Mare. Al Lādhiqīyah, W Syria
Allahābād 135 E3 Uttar Pradesh, N India
Allanmyo *see* Aunglan
Allegheny Plateau 41 E3 *mountain range* New York/Pennsylvania, NE USA
Allenstein *see* Olsztyn
Allentown 41 F4 Pennsylvania, NE USA
Alleppey 132 C3 *var.* Alappuzha. Kerala, SW India
Alliance 44 D3 Nebraska, C USA
Al Lîth 121 B5 Makkah, SW Saudi Arabia
Al Lubnān *see* Lebanon
Alma-Ata *see* Almaty
Almada 92 B4 Setúbal, W Portugal
Al Madīnah 121 A5 *Eng.* Medina. Al Madīnah, W Saudi Arabia
Al Mafraq 119 B6 *var.* Mafraq. Al Mafraq, N Jordan
Al Mahdīyah *see* Mahdia
Al Mahrah 121 C6 *mountain range* E Yemen
Al Majma'ah 120 B4 Ar Riyāḍ, C Saudi Arabia
Al Mālikīyah 118 E1 *var.* Malkiye. Al Ḥasakah, N Syria
Almalyk *see* Olmaliq
Al Mamlakah *see* Morocco
Al Mamlaka al Urdunīya al Hashemīyah *see* Jordan
Al Manāmah 120 C4 *Eng.* Manama. *country capital* (Bahrain) (Bahrain) N Bahrain
Al Manāşif 118 E3 *mountain range* E Syria
Almansa 93 F4 Castilla-La Mancha, C Spain
Al-Mariyya *see* Almería
Al Marj 71 G2 *var.* Barka, *It.* Barce. NE Libya
Almaty 114 C5 *var.* Alma-Ata. Almaty, SE Kazakhstan
Al Mawşil 120 B2 *Eng.* Mosul. Nīnawá, N Iraq
Al Mayādīn 118 D3 *var.* Mayadin, *Fr.* Meyadine. Dayr az Zawr, E Syria
Al Mazra' *see* Al Mazra'ah
Al Mazra'ah 119 B6 *var.* Al Mazra', Mazra'a. Al Karak, W Jordan
Almelo 86 E3 Overijssel, E Netherlands
Almendra, Embalse de 92 C2 *reservoir* Castilla-León, NW Spain
Almendralejo 92 C4 Extremadura, W Spain
Almere 86 C3 *var.* Almere-stad. Flevoland, C Netherlands
Almere-stad *see* Almere
Almería 93 E5 *Ar.* Al-Mariyya; *anc.* Unci, *Lat.* Portus Magnus. Andalucía, S Spain
Al'met'yevsk 111 D5 Respublika Tatarstan, W Russian Federation
Al Minā' *see* El Mina
Al Minyā 72 B2 *var.* El Minya, Minya. C Egypt
Almirante 53 E4 Bocas del Toro, NW Panama
Al Mudawwarah 119 B8 Ma'ān, SW Jordan
Al Mukallā 121 C6 *var.* Mukalla. SE Yemen
Al Obayyid *see* El Obeid
Alofi 145 F4 *dependent territory capital* (Niue) W Niue
Aloha State *see* Hawai'i
Aloja 106 D3 Limbaži, N Latvia
Alónnisos 105 C5 *island* Vóreies Sporádes, Greece, Aegean Sea
Álora 92 D5 Andalucía, S Spain
Alor, Kepulauan 139 E5 *island group* E Indonesia
Al Oued *see* El Oued
Alpen *see* Alps

Alpena 40 D2 Michigan, N USA
Alpes *see* Alps
Alpha Cordillera 155 B3 *var.* Alpha Ridge. *seamount range* Arctic Ocean
Alpha Ridge *see* Alpha Cordillera
Alpheius *see* Alfeiós
Alphen *see* Alphen aan den Rijn
Alphen aan den Rijn 86 C3 *var.* Alphen. Zuid-Holland, C Netherlands
Alpheus *see* Alfeiós
Alpi *see* Alps
Alpine 49 E4 Texas, SW USA
Alps 102 C1 *Fr.* Alpes, *Ger.* Alpen, *It.* Alpi. *mountain range* C Europe
Al Qaḍārif *see* Gedaref
Al Qāhirah *see* Cairo
Al Qāmishlī 118 E1 *var.* Kamishli, Qamishly. Al Ḥasakah, NE Syria
Al Qaşrayn *see* Kasserine
Al Qayrawān *see* Kairouan
Al-Qsar al-Kbir *see* Ksar-el-Kebir
Al Qubayyāt *see* Qoubaïyât
Al Quds/Al Quds ash Sharīf *see* Jerusalem
Alqueva, Barragem do 92 C4 *reservoir* Portugal/Spain
Al Qunayţirah 119 B5 *var.* El Kuneitra, El Quneitra, Kuneitra, Qunaytra. Al Qunayţirah, SW Syria
Al Quşayr 118 B4 *var.* El Quseir, Quşayr, *Fr.* Kousseir. Ḥimş, W Syria
Al Quwayrah 119 B8 *var.* El Quweira. Al 'Aqabah, SW Jordan
Alsace 90 E3 *Ger.* Elsass; *anc.* Alsatia. *cultural region* NE France
Alsatia *see* Alsace
Alsdorf 94 A4 Nordrhein-Westfalen, W Germany
Alt *see* Olt
Alta 84 D2 *Fin.* Alattio. Finnmark, N Norway
Altai *see* Altai Mountains
Altai Mountains 126 C2 *var.* Altai, *Chin.* Altay Shan, *Rus.* Altay. *mountain range* Asia/Europe
Altamaha River 43 E3 *river* Georgia, SE USA
Altamira 63 E2 Pará, NE Brazil
Altamura 97 E5 *anc.* Lupatia. Puglia, SE Italy
Altar, Desierto de 50 A1 *var.* Sonoran Desert. *desert* Mexico/USA
Altar, Desierto de *see* Sonoran Desert
Altay 126 C2 Xinjiang Uygur Zizhiqu, NW China
Altay 126 D2 *prev.* Yösönbulag. Govĭ-Altay, W Mongolia
Altay Altai Mountains, Asia/Europe
Altay Shan *see* Altai Mountains
Altbetsche *see* Bečej
Altenburg *see* Bucureşti, Romania
Altin Köprü 120 B3 *var.* Altun Kupri. At Ta'mīn, N Iraq
Altiplano 61 F4 *physical region* W South America
Altkanischa *see* Kanjiža
Alton 40 B5 Illinois, N USA
Alton 40 B4 Missouri, C USA
Altoona 41 E4 Pennsylvania, NE USA
Alto Paraná *see* Paraná
Altpasua *see* Stara Pazova
Alt-Schwanenburg *see* Gulbene
Altsohl *see* Zvolen
Altun Kupri *see* Altin Köprü
Altun Shan 126 C3 *var.* Altyn Tagh. *mountain range* NW China
Altus 49 F2 Oklahoma, C USA
Altyn Tagh *see* Altun Shan
Al Ubayyid *see* El Obeid
Alūksne 106 D3 *Ger.* Marienburg. Alūksne, NE Latvia
Al 'Ulā 120 A4 Al Madīnah, NW Saudi Arabia
Al 'Umarī 119 C6 'Ammān, E Jordan
Alupka 109 F5 Respublika Krym, S Ukraine
Al Uqşur *see* Luxor
Al Urdunn *see* Jordan
Alushta 109 F5 Respublika Krym, S Ukraine
Al 'Uwaynāt 71 F4 *var.* Al Awaynāt. SW Libya
Alva 49 F1 Oklahoma, C USA
Alvarado 51 F4 Veracruz-Llave, E Mexico
Alvin 49 H4 Texas, SW USA

Al Wajh *120 A4* Tabūk, NW Saudi Arabia
Alwar *134 D3* Rājasthān, N India
Al Wari'ah *120 C4* Ash Sharqīyah, N Saudi Arabia
Al Yaman *see* Yemen
Alykí *104 C4 var.* Aliki. Thásos, N Greece
Alytus *107 B5 Pol.* Olita. Alytus, S Lithuania
Alzette *87 D8 river* S Luxembourg
Amadeus, Lake *147 D5 seasonal lake* Northern Territory, C Australia
Amadi *73 B5* Western Equatoria, SW Sudan
Amadjuak Lake *37 G3 lake* Baffin Island, Nunavut, N Canada
Amakusa-nada *131 A7 gulf* SW Japan
Åmål *85 B6* Västra Götaland, S Sweden
Amami-gunto *130 A3 island group* SW Japan
Amami-o-shim *130 A3 island* S Japan
Amantea *97 D6* Calabria, SW Italy
Amapá *63 E1 off.* Estado de Amapá; *prev.* Território de Amapá. *state* NE Brazil
Amapá *63 E1 off.* Estado de Amapá; *prev.* Território de Amapá. *region* NE Brazil
Amapá, Estado de *see* Amapá
Amapá, Território de *see* Amapá
Amara *see* Al 'Amārah
Amarapura *136 B3* Mandalay, C Burma (Myanmar)
Amarillo *49 E2* Texas, SW USA
Amay *87 C6* Liège, E Belgium
Amazon *63 E1 Sp.* Amazonas. *river* Brazil/Peru
Amazonas *see* Amazon
Amazon Basin *62 D2 basin* N South America
Amazon, Mouths of the *63 F1 delta* NE Brazil
Ambam *77 B5* Sud, S Cameroon
Ambanja *79 G2* Antsirañana, N Madagascar
Ambarchik *115 G2* Respublika Sakha (Yakutiya), NE Russian Federation
Ambato *60 B1* Tungurahua, C Ecuador
Ambérieu-en-Bugey *91 D5* Ain, E France
Ambianum *see* Amiens
Amboasary *79 F4* Toliara, S Madagascar
Amboina *see* Ambon
Ambon *139 F4 prev.* Amboina, Amboyna. Pulau Ambon, E Indonesia
Ambositra *79 G3* Fianarantsoa, SE Madagascar
Amboyna *see* Ambon
Ambracia *see* Árta
Ambre, Cap d' *see* Bobaomby, Tanjona
Ambrim *see* Ambrym
Ambriz *78 A1* Bengo, NW Angola
Ambrym *144 D4 var.* Ambrim. *island* C Vanuatu
Amchitka Island *36 A2 island* Aleutian Islands, Alaska, USA
Amdo *126 C5* Xizang Zizhiqu, W China
Ameland *86 D1 Fris.* It Amelân. *island* Waddeneilanden, N Netherlands
Amelân, It *see* Ameland
America *see* United States of America
America-Antarctica Ridge *67 C7 undersea ridge* S Atlantic Ocean
America in Miniature *see* Maryland
American Falls Reservoir *46 E4 reservoir* Idaho, NW USA
American Samoa *145 E4 US unincorporated territory* W Polynesia
Amersfoort *86 D3* Utrecht, C Netherlands
Ames *45 F3* Iowa, C USA
Amfilochía *105 A5 var.* Amfilokhía. Dytikí Ellás, C Greece
Amfilokhía *see* Amfilochía
Amga *115 F3 river* NE Russian Federation
Amherst *39 F4* Nova Scotia, SE Canada
Amherst *see* Kyaikkami
Amida *see* Diyarbakır
Amiens *90 C3 anc.* Ambianum, Samarobriva. Somme, N France
Amíndaion/Amýntaio *see* Amýntaio
Amindivi Islands *132 A2 island group* Lakshadweep, India, N Indian Ocean
Amirante Islands *79 G1 var.* Amirantes Group. *island group* C Seychelles

Amirantes Group *see* Amirante Islands
Amistad, Presa de la *see* Amistad Reservoir
Amistad Reservoir *49 F4 var.* Presa de la Amistad. *reservoir* Mexico/USA
Amisus *see* Samsun
Ammaia *see* Portalegre
'Ammān *119 B6 var.* Amman; *anc.* Philadelphia, *Bibl.* Rabbah Ammon, Rabbath Ammon. *country capital* (Jordan) (Jordan) 'Ammān, NW Jordan
Ammassalik *82 D4 var.* Angmagssalik. Tunu, S Greenland
Ammóchostos *see* Gazimağusa
Ammóchostos, Kólpos *see* Gazimağusa Körfezi
Amnok-kang *see* Yalu
Amoea *see* Portalegre
Amoentai *see* Amuntai
Åmol *120 D2 var.* Amul. Māzandarān, N Iran
Amorgós *105 D6* Amorgós, Kykládes, Greece, Aegean Sea
Amorgós *105 D6 island* Kykládes, Greece, Aegean Sea
Amos *38 D4* Québec, SE Canada
Amourj *74 D3* Hodh ech Chargui, SE Mauritania
Amoy *see* Xiamen
Ampato, Nevado *61 E4 mountain* S Peru
Amposta *93 F2* Cataluña, NE Spain
Amraoti *see* Amrāvati
Amrāvati *134 D4 prev.* Amraoti. Mahārāshtra, C India
Amritsar *134 D2* Punjab, N India
Amstelveen *86 C3* Noord-Holland, C Netherlands
Amsterdam *86 C3 country capital* (Netherlands) (Netherlands) Noord-Holland, C Netherlands
Amsterdam Island *141 C6 island* NE French Southern and Antarctic Territories
Am Timan *76 C3* Salamat, SE Chad
Amu Darya *122 D2 Rus.* Amudar'ya, *Taj.* Dar'yoi Amu, *Turkm.* Amyderya, *Uzb.* Amudaryo; *anc.* Oxus. *river* C Asia
Amu-Dar'ya *see* Amyderÿa
Amudar'ya/Amudaryo/Amu, Dar"yoi *see* Amu Darya
Amul *see* Åmol
Amund Ringnes Island *37 F2 Island* Nunavut, N Canada
Amundsen Basin *see* Fram Basin
Amundsen Plain *154 A4 abyssal plain* S Pacific Ocean
Amundsen-Scott *154 B3 US research station* Antarctica
Amundsen Sea *154 A4 sea* S Pacific Ocean
Amuntai *138 D4 prev.* Amoentai. Borneo, C Indonesia
Amur *115 G4 Chin.* Heilong Jiang. *river* China/Russian Federation
Amvrosiyevka *see* Amvrosiyivka
Amvrosiyivka *109 H3 Rus.* Amvrosiyevka. Donets'ka Oblast', SE Ukraine
Amyderÿa *123 E3 Rus.* Amu-Dar'ya. Lebap Welaýaty, NE Turkmenistan
Amyderya *see* Amu Darya
Amýntaio *104 B4 var.* Amindeo; *prev.* Amíndaion. Dytikí Makedonía, N Greece
Anabar *115 E2 river* NE Russian Federation
An Abhainn Mhór *see* Blackwater
Anaco *59 E2* Anzoátegui, NE Venezuela
Anaconda *44 B2* Montana, NW USA
Anacortes *46 B1* Washington, NW USA
Anadolu Dağları *see* Doğu Karadeniz Dağları
Anadyr' *115 H1* Chukotskiy Avtonomnyy Okrug, NE Russian Federation
Anadyr' *115 G1 river* NE Russian Federation
Anadyr, Gulf of *115 H1 Eng.* Gulf of Anadyr. *gulf* NE Russian Federation
Anadyr, Gulf of *see* Anadyrskiy Zaliv
Anáfi *105 D6 var.* Anaphe. *island* Kykládes, Greece, Aegean Sea
'Ānah *see* 'Annah
Anaheim *46 E2* California, W USA
Anaiza *see* 'Unayzah

Analalava *79 G2* Mahajanga, NW Madagascar
Anamur *116 C5* İçel, S Turkey
Anantapur *132 C2* Andhra Pradesh, S India
Anaphe *see* Anáfi
Anápolis *63 F3* Goiás, C Brazil
Anār *120 D3* Kermān, C Iran
Anatolia *116 C4 plateau* C Turkey
Anatom *see* Aneityum
Añatuya *64 C3* Santiago del Estero, N Argentina
Anchorage *36 C3* Alaska, USA
Ancud *65 B6 prev.* San Carlos de Ancud. Los Lagos, S Chile
Ancyra *see* Ankara
Åndalsnes *85 A5* Møre og Romsdal, S Norway
Andalucía *92 D4 cultural region* S Spain
Andalusia *42 C3* Alabama, S USA
Andaman Islands *124 B4 island group* India, NE Indian Ocean
Andaman Sea *124 C4 sea* NE Indian Ocean
Andenne *87 C6* Namur, SE Belgium
Anderson *36 C3* Alaska, USA
Anderlues *87 B7* Hainaut, S Belgium
Anderson *40 C4* Indiana, N USA
Andes *64 B3 mountain range* W South America
Andhra Pradesh *135 E5 cultural region* E India
Andijon *123 F2 Rus.* Andizhan. Andijon Viloyati, E Uzbekistan
Andikíthira *see* Antikýthira
Andipaxi *see* Antípaxoi
Andípsara *see* Antípsara
Ándissa *see* Antissa
Andizhan *see* Andijon
Andkhvoy *122 D3* Fāryāb, N Afghanistan
Andorra *91 A7 off.* Principality of Andorra, *Cat.* Valls d'Andorra, *Fr.* Vallée d'Andorre. *country* SW Europe

ANDORRA
Southwest Europe

Official name Principality of Andorra
Formation 1278 / 1278
Capital Andorra la Vella
Population 71,822 / 399 people per sq mile (154 people per sq km) / 91%
Total area 181 sq. miles (468 sq. km)
Languages Spanish, Catalan*, French, Portuguese
Religions Roman Catholic 94%, Other 6%
Ethnic mix Spanish 46%, Andorran 28%, Other 18%, French 8%
Government Parliamentary system
Currency Euro = 100 cents
Literacy rate 99%
Calorie consumption Not available

Andorra *see* Andorra la Vella
Andorra la Vella *91 A8 var.* Andorra, *Fr.* Andorre la Vielle, *Sp.* Andorra la Vieja. *country capital* (Andorra) (Andorra) C Andorra
Andorra la Vieja *see* Andorra la Vella
Andorra, Principality of *see* Andorra
Andorra, Valls d'/Andorra, Vallée d' *see* Andorra
Andorre la Vielle *see* Andorra la Vella
Andover *89 D7* S England, United Kingdom
Andoya *84 C3 island* C Norway
Andreanof Islands *36 A3 island group* Aleutian Islands, Alaska, USA
Andrews *49 E3* Texas, SW USA
Andrew Tablemount *140 A4 var.* Gora Andryu. *seamount* W Indian Ocean
Andria *97 D5* Puglia, SE Italy
An Droicheal Nua *see* Newbridge
Andropov *see* Rybinsk
Ándros *105 D6* Ándros, Kykládes, Greece, Aegean Sea
Ándros *105 C6 island* Kykládes, Greece, Aegean Sea
Andros Island *54 B2 island* NW Bahamas
Andros Town *54 C1* Andros Island, NW Bahamas
Andryu, Gora *see* Andrew Tablemount
Aneityum *144 D5 var.* Anatom; *prev.* Kéamu. *island* S Vanuatu

Ānewetak *see* Enewetak Atoll
Angara *115 E4 river* C Russian Federation
Angarsk *115 E4* Irkutskaya Oblast', S Russian Federation
Ånge *85 C5* Västernorrland, C Sweden
Ángel de la Guarda, Isla *50 B2 island* NW Mexico
Angeles *139 E1 off.* Angeles City. Luzon, N Philippines
Angeles City *see* Angeles
Angel Falls *59 E3 Eng.* Angel Falls. *waterfall* E Venezuela
Ángel Falls *see* Ángel, Salto
Angerburg *see* Węgorzewo
Ångermanälven *84 C4 river* N Sweden
Angermünde *94 D3* Brandenburg, NE Germany
Angers *90 B4 anc.* Juliomagus. Maine-et-Loire, NW France
Anglesey *89 C5 island* NW Wales, United Kingdom
Anglet *91 A6* Pyrénées-Atlantiques, SW France
Angleton *49 H4* Texas, SW USA
Anglia *see* England
Anglo-Egyptian Sudan *see* Sudan
Angmagssalik *see* Ammassalik
Ang Nam Ngum *136 C4 lake* C Laos
Angola *78 B2 off.* Republic of Angola; *prev.* People's Republic of Angola, Portuguese West Africa. *country* SW Africa

ANGOLA
Southern Africa

Official name Republic of Angola
Formation 1975 / 1975
Capital Luanda
Population 16.9 million / 35 people per sq mile (14 people per sq km) / 36%
Total area 481,351 sq. miles (1,246,700 sq. km)
Languages Portuguese*, Umbundu, Kimbundu, Kikongo
Religions Roman Catholic 50%, Other 30%, Protestant 20%
Ethnic mix Ovimbundu 37%, Other 25%, Kimbundu 25%, Bakongo 13%
Government Presidential system
Currency Readjusted kwanza = 100 lwei
Literacy rate 67%
Calorie consumption 2083 calories

Angola Basin *69 B5 undersea basin* E Atlantic Ocean
Angola, People's Republic of *see* Angola
Angola, Republic of *see* Angola
Angora *see* Ankara
Angostura *see* Ciudad Bolívar
Angostura, Presa de la *51 G5 reservoir* SE Mexico
Angoulême *91 B5 anc.* Iculisma. Charente, W France
Angoumois *91 B5 cultural region* W France
Angra Pequena *see* Lüderitz
Angren *123 F2* Toshkent Viloyati, E Uzbekistan
Anguilla *55 G3 UK dependent territory* E West Indies
Anguilla Cays *54 B2 islets* SW Bahamas
Anhui *128 C5 var.* Anhui Sheng, Anhwei, Wan. *province* E China
AnhuiSheng/Anhwei Wan *see* Anhui
Anicium *see* le Puy
Anina *108 A4 Ger.* Steierdorf, *Hung.* Stájerlakanina; *prev.* Stájerlak-Anina, Steierdorf-Anina, Steyerlak-Anina. Caraş-Severin, SW Romania
Anjou *90 B4 cultural region* NW France
Anjouan *79 F2 var.* Ndzouani, Nzwani. *island* SE Comoros
Ankara *116 C3 prev.* Angora; *anc.* Ancyra. *country capital* (Turkey) (Turkey) Ankara, C Turkey
Ankeny *45 F3* Iowa, C USA
Anklam *94 D2* Mecklenburg-Vorpommern, NE Germany
An Mhuir Cheilteach *see* Celtic Sea
Annaba *71 E1 prev.* Bône. NE Algeria
An Nafud *120 B4 desert* NW Saudi Arabia
'Annah *120 B3 var.* 'Ānah. Al Anbār, NW Iraq

An Najaf *120 B3 var.* Najaf. An Najaf,
S Iraq
Annamitique, Chaîne *136 D4 mountain range* C Laos
Annapolis *41 F4 state capital* Maryland, NE USA
Annapurna *135 E3 mountain* C Nepal
An Nâqûrah *see* En Nâqoûra
Ann Arbor *40 C3* Michigan, N USA
An Nâsiriyah *120 C3 var.* Nasiriya. Dhî Qâr, SE Iraq
Anneciacum *see* Annecy
Annecy *91 D5 anc.* Anneciacum. Haute-Savoie, E France
An Nil al Abyad *see* White Nile
An Nîl al Azraq *see* Blue Nile
Anniston *42 D2* Alabama, S USA
Annotto Bay *54 B4* C Jamaica
An Ómaigh *see* Omagh
Anqing *128 D5* Anhui, E China
Anse La Raye *55 F1* NW Saint Lucia
Anshun *128 B6* Guizhou, S China
Ansongo *75 E3* Gao, E Mali
An Srath Bán *see* Strabane
Antakya *116 D4 anc.* Antioch, Antiochia. Hatay, S Turkey
Antalaha *79 G2* Antsirañana, NE Madagascar
Antalya *116 B4 prev.* Adalia; *anc.* Attaleia, *Bibl.* Attalia. Antalya, SW Turkey
Antalya, Gulf of *116 B4 var.* Gulf of Adalia, *Eng.* Gulf of Antalya. *gulf* SW Turkey
Antalya, Gulf of *see* Antalya Körfezi
Antananarivo *79 G3 prev.* Tananarive. *country capital* (Madagascar) (Madagascar) Antananarivo, C Madagascar
Antarctica *154 B3 continent*
Antarctic Peninsula *154 A2 peninsula* Antarctica
Antep *see* Gaziantep
Antequera *92 D5 anc.* Anticaria, Antiquaria. Andalucía, S Spain
Antequera *see* Oaxaca
Antibes *91 D6 anc.* Antipolis. Alpes-Maritimes, SE France
Anticaria *see* Antequera
Anticosti, Île d' *39 F3 Eng.* Anticosti Island. *island* Québec, E Canada
Anticosti Island *see* Anticosti, Île d'
Antigua *55 G3 island* S Antigua and Barbuda, Leeward Islands
Antigua and Barbuda *55 G3 country* E West Indies

ANTIGUA & BARBUDA
West Indies

Official name Antigua and Barbuda
Formation 1981 / 1981
Capital St. John's
Population 69,481 / 409 people per sq mile (158 people per sq km) / 38%
Total area 170 sq. miles (442 sq. km)
Languages English*, English patois
Religions Anglican 45%, Other Protestant 42%, Roman Catholic 10%, Other 2%, Rastafarian 1%
Ethnic mix Black African 95%, Other 5%
Government Parliamentary system
Currency Eastern Caribbean dollar = 100 cents
Literacy rate 86%
Calorie consumption 2349 calories

Antikythira *105 B7 var.* Andikíthira. *island* S Greece
Anti-Lebanon *118 B4 var.* Jebel esh Sharqi, *Ar.* Al Jabal ash Sharqi, *Fr.* Anti-Liban. *mountain range* Lebanon/Syria
Anti-Liban *see* Anti-Lebanon
Antioch *see* Antakya
Antiochia *see* Antakya
Antipaxoí *105 A5 var.* Andípaxi. *island* Iónia Nísiá, Greece, C Mediterranean Sea
Antipodes Islands *142 D5 island group* S New Zealand
Antipolis *see* Antibes
Antípsara *105 D5 var.* Andípsara. *island* E Greece
Antiquaria *see* Antequera
Antissa *105 D5 var.* Ándissa. Lésvos, E Greece
An tIúr *see* Newry
Antivari *see* Bar
Antofagasta *64 B2* Antofagasta, N Chile
Antony *90 E2* Hauts-de-Seine, N France
An tSionainn *see* Shannon
Antsirañana *79 G2 province* N Madagascar
Antsohihy *79 G2* Mahajanga, NW Madagascar
An-tung *see* Dandong
Antwerpen *87 C5 Eng.* Antwerp, *Fr.* Anvers. Antwerpen, N Belgium
Anuradhapura *132 D3* North Central Province, C Sri Lanka
Anvers *see* Antwerpen
Anyang *120 C1* Henan, C China
A'nyêmaqên Shan *126 D4 mountain range* C China
Anykščiai *106 C4* Utena, E Lithuania
Anzio *97 C5* Lazio, C Italy
Ao Krung Thep *137 C5 var.* Krung Thep Mahanakhon, *Eng.* Bangkok. *country capital* (Thailand) (Thailand) Bangkok, C Thailand
Aomen *see* Macao
Aomori *130 D3* Aomori, Honshû, C Japan
Aóos *see* Vjosës, Lumi i
Aoraki *151 B6 prev.* Aorangi, Mount Cook. *mountain* South Island, New Zealand
Aorangi *see* Aoraki
Aosta *96 A1 anc.* Augusta Praetoria. Valle d'Aosta, NW Italy
Aoukâr *74 D3 var.* Aouker. *plateau* C Mauritania
Aouk, Bahr *76 C4 river* Central African Republic/Chad
Aouker *see* Aoukâr
Aozou *76 C1* Borkou-Ennedi-Tibesti, N Chad
Apalachee Bay *42 D3 bay* Florida, SE USA
Apalachicola River *42 D3 river* Florida, SE USA
Apamama *see* Abemama
Apaporis, Río *58 C4 river* Brazil/Colombia
Apatity *110 C2* Murmanskaya Oblast', NW Russian Federation
Ape *106 C3* Alûksne, NE Latvia
Apeldoorn *86 D3* Gelderland, E Netherlands
Apennines *96 E2 Eng.* Apennines. *mountain range* Italy/San Marino
Apennines *see* Apennines
Äpia *145 F4 country capital* (Samoa) (Samoa) Upolu, SE Samoa
Ap'khazet'i *117 E1 var.* Abkhazia. *autonomous republic* NW Georgia
Apoera *59 G3* Sipaliwini, NW Suriname
Apostle Islands *40 B1 island group* Wisconsin, N USA
Appalachian Mountains *35 D5 mountain range* E USA
Appingedam *86 E1* Groningen, NE Netherlands
Appleton *40 B2* Wisconsin, N USA
Apulia *see* Puglia
Apure, Río *58 C2 river* W Venezuela
Apurímac, Río *60 D3 river* S Peru
Apuseni, Munţii *108 A4 mountain range* W Romania
Aqaba/'Aqaba *see* Al 'Aqabah
Aqaba, Gulf of *120 A4 var.* Gulf of Elat, *Ar.* Khalij al 'Aqabah; *anc.* Sinus Aelaniticus. *gulf* NE Red Sea
'Aqaba, Khalij al *see* Aqaba, Gulf of
Äqchah *123 E3 var.* Aqcheh. Jowzjân, N Afghanistan
Äqcheh *see* Äqchah
Aqmola *see* Astana
Aqtöbe *see* Aktobe
Aquae Augustae *see* Dax
Aquae Calidae *see* Bath
Aquae Flaviae *see* Chaves
Aquae Grani *see* Aachen
Aquae Sextiae *see* Aix-en-Provence
Aquae Solis *see* Bath
Aquae Tarbelicae *see* Dax
Aquidauana *63 E4* Mato Grosso do Sul, S Brazil
Aquila/Aquila degli Abruzzi *see* L'Aquila
Aquisgranum *see* Aachen
Aquitaine *91 B6 cultural region* SW France
'Arabah, Wadi al *119 B7 Heb.* Ha'Arava. *dry watercourse* Israel/Jordan
Arabian Basin *124 A4 undersea basin* N Arabian Sea
Arabian Desert *see* Sahara el Sharqîya
Arabian Peninsula *121 B5 peninsula* SW Asia
Arabian Sea *124 A3 sea* NW Indian Ocean
Arabicus, Sinus *see* Red Sea
'Arabi, Khalij al *see* Gulf, The
'Arabîyah as Su'ûdîyah, Al Mamlakah al *see* Saudi Arabia
'Arabîyah Jumhûrîyah, Mişr al *see* Egypt
Arab Republic of Egypt *see* Egypt
Araçagi *63 F3* Minas Gerais, SE Brazil
Araçuaí *63 F3* Minas Gerais, SE Brazil
Arad *119 B7* Southern, S Israel
Arad *108 A4* Arad, W Romania
Arafura Sea *142 A3 Ind.* Laut Arafuru. *sea* W Pacific Ocean
Arafuru, Laut *see* Arafura Sea
Aragón *93 E2 autonomous community* E Spain
Araguaia, Río *63 E3 var.* Araguaya. *river* C Brazil
Araguari *63 F3* Minas Gerais, SE Brazil
Araguaya *see* Araguaia, Río
Ara Jovis *see* Aranjuez
Äräk *120 C3 prev.* Sultânâbâd. Markazi, W Iran
Arakan Yoma *136 A3 mountain range* W Burma (Myanmar)
Araks/Arak's *see* Aras
Aral *see* Aralsk, Kazakhstan
Aral *122 C1 Kaz.* Aral Tengizi, *Rus.* Aral'skoye More, *Uzb.* Orol Dengizi. *inland sea* Kazakhstan/Uzbekistan
Aral'sk *114 B4 Kaz.* Aral. Kzylorda, SW Kazakhstan
Aral'skoye More/Aral Tengizi *see* Aral Sea
Aranda de Duero *92 D2* Castilla-León, N Spain
Arandelovac *100 D1 prev.* Arandjelovac. Serbia, C Serbia
Arandjelovac *see* Arandelovac
Aranjuez *92 D3 anc.* Ara Jovis. Madrid, C Spain
Araouane *75 E2* Tombouctou, N Mali
'Ar'ar *120 B3* Al Ḥudûd ash Shamâlîyah, NW Saudi Arabia
Mount Ararat *117 F3 var.* Aghri Dagi, Agri Dagi, Koh I Noh, Masis, *Eng.* Great Ararat, Mount Ararat. *mountain* E Turkey
Ararat, Mount *see* Büyükağri Dağı
Aras *117 G3 Arm.* Arak's, *Az.* Araz Nehri, *Per.* Rûd-e Aras, *Rus.* Araks; *prev.* Araxes. *river* SW Asia
Arauca *58 C2* Arauca, NE Colombia
Arauca, Río *58 C2 river* Colombia/Venezuela
Arausio *see* Orange
Araxes *see* Aras
Araz Nehri *see* Aras
Arbela *see* Arbil
Arbil *120 B2 var.* Erbil, Irbil, *Kurd.* Hawlêr; *anc.* Arbela. Arbil, N Iraq
Arbroath *88 D3 anc.* Aberbrothock. E Scotland, United Kingdom
Arbuzinka *see* Arbuzynka
Arbuzynka *109 E3 Rus.* Arbuzinka. Mykolayivs'ka Oblast', S Ukraine
Arcachon *91 B5* Gironde, SW France
Arcae Remorum *see* Châlons-en-Champagne
Arcata *46 A4* California, W USA
Archangel *see* Arkhangel'sk
Archangel Bay *see* Chëshskaya Guba
Archidona *92 D5* Andalucía, S Spain
Arco *96 C2* Trentino-Alto Adige, N Italy
Arctic Mid Oceanic Ridge *see* Nansen Cordillera
Arctic Ocean *155 B3 ocean*
Arda *104 C3 var.* Ardhas, *Gk.* Ardas. *river* Bulgaria/Greece
Ardabil *120 C2 var.* Ardebil. Ardabîl, NW Iran
Ardakân *120 D3* Yazd, C Iran
Ardas *104 C3 var.* Ardhas, *Bul.* Arda. *river* Bulgaria/Greece
Arḑ aş Şawwân *119 C7 var.* Ardh es Suwwân. *plain* S Jordan
Ardebil *see* Ardabîl
Ardèche *91 C5 cultural region* E France
Ardennes *87 C8 physical region* Belgium/France
Ardhas *see* Arda/Ardas
Ardh es Suwwân *see* Arḑ aş Şawwân
Ardino *104 D3* Kürdzhali, S Bulgaria
Ard Mhacha *see* Armagh
Ardmore *49 G2* Oklahoma, C USA
Arel *see* Arlon
Arelas/Arelate *see* Arles
Arendal *85 A6* Aust-Agder, S Norway
Arensburg *see* Kuressaare
Arenys de Mar *93 G2* Cataluña, NE Spain
Areópoli *105 B7 prev.* Areópolis. Pelopónnisos, S Greece
Areópolis *see* Areópoli
Arequipa *61 E4* Arequipa, SE Peru
Arezzo *96 C3 anc.* Arretium. Toscana, C Italy
Argalasti *105 C5* Thessalía, C Greece
Argenteuil *90 D1* Val-d'Oise, N France
Argentina *65 B5 off.* Argentine Republic. *country* S South America

ARGENTINA
South America

Official name The Argentine Republic
Formation 1816 / 1816
Capital Buenos Aires
Population 39.5 million / 37 people per sq mile (14 people per sq km) / 90%
Total area 1,068,296 sq. miles (2,766,890 sq. km)
Languages Spanish*, Italian, Amerindian languages
Religions Roman Catholic 90%, Other 6%, Protestant 2%, Jewish 2%
Ethnic mix Indo-European 83%, Mestizo 14%, Jewish 2%, Amerindian 1%
Government Presidential system
Currency new Argentine peso = 100 centavos
Literacy rate 97%
Calorie consumption 2992 calories

Argentina Basin *see* Argentine Basin
Argentine Basin *57 C7 var.* Argentina Basin. *undersea basin* SW Atlantic Ocean
Argentine Republic *see* Argentina
Argentine Rise *see* Falkland Plateau
Argentoratum *see* Strasbourg
Darya-ye Arghandab *123 E5 river* SE Afghanistan
Argirocastro *see* Gjirokastër
Argo *72 B3* Northern, N Sudan
Argo Fracture Zone *141 C5 tectonic Feature* C Indian Ocean
Árgos *105 B6* Pelopónnisos, S Greece
Argostóli *105 A5 var.* Argostólion. Kefallonía, Iónia Nísiá, Greece, C Mediterranean Sea
Argostólion *see* Argostóli
Argun *125 E1 Chin.* Ergun He, *Rus.* Argun'. *river* China/Russian Federation
Argyrokastron *see* Gjirokastër
Århus *85 B7 var.* Aarhus. Århus, C Denmark
Aria *see* Herât
Ari Atoll *132 A4 var.* Alifu Atoll. *atoll* C Maldives
Arica *64 B1 hist.* San Marcos de Arica. Tarapacá, N Chile
Aridaía *104 B3 var.* Aridea, Aridhaía. Dytikí Makedonía, N Greece
Aridea *see* Aridaía
Aridhaía *see* Aridaía
Arîhâ *118 B3* Al Karak, W Jordan
Arîḩâ *see* Jericho
Ariminum *see* Rimini
Arinsal *91 A7* NW Andorra Europe
Arizona *48 A2 off.* State of Arizona, *also known as* Copper State, Grand Canyon State. *state* SW USA
Arkansas *42 A1 off.* State of Arkansas, *also known as* The Land of Opportunity. *state* S USA
Arkansas City *45 F5* Kansas, C USA
Arkansas River *49 G1 river* C USA
Arkhangel'sk *114 B2 Eng.* Archangel. Arkhangel'skaya Oblast', NW Russian Federation
Arkoí *105 E6 island* Dodekánisa, Greece, Aegean Sea

Arles 91 D6 var. Arles-sur-Rhône; anc. Arelas, Arelate. Bouches-du-Rhône, SE France
Arles-sur-Rhône see Arles
Arlington 49 G2 Texas, SW USA
Arlington 41 E4 Virginia, NE USA
Arlon 87 D8 Dut. Aarlen, Ger. Arel, Lat. Orolaunum. Luxembourg, SE Belgium
Armagh 89 B5 Ir. Ard Mhacha. S Northern Ireland, United Kingdom
Armagnac 91 B6 cultural region S France
Armenia 58 B3 Quindío, W Colombia
Armenia 117 F3 off. Republic of Armenia, var. Ajastan, Arm. Hayastani Hanrapetut'yun; prev. Armenian Soviet Socialist Republic. country SW Asia

ARMENIA
Southwest Asia

Official name Republic of Armenia
Formation 1991 / 1991
Capital Yerevan
Population 3 million / 261 people per sq mile (101 people per sq km) / 64%
Total area 11,506 sq. miles (29,800 sq. km)
Languages Armenian*, Azeri, Russian
Religions Armenian Apostolic Church (Orthodox) 88%, Other 6%, Armenian Catholic Church 6%
Ethnic mix Armenian 98%, Other 1%, Yezidi 1%
Government Parliamentary system
Currency Dram = 100 luma
Literacy rate 99%
Calorie consumption 2268 calories

Armenian Soviet Socialist Republic see Armenia
Armenia, Republic of see Armenia
Armidale 149 D6 New South Wales, SE Australia
Armstrong 38 B3 Ontario, S Canada
Armyans'k 109 F4 Rus. Armyansk. Respublika Krym, S Ukraine
Arnaía 104 C4 Cont. Arnea. Kentrikí Makedonía, N Greece
Arnaud 82 A3 river Québec, E Canada
Arnea see Arnaía
Arnedo 93 E2 La Rioja, N Spain
Arnhem 86 D4 Gelderland, SE Netherlands
Arnhem Land 148 A2 physical region Northern Territory, N Australia
Arno 96 B3 river C Italy
Arnold 45 G4 Missouri, C USA
Arnswalde see Choszczno
Aroe Islands see Aru, Kepulauan
Arorae 145 E3 atoll Tungaru, W Kiribati
Arrabona see Győr
Ar Rahad see Er Rahad
Ar Ramādī 120 B3 var. Ramadi, Rumadiya. Al Anbār, SW Iraq
Ar Rāmī 118 C4 Ḥimṣ, C Syria
Ar Ramthā 119 B5 var. Ramtha. Irbid, N Jordan
Arran, Isle of 88 C4 island SW Scotland, United Kingdom
Ar Raqqah 118 C2 var. Rakka; anc. Nicephorium. Ar Raqqah, N Syria
Arras 90 C2 anc. Nemetocenna. Pas-de-Calais, N France
Ar Rawḍatayn 120 C4 var. Raudhatain. N Kuwait
Arretium see Arezzo
Arriaca see Guadalajara
Arriaga 51 G5 Chiapas, SE Mexico
Ar Riyāḍ 121 C5 Eng. Riyadh. country capital (Saudi Arabia) (Saudi Arabia) Ar Riyāḍ, C Saudi Arabia
Ar Rub 'al Khali 121 C6 Eng. Empty Quarter, Great Sandy Desert. desert SW Asia
Ar Rustāq 121 E5 var. Rostak, Rustaq. N Oman
Ar Ruṭbah 120 B3 var. Rutba. Al Anbār, SW Iraq
Árta 105 A5 anc. Ambracia. Ípeiros, W Greece
Artashat 117 F3 S Armenia
Artemisa 54 B2 La Habana, W Cuba
Artesia 48 D3 New Mexico, SW USA
Arthur's Pass 151 C6 pass South Island, New Zealand
Artigas 64 D3 prev. San Eugenio, San Eugenio del Cuareim. Artigas, N Uruguay

Art'ik 117 F2 W Armenia
Artois 90 C2 cultural region N France
Artsiz see Artsyz
Artsyz 108 D4 Rus. Artsiz. Odes'ka Oblast', SW Ukraine
Artvin 117 F2 Artvin, NE Turkey
Arua 73 B6 NW Uganda
Aruba 58 C1 var. Oruba. Dutch autonomous region S West Indies
Aru Islands see Aru, Kepulauan
Aru, Kepulauan 139 G4 Eng. Aru Islands; prev. Aroe Islands. island group E Indonesia
Arunāchal Pradesh 135 G3 prev. North East Frontier Agency, North East Frontier Agency of Assam. cultural region NE India
Arusha 73 C7 Arusha, N Tanzania
Arviat 37 G4 prev. Eskimo Point. Nunavut, C Canada
Arvidsjaur 84 C4 Norrbotten, N Sweden
Arys' 114 B5 Kaz. Arys. Yuzhnyy Kazakhstan, S Kazakhstan
Arys see Arys'
Asadābād 123 F4 var. Asaḍābād; prev. Chaghasaráy. Konar, E Afghanistan
Asaḍābād see Asadābād
Asahi-dake 130 D2 mountain Hokkaidō, N Japan
Asahikawa 130 D2 Hokkaidō, N Japan
Asamankese 75 E5 SE Ghana
Āsansol 135 F4 West Bengal, NE India
Asben see Aïr, Massif de l'
Ascension Fracture Zone 69 A5 tectonic Feature C Atlantic Ocean
Ascension Island 67 C5 dependency of St.Helena C Atlantic Ocean
Ascoli Piceno 96 C4 anc. Asculum Picenum. Marche, C Italy
Asculum Picenum see Ascoli Piceno
'Aseb 72 D4 var. Āseb, Amh. Āseb. SE Eritrea
Assen 86 E2 Drenthe, NE Netherlands
Aşgabat 122 C3 prev. Ashgabat, Ashkhabad, Poltoratsk. country capital (Turkmenistan) (Turkmenistan) Ahal Welayaty, C Turkmenistan
Ashara see Al 'Ashārah
Ashburton 151 C6 Canterbury, South Island, New Zealand
Ashburton River 146 A4 river Western Australia
Ashdod 119 A6 anc. Azotos, Lat. Azotus. Central, W Israel
Asheville 43 E1 North Carolina, SE USA
Ashgabat see Aşgabat
Ashkelon 119 A6 prev. Ashqelon. Southern, C Israel
Ashkhabad see Aşgabat
Ashland 46 B4 Oregon, NW USA
Ashland 40 B1 Wisconsin, N USA
Ashmore and Cartier Islands 142 A3 Australian external territory E Indian Ocean
Ashmyany 107 C5 Rus. Oshmyany. Hrodzyenskaya Voblasts', W Belarus
Ashqelon see Ashkelon
Ash Shaddādah 118 D2 var. Ash Shaddādah, Jisr ash Shadadi, Shaddādī, Shedadi, Tell Shedadi. Al Ḥasakah, NE Syria
Ash Shaddādah see Ash Shaddādah
Ash Sharah 119 B7 var. Esh Sharā. mountain range W Jordan
Ash Shāriqah 120 D4 Eng. Sharjah. Ash Shāriqah, NE United Arab Emirates
Ash Shawbak 119 B7 Ma'ān, W Jordan
Ash Shiḥr 121 C6 SE Yemen
Asia 112 continent
Asinara 96 A4 island W Italy
Asipovichy 107 D6 Rus. Osipovichi. Mahilyowskaya Voblasts', C Belarus
Aşkale 117 E3 Erzurum, NE Turkey
Askersund 85 C6 Örebro, C Sweden
Asmara see Asmera
Asmera 72 C4 var. Asmara. country capital (Eritrea) (Eritrea) C Eritrea
Aspadana see Eşfahān
Asphaltites, Lacus see Dead Sea
Aspinwall see Colón
Assab see Aseb
As Sabkhah 118 D2 var. Sabkha. Ar Raqqah, NE Syria
Assad, Lake 118 C2 Eng. Lake Assad. lake N Syria
Assad, Lake see Asad, Buḩayrat al
Aş Şafāwī 119 C6 Al Mafraq, N Jordan

Aş Şaḥrā' ash Sharqīyah see Sahara el Sharqīya
As Salamīyah see Salamīyah
'Assal, Lac 68 E4 lake C Djibouti
As Salt 119 B6 var. Salt. Al Balqā', NW Jordan
Assamaka see Assamakka
Assamakka 75 F2 var. Assamaka. Agadez, NW Niger
As Samāwah 120 B3 var. Samawa. Al Muthanná, S Iraq
Assende 87 B5 Oost-Vlaanderen, NW Belgium
Assiout see Asyūṭ
Assiut see Asyūṭ
Assling see Jesenice
Assouan see Aswān
Assu see Açu
Assuan see Aswān
As Sukhnah 118 C3 var. Sukhne, Fr. Soukhné. Ḥimṣ, C Syria
As Sulaymānīyah 120 C3 var. Sulaimaniya, Kurd. Slēmāni. As Sulaymānīyah, NE Iraq
As Sulayyil 121 B5 Ar Riyāḍ, S Saudi Arabia
Aş Şuwār 118 D2 var. Şuwār. Dayr az Zawr, E Syria
As Suwaydā' 119 B5 var. El Suweida, Es Suweida, Suweida, Fr. Soueida. As Suwaydā', SW Syria
As Suways see Suez
Asta Colonia see Asti
Astacus see Izmit
Astana 114 C4 prev. Akmola, Akmolinsk, Tselinograd, Aqmola. country capital (Kazakhstan) (Kazakhstan) Akmola, N Kazakhstan
Asta Pompeia see Asti
Astarabad see Gorgān
Asterābād see Gorgān
Asti 96 A2 anc. Asta Colonia, Asta Pompeia, Hasta Colonia, Hasta Pompeia. Piemonte, NW Italy
Astigi see Ecija
Astipálaia see Astypálaia
Astorga 92 C1 anc. Asturica Augusta. Castilla-León, N Spain
Astrabad see Gorgān
Astrakhan' 111 C7 Astrakhanskaya Oblast', SW Russian Federation
Asturias 92 C1 autonomous community NW Spain
Asturias see Oviedo
Asturica Augusta see Astorga
Astypálaia 105 D7 var. Astipálaia, It. Stampalia. island Kykládes, Greece, Aegean Sea
Asunción 64 D2 country capital (Paraguay) (Paraguay) Central, S Paraguay
Aswān 72 B2 var. Assouan, Assuan, Aswân; anc. Syene. SE Egypt
Aswân see Aswān
Asyūṭ 72 B2 var. Assiout, Assiut, Asyût, Siut; anc. Lycopolis. C Egypt
Asyût see Asyūṭ
Atacama Desert 64 B2 Eng. Atacama Desert. desert N Chile
Atacama Desert see Atacama, Desierto de
Atafu Atoll 145 E3 island NW Tokelau
Atamyrat 122 D3 prev. Kerki. Lebap Welayaty, E Turkmenistan
Aṭār 74 C2 Adrar, W Mauritania
Atas Bogd 126 D3 mountain SW Mongolia
Atascadero 47 B7 California, W USA
Atatürk Baraji 117 E4 reservoir S Turkey
Atbara 72 C3 var. 'Aṭbārah. River Nile, NE Sudan
'Aṭbārah/'Aṭbarah, Nahr see Atbara
Atbasar 114 C4 Akmola, N Kazakhstan
Atchison 45 F4 Kansas, C USA
Aternum see Pescara
Ath 87 B6 var. Aat. Hainaut, SW Belgium
Athabasca 37 E5 Alberta, SW Canada
Athabasca 37 E5 var. Athabaska. river Alberta, SW Canada
Athabasca, Lake 37 F4 lake Alberta / Saskatchewan, SW Canada
Athabaska see Athabasca
Athenae see Athína
Athens 43 E2 Georgia, SE USA
Athens 40 D4 Ohio, N USA
Athens 49 G3 Texas, SW USA
Athens see Athína

Atherton 148 D3 Queensland, NE Australia
Athína 105 C6 Eng. Athens, prev. Athínai; anc. Athenae. country capital (Greece) (Greece) Attikí, C Greece
Athínai see Athína
Athlone 89 B5 Ir. Baile Átha Luain. C Ireland
Ath Thawrah see Madīnat ath Thawrah
Ati 76 C3 Batha, C Chad
Atikokan 38 B4 Ontario, S Canada
Atka 115 G3 Magadanskaya Oblast', E Russian Federation
Atka 36 A3 Atka Island, Alaska, USA
Atlanta 42 D2 state capital Georgia, SE USA
Atlanta 49 H2 Texas, SW USA
Atlantic City 41 F4 New Jersey, NE USA
Atlantic-Indian Basin 67 D7 undersea basin SW Indian Ocean
Atlantic-Indian Ridge 69 B8 undersea ridge SW Indian Ocean
Atlantic Ocean 66 B4 ocean
Atlas Mountains 70 C2 mountain range NW Africa
Atlasovo 115 H3 Kamchatskaya Oblast', E Russian Federation
Atlas, Tell 102 C3 Eng. Tell Atlas. mountain range N Algeria
Atlas, Tell see Atlas Tellien
Atlin 36 D4 British Columbia, W Canada
At Tafilah 119 B7 var. Et Tafila, Tafila. Aṭ Ṭafīlah, W Jordan
Aṭ Ṭafīlah see At Tafilah
Aṭ Ṭā'if 121 B5 Makkah, W Saudi Arabia
Attaleia/Attalia see Antalya
At Tall al Abyaḍ 118 C2 var. Tall al Abyaḍ, Tell Abyad, Fr. Tell Abiad. Ar Raqqah, N Syria
Aṭ Ṭanf 118 D4 Ḥimṣ, S Syria
Attapu see Samakhixai
Attawapiskat 38 C3 Ontario, C Canada
Attawapiskat 38 C3 river Ontario, S Canada
At Tibnī 118 D2 var. Tibnī. Dayr az Zawr, NE Syria
Attopeu see Samakhixai
Attu Island 36 A2 island Aleutian Islands, Alaska, USA
Atyrau 114 B4 prev. Gur'yev. Atyrau, W Kazakhstan
Aubagne 91 D6 anc. Albania. Bouches-du-Rhône, SE France
Aubange 87 D8 Luxembourg, SE Belgium
Aubervilliers 90 E1 Seine-St-Denis, Île-de-France, N France Europe
Auburn 46 B2 Washington, NW USA
Auch 91 B6 Lat. Augusta Auscorum, Elimberrum. Gers, S France
Auckland 150 D2 Auckland, North Island, New Zealand
Auckland Islands 142 C5 island group S New Zealand
Audern see Audru
Audincourt 90 E4 Doubs, E France
Audru 106 D2 Ger. Audern. Pärnumaa, SW Estonia
Augathella 149 D5 Queensland, E Australia
Augsbourg see Augsburg
Augsburg 95 C6 Fr. Augsbourg; anc. Augusta Vindelicorum. Bayern, S Germany
Augusta 147 A7 Western Australia
Augusta 43 E2 Georgia, SE USA
Augusta 41 G2 state capital Maine, NE USA
Augusta see London
Augusta Auscorum see Auch
Augusta Emerita see Mérida
Augusta Praetoria see Aosta
Augusta Trajana see Stara Zagora
Augusta Treverorum see Trier
Augusta Vangionum see Worms
Augusta Vindelicorum see Augsburg
Augustobona Tricassium see Troyes
Augustodurum see Bayeux
Augustoritum Lemovicensium see Limoges
Augustów 98 E2 Rus. Avgustov. Podlaskie, NE Poland
Aulie Ata/Auliye-Ata see Taraz
Aunglan 136 B4 var. Allanmyo, Myaydo. Magway, C Burma (Myanmar)
Auob 78 B4 var. Oup. river Namibia / South Africa

Aurangābād *134 D5* Mahārāshtra, C India
Auray *90 A3* Morbihan, NW France
Aurelia Aquensis *see* Baden-Baden
Aurelianum *see* Orléans
Aurès, Massif de l' *102 C4 mountain range* NE Algeria
Aurillac *91 C5* Cantal, C France
Aurium *see* Ourense
Aurora *59 F2* NW Guyana
Aurora *44 D4* Colorado, C USA
Aurora *40 B3* Illinois, N USA
Aurora *45 G5* Missouri, C USA
Aurora *see* Maéwo, Vanuatu
Aus *78 B4* Karas, SW Namibia
Ausa *see* Vic
Aussig *see* Ústí nad Labem
Austin *45 G3* Minnesota, N USA
Austin *49 G3 state capital* Texas, SW USA
Australes, Archipel des *see* Australes, Îles
Australes et Antarctiques Françaises, Terres *see* French Southern and Antarctic Territories
Australes, Îles *143 F4 var.* Archipel des Australes, Îles Tubuai, Tubuai Islands, *Eng.* Austral Islands. *island group* SW French Polynesia
Austral Fracture Zone *143 H4 tectonic feature* S Pacific Ocean
Australia *142 A4 off.* Commonwealth of Australia. *country*

AUSTRALIA
Australasia & Oceania

Official name Commonwealth of Australia
Formation 1901 / 1901
Capital Canberra
Population 20.9 million / 7 people per sq mile (3 people per sq km) / 92%
Total area 2,967,893 sq. miles (7,686,850 sq. km)
Languages English*, Italian, Cantonese, Greek, Arabic, Vietnamese, Aboriginal languages
Religions Roman Catholic 26%, Anglican 24%, Other 23%, Nonreligious 13%, United Church 8%, Other Protestant 6%
Ethnic mix European 92%, Asian 5%, Aboriginal 2%, Other 1%
Government Parliamentary system
Currency Australian dollar = 100 cents
Literacy rate 99%
Calorie consumption 3054 calories

Australia, Commonwealth of *see* Australia
Australian Alps *149 C7 mountain range* SE Australia
Australian Capital Territory *149 D7 prev.* Federal Capital Territory *territory* SE Australia
Australie, Bassin Nord de l' *see* North Australian Basin
Austral Islands *see* Australes, Îles
Austrava *see* Ostrov
Austria *95 D7 off.* Republic of Austria, *Ger.* Österreich. *country* C Europe

AUSTRIA
Central Europe

Official name Republic of Austria
Formation 1918 / 1919
Capital Vienna
Population 8.2 million / 257 people per sq mile (99 people per sq km) / 66%
Total area 32,378 sq. miles (83,858 sq. km)
Languages German*, Croatian, Slovenian, Hungarian (Magyar)
Religions Roman Catholic 78%, Nonreligious 9%, Other (including Jewish and Muslim) 8%, Protestant 5%
Ethnic mix Austrian 93%, Croat, Slovene, and Hungarian 6%, Other 1%
Government Parliamentary system
Currency Euro = 100 cents
Literacy rate 99%
Calorie consumption 3673 calories

Austria, Republic of *see* Austria
Autesiodorum *see* Auxerre
Autissiodorum *see* Auxerre
Autricum *see* Chartres
Auvergne *91 C5 cultural region* C France

Auxerre *90 C4 anc.* Autesiodorum, Autissiodorum. Yonne, C France
Avaricum *see* Bourges
Avarua *145 G5 dependent territory capital* (Cook Islands) Rarotonga, S Cook Islands
Avasfelsőfalu *see* Negreşti-Oaş
Avdira *104 C3* Anatolikí Makedonía kai Thráki, NE Greece
Aveiro *92 B3 anc.* Talabriga. Aveiro, W Portugal
Avela *see* Ávila
Avellino *97 D5 anc.* Abellinum. Campania, S Italy
Avenio *see* Avignon
Avesta *85 C6* Dalarna, C Sweden
Aveyron *91 C6 river* S France
Avezzano *96 C4* Abruzzo, C Italy
Avgustov *see* Augustów
Aviemore *88 C3* N Scotland, United Kingdom
Avignon *91 D6 anc.* Avenio. Vaucluse, SE France
Ávila *92 D3 var.* Avila; *anc.* Abela, Abula, Abyla, Avela. Castilla-León, C Spain
Avilés *92 C1* Asturias, NW Spain
Avranches *90 B3* Manche, N France
Avveel *see* Ivalo, Finland
Avvil *see* Ivalo
Awaji-shima *131 C6 island* SW Japan
Āwash *73 D5* Āfar, NE Ethiopia
Awbārī *71 F3* SW Libya
Ax *see* Dax
Axel *87 B5* Zeeland, SW Netherlands
Axel Heiburg Island *27 E1 var.* Axel Heiburg. *island* Nunavut, N Canada
Axel Heiburg *see* Axel Heiberg Island
Axiós *see* Vardar
Ayacucho *60 D4* Ayacucho, S Peru
Ayagoz *114 C5 var.* Ayaguz, Kaz. Ayakoz. *river* E Kazakhstan
Ayamonte *92 C4* Andalucía, S Spain
Ayaviri *61 E4* Puno, S Peru
Aydarko'l Ko'li *123 E2 Rus.* Ozero Aydarkul'. *lake* C Uzbekistan
Aydarkul', Ozero *see* Aydarko'l Ko'li
Aydın *116 A4 var.* Aidin; *anc.* Tralles Aydin. Aydın, SW Turkey
Ayers Rock *see* Uluru
Ayeyarwady *see* Irrawaddy
Ayiá *see* Agiá
Áyios Evstrátios *see* Ágios Efstrátios
Áyios Nikólaos *see* Ágios Nikólaos
Ayorou *75 E3* Tillabéri, W Niger
'Ayoûn el 'Atroûs *74 D3 var.* Aïoun el Atrous, Aïoun el Atroûss. Hodh el Gharbi, SE Mauritania
Ayr *88 C4* W Scotland, United Kingdom
Ayteke Bi *114 B4 Kaz.* Zhangaqazaly; *prev.* Novokazalinsk. Kzylorda, SW Kazakhstan
Aytos *104 E2* Burgas, E Bulgaria
Ayutthaya *137 C5 var.* Phra Nakhon Si Ayutthaya. Phra Nakhon Si Ayutthaya, C Thailand
Ayvalık *116 A3* Balıkesir, W Turkey
Azahar, Costa del *93 F3 coastal region* E Spain
Azaouâd *75 E3 desert* C Mali
Azärbaycan/Azärbaycan Respublikası *see* Azerbaijan
A'zāz *118 B2* Ḩalab, NW Syria
Azerbaijan *117 G2 off.* Azerbaijani Republic, *Az.* Azärbaycan, Azärbaycan Respublikası; *prev.* Azerbaijan SSR. *country* SE Asia

AZERBAIJAN
Southwest Asia

Official name Republic of Azerbaijan
Formation 1991 / 1991
Capital Baku
Population 8.5 million / 254 people per sq mile (98 people per sq km) / 50%
Total area 33,436 sq. miles (86,600 sq. km)
Languages Azeri*, Russian
Religions Shi'a Muslim 68%, Sunni Muslim 26%, Russian Orthodox 3%, Armenian Apostolic Church (Orthodox) 2%, Other 1%
Ethnic mix Azeri 90%, Other 3%, Lazs 2%, Armenian 2%, Russian 2%
Government Presidential system

AZERBAIJAN
(continued)

Currency New manat = 100 gopik
Literacy rate 99%
Calorie consumption 2575 calories

Azerbaijani Republic *see* Azerbaijan
Azerbaijan SSR *see* Azerbaijan
Azimabad *see* Patna
Azizie *see* Telish
Azogues *60 B2* Cañar, S Ecuador
Azores *92 A4 var.* Açores, Ilhas dos Açores, *Port.* Arquipélago dos Açores. *island group* Portugal. NE Atlantic Ocean
Azores-Biscay Rise *80 A3 undersea rise* E Atlantic Ocean
Azotos/Azotus *see* Ashdod
Azoum, Bahr *76 C3 seasonal river* SE Chad
Azov, Sea of *103 H1 Rus.* Azovskoye More, *Ukr.* Azovs'ke More. *sea* NE Black Sea
Azovs'ke More/Azovskoye More *see* Azov, Sea of
Azraq, Wāḩat al *119 C6 oasis* N Jordan
Aztec *48 C1* New Mexico, SW USA
Azuaga *92 C4* Extremadura, W Spain
Azuero, Península de *53 F5 peninsula* S Panama
Azul *65 D5* Buenos Aires, E Argentina
Azur, Côte d' *91 E6 coastal region* SE France
'Azza *see* Gaza
Az Zaqāzīq *72 B1 var.* Zagazig *var.* Az Zaqāzīq. N Egypt
Az Zaqāzīq *see* Az Zaqāzīq
Az Zarqā' *119 B6 var.* Zarqa. Az Zarqā', NW Jordan
Az Zāwiyah *71 F2 var.* Zawia. NW Libya
Az Zilfi *120 B4* Ar Riyāḑ, N Saudi Arabia

B

Baalbek *118 B4 var.* Ba'labakk; *anc.* Heliopolis. E Lebanon
Baardheere *73 D6 var.* Bardere, *It.* Bardera. Gedo, SW Somalia
Baarle-Hertog *87 C5* Antwerpen, N Belgium
Baarn *86 C3* Utrecht, C Netherlands
Babadag *108 D5* Tulcea, SE Romania
Babahoyo *60 B2 prev.* Bodegas. Los Ríos, C Ecuador
Bābā, Kūh-e *123 E4 mountain range* C Afghanistan
Babayevo *110 B4* Vologodskaya Oblast', NW Russian Federation
Babeldaob *144 A1 var.* Babeldaop, Babelthuap. *island* N Palau
Babeldaop *see* Babeldaob
Bab el Mandeb *121 B7 strait* Gulf of Aden/Red Sea
Babelthuap *see* Babeldaob
Babian Jiang *see* Black River
Babruysk *107 D7 Rus.* Bobruysk. Mahilyowskaya Voblasts', E Belarus
Babuyan Channel *139 E1 channel* N Philippines
Babuyan Islands *139 E1 island group* N Philippines
Bacabal *63 F2* Maranhão, E Brazil
Bacău *108 C4 Hung.* Bákó. Bacău, NE Romania
Bắc Bộ, Vịnh *see* Tongking, Gulf of
Bắc Giang *136 D3* Ha Bắc, N Vietnam
Bacheykava *107 D5 Rus.* Bocheykovo. Vitsyebskaya Voblasts', N Belarus
Back *37 F3 river* Nunavut, N Canada
Bačka Palanka *100 D3 prev.* Palanka. Serbia, NW Serbia
Bačka Topola *100 D3 Hung.* Topolya; *prev. Hung.* Bácstopolya. Vojvodina, N Serbia
Bạc Liêu *137 D6 var.* Vinh Loi. Minh Hai, S Vietnam
Bacolod *125 E4 off.* Bacolod City. Negros, C Philippines
Bacolod City *see* Bacolod
Bácsszenttamás *see* Srbobran
Bácstopolya *see* Bačka Topola
Bactra *see* Balkh
Badajoz *92 C4 anc.* Pax Augusta. Extremadura, W Spain

Baden-Baden *95 B6 anc.* Aurelia Aquensis. Baden-Württemberg, SW Germany
Bad Freienwalde *94 D3* Brandenburg, NE Germany
Badger State *see* Wisconsin
Bad Hersfeld *94 B4* Hessen, C Germany
Bad Homburg *see* Bad Homburg vor der Höhe
Bad Homburg vor der Höhe *95 B5 var.* Bad Homburg. Hessen, W Germany
Bad Ischl *95 D7* Oberösterreich, N Austria
Bad Krozingen *95 A6* Baden-Württemberg, SW Germany
Badlands *44 D2 physical region* North Dakota/South Dakota, N USA
Badu Island *148 C1 island* Queensland, NE Australia
Bad Vöslau *95 E6* Niederösterreich, NE Austria
Baeterrae/Baeterrae Septimanorum *see* Béziers
Baetic Cordillera/Baetic Mountains *see* Béticos, Sistema
Bafatá *74 C4* C Guinea-Bissau
Baffin Bay *37 G2 bay* Canada/Greenland
Baffin Island *37 G2 island* Nunavut, NE Canada
Bafing *74 C3 river* W Africa
Bafoussam *76 A4* Ouest, W Cameroon
Bafra *116 D2* Samsun, N Turkey
Bāft *120 D4* Kermān, S Iran
Bagaces *52 D4* Guanacaste, NW Costa Rica
Bagdad *see* Baghdād
Bagé *63 F5* Rio Grande do Sul, S Brazil
Baghdād *120 B3 var.* Bagdad, *Eng.* Baghdad. *country capital* (Iraq) Baghdād, C Iraq
Baghdad *see* Baghdād
Baghlān *123 E3* Baghlān, NE Afghanistan
Bago *136 B4 var.* Pegu. Bago, SW Burma (Myanmar)
Bagoé *74 D4 river* Côte d'Ivoire/Mali
Bagrationovsk *106 A4* Ger. Preussisch Eylau. Kaliningradskaya Oblast', W Russian Federation
Bagrax Hu *see* Bosten Hu
Baguio *139 E1 off.* Baguio City. Luzon, N Philippines
Baguio City *see* Baguio
Bagzane, Monts *75 F3 mountain* N Niger
Bahama Islands *see* Bahamas
Bahamas *54 C2 off.* Commonwealth of the Bahamas. *country* N West Indies

BAHAMAS
West Indies

Official name Commonwealth of the Bahamas
Formation 1973 / 1973
Capital Nassau
Population 305,655 / 79 people per sq mile (31 people per sq km) / 90%
Total area 5382 sq. miles (13,940 sq. km)
Languages English*, English Creole, French Creole
Religions Baptist 32%, Anglican 20%, Roman Catholic 19%, Other 17%, Methodist 6%, Church of God 6%
Ethnic mix Black African 85%, Other 15%
Government Parliamentary system
Currency Bahamian dollar = 100 cents
Literacy rate 96%
Calorie consumption 2755 calories

Bahamas *35 D6 var.* Bahama Islands. *island group* N West Indies
Bahamas, Commonwealth of the *see* Bahamas
Baharly *122 C3 var.* Bäherden, *Rus.* Bakharden; *prev.* Bakherden. Ahal Welaýaty, C Turkmenistan
Bahāwalpur *134 C2* Punjab, E Pakistan
Bäherden *see* Baharly
Bahia *63 F3 off.* Estado da Bahia. *state* E Brazil
Bahia *63 F3 off.* Estado da Bahia. *region* E Brazil
Bahía Blanca *65 C5* Buenos Aires, E Argentina
Bahia, Estado da *see* Bahia
Bahir Dar *72 C4 var.* Bahr Dar, Bahrdar Giyorgis. Āmara, N Ethiopia

Bahraich *135 E3* Uttar Pradesh, N India
Bahrain *120 C4 off.* State of Bahrain,
  Dawlat al Bahrayn, *Ar.* Al Baḥrayn,
  prev. Bahrein; *anc.* Tylos, Tyros.
  country SW Asia

BAHRAIN
Southwest Asia

Official name Kingdom of Bahrain
Formation 1971 / 1971
Capital Manama
Population 708,573 / 2596 people per
sq mile (1004 people per sq km) / 90%
Total area 239 sq. miles (620 sq. km)
Languages Arabic
Religions Muslim (mainly Shi'a) 99%,
Other 1%
Ethnic mix Bahraini 70%, Iranian, Indian,
and Pakistani 24%, Other Arab 4%,
European 2%
Government Mixed monarchical–
parliamentary system
Currency Bahraini dinar = 1000 fils
Literacy rate 87%
Calorie consumption Not available

Bahrain, State of *see* Bahrain
Bahrayn, Dawlat al *see* Bahrain
Bahr Dar/Bahrdar Giyorgis *see*
  Bahir Dar
Bahrein *see* Bahrain
Bahr el, Azraq *see* Blue Nile
Bahr Tabariya, Sea of *see* Tiberias, Lake
Bahushewsk *107 E6 Rus.* Bogushëvsk.
  Vitsyebskaya Voblasts', NE Belarus
Baia Mare *108 B3 Ger.* Frauenbach,
  Hung. Nagybánya; *prev.* Neustadt.
  Maramureş, NW Romania
Baia Sprie *108 B3 Ger.* Mittelstadt,
  Hung. Felsőbánya. Maramureş,
  NW Romania
Baïbokoum *76 B4* Logone-Oriental,
  SW Chad
Baidoa *see* Baydhabo
Baie-Comeau *39 E3* Québec, SE Canada
Baikal, Lake *115 E4 Eng.* Lake Baikal.
  lake S Russian Federation
Baikal, Lake *see* Baykal, Ozero
Baile Átha Cliath *see* Dublin
Baile Átha Luain *see* Athlone
Bailén *92 D4* Andalucía, S Spain
Baile na Mainistreach *see* Newtownabbey
Băileşti *108 B5* Dolj, SW Romania
Ba Illi *76 B3* Chari-Baguirmi, SW Chad
Bainbridge *42 D3* Georgia, SE USA
Bā'ir *see* Bāyir
Baireuth *see* Bayreuth
Bairiki *144 D2* country capital (Kiribati)
  (Kiribati) Tarawa, NW Kiribati
Bairnsdale *149 C7* Victoria, SE Australia
Baishan *129 E3 prev.* Hunjiang. Jilin,
  NE China
Baiyin *128 B4* Gansu, C China
Baja *99 C7* Bács-Kiskun, S Hungary
Baja California Norte *50 B2 state*
  NW Mexico
Bajo Boquete *see* Boquete
Bajram Curri *101 D5* Kukës, N Albania
Bakala *76 C4* Ouaka, C Central African
  Republic
Bakan *see* Shimonoseki
Baker *46 C3* Oregon, NW USA
Baker and Howland Islands *145 E2 US
  unincorporated territory* W Polynesia
Baker Lake *37 F3* Nunavut, N Canada
Bakersfield *47 C7* California, W USA
Bakharden *see* Baharly
Bakhchisaray *see* Bakhchysaray
Bakhchysaray *109 F5 Rus.* Bakhchisaray.
  Respublika Krym, S Ukraine
Bakherden *see* Baharly
Bakhmach *109 F1* Chernihivs'ka Oblast',
  N Ukraine
Bākhtarān *see* Kermānshāh
Bakı *117 H2 Eng.* Baku. *country capital*
  (Azerbaijan) (Azerbaijan) E Azerbaijan
Bákó *see* Bacău
Bakony *99 C7 Eng.* Bakony Mountains,
  Ger. Bakonywald. *mountain range*
  W Hungary
Bakony Mountains/Bakonywald *see*
  Bakony
Baku *see* Bakı
Bakwanga *see* Mbuji-Mayi
Balabac Island *129 C8 island*
  W Philippines

Balabac, Selat *see* Balabac Strait
Balabac Strait *138 D2 var.* Selat Balabac.
  strait Malaysia/Philippines
Ba'labakk *see* Baalbek
Balaguer *93 F2* Cataluña, NE Spain
Balakovo *111 C6* Saratovskaya Oblast',
  W Russian Federation
Bālā Morghāb *122 D4* Laghmān,
  NW Afghanistan
Balashov *111 B6* Saratovskaya Oblast',
  W Russian Federation
Balasore *see* Bāleshwar
Balaton, Lake *99 C7 var.* Lake Balaton,
  Ger. Plattensee. *lake* W Hungary
Balaton, Lake *see* Balaton
Balbina, Represa *62 D1 reservoir*
  NW Brazil
Balboa *53 G4* Panamá, C Panama
Balcarce *65 D5* Buenos Aires,
  E Argentina
Balclutha *151 B7* Otago, South Island,
  New Zealand
Baldy Mountain *44 C1 mountain*
  Montana, NW USA
Bâle *see* Basel
Balearic Plain *see* Algerian Basin
Baleares Major *see* Mallorca
Balearic Islands *93 G3 Eng.* Balearic
  Islands. *island group* Spain,
  W Mediterranean Sea
Balearic Islands *see* Baleares, Islas
Balearis Minor *see* Menorca
Baleine, Rivière à la *39 E2 river* Québec,
  E Canada
Balen *87 C5* Antwerpen, N Belgium
Bāleshwar *135 F4 prev.* Balasore. Orissa,
  E India
Bălgrad *see* Alba Iulia
Bali *138 D5 island* C Indonesia
Balıkesir *116 A3* Balıkesir, W Turkey
Balıkh, Nahr *118 C2 river* N Syria
Balikpapan *138 D4* Borneo, C Indonesia
Balkanabat *122 B2 Rus.* Nebitdag.
  Balkan Welaýaty, W Turkmenistan
Balkan Mountains *104 C2 Bul./
  SCr.* Stara Planina. *mountain range*
  Bulgaria/Serbia
Balkh *123 E3 anc.* Bactra. Balkh,
  N Afghanistan
Balkhash *114 C5 Kaz.* Balqash.
  Karaganda, SE Kazakhstan
Lake Balkhash *114 C5 Eng.* Lake
  Balkhash, *Kaz.* Balqash. *lake*
  SE Kazakhstan
Balkhash, Lake *see* Balkhash, Ozero
Balladonia *147 C6* Western Australia
Ballarat *149 C7* Victoria,
  SE Australia
Balleny Islands *154 B5 island group*
  Antarctica
Ballinger *49 F3* Texas, SW USA
Balochistān *see* Baluchistān
Balqash *see* Balkhash/Balkhash, Ozero
Balş *108 B5* Olt, S Romania
Balsas *63 F2* Maranhão, E Brazil
Balsas, Río *51 E5 var.* Río Mexcala. *river*
  S Mexico
Bal'shavik *107 D7 Rus.* Bol'shevik.
  Homyel'skaya Voblasts', SE Belarus
Balta *108 D3 Rus.* Odes'ka Oblast',
  SW Ukraine
Bălţi *108 D3 Rus.* Bel'tsy. N Moldova
Baltic Port *see* Paldiski
Baltic Sea *85 C7 Ger.* Ostee, *Rus.*
  Baltiskoye More. *sea* N Europe
Baltimore *41 F4* Maryland, NE USA
Baltischport/Baltiski *see* Paldiski
Baltiskoye More *see* Baltic Sea
Baltkrievija *see* Belarus
Baluchistān *134 B3 var.* Balochistān,
  Beluchistan. *province* SW Pakistan
Balvi *106 D4* Balvi, NE Latvia
Balykchy *123 G2 Kir.* Ysyk-Köl; *prev.*
  Issyk-Kul', Rybach'ye. Issyk-Kul'skaya
  Oblast', NE Kyrgyzstan
Balzers *94 E2* S Liechtenstein
Bam *120 E4* Kermān, SE Iran
Bamako *74 D4 country capital* (Mali)
  (Mali) Capital District, SW Mali
Bambari *76 C4* Ouaka, C Central African
  Republic
Bamberg *95 C5* Bayern, SE Germany
Bamenda *76 A4* Nord-Ouest,
  W Cameroon
Banaba *144 D2 var.* Ocean Island. *island*
  Tungaru, W Kiribati
Banaras *see* Vārānasi

Bandaaceh *138 A3 var.* Banda Atjeh;
  prev. Koetaradja, Kutaradja, Kutaraja.
  Sumatera, W Indonesia
Banda Atjeh *see* Bandaaceh
Banda, Laut *see* Banda Sea
Bandama *74 D5 var.* Bandama Fleuve.
  river S Côte d'Ivoire
Bandama Fleuve *see* Bandama
Bandar 'Abbās *see* Bandar-e 'Abbās
Bandarbeyla *73 E5 var.* Bender Beila,
  Bender Beyla. Bari, NE Somalia
Bandar-e 'Abbās *120 D4 var.* Bandar
  'Abbās; *prev.* Gombroon. Hormozgān,
  S Iran
Bandar-e Būshehr *120 C4 var.* Būshehr,
  Eng. Bushire. Būshehr, S Iran
Bandar-e Kangān *120 D4 var.* Kangān.
  Būshehr, S Iran
Bandar-e Khamīr *120 D4* Hormozgān,
  S Iran
Bandar-e Langeh *see* Bandar-e
  Lengeh
Bandar-e Lengeh *120 D4 var.*
  Bandar-e Langeh, Lingeh. Hormozgān,
  S Iran
Bandar Kassim *see* Boosaaso
Bandar Lampung *138 C4 var.*
  Bandarlampung, Tanjungkarang-
  Telukbetung; *prev.* Tandjoengkarang,
  Tanjungkarang, Teloekbetoeng,
  Telukbetung. Sumatera,
  W Indonesia
Bandarlampung *see* Bandar Lampung
Bandar Maharani *see* Muar
Bandar Masulipatnam *see*
  Machilipatnam
Bandar Penggaram *see* Batu Pahat
Bandar Seri Begawan *138 D3 prev.*
  Brunei Town. *country capital* (Brunei)
  (Brunei) N Brunei
Banda Sea *139 F5 var.* Laut Banda. *sea*
  E Indonesia
Bandiagara *75 E3* Mopti, C Mali
Bandırma *116 A3 var.* Penderma.
  Balıkesir, NW Turkey
Bandjarmasin *see* Banjarmasin
Bandoeng *see* Bandung
Bandundu *77 C6 prev.* Banningville.
  Bandundu, W Dem. Rep. Congo
Bandung *138 C5 prev.* Bandoeng. Jawa,
  C Indonesia
Bangalore *132 C2 var.* Bengalooru. *state
  capital* Karnātaka, S India
Bangassou *76 D4* Mbomou, SE Central
  African Republic
Banggai, Kepulauan *139 E4 island
  group* C Indonesia
Banghāzī *71 G2 Eng.* Bengazi, Benghazi,
  It. Bengasi. NE Libya
Bangka, Pulau *138 C4 island*
  W Indonesia
Bangkok *see* Ao Krung Thep
Bangkok, Bight of *see* Krung Thep, Ao
Bangladesh *135 G3 off.* People's
  Republic of Bangladesh; *prev.* East
  Pakistan. *country* S Asia

BANGLADESH
South Asia

Official name People's Republic
of Bangladesh
Formation 1971 / 1971
Capital Dhaka
Population 147 million / 2845 people
per sq mile (1098 people per sq km) / 25%
Total area 55,598 sq. miles
(144,000 sq. km)
Languages Bengali*, Urdu, Chakma,
Marma (Magh), Garo, Khasi, Santhali,
Tripuri, Mro
Religions Muslim (mainly Sunni) 87%,
Hindu 12%, Other 1%
Ethnic mix Bengali 98%, Other 2%
Government Transitional regime
Currency Taka = 100 poisha
Literacy rate 41%
Calorie consumption 2205 calories

Bangladesh, People's Republic of *see*
  Bangladesh
Bangor *89 C6* NW Wales, United
  Kingdom
Bangor *89 B5 Ir.* Beannchar. E Northern
  Ireland, United Kingdom
Bangor *41 G2* Maine, NE USA
Bang Pla Soi *see* Chon Buri

Bangui *77 B5 country capital* (Central
  African Republic) (Central African
  Republic) Ombella-Mpoko, SW Central
  African Republic
Bangweulu, Lake *73 B8 var.* Lake
  Bengweulu. *lake* N Zambia
Ban Hat Yai *see* Hat Yai
Ban Hin Heup *136 C4* Viangchan,
  C Laos
Ban Houayxay/Ban Houei Sai *see*
  Houayxay
Ban Hua Hin *137 C6 var.* Hua Hin.
  Prachuap Khiri Khan, SW Thailand
Bani *74 D3 river* S Mali
Banias *see* Bāniyās
Banijska Palanka *see* Glina
Bani Suwayf *72 B2 var.* Beni Suef.
  N Egypt
Bāniyās *118 B3 var.* Banias, Baniyas,
  Paneas. Ṭarṭūs, W Syria
Banjak, Kepulauan *see* Banyak,
  Kepulauan
Banja Luka *100 B3* Republika Srpska,
  NW Bosnia and Herzegovina
Banjarmasin *138 D4 prev.*
  Bandjarmasin. Borneo, C Indonesia
Banjul *74 B3 prev.* Bathurst. *country
  capital* (Gambia) (Gambia) W Gambia
Banks, Îles *see* Banks Islands
Banks Island *37 E2 island* Northwest
  Territories, NW Canada
Banks Islands *144 D4 Fr.* Îles Banks.
  island group N Vanuatu
Banks Lake *46 B1 reservoir* Washington,
  NW USA
Banks Peninsula *151 C6 peninsula*
  South Island, New Zealand
Banks Strait *149 C8 strait* SW Tasman
  Sea
Bānkura *135 F4* West Bengal, NE India
Ban Mak Khaeng *see* Udon Thani
Banmo *see* Bhamo
Banningville *see* Bandundu
Bañolas *see* Banyoles
Ban Pak Phanang *see* Pak Phanang
Ban Sichon *see* Sichon
Banská Bystrica *99 C6 Ger.*
  Neusohl, *Hung.* Besztercebánya.
  Banskobystrický Kraj, C Slovakia
Bantry Bay *89 A7 Ir.* Bá Bheanntraí. *bay*
  SW Ireland
Banya *104 E2* Burgas, E Bulgaria
Banyak, Kepulauan *138 A3 prev.*
  Kepulauan Banjak. *island group*
  NW Indonesia
Banyo *76 B4* Adamaoua, NW Cameroon
Banyoles *93 G2 var.* Bañolas. Cataluña,
  NE Spain
Banzare Seamounts *141 C7 seamount
  range* S Indian Ocean
Banzart *see* Bizerte
Baoji *128 B4 var.* Pao-chi, Paoki.
  Shaanxi, C China
Baoro *76 B4* Nana-Mambéré, W Central
  African Republic
Baoshan *128 A6 var.* Pao-shan. Yunnan,
  SW China
Baotou *127 F3 var.* Pao-t'ou, Paotow.
  Nei Mongol Zizhiqu, N China
Ba'qūbah *120 B3 var.* Qubba. Diyālá,
  C Iraq
Baquerizo Moreno *see* Puerto Baquerizo
  Moreno
Bar *101 C5 It.* Antivari. S Montenegro
Baraawe *73 D6 It.* Brava. Shabeellaha
  Hoose, S Somalia
Bārāmati *134 C5* Mahārāshtra, W India
Baranavichy *107 B6 Pol.* Baranowicze,
  Rus. Baranovichi. Brestskaya Voblasts',
  SW Belarus
Baranovichi/Baranowicze *see*
  Baranavichy
Barbados *55 G1 country* SE West Indies

BARBADOS
West Indies

Official name Barbados
Formation 1966 / 1966
Capital Bridgetown
Population 280,946 / 1692 people
per sq mile (653 people per sq km) / 52%
Total area 166 sq. miles (430 sq. km)
Languages English*, Bajan
(Barbadian English)
Religions Anglican 40%, Other 24%,
Nonreligious 17%, Pentecostal 8%,

BARBADOS
(continued)

Methodist 7%, Roman Catholic 4%
Ethnic mix Black African 92%, White 3%,
Other 3%, Mixed race 2%
Government Parliamentary system
Currency Barbados dollar = 100 cents
Literacy rate 99%
Calorie consumption 3091 calories

Barbastro 93 F2 Aragón, NE Spain
Barbate de Franco 92 C5 Andalucía,
S Spain
Barbuda 55 G3 *island* N Antigua and
Barbuda
Barcaldine 148 C4 Queensland,
E Australia
Barcarozsnyó *see* Râşnov
Barcău *see* Berettyó
Barce *see* Al Marj
Barcelona 93 G2 *anc.* Barcino,
Barcinona. Cataluña, E Spain
Barcelona 59 E2 Anzoátegui,
NE Venezuela
Barcino/Barcinona *see* Barcelona
Barcoo *see* Cooper Creek
Barcs 99 C7 Somogy, SW Hungary
Bardaï 76 C1 Borkou-Ennedi-Tibesti,
N Chad
Bardejov 99 D5 Ger. Bartfeld, *Hung.*
Bártfa. Presovský Kraj, E Slovakia
Bardera/Bardere *see* Baardheere
Barduli *see* Barletta
Bareilly 135 E3 *var.* Bareli. Uttar
Pradesh, N India
Bareli *see* Bareilly
Barendrecht 86 C4 Zuid-Holland,
SW Netherlands
Barentin 90 C3 Seine-Maritime,
N France
Barentsburg 83 G2 Spitsbergen,
W Svalbard
Barentsøeva More/Barents Havet *see*
Barents Sea
Barentsøya 83 G2 *island* E Svalbard
Barents Sea 110 C2 *Nor.* Barents Havet,
Rus. Barentsevo More. *sea* Arctic
Ocean
Bar Harbor 41 H2 Mount Desert Island,
Maine, NE USA
Bari 97 E5 *var.* Bari delle Puglie; *anc.*
Barium. Puglia, SE Italy
Báridah *see* Al Bāridah
Bari delle Puglie *see* Bari
Barikot *see* Barīkowṭ
Barīkowṭ 123 F4 *var.* Barikot. Konar,
NE Afghanistan
Barlllas 52 A2 *var.* Santa Cruz Barlllas.
Huehuetenango, NW Guatemala
Barinas 58 C2 Barinas, W Venezuela
Barisal 135 G4 Barisal, S Bangladesh
Barisan, Pegunungan 138 B4 *mountain
range* Sumatera, W Indonesia
Barito, Sungai 138 D4 *river* Borneo,
C Indonesia
Barium *see* Bari
Barka *see* Al Marj
Barkly Tableland 148 B3 *plateau*
Northern Territory/Queensland,
N Australia
Bârlad 108 D4 *prev.* Bîrlad. Vaslui,
E Romania
Barlavento, Ilhas de 74 A2 *var.*
Windward Islands. *island group*
N Cape Verde
Bar-le-Duc 90 D3 *var.* Bar-sur-Ornain.
Meuse, NE France
Barlee, Lake 147 B6 *lake* Western
Australia
Barlee Range 146 A4 *mountain range*
Western Australia
Barletta 97 D5 *anc.* Barduli. Puglia,
SE Italy
Barlinek 98 B3 *Ger.* Berlinchen.
Zachodnio-pomorskie,
NW Poland
Barmen-Elberfeld *see* Wuppertal
Barmouth 89 C6 NW Wales, United
Kingdom
Barnaul 114 D4 Altayskiy Kray,
C Russian Federation
Barnet 89 A7 United Kingdom
Barnstaple 89 C7 SW England, United
Kingdom
Baroda *see* Vadodara

Baroghil Pass 123 F3 *var.* Kowtal-e
Barowghīl. *pass* Afghanistan/Pakistan
Baron'ki 107 E7 *Rus.* Boron'ki.
Mahilyowskaya Voblasts', E Belarus
Barowghīl, Kowtal-e *see* Baroghil Pass
Barquisimeto 58 C2 Lara,
NW Venezuela
Barra 88 B3 *island* NW Scotland, United
Kingdom
Barra de Río Grande 53 E3 Región
Autónoma Atlántico Sur, E Nicaragua
Barranca 60 C3 Lima, W Peru
Barrancabermeja 58 B2 Santander,
N Colombia
Barranquilla 58 B1 Atlántico,
N Colombia
Barreiro 92 B4 Setúbal, W Portugal
Barrier Range 149 C6 *hill range* New
South Wales, SE Australia
Barrow 36 D2 Alaska, USA
Barrow 89 B6 *Ir.* An Bhearú. *river*
SE Ireland
Barrow-in-Furness 89 C5 NW England,
United Kingdom
Barrow Island 146 A4 *island* Western
Australia
Barstow 47 C7 California, W USA
Bar-sur-Ornain *see* Bar-le-Duc
Bartang 123 F3 *river* SE Tajikistan
Bartenstein *see* Bartoszyce
Bártfa/Bartfeld *see* Bardejov
Bartica 59 F3 N Guyana
Bartın 116 C2 Bartın, NW Turkey
Bartlesville 49 G1 Oklahoma, C USA
Bartoszyce 98 D2 *Ger.* Bartenstein.
Warmińsko-mazurskie, NE Poland
Baruun-Urt 127 E2 Sühbaatar,
E Mongolia
Barú, Volcán 53 E5 *var.* Volcán de
Chiriquí. *volcano* W Panama
Barwon River 149 D5 *river* New South
Wales, SE Australia
Barysaw 107 D6 *Rus.* Borisov. Minskaya
Voblasts', NE Belarus
Basarabeasca 108 D4 *Rus.* Bessarabka.
SE Moldova
Basel 95 A7 *Eng.* Basle, *Fr.* Bâle. Basel-
Stadt, NW Switzerland
Basilan 139 E3 *island* Sulu Archipelago,
SW Philippines
Basle *see* Basel
Basra *see* Al Başrah
Bassano del Grappa 96 C2 Veneto,
NE Italy
Bassein *see* Pathein
Basseterre 55 G4 *country capital* (Saint
Kitts and Nevis) (Saint Kitts and Nevis)
Saint Kitts, Saint Kitts and Nevis
Basse-Terre 55 G3 *dependent territory
capital* (Guadeloupe) Basse Terre,
SW Guadeloupe
Basse Terre 55 G4 *island* W Guadeloupe
Bassikounou 74 D3 Hodh ech Chargui,
SE Mauritania
Bass, Îlots de *see* Marotiri
Bass Strait 149 C7 *strait* SE Australia
Bassum 94 B3 Niedersachsen,
NW Germany
Bastia 91 E7 Corse, France,
C Mediterranean Sea
Bastogne 87 D7 Luxembourg,
SE Belgium
Bastrop 42 B2 Louisiana, S USA
Bastyn' 107 B7 *Rus.* Bostyn'. Brestskaya
Voblasts', SW Belarus
Basuo *see* Dongfang
Basutoland *see* Lesotho
Bata 77 A5 NW Equatorial Guinea
Batae Coritanorum *see* Leicester
Batajnica 100 D3 Vojvodina, N Serbia
Batangas 139 E2 *off.* Batangas City.
Luzon, N Philippines
Batangas City *see* Batangas
Batavia *see* Jakarta
Bătdâmbâng 137 C5 *prev.* Battambang.
Bătdâmbâng, NW Cambodia
Batéké, Plateaux 77 B6 *plateau* S Congo
Bath 89 D7 *hist.* Akermancester;
anc. Aquae Calidae, Aquae Solis.
SW England, United Kingdom
Bathinda 134 D2 Punjab, NW India
Bathsheba 55 G1 E Barbados
Bathurst 149 D6 New South Wales,
SE Australia
Bathurst 39 F4 New Brunswick,
SE Canada
Bathurst *see* Banjul

Bathurst Island 146 D2 *island* Northern
Territory, N Australia
Bathurst Island 37 F2 *island* Parry
Islands, Nunavut, N Canada
Wadi al Batin 120 C4 *dry watercourse*
SW Asia
Batman 117 E4 *var.* İluh. Batman,
SE Turkey
Batna 71 E2 NE Algeria
Baton Rouge 42 B3 *state capital*
Louisiana, S USA
Batroûn 118 A4 *var.* Al Batrūn.
N Lebanon
Battambang *see* Bătdâmbâng
Batticaloa 132 D3 Eastern Province,
E Sri Lanka
Battipaglia 97 D5 Campania, S Italy
Battle Born State *see* Nevada
Bat'umi 117 F2 W Georgia
Batu Pahat 138 B3 *prev.* Bandar
Penggaram. Johor, Peninsular Malaysia
Bauchi 75 G4 Bauchi, NE Nigeria
Bauer Basin 153 F3 *undersea basin*
E Pacific Ocean
Bauska 106 C3 *Ger.* Bauske. Bauska,
S Latvia
Bauske *see* Bauska
Bautzen 94 D4 *Lus.* Budyšin. Sachsen,
E Germany
Bauzanum *see* Bolzano
Bavaria *see* Bayern
Bavarian Alps 95 C7 *Ger.* Bayrische
Alpen. *mountain range* Austria/
Germany
Bavière *see* Bayern
Bavispe, Río 50 C2 *river* NW Mexico
Bawiti 72 B2 *var.* Bawîti. N Egypt
Bawku 75 E4 N Ghana
Bayamo 54 C3 Granma, E Cuba
Bayan Har Shan 126 D4 *var.* Bayan
Khar. *mountain range* C China
Bayanhongor 126 D2 Bayanhongor,
C Mongolia
Bayan Khar *see* Bayan Har Shan
Bayano, Lago 53 G4 *lake* E Panama
Bay City 40 C3 Michigan, N USA
Bay City 49 G4 Texas, SW USA
Baydhabo 73 D6 *var.* Baydhowa, Isha
Baydhabo, *It.* Baidoa. Bay, SW Somalia
Baydhowa *see* Baydhabo
Bayern 95 C6 *Eng.* Bavaria, *Fr.* Bavière.
state SE Germany
Bayeux 90 B3 *anc.* Augustodurum.
Calvados, N France
Bāyir 119 C7 *var.* Bā'ir. Ma'ān, S Jordan
Bay Islands 52 C1 *Eng.* Bay Islands.
island group N Honduras
Bay Islands *see* Bahía, Islas de la
Baymak 111 D6 Respublika
Bashkortostan, W Russian Federation
Bayonne 91 A6 *anc.* Lapurdum.
Pyrénées-Atlantiques, SW France
Bayou State *see* Mississippi
Bayram-Ali *see* Bayramaly
Baýramaly 122 D3 *var.* Bayramaly;
prev. Bayram-Ali. Mary Welaýaty,
S Turkmenistan
Bayreuth 95 C5 *var.* Baireuth. Bayern,
SE Germany
Bayrische Alpen *see* Bavarian Alps
Bayrūt *see* Beyrouth
Bay State *see* Massachusetts
Baysun *see* Boysun
Bayt Laḥm *see* Bethlehem
Baytown 49 H4 Texas, SW USA
Baza 93 E4 Andalucía, S Spain
Bazargic *see* Dobrich
Bazin *see* Pezinok
Beagle Channel 65 C8 *channel*
Argentina/Chile
Béal Feirste *see* Belfast
Beannchar *see* Bangor, Northern
Ireland, UK
Bear Island *see* Bjørnøya
Bear Lake 46 E4 *lake* Idaho/Utah,
NW USA
Beas de Segura 93 E4 Andalucía, S Spain
Beata, Isla 55 E3 *island* SW Dominican
Republic
Beatrice 45 F4 Nebraska, C USA
Beaufort Sea 36 D2 *sea* Arctic Ocean
Beaufort-Wes *see* Beaufort West
Beaufort West 78 C5 *Afr.* Beaufort-Wes.
Western Cape, SW South Africa
Beaumont 49 H3 Texas, SW USA
Beaune 90 D4 Côte d'Or, C France

Beauvais 90 C3 *anc.* Bellovacum,
Caesaromagus. Oise, N France
Beaver Island 40 C2 *island* Michigan,
N USA
Beaver Lake 49 H1 *reservoir* Arkansas,
C USA
Beaver River 49 F1 *river* Oklahoma,
C USA
Beaver State *see* Oregon
Beäwar 134 C3 Rājasthān, N India
Bečej 100 D3 *Ger.* Altbetsche, *Hung.*
Óbecse, Rácz-Becse; *prev.* Magyar-
Becse, Stari Bečej. Vojvodina, N Serbia
Béchar 70 D2 *prev.* Colomb-Béchar.
W Algeria
Beckley 40 D5 West Virginia, NE USA
Bécs *see* Wien
Bedford 89 D6 E England, United
Kingdom
Bedum 86 E1 Groningen,
NE Netherlands
Beehive State *see* Utah
Be'er Menuha 119 B7 *prev.* Be'ér
Menuẖa. Southern, S Israel
Be'ér Menuẖa *see* Be'er Menuha
Beernem 87 A5 West-Vlaanderen,
NW Belgium
Beersheba *see* Be'er Sheva
Be'er Sheva 119 A7 *var.* Beersheba,
Ar. Bir es Saba; *prev.* Be'ér Sheva'.
Southern, S Israel
Be'ér Sheva' *see* Be'er Sheva
Beesel 87 D5 Limburg, SE Netherlands
Beeville 49 G4 Texas, SW USA
Bega 149 D7 New South Wales,
SE Australia
Begoml' *see* Byahoml'
Begovat *see* Bekobod
Behagle *see* Laï
Behar *see* Bihār
Beibu Wan *see* Tongking, Gulf of
Beida *see* Al Bayḍā'
Beihai 128 B6 Guangxi Zhuangzu
Zizhiqu, S China
Beijing 128 C3 *var.* Pei-ching, *Eng.*
Peking; *prev.* Pei p'ing. *country
capital* (China) (China) Beijing Shi,
E China
Beilen 86 E2 Drenthe, NE Netherlands
Beira 79 E3 Sofala, C Mozambique
Beirut *see* Beyrouth
Beit Lekhem *see* Bethlehem
Beiuş 108 B3 *Hung.* Belényes. Bihor,
NW Romania
Beja 92 B4 *anc.* Pax Julia. Beja,
SE Portugal
Béjar 92 C3 Castilla-León, N Spain
Bejraburi *see* Phetchaburi
Bekabad *see* Bekobod
Békás *see* Bicaz
Bek-Budi *see* Qarshi
Békéscsaba 99 D7 *Rom.* Bichiş-Ciaba.
Békés, SE Hungary
Bekobod 123 E2 *Rus.* Bekabad;
prev. Begovat. Toshkent Viloyati,
E Uzbekistan
Bela Crkva 100 E3 *Ger.* Weisskirchen,
Hung. Fehértemplom. Vojvodina,
W Serbia
Belarus 107 B6 *off.* Republic of Belarus,
var. Belorussia, *Latv.* Baltkrievija; *prev.*
Belorussian SSR, *Rus.* Belorusskaya
SSR. *country* E Europe

BELARUS
Eastern Europe

Official name Republic of Belarus
Formation 1991 / 1991
Capital Minsk
Population 9.6 million / 120 people
per sq mile (46 people per sq km) / 71%
Total area 80,154 sq. miles
(207,600 sq. km)
Languages Belorussian*, Russian*
Religions Orthodox Christian 60%,
Other 32%, Roman Catholic 8%
Ethnic mix Belorussian 81%, Russian 11%,
Polish 4%, Other 2%, Ukrainian 2%
Government Presidential system
Currency Belorussian rouble = 100 kopeks
Literacy rate 99%
Calorie consumption 3000 calories

Belarus, Republic of *see* Belarus
Belau *see* Palau
Belaya Tserkov' *see* Bila Tserkva

Bełchatów *98 C4 var.* Belchatow.
Łódzkis, C Poland
Belchatow *see* Bełchatów
Belcher, Îles *see* Belcher Islands
Belcher Islands *38 C2 Fr.* Îles Belcher.
island group Nunavut, SE Canada
Beledweyne *73 D5 var.* Belet Huen, *It.*
Belet Uen. Hiiraan, C Somalia
Belém *63 F1 var.* Pará. *state capital* .
Pará, N Brazil
Belén *52 D4* Rivas, SW Nicaragua
Belen *48 D2* New Mexico, SW USA
Belényes *see* Beiuş
Belet Huen/Belet Uen *see* Beledweyne
Belfast *89 B5 Ir. Béal Feirste. national
capital* E Northern Ireland, United
Kingdom
Belfield *44 D2* North Dakota, N USA
Belfort *90 E4* Territoire-de-Belfort,
E France
Belgard *see* Białogard
Belgaum *132 B1* Karnātaka, W India
Belgian Congo *see* Congo (Democratic
Republic of)
België/Belgique *see* Belgium
Belgium *87 B6 off.* Kingdom of Belgium,
Dut. België, *Fr.* Belgique. *country*
NW Europe

BELGIUM
Northwest Europe

Official name Kingdom of Belgium
Formation 1830 / 1919
Capital Brussels
Population 10.5 million / 829 people
per sq mile (320 people per sq km) / 97%
Total area 11,780 sq. miles (30,510 sq. km)
Languages Dutch*, French*, German*
Religions Roman Catholic 88%,
Other 10%, Muslim 2%
Ethnic mix Fleming 58%, Walloon 33%,
Other 6%, Italian 2%, Moroccan 1%
Government Parliamentary system
Currency Euro = 100 cents
Literacy rate 99%
Calorie consumption 3584 calories

Belgium, Kingdom of *see* Belgium
Belgorod *111 A6* Belgorodskaya Oblast',
W Russian Federation
Belgrano II *154 A2 Argentinian research
station* Antarctica
Belice *see* Belize/Belize City
Beligrad *see* Berat
Beli Manastir *100 C3 Hung.*
Pélmonostor; *prev.* Monostor. Osijek-
Baranja, NE Croatia
Bélinga *77 B5* Ogooué-Ivindo,
NE Gabon
Belitung, Pulau *138 C4 island*
W Indonesia
Belize *52 B1 Sp.* Belice; *prev.* British
Honduras, Colony of Belize. *country*
Central America

BELIZE
Central America

Official name Belize
Formation 1981 / 1981
Capital Belmopan
Population 294,385 / 33 people
per sq mile (13 people per sq km) / 48%
Total area 8867 sq. miles (22,966 sq. km)
Languages English*, English Creole,
Spanish, Mayan, Garifuna (Carib)
Religions Roman Catholic 62%,
Other 13%, Anglican 12%,
Methodist 6%, Mennonite 4%,
Seventh-day Adventist 3%
Ethnic mix Mestizo 49%, Creole 25%,
Maya 11%, Other 6%, Garifuna 6%,
Asian Indian 3%
Government Parliamentary system
Currency Belizean dollar = 100 cents
Literacy rate 75%
Calorie consumption 2869 calories

Belize *52 B1 river* Belize/Guatemala
Belize *see* Belize City
Belize City *52 C1 var.* Belize, *Sp.* Belice.
Belize, NE Belize
Belize, Colony of *see* Belize
Beljak *see* Villach
Belkofski *36 B3* Alaska, USA
Belle Île *90 A4 island* NW France

Belle Isle, Strait of *39 G3 strait*
Newfoundland and Labrador, E Canada
Bellenz *see* Bellinzona
Belleville *40 B4* Illinois, N USA
Bellevue *45 F4* Iowa, C USA
Bellevue *46 B2* Washington, NW USA
Bellingham *46 B1* Washington,
NW USA
Belling Hausen Mulde *see* Southeast
Pacific Basin
Bellingshausen Abyssal Plain *see*
Bellingshausen Plain
Bellingshausen Plain *153 F5 var.*
Bellingshausen Abyssal Plain. *abyssal
plain* SE Pacific Ocean
Bellingshausen Sea *154 A3 sea*
Antarctica
Bellinzona *95 B8 Ger.* Bellenz. Ticino,
S Switzerland
Bello *58 B2* Antioquia, W Colombia
Bello Horizonte *see* Belo Horizonte
Bellovacum *see* Beauvais
Bellville *78 B5* Western Cape, SW South
Africa
Belmopan *52 C1 country capital* (Belize)
(Belize) Cayo, C Belize
Belogradchik *104 B1* Vidin,
NW Bulgaria
Belo Horizonte *63 F4 prev.* Bello
Horizonte. *state capital* Minas Gerais,
SE Brazil
Belomorsk *110 B3* Respublika Kareliya,
NW Russian Federation
Beloretsk *111 D6* Respublika
Bashkortostan, W Russian Federation
Belorussia/Belorussian SSR *see* Belarus
Belorusskaya Gryada *see* Byelaruskaya
Hrada
Beloslav *104 D2* Varna, E Bulgaria
Belostok *see* Białystok
Belovár *see* Bjelovar
Belozërsk *110 B4* Vologodskaya Oblast',
NW Russian Federation
Belton *49 G3* Texas, SW USA
Bel'tsy *see* Bălți
Beluchistan *see* Baluchistän
Belukha, Gora *114 D5 mountain*
Kazakhstan/Russian Federation
Belynichi *see* Byalynichy
Belyy, Ostrov *114 D2 island* N Russian
Federation
Bemaraha *79 F3 var.* Plateau du
Bemaraha. *mountain range*
W Madagascar
Bemaraha, Plateau du *see* Bemaraha
Bemidji *45 F1* Minnesota, N USA
Bemmel *86 D4* Gelderland,
SE Netherlands
Benaco *see* Garda, Lago di
Benares *see* Vārānasi
Benavente *92 D2* Castilla-León, N Spain
Bend *46 B3* Oregon, NW USA
Bender *see* Tighina
Bender Beila/Bender Beyla *see*
Bandarbeyla
Bender Cassim/Bender Qaasim *see*
Boosaaso
Bendern *94 E1* NW Liechtenstein Europe
Bendery *see* Tighina
Bendigo *149 C7* Victoria, SE Australia
Beneschau *see* Benešov
Beneški Zaliv *see* Venice, Gulf of
Benešov *99 B5 Ger.* Beneschau.
Středočeský Kraj, W Czech Republic
Benevento *97 D5 anc.* Beneventum,
Malventum. Campania, S Italy
Beneventum *see* Benevento
Bengal, Bay of *124 C4 bay* N Indian
Ocean
Bengalooru *see* Bangalore
Bengasi *see* Banghāzī
Bengazi *see* Banghāzī
Bengbu *128 D5 var.* Peng-pu. Anhui,
E China
Benghazi *see* Banghāzī
Bengkulu *138 B4 prev.* Bengkoeloe,
Benkoelen, Benkulen. Sumatera,
W Indonesia
Benguela *78 A2 var.* Benguella.
Benguela, W Angola
Benguella *see* Benguela
Bengweulu, Lake *see* Bangweulu, Lake
Ben Hope *88 B2 mountain* N Scotland,
United Kingdom
Beni *77 E5* Nord-Kivu, NE Dem. Rep.
Congo

Benidorm *93 F4* País Valenciano,
SE Spain
Beni-Mellal *70 C2* C Morocco
Benin *75 F4 off.* Republic of Benin; *prev.*
Dahomey. *country* W Africa

BENIN
West Africa

Official name Republic of Benin
Formation 1960 / 1960
Capital Porto-Novo
Population 9 million / 211 people
per sq mile (81 people per sq km) / 45%
Total area 43,483 sq. miles (112,620 sq. km)
Languages French*, Fon, Bariba, Yoruba,
Adja, Houeda, Somba
Religions Voodoo 50%, Muslim 30%,
Christian 20%
Ethnic mix Fon 41%, Other 21%, Adja 16%,
Yoruba 12%, Bariba 10%
Government Presidential system
Currency CFA franc = 100 centimes
Literacy rate 35%
Calorie consumption 2548 calories

Benin, Bight of *75 F5 gulf* W Africa
Benin City *75 F5* Edo, SW Nigeria
Benin, Republic of *see* Benin
Beni, Río *61 E3 river* N Bolivia
Beni Suef *see* Banī Suwayf
Ben Nevis *88 C3 mountain* N Scotland,
United Kingdom
Benson *48 B3* Arizona, SW USA
Bent Jbaïl *119 A5 var.* Bint Jubayl.
S Lebanon
Benton *42 B1* Arkansas, C USA
Benue *76 B4 Fr.* Bénoué. *river*
Cameroon/Nigeria
Beograd *100 D3 Eng.* Belgrade. Serbia,
N Serbia
Berane *101 D5 prev.* Ivangrad.
E Montenegro
Berat *101 C6 var.* Berati, *SCr.* Beligrad.
Berat, C Albania
Berătău *see* Berettyó
Berati *see* Berat
Berau, Teluk *139 G4 var.* MacCluer Gulf.
bay Papua, E Indonesia
Berbera *72 D4* Sahil, NW Somalia
Berbérati *77 B5* Mambéré-Kadéï,
SW Central African Republic
Berck-Plage *90 C2* Pas-de-Calais,
N France
Berdichev *see* Berdychiv
Berdyans'k *109 G4 Rus.* Berdyansk;
prev. Osipenko. Zaporiz'ka Oblast',
SE Ukraine
Berdychiv *108 D2 Rus.* Berdichev.
Zhytomyrs'ka Oblast', N Ukraine
Beregovo/Beregszász *see* Berehove
Berehove *108 B3 Cz.* Berehovo,
Hung. Beregszász, *Rus.* Beregovo.
Zakarpats'ka Oblast', W Ukraine
Berehovo *see* Berehove
Bereket *122 B2 prev. Rus.* Gazandzhyk,
Kazandzhik, Gazanjyk. Balkan
Welaýaty, W Turkmenistan
Berettyó *99 D7 Rom.* Barcău; *prev.*
Berătău, Beretău. *river* Hungary/
Romania
Berettyóújfalu *99 D6* Hajdú-Bihar,
E Hungary
Berezhany *108 C2 Pol.* Brzeżany.
Ternopil's'ka Oblast', W Ukraine
Berezina *see* Byerezino
Berezniki *111 D5* Permskaya Oblast',
NW Russian Federation
Berga *93 G2* Cataluña, NE Spain
Bergamo *96 B2 anc.* Bergomum.
Lombardia, N Italy
Bergara *93 E1* País Vasco, N Spain
Bergen *94 D2* Mecklenburg-
Vorpommern, NE Germany
Bergen *86 C2* Noord-Holland,
NW Netherlands
Bergen *85 A5* Hordaland, S Norway
Bergen *see* Mons
Bergerac *91 B5* Dordogne, SW France
Bergeyk *87 C5* Noord-Brabant,
S Netherlands
Bergomum *see* Bergamo
Bergse Maas *86 D4 river* S Netherlands
Beringen *87 C5* Limburg, NE Belgium
Beringov Proliv *see* Bering Strait

Bering Sea *36 A2 sea* N Pacific Ocean
Bering Strait *36 C2 Rus.* Beringov Proliv.
strait Bering Sea/Chukchi Sea
Berja *93 E5* Andalucía, S Spain
Berkeley *47 B6* California, W USA
Berkner Island *154 A2 island* Antarctica
Berkovitsa *104 C2* Montana,
NW Bulgaria
Berlin *94 D3 country capital* (Germany)
(Germany) Berlin, NE Germany
Berlin *41 G2* New Hampshire, NE USA
Berlinchen *see* Barlinek
Bermejo, Río *64 C2 river* N Argentina
Bermeo *93 E1* País Vasco, N Spain
Bermuda *35 D6 var.* Bermuda Islands,
Bermudas; *prev.* Somers Islands. *UK
crown colony* NW Atlantic Ocean
Bermuda Islands *see* Bermuda
Bermuda Rise *35 E6 undersea rise*
C Sargasso Sea
Bermudas *see* Bermuda
Bern *95 A7 Fr.* Berne. *country capital*
(Switzerland) (Switzerland) Bern,
W Switzerland
Bernau *94 D3* Brandenburg,
NE Germany
Bernburg *94 C4* Sachsen-Anhalt,
C Germany
Berne *see* Bern
Berner Alpen *95 A7 var.* Berner
Oberland, *Eng.* Bernese Oberland.
mountain range SW Switzerland
Berner Oberland/Bernese Oberland *see*
Berner Alpen
Bernier Island *147 A5 island* Western
Australia
Beroea *see* Ḥalab
Berry *90 C4 cultural region* C France
Berry Islands *54 C1 island group*
N Bahamas
Bertoua *77 B5* Est, E Cameroon
Beru *145 E2 var.* Peru. *atoll* Tungaru,
W Kiribati
Berwick-upon-Tweed *88 D4* N England,
United Kingdom
Berytus *see* Beyrouth
Besançon *90 D4 anc.* Besontium,
Vesontio. Doubs, E France
Beskra *see* Biskra
Besontium *see* Besançon
Bessarabka *see* Basarabeasca
Besztercze *see* Bistrița
Besztercebánya *see* Banská Bystrica
Betafo *79 G3* Antananarivo,
C Madagascar
Betanzos *92 B1* Galicia, NW Spain
Bethlehem *78 D4* Free State, C South
Africa
Bethlehem *119 B6 var.* Beit Lekhem,
Ar. Bayt Laḥm, *Heb.* Bet Leḥem.
C West Bank
Béticos, Sistemas *92 D4 var.* Sistema
Penibético, *Eng.* Baetic Cordillera,
Baetic Mountains. *mountain range*
S Spain
Bet Leḥem *see* Bethlehem
Bétou *77 C5* Likouala, N Congo
Bette, Picco *71 G4 var.* Bikkū Bittī, *It.*
Picco Bette. *mountain* S Libya
Bette, Picco *see* Bette, Picco
Beulah *40 C2* Michigan, N USA
Beuthen *see* Bytom
Beveren *87 B5* Oost-Vlaanderen,
N Belgium
Beverley *89 D5* E England, United
Kingdom
Bexley *89 B8* Bexley, SE England, United
Kingdom
Beyla *74 D4* SE Guinea
Beyrouth *118 A4 var.* Bayrūt, *Eng.*
Beirut; *anc.* Berytus. *country capital*
(Lebanon) (Lebanon) W Lebanon
Beyşehir *116 B4* Konya, SW Turkey
Beyşehir Gölü *116 B4 lake* C Turkey
Béziers *91 C6 anc.* Baeterrae, Baeterrae
Septimanorum, Julia Beterrae. Hérault,
S France
Bezmein *see* Abadan
Bezwada *see* Vijayawāda
Bhadrāvati *132 C2* Karnātaka, SW India
Bhāgalpur *135 F3* Bihār, NE India
Bhaktapur *135 F3* Central, C Nepal
Bhamo *136 B2 var.* Banmo. Kachin
State, N Burma (Myanmar)
Bhārat *see* India
Bharūch *134 C4* Gujarāt, W India
Bhaunagar *see* Bhāvnagar

INDEX – GAZETTEER: **Bhāvnagar – Bogor**

Bhāvnagar *134 C4 prev.* Bhaunagar. Gujarāt, W India
Bheanntraí, Bá *see* Bantry Bay
Bhopāl *134 D4 state capital* Madhya Pradesh, C India
Bhubaneshwar *135 F5 prev.* Bhubaneswar, Bhuvaneshwar. *state capital* Orissa, E India
Bhubaneswar *see* Bhubaneshwar
Bhuket *see* Phuket
Bhusaval *see* Bhusāwal
Bhusāwal *134 D4 prev.* Bhusaval. Mahārāshtra, C India
Bhutan *135 G3 off.* Kingdom of Bhutan, *var.* Druk-yul. *country* S Asia

BHUTAN
South Asia

Official name Kingdom of Bhutan
Formation 1656 / 1865
Capital Thimphu
Population 2.3 million / 127 people per sq mile (49 people per sq km) / 9%
Total area 18,147 sq. miles (47,000 sq. km)
Languages Dzongkha*, Nepali, Assamese
Religions Mahayana Buddhist 70%, Hindu 24%, Other 6%
Ethnic mix Bhute 50%, Other 25%, Nepalese 25%
Government Mixed monarchical–parliamentary system
Currency Ngultrum = 100 chetrum
Literacy rate 47%
Calorie consumption Not available

Bhutan, Kingdom of *see* Bhutan
Bhuvaneshwar *see* Bhubaneshwar
Biak, Pulau *139 G4 island* E Indonesia
Biała Podlaska *98 E3* Lubelskie, E Poland
Białogard *98 B2 Ger.* Belgard. Zachodnio-pomorskie, NW Poland
Białystok *98 E3 Rus.* Belostok, Bielostok. Podlaskie, NE Poland
Blanco, Monte *see* Blanc, Mont
Biarritz *91 A6* Pyrénées-Atlantiques, SW France
Bicaz *108 C3 Hung.* Békás. Neamţ, NE Romania
Bichiş-Ciaba *see* Békéscsaba
Biddeford *41 G2* Maine, NE USA
Bideford *89 C7* SW England, United Kingdom
Biel *95 A7 Fr.* Bienne. Bern, W Switzerland
Bielefeld *94 B4* Nordrhein-Westfalen, NW Germany
Bielitz/Bielitz-Biala *see* Bielsko-Biała
Bielostok *see* Białystok
Bielsko-Biała *99 C5 Ger.* Bielitz, Bielitz-Biala. Śląskie, S Poland
Bielsk Podlaski *98 E3* Białystok, E Poland
Bien Bien *see* Điện Biên
Biển Đông *see* South China Sea
Biên Hoa *137 E6* Đông Nai, S Vietnam
Bienne *see* Biel
Bienville, Lac *38 D2 lake* Québec, C Canada
Bié Plateau *78 B2 var.* Bié Plateau. *plateau* C Angola
Bié Plateau *see* Bié, Planalto do
Big Cypress Swamp *43 E5 wetland* Florida, SE USA
Bigge Island *146 C2 island* Western Australia
Bighorn Mountains *44 C2 mountain range* Wyoming, C USA
Bighorn River *44 C2 river* Montana/Wyoming, NW USA
Bignona *74 B3* SW Senegal
Bigorra *see* Tarbes
Bigosovo *see* Bihosava
Big Sioux River *45 E2 river* Iowa/South Dakota, N USA
Big Spring *49 E3* Texas, SW USA
Bihać *100 B3* Federacija Bosna I Hercegovina, NW Bosnia and Herzegovina
Bihār *135 F3 prev.* Behar. *cultural region* N India
Bihār *see* Bihār Sharīf
Biharamulo *73 B7* Kagera, NW Tanzania
Bihār Sharīf *135 F3 var.* Bihār. Bihār, N India
Bihosava *107 D5 Rus.* Bigosovo. Vitsyebskaya Voblasts', NW Belarus
Bijeljina *100 C3* Republika Srpska, NE Bosnia and Herzegovina
Bijelo Polje *101 D5* E Montenegro
Bīkāner *134 C3* Rājasthān, NW India
Bikin *115 G4* Khabarovskiy Kray, SE Russian Federation
Bikini Atoll *144 C1 var.* Pikinni. *atoll* Ralik Chain, NW Marshall Islands
Bīkkū Bīttī *see* Bette, Picco
Bilāspur *135 E4* Chhattīsgarh, C India
Biläsuvar *117 H3 Rus.* Bilyasuvar; *prev.* Pushkino. SE Azerbaijan
Bila Tserkva *109 E2 Rus.* Belaya Tserkov'. Kyyivs'ka Oblast', N Ukraine
Bilauktaung Range *137 C6 var.* Thanintari Taungdan. *mountain range* Burma (Myanmar)/Thailand
Bilbao *93 E1 Basq.* Bilbo. País Vasco, N Spain
Bilbo *see* Bilbao
Bilecik *116 B3* Bilecik, NW Turkey
Billings *44 C2* Montana, NW USA
Bilma, Grand Erg de *75 H3 desert* NE Niger
Biloela *148 D4* Queensland, E Australia
Biloxi *42 C3* Mississippi, S USA
Biltine *76 C3* Biltine, E Chad
Bilwi *see* Puerto Cabezas
Bilyasuvar *see* Biläsuvar
Bilzen *87 D6* Limburg, NE Belgium
Bimini Islands *54 C1 island group* W Bahamas
Binche *87 B7* Hainaut, S Belgium
Bindloe Island *see* Marchena, Isla
Bin Ghalfān, Jazā'ir *see* Ḥalāniyāt, Juzur al
Binghamton *41 F3* New York, NE USA
Bingöl *117 E3* Bingöl, E Turkey
Bint Jubayl *see* Bent Jbaïl
Bintulu *138 D3* Sarawak, East Malaysia
Binzhou *128 D4* Shandong, E China
Bío Bío, Río *65 B5 river* C Chile
Bioco, Isla de *77 A5 var.* Bioko, *Eng.* Fernando Po, *Sp.* Fernando Póo; *prev.* Macías Nguema Biyogo. *island* NW Equatorial Guinea
Bioko *see* Bioco, Isla de
Birāk *71 F3 var.* Brak. C Libya
Birao *76 D3* Vakaga, NE Central African Republic
Birātnagar *135 F3* Eastern, SE Nepal
Bir es Saba *see* Be'er Sheva
Bīrjand *120 E3* Khorāsān-e Janūbī, E Iran
Birkenfeld *95 A5* Rheinland-Pfalz, SW Germany
Birkenhead *89 C5* NW England, United Kingdom
Bîrlad *see* Bârlad
Birmingham *89 C6* C England, United Kingdom
Birmingham *42 C2* Alabama, S USA
Bir Moghrein *see* Bîr Mogreïn
Bîr Mogreïn *74 C1 var.* Bir Moghrein; *prev.* Fort-Trinquet. Tiris Zemmour, N Mauritania
Birnie Island *145 E3 atoll* Phoenix Islands, C Kiribati
Birnin Konni *75 F3 var.* Birni-Nkonni. Tahoua, SW Niger
Birni-Nkonni *see* Birnin Konni
Birobidzhan *115 G4* Yevreyskaya Avtonomnaya Oblast', SE Russian Federation
Birsen *see* Biržai
Birsk *111 D5* Respublika Bashkortostan, W Russian Federation
Biržai *106 C4 Ger.* Birsen. Panevėžys, NE Lithuania
Birżebbuġa *102 B5* SE Malta
Bisanthe *see* Tekirdağ
Bisbee *48 B3* Arizona, SW USA
Biscaia, Baía de *see* Biscay, Bay of
Biscay, Bay of *80 B4 Sp.* Golfo de Vizcaya, *Port.* Baía de Biscaia. *bay* France/Spain
Biscay Plain *80 B3 abyssal plain* SE Bay of Biscay
Bischofsburg *see* Biskupiec
Bishah, Wadi *121 B5 dry watercourse* C Saudi Arabia
Bishkek *123 G2 var.* Pishpek; *prev.* Frunze. *country capital* (Kyrgyzstan) (Kyrgyzstan) Chuyskaya Oblast', N Kyrgyzstan
Bishop's Lynn *see* King's Lynn
Bishrī, Jabal *118 D3 mountain range* E Syria
Biskara *see* Biskra
Biskra *71 E2 var.* Beskra, Biskara. NE Algeria
Biskupiec *98 D2 Ger.* Bischofsburg. Warmińsko-Mazurskie, NE Poland
Bislig *139 F2* Mindanao, S Philippines
Bismarck *45 E2 state capital* North Dakota, N USA
Bismarck Archipelago *144 B3 island group* NE Papua New Guinea
Bismarck Sea *144 B3 sea* W Pacific Ocean
Bisnulok *see* Phitsanulok
Bissau *74 B4 country capital* (Guinea-Bissau) (Guinea-Bissau) W Guinea-Bissau
Bistriţa *108 B3 Ger.* Bistritz, *Hung.* Beszterce; *prev.* Nösen. Bistriţa-Năsăud, N Romania
Bistritz *see* Bistriţa
Bitam *77 B5* Woleu-Ntem, N Gabon
Bitburg *95 A5* Rheinland-Pfalz, SW Germany
Bitlis *117 F3* Bitlis, SE Turkey
Bitoeng *see* Bitung
Bitola *101 D6 Turk.* Monastir; *prev.* Bitolj. S FYR Macedonia
Bitolj *see* Bitola
Bitonto *97 D5 anc.* Butuntum. Puglia, SE Italy
Bitterroot Range *46 D2 mountain range* Idaho/Montana, NW USA
Bitung *139 F3 prev.* Bitoeng. Sulawesi, C Indonesia
Biu *75 H4* Borno, E Nigeria
Biwa-ko *131 C6 lake* Honshū, SW Japan
Bizerta *see* Bizerte
Bizerte *71 E1 Ar.* Banzart, *Eng.* Bizerta. N Tunisia
Bjelovar *100 B2 Hung.* Belovár. Bjelovar-Bilogora, N Croatia
Bjeshkët e Namuna *see* North Albanian Alps
Björneborg *see* Pori
Bjørnøya *83 F3 Eng.* Bear Island. *island* N Norway
Blackall *148 C4* Queensland, E Australia
Black Drin *101 D6 Alb.* Lumi i Drinit të Zi, *SCr.* Crni Drim. *river* Albania/FYR Macedonia
Blackfoot *46 E4* Idaho, NW USA
Black Forest *95 B6 Eng.* Black Forest. *mountain range* SW Germany
Black Forest *see* Schwarzwald
Black Hills *44 D3 mountain range* South Dakota/Wyoming, N USA
Blackpool *89 C5* NW England, United Kingdom
Black Range *48 C2 mountain range* New Mexico, SW USA
Black River *54 A5* W Jamaica
Black River *136 C3 Chin.* Babian Jiang, Lixian Jiang, *Fr.* Rivière Noire, *Vtn.* Sông Đa. *river* China/Vietnam
Black Rock Desert *47 C5 desert* Nevada, W USA
Black Sand Desert *see* Garagum
Black Sea *116 B1 var.* Euxine Sea, *Bul.* Cherno More, *Rom.* Marea Neagră, *Rus.* Chernoye More, *Turk.* Karadeniz, *Ukr.* Chorne More. *sea* Asia/Europe
Black Sea Lowland *109 E4 Ukr.* Prychornomor'ska Nyzovyna. *depression* SE Europe
Black Volta *75 E4 var.* Borongo, Mouhoun, Moun Hou, *Fr.* Volta Noire. *river* W Africa
Blackwater *89 A6 Ir.* An Abhainn Mhór. *river* S Ireland
Blackwater State *see* Nebraska
Blagoevgrad *104 C3 prev.* Gorna Dzhumaya. Blagoevgrad, W Bulgaria
Blagoveshchensk *115 G4* Amurskaya Oblast', SE Russian Federation
Blake Plateau *35 D6 var.* Blake Terrace. *undersea plateau* W Atlantic Ocean
Blake Terrace *see* Blake Plateau
Blanca, Bahía *65 C5 bay* E Argentina
Blanca, Costa *93 F4 physical region* SE Spain
Blanche, Lake *149 B5 lake* South Australia
Blanc, Mont *91 D5 It.* Monte Bianco. *mountain* France/Italy
Blanco, Cape *46 A4 headland* Oregon, NW USA
Blanes *93 G2* Cataluña, NE Spain
Blankenberge *87 A5* West-Vlaanderen, NW Belgium
Blankenheim *95 A5* Nordrhein-Westfalen, W Germany
Blanquilla, Isla *59 E1 var.* La Blanquilla. *island* N Venezuela
Blanquilla, La *see* Blanquilla, Isla
Blantyre *79 E2 var.* Blantyre-Limbe. Southern, S Malawi
Blantyre-Limbe *see* Blantyre
Blaricum *86 C3* Noord-Holland, C Netherlands
Blatnitsa *see* Durankulak
Blenheim *151 C5* Marlborough, South Island, New Zealand
Blesae *see* Blois
Blida *70 D2 var.* El Boulaida, El Boulaïda. N Algeria
Bloemfontein *78 C4 var.* Mangaung. *country capital* (South Africa-judicial capital) (South Africa-judicial capital) Free State, C South Africa
Blois *90 C4 anc.* Blesae. Loir-et-Cher, C France
Bloomfield *48 C1* New Mexico, SW USA
Bloomington *40 B4* Illinois, N USA
Bloomington *40 C4* Indiana, N USA
Bloomington *45 F2* Minnesota, N USA
Bloomsbury *148 D3* Queensland, NE Australia
Bluefield *40 D5* West Virginia, NE USA
Bluefields *53 E3* Región Autónoma Atlántico Sur, SE Nicaragua
Bluegrass State *see* Kentucky
Blue Hen State *see* Delaware
Blue Law State *see* Connecticut
Blue Mountain Peak *54 B5 mountain* E Jamaica
Blue Mountains *46 C3 mountain range* Oregon/Washington, NW USA
Blue Nile *72 C4 var.* Abai, Bahr el, Azraq, *Amh.* Ābay Wenz, *Ar.* An Nīl al Azraq. *river* Ethiopia/Sudan
Blumenau *63 E5* Santa Catarina, S Brazil
Blythe *47 D8* California, W USA
Blytheville *42 C1* Arkansas, C USA
Bo *74 C4* S Sierra Leone
Boaco *52 D3* Boaco, S Nicaragua
Boa Vista *62 D1 state capital* Roraima, NW Brazil
Boa Vista *74 A3 island* Ilhas de Barlavento, E Cape Verde
Bobaomby, Tanjona *79 G2 Fr.* Cap d'Ambre. *headland* N Madagascar
Bobigny *90 E1* Seine-St-Denis, N France
Bobo-Dioulasso *74 D4* SW Burkina Faso
Bobrinets *see* Bobrynets'
Bobruysk *see* Babruysk
Bobrynets' *109 E3 Rus.* Bobrinets. Kirovohrads'ka Oblast', C Ukraine
Boca Raton *43 F5* Florida, SE USA
Bocay *52 D2* Jinotega, N Nicaragua
Bocheykovo *see* Bacheykava
Bocholt *94 A4* Nordrhein-Westfalen, W Germany
Bochum *94 A4* Nordrhein-Westfalen, W Germany
Bocşa *108 A4 Ger.* Bokschen, *Hung.* Boksánbánya. Caraş-Severin, SW Romania
Bodaybo *115 F4* Irkutskaya Oblast', E Russian Federation
Bodegas *see* Babahoyo
Boden *84 D4* Norrbotten, N Sweden
Bodensee *see* Constance, Lake, C Europe
Bodmin *89 C7* SW England, United Kingdom
Bodø *84 C3* Nordland, C Norway
Bodrum *116 A4* Muğla, SW Turkey
Boeloekoemba *see* Bulukumba
Boende *77 C5* Equateur, C Dem. Rep. Congo
Boeroe *see* Buru, Pulau
Boetoeng *see* Buton, Pulau
Bogale *136 B4* Ayeyarwady, SW Burma (Myanmar)
Bogalusa *42 B3* Louisiana, S USA
Bogatynia *98 B4 Ger.* Reichenau. Dolnośląskie, SW Poland
Boğazlıyan *116 D3* Yozgat, C Turkey
Bogendorf *see* Łuków
Bogor *138 C5 Dut.* Buitenzorg. Jawa, C Indonesia

Bogotá 58 B3 prev. Santa Fe, Santa
Fe de Bogotá. country capital
(Colombia) (Colombia) Cundinamarca,
C Colombia
Bogushëvsk see Bahushewsk
Boguslav see Bohuslav
Bo Hai 128 D4 var. Gulf of Chihli. gulf
NE China
Bohemia 99 A5 Cz. Čechy, Ger. Böhmen.
W Czech Republic
Bohemian Forest 95 C5 Cz. Český Les,
Šumava, Ger. Böhmerwald. mountain
range C Europe
Böhmen see Bohemia
Böhmerwald see Bohemian Forest
Böhmisch-Krumau see Český Krumlov
Bohol Sea 139 E2 var. Mindanao Sea. sea
S Philippines
Bohuslav 109 E2 Rus. Boguslav.
Kyyïvs'ka Oblast', N Ukraine
Boise 46 D3 var. Boise City. state capital
Idaho, NW USA
Boise City 49 E1 Oklahoma, C USA
Boise City see Boise
Bois, Lac des see Woods, Lake of the
Bois-le-Duc see 's-Hertogenbosch
Boizenburg 94 C3 Mecklenburg-
Vorpommern, N Germany
Bojador see Boujdour
Bojnûrd 120 D2 var. Bujnurd.
Khorāsān-e Shemālī, N Iran
Bokāro 135 F4 Jhārkhand, N India
Boké 74 C4 W Guinea
Bokhara see Buxoro
Boknafjorden 85 A6 fjord S Norway
Boksánbánya/Bokschen see Bocşa
Bol 76 B3 Lac, W Chad
Bolgatanga 75 E4 N Ghana
Bolgrad see Bolhrad
Bolhrad 108 D4 Rus. Bolgrad. Odes'ka
Oblast', SW Ukraine
Bolívar, Pico 58 C2 mountain
W Venezuela
Bolivia 61 F3 off. Republic of Bolivia.
country W South America

BOLIVIA
South America

Official name Republic of Bolivia
Formation 1825 / 1938
Capital La Paz (administrative);
Sucre (judicial)
Population 9.5 million / 23 people
per sq mile (9 people per sq km) / 64%
Total area 424,162 sq. miles
(1,098,580 sq. km)
Languages Aymara*, Quechua*, Spanish*
Religions Roman Catholic 93%, Other 7%
Ethnic mix Quechua 37%, Aymara 32%,
Mixed race 13%, European 10%, Other 8%
Government Presidential system
Currency Boliviano = 100 centavos
Literacy rate 87%
Calorie consumption 2235 calories

Bolivia, Republic of see Bolivia
Bollène 91 D6 Vaucluse, SE France
Bollnäs 85 C5 Gävleborg, C Sweden
Bollon 149 D5 Queensland, C Australia
Bologna 96 C3 Emilia-Romagna,
N Italy
Bol'shevik see Bal'shavik
Bol'shevik, Ostrov 115 E2 island
Severnaya Zemlya, N Russian
Federation
Bol'shezemel'skaya Tundra 110 E3
physical region N Russian Federation
Bol'shoy Lyakhovskiy, Ostrov 115 F2
island NE Russian Federation
Bolton 89 D5 prev. Bolton-le-Moors.
NW England, United Kingdom
Bolton-le-Moors see Bolton
Bolu 116 B3 Bolu, NW Turkey
Bolungarvík 83 E4 Vestfirðhir,
NW Iceland
Bolyarovo 104 D3 prev. Pashkeni.
Yambol, E Bulgaria
Bolzano 96 C1 Ger. Bozen; anc.
Bauzanum. Trentino-Alto Adige,
N Italy
Boma 77 B6 Bas-Congo, W Dem. Rep.
Congo
Bombay see Mumbai
Bomu 76 D4 var. Mbomou, Mbomu,
M'Bomu. river Central African
Republic/Dem. Rep. Congo

Bonaire 55 F5 Dutch autonomous region
S Caribbean Sea
Bonanza 52 D2 Región Autónoma
Atlántico Norte, NE Nicaragua
Bonaparte Archipelago 146 C2 island
group Western Australia
Bon, Cap 102 D3 headland N Tunisia
Bonda 77 B6 Ogooué-Lolo, C Gabon
Bondoukou 75 E4 E Côte d'Ivoire
Bône see Watampone, Indonesia
Bone, Teluk 139 E4 bay Sulawesi,
C Indonesia
Bongaigaon 135 G3 Assam, NE India
Bongo, Massif des 76 D4 var. Chaîne des
Mongos. mountain range NE Central
African Republic
Bongor 76 B3 Mayo-Kébbi, SW Chad
Bonifacio 91 E7 Corse, France,
C Mediterranean Sea
**Bonifacio, Bocche de/Bonifacio,
Bouches de** see Bonifacio, Strait of
Bonifacio, Strait of 96 A4 Fr. Bouches
de Bonifacio, It. Bocche di Bonifacio.
strait C Mediterranean Sea
Bonn 95 A5 Nordrhein-Westfalen,
W Germany
Bononia see Vidin, Bulgaria
Bononia see Boulogne-sur-Mer, France
Boosaaso 72 E4 var. Bandar Kassim,
Bender Qaasim, Bosaso, It. Bender
Cassim. Bari, N Somalia
Boothia Felix see Boothia Peninsula
Boothia, Gulf of 37 F2 gulf Nunavut,
NE Canada
Boothia Peninsula 37 F2 prev. Boothia
Felix. peninsula Nunavut, NE Canada
Boppard 95 A5 Rheinland-Pfalz,
W Germany
Boquete 53 E5 var. Bajo Boquete.
Chiriquí, W Panama
Boquillas 50 D2 var. Boquillas del
Carmen. Coahuila, NE Mexico
Boquillas del Carmen see Boquillas
Bor 100 E4 Serbia, E Serbia
Bor 73 B5 Jonglei, S Sudan
Borås 85 B7 Västra Götaland, S Sweden
Borbetomagus see Worms
Borborema, Planalto da 56 E3 plateau
NE Brazil
Bordeaux 91 B5 anc. Burdigala.
Gironde, SW France
Bordj Omar Driss 71 E3 E Algeria
Borgå see Porvoo
Børgefjell 84 C4 mountain range
C Norway
Borger 86 E2 Drenthe, NE Netherlands
Borger 49 E1 Texas, SW USA
Borgholm 85 C7 Kalmar, S Sweden
Borgo Maggiore 96 E1 NW San Marino
Borislav see Boryslav
Borisoglebsk 111 B6 Voronezhskaya
Oblast', W Russian Federation
Borisov see Barysaw
Borlänge 85 C6 Dalarna, C Sweden
Borne 86 E3 Overijssel, E Netherlands
Borneo 138 C4 island Brunei/Indonesia/
Malaysia
Bornholm 85 B8 island E Denmark
Borohoro Shan 126 B2 mountain range
NW China
Borongo see Black Volta
Boron'ki see Baron'ki
Borosjenő see Ineu
Borovan 104 C2 Vratsa, NW Bulgaria
Borovichi 110 B4 Novgorodskaya
Oblast', W Russian Federation
Borovo 100 C3 Vukovar-Srijem,
NE Croatia
Borşa 108 C3 Hung. Borsa. Maramureş,
N Romania
Boryslav 108 B2 Pol. Borysław, Rus.
Borislav. L'vivs'ka Oblast', NW Ukraine
Borysław see Boryslav
Bosanska Dubica 100 B3 var. Kozarska
Dubica. Republika Srpska, NW Bosnia
and Herzegovina
Bosanska Gradiška 100 B3 var.
Gradiška. Republika Srpska, N Bosnia
and Herzegovina
Bosanski Novi 100 B3 var. Novi Grad.
Republika Srpska, NW Bosnia and
Herzegovina
Bosanski Šamac 100 C3 var. Šamac.
Republika Srpska, N Bosnia and
Herzegovina
Bosaso see Boosaaso

Bösing see Pezinok
Boskovice 99 B5 Ger. Boskowitz.
Jihomoravský Kraj, SE Czech Republic
Boskowitz see Boskovice
Bosna 100 C4 river N Bosnia and
Herzegovina
Bosnia and Herzegovina 100 B3 off.
Republic of Bosnia and Herzegovina.
country SE Europe

BOSNIA & HERZEGOVINA
Southeast Europe

Official name Bosnia and Herzegovina
Formation 1992 / 1992
Capital Sarajevo
Population 3.9 million / 198 people
per sq mile (76 people per sq km) / 45%
Total area 19,741 sq. miles (51,129 sq. km)
Languages Bosnian*, Croatian*, Serbian*
Religions Muslim (mainly Sunni) 40%,
Orthodox Christian 31%, Roman
Catholic 15%, Other 10%, Protestant 4%
Ethnic mix Bosniak 44%, Serb 31%,
Croat 17%, Other 8%
Government Parliamentary system
Currency Marka = 100 pfeninga
Literacy rate 97%
Calorie consumption 2894 calories

Bosnia and Herzegovina, Republic of
see Bosnia and Herzegovina
Boso-hanto 131 D6 peninsula Honshū,
S Japan
Bosphorus/Bosporus see İstanbul Boğazı
Bosporus 116 B2 var. Bosporus
Thracius, Eng. Bosphorus, Bosporus,
Turk. Karadeniz Boğazı. strait
NW Turkey
Bosporus Cimmerius see Kerch Strait
Bosporus Thracius see İstanbul Boğazı
Bossangoa 76 C4 Ouham, C Central
African Republic
Bossembélé 76 C4 Ombella-Mpoko,
C Central African Republic
Bossier City 42 A2 Louisiana, S USA
Bosten Hu 126 C3 var. Bagrax Hu. lake
NW China
Boston 89 E6 prev. St.Botolph's Town.
E England, United Kingdom
Boston 41 G3 state capital Massachusetts,
NE USA
Boston Mountains 42 B1 mountain
range Arkansas, C USA
Bostyn' see Bastyn'
Botany 148 E2 New South Wales,
E Australia
Botany Bay 148 E2 inlet New South
Wales, SE Australia
Boteti 78 C3 var. Botletle. river
N Botswana
Bothnia, Gulf of 85 D5 Fin. Pohjanlahti,
Swe. Bottniska Viken. gulf N Baltic Sea
Botletle see Boteti
Botoşani 108 C3 Hung. Botosány.
Botoşani, NE Romania
Botosány see Botoşani
Botou 128 C4 prev. Bozhen. Hebei,
E China
Botrange 87 D6 mountain E Belgium
Botswana 78 C3 off. Republic of
Botswana. country S Africa

BOTSWANA
Southern Africa

Official name Republic of Botswana
Formation 1966 / 1966
Capital Gaborone
Population 1.8 million / 8 people
per sq mile (3 people per sq km) / 52%
Total area 231,803 sq. miles
(600,370 sq. km)
Languages English*, Setswana, Shona,
San, Khoikhoi, isiNdebele
Religions Traditional beliefs 50%,
Christian (mainly Protestant) 30%,
Other (including Muslim) 20%
Ethnic mix Tswana 98%, Other 2%
Government Presidential system
Currency Pula = 100 thebe
Literacy rate 81%
Calorie consumption 2151 calories

Botswana, Republic of see
Botswana
Bottniska Viken see Bothnia, Gulf of

Bouar 76 B4 Nana-Mambéré, W Central
African Republic
Bou Craa 70 B3 var. Bu Craa.
NW Western Sahara
Bougainville Island 142 B3 island
NE Papua New Guinea
Bougaroun, Cap 102 C3 headland
NE Algeria
Bougouni 74 D4 Sikasso, SW Mali
Boujdour 70 A3 var. Bojador.
W Western Sahara
Boulder 44 C4 Colorado, C USA
Boulder 44 B2 Montana, NW USA
Boulogne see Boulogne-sur-Mer
Boulogne-Billancourt 90 D1 Île-de-
France, N France Europe
Boulogne-sur-Mer 90 C2 var.
Boulogne; anc. Bononia, Gesoriacum,
Gessoriacum. Pas-de-Calais, N France
Boûmdeïd 74 C3 var. Boumdeït. Assaba,
S Mauritania
Boumdeït see Boûmdeïd
Boundiali 74 D4 N Côte d'Ivoire
Bountiful 44 B4 Utah, W USA
Bounty Basin see Bounty Trough
Bounty Islands 142 D5 island group
S New Zealand
Bounty Trough 152 C5 var. Bounty
Basin. trough S Pacific Ocean
Bourbonnais 90 C4 cultural region
C France
Bourbon Vendée see la Roche-sur-Yon
Bourg see Bourg-en-Bresse
Bourgas see Burgas
Bourge-en-Bresse see Bourg-en-Bresse
Bourg-en-Bresse 91 D5 var. Bourg,
Bourge-en-Bresse. Ain, E France
Bourges 90 C4 anc. Avaricum. Cher,
C France
Bourgogne 90 C4 Eng. Burgundy.
cultural region E France
Bourke 149 C5 New South Wales,
SE Australia
Bournemouth 89 D7 S England, United
Kingdom
Boutilimit 74 C3 Trarza, SW Mauritania
Bouvet Island 67 D7 Norwegian
dependency S Atlantic Ocean
Bowen 148 D3 Queensland, NE Australia
Bowling Green 40 B5 Kentucky, S USA
Bowling Green 40 C3 Ohio, N USA
Boxmeer 86 D4 Noord-Brabant,
SE Netherlands
Boyarka 109 E2 Kyyivs'ka Oblast',
N Ukraine
Boysun 123 E3 Rus. Baysun.
Surkhondaryo Viloyati, S Uzbekistan
Bozeman 44 B2 Montana, NW USA
Bozen see Bolzano
Bozhen see Botou
Bozüyük 116 B3 Bilecik, NW Turkey
Brač 100 B4 var. Brach, It. Brazza; anc.
Brattia. island S Croatia
Bracara Augusta see Braga
Brach see Brač
Bradford 89 D5 N England, United
Kingdom
Brady 49 F3 Texas, SW USA
Braga 92 B2 anc. Bracara Augusta.
Braga, NW Portugal
Bragança 92 C2 Eng. Braganza; anc. Julio
Briga. Bragança, NE Portugal
Braganza see Bragança
Brahestad see Raahe
Brahmanbaria 135 G4 Chittagong,
E Bangladesh
Brahmapur 135 F5 Orissa, E India
Brahmaputra 135 H3 var. Padma,
Tsangpo, Ben. Jamuna, Chin. Yarlung
Zangbo Jiang, Ind. Bramaputra,
Dihang, Siang. river S Asia
Bräila 108 D4 Bräila, E Romania
Braine-le-Comte 87 B6 Hainaut,
SW Belgium
Brainerd 45 F2 Minnesota, N USA
Brak see Birāk
Bramaputra see Brahmaputra
Brampton 38 D5 Ontario, S Canada
Branco, Rio 56 C2 river N Brazil
Brandberg 78 A3 mountain
NW Namibia
Brandenburg 94 C3 var. Brandenburg
an der Havel. Brandenburg,
NE Germany
Brandenburg an der Havel see
Brandenburg
Brandon 37 F5 Manitoba, S Canada

Braniewo *98 D2 Ger.* Braunsberg. Warmińsko-mazurskie, N Poland
Brasil *see* Brazil
Brasília *63 F3 country capital* (Brazil) (Brazil) Distrito Federal, C Brazil
Brasil, República Federativa do *see* Brazil
Braşov *108 C4 Ger.* Kronstadt, *Hung.* Brassó; *prev.* Oraşul Stalin. Braşov, C Romania
Brassó *see* Braşov
Bratislava *99 C6 Ger.* Pressburg, *Hung.* Pozsony. *country capital* (Slovakia) (Slovakia) Bratislavský Kraj, W Slovakia
Bratsk *115 E4* Irkutskaya Oblast', C Russian Federation
Brattia *see* Brač
Braunsberg *see* Braniewo
Braunschweig *94 C4 Eng./Fr.* Brunswick. Niedersachsen, N Germany
Brava *see* Baraawe
Brava, Costa *93 H2 coastal region* NE Spain
Bravo del Norte, Río/Bravo, Río *see* Grande, Rio
Bravo, Río *50 C1 river* Mexico/USA North America
Brawley *47 D8* California, W USA
Brazil *62 C2 off.* Federative Republic of Brazil, *Port.* República Federativa do Brasil, *Sp.* Brasil; *prev.* United States of Brazil. *country* South America
Brazil Basin *67 C5 var.* Brazilian Basin, Brazil'skaya Kotlovina. *undersea basin* W Atlantic Ocean

BRAZIL
South America

Official name Federative Republic of Brazil
Formation 1822 / 1828
Capital Brasília
Population 191 million / 59 people per sq mile (23 people per sq km) / 84%
Total area 3,286,470 sq. miles (8,511,965 sq. km)
Languages Portuguese*, German, Italian, Spanish, Polish, Japanese, Amerindian languages
Religions Roman Catholic 74%, Protestant 15%, Atheist 7%, Other 4%
Ethnic mix White 54%, Mixed race 38%, Black 6%, Other 2%
Government Presidential system
Currency Real = 100 centavos
Literacy rate 89%
Calorie consumption 3049 calories

Brazil, Federative Republic of *see* Brazil
Brazilian Basin *see* Brazil Basin
Brazilian Highlands *63 F3 var.* Brazilian Highlands. *mountain range* E Brazil
Brazilian Highlands *see* Central, Planalto
Brazil'skaya Kotlovina *see* Brazil Basin
Brazil, United States of *see* Brazil
Brazos River *49 G3 river* Texas, SW USA
Brazza *see* Brač
Brazzaville *77 B6 country capital* (Congo) (Congo) Capital District, S Congo
Brčko *100 C3* Republika Srpska, NE Bosnia and Herzegovina
Brecht *87 C5* Antwerpen, N Belgium
Brecon Beacons *89 C6 mountain range* S Wales, United Kingdom
Breda *86 C4* Noord-Brabant, S Netherlands
Bree *87 D5* Limburg, NE Belgium
Bregalnica *101 E6 river* E FYR Macedonia
Bregenz *57 B7 anc.* Brigantium. Vorarlberg, W Austria
Bregovo *104 B1* Vidin, NW Bulgaria
Bremen *94 B3 Fr.* Brême. Bremen, NW Germany
Bremerhaven *94 B3* Bremen, NW Germany
Bremerton *46 B2* Washington, NW USA
Brenham *49 G3* Texas, SW USA
Brenner, Col de/Brennero, Passo del *see* Brenner Pass
Brenner Pass *96 C1 var.* Brenner Sattel, *Fr.* Col du Brenner, *Ger.* Brennerpass, *It.* Passo del Brennero. *pass* Austria/Italy
Brennerpass *see* Brenner Pass

Brenner Sattel *see* Brenner Pass
Brescia *96 B2 anc.* Brixia. Lombardia, N Italy
Breslau *see* Wrocław
Bressanone *96 C1 Ger.* Brixen. Trentino-Alto Adige, N Italy
Brest *107 A6 Pol.* Brześć nad Bugiem, *Rus.* Brest-Litovsk; *prev.* Brześć Litewski. Brestskaya Voblasts', SW Belarus
Brest *90 A3* Finistère, NW France
Brest-Litovsk *see* Brest
Bretagne *90 A3 Eng.* Brittany, *Lat.* Britannia Minor. *cultural region* NW France
Breukelen, Kap *see* Yangikishlaf
Brewton *42 C3* Alabama, S USA
Brezhnev *see* Naberezhnyye Chelny
Brezovo *104 D2 prev.* Abrashlare. Plovdiv, C Bulgaria
Bria *76 D4* Haute-Kotto, C Central African Republic
Briançon *91 D5 anc.* Brigantio. Hautes-Alpes, SE France
Bricgstow *see* Bristol
Bridgeport *41 F3* Connecticut, NE USA
Bridgetown *55 G2 country capital* (Barbados) (Barbados) SW Barbados
Bridlington *89 D5* E England, United Kingdom
Bridport *89 D7* S England, United Kingdom
Brieg *see* Brzeg
Brig *95 A7 Fr.* Brigue, *It.* Briga. Valais, SW Switzerland
Briga *see* Brig
Brigantio *see* Briançon
Brigantium *see* Bregenz
Brigham City *44 B3* Utah, W USA
Brighton *89 E7* SE England, United Kingdom
Brighton *44 D4* Colorado, C USA
Brigue *see* Brig
Brindisi *97 E5 anc.* Brundisium, Brundusium. Puglia, SE Italy
Briovera *see* St-Lô
Brisbane *149 E5 state capital* Queensland, E Australia
Bristol *89 D7 anc.* Bricgstow. SW England, United Kingdom
Bristol *41 F3* Connecticut, NE USA
Bristol *40 D5* Tennessee, S USA
Bristol Bay *36 B3 bay* Alaska, USA
Bristol Channel *89 C7 inlet* England/Wales, United Kingdom
Britain *80 C3 var.* Great Britain. *island* United Kingdom
Britannia Minor *see* Bretagne
British Columbia *36 D4 Fr.* Colombie-Britannique. *province* SW Canada
British Guiana *see* Guyana
British Honduras *see* Belize
British Indian Ocean Territory *141 B5 UK dependent territory* C Indian Ocean
British Isles *89 island group* NW Europe
British North Borneo *see* Sabah
British Solomon Islands Protectorate *see* Solomon Islands
British Virgin Islands *55 F3 var.* Virgin Islands. *UK dependent territory* E West Indies
Brittany *see* Bretagne
Briva Curretia *see* Brive-la-Gaillarde
Briva Isarae *see* Pontoise
Brive *see* Brive-la-Gaillarde
Brive-la-Gaillarde *91 C5 prev.* Brive; *anc.* Briva Curretia. Corrèze, C France
Brixen *see* Bressanone
Brixia *see* Brescia
Brno *99 B5 Ger.* Brünn. Jihomoravský Kraj, SE Czech Republic
Brocēni *106 B3* Saldus, SW Latvia
Brod/Bród *see* Slavonski Brod
Brodeur Peninsula *37 F2 peninsula* Baffin Island, Nunavut, NE Canada
Brod na Savi *see* Slavonski Brod
Brodnica *98 C3 Ger.* Buddenbrock. Kujawski-pomorskie, C Poland
Broek-in-Waterland *86 C3* Noord-Holland, C Netherlands
Broken Arrow *49 G1* Oklahoma, C USA
Broken Bay *148 E1 bay* New South Wales, SE Australia
Broken Hill *149 B6* New South Wales, SE Australia
Broken Ridge *141 D6 undersea plateau* S Indian Ocean

Bromberg *see* Bydgoszcz
Bromley *89 B8* United Kingdom
Brookhaven *42 B3* Mississippi, S USA
Brookings *45 F3* South Dakota, N USA
Brooks Range *36 D2 mountain range* Alaska, USA
Brookton *147 B6* Western Australia
Broome *146 B3* Western Australia
Broomfield *44 D4* Colorado, C USA
Broucsella *see* Brussel/Bruxelles
Brovary *109 E2* Kyyivs'ka Oblast', N Ukraine
Brownfield *49 E2* Texas, SW USA
Brownsville *49 G5* Texas, SW USA
Brownwood *49 F3* Texas, SW USA
Brozha *107 D7* Mahilyowskaya Voblasts' E Belarus
Bruges *see* Brugge
Brugge *87 A5 Fr.* Bruges. West-Vlaanderen, NW Belgium
Brummen *86 D3* Gelderland, E Netherlands
Brundisium/Brundusium *see* Brindisi
Brunei *138 D3 off.* Brunei Darussalam, *Mal.* Negara Brunei Darussalam. *country* SE Asia

BRUNEI
Southeast Asia

Official name Brunei Darussalam
Formation 1984 / 1984
Capital Bandar Seri Begawan
Population 374,577 / 184 people per sq mile (71 people per sq km) / 77%
Total area 2228 sq. miles (5770 sq. km)
Languages Malay*, English, Chinese
Religions Muslim (mainly Sunni) 66%, Buddhist 14%, Other 10%, Christian 10%
Ethnic mix Malay 67%, Chinese 16%, Other 11%, Indigenous 6%
Government Monarchy
Currency Brunei dollar = 100 cents
Literacy rate 93%
Calorie consumption 2855 calories

Brunei Darussalam *see* Brunei
Brunei Town *see* Bandar Seri Begawan
Brünn *see* Brno
Brunner, Lake *151 C5 lake* South Island, New Zealand
Brunswick *43 E3* Georgia, SE USA
Brunswick *see* Braunschweig
Brusa *see* Bursa
Brus Laguna *52 D2* Gracias a Dios, E Honduras
Brussa *see* Bursa
Brussel *87 C6 var.* Brussels, *Fr.* Bruxelles, *Ger.* Brüssel; *anc.* Broucsella. *country capital* (Belgium) (Belgium) Brussels, C Belgium
Brüssel/Brussels *see* Brussel/Bruxelles
Brüx *see* Most
Bruxelles *see* Brussel
Bryan *49 G3* Texas, SW USA
Bryansk *111 A5* Bryanskaya Oblast', W Russian Federation
Brzeg *98 C4 Ger.* Brieg; *anc.* Civitas Altae Ripae. Opolskie, S Poland
Brześć Litewski/Brześć nad Bugiem *see* Brest
Brześćany *see* Berezhany
Bucaramanga *58 B2* Santander, N Colombia
Buchanan *74 C5* prev. Grand Bassa. SW Liberia
Buchanan, Lake *49 F3 reservoir* Texas, SW USA
Bucharest *see* Bucureşti
Buckeye State *see* Ohio
Bu Craa *see* Bou Craa
Bucureşti *108 C5 Eng.* Bucharest, *Ger.* Bukarest; *prev.* Altenburg; *anc.* Cetatea Damboviţei. *country capital* (Romania) (Romania) Bucureşti, S Romania
Buda-Kashalyova *107 D7 Rus.* Buda-Koshelëvo. Homyel'skaya Voblasts', SE Belarus
Buda-Koshelëvo *see* Buda-Kashalyova
Budapest *99 C6 off.* Budapest Főváros, *SCr.* Budimpešta. *country capital* (Hungary) (Hungary) Pest, N Hungary
Budapest Főváros *see* Budapest
Budaun *133 D3* Uttar Pradesh, N India
Buddenbrock *see* Brodnica
Budimpešta *see* Budapest
Budweis *see* České Budějovice

Budýšin *see* Bautzen
Buena Park *46 E2* California, W USA North America
Buenaventura *58 A3* Valle del Cauca, W Colombia
Buena Vista *61 G4* Santa Cruz, C Bolivia
Buena Vista *93 H5* S Gibraltar Europe
Buena Vista *93 H5* S Gibraltar Europe
Buenavista *93 H5* Baja California Sur, NW Mexico
Buena Vista *93 H5* Sonora, NW Mexico
Buena Vista *93 H5* Cerro Largo, Uruguay
Buena Vista *93 H5* Colorado, C USA
Buena Vista *93 H5* Georgia, SE USA
Buena Vista *93 H5* Virginia, NE USA
Buenos Aires *61 D4 hist.* Santa María del Buen Aire. *country capital* (Argentina) (Argentina) Buenos Aires, E Argentina
Buenos Aires *53 E5* Puntarenas, SE Costa Rica
Buenos Aires, Lago *65 B6 var.* Lago General Carrera. *lake* Argentina/Chile
Buffalo *41 E3* New York, NE USA
Buffalo Narrows *37 F4* Saskatchewan, C Canada
Buff Bay *54 B5* E Jamaica
Buftea *108 C5* Ilfov, S Romania
Bug *81 E3 Bel.* Zakhodni Buh, *Eng.* Western Bug, *Rus.* Zapadnyy Bug, *Ukr.* Zakhidnyy Buh. *river* E Europe
Buga *58 B3* Valle del Cauca, W Colombia
Bughotu *see* Santa Isabel
Buguruslan *111 D6* Orenburgskaya Oblast', W Russian Federation
Buitenzorg *see* Bogor
Bujalance *92 D4* Andalucía, S Spain
Bujanovac *101 E5* SE Serbia
Bujnurd *see* Bojnūrd
Bujumbura *73 B7 prev.* Usumbura. *country capital* (Burundi) (Burundi) W Burundi
Bukarest *see* Bucureşti
Bukavu *77 E6 prev.* Costermansville. Sud-Kivu, E Dem. Rep. Congo
Bukhara *see* Buxoro
Bukoba *73 B6* Kagera, NW Tanzania
Bülach *95 B7* Zürich, NW Switzerland
Bulawayo *78 D3* Matabeleland North, SW Zimbabwe
Bulgan *127 E2* Bulgan, N Mongolia
Bulgaria *104 C2 off.* Republic of Bulgaria, *Bul.* Bŭlgariya; *prev.* People's Republic of Bulgaria. *country* SE Europe

BULGARIA
Southeast Europe

Official name Republic of Bulgaria
Formation 1908 / 1947
Capital Sofia
Population 7.6 million / 178 people per sq mile (69 people per sq km) / 70%
Total area 42,822 sq. miles (110,910 sq. km)
Languages Bulgarian*, Turkish, Romani
Religions Orthodox Christian 83%, Muslim 12%, Other 4%, Roman Catholic 1%
Ethnic mix Bulgarian 84%, Turkish 9%, Roma 5%, Other 2%
Government Parliamentary system
Currency Lev = 100 stotinki
Literacy rate 98%
Calorie consumption 2848 calories

Bulgaria, People's Republic of *see* Bulgaria
Bulgaria, Republic of *see* Bulgaria
Bŭlgariya *see* Bulgaria
Bullion State *see* Missouri
Bull Shoals Lake *42 B1 reservoir* Arkansas/Missouri, C USA
Bulukumba *139 E4 prev.* Boeloekoemba. Sulawesi, C Indonesia
Bumba *77 D5* Equateur, N Dem. Rep. Congo
Bunbury *147 A7* Western Australia
Bundaberg *148 E4* Queensland, E Australia
Bungo-suido *131 B7 strait* SW Japan
Bunia *77 E5* Orientale, NE Dem. Rep. Congo
Bünyan *116 D3* Kayseri, C Turkey
Buraida *see* Buraydah
Buraydah *120 B4 var.* Buraida. Al Qaşīm, N Saudi Arabia
Burdigala *see* Bordeaux

Burdur *116 B4 var.* Buldur. Burdur, SW Turkey
Burdur Gölü *116 B4 salt lake* SW Turkey
Buré *72 C4* Âmara, N Ethiopia
Burgas *104 E2 var.* Bourgas. Burgas, E Bulgaria
Burgaski Zaliv *104 E2 gulf* E Bulgaria
Burgos *92 D2* Castilla-León, N Spain
Burgundy *see* Bourgogne
Burhan Budai Shan *126 D4 mountain range* C China
Buriram *137 D5 var.* Buri Ram, Puriramya. Buri Ram, E Thailand
Buri Ram *see* Buriram
Burjassot *93 F3* País Valenciano, E Spain
Burkburnett *49 F2* Texas, SW USA
Burketown *148 B3* Queensland, NE Australia
Burkina *see* Burkina Faso
Burkina Faso *72 E4 off.* Burkina Faso; *prev.* Upper Volta. *country* W Africa

---

BURKINA FASO
West Africa

Official name Burkina Faso
Formation 1960 / 1960
Capital Ouagadougou
Population 14 million / 132 people per sq mile (51 people per sq km) / 18%
Total area 105,869 sq. miles (274,200 sq. km)
Languages French*, Mossi, Fulani, Tuareg, Dyula, Songhai
Religions Muslim 55%, Traditional beliefs 35%, Roman Catholic 9%, Other Christian 1%
Ethnic mix Mossi 48%, Other 21%, Peul 10%, Lobi 7%, Bobo 7%, Mandé 7%
Government Presidential system
Currency CFA franc = 100 centimes
Literacy rate 22%
Calorie consumption 2462 calories

Burley *46 D4* Idaho, NW USA
Burlington *45 G4* Iowa, C USA
Burlington *41 F2* Vermont, NE USA
Burma *136 A3 off.* Union of Myanmar. *country* SE Asia. *see also* Myanmar
Burnie *149 C8* Tasmania, SE Australia
Burns *46 C3* Oregon, NW USA
Burnside *37 F3 river* Nunavut, NW Canada
Burnsville *45 F2* Minnesota, N USA
Burrel *101 D6 var.* Burreli. Dibër, C Albania
Burreli *see* Burrel
Burriana *93 F3* País Valenciano, E Spain
Bursa *116 B3 var.* Brussa, *prev.* Brusa; *anc.* Prusa. Bursa, NW Turkey
Burtnieks Ezers *see* Burtnieks
Burtnieks *106 C3 var.* Burtnieks Ezers. *lake* N Latvia
Burundi *73 B7 off.* Republic of Burundi; *prev.* Kingdom of Burundi, Urundi. *country* C Africa

---

BURUNDI
Central Africa

Official name Republic of Burundi
Formation 1962 / 1962
Capital Bujumbura
Population 8.1 million / 818 people per sq mile (316 people per sq km) / 10%
Total area 10,745 sq. miles (27,830 sq. km)
Languages Kirundi*, French*, Kiswahili
Religions Christian (mainly Roman Catholic) 60%, Traditional beliefs 39%, Muslim 1%
Ethnic mix Hutu 85%, Tutsi 14%, Twa 1%
Government Presidential system
Currency Burundian franc = 100 centimes
Literacy rate 59%
Calorie consumption 1649 calories

Burundi, Kingdom of *see* Burundi
Burundi, Republic of *see* Burundi
Buru, Pulau *139 F4 prev.* Boeroe. *island* E Indonesia
Busan *see* Pusan
Buşayrah *118 D3* Dayr az Zawr, E Syria
Büshehr/Bushire *see* Bandar-e Büshehr
Busra *see* Al Başrah, Iraq
Busselton *147 A7* Western Australia
Bussora *see* Al Başrah

Buta *77 D5* Orientale, N Dem. Rep. Congo
Butembo *77 E5* Nord-Kivu, NE Dem. Rep. Congo
Butler *41 E4* Pennsylvania, NE USA
Buton, Pulau *139 E4 var.* Pulau Butung; *prev.* Boetoeng. *island* C Indonesia
Bütow *see* Bytów
Butte *44 B2* Montana, NW USA
Butterworth *138 B3* Pinang, Peninsular Malaysia
Button Islands *39 E1 island group* Nunavut, NE Canada
Butuan *139 F2 off.* Butuan City. Mindanao, S Philippines
Butuan City *see* Butuan
Butung, Pulau *see* Buton, Pulau
Butuntum *see* Bitonto
Buulobarde *73 D5 var.* Buulo Berde. Hiiraan, C Somalia
Buulo Berde *see* Buulobarde
Buur Gaabo *73 D6* Jubbada Hoose, S Somalia
Buxoro *122 D2 var.* Bokhara, *Rus.* Bukhara. Buxoro Viloyati, C Uzbekistan
Buynaksk *111 B8* Respublika Dagestan, SW Russian Federation
Büyükmenderes Nehri *116 A4 river* SW Turkey
Buzău *108 C4* Buzău, SE Romania
Büzmeýin *see* Abadan
Buzuluk *111 D6* Orenburgskaya Oblast', W Russian Federation
Byahoml' *107 D5 Rus.* Begoml'. Vitsyebskaya Voblasts', N Belarus
Byalynichy *107 D6 Rus.* Belynichi. Mahilyowskaya Voblasts', E Belarus
Byan Tumen *see* Choybalsan
Bydgoszcz *98 C3 Ger.* Bromberg. Kujawski-pomorskie, C Poland
Byelaruskaya Hrada *107 B6 Rus.* Belorusskaya Gryada. *ridge* N Belarus
Byerazino *107 D6 Rus.* Berezina. *river* C Belarus
Byron Island *see* Nikunau
Bystrovka *see* Kemin
Bytča *99 C5* Žilinský Kraj, N Slovakia
Bytom *99 C5 Ger.* Beuthen. Śląskie, S Poland
Bytów *98 C2 Ger.* Bütow. Pomorskie, N Poland
Byuzmeýin *see* Abadan
Byval'ki *107 D8* Homyel'skaya Voblasts', SE Belarus
Byzantium *see* Istanbul

C

Caála *78 B2 var.* Kaala, Robert Williams, *Port.* Vila Robert Williams. Huambo, C Angola
Caazapá *64 D3* Caazapá, S Paraguay
Caballo Reservoir *48 C3 reservoir* New Mexico, SW USA
Cabañaquinta *92 D1* Asturias, N Spain
Cabanatuan *139 E1 off.* Cabanatuan City. Luzon, N Philippines
Cabanatuan City *see* Cabanatuan
Cabillonum *see* Chalon-sur-Saône
Cabimas *58 C1* Zulia, NW Venezuela
Cabinda *78 A1 var.* Kabinda. Cabinda, NW Angola
Cabinda *78 A1 var.* Kabinda. *province* NW Angola
Lake Cabora Bassa *78 D2 var.* Lake Cabora Bassa. *reservoir* NW Mozambique
Cabora Bassa, Lake *see* Cahora Bassa, Albufeira de
Caborca *50 B1* Sonora, NW Mexico
Cabot Strait *39 G4 strait* E Canada
Cabo Verde, Ilhas do *see* Cape Verde
Cabras, Ilha *76 E2 island* S Sao Tome and Principe, Africa, E Atlantic Ocean
Cabrera *93 G3 river* NW Spain
Cáceres *92 C3 Ar.* Qazris. Extremadura, W Spain
Cachimbo, Serra do *63 E2 mountain range* C Brazil
Caconda *78 B2* Huíla, C Angola
Čadca *99 C5 Hung.* Csaca. Žilinský Kraj, N Slovakia
Cadillac *40 C2* Michigan, N USA

Cadiz *139 E2 off.* Cadiz City. Negros, C Philippines
Cádiz *92 C5 anc.* Gades, Gadier, Gadir, Gadire. Andalucía, SW Spain
Cadiz City *see* Cadiz
Gulf of Cadiz *92 B5 Eng.* Gulf of Cadiz. *gulf* Portugal/Spain
Cadiz, Gulf of *see* Cadiz, Golfo de
Cadurcum *see* Cahors
Caen *90 B3* Calvados, N France
Caene/Caenepolis *see* Qinã
Caerdydd *see* Cardiff
Caer Glou *see* Gloucester
Caer Gybi *see* Holyhead
Caerleon *see* Chester
Caer Luel *see* Carlisle
Caesaraugusta *see* Zaragoza
Caesarea Mazaca *see* Kayseri
Caesarobriga *see* Talavera de la Reina
Caesarodunum *see* Tours
Caesaromagus *see* Beauvais
Caesena *see* Cesena
Cafayate *64 C2* Salta, N Argentina
Cagayan de Oro *139 E2 off.* Cagayan de Oro City. Mindanao, S Philippines
Cagayan de Oro City *see* Cagayan de Oro
Cagliari *97 A6 anc.* Caralis. Sardegna, Italy, C Mediterranean Sea
Caguas *55 F3* E Puerto Rico
Cahors *91 C5 anc.* Cadurcum. Lot, S France
Cahul *108 D4 Rus.* Kagul. S Moldova
Caicos Passage *54 D2 strait* Bahamas/Turks and Caicos Islands
Caiffa *see* Hefa
Cailungo *96 E1* N San Marino
Caiphas *see* Hefa
Cairns *148 D3* Queensland, NE Australia
Cairo *72 B2 var.* El Qãhira, *Ar.* Al Qãhirah. *country capital* (Egypt) (Egypt) N Egypt
Caisleán an Bharraigh *see* Castlebar
Cajamarca *60 B3 prev.* Caxamarca. Cajamarca, N Peru
Čakovec *100 B2 prev.* Csakathurn, *Hung.* Csáktornya; *prev. Ger.* Tschakathurn. Medimurje, N Croatia
Calabar *75 G5* Cross River, S Nigeria
Calabozo *58 D2* Guárico, C Venezuela
Calafat *108 B5* Dolj, SW Romania
Calafate *see* El Calafate
Calahorra *93 E2* La Rioja, N Spain
Calais *90 C2* Pas-de-Calais, N France
Calais *41 H2* Maine, NE USA
Calais, Pas de *see* Dover, Strait of
Calama *64 B2* Antofagasta, N Chile
Cãlãras *see* Cãlãrasi
Cãlãrasi *108 D5 var.* Cãlãrasi, SE Romania
Cãlãrasi *108 D3 var.* Cãlãrasi, *Rus.* Kalarash. C Moldova
Calatayud *93 E2* Aragón, NE Spain
Calbayog *139 E2 off.* Calbayog City. Samar, C Philippines
Calbayog City *see* Calbayog
Calcutta *135 G4* West Bengal, NE India
Caldas da Rainha *92 B3* Leiria, W Portugal
Caldera *64 B3* Atacama, N Chile
Caldwell *46 C3* Idaho, NW USA
Caledonia *52 C1* Corozal, N Belize
Caleta Olivia *65 B6* Santa Cruz, SE Argentina
Calgary *37 E5* Alberta, SW Canada
Cali *58 B3* Valle del Cauca, W Colombia
Calicut *132 C2 var.* Kozhikode. Kerala, SW India
California *47 B7 off.* State of California, *also known as* El Dorado, The Golden State. *state* W USA
Gulf of California *50 B2 Eng.* Gulf of California; *prev.* Sea of Cortez. *gulf* W Mexico
California, Gulf of *see* California, Golfo de
Cãlimãnesti *108 B4* Vâlcea, SW Romania
Calisia *see* Kalisz
Callabonna, Lake *149 B5 lake* South Australia
Callao *60 C4* Callao, W Peru
Callatis *see* Mangalia
Callosa de Segura *93 F4* País Valenciano, E Spain
Calmar *see* Kalmar

Caloundra *149 E5* Queensland, E Australia
Caltanissetta *97 C7* Sicilia, Italy, C Mediterranean Sea
Caluula *72 E4* Bari, NE Somalia
Camabatela *78 B1* Cuanza Norte, NW Angola
Camacupa *78 B2 var.* General Machado, *Port.* Vila General Machado. Bié, C Angola
Camagüey *54 C2 prev.* Puerto Príncipe. Camagüey, C Cuba
Camagüey, Archipiélago de *54 C2 island group* C Cuba
Camana *61 E4 var.* Camaná. Arequipa, SW Peru
Camargue *91 D6 physical region* SE France
Ca Mau *137 D6 var.* Quan Long. Minh Hai, S Vietnam
Cambay, Gulf of *see* Khambhãt, Gulf of
Camberia *see* Chambéry
Cambodia *137 D5 off.* Kingdom of Cambodia, *var.* Democratic Kampuchea, Roat Kampuchea, Cam. Kampuchea; *prev.* People's Democratic Republic of Kampuchea. *country* SE Asia

---

CAMBODIA
Southeast Asia

Official name Kingdom of Cambodia
Formation 1953 / 1953
Capital Phnom Penh
Population 14.6 million / 214 people per sq mile (83 people per sq km) / 19%
Total area 69,900 sq. miles (181,040 sq. km)
Languages Khmer*, French, Chinese, Vietnamese, Cham
Religions Buddhist 93%, Muslim 6%, Christian 1%
Ethnic mix Khmer 90%, Other 5%, Vietnamese 4%, Chinese 1%
Government Parliamentary system
Currency Riel = 100 sen
Literacy rate 74%
Calorie consumption 2046 calories

Cambodia, Kingdom of *see* Cambodia
Cambrai *90 C2 Flem.* Kambryk, *prev.* Cambray; *anc.* Cameracum. Nord, N France
Cambray *see* Cambrai
Cambrian Mountains *89 C6 mountain range* C Wales, United Kingdom
Cambridge *54 A4* W Jamaica
Cambridge *150 D3* Waikato, North Island, New Zealand
Cambridge *89 E6 Lat.* Cantabrigia. E England, United Kingdom
Cambridge *41 F4* Maryland, NE USA
Cambridge *40 D4* Ohio, NE USA
Cambridge Bay *37 F3 var.* Ikaluktutiak. Victoria Island, Nunavut, NW Canada
Camden *42 B2* Arkansas, C USA
Camellia State *see* Alabama
Cameracum *see* Cambrai
Cameroon *76 A4 off.* Republic of Cameroon, *Fr.* Cameroun. *country* W Africa

---

CAMEROON
Central Africa

Official name Republic of Cameroon
Formation 1960 / 1961
Capital Yaoundé
Population 16.3 million / 94 people per sq mile (36 people per sq km) / 52%
Total area 183,567 sq. miles (475,400 sq. km)
Languages English*, French*, Bamileke, Fang, Fulani
Religions Roman Catholic 35%, Traditional beliefs 25%, Muslim 22%, Protestant 18%
Ethnic mix Cameroon highlanders 31%, Other 21%, Equatorial Bantu 19%, Kirdi 11%, Fulani 10%, Northwestern Bantu 8%
Government Presidential system
Currency CFA franc = 100 centimes
Literacy rate 68%
Calorie consumption 2273 calories

Cameroon, Republic of see Cameroon
Cameroun see Cameroon
Camocim 63 F2 Ceará, E Brazil
Camopi 59 H3 E French Guiana
Campamento 52 C2 Olancho, C Honduras
Campania 97 D5 *Eng.* Champagne. *region* S Italy
Campbell, Cape 151 D5 *headland* South Island, New Zealand
Campbell Island 142 D5 *island* S New Zealand
Campbell Plateau 142 D5 *undersea plateau* SW Pacific Ocean
Campbell River 36 D5 Vancouver Island. British Columbia, SW Canada
Campeche 51 G4 Campeche, SE Mexico
Bay of Campeche 51 F4 *Eng.* Bay of Campeche. *bay* E Mexico
Campeche, Bay of see Campeche, Bahía de
Cam Pha 136 E3 Quang Ninh, N Vietnam
Câmpina 108 C4 *prev.* Cîmpina. Prahova, SE Romania
Campina Grande 63 G2 Paraíba, E Brazil
Campinas 63 F4 São Paulo, S Brazil
Campobasso 97 D5 Molise, C Italy
Campo Criptana see Campo de Criptana
Campo de Criptana 93 E3 *var.* Campo Criptana. Castilla-La Mancha, C Spain
Campo dos Goitacazes see Campos
Campo Grande 63 E4 *state capital* Mato Grosso do Sul, SW Brazil
Campos 63 F4 *var.* Campo dos Goitacazes. Rio de Janeiro, SE Brazil
Câmpulung 108 B4 *prev.* Câmpulung-Muşcel, Cîmpulung. Argeş, S Romania
Câmpulung-Muşcel see Câmpulung
Campus Stellae see Santiago
Cam Ranh 137 E6 Khanh Hoa, S Vietnam
Canada 34 *country* N North America

CANADA
North America

Official name Canada
Formation 1867 / 1949
Capital Ottawa
Population 32.9 million / 9 people per sq mile (4 people per sq km) / 81%
Total area 3,854,085 sq. miles (9,984,670 sq. km)
Languages English*, French*, Chinese, Italian, German, Ukrainian, Portuguese, Inuktitut, Cree
Religions Roman Catholic 44%, Protestant 29%, Other and nonreligious 27%
Government Parliamentary system
Currency Canadian dollar = 100 cents
Literacy rate 99%
Calorie consumption 3589 calories

Canada Basin 34 C2 *undersea basin* Arctic Ocean
Canadian River 49 E2 river USA
Çanakkale 116 A3 *var.* Dardanelli; *prev.* Chanak, Kale Sultanie. Çanakkale, W Turkey
Cananea 50 B1 Sonora, NW Mexico
Canarreos, Archipiélago de los 54 B2 *island group* W Cuba
Canary Islands 70 A2 *Eng.* Canary Islands. *island group* Spain, NE Atlantic Ocean
Canary Islands see Canarias, Islas
Cañas 52 D4 Guanacaste, NW Costa Rica
Canaveral, Cape 43 E4 *headland* Florida, SE USA
Canavieiras 63 G3 Bahia, E Brazil
Canberra 142 *country capital* (Australia) (Australia) Australian Capital Territory, SE Australia
Cancún 51 H3 Quintana Roo, SE Mexico
Candia see Irákleio
Canea see Chaniá
Cangzhou 128 D4 Hebei, E China
Caniapiscau 39 E2 river Québec, E Canada
Caniapiscau, Réservoir de 38 D3 *reservoir* Québec, C Canada
Canik Dağları 116 D2 *mountain range* N Turkey
Canillo 91 A7 Canillo, C Andorra Europe

Çankırı 116 C3 *var.* Chankiri; *anc.* Gangra, Germanicopolis. Çankırı, N Turkey
Cannanore 132 B2 *var.* Kannur. Kerala, SW India
Cannes 91 D6 Alpes-Maritimes, SE France
Canoas 63 E5 Rio Grande do Sul, S Brazil
Canon City 44 C5 Colorado, C USA
Cantabria 92 D1 *autonomous community* N Spain
Cantábrica, Cordillera 92 C1 *mountain range* N Spain
Cantabrigia see Cambridge
Cantaura 59 E2 Anzoátegui, NE Venezuela
Canterbury 89 E7 *hist.* Cantwaraburh; *anc.* Durovernum, *Lat.* Cantuaria. SE England, United Kingdom
Canterbury Bight 151 C6 *bight* South Island, New Zealand
Canterbury Plains 151 C6 *plain* South Island, New Zealand
Cần Thơ 137 E6 Cân Thơ, S Vietnam
Canton 42 B2 Mississippi, S USA
Canton 40 D4 Ohio, N USA
Canton see Guangzhou
Canton Island see Kanton
Cantuaria/Cantwaraburh see Canterbury
Canyon 49 E2 Texas, SW USA
Cao Bằng 136 D3 *var.* Caobang. Cao Bằng, N Vietnam
Caobang see Cao Bằng
Cap-Breton, Île du see Cape Breton Island
Cape Barren Island 149 C8 *island* Furneaux Group, Tasmania, SE Australia
Cape Basin 69 B7 *undersea basin* S Atlantic Ocean
Cape Breton Island 39 G4 *Fr.* Île du Cap-Breton. *island* Nova Scotia, SE Canada
Cape Charles 41 F5 Virginia, NE USA
Cape Coast 75 E5 *prev.* Cape Coast Castle. S Ghana
Cape Coast Castle see Cape Coast
Cape Girardeau 45 H5 Missouri, C USA
Capelle aan den IJssel 86 C4 Zuid-Holland, SW Netherlands
Cape Palmas see Harper
Cape Saint Jacques see Vung Tau
Cape Town 78 B5 *var.* Ekapa, *Afr.* Kaapstad, Kapstad. *country capital* (South Africa-legislative capital) (South Africa-legislative capital) Western Cape, SW South Africa
Cape Verde 74 A2 *off.* Republic of Cape Verde, *Port.* Cabo Verde, Ilhas do Cabo Verde. *country* E Atlantic Ocean

CAPE VERDE
Atlantic Ocean

Official name Republic of Cape Verde
Formation 1975 / 1975
Capital Praia
Population 423,613 / 272 people per sq mile (105 people per sq km) / 57%
Total area 1557 sq. miles (4033 sq. km)
Languages Portuguese*, Portuguese CreoleReligions Roman Catholic 97%, Other 2%, Protestant (Church of the Nazarene) 1%
Ethnic mix Mestiço 60%, African 30%, Other 10%
Government Mixed presidential–parliamentary system
Currency Cape Verde escudo = 100 centavos
Literacy rate 76%
Calorie consumption 3243 calories

Cape Verde Basin 66 C4 *undersea basin* E Atlantic Ocean
Cape Verde Plain 66 C4 *abyssal plain* E Atlantic Ocean
Cape Verde, Republic of see Cape Verde
Cape York Peninsula 148 C2 *peninsula* Queensland, N Australia
Cap-Haïtien 54 D3 *var.* Le Cap. N Haiti
Capira 53 G5 Panamá, C Panama
Capitán Arturo Prat 154 A2 *Chilean research station* South Shetland Islands, Antarctica

Capitán Pablo Lagerenza 64 D1 *var.* Mayor Pablo Lagerenza. Chaco, N Paraguay
Capodistria see Koper
Capri 97 C5 *island* S Italy
Caprivi Concession see Caprivi Strip
Caprivi Strip 78 C3 *Ger.* Caprivizipfel; *prev.* Caprivi Concession. *cultural region* NE Namibia
Caprivizipfel see Caprivi Strip
Cap Saint-Jacques see Vung Tau
Caquetá, Río 58 C5 *var.* Rio Japurá, Yapurá. *river* Brazil/Colombia
Caquetá, Río see Japurá, Rio
CAR see Central African Republic
Caracal 108 B5 Olt, S Romania
Caracarai 62 D1 Rondônia, W Brazil
Caracas 58 D1 *country capital* (Venezuela) (Venezuela) Distrito Federal, N Venezuela
Caralis see Cagliari
Caratasca, Laguna de 53 E2 *lagoon* NE Honduras
Carballiño see O Carballiño
Carbondale 40 B5 Illinois, N USA
Carbonia 97 A6 *var.* Carbonia Centro. Sardegna, Italy, C Mediterranean Sea
Carbonia Centro see Carbonia
Carcaso see Carcassonne
Carcassonne 91 C6 *anc.* Carcaso. Aude, S France
Cardamomes, Chaîne des see Krâvanh, Chuŏr Phnum
Cardamom Mountains see Krâvanh, Chuŏr Phnum
Cárdenas 54 B2 Matanzas, W Cuba
Cardiff 89 C7 *Wel. Caerdydd. national capital* S Wales, United Kingdom
Cardigan Bay 89 C6 *bay* W Wales, United Kingdom
Carei 108 B3 *Ger.* Gross-Karol, Karol, *Hung.* Nagykároly; *prev.* Careii-Mari. Satu Mare, NW Romania
Careii-Mari see Carei
Carey, Lake 147 B6 *lake* Western Australia
Cariaco 59 E1 Sucre, NE Venezuela
Caribbean Sea 54 C4 *sea* W Atlantic Ocean
Caribrod see Dimitrovgrad
Carlisle 88 C4 *anc.* Caer Luel, Luguvallium, Luguvallum. NW England, United Kingdom
Carlow 89 B6 *Ir.* Ceatharlach. SE Ireland
Carlsbad 48 D3 New Mexico, SW USA
Carlsbad see Karlovy Vary
Carlsberg Ridge 140 B4 *undersea ridge* S Arabian Sea
Carlsruhe see Karlsruhe
Carmana/Carmania see Kermān
Carmarthen 89 C6 SW Wales, United Kingdom
Carmaux 91 C6 Tarn, S France
Carmel 40 C4 Indiana, N USA
Carmelita 52 B1 Petén, N Guatemala
Carmen 51 G4 *var.* Ciudad del Carmen. Campeche, SE Mexico
Carmona 92 C4 Andalucía, S Spain
Carmona see Uíge
Carnaro see Kvarner
Carnarvon 147 A5 Western Australia
Carnegie, Lake 147 B5 *salt lake* Western Australia
Car Nicobar 133 F3 *island* Nicobar Islands, India, NE Indian Ocean
Caroço, Ilha 76 E1 *island* N Sao Tome and Principe, Africa, E Atlantic Ocean
Carolina 63 F2 Maranhão, E Brazil
Caroline Island see Millennium Island
Caroline Islands 144 B2 *island group* C Micronesia
Carolopois see Châlons-en-Champagne
Caroní, Río 59 E3 river E Venezuela
Caronium see A Coruña
Carora 58 C1 Lara, N Venezuela
Carpathian Mountains 81 E4 *var.* Carpathians, *Cz./Pol.* Karpaty, *Ger.* Karpaten. *mountain range* E Europe
Carpathians see Carpathian Mountains
Carpathos/Carpathus see Kárpathos
Carpaţii Sudici see Carpaţii Meridionali
Carpentaria, Gulf of 148 B2 *gulf* N Australia
Carpi 96 C2 Emilia-Romagna, N Italy
Carrara 96 B3 Toscana, C Italy
Carson City 47 C5 *state capital* Nevada, W USA

Carson Sink 47 C5 *salt flat* Nevada, W USA
Carstensz, Puntjak see Jaya, Puncak
Cartagena 58 B1 *var.* Cartagena de los Indes. Bolívar, NW Colombia
Cartagena 93 F4 *anc.* Carthago Nova. Murcia, SE Spain
Cartagena de los Indes see Cartagena
Cartago 53 E4 Cartago, C Costa Rica
Carthage 45 F5 Missouri, C USA
Carthago Nova see Cartagena
Cartwright 39 F2 Newfoundland and Labrador, E Canada
Carúpano 59 E1 Sucre, NE Venezuela
Carusbur see Cherbourg
Caruthersville 45 H5 Missouri, C USA
Cary 43 F1 North Carolina, SE USA
Casablanca 70 C2 *Ar.* Dar el Beida. NW Morocco
Casa Grande 48 B2 Arizona, SW USA
Cascade Range 46 B3 *mountain range* Oregon/Washington, NW USA
Cascadia Basin 34 A4 *undersea basin* NE Pacific Ocean
Cascais 92 B4 Lisboa, C Portugal
Caserta 97 D5 Campania, S Italy
Casey 154 D4 *Australian research station* Antarctica
Čáslav 99 B5 *Ger.* Tschaslau. Střední Čechy, C Czech Republic
Casper 44 C3 Wyoming, C USA
Caspian Depression 111 B7 *Kaz.* Kaspiy Mangy Oypaty, *Rus.* Prikaspiyskaya Nizmennost'. *depression* Kazakhstan/Russian Federation
Caspian Sea 114 A4 *Az.* Xäzär Dänizi, *Kaz.* Kaspiy Tengizi, *Per.* Bahr-e Khazar, Daryā-ye Khazar, *Rus.* Kaspiyskoye More. *inland sea* Asia/Europe
Cassai see Kasai
Cassel see Kassel
Castamoni see Kastamonu
Casteggio 96 B2 Lombardia, N Italy
Castelló de la Plana see Castellón de la Plana
Castellón see Castellón de la Plana
Castellón de la Plana 93 F3 *var.* Castellón, *Cat.* Castelló de la Plana. País Valenciano, E Spain
Castelnaudary 91 C6 Aude, S France
Castelo Branco 92 C3 Castelo Branco, C Portugal
Castelsarrasin 91 B6 Tarn-et-Garonne, S France
Castelvetrano 97 C7 Sicilia, Italy, C Mediterranean Sea
Castilla-La Mancha 93 E3 *autonomous community* NE Spain
Castilla-León 92 C2 *var.* Castilla y León. *autonomous community* NW Spain
Castilla y Leon see Castilla-León
Castlebar 89 A5 *Ir.* Caisleán an Bharraigh. W Ireland
Castleford 89 D5 N England, United Kingdom
Castle Harbour 42 B5 *inlet* Bermuda, NW Atlantic Ocean
Castra Regina see Regensburg
Castricum 86 C3 Noord-Holland, W Netherlands
Castries 55 F1 *country capital* (Saint Lucia) (Saint Lucia) N Saint Lucia
Castro 65 B6 Los Lagos, W Chile
Castrovillari 97 D6 Calabria, SW Italy
Castuera 92 D4 Extremadura, W Spain
Caswell Sound 151 A7 *sound* South Island, New Zealand
Catacamas 52 D2 Olancho, C Honduras
Catacaos 60 B3 Piura, NW Peru
Catalan Bay 93 H4 *bay* E Gibraltar, Mediterranean Sea
Cataluña 93 G2 N Spain
Catamarca see San Fernando del Valle de Catamarca
Catania 97 D7 Sicilia, Italy, C Mediterranean Sea
Catanzaro 97 D6 Calabria, SW Italy
Catarroja 93 F3 País Valenciano, E Spain
Cat Island 54 C1 *island* C Bahamas
Catskill Mountains 41 F3 *mountain range* New York, NE USA
Cattaro see Kotor
Cauca, Río 58 B2 river N Colombia
Caucasia 58 B2 Antioquia, NW Colombia

Caucasus 81 G4 *Rus.* Kavkaz. *mountain range* Georgia/Russian Federation
Caura, Río 59 E3 *river* C Venezuela
Cavaia *see* Kavajë
Cavalla 74 D5 *var.* Cavally, Cavally Fleuve. *river* Côte d'Ivoire/Liberia
Cavally/Cavally Fleuve *see* Cavalla
Caviana de Fora, Ilha 63 E1 *var.* Ilha Caviana. *island* N Brazil
Caviana, Ilha *see* Caviana de Fora, Ilha
Cawnpore *see* Kānpur
Caxamarca *see* Cajamarca
Caxito 78 B1 Bengo, NW Angola
Cayenne 59 H3 *dependent territory/ arrondissement capital* (French Guiana) NE French Guiana
Cayes 54 D3 *var.* Les Cayes. SW Haiti
Cayman Brac 54 B3 *island* E Cayman Islands
Cayman Islands 54 B3 *UK dependent territory* W West Indies
Cayo *see* San Ignacio
Cay Sal 54 B2 *islet* SW Bahamas
Cazin 100 B3 Federacija Bosna I Hercegovina, NW Bosnia and Herzegovina
Cazorla 93 E4 Andalucía, S Spain
Ceadâr-Lunga *see* Ciadîr-Lunga
Ceará 63 F2 *off.* Estado do Ceará. *region* C Brazil
Ceará 63 F2 *off.* Estado do Ceará. *state* C Brazil
Ceará *see* Fortaleza
Ceara Abyssal Plain *see* Ceará Plain
Ceará, Estado do *see* Ceará
Ceará Plain 56 E3 *var.* Ceara Abyssal Plain. *abyssal plain* W Atlantic Ocean
Ceathlarlach *see* Carlow
Cébaco, Isla 53 F5 *island* SW Panama
Cebu 139 E2 *off.* Cebu City. Cebu, C Philippines
Cebu City *see* Cebu
Čechy *see* Bohemia
Cecina 96 B3 Toscana, C Italy
Cedar City 44 A5 Utah, W USA
Cedar Falls 45 G3 Iowa, C USA
Cedar Lake 38 A2 *lake* Manitoba, C Canada
Cedar Rapids 45 G3 Iowa, C USA
Cedros, Isla 50 A3 *island* W Mexico
Ceduna 149 A6 South Australia
Cefalù 97 C7 *anc.* Cephaloedium. Sicilia, Italy, C Mediterranean Sea
Celebes 139 E4 *Eng.* Celebes. *island* C Indonesia
Celebes *see* Sulawesi
Celebes Sea 139 E3 *Ind.* Laut Sulawesi. *sea* Indonesia/Philippines
Celje 95 E7 *Ger.* Cilli. S Slovenia
Celldömölk 99 C6 Vas, W Hungary
Celle 94 B3 *var.* Zelle. Niedersachsen, N Germany
Celovec *see* Klagenfurt
Celtic Sea 89 B7 *Ir.* An Mhuir Cheilteach. *sea* SW British Isles
Celtic Shelf 80 B3 *continental shelf* E Atlantic Ocean
Cenderawasih, Teluk 139 G4 *var.* Teluk Irian, Teluk Sarera. *bay* W Pacific Ocean
Cenon 91 B5 Gironde, SW France
Centennial State *see* Colorado
Centrafricaine, République *see* Central African Republic
Central African Republic 76 C4 *var.* République Centrafricaine, *abbrev.* CAR; *prev.* Ubangi-Shari, Oubangui-Chari, Territoire de l'Oubangui-Chari. *country* C Africa

CENTRAL AFRICAN REPUBLIC
Central Africa

Official name Central African Republic
Formation 1960 / 1960
Capital Bangui
Population 4.2 million / 17 people per sq mile (7 people per sq km) / 43%
Total area 240,534 sq. miles (622,984 sq. km)
Languages French*, Sango, Banda, Gbaya
Religions Traditional beliefs 60%, Christian (mainly Roman Catholic) 35%, Muslim 5%
Ethnic mix Baya 34%, Banda 27%, Mandjia 21%, Sara 10%, Other 8%
Government Presidential system

CENTRAL AFRICAN REPUBLIC
(continued)

Currency CFA franc = 100 centimes
Literacy rate 49%
Calorie consumption 1980 calories

Central, Cordillera 58 B3 *mountain range* W Colombia
Cordillera Central 55 E3 *mountain range* C Dominican Republic
Cordillera Central 53 F5 *mountain range* C Panama
Central, Cordillera 139 E1 *mountain range* Luzon, N Philippines
Central Group *see* Inner Islands
Centralia 46 B2 Washington, NW USA
Central Indian Ridge *see* Mid-Indian Ridge
Central Makran Range 134 A3 *mountain range* W Pakistan
Central Pacific Basin 142 D1 *undersea basin* C Pacific Ocean
Central Provinces and Berar *see* Madhya Pradesh
Central Range 144 B3 *mountain range* NW Papua New Guinea
Central Russian Upland 109 G1 *Eng.* Central Russian Upland. *mountain range* W Russian Federation
Central Russian Upland *see* Srednerusskaya Vozvyshennost'
Central Siberian Plateau 114 D3 *var.* Central Siberian Uplands, *Eng.* Central Siberian Plateau. *mountain range* N Russian Federation
Central Siberian Plateau/Central Siberian Uplands *see* Srednesibirskoye Ploskogor'ye
Central, Sistema 92 D3 *mountain range* C Spain
Central Valley 47 B6 *valley* California, W USA
Centum Cellae *see* Civitavecchia
Ceos *see* Tziá
Cephaloedium *see* Cefalù
Ceram *see* Seram, Pulau
Ceram Sea 139 F4 *Ind.* Laut Seram. *sea* E Indonesia
Cerasus *see* Giresun
Cereté 58 B2 Córdoba, NW Colombia
Cergy-Pontoise *see* Pontoise
Cerignola 97 D5 Puglia, SE Italy
Çerkeş 116 C2 Çankın, N Turkey
Cernăuţi *see* Chernivtsi
Cernay 90 E4 Haut-Rhin, NE France
Cerro de Pasco 60 C3 Pasco, C Peru
Cervera 93 F2 Cataluña, NE Spain
Cervino, Monte *see* Matterhorn
Cesena 96 C3 *anc.* Caesena. Emilia-Romagna, N Italy
Cēsis 106 D3 *Ger.* Wenden. Cēsis, C Latvia
Česká Republika *see* Czech Republic
České Budějovice 99 B5 *Ger.* Budweis. Jihočeský Kraj, S Czech Republic
Český Krumlov 99 A5 *var.* Böhmisch-Krumau, *Ger.* Krummau. Jihočeský Kraj, S Czech Republic
Český Les *see* Bohemian Forest
Cetatea Damboviţei *see* Bucureşti
Cetinje 101 C5 *It.* Cettigne. S Montenegro
Cette *see* Sète
Cettigne *see* Cetinje
Ceuta 70 C2 *enclave* Spain, N Africa
Cévennes 91 C6 *mountain range* S France
Ceyhan 116 D4 Adana, S Turkey
Ceylanpınar 117 E4 Şanlıurfa, SE Turkey
Ceylon *see* Sri Lanka
Ceylon Plain 124 B4 *abyssal plain* N Indian Ocean
Ceyre to the Caribs *see* Marie-Galante
Chachapoyas 60 B2 Amazonas, NW Peru
Chachevichy 107 D6 *Rus.* Chechevichi. Mahilyowskaya Voblasts', E Belarus
Chaco *see* Gran Chaco
Chad 76 C3 *off.* Republic of Chad, *Fr.* Tchad. *country* C Africa

CHAD
Central Africa

Official name Republic of Chad
Formation 1960 / 1960
Capital N'Djamena

CHAD
(continued)

Population 10.3 million / 21 people per sq mile (8 people per sq km) / 25%
Total area 495,752 sq. miles (1,284,000 sq. km)
Languages Arabic*, French*, Sara, Maba
Religions Muslim 55%, Traditional beliefs 35%, Christian 10%
Ethnic mix Other 30%, Sara 28%, Mayo-Kebbi 12%, Arab 12%, Ouaddai 9%, Kanem-Bornou 9%
Government Presidential system
Currency CFA franc = 100 centimes
Literacy rate 26%
Calorie consumption 2114 calories

Chad, Lake 76 B3 *Fr.* Lac Tchad. *lake* C Africa
Chad, Republic of *see* Chad
Chadron 44 D3 Nebraska, C USA
Chadyr-Lunga *see* Ciadîr-Lunga
Chagai Hills 134 A2 *var.* Chāh Gay. *mountain range* Afghanistan/Pakistan
Chaghasarāy *see* Asadābād
Chagos-Laccadive Plateau 124 B4 *undersea plateau* N Indian Ocean
Chagos Trench 141 C5 *trench* N Indian Ocean
Chāh Gay *see* Chāgai Hills
Chaillu, Massif du 77 B6 *mountain range* C Gabon
Chain Ridge 140 B4 *undersea ridge* W Indian Ocean
Chajul 52 B2 Quiché, W Guatemala
Chakhānsūr 122 D5 Nīmrūz, SW Afghanistan
Chala 60 D4 Arequipa, SW Peru
Chalatenango 52 C3 Chalatenango, N El Salvador
Chalcidice *see* Chalkidikí
Chalcis *see* Chalkída
Chalki 105 E7 *island* Dodekánisa, Greece, Aegean Sea
Chalkída 105 C5 *var.* Halkida, *prev.* Khalkís; *anc.* Chalcis. Evvoia, E Greece
Chalkidikí 104 C4 *var.* Khalkidhikí; *anc.* Chalcidice. *peninsula* NE Greece
Challans 90 B4 Vendée, NW France
Challapata 61 F4 Oruro, SW Bolivia
Challenger Deep 152 B3 *trench* W Pacific Ocean
Challenger Deep *see* Mariana Trench
Challenger Fracture Zone 153 F4 *tectonic feature* SE Pacific Ocean
Châlons-en-Champagne 90 D3 *prev.* Châlons-sur-Marne, *hist.* Arcae Remorum; *anc.* Carolopois. Marne, NE France
Châlons-sur-Marne *see* Châlons-en-Champagne
Chalon-sur-Saône 90 D4 *anc.* Cabillonum. Saône-et-Loire, C France
Cha Mai *see* Thung Song
Chaman 134 B2 Baluchistān, SW Pakistan
Chambéry 91 D5 *anc.* Camberia. Savoie, E France
Champagne 90 D3 *cultural region* N France
Champagne *see* Campania
Champaign 40 B4 Illinois, N USA
Champasak 137 D5 Champasak, S Laos
Champlain, Lake 41 F2 *lake* Canada/ USA
Champotón 51 G4 Campeche, SE Mexico
Chanak *see* Çanakkale
Chañaral 64 B3 Atacama, N Chile
Chan-chiang/Chanchiang *see* Zhanjiang
Chandeleur Islands 42 C3 *island group* Louisiana, S USA
Chandigarh 134 D2 *state capital* Punjab, N India
Chandrapur 135 E5 Mahārāshtra, C India
Changan *see* Xi'an, Shaanxi, C China
Changane 79 E3 *river* S Mozambique
Changchun 128 D3 *var.* Ch'angch'un, Ch'ang-ch'un; *prev.* Hsinking. *province capital* Jilin, NE China
Ch'angch'un/Ch'ang-ch'un *see* Changchun
Changkiakow *see* Zhangjiakou
Chang, Ko 137 C6 *island* S Thailand

Changsha 128 C5 *var.* Ch'angsha, Ch'ang-sha. *province capital* Hunan, S China
Ch'angsha/Ch'ang-sha *see* Changsha
Changzhi 128 C4 Shanxi, C China
Chaniá 105 C7 *var.* Hania, Khaniá, *Eng.* Canea; *anc.* Cydonia. Kríti, Greece, E Mediterranean Sea
Chañi, Nevado de 64 B2 *mountain* NW Argentina
Chankiri *see* Çankırı
Channel Islands 89 C8 *Fr.* Iles Normandes. *island group* S English Channel
Channel Islands 47 B8 *island group* California, W USA
Channel-Port aux Basques 39 G4 Newfoundland and Labrador, SE Canada
Channel, The *see* English Channel
Channel Tunnel 90 C2 *tunnel* France/ United Kingdom
Chantabun/Chantaburi *see* Chanthaburi
Chantada 92 C1 Galicia, NW Spain
Chanthaburi 137 C6 *var.* Chantabun, Chantaburi. Chantaburi, S Thailand
Chanute 45 F5 Kansas, C USA
Chaouèn *see* Chefchaouen
Chaoyang 128 D3 Liaoning, NE China
Chapala, Lago de 50 D4 *lake* C Mexico
Chapan, Gora 122 B3 *mountain* C Turkmenistan
Chapayevsk 111 C6 Samarskaya Oblast', W Russian Federation
Chaplynka 109 F4 Khersons'ka Oblast', S Ukraine
Chapra *see* Chhapra
Charcot Seamounts 80 B3 *seamount range* E Atlantic Ocean
Chardzhev *see* Türkmenabat
Chardzhou/Chardzhui *see* Türkmenabat
Charente 91 B5 *cultural region* W France
Charente 91 B5 *river* W France
Chari 76 B3 *var.* Shari. *river* Central African Republic/Chad
Chārīkār 123 E4 Parvān, NE Afghanistan
Charity 59 F2 NW Guyana
Chärjew *see* Türkmenabat
Charkhlik/Charkhliq *see* Ruoqiang
Charleroi 87 C7 Hainaut, S Belgium
Charlesbourg 39 E4 Québec, SE Canada
Charles de Gaulle 90 E1 (Paris) Seine-et-Marne, N France
Charles Island 38 D1 *island* Nunavut, NE Canada
Charles Island *see* Santa María, Isla
Charleston 43 F2 South Carolina, SE USA
Charleston 40 D5 *state capital* West Virginia, NE USA
Charleville 149 D5 Queensland, E Australia
Charleville-Mézières 90 D3 Ardennes, N France
Charlie-Gibbs Fracture Zone 66 C2 *tectonic feature* N Atlantic Ocean
Charlotte 43 E1 North Carolina, SE USA
Charlotte Amalie 55 F3 *prev.* Saint Thomas. *dependent territory capital* (Virgin Islands (US)) Saint Thomas, N Virgin Islands (US)
Charlotte Harbor 43 E5 *inlet* Florida, SE USA
Charlottenhof *see* Aegviidu
Charlottesville 41 E5 Virginia, NE USA
Charlottetown 39 F4 *province capital* Prince Edward Island, Prince Edward Island, SE Canada
Charlotte Town *see* Roseau, Dominica
Charsk *see* Shar
Charters Towers 148 D3 Queensland, NE Australia
Chartres 90 C3 *anc.* Autricum, Civitas Carnutum. Eure-et-Loir, C France
Chashniki 107 D5 Vitsyebskaya Voblasts', N Belarus
Châteaubriant 90 B3 Loire-Atlantique, NW France
Châteaudun 90 C3 Eure-et-Loir, C France
Châteauroux 90 C4 *prev.* Indreville. Indre, C France
Château-Thierry 90 C3 Aisne, N France
Châtelet 87 C7 Hainaut, S Belgium
Châtellerault 90 B4 *var.* Châtelherault. Vienne, W France

INDEX – GAZETTEER: **Chatham Island – Chorne More**

Chatham Island *see* San Cristóbal, Isla
Chatham Island Rise *see* Chatham Rise
Chatham Islands *143 E5 island group* New Zealand, SW Pacific Ocean
Chatham Rise *142 D5 var.* Chatham Island Rise. *undersea rise* S Pacific Ocean
Chatkal Range *123 F2 Rus.* Chatkal'skiy Khrebet. *mountain range* Kyrgyzstan/Uzbekistan
Chatkal'skiy Khrebet *see* Chatkal Range
Chāttagām *see* Chittagong
Chattahoochee River *42 D3 river* SE USA
Chattanooga *42 D1* Tennessee, S USA
Chatyr-Tash *123 G2* Narynskaya Oblast', C Kyrgyzstan
Châu Đôc *137 D6 var.* Chauphu, Chau Phu. An Giang, S Vietnam
Chauk *136 A3* Magway, W Burma (Myanmar)
Chaumont *90 D4 prev.* Chaumont-en-Bassigny. Haute-Marne, N France
Chaumont-en-Bassigny *see* Chaumont
Chau Phu *see* Châu Đôc
Chausy *see* Chavusy
Chaves *92 C2 anc.* Aquae Flaviae. Vila Real, N Portugal
Chávez, Isla *see* Santa Cruz, Isla
Chavusy *107 E6 Rus.* Chausy. Mahilyowskaya Voblasts', E Belarus
Chaykovskiy *111 D5* Permskaya Oblast', NW Russian Federation
Cheb *99 A5 Ger.* Eger. Karlovarský Kraj, W Czech Republic
Cheboksary *111 C5* Chuvashskaya Respublika, W Russian Federation
Cheboygan *40 C2* Michigan, N USA
Chechaouèn *see* Chefchaouen
Chech, Erg *74 D1 desert* Algeria/Mali
Chechevichi *see* Chachevichy
Che-chiang *see* Zhejiang
Cheduba Island *136 A4 island* W Burma (Myanmar)
Chefchaouen *70 C2 var.* Chaouèn, Chechaouèn, *Sp.* Xauen. N Morocco
Chefoo *see* Yantai
Cheju-do *129 E4 Jap.* Saishū; *prev.* Quelpart. *island* S South Korea
Cheju Strait *129 E4 Eng.* Cheju Strait. *strait* S South Korea
Cheju Strait *see* Cheju-haehyŏp
Chekiang *see* Zhejiang
Cheleken *see* Hazar
Chelkar *see* Shalkar
Chełm *98 E4 Rus.* Kholm. Lubelskie, SE Poland
Chełmno *98 C3 Ger.* Culm, Kulm. Kujawski-pomorskie, C Poland
Chełmża *98 C3 Ger.* Culmsee, Kulmsee. Kujawski-pomorskie, C Poland
Cheltenham *89 D6* C England, United Kingdom
Chelyabinsk *114 C3* Chelyabinskaya Oblast', C Russian Federation
Chemnitz *94 D4 prev.* Karl-Marx-Stadt. Sachsen, E Germany
Chemulpo *see* Inch'ŏn
Chenāb *134 C2 river* India/Pakistan
Chengchiatun *see* Liaoyuan
Ch'eng-chou/Chengchow *see* Zhengzhou
Chengde *128 D3 var.* Jehol. Hebei, E China
Chengdu *128 B5 var.* Chengtu, Ch'eng-tu. *province capital* Sichuan, C China
Chenghsien *see* Zhengzhou
Chengtu/Ch'eng-tu *see* Chengdu
Chennai *132 D2 prev.* Madras. *state capital* Tamil Nādu, S India
Chenstokhov *see* Częstochowa
Chen Xian/Chenxian/Chen Xiang *see* Chenzhou
Chenzhou *128 C6 var.* Chenxian, Chen Xian, Chen Xiang. Hunan, S China
Chepelare *104 C3* Smolyan, S Bulgaria
Chepén *60 B3* La Libertad, C Peru
Cher *90 C4 river* C France
Cherbourg *90 B3 anc.* Carusbur. Manche, N France
Cherepovets *110 B4* Vologodskaya Oblast', NW Russian Federation
Chergui, Chott ech *70 D2 salt lake* NW Algeria
Cherikov *see* Cherykaw
Cherkassy *see* Cherkasy
Cherkasy *109 E2 Rus.* Cherkassy. Cherkas'ka Oblast', C Ukraine
Cherkessk *111 B7* Karachayevo-Cherkesskaya Respublika, SW Russian Federation
Chernigov *see* Chernihiv
Chernihiv *109 E1 Rus.* Chernigov. Chernihivs'ka Oblast', NE Ukraine
Chernivtsi *108 C3 Ger.* Czernowitz, *Rom.* Cernăuţi, *Rus.* Chernovtsy. Chernivets'ka Oblast', W Ukraine
Cherno More *see* Black Sea
Chernomorskoye *see* Chornomors'ke
Chernovtsy *see* Chernivtsi
Chernoye More *see* Black Sea
Chernyakhovsk *106 A1 Ger.* Insterburg. Kaliningradskaya Oblast', W Russian Federation
Cherry Hill *41 F4* New Jersey, NE USA
Cherski Range *see* Cherskogo, Khrebet
Cherskiy *115 G2* Respublika Sakha (Yakutiya), NE Russian Federation
Cherskogo, Khrebet *115 F2 var.* Cherski Range. *mountain range* NE Russian Federation
Cherso *see* Cres
Cherven' *see* Chervyen'
Chervonograd *see* Chervonohrad
Chervonohrad *108 C2 Rus.* Chervonograd. L'vivs'ka Oblast', NW Ukraine
Chervyen' *107 D6 Rus.* Cherven'. Minskaya Voblasts', C Belarus
Cherykaw *107 E7 Rus.* Cherikov. Mahilyowskaya Voblasts', E Belarus
Chesapeake Bay *41 F5 inlet* NE USA
Chesha Bay *see* Chëshskaya Guba
Chëshskaya Guba *155 D5 var.* Archangel Bay, Chesha Bay, Dvina Bay. *bay* NW Russian Federation
Chester *89 C6 Wel.* Caerleon, *hist.* Legaceaster, *Lat.* Deva, Devana Castra. C England, United Kingdom
Chetumal *51 H4 var.* Payo Obispo. Quintana Roo, SE Mexico
Cheviot Hills *88 D4 hill range* England/Scotland, United Kingdom
Cheyenne *44 D4 state capital* Wyoming, C USA
Cheyenne River *44 D3 river* South Dakota/Wyoming, N USA
Chezdi-Oşorheiu *see* Târgu Secuiesc
Chhapra *135 F3 prev.* Chapra. Bihār, N India
Chhattīsgarh *135 E4 cultural region* E India
Chiai *128 D6 var.* Chia-i, Chiayi, Kiayi, Jiayi, *Jap.* Kagi. C Taiwan
Chia-i *see* Chiai
Chiang-hsi *see* Jiangxi
Chiang Mai *136 B4 var.* Chiangmai, Chiengmai, Kiangmai. Chiang Mai, NW Thailand
Chiangmai *see* Chiang Mai
Chiang Rai *136 C3 var.* Chianpai, Chienrai, Muang Chiang Rai. Chiang Rai, NW Thailand
Chiang-su *see* Jiangsu
Chianning/Chian-ning *see* Nanjing
Chianpai *see* Chiang Rai
Chianti *96 C3 cultural region* C Italy
Chiapa *see* Chiapa de Corzo
Chiapa de Corzo *51 G5 var.* Chiapa. Chiapas, SE Mexico
Chiayi *see* Chiai
Chiba *130 B1 var.* Tiba. Chiba, Honshū, S Japan
Chibougamau *38 D3* Québec, SE Canada
Chicago *40 B3* Illinois, N USA
Ch'i-ch'i-ha-erh *see* Qiqihar
Chickasha *49 G2* Oklahoma, C USA
Chiclayo *60 B3* Lambayeque, NW Peru
Chico *47 B5* California, W USA
Chico, Río *65 B7 river* SE Argentina
Chico, Río *65 B6 river* S Argentina
Chicoutimi *39 E4* Québec, SE Canada
Chiengmai *see* Chiang Mai
Chienrai *see* Chiang Rai
Chiesanuova *96 D2* SW San Marino
Chieti *96 D4 var.* Teate. Abruzzo, C Italy
Chifeng *127 G2 var.* Ulanhad. Nei Mongol Zizhiqu, N China
Chigirin *see* Chyhyryn
Chih-fu *see* Yantai
Chihli *see* Hebei
Chihli, Gulf of *see* Bo Hai
Chihuahua *50 C2* Chihuahua, NW Mexico
Childress *49 F2* Texas, SW USA
Chile *64 B3 off.* Republic of Chile. *country* SW South America

CHILE
South America

Official name Republic of Chile
Formation 1818 / 1883
Capital Santiago
Population 16.6 million / 57 people per sq mile (22 people per sq km) / 87%
Total area 292,258 sq. miles (756,950 sq. km)
Languages Spanish*, Amerindian languages
Religions Roman Catholic 80%, Other and nonreligious 20%
Ethnic mix Mixed race and European 90%, Other Amerindian 9%, Mapuche 1%
Government Presidential system
Currency Chilean peso = 100 centavos
Literacy rate 96%
Calorie consumption 2863 calories

Chile Basin *57 A5 undersea basin* E Pacific Ocean
Chile Chico *65 B6* Aisén, W Chile
Chile, Republic of *see* Chile
Chile Rise *57 A7 undersea rise* SE Pacific Ocean
Chilia-Nouă *see* Kiliya
Chililabombwe *78 D2* Copperbelt, C Zambia
Chi-lin *see* Jilin
Chillán *65 B5* Bío Bío, C Chile
Chillicothe *40 D4* Ohio, N USA
Chill Mhantáin, Sléibhte *see* Wicklow Mountains
Chiloé, Isla de *65 A6 var.* Isla Grande de Chiloé. *island* W Chile
Chilpancingo *51 E5 var.* Chilpancingo de los Bravos. Guerrero, S Mexico
Chilpancingo de los Bravos *see* Chilpancingo
Chilung *128 D6 var.* Keelung, *Jap.* Kirun, Kirun'; *prev. Sp.* Santissima Trinidad. N Taiwan
Chimán *53 G5* Panamá, E Panama
Chimbay *see* Chimboy
Chimborazo *60 A1 volcano* C Ecuador
Chimbote *60 C3* Ancash, W Peru
Chimboy *122 D1 Rus.* Chimbay. Qoraqalpog'iston Respublikasi, NW Uzbekistan
Chimkent *see* Shymkent
Chimoio *79 E3* Manica, C Mozambique
China *124 C2 off.* People's Republic of China, *Chin.* Chung-hua Jen-min Kung-ho-kuo, Zhonghua Renmin Gongheguo; *prev.* Chinese Empire. *country* E Asia

CHINA
East Asia

Official name People's Republic of China
Formation 960 / 1999
Capital Beijing
Population 1.33 billion / 370 people per sq mile (143 people per sq km) / 40%
Total area 3,705,386 sq. miles (9,596,960 sq. km)
Languages Mandarin*, Wu, Cantonese, Hsiang, Min, Hakka, Kan
Religions Nonreligious 59%, Traditional beliefs 20%, Other 13%, Buddhist 6%, Muslim 2%
Ethnic mix Han 92%, Other 4%, Hui 1%, Miao 1%, Manchu 1%, Zhuang 1%
Government One-party state
Currency Renminbi (known as yuan) = 10 jiao = 100 fen
Literacy rate 91%
Calorie consumption 2951 calories

Chi-nan/Chinan *see* Jinan
Chinandega *52 C3* Chinandega, NW Nicaragua
China, People's Republic of *see* China
China, Republic of *see* Taiwan
Chincha Alta *60 D4* Ica, SW Peru
Chin-chiang *see* Quanzhou
Chin-chou/Chinchow *see* Jinzhou
Chindwin *see* Chindwinn
Chindwinn *136 B2 var.* Chindwin. *river* N Burma (Myanmar)
Chinese Empire *see* China
Chinghai *see* Qinghai
Ch'ing Hai *see* Qinghai Hu, China
Chingola *78 D2* Copperbelt, C Zambia
Ching-Tao/Ch'ing-tao *see* Qingdao
Chinguețți *74 C2 var.* Chinguetti. Adrar, C Mauritania
Chin Hills *136 A3 mountain range* W Burma (Myanmar)
Chinhsien *see* Jinzhou
Chinnereth *see* Tiberias, Lake
Chinook Trough *113 H4 trough* N Pacific Ocean
Chioggia *96 C2 anc.* Fossa Claudia. Veneto, NE Italy
Chíos *105 D5 var.* Hios, Khíos, *It.* Scio, *Turk.* Sakiz-Adasi. Chíos, E Greece
Chíos *105 D5 var.* Khíos. *island* E Greece
Chipata *78 D2 prev.* Fort Jameson. Eastern, E Zambia
Chiquián *60 C3* Ancash, W Peru
Chiquimula *52 B2* Chiquimula, SE Guatemala
Chīrāla *132 D1* Andhra Pradesh, E India
Chirchik *see* Chirchiq
Chirchiq *123 E2 Rus.* Chirchik. Toshkent Viloyati, E Uzbekistan
Chiriqui Gulf *53 E5 Eng.* Chiriqui Gulf. *gulf* SW Panama
Chiriqui Gulf *see* Chiriquí, Golfo de
Chiriquí, Laguna de *53 E5 lagoon* NW Panama
Chiriquí, Volcán de *see* Barú, Volcán
Chirripó, Cerro *see* Chirripó Grande, Cerro
Chirripó Grande, Cerro *52 D4 var.* Cerro Chirripó. *mountain* SE Costa Rica
Chisec *52 B2* Alta Verapaz, C Guatemala
Chisholm *45 F1* Minnesota, N USA
Chisimaio/Chisimayu *see* Kismaayo
Chişinău *108 D4 Rus.* Kishinev. *country capital* (Moldova) (Moldova) C Moldova
Chita *115 F4* Chitinskaya Oblast', S Russian Federation
Chitangwiza *see* Chitungwiza
Chitato *78 C1* Lunda Norte, NE Angola
Chitina *36 D3* Alaska, USA
Chitose *130 D2 var.* Titose. Hokkaidō, NE Japan
Chitré *53 F5* Herrera, S Panama
Chittagong *135 G4 Ben.* Chāttagām. Chittagong, SE Bangladesh
Chitungwiza *78 D3 prev.* Chitangwiza. Mashonaland East, NE Zimbabwe
Chkalov *see* Orenburg
Chlef *70 D2 var.* Ech Cheliff, Ech Chleff; *prev.* Al-Asnam, El Asnam, Orléansville. NW Algeria
Chocolate Mountains *47 D8 mountain range* California, W USA
Chodorów *see* Khodoriv
Chodzież *98 C3* Wielkopolskie, C Poland
Choele Choel *65 C5* Río Negro, C Argentina
Choiseul *144 C3 var.* Lauru. *island* NW Solomon Islands
Chojnice *98 C2 Ger.* Konitz. Pomorskie, N Poland
Ch'ok'ē *72 C4 var.* Choke Mountains. *mountain range* NW Ethiopia
Choke Mountains *see* Ch'ok'ē
Cholet *90 B4* Maine-et-Loire, NW France
Choluteca *52 C3* Choluteca, S Honduras
Choluteca, Río *52 C3 river* SW Honduras
Choma *78 D2* Southern, S Zambia
Chomutov *98 A4 Ger.* Komotau. Ústecký Kraj, NW Czech Republic
Chona *113 E2 river* C Russian Federation
Chon Buri *137 C5 prev.* Bang Pla Soi. Chon Buri, S Thailand
Chone *60 A1* Manabí, W Ecuador
Ch'ŏngjin *129 E3* NE North Korea
Chongqing *128 B5 var.* Ch'ung-ching, Ch'ung-ch'ing, Chungking, Pahsien, Tchongking, Yuzhou. Chongqing Shi, C China
Chonnacht *see* Connaught
Chonos, Archipiélago de los *65 A6 island group* S Chile
Chóra Sfakíon *105 C8 var.* Sfákia. Kríti, Greece, E Mediterranean Sea
Chorne More *see* Black Sea

Chornomors'ke 109 E4 Rus.
Chernomorskoye. Respublika Krym,
S Ukraine
Chorokh/Chorokhi see Çoruh Nehri
Chortkiv 108 C2 Rus. Chortkov.
Ternopil's'ka Oblast', W Ukraine
Chortkov see Chortkiv
Chorzów 99 C5 Ger. Königshütte; prev.
Królewska Huta. Śląskie, S Poland
Chośebuz see Cottbus
Chōsen-kaikyō see Korea Strait
Chōshi 131 D5 var. Tyôsi. Chiba,
Honshū, S Japan
Chosŏn-minjujuŭi-inmin-kanghwaguk
see North Korea
Choszczno 98 B3 Ger. Arnswalde.
Zachodnio-pomorskie, NW Poland
Chota Nagpur 135 E4 plateau N India
Choûm 74 C2 Adrar, C Mauritania
Choybalsan 127 F2 prev. Byan Tumen.
Dornod, E Mongolia
Christchurch 151 C6 Canterbury, South
Island, New Zealand
Christiana 54 B5 C Jamaica
Christiania see Oslo
Christiansand see Kristiansand
Christianshåb see Qasigiannguit
Christiansund see Kristiansand
Christmas Island 141 D5 Australian
external territory E Indian Ocean
Christmas Island see Kiritimati
Christmas Ridge 143 E1 undersea ridge
C Pacific Ocean
Chuan see Sichuan
Ch'uan-chou see Quanzhou
Chubek see Moskva
Chubut, Río 65 B6 river SE Argentina
Ch'u-chiang see Shaoguan
Chudskoye Ozero see Peipus, Lake
Chugoku-sanchi 131 B6 mountain range
Honshū, SW Japan
Chui see Chuy
Chukai see Cukai
Chukchi Plain 155 B2 abyssal plain
Arctic Ocean
Chukchi Plateau 34 C2 undersea plateau
Arctic Ocean
Chukchi Sea 34 B2 Rus. Chukotskoye
More. sea Arctic Ocean
Chukotskoye More see Chukchi Sea
Chula Vista 47 C8 California, W USA
Chulucanas 60 B2 Piura, NW Peru
Chulym 114 D4 river C Russian
Federation
Chumphon 137 C6 var. Jumporn.
Chumphon, SW Thailand
Ch'unch'ŏn 129 E4 Jap. Shunsen.
N South Korea
Ch'ung-ch'ing/Ch'ung-ching see
Chongqing
Chung-hua Jen-min Kung-ho-kuo
see China
Chungking see Chongqing
Chunya 115 E3 river C Russian
Federation
Chuquicamata 64 B2 Antofagasta,
N Chile
Chuquisaca see Sucre
Chur 95 B7 Fr. Coire, It. Coira, Rmsch.
Cuera, Quera; anc. Curia Rhaetorum.
Graubünden, E Switzerland
Churchill 37 G4 Manitoba,
C Canada
Churchill 38 B2 river Manitoba/
Saskatchewan, C Canada
Churchill 39 F2 river Newfoundland and
Labrador, E Canada
Chuska Mountains 48 C1 mountain
range Arizona/New Mexico, SW USA
Chusovoy 111 D5 Permskaya Oblast',
NW Russian Federation
Chust see Khust
Chuuk Islands 144 B2 var. Hogoley
Islands; prev. Truk Islands. island
group Caroline Islands, C Micronesia
Chuy 64 E4 var. Chuí. Rocha, E Uruguay
Chyhyryn 109 E2 Rus. Chigirin.
Cherkas'ka Oblast', N Ukraine
Ciadâr-Lunga 108 D4 var. Ceadâr-
Lunga, Rus. Chadyr-Lunga. S Moldova
Cide 116 C2 Kastamonu, N Turkey
Ciechanów 98 D3 prev. Zichenau.
Mazowieckie, C Poland
Ciego de Ávila 54 C2 Ciego de Ávila,
C Cuba
Ciénaga 58 B1 Magdalena, N Colombia
Cienfuegos 54 B2 Cienfuegos, C Cuba

Cieza 93 E4 Murcia, SE Spain
Cihanbeyli 116 C3 Konya, C Turkey
Cikobia 145 E4 prev. Thikombia.
island N Fiji
Cilacap 138 C5 prev. Tjilatjap. Jawa,
C Indonesia
Cill Airne see Killarney
Cill Chainnigh see Kilkenny
Cilli see Celje
Cill Mhantáin see Wicklow
Címpina see Câmpina
Cîmpulung see Câmpulung
Cina Selatan, Laut see South China Sea
Cincinnati 40 C4 Ohio, N USA
Ciney 87 C7 Namur, SE Belgium
Cinto, Monte 91 E7 mountain Corse,
France, C Mediterranean Sea
Cintra see Sintra
Cipolletti 65 B5 Río Negro, C Argentina
Cirebon 138 C4 prev. Tjirebon. Jawa,
S Indonesia
Cirkvenica see Crikvenica
Ciro Marino 97 E6 Calabria, S Italy
Cirquenizza see Crikvenica
Cisnădie 108 B4 Ger. Heltau, Hung.
Nagydisznód. Sibiu, SW Romania
Citharista see la Ciotat
Citlaltépetl see Orizaba, Volcán Pico de
Citrus Heights 47 B5 California, W USA
Ciudad Acuña see Villa Acuña
Ciudad Bolívar 59 E2 prev. Angostura.
Bolívar, E Venezuela
Ciudad Camargo 50 D2 Chihuahua,
N Mexico
Ciudad Cortés see Cortés
Ciudad Darío 52 D3 var. Dario.
Matagalpa, W Nicaragua
Ciudad de Dolores Hidalgo see Dolores
Hidalgo
Ciudad de Guatemala 52 B2 Eng.
Guatemala City; prev. Santiago
de los Caballeros. country capital
(Guatemala) (Guatemala) Guatemala,
C Guatemala
Ciudad del Carmen see Carmen
Ciudad del Este 64 E2 prev. Ciudad
Presidente Stroessner, Presidente
Stroessner, Puerto Presidente
Stroessner. Alto Paraná, SE Paraguay
Ciudad Delicias see Delicias
Ciudad de México see México
Ciudad de Panamá see Panamá
Ciudad Guayana 59 E2 prev. San Tomé
de Guayana, Santo Tomé de Guayana.
Bolívar, NE Venezuela
Ciudad Guzmán 50 D4 Jalisco,
SW Mexico
Ciudad Hidalgo 51 G5 Chiapas,
SE Mexico
Ciudad Juárez 50 C1 Chihuahua,
N Mexico
Ciudad Lerdo 50 D3 Durango, C Mexico
Ciudad Madero 51 E3 var. Villa Cecilia.
Tamaulipas, C Mexico
Ciudad Mante 51 E3 Tamaulipas,
C Mexico
Ciudad Miguel Alemán 51 E2
Tamaulipas, C Mexico
Ciudad Obregón 50 B2 Sonora,
NW Mexico
Ciudad Ojeda 58 C1 Zulia,
NW Venezuela
Cobán 52 B2 Alta Verapaz, C Guatemala
Ciudad Porfirio Díaz see Piedras Negras
Ciudad Presidente Stroessner see
Ciudad del Este
Ciudad Quesada see Quesada
Ciudad Real 92 D3 Castilla-La Mancha,
C Spain
Ciudad-Rodrigo 92 C3 Castilla-León,
N Spain
Ciudad Trujillo see Santo Domingo
Ciudad Valles 51 E3 San Luis Potosí,
C Mexico
Ciudad Victoria 51 E3 Tamaulipas,
C Mexico
Ciutadella 93 H3 var. Ciutadella
de Menorca. Menorca, Spain,
W Mediterranean Sea
Ciutadella Ciutadella de Menorca see
Ciutadella
Civitanova Marche 96 D3 Marche,
C Italy
Civitas Altae Ripae see Brzeg
Civitas Carnutum see Chartres
Civitas Eburovicum see Évreux
Civitavecchia 96 C4 anc. Centum Cellae,
Trajani Portus. Lazio, C Italy

Claremore 49 G1 Oklahoma, C USA
Clarence 151 C5 Canterbury, South
Island, New Zealand
Clarence 151 C5 river South Island,
New Zealand
Clarence Town 54 D2 Long Island,
C Bahamas
Clarinda 45 F4 Iowa, C USA
Clarion Fracture Zone 153 E2 tectonic
feature NE Pacific Ocean
Clarión, Isla 50 A5 island W Mexico
Clark Fork 44 A1 river Idaho/Montana,
NW USA
Clark Hill Lake 43 E2 var. J.Storm
Thurmond Reservoir. reservoir
Georgia/South Carolina, SE USA
Clarksburg 40 D4 West Virginia,
NE USA
Clarksdale 42 B2 Mississippi, S USA
Clarksville 42 C1 Tennessee, S USA
Clausentum see Southampton
Clayton 49 E1 New Mexico, SW USA
Clearwater 43 E4 Florida, SE USA
Clearwater Mountains 46 D2 mountain
range Idaho, NW USA
Cleburne 49 G3 Texas, SW USA
Clermont 148 D4 Queensland,
E Australia
Clermont-Ferrand 91 C5 Puy-de-Dôme,
C France
Cleveland 40 D3 Ohio, N USA
Cleveland 42 D1 Tennessee, S USA
Clifton 48 C2 Arizona, SW USA
Clinton 42 B2 Mississippi, S USA
Clinton 49 F1 Oklahoma, C USA
Clipperton Fracture Zone 153 E3
tectonic feature E Pacific Ocean
Clipperton Island 35 A7 French
dependency of French Polynesia
E Pacific Ocean
Cloncurry 148 B3 Queensland,
C Australia
Clonmel 89 B6 Ir. Cluain Meala.
S Ireland
Cloppenburg 94 B3 Niedersachsen,
NW Germany
Cloquet 45 G2 Minnesota, N USA
Cloud Peak 44 C3 mountain Wyoming,
C USA
Clovis 49 E2 New Mexico, SW USA
Cluain Meala see Clonmel
Cluj see Cluj-Napoca
Cluj-Napoca 108 B3 Ger. Klausenburg,
Hung. Kolozsvár; prev. Cluj. Cluj,
NW Romania
Clutha 151 B7 river South Island, New
Zealand
Clyde 88 C4 river W Scotland, United
Kingdom
Coari 62 D2 Amazonas, N Brazil
Coast Mountains 36 D4 Fr. Chaîne
Côtière. mountain range Canada/USA
Coast Ranges 46 A4 mountain range
W USA
Coats Island 37 G3 island Nunavut,
NE Canada
Coats Land 154 B2 physical region
Antarctica
Coatzacoalcos 51 G4 var. Quetzalcoalco;
prev. Puerto México. Veracruz-Llave,
E Mexico
Cobija 61 E5 Pando, NW Bolivia
Coblence/Coblenz see Koblenz
Coburg 95 C5 Bayern, SE Germany
Cocanada see Kākināda
Cochabamba 61 F4 hist. Oropeza.
Cochabamba, C Bolivia
Cochin 132 C4 var. Kochchi, Kochi.
Kerala, SW India
Cochrane 38 C4 Ontario, S Canada
Cochrane 65 B7 Aisén, S Chile
Cocibolca see Nicaragua, Lago de
Cockade State see Maryland
Cockburn Town 55 E2 San Salvador,
E Bahamas
Cockpit Country, The 54 A4 physical
region W Jamaica
Cocobeach 77 A5 Estuaire, NW Gabon
Coconino Plateau 48 B1 plain Arizona,
SW USA
Coco, Río 53 E2 var. Río Wanki,
Segoviao Wangkí. river Honduras/
Nicaragua

Cocos Basin 124 C5 undersea basin
E Indian Ocean
Cocos Island Ridge see Cocos Ridge
Cocos Islands 141 D5 island group
E Indian Ocean
Cocos Ridge 35 C8 var. Cocos Island
Ridge. undersea ridge E Pacific Ocean
Cod, Cape 41 G3 headland
Massachusetts, NE USA
Codfish Island 151 A8 island SW New
Zealand
Codlea 108 C4 Ger. Zeiden, Hung.
Feketehalom. Braşov, C Romania
Cody 44 C2 Wyoming, C USA
Coeur d'Alene 46 C2 Idaho, NW USA
Coevorden 86 E2 Drenthe,
NE Netherlands
Coffs Harbour 149 E6 New South Wales,
SE Australia
Cognac 91 B5 anc. Compniacum.
Charente, W France
Cohalm see Rupea
Coihaique 65 B6 var. Coyhaique. Aisén,
S Chile
Coimbatore 132 C3 Tamil Nādu, S India
Coimbra 92 B3 anc. Conimbria,
Conimbriga. Coimbra, W Portugal
Coín 92 D5 Andalucía, S Spain
Coira/Coire see Chur
Coirib, Loch see Corrib, Lough
Colby 45 E4 Kansas, C USA
Colchester 89 E6 Connecticut, NE USA
Coleman 49 F3 Texas, SW USA
Coleraine 88 B4 Ir. Cúil Raithin.
N Northern Ireland, United Kingdom
Colesberg 78 C5 Northern Cape,
C South Africa
Colima 50 D4 Colima, S Mexico
Coll 88 B3 island W Scotland, United
Kingdom
College Station 49 G3 Texas, SW USA
Collie 147 A7 Western Australia
Collipo see Leiria
Colmar 90 E4 Ger. Kolmar. Haut-Rhin,
NE France
Cöln see Köln
Cologne see Köln
Colomb-Béchar see Béchar
Colombia 58 B3 off. Republic of
Colombia. country N South America

COLOMBIA
South America

Official name Republic of Colombia
Formation 1819 / 1903
Capital Bogotá
Population 47 million / 117 people
per sq mile (45 people per sq km) / 77%
Total area 439,733 sq. miles
(1,138,910 sq. km)
Languages Spanish*, Wayuu, Páez, and
other Amerindian languages
Religions Roman Catholic 95%, Other 5%
Ethnic mix Mestizo 58%, White 20%,
European–African 14%, African 4%,
African–Amerindian 3%, Amerindian 1%
Government Presidential system
Currency Colombian peso = 100 centavos
Literacy rate 93%
Calorie consumption 2585 calories

Colombian Basin 56 A1 undersea basin
SW Caribbean Sea
Colombia, Republic of see Colombia
Colombie-Britannique see British
Columbia
Colombo 132 C4 country capital (Sri
Lanka) (Sri Lanka) Western Province,
W Sri Lanka
Colón 53 G4 prev. Aspinwall. Colón,
C Panama
Colonia Agrippina see Köln
Colón Ridge 35 B8 undersea ridge
E Pacific Ocean
Colorado 44 C4 off. State of Colorado,
also known as Centennial State, Silver
State. state C USA
Colorado City 49 F3 Texas, SW USA
Colorado Plateau 44 B4 plateau W USA
Colorado, Río 65 C5 river E Argentina
Colorado, Río see Colorado River
Colorado River 35 B5 var. Río Colorado.
river Mexico/USA
Colorado River 49 G4 river Texas,
SW USA

Colorado Springs *44 D5* Colorado, C USA
Columbia *41 E4* Maryland, NE USA
Columbia *45 G4* Missouri, C USA
Columbia *43 E2 state capital* South Carolina, SE USA
Columbia *42 C1* Tennessee, S USA
Columbia River *46 B3 river* Canada/ USA
Columbia Plateau *46 C3 plateau* Idaho/ Oregon, NW USA
Columbus *42 D2* Georgia, SE USA
Columbus *40 C4* Indiana, N USA
Columbus *42 C2* Mississippi, S USA
Columbus *45 F4* Nebraska, C USA
Columbus *40 D4 state capital* Ohio, N USA
Colville Channel *150 D2 channel* North Island, New Zealand
Colville River *36 D2 river* Alaska, USA
Comacchio *96 C3 var.* Commachio; *anc.* Comactium. Emilia-Romagna, N Italy
Comactium *see* Comacchio
Comalcalco *51 G4* Tabasco, SE Mexico
Coma Pedrosa, Pic de *91 A7 mountain* NW Andorra
Comarapa *61 F4* Santa Cruz, C Bolivia
Comayagua *52 C2* Comayagua, W Honduras
Comer See *see* Como, Lago di
Comilla *135 G4 Ben.* Kumillã. Chittagong, E Bangladesh
Comino *102 A5 Malt.* Kemmuna. *island* C Malta
Comitán *51 G5 var.* Comitán de Domínguez. Chiapas, SE Mexico
Comitán de Domínguez *see* Comitán
Commachio *see* Comacchio
Commissioner's Point *42 A5 headland* W Bermuda
Communism Peak *123 F3 prev.* Qullai Kommunizm. *mountain* E Tajikistan
Como *96 B2 anc.* Comum. Lombardia, N Italy
Comodoro Rivadavia *65 B6* Chubut, SE Argentina
Como, Lake *96 B2 var.* Lario, *Eng.* Lake Como, *Ger.* Comer See. *lake* N Italy
Como, Lake *see* Como, Lago di
Comores, République Fédérale Islamique des *see* Comoros
Comoros *79 F2 off.* Federal Islamic Republic of the Comoros, *Fr.* République Fédérale Islamique des Comores. *country* W Indian Ocean

COMOROS
Indian Ocean

Official name Union of the Comoros
Formation 1975 / 1975
Capital Moroni
Population 711,417 / 826 people per sq mile (319 people per sq km) / 36%
Total area 838 sq. miles (2170 sq. km)
Languages Arabic*, Comoran*, French*
Religions Muslim (mainly Sunni) 98%, Other 1%, Roman Catholic 1%
Ethnic mix Comoran 97%, Other 3%
Government Presidential system
Currency Comoros franc = 100 centimes
Literacy rate 56%
Calorie consumption 1754 calories

Comoros, Federal Islamic Republic of the *see* Comoros
Compiègne *90 C3* Oise, N France
Complutum *see* Alcalá de Henares
Compniacum *see* Cognac
Compostella *see* Santiago
Comrat *108 D4 Rus.* Komrat. S Moldova
Comum *see* Como
Conakry *74 C4 country capital* (Guinea) (Guinea) SW Guinea
Conca *see* Cuenca
Concarneau *90 A3* Finistère, NW France
Concepción *61 G3* Santa Cruz, E Bolivia
Concepción *65 B5* Bío Bío, C Chile
Concepción *64 D2 var.* Villa Concepción. Concepción, C Paraguay
Concepción *see* La Concepción
Concepción de la Vega *see* La Vega
Conchos, Río *48 D4 river* NW Mexico
Conchos, Río *50 D2 river* C Mexico
Concord *41 G3 state capital* New Hampshire, NE USA
Concordia *64 D4* Entre Ríos, E Argentina
Concordia *45 E4* Kansas, C USA
Côn Đảo *137 E7 var.* Con Son. *island* S Vietnam
Condate *see* Rennes, Ille-et-Vilaine, France
Condate *see* St-Claude, Jura, France
Condega *52 D1* Estelí, NW Nicaragua
Condivincum *see* Nantes
Confluentes *see* Koblenz
Công Hoa Xa Hôi Chu Nghia Viêt Nam *see* Vietnam
Congo *77 D5 off.* Republic of the Congo, *Fr. Moyen Congo; prev.* Middle Congo. *country* C Africa

CONGO
Central Africa

Official name Republic of the Congo
Formation 1960 / 1960
Capital Brazzaville
Population 4.2 million / 32 people per sq mile (12 people per sq km) / 54%
Total area 132,046 sq. miles (342,000 sq. km)
Languages French*, Kongo, Teke, Lingala
Religions Traditional beliefs 50%, Roman Catholic 25%, Protestant 23%, Muslim 2%
Ethnic mix Bakongo 51%, Teke 17%, Other 16%, Mbochi 11%, Mbédé 5%
Government Presidential system
Currency CFA franc = 100 centimes
Literacy rate 83%
Calorie consumption 2162 calories

Congo *77 C6 off.* Democratic Republic of Congo; *prev.* Zaire, Belgian Congo, Congo (Kinshasa). *country* C Africa

CONGO, DEM. REP.
Central Africa

Official name Democratic Republic of the Congo
Formation 1960 / 1960
Capital Kinshasa
Population 61.2 million / 70 people per sq mile (27 people per sq km) / 33%
Total area 905,563 sq. miles (2,345,410 sq. km)
Languages French*, Kiswahili, Tshiluba, Kikongo, Lingala
Religions Roman Catholic 50%, Protestant 20%, Traditional beliefs and other 10%, Muslim 10%, Kimbanguist 10%
Ethnic mix Other 55%, Mongo, Luba, Kongo, and Mangbetu-Azande 45%
Government Presidential system
Currency Congolese franc = 100 centimes
Literacy rate 67%
Calorie consumption 1599 calories

Congo *77 C6 var.* Kongo, *Fr.* Zaire. *river* C Africa
Congo Basin *77 C6 drainage basin* W Dem. Rep. Congo
Congo/Congo (Kinshasa) *see* Congo (Democratic Republic of)
Coni *see* Cuneo
Conimbria/Conimbriga *see* Coimbra
Conjeeveram *see* Kânchipuram
Connacht *see* Connaught
Connaught *89 A5 var.* Connacht, *Ir.* Chonnacht, Cúige. *province* W Ireland
Connecticut *41 F3 off.* State of Connecticut, *also known as* Blue Law State, Constitution State, Land of Steady Habits, Nutmeg State. *state* NE USA
Connecticut *41 G3 river* Canada/USA
Conroe *49 G3* Texas, SW USA
Consentia *see* Cosenza
Consolación del Sur *54 A2* Pinar del Río, W Cuba
Con Son *see* Côn Đảo
Constance *see* Konstanz
Constance, Lake *95 B7 Ger.* Bodensee. *lake* C Europe
Constanţa *108 D5 var.* Küstendje, *Eng.* Constanza, *Ger.* Konstanza, *Turk.* Küstence. Constanţa, SE Romania
Constantia *see* Coutances
Constantia *see* Konstanz
Constantine *71 E2 var.* Qacentina, *Ar.* Qoussantîna. NE Algeria
Constantinople *see* Istanbul
Constantiola *see* Oltenița
Constanz *see* Konstanz
Constanza *see* Constanţa
Constitution State *see* Connecticut
Çuu *see* Kus
Coober Pedy *149 A5* South Australia
Cookeville *42 D1* Tennessee, S USA
Cook Islands *145 F4 territory in free association with New Zealand* S Pacific Ocean
Cook, Mount *see* Aoraki
Cook Strait *151 D5 var.* Raukawa. *strait* New Zealand
Cooktown *148 D2* Queensland, NE Australia
Coolgardie *147 B6* Western Australia
Cooma *149 D7* New South Wales, SE Australia
Coomassie *see* Kumasi
Coon Rapids *45 F2* Minnesota, N USA
Cooper Creek *148 C4 var.* Barcoo, Cooper's Creek. *seasonal river* Queensland/South Australia
Cooper's Creek *see* Cooper Creek
Coos Bay *46 A3* Oregon, NW USA
Cootamundra *149 D6* New South Wales, SE Australia
Copacabana *61 E4* La Paz, W Bolivia
Copenhagen *see* København
Copiapó *64 B3* Atacama, N Chile
Copperas Cove *49 G3* Texas, SW USA
Coppermine *see* Kugluktuk
Copper State *see* Arizona
Coquilhatville *see* Mbandaka
Coquimbo *64 B3* Coquimbo, N Chile
Corabia *108 B5* Olt, S Romania
Coral Harbour *37 G3* Southampton Island, Nunavut, NE Canada
Coral Sea *142 B3 sea* SW Pacific Ocean
Coral Sea Islands *144 B4 Australian external territory* SW Pacific Ocean
Corantijn Rivier *see* Courantyne River
Corcovado, Golfo *65 B6 gulf* S Chile
Corcyra Nigra *see* Korčula
Cordele *42 D3* Georgia, SE USA
Córdoba *64 C3* Córdoba, C Argentina
Córdoba *51 F4* Veracruz-Llave, E Mexico
Córdoba *92 D4 var.* Cordoba, *Eng.* Cordova; *anc.* Corduba. Andalucía, SW Spain
Cordova *36 C3* Alaska, USA
Cordova/Cordoba *see* Córdoba
Corduba *see* Córdoba
Corentyne River *see* Courantyne River
Corfu *104 A4 var.* Kérkira, Greece, *Corfu.* *island* Iónia Nisiá, Greece, C Mediterranean Sea
Corfu *see* Kérkyra
Coria *92 C3* Extremadura, W Spain
Corinth *42 C1* Mississippi, S USA
Corinth, Gulf of *105 B5 Eng.* Gulf of Corinth; *anc.* Corinthiacus Sinus. *gulf* C Greece
Corinth, Gulf of/Corinthiacus Sinus *see* Korinthiakós Kólpos
Corinthus *see* Kórinthos
Corinto *52 C3* Chinandega, NW Nicaragua
Cork *89 A6 Ir.* Corcaigh. S Ireland
Çorlu *116 A2* Tekirdağ, NW Turkey
Corner Brook *39 G3* Newfoundland, Newfoundland and Labrador, E Canada
Cornhusker State *see* Nebraska
Corn Islands *53 E3 var.* Corn Islands. *island group* SE Nicaragua
Corn Islands *see* Maíz, Islas del
Cornwallis Island *37 F2 Island* Nunavut, N Canada
Coro *58 C1 prev.* Santa Ana de Coro. Falcón, NW Venezuela
Corocoro *61 F4* La Paz, W Bolivia
Coromandel *150 D2* Waikato, North Island, New Zealand
Coromandel Coast *132 D2 coast* E India
Coromandel Peninsula *150 D2 peninsula* North Island, New Zealand
Coronado, Bahía de *52 D5 bay* S Costa Rica
Coronel Dorrego *65 C5* Buenos Aires, E Argentina
Coronel Oviedo *64 D2* Caaguazú, SE Paraguay
Corozal *52 C1* Corozal, N Belize
Corpus Christi *49 G4* Texas, SW USA
Corrales *48 D2* New Mexico, SW USA
Corrib, Lough *89 A5 Ir.* Loch Coirib. *lake* W Ireland
Corrientes *64 D3* Corrientes, NE Argentina
Corriza *see* Korçë
Corsica *91 E7 Eng.* Corsica. *island* France, C Mediterranean Sea
Corsica *see* Corse
Corsicana *49 G3* Texas, SW USA
Cortegana *92 C4* Andalucía, S Spain
Cortés *53 E5 var.* Ciudad Cortés. Puntarenas, SE Costa Rica
Cortez, Sea of *see* California, Golfo de
Cortina d'Ampezzo *96 C1* Veneto, NE Italy
Coruche *92 B3* Santarém, C Portugal
Çoruh Nehri *117 E3 Geor.* Chorokhi, *Rus.* Chorokhi. *river* Georgia/Turkey
Çorum *116 D3 var.* Chorum. Çorum, N Turkey
Corunna *see* A Coruña
Corvallis *46 B3* Oregon, NW USA
Corvo *92 A5 var.* Ilha do Corvo. *island* Azores, Portugal, NE Atlantic Ocean
Corvo, Ilha do *see* Corvo
Cos *see* Kos
Cosenza *97 D6 anc.* Consentia. Calabria, SW Italy
Cosne-Cours-sur-Loire *90 C4* Nièvre, Bourgogne, C France Europe
Costa Mesa *46 D2* California, W USA North America
Costa Rica *53 E4 off.* Republic of Costa Rica, *country* Central America

COSTA RICA
Central America

Official name Republic of Costa Rica
Formation 1838 / 1838
Capital San José
Population 4.5 million / 228 people per sq mile (88 people per sq km) / 61%
Total area 19,730 sq. miles (51,100 sq. km)
Languages Spanish*, English Creole, Bribri, Cabecar
Religions Roman Catholic 76%, Other (including Protestant) 24%
Ethnic mix Mestizo and European 96%, Black 2%, Chinese 1%, Amerindian 1%
Government Presidential system
Currency Costa Rican colón = 100 céntimos
Literacy rate 95%
Calorie consumption 2876 calories

Costa Rica, Republic of *see* Costa Rica
Costermansville *see* Bukavu
Cotagaita *61 F5* Potosí, S Bolivia
Côte d'Ivoire *74 D4 off.* Republic of Côte d'Ivoire, *Fr.* Côte d'Ivoire, République de la Côte d'Ivoire, *Eng.* Ivory Coast. *country* W Africa

CÔTE D'IVOIRE (IVORY COAST)
West Africa

Official name Republic of Côte d'Ivoire
Formation 1960 / 1960
Capital Yamoussoukro
Population 18.8 million / 153 people per sq mile (59 people per sq km) / 45%
Total area 124,502 sq. miles (322,460 sq. km)
Languages Akan, French*, Krou, Voltaique
Religions Muslim 38%, Traditional beliefs 25%, Roman Catholic 25%, Other 6%, Protestant 6%
Ethnic mix Akan 42%, Voltaique 18%, Mandé du Nord 17%, Krou 11%, Mandé du Sud 10%, Other 2%
Government Presidential system
Currency CFA franc = 100 centimes
Literacy rate 49%
Calorie consumption 2631 calories

Côte d'Ivoire, République de la *see* Côte d'Ivoire
Côte d'Or *90 D4 cultural region* C France
Côtière, Chaine *see* Coast Mountains
Côte Française des Somalis *see* Djibouti
Cotonou *75 F5 var.* Kotonu. S Benin
Cotrone *see* Crotone

Cotswold Hills 89 *D6 var.* Cotswolds.
  hill range S England, United Kingdom
Cotswolds *see* Cotswold Hills
Cottbus 94 *D4 Lus.* Chośebuz; *prev.*
  Kottbus. Brandenburg, E Germany
Cotton State, The *see* Alabama
Cotyora *see* Ordu
Couentrey *see* Coventry
Council Bluffs 45 *F4* Iowa, C USA
Courantyne River 59 *G4 var.* Corantijn
  Rivier, Corentyne River. *river* Guyana/
  Suriname
Courland Lagoon 106 *A4 Ger.* Kurisches
  Haff, *Rus.* Kurskiy Zaliv. *lagoon*
  Lithuania/Russian Federation
Courtrai *see* Kortrijk
Coutances 90 *B3 anc.* Constantia.
  Manche, N France
Couvin 87 *C7* Namur, S Belgium
Coventry 89 *D6 anc.* Couentrey.
  C England, United Kingdom
Covilhã 92 *C3* Castelo Branco, E Portugal
Cowan, Lake 147 *B6 lake* Western
  Australia
Coxen Hole *see* Roatán
Coxin Hole *see* Roatán
Coyhaique *see* Coíhaique
Coyote State, The *see* South Dakota
Cozhë 126 *C5* Xizang Zizhiqu, W China
Cozumel, Isla 51 *H3 island* SE Mexico
Cracovia/Cracow *see* Kraków
Cradock 78 *C5* Eastern Cape, S South
  Africa
Craig 44 *C4* Colorado, C USA
Craiova 108 *B5* Dolj, SW Romania
Cranbrook 37 *E5* British Columbia,
  SW Canada
Crane *see* The Crane
Cranz *see* Zelenogradsk
Crawley 89 *E7* SE England, United
  Kingdom
Cremona 96 *B2* Lombardia, N Italy
Creole State *see* Louisiana
Cres 100 *A3 It.* Cherso; *anc.* Crexa.
  island W Croatia
Crescent City 46 *A4* California, W USA
Crescent Group 128 *C7 island group*
  C Paracel Islands
Creston 45 *F4* Iowa, C USA
Crestview 42 *D3* Florida, SE USA
Crete 105 *C7 Eng.* Crete. *island* Greece,
  Aegean Sea
Créteil 90 *E2* Val-de-Marne, N France
Sea of Crete 105 *D7 var.* Kretikon
  Delagos, *Eng.* Sea of Crete; *anc.* Mare
  Creticum. *sea* Greece, Aegean Sea
Crete, Sea of/Creticum, Mare *see* Kritikó
  Pélagos
Creuse 90 *B4 river* C France
Crewe 89 *D6* C England, United
  Kingdom
Crexa *see* Cres
Crikvenica 100 *A3 It.* Cirquenizza; *prev.*
  Cirkvenica, Crjkvenica. Primorje-
  Gorski Kotar, NW Croatia
Crimea 81 *F4 peninsula* SE Ukraine
  Europe
Cristóbal 53 *G4* Colón, C Panama
Cristóbal Colón, Pico 58 *B1 mountain*
  N Colombia
Cristur/Cristuru Săcuiesc *see* Cristuru
  Secuiesc
Cristuru Secuiesc 108 *C4 prev.* Cristur,
  Cristuru Săcuiesc; Sitaş Cristuru, *Ger.*
  Kreutz, *Hung.* Székelykeresztúr, Szitás-
  Keresztúr. Harghita, C Romania
Crjkvenica *see* Crikvenica
Crna Gora *see* Montenegro
Crna Reka 101 *D6 river* S FYR
  Macedonia
Crni Drim *see* Black Drin
Croatia 100 *B3 off.* Republic of Croatia,
  Ger. Kroatien, *SCr.* Hrvatska. *country*
  SE Europe

CROATIA
Southeast Europe

Official name Republic of Croatia
Formation 1991 / 1991
Capital Zagreb
Population 4.6 million / 211 people
per sq mile (81 people per sq km) / 59%
Total area 21,831 sq. miles (56,542 sq. km)
Languages Croatian*
Religions Roman Catholic 88%, Other 7%,
Orthodox Christian 4%, Muslim 1%

CROATIA
(continued)

Ethnic mix Croat 90%, Other 5%, Serb 5%
Government Parliamentary system
Currency Kuna = 100 lipa
Literacy rate 98%
Calorie consumption 2799 calories

Croatia, Republic of *see* Croatia
Crocodile *see* Limpopo
Croia *see* Krujë
Croker Island 146 *E2 island* Northern
  Territory, N Australia
Cromwell 151 *B7* Otago, South Island,
  New Zealand
Crooked Island 54 *D2 island* SE Bahamas
Crooked Island Passage 54 *D2 channel*
  SE Bahamas
Crookston 45 *F1* Minnesota, N USA
Crossen *see* Krosno Odrzańskie
Croton/Crotona *see* Crotone
Crotone 97 *E6 var.* Cotrone; *anc.* Croton,
  Crotona. Calabria, SW Italy
Croydon 89 *A8* SE England, United
  Kingdom
Crozet Basin 141 *B6 undersea basin*
  S Indian Ocean
Crozet Islands 141 *B7 island group*
  French Southern and Antarctic
  Territories
Crozet Plateau 141 *B7 var.* Crozet
  Plateaus. *undersea plateau* SW Indian
  Ocean
Crozet Plateaus *see* Crozet Plateau
Crystal Brook 149 *B6* South Australia
Csaca *see* Čadca
Csakathurn/Csáktornya *see* Čakovec
Csíkszereda *see* Miercurea-Ciuc
Csorna 99 *C6* Győr-Moson-Sopron,
  NW Hungary
Csurgó 99 *C7* Somogy, SW Hungary
Cuando 78 *C2 var.* Kwando. *river*
  S Africa
Cuango 78 *B1 var.* Kwango. *river*
  Angola/Dem. Rep. Congo
Cuango *see* Kwango
Cuanza 78 *B1 var.* Kwanza. *river*
  C Angola
Cuauhtémoc 50 *C2* Chihuahua,
  N Mexico
Cuautla 51 *E4* Morelos, S Mexico
Cuba 54 *B2 off.* Republic of Cuba.
  country W West Indies

CUBA
West Indies

Official name Republic of Cuba
Formation 1902 / 1902
Capital Havana
Population 11.3 million / 264 people
per sq mile (102 people per sq km) / 76%
Total area 42,803 sq. miles (110,860 sq. km)
Languages Spanish
Religions Nonreligious 49%, Roman
Catholic 40%, Atheist 6%, Other 4%,
Protestant 1%
Ethnic mix White 66%, European–African
22%, Black 12%
Government One-party state
Currency Cuban peso = 100 centavos
Literacy rate 99%
Calorie consumption 3152 calories

Cubal 78 *B2* Benguela, W Angola
Cubango 78 *B2 var.* Kuvango, *Port.* Vila
  Artur de Paiva, Vila da Ponte. Huíla,
  SW Angola
Cubango 78 *B2 var.* Kavango, Kavengo,
  Kubango, Okavango, Okavanggo.
  river S Africa
Cuba, Republic of *see* Cuba
Cúcuta 58 *C2 var.* San José de Cúcuta.
  Norte de Santander, N Colombia
Cuddapah 132 *C2* Andhra Pradesh,
  S India
Cuenca 60 *B2* Azuay, S Ecuador
Cuenca 93 *E3 anc.* Conca. Castilla-La
  Mancha, C Spain
Cuera *see* Chur
Cuernavaca 51 *E4* Morelos, S Mexico
Cuiabá 63 *E3 prev.* Cuyabá. *state capital*
  Mato Grosso, SW Brazil
Cúige *see* Connaught

Cúige Laighean *see* Leinster
Cúige Mumhan *see* Munster
Cuijck 86 *D4* Noord-Brabant,
  SE Netherlands
Cúil Raithin *see* Coleraine
Cuito 78 *B2 var.* Kwito. *river* SE Angola
Cukai 138 *B3 var.* Chukai, Kemaman.
  Terengganu, Peninsular Malaysia
Cularo *see* Grenoble
Culiacán 50 *C3 var.* Culiacán Rosales,
  Culiacán-Rosales. Sinaloa, C Mexico
Culiacán-Rosales/Culiacán Rosales
  see Culiacán
Cullera 93 *F3* País Valenciano, E Spain
Cullman 42 *C2* Alabama, S USA
Culm *see* Chełmno
Culmsee *see* Chełmża
Cumaná 59 *E1* Sucre, NE Venezuela
Cumbal, Nevado de 58 *A4 elevation*
  S Colombia
Cumberland 41 *E4* Maryland, NE USA
Cumberland Plateau 42 *D1 plateau*
  E USA
Cumberland Sound 37 *H3 inlet* Baffin
  Island, Nunavut, NE Canada
Cumpas 50 *B2* Sonora, NW Mexico
Cuneo 96 *A2 Fr.* Coni. Piemonte,
  NW Italy
Cunnamulla 149 *C5* Queensland,
  E Australia
Ćuprija 100 *E4* Serbia, E Serbia
Curaçao 55 *E5 Dutch autonomous region*
  S Caribbean Sea
Curia Rhaetorum *see* Chur
Curicó 64 *B4* Maule, C Chile
Curieta *see* Krk
Curitiba 63 *E4 prev.* Curytiba. *state
  capital* Paraná, S Brazil
Curtbunar *see* Tervel
Curtea de Argeş 108 *C4 var.* Curtea-de-
  Arges. Arges, S Romania
Curtea-de-Arges *see* Curtea de Argeş
Curtici 108 *A4 Ger.* Kurtitsch, *Hung.*
  Kürtős. Arad, W Romania
Curtis Island 148 *E4 island* Queensland,
  SE Australia
Curytiba *see* Curitiba
Curzola *see* Korčula
Cusco 61 *E4 var.* Cuzco. Cusco, C Peru
Cusset 91 *C5* Allier, C France
Cutch, Gulf of *see* Kachchh, Gulf of
Cuttack 135 *F4* Orissa, E India
Cuvier Plateau 141 *E6 undersea plateau*
  E Indian Ocean
Cuxhaven 94 *B2* Niedersachsen,
  NW Germany
Cuyabá *see* Cuiabá
Cuyuni, Río *see* Cuyuni River
Cuyuni River 59 *F3 var.* Río Cuyuni.
  river Guyana/Venezuela
Cuzco *see* Cusco
Cyclades 105 *D6 var.* Kikládhes, *Eng.*
  Cyclades. *island group* SE Greece
Cyclades *see* Kykládes
Cydonia *see* Chaniá
Cymru *see* Wales
Cyprus 102 *C4 off.* Republic of
  Cyprus, *Gk.* Kypros, *Turk.* Kıbrıs,
  Kıbrıs Cumhuriyeti. *country*
  E Mediterranean Sea

CYPRUS
Southeast Europe

Official name Republic of Cyprus
Formation 1960 / 1960
Capital Nicosia
Population 788,457 / 221 people
per sq mile (85 people per sq km) / 69%
Total area 3571 sq. miles (9250 sq. km)
Languages Greek*, Turkish*
Religions Orthodox Christian 78%,
Muslim 18%, Other 4%
Ethnic mix Greek 81%, Turkish 11%,
Other 8%
Government Presidential system
Currency Euro (Turkish lira in TRNC) = 100
cents (euro); 100 kurus (Turkish lira)
Literacy rate 97%
Calorie consumption 3255 calories

Cyprus, Republic of *see* Cyprus
Cythnos *see* Kýthnos
Czech Republic 99 *A5 Cz.* Česká
  Republika. *country* C Europe

CZECH REPUBLIC
Central Europe

Official name Czech Republic
Formation 1993 / 1993
Capital Prague
Population 10.2 million / 335 people
per sq mile (129 people per sq km) / 74%
Total area 30,450 sq. miles (78,866 sq. km)
Languages Czech*, Slovak,
Hungarian (Magyar)
Religions Roman Catholic 39%,
Atheist 38%, Other 18%, Protestant 3%,
Hussite 2%
Ethnic mix Czech 90%, Other 4%,
Moravian 4%, Slovak 2%
Government Parliamentary system
Currency Czech koruna = 100 haleru
Literacy rate 99%
Calorie consumption 3171 calories

Czenstochau *see* Częstochowa
Czernowitz *see* Chernivtsi
Częstochowa 98 *C4 Ger.* Czenstochau,
  Tschenstochau, *Rus.* Chenstokhov.
  Śląskie, S Poland
Człuchów 98 *C3 Ger.* Schlochau.
  Pomorskie, NW Poland

D

Dabajuro 58 *C1* Falcón, NW Venezuela
Dabeiba 58 *B2* Antioquia, NW Colombia
Dąbrowa Tarnowska 99 *D5*
  Małopolskie, S Poland
Dabryn' 107 *C8 Rus.* Dobryn'.
  Homyel'skaya Voblasts', SE Belarus
Dacca *see* Dhaka
Daegu *see* Taegu
Dagana 74 *B3* N Senegal
Dagda 106 *D4* Krāslava, SE Latvia
Dagden *see* Hiiumaa
Dagenham 89 *B8* United Kingdom
Dağlıq Quarabağ *see* Nagorno-Karabakh
Dagö *see* Hiiumaa
Dagupan 139 *E1 off.* Dagupan City.
  Luzon, N Philippines
Dagupan City *see* Dagupan
Dahm, Ramlat 121 *B6 desert* NW Yemen
Dahomey *see* Benin
Daihoku *see* T'aipei
Daimiel 92 *D3* Castilla-La Mancha,
  C Spain
Daimonia 105 *B7* Pelopónnisos, S Greece
Dainan *see* T'ainan
Daingin, Bá an *see* Dingle Bay
Dairen *see* Dalian
Dakar 74 *B3 country capital* (Senegal)
  (Senegal) W Senegal
Dakhla *see* Ad Dakhla
Dakoro 75 *G3* Maradi, S Niger
Đakovica *see* Gjakovë
Đakovo 100 *C3 var.* Djakovo, *Hung.*
  Diakovár. Osijek-Baranja, E Croatia
Dakshin *see* Deccan
Dalain Hob 126 *D3 var.* Ejin Qi. Nei
  Mongol Zizhiqu, N China
Dalai Nor *see* Hulun Nur
Dalaman 116 *A4* Muğla, SW Turkey
Dalandzadgad 127 *E3* Ömnögovĭ,
  S Mongolia
Đa Lat 137 *E6* Lâm Đông, S Vietnam
Dalby 149 *D5* Queensland, E Australia
Dale City 41 *E4* Virginia, NE USA
Dalhart 49 *E1* Texas, SW USA
Dali 128 *A6 var.* Xiaguan. Yunnan,
  SW China
Dalian 128 *D4 var.* Dairen, Dalien, Jay
  Dairen, Lüda, Ta-lien, *Rus.* Dalny.
  Liaoning, NE China
Dalien *see* Dalian
Dallas 49 *G2* Texas, SW USA
Dalmacija 100 *B4 Eng.* Dalmatia, *Ger.*
  Dalmatien, *It.* Dalmazia. *cultural region*
  S Croatia
Dalmatia/Dalmatien/Dalmazia *see*
  Dalmacija
Dalny *see* Dalian
Dalton 42 *D1* Georgia, SE USA
Dálvvadis *see* Jokkmokk
Daly Waters 148 *A2* Northern Territory,
  N Australia
Damachava 107 *A6 var.* Damachova,
  Pol. Domaczewo, *Rus.* Domachëvo.
  Brestskaya Voblasts', SW Belarus

Damachova see Damachava
Damān 134 C4 Damän and Diu, W India
Damara 76 C4 Ombella-Mpoko, S Central African Republic
Damas see Dimashq
Damasco see Dimashq
Damascus see Dimashq
Qolleh-ye Damavand 120 D3 mountain N Iran
Damietta see Dumyät
Dammām see Ad Dammän
Damoûr 119 A5 var. Ad Dämûr. W Lebanon
Dampier 146 A4 Western Australia
Dampier, Selat 139 F4 strait Papua, E Indonesia
Damqawt 121 D6 var. Damqut. E Yemen
Damqut see Damqawt
Damxung 126 C5 var. Gongtang. Xizang Zizhiqu, W China
Danakil Desert 72 D4 var. Afar Depression, Danakil Plain. desert E Africa
Danakil Plain see Danakil Desert
Danané 74 D5 W Côte d'Ivoire
Đà Nẵng 137 E5 prev. Tourane. Quang Nam-Đa Nẵng, C Vietnam
Danborg see Daneborg
Dandong 128 D3 var. Tan-tung; prev. An-tung. Liaoning, NE China
Daneborg 83 E3 var. Danborg. Tunu, N Greenland
Dänew see Galkynyş
Dangara see Danghara
Dangerous Archipelago see Tuamotu, Îles
Danghara 123 E3 Rus. Dangara. SW Tajikistan
Danghe Nanshan 126 D3 mountain range W China
Dang Raek, Phanom/Dangrek, Chaine des see Dângrêk, Chuör Phnum
Chuor Phnum Dangrek 137 D5 var. Phanom Dang Raek, Phanom Dong Rak, Fr. Chaine des Dangrek. mountain range Cambodia/Thailand
Dangriga 42 C1 prev. Stann Creek. Stann Creek, E Belize
Danish West Indies see Virgin Islands (US)
Danli 52 D2 El Paraíso, S Honduras
Danmark see Denmark
Danmarksstraedet see Denmark Strait
Dannenberg 94 C3 Niedersachsen, N Germany
Dannevirke 150 D4 Manawatu-Wanganui, North Island, New Zealand
Dantzig see Gdańsk
Danube 81 E4 Bul. Dunav, Cz. Dunaj, Ger. Donau, Hung. Duna, Rom. Dunărea. river C Europe
Danubian Plain 104 C2 Eng. Danubian Plain. lowlands N Bulgaria
Danubian Plain see Dunavska Ravnina
Danum see Doncaster
Danville 41 E5 Virginia, NE USA
Danxian/Dan Xian see Danzhou
Danzhou 128 C2 prev. Danxian, Dan Xian, Nada. Hainan, S China
Danzig see Gdańsk
Danziger Bucht see Danzig, Gulf of
Danzig, Gulf of 98 C2 var. Gulf of Gdańsk, Ger. Danziger Bucht, Pol. Zakota Gdańska, Rus. Gdan'skaya Bukhta. gulf N Poland
Daqm see Duqm
Dar'ā 119 B5 var. Der'a, Fr. Déraa. Dar'ā, SW Syria
Darabani 108 C3 Botoşani, NW Romania
Daraut-Kurgan see Daroot-Korgon
Dardanelles 116 A2 Eng. Dardanelles. strait NW Turkey
Dardanelles see Çanakkale Boğazı
Dardanelli see Çanakkale
Dar-el-Beida see Casablanca
Dar es Salaam 73 C7 Dar es Salaam, E Tanzania
Darfield 151 C6 Canterbury, South Island, New Zealand
Darfur 72 A4 var. Darfur Massif. cultural region W Sudan
Darfur Massif see Darfur
Darhan 127 E2 Darhan Uul, N Mongolia
Darién, Golfo del see Darien, Gulf of
Darien, Gulf of 58 A2 Sp. Golfo del Darién. gulf S Caribbean Sea

Darien, Isthmus of see Panama, Istmo de
Darién, Serranía del 53 H5 mountain range Colombia/Panama
Dario see Ciudad Darío
Dariorigum see Vannes
Darjeeling see Därjiling
Därjiling 135 F3 prev. Darjeeling. West Bengal, NE India
Darling River 149 C6 river New South Wales, SE Australia
Darlington 89 D5 N England, United Kingdom
Darmstadt 95 B5 Hessen, SW Germany
Darnah 71 G2 var. Dérna. NE Libya
Darnley, Cape 154 D2 cape Antarctica
Daroca 93 E2 Aragón, NE Spain
Daroot-Korgon 123 F3 var. Daraut-Kurgan. Oshskaya Oblast', SW Kyrgyzstan
Dartford 89 B8 SE England, United Kingdom
Dartmoor 89 C7 moorland SW England, United Kingdom
Dartmouth 39 F4 Nova Scotia, SE Canada
Darvaza see Derweze, Turkmenistan
Darwin 146 D2 prev. Palmerston, Port Darwin. territory capital Northern Territory, N Australia
Darwin, Isla 60 A4 island Galápagos, Galapagos Islands, W Ecuador
Dashhowuz see Daşoguz
Dashkawka 107 D6 Rus. Dashkovka. Mahilyowskaya Voblasts', E Belarus
Dashkovka see Dashkawka
Daşoguz 122 C2 Rus. Dashkhovuz, Turkm. Dashhowuz; prev. Tashauz. Daşoguz Welaýaty, N Turkmenistan
Đa, Sông see Black River
Datong 128 C3 var. Tatung, Ta-t'ung. Shanxi, C China
Daugava see Western Dvina
Daugavpils 106 D4 Ger. Dünaburg; prev. Rus. Dvinsk. Daugvapils, SE Latvia
Daung Kyun 137 B6 island S Burma (Myanmar)
Dauphiné 91 D5 cultural region E France
Dāvangere 132 C2 Karnātaka, W India
Davao 139 F3 off. Davao City. Mindanao, S Philippines
Davao City see Davao
Davao Gulf 139 F3 gulf Mindanao, S Philippines
Davenport 45 G3 Iowa, C USA
David 53 E5 Chiriquí, W Panama
Davie Ridge 141 A5 undersea ridge W Indian Ocean
Davis 154 D3 Australian research station Antarctica
Davis Sea 154 D3 sea Antarctica
Davis Strait 82 B3 strait Baffin Bay/ Labrador Sea
Dawei 137 B5 var. Tavoy, Htawei. Tanintharyi, S Burma (Myanmar)
Dawlat Qatar see Qatar
Dax 91 B6 var. Ax; anc. Aquae Augustae, Aquae Tarbelicae. Landes, SW France
Dayr az Zawr 118 D3 var. Deir ez Zor. Dayr az Zawr, E Syria
Dayton 40 C4 Ohio, N USA
Daytona Beach 43 E4 Florida, SE USA
De Aar 78 C5 Northern Cape, C South Africa
Dead Sea 119 B6 var. Bahret Lut, Lacus Asphaltites, Ar. Al Baḥr al Mayyit, Baḥrat Lūt, Heb. Yam HaMelaḥ. salt lake Israel/Jordan
Deán Funes 64 C3 Córdoba, C Argentina
Death Valley 47 C7 valley California, W USA
Deatnu 84 D2 Fin. Tenojoki, Nor. Tana. river Finland/Norway
Debar 101 D6 Ger. Dibra, Turk. Debre. W FYR Macedonia
De Behagle see Laï
Dębica 99 D5 Podkarpackie, SE Poland
De Bildt see De Bilt
De Bilt 86 D3 var. De Bildt. Utrecht, C Netherlands
Dębno 98 B3 Zachodnio-pomorskie, NW Poland
Debre see Debar
Debrecen 99 D6 Ger. Debreczin, Rom. Debreţin; prev. Debreczen. Hajdú-Bihar, E Hungary
Debrecen/Debreczin see Debrecen
Debreţin see Debrecen
Decatur 42 C1 Alabama, S USA

Decatur 40 B4 Illinois, N USA
Deccan 134 D5 Hind. Dakshin. plateau C India
Děčín 98 B4 Ger. Tetschen. Ústecký Kraj, NW Czech Republic
Dedeagaç/Dedeagach see Alexandroúpoli
Dedemsvaart 86 E3 Overijssel, E Netherlands
Dee 88 C3 river NE Scotland, United Kingdom
Deering 36 C2 Alaska, USA
Deés see Dej
Deggendorf 95 D6 Bayern, SE Germany
Değirmenlik 102 C5 Gk. Kythréa. N Cyprus
Deh Bid see Şafāshahr
Dehli see Delhi
Deh Shū 122 D5 var. Deshu. Helmand, S Afghanistan
Deinze 87 B5 Oost-Vlaanderen, NW Belgium
Deir ez Zor see Dayr az Zawr
Deirgeirt, Loch see Derg, Lough
Dej 108 B3 Hung. Dés; prev. Deés. Cluj, NW Romania
De Jouwer see Joure
Dekélea see Dhekélia
Dékoa 76 C4 Kémo, C Central African Republic
De Land 43 E4 Florida, SE USA
Delano 47 C7 California, W USA
Delārām 122 D5 Nīmrūz, SW Afghanistan
Delaware 40 D4 Ohio, N USA
Delaware 41 F4 off. State of Delaware, also known as Blue Hen State, Diamond State, First State. state NE USA
Delft 86 B4 Zuid-Holland, W Netherlands
Delfzijl 86 E1 Groningen, NE Netherlands
Delgo 72 B3 Northern, N Sudan
Delhi 134 D3 var. Dehli, Hind. Dilli, hist. Shahjahanabad. union territory capital Delhi, N India
Delicias 50 D2 var. Ciudad Delicias. Chihuahua, N Mexico
Déli-Kárpátok see Carpaţii Meridionalii
Delmenhorst 94 B3 Niedersachsen, NW Germany
Del Rio 49 F4 Texas, SW USA
Deltona 43 E4 Florida, SE USA
Demba 77 D6 Kasai-Occidental, C Dem. Rep. Congo
Dembia 76 D4 Mbomou, SE Central African Republic
Demchok 126 A5 var. Dêmqog. disputed region China/India
Demerara Plain 56 C2 abyssal plain W Atlantic Ocean
Deming 48 C3 New Mexico, SW USA
Demmin 94 C2 Mecklenburg-Vorpommern, NE Germany
Demopolis 42 C2 Alabama, S USA
Dêmqog 126 A5 var. Demchok. China/ India
Denali see McKinley, Mount
Denau see Denov
Dender 87 B6 Fr. Dendre. river W Belgium
Dendre see Dender
Denekamp 86 E3 Overijssel, E Netherlands
Den Haag see 's-Gravenhage
Denham 147 A5 Western Australia
Den Ham 86 E3 Overijssel, E Netherlands
Den Helder 86 C2 Noord-Holland, NW Netherlands
Dénia 93 F4 País Valenciano, E Spain
Deniliquin 149 C7 New South Wales, SE Australia
Denison 45 F3 Iowa, C USA
Denison 49 G2 Texas, SW USA
Denizli 116 B4 Denizli, SW Turkey
Denmark 85 A7 off. Kingdom of Denmark, Dan. Danmark; anc. Hafnia. country N Europe

Denmark, Kingdom of see Denmark
Denmark Strait 82 D4 var. Danmarksstraedet. strait Greenland/ Iceland
Dennery 55 F1 E Saint Lucia
Denov 123 E3 Rus. Denau. Surkhondaryo Viloyati, S Uzbekistan
Denpasar 138 D5 prev. Paloe. Bali, C Indonesia
Denton 49 G2 Texas, SW USA
D'Entrecasteaux Islands 144 B3 island group SE Papua New Guinea
Denver 44 D4 state capital Colorado, C USA
Der'a/Derá/Déraa see Dar'ā
Dera Ghāzi Khān 134 C2 var. Dera Ghāzikhān. Punjab, C Pakistan
Dera Ghāzikhān see Dera Ghāzi Khān
Đeravica 101 D5 mountain S Serbia
Derbent 111 B8 Respublika Dagestan, SW Russian Federation
Derby 89 D6 C England, United Kingdom
Dereli see Gónnoi
Dergachi see Derhachi
Derg, Lough 89 A6 Ir. Loch Deirgeirt. lake W Ireland
Derhachi 109 G2 Rus. Dergachi. Kharkivs'ka Oblast', E Ukraine
De Ridder 42 A3 Louisiana, S USA
Dérna see Darnah
Derry see Londonderry
Dertosa see Tortosa
Derventa 100 B3 Republika Srpska, N Bosnia and Herzegovina
Derweze 122 C2 Rus. Darvaza. Ahal Welaýaty, C Turkmenistan
Dés see Dej
Deschutes River 46 B3 river Oregon, NW USA
Desé 72 C4 var. Desse, It. Dessie. Āmara, N Ethiopia
Deseado, Río 65 B7 river S Argentina
Desertas, Ilhas 70 A2 island group Madeira, Portugal, NE Atlantic Ocean
Deshu see Deh Shū
Des Moines 45 F3 state capital Iowa, C USA
Desna 109 E2 river Russian Federation/ Ukraine
Dessau 94 C4 Sachsen-Anhalt, E Germany
Desse see Desé
Dessie see Desé
Destêrro see Florianópolis
Detroit 40 D3 Michigan, N USA
Detroit Lakes 45 F2 Minnesota, N USA
Deurne 87 D5 Noord-Brabant, SE Netherlands
Deutschendorf see Poprad
Deutsch-Eylau see Iława
Deutsch Krone see Wałcz
Deutschland/Deutschland, Bundesrepublik see Germany
Deutsch-Südwestafrika see Namibia
Deva 108 B4 Ger. Diemrich, Hung. Déva. Hunedoara, W Romania
Déva see Deva
Deva see Chester
Devana see Aberdeen
Devana Castra see Chester
Đevđelija see Gevgelija
Deventer 86 D3 Overijssel, E Netherlands
Devils Lake 45 E1 North Dakota, N USA
Devoll 99 C7 Devollit, Lumi i
Devollit, Lumi i 101 D6 var. Devoll. river SE Albania
Devon Island 37 F2 prev. North Devon Island. island Parry Islands, Nunavut, NE Canada
Devonport 149 C8 Tasmania, SE Australia

Devrek 116 C2 Zonguldak, N Turkey
Dexter 45 H5 Missouri, C USA
Deynau see Galkynyş
Dezfül 120 C3 var. Dizful. Khüzestän,
SW Iran
Dezhou 128 D4 Shandong, E China
Dhaka 135 G4 prev. Dacca. country
capital (Bangladesh) (Bangladesh)
Dhaka, C Bangladesh
Dhanbād 135 F4 Jhärkhand, NE India
Dhekélia 102 C5 Eng. Dhekelia, Gk.
Dekéleia. UK air base SE Cyprus
see Dhekélia
Dhidhimótikhon see Didymóteicho
Dhíkti Ori see Díkti
Dhodhekánisos see Dodekánisa
Dhomokós see Domokós
Dhráma see Dráma
Dhrepanon, Akrotírio see Drépano,
Akrotírio
Dhún na nGall, Bá see Donegal Bay
Dhuusa Marreeb 73 E5 var. Dusa
Marreb, It. Dusa Mareb. Galguduud,
C Somalia
Diakovár see Đakovo
Diamantina, Chapada 63 F3 mountain
range E Brazil
Diamantina Fracture Zone 141 E6
tectonic feature E Indian Ocean
Diamond State see Delaware
Diarbekr see Diyarbakır
Dibio see Dijon
Dibra see Debar
Dibrugarh 135 H3 Assam, NE India
Dickinson 44 D2 North Dakota, N USA
Dicle see Tigris
Didimotiho see Didymóteicho
Didymóteicho 104 D3 var.
Dhidhimótikhon, Didimotího.
Anatolikí Makedonía kai Thráki,
NE Greece
Diedenhofen see Thionville
Diekirch 87 D7 Diekirch, C Luxembourg
Diemrich see Deva
Điện Biên 136 D3 var. Bien Bien, Dien
Bien Phu. Lai Châu, N Vietnam
Dien Bien Phu see Điện Biên
Diepenbeek 87 D6 Limburg, NE Belgium
Diepholz 94 B3 Niedersachsen,
NW Germany
Dieppe 90 C2 Seine-Maritime, N France
Dieren 86 D4 Gelderland, E Netherlands
Differdange 87 D8 Luxembourg,
SW Luxembourg
Digne 91 D6 var. Digne-les-Bains.
Alpes-de-Haute-Provence, SE France
Digne-les-Bains see Digne
Digoel see Digul, Sungai
Digoin 90 C4 Saône-et-Loire, C France
Digul, Sungai 139 H5 prev. Digoel. river
Papua, E Indonesia
Dihang see Brahmaputra
Dijlah see Tigris
Dijon 90 D4 anc. Dibio. Côte d'Or,
C France
Dikhil 72 D4 SW Djibouti
Dikson 114 D2 Taymyrskiy (Dolgano-
Nenetskiy) Avtonomnyy Okrug,
N Russian Federation
Díkti 105 D8 var. Dhíkti Ori.
mountain range Kríti, Greece,
E Mediterranean Sea
Dili 139 F5 var. Dilli, Dilly. country
capital (East Timor) (East Timor)
N East Timor
Dilia 75 G3 var. Dillia. river SE Niger
Di Linh 137 E6 Lâm Đông, S Vietnam
Dilli see Dili, East Timor
Dilli see Delhi, India
Dillia see Dilia
Dilling 72 B4 var. Ad Dalanj. Southern
Kordofan, C Sudan
Dillon 44 B2 Montana, NW USA
Dilly see Dili
Dilolo 77 D7 Katanga, S Dem. Rep. Congo
Dimashq 119 B5 var. Ash Shām, Esh
Sham, Eng. Damascus, Fr. Damas,
It. Damasco. country capital (Syria)
Dimashq, SW Syria
Dimitrovgrad 104 D3 Khaskovo,
S Bulgaria
Dimitrovgrad 111 C6 prev. Caribrod.
Serbia, SE Serbia
Dimitrovo see Pernik
Dimovo 104 B1 Vidin, NW Bulgaria
Dinajpur 135 F3 Rajshahi,
NW Bangladesh

Dinan 90 B3 Côtes d'Armor, NW France
Dinant 87 C7 Namur, S Belgium
Dinar 116 B4 Afyon, SW Turkey
Dinara see Dinaric Alps
Dinaric Alps 100 C4 var. Dinara.
mountain range Bosnia and
Herzegovina/Croatia
Dindigul 132 C3 Tamil Nādu, SE India
Dingle Bay 89 A6 Ir. Bá an Daingin. bay
SW Ireland
Dinguiraye 74 C4 N Guinea
Diourbel 74 B3 W Senegal
Diré Dawa 73 D5 Diré Dawa, E Ethiopia
Dirk Hartog Island 147 A5 island
Western Australia
Dirschau see Tczew
Disappointment, Lake 146 C4 salt lake
Western Australia
Discovery Bay 54 B4 Middlesex,
Jamaica, Greater Antilles, C Jamaica
Caribbean Sea
Disko Bugt see Qeqertarsuup Tunua
Dispur 135 G3 state capital Assam,
NE India
Divinópolis 63 F4 Minas Gerais, SE Brazil
Divo 74 D5 S Côte d'Ivoire
Divodurum Mediomatricum see Metz
Diyarbakır 117 F4 var. Diarbekr; anc.
Amida. Diyarbakır, SE Turkey
Dizful see Dezfül
Djailolo see Halmahera, Pulau
Djajapura see Jayapura
Djakarta see Jakarta
Djakovo see Đakovo
Djambala 77 B6 Plateaux, C Congo
Djambi see Jambi
Djambi see Hari, Batang
Djanet 71 E4 prev. Fort Charlet.
SE Algeria
Djéblé see Jablah
Djelfa 70 D2 var. El Djelfa. N Algeria
Djéma 76 D4 Haut-Mbomou, E Central
African Republic
Djember see Jember
Djérablous see Jarābulus
Djerba 71 F2 var. Djerba, Jazīrat Jarbah.
island E Tunisia
Djerba see Jerba, Île de
Djérem 76 B4 river C Cameroon
Djevdjelija see Gevgelija
Djibouti 72 D4 var. Jibuti. country
capital (Djibouti) (Djibouti) E Djibouti
Djibouti 72 D4 off. Republic of Djibouti,
var. Jibuti; prev. French Somaliland,
French Territory of the Afars and
Issas, Fr. Côte Française des Somalis,
Territoire Français des Afars et des
Issas. country E Africa

DJIBOUTI
East Africa

Official name Republic of Djibouti
Formation 1977 / 1977
Capital Djibouti
Population 496,374 / 55 people
per sq mile (21 people per sq km) / 84%
Total area 8494 sq. miles (22,000 sq. km)
Languages Arabic*, French*, Somali, Afar
Religions Muslim (mainly Sunni) 94%,
Christian 6%
Ethnic mix Issa 60%, Afar 35%, Other 5%
Government Presidential system
Currency Djibouti franc = 100 centimes
Literacy rate 66%
Calorie consumption 2220 calories

Djibouti, Republic of see Djibouti
Djokjakarta see Yogyakarta
Djourab, Erg du 76 C2 desert N Chad
Djúpivogur 83 E5 Austurland,
SE Iceland
Dmitriyevsk see Makiyivka
Dnepr see Dnieper
Dneprodzerzhinsk see Romaniv
Dneprodzerzhinskoye
Vodokhranilishche
Dniprodzerzhyns'ke Vodokhvovyshche
Dnepropetrovsk see Dnipropetrovs'k
Dneprorudnoye see Dniprorudne
Dnestr see Dniester
Dnieper 81 E4 Bel. Dnyapro, Rus. Dnepr,
Ukr. Dnipro. river E Europe
Dnieper Lowland 109 E2 Bel.
Prydnyaprowskaya Nizina, Ukr.
Prydniprovs'ka Nyzovyna. lowlands
Belarus/Ukraine

Dniester 81 E4 Rom. Nistru, Rus.
Dnestr, Ukr. Dnister; anc. Tyras. river
Moldova/Ukraine
Dnipro see Dnieper
Dniprodzerzhyns'k see Romaniv
Dniprodzerzhyns'ke Vodokhovyshche
109 F3 Rus. Dneprodzerzhinskoye
Vodokhranilishche. reservoir
C Ukraine
Dnipropetrovs'k 109 F3 Rus.
Dnepropetrovsk; prev. Yekaterinoslav.
Dnipropetrovs'ka Oblast', E Ukraine
Dniprorudne 109 F3 Rus.
Dneprorudnoye. Zaporiz'ka Oblast',
SE Ukraine
Dnister see Dniester
Dnyapro see Dnieper
Doba 76 C4 Logone-Oriental, S Chad
Döbeln 94 D4 Sachsen, E Germany
Doberai Peninsula 139 G4 Dut.
Vogelkop. peninsula Papua,
E Indonesia
Doboj 100 C3 Republiks Srpska,
N Bosnia and Herzegovina
Dobre Miasto 98 D2 Ger. Guttstadt.
Warmińsko-mazurskie, NE Poland
Dobrich 104 E1 Rom. Bazargic; prev.
Tolbukhin. Dobrich, NE Bulgaria
Dobrush 107 D7 Homyel'skaya
Voblasts', SE Belarus
Dobryn' see Dabryn'
Dodecanese 105 D6 var. Nóties
Sporádes, Eng. Dodecanese; prev.
Dhodhekánisos, Dodekanisos. island
group SE Greece
Dodecanese see Dodekánisa
Dodekanisos see Dodekánisa
Dodge City 45 E5 Kansas, C USA
Dodoma 69 D5 country capital
(Tanzania) (Tanzania) Dodoma,
C Tanzania
Dogana 96 E1 NE San Marino Europe
Dogo 131 B6 island Oki-shotō, SW Japan
Dogondoutchi 75 F3 Dosso, SW Niger
Dogrular see Pravda
Doğubayazıt 117 F3 Ağrı, E Turkey
Doğu Karadeniz Dağları 117 E3 var.
Anadolu Dağları. mountain range
NE Turkey
Doha see Ad Dawhah
Doire see Londonderry
Dokkum 86 D1 Friesland, N Netherlands
Dokuchayevs'k 109 G3 var.
Dokuchayevsk. Donets'ka Oblast',
SE Ukraine
Dokuchayevsk see Dokuchayevs'k
Doldrums Fracture Zone 66 C4 fracture
zone W Atlantic Ocean
Dôle 90 D4 Jura, E France
Dolina see Dolyna
Dolinskaya see Dolyns'ka
Dolisie 77 B6 prev. Loubomo. Niari,
S Congo
Dolomites 96 C1 var. Dolomiti, Eng.
Dolomites. mountain range NE Italy
Dolomites/Dolomiti see Dolomites,
Alpi
Dolores 64 D4 Buenos Aires, E Argentina
Dolores 52 B1 Petén, N Guatemala
Dolores 64 D4 Soriano, SW Uruguay
Dolores Hidalgo 51 E4 var. Ciudad
de Dolores Hidalgo. Guanajuato,
C Mexico
Dolyna 108 B2 Rus. Dolina. Ivano-
Frankivs'ka Oblast', W Ukraine
Dolyns'ka 109 E3 Rus. Dolinskaya.
Kirovohrads'ka Oblast', S Ukraine
Domachëvo/Domaczewo see Damachava
Dombås 85 B5 Oppland, S Norway
Domel Island see Letsók-aw Kyun
Domesnes, Cape see Kolkasrags
Domeyko 64 B3 Atacama, N Chile
Dominica 55 H4 off. Commonwealth of
Dominica. country E West Indies

DOMINICA
West Indies

Official name Commonwealth
of Dominica
Formation 1978 / 1978
Capital Roseau
Population 72,386 / 250 people
per sq mile (97 people per sq km) / 72%
Total area 291 sq. miles (754 sq. km)
Languages English*, French Creole
Religions Roman Catholic 77%, Dominica

DOMINICA
(continued)

Protestant 15%, Other 8%
Ethnic mix Black 87%, Mixed race 9%,
Carib 3%, Other 1%
Government Parliamentary system
Currency Eastern Caribbean dollar
= 100 cents
Literacy rate 88%
Calorie consumption 2763 calories

Dominica Channel see Martinique
Passage
Dominica, Commonwealth of see
Dominica
Dominican Republic 55 E2 country
C West Indies

DOMINICAN REPUBLIC
West Indies

Official name Dominican Republic
Formation 1865 / 1865
Capital Santo Domingo
Population 9.1 million / 487 people
per sq mile (188 people per sq km) / 60%
Total area 18,679 sq. miles (48,380 sq. km)
Languages Spanish*, French Creole
Religions Roman Catholic 92%,
Other and nonreligious 8%
Ethnic mix Mixed race 75%, White 15%,
Black 10%
Government Presidential system
Currency Dominican Republic peso
= 100 centavos
Literacy rate 87%
Calorie consumption 2347 calories

Domokós 105 B5 var. Dhomokós. Stereá
Ellás, C Greece
Don 111 B6 var. Duna, Tanais. river
SW Russian Federation
Donau see Danube
Donauwörth 95 C6 Bayern, S Germany
Don Benito 92 C3 Extremadura,
W Spain
Doncaster 89 D5 anc. Danum.
N England, United Kingdom
Dondo 78 B1 Cuanza Norte, NW Angola
Donegal 89 B5 Ir. Dún na nGall.
Donegal, NW Ireland
Donegal Bay 89 A5 Ir. Bá Dhún na nGall.
bay NW Ireland
Donets 109 G2 river Russian Federation/
Ukraine
Donets'k 109 G3 Rus. Donetsk; prev.
Stalino. Donets'ka Oblast', E Ukraine
Dongfang 128 B7 var. Basuo. Hainan,
S China
Dongguan 128 C6 Guangdong, S China
Dong Hai see East China Sea
Đông Ha 136 E4 Quang Tri, C Vietnam
Đông Hoi 136 D4 Quang Binh,
C Vietnam
Dongliao see Liaoyuan
Dongola 72 B3 var. Donqola, Dunqulah.
Northern, N Sudan
Dongou 77 C5 Likouala, NE Congo
Dong Rak, Phanom see Dângrêk, Chuŏr
Phnum
Dongting Hu 128 C5 var. Tung-t'ing
Hu. lake S China
Donostia-San Sebastián 93 E1 País
Vasco, N Spain
Donqola see Dongola
Doolow 73 D5 Sumalé, E Ethiopia
Doornik see Tournai
Door Peninsula 40 C2 peninsula
Wisconsin, N USA
Dooxo Nugaaleed 73 E5 var. Nogal
Valley. valley E Somalia
Dordogne 91 B5 cultural region
SW France
Dordogne 91 B5 river W France
Dordrecht 86 C4 var. Dordt, Dort.
Zuid-Holland, SW Netherlands
Dordt see Dordrecht
Dorohoi 108 C3 Botoşani, NE Romania
Dorotea 84 C4 Västerbotten, N Sweden
Dorpat see Tartu
Dorre Island 147 A5 island Western
Australia
Dort see Dordrecht
Dortmund 94 A4 Nordrhein-Westfalen,
W Germany

Dos Hermanas *92 C4* Andalucía, S Spain
Dospad Dagh *see* Rhodope Mountains
Dospat *104 C3* Smolyan, S Bulgaria
Dothan *42 D3* Alabama, S USA
Dotnuva *106 B4* Kaunas, C Lithuania
Douai *90 C2 prev.* Douay; *anc.* Duacum. Nord, N France
Douala *77 A5 var.* Duala. Littoral, W Cameroon
Douay *see* Douai
Douglas *89 C5 dependent territory capital* (Isle of Man) E Isle of Man
Douglas *48 C3* Arizona, SW USA
Douglas *44 D3* Wyoming, C USA
Douma *see* Dūmā
Douro *see* Duero
Douvres *see* Dover
Dover *89 E7 Fr.* Douvres, *Lat.* Dubris Portus. SE England, United Kingdom
Dover *41 F4 state capital* Delaware, NE USA
Dover, Strait of *90 C2 var.* Straits of Dover, *Fr.* Pas de Calais. *strait* England, United Kingdom/France
Dover, Straits of *see* Dover, Strait of
Dovrefjell *85 B5 plateau* S Norway
Downpatrick *89 B5 Ir.* Dún Pádraig. SE Northern Ireland, United Kingdom
Dozen *131 B6 island* Oki-shotō, SW Japan
Drâa, Hammada du *see* Dra, Hamada du
Drač/Draç *see* Durrës
Drachten *86 D2* Friesland, N Netherlands
Drăgăşani *108 B5* Vâlcea, SW Romania
Dragoman *104 B2* Sofiya, W Bulgaria
Dra, Hamada du *70 C3 var.* Hammada du Drâa, Haut Plateau du Dra. *plateau* W Algeria
Dra, Haut Plateau du *see* Dra, Hamada du
Drahichyn *107 B6 Pol.* Drohiczyn Poleski, *Rus.* Drogichin. Brestskaya Voblasts', SW Belarus
Drakensberg *78 D5 mountain range* Lesotho/South Africa
Drake Passage *57 B8 passage* Atlantic Ocean/Pacific Ocean
Dralfa *104 D2* Türgovishte, N Bulgaria
Dráma *104 C3 var.* Dhráma. Anatolikí Makedonía kai Thráki, NE Greece
Dramburg *see* Drawsko Pomorskie
Drammen *85 B6* Buskerud, S Norway
Drau *see* Drava
Drava *100 C3 var.* Drau, *Eng.* Drave, *Hung.* Dráva. *river* C Europe
Dráva/Drave *see* Drau/Drava
Drawsko Pomorskie *98 B3 Ger.* Dramburg. Zachodnio-pomorskie, NW Poland
Drépano, Akrotírio *104 C4 var.* Akrotirio Dhrepanon. *headland* N Greece
Drepanum *see* Trapani
Dresden *94 D4* Sachsen, E Germany
Drin *see* Drinit, Lumi i
Drina *100 C3 river* Bosnia and Herzegovina/Serbia
Drinit, Lumi i *101 D5 var.* Drin. *river* NW Albania
Drinit te Zi, Lumi i *see* Black Drin
Drissa *see* Drysa
Drobeta-Turnu Severin *108 B5 prev.* Turnu Severin. Mehedinţi, SW Romania
Drogheda *89 B5 Ir.* Droichead Átha. NE Ireland
Drogichin *see* Drahichyn
Drogobych *see* Drohobych
Drohiczyn Poleski *see* Drahichyn
Drohobych *108 B2 Pol.* Drohobycz, *Rus.* Drogobych. L'vivs'ka Oblast', NW Ukraine
Drohobycz *see* Drohobych
Droichead Átha *see* Drogheda
Drôme *91 D5 cultural region* E France
Dronning Maud Land *154 B2 physical region* Antarctica
Drontheim *see* Trondheim
Drug *see* Durg
Druk-yul *see* Bhutan
Drummondville *39 E4* Québec, SE Canada
Druskienniki *see* Druskininkai
Druskininkai *107 B5 Pol.* Druskienniki. Alytus, S Lithuania
Dryden *38 B3* Ontario, C Canada

Drysa *107 D5 Rus.* Drissa. *river* N Belarus
Duacum *see* Douai
Duala *see* Douala
Dubai *see* Dubayy
Dubăsari *108 D3 Rus.* Dubossary. NE Moldova
Dubawnt *37 F4 river* Nunavut, NW Canada
Dubayy *120 D4 Eng.* Dubai. Dubayy, NE United Arab Emirates
Dubbo *149 D6* New South Wales, SE Australia
Dublin *89 B5 Ir.* Baile Átha Cliath; *anc.* Eblana. *country capital* (Ireland) (Ireland) Dublin, E Ireland
Dublin *43 E2* Georgia, SE USA
Dubno *108 C2* Rivnens'ka Oblast', NW Ukraine
Dubossary *see* Dubăsari
Dubris Portus *see* Dover
Dubrovnik *101 B5 It.* Ragusa. Dubrovnik-Neretva, SE Croatia
Dubuque *45 G3* Iowa, C USA
Dudelange *87 D8 var.* Forge du Sud, *Ger.* Dudelingen. Luxembourg, S Luxembourg
Dudelingen *see* Dudelange
Duero *92 D2 Port.* Douro. *river* Portugal/Spain
Duesseldorf *see* Düsseldorf
Duffel *87 C5* Antwerpen, C Belgium
Dugi Otok *100 A4 var.* Isola Grossa, *It.* Isola Lunga. *island* W Croatia
Duinekerke *see* Dunkerque
Duisburg *94 A4 prev.* Duisburg-Hamborn. Nordrhein-Westfalen, W Germany
Duisburg-Hamborn *see* Duisburg
Duiven *86 D4* Gelderland, E Netherlands
Duk Faiwil *73 B5* Jonglei, SE Sudan
Dulan *126 D4 var.* Qagan Us. Qinghai, C China
Dulce, Golfo *53 E5 gulf* S Costa Rica
Dulce, Golfo *see* Izabal, Lago de
Dülmen *94 A4* Nordrhein-Westfalen, W Germany
Dulovo *104 E1* Silistra, NE Bulgaria
Duluth *45 G2* Minnesota, N USA
Dūmā *119 B5 Fr.* Douma. Dimashq, SW Syria
Dumas *49 E1* Texas, SW USA
Dumfries *88 C4* S Scotland, United Kingdom
Dumont d'Urville *154 C4 French research station* Antarctica
Dumyât *72 B1 var.* Dumyât, *Eng.* Damietta. N Egypt
Duna *see* Danube, C Europe
Düna *see* Western Dvina
Duna *see* Don, Russian Federation
Dünaburg *see* Daugavpils
Dunaj *see* Wien, Austria
Dunaj *see* Danube, C Europe
Dunapentele *see* Dunaújváros
Dunărea *see* Danube
Dunaújváros *99 C7 prev.* Dunapentele, Sztálinváros. Fejér, C Hungary
Dunav *see* Danube
Duncan *49 G2* Oklahoma, C USA
Dundalk *89 B5 Ir.* Dún Dealgan. Louth, NE Ireland
Dún Dealgan *see* Dundalk
Dundee *78 D4* KwaZulu/Natal, E South Africa
Dundee *88 C4* E Scotland, United Kingdom
Dunedin *151 B7* Otago, South Island, New Zealand
Dunfermline *88 C4* C Scotland, United Kingdom
Dungu *77 E5* Orientale, NE Dem. Rep. Congo
Dungun *138 B3 var.* Kuala Dungun. Terengganu, Peninsular Malaysia
Dunholme *see* Durham
Dunkerque *90 C2 Eng.* Dunkirk, *Flem.* Duinekerke; *prev.* Dunquerque. Nord, N France
Dunkirk *see* Dunkerque
Dún Laoghaire *89 B6 Eng.* Dunleary; *prev.* Kingstown. E Ireland
Dunleary *see* Dún Laoghaire
Dún Pádraig *see* Downpatrick
Dunquerque *see* Dunkerque
Dunqulah *see* Dongola

Dupnitsa *104 C2 prev.* Marek, Stanke Dimitrov. Kyustendil, W Bulgaria
Duqm *121 E5 var.* Daqm. E Oman
Durance *91 D6 river* SE France
Durango *50 D3 var.* Victoria de Durango. Durango, W Mexico
Durango *44 C5* Colorado, C USA
Durankulak *104 E1 Rom.* Răcari; *prev.* Blatnitsa, Duranulac. Dobrich, NE Bulgaria
Durant *49 G2* Oklahoma, C USA
Duranulac *see* Durankulak
Durazzo *see* Durrës
Durban *78 D4 var.* Port Natal. KwaZulu/Natal, E South Africa
Durbe *106 B3 Ger.* Durben. Liepāja, W Latvia
Durben *see* Durbe
Durg *135 F4 prev.* Drug. Chhattisgarh, C India
Durham *89 D5 hist.* Dunholme. N England, United Kingdom
Durham *43 F1* North Carolina, SE USA
Durocortorum *see* Reims
Durostorum *see* Silistra
Durovernum *see* Canterbury
Durrës *101 C6 var.* Durrësi, Dursi, *It.* Durazzo, *SCr.* Drač, *Turk.* Draç. Durrës, W Albania
Durrësi *see* Durrës
Dursi *see* Durrës
Durūz, Jabal ad *119 C5 mountain* S Syria
D'Urville Island *150 C4 island* C New Zealand
Dusa Mareb/Dusa Marreb *see* Dhuusa Marreeb
Dushanbe *123 E3 var.* Dyushambe; *prev.* Stalinabad, *Taj.* Stalinobod. *country capital* (Tajikistan) (Tajikistan) W Tajikistan
Düsseldorf *94 A4 var.* Duessedorf. Nordrhein-Westfalen, W Germany
Dústi *123 E3 Rus.* Dusti. SW Tajikistan
Dutch East Indies *see* Indonesia
Dutch Guiana *see* Suriname
Dutch Harbor *36 B3* Unalaska Island, Alaska, USA
Dutch New Guinea *see* Papua
Dutch West Indies *see* Netherlands Antilles
Duzdab *see* Zāhedān
Dvina Bay *see* Chëshskaya Guba
Dvinsk *see* Daugavpils
Dyanev *see* Galkynyş
Dyersburg *42 C1* Tennessee, S USA
Dyushambe *see* Dushanbe
Dza Chu *see* Mekong
Dzaudzhikau *see* Vladikavkaz
Dzerzhinsk *111 C5* Nizhegorodskaya Oblast', W Russian Federation
Dzerzhinskiy *see* Nar'yan-Mar
Dzhalal-Abad *123 F2 Kir.* Jalal-Abad. Dzhalal-Abadskaya Oblast', W Kyrgyzstan
Dzhambul *see* Taraz
Dzhankoy *109 F4* Respublika Krym, S Ukraine
Dzharkurgan *see* Jarqo'rg'on
Dzhelandy *123 F3* SE Tajikistan
Dzhergalan *123 G2 Kir.* Jyrgalan. Issyk-Kul'skaya Oblast', NE Kyrgyzstan
Dzhezkazgan *see* Zhezkazgan
Dzhizak *see* Jizzax
Dzhugdzhur, Khrebet *115 G3 mountain range* E Russian Federation
Dzhusaly *114 B4 Kaz.* Zhosaly. Kzylorda, SW Kazakhstan
Działdowo *98 D3* Warmińsko-Mazurskie, C Poland
Dzuunmod *127 E2 Töv,* C Mongolia
Dzüün Soyonï Nuruu *see* Eastern Sayans
Dzvina *see* Western Dvina

E

Eagle Pass *49 F4* Texas, SW USA
East Açores Fracture Zone *see* East Azores Fracture Zone
East Antarctica *154 C3 var.* Greater Antarctica. *physical region* Antarctica
East Australian Basin *see* Tasman Basin
East Azores Fracture Zone *66 C3 var.* East Açores Fracture Zone. *tectonic feature* E Atlantic Ocean

Eastbourne *89 E7* SE England, United Kingdom
East Cape *150 E3 headland* North Island, New Zealand
East China Sea *125 E2 Chin.* Dong Hai. *sea* W Pacific Ocean
Easter Fracture Zone *153 G4 tectonic feature* E Pacific Ocean
Easter Island *153 F4 var.* Rapa Nui, Easter Island. *island* E Pacific Ocean
Easter Island *see* Pascua, Isla de
Eastern Desert *68 D3 var.* Aş Şaḥrā' ash Sharqīyah, *Eng.* Arabian Desert, Eastern Desert. *desert* E Egypt
Eastern Desert *see* Sahara el Sharqīya
Eastern Ghats *124 D3 mountain range* SE India
Eastern Sayans *115 F4 Mong.* Dzüün Soyonï Nuruu, *Rus.* Vostochnyy Sayan. *mountain range* Mongolia/Russian Federation
Eastern Sierra Madre *see* Madre Oriental, Sierra
East Falkland *65 D8 var.* Isla Soledad. *island* E Falkland Islands
East Frisian Islands *94 A3 Eng.* East Frisian Islands. *island group* NW Germany
East Frisian Islands *see* Ostfriesische Inseln
East Grand Forks *45 E1* Minnesota, N USA
East Indiaman Ridge *141 D6 undersea ridge* E Indian Ocean
East Indies *152 A3 island group* SE Asia
East Kilbride *88 C4* S Scotland, United Kingdom
East Korea Bay *129 E3 bay* E North Korea
Eastleigh *89 D7* S England, United Kingdom
East London *78 D5 Afr.* Oos-Londen; *prev.* Emonti, Port Rex. Eastern Cape, S South Africa
Eastmain *38 D3 river* Québec, C Canada
East Mariana Basin *142 B1 undersea basin* W Pacific Ocean
East Novaya Zemlya Trough *112 C1 var.* Novaya Zemlya Trough. *trough* W Kara Sea
East Pacific Rise *153 F4 undersea rise* E Pacific Ocean
East Pakistan *see* Bangladesh
East Saint Louis *40 B4* Illinois, N USA
East Scotia Basin *67 C7 undersea basin* SE Scotia Sea
East Sea *130 A4 var.* Sea of Japan, *Rus.* Yaponskoye More. *sea* NW Pacific Ocean
East Siberian Sea *115 F1 Eng.* East Siberian Sea. *sea* Arctic Ocean
East Siberian Sea *see* Vostochno-Sibirskoye More
East Timor *139 F5 var.* Loro Sae; *prev.* Portuguese Timor, Timor Timur. *country* S Indonesia

EAST TIMOR
Southeast Asia

Official name Democratic Republic of Timor-Leste
Formation 2002 / 2002
Capital Dili
Population 1.1 million / 192 people per sq mile (74 people per sq km) / 8%
Total area 5756 sq. miles (14,874 sq. km)
Languages Tetum (Portuguese/Austronesian)*, Bahasa Indonesia, and Portuguese*
Religions Roman Catholic 95%, Other (including Muslim and Protestant) 5%
Government Parliamentary system
Currency US dollar = 100 cents
Literacy rate 59%
Calorie consumption 2806 calories

Eau Claire *40 A2* Wisconsin, N USA
Eau Claire, Lac à L' *see* St. Clair, Lake
Eauripik Rise *142 B2 undersea rise* W Pacific Ocean
Ebensee *95 D6* Oberösterreich, N Austria
Eberswalde-Finow *94 D3* Brandenburg, E Germany
Ebetsu *130 D2 var.* Ebetu. Hokkaidō, NE Japan

Ebetu *see* Ebetsu
Eblana *see* Dublin
Ebolowa 77 A5 Sud, S Cameroon
Ebon Atoll 144 D2 *var.* Epoon. *atoll* Ralik Chain, S Marshall Islands
Ebora *see* Évora
Eboracum *see* York
Ebro 93 E2 *river* NE Spain
Eburacum *see* York
Ebusus *see* Eivissa
Ebusus *see* Eivissa
Ebusus *see* Eivissa
Ecbatana *see* Hamadān
Ech Cheliff/Ech Chleff *see* Chlef
Echo Bay 37 E3 Northwest Territories, NW Canada
Echt 87 D5 Limburg, SE Netherlands
Ecija 92 D4 *anc.* Astigi. Andalucía, SW Spain
Eckengraf *see* Viesīte
Ecuador 60 B1 *off.* Republic of Ecuador. *country* NW South America

ECUADOR
South America

Official name Republic of Ecuador
Formation 1830 / 1942
Capital Quito
Population 13.6 million / 127 people per sq mile (49 people per sq km) / 62%
Total area 109,483 sq. miles (283,560 sq. km)
Languages Spanish*, Quechua, other Amerindian languages
Religions Roman Catholic 93%, Protestant, Jewish, and other 7%
Ethnic mix Mestizo 55%, Amerindian 25%, White 10%, Black 10%
Government Presidential system
Currency US dollar = 100 cents
Literacy rate 91%
Calorie consumption 2754 calories

Ecuador, Republic of *see* Ecuador
Ed Da'ein 72 A4 Southern Darfur, W Sudan
Ed Damazin 72 C4 *var.* Ad Damazīn. Blue Nile, E Sudan
Ed Damer 72 C3 *var.* Ad Dāmir, Ad Damar. River Nile, NE Sudan
Ed Debba 72 B3 Northern, N Sudan
Ede 86 D4 Gelderland, C Netherlands
Ede 75 F5 Osun, SW Nigeria
Edéa 77 A5 Littoral, SW Cameroon
Edessa *see* Şanlıurfa
Edfu *see* Idfū
Edgeoya 83 G2 *island* S Svalbard
Edgware 89 A7 Harrow, SE England, United Kingdom
Edinburg 49 G5 Texas, SW USA
Edinburgh 88 C4 *national capital* S Scotland, United Kingdom
Edingen *see* Enghien
Edirne 116 A2 *Eng.* Adrianople; *anc.* Adrianopolis, Hadrianopolis. Edirne, NW Turkey
Edmonds 46 B2 Washington, NW USA
Edmonton 37 E5 *province capital* Alberta, SW Canada
Edmundston 39 E4 New Brunswick, SE Canada
Edna 49 G4 Texas, SW USA
Edolo 96 B1 Lombardia, N Italy
Edremit 116 A3 Balıkesir, NW Turkey
Edward, Lake 77 E5 *var.* Albert Edward Nyanza, Edward Nyanza, Lac Idi Amin, Lake Rutanzige. *lake* Uganda/Dem. Rep. Congo
Edward Nyanza *see* Edward, Lake
Edwards Plateau 49 F3 *plain* Texas, SW USA
Edzo 53 E4 *prev.* Rae-Edzo. Northwest Territories, NW Canada
Eeklo 87 B5 *var.* Eekloo. Oost-Vlaanderen, NW Belgium
Eekloo *see* Eeklo
Eems *see* Ems
Eersel 87 C5 Noord-Brabant, S Netherlands
Eesti Vabariik *see* Estonia
Efate 144 D4 *var.* Efate, Fr. Vaté; *prev.* Sandwich Island. *island* C Vanuatu
Efate *see* Efate
Effingham 40 B4 Illinois, N USA
Eforie Sud 108 D5 Constanţa, E Romania
Egadi Is. 97 B7 *island group* S Italy

Ege Denizi *see* Aegean Sea
Eger 99 D6 *Ger.* Erlau. Heves, NE Hungary
Eger *see* Cheb, Czech Republic
Egeria Fracture Zone 141 C5 *tectonic feature* W Indian Ocean
Éghezée 87 C6 Namur, C Belgium
Egina *see* Aígina
Egio *see* Aígio
Egmont *see* Taranaki, Mount
Egmont, Cape 150 C4 *headland* North Island, New Zealand
Egoli *see* Johannesburg
Egypt 72 B2 *off.* Arab Republic of Egypt, *Ar.* Jumhūrīyah Miṣr al 'Arabīyah, *prev.* United Arab Republic; *anc.* Aegyptus. *country* NE Africa

EGYPT
North Africa

Official name Arab Republic of Egypt
Formation 1936 / 1982
Capital Cairo
Population 76.9 million / 200 people per sq mile (77 people per sq km) / 42%
Total area 386,660 sq. miles (1,001,450 sq. km)
Languages Arabic*, French, English, Berber
Religions Muslim (mainly Sunni) 94%, Coptic Christian and other 6%
Ethnic mix Egyptian 99%, Nubian, Armenian, Greek, and Berber 1%
Government Presidential system
Currency Egyptian pound = 100 piastres
Literacy rate 71%
Calorie consumption 3338 calories

Eibar 93 E1 País Vasco, N Spain
Eibergen 86 E3 Gelderland, E Netherlands
Eidfjord 85 A5 Hordaland, S Norway
Eier-Berg *see* Suur Munamägi
Eifel 95 A5 *plateau* W Germany
Eiger 95 B7 *mountain* C Switzerland
Eigg 88 B3 *island* W Scotland, United Kingdom
Eight Degree Channel 132 B3 *channel* India/Maldives
Eighty Mile Beach 146 B4 *beach* Western Australia
Eijsden 87 D6 Limburg, SE Netherlands
Eilat *see* Elat
Eindhoven 87 D5 Noord-Brabant, S Netherlands
Eipel *see* Ipel'
Éire *see* Ireland
Éireannn, Muir *see* Irish Sea
Eisenhüttenstadt 94 D4 Brandenburg, E Germany
Eisenmarkt *see* Hunedoara
Eisenstadt 95 E6 Burgenland, E Austria
Eisleben 94 C4 Sachsen-Anhalt, C Germany
Eivissa 93 G3 *var.* Iviza, *Cast.* Ibiza; *anc.* Ebusus. Ibiza, Spain, W Mediterranean Sea
Eivissa 93 G3 *var.* Iviza, *Cast.* Ibiza; *anc.* Ebusus. Ibiza, Spain, W Mediterranean Sea
Eivissa 93 G3 *var.* Iviza, *Cast.* Ibiza; *anc.* Ebusus. Ibiza, Spain, W Mediterranean Sea
Ejea de los Caballeros 93 E2 Aragón, NE Spain
Ejin Qi *see* Dalain Hob
Ekapa *see* Cape Town
Ekaterinodar *see* Krasnodar
Ekvytvatapskiy Khrebet 115 G1 *mountain range* NE Russian Federation
El 'Alamein *see* Al 'Alamayn
El Asnam *see* Chlef
Elat 119 B8 *var.* Eilat, Elath. Southern, S Israel
Elat, Gulf of *see* Aqaba, Gulf of
Elath *see* Elat, Israel
Elath *see* Al 'Aqabah, Jordan
El'Atrun 72 B3 Northern Darfur, NW Sudan
Elâziğ 117 E3 *var.* Elâzig, Elâziz. Elâziğ, E Turkey
Elba 96 B4 *island* Archipelago Toscano, C Italy
Elbasan 101 D6 *var.* Elbasani. Elbasan, C Albania
Elbasani *see* Elbasan

Elbe 80 D3 *Cz.* Labe. *river* Czech Republic/Germany
Elbert, Mount 44 C4 *mountain* Colorado, C USA
Elbing *see* Elbląg
Elbląg 98 C2 *var.* Elblag, *Ger.* Elbing. Warmińsko-Mazurskie, NE Poland
El Boulaïda/El Boulaïda *see* Blida
El'brus 111 A8 *var.* Gora El'brus. *mountain* SW Russian Federation
El'brus, Gora *see* El'brus
El Burgo de Osma 93 E2 Castilla-León, C Spain
Elburz Mountains 120 C2 *Eng.* Elburz Mountains. *mountain range* N Iran
Elburz Mountains *see* Alborz, Reshteh-ye Kūhhā-ye
El Cajon 47 C8 California, W USA
El Calafate 65 B7 *var.* Calafate. Santa Cruz, S Argentina
El Callao 59 E2 Bolívar, E Venezuela
El Campo 49 G4 Texas, SW USA
El Carmen de Bolívar 58 B2 Bolívar, NW Colombia
El Cayo *see* San Ignacio
El Centro 47 D8 California, W USA
Elche 93 F4 *Cat.* Elx; *anc.* Ilici, *Lat.* Illicis. País Valenciano, E Spain
Elda 93 F4 País Valenciano, E Spain
El Djazaïr *see* Alger
El Djelfa *see* Djelfa
Eldorado 64 E3 Misiones, NE Argentina
El Dorado 50 C3 Sinaloa, C Mexico
El Dorado 42 B2 Arkansas, C USA
El Dorado 45 F5 Kansas, C USA
El Dorado 59 F2 Bolívar, E Venezuela
El Dorado *see* California
Eldoret 73 C6 Rift Valley, W Kenya
Elektrostal' 111 B5 Moskovskaya Oblast', W Russian Federation
Elemi Triangle 73 B5 *disputed region* Kenya/Sudan
Elephant Butte Reservoir 48 C2 *reservoir* New Mexico, SW USA
Élesd *see* Aleşd
Eleuthera Island 54 C1 *island* N Bahamas
El Fasher 72 A4 *var.* Al Fāshir. Northern Darfur, W Sudan
El Ferrol/El Ferrol del Caudillo *see* Ferrol
El Gedaref *see* Gedaref
El Geneina 72 A4 *var.* Ajjinena, Al-Genain, Al Junaynah. Western Darfur, W Sudan
Elgin 88 C3 NE Scotland, United Kingdom
Elgin 40 B3 Illinois, N USA
El Gîza *see* Gîza
El Goléa 70 D3 *var.* Al Golea. C Algeria
El Hank 74 D1 *cliff* N Mauritania
El Haseke *see* Al Ḥasakah
Elimberrum *see* Auch
Elioccoca *see* Lorca
Élisabethville *see* Lubumbashi
Elista 111 B7 Respublika Kalmykiya, SW Russian Federation
Elizabeth 149 B6 South Australia
Elizabeth City 43 G1 North Carolina, SE USA
Elizabethtown 40 C5 Kentucky, S USA
El-Jadida 70 C2 *prev.* Mazagan. W Morocco
Elk 98 E2 *Ger.* Lyck. Warmińsko-mazurskie, NE Poland
Elk City 49 F1 Oklahoma, C USA
El Khalil *see* Hebron
El Khârga *see* Al Khārijah
Elkhart 40 C3 Indiana, N USA
El Khartum *see* Khartoum
Elk River 45 F2 Minnesota, N USA
El Kuneitra *see* Al Qunayţirah
Ellás *see* Greece
Ellef Ringnes Island 37 E1 *island* Nunavut, N Canada
Ellen, Mount 44 B5 *mountain* Utah, W USA
Ellensburg 46 B2 Washington, NW USA
Ellesmere Island 37 F1 *island* Queen Elizabeth Islands, Nunavut, N Canada
Ellesmere, Lake 151 C6 *lake* South Island, New Zealand
Ellice Islands *see* Tuvalu
Elliston 149 A6 South Australia
Ellsworth Land 154 A3 *physical region* Antarctica

El Mahbas 70 B3 *var.* Mahbés. SW Western Sahara
El Mina 118 B4 *var.* Al Mīnā'. N Lebanon
El Minya *see* Al Minyā
Elmira 41 E3 New York, NE USA
El Mreyyé 74 D2 *desert* E Mauritania
Elmshorn 94 B3 Schleswig-Holstein, N Germany
El Muglad 72 B4 Western Kordofan, C Sudan
El Obeid 72 B4 *var.* Al Obayyid, Al Ubayyiḍ. Northern Kordofan, C Sudan
El Ouâdi *see* El Oued
El Oued 71 E2 *var.* Al Oued, El Ouâdi, El Wad. NE Algeria
Eloy 48 B2 Arizona, SW USA
El Paso 48 D3 Texas, SW USA
El Porvenir 53 G4 Kuna Yala, N Panama
El Progreso 52 C2 Yoro, NW Honduras
El Puerto de Santa María 92 C5 Andalucía, S Spain
El Qâhira *see* Cairo
El Quneitra *see* Al Qunayţirah
El Quseir *see* Al Quşayr
El Quweira *see* Al Quwayrah
El Rama 53 E3 Región Autónoma Atlántico Sur, SE Nicaragua
El Real 53 H5 *var.* El Real de Santa María. Darién, SE Panama
El Real de Santa María *see* El Real
El Reno 49 F1 Oklahoma, C USA
El Salvador 52 B3 *off.* Republica de El Salvador. *country* Central America

EL SALVADOR
Central America

Official name Republic of El Salvador
Formation 1841 / 1841
Capital San Salvador
Population 7.1 million / 888 people per sq mile (343 people per sq km) / 60%
Total area 8124 sq. miles (21,040 sq. km)
Languages Spanish
Religions Roman Catholic 80%, Evangelical 18%, Other 2%
Ethnic mix Mestizo 94%, Amerindian 5%, White 1%
Government Presidential system
Currency Salvadorean colón & US dollar = 100 centavos (colón): 100 cents (US dollar)
Literacy rate 80%
Calorie consumption 2584 calories

El Salvador, Republica de *see* El Salvador
Elsass *see* Alsace
El Sáuz 50 C2 Chihuahua, N Mexico
El Serrat 91 A7 N Andorra Europe
Elst 86 D4 Gelderland, E Netherlands
El Sueco 50 C2 Chihuahua, N Mexico
El Suweida *see* As Suwaydā'
El Suweis *see* Suez
Eltanin Fracture Zone 153 E5 *tectonic feature* SE Pacific Ocean
El Tigre 59 E2 Anzoátegui, NE Venezuela
Elvas 92 C4 Portalegre, C Portugal
El Vendrell 93 G2 Cataluña, NE Spain
El Vigía 58 C2 Mérida, NW Venezuela
El Wad *see* El Oued
Elwell, Lake 44 B1 *reservoir* Montana, NW USA
Elx *see* Elche
Ely 47 D5 Nevada, W USA
El Yopal *see* Yopal
Emajõgi 106 D3 *Ger.* Embach. *river* SE Estonia
Emämrüd *see* Shāhrüd
Emämshahr *see* Shāhrüd
Emba 114 B4 *Kaz.* Embi. Aktyubinsk, W Kazakhstan
Embach *see* Emajõgi
Embi *see* Emba
Emden 94 A3 Niedersachsen, NW Germany
Emerald 148 D4 Queensland, E Australia
Emerald Isle *see* Montserrat
Emesa *see* Ḥimş
Emmaste 106 C2 Hiiumaa, W Estonia
Emmeloord 86 D2 Flevoland, N Netherlands
Emmen 86 E2 Drenthe, NE Netherlands
Emmendingen 95 A6 Baden-Württemberg, SW Germany
Emona *see* Ljubljana
Emonti *see* East London

Emory Peak 49 E4 *mountain* Texas, SW USA
Empalme 50 B2 Sonora, NW Mexico
Emperor Seamounts 113 G3 *seamount range* NW Pacific Ocean
Empire State of the South *see* Georgia
Emporia 45 F5 Kansas, C USA
Empty Quarter *see* Ar Rub 'al Khālī
Ems 94 A3 *Dut.* Eems. *river* NW Germany
Enареträsk *see* Inarijärvi
Encamp 91 A8 Encamp, C Andorra Europe
Encarnación 64 D3 Itapúa, S Paraguay
Encinitas 47 C8 California, W USA
Encs 99 D6 Borsod-Abaúj-Zemplén, NE Hungary
Endeavour Strait 148 C1 *strait* Queensland, NE Australia
Enderbury Island 145 F3 *atoll* Phoenix Islands, C Kiribati
Enderby Land 154 C2 *physical region* Antarctica
Enderby Plain 154 D2 *abyssal plain* S Indian Ocean
Endersdorf *see* Jędrzejów
Enewetak Atoll 144 C1 *var.* Änewetak, Eniwetok. *atoll* Ralik Chain, W Marshall Islands
Enfield 89 A7 United Kingdom
Engeten *see* Aiud
Enghien 87 B6 *Dut.* Edingen. Hainaut, SW Belgium
England 89 D5 *Lat.* Anglia. *cultural region* England, United Kingdom
Englewood 44 D4 Colorado, C USA
English Channel 89 D8 *var.* The Channel, *Fr.* la Manche. *channel* NW Europe
Engure 106 C3 Tukums, W Latvia
Engures Ezers 106 B3 *lake* NW Latvia
Enguri 117 F1 *Rus.* Inguri. *river* NW Georgia
Enid 49 F1 Oklahoma, C USA
Enikale Strait *see* Kerch Strait
Eniwetok *see* Enewetak Atoll
En Nâqoûra 119 A5 *var.* An Nāqūrah. SW Lebanon
En Nazira *see* Natzrat
Ennedi 76 D2 *plateau* E Chad
Ennis 89 A6 *Ir.* Inis. Clare, W Ireland
Ennis 49 G3 Texas, SW USA
Enniskillen 89 B5 *var.* Inniskilling, *Ir.* Inis Ceithleann. SW Northern Ireland, United Kingdom
Enns 95 D6 *river* C Austria
Enschede 86 E3 Overijssel, E Netherlands
Ensenada 50 A1 Baja California Norte, NW Mexico
Entebbe 73 B6 S Uganda
Entroncamento 92 B3 Santarém, C Portugal
Enugu 75 G5 Enugu, S Nigeria
Epanomí 104 B4 Kentrikí Makedonía, N Greece
Epéna 77 B5 Likouala, NE Congo
Eperies/Eperjes *see* Prešov
Epi 144 D4 *var.* Épi. *island* C Vanuatu
Épi *see* Epi
Épinal 90 D4 Vosges, NE France
Epiphania *see* Ḥamāh
Epitoli *see* Tshwane
Epoon *see* Ebon Atoll
Epsom 89 A8 United Kingdom
Equality State *see* Wyoming
Equatorial Guinea 77 A5 *off.* Equatorial Guinea, Republic of. *country* C Africa
Equatorial Guinea, Republic of *see* Equatorial Guinea

EQUATORIAL GUINEA
Central Africa

Official name Republic of Equatorial Guinea
Formation 1968 / 1968
Capital Malabo
Population 551,201 / 51 people per sq mile (20 people per sq km) / 49%
Total area 10,830 sq. miles (28,051 sq. km)
Languages French*, Spanish*, Fang, Bubi
Religions Roman Catholic 90%, Other 10%
Ethnic mix Fang 85%, Other 11%, Bubi 4%
Government Presidential system
Currency CFA franc = 100 centimes
Literacy rate 87%
Calorie consumption Not-available

Erautini *see* Johannesburg
Erbil *see* Arbil
Erciş 117 F3 Van, E Turkey
Erdély *see* Transylvania
Erdélyi-Havasok *see* Carpaţii Meridionalii
Erdenet 127 E2 Orhon, N Mongolia
Erdi 76 C2 *plateau* NE Chad
Erdi Ma 76 D2 *desert* NE Chad
Erebus, Mount 154 B4 *volcano* Ross Island, Antarctica
Ereğli 116 C4 Konya, S Turkey
Erenhot 127 F2 *var.* Erlian. Nei Mongol Zizhiqu, NE China
Erfurt 94 C4 Thüringen, C Germany
Ergene Çayı *see* Ergene Irmağı
Ergene Irmağı 116 A2 *var.* Ergene Çayı *river* NW Turkey
Ergun 127 F1 *var.* Labudalin; *prev.* Ergun Youqi. Nei Mongol Zizhiqu, N China
Ergun He *see* Ergun
Ergun Youqi *see* Ergun
Erie 40 D3 Pennsylvania, NE USA
Érié, Lac *see* Erie, Lake
Erie, Lake 40 D3 *Fr.* Lac Érié. *lake* Canada/USA
Eritrea 72 C4 *off.* State of Eritrea, Ērtra. *country* E Africa

ERITREA
East Africa

Official name State of Eritrea
Formation 1993 / 2002
Capital Asmera
Population 4.7 million / 104 people per sq mile (40 people per sq km) / 20%
Total area 46,842 sq. miles (121,320 sq. km)
Languages Tigrinya*, English*, Tigre, Afar, Arabic*, Bilen, Kunama, Nara, Saho, Hadareb
Religions Christian 45%, Muslim 45%, Other 10%
Ethnic mix Tigray 50%, Tigray and Kunama 40%, Afar 4%, Other 3%, Saho 3%
Government Transitional regime
Currency Nakfa = 100 cents
Literacy rate 57%
Calorie consumption 1513 calories

Eritrea, State of *see* Eritrea
Erivan *see* Yerevan
Erlangen 95 C5 Bayern, S Germany
Erlau *see* Eger
Erlian *see* Erenhot
Ermelo 86 D3 Gelderland, C Netherlands
Ermióni 105 C6 Pelopónnisos, S Greece
Ermoúpoli 105 D6 *var.* Hermoupolis; *prev.* Ermoúpolis. Sýros, Kykládes, Greece, Aegean Sea
Ermoúpolis *see* Ermoúpoli
Ernakulam 132 C3 Kerala, SW India
Erode 132 C2 Tamil Nādu, SE India
Erquelinnes 87 B7 Hainaut, S Belgium
Er-Rachidia 70 C2 *var.* Ksar al Soule. E Morocco
Er Rahad 72 B4 *var.* Ar Rahad. Northern Kordofan, C Sudan
Erromango 144 D4 *island* S Vanuatu
Ertis *see* Irtysh, C Asia
Ērtra *see* Eritrea
Erzerum *see* Erzurum
Erzincan 117 E3 *var.* Erzinjan. Erzincan, E Turkey
Erzinjan *see* Erzincan
Erzurum 117 F3 *prev.* Erzerum. Erzurum, NE Turkey
Esbjerg 85 A7 Ribe, W Denmark
Esbo *see* Espoo
Escaldes 91 A8 Escaldes Engordany, C Andorra Europe
Escanaba 40 C2 Michigan, N USA
Escaut *see* Scheldt
Esch-sur-Alzette 87 D8 Luxembourg, S Luxembourg
Esclaves, Grand Lac des *see* Great Slave Lake
Escondido 47 C8 California, W USA
Escuinapa 50 D3 *var.* Escuinapa de Hidalgo. Sinaloa, C Mexico
Escuinapa de Hidalgo *see* Escuinapa
Escuintla 52 B2 Escuintla, S Guatemala
Escuintla 51 G5 Chiapas, SE Mexico
Esenguly 122 B3 *Rus.* Gasan-Kuli. Balkan Welaýaty, W Turkmenistan
Eşfahān 120 C3 *Eng.* Isfahan; *anc.* Aspadana. Eşfahān, C Iran
Esh Sharā *see* Ash Sharāh

Esil *see* Ishim, Kazakhstan/Russian Federation
Eskimo Point *see* Arviat
Eskişehir 116 B3 *var.* Eskishehr. Eskişehir, W Turkey
Eskishehr *see* Eskişehir
Eslāmābād 120 C3 *var.* Eslāmābād-e Gharb; *prev.* Harunabad, Shāhābād. Kermānshāhān, W Iran
Eslāmābād-e Gharb *see* Eslāmābād
Esmeraldas 60 A1 Esmeraldas, N Ecuador
Esna *see* Isnā
España *see* Spain
Espanola 48 D1 New Mexico, SW USA
Esperance 147 B7 Western Australia
Esperanza 50 B2 Sonora, NW Mexico
Esperanza 154 A2 *Argentinian research station* Antarctica
Espinal 58 B3 Tolima, C Colombia
Espinhaço, Serra do 56 D4 *mountain range* SE Brazil
Espírito Santo 63 F4 *off.* Estado do Espírito Santo. *state* E Brazil
Espírito Santo 63 F4 *off.* Estado do Espírito Santo. *region* E Brazil
Espírito Santo, Estado do *see* Espírito Santo
Espíritu Santo 144 C4 *var.* Santo. *island* W Vanuatu
Espoo 85 D6 *Swe.* Esbo. Etelä-Suomi, S Finland
Esquel 65 B6 Chubut, SW Argentina
Essaouira 70 B2 *prev.* Mogador. W Morocco
Esseg *see* Osijek
Es Senia *see* Oran
Essen 87 C5 Antwerpen, N Belgium
Essen 94 A4 *var.* Essen an der Ruhr. Nordrhein-Westfalen, W Germany
Essen an der Ruhr *see* Essen
Essequibo River 59 F3 *river* C Guyana
Es Suweida *see* As Suwaydā'
Estacado, Llano 49 E2 *plain* New Mexico/Texas, SW USA
Estados, Isla de los 65 C8 *prev. Eng.* Staten Island. *island* S Argentina
Estância 63 G3 Sergipe, E Brazil
Estelí 52 D3 Estelí, NW Nicaragua
Estella 93 E1 *Bas.* Lizarra. Navarra, N Spain
Estepona 92 D5 Andalucía, S Spain
Estevan 37 F5 Saskatchewan, S Canada
Estland *see* Estonia
Estonia 106 D2 *off.* Republic of Estonia, *Est.* Eesti Vabariik, *Ger.* Estland, *Latv.* Igaunija; *prev.* Estonian SSR, *Rus.* Estonskaya SSR. *country* NE Europe

ESTONIA
Northeast Europe

Official name Republic of Estonia
Formation 1991 / 1991
Capital Tallinn
Population 1.3 million / 75 people per sq mile (29 people per sq km) / 70%
Total area 17,462 sq. miles (45,226 sq. km)
Languages Estonian*, Russian
Religions Evangelical Lutheran 56%, Orthodox Christian 25%, Other 19%
Ethnic mix Estonian 68%, Russian 26%, Other 4%, Ukrainian 2%
Government Parliamentary system
Currency Euro = 100 cents
Literacy rate 99%
Calorie consumption 3002 calories

Estonian SSR *see* Estonia
Estonia, Republic of *see* Estonia
Estonskaya SSR *see* Estonia
Estrela, Serra da 92 C3 *mountain range* C Portugal
Estremadura *see* Extremadura
Estremoz 92 C4 Évora, S Portugal
Eszék *see* Osijek
Esztergom 99 C6 *Ger.* Gran; *anc.* Strigonium. Komárom-Esztergom, N Hungary
Étalle 87 D8 Luxembourg, SE Belgium
Etāwah 134 D3 Uttar Pradesh, N India
Ethiopia 73 C5 *off.* Federal Democratic Republic of Ethiopia; *prev.* Abyssinia, People's Democratic Republic of Ethiopia. *country* E Africa

ETHIOPIA
East Africa

Official name Federal Democratic Republic of Ethiopia
Formation 1896 / 2002
Capital Addis Ababa
Population 81.2 million / 189 people per sq mile (73 people per sq km) / 16%
Total area 435,184 sq. miles (1,127,127 sq. km)
Languages Amharic*, Tigrinya, Galla, Sidamo, Somali, English, Arabic
Religions Orthodox Christian 40%, Muslim 40%, Traditional beliefs 15%, Other 5%
Ethnic mix Oromo 32%, Amhara 30%, Other 22%, Tigrean 6%, Somali 6%, Gurage 4%
Government Parliamentary system
Currency Ethiopian birr = 100 cents
Literacy rate 42%
Calorie consumption 1857 calories

Ethiopia, Federal Democratic Republic of *see* Ethiopia
Ethiopian Highlands 73 C5 *var.* Ethiopian Plateau. *plateau* N Ethiopia
Ethiopian Plateau *see* Ethiopian Highlands
Ethiopia, People's Democratic Republic of *see* Ethiopia
Mount Etna 97 D7 *Eng.* Mount Etna. *volcano* Sicilia, Italy, C Mediterranean Sea
Etna, Mount *see* Etna, Monte
Etosha Pan 78 B3 *salt lake* N Namibia
Étoumbi 77 B5 Cuvette-Ouest, NW Congo
Etsch *see* Adige
Et Tafila *see* At Ṭafilah
Ettelbrück 87 D8 Diekirch, C Luxembourg
'Eua 145 E5 *prev.* Middleburg Island. *island* Tongatapu Group, SE Tonga
Euboea 105 C5 *Lat.* Euboea. *island* C Greece
Euboea *see* Évvoia
Eucla 147 D6 Western Australia
Euclid 40 D3 Ohio, N USA
Eufaula Lake 49 G1 *var.* Eufaula Reservoir. *reservoir* Oklahoma, C USA
Eufaula Reservoir *see* Eufaula Lake
Eugene 46 B3 Oregon, NW USA
Eumolpias *see* Plovdiv
Eupen 87 D6 Liège, E Belgium
Euphrates 112 B4 *Ar.* Al-Furāt, *Turk.* Fırat Nehri. *river* SW Asia
Eureka 47 A5 California, W USA
Eureka 44 A1 Montana, NW USA
Europa Point 93 H5 *headland* S Gibraltar
Europe 80 *continent*
Eutin 94 C2 Schleswig-Holstein, N Germany
Euxine Sea *see* Black Sea
Evansdale 45 G3 Iowa, C USA
Evanston 40 B3 Illinois, N USA
Evanston 44 B4 Wyoming, C USA
Evansville 40 B5 Indiana, N USA
Eveleth 45 G1 Minnesota, N USA
Everard, Lake 149 A6 *salt lake* South Australia
Everest, Mount 126 B5 *Chin.* Qomolangma Feng, *Nep.* Sagarmāthā. *mountain* China/Nepal
Everett 46 B2 Washington, NW USA
Everglades, The 43 F5 *wetland* Florida, SE USA
Evje 85 A6 Aust-Agder, S Norway
Evmolpia *see* Plovdiv
Évora 92 B4 *anc.* Ebora, *Lat.* Liberalitas Julia. Évora, C Portugal
Évreux 90 C3 *anc.* Civitas Eburovicum. Eure, N France
Évros *see* Maritsa
Évry 90 E2 Essonne, N France
Ewarton 54 B5 C Jamaica
Excelsior Springs 45 F4 Missouri, C USA
Exe 89 C7 *river* SW England, United Kingdom
Exeter 89 C7 *anc.* Isca Damnoniorum. SW England, United Kingdom
Exmoor 89 C7 *moorland* SW England, United Kingdom

Exmouth 146 A4 Western Australia
Exmouth 89 C7 SW England, United Kingdom
Exmouth Gulf 146 A4 *gulf* Western Australia
Exmouth Plateau 141 E5 *undersea plateau* E Indian Ocean
Extremadura 92 C3 *var.* Estremadura. *autonomous community* W Spain
Exuma Cays 54 C1 *islets* C Bahamas
Exuma Sound 54 C1 *sound* C Bahamas
Eyre Mountains 151 A7 *mountain range* South Island, New Zealand
Eyre North, Lake 149 A5 *salt lake* South Australia
Eyre Peninsula 149 A6 *peninsula* South Australia
Eyre South, Lake 149 A5 *salt lake* South Australia
Ezo *see* Hokkaidō

F

Faadhippolhu Atoll 132 B4 *var.* Fadiffolu, Lhaviyani Atoll. *atoll* N Maldives
Fabens 48 D3 Texas, SW USA
Fada 76 C2 Borkou-Ennedi-Tibesti, E Chad
Fada-Ngourma 75 E4 E Burkina Faso
Fadiffolu *see* Faadhippolhu Atoll
Faenza 96 C3 *anc.* Faventia. Emilia-Romagna, N Italy
Faeroe-Iceland Ridge 80 C1 *undersea ridge* NW Norwegian Sea
Faeroe Islands 83 E5 *Dan.* Færøerne, *Faer.* Føroyar. *Danish external territory* N Atlantic Ocean
Færøerne *see* Faeroe Islands
Faeroe-Shetland Trough 80 C2 *trough* NE Atlantic Ocean
Faetano 96 E2 E San Marino
Făgăraş 108 C4 *Ger.* Fogarasch, *Hung.* Fogaras. Brașov, C Romania
Fagibina, Lake *see* Faguibine, Lac
Fagne 87 C7 *hill range* S Belgium
Faguibine, Lac 75 E3 *var.* Lake Fagibina. *lake* NW Mali
Fahlun *see* Falun
Fahraj 120 E4 Kermän, SE Iran
Faial 92 A5 *var.* Ilha do Faial. *island* Azores, Portugal, NE Atlantic Ocean
Faial, Ilha do *see* Faial
Faifo *see* Hôi An
Fairbanks 36 D3 Alaska, USA
Fairfield 47 B6 California, W USA
Fair Isle 88 D2 *island* NE Scotland, United Kingdom
Fairlie 151 B6 Canterbury, South Island, New Zealand
Fairmont 45 F3 Minnesota, N USA
Faisalábád 134 C2 *prev.* Lyallpur. Punjab, NE Pakistan
Faizábád 135 E3 Uttar Pradesh, N India
Faizabad/Faizābād *see* Feyzābād
Fakaofo Atoll 145 F3 *island* SE Tokelau
Falam 136 A3 Chin State, W Burma (Myanmar)
Falconara Marittima 96 C3 Marche, C Italy
Falkenau an der Eger *see* Sokolov
Falkland Islands 65 D7 *var.* Falklands, Islas Malvinas. *UK dependent territory* SW Atlantic Ocean
Falkland Plateau 57 D7 *var.* Argentine Rise. *undersea feature* SW Atlantic Ocean
Falklands *see* Falkland Islands
Falknov nad Ohří *see* Sokolov
Fallbrook 47 C8 California, W USA
Falmouth 54 A4 W Jamaica
Falmouth 89 C7 SW England, United Kingdom
Falster 85 B8 *island* SE Denmark
Fălticeni 108 C3 *Hung.* Falticsén. Suceava, NE Romania
Falun 85 C6 *var.* Fahlun. Kopparberg, C Sweden
Famagusta *see* Gazimağusa
Famagusta Bay 102 D5 *var.* Famagusta Bay, *Gk.* Kólpos Ammóchostos. *bay* E Cyprus
Famagusta Bay *see* Gazimağusa Körfezi

Famenne 87 C7 *physical region* SE Belgium
Fang 136 C3 Chiang Mai, NW Thailand
Fanning Island *see* Tabuaeran
Fanø 96 C3 *island* W Denmark
Farafangana 79 G4 Fianarantsoa, SE Madagascar
Faräh 122 D4 *var.* Farah, Fararud. Faräh, W Afghanistan
Farah Rud 122 D4 *river* W Afghanistan
Faranah 74 C4 Haute-Guinée, S Guinea
Fararud *see* Faräh
Farasan, Jaza'ir 121 A6 *island group* SW Saudi Arabia
Farewell, Cape 150 C4 *headland* South Island, New Zealand
Farewell, Cape *see* Nunap Isua
Fargo 45 F2 North Dakota, N USA
Farg'ona 123 F2 *Rus.* Fergana; *prev.* Novyy Margilan. Farg'ona Viloyati, E Uzbekistan
Faribault 45 F2 Minnesota, N USA
Farīdābād 134 D3 Haryāna, N India
Farkhor 123 E3 *Rus.* Parkhar. SW Tajikistan
Farmington 45 G5 Missouri, C USA
Farmington 48 C1 New Mexico, SW USA
Faro 92 B5 Faro, S Portugal
Farquhar Group 79 G2 *island group* S Seychelles
Fars, Khalīj-e *see* Gulf, The
Farvel, Kap *see* Nunap Isua
Fastiv 109 E2 *Rus.* Fastov. Kyyivs'ka Oblast', NW Ukraine
Fastov *see* Fastiv
Fauske 84 C3 Nordland, C Norway
Faventia *see* Faenza
Faxa Bay *see* Faxaflói
Faxaflói 82 D5 *Eng.* Faxa Bay. *bay* W Iceland
Faya 76 C2 *prev.* Faya-Largeau, Largeau. Borkou-Ennedi-Tibesti, N Chad
Faya-Largeau *see* Faya
Fayetteville 42 A1 Arkansas, C USA
Fayetteville 43 F1 North Carolina, SE USA
Fdérick *see* Fdérik
Fdérik 74 C2 *var.* Fdérick, *Fr.* Fort Gouraud. Tiris Zemmour, NW Mauritania
Fear, Cape 43 F2 *headland* Bald Head Island, North Carolina, SE USA
Fécamp 90 B3 Seine-Maritime, N France
Fédala *see* Mohammedia
Federal Capital Territory *see* Australian Capital Territory
Fehérgyarmat 99 E6 Szabolcs-Szatmár-Bereg, E Hungary
Fehértemplom *see* Bela Crkva
Fehmarn 94 C2 *island* N Germany
Fehmarn Belt 94 C2 *Dan.* Femern Bælt, *Ger.* Fehmarnbelt. *strait* Denmark/Germany
Fehmarnbelt *see* Fehmarn Belt/Femer Bælt
Feijó 62 C2 Acre, W Brazil
Feilding 150 D4 Manawatu-Wanganui, North Island, New Zealand
Feira *see* Feira de Santana
Feira de Santana 63 G3 *var.* Feira. Bahia, E Brazil
Feketehalom *see* Codlea
Felanitx 93 G3 Mallorca, Spain, W Mediterranean Sea
Felicitas Julia *see* Lisboa
Felidhu Atoll 132 B4 *atoll* C Maldives
Felipe Carrillo Puerto 51 H4 Quintana Roo, SE Mexico
Felixstowe 89 E6 E England, United Kingdom
Fellin *see* Viljandi
Felsőbánya *see* Baia Sprie
Felsőmuzslya *see* Mužlja
Femunden 85 B5 *lake* S Norway
Fénérive *see* Fenoarivo Atsinanana
Fengcheng 128 D3 *var.* Feng-cheng, Fenghwangcheng. Liaoning, NE China
Feng-cheng *see* Fengcheng
Fenghwangcheng *see* Fengcheng
Fengtien *see* Liaoning, China
Fengtien *see* Shenyang, China
Fenoarivo Atsinanana 79 G3 *Fr.* Fénérive. Toamasina, E Madagascar
Fens, The 89 E6 *wetland* E England, United Kingdom
Feodosiya 109 F5 *var.* Kefe, *It.* Kaffa; *anc.* Theodosia. Respublika Krym, S Ukraine

Ferdinand *see* Montana, Bulgaria
Ferdinandsberg *see* Oţelu Roşu
Féres 104 D3 Anatolikí Makedonía kai Thráki, NE Greece
Fergana *see* Farg'ona
Fergus Falls 45 F2 Minnesota, N USA
Ferizaj 101 D5 *Serb.* Uroševac. C Kosovo
Ferkessédougou 74 D4 N Côte d'Ivoire
Fermo 96 C4 *anc.* Firmum Picenum. Marche, C Italy
Fernandina, Isla 60 A5 *var.* Narborough Island. *island* Galapagos Islands, Ecuador, E Pacific Ocean
Fernando de Noronha 63 H2 *island* E Brazil
Fernando Po/Fernando Póo *see* Bioco, Isla de
Ferrara 96 C2 *anc.* Forum Alieni. Emilia-Romagna, N Italy
Ferreñafe 60 B3 Lambayeque, W Peru
Ferro *see* Hierro
Ferrol 92 B1 *var.* El Ferrol; *prev.* El Ferrol del Caudillo. Galicia, NW Spain
Fertő *see* Neusiedler See
Ferwerd 86 D1 *Fris.* Ferwert. Friesland, N Netherlands
Ferwert *see* Ferwerd
Fès 70 C2 *Eng.* Fez. N Morocco
Feteşti 108 D5 Ialomiţa, SE Romania
Fethiye 116 B4 Muğla, SW Turkey
Fetlar 88 D1 *island* NE Scotland, United Kingdom
Feyzābād 123 F3 *var.* Faizabad, Faizābād, Feyzābād, Fyzabad. Badakhshān, NE Afghanistan
Feyzābād *see* Feyzābād
Fez *see* Fès
Fianarantsoa 79 F3 Fianarantsoa, C Madagascar
Fianga 76 B4 Mayo-Kébbi, SW Chad
Fier 101 C6 *var.* Fieri. Fier, SW Albania
Fieri *see* Fier
Figeac 91 C5 Lot, S France
Figig *see* Figuig
Figueira da Foz 92 B3 Coimbra, W Portugal
Figueres 93 G2 Cataluña, E Spain
Figuig 70 D2 *var.* Figig. E Morocco
Fiji 145 E5 *off.* Sovereign Democratic Republic of Fiji, *Fij.* Viti. *country* SW Pacific Ocean

FIJI
Australasia & Oceania

Official name Republic of the Fiji Islands
Formation 1970 / 1970
Capital Suva
Population 893,675 / 130 people per sq mile (50 people per sq km) / 52%
Total area 7054 sq. miles (18,270 sq km)
Languages Fijian, English*, Hindi, Urdu, Tamil, Telugu
Religions Hindu 38%, Methodist 37%, Roman Catholic 9%, Other 8%, Muslim 8%
Ethnic mix Melanesian 51%, Indian 44%, Other 5%
Government Transitional regime
Currency Fiji dollar = 100 cents
Literacy rate 93%
Calorie consumption 2894 calories

Fiji, Sovereign Democratic Republic of *see* Fiji
Filadelfia 52 D4 Guanacaste, W Costa Rica
Filiaşi 108 B5 Dolj, SW Romania
Filipstad 85 B6 Värmland, C Sweden
Finale Ligure 96 A3 Liguria, NW Italy
Finchley 89 A7 United Kingdom
Findlay 40 C4 Ohio, N USA
Finike 116 B4 Antalya, SW Turkey
Finland 84 D4 *off.* Republic of Finland, *Fin.* Suomen Tasavalta, Suomi. *country* N Europe

FINLAND
Northern Europe

Official name Republic of Finland
Formation 1917 / 1947
Capital Helsinki
Population 5.3 million / 45 people per sq mile (17 people per sq km) / 61%
Total area 130,127 sq. miles (337,030 sq. km)

FINLAND
(continued)

Languages Finnish*, Swedish*, Sámi
Religions Evangelical Lutheran 89%, Other 9%, Orthodox Christian 1%, Roman Catholic 1%
Ethnic mix Finnish 93%, Other (including Sámi) 7%
Government Parliamentary system
Currency Euro = 100 cents
Literacy rate 99%
Calorie consumption 3100 calories

Finland, Gulf of 85 D6 *Est.* Soome Laht, *Fin.* Suomenlahti, *Ger.* Finnischer Meerbusen, *Rus.* Finskiy Zaliv, *Swe.* Finska Viken. *gulf* E Baltic Sea
Finland, Republic of *see* Finland
Finnischer Meerbusen *see* Finland, Gulf of
Finnmarksvidda 84 D2 *physical region* N Norway
Finska Viken/Finskiy Zaliv *see* Finland, Gulf of
Finsterwalde 94 D4 Brandenburg, E Germany
Fiordland 151 A7 *physical region* South Island, New Zealand
Fiorina 96 E1 NE San Marino
Firat Nehri *see* Euphrates
Firenze 96 C3 *Eng.* Florence; *anc.* Florentia. Toscana, C Italy
Firmum Picenum *see* Fermo
First State *see* Delaware
Fischbacher Alpen 95 E7 *mountain range* E Austria
Fischhausen *see* Primorsk
Fish 78 B4 *var.* Vis. *river* S Namibia
Fishguard 89 C6 *Wel.* Abergwaun. SW Wales, United Kingdom
Fisterra, Cabo 92 B1 *headland* NW Spain
Fitzroy Crossing 146 C3 Western Australia
Fitzroy River 146 C3 *river* Western Australia
Fiume *see* Rijeka
Flagstaff 48 B2 Arizona, SW USA
Flanders 87 A6 *Dut.* Vlaanderen, *Fr.* Flandre. *cultural region* Belgium/France
Flandre *see* Flanders
Flathead Lake 44 B1 *lake* Montana, NW USA
Flat Island 128 C8 *island* NE Spratly Islands
Flatts Village 42 B5 *var.* The Flatts Village. C Bermuda
Flensburg 94 B2 Schleswig-Holstein, N Germany
Flessingue *see* Vlissingen
Flickertail State *see* North Dakota
Flinders Island 149 C6 *island* Furneaux Group, Tasmania, SE Australia
Flinders Ranges 149 B6 *mountain range* South Australia
Flinders River 148 C3 *river* Queensland, NE Australia
Flin Flon 37 F5 Manitoba, C Canada
Flint 40 C3 Michigan, N USA
Flint Island 145 G4 *island* Line Islands, E Kiribati
Floreana, Isla *see* Santa María, Isla
Florence 42 C1 Alabama, S USA
Florence 43 F2 South Carolina, SE USA
Florence *see* Firenze
Florencia 58 B4 Caquetá, S Colombia
Florentia *see* Firenze
Flores 52 B1 Petén, N Guatemala
Flores 139 E5 *island* Nusa Tenggara, C Indonesia
Flores 92 A5 *island* Azores, Portugal, NE Atlantic Ocean
Flores, Laut *see* Flores Sea
Flores Sea 138 D5 *Ind.* Laut Flores. *sea* C Indonesia
Floriano 63 F2 Piauí, E Brazil
Florianópolis 63 F5 *prev.* Destêrro. *state capital* Santa Catarina, S Brazil
Florida 43 E4 *off.* State of Florida, *also known as* Peninsular State, Sunshine State. *state* SE USA
Florida Bay 43 E5 *bay* Florida, SE USA
Florida Keys 43 E5 *island group* Florida, SE USA

Florida, Straits of *54 B1 strait* Atlantic Ocean/Gulf of Mexico
Flórina *104 B4 var.* Phlórina. Dytikí Makedonía, N Greece
Florissant *45 G4* Missouri, C USA
Floúda, Akrotírio *105 D7 headland* Astypálaia, Kykládes, Greece, Aegean Sea
Flushing *see* Vlissingen
Flylân *see* Vlieland
Foča *100 C4 var.* Srbinje. SE Bosnia and Herzegovina
Focşani *108 C4* Vrancea, E Romania
Fogaras/Fogarasch *see* Făgăraş
Foggia *97 D5* Puglia, SE Italy
Fogo *74 A3 island* Ilhas de Sotavento, SW Cape Verde
Foix *91 B6* Ariège, S France
Folégandros *105 C7 island* Kykládes, Greece, Aegean Sea
Foleyet *38 C4* Ontario, S Canada
Foligno *96 C4* Umbria, C Italy
Folkestone *89 E7* SE England, United Kingdom
Fond du Lac *40 B2* Wisconsin, N USA
Fongafale *145 E3 var.* Funafuti. *country capital* (Tuvalu) (Tuvalu) Funafuti Atoll, SE Tuvalu
Fonseca, Golfo de *see* Fonseca, Gulf of
Fonseca, Gulf of *52 C3 Sp.* Golfo de Fonseca. *gulf* C Central America
Fontainebleau *90 C3* Seine-et-Marne, N France
Fontenay-le-Comte *90 B4* Vendée, NW France
Fontvieille *91 B8* SW Monaco Europe
Fonyód *99 C7* Somogy, W Hungary
Foochow *see* Fuzhou
Foochow *see* Fuzhou
Forchheim *95 C5* Bayern, SE Germany
Forel, Mont *82 D4 mountain* SE Greenland
Forfar *88 C3* E Scotland, United Kingdom
Forge du Sud *see* Dudelange
Forlì *96 C3 anc.* Forum Livii. Emilia-Romagna, N Italy
Formentera *93 G4 anc.* Ophiusa, *Lat.* Frumentum. *island* Islas Baleares, Spain, W Mediterranean Sea
Formosa *64 D2* Formosa, NE Argentina
Formosa/Formo'sa *see* Taiwan
Formosa, Serra *63 E3 mountain range* C Brazil
Formosa Strait *see* Taiwan Strait
Føroyar *see* Faeroe Islands
Forrest City *42 B1* Arkansas, C USA
Fortaleza *61 F2* Pando, N Bolivia
Fortaleza *63 G2 prev.* Ceará. *state capital* Ceará, NE Brazil
Fort-Archambault *see* Sarh
Fort-Bayard *see* Zhanjiang
Fort-Cappolani *see* Tidjikja
Fort Charlet *see* Djanet
Fort-Chimo *see* Kuujjuaq
Fort Collins *44 D4* Colorado, C USA
Fort-Crampel *see* Kaga Bandoro
Fort Davis *49 E3* Texas, SW USA
Fort-de-France *55 H4 prev.* Fort-Royal. *dependent territory capital* (Martinique) W Martinique
Fort Dodge *45 F3* Iowa, C USA
Fortescue River *146 A4 river* Western Australia
Fort-Foureau *see* Kousséri
Fort Frances *38 B4* Ontario, S Canada
Fort Good Hope *37 E4 var.* Rádeyilikóé. Northwest Territories, NW Canada
Fort Gouraud *see* Fdérik
Forth *88 C4 river* C Scotland, United Kingdom
Forth, Firth of *88 C4 estuary* E Scotland, United Kingdom
Fortín General Eugenio Garay *see* General Eugenio A. Garay
Fort Jameson *see* Chipata
Fort-Lamy *see* Ndjamena
Fort Lauderdale *43 F5* Florida, SE USA
Fort Liard *37 E4 var.* Liard. Northwest Territories, W Canada
Fort Madison *45 G4* Iowa, C USA
Fort McMurray *37 F3* Alberta, C Canada
Fort McPherson *36 D3 var.* McPherson. Northwest Territories, NW Canada
Fort Morgan *44 D4* Colorado, C USA
Fort Myers *43 E5* Florida, SE USA

Fort Nelson *37 E4* British Columbia, W Canada
Fort Peck Lake *44 C1 reservoir* Montana, NW USA
Fort Pierce *43 F4* Florida, SE USA
Fort Providence *37 E4 var.* Providence. Northwest Territories, W Canada
Fort-Repoux *see* Akjoujt
Fort Rosebery *see* Mansa
Fort Rousset *see* Owando
Fort-Royal *see* Fort-de-France
Fort St. John *37 E4* British Columbia, W Canada
Fort Scott *45 F5* Kansas, C USA
Fort Severn *38 C2* Ontario, C Canada
Fort-Shevchenko *114 A4* Mangistau, W Kazakhstan
Fort-Sibut *see* Sibut
Fort Simpson *37 E4 var.* Simpson. Northwest Territories, W Canada
Fort Smith *42 B1* Arkansas, C USA
Fort Smith *37 E3* Northwest Territories, W Canada
Fort Stockton *49 E3* Texas, SW USA
Fort-Trinquet *see* Bir Mogreïn
Fort Vermilion *37 E4* Alberta, W Canada
Fort Victoria *see* Masvingo
Fort Walton Beach *42 C3* Florida, SE USA
Fort Wayne *40 C4* Indiana, N USA
Fort William *88 C3* N Scotland, United Kingdom
Fort Worth *49 G2* Texas, SW USA
Fort Yukon *36 D3* Alaska, USA
Forum Alieni *see* Ferrara
Forum Livii *see* Forlì
Fossa Claudia *see* Chioggia
Fougamou *77 A6* Ngounié, C Gabon
Fougères *90 B3* Ille-et-Vilaine, NW France
Fou-hsin *see* Fuxin
Foulwind, Cape *151 B5 headland* South Island, New Zealand
Foumban *76 A4* Ouest, NW Cameroon
Fou-shan *see* Fushun
Foveaux Strait *151 A8 strait* S New Zealand
Foxe Basin *37 G3 sea* Nunavut, N Canada
Fox Glacier *151 B6* West Coast, South Island, New Zealand
Fraga *93 F2* Aragón, NE Spain
Fram Basin *155 C3 var.* Amundsen Basin. *undersea basin* Arctic Ocean
France *90 B4 off.* French Republic, *It./Sp.* Francia; *prev.* Gaul, Gaule, *Lat.* Gallia. *country* W Europe

FRANCE
Western Europe
Official name French Republic
Formation 987 / 1919
Capital Paris
Population 60.9 million / 287 people per sq mile (111 people per sq km) / 76%
Total area 211,208 sq. miles (547,030 sq. km)
Languages French*, Provençal, German, Breton, Catalan, Basque
Religions Roman Catholic 88%, Muslim 8%, Protestant 2%, Buddhist 1%, Jewish 1%
Ethnic mix French 90%, North African (mainly Algerian) 6%, German (Alsace) 2%, Breton 1%, Other (including Corsicans) 1%
Government Mixed presidential–parliamentary system
Currency Euro = 100 cents
Literacy rate 99%
Calorie consumption 3654 calories

Franceville *77 B6 var.* Massoukou, Masuku. Haut-Ogooué, E Gabon
Francfort *see* Frankfurt am Main
Franche-Comté *90 D4 cultural region* E France
Francia *see* France
Francis Case, Lake *45 E3 reservoir* South Dakota, N USA
Francisco Escárcega *51 G4* Campeche, SE Mexico
Francistown *78 D3* North East, NE Botswana
Franconian Jura *see* Fränkische Alb

Frankenalb *see* Fränkische Alb
Frankenstein/Frankenstein in Schlesien *see* Ząbkowice Śląskie
Frankfort *40 C5 state capital* Kentucky, S USA
Frankfort on the Main *see* Frankfurt am Main
Frankfurt *see* Frankfurt am Main, Germany
Frankfurt *see* Słubice, Poland
Frankfort on the Main. Hessen, SW Germany
Frankfurt am Main *95 B5 var.* Frankfurt, *Fr.* Francfort; *prev. Eng.* Frankfort on the Main. Hessen, SW Germany
Frankfurt an der Oder *94 D3* Brandenburg, E Germany
Fränkische Alb *95 C6 var.* Frankenalb, *Eng.* Franconian Jura. *mountain range* S Germany
Franklin *42 C1* Tennessee, S USA
Franklin D. Roosevelt Lake *46 C1 reservoir* Washington, NW USA
Franz Josef Land *114 D1 Eng.* Franz Josef Land. *island group* N Russian Federation
Franz Josef Land *see* Frantsa-Iosifa, Zemlya
Fraserburgh *88 D3* NE Scotland, United Kingdom
Fraser Island *148 E4 var.* Great Sandy Island. *island* Queensland, E Australia
Frauenbach *see* Baia Mare
Frauenburg *see* Saldus, Latvia
Fredericksburg *41 E5* Virginia, NE USA
Fredericton *39 F4 province capital* New Brunswick, SE Canada
Frederikshåb *see* Paamiut
Frederikshald *see* Halden
Fredrikstad *85 B6* Østfold, S Norway
Freeport *54 C1* Grand Bahama Island, N Bahamas
Freeport *49 H4* Texas, SW USA
Free State *see* Maryland
Freetown *74 C4 country capital* (Sierra Leone) (Sierra Leone) W Sierra Leone
Freiburg *see* Freiburg im Breisgau, Germany
Freiburg im Breisgau *95 A6 var.* Freiburg, *Fr.* Fribourg-en-Brisgau. Baden-Württemberg, SW Germany
Freiburg in Schlesien *see* Świebodzice
Fremantle *147 A6* Western Australia
Fremont *45 F4* Nebraska, C USA
French Guiana *59 H3 var.* Guiana, Guyane. *French overseas department* N South America
French Guinea *see* Guinea
French Polynesia *143 F4 French overseas territory* S Pacific Ocean
French Republic *see* France
French Somaliland *see* Djibouti
French Southern and Antarctic Territories *141 B7 Fr.* Terres Australes et Antarctiques Françaises. *French overseas territory* S Indian Ocean
French Sudan *see* Mali
French Territory of the Afars and Issas *see* Djibouti
French Togoland *see* Togo
Fresnillo *50 D3 var.* Fresnillo de González Echeverría. Zacatecas, C Mexico
Fresnillo de González Echeverría *see* Fresnillo
Fresno *47 C6* California, W USA
Frías *64 C3* Catamarca, N Argentina
Fribourg-en-Brisgau *see* Freiburg im Breisgau
Friedek-Mistek *see* Frýdek-Místek
Friedrichshafen *95 B7* Baden-Württemberg, S Germany
Friendly Islands *see* Tonga
Frisches Haff *see* Vistula Lagoon
Frobisher Bay *82 B3 inlet* Baffin Island, Nunavut, NE Canada
Frobisher Bay *see* Iqaluit
Frohavet *84 B4 sound* C Norway
Frome, Lake *149 B6 salt lake* South Australia
Frontera *51 G4* Tabasco, SE Mexico
Frontignan *91 C6* Hérault, S France
Frostviken *see* Kvarnbergsvattnet
Frøya *84 A4 island* W Norway
Frumentum *see* Formentera
Frunze *see* Bishkek

Frýdek-Místek *99 C5 Ger.* Friedek-Mistek. Moravskoslezský Kraj, E Czech Republic
Fu-chien *see* Fujian
Fu-chou *see* Fuzhou
Fu-chou *see* Fuzhou
Fuengirola *92 D5* Andalucía, S Spain
Fuerte Olimpo *64 D2 var.* Olimpo. Alto Paraguay, NE Paraguay
Fuerte, Río *48 C3 river* C Mexico
Fuerteventura *70 B3 island* Islas Canarias, Spain, NE Atlantic Ocean
Fuhkien *see* Fujian
Fu-hsin *see* Fuxin
Fuji *131 D6 var.* Huzi. Shizuoka, Honshū, S Japan
Fujian *128 D6 var.* Fu-chien, Fuhkien, *Eng.* Fukien, Min, Fujian Sheng. *province* SE China
Fujian Sheng *see* Fujian
Mount Fuji *131 C6 var.* Fujiyama, *Eng.* Mount Fuji. *mountain* Honshū, SE Japan
Fuji, Mount/Fujiyama *see* Fuji-san
Fukang *126 C2* Xinjiang Uygur Zizhiqu, W China
Fukien *see* Fujian
Fukui *131 C6 var.* Hukui. Fukui, Honshū, SW Japan
Fukuoka *131 A7 var.* Hukuoka, *hist.* Najima. Fukuoka, Kyūshū, SW Japan
Fukushima *130 D4 var.* Hukusima. Fukushima, Honshū, C Japan
Fulda *95 B5* Hessen, C Germany
Funafuti *see* Fongafale
Funafuti Atoll *145 E3 atoll* C Tuvalu
Funchal *70 A2* Madeira, Portugal, NE Atlantic Ocean
Fundy, Bay of *39 F5 bay* Canada/USA
Fünen *see* Fyn
Fünfkirchen *see* Pécs
Furnes *see* Veurne
Fürth *95 C5* Bayern, S Germany
Furukawa *130 D4 var.* Hurukawa, Ōsaki. Miyagi, Honshū, C Japan
Pusan *see* Busan
Fushë Kosovë *101 D5 Serb.* Kosovo Polje. C Kosovo
Fushun *128 D3 var.* Fou-shan, Fu-shun. Liaoning, NE China
Fu-shun *see* Fushun
Fusin *see* Fuxin
Füssen *95 C7* Bayern, S Germany
Futog *100 D3* Vojvodina, NW Serbia
Futuna, Île *145 E4 island* S Wallis and Futuna
Fuxin *128 D3 var.* Fou-hsin, Fu-hsin, Fusin. Liaoning, NE China
Fuzhou *128 D6 var.* Foochow, Fu-chou. *province capital* Fujian, SE China
Fuzhou *128 D6 var.* Foochow, Fu-chou. *province capital* Fujian, SE China
Fyn *85 B8 Ger.* Fünen. *island* C Denmark
FYR Macedonia/FYROM *see* Macedonia, FYR
Fyzabad *see* Feyzābād

G

Gaafu Alifu Atoll *see* North Huvadhu Atoll
Gaalkacyo *73 E5 var.* Galka'yo, *It.* Galcaio. Mudug, C Somalia
Gabela *78 B2* Cuanza Sul, W Angola
Gaberones *see* Gaborone
Gabès *71 E2 var.* Qābis. E Tunisia
Gabès, Golfe de *71 F2 Ar.* Khalīj Qābis. *gulf* E Tunisia
Gabon *77 B6 off.* Gabonese Republic. *country* C Africa

GABON
Central Africa
Official name Gabonese Republic
Formation 1960 / 1960
Capital Libreville
Population 1.4 million / 14 people per sq mile (5 people per sq km) / 84%
Total area 103,346 sq. miles (267,667 sq. km)
Languages Fang, French*, Punu, Sira, Nzebi, Mpongwe
Religions Christian (mainly Roman Catholic) 55%, Traditional beliefs 40%, Other 4%, Muslim 1%

GABON
(continued)

Ethnic mix Fang 26%, Shira-punu 24%, Other 16%, Foreign residents 15%, Nzabi-duma 11%, Mbédé-Teke 8%
Government Presidential system
Currency CFA franc = 100 centimes
Literacy rate 71%
Calorie consumption 2637 calories

Gabonese Republic see Gabon
Gaborone 78 C4 prev. Gaberones. country capital (Botswana) (Botswana) South East, SE Botswana
Gabrovo 104 D2 Gabrovo, N Bulgaria
Gadag 132 C1 Karnātaka, W India
Gades/Gadier/Gadir/Gadire see Cádiz
Gadsden 42 D2 Alabama, S USA
Gaeta 97 C5 Lazio, C Italy
Gaeta, Gulf of 97 C5 var. Gulf of Gaeta. gulf C Italy
Gaeta, Gulf of see Gaeta, Golfo di
Gäfle see Gävle
Gafsa 71 E2 var. Qafşah. W Tunisia
Gagnoa 74 D5 C Côte d'Ivoire
Gagra 117 E1 NW Georgia
Gaillac 91 C6 var. Gaillac-sur-Tarn. Tarn, S France
Gaillac-sur-Tarn see Gaillac
Gaillimh see Galway
Gaillimhe, Cuan na see Galway Bay
Gainesville 43 E3 Florida, SE USA
Gainesville 42 D2 Georgia, SE USA
Gainesville 49 G2 Texas, SW USA
Lake Gairdner 149 A6 salt lake South Australia
Gaizina Kalns see Gaiziņkalns
Gaiziņkalns 106 C3 var. Gaizina Kalns. mountain E Latvia
Galán, Cerro 64 B3 mountain NW Argentina
Galanta 99 C6 Hung. Galánta. Trnavský Kraj, W Slovakia
Galapagos Fracture Zone 153 E3 tectonic feature E Pacific Ocean
Galapagos Islands 153 F3 var. Islas de los Galápagos, Eng. Galapagos Islands, Tortoise Islands. island group Ecuador, E Pacific Ocean
Galapagos Islands see Colón, Archipiélago de
Galápagos, Islas de los see Colón, Archipiélago de
Galapagos Rise 153 F3 undersea rise E Pacific Ocean
Galashiels 88 C4 SE Scotland, United Kingdom
Galaţi 108 D4 Ger. Galatz. Galaţi, E Romania
Galatz see Galaţi
Galcaio see Gaalkacyo
Galesburg 40 B3 Illinois, N USA
Galicia 92 B1 anc. Gallaecia. autonomous community NW Spain
Galicia Bank 80 B4 undersea bank E Atlantic Ocean
Galilee, Sea of see Tiberias, Lake
Galka'yo see Gaalkacyo
Galkynyş 122 D3 prev. Rus. Deynau, Dyanev, Turkm. Dänew. Lebap Welaýaty, NE Turkmenistan
Gallaecia see Galicia
Galle 132 D4 prev. Point de Galle. Southern Province, SW Sri Lanka
Gallego Rise 153 F3 undersea rise E Pacific Ocean
Gallegos see Río Gallegos
Gallia see France
Gallipoli 97 E6 Puglia, SE Italy
Gällivare 84 C3 Lapp. Váhtjer. Norrbotten, N Sweden
Gallup 48 C1 New Mexico, SW USA
Galtat-Zemmour 70 B3 C Western Sahara
Galveston 49 H4 Texas, SW USA
Galway 89 A5 Ir. Gaillimh. W Ireland
Galway Bay 89 A6 Ir. Cuan na Gaillimhe. bay W Ireland
Gámas see Kaamanen
Gambell 36 C2 Saint Lawrence Island, Alaska, USA
Gambia 74 B3 off. Republic of The Gambia, The Gambia. country W Africa

GAMBIA
West Africa

Official name Republic of the Gambia
Formation 1965 / 1965
Capital Banjul
Population 1.6 million / 414 people per sq mile (160 people per sq km) / 26%
Total area 4363 sq. miles (11,300 sq. km)
Languages English*, Mandinka, Fulani, Wolof, Jola, Soninke
Religions Sunni Muslim 90%, Christian 9%, Traditional beliefs 1%
Ethnic mix Mandinka 40%, Fulani 19%, Wolof 15%, Jola 11%, Serahuli 9%, Other 6%
Government Presidential system
Currency Dalasi = 100 butut
Literacy rate 38%
Calorie consumption 2273 calories

Gambia 74 C3 Fr. Gambie. river W Africa
Gambia, Republic of The see Gambia
Gambia, The see Gambia
Gambie see Gambia
Gambier, Îles 143 G4 island group E French Polynesia
Gamboma 77 B6 Plateaux, E Congo
Gamlakarleby see Kokkola
Gan 132 B5 Addu Atoll, C Maldives
Gan see Gansu, China
Gan see Jiangxi, China
Ganaane see Juba
Gäncä 117 G2 Rus. Gyandzha; prev. Kirovabad, Yelisavetpol. W Azerbaijan
Gand see Gent
Gandajika 77 D7 Kasai-Oriental, S Dem. Rep. Congo
Gander 39 G3 Newfoundland and Labrador, SE Canada
Gāndhīdhām 134 C4 Gujarāt, W India
Gandía 93 F3 País Valenciano, E Spain
Ganges 135 F3 Ben. Padma. river Bangladesh/India
Ganges Cone see Ganges Fan
Ganges Fan 140 D3 var. Ganges Cone. undersea fan N Bay of Bengal
Ganges, Mouths of the 135 G4 delta Bangladesh/India
Gangra see Çankırı
Gangtok 135 F3 state capital Sikkim, N India
Gansos, Lago dos see Goose Lake
Gansu 128 B4 var. Gan, Gansu Sheng, Kansu. province N China
Gansu Sheng see Gansu
Gantsevichi see Hantsavichy
Ganzhou 128 D6 Jiangxi, S China
Gao 75 E3 Gao, E Mali
Gaocheng see Litang
Gaoual 74 C4 N Guinea
Gaoxiong see Kaohsiung
Gap 91 D5 anc. Vapincum. Hautes-Alpes, SE France
Gaplaňgyr Platosy 122 C2 Rus. Plato Kaplangky. ridge Turkmenistan/ Uzbekistan
Gar see Gar Xincun
Garabil Belentligi 122 D3 Rus. Vozvyshennost' Karabil'. mountain range S Turkmenistan
Garabogaz Aylagy 122 B2 Rus. Zaliv Kara-Bogaz-Gol. bay NW Turkmenistan
Garachiné 53 G5 Darién, SE Panama
Garagum 122 C3 var. Garagumy, Qara Qum, Eng. Black Sand Desert, Kara Kum; prev. Peski Karakumy. desert C Turkmenistan
Garagum Canal 122 D3 var. Kara Kum Canal, Rus. Karagumskiy Kanal, Karakumskiy Kanal. canal C Turkmenistan
Garagumy see Garagum
Gara Khitrino 104 D2 Shumen, NE Bulgaria
Gárassavon see Kaaresuvanto
Garda, Lake 96 C2 var. Benaco, Eng. Lake Garda, Ger. Gardasee. lake NE Italy
Garda, Lake see Garda, Lago di
Gardasee see Garda, Lago di
Garden City 45 E5 Kansas, C USA
Garden State, The see New Jersey
Gardner Island see Nikumaroro
Garegegasnjárga see Karigasniemi

Gargždai 106 B3 Klaipėda, W Lithuania
Garissa 73 D6 Coast, E Kenya
Garland 49 G2 Texas, SW USA
Garoe see Garoowe
Garonne 91 B5 anc. Garumna. river S France
Garoowe 73 E5 var. Garoe. Nugaal, N Somalia
Garoua 76 B4 var. Garua. Nord, N Cameroon
Garry Lake 37 F3 lake Nunavut, N Canada
Garsen 73 D6 Coast, S Kenya
Garua see Garoua
Garumna see Garonne
Garwolin 98 D4 Mazowieckie, E Poland
Gar Xincun 126 A4 prev. Gar. Xizang Zizhiqu, W China
Gary 40 B3 Indiana, N USA
Garzón 58 B4 Huila, S Colombia
Gasan-Kuli see Esenguly
Gascogne 91 B6 Eng. Gascony. cultural region S France
Gascony see Gascogne
Gascoyne River 147 A5 river Western Australia
Gaspé 39 F3 Québec, SE Canada
Gaspé, Péninsule de 39 E4 var. Péninsule de la Gaspésie. peninsula Québec, SE Canada
Gaspésie, Péninsule de la see Gaspé, Péninsule de
Gastonia 43 E1 North Carolina, SE USA
Gastoúni 105 B6 Dytikí Ellás, S Greece
Gatchina 110 B4 Leningradskaya Oblast', NW Russian Federation
Gatineau 38 D4 Québec, SE Canada
Gatooma see Kadoma
Gatún, Lake 53 F4 reservoir C Panama
Gauhāti see Guwāhāti
Gauja 106 D3 Ger. Aa. river Estonia/ Latvia
Gaul/Gaule see France
Gauteng 78 D4 off. Gauteng Province; prev. Pretoria-Witwatersrand-Vereeniging. province NE South Africa
Gävbandī 120 D4 Hormozgān, S Iran
Gávdos 105 D8 island SE Greece
Gavere 87 B6 Oost-Vlaanderen, NW Belgium
Gävle 85 C6 var. Gäfle; prev. Gefle. Gävleborg, C Sweden
Gawler 149 B6 South Australia
Gaya 135 F3 Bihār, N India
Gaya see Kyjov
Gayndah 149 E5 Queensland, E Australia
Gaysin see Haysyn
Gaza 119 A6 Ar. Ghazzah, Heb. 'Azza. NE Gaza Strip
Gaz-Achak see Gazojak
Gazandzhyk/Gazanjyk see Bereket
Gaza Strip 119 A7 Ar. Qita Ghazzah. disputed region SW Asia
Gaziantep 116 D4 var. Gazi Antep; prev. Aintab, Antep. Gaziantep, S Turkey
Gazi Antep see Gaziantep
Gazimağusa 102 C5 var. Famagusta, Gk. Ammóchostos. E Cyprus
Gazli 122 D2 Buxoro Viloyati, C Uzbekistan
Gazojak 122 D2 Rus. Gaz Achak. Lebap Welaýaty, NE Turkmenistan
Gbanga 74 D5 var. Gbarnga. N Liberia
Gbarnga see Gbanga
Gdańsk 98 C2 Fr. Dantzig, Ger. Danzig. Pomorskie, N Poland
Gdan'skaya Bukhta/Gdańsk, Gulf of see Danzig, Gulf of
Gdańska, Zakota see Danzig, Gulf of
Gdingen see Gdynia
Gdynia 98 C2 Ger. Gdingen. Pomorskie, N Poland
Gedaref 72 C4 var. Al Qaḑārif, El Gedaref. Gedaref, E Sudan
Gediz 116 B3 Kütahya, W Turkey
Gediz Nehri 116 A3 river W Turkey
Geel 87 C5 var. Gheel. Antwerpen, N Belgium
Geelong 149 C7 Victoria, SE Australia
Ge'e'mu see Golmud
Geilo 85 A5 Buskerud, S Norway
Gejiu 128 B6 var. Kochiu. Yunnan, S China
Gëkdepe see Gökdepe
Gela 97 C7 prev. Terranova di Sicilia. Sicilia, Italy, C Mediterranean Sea

Geldermalsen 86 C4 Gelderland, C Netherlands
Geleen 87 D6 Limburg, SE Netherlands
Gelib see Jilib
Gellinsor 73 E5 Mudug, C Somalia
Gembloux 87 C6 Namur, Belgium
Gemena 77 C5 Equateur, NW Dem. Rep. Congo
Gem of the Mountains see Idaho
Gemona del Friuli 96 D2 Friuli-Venezia Giulia, NE Italy
Gem State see Idaho
Genalē Wenz see Juba
Genck see Genk
General Alvear 64 B4 Mendoza, W Argentina
General Carrera, Lago see Buenos Aires, Lago
General Eugenio A. Garay 64 C1 var. Fortín General Eugenio Garay; prev. Yrendagüé. Nueva Asunción, NW Paraguay
General José F.Uriburu see Zárate
General Machado see Camacupa
General Santos 139 F3 off. General Santos City. Mindanao, S Philippines
General Santos City see General Santos
Gênes see Genova
Geneva see Genève
Geneva, Lake 95 A7 Fr. Lac de Genève, Lac Léman, Ger. Léman, Der. Genfer See. lake France/Switzerland
Genève 95 A7 Eng. Geneva, Ger. Genf, It. Ginevra. Genève, SW Switzerland
Genève, Lac de see Geneva, Lake
Genf see Genève
Genfer See see Geneva, Lake
Genichesk see Heniches'k
Genk 87 D6 var. Genck. Limburg, NE Belgium
Gennep 86 D4 Limburg, SE Netherlands
Genoa see Genova
Genoa, Gulf of 96 A3 Eng. Gulf of Genoa. gulf NW Italy
Genoa, Gulf of see Genova, Golfo di
Genova 102 D1 Eng. Genoa; anc. Genua, Fr. Gênes. Liguria, NW Italy
Genovesa, Isla 60 B5 var. Tower Island. island Galapagos Islands, Ecuador, E Pacific Ocean
Gent 87 B5 Eng. Ghent, Fr. Gand. Oost-Vlaanderen, NW Belgium
Genua see Genova
Geok-Tepe see Gökdepe
George 78 C5 Western Cape, S South Africa
George 82 A4 river Newfoundland and Labrador/Québec, E Canada
George, Lake 43 E3 lake Florida, SE USA
Georgenburg see Jurbarkas
Georges Bank 35 D5 undersea bank W Atlantic Ocean
George Sound 151 A7 sound South Island, New Zealand
Georges River 148 D2 river New South Wales, E Australia
Georgetown 59 F2 country capital (Guyana) (Guyana) N Guyana
George Town 54 C2 Great Exuma Island, C Bahamas
George Town 54 B3 var. Georgetown. dependent territory capital (Cayman Islands) Grand Cayman, SW Cayman Islands
George Town 138 B3 var. Penang, Pinang. Pinang, Peninsular Malaysia
Georgetown 43 F2 South Carolina, SE USA
Georgetown see George Town
George V Land 154 C4 physical region Antarctica
Georgia 117 F2 off. Republic of Georgia, Geor. Sak'art'velo, Rus. Gruzinskaya SSR, Gruziya. country SW Asia

GEORGIA
Southwest Asia

Official name Georgia
Formation 1991 / 1991
Capital Tbilisi
Population 4.4 million / 164 people per sq mile (63 people per sq km) / 52%
Total area 26,911 sq. miles (69,700 sq. km)
Languages Georgian*, Russian, Azeri, Armenian, Mingrelian, Ossetian, Abkhazian* (in Abkhazia)

GEORGIA
(continued)

Religions Georgian Orthodox 65%,
Muslim 11%, Russian Orthodox 10%,
Armenian Apostolic Church
(Orthodox) 8%, Other 6%
Ethnic mix Georgian 84%, Armenian 6%,
Azeri 6%, Russian 2%, Other 1%,
Ossetian 1%
Government Presidential system
Currency Lari = 100 tetri
Literacy rate 99%
Calorie consumption 2354 calories

Georgia *42 D2 off.* State of Georgia, *also
known as* Empire State of the South,
Peach State. *state* SE USA
Georgian Bay *40 D2 lake bay* Ontario,
S Canada
Georgia, Republic of *see* Georgia
Georgia, Strait of *46 A1 strait* British
Columbia, W Canada
Georgi Dimitrov *see* Kostenets
Georgiu-Dezh *see* Liski
Georg von Neumayer *154 A2 German
research station* Antarctica
Gera *94 C4* Thüringen, E Germany
Geráki *105 B6* Pelopónnisos, S Greece
Geraldine *151 B6* Canterbury, South
Island, New Zealand
Geraldton *147 A6* Western Australia
Geral, Serra *57 D5 mountain range*
S Brazil
Gerede *116 C2* Bolu, N Turkey
Gereshk *122 D3* Helmand,
SW Afghanistan
Gering *44 D3* Nebraska, C USA
German East Africa *see* Tanzania
Germanicopolis *see* Çankırı
Germanicum, Mare/German Ocean
see North Sea
German Southwest Africa *see* Namibia
Germany *94 B4 off.* Federal Republic
of Germany, Bundesrepublik
Deutschland, *Ger.* Deutschland.
country N Europe

GERMANY
Northern Europe

Official name Federal Republic
of Germany
Formation 1871 / 1990
Capital Berlin
Population 82.7 million / 613 people
per sq mile (237 people per sq km) / 88%
Total area 137,846 sq. miles
(357,021 sq. km)
Languages German*, Turkish
Religions Protestant 34%, Roman
Catholic 33%, Other 30%, Muslim 3%
Ethnic mix German 92%, Other
European 3%, Other 3%, Turkish 2%
Government Parliamentary system
Currency Euro = 100 cents
Literacy rate 99%
Calorie consumption 3496 calories

Germany, Federal Republic of *see*
Germany
Geroliménas *105 B7* Pelopónnisos,
S Greece
Gerona *see* Girona
Gerpinnes *87 C7* Hainaut, S Belgium
Gerunda *see* Girona
Gerze *116 D2* Sinop, N Turkey
Gesoriacum *see* Boulogne-sur-Mer
Gessoriacum *see* Boulogne-sur-Mer
Getafe *92 D3* Madrid, C Spain
Gevaş *117 F3* Van, SE Turkey
Gevgeli *see* Gevgelija
Gevgelija *101 E6 var.* Đevđelija,
Djevdjelija, *Turk.* Gevgeli.
SE Macedonia
Ghaba *see* Al Ghābah
Ghana *75 E5 off.* Republic of Ghana.
country W Africa

GHANA
West Africa

Official name Republic of Ghana
Formation 1957 / 1957
Capital Accra
Population 23 million / 259 people
per sq mile (100 people per sq km) / 46%

GHANA
(continued)

Total area 92,100 sq. miles (238,540 sq. km)
Languages English*, Twi, Fanti, Ewe, Ga,
Adangbe, Gurma, Dagomba (Dagbani)
Religions Christian 69%, Muslim 16%,
Traditional beliefs 9%, Other 6%
Ethnic mix Akan 49%, Mole-Dagbani 17%,
Ewe 13%, Other 9%, Ga and
Ga-Adangbe 8%, Guan 4%
Government Presidential system
Currency Cedi = 100 pesewas
Literacy rate 58%
Calorie consumption 2667 calories

Ghanzi *78 C3 var.* Khanzi. Ghanzi,
W Botswana
Gharandal *119 B7* Al'Aqabah,
SW Jordan
Gharbt, Jabal al *see* Lībiya, Jebel
Ghardaïa *70 D2* N Algeria
Gharvān *see* Gharyān
Gharyān *71 F2 var.* Gharvān. NW Libya
Ghawdex *see* Gozo
Ghaznī *123 E4 var.* Ghazni. Ghaznī,
E Afghanistan
Ghazzah *see* Gaza
Gheel *see* Geel
Ghent *see* Gent
Gheorgheni *108 C4 prev.* Gheorghieni,
Sin-Miclâuş, *Ger.* Niklasmarkt, *Hung.*
Gyergyószentmiklós. Harghita,
C Romania
Gheorghieni *see* Gheorgheni
Ghūdara *123 F3 var.* Gudara *Rus.*
Kudara. SE Tajikistan
Ghurdaqah *see* Hurghada
Ghūrīān *122 D4* Herāt, W Afghanistan
Giamame *see* Jamaame
Giannitsá *104 B4 var.* Yiannitsá.
Kentrikí Makedonía, N Greece
Gibraltar *93 G4 UK dependent territory*
SW Europe
Gibraltar, Bay of *93 G5 bay* Gibraltar/
Spain Europe Mediterranean Sea
Atlantic Ocean
**Gibraltar, Détroit de/Gibraltar,
Estrecho de** *see* Gibraltar, Strait of
Gibraltar, Strait of *92 C5 Fr.* Détroit de
Gibraltar, *Sp.* Estrecho de Gibraltar.
strait Atlantic Ocean/Mediterranean Sea
Gibson Desert *147 B5 desert* Western
Australia
Giedraičiai *107 C5* Utena, E Lithuania
Giessen *95 B5* Hessen, W Germany
Gifu *131 C6 var.* Gihu. Gifu, Honshū,
SW Japan
Giganta, Sierra de la *50 B3 mountain
range* NW Mexico
Gihu *see* Gifu
G'ijduvon *122 D2 Rus.* Gizhduvon.
Buxoro Viloyati, C Uzbekistan
Gijón *92 D1 var.* Xixón. Asturias,
NW Spain
Gila River *48 A2 river* Arizona, SW USA
Gilbert Islands *see* Tungaru
Gilbert River *148 C3 river* Queensland,
NE Australia
Gilf Kebir Plateau *see* Haḍabat al Jilf
al Kabīr
Gillette *44 D3* Wyoming, C USA
Gilolo *see* Halmahera, Pulau
Gilroy *47 B6* California, W USA
Gimie, Mount *55 F1 mountain* C Saint
Lucia
Gimma *see* Jīma
Ginevra *see* Genève
Gingin *147 A6* Western Australia
Giohar *see* Jawhar
Gipeswic *see* Ipswich
Girardot *58 B3* Cundinamarca,
C Colombia
Giresun *117 E2 var.* Kerasunt; *anc.*
Cerasus, Pharnacia. Giresun, NE Turkey
Girgenti *see* Agrigento
Girin *see* Jilin
Girne *102 C5 Gk.* Kerýneia, Kyrenia.
N Cyprus
Giron *see* Kiruna
Girona *93 G2 var.* Gerona; *anc.* Gerunda.
Cataluña, NE Spain
Gisborne *150 E3* Gisborne, North Island,
New Zealand
Gissar Range *123 E3 Rus.* Gissarskiy
Khrebet. *mountain range* Tajikistan/
Uzbekistan

Gissarskiy Khrebet *see* Gissar Range
Githio *see* Gýtheio
Giulianova *96 D4* Abruzzi, C Italy
Giumri *see* Gyumri
Giurgiu *108 C5* Giurgiu, S Romania
Giza *72 B1 var.* Al Jīzah, El Gîza, Gizeh.
N Egypt
Gizhduvon *see* G'ijduvon
Giżycko *98 D2 Ger.* Lötzen. Warmińsko-
Mazurskie, NE Poland
Gjakovë *101 D5 Serb.* Đakovica.
W Kosovo
Gjilan *101 D5 Serb.* Gnjilane. E Kosovo
Gjinokastër *see* Gjirokastër
Gjirokastër *101 C7 var.* Gjirokastra;
prev. Gjinokastër, Gk. Argyrokastron,
It. Argirocastro. Gjirokastër, S Albania
Gjirokastra *see* Gjirokastër
Gjoa Haven *37 F3 var.* Uqsuqtuuq. King
William Island, Nunavut, NW Canada
Gjøvik *85 B5* Oppland, S Norway
Glace Bay *39 G4* Cape Breton Island,
Nova Scotia, SE Canada
Gladstone *148 E4* Queensland,
E Australia
Gláma *83 B5 var.* Glommen. *river*
S Norway
Glasgow *88 C4* S Scotland, United
Kingdom
Glavn'a Morava *see* Velika Morava
Glazov *111 D5* Udmurtskaya Respublika,
NW Russian Federation
Gleiwitz *see* Gliwice
Glendale *48 B2* Arizona, SW USA
Glendive *44 D2* Montana, NW USA
Glens Falls *41 F3* New York, NE USA
Glevum *see* Gloucester
Glina *100 B3 var.* Banijska Palanka.
Sisak-Moslavina, NE Croatia
Glittertind *85 A5 mountain* S Norway
Gliwice *99 C5 Ger.* Gleiwitz. Śląskie,
S Poland
Globe *48 B2* Arizona, SW USA
Globino *see* Hlobyne
Głogau *see* Głogów
Głogów *98 B4 Ger.* Glogau, Glogow.
Dolnośląskie, SW Poland
Glogow *see* Głogów
Glomma *see* Gláma
Glommen *see* Gláma
Gloucester *89 D6 hist.* Caer Glou, *Lat.*
Glevum. C England, United Kingdom
Głowno *98 D4* Łódź, C Poland
Glubokoye *see* Hlybokaye
Glukhov *see* Hlukhiv
Gnesen *see* Gniezno
Gniezno *98 C3 Ger.* Gnesen.
Weilkopolskie, C Poland
Gnjilane *see* Gjilan
Gobabis *78 B3* Omaheke, E Namibia
Gobi *126 D3 desert* China/Mongolia
Gobō *131 C6* Wakayama, Honshū,
SW Japan
Godavari *124 B3 var.* Godavari. *river*
C India
Godavari *see* Godāvari
Godhavn *see* Qeqertarsuaq
Godhra *134 C4* Gujarāt, W India
Gōding *see* Hodonín
Godoy Cruz *64 B4* Mendoza,
W Argentina
Godthaab/Godthåb *see* Nuuk
Godwin Austen, Mount *see* K2
Goede Hoop, Kaap de *see* Good Hope,
Cape of
Goeie Hoop, Kaap die *see* Good Hope,
Cape of
Goeree *86 B4 island* SW Netherlands
Goes *87 B5* Zeeland, SW Netherlands
Goettingen *see* Göttingen
Gogebic Range *40 B1 hill range*
Michigan/Wisconsin, N USA
Goiânia *63 E3 prev.* Goyania. *state
capital* Goiás, C Brazil
Goiás *63 E3 off.* Estado de Goiás; *prev.*
Goiaz, Goyaz. *region* C Brazil
Goiás *63 E3 off.* Estado de Goiás; *prev.*
Goiaz, Goyaz. *state* C Brazil
Goiás, Estado de *see* Goiás
Goidhoo Atoll *see* Horsburgh Atoll
Gojōme *130 D4 var.* Akita, Honshū,
NW Japan
Gökçeada *104 D4 var.* Imroz Adasi, *Gk.*
Imbros. *island* NW Turkey
Gökdepe *122 C3 Rus.* Gökdepe, Geok-
Tepe. Ahal Welaýaty, C Turkmenistan

Göksun *116 D4* Kahramanmaraş,
C Turkey
Gol *85 A5* Buskerud, S Norway
Golan Heights *119 B5 Ar.* Al Jawlān,
Heb. HaGolan. *mountain range*
SW Syria
Golaya Pristan *see* Hola Prystan'
Gołdap *98 E2 Ger.* Goldap. Warmińsko-
Mazurskie, NE Poland
Gold Coast *149 E5 cultural region*
Queensland, E Australia
Golden Bay *150 C4 bay* South Island,
New Zealand
Golden State, The *see* California
Goldingen *see* Kuldīga
Goldsboro *43 F1* North Carolina,
SE USA
Goleniów *98 B3 Ger.* Gollnow.
Zachodnio-pomorskie, NW Poland
Gollnow *see* Goleniów
Golmo *see* Golmud
Golmud *126 D4 var.* Ge'e'mu, Golmo,
Chin. Ko-erh-mu. Qinghai, C China
Golovanevsk *see* Holovanivs'k
Golub-Dobrzyń *98 C3* Kujawsko-
pomorskie, C Poland
Goma *77 E6* Nord-Kivu, NE Dem.
Rep. Congo
Gombi *75 H4* Adamawa, E Nigeria
Gombroon *see* Bandar-e 'Abbās
Gomel' *see* Homyel'
Gomera *70 A3 island* Islas Canarias,
Spain, NE Atlantic Ocean
Gómez Palacio *50 D3* Durango,
C Mexico
Gonaïves *54 D3 var.* Les Gonaïves.
N Haiti
Gonâve, Île de la *54 D3 island* C Haiti
Gondar *see* Gonder
Gonder *72 C4 var.* Gondar. Āmara,
NW Ethiopia
Gondia *135 E4* Mahārāshtra, C India
Gonggar *126 C5 var.* Gyixong. Xizang
Zizhiqu, W China
Gongola *75 G4 river* E Nigeria
Gongtang *see* Damxung
Gonni/Gónnos *see* Gónnoi
Gónnoi *104 B4 var.* Gonni, Gónnos;
prev. Derelí. Thessalía, C Greece
Good Hope, Cape of *78 B5 Afr.* Kaap de
Goede Hoop, Kaap die Goeie Hoop.
headland SW South Africa
Goodland *44 D4* Kansas, C USA
Goondiwindi *149 D5* Queensland,
E Australia
Goor *86 E3* Overijssel, E Netherlands
Goose Green *65 D7 var.* Prado del
Ganso. East Falkland, Falkland Islands
Goose Lake *46 B4 var.* Lago dos Gansos.
lake California/Oregon, W USA
Gopher State *see* Minnesota
Göppingen *95 B6* Baden-Württemberg,
SW Germany
Góra Kalwaria *114 D4* Mazowieckie,
C Poland
Gorakhpur *135 E3* Uttar Pradesh,
N India
Gorany *see* Harany
Goražde *100 C4* Federacija Bosna
I Hercegovina, SE Bosnia and
Herzegovina
Gorbovichi *see* Harbavichy
Goré *76 C4* Logone-Oriental, S Chad
Gorē *73 C5* Oromīya, C Ethiopia
Gore *151 B7* Southland, South Island,
New Zealand
Gorgān *120 D2 var.* Astarabad,
Astrabad, Gurgan, *prev.* Asterābād;
anc. Hyrcania. Golestán, N Iran
Gori *117 F2* C Georgia
Gorinchem *86 C4 var.* Gorkum. Zuid-
Holland, C Netherlands
Goris *117 G3* SE Armenia
Gorki *see* Horki
Gor'kiy *see* Nizhniy Novgorod
Gorkum *see* Gorinchem
Görlitz *94 D4* Sachsen, E Germany
Görlitz *see* Zgorzelec
Gorlovka *see* Horlivka
Gorna Dzhumaya *see* Blagoevgrad
Gornja Mužlja *see* Mužlja
Gornji Milanovac *100 C4* Serbia,
C Serbia
Gorodets *see* Haradzyets
Gorodishche *see* Horodyshche
Gorodnya *see* Horodnya
Gorodok *see* Haradok

Gorodok/Gorodok Yagellonski see
Horodok
Gorontalo *139 E4* Sulawesi, C Indonesia
Gorontalo, Teluk see Tomini, Gulf of
Gorssel *86 D3* Gelderland, E Netherlands
Goryn see Horyn'
Gorzów Wielkopolski *98 B3* Ger.
Landsberg, Landsberg an der Warthe.
Lubuskie, W Poland
Gosford *149 D6* New South Wales,
SE Australia
Goshogawara *130 D3* var. Gosyogawara.
Aomori, Honshū, C Japan
Gospić *100 A3* Lika-Senj, C Croatia
Gostivar *101 D6* W FYR Macedonia
Gosyogawara see Goshogawara
Göteborg *85 B7* Eng. Gothenburg.
Västra Götaland, S Sweden
Gotel Mountains *75 G5* mountain range
E Nigeria
Gotha *94 C4* Thüringen, C Germany
Gothenburg see Göteborg
Gotland *85 C7* island SE Sweden
Goto-retto *131 A7* island group
SW Japan
Gotska Sandön *106 B1* island SE Sweden
Gōtsu *131 B6* var. Gôtu. Shimane,
Honshū, SW Japan
Göttingen *94 B4* var. Goettingen.
Niedersachsen, C Germany
Gottschee see Kočevje
Gottwaldov see Zlín
Gôtu see Gōtsu
Gouda *86 C4* Zuid-Holland,
C Netherlands
Gough Fracture Zone *67 C6* tectonic
feature S Atlantic Ocean
Gough Island *69 B8* island Tristan da
Cunha, S Atlantic Ocean
Gouin, Réservoir *38 D4* reservoir
Québec, SE Canada
Goulburn *149 D6* New South Wales,
SE Australia
Goundam *75 E3* Tombouctou, NW Mali
Gouré *75 G3* Zinder, SE Niger
Goverla, Gora see Hoverla, Hora
Governador Valadares *63 F4* Minas
Gerais, SE Brazil
Govi Altayn Nuruu *127 E3* mountain
range S Mongolia
Goya *64 D3* Corrientes, NE Argentina
Goyania see Goiânia
Goyaz see Goiás
Goz Beïda *76 C3* Ouaddaï, SE Chad
Gozo *97 C8* var. Ghawdex. island
N Malta
Graciosa *92 A5* var. Ilha Graciosa. island
Azores, Portugal, NE Atlantic Ocean
Graciosa, Ilha see Graciosa
Gradačac *100 C3* Federacija Bosna
I Hercegovina, N Bosnia and
Herzegovina
Gradaús, Serra dos *63 E3* mountain
range C Brazil
Gradiška see Bosanska Gradiška
Grafton *149 E5* New South Wales,
SE Australia
Grafton *45 E1* North Dakota, N USA
Graham Land *154 A2* physical region
Antarctica
Grajewo *98 E3* Podlaskie, NE Poland
Grampian Mountains *88 C3* mountain
range C Scotland, United Kingdom
Gran see Esztergom, Hungary
Granada *52 D3* Granada, SW Nicaragua
Granada *92 D5* Andalucía, S Spain
Gran Canaria *70 A3* var. Grand Canary.
island Islas Canarias, Spain, NE Atlantic
Ocean
Gran Chaco *64 D2* var. Chaco. lowland
plain South America
Grand Bahama Island *54 B1* island
N Bahamas
Grand Banks of Newfoundland *34 E4*
undersea basin NW Atlantic Ocean
Grand Bassa see Buchanan
Grand Canary see Gran Canaria
Grand Canyon *48 A1* canyon Arizona,
SW USA
Grand Canyon State see Arizona
Grand Cayman *54 B3* island
SW Cayman Islands
Grand Duchy of Luxembourg see
Luxembourg
Grande, Bahía *65 B7* bay S Argentina
Grande-Comor see Ngazidja
Grande de Chiloé, Isla see Chiloé, Isla de

Grande Prairie *37 E4* Alberta, W Canada
Grand Erg Occidental *70 D3* desert
W Algeria
Grand Erg Oriental *71 E3* desert
Algeria/Tunisia
Río Grande *51 E2* var. Río Bravo, Sp. Río
Bravo del Norte, Bravo del Norte. river
Mexico/USA
Grande Terre *55 G3* island E West Indies
Grand Falls *39 G3* Newfoundland,
Newfoundland and Labrador,
SE Canada
Grand Forks *45 E1* North Dakota,
N USA
Grandichi see Hrandzichy
Grand Island *45 E4* Nebraska, C USA
Grand Junction *44 C4* Colorado, C USA
Grand Paradis see Gran Paradiso
Grand Rapids *40 C3* Michigan, N USA
Grand Rapids *45 F1* Minnesota, N USA
Grand-Saint-Bernard, Col du see Great
Saint Bernard Pass
Grand-Santi *59 G3* W French Guiana
Granite State see New Hampshire
Gran Lago see Nicaragua, Lago de
Gran Malvina see West Falkland
Gran Paradiso *96 A2* Fr. Grand Paradis.
mountain NW Italy
Gran San Bernardo, Passo di see Great
Saint Bernard Pass
Gran Santiago see Santiago
Grants *48 C2* New Mexico, SW USA
Grants Pass *46 B4* Oregon, NW USA
Granville *90 B3* Manche, N France
Gratianopolis see Grenoble
Gratz see Graz
Graudenz see Grudziądz
Graulhet *91 C6* Tarn, S France
Grave *86 D4* Noord-Brabant,
SE Netherlands
Grayling *36 C2* Alaska, USA
Graz *95 E7* prev. Gratz. Steiermark,
SE Austria
Great Abaco *54 C1* var. Abaco Island.
island N Bahamas
Great Alfold see Great Hungarian Plain
Great Ararat see Büyükağrı Dağı
Great Australian Bight *147 D7* bight
S Australia
Great Barrier Island *150 D2* island
N New Zealand
Great Barrier Reef *148 D2* reef
Queensland, NE Australia
Great Basin *47 C5* basin W USA
Great Bear Lake *37 E3* Fr. Grand Lac
de l'Ours. lake Northwest Territories,
NW Canada
Great Belt *85 B8* var. Store Bælt, Eng.
Great Belt, Storebælt. channel Baltic
Sea/Kattegat
Great Belt see Storebælt
Great Bend *45 E5* Kansas, C USA
Great Britain see Britain
Great Dividing Range *148 D4* mountain
range NE Australia
Greater Antilles *54 D3* island group
West Indies
Greater Caucasus *117 G2* mountain
range Azerbaijan/Georgia/Russian
Federation Asia/Europe
Greater Sunda Islands *124 D5* var.
Sunda Islands. island group Indonesia
Great Exhibition Bay *150 C1* inlet North
Island, New Zealand
Great Exuma Island *54 C2* island
C Bahamas
Great Falls *44 B1* Montana, NW USA
Great Grimsby see Grimsby
Great Hungarian Plain *99 C7* var. Great
Alfold, Plain of Hungary, Hung. Alföld.
plain SE Europe
Great Inagua *54 D2* var. Inagua Islands.
island S Bahamas
Great Indian Desert see Thar Desert
Great Khingan Range *127 G1* Eng.
Great Khingan Range. mountain range
NE China
Great Khingan Range see Da Hinggan
Ling
Great Lake see Tônlé Sap
Great Lakes *35 C5* lakes Ontario,
Canada/USA
Great Lakes State see Michigan
Great Meteor Seamount see Great
Meteor Tablemount
Great Meteor Tablemount *66 B3* var.
Great Meteor Seamount. seamount
E Atlantic Ocean

Great Nicobar *133 G3* island Nicobar
Islands, India, NE Indian Ocean
Great Plain of China *125 E2* plain
E China
Great Plains *45 E3* var. High Plains.
plains Canada/USA
Great Rift Valley *73 C5* var. Rift Valley.
depression Asia/Africa
Great Ruaha *73 C7* river S Tanzania
Great Saint Bernard Pass *96 A1* Fr.
Col du Grand-Saint-Bernard, It. Passo
del Gran San Bernardo. pass Italy/
Switzerland
Great Salt Desert see Kavīr, Dasht-e
Great Salt Lake *44 A3* salt lake Utah,
W USA
Great Salt Lake Desert *44 A4* plain
Utah, W USA
Great Sand Sea *71 H3* desert Egypt/Libya
Great Sandy Desert *146 C4* desert
Western Australia
Great Sandy Desert see Ar Rub 'al Khālī
Great Sandy Island see Fraser Island
Great Slave Lake *37 E4* Fr. Grand
Lac des Esclaves. lake Northwest
Territories, NW Canada
**Great Socialist People's Libyan Arab
Jamahiriya** see Libya
Great Sound *42 A5* sound Bermuda,
NW Atlantic Ocean
Great Victoria Desert *147 C5* desert
South Australia/Western Australia
Great Wall of China *128 C4* ancient
monument N China Asia
Great Yarmouth *89 E6* var. Yarmouth.
E England, United Kingdom
Grebenka see Hrebinka
Gredos, Sierra de *92 D3* mountain
range W Spain
Greece *105 A5* off. Hellenic Republic, Gk.
Ellás; anc. Hellas. country SE Europe

GREECE
Southeast Europe

Official name Hellenic Republic
Formation 1829 / 1947
Capital Athens
Population 11.2 million / 222 people
per sq mile (86 people per sq km) / 61%
Total area 50,942 sq. miles (131,940 sq. km)
Languages Greek*, Turkish, Macedonian,
Albanian
Religions Orthodox Christian 98%,
Other 1%, Muslim 1%
Ethnic mix Greek 98%, Other 2%
Government Parliamentary system
Currency Euro = 100 cents
Literacy rate 96%
Calorie consumption 3721 calories

Greeley *44 D4* Colorado, C USA
Green Bay *40 B2* Wisconsin, N USA
Green Bay *40 B2* lake bay Michigan/
Wisconsin, N USA
Greeneville *43 E1* Tennessee, S USA
Greenland *82 D3* Dan. Grønland, Inuit
Kalaallit Nunaat. Danish external
territory NE North America
Greenland Sea *83 F2* sea Arctic Ocean
Green Mountains *41 G2* mountain
range Vermont, NE USA
Green Mountain State see Vermont
Greenock *88 C4* W Scotland, United
Kingdom
Green River *44 B3* Wyoming, C USA
Green River *40 C5* river Kentucky,
C USA
Green River *44 B4* river Utah, W USA
Greensboro *43 F1* North Carolina,
SE USA
Greenville *42 B2* Mississippi, S USA
Greenville *43 F1* North Carolina, SE USA
Greenville *43 E1* South Carolina, SE USA
Greenville *49 G2* Texas, SW USA
Greenwich *89 B8* United Kingdom
Greenwood *42 B2* Mississippi, S USA
Greenwood *43 E2* South Carolina,
SE USA
Gregory Range *148 C3* mountain range
Queensland, E Australia
Greifenberg/Greifenberg in Pommern
see Gryfice
Greifswald *94 D2* Mecklenburg-
Vorpommern, NE Germany
Grenada *42 C2* Mississippi, S USA

Grenada *55 G5* country SE West Indies

GRENADA
West Indies

Official name Grenada
Formation 1974 / 1974
Capital St. George's
Population 89,971 / 687 people
per sq mile (265 people per sq km) / 41%
Total area 131 sq. miles (340 sq. km)
Languages English*, English Creole
Religions Roman Catholic 68%,
Anglican 17%, Other 15%
Ethnic mix Black African 82%, Mulatto
(mixed race) 13%, East Indian 3%,
Other 2%
Government Parliamentary system
Currency Eastern Caribbean dollar
= 100 cents
Literacy rate 96%
Calorie consumption 2932 calories

Grenadines, The *55 H4* island group
Grenada/St Vincent and the
Grenadines
Grenoble *91 D5* anc. Cularo,
Gratianopolis. Isère, E France
Gresham *46 B3* Oregon, NW USA
Grevená *104 B4* Dytiki Makedonía,
N Greece
Grevenmacher *87 E8* Grevenmacher,
E Luxembourg
Greymouth *151 B5* West Coast, South
Island, New Zealand
Grey Range *149 C5* mountain range New
South Wales/Queensland, E Australia
Greytown see San Juan del Norte
Griffin *42 D2* Georgia, SE USA
Grimari *76 C4* Ouaka, C Central African
Republic
Grimsby *89 E5* prev. Great Grimsby.
E England, United Kingdom
Grobin see Grobiņa
Grobiņa *106 B3* Ger. Grobin. Liepāja,
W Latvia
Gródek Jagielloński see Horodok
Grodno see Hrodna
Grodzisk Wielkopolski *98 B3*
Wielkopolskie, C Poland
Groesbeek *86 D4* Gelderland,
SE Netherlands
Grójec *98 D4* Mazowieckie, C Poland
Groningen *86 E1* Groningen,
NE Netherlands
Grønland see Greenland
Groote Eylandt *148 B2* island Northern
Territory, N Australia
Grootfontein *78 B3* Otjozondjupa,
N Namibia
Groot Karasberge *78 B4* mountain
range S Namibia
Gros Islet *55 F1* N Saint Lucia
Grossa, Isola see Dugi Otok
Grossbetschkerek see Zrenjanin
Grosse Morava see Velika Morava
Grosser Sund see Suur Väin
Grosseto *96 B4* Toscana, C Italy
Grossglockner *95 C7* mountain
W Austria
Grosskanizsa see Nagykanizsa
Gross-Karol see Carei
Grosskikinda see Kikinda
Grossmichel see Michalovce
Gross-Schlatten see Abrud
Grosswardein see Oradea
Groznyy *111 B8* Chechenskaya
Respublika, SW Russian Federation
Grudovo see Sredets
Grudziądz *98 C3* Ger. Graudenz.
Kujawsko-pomorskie, C Poland
Grums *85 B6* Värmland, C Sweden
Grünberg/Grünberg in Schlesien see
Zielona Góra
Grüneberg see Zielona Góra
Gruzinskaya SSR/Gruziya see Georgia
Gryazi *111 B6* Lipetskaya Oblast',
W Russian Federation
Gryfice *98 B2* Ger. Greifenberg,
Greifenberg in Pommern. Zachodnio-
pomorskie, NW Poland
Guabito *53 E4* Bocas del Toro,
NW Panama
Guadalajara *50 D4* Jalisco, C Mexico
Guadalajara *93 E3* Ar. Wad Al-Hajarah;
anc. Arriaca. Castilla-La Mancha,
C Spain

Guadalcanal *144 C3 island* C Solomon Islands
Guadalquivir *92 D4 river* W Spain
Guadalupe *50 D3* Zacatecas, C Mexico
Guadalupe Peak *48 D3 mountain* Texas, SW USA
Guadalupe River *49 G4 river* SW USA
Guadarrama, Sierra de *93 E2 mountain range* C Spain
Guadeloupe *55 H3 French overseas department* E West Indies
Guadiana *92 C4 river* Portugal/Spain
Guadix *93 E4* Andalucía, S Spain
Guaimaca *52 C2* Francisco Morazán, C Honduras
Guajira, Península de la *38 B1 peninsula* N Colombia
Gualaco *52 D2* Olancho, C Honduras
Gualán *52 B2* Zacapa, C Guatemala
Gualdicciolo *96 D1* NW San Marino
Gualeguaychú *64 D4* Entre Ríos, E Argentina
Guam *144 B1 US unincorporated territory* W Pacific Ocean
Guamúchil *50 C3* Sinaloa, C Mexico
Guanabacoa *54 B2* La Habana, W Cuba
Guanajuato *51 E4* Guanajuato, C Mexico
Guanare *58 C2* Portuguesa, N Venezuela
Guanare, Río *58 D2 river* W Venezuela
Guangdong *128 C6 var.* Guangdong Sheng, Kuang-tung, Kwangtung, Yue. *province* S China
Guangdong Sheng *see* Guangdong
Guangju *see* Kwangju
Guangxi *see* Guangxi Zhuangzu Zizhiqu
Guangxi Zhuangzu Zizhiqu *128 C6 var.* Guangxi, Gui, Kuang-hsi, Kwangsi, *Eng.* Kwangsi Chuang Autonomous Region. *autonomous region* S China
Guangyuan *128 B5 var.* Kuang-yuan, Kwangyuan. Sichuan, C China
Guangzhou *128 C6 var.* Kuang-chou, Kwangchow, *Eng.* Canton. *province capital* Guangdong, S China
Guantánamo *54 D3* Guantánamo, SE Cuba
Guantánamo, Bahía de *54 D3 Eng.* Guantanamo Bay. *US military base* SE Cuba
Guantanamo Bay *see* Guantánamo, Bahía de
Guaporé, Río *62 D3 var.* Río Iténez. *river* Bolivia/Brazil
Guarda *92 C3* Guarda, N Portugal
Guarumal *53 F5* Veraguas, S Panama
Guasave *50 C3* Sinaloa, C Mexico
Guatemala *52 A2 off.* Republic of Guatemala. *country* Central America

GUATEMALA
Central America

Official name Republic of Guatemala
Formation 1838 / 1838
Capital Guatemala City
Population 13.2 million / 315 people per sq mile (122 people per sq km) / 47%
Total area 42,042 sq. miles (108,890 sq. km)
Languages Spanish*, Quiché, Mam, Cakchiquel, Kekchí
Religions Roman Catholic 65%, Protestant 33%, Other and nonreligious 2%
Ethnic mix Amerindian 60%, Mestizo 30%, Other 10%
Government Presidential system
Currency Quetzal = 100 centavos
Literacy rate 69%
Calorie consumption 2219 calories

Guatemala Basin *35 B7 undersea basin* E Pacific Ocean
Guatemala City *see* Ciudad de Guatemala
Guatemala, Republic of *see* Guatemala
Guaviare *56 B2 off.* Comisaría Guaviare. *province* S Colombia
Guaviare, Comisaría *see* Guaviare
Guaviare, Río *58 D3 river* E Colombia
Guayanas, Macizo de las *see* Guiana Highlands
Guayaquil *60 A2 var.* Santiago de Guayaquil. Guayas, SW Ecuador
Guayaquil, Gulf of *60 A2 var.* Gulf of Guayaquil. *gulf* SW Ecuador

Guayaquil, Gulf of *see* Guayaquil, Golfo de
Guayaquil, Golfo de *see* Guayaquil, Gulf of
Guaymas *50 B2* Sonora, NW Mexico
Gubadag *122 C2 Turkm.* Tel'man; *prev.* Tel'mansk. Daşoguz Welaýaty, N Turkmenistan
Guben *94 D4 var.* Wilhelm-Pieck-Stadt. Brandenburg, E Germany
Gudara *see* Ghūdara
Gudaut'a *117 E1* NW Georgia
Guéret *90 C4* Creuse, C France
Guernsey *89 D8 island* Channel Islands, NW Europe
Guerrero Negro *50 A2* Baja California Sur, NW Mexico
Gui *see* Guangxi Zhuangzu Zizhiqu
Guiana *see* French Guiana
Guiana Highlands *62 D1 var.* Macizo de las Guayanas. *mountain range* N South America
Guiba *see* Juba
Guidder *see* Guider
Guider *76 B4 var.* Guidder. Nord, N Cameroon
Guidimouni *75 G3* Zinder, S Niger
Guildford *89 D7* SE England, United Kingdom
Guilin *128 C6 var.* Kuei-lin, Kweilin. Guangxi Zhuangzu Zizhiqu, S China
Guimarães *92 B2 var.* Guimarães. Braga, N Portugal
Guimaráes *see* Guimarães
Guinea *74 C4 off.* Republic of Guinea, *var.* Guinée; *prev.* French Guinea, People's Revolutionary Republic of Guinea. *country* W Africa

GUINEA
West Africa

Official name Republic of Guinea
Formation 1958 / 1958
Capital Conakry
Population 9.8 million / 103 people per sq mile (40 people per sq km) / 36%
Total area 94,925 sq. miles (245,857 sq. km)
Languages French*, Pulaar, Malinke, Soussou
Religions Muslim 65%, Traditional beliefs 33%, Christian 2%
Ethnic mix Peul 39%, Malinké 23%, Other 16%, Soussou 11%, Kissi 6%, Kpellé 5%
Government Presidential system
Currency Guinea franc = 100 centimes
Literacy rate 30%
Calorie consumption 2409 calories

Guinea Basin *69 A5 undersea basin* E Atlantic Ocean
Guinea-Bissau *74 B4 off.* Republic of Guinea-Bissau, *Fr.* Guinée-Bissau, *Port.* Guiné-Bissau; *prev.* Portuguese Guinea. *country* W Africa

GUINEA-BISSAU
West Africa

Official name Republic of Guinea-Bissau
Formation 1974 / 1974
Capital Bissau
Population 1.7 million / 157 people per sq mile (61 people per sq km) / 35%
Total area 13,946 sq. miles (36,120 sq. km)
Languages Portuguese*, Portuguese Creole, Balante, Fulani, Malinke
Religions Traditional beliefs 52%, Muslim 40%, Christian 8%
Ethnic mix Balante 30%, Fulani 20%, Other 17%, Mandyako 14%, Mandinka 12%, Papel 7%
Government Presidential system
Currency CFA franc = 100 centimes
Literacy rate 40%
Calorie consumption 2024 calories

Guinea-Bissau, Republic of *see* Guinea-Bissau
Guinea, Gulf of *68 B4 Fr.* Golfe de Guinée. *gulf* E Atlantic Ocean
Guinea, People's Revolutionary Republic of *see* Guinea
Guinea, Republic of *see* Guinea
Guiné-Bissau *see* Guinea-Bissau
Guinée *see* Guinea
Guinée-Bissau *see* Guinea-Bissau

Guinée, Golfe de *see* Guinea, Gulf of
Güiria *59 E1* Sucre, NE Venezuela
Guiyang *128 B6 var.* Kuei-Yang, Kuei-yang, Kueyang, Kweiyang; *prev.* Kweichu. *province capital* Guizhou, S China
Guizhou *128 B6* Guangdong, SE China
Gujarāt *134 C4 var.* Gujerat. *cultural region* W India
Gujerat *see* Gujarāt
Gujrānwāla *134 D2* Punjab, NE Pakistan
Gujrāt *134 D2* Punjab, E Pakistan
Gulbarga *132 C1* Karnātaka, C India
Gulbene *106 D3 Ger.* Alt-Schwanenburg. Gulbene, NE Latvia
Gulf of Liaotung *see* Liaodong Wan
Gulfport *42 C3* Mississippi, S USA
Gulf, The *see* Persian Gulf
Gulistan *see* Guliston
Guliston *123 E2 Rus.* Gulistan. Sirdaryo Viloyati, E Uzbekistan
Gulja *see* Yining
Gulkana *36 D3* Alaska, USA
Gulu *73 B6* N Uganda
Gulyantsi *104 C1* Pleven, N Bulgaria
Guma *see* Pishan
Gumbinnen *see* Gusev
Gumpolds *see* Humpolec
Gümülcine/Gümüljina *see* Komotiní
Gümüşane *see* Gümüşhane
Gümüşhane *117 E3 var.* Gümüşane, Gumushkhane. Gümüşhane, NE Turkey
Gumushkhane *see* Gümüşhane
Güney Doğu Toroslar *117 E4 mountain range* SE Turkey
Gunnbjørn Fjeld *82 D4 var.* Gunnbjørns Bjerge. *mountain* C Greenland
Gunnbjørns Bjerge *see* Gunnbjørn Fjeld
Gunnedah *149 D6* New South Wales, SE Australia
Gunnison *44 C5* Colorado, C USA
Gurbansoltan Eje *122 C2 prev.* Ýylanly, *Rus.* Il'yaly. Daşoguz Welaýaty, N Turkmenistan
Gurbantünggüt Shamo *126 B2 desert* W China
Gurgan *see* Gorgān
Guri, Embalse de *59 E2 reservoir* E Venezuela
Gurkfeld *see* Krško
Gurktaler Alpen *95 D7 mountain range* S Austria
Gürün *116 D3* Sivas, C Turkey
Gur'yev/Gur'yevskaya Oblast' *see* Atyrau
Gusau *75 G4* Zamfara, NW Nigeria
Gusev *106 B4 Ger.* Gumbinnen. Kaliningradskaya Oblast', W Russian Federation
Gustavus *36 D4* Alaska, USA
Güstrow *94 C3* Mecklenburg-Vorpommern, NE Germany
Guta/Gúta *see* Kolárovo
Gütersloh *94 B4* Nordrhein-Westfalen, W Germany
Gutta *see* Kolárovo
Guttstadt *see* Dobre Miasto
Guwāhāti *135 G3 prev.* Gauhāti. Assam, NE India
Guyana *59 F3 off.* Co-operative Republic of Guyana; *prev.* British Guiana. *country* N South America

GUYANA
South America

Official name The Co-operative Republic of Guyana
Formation 1966 / 1966
Capital Georgetown
Population 769,095 / 10 people per sq mile (4 people per sq km) / 38%
Total area 83,000 sq. miles (214,970 sq. km)
Languages English*, English Creole, Hindi, Tamil, Amerindian languages
Religions Christian 57%, Hindu 33%, Muslim 9%, Other 1%
Ethnic mix East Indian 43%, Black African 30%, Mixed race 17%, Amerindian 9%, Other 1%
Government Presidential system
Currency Guyanese dollar = 100 cents
Literacy rate 97%
Calorie consumption 2692 calories

Guyana, Co-operative Republic of *see* Guyana
Guyane *see* French Guiana
Guymon *49 E1* Oklahoma, C USA
Güzelyurt *102 C5 Gk.* Kólpos Mórfu, Morphou. W Cyprus
Gvardeysk *106 A4 Ger.* Tapiau. Kaliningradskaya Oblast', W Russian Federation
Gwādar *134 A3 var.* Gwadur. Baluchistān, SW Pakistan
Gwadur *see* Gwādar
Gwalior *134 D3* Madhya Pradesh, C India
Gwanda *78 D3* Matabeleland South, SW Zimbabwe
Gwy *see* Wye
Gyandzha *see* Gäncä
Gyangzê *126 C5* Xizang Zizhiqu, W China
Gyaring Co *126 C5 lake* W China
Gyêgu *see* Yushu
Gyergyószentmiklós *see* Gheorgheni
Gyixong *see* Gonggar
Gympie *149 E5* Queensland, E Australia
Gyomaendrőd *99 D7* Békés, SE Hungary
Gyöngyös *99 D6* Heves, NE Hungary
Győr *99 C6 Ger.* Raab, *Lat.* Arrabona. Győr-Moson-Sopron, NW Hungary
Gýtheio *105 B6 var.* Githio; *prev.* Yíthion. Pelopónnisos, S Greece
Gyulafehérvár *see* Alba Iulia
Gyumri *117 F2 var.* Giumri, *Rus.* Kumayri; *prev.* Aleksandropol', Leninakan. W Armenia
Gyzylarbat *see* Serdar

H

Haabai *see* Ha'apai Group
Haacht *87 C6* Vlaams Brabant, C Belgium
Haaksbergen *86 E3* Overijssel, E Netherlands
Ha'apai Group *145 F4 var.* Haabai. *island group* C Tonga
Haapsalu *106 D2 Ger.* Hapsal. Läänemaa, W Estonia
Ha'Arava *see* 'Arabah, Wādī al
Haarlem *86 C3 prev.* Harlem. Noord-Holland, W Netherlands
Haast *151 B6* West Coast, South Island, New Zealand
Hachijō-jima *131 D6 island* Izu-shotō, SE Japan
Hachinohe *130 D3* Aomori, Honshū, C Japan
Ḥaḍabat al Jilf al Kabīr *72 A2 var.* Gilf Kebir Plateau. *plateau* SW Egypt
Hadama *see* Nazrēt
Hadejia *75 G4* Jigawa, N Nigeria
Hadejia *75 G3 river* N Nigeria
Hadera *119 A6 var.* Khadera; *prev.* Ḥadera. Haifa, C Israel
Ḥadera *see* Hadera
Hadhdhunmathi Atoll *132 A5 atoll* S Maldives
Ha Đông *136 D3 var.* Hadong. Ha Tây, N Vietnam
Hadong *see* Ha Đông
Hadramaut *121 C6 Eng.* Hadramaut. *mountain range* S Yemen
Hadramaut *see* Ḥaḍramawt
Hadrianopolis *see* Edirne
Haerbin/Haerhpin/Ha-erh-pin *see* Harbin
Hafnia *see* Denmark
Hafnia *see* København
Hafren *see* Severn
Hafun, Ras *see* Xaafuun, Raas
Hagåtña *144 B1 var.* Agaña. *dependent territory capital* (Guam) NW Guam
Hagerstown *41 F4* Maryland, NE USA
Ha Giang *136 D3* Ha Giang, N Vietnam
Hagios Evstrátios *see* Ágios Efstrátios
HaGolan *see* Golan Heights
Hagondange *90 D3* Moselle, NE France
Haguenau *90 E3* Bas-Rhin, NE France
Haibowan *see* Wuhai
Haicheng *128 D3* Liaoning, NE China
Haidarabad *see* Hyderābād
Haifa *see* Hefa
Haifa, Bay of *see* Mifrats Hefa
Haifong *see* Hai Phong
Haikou *128 C7 var.* Hai-k'ou, Hoihow, *Fr.* Hoï-Hao. *province capital* Hainan, S China

Hai-k'ou see Haikou
Ḥā'il 120 B4 Ḥā'il, NW Saudi Arabia
Hailuoto 84 D4 Swe. Karlö. island
W Finland
Hainan 128 B7 var. Hainan Sheng,
Qiong. province S China
Hainan Dao 128 C7 island S China
Hainan Sheng see Hainan
Hainasch see Ainaži
Haines 36 D4 Alaska, USA
Hainichen 94 D4 Sachsen, E Germany
Hai Phong 136 D3 var. Haifong,
Haiphong. N Vietnam
Haiphong see Hai Phong
Haiti 54 D3 off. Republic of Haiti.
country C West Indies

HAITI
West Indies

Official name Republic of Haiti
Formation 1804 / 1844
Capital Port-au-Prince
Population 8.8 million / 827 people
per sq mile (319 people per sq km) / 38%
Total area 10,714 sq. miles (27,750 sq. km)
Languages French*, French Creole*
Religions Roman Catholic 80%,
Protestant 16%, Other (including
Voodoo) 3%, Nonreligious 1%
Ethnic mix Black African 95%,
Mulatto (mixed race) and European 5%
Government Presidential system
Currency Gourde = 100 centimes
Literacy rate 52%
Calorie consumption 2086 calories

Haiti, Republic of see Haiti
Haiya 72 C3 Red Sea, NE Sudan
Hajdúhadház 99 D6 Hajdú-Bihar,
E Hungary
Hajine see Abū Ḥardān
Hajnówka 98 E3 Ger. Hermhausen.
Podlaskie, NE Poland
Hakodate 130 D3 Hokkaidō, NE Japan
Hal see Halle
Ḥalab 118 B2 Eng. Aleppo, Fr. Alep; anc.
Beroea. Ḥalab, NW Syria
Ḥalāniyāt, Juzur al 121 D6 var. Jazā'ir
Bin Ghalfān, Eng. Kuria Muria Islands.
island group S Oman
Halberstadt 94 C4 Sachsen-Anhalt,
C Germany
Halden 85 B6 prev. Fredrikshald.
Østfold, S Norway
Halfmoon Bay 151 A8 var. Oban.
Stewart Island, Southland, New Zealand
Haliacmon see Aliákmonas
Halifax 39 F4 province capital Nova
Scotia, SE Canada
Halkida see Chalkída
Halle 87 B6 Fr. Hal. Vlaams Brabant,
C Belgium
Halle 94 C4 var. Halle an der Saale.
Sachsen-Anhalt, C Germany
Halle an der Saale see Halle
Halle-Neustadt 94 C4 Sachsen-Anhalt,
C Germany
Halley 154 B2 UK research station
Antarctica
Hall Islands 142 B2 island group
C Micronesia
Halls Creek 146 C3 Western Australia
Halmahera, Laut see Halmahera Sea
Halmahera, Pulau 139 F3 prev. Djailolo,
Gilolo, Jailolo. island E Indonesia
Halmahera Sea 139 F4 Ind. Laut
Halmahera. sea E Indonesia
Halmstad 85 B7 Halland, S Sweden
Hälsingborg see Helsingborg
Hamada 131 B6 Shimane, Honshū,
SW Japan
Hamadān 120 C3 anc. Ecbatana.
Hamadān, W Iran
Ḥamāh 118 B3 var. Hama; anc. Epiphania,
Bibl. Hamath. Ḥamāh, W Syria
Hamamatsu 131 D6 var. Hamamatu.
Shizuoka, Honshū, S Japan
Hamamatu see Hamamatsu
Hamar 85 B5 prev. Storhammer.
Hedmark, S Norway
Hamath see Ḥamāh
Hamburg 94 B3 Hamburg, N Germany
Hamd, Wadi al 120 A4 dry watercourse
W Saudi Arabia
Hämeenlinna 85 D5 Swe. Tavastehus.
Etelä-Suomi, S Finland

HaMela h, Yam see Dead Sea
Hamersley Range 146 A4 mountain
range Western Australia
Hamhŭng 129 E3 C North Korea
Hami 126 C3 var. Ha-mi, Uigh. Kumul,
Qomul. Xinjiang Uygur Zizhiqu,
NW China
Ha-mi see Hami
Hamilton 42 A5 dependent territory
capital (Bermuda) C Bermuda
Hamilton 38 D5 Ontario, S Canada
Hamilton 150 D3 Waikato, North Island,
New Zealand
Hamilton 88 C4 S Scotland, United
Kingdom
Hamilton 42 C2 Alabama, S USA
Hamim, Wadi al 71 G2 river NE Libya
Hamīs Musait see Khamīs Mushayt
Hamm 94 B4 var. Hamm in Westfalen.
Nordrhein-Westfalen, W Germany
Ḩammāmāt, Khalīj al see Hammamet,
Golfe de
Hammamet, Golfe de 102 D3 Ar. Khalīj
al Ḩammāmāt. gulf NE Tunisia
Hammar, Hawr al 120 C3 lake SE Iraq
Hamm in Westfalen see Hamm
Hampden 151 B7 Otago, South Island,
New Zealand
Hampstead 89 A7 Maryland, USA
Hamrun 102 B5 C Malta
Hāmūn, Daryācheh-ye see Şāberī,
Hāmūn-e/Sīstān, Daryācheh-ye
Hamwih see Southampton
Hăncești see Hîncești
Hancewicze see Hantsavichy
Handan 128 C4 var. Han-tan. Hebei,
E China
Haneda 130 A2 (Tōkyō) Tōkyō, Honshū,
S Japan
Hanford 47 C6 California, W USA
Hangayn Nuruu 126 D2 mountain
range C Mongolia
Hang-chou/Hangchow see Hangzhou
Hangö see Hanko
Hangzhou 128 D5 var. Hang-chou,
Hangchow. province capital Zhejiang,
SE China
Hania see Chaniá
Hanka, Lake see Khanka, Lake
Hanko 85 D6 Swe. Hangö. Etelä-Suomi,
SW Finland
Han-kou/Han-k'ou/Hankow see Wuhan
Hanmer Springs 151 C5 Canterbury,
South Island, New Zealand
Hannibal 45 G4 Missouri, C USA
Hannover 94 B3 Eng. Hanover.
Niedersachsen, NW Germany
Hanöbukten 85 B7 bay S Sweden
Ha Nôi 136 D3 Eng. Hanoi, Fr. Hanoï.
country capital (Vietnam) (Vietnam)
N Vietnam
Hanover see Hannover
Han Shui 127 E4 river C China
Han-tan see Handan
Hantsavichy 107 B6 Pol. Hancewicze,
Rus. Gantsevichi. Brestskaya Voblasts',
SW Belarus
Hanyang see Wuhan
Hanzhong 128 B5 Shaanxi, C China
Hāora 135 F4 prev. Howrah. West
Bengal, NE India
Hapsal see Haapsalu
Haradok 107 E5 Rus. Gorodok.
Vitsyebskaya Voblasts', N Belarus
Haradzyets 107 B6 Rus. Gorodets.
Brestskaya Voblasts', SW Belarus
Haramachi 130 D4 Fukushima, Honshū,
E Japan
Harany 107 D5 Rus. Gorany.
Vitsyebskaya Voblasts', N Belarus
Harare 78 D3 prev. Salisbury. country
capital (Zimbabwe) (Zimbabwe)
Mashonaland East, NE Zimbabwe
Harbavichy 107 E6 Rus. Gorbovichi.
Mahilyowskaya Voblasts', E Belarus
Harbel 74 C5 W Liberia
Harbin 129 E2 var. Haerbin, Ha-
erh-pin, Kharbin; prev. Haerhpin,
Pingkiang, Pinkiang. province capital
Heilongjiang, NE China
Hardangerfjorden 85 A6 fjord S Norway
Hardangervidda 85 A6 plateau S Norway
Hardenberg 86 E3 Overijssel,
E Netherlands
Harelbeke 87 A6 var. Harlebeke. West-
Vlaanderen, W Belgium

Harem see Ḩārim
Haren 86 E2 Groningen, NE Netherlands
Härer 73 D5 E Ethiopia
Hargeisa see Hargeysa
Hargeysa 73 D5 var. Hargeisa. Woqooyi
Galbeed, NW Somalia
Hariana see Haryāna
Hari, Batang 138 B4 prev. Djambi. river
Sumatera, W Indonesia
Ḩārim 118 B2 var. Harem. Idlib, W Syria
Harima-nada 131 B6 sea S Japan
Harirud 123 E4 var. Tedzhen, Turkm.
Tejen. river Afghanistan/Iran
Harlan 45 F3 Iowa, C USA
Harlebeke see Harelbeke
Harlem see Haarlem
Harlingen 86 D2 Fris. Harns. Friesland,
N Netherlands
Harlingen 49 G5 Texas, SW USA
Harlow 89 E6 E England, United
Kingdom
Harney Basin 46 B4 basin Oregon,
NW USA
Härnösand 85 C5 var. Hernösand.
Västernorrland, C Sweden
Harns see Harlingen
Harper 74 D5 var. Cape Palmas.
NE Liberia
Harricana 38 D3 river Québec,
SE Canada
Harris 88 B3 physical region
NW Scotland, United Kingdom
Harrisburg 41 E4 state capital
Pennsylvania, NE USA
Harrison, Cape 39 F2 headland
Newfoundland and Labrador, E Canada
Harris Ridge see Lomonosov Ridge
Harrogate 89 D5 N England, United
Kingdom
Hârșova 108 D5 prev. Hîrșova.
Constanța, SE Romania
Harstad 84 C2 Troms, N Norway
Hartford 41 G3 state capital Connecticut,
NE USA
Hartlepool 89 D5 N England, United
Kingdom
Harunabad see Eslāmābād
Har Us Gol 126 C2 lake Hovd,
W Mongolia
Har Us Nuur 126 C2 lake NW Mongolia
Harwich 89 E6 E England, United
Kingdom
Haryāna 134 D2 var. Hariana. cultural
region N India
Hashemite Kingdom of Jordan see
Jordan
Hasselt 87 C6 Limburg, NE Belgium
Hassetché see Al Ḩasakah
Hasta Colonia/Hasta Pompeia see Asti
Hastings 150 E4 Hawke's Bay, North
Island, New Zealand
Hastings 89 E7 SE England, United
Kingdom
Hastings 45 E4 Nebraska, C USA
Haṭeg 108 B4 Ger. Wallenthal, Hung.
Hátszeg; prev. Hatzeg, Hötzing.
Hunedoara, SW Romania
Hátszeg see Haṭeg
Hattem 86 D3 Gelderland, E Netherlands
Hatteras, Cape 43 G1 headland North
Carolina, SE USA
Hatteras Plain 35 D6 abyssal plain
W Atlantic Ocean
Hattiesburg 42 C3 Mississippi, S USA
Hatton Bank see Hatton Ridge
Hatton Ridge 80 B2 var. Hatton Bank.
undersea ridge N Atlantic Ocean
Hat Yai 137 C7 var. Ban Hat Yai.
Songkhla, SW Thailand
Hatzeg see Haṭeg
Hatzfeld see Jimbolia
Haugesund 85 A6 Rogaland, S Norway
Haukeligrend 85 A6 Telemark,
S Norway
Haukivesi 85 E5 lake SE Finland
Hauraki Gulf 150 D2 gulf North Island,
N New Zealand
Hauroko, Lake 151 A7 lake South
Island, New Zealand
Hautes Fagnes 87 D6 Ger. Hohes Venn.
mountain range E Belgium
Hauts Plateaux 70 D2 plateau Algeria/
Morocco
Hauzenberg 95 D6 Bayern, SE Germany
Havana 35 D6 Illinois, N USA
Havana see La Habana

Havant 89 D7 S England, United
Kingdom
Havelock 43 F1 North Carolina, SE USA
Havelock North 150 E4 Hawke's Bay,
North Island, New Zealand
Haverfordwest 89 C6 SW Wales, United
Kingdom
Havířov 99 C5 Moravskoslezský Kraj,
E Czech Republic
Havre 44 C1 Montana, NW USA
Havre see le Havre
Havre-St-Pierre 39 F3 Québec,
E Canada
Hawai'i 47 A8 off. State of Hawai'i,
also known as Aloha State, Paradise
of the Pacific, var. Hawaii. state USA,
C Pacific Ocean
Hawai'i 47 B8 var. Hawaii. island
Hawaiian Islands, USA, C Pacific Ocean
Hawaiian Islands 152 D2 prev.
Sandwich Islands. island group
Hawaii, USA
Hawaiian Ridge 152 H4 undersea ridge
N Pacific Ocean
Hawea, Lake 151 B6 lake South Island,
New Zealand
Hawera 150 D4 Taranaki, North Island,
New Zealand
Hawick 88 C4 SE Scotland, United
Kingdom
Hawke Bay 150 E4 bay North Island,
New Zealand
Hawkeye State see Iowa
Hawlēr see Arbīl
Hawthorne 47 C6 Nevada, W USA
Hay 149 C6 New South Wales,
SE Australia
HaYarden see Jordan
Hayastani Hanrapetut'yun see Armenia
Hayes 38 B2 river Manitoba, C Canada
Hay River 37 E4 Northwest Territories,
W Canada
Hays 45 E5 Kansas, C USA
Haysyn 108 D3 Rus. Gaysin. Vinnyts'ka
Oblast', C Ukraine
Hazar 122 B2 prev. Rus. Cheleken.
Balkan Welaýaty, W Turkmenistan
Heard and McDonald Islands 141 B7
Australian external territory S Indian
Ocean
Hearst 38 C4 Ontario, S Canada
Heart of Dixie see Alabama
Heathrow 89 A8 (London) SE England,
United Kingdom
Hebei 128 C4 var. Hebei Sheng, Hopeh,
Hopei, Ji; prev. Chihli. province
E China
Hebei Sheng see Hebei
Hebron 119 A6 var. Al Khalīl, El Khalil,
Heb. Hevron; anc. Kiriath-Arba.
S West Bank
Heemskerk 86 C3 Noord-Holland,
W Netherlands
Heerde 86 D3 Gelderland, E Netherlands
Heerenveen 86 D2 Fris. It Hearrenfean.
Friesland, N Netherlands
Heerhugowaard 86 C2 Noord-Holland,
NW Netherlands
Heerlen 87 D6 Limburg, SE Netherlands
Heerwegen see Polkowice
Hefa 119 A5 var. Haifa, hist. Caiffa,
Caiphas; anc. Sycaminum. Haifa, N Israel
Hefa, Mifraz see Mifrats Hefa
Hefei 128 D5 var. Hofei, hist. Luchow.
province capital Anhui, E China
Hegang 129 F2 Heilongjiang, NE China
Hei see Heilongjiang
Heide 94 B2 Schleswig-Holstein,
N Germany
Heidelberg 95 B5 Baden-Württemberg,
SW Germany
Heidenheim see Heidenheim an der
Brenz
Heidenheim an der Brenz 95 B6 var.
Heidenheim. Baden-Württemberg,
S Germany
Hei-ho see Nagqu
Heilbronn 95 B6 Baden-Württemberg,
SW Germany
Heiligenbeil see Mamonovo
Heilongjiang 128 D2 var. Hei,
Heilongjiang Sheng, Hei-lung-chiang,
Heilungkiang. province NE China
Heilong Jiang see Amur
Heilongjiang Sheng see Heilongjiang
Heiloo 86 C3 Noord-Holland,
NW Netherlands

Heilsberg see Lidzbark Warmiński
Hei-lung-chiang/Heilungkiang see Heilongjiang
Heimdal 85 B5 Sør-Trøndelag, S Norway
Heinaste see Ainaži
Hekimhan 116 D3 Malatya, C Turkey
Helena 44 B2 state capital Montana, NW USA
Helensville 150 D2 Auckland, North Island, New Zealand
Helgoland Bay see Helgoländer Bucht
Helgoländer Bucht 94 A2 var. Helgoland Bay, Heligoland Bight. bay NW Germany
Heligoland Bight see Helgoländer Bucht
Heliopolis see Baalbek
Hellas see Greece
Hellenic Republic see Greece
Hellevoetsluis 86 B4 Zuid-Holland, SW Netherlands
Hellín 93 E4 Castilla-La Mancha, C Spain
Darya-ye Helmand 122 D5 var. Rūd-e Hirmand. river Afghanistan/Iran
Helmantica see Salamanca
Helmond 87 D5 Noord-Brabant, S Netherlands
Helsingborg 85 B7 prev. Hälsingborg. Skåne, S Sweden
Helsingfors see Helsinki
Helsinki 85 D6 Swe. Helsingfors. country capital (Finland) (Finland) Etelä-Suomi, S Finland
Heltau see Cisnădie
Helvetia see Switzerland
Henan 128 C5 var. Henan Sheng, Honan, Yu. province C China
Henderson 40 B5 Kentucky, S USA
Henderson 47 D7 Nevada, W USA
Henderson 49 H3 Texas, SW USA
Hendū Kosh see Hindu Kush
Hengchow see Hengyang
Hengduan Shan 128 A5 mountain range SW China
Hengelo 86 E3 Overijssel, E Netherlands
Hengnan see Hengyang
Hengyang 128 C6 var. Hengnan, Heng-yang; prev. Hengchow. Hunan, S China
Heng-yang see Hengyang
Henichesk 109 F4 Rus. Genichesk. Khersons'ka Oblast', S Ukraine
Hennebont 90 A3 Morbihan, NW France
Henrique de Carvalho see Saurimo
Henzada see Hinthada
Herakleion see Irákleio
Herāt 122 D4 var. Herat; anc. Aria. Herāt, W Afghanistan
Heredia 53 E4 Heredia, C Costa Rica
Hereford 49 E2 Texas, SW USA
Herford 94 B4 Nordrhein-Westfalen, NW Germany
Héristal see Herstal
Herk-de-Stad 87 C6 Limburg, NE Belgium
Herlen Gol/Herlen He see Kerulen
Hermannstadt see Sibiu
Hermansverk 85 A5 Sogn Og Fjordane, S Norway
Hermhausen see Hajnówka
Hermiston 46 C2 Oregon, NW USA
Hermon, Mount 119 B5 Ar. Jabal ash Shaykh. mountain S Syria
Hermosillo 50 B2 Sonora, NW Mexico
Hermoupolis see Ermoúpoli
Hernösand see Härnösand
Herrera del Duque 92 D3 Extremadura, W Spain
Herselt 87 C5 Antwerpen, C Belgium
Herstal 87 D6 Fr. Héristal. Liège, E Belgium
Herzogenbusch see 's-Hertogenbosch
Hesse see Hessen
Hessen 95 B5 Eng./Fr. Hesse. state C Germany
Hevron see Hebron
Heydebreck see Kędzierzyn-Kozle
Heydekrug see Šilutė
Heywood Islands 146 C3 island group Western Australia
Hibbing 45 F1 Minnesota, N USA
Hibernia see Ireland
Hidalgo del Parral 50 C2 var. Parral. Chihuahua, N Mexico
Hida-sanmyaku 131 C5 mountain range Honshū, S Japan
Hierosolyma see Jerusalem
Hierro 70 A3 var. Ferro. island Islas Canarias, Spain, NE Atlantic Ocean

High Atlas 70 C2 Eng. High Atlas. mountain range C Morocco
High Atlas see Haut Atlas
High Plains see Great Plains
High Point 43 E1 North Carolina, SE USA
Hiiumaa 106 C2 Ger. Dagden, Swe. Dagö. island W Estonia
Hikurangi 150 D2 Northland, North Island, New Zealand
Hildesheim 94 B4 Niedersachsen, N Germany
Hilla see Al Ḩillah
Hillaby, Mount 55 G1 mountain N Barbados
Hill Bank 52 C1 Orange Walk, N Belize
Hillegom 86 C3 Zuid-Holland, W Netherlands
Hilo 47 B8 Hawai'i, USA, C Pacific Ocean
Hilton Head Island 43 E2 South Carolina, SE USA
Hilversum 86 C3 Noord-Holland, C Netherlands
Himalaya/Himalaya Shan see Himalayas
Himalayas 135 E2 var. Himalaya, Chin. Himalaya Shan. mountain range S Asia
Himeji 131 C6 var. Himezi. Hyōgo, Honshū, SW Japan
Himezi see Himeji
Ḩimş 118 B4 var. Homs; anc. Emesa. Ḩimş, C Syria
Hînceşti 108 D4 var. Hânceşti; prev. Kotovsk. C Moldova
Hinchinbrook Island 148 D3 island Queensland, NE Australia
Hinds 151 C6 Canterbury, South Island, New Zealand
Hindu Kush 123 F4 Per. Hendū Kosh. mountain range Afghanistan/Pakistan
Hinesville 43 E3 Georgia, SE USA
Hinnøya 84 C3 Lapp. Iinnasuolu. island C Norway
Hinson Bay 42 A5 bay W Bermuda
Hinthada 136 B4 var. Henzada. Ayeyarwady, SW Burma (Myanmar)
Hios see Chíos
Hirfanlı Barajı 116 C3 reservoir C Turkey
Hîrmand, Rūd-e see Helmand, Daryā-ye
Hirosaki 130 D3 Aomori, Honshū, C Japan
Hiroshima 131 B6 var. Hirosima. Hiroshima, Honshū, SW Japan
Hirschberg/Hirschberg im Riesengebirge/Hirschberg in Schlesien see Jelenia Góra
Hirson 90 D3 Aisne, N France
Hîrşova see Hârşova
Hispalis see Sevilla
Hispana/Hispania see Spain
Hispaniola 56 B1 island Dominion Republic/Haiti
Hitachi 131 D5 var. Hitati. Ibaraki, Honshū, S Japan
Hitati see Hitachi
Hitra 84 A4 prev. Hitteren. island S Norway
Hitteren see Hitra
Hjälmaren 85 C6 Eng. Lake Hjalmar. lake C Sweden
Hjalmar, Lake see Hjälmaren
Hjørring 85 B7 Nordjylland, N Denmark
Hkakabo Razi 136 B1 mountain Burma (Myanmar)/China
Hlobyne 109 F2 Rus. Globino. Poltavs'ka Oblast', NE Ukraine
Hlukhiv 109 F1 Rus. Glukhov. Sums'ka Oblast', NE Ukraine
Hlybokaye 107 D5 Rus. Glubokoye. Vitsyebskaya Voblasts', N Belarus
Hoa Binh 136 D3 Hoa Binh, N Vietnam
Hoang Lien Son 136 D3 mountain range N Vietnam
Hobart 149 C8 prev. Hobarton, Hobart Town. state capital Tasmania, SE Australia
Hobarton/Hobart Town see Hobart
Hobbs 49 E3 New Mexico, SW USA
Hobro 85 A7 Nordjylland, N Denmark
Hô Chi Minh 137 E6 var. Ho Chi Minh City; prev. Saigon. S Vietnam
Ho Chi Minh City see Hô Chi Minh
Hodeida see Al Ḩudaydah
Hódmezővásárhely 99 D7 Csongrád, SE Hungary

Hodna, Chott El 102 C4 var. Chott el-Hodna, Ar. Shatt al-Hodna. salt lake N Algeria
Hodna, Chott el-/Hodna, Shatt al- see Hodna, Chott El
Hodonín 99 C5 Ger. Göding. Jihomoravský Kraj, SE Czech Republic
Hoei see Huy
Hoey see Huy
Hof 95 C5 Bayern, SE Germany
Hofei see Hefei
Hōfu 131 B7 Yamaguchi, Honshū, SW Japan
Hofuf see Al Hufūf
Hogoley Islands see Chuuk Islands
Hohensalza see Inowrocław
Hohenstadt see Zábřeh
Hohes Venn see Hautes Fagnes
Hohe Tauern 95 C7 mountain range W Austria
Hohhot 127 F3 var. Huhehot, Huhohaote, Mong. Kukukhoto; prev. Kweisui, Kwesui. Nei Mongol Zizhiqu, N China
Hôi An 137 E5 prev. Faifo. Quang Nam-Đa Nẵng, C Vietnam
Hoï-Hao/Hoihow see Haikou
Hokianga Harbour 150 C2 inlet SE Tasman Sea
Hokitika 151 B5 West Coast, South Island, New Zealand
Hokkaidō 130 C2 prev. Ezo, Yeso, Yezo. island NE Japan
Hola Prystan' 109 E4 Rus. Golaya Pristan. Khersons'ka Oblast', S Ukraine
Holbrook 48 B2 Arizona, SW USA
Holetown 33 G1 prev. Jamestown. W Barbados
Holguín 54 C2 Holguín, SE Cuba
Hollabrunn 95 E6 Niederösterreich, NE Austria
Holland see Netherlands
Hollandia see Jayapura
Holly Springs 42 C1 Mississippi, S USA
Holman 37 E3 Victoria Island, Northwest Territories, N Canada
Holmsund 84 D4 Västerbotten, N Sweden
Holon 119 A6 var. Kholon; prev. Ḩolon. Tel Aviv, C Israel
Ḩolon see Holon
Holovanivs'k 109 E3 Rus. Golovanevsk. Kirovohrads'ka Oblast', C Ukraine
Holstebro 85 A7 Ringkøbing, W Denmark
Holsteinborg/Holsteinsborg/ Holstenborg/Holstensborg see Sisimiut
Holyhead 89 C5 Wel. Caer Gybi. NW Wales, United Kingdom
Hombori 75 E3 Mopti, S Mali
Homs see Al Khums, Libya
Homs see Ḩimş
Homyel' 107 D7 Rus. Gomel'. Homyel'skaya Voblasts', SE Belarus
Honan see Luoyang, China
Honan see Henan, China
Hondo 49 F4 Texas, SW USA
Hondo see Honshū
Honduras 52 C2 off. Republic of Honduras. country Central America

HONDURAS
Central America

Official name Republic of Honduras
Formation 1838 / 1838
Capital Tegucigalpa
Population 7.5 million / 174 people per sq mile (67 people per sq km) / 46%
Total area 43,278 sq. miles (112,090 sq. km)
Languages Spanish*, Garífuna (Carib), English Creole
Religions Roman Catholic 97%, Protestant 3%
Ethnic mix Mestizo 90%, Black African 5%, Amerindian 4%, White 1%
Government Presidential system
Currency Lempira = 100 centavos
Literacy rate 80%
Calorie consumption 2356 calories

Honduras, Golfo de see Honduras, Gulf of
Honduras, Gulf of 52 C2 Sp. Golfo de Honduras. gulf W Caribbean Sea
Honduras, Republic of see Honduras
Hønefoss 85 B6 Buskerud, S Norway

Honey Lake 47 B5 lake California, W USA
Hon Gai see Hông Gai
Hongay see Hông Gai
Hông Gai 136 E3 var. Hon Gai, Hongay. Quang Ninh, N Vietnam
Hông Hà, Sông see Red River
Hong Kong 128 A1 Chin. Xianggang. Hong Kong, S China
Hong Kong Island 128 B2 island S China Asia
Honiara 144 C3 country capital (Solomon Islands) (Solomon Islands) Guadalcanal, C Solomon Islands
Honjō 130 D4 var. Honzyō, Yurihonjō. Akita, Honshū, C Japan
Honolulu 47 A8 state capital O'ahu, Hawaii, USA, C Pacific Ocean
Honshū 131 E5 var. Hondo, Honsyū. island SW Japan
Honsyū see Honshū
Honte see Westerschelde
Honzyō see Honjō
Hoogeveen 86 E2 Drenthe, NE Netherlands
Hoogezand-Sappemeer 86 E2 Groningen, NE Netherlands
Hoorn 86 C2 Noord-Holland, NW Netherlands
Hoosier State see Indiana
Hopa 117 E2 Artvin, NE Turkey
Hope 36 C3 British Columbia, SW Canada
Hopedale 39 F2 Newfoundland and Labrador, NE Canada
Hopeh/Hopei see Hebei
Hopkinsville 40 B5 Kentucky, S USA
Horasan 117 F3 Erzurum, NE Turkey
Horizon Deep 152 D4 trench W Pacific Ocean
Horki 107 E6 Rus. Gorki. Mahilyowskaya Voblasts', E Belarus
Horlivka 109 G3 Rom. Adâncata, Rus. Gorlovka. Donets'ka Oblast', E Ukraine
Hormoz, Tangeh-ye see Hormuz, Strait of
Hormuz, Strait of 120 D4 var. Strait of Ormuz, Per. Tangeh-ye Hormoz. strait Iran/Oman
Cape Horn 65 C8 Eng. Cape Horn. headland S Chile
Horn, Cape see Hornos, Cabo de
Hornsby 148 E1 New South Wales, SE Australia
Horodnya 109 E1 Rus. Gorodnya. Chernihivs'ka Oblast', NE Ukraine
Horodok 108 B2 Pol. Gródek Jagielloński, Rus. Gorodok, Gorodok Yagellonski. L'vivs'ka Oblast', NW Ukraine
Horodyshche 109 E2 Rus. Gorodishche. Cherkas'ka Oblast', C Ukraine
Horoshiri-dake 130 D2 var. Horosiri Dake. mountain Hokkaidō, N Japan
Horosiri Dake see Horoshiri-dake
Horsburgh Atoll 132 A4 var. Goidhoo Atoll. atoll N Maldives
Horseshoe Bay 42 A5 bay W Bermuda W Atlantic Ocean
Horseshoe Seamounts 80 A4 seamount range E Atlantic Ocean
Horsham 149 B7 Victoria, SE Australia
Horst 87 D5 Limburg, SE Netherlands
Horten 85 B6 Vestfold, S Norway
Horyn' 107 B7 Rus. Goryn. river NW Ukraine
Hosingen 87 D7 Diekirch, NE Luxembourg
Hospitalet see L'Hospitalet de Llobregat
Hotan 126 B4 var. Hotien, Khotan, Chin. Ho-t'ien. Xinjiang Uygur Zizhiqu, NW China
Ho-t'ien see Hotan
Hoting 84 C4 Jämtland, C Sweden
Hot Springs 42 B1 Arkansas, C USA
Hötzing see Hateg
Houayxay 136 C3 var. Ban Houayxay. Bokèo, N Laos
Houghton 40 B1 Michigan, N USA
Houilles 91 B5 Yvelines, Île-de-France, N France Europe
Houlton 41 H1 Maine, NE USA
Houma 42 B3 Louisiana, S USA
Houston 49 H4 Texas, SW USA
Hovd 126 C2 var. Khovd, Kobdo; prev. Jirgalanta. Hovd, W Mongolia
Hove 89 E7 SE England, United Kingdom

Hoverla, Hora *108 C3 Rus.* Gora Goverla. *mountain* W Ukraine
Hovsgol, Lake *see* Hövsgöl Nuur
Hövsgöl Nuur *126 D1 var.* Lake Hovsgol. *lake* N Mongolia
Howa, Ouadi *see* Howar, Wâdi
Howar, Wâdi *72 A3 var.* Ouadi Howa. *river* Chad/Sudan
Howrah *see* Hāora
Hoy *88 C2 island* N Scotland, United Kingdom
Hoyerswerda *94 D4 Lus.* Wojerecy. Sachsen, E Germany
Hpa-an *136 B4 var.* Pa-an. *S* Burma (Myanmar)
Hpyu *see* Phyu
Hradec Králové *99 B5 Ger.* Königgrätz. Královéhradecký Kraj, N Czech Republic
Hrandzichy *107 B5 Rus.* Grandichi. Hrodzyenskaya Voblasts', W Belarus
Hranice *99 C5 Ger.* Mährisch-Weisskirchen. Olomoucký Kraj, E Czech Republic
Hrebinka *109 E2 Rus.* Grebenka. Poltavs'ka Oblast', NE Ukraine
Hrodna *107 B5 Pol.* Grodno. Hrodzyenskaya Voblasts', W Belarus
Hrvatska *see* Croatia
Hsia-men *see* Xiamen
Hsiang-t'an *see* Xiangtan
Hsi Chiang *see* Xi Jiang
Hsing-K'ai Hu *see* Khanka, Lake
Hsi-ning/Hsining *see* Xining
Hsinking *see* Changchun
Hsin-yang *see* Xinyang
Hsu-chou *see* Xuzhou
Htawei *see* Dawei
Huacho *60 C4* Lima, W Peru
Hua Hin *see* Ban Hua Hin
Huaihua *128 C5* Hunan, S China
Huailai *128 C3 var.* Shacheng. Hebei, E China
Huainan *128 D3 var.* Huai-nan, Hwainan. Anhui, E China
Huai-nan *see* Huainan
Huajuapan *51 F5 var.* Huajuapan de León. Oaxaca, SE Mexico
Huajuapan de León *see* Huajuapan
Hualapai Peak *48 A2 mountain* Arizona, SW USA
Huallaga, Río *60 C3 river* N Peru
Huambo *78 B2 Port.* Nova Lisboa. Huambo, C Angola
Huancavelica *60 D4* Huancavelica, SW Peru
Huancayo *60 D3* Junín, C Peru
Huangshi *128 C5 var.* Huang-shih, Hwangshih. Hubei, C China
Huang-shih *see* Huangshi
Huanta *60 D4* Ayacucho, C Peru
Huánuco *60 C3* Huánuco, C Peru
Huanuni *61 F4* Oruro, W Bolivia
Huaral *60 C4* Lima, W Peru
Huarás *see* Huaraz
Huaraz *60 C3 var.* Huarás. Ancash, W Peru
Huarmey *60 C3* Ancash, W Peru
Huatabampo *50 C2* Sonora, NW Mexico
Hubli *124 B3* Karnātaka, SW India
Huddersfield *89 D5* N England, United Kingdom
Hudiksvall *85 C5* Gävleborg, C Sweden
Hudson Bay *37 G4 bay* NE Canada
Hudson, Détroit d' *see* Hudson Strait
Hudson Strait *37 H3 Fr.* Détroit d'Hudson. *strait* Northwest Territories/Québec, NE Canada
Hudur *see* Xuddur
Huê *136 E4 Tha,n* Thiên-Huê, C Vietnam
Huehuetenango *52 A2* Huehuetenango, W Guatemala
Huelva *92 C4 anc.* Onuba. Andalucía, SW Spain
Huesca *93 F2 anc.* Osca. Aragón, NE Spain
Huéscar *93 E4* Andalucía, S Spain
Hughenden *148 C3* Queensland, NE Australia
Hugo *49 G2* Oklahoma, C USA
Huehot/Huhohaote *see* Hohhot
Huila Plateau *78 B2 plateau* S Angola
Huixtla *51 G5* Chiapas, SE Mexico
Hulingol *127 G2 prev.* Huolin Gol. Nei Mongol Zizhiqu, N China
Hull *38 D4* Québec, SE Canada
Hull *see* Kingston upon Hull

Hull Island *see* Orona
Hulst *87 B5* Zeeland, SW Netherlands
Hulun *see* Hulun Buir
Hulun Buir *127 F1 var.* Hailar; *prev.* Hulun. Nei Mongol Zizhiqu, N China
Hu-lun Ch'ih *see* Hulun Nur
Hulun Nur *127 F1 var.* Hu-lun Ch'ih; *prev.* Dalai Nor. *lake* NE China
Humaitá *62 D2* Amazonas, N Brazil
Humboldt River *47 C5 river* Nevada, W USA
Humphreys Peak *48 B1 mountain* Arizona, SW USA
Humpolec *99 B5 Ger.* Gumpolds, Humpoletz. Vysočina, C Czech Republic
Humpoletz *see* Humpolec
Hunan *128 C6 var.* Hunan Sheng, Xiang. *province* S China
Hunan Sheng *see* Hunan
Hunedoara *108 B4 Ger.* Eisenmarkt, *Hung.* Vajdahunyad. Hunedoara, SW Romania
Hünfeld *95 B5* Hessen, C Germany
Hungarian People's Republic *see* Hungary
Hungary *99 C6 off.* Republic of Hungary, *Ger.* Ungarn, *Hung.* Magyarország, *Rom.* Ungaria, *SCr.* Mađarska, *Ukr.* Uhorshchyna; *prev.* Hungarian People's Republic. *country* C Europe

HUNGARY	
Central Europe	
Official name	Republic of Hungary
Formation	1918 / 1947
Capital	Budapest
Population	10 million / 280 people per sq mile (108 people per sq km) / 66%
Total area	35,919 sq. miles (93,030 sq. km)
Languages	Hungarian (Magyar)*
Religions	Roman Catholic 52%, Calvinist 16%, Other 15%, Nonreligious 14%, Lutheran 3%
Ethnic mix	Magyar 94%, Other 5%, Roma 1%
Government	Parliamentary system
Currency	Forint = 100 fillér
Literacy rate	99%
Calorie consumption	3483 calories

Hungary, Plain of *see* Great Hungarian Plain
Hungary, Republic of *see* Hungary
Hunjiang *see* Baishan
Hunter Island *149 B8 island* Tasmania, SE Australia
Huntington *40 D4* West Virginia, NE USA
Huntington Beach *47 B8* California, W USA
Huntly *150 D3* Waikato, North Island, New Zealand
Huntsville *42 D1* Alabama, S USA
Huntsville *49 G3* Texas, SW USA
Huolin Gol *see* Hulingol
Hurghada *72 C2 var.* Al Ghurdaqah, Ghurdaqah. E Egypt
Huron *45 E3* South Dakota, N USA
Huron, Lake *40 D2 lake* Canada/USA
Hurukawa *see* Furukawa
Hurunui *151 C5 river* South Island, New Zealand
Húsavík *83 E4* Nordhurland Eystra, NE Iceland
Husté *see* Khust
Husum *94 B2* Schleswig-Holstein, N Germany
Huszt *see* Khust
Hutchinson *45 E5* Kansas, C USA
Hutchinson Island *43 F4 island* Florida, SE USA
Huy *87 C6 Dut.* Hoei, Hoey. Liège, E Belgium
Huzi *see* Fuji
Hvannadalshnúkur *83 E5 volcano* S Iceland
Hvar *100 B4 It.* Lesina; *anc.* Pharus. *island* S Croatia
Hwainan *see* Huainan
Hwange *78 D3 prev.* Wankie. Matabeleland North, W Zimbabwe
Hwang-Hae *see* Yellow Sea
Hwangshih *see* Huangshi
Hyargas Nuur *126 C2 lake* NW Mongolia
Hyderābād *134 D5 var.* Haidarabad. *state capital* Andhra Pradesh, C India

Hyderābād *134 B3 var.* Haidarabad. Sind, SE Pakistan
Hyères *91 D6* Var, SE France
Hyères, Îles d' *91 D6 island group* S France
Hypanis *see* Kuban'
Hyrcania *see* Gorgān
Hyvinge *see* Hyvinkää
Hyvinkää *85 D5 Swe.* Hyvinge. Etelä-Suomi, S Finland

I

Iader *see* Zadar
Ialomiţa *108 C5 river* SE Romania
Iaşi *108 D3 Ger.* Jassy. Iaşi, NE Romania
Ibadan *75 F5* Oyo, SW Nigeria
Ibagué *58 B3* Tolima, C Colombia
Ibar *100 D4 Alb.* Ibër. *river* C Serbia
Ibarra *60 B1 var.* San Miguel de Ibarra. Imbabura, N Ecuador
Ibër *see* Ibar
Iberia *see* Spain
Iberian Mountains *see* Ibérico, Sistema
Iberian Peninsula *80 B4 physical region* Portugal/Spain
Iberian Plain *80 B4 abyssal plain* E Atlantic Ocean
Ibérica, Cordillera *see* Ibérico, Sistema
Ibérico, Sistema *93 E2 var.* Cordillera Ibérica, *Eng.* Iberian Mountains. *mountain range* NE Spain
Ibiza *see* Eivissa
Ibiza *see* Eivissa
Ibiza *see* Eivissa
Ibo *see* Sassandra
Ica *60 D4* Ica, SW Peru
Icaria *see* Ikaría
Içá, Rio *62 C2 var.* Río Putumayo. *river* NW South America
Içá, Rio *see* Putumayo, Río
İçel *see* Mersin
Iceland *83 E4 off.* Republic of Iceland, *Dan.* Island, *Icel.* Ísland. *country* N Atlantic Ocean

ICELAND	
Northwest Europe	
Official name	Republic of Iceland
Formation	1944 / 1944
Capital	Reykjavik
Population	301,931 / 8 people per sq mile (3 people per sq km) / 93%
Total area	39,768 sq. miles (103,000 sq. km)
Languages	Icelandic*
Religions	Evangelical Lutheran 93%, Nonreligious 6%, Other (mostly Christian) 1%
Ethnic mix	Icelandic 94%, Other 5%, Danish 1%
Government	Parliamentary system
Currency	Icelandic króna = 100 aurar
Literacy rate	99%
Calorie consumption	3249 calories

Iceland Basin *80 B1 undersea basin* N Atlantic Ocean
Icelandic Plateau *see* Iceland Plateau
Iceland Plateau *155 B6 var.* Icelandic Plateau. *undersea plateau* S Greenland Sea
Iceland, Republic of *see* Iceland
Iconium *see* Konya
Iculisma *see* Angoulême
Idabel *49 H2* Oklahoma, C USA
Idaho *46 D3 off.* State of Idaho, *also known as* Gem of the Mountains, Gem State. *state* NW USA
Idaho Falls *46 E3* Idaho, NW USA
Idensalmi *see* Iisalmi
Idfu *72 B2 var.* Edfu. SE Egypt
Idi Amin, Lac *see* Edward, Lake
Idini *74 B2* Trarza, W Mauritania
Idlib *118 B3* Idlib, NW Syria
Idre *85 B5* Dalarna, C Sweden
Iecava *106 C3* Bauska, S Latvia
Ieper *87 A6 Fr.* Ypres. West-Vlaanderen, W Belgium
Ierápetra *105 D8* Kríti, Greece, E Mediterranean Sea
Ierisós *see* Ierissós
Ierissós *104 C4 var.* Ierisós. Kentrikí Makedonía, N Greece
Iferouâne *75 G2* Agadez, N Niger

Ifôghas, Adrar des *75 E2 var.* Adrar des Iforas. *mountain range* NE Mali
Iforas, Adrar des *see* Ifôghas, Adrar des
Igarka *114 D3* Krasnoyarskiy Kray, N Russian Federation
Igaunija *see* Estonia
Iglau/Iglawa/Iglawa *see* Jihlava
Iglesias *97 A5* Sardegna, Italy, C Mediterranean Sea
Igloolik *37 G2* Nunavut, N Canada
Igoumenítsa *104 A4* Ípeiros, W Greece
Iguaçu, Rio *61 E4 Sp.* Río Iguazú. *river* Argentina/Brazil
Iguaçu, Salto do *63 E4 Sp.* Cataratas del Iguazú; *prev.* Victoria Falls. *waterfall* Argentina/Brazil
Iguala *51 E4 var.* Iguala de la Independencia. S Mexico
Iguala de la Independencia *see* Iguala
Iguazú, Cataratas del *see* Iguaçu, Salto do
Iguazú, Río *see* Iguaçu, Rio
Iguid, 'Erg *see* Iguidi, 'Erg
Iguidi, 'Erg *70 C3 var.* Erg Iguid. *desert* Algeria/Mauritania
Ihavandhippolhu Atoll *132 A3 var.* Ihavandiffulu Atoll. *atoll* N Maldives
Ihavandiffulu Atoll *see* Ihavandhippolhu Atoll
Ihosy *79 F4* Fianarantsoa, S Madagascar
Iinnasuolu *see* Hinnøya
Iisalmi *84 E4 var.* Idensalmi. Itä-Suomi, C Finland
IJmuiden *86 C3* Noord-Holland, W Netherlands
IJssel *86 D3 var.* Yssel. *river* Netherlands
IJsselmeer *86 C2 prev.* Zuider Zee. *lake* N Netherlands
IJsselmuiden *86 D3* Overijssel, E Netherlands
Ijzer *87 A6 river* W Belgium
Ikaahuk *see* Sachs Harbour
Ikalukutiak *see* Cambridge Bay
Ikaría *105 D6 var.* Kariot, Nicaria, Nikariá; *anc.* Icaria. *island* Dodekánisa, Greece, Aegean Sea
Ikela *77 D6* Equateur, C Dem. Rep. Congo
Iki *131 A7 island* SW Japan
Ilagan *139 E1* Luzon, N Philippines
Ilave *61 E4* Puno, S Peru
Iława *98 D3 Ger.* Deutsch-Eylau. Warmińsko-Mazurskie, NE Poland
Ilebo *77 C6 prev.* Port-Francqui. Kasai-Occidental, W Dem. Rep. Congo
Île-de-France *90 C3 cultural region* N France
Ilerda *see* Lleida
Ilfracombe *89 C7* SW England, United Kingdom
Ílhavo *92 B2* Aveiro, N Portugal
Iliamna Lake *36 C3 lake* Alaska, USA
Il'ichevsk *see* Illichivs'k, Ukraine
Ilici *see* Elche
Iligan *139 E2 off.* Iligan City. Mindanao, S Philippines
Iligan City *see* Iligan
Illapel *64 B4* Coquimbo, C Chile
Illichivs'k *109 E4 Rus.* Il'ichevsk. Odes'ka Oblast', SW Ukraine
Illicis *see* Elche
Illinois *40 A4 off.* State of Illinois, *also known as* Prairie State, Sucker State. *state* C USA
Illinois River *40 B4 river* Illinois, N USA
Illurco *see* Lorca
Illuro *see* Mataró
Ilo *61 E4* Moquegua, SW Peru
Iloilo *139 E2 off.* Iloilo City. Panay Island, C Philippines
Iloilo City *see* Iloilo
Ilorin *75 F4* Kwara, W Nigeria
Ilovlya *111 B6* Volgogradskaya Oblast', SW Russian Federation
Iluh *see* Batman
Il'yaly *see* Gurbansoltan Eje
Imatra *85 E5* Etelä-Suomi, SE Finland
Imbros *see* Gökçeada
Imishli *see* İmişli
İmişli *117 H3 Rus.* Imishli. C Azerbaijan
Imola *96 C3* Emilia-Romagna, N Italy
Imperatriz *63 F2* Maranhão, NE Brazil
Imperia *96 A3* Liguria, NW Italy
Impfondo *77 C5* Likouala, NE Congo
Imphâl *135 H3 state capital* Manipur, NE India
Imroz Adası *see* Gökçeada
Inagua Islands *see* Great Inagua

Inagua Islands see Little Inagua
Inarijärvi 84 D2 *Lapp.* Aanaarjävri, *Swe.*
   Enareträsk. *lake* N Finland
Ináu see Ineu
Inawashiro-ko 131 D5 *var.* Inawasiro
   Ko. *lake* Honshū, C Japan
Inawasiro Ko see Inawashiro-ko
Incesu 116 D3 Kayseri, Turkey Asia
Inch'ŏn 129 E4 *off.* Inch'ŏn gwangyŏksi,
   Jap. Jinsen; *prev.* Chemulpo. NW South
   Korea
Inch'ŏn-gwangyŏksi see Inch'ŏn
Incudine, Monte 91 E7 *mountain* Corse,
   France, C Mediterranean Sea
Indefatigable Island see Santa Cruz, Isla
Independence 43 F4 Missouri, C USA
Independence Fjord 83 E1 *fjord*
   N Greenland
Independence Island see Malden Island
Independence Mountains 46 C4
   mountain range Nevada, W USA
India 124 B3 *off.* Republic of India, *var.*
   Indian Union, Union of India, *Hind.*
   Bhārat. *country* S Asia

INDIA
South Asia

Official name Republic of India
Formation 1947 / 1947
Capital New Delhi
Population 1.14 billion / 989 people
   per sq mile (382 people per sq km) / 29%
Total area 1,269,338 sq. miles
   (3,287,590 sq. km)
Languages Hindi*, English*, Urdu,
   Bengali, Marathi, Telugu, Tamil, Bihari,
   Gujarati, Kanarese
Religions Hindu 81%, Muslim 13%,
   Christian 2%, Sikh 2%, Other 1%,
   Buddhist 1%
Ethnic mix Indo-Aryan 72%,
   Dravidian 25%, Mongoloid and other 3%
Government Parliamentary system
Currency Indian rupee = 100 paise
Literacy rate 61%
Calorie consumption 2459 calories

India see Indija
Indiana 40 B4 *off.* State of Indiana, *also
   known as* Hoosier State. *state* N USA
Indianapolis 40 C4 *state capital* Indiana,
   N USA
Indian Church 52 C1 Orange Walk,
   N Belize
Indian Desert see Thar Desert
Indianola 45 F4 Iowa, C USA
Indian Union see India
India, Republic of see India
India, Union of see India
Indigirka 115 F2 *river* NE Russian
   Federation
Indija 100 D3 *Hung.* India; *prev.* Indjija.
   Vojvodina, N Serbia
Indira Point 132 G3 *headland* Andaman
   and Nicobar Island, India, NE Indian
   Ocean
Indjija see Indija
Indomed Fracture Zone 141 B6 *tectonic
   feature* SW Indian Ocean
Indonesia 138 B4 *off.* Republic of
   Indonesia, *Ind.* Republik Indonesia;
   prev. Dutch East Indies, Netherlands
   East Indies, United States of Indonesia.
   country SE Asia

INDONESIA
Southeast Asia

Official name Republic of Indonesia
Formation 1949 / 1999
Capital Jakarta
Population 231 million / 329 people
   per sq mile (127 people per sq km) / 47%
Total area 741,096 sq. miles
   (1,919,440 sq. km)
Languages Bahasa Indonesia*, Javanese,
   Sundanese, Madurese, Dutch
Religions Sunni Muslim 87%,
   Protestant 6%, Roman Catholic 3%,
   Hindu 2%, Other 1%, Buddhist 1%
Ethnic mix Javanese 42%, Sundanese 15%,
   Coastal Malays 12%, Madurese 4%,
   Other 28%
Government Presidential system
Currency Rupiah = 100 sen
Literacy rate 90%
Calorie consumption 2904 calories

Indonesian Borneo see Kalimantan
Indonesia, Republic of see Indonesia
Indonesia, Republik see Indonesia
Indonesia, United States of see
   Indonesia
Indore 134 D4 Madhya Pradesh, C India
Indreville see Châteauroux
Indus 134 C2 *Chin.* Yindu He; *prev.*
   Yin tu Ho. *river* S Asia
Indus Cone see Indus Fan
Indus Fan 112 C5 *var.* Indus Cone.
   undersea fan N Arabian Sea
Indus, Mouths of the 134 B4 *delta*
   S Pakistan
Inebolu 116 C2 Kastamonu, N Turkey
Ineu 108 A4 *Hung.* Borosjenő, *prev.* Ináu.
   Arad, W Romania
Infiernillo, Presa del 51 E4 *reservoir*
   S Mexico
Inglewood 46 D2 California, W USA
Ingolstadt 95 C6 Bayern, S Germany
Ingulets see Inhulets'
Inguri see Enguri
Inhambane 79 E4 Inhambane,
   SE Mozambique
Inhulets' 109 F3 *Rus.* Ingulets.
   Dnipropetrovs'ka Oblast', E Ukraine
I-ning see Yining
Inis see Ennis
Inis Ceithleann see Enniskillen
Inn 95 C6 *river* C Europe
Innaanganeq 82 C1 *var.* Kap York.
   headland NW Greenland
Inner Hebrides 88 B4 *island group*
   W Scotland, United Kingdom
Inner Islands 79 H1 *var.* Central Group.
   island group NE Seychelles
Innisfail 148 D3 Queensland, NE Australia
Inniskilling see Enniskillen
Innsbruck see Innsbruck
Innsbruck 95 C7 *var.* Innsbruch. Tirol,
   W Austria
Inoucdjouac see Inukjuak
Inowrazlaw see Inowrocław
Inowrocław 98 C3 *Ger.* Hohensalza;
   prev. Inowrazlaw. Kujawski-
   pomorskie, C Poland
I-n-Sakane, 'Erg 75 E2 *desert* N Mali
I-n-Salah 70 D3 *var.* In Salah. C Algeria
Insterburg see Chernyakhovsk
Insula see Lille
Inta 110 E3 Respublika Komi,
   NW Russian Federation
Interamna see Teramo
Interamna Nahars see Terni
International Falls 45 F1 Minnesota,
   N USA
Inukjuak 38 D2 *var.* Inoucdjouac; *prev.*
   Port Harrison. Québec, NE Canada
Inuuvik see Inuvik
Inuvik 36 D3 *var.* Inuuvik. Northwest
   Territories, NW Canada
Invercargill 151 A7 Southland, South
   Island, New Zealand
Inverness 88 C3 N Scotland, United
   Kingdom
Investigator Ridge 141 D5 *undersea
   ridge* E Indian Ocean
Investigator Strait 149 B7 *strait* South
   Australia
Inyangani 78 D3 *mountain* NE Zimbabwe
Ioánnina 104 A4 *var.* Janina, Yannina.
   Ípeiros, W Greece
Iola 45 F5 Kansas, C USA
Ionia Basin see Ionian Basin
Ionian Basin 80 D5 *var.* Ionia
   Basin. *undersea basin* Ionian Sea,
   C Mediterranean Sea
Ionian Sea 103 E3 *Gk.* Iónio Pélagos, *It.*
   Mar Ionio. *sea* C Mediterranean Sea
Iónioi Nísoi 105 A5 *Eng.* Ionian Islands.
   region W Greece
Ionio, Mar/Iónio Pélagos see Ionian Sea
Íos 105 D6 *var.* Nio. *island* Kykládes,
   Greece, Aegean Sea
Íos 105 D6 *var.* Nio. *island* Kykládes,
   Greece, Aegean Sea
Íos 105 D6 *var.* Nio. *island* Kykládes,
   Greece, Aegean Sea
Ioulís 105 C6 *prev.* Kéa. Tziá, Kykládes,
   Greece, Aegean Sea
Iowa 45 F3 *off.* State of Iowa, *also known
   as* Hawkeye State. *state* C USA
Iowa City 45 G3 Iowa, C USA
Iowa Falls 45 G3 Iowa, C USA
Ipel' 99 C6 *var.* Ipoly, *Ger.* Eipel. *river*
   Hungary/Slovakia

Ipiales 58 A4 Nariño, SW Colombia
Ipoh 138 B3 Perak, Peninsular Malaysia
Ipoly see Ipel'
Ippy 76 C4 Ouaka, C Central African
   Republic
Ipswich 149 E5 Queensland, E Australia
Ipswich 89 E6 *hist.* Gipeswic. E England,
   United Kingdom
Iqaluit 37 H3 *prev.* Frobisher Bay.
   province capital Baffin Island, Nunavut,
   NE Canada
Iquique 64 B1 Tarapacá, N Chile
Iquitos 60 C1 Loreto, N Peru
Irákleio 105 D7 *var.* Heraklion, *Eng.*
   Candia; *prev.* Iráklion. Kríti, Greece,
   E Mediterranean Sea
Iráklion see Irákleio
Iran 120 C3 *off.* Islamic Republic of Iran;
   prev. Persia. *country* SW Asia

IRAN
Southwest Asia

Official name Islamic Republic of Iran
Formation 1502 / 1990
Capital Tehran
Population 71.2 million / 113 people
   per sq mile (44 people per sq km) / 67%
Total area 636,293 sq. miles
   (1,648,000 sq. km)
Languages Farsi*, Azeri, Luri, Gilaki,
   Kurdish, Mazanderani, Turkmen,
   Arabic, Baluchi
Religions Shi'a Muslim 93%, Sunni
   Muslim 6%, Other 1%
Ethnic mix Persian 50%, Azari 24%,
   Other 10%, Kurdish 8%, Lur and
   Bakhtiari 8%
Government Islamic theocracy
Currency Iranian rial = 100 dinars
Literacy rate 77%
Calorie consumption 3085 calories

Iranian Plateau 120 D3 *var.* Plateau of
   Iran. *plateau* N Iran
Iran, Islamic Republic of see Iran
Iran, Plateau of see Iranian Plateau
Irapuato 51 E4 Guanajuato, C Mexico
Iraq 120 B3 *off.* Republic of Iraq, *Ar.*
   'Iráq. *country* SW Asia

IRAQ
Southwest Asia

Official name Republic of Iraq
Formation 1932 / 1990
Capital Baghdad
Population 30.3 million / 179 people
   per sq mile (69 people per sq km) / 67%
Total area 168,753 sq. miles
   (437,072 sq. km)
Languages Arabic*, Kurdish*, Turkic
   languages, Armenian, Assyrian
Religions Shi'a Muslim 60%,
   Sunni Muslim 35%, Other (including
   Christian) 5%
Ethnic mix Arab 80%, Kurdish 15%,
   Turkmen 3%, Other 2%
Government Parliamentary system
Currency New Iraqi dinar = 1000 fils
Literacy rate 74%
Calorie consumption 2197 calories

'Iráq see Iraq
Iraq, Republic of see Iraq
Irbid 119 B5 Irbid, N Jordan
Irbil see Arbil
Ireland 89 A5 *off.* Republic of Ireland, *Ir.*
   Éire. *country* NW Europe

IRELAND
Northwest Europe

Official name Ireland
Formation 1922 / 1922
Capital Dublin
Population 4.3 million / 162 people
   per sq mile (63 people per sq km) / 60%
Total area 27,135 sq. miles (70,280 sq. km)
Languages English*, Irish Gaelic*
Religions Roman Catholic 88%,
   Other and nonreligious 9%, Anglican 3%
Ethnic mix Irish 90%, Other 1%
Government Parliamentary system
Currency Euro = 100 cents
Literacy rate 99%
Calorie consumption 3656 calories

Ireland 80 C3 *Lat.* Hibernia. *island*
   Ireland/United Kingdom
Ireland, Republic of see Ireland
Irian see New Guinea
Irian Barat see Papua
Irian Jaya see Papua
Irian, Teluk see Cenderawasih, Teluk
Iringa 73 C7 Iringa, C Tanzania
Iriomote-jima 130 A4 *island* Sakishima-
   shotō, SW Japan
Iriona 52 D2 Colón, NE Honduras
Irish Sea 89 C5 *Ir.* Muir Éireann. *sea*
   C British Isles
Irkutsk 115 E4 Irkutskaya Oblast',
   S Russian Federation
Irminger Basin see Reykjanes Basin
Iroise 90 A3 *sea* NW France
Iron Mountain 40 B2 Michigan,
   N USA
Ironwood 40 B1 Michigan, N USA
Irrawaddy 136 B2 *var.* Ayeyarwady.
   river W Burma (Myanmar)
Irrawaddy, Mouths of the 137 A5 *delta*
   SW Burma (Myanmar)
Irtish see Irtysh
Irtysh 114 C4 *var.* Irtish, *Kaz.* Ertis.
   river C Asia
Irun 93 E1 *Cast.* Irún. País Vasco,
   N Spain
Irún see Irun
Iruña see Pamplona
Isabela, Isla 60 A5 *var.* Albemarle Island.
   island Galapagos Islands, Ecuador,
   E Pacific Ocean
Isaccea 108 D4 Tulcea, E Romania
Isachsen 37 F1 Ellef Ringnes Island,
   Nunavut, N Canada
Ísafjördhur 83 E4 Vestfirdhir,
   NW Iceland
Isbarta see Isparta
Isca Damnoniorum see Exeter
Ise 131 C6 Mie, Honshū, SW Japan
Iseghem see Izegem
Isère 91 D5 *river* E France
Isernia 97 D5 *var.* Æsernia. Molise,
   C Italy
Ise-wan 131 C6 *bay* S Japan
Isfahan see Esfahān
Isha Baydhabo see Baydhabo
Ishigaki-jima 130 A4 *island* Sakishima-
   shotō, SW Japan
Ishikari-wan 130 C2 *bay* Hokkaidō,
   NE Japan
Ishim 114 C4 Tyumenskaya Oblast',
   C Russian Federation
Ishim 114 C4 *Kaz.* Esil. *river*
   Kazakhstan/Russian Federation
Ishinomaki 130 D4 *var.* Isinomaki.
   Miyagi, Honshū, C Japan
Ishkashim see Ishkoshim
Ishkoshim 123 F3 *Rus.* Ishkashim.
   S Tajikistan
Isinomaki see Ishinomaki
Isiro 77 E5 Orientale, NE Dem. Rep.
   Congo
Iskår see Iskŭr
İskenderun 116 D4 *Eng.* Alexandretta.
   Hatay, S Turkey
İskenderun Körfezi 118 A2 *Eng.* Gulf of
   Alexandretta. *gulf* S Turkey
Iskur 104 C2 *var.* Iskår. *river*
   NW Bulgaria
Yazovir Iskur 104 B2 *prev.* Yazovir
   Stalin. *reservoir* W Bulgaria
Isla Cristina 92 C4 Andalucía, S Spain
Isla de León see San Fernando
Islāmābād 134 C1 *country capital*
   (Pakistan) (Pakistan) Federal Capital
   Territory Islāmābād, NE Pakistan
Island/Island see Iceland
Islay 88 B4 *island* SW Scotland, United
   Kingdom
Isle 91 B5 *river* W France
Isle of Man 89 B5 *UK crown dependency*
   NW Europe
Isles of Scilly 89 B8 *island group*
   SW England, United Kingdom
Ismailia see Al Ismā'īliya
Ismā'īliya see Al Ismā'īliya
Ismid see Izmit
Isnā 72 B2 *var.* Esna. SE Egypt
Isoka 78 D1 Northern, NE Zambia
Isparta 116 B4 *var.* Isbarta. Isparta,
   SW Turkey
Ispir 117 E3 Erzurum, NE Turkey

Israel *119 A7 off.* State of Israel, *var.*
Medinat Israel, *Heb.* Yisrael, Yisra'el.
country SW Asia

ISRAEL
Southwest Asia

Official name State of Israel
Formation 1948 / 1994
Capital Jerusalem (not internationally
recognized)
Population 7 million / 892 people
per sq mile (344 people per sq km) / 92%
Total area 8019 sq. miles (20,770 sq. km)
Languages Hebrew*, Arabic*,
Yiddish, German, Russian, Polish,
Romanian, Persian
Religions Jewish 76%, Muslim (mainly
Sunni) 16%, Other 4%, Druze 2%,
Christian 2%
Ethnic mix Jewish 76%, Other
(mostly Arab) 24%
Government Parliamentary system
Currency Shekel = 100 agorot
Literacy rate 97%
Calorie consumption 3666 calories

Israel, State of *see* Israel
Issa *see* Vis
Issiq Köl *see* Issyk-Kul', Ozero
Issoire *91 C5* Puy-de-Dôme, C France
Issyk-Kul' *see* Balykchy
Issyk-Kul', Ozero *123 G2 var.* Issiq Köl,
Kir. Ysyk-Köl. *lake* E Kyrgyzstan
İstanbul *116 B2 Bul.* Tsarigrad, *Eng.*
Istanbul, *prev.* Constantinople; *anc.*
Byzantium. Istanbul, NW Turkey
Istarska Županija *see* Istra
Istra *100 A3 off.* Istarska Županija.
province NW Croatia
Istra *100 A3 Eng.* Istria, *Ger.* Istrien.
cultural region NW Croatia
Istria/Istrien *see* Istra
Itabuna *63 G3* Bahia, E Brazil
Itagüí *58 B3* Antioquia, W Colombia
Itaipú, Represa de *63 E4 reservoir* Brazil/
Paraguay
Itaituba *63 E2* Pará, NE Brazil
**Italia/Italiana, Republica/Italian
Republic, The** *see* Italy
Italian Somaliland *see* Somalia
Italy *96 C3 off.* The Italian Republic, *It.*
Italia, Repubblica Italiana. *country*
S Europe

ITALY
Southern Europe

Official name Italian Republic
Formation 1861 / 1947
Capital Rome
Population 58.2 million / 513 people
per sq mile (198 people per sq km) / 67%
Total area 116,305 sq. miles
(301,230 sq. km)
Languages Italian*, German, French,
Rhaeto-Romanic, Sardinian
Religions Roman Catholic 85%,
Other and nonreligious 13%, Muslim 2%
Ethnic mix Italian 94%, Other 4%,
Sardinian 2%
Government Parliamentary system
Currency Euro = 100 cents
Literacy rate 98%
Calorie consumption 3671 calories

Iténez, Rio *see* Guaporé, Rio
Ithaca *41 E3* New York, NE USA
It Hearrenfean *see* Heerenveen
Itoigawa *131 C5* Niigata, Honshū,
C Japan
Itseqqortoormiit *see* Ittoqqortoormiit
Ittoqqortoormiit *83 E3 var.*
Itseqqortoormiit, *Dan.* Scoresbysund,
Eng. Scoresby Sound. Tunu,
C Greenland
Iturup, Ostrov *130 E1 island* Kuril'skiye
Ostrova, SE Russian Federation
Itzehoe *94 B2* Schleswig-Holstein,
N Germany
Ivalo *84 D2 Lapp.* Avveel, Avvil. Lappi,
N Finland
Ivanava *107 B7 Pol.* Janów, Janów
Poleski, *Rus.* Ivanovo. Brestskaya
Voblasts', SW Belarus
Ivangrad *see* Berane

Ivanhoe *149 C6* New South Wales,
SE Australia
Ivano-Frankivs'k *108 C2 Ger.* Stanislau,
Pol. Stanisławów, *Rus.* Ivano-
Frankovsk; *prev.* Stanislav. Ivano-
Frankivs'ka Oblast', W Ukraine
Ivano-Frankovsk *see* Ivano-Frankivs'k
Ivanovo *111 B5* Ivanovskaya Oblast',
W Russian Federation
Ivanovo *see* Ivanava
Ivantsevichi/Ivatsevichi *see* Ivatsevichy
Ivatsevichy *107 B6 Pol.* Iwacewicze, *Rus.*
Ivantsevichi, Ivatsevichi. Brestskaya
Voblasts', SW Belarus
Ivigtut *see* Ivittuut
Ivittuut *82 B4 var.* Ivigtut. Kitaa,
S Greenland
Iviza *see* Eivissa\Ibiza
Iviza *see* Eivissa\Ibiza
Iviza *see* Eivissa\Ibiza
Ivory Coast *see* Côte d'Ivoire
Ivory Coast, Republic of the *see* Côte
d'Ivoire
Ivujivik *38 D1* Québec, NE Canada
Iwacewicze *see* Ivatsevichy
Iwaki *131 D5* Fukushima, Honshū,
N Japan
Iwakuni *131 B7* Yamaguchi, Honshū,
SW Japan
Iwanai *130 C2* Hokkaidō, NE Japan
Iwate *130 D3* Iwate, Honshū, N Japan
Ixtapa *51 E5* Guerrero, S Mexico
Ixtepec *51 F5* Oaxaca, SE Mexico
Iyo-nada *131 B7 sea* S Japan
Izabal, Lago de *52 B2 prev.* Golfo Dulce.
lake E Guatemala
İzad Khvāst *120 D3* Fārs, C Iran
Izegem *87 A6 prev.* Iseghem. West-
Vlaanderen, W Belgium
Izhevsk *111 D5 prev.* Ustinov.
Udmurtskaya Respublika, NW Russian
Federation
Izmail *see* Izmayil
Izmayil *108 D4 Rus.* Izmail. Odes'ka
Oblast', SW Ukraine
İzmir *116 A3 prev.* Smyrna. İzmir,
W Turkey
İzmit *116 B2 var.* Ismid; *anc.* Astacus.
Kocaeli, NW Turkey
İznik Gölü *116 B3 lake* NW Turkey
Izu-hantō *131 D6 peninsula* Honshū,
S Japan
Izu Shichito *see* Izu-shotō
Izu-shoto *131 D6 var.* Izu Shichito.
island group S Japan
Izvor *104 B2* Pernik, W Bulgaria
Izyaslav *108 C2* Khmel'nyts'ka Oblast',
W Ukraine
Izyum *109 G2* Kharkiv'ska Oblast',
E Ukraine

J

Jabal ash Shifa *120 A4 desert* NW Saudi
Arabia
Jabalpur *135 E4 prev.* Jubbulpore.
Madhya Pradesh, C India
Jabbūl, Sabkhat al *118 B2 sabkha*
NW Syria
Jablah *118 A3 var.* Jeble, *Fr.* Djéblé. Al
Lādhiqiyah, W Syria
Jaca *93 F1* Aragón, NE Spain
Jacaltenango *52 A2* Huehuetenango,
W Guatemala
Jackson *42 B2 state capital* Mississippi,
S USA
Jackson *45 H5* Missouri, C USA
Jackson *42 C1* Tennessee, S USA
Jackson Head *151 A6 headland* South
Island, New Zealand
Jacksonville *43 E3* Florida, SE USA
Jacksonville *40 B4* Illinois, N USA
Jacksonville *43 F1* North Carolina,
SE USA
Jacksonville *49 G3* Texas, SW USA
Jacmel *54 D3 var.* Jaquemel. S Haiti
Jacob *see* Nkayi
Jacobābād *134 B3* Sind, SE Pakistan
Jadotville *see* Likasi
Jadransko More/Jadransko Morje *see*
Adriatic Sea
Jaén *60 B2* Cajamarca, N Peru
Jaén *92 D4* Andalucía, SW Spain
Jaffna *132 D3* Northern Province,
N Sri Lanka
Jagannath *see* Puri

Jagdalpur *135 E5* Chhattisgarh, C India
Jagdaqi *127 G1* Nei Mongol Zizhiqu,
N China
Jagodina *100 D4 prev.* Svetozarevo.
Serbia, C Serbia
Jahra *see* Al Jahrā'
Jailolo *see* Halmahera, Pulau
Jaipur *134 D3 prev.* Jeypore. *state capital*
Rājasthān, N India
Jaisalmer *134 C3* Rājasthān, NW India
Jajce *100 B3* Federacija Bosna
I Hercegovina, W Bosnia and
Herzegovina
Jakarta *138 C5 prev.* Djakarta, *Dut.*
Batavia. *country capital* (Indonesia)
(Indonesia) Jawa, C Indonesia
Jakobstad *84 D4 Fin.* Pietarsaari. Länsi-
Suomi, W Finland
Jakobstadt *see* Jēkabpils
Jalālābād *123 F4 var.* Jalalabad,
Jelalabad. Nangarhār, E Afghanistan
Jalal-Abad *see* Dzhalal-Abad, Dzhalal-
Abadskaya Oblast', Kyrgyzstan
Jalandhar *134 D2 prev.* Jullundur.
Punjab, N India
Jalapa *52 D3* Nueva Segovia,
NW Nicaragua
Jalpa *50 D4* Zacatecas, C Mexico
Jālū *71 G3 var.* Jālū. NE Libya
Jaluit Atoll *144 D2 var.* Jālwōj. *atoll*
Ralik Chain, S Marshall Islands
Jālwōj *see* Jaluit Atoll
Jamaame *73 D6 It.* Giamame; *prev.*
Margherita. Jubbada Hoose, S Somalia
Jamaica *54 A4 country* W West Indies

JAMAICA
West Indies

Official name Jamaica
Formation 1962 / 1962
Capital Kingston
Population 2.7 million / 646 people
per sq mile (249 people per sq km) / 52%
Total area 4243 sq. miles (10,990 sq. km)
Languages English*, English Creole
Religions Other and nonreligious 45%,
Other Protestant 20%, Church
of God 18%, Baptist 10%, Anglican 7%
Ethnic mix Black African 92%,
Mulatto (mixed race) 6%, East Indian 1%,
European and Chinese 1%
Government Parliamentary system
Currency Jamaican dollar = 100 cents
Literacy rate 80%
Calorie consumption 2685 calories

Jamaica *56 A1 island* W West Indies
Jamaica Channel *54 D3 channel* Haiti/
Jamaica
Jamālpur *135 F3* Bihār, NE India
Jambi *138 B4 var.* Telanaipura; *prev.*
Djambi. Sumatera, W Indonesia
Jamdena *see* Yamdena, Pulau
James Bay *38 C3 bay* Ontario/Québec,
E Canada
James River *45 E2 river* North Dakota/
South Dakota, N USA
James River *41 E5 river* Virginia,
NE USA
Jamestown *41 E3* New York, NE USA
Jamestown *45 E2* North Dakota,
N USA
Jamestown *see* Holetown
Jammu *134 D2 prev.* Jummoo. *state
capital* Jammu and Kashmir,
NW India
Jammu and Kashmir *134 D1 disputed
region* India/Pakistan
Jāmnagar *134 C4 prev.* Navanagar.
Gujarāt, W India
Jamshedpur *135 F4* Jhārkhand, NE India
Jamuna *see* Brahmaputra
Janaúba *63 F3* Minas Gerais, SE Brazil
Janesville *40 B3* Wisconsin, N USA
Janina *see* Ioánnina
Janischken *see* Joniškis
Jankovac *see* Jánoshalma
Jan Mayen *83 F4 Norwegian dependency*
N Atlantic Ocean
Jánoshalma *99 C7 SCr.* Jankovac. Bács-
Kiskun, S Hungary
Janów *see* Ivanava, Belarus
Janów/Janów *see* Jonava, Lithuania
Janów Poleski *see* Ivanava

JAPAN
East Asia

Official name Japan
Formation 1590 / 1972
Capital Tokyo
Population 128 million / 883 people
per sq mile (341 people per sq km) / 66%
Total area 145,882 sq. miles
(377,835 sq. km)
Languages Japanese*, Korean, Chinese
Religions Shinto and Buddhist 76%,
Buddhist 16%, Other (including
Christian) 8%
Ethnic mix Japanese 99%, Other
(mainly Korean) 1%
Government Parliamentary system
Currency Yen = 100 sen
Literacy rate 99%
Calorie consumption 2761 calories

Japan *130 C4 var.* Nippon, *Jap.* Nihon.
country E Asia
Japan, Sea of *130 A4 var.* East Sea, *Rus.*
Yapanskoye More. *sea* NW Pacific
Ocean
Japan Trench *125 F1 trench* NW Pacific
Ocean
Japen *see* Yapen, Pulau
Japiim *62 C2 var.* Máncio Lima. Acre,
W Brazil
Japurá, Rio *62 C2 var.* Río Caquetá,
Yapurá. *river* Brazil/Colombia
Japurá, Rio *see* Caquetá, Río
Jaqué *53 G5* Darién, SE Panama
Jaquemel *see* Jacmel
Jarablos *see* Jarābulus
Jarābulus *118 C2 var.* Jarablos, Jerablus,
Fr. Djérablous. Ḥalab, N Syria
Jarbah, Jazīrat *see* Jerba, Île de
**Jardines de la Reina, Archipiélago de
los** *54 B2 island group* C Cuba
Jarid, Shaṭṭ al *see* Jerid, Chott el
Jarocin *98 C4* Wielkopolskie, C Poland
Jarosław *see* Jarosław
Jarosław *99 E5 Ger.* Jaroslau, *Rus.*
Yaroslav. Podkarpackie, SE Poland
Jarqo'rg'on *123 E3 Rus.* Dzharkurgan.
Surkhondaryo Viloyati, S Uzbekistan
Jarvis Island *145 G2 US unincorporated
territory* C Pacific Ocean
Jasło *99 D5* Podkarpackie, SE Poland
Jastrzębie-Zdrój *99 C5* Śląskie, S Poland
Jataí *63 E3* Goiás, C Brazil
Jativa *see* Xàtiva
Jauf *see* Al Jawf
Jaunpiebalga *106 D3* Gulbene, NE Latvia
Jaunpur *135 E3* Uttar Pradesh, N India
Java *152 A3* South Dakota, N USA
Javalambre *93 E3 mountain* E Spain
Java Sea *138 D4 Ind.* Laut Jawa. *sea*
W Indonesia
Java Trench *124 D5 var.* Sunda Trench.
trench E Indian Ocean
Jawa, Laut *see* Java Sea
Jawhar *73 D6 var.* Jowhar, *It.* Giohar.
Shabeellaha Dhexe, S Somalia
Jaworów *see* Yavoriv
Jaya, Puncak *139 G4 prev.* Puntjak
Carstensz, Puntjak Sukarno. *mountain*
Papua, E Indonesia
Jayapura *139 H4 var.* Djajapura,
Dut. Hollandia; *prev.* Kotabaru,
Sukarnapura. Papua, E Indonesia
Jay Dairen *see* Dalian
Jayhawker State *see* Kansas
Jaz Murian, Hamun-e *120 E4 lake*
SE Iran
Jebba *75 F4* Kwara, W Nigeria
Jebel, Bahr el *see* White Nile
Jeble *see* Jablah
Jedda *see* Jiddah
Jędrzejów *98 D4 Ger.* Endersdorf.
Świętokrzyskie, C Poland
Jefferson City *45 G5 state capital*
Missouri, C USA
Jega *75 F4* Kebbi, NW Nigeria
Jehol *see* Chengde
Jēkabpils *106 C4 Ger.* Jakobstadt.
Jēkabpils, S Latvia
Jelalabad *see* Jalālābād
Jelenia Góra *98 B4 Ger.* Hirschberg,
Hirschberg im Riesengebirge,
Hirschberg in Riesengebirge, Hirschberg
in Schlesien. Dolnośląskie, SW Poland
Jelgava *106 C3 Ger.* Mitau. Jelgava,
C Latvia

Jemappes *87 B6* Hainaut, S Belgium
Jember *138 D5 prev.* Djember.
C Indonesia
Jena *94 C4* Thüringen, C Germany
Jenin *119 A6* N West Bank
Jerablus *see* Jarãblus
Jerada *70 D2* NE Morocco
Jérémie *54 D3* SW Haiti
Jerez *see* Jeréz de la Frontera, Spain
Jeréz de la Frontera *92 C5 var.* Jerez;
prev. Xeres. Andalucía, SW Spain
Jeréz de los Caballeros *92 C4*
Extremadura, W Spain
Jericho *119 B6 Ar.* Arīḥā, *Heb.* Yeriḥo.
F West Bank
Jerid, Chott el *71 E2 var.* Shaṭṭ al Jarīd.
salt lake SW Tunisia
Jersey *89 D8 uk crown dependency*
Channel Islands, NW Europe
Jerusalem *103 H4 Ar.* Al Quds, Al Quds
ash Sharif, *Heb.* Yerushalayim; *anc.*
Hierosolyma. *country capital* (Israel)
(Israel) Jerusalem, NE Israel
Jesenice *95 D7 Ger.* Assling. NW Slovenia
Jesselton *see* Kota Kinabalu
Jessore *135 G4* Khulna, W Bangladesh
Jesús María *64 C3* Córdoba, C Argentina
Jeypore *see* Jaipur, Rājasthãn, India
Jhãnsi *134 D3* Uttar Pradesh, N India
Jhãrkhand *135 F4 cultural region*
NE India
Jhelum *134 C2* Punjab, NE Pakistan
Ji *see* Hebei, China
Ji *see* Jilin, China
Jiangmen *128 C6* Guangdong, S China
Jiangsu *128 D4 var.* Chiang-su, Jiangsu
Sheng, Kiangsu, Su. *province* E China
Jiangsu *see* Nanjing
Jiangsu Sheng *see* Jiangsu
Jiangxi *128 C6 var.* Chiang-hsi, Gan,
Jiangxi Sheng, Kiangsi. *province*
S China
Jiangxi Sheng *see* Jiangxi
Jiaxing *128 D5* Zhejiang, SE China
Jiayi *see* Chiai
Jibuti *see* Djibouti
Jiddah *121 A5 Eng.* Jedda. (Saudi
Arabia) Makkah, W Saudi Arabia
Jih-k'a-tse *see* Xigazê
Jihlava *99 B5 Ger.* Iglau, *Pol.* Igława.
Vysocina, S Czech Republic
Jilib *73 D6 It.* Gelib. Jubbada Dhexe,
S Somalia
Jilin *128 E3 var.* Chi-lin, Girin, Kirin;
prev. Yungki, Yunki. Jilin, NE China
Jilin *128 E3 var.* Chi-lin, Girin, Ji, Jilin
Sheng, Kirin. *province* NE China
Jilin Sheng *see* Jilin
Jima *73 C5 var.* Jimma, *It.* Gimma.
Oromīya, C Ethiopia
Jimbolia *108 A4 Ger.* Hatzfeld, *Hung.*
Zsombolya. Timiş, W Romania
Jimma *see* Jima
Jiménez *50 D2* Chihuahua, N Mexico
Jimsar *126 C3* Xinjiang Uygur Zizhiqu,
NW China
Jin *see* Shanxi
Jin *see* Tianjin Shi
Jinan *128 C4 var.* Chinan, Chi-nan,
Tsinan. *province capital* Shandong,
E China
Jingdezhen *128 C5* Jiangxi, S China
Jinghong *128 A6 var.* Yunjinghong.
Yunnan, SW China
Jinhua *128 D5* Zhejiang, SE China
Jining *127 F3* Shandong, E China
Jinja *73 C6* S Uganda
Jinotega *52 D3* Jinotega, NW Nicaragua
Jinotepe *52 D3* Carazo, SW Nicaragua
Jinsen *see* Inch'ŏn
Jinsha Jiang *128 A5 Eng.* Yangtze. *river*
SW China
Jinzhong *128 C4 var.* Yuci. Shanxi,
C China
Jinzhou *128 D3 var.* Chin-chou,
Chinchow; *prev.* Chinhsien. Liaoning,
NE China
Jirgalanta *see* Hovd
Jisr ash Shadadi *see* Ash Shadãdah
Jiu *108 B5 Ger.* Schil, Schyl, *Hung.* Zsil,
Zsily. *river* S Romania
Jiujiang *128 C5* Jiangxi, S China
Jixi *128 E2* Heilongjiang, NE China
Jīzãn *121 B6 var.* Qîzãn. Jīzãn, SW Saudi
Arabia
Jizzax *123 E2 Rus.* Dzhizak. Jizzax
Viloyati, C Uzbekistan

João Belo *see* Xai-Xai
João Pessoa *63 G2 prev.* Paraíba. *state
capital* Paraíba, E Brazil
Joazeiro *see* Juazeiro
Job'urg *see* Johannesburg
Jo-ch'iang *see* Ruoqiang
Jodhpur *134 C3* Rājasthãn, NW India
Joensuu *85 E5* Itä-Suomi, SE Finland
Jōetsu *131 C5 var.* Zyôetu. Niigata,
Honshū, C Japan
Jogjakarta *see* Yogyakarta
Johannesburg *78 D4 var.* Egoli,
Erautini, Gauteng, *abbrev.* Job'urg.
Gauteng, NE South Africa
Johannisburg *see* Pisz
John Day River *46 C3 river* Oregon,
NW USA
John o'Groats *88 C2* N Scotland, United
Kingdom
Johnston Atoll *143 E1 US unincorporated
territory* C Pacific Ocean
Johor Baharu *see* Johor Bahru
Johor Bahru *138 B3 var.* Johor Baharu,
Johore Bahru. Johor, Peninsular
Malaysia
Johore Bahru *see* Johor Bahru
Johore Strait *138 A1 strait* Johor,
Peninsular Malaysia, Malaysia/Singapore
Asia Andaman Sea/South China Sea
Joinville *see* Joinville
Joinville *63 E4 var.* Joinvile. Santa
Catarina, S Brazil
Jokkmokk *84 C3 Lapp.* Dálvvadis.
Norrbotten, N Sweden
Jokyakarta *see* Yogyakarta
Joliet *40 B3* Illinois, N USA
Joniava *106 B4 Ger.* Janova, *Pol.* Janów.
Kaunas, C Lithuania
Jonesboro *42 B1* Arkansas, C USA
Joniškis *106 C3 Ger.* Janischken. Šiauliai,
N Lithuania
Jönköping *85 B7* Jönköping, S Sweden
Jonquière *39 E4* Québec, SE Canada
Joplin *45 F5* Missouri, C USA
Jordan *119 B6 off.* Hashemite Kingdom
of Jordan, *Ar.* Al Mamlaka al Urdunīya
al Hashemīyah, Al Urdunn; *prev.*
Transjordan. *country* SW Asia

JORDAN
Southwest Asia

Official name Hashemite Kingdom
of Jordan
Formation 1946 / 1967
Capital Amman
Population 6 million / 175 people
per sq mile (67 people per sq km) / 79%
Total area 35,637 sq. miles (92,300 sq. km)
Languages Arabic*
Religions Muslim (mainly Sunni) 92%,
Other (mostly Christian) 8%
Ethnic mix Arab 98%, Circassian 1%,
Armenian 1%
Government Monarchy
Currency Jordanian dinar = 1000 fils
Literacy rate 90%
Calorie consumption 2673 calories

Jordan *119 B6 Ar.* Urdunn, *Heb.*
HaYarden. *river* SW Asia
Jorhãt *135 H3* Assam, NE India
Jos *75 G4* Plateau, C Nigeria
Joseph Bonaparte Gulf *146 D2 gulf*
N Australia
Jos Plateau *75 G4 plateau* C Nigeria
Jotunheimen *85 A5 mountain range*
S Norway
Joûnié *118 A4 var.* Juniyah. W Lebanon
Joure *86 D2 Fris.* De Jouwer. Friesland,
N Netherlands
Joutseno *85 E5* Etelä-Suomi, SE Finland
Jowhar *see* Jawhar
J.Storm Thurmond Reservoir *see* Clark
Hill Lake
Juan Aldama *50 D3* Zacatecas, C Mexico
Juan de Fuca, Strait of *46 A1 strait*
Canada/USA
Juan Fernandez Islands *57 A6 Eng.*
Juan Fernandez Islands. *island group*
W Chile
Juan Fernandez Islands *see* Juan
Fernández, Islas
Juazeiro *63 G2 prev.* Joazeiro. Bahia,
E Brazil
Juazeiro do Norte *63 G2* Ceará, E Brazil

Juba *73 B5 var.* Jūbã. Bahr el Gabel,
S Sudan
Juba *73 D6 Amh.* Genalê Wenz, *It.* Guiba,
Som. Ganaane, Webi Jubba. *river*
Ethiopia/Somalia
Jubba, Webi *see* Juba
Jubbulpore *see* Jabalpur
Júcar *93 E3 var.* Jucar. *river* C Spain
Juchitán *51 F5 var.* Juchitán de Zaragosa.
Oaxaca, SE Mexico
Juchitán de Zaragosa *see* Juchitán
Judayyidat Hãmir *120 B3* Al Anbãr,
S Iraq
Judenburg *95 D7* Steiermark, C Austria
Jugoslavija *see* Serbia
Juigalpa *52 D3* Chontales, S Nicaragua
Juist *94 B2 island* NW Germany
Juiz de Fora *63 F4* Minas Gerais,
SE Brazil
Jujuy *see* San Salvador de Jujuy
Jūlã *see* Jãlū, Libya
Julia Betterae *see* Béziers
Juliaca *61 F4* Puno, SE Peru
Juliana Top *59 G3 mountain* C Suriname
Julianehãb *see* Qaqortoq
Julio Briga *see* Bragança
Juliobriga *see* Logroño
Juliomagus *see* Angers
Jullundur *see* Jalandhar
Jumilla *93 E4* Murcia, SE Spain
Jummoo *see* Jammu
Jumna *see* Yamuna
Jumporn *see* Chumphon
Junction City *45 F4* Kansas, C USA
Juneau *36 D4 state capital* Alaska, USA
Junín *64 C4* Buenos Aires, E Argentina
Juniyah *see* Joûnié
Junkseylon *see* Phuket
Jur *73 B5 river* C Sudan
Jura *90 D4 cultural region* E France
Jura *95 A7 var.* Jura Mountains.
mountain range France/Switzerland
Jura *88 B4 island* SW Scotland, United
Kingdom
Jura Mountains *see* Jura
Jurbarkas *106 B4 Ger.* Georgenburg,
Jurburg. Tauragé, W Lithuania
Jurburg *see* Jurbarkas
Jūrmala *106 C3* Rīga, C Latvia
Juruá, Rio *62 C2 var.* Rio Yuruá. *river*
Brazil/Peru
Juruena, Rio *62 D3 river*
W Brazil
Jutiapa *52 B2* Jutiapa, S Guatemala
Juticalpa *52 D2* Olancho, C Honduras
Jutland *85 A7 Eng.* Jutland. *peninsula*
W Denmark
Jutland *see* Jylland
Juvavum *see* Salzburg
Južna Morava *101 E5 Ger.* Südliche
Morava. *river* SE Serbia
Jwaneng *78 C4* Southern, S Botswana
Jyrgalan *see* Dzhergalan
Jyväskylä *85 D5* Länsi-Suomi, C Finland

K

K2 *126 A4 Chin.* Qogir Feng, *Eng.* Mount
Godwin Austen. *mountain* China/
Pakistan
Kaafu Atoll *see* Male' Atoll
Kaaimanston *59 G3* Sipaliwini,
N Suriname
Kaahka *see* Kaka
Kaala *see* Caála
Kaamanen *84 D2 Lapp.* Gámas. Lappi,
N Finland
Kaapstad *see* Cape Town
Kaaresuvanto *84 C3 Lapp.* Gárassavon.
Lappi, N Finland
Kabale *73 B6* SW Uganda
Kabinda *77 D7* Kasai-Oriental, SE Dem.
Rep. Congo
Kabinda *see* Cabinda
Kãbol *123 E4 var.* Kabul, *Pash.*
Kãbul. *country capital* (Afghanistan)
(Afghanistan) Kãbul, E Afghanistan
Kabompo *78 C2 river* W Zambia
Kabul *123 E4 var.* Daryã-ye Kãbul. *river*
Afghanistan/Pakistan
Kãbul *see* Kãbol
Kãbul, Daryã-ye *see* Kabul
Kabwe *78 D2* Central, C Zambia
Kachchh, Gulf of *134 B4 var.* Gulf of
Cutch, Gulf of Kutch. *gulf* W India
Kachchh, Rann of *134 B4 var.* Rann
of Kach, Rann of Kutch. *salt marsh*
India/Pakistan

Kachch, Rann of *see* Kachchh, Rann of
Kadan Kyun *137 B5 prev.* King Island.
island Mergui Archipelago, S Burma
(Myanmar)
Kadavu *145 E4 prev.* Kandavu. *island*
S Fiji
Kadoma *78 D3 prev.* Gatooma.
Mashonaland West, C Zimbabwe
Kadugli *72 B4* Southern Kordofan,
S Sudan
Kaduna *75 G4* Kaduna, C Nigeria
Kadzhi-Say *123 G2 Kir.* Kajisay. Issyk-
Kul'skaya Oblast', NE Kyrgyzstan
Kaédi *74 C3* Gorgol, S Mauritania
Kaffa *see* Feodosiya
Kafue *78 D2* Lusaka, SE Zambia
Kafue *78 C2 river* C Zambia
Kaga Bandoro *76 C4 prev.* Fort-
Crampel. Nana-Grébizi, C Central
African Republic
Kagan *see* Kogon
Kãghet *74 D1 var.* Karet. *physical region*
N Mauritania
Kagi *see* Chiai
Kagoshima *131 B8 var.* Kagosima.
Kagoshima, Kyūshū, SW Japan
Kagoshima-wan *131 A8 bay* SW Japan
Kagosima *see* Kagoshima
Kagul *see* Cahul
Darya-ye Kahmard *123 E4 prev.* Darya-
i-surkhab. *river* NE Afghanistan
Kahmanmaraş *116 D4 var.*
Kahraman Maraş, Maraş, Marash.
Kahramanmaraş, S Turkey
Kaiapoi *151 C6* Canterbury, South
Island, New Zealand
Kaifeng *128 C4* Henan, C China
Kai, Kepulauan *139 F4 prev.* Kei Islands.
island group Maluku, SE Indonesia
Kaikohe *150 C2* Northland, North
Island, New Zealand
Kaikoura *151 C5* Canterbury, South
Island, New Zealand
Kaikoura Peninsula *151 C5 peninsula*
South Island, New Zealand
Kainji Lake *see* Kainji Reservoir
Kainji Reservoir *75 F4 var.* Kainji Lake.
reservoir W Nigeria
Kalpara Harbour *150 C2 harbour* North
Island, New Zealand
Kairouan *71 E2 var.* Al Qayrawãn.
E Tunisia
Kaisaria *see* Kayseri
Kaiserslautern *95 A5* Rheinland-Pfalz,
SW Germany
Kaišiadorys *107 B5* Kaunas,
S Lithuania
Kaitaia *150 C2* Northland, North Island,
New Zealand
Kajaani *84 E4 Swe.* Kajana. Oulu,
C Finland
Kajan *see* Kayan, Sungai
Kajana *see* Kajaani
Kajisay *see* Kadzhi-Say
Kaka *122 C2 Rus.* Kaakhka. Ahal
Welaýaty, S Turkmenistan
Kake *36 D4* Kupreanof Island, Alaska,
USA
Kakhovka *109 F4* Khersons'ka Oblast',
S Ukraine
Kakhovs'ke Vodoskhovyshche *109 F4
Rus.* Kakhovskoye Vodokhranilishche.
reservoir SE Ukraine
Kakhovskoye Vodokhranilishche *see*
Kakhovs'ke Vodoskhovyshche
Kãkinãda *132 D1 prev.* Cocanada.
Andhra Pradesh, E India
Kakshaal-Too, Khrebet *see*
Kokshaal-Tau
Kaktovik *36 D2* Alaska, USA
Kalaallit Nunaat *see* Greenland
Kalahari Desert *78 B4 desert* Southern
Africa
Kalaikhum *see* Qal'aikhum
Kalámai *see* Kalámata
Kalamariá *104 B4* Kentrikí Makedonía,
N Greece
Kalámas *104 A4 var.* Thiamis; *prev.*
Thýamis. *river* W Greece
Kalámata *105 B6 prev.* Kalámai.
Pelopónnisos, S Greece
Kalamazoo *40 C3* Michigan, N USA
Kalambaka *see* Kalampáka
Kálamos *105 C5* Attikí, C Greece
Kalampáka *104 B4 var.* Kalambaka.
Thessalía, C Greece

Kalanchak *109 F4* Khersons'ka Oblast', S Ukraine
Kalarash *see* Călăraşi
Kalasin *136 D4 var.* Muang Kalasin. Kalasin, E Thailand
Kālat *134 B2 var.* Kelat, Khelat. Baluchistān, SW Pakistan
Kalāt *see* Qalāt
Kalbarri *147 A5* Western Australia
Kalecik *116 C3* Ankara, N Turkey
Kalemie *77 E6 prev.* Albertville. Katanga, SE Dem. Rep. Congo
Kale Sultanie *see* Çanakkale
Kalgan *see* Zhangjiakou
Kalgoorlie *147 B6* Western Australia
Kalima *77 D6* Maniema, E Dem. Rep. Congo
Kalimantan *138 D4 Eng.* Indonesian Borneo. *geopolitical region* Borneo, C Indonesia
Kalinin *see* Tver'
Kaliningrad *106 A4* Kaliningradskaya Oblast', W Russian Federation
Kaliningrad *see* Kaliningradskaya Oblast'
Kaliningradskaya Oblast' *106 B4 var.* Kaliningrad. *province and enclave* W Russian Federation
Kalinkavichy *107 C7 Rus.* Kalinkovichi. Homyel'skaya Voblasts', SE Belarus
Kalinkovichi *see* Kalinkavichy
Kalisch/Kalish *see* Kalisz
Kalispell *44 B1* Montana, NW USA
Kalisz *98 C4 Ger.* Kalisch, *Rus.* Kalish; *anc.* Calisia. Wielkopolskie, C Poland
Kalix *84 D4* Norrbotten, N Sweden
Kalixälven *84 D3 river* N Sweden
Kallaste *106 E3 Ger.* Krasnogor. Tartumaa, SE Estonia
Kallavesi *85 E5* lake SE Finland
Kalloní *105 D5* Lésvos, E Greece
Kalmar *85 C7 var.* Calmar. Kalmar, S Sweden
Kalmthout *87 C5* Antwerpen, N Belgium
Kalpáki *104 A4* Ípeiros, W Greece
Kalpeni Island *132 B3 island* Lakshadweep, India, N Indian Ocean
Kaltdorf *see* Pruszków
Kaluga *111 B5* Kaluzhskaya Oblast', W Russian Federation
Kalush *108 C2 Pol.* Kałusz. Ivano-Frankivs'ka Oblast', W Ukraine
Kałusz *see* Kalush
Kalutara *132 D4* Western Province, SW Sri Lanka
Kalvarija *107 B5 Pol.* Kalwaria. Marijampolė, S Lithuania
Kalwaria *see* Kalvarija
Kalyān *134 C5* Mahārāshtra, W India
Kálymnos *105 D6 var.* Kálimnos. *island* Dodekánisa, Greece, Aegean Sea
Kama *110 D4 river* NW Russian Federation
Kamarang *59 F3* W Guyana
Kambryk *see* Cambrai
Kamchatka *115 G3 Eng.* Kamchatka. *peninsula* E Russian Federation
Kamchatka *see* Kamchatka, Poluostrov
Kamenets-Podol'skiy *see* Kam″yanets'-Podil's'kyy
Kamenka Dneprovskaya *see* Kam″yanka-Dniprovs'ka
Kamenskoye *see* Romaniv
Kamensk-Shakhtinskiy *111 B6* Rostovskaya Oblast', SW Russian Federation
Kamina *77 D7* Katanga, S Dem. Rep. Congo
Kamishli *see* Al Qāmishlī
Kamloops *37 E5* British Columbia, SW Canada
Kammu Seamount *152 C2 guyot* N Pacific Ocean
Kampala *73 B6 country capital* (Uganda) (Uganda) S Uganda
Kâmpóng Cham *137 D6 prev.* Kompong Cham. Kâmpóng Cham, C Cambodia
Kâmpóng Chhnăng *137 D6 prev.* Kompong. Kâmpóng Chhnăng, C Cambodia
Kâmpóng Saôm *137 D6 prev.* Kompong Som, Sihanoukville. Kâmpóng Saôm, SW Cambodia
Kâmpóng Spœ *137 D6 prev.* Kompong Speu. Kâmpóng Spœ, S Cambodia
Kâmpôt *137 D6 prev.* Kâmpôt, SW Cambodia
Kampuchea *see* Cambodia
Kampuchea, Democratic *see* Cambodia

Kampuchea, People's Democratic Republic of *see* Cambodia
Kam″yanets'-Podil''s'kyy *108 C3 Rus.* Kamenets-Podol'skiy. Khmel'nyts'ka Oblast', W Ukraine
Kam″yanka-Dniprovs'ka *109 F3 Rus.* Kamenka Dneprovskaya. Zaporiz'ka Oblast', SE Ukraine
Kamyshin *111 B6* Volgogradskaya Oblast', SW Russian Federation
Kanaky *see* New Caledonia
Kananga *77 D6 prev.* Luluabourg. Kasai-Occidental, S Dem. Rep. Congo
Kanara *see* Karnātaka
Kanash *111 C5* Chuvashskaya Respublika, W Russian Federation
Kanazawa *131 C5* Ishikawa, Honshū, SW Japan
Kanbe *136 B4* Yangon, SW Burma (Myanmar)
Kānchīpuram *132 C2 prev.* Conjeeveram. Tamil Nādu, SE India
Kandahār *123 E5 Per.* Qandahār. Kandahār, S Afghanistan
Kandalakša *see* Kandalaksha
Kandalaksha *110 B2 var.* Kandalakša, *Fin.* Kantalahti. Murmanskaya Oblast', NW Russian Federation
Kandangan *138 D4* Borneo, C Indonesia
Kandau *see* Kandava
Kandava *106 C3 Ger.* Kandau. Tukums, W Latvia
Kandavu *see* Kadavu
Kandi *75 F4* N Benin
Kandy *132 D3* Central Province, C Sri Lanka
Kane Fracture Zone *66 B4 fracture zone* NW Atlantic Ocean
Kāne'ohe *47 A8 var.* Kaneohe. O'ahu, Hawaii, USA, C Pacific Ocean
Kanestron, Akrotírio *see* Palioúri, Akrotírio
Kanëv *see* Kaniv
Kanevskoye Vodokhranilishche *see* Kanivs'ke Vodoskhovyshche
Kangān *see* Bandar-e Kangān
Kangaroo Island *149 A7 island* South Australia
Kangertittivaq *83 E4 Dan.* Scoresby Sund. *fjord* E Greenland
Kangikajik *83 E4 var.* Kap Brewster. *headland* E Greenland
Kaniv *109 E2 Rus.* Kanëv. Cherkas'ka Oblast', C Ukraine
Kanivs'ke Vodoskhovyshche *109 E2 Rus.* Kanevskoye Vodokhranilishche. *reservoir* C Ukraine
Kanjiža *100 D2 Ger.* Altkanischa, *Hung.* Magyarkanizsa, Ókanizsa; *prev.* Stara Kanjiža. Vojvodina, N Serbia
Kankaanpää *85 D5* Länsi-Suomi, SW Finland
Kankakee *40 B3* Illinois, N USA
Kankan *74 D4* E Guinea
Kano *75 G4* Kano, N Nigeria
Kānpur *135 E3 Eng.* Cawnpore. Uttar Pradesh, N India
Kansas *45 F5 off.* State of Kansas, *also known as* Jayhawker State, Sunflower State. *state* C USA
Kansas City *45 F4* Kansas, C USA
Kansas City *45 F4* Missouri, C USA
Kansas River *45 F5 river* Kansas, C USA
Kansk *115 E4* Krasnoyarskiy Kray, S Russian Federation
Kansu *see* Gansu
Kantalahti *see* Kandalaksha
Kántanos *105 C7* Kríti, Greece, E Mediterranean Sea
Kantemirovka *111 B6* Voronezhskaya Oblast', W Russian Federation
Kantipur *see* Kathmandu
Kanton *145 F3 var.* Abariringa, Canton Island; *prev.* Mary Island. *atoll* Phoenix Islands, C Kiribati
Kanye *78 C4* Southern, SE Botswana
Kaohsiung *128 D6 var.* Gaoxiong, *Jap.* Takao, Takow. S Taiwan
Kaolack *74 B3 var.* Kaolak. W Senegal
Kaolak *see* Kaolack
Kaolan *see* Lanzhou
Kaoma *78 C2* Western, W Zambia
Kapelle *87 B5* Zeeland, SW Netherlands
Kapellen *87 C5* Antwerpen, N Belgium
Kapka, Massif du *76 C2 mountain range* E Chad
Kaplangky, Plato *see* Gaplañgyr Platosy
Kapoeas *see* Kapuas, Sungai

Kapoeta *73 C5* Eastern Equatoria, SE Sudan
Kaposvár *99 C7* Somogy, SW Hungary
Kappeln *94 B2* Schleswig-Holstein, N Germany
Kaproncza *see* Koprivnica
Kapstad *see* Cape Town
Kapsukas *see* Marijampolė
Kaptsevichy *107 C7 Rus.* Koptsevichi. Homyel'skaya Voblasts', SE Belarus
Kapuas, Sungai *138 C4 prev.* Kapoeas. *river* Borneo, C Indonesia
Kapuskasing *38 C4* Ontario, S Canada
Kapyl' *107 C6 Rus.* Kopyl'. Minskaya Voblasts', C Belarus
Kara-Balta *123 F2* Chuyskaya Oblast', N Kyrgyzstan
Karabil', Vozvyshennost' *see* Garabil Belentligi
Kara-Bogaz-Gol, Zaliv *see* Garabogaz Aylagy
Karabük *116 C2* Karabük, NW Turkey
Karāchi *134 B3* Sind, SE Pakistan
Karácsonkő *see* Piatra-Neamţ
Karadeniz *see* Black Sea
Karadeniz Boğazı *see* İstanbul Boğazı
Karaferiye *see* Véroia
Karaganda *114 C4 Kaz.* Qaraghandy. Karaganda, C Kazakhstan
Karaginskiy, Ostrov *115 H2 island* E Russian Federation
Karagumskiy Kanal *see* Garagum Kanaly
Karak *see* Al Karak
Karakax *see* Moyu
Karakılısse *see* Ağrı
Karakol *123 G2 prev.* Przheval'sk. Issyk-Kul'skaya Oblast', NE Kyrgyzstan
Karakol *123 G2 var.* Karakolka. Issyk-Kul'skaya Oblast', NE Kyrgyzstan
Karakolka *see* Karakol
Karakoram Range *134 D1 mountain range* C Asia
Karaköse *see* Ağrı
Karakul' *see* Qarokŭl, Tajikistan
Kara Kum *see* Garagum
Kara Kum Canal/Karakumskiy Kanal *see* Garagum Kanaly
Karakumy, Peski *see* Garagum
Karamai *see* Karamay
Karaman *116 C4* Karaman, S Turkey
Karamay *126 B2 var.* Karamai, Kelamayi; *prev. Chin.* K'o-la-ma-i. Xinjiang Uygur Zizhiqu, NW China
Karamea Bight *151 B5 gulf* South Island, New Zealand
Karapelit *104 E1 Rom.* Stejarul. Dobrich, NE Bulgaria
Kara-Say *123 G2* Issyk-Kul'skaya Oblast', NE Kyrgyzstan
Karasburg *78 B4* Karas, S Namibia
Kara Sea *114 D2 Eng.* Kara Sea. *sea* Arctic Ocean
Kara Sea *see* Karskoye More
Kara Strait *110 E2 Eng.* Kara Strait. *strait* N Russian Federation
Kara Strait *see* Karskiye Vorota, Proliv
Karatau *114 C5 Kaz.* Qarataū. Zhambyl, S Kazakhstan
Karavás *85 B7* Kýthira, S Greece
Karbalā' *120 B3 var.* Kerbala, Kerbela. Karbalā', S Iraq
Kardeljevo *see* Ploče
Kardhítsa *see* Karditsa
Karditsa *105 B5 var.* Kardhítsa. Thessalía, C Greece
Kärdla *106 C2 Ger.* Kertel. Hiiumaa, W Estonia
Karet *see* Kâghet
Kargı *116 C2* Çorum, N Turkey
Kargılık *see* Yecheng
Kariba *78 D2* Mashonaland West, N Zimbabwe
Kariba, Lake *78 D3 reservoir* Zambia/Zimbabwe
Karibib *78 B3* Erongo, C Namibia
Karies *see* Karyés
Karigasniemi *84 D2 Lapp.* Garegasnjárga. Lappi, N Finland
Karīmnagar *134 D5* Andhra Pradesh, C India
Karin *72 D4* Sahil, N Somalia
Kariot *see* Ikaría
Káristos *see* Kárystos

Karkinitskiy Zaliv *see* Karkinits'ka Zatoka
Karkük *see* Kirkük
Karleby *see* Kokkola
Karl-Marx-Stadt *see* Chemnitz
Karló *see* Hailuoto
Karlovac *100 B3 Ger.* Karlstadt, *Hung.* Károlyváros. Karlovac, C Croatia
Karlovy Vary *99 A5 Ger.* Karlsbad; *prev.* Carlsbad. Karlovarský Kraj, W Czech Republic
Karlsbad *see* Karlovy Vary
Karlsburg *see* Alba Iulia
Karlskrona *85 C7* Blekinge, S Sweden
Karlsruhe *95 B6 var.* Carlsruhe. Baden-Württemberg, SW Germany
Karlstad *85 B6* Värmland, C Sweden
Karlstadt *see* Karlovac
Karnāl *134 D2* Haryāna, N India
Karnātaka *132 C1 var.* Kanara; *prev.* Maisur, Mysore. *cultural region* W India
Karnobat *104 D2* Burgas, E Bulgaria
Karnul *see* Kurnool
Karol *see* Carei
Károly-Fehérvár *see* Alba Iulia
Karpaten *see* Carpathian Mountains
Kárpathos *105 E7* Kárpathos, SE Greece
Kárpathos *105 E7 It.* Scarpanto; *anc.* Carpathos, Carpathus. *island* SE Greece
Karpaty *see* Carpathian Mountains
Karpenísi *105 B5 prev.* Karpenision. Stereá Ellás, C Greece
Karpenision *see* Karpenísi
Karpilovka *see* Aktsyabrski
Kars *117 F2 var.* Qars. Kars, NE Turkey
Karsau *see* Kārsava
Kārsava *106 D4 Ger.* Karsau; *prev. Rus.* Korsovka. Ludza, E Latvia
Karshi *see* Qarshi, Uzbekistan
Karyés *104 C4 var.* Karies. Ágion Óros, N Greece
Kárystos *105 C6 var.* Káristos. Évvoia, C Greece
Kasai *77 C6 var.* Cassai, Kassai. *river* Angola/Dem. Rep. Congo
Kasaji *77 D7* Katanga, S Dem. Rep. Congo
Kasama *78 D1* Northern, N Zambia
Kasan *see* Koson
Kāsaragod *132 B2* Kerala, SW India
Kaschau *see* Košice
Kāshān *120 C3* Eşfahān, C Iran
Kashgar *see* Kashi
Kashi *126 A3 Chin.* Kaxgar, K'o-shih, *Uigh.* Kashgar. Xinjiang Uygur Zizhiqu, NW China
Kasi *see* Vārānasi
Kasongo *77 D6* Maniema, E Dem. Rep. Congo
Kasongo-Lunda *77 C7* Bandundu, SW Dem. Rep. Congo
Kásos *105 D7 island* S Greece
Kaspiy Mangy Oypaty *see* Caspian Depression
Kaspiysk *111 B8* Respublika Dagestan, SW Russian Federation
Kaspiyskoye More/Kaspiy Tengizi *see* Caspian Sea
Kassa *see* Košice
Kassai *see* Kasai
Kassala *72 C4* Kassala, E Sudan
Kassel *94 B4 prev.* Cassel. Hessen, C Germany
Kasserine *71 E2 var.* Al Qaşrayn. W Tunisia
Kastamonu *116 C2 var.* Castamoni, Kastamuni. Kastamonu, N Turkey
Kastamuni *see* Kastamonu
Kastaneá *104 B4* Kentrikí Makedonía, N Greece
Kastélli *see* Kíssamos
Kastoría *104 B4* Dytikí Makedonía, N Greece
Kástro *105 C6* Sífnos, Kykládes, Greece, Aegean Sea
Kastsyukovichy *107 E7 Rus.* Kostyukovichi. Mahilyowskaya Voblasts', E Belarus
Kastsyukowka *107 D7 Rus.* Kostyukovka. Homyel'skaya Voblasts', SE Belarus
Kasulu *73 B7* Kigoma, W Tanzania
Kasumiga-ura *131 D5 lake* Honshū, S Japan
Katahdin, Mount *41 G1 mountain* Maine, NE USA

Katalla 36 C3 Alaska, USA
Katana see Qaṭanā
Katanning 147 B7 Western Australia
Katawaz see Zarghūn Shahr
Katchall Island 133 F3 island Nicobar Islands, India, NE Indian Ocean
Kateríni 104 B4 Kentrikí Makedonía, N Greece
Katha 136 B2 Sagaing, N Burma (Myanmar)
Katherine 148 A2 Northern Territory, N Australia
Kathmandu 124 C3 prev. Kantipur. country capital (Nepal) (Nepal) Central, C Nepal
Katikati 150 D3 Bay of Plenty, North Island, New Zealand
Katima Mulilo 78 C3 Caprivi, NE Namibia
Katiola 74 D4 C Côte d'Ivoire
Káto Achaḯa 105 B5 var. Kato Ahaia, Káto Akhaḯa. Dytikí Ellás, S Greece
Kato Ahaia/Kato Akhaïa see Káto Achaḯa
Katoúna 105 A5 Dytikí Ellás, C Greece
Katowice 99 C5 Ger. Kattowitz. Śląskie, S Poland
Katsina 75 G3 Katsina, N Nigeria
Kattakurgan see Kattaqo'rg'on
Kattaqo'rg'on 123 E2 Rus. Kattakurgan. Samarqand Viloyati, C Uzbekistan
Kattavía 105 E7 Ródos, Dodekánisa, Greece, Aegean Sea
Kattegat 85 B7 Dan. Kattegatt. strait N Europe
Kattegatt see Kattegat
Kattowitz see Katowice
Kaua'i 47 A7 var. Kauai. island Hawaiian Islands, Hawai'i, USA, C Pacific Ocean
Kauai see Kaua'i
Kauen see Kaunas
Kaufbeuren 95 C6 Bayern, S Germany
Kaunas 106 B4 Ger. Kauen, Pol. Kowno; prev. Rus. Kovno. Kaunas, C Lithuania
Kavadar see Kavadarci
Kavadarci 101 E6 Turk. Kavadar. C Macedonia
Kavaja see Kavajë
Kavajë 101 C6 It. Cavaia, Kavaja. Tiranë, W Albania
Kavakli see Topolovgrad
Kavála 104 C3 prev. Kaválla. Anatolikí Makedonía kai Thráki, NE Greece
Kāvali 132 D2 Andhra Pradesh, E India
Kaválla see Kavála
Kavango see Cubango/Okavango
Kavaratti Island 132 A3 island Lakshadweep, Lakshadweep, SW India Asia N Indian Ocean
Kavarna 104 E2 Dobrich, NE Bulgaria
Kavengo see Cubango/Okavango
Kavir, Dasht-e 120 D3 var. Great Salt Desert. salt pan N Iran
Kavkaz see Caucasus
Kawagoe 131 D5 Saitama, Honshū, S Japan
Kawasaki 130 A2 Kanagawa, Honshū, S Japan
Kawerau 150 E3 Bay of Plenty, North Island, New Zealand
Kaxgar see Kashi
Kaya 75 E3 C Burkina Faso
Kayan 136 B4 Yangon, SW Burma (Myanmar)
Kayan, Sungai 138 D3 prev. Kajan. river Borneo, C Indonesia
Kayes 74 C3 Kayes, W Mali
Kayseri 116 D3 var. Kaisaria; anc. Caesarea Mazaca, Mazaca. Kayseri, C Turkey
Kazach'ye 115 F2 Respublika Sakha (Yakutiya), NE Russian Federation
Kazakhskaya SSR/Kazakh Soviet Socialist Republic see Kazakhstan
Kazakhstan 114 B4 off. Republic of Kazakhstan, var. Kazakstan, Kaz. Qazaqstan, Qazaqstan Respublikasy; prev. Kazakh Soviet Socialist Republic, Rus. Kazakhskaya SSR. country C Asia

KAZAKHSTAN
Central Asia

Official name Republic of Kazakhstan
Formation 1991 / 1991
Capital Astana

KAZAKHSTAN
(continued)

Population 14.8 million / 14 people per sq mile (5 people per sq km) / 56%
Total area 1,049,150 sq. miles (2,717,300 sq. km)
Languages Kazakh*, Russian, Ukrainian, German, Uzbek, Tatar, Uighur
Religions Muslim (mainly Sunni) 47%, Orthodox Christian 44%, Other 9%
Ethnic mix Kazakh 57%, Russian 27%, Other 8%, Uzbek 3%, Ukrainian 3%, German 2%
Government Presidential system
Currency Tenge = 100 tiyn
Literacy rate 99%
Calorie consumption 2677 calories

Kazakhstan, Republic of see Kazakhstan
Kazakh Uplands 114 C4 Eng. Kazakh Uplands, Kirghiz Steppe, Kaz. Saryarqa. uplands C Kazakhstan
Kazakh Uplands see Kazakhskiy Melkosopochnik
Kazakstan see Kazakhstan
Kazan' 111 C5 Respublika Tatarstan, W Russian Federation
Kazandzhik see Bereket
Kazanlik see Kazanlŭk
Kazanlŭk 104 D2 prev. Kazanlik. Stara Zagora, C Bulgaria
Kazatin see Kozyatyn
Kazbegi see Kazbek
Kazbek 117 F1 var. Kazbegi, Geor. Mqinvartsveri. mountain N Georgia
Kazerún 120 D4 Fārs, S Iran
Kazi Magomed see Qazimämmäd
Kazvin see Qazvin
Kéa see Tziá
Kéa see Ioulís
Kea, Mauna 47 B8 mountain Hawai'i, USA
Kéamu see Aneityum
Kearney 45 E4 Nebraska, C USA
Keban Barajı 117 E3 reservoir C Turkey
Kebkabiya 72 A4 Northern Darfur, W Sudan
Kebnekaise 84 C3 mountain N Sweden
Kecskemét 99 D7 Bács-Kiskun, C Hungary
Kediri 138 D5 Jawa, C Indonesia
Kędzierzyn-Kozle 99 C5 Ger. Heydebrech. Opolskie, S Poland
Keelung see Chilung
Keetmanshoop 78 B4 Karas, S Namibia
Kefallinía see Kefallonía
Kefallonía 105 A5 var. Kefallinía. island Iónia Nisiá, Greece, C Mediterranean Sea
Kefe see Feodosiya
Kegel see Keila
Kehl 95 A6 Baden-Württemberg, SW Germany
Kei Islands see Kai, Kepulauan
Keijō see Sŏul
Keila 106 D2 Ger. Kegel. Harjumaa, NW Estonia
Keïta 75 F3 Tahoua, C Niger
Keith 149 B7 South Australia
Kёk-Art 123 G2 prev. Alaykel', Alay-Kuu. Oshskaya Oblast', SW Kyrgyzstan
Kékes 99 C6 mountain N Hungary
Kelamayi see Karamay
Kelang see Klang
Kelat see Kālat
Kelifskiy Uzboy see Kelif Uzboŷy
Kelif Uzboŷy 122 D3 Rus. Kelifskiy Uzboy. salt marsh E Turkmenistan
Kelkit Çayı 117 E3 river N Turkey
Kelmė 106 B4 Šiaulai, C Lithuania
Kélo 76 B4 Tandjilé, SW Chad
Kelowna 37 E5 British Columbia, SW Canada
Kelso 46 B2 Washington, NW USA
Keltsy see Kielce
Keluang 138 B3 var. Kluang. Johor, Peninsular Malaysia
Kem' 110 B3 Respublika Kareliya, NW Russian Federation
Kemah 117 E3 Erzincan, E Turkey
Kemaman see Cukai
Kemerovo 114 D4 prev. Shcheglovsk. Kemerovskaya Oblast', C Russian Federation

Kemi 84 D4 Lappi, NW Finland
Kemijärvi 84 D3 Swe. Kemiträsk. Lappi, N Finland
Kemijoki 84 D3 river NW Finland
Kemin 123 G2 prev. Bystrovka. Chuyskaya Oblast', N Kyrgyzstan
Kemins Island see Nikumaroro
Kemiträsk see Kemijärvi
Kemmuna see Comino
Kempele 84 D4 Oulu, C Finland
Kempten 95 B7 Bayern, S Germany
Kendal 89 D5 NW England, United Kingdom
Kendari 139 E4 Sulawesi, C Indonesia
Kenedy 49 G4 Texas, SW USA
Kenema 74 C4 SE Sierra Leone
Këneurgench see Köneürgenç
Kenge 77 C6 Bandundu, SW Dem. Rep. Congo
Keng Tung 136 C3 var. Kentung. Shan State, E Burma (Myanmar)
Kénitra 70 C2 prev. Port-Lyautey. NW Morocco
Kennett 45 H5 Missouri, C USA
Kennewick 46 C2 Washington, NW USA
Kenora 38 A3 Ontario, S Canada
Kenosha 40 B3 Wisconsin, N USA
Kentau 114 B5 Yuzhnyy Kazakhstan, S Kazakhstan
Kentucky 40 C5 off. Commonwealth of Kentucky, also known as Bluegrass State. state C USA
Kentucky Lake 40 B5 reservoir Kentucky/Tennessee, S USA
Kentung see Keng Tung
Kenya 73 C6 off. Republic of Kenya. country E Africa

KENYA
East Africa

Official name Republic of Kenya
Formation 1963 / 1963
Capital Nairobi
Population 36 million / 164 people per sq mile (63 people per sq km) / 40%
Total area 224,961 sq. miles (582,650 sq. km)
Languages Kiswahili*, English*, Kikuyu, Luo, Kalenjin, Kamba
Religions Christian 60%, Traditional beliefs 25%, Other 9%, Muslim 6%
Ethnic mix Other 34%, Kikuyu 20%, Luhya 14%, Luo 13%, Kalenjin 11%, Kamba 11%
Government Mixed Presidential–Parliamentary system
Currency Kenya shilling = 100 cents
Literacy rate 74%
Calorie consumption 2090 calories

Kenya, Mount see Kirinyaga
Kenya, Republic of see Kenya
Keokuk 45 G4 Iowa, C USA
Kéos see Tziá
Kępno 98 C4 Wielkopolskie, C Poland
Keppel Island see Niuatoputapu
Kerak see Al Karak
Kerala 132 C2 cultural region S India
Kerasunt see Giresun
Keratéa 105 C6 var. Keratea. Attikí, C Greece
Keratea see Keratéa
Kerbala/Kerbela see Karbalā'
Kerch 109 G5 Rus. Kerch'. Respublika Krym, SE Ukraine
Kerch' see Kerch
Kerchens'ka Protska/Kerchenskiy Proliv see Kerch Strait
Kerch Strait 109 G4 var. Bosporus Cimmerius, Enikale Strait, Rus. Kerchenskiy Proliv, Ukr. Kerchens'ka Protska. strait Black Sea/Sea of Azov
Keremitlik see Lyulyakovo
Kerguelen 141 C7 island C French Southern and Antarctic Territories
Kerguelen Plateau 141 C7 undersea plateau S Indian Ocean
Keri 105 A6 Zákynthos, Iónia Nisiá, Greece, C Mediterranean Sea
Kerikeri 150 D2 Northland, North Island, New Zealand
Kerkenah, Îles de 102 D4 var. Kerkenna Islands, Ar. Juzur Qarqannah. island group E Tunisia

Kerkenna Islands see Kerkenah, Îles de
Kerki see Atamyrat
Kérkira see Kérkyra
Kerkrade 87 D6 Limburg, SE Netherlands
Kerkuk see Kirkūk
Kérkyra 104 A4 var. Kérkira, Eng. Corfu. Kérkyra, Iónia Nisiá, Greece, C Mediterranean Sea
Kermadec Islands 152 C4 island group New Zealand, SW Pacific Ocean
Kermadec Trench 143 E4 trench SW Pacific Ocean
Kermān 120 D3 var. Kirman; anc. Carmana. Kermān, C Iran
Kermānshāh 120 C3 var. Qahremānshahr; prev. Bākhtarān. Kermānshāhān, W Iran
Kerrville 49 F4 Texas, SW USA
Kertel see Kärdla
Kerulen 127 E2 Chin. Herlen He, Mong. Herlen Gol. river China/Mongolia
Kerýneia see Girne
Kesennuma 130 D4 Miyagi, Honshū, C Japan
Keszthely 99 C7 Zala, SW Hungary
Ketchikan 36 D4 Revillagigedo Island, Alaska, USA
Kętrzyn 98 D2 Ger. Rastenburg. Warmińsko-Mazurskie, NE Poland
Kettering 89 D6 C England, United Kingdom
Kettering 40 C4 Ohio, N USA
Keupriya see Primorsko
Keuruu 85 D5 Länsi-Suomi, C Finland
Keweenaw Peninsula 40 B1 peninsula Michigan, N USA
Key Largo 43 F5 Key Largo, Florida, SE USA
Keystone State see Pennsylvania
Key West 43 E5 Florida Keys, Florida, SE USA
Kezdivásárhely see Târgu Secuiesc
Khabarovsk 115 G4 Khabarovskiy Kray, SE Russian Federation
Khachmas see Xaçmaz
Khadera see Hadera
Khairpur 134 B3 Sind, SE Pakistan
Khalij as Suways 72 B2 var. Suez, Gulf of. gulf NE Egypt
Khalkidhikí see Chalkidikí
Khalkís see Chalkída
Gulf of Khambhat 134 C4 Eng. Gulf of Cambay. gulf W India
Khamis Mushayt 121 B6 var. Hamīs Musait. 'Asīr, SW Saudi Arabia
Khānābād 123 E3 Kunduz, NE Afghanistan
Khān al Baghdādī see Al Baghdādī
Khandwa 134 D4 Madhya Pradesh, C India
Khanh Hung see Soc Trăng
Khaniá see Chaniá
Khanka, Lake 129 E2 var. Hsing-K'ai Hu, Lake Hanka, Chin. Xingkai Hu, Rus. Ozero Khanka. lake China/Russian Federation
Khanka, Ozero see Khanka, Lake
Khankendi see Xankändi
Khanthabouli 136 D4 prev. Savannakhét. Savannakhét, S Laos
Khanty-Mansiysk 114 C3 prev. Ostyako-Voguls'k. Khanty-Mansiyskiy Avtonomnyy Okrug-Yugra, C Russian Federation
Khān Yūnis 119 A7 var. Khān Yūnus. S Gaza Strip
Khān Yūnus see Khān Yūnis
Khanzi see Ghanzi
Kharagpur 135 F4 West Bengal, NE India
Harbin see Harbin
Kharkiv 109 G2 Rus. Khar'kov. Kharkivs'ka Oblast', NE Ukraine
Khar'kov see Kharkiv
Kharmanli 104 D3 Khaskovo, S Bulgaria
Khartoum 72 B4 var. El Khartûm, Khartum. country capital (Sudan) (Sudan) Khartoum, C Sudan
Khartum see Khartoum
Khasavyurt 111 B8 Respublika Dagestan, SW Russian Federation
Khash, Dasht-e 122 D5 Eng. Khash Desert. desert SW Afghanistan
Khash Desert see Khash, Dasht-e
Khashim Al Qirba/Khashm al Qirbah see Khashm el Girba

Khashm el Girba *72 C4 var.* Khashim Al Qirba, Khashm al Qirbah. Kassala, E Sudan
Khaskovo *104 D3* Khaskovo, S Bulgaria
Khaybar, Kowtal-e *see* Khyber Pass
Khaydarkan *123 F2 var.* Khaydarken. Batkenskaya Oblast', SW Kyrgyzstan
Khaydarken *see* Khaydarkan
Khazar, Baḥr-e/Khazar, Daryā-ye *see* Caspian Sea
Khelat *see* Kālat
Kherson *109 E4* Khersons'ka Oblast', S Ukraine
Kheta *115 E2 river* N Russian Federation
Khíos *see* Chíos
Khirbet el 'Aujâ et Taḥtâ *119 E7* E West Bank Asia
Khiva/Khiwa *see* Xiva
Khmel'nitskiy *see* Khmel 'nyts'kyy
Khmel 'nyts'kyy *108 C2 Rus.* Khmel'nitskiy; *prev.* Proskurov. Khmel'nyts'ka Oblast', W Ukraine
Khodasy *107 E6 Rus.* Khodosy. Mahilyowskaya Voblasts', E Belarus
Khodoriv *108 C2 Pol.* Chodorów, *Rus.* Khodorov. L'vivs'ka Oblast', NW Ukraine
Khodorov *see* Khodoriv
Khodosy *see* Khodasy
Khodzhent *see* Khujand
Khoi *see* Khvoy
Khojend *see* Khujand
Khokand *see* Qo'qon
Kholm *123 E3 var.* Tashqurghan, *Pash.* Khulm. Balkh, N Afghanistan
Kholm *see* Chełm
Kholon *see* Holon
Khoms *see* Al Khums
Khong Sedone *see* Muang Khôngxédôn
Khon Kaen *136 D4 var.* Muang Khon Kaen. Khon Kaen, E Thailand
Khor *115 G4* Khabarovskiy Kray, SE Russian Federation
Khorat *see* Nakhon Ratchasima
Khorog *see* Khorugh
Khorugh *123 F3 Rus.* Khorog. S Tajikistan
Khotan *see* Hotan
Khouribga *70 B2* C Morocco
Khovd *see* Hovd
Khowst *123 F4* Khowst, E Afghanistan
Khoy *see* Khvoy
Khoyniki *107 D8* Homyel'skaya Voblasts', SE Belarus
Khudzhand *see* Khujand
Khujand *123 E2 var.* Khodzhent, Khojend, *Rus.* Khudzhand; *prev.* Leninabad, *Taj.* Leninobod. N Tajikistan
Khulm *see* Kholm
Khulna *135 G4* Khulna, SW Bangladesh
Khums *see* Al Khums
Khust *108 B3 var.* Husté, *Cz.* Chust, *Hung.* Huszt. Zakarpats'ka Oblast', W Ukraine
Khvoy *120 C2 var.* Khoi, Khoy. Āzarbāyjān-e Bākhtarī, NW Iran
Khyber Pass *134 C1 var.* Kowtal-e Khaybar. *pass* Afghanistan/Pakistan
Kiangmai *see* Chiang Mai
Kiang-ning *see* Nanjing
Kiangsi *see* Jiangxi
Kiangsu *see* Jiangsu
Kiáto *105 B6 prev.* Kiáton. Pelopónnisos, S Greece
Kiáton *see* Kiáto
Kiayi *see* Chiai
Kibangou *77 B6* Niari, SW Congo
Kibombo *77 D6* Maniema, E Dem. Rep. Congo
Kibris/Kıbrıs Cumhuriyeti *see* Cyprus
Kičevo *101 D6* SW FYR Macedonia
Kidderminster *89 D6* C England, United Kingdom
Kiel *94 B2* Schleswig-Holstein, N Germany
Kielce *98 D4 Rus.* Keltsy. Świętokrzyskie, C Poland
Kieler Bucht *94 B2 bay* N Germany
Kiev *see* Kyyiv
Kiev Reservoir *109 E1 Eng.* Kiev Reservoir, *Rus.* Kiyevskoye Vodokhranilishche. *reservoir* N Ukraine
Kiev Reservoir *see* Kyyivs'ke Vodokhovyshche
Kiffa *74 C3* Assaba, S Mauritania

Kigali *73 B6 country capital* (Rwanda) (Rwanda) C Rwanda
Kigoma *73 B7* Kigoma, W Tanzania
Kihnu *106 C2 var.* Kihnu Saar, *Ger.* Kühnö. *island* SW Estonia
Kihnu Saar *see* Kihnu
Kii-suido *131 C7 strait* S Japan
Kikinda *100 D3 Ger.* Grosskikinda, *Hung.* Nagykikinda; *prev.* Velika Kikinda. Vojvodina, N Serbia
Kikládhes *see* Kykládes
Kikwit *77 C6* Bandundu, W Dem. Rep. Congo
Kilien Mountains *see* Qilian Shan
Kilimane *see* Quelimane
Kilimanjaro *69 E5 region* E Tanzania
Kilimanjaro *73 C7 var.* Uhuru Peak. *volcano* NE Tanzania
Kilingi-Nõmme *106 D3 Ger.* Kurkund. Pärnumaa, SW Estonia
Kilis *116 D4* Kilis, S Turkey
Kiliya *108 D4 Rom.* Chilia-Nouă. Odes'ka Oblast', SW Ukraine
Kilkenny *89 B6 Ir.* Cill Chainnigh. Kilkenny, S Ireland
Kilkís *104 B3* Kentrikí Makedonía, N Greece
Killarney *89 A6 Ir.* Cill Airne. Kerry, SW Ireland
Killeen *49 G3* Texas, SW USA
Kilmain *see* Quelimane
Kilmarnock *88 C4* W Scotland, United Kingdom
Kilwa *see* Kilwa Kivinje
Kilwa Kivinje *73 C7 var.* Kilwa. Lindi, SE Tanzania
Kimberley *78 C4* Northern Cape, C South Africa
Kimberley Plateau *146 C3 plateau* Western Australia
Kimch'aek *129 E3 prev.* Sŏngjin. E North Korea
Kími *see* Kými
Kinabalu, Gunung *138 D3 mountain* East Malaysia
Kindersley *37 F5* Saskatchewan, S Canada
Kindia *74 C4* Guinée-Maritime, SW Guinea
Kindley Field *42 A4 air base* E Bermuda
Kindu *77 D6 prev.* Kindu-Port-Empain. Maniema, C Dem. Rep. Congo
Kindu-Port-Empain *see* Kindu
Kineshma *111 C5* Ivanovskaya Oblast', W Russian Federation
King Charles Islands *see* Kong Karls Land
King Christian IX Land *see* Kong Christian IX Land
King Frederik VI Coast *see* Kong Frederik VI Kyst
King Frederik VIII Land *see* Kong Frederik VIII Land
King Island *149 B8 island* Tasmania, SE Australia
King Island *see* Kadan Kyun
Kingissepp *see* Kuressaare
Kingman *48 A1* Arizona, SW USA
Kingman Reef *145 E2 US territory* C Pacific Ocean
Kingsford Smith *148 E2* (Sydney) New South Wales, SE Australia
King's Lynn *89 E6 var.* Bishop's Lynn, Kings Lynn, Lynn, Lynn Regis. E England, United Kingdom
Kings Lynn *see* King's Lynn
King Sound *146 B3 sound* Western Australia
Kingsport *43 E1* Tennessee, S USA
Kingston *54 B5 country capital* (Jamaica) (Jamaica) E Jamaica
Kingston *38 D5* Ontario, SE Canada
Kingston *41 F3* New York, NE USA
Kingston upon Hull *89 D5 var.* Hull. E England, United Kingdom
Kingston upon Thames *89 A8* SE England, United Kingdom
Kingstown *55 H4 country capital* (Saint Vincent and the Grenadines) (Saint Vincent and the Grenadines) Saint Vincent, Saint Vincent and the Grenadines
Kingstown *see* Dún Laoghaire
Kingsville *49 G5* Texas, SW USA
King William Island *37 F3 island* Nunavut, N Canada
Kinneret, Yam *see* Tiberias, Lake

Kinrooi *87 D5* Limburg, NE Belgium
Kinshasa *77 B6 prev.* Léopoldville. *country capital* (Dem. Rep. Congo) Kinshasa, W Dem. Rep. Congo
Kintyre *88 B4 peninsula* W Scotland, United Kingdom
Kinyeti *73 B5 mountain* S Sudan
Kiparissía *see* Kyparissía
Kipili *73 B7* Rukwa, W Tanzania
Kipushi *77 D8* Katanga, SE Dem. Rep. Congo
Kirdzhali *see* Kŭrdzhali
Kirghizia *see* Kyrgyzstan
Kirghiz Range *123 F2 Rus.* Kirgizskiy Khrebet; *prev.* Alexander Range. *mountain range* Kazakhstan/Kyrgyzstan
Kirghiz SSR *see* Kyrgyzstan
Kirghiz Steppe *see* Kazakhskiy Melkosopochnik
Kirgizskaya SSR *see* Kyrgyzstan
Kirgizskiy Khrebet *see* Kirghiz Range
Kiriath-Arba *see* Hebron
Kiribati *145 F2 off.* Republic of Kiribati. *country* C Pacific Ocean

---

KIRIBATI
Australasia & Oceania

Official name Republic of Kiribati
Formation 1979 / 1979
Capital Bairiki (Tarawa Atoll)
Population 107,817 / 393 people per sq mile (152 people per sq km) / 49%
Total area 277 sq. miles (717 sq. km)
Languages English*, Kiribati
Religions Roman Catholic 53%, Kiribati Protestant Church 39%, Other 8%
Ethnic mix Micronesian 99%, Other 1%
Government Nonparty system
Currency Australian dollar = 100 cents
Literacy rate 99%
Calorie consumption 2859 calories

Kiribati, Republic of *see* Kiribati
Kırıkhan *116 D4* Hatay, S Turkey
Kırıkkale *116 C3 province* C Turkey
Kirin *see* Jilin
Kirinyaga *73 C6 prev.* Mount Kenya. *volcano* C Kenya
Kirishi *110 B4 var.* Kirisi. Leningradskaya Oblast', NW Russian Federation
Kirisi *see* Kirishi
Kiritimati *145 G2 prev.* Christmas Island. *atoll* Line Islands, E Kiribati
Kirkenes *84 E2 Fin.* Kirkkoniemi. Finnmark, N Norway
Kirk-Kilissa *see* Kırklareli
Kirkkoniemi *see* Kirkenes
Kirkland Lake *38 D4* Ontario, S Canada
Kırklareli *116 A2 prev.* Kirk-Kilissa. Kırklareli, NW Turkey
Kirkpatrick, Mount *154 B3 mountain* Antarctica
Kirksville *45 G4* Missouri, C USA
Kirkūk *120 B3 var.* Karkūk, Kerkuk. At Ta'mīn, N Iraq
Kirkwall *88 C2* NE Scotland, United Kingdom
Kirkwood *45 G4* Missouri, C USA
Kir Moab/Kir of Moab *see* Al Karak
Kirov *111 C5 prev.* Vyatka. Kirovskaya Oblast', NW Russian Federation
Kirovabad *see* Gäncä
Kirovakan *see* Vanadzor
Kirovo-Chepetsk *111 D5* Kirovskaya Oblast', NW Russian Federation
Kirovohrad *109 E3 Rus.* Kirovograd; *prev.* Kirovo, Yelizavetgrad, Zinov'yevsk. Kirovohrads'ka Oblast', C Ukraine
Kirovo/Kirovograd *see* Kirovohrad
Kŭrthar Range *134 B3 mountain range* S Pakistan
Kiruna *84 C3 Lapp.* Giron. Norrbotten, N Sweden
Kirun/Kirun' *see* Chilung
Kisalföld *see* Little Alföld
Kisangani *77 D5 prev.* Stanleyville. Orientale, NE Dem. Rep. Congo
Kishinev *see* Chişinău
Kislovodsk *111 B7* Stavropol'skiy Kray, SW Russian Federation
Kismaayo *73 D6 var.* Chisimayu, Kismayu, *It.* Chisimaio. Jubbada Hoose, S Somalia
Kismayu *see* Kismaayo

Kíssamos *105 C7 prev.* Kastélli. Kríti, Greece, E Mediterranean Sea
Kissidougou *74 C4* Guinée-Forestière, S Guinea
Kissimmee, Lake *43 E4* lake Florida, SE USA
Kistna *see* Krishna
Kisumu *73 C6 prev.* Port Florence. Nyanza, W Kenya
Kisvárda *99 E6 Ger.* Kleinwardein. Szabolcs-Szatmár-Bereg, E Hungary
Kita *74 D3* Kayes, W Mali
Kitab *see* Kitob
Kitakyūshū *131 A7 var.* Kitakyūsyū. Fukuoka, Kyūshū, SW Japan
Kitakyūsyū *see* Kitakyūshū
Kitami *130 D2* Hokkaidō, NE Japan
Kitchener *38 C5* Ontario, S Canada
Kíthnos *see* Kýthnos
Kitimat *36 D4* British Columbia, SW Canada
Kitinen *84 D3 river* N Finland
Kitob *123 E3 Rus.* Kitab. Qashqadaryo Viloyati, S Uzbekistan
Kitwe *78 D2 var.* Kitwe-Nkana. Copperbelt, C Zambia
Kitwe-Nkana *see* Kitwe
Kitzbüheler Alpen *95 C7 mountain range* W Austria
Kivalina *36 C2* Alaska, USA
Kivalo *84 D3 ridge* C Finland
Kivertsi *108 C1 Pol.* Kiwerce, *Rus.* Kivertsy. Volyns'ka Oblast', NW Ukraine
Kivertsy *see* Kivertsi
Kivu, Lac *see* Kivu, Lake
Kivu, Lake *77 E6 Fr.* Lac Kivu. *lake* Rwanda/Dem. Rep. Congo
Kiwerce *see* Kivertsi
Kiyev *see* Kyyiv
Kiyevskoye Vodokhranilishche *see* Kyyivs'ke Vodokhovyshche
Kızıl Irmak *116 C3 river* C Turkey
Kizil Kum *see* Kyzyl Kum
Kizyl-Arvat *see* Serdar
Kjølen *see* Kölen
Kladno *99 A5* Středočeský, NW Czech Republic
Klagenfurt *95 D7 Slvn.* Celovec. Kärnten, S Austria
Klaipėda *106 B3 Ger.* Memel. Klaipėda, NW Lithuania
Klamath Falls *46 B4* Oregon, NW USA
Klamath Mountains *46 A4 mountain range* California/Oregon, W USA
Klang *138 B3 var.* Kelang; *prev.* Port Swettenham. Selangor, Peninsular Malaysia
Klarälven *85 B6 river* Norway/Sweden
Klatovy *99 A5 Ger.* Klattau. Plzeňský Kraj, W Czech Republic
Klattau *see* Klatovy
Klausenburg *see* Cluj-Napoca
Klazienaveen *86 E2* Drenthe, NE Netherlands
Kleines Ungarisches Tiefland *see* Little Alföld
Klein Karas *78 B4* Karas, S Namibia
Kleinwardein *see* Kisvárda
Kleisoúra *105 A5* Ípeiros, W Greece
Klerksdorp *78 D4* North-West, N South Africa
Klimavichy *107 E7 Rus.* Klimovichi. Mahilyowskaya Voblasts', E Belarus
Klimovichi *see* Klimavichy
Klintsy *111 A5* Bryanskaya Oblast', W Russian Federation
Klisura *104 D2* Plovdiv, C Bulgaria
Ključ *100 B3* Federacija Bosna I Hercegovina, NW Bosnia and Herzegovina
Kłobuck *98 C4* Śląskie, S Poland
Klosters *95 B7* Graubünden, SE Switzerland
Kluang *see* Keluang
Kluczbork *98 C4 Ger.* Kreuzburg, Kreuzburg in Oberschlesien. Opolskie, S Poland
Klyuchevskaya Sopka, Vulkan *115 H3 volcano* E Russian Federation
Knin *100 B4* Šibenik-Knin, S Croatia
Knjaževac *100 E4* Serbia, E Serbia
Knokke-Heist *87 A5* West-Vlaanderen, NW Belgium
Knoxville *42 D1* Tennessee, S USA
Knud Rasmussen Land *82 D1 physical region* N Greenland
Kobdo *see* Hovd

Kōbe *131 C6* Hyōgo, Honshū, SW Japan
København *85 B7* Eng. Copenhagen; anc. Hafnia. *country capital* (Denmark) (Denmark) Sjælland, København, E Denmark
Kobenni *74 D3* Hodh el Gharbi, S Mauritania
Koblenz *95 A5* prev. Coblenz, Fr. Coblence; anc. Confluentes. Rheinland-Pfalz, W Germany
Kobrin *see* Kobryn
Kobryn *107 A6* Rus. Kobrin. Brestskaya Voblasts', SW Belarus
K'obulet'i *117 F2* W Georgia
Kočani *101 E6* NE FYR Macedonia
Kočevje *95 D8* Ger. Gottschee. S Slovenia
Koch Bihār *135 G3* West Bengal, NE India
Kochchi Cochin/Kochi
Kōchi *131 B7* var. Kôti. Kōchi, Shikoku, SW Japan
Kochiu *see* Gejiu
Kodiak *36 C3* Kodiak Island, Alaska, USA
Kodiak Island *36 C3* island Alaska, USA
Koedoes *see* Kudus
Koeln *see* Köln
Koepang *see* Kupang
Ko-erh-mu *see* Golmud
Koetai *see* Mahakam, Sungai
Koetaradja *see* Bandaaceh
Kōfu *131 D5* var. Kôhu. Yamanashi, Honshū, S Japan
Kogarah *148 E2* New South Wales, E Australia
Kogon *122 D2* Rus. Kagan. Buxoro Viloyati, C Uzbekistan
Kōhalom *see* Rupea
Kohīma *135 H3* state capital Nāgāland, E India
Koh I Noh *see* Büyükağrı Dağı
Kohtla-Järve *106 E2* Ida-Virumaa, NE Estonia
Kôhu *see* Kōfu
Kokand *see* Qo'qon
Kokchetav *see* Kokshetau
Kokkola *84 D4* Swe. Karleby; prev. Swe. Gamlakarleby. Länsi-Suomi, W Finland
Koko *75 F4* Kebbi, W Nigeria
Kokomo *40 C4* Indiana, N USA
Koko Nor *see* Qinghai, China
Koko Nor *see* Qinghai Hu, China
Kokrines *36 C2* Alaska, USA
Kokshaal-Tau *123 G2* Rus. Khrebet Kakshaal-Too. mountain range China/Kyrgyzstan
Kokshetau *114 C4* Kaz. Kökshetaü; prev. Kokchetav. Kokshetau, N Kazakhstan
Kökshetaü *see* Kokshetau
Koksijde *87 A5* West-Vlaanderen, W Belgium
Koksoak *38 D2* river Québec, E Canada
Kokstad *78 D5* KwaZulu/Natal, E South Africa
Kolaka *139 E4* Sulawesi, C Indonesia
K'o-la-ma-i *see* Karamay
Kola Peninsula *110 E2* Eng. Kola Peninsula. peninsula NW Russian Federation
Kola Peninsula *see* Kol'skiy Poluostrov
Kolari *84 D3* Lappi, NW Finland
Kolárovo *99 C6* Ger. Gutta; prev. Guta, Hung. Gúta. Nitriansky Kraj, SW Slovakia
Kolberg *see* Kołobrzeg
Kolda *74 C3* S Senegal
Kolding *85 A7* Vejle, C Denmark
Kölen *81 E1* Nor. Kjølen. mountain range Norway/Sweden
Kolguyev, Ostrov *110 C2* island NW Russian Federation
Kolhāpur *132 B1* Mahārāshtra, SW India
Kolhumadulu *132 A5* var. Thaa Atoll. atoll S Maldives
Kolín *99 B5* Ger. Kolin. Středni Čechy, C Czech Republic
Kolka *106 C2* Talsi, NW Latvia
Kolkasrags *106 C2* prev. Eng. Cape Domesnes. headland NW Latvia
Kolmar *see* Colmar
Köln *94 A4* var. Koeln, Eng./Fr. Cologne, prev. Cöln; anc. Colonia Agrippina, Oppidum Ubiorum. Nordrhein-Westfalen, W Germany
Koło *98 C3* Wielkopolskie, C Poland

Kołobrzeg *98 B2* Ger. Kolberg. Zachodnio-pomorskie, NW Poland
Kolokani *74 D3* Koulikoro, W Mali
Kolomea *see* Kolomyya
Kolomna *111 B5* Moskovskaya Oblast', W Russian Federation
Kolomyya *108 C3* Ger. Kolomea. Ivano-Frankivs'ka Oblast', W Ukraine
Kolosjoki *see* Nikel
Kolozsvár *see* Cluj-Napoca
Kolpa *100 A2* Ger. Kulpa, SCr. Kupa. river Croatia/Slovenia
Kolpino *110 B4* Leningradskaya Oblast', NW Russian Federation
Kólpos Mórfu *see* Güzelyurt
Kolwezi *77 D7* Katanga, S Dem. Rep. Congo
Kolyma *115 G2* river NE Russian Federation
Komatsu *131 C5* var. Komatu. Ishikawa, Honshū, SW Japan
Komatu *see* Komatsu
Kommunizm, Qullai *see* Ismoili Somoní, Qullai
Komoé *75 E4* var. Komoé Fleuve. river E Côte d'Ivoire
Komoé Fleuve *see* Komoé
Komotau *see* Chomutov
Komotiní *104 D3* var. Gümüljina, Turk. Gümülcine. Anatolikí Makedonía kai Thráki, NE Greece
Kompong *see* Kâmpóng Chhnāng
Kompong Cham *see* Kâmpóng Cham
Kompong Som *see* Kâmpóng Saôm
Kompong Speu *see* Kâmpóng Spoe
Komrat *see* Comrat
Komsomolets, Ostrov *115 E1* island Severnaya Zemlya, N Russian Federation
Komsomol'sk-na-Amure *115 G4* Khabarovskiy Kray, SE Russian Federation
Kondolovo *104 E3* Burgas, E Bulgaria
Kondopoga *110 B3* Respublika Kareliya, NW Russian Federation
Kondoz *123 E3* Pash. Kunduz. province NE Afghanistan
Köneürgenç *122 C2* var. Köneürgench, Rus. Këneurgench; prev. Kunya-Urgench. Daşoguz Welayaty, N Turkmenistan
Kong Christian IX Land *82 D4* Eng. King Christian IX Land. physical region SE Greenland
Kong Frederik IX Land *82 C3* physical region SW Greenland
Kong Frederik VIII Land *83 E2* Eng. King Frederik VIII Land. physical region NE Greenland
Kong Frederik VI Kyst *82 C4* Eng. King Frederik VI Coast. physical region SE Greenland
Kong Karls Land *83 G2* Eng. King Charles Islands. island group SE Svalbard
Kongo *see* Congo (river)
Kongolo *77 D6* Katanga, E Dem. Rep. Congo
Kongor *73 B5* Jonglei, SE Sudan
Kong Oscar Fjord *83 E3* fjord E Greenland
Kongsberg *85 B6* Buskerud, S Norway
Kông, Tônle *137 E5* var. Xê Kong. river Cambodia/Laos
Kong, Xê *see* Kông, Tônle
Königgrätz *see* Hradec Králové
Königshütte *see* Chorzów
Konin *98 C4* Ger. Kuhnau. Weilkopolskie, C Poland
Koninkrijk der Nederlanden *see* Netherlands
Konispol *101 C7* var. Konispoli. Vlorë, S Albania
Konispoli *see* Konispol
Kónitsa *104 A4* Ípeiros, W Greece
Konitz *see* Chojnice
Konjic *100 C4* Federacija Bosna I Hercegovina, S Bosnia and Herzegovina
Konosha *111 C4* Arkhangel'skaya Oblast', NW Russian Federation
Konotop *109 F1* Sums'ka Oblast', NE Ukraine
Konstantinovka *see* Kostyantynivka
Konstanz *95 B7* var. Constanz, Eng. Constance, hist. Kostnitz; anc. Constantia. Baden-Württemberg, S Germany

Konstanza *see* Constanţa
Konya *116 C4* var. Konieh, prev. Konia; anc. Iconium. Konya, C Turkey
Kopaonik *101 D5* mountain range S Serbia
Kopar *see* Koper
Koper *95 D8* It. Capodistria; prev. Kopar. SW Slovenia
Köpetdag Gershi *122 C3* mountain range Iran/Turkmenistan
Köpetdag Gershi/Kopetdag, Khrebet *see* Koppeh Dagh
Koppeh Dagh *120 D2* Rus. Khrebet Kopetdag, Turkm. Köpetdag Gershi. mountain range Iran/Turkmenistan
Köprili *see* Koprivnica
Koprivnica *100 B2* Ger. Kopreinitz, Hung. Kaproncza. Koprivnica-Križevci, N Croatia
Köprülü *see* Veles
Koptsevichi *see* Kaptsevichy
Kopyl' *see* Kapyl'
Korat *see* Nakhon Ratchasima
Korat Plateau *136 D4* plateau E Thailand
Korba *135 E4* Chhattisgarh, C India
Korça *see* Korçë
Korçë *101 D6* var. Korça, Gk. Korytsa, It. Corriza; prev. Koritsa. Korçë, SE Albania
Korčula *100 B4* It. Curzola; anc. Corcyra Nigra. island S Croatia
Korea Bay *127 G3* bay China/North Korea
Korea, Democratic People's Republic of *see* North Korea
Korea, Republic of *see* South Korea
Korea Strait *131 A7* Jap. Chōsen-kaikyō, Kor. Taehan-haehyŏp. channel Japan/South Korea
Korhogo *74 D4* N Côte d'Ivoire
Kórinthos *105 B6* Eng. Corinth anc. Corinthus. Pelopónnisos, S Greece
Koritsa *see* Korçë
Kōriyama *131 D5* Fukushima, Honshū, C Japan
Korla *126 C3* Chin. K'u-erh-lo. Xinjiang Uygur Zizhiqu, NW China
Körmend *99 B7* Vas, W Hungary
Koróni *105 B6* Pelopónnisos, S Greece
Koror *144 A2* (Palau) Oreor, N Palau
Körös *see* Crişul
Korosten' *108 D1* Zhytomyrs'ka Oblast', NW Ukraine
Koro Toro *76 C2* Borkou-Ennedi-Tibesti, N Chad
Korsovka *see* Kārsava
Kortrijk *87 A6* Fr. Courtrai. West-Vlaanderen, W Belgium
Koryak Range *115 H2* var. Koryakskiy Khrebet, Eng. Koryak Range. mountain range NE Russian Federation
Koryak Range *see* Koryakskoye Nagor'ye
Koryakskiy Khrebet *see* Koryakskoye Nagor'ye
Koryazhma *111 C4* Arkhangel'skaya Oblast', NW Russian Federation
Korytsa *see* Korçë
Kos *105 E6* Kos, Dodekánisa, Greece, Aegean Sea
Kos *105 E6* It. Coo; anc. Cos. island Dodekánisa, Greece, Aegean Sea
Ko-saki *131 A7* headland Nagasaki, Tsushima, SW Japan
Kościan *98 B4* Ger. Kosten. Wielkopolskie, C Poland
Kościerzyna *98 C2* Pomorskie, NW Poland
Kosciuszko, Mount *see* Kosciuszko, Mount
Kosciuszko, Mount *149 C7* prev. Mount Kosciusko. mountain New South Wales, SE Australia
K'o-shih *see* Kashi
Koshikijima-rettō *131 A8* var. Kosikizima Rettō. island group SW Japan
Kōshū *see* Kwangju
Košice *99 D6* Ger. Kaschau, Hung. Kassa. Košický Kraj, E Slovakia
Kosikizima Rettō *see* Koshikijima-rettō
Köslin *see* Koszalin
Koson *123 E3* Rus. Kasan. Qashqadaryo Viloyati, S Uzbekistan
Kosovo *101 D5* prev. Autonomous Province of Kosovo and Metohija. country SE Europe

KOSOVO (not yet fully recognized)
Southeast Europe

Official name Republic of Kosovo
Formation 2008 / 2008
Capital Pristina
Population 2.1 million / 499 people per sq mile (193 people per sq km) / 40%
Total area 4212 sq miles (10 908 sq km)
Languages Albanian*, Serbian*, Bosniak, Gorani, Roma, Turkish
Religions Muslim 92%, Roman Catholic 4%, Orthodox Christian 4%
Ethnic mix Albanian 92%, Serb 4%, Bosniak and Gorani 2%, Turkish 1%, Roma 1%
Government Parliamentary system
Currency Euro = 100 cents
Literacy rate 92%
Calorie consumption Not available

Kosovo and Metohija, Autonomous Province of *see* Kosovo
Kosovo Polje *see* Fushë Kosovë
Kosovska Mitrovica *see* Mitrovicë
Kosrae *144 C2* prev. Kusaie. island Caroline Islands, E Micronesia
Kossou, Lac de *74 D5* lake C Ivory Coast
Kostanay *114 C4* var. Kustanay, Kaz. Qostanay. Kostanay, N Kazakhstan
Kosten *see* Kościan
Kostenets *104 C2* prev. Georgi Dimitrov. Sofiya, W Bulgaria
Kostnitz *see* Konstanz
Kostroma *110 B4* Kostromskaya Oblast', NW Russian Federation
Kostyantynivka *109 G3* Rus. Konstantinovka. Donets'ka Oblast', SE Ukraine
Kostyukovichi *see* Kastsyukovichy
Kostyukovka *see* Kastsyukowka
Koszalin *98 B2* Ger. Köslin. Zachodnio-pomorskie, NW Poland
Kota *134 D3* prev. Kotah. Rājasthān, N India
Kota Baharu *see* Kota Bharu
Kota Bahru *see* Kota Bharu
Kotabaru *see* Jayapura
Kota Bharu *138 B3* var. Kota Baharu, Kota Bahru. Kelantan, Peninsular Malaysia
Kotaboemi *see* Kotabumi
Kotabumi *138 B4* prev. Kotaboemi. Sumatera, W Indonesia
Kotah *see* Kota
Kota Kinabalu *138 D3* prev. Jesselton. Sabah, East Malaysia
Kotel'nyy, Ostrov *115 E2* island Novosibirskiye Ostrova, N Russian Federation
Kotka *85 E5* Etelä-Suomi, S Finland
Kotlas *110 C4* Arkhangel'skaya Oblast', NW Russian Federation
Kotonu *see* Cotonou
Kotor *101 C5* It. Cattaro. SW Montenegro
Kotovs'k *108 D3* Rus. Kotovsk. Odes'ka Oblast', SW Ukraine
Kotovsk *see* Hînceşti
Kottbus *see* Cottbus
Kotto *76 D4* river Central African Republic/Dem. Rep. Congo
Kotuy *115 E2* river N Russian Federation
Koudougou *75 E4* C Burkina Faso
Koulamoutou *77 B6* Ogooué-Lolo, C Gabon
Koulikoro *74 D3* Koulikoro, SW Mali
Koumra *76 C4* Moyen-Chari, S Chad
Kourou *59 H3* N French Guiana
Kousséier *see* Al Quşayr
Kousséri *76 B3* prev. Fort-Foureau. Extrême-Nord, NE Cameroon
Koutiala *74 D4* Sikasso, S Mali
Kouvola *85 E5* Etelä-Suomi, S Finland
Kovel' *108 C1* Pol. Kowel. Volyns'ka Oblast', NW Ukraine
Kovno *see* Kaunas
Koweit *see* Kuwait
Kowel *see* Kovel'
Kowloon *128 A2* Hong Kong, S China
Kowno *see* Kaunas
Kozáni *104 B4* Dytikí Makedonía, N Greece
Kozara *100 B3* mountain range NW Bosnia and Herzegovina

Kozarska Dubica *see* Bosanska Dubica
Kozu-shima *131 D6 island* E Japan
Kozyatyn *108 D2 Rus.* Kazatin.
Vinnyts'ka Oblast', C Ukraine
Kpalimé *75 E5 var.* Palimé. SW Togo
Krâchéh *137 D6 prev.* Kratie. Krâchéh,
E Cambodia
Kragujevac *100 D4* Serbia, C Serbia
Krainburg *see* Kranj
Kra, Isthmus of *137 B6 isthmus*
Malaysia/Thailand
Krakau *see* Kraków
Kraków *99 D5 Eng.* Cracow, Ger.
Krakau; *anc.* Cracovia. Małopolskie,
S Poland
Krâlänh *137 D5* Siĕmréab,
NW Cambodia
Kraljevo *100 D4 prev.* Rankovićevo.
Serbia, C Serbia
Kramators'k *109 G3 Rus.* Kramatorsk.
Donets'ka Oblast', SE Ukraine
Kramatorsk *see* Kramators'k
Kramfors *85 C5* Västernorrland,
C Sweden
Kranéa *see* Kraniá
Kraniá *104 B4 var.* Kranéa. Dytikí
Makedonía, N Greece
Kranj *95 D7 Ger.* Krainburg.
NW Slovenia
Kranz *see* Zelenogradsk
Kräslava *106 D4* Krāslava, SE Latvia
Krasnaye *107 C5 Rus.* Krasnoye.
Minskaya Voblasts', C Belarus
Krasnoarmeysk *111 C6* Saratovskaya
Oblast', W Russian Federation
Krasnodar *111 A7 prev.* Ekaterinodar,
Yekaterinodar. Krasnodarskiy Kray,
SW Russian Federation
Krasnodon *109 H3* Luhans'ka Oblast',
E Ukraine
Krasnogor *see* Kallaste
Krasnogvardeyskoye *see*
Krasnohvardiys'ke
Krasnohvardiys'ke *109 F4 Rus.*
Krasnogvardeyskoye. Respublika
Krym, S Ukraine
Krasnokamensk *115 F4* Chitinskaya
Oblast', S Russian Federation
Krasnokamsk *111 D5* Permskaya
Oblast', W Russian Federation
Krasnoperekops'k *109 F4 Rus.*
Krasnoperekopsk. Respublika Krym,
S Ukraine
Krasnoperekopsk *see* Krasnoperekops'k
Krasnostav *see* Krasnystaw
Krasnovodsk *see* Türkmenbaşy
Krasnovodskiy Zaliv *see* Türkmenbaşy
Aylagy
Krasnowodsk Aylagy *see* Türkmenbaşy
Aylagy
Krasnoyarsk *114 D4* Krasnoyarskiy
Kray, S Russian Federation
Krasnoye *see* Krasnaye
Krasnystaw *98 E4 Rus.* Krasnostav.
Lubelskie, SE Poland
Krasnyy Kut *111 C6* Saratovskaya
Oblast', W Russian Federation
Krasnyy Luch *109 H3 prev.*
Krindachevka. Luhans'ka Oblast',
E Ukraine
Kratie *see* Krâchéh
Krăvanh, Chuŏr Phnum *137 C6 Eng.*
Cardamom Mountains, *Fr.* Chaîne
des Cardamomes. *mountain range*
W Cambodia
Krefeld *94 A4* Nordrhein-Westfalen,
W Germany
Kreisstadt *see* Krosno Odrzańskie
Kremenchug *see* Kremenchuk
**Kremenchugskoye Vodokhranilishche/
Kremenchuk Reservoir** *see*
Kremenchuts'ke Vodokhovyshche
Kremenchuk *109 F2 Rus.* Kremenchug.
Poltavs'ka Oblast', NE Ukraine
Kremenchuk Reservoir *109 F2*
Eng. Kremenchuk Reservoir, *Rus.*
Kremenchugskoye Vodokhranilishche.
reservoir C Ukraine
Kremenets' *108 C2 Pol.* Krzemieniec,
Rus. Kremenets. Ternopil's'ka Oblast',
W Ukraine
Kremennaya *see* Kreminna
Kreminna *109 G2 Rus.* Kremennaya.
Luhans'ka Oblast', E Ukraine
Kresena *see* Kresna
Kresna *104 C3 var.* Kresena.
Blagoevgrad, SW Bulgaria

Kretikon Delagos *see* Kritikó Pélagos
Kretinga *106 B3 Ger.* Krottingen.
Klaipėda, NW Lithuania
Kreutz *see* Cristuru Secuiesc
Kreuz *see* Križevci, Croatia
Kreuz *see* Risti, Estonia
**Kreuzburg/Kreuzburg in
Oberschlesien** *see* Kluczbork
Krichëv *see* Krychaw
Krievija *see* Russian Federation
Krindachevka *see* Krasnyy Luch
Krishna *132 C1 prev.* Kistna. *river*
C India
Krishnagiri *132 C2* Tamil Nādu,
SE India
Kristiania *see* Oslo
Kristiansand *85 A6 var.* Christiansand.
Vest-Agder, S Norway
Kristianstad *85 B7* Skåne, S Sweden
Kristiansund *84 A4 var.* Christiansund.
Møre og Romsdal, S Norway
Krivoy Rog *see* Kryvyy Rih
Križevci *100 B2 Ger.* Kreuz, *Hung.*
Kőrös. Varaždin, NE Croatia
Krk *100 A3 It.* Veglia; *anc.* Curieta.
island NW Croatia
Kroatien *see* Croatia
Krolevets' *109 F1 Rus.* Krolevets.
Sums'ka Oblast', NE Ukraine
Krolevets *see* Krolevets'
Królewska Huta *see* Chorzów
Kronach *95 C5* Bayern, E Germany
Kronstadt *see* Braşov
Kroonstad *78 D4* Free State, C South
Africa
Kropotkin *111 A7* Krasnodarskiy Kray,
SW Russian Federation
Krosno *99 D5 Ger.* Krossen.
Podkarpackie, SE Poland
Krosno Odrzańskie *98 B3 Ger.* Crossen,
Kreisstadt. Lubuskie, W Poland
Krossen *see* Krosno
Krottingen *see* Kretinga
Krško *95 E8 Ger.* Gurkfeld; *prev.* Videm-
Krško. E Slovenia
Krugloye *see* Kruhlaye
Kruhlaye *107 D6 Rus.* Krugloye.
Mahilyowskaya Voblasts', E Belarus
Kruja *see* Krujë
Krujë *101 C6 var.* Kruja, *It.* Croia.
Durrës, C Albania
Krummau *see* Český Krumlov
Krung Thep, Ao *137 C5 var.* Bight of
Bangkok. *bay* S Thailand
Krung Thep Mahanakhon *see* Ao
Krung Thep
Krupki *107 D6* Minskaya Voblasts',
C Belarus
Krušné Hory *see* Erzgebirge
Krychaw *107 E7 Rus.* Krichëv.
Mahilyowskaya Voblasts', E Belarus
Kryms'ki Hory *109 F5 mountain range*
S Ukraine
Kryms'kyy Pivostriv *109 F5 peninsula*
S Ukraine
Krynica *99 D5 Ger.* Tannenhof.
Małopolskie, S Poland
Kryve Ozero *109 E3* Odes'ka Oblast',
SW Ukraine
Kryvyy Rih *109 F3 Rus.* Krivoy Rog.
Dnipropetrovs'ka Oblast', SE Ukraine
Krzemieniec *see* Kremenets'
Ksar al Kabir *see* Ksar-el-Kebir
Ksar al Soule *see* Er-Rachidia
Ksar-el-Kebir *70 C2 var.* Alcázar,
Ksar al Kabir, Ksar-el-Kébir, *Ar.*
Al-Kasr al-Kebir, Al-Qsar al-Kbir, *Sp.*
Alcazarquivir. NW Morocco
Ksar-el-Kébir *see* Ksar-el-Kebir
Kuala Dungun *see* Dungun
Kuala Lumpur *138 B3 country capital*
(Malaysia) (Malaysia) Kuala Lumpur,
Peninsular Malaysia
Kuala Terengganu *138 B3 var.* Kuala
Trengganu, Trengganu, Peninsular
Malaysia
Kualatungkal *138 B4* Sumatera,
W Indonesia
Kuang-chou *see* Guangzhou
Kuang-hsi *see* Guangxi Zhuangzu Zizhiqu
Kuang-tung *see* Guangdong
Kuang-yuan *see* Guangyuan
Kuantan *138 B3* Pahang, Peninsular
Malaysia
Kuba *see* Quba
Kuban' *109 G5 var.* Hypanis. *river*
SW Russian Federation

Kubango *see* Cubango/Okavango
Kuching *138 C3 prev.* Sarawak. Sarawak,
East Malaysia
Kŭchnay Darweyshān *122 D5* Helmand,
S Afghanistan
Kuçova *see* Kuçovë
Kuçovë *101 C6 var.* Kuçova; *prev.* Qyteti
Stalin. Berat, C Albania
Kudara *see* Ghüdara
Kudus *138 C5 prev.* Koedoes. Jawa,
C Indonesia
Kuei-lin *see* Guilin
Kuei-Yang/Kuei-yang *see* Guiyang
K'u-erh-lo *see* Korla
Kueyang *see* Guiyang
Kugaaruk *37 G3 prev.* Pelly Bay.
Nunavut, N Canada
Kugluktuk *53 E3 var.* Qurlurtuuq; *prev.*
Coppermine. Nunavut, NW Canada
Kuhmo *84 E4* Oulu, E Finland
Kuhnau *see* Konin
Kühnö *see* Kihnu
Kuibyshev *see* Kuybyshevskoye
Vodokhranilishche
Kuito *78 B2 Port.* Silva Porto. Bié,
C Angola
Kuji *130 D3 var.* Kuzi. Iwate, Honshū,
C Japan
Kukës *101 D5 var.* Kukësi. Kukës,
NE Albania
Kukësi *see* Kukës
Kukong *see* Shaoguan
Kukukhoto *see* Hohhot
Kula Kangri *135 G3 var.* Kulhakangri.
mountain Bhutan/China
Kuldiga *106 B3 Ger.* Goldingen. Kuldīga,
W Latvia
Kuldja *see* Yining
Kulhakangri *see* Kula Kangri
Kullorsuaq *82 D2 var.* Kuvdlorssuak.
Kitaa, C Greenland
Kulm *see* Chełmno
Kulmsee *see* Chełmża
Külob *123 F3 Rus.* Kulyab.
SW Tajikistan
Kulpa *see* Kolpa
Kulu *116 C3* Konya, W Turkey
Kulunda Steppe *114 C4 Kaz.* Qulyndy
Zhazyghy, *Rus.* Kulundinskaya
Ravnina. *grassland* Kazakhstan/
Russian Federation
Kulundinskaya Ravnina *see* Kulunda
Steppe
Kulyab *see* Külob
Kum *see* Qom
Kuma *111 B7 river* SW Russian
Federation
Kumamoto *131 A7* Kumamoto, Kyūshū,
SW Japan
Kumanova *see* Kumanovo
Kumanovo *101 E5 Turk.* Kumanova.
N Macedonia
Kumasi *75 E5 prev.* Coomassie. C Ghana
Kumayri *see* Gyumri
Kumba *77 A5* Sud-Ouest, W Cameroon
Kumertau *111 D6* Respublika
Bashkortostan, W Russian Federation
Kumillã *see* Comilla
Kumo *75 G4* Gombe, E Nigeria
Kumon Range *136 B2 mountain range*
N Burma (Myanmar)
Kumul *see* Hami
Kunashiri *see* Kunashir, Ostrov
Kunashir, Ostrov *130 E1 var.* Kunashiri.
island Kuril'skiye Ostrova, SE Russian
Federation
Kunda *106 E2* Lääne-Virumaa, NE Estonia
Kunduz *see* Kondoz
Kunene *69 C6 var.* Kunene. *river*
Angola/Namibia
Kunene *see* Cunene
Kungsbacka *85 B7* Halland, S Sweden
Kungur *111 D5* Permskaya Oblast',
NW Russian Federation
Kunlun Mountains *see* Kunlun Shan
Kunlun Shan *126 B4 Eng.* Kunlun
Mountains. *mountain range* NW China
Kunming *128 B6 var.* K'un-ming; *prev.*
Yunnan. *province capital* Yunnan,
SW China
K'un-ming *see* Kunming
Kununurra *146 D3* Western Australia
Kunya-Urgench *see* Köneürgenç
Kuopio *85 E5* Itä-Suomi, C Finland
Kupa *see* Kolpa
Kupang *139 E5 prev.* Koepang. Timor,
C Indonesia

Kup"yans'k *109 G2 Rus.* Kupyansk.
Kharkivs'ka Oblast', E Ukraine
Kupyansk *see* Kup"yans'k
Kür *see* Kura
Kura *117 H3 Az.* Kür, *Geor.* Mtkvari,
Turk. Kura Nehri. *river* SW Asia
Kura Nehri *see* Kura
Kurashiki *131 B6 var.* Kurasiki.
Okayama, Honshū, SW Japan
Kurasiki *see* Kurashiki
Kurdistan *117 F4 cultural region* SW Asia
Kürdzhali *104 D3 var.* Kirdzhali.
Kürdzhali, S Bulgaria
Kure *131 B7* Hiroshima, Honshū,
SW Japan
Küre Dağları *116 C2 mountain range*
N Turkey
Kuressaare *106 C2 Ger.* Arensburg; *prev.*
Kingissepp. Saaremaa, W Estonia
Kureyka *112 D2 river* N Russian
Federation
Kurgan-Tyube *see* Qürghonteppa
Kuria Muria Islands *see* Ḩalāniyät,
Juzur al
Kurile Islands *115 H4 Eng.* Kurile
Islands. *island group* SE Russian
Federation
Kurile Islands *see* Kuril'skiye Ostrova
Kurile-Kamchatka Depression *see*
Kurile Trench
Kurile Trench *113 F3 var.* Kurile-
Kamchatka Depression. *trench*
NW Pacific Ocean
Kuril'sk *130 E1 Jap.* Shana. Kuril'skiye
Ostrova, Sakhalinskaya Oblats',
SE Russian Federation
Kurisches Haff *see* Courland Lagoon
Kurkund *see* Kilingi-Nõmme
Kurnool *132 C1 var.* Karnul. Andhra
Pradesh, S India
Kursk *111 A6* Kurskaya Oblast',
W Russian Federation
Kurskiy Zaliv *see* Courland Lagoon
Kuršumlija *101 D5* Serbia, S Serbia
Kurtbunar *see* Tervel
Kurtitsch/Kürtös *see* Curtici
Kuruktag *126 C3 mountain range*
NW China
Kurume *131 A7* Fukuoka, Kyūshū,
SW Japan
Kurupukari *59 F3* C Guyana
Kusaie *see* Kosrae
Kushiro *130 D2 var.* Kusiro. Hokkaidō,
NE Japan
Kushka *see* Serhetabat
Kusiro *see* Kushiro
Kuskokwim Mountains *36 C3*
mountain range Alaska, USA
Kustanay *see* Kostanay
Küstence/Küstendje *see* Constanţa
Kütahya *116 B3 prev.* Kutaia. Kütahya,
W Turkey
Kutai *see* Mahakam, Sungai
K'ut'aisi *117 F2* W Georgia
Kūt al 'Amārah *see* Al Kūt
Kut al Imara *see* Al Kūt
Kutaradja/Kutaraja *see* Bandaaceh
Kutch, Gulf of *see* Kachchh, Gulf of
Kutch, Rann of *see* Kachchh, Rann of
Kutina *100 B3* Sisak-Moslavina, NE Croatia
Kutno *98 C3* Łódzkie, C Poland
Kuujjuaq *39 E2 prev.* Fort-Chimo.
Québec, E Canada
Kuusamo *84 E3* Oulu, E Finland
Kuvango *see* Cubango
Kuvdlorssuak *see* Kullorsuaq
Kuwait *120 C4 off.* State of Kuwait, *var.*
Dawlat al Kuwait, Koweit, Kuwayt.
country SW Asia

KUWAIT
Southwest Asia

Official name State of Kuwait
Formation 1961 / 1961
Capital Kuwait City
Population 2.8 million / 407 people
per sq mile (157 people per sq km) / 96%
Total area 6880 sq. miles (17,820 sq. km)
Languages Arabic*, English
Religions Sunni Muslim 45%, Shi'a
Muslim 40%, Christian, Hindu,
and other 15%
Ethnic mix Kuwaiti 45%, Other Arab 35%,
South Asian 9%, Other 7%, Iranian 4%

KUWAIT
(continued)

Government Monarchy
Currency Kuwaiti dinar = 1000 fils
Literacy rate 93%
Calorie consumption 3010 calories

Kuwait *see* Al Kuwayt
Kuwait City *see* Al Kuwayt
Kuwait, Dawlat al *see* Kuwait
Kuwait, State of *see* Kuwait
Kuwajleen *see* Kwajalein Atoll
Kuwayt *120 C3* Maysān, E Iraq
Kuweit *see* Kuwait
Kuybyshev *see* Samara
Kuybyshev Reservoir *111 C5 var.*
Kuibyshev, *Eng.* Kuybyshev
Reservoir. *reservoir* W Russian
Federation
Kuybyshev Reservoir *see*
Kuybyshevskoye
Vodokhranilishche
Kuytun *126 B2* Xinjiang Uygur Zizhiqu,
NW China
Kuzi *see* Kuji
Kuznetsk *111 B6* Penzenskaya Oblast',
W Russian Federation
Kuźnica *98 E2* Białystok, NE Poland
Europe
Kvaløya *84 C2 island* N Norway
Kvarnbergsvattnet *84 B4 var.*
Frostviken. *lake* N Sweden
Kvarner *100 A3 var.* Carnaro, It.
Quarnero. *gulf* W Croatia
Kvitøya *83 G1 island* NE Svalbard
Kwajalein Atoll *144 C1 var.*
Kuwajleen. *atoll* Ralik Chain,
C Marshall Islands
Kwando *see* Cuando
Kwangchow *see* Guangzhou
Kwangchu *see* Kwangju
Kwangju *129 E4 off.* Kwangju-
gwangyŏksi, *var.* Guangju, Kwangchu,
Jap. Kōshū. SW South Korea
Kwangju gwangyŏksi *see* Kwangju
Kwango *77 C7* Port. Cuango. *river*
Angola/Dem. Rep. Congo
Kwango *see* Cuango
Kwangsi/Kwangsi Chuang
Autonomous Region *see* Guangxi
Zhuangzu Zizhiqu
Kwangtung *see* Guangdong
Kwangyuan *see* Guangyuan
Kwanza *see* Cuanza
Kweichow *see* Guiyang
Kweilin *see* Guilin
Kweisui *see* Hohhot
Kweiyang *see* Guiyang
Kwekwe *78 D3 prev.* Que Que. Midlands,
C Zimbabwe
Kwesui *see* Hohhot
Kwidzyń *98 C2 Ger.* Marienwerder.
Pomorskie, N Poland
Kwigillingok *36 C3* Alaska, USA
Kwilu *77 C6 river* W Dem. Rep.
Congo
Kwito *see* Cuito
Kyabé *76 C4* Moyen-Chari, S Chad
Kyaikkami *137 B5 prev.* Amherst. Mon
State, S Burma (Myanmar)
Kyaiklat *136 B4* Ayeyarwady, SW Burma
(Myanmar)
Kyaikto *136 B4* Mon State, S Burma
(Myanmar)
Kyakhta *115 E5* Respublika Buryatiya,
S Russian Federation
Kyaukse *136 B3* Mandalay, C Burma
(Myanmar)
Kyjov *99 C5 Ger.* Gaya. Jihomoravský
Kraj, SE Czech Republic
Kými *105 C5 prev.* Kími. Évvoia,
C Greece
Kyōngsŏng *see* Sŏul
Kyōto *131 C6* Kyōto, Honshū, SW Japan
Kyparissía *105 B6 var.* Kiparissía.
Pelopónnisos, S Greece
Kypros *see* Cyprus
Kyrá Panagía *105 C5 island* Vóreies
Sporádes, Greece, Aegean Sea
Kyrenia *see* Girne
Kyrgyz Republic *see* Kyrgyzstan
Kyrgyzstan *123 F2 off.* Kyrgyz Republic,
var. Kirghizia; *prev.* Kirgizskaya SSR,
Kirghiz SSR, Republic of Kyrgyzstan.
country C Asia

KYRGYZSTAN
Central Asia

Official name Kyrgyz Republic
Formation 1991 / 1991
Capital Bishkek
Population 5.4 million / 70 people
per sq mile (27 people per sq km) / 34%
Total area 76,641 sq. miles (198,500 sq. km)
Languages Kyrgyz*, Russian*, Uzbek,
Tatar, Ukrainian
Religions Muslim (mainly Sunni) 70%,
Orthodox Christian 30%
Ethnic mix Kyrgyz 65%, Uzbek 14%,
Russian 13%, Other 6%,
Dungan 1%, Ukrainian 1%
Government Presidential system
Currency Som = 100 tyiyn
Literacy rate 99%
Calorie consumption 2999 calories

Kyrgyzstan, Republic of *see* Kyrgyzstan
Kythira *105 C7 var.* Kíthira, *It.* Cerigo,
Lat. Cythera. *island* S Greece
Kýthnos *105 C6* Knýthnos, Kykládes,
Greece, Aegean Sea
Kythnos *105 C6 var.* Kíthnos, Thermiá,
It. Termia; *anc.* Cythnos. *island*
Kykládes, Greece, Aegean Sea
Kythréa *see* Değirmenlik
Kyushu *131 B7 var.* Kyūsyū. *island*
SW Japan
Kyushu-Palau Ridge *125 F3 var.*
Kyusyu-Palau Ridge. *undersea ridge*
W Pacific Ocean
Kyustendil *104 B2 anc.* Pautalia.
Kyustendil, W Bulgaria
Kyûsyû *see* Kyūshū
Kyusyu-Palau Ridge *see* Kyushu-Palau
Ridge
Kyyiv *109 E2 Eng.* Kiev, *Rus.* Kiyev.
country capital (Ukraine) (Ukraine)
Kyyivs'ka Oblast', N Ukraine
Kyzyl *114 D4* Respublika Tyva, C Russian
Federation
Kyzyl Kum *122 D2 var.* Kizil Kum,
Qizil Qum, *Uzb.* Qizilqum. *desert*
Kazakhstan/Uzbekistan
Kyzylrabot *see* Qizilrabot
Kyzyl-Suu *123 G2 prev.* Pokrovka.
Issyk-Kul'skaya Oblast', NE Kyrgyzstan
Kzylorda *114 B5 var.* Kzyl-Orda, Qizil
Orda, Qyzylorda; *prev.* Perovsk.
Kyzylorda, S Kazakhstan
Kzyl-Orda *see* Kzylorda

L

Laaland *see* Lolland
La Algaba *92 C4* Andalucía, S Spain
Laarne *87 B5* Oost-Vlaanderen,
NW Belgium
La Asunción *59 E1* Nueva Esparta,
NE Venezuela
Laatokka *see* Ladozhskoye, Ozero
Laâyoune *70 B3 var.* Aaiún. *country
capital* (Western Sahara) (Western
Sahara) NW Western Sahara
La Banda Oriental *see* Uruguay
la Baule-Escoublac *90 A4* Loire-
Atlantique, NW France
Labé *74 C4* NW Guinea
Labe *see* Elbe
Laborca *see* Laborec
Laborec *99 E5 Hung.* Laborca. *river*
E Slovakia
Labrador *39 F2 cultural region*
Newfoundland and Labrador,
SW Canada
Labrador Basin *34 E3 var.* Labrador Sea
Basin. *undersea basin* Labrador Sea
Labrador Sea *82 A4 sea* NW Atlantic
Ocean
Labrador Sea Basin *see* Labrador Basin
Labudalin *see* Ergun
Labutta *137 A5* Ayeyarwady, SW Burma
(Myanmar)
Laç *101 C6 var.* Laci. Lezhë, C Albania
La Calera *64 B4* Valparaíso, C Chile
La Carolina *92 D4* Andalucía, S Spain
Laccadive Islands *132 A3 Eng.* Laccadive
Islands. *island group* India, N Indian
Ocean
**Laccadive Islands/Laccadive Minicoy
and Amindivi Islands, the** *see*
Lakshadweep

La Ceiba *52 D2* Atlántida, N Honduras
Lachanás *104 B3* Kentrikí Makedonía,
N Greece
La Chaux-de-Fonds *95 A7* Neuchâtel,
W Switzerland
Lachlan River *149 C6 river* New South
Wales, SE Australia
Laci *see* Laç
la Ciotat *91 D6 anc.* Citharista. Bouches-
du-Rhône, SE France
Lacobriga *see* Lagos
La Concepción *53 E5 var.* Concepción.
Chiriquí, W Panama
La Concepción *58 C1* Zulia,
NW Venezuela
Laconia *41 G2* New Hampshire, NE USA
La Crosse *40 A2* Wisconsin, N USA
La Cruz *52 D4* Guanacaste, NW Costa
Rica
Lake Ladoga *110 B3 Eng.* Lake Ladoga,
Fin. Laatokka. *lake* NW Russian
Federation
Ladoga, Lake *see* Ladozhskoye, Ozero
Ladysmith *40 B2* Wisconsin, N USA
Lae *144 B3* Morobe, W Papua New
Guinea
La Esperanza *52 C2* Intibucá,
SW Honduras
Lafayette *40 C4* Indiana, N USA
Lafayette *42 B3* Louisiana, S USA
La Fé *54 A2* Pinar del Río, W Cuba
Lafia *75 G4* Nassarawa, C Nigeria
la Flèche *90 B4* Sarthe, NW France
Lagdo, Lac de *76 B4 lake* N Cameroon
Laghouat *70 D2* N Algeria
Lagos *75 F5 Yor.* Lagos, W Nigeria
Lagos *92 B5 anc.* Lacobriga. Faro,
S Portugal
Lagos de Moreno *51 E4* Jalisco,
SW Mexico
Lagouira *70 A4* SW Western Sahara
La Grande *46 C3* Oregon, NW USA
La Guaira *58 D1* Distrito Federal,
N Venezuela
Lagunas *64 B1* Tarapacá, N Chile
Lagunillas *61 G4* Santa Cruz, SE Bolivia
La Habana *54 B2 var.* Havana. *country
capital* (Cuba) (Cuba) Ciudad de La
Habana, W Cuba
Lahat *138 B4* Sumatera, W Indonesia
La Haye *see* 's-Gravenhage
Laholm *85 B7* Halland, S Sweden
Lahore *134 D2* Punjab, NE Pakistan
Lahr *95 A6* Baden-Württemberg,
S Germany
Lahti *85 D5 Swe.* Lahtis. Etelä-Suomi,
S Finland
Lahtis *see* Lahti
Laï *76 B4 prev.* Behagle, De Behagle.
Tandjilé, S Chad
Laibach *see* Ljubljana
Lai Châu *136 D3* Lai Châu, N Vietnam
Laila *see* Laylā
La Junta *44 D5* Colorado, C USA
Lake Charles *42 A3* Louisiana, S USA
Lake City *43 E3* Florida, SE USA
Lake District *89 C5 physical region*
NW England, United Kingdom
Lake Havasu City *48 A2* Arizona,
SW USA
Lake Jackson *49 H4* Texas, SW USA
Lakeland *43 E4* Florida, SE USA
Lakeside *47 C8* California, W USA
Lake State *see* Michigan
Lakewood *44 C4* Colorado, C USA
Lakhnau *see* Lucknow
Lakonikós Kólpos *105 B7 gulf* S Greece
Laksely *84 D2* Lapp. Leavdnja.
Finnmark, N Norway
la Laon *see* Laon
Lalibela *72 C4* Āmara, Ethiopia
La Libertad *52 B1* Petén, N Guatemala
La Ligua *64 B4* Valparaíso, C Chile
Lalín *92 B2* Galicia, NW Spain
Lalitpur *135 F3* Central, C Nepal
La Louvière *87 B6* Hainaut, S Belgium
La Maddalena *96 A4* Sardegna, Italy,
C Mediterranean Sea
la Manche *see* English Channel
Lamar *44 D5* Colorado, C USA
La Marmora, Punta *97 A5 mountain*
Sardegna, Italy, C Mediterranean Sea
La Massana *91 A8* La Massana,
W Andorra Europe
Lambaréné *77 A6* Moyen-Ogooué,
W Gabon

Lamego *92 C2* Viseu, N Portugal
Lamesa *49 E3* Texas, SW USA
Lamezia Terme *97 D6* Calabria, SE Italy
Lamía *105 B5* Stereá Ellás, C Greece
Lamoni *45 F4* Iowa, C USA
Lampang *136 C4 var.* Muang Lampang.
Lampang, NW Thailand
Lámpeia *105 B6* Dytikí Ellás, S Greece
Lanbi Kyun *137 B6 prev.* Sullivan Island.
island Mergui Archipelago, S Burma
(Myanmar)
Lancang Jiang *see* Mekong
Lancaster *89 D5* NW England, United
Kingdom
Lancaster *47 C7* California, W USA
Lancaster *41 F4* Pennsylvania, NE USA
Lancaster Sound *37 F2 sound* Nunavut,
N Canada
Lan-chou/Lan-chow/Lanchow *see*
Lanzhou
Landao *see* Lantau Island
Landen *87 C6* Vlaams Brabant, C Belgium
Lander *44 C3* Wyoming, C USA
Landerneau *90 A3* Finistère, NW France
Landes *91 B5 cultural region* SW France
Land of Enchantment *see* New Mexico
The Land of Opportunity *see* Arkansas
Land of Steady Habits *see* Connecticut
Land of the Midnight Sun *see* Alaska
Landsberg *see* Gorzów Wielkopolski,
Lubuskie, Poland
Landsberg an der Warthe *see* Gorzów
Wielkopolski
Land's End *89 B8 headland* SW England,
United Kingdom
Landshut *95 C6* Bayern, SE Germany
Langar *123 F2 Rus.* Lyangar. Navoiy
Viloyati, C Uzbekistan
Langfang *128 D4* Hebei, E China
Langkawi, Pulau *137 B7 island*
Peninsular Malaysia
Langres *90 D4* Haute-Marne, N France
Langsa *138 A3* Sumatera, W Indonesia
Lang Shan *127 E3 mountain range*
N China
Lang Son *136 D3 var.* Langson. Lang
Son, N Vietnam
Langson *see* Lang Son
Lang Suan *137 B6* Chumphon,
SW Thailand
Languedoc *91 C6 cultural region* S France
Länkäran *117 H3 Rus.* Lenkoran'.
S Azerbaijan
Lansing *40 C3 state capital* Michigan,
N USA
Lanta, Ko *137 B7 island* S Thailand
Lantau Island *128 A2 Cant.* Tai Yue
Shan, *Chin.* Landao. *island* Hong
Kong, S China
Lan-ts'ang Chiang *see* Mekong
Lantung, Gulf of *see* Liaodong Wan
Lanzarote *70 B3 island* Islas Canarias,
Spain, NE Atlantic Ocean
Lanzhou *128 B4 var.* Lan-chou,
Lanchow, Lan-chow; *prev.* Kaolan.
province capital Gansu, C China
Lao Cai *136 D3* Lao Cai, N Vietnam
Laodicea/Laodicea ad Mare *see* Al
Lādhiqīyah
Laoet *see* Laut, Pulau
Laojunmiao *128 A3 prev.* Yumen.
Gansu, N China
Laon *90 D3 var.* la Laon; *anc.* Laudunum.
Aisne, N France
Lao People's Democratic Republic
see Laos
La Orchila, Isla *58 D1 island*
N Venezuela
La Oroya *60 C3* Junín, C Peru
Laos *136 D4 off.* Lao People's Democratic
Republic. *country* SE Asia

LAOS
Southeast Asia

Official name Lao People's Democratic
Republic
Formation 1953 / 1953
Capital Vientiane
Population 6.2 million / 70 people
per sq mile (27 people per sq km) / 21%
Total area 91,428 sq. miles
(236,800 sq. km)
Languages Lao*, Mon-Khmer, Yao,
Vietnamese, Chinese, French
Religions Buddhist 85%,
Other (including animist) 15%

LAOS
(continued)

Ethnic mix Lao Loum 66%, Lao Theung 30%, Other 2%, Lao Soung 2%
Government One-party state
Currency New kip = 100 at
Literacy rate 69%
Calorie consumption 2312 calories

La Palma 53 G5 Darién, SE Panama
La Palma 70 A3 *island* Islas Canarias, Spain, NE Atlantic Ocean
La Paz 61 F4 *var.* La Paz de Ayacucho. *country capital* (Bolivia-legislative and administrative capital) (Bolivia-legislative and administrative capital) La Paz, W Bolivia
La Paz 50 B3 Baja California Sur, NW Mexico
La Paz, Bahía de 50 B3 *bay* NW Mexico
La Paz de Ayacucho *see* La Paz
La Perouse Strait 130 D1 *Jap.* Sóyakaikyō, *Rus.* Proliv Laperuza. *strait* Japan/Russian Federation
Laperuza, Proliv *see* La Perouse Strait
Lápithos *see* Lápithos
Lapland 84 D3 *Fin.* Lappi, *Swe.* Lappland. *cultural region* N Europe
La Plata 64 D4 Buenos Aires, E Argentina
La Plata *see* Sucre
Lappeenranta 85 E5 *Swe.* Villmanstrand. Etelä-Suomi, SE Finland
Lappi/Lappland *see* Lapland
Lappo *see* Lapua
Lapta 102 C5 *Gk.* Lápithos. NW Cyprus
Laptev Sea 115 F2 *Eng.* Laptev Sea. *sea* Arctic Ocean
Laptev Sea *see* Laptevykh, More
Lapua 85 D5 *Swe.* Lappo. Länsi-Suomi, W Finland
Lapurdum *see* Bayonne
Łapy 98 E3 Podlaskie, NE Poland
La Quiaca 64 C2 Jujuy, N Argentina
L'Aquila 96 C4 *var.* Aquila, Aquila degli Abruzzi. Abruzzo, C Italy
Laracha 92 B1 Galicia, NW Spain
Laramie 44 C4 Wyoming, C USA
Laramie Mountains 44 C3 *mountain range* Wyoming, C USA
Laredo 93 E1 Cantabria, N Spain
Laredo 49 F5 Texas, SW USA
La Réunion *see* Réunion
Largeau *see* Faya
Largo 43 E4 Florida, SE USA
Largo, Cayo 54 B2 *island* W Cuba
Lario *see* Como, Lago di
La Rioja 64 C3 La Rioja, NW Argentina
La Rioja 93 E2 *autonomous community* N Spain
Lárisa 104 B4 *var.* Larissa. Thessalía, C Greece
Larissa *see* Lárisa
Lārkāna 134 B3 *var.* Larkhana. Sind, SE Pakistan
Larkhana *see* Lārkāna
Larnaca *see* Lárnaka
Lárnaka 102 C5 *var.* Larnaca, Larnax. SE Cyprus
Larnax *see* Lárnaka
la Rochelle 90 B4 *anc.* Rupella. Charente-Maritime, W France
la Roche-sur-Yon 90 B4 *prev.* Bourbon Vendée, Napoléon-Vendée. Vendée, NW France
La Roda 93 E3 Castilla-La Mancha, C Spain
La Romana 55 E3 E Dominican Republic
Larvotto 91 C8 N Monaco Europe
La-sa *see* Lhasa
Las Cabezas de San Juan 92 C5 Andalucía, S Spain
Las Cruces 48 D3 New Mexico, SW USA
La See d'Urgel 93 G1 *var.* La Seu d'Urgell, Seo de Urgel. Cataluña, NE Spain
La Serena 64 B3 Coquimbo, C Chile
La Seu d'Urgell *see* La See d'Urgel
la Seyne-sur-Mer 91 D6 *Var.* SE France
Lashio 136 B3 Shan State, E Burma (Myanmar)
Lashkar Gāh 122 D5 *var.* Lash-Kar-Gar'. Helmand, S Afghanistan
Lash-Kar-Gar' *see* Lashkar Gāh
La Sila 97 D6 *mountain range* SW Italy
La Sirena 51 D6 Región Autónoma Atlántico Sur, E Nicaragua

Łask 98 C4 Łódzkie, C Poland
Las Lomitas 64 D2 Formosa, N Argentina
La Solana 93 E4 Castilla-La Mancha, C Spain
Las Palmas 70 A3 *var.* Las Palmas de Gran Canaria. Gran Canaria, Islas Canarias, Spain, NE Atlantic Ocean
Las Palmas de Gran Canaria *see* Las Palmas
La Spezia 96 B3 Liguria, NW Italy
Lassa *see* Lhasa
Las Tablas 53 F5 Los Santos, S Panama
Last Frontier, The *see* Alaska
Las Tunas 54 C2 *var.* Victoria de las Tunas. Las Tunas, E Cuba
La Suisse *see* Switzerland
Las Vegas 47 D7 Nevada, W USA
Latacunga 60 B1 Cotopaxi, C Ecuador
la Teste 91 B5 Gironde, SW France
Latina 97 C5 *prev.* Littoria. Lazio, C Italy
La Tortuga, Isla 59 E1 *var.* Isla Tortuga. *island* N Venezuela
La Tuque 39 E4 Québec, SE Canada
Latvia 106 C3 *off.* Republic of Latvia, *Ger.* Lettland, *Latv.* Latvija, Latvijas Republika; *prev.* Latvian SSR, *Rus.* Latviyskaya SSR. *country* NE Europe

LATVIA
Northeast Europe

Official name Republic of Latvia
Formation 1991 / 1991
Capital Riga
Population 2.3 million / 92 people per sq mile (36 people per sq km) / 66%
Total area 24,938 sq. miles (64,589 sq. km)
Languages Latvian*, Russian
Religions Lutheran 55%, Roman Catholic 24%, Other 12%, Orthodox Christian 9%
Ethnic mix Latvian 58%, Russian 29%, Belarussian 4%, Polish 3%, Ukrainian 3%, Other 2%
Government Parliamentary system
Currency Lats = 100 santimi
Literacy rate 99%
Calorie consumption 2938 calories

Latvian SSR/Latvija/Latvijas Republika/Latviyskaya SSR *see* Latvia
Latvia, Republic of *see* Latvia
Laudunum *see* Laon
Laudus *see* St-Lô
Lauenburg/Lauenburg in Pommern *see* Lębork
Lau Group 145 E4 *island group* E Fiji
Lauis *see* Lugano
Launceston 149 C8 Tasmania, SE Australia
La Unión 52 C2 Olancho, C Honduras
La Unión 93 F4 Murcia, SE Spain
Laurel 42 C3 Mississippi, S USA
Laurel 44 C2 Montana, NW USA
Laurentian Highlands *see* Laurentian Mountains
Laurentian Mountains 39 E3 *var.* Laurentian Highlands, *Fr.* Les Laurentides. *plateau* Newfoundland and Labrador/Québec, Canada
Laurentides, Les *see* Laurentian Mountains
Lauria 97 D6 Basilicata, S Italy
Laurinburg 43 F1 North Carolina, SE USA
Lauru *see* Choiseul
Lausanne 95 A7 *It.* Losanna. Vaud, SW Switzerland
Laut, Pulau 138 D4 *prev.* Laoet. *island* Borneo, C Indonesia
Laval 38 D4 Québec, SE Canada
Laval 90 B3 Mayenne, NW France
La Vall d'Uixó 93 F3 *var.* Vall D'Uxó. País Valenciano, E Spain
La Vega 55 E3 *var.* Concepción de la Vega. C Dominican Republic
La Vila Joĩosa *see* Villajoyosa
Lávrio 105 C6 *prev.* Lávrion. Attikí, C Greece
Lávrion *see* Lávrio
Lawrence 41 G3 Massachusetts, NE USA
Lawrenceburg 42 C1 Tennessee, S USA
Lawton 49 F2 Oklahoma, C USA
La Yarada 61 E4 Tacna, SW Peru
Laylā 121 C5 *var.* Laila. Ar Riyāḍ, C Saudi Arabia

Lazarev Sea 154 B1 *sea* Antarctica
Lázaro Cárdenas 51 E5 Michoacán, SW Mexico
Leal *see* Lihula
Leamhcán *see* Lucan
Leamington 38 C5 Ontario, S Canada
Leavdnja *see* Lakselv
Lebak 139 E3 Mindanao, S Philippines
Lebanese Republic *see* Lebanon
Lebanon 45 G5 Missouri, C USA
Lebanon 41 G2 New Hampshire, NE USA
Lebanon 46 B3 Oregon, NW USA
Lebanon 118 A4 *off.* Lebanese Republic, *Ar.* Al Lubnān, *Fr.* Liban. *country* SW Asia

LEBANON
Southwest Asia

Official name The Lebanese Republic
Formation 1941 / 1941
Capital Beirut
Population 3.7 million / 937 people per sq mile (362 people per sq km) / 88%
Total area 4015 sq. miles (10,400 sq. km)
Languages Arabic*, French, Armenian, Assyrian
Religions Muslim 70%, Christian 30%
Ethnic mix Arab 94%, Armenian 4%, Other 2%
Government Parliamentary system
Currency Lebanese pound = 100 piastres
Literacy rate 86%
Calorie consumption 3196 calories

Lebanon, Mount *see* Liban, Jebel
Lebap 122 D2 Lebapskiy Velayat, NE Turkmenistan
Lebedin *see* Lebedyn
Lebedyn 109 F2 *Rus.* Lebedin. Sums'ka Oblast', NE Ukraine
Lębork 98 C2 *var.* Lębórk, *Ger.* Lauenburg, Lauenburg in Pommern. Pomorskie, N Poland
Lebrija 92 C5 Andalucía, S Spain
Lebu 65 A5 Bío Bío, C Chile
le Cannet 91 D6 Alpes-Maritimes, SE France
Le Cap *see* Cap-Haïtien
Lecce 97 E6 Puglia, SE Italy
Lechainá 105 B6 *var.* Lehena, Lekhainá. Dytikí Ellás, S Greece
Ledo Salinarius *see* Lons-le-Saunier
Leduc 37 E5 Alberta, SW Canada
Leech Lake 45 F2 *lake* Minnesota, N USA
Leeds 89 D5 N England, United Kingdom
Leek 86 E2 Groningen, NE Netherlands
Leer 94 A3 Niedersachsen, NW Germany
Leeuwarden 86 D1 *Fris.* Ljouwert. Friesland, N Netherlands
Leeuwin, Cape 142 A5 *headland* Western Australia
Leeward Islands 55 G3 *island group* E West Indies
Leeward Islands *see* Sotavento, Ilhas de
Lefkáda 105 A5 *prev.* Levkás. Lefkáda, Iónia Nisiá, Greece, C Mediterranean Sea
Lefkáda 105 A5 *It.* Santa Maura, *prev.* Levkás; *anc.* Leucas. *island* Iónia Nisiá, Greece, C Mediterranean Sea
Lefká Óri 105 C7 *mountain range* Kríti, Greece, E Mediterranean Sea
Lefkímmi 105 A5 *var.* Levkímmi. Kérkyra, Iónia Nisiá, Greece, C Mediterranean Sea
Lefkosía/Lefkoşa *see* Nicosia
Legaceaster *see* Chester
Legaspi *see* Legazpi City
Leghorn *see* Livorno
Legnica 98 B4 *Ger.* Liegnitz. Dolnośląskie, SW Poland
le Havre 90 B3 *Eng.* Havre; *prev.* le Havre-de-Grâce. Seine-Maritime, N France
le Havre-de-Grâce *see* le Havre
Lehena *see* Lechainá
Leicester 89 D6 *Lat.* Batae Coritanorum. C England, United Kingdom
Leiden 86 C3 *prev.* Leyden; *anc.* Lugdunum Batavorum. Zuid-Holland, W Netherlands
Leie 90 D2 *Fr.* Lys. *river* Belgium/France
Leinster 89 B6 *Ir.* Cúige Laighean. *cultural region* E Ireland
Leipsic *see* Leipzig

Leipsoí 105 E6 *island* Dodekánisa, Greece, Aegean Sea
Leipzig 94 C4 *Pol.* Lipsk, *hist.* Leipsic; *anc.* Lipsia. Sachsen, E Germany
Leiria 92 B3 *anc.* Collipo. Leiria, C Portugal
Leirvik 85 A6 Hordaland, S Norway
Lek 86 C4 *river* NE Netherlands
Lekhainá *see* Lechainá
Lekhchevo 104 C2 Montana, NW Bulgaria
Leksand 85 C5 Dalarna, C Sweden
Lel'chitsy *see* Lyel'chytsy
le Léman *see* Geneva, Lake
Lelystad 86 D3 Flevoland, C Netherlands
Léman, Lac *see* Geneva, Lake
le Mans 90 B3 Sarthe, NW France
Lemberg *see* L'viv
Lemesós 102 C5 *var.* Limassol. SW Cyprus
Lemhi Range 46 D3 *mountain range* Idaho, C USA North America
Lemnos *see* Límnos
Lemovices *see* Limoges
Lena 115 F3 *river* NE Russian Federation
Lena Tablemount 141 B7 *seamount* S Indian Ocean
Len Dao 128 C8 *island* S Spratly Islands
Lengshuitan *see* Yongzhou
Leninabad *see* Khujand
Leninakan *see* Gyumri
Lenine 109 G5 *Rus.* Lenino. Respublika Krym, S Ukraine
Leningor *see* Ridder
Leningrad *see* Sankt-Peterburg
Leningradskaya 154 B4 *Russian research station* Antarctica
Lenino *see* Lenine, Ukraine
Leninobod *see* Khujand
Leninpol' 123 F2 Talasskaya Oblast', NW Kyrgyzstan
Lenin-Turkmenski *see* Türkmenabat
Lenkoran' *see* Länkäran
Lenti 99 B7 Zala, SW Hungary
Lentia *see* Linz
Leoben 95 E7 Steiermark, C Austria
León 51 E4 *var.* León de los Aldamas. Guanajuato, C Mexico
León 52 C3 León, NW Nicaragua
León 92 D1 Castilla-León, NW Spain
León de los Aldamas *see* León
Leonídi *see* Leonídio
Leonídio 105 B6 *var.* Leonídi. Pelopónnisos, S Greece
Léopold II, Lac *see* Mai-Ndombe, Lac
Léopoldville *see* Kinshasa
Lepe 92 C4 Andalucía, S Spain
Lepel' *see* Lyepyel'
le Portel 90 C2 Pas-de-Calais, N France
Le Puglie *see* Puglia
le Puy 91 C5 *prev.* le Puy-en-Velay, *hist.* Anicium, Podium Anicensis. Haute-Loire, C France
le Puy-en-Velay *see* le Puy
Léré 76 B4 Mayo-Kébbi, SW Chad
Lérida *see* Lleida
Lerma 92 D2 Castilla-León, N Spain
Leros 105 D6 *island* Dodekánisa, Greece, Aegean Sea
Lerrnayin Gharabakh *see* Nagorno-Karabakh
Lerwick 88 D1 NE Scotland, United Kingdom
Lesbos 116 A3 *anc.* Lesbos. *island* E Greece
Lesbos *see* Lésvos
Les Cayes *see* Cayes
Les Gonaïves *see* Gonaïves
Leshan 128 B5 Sichuan, C China
les Herbiers 90 B4 Vendée, NW France
Lesh/Leshi *see* Lezhë
Lesina *see* Hvar
Leskovac 101 E5 Serbia, SE Serbia
Lesnoy 114 C3 Sverdlovskaya Oblast', C Russian Federation
Lesotho 78 D4 *off.* Kingdom of Lesotho; *prev.* Basutoland. *country* S Africa

LESOTHO
Southern Africa

Official name Kingdom of Lesotho
Formation 1966 / 1966
Capital Maseru
Population 1.8 million / 154 people per sq mile (59 people per sq km) / 18%
Total area 11,720 sq. miles (30,355 sq. km)

LESOTHO
(continued)

Languages English*, Sesotho*, isiZulu
Religions Christian 90%, Traditional
beliefs 10%
Ethnic mix Sotho 97%, European
and Asian 3%
Government Parliamentary system
Currency Loti = 100 lisente
Literacy rate 82%
Calorie consumption 2638 calories

Lesotho, Kingdom of *see* Lesotho
les Sables-d'Olonne *90 B4* Vendée,
 NW France
Lesser Antarctica *see* West Antarctica
Lesser Antilles *55 G4 island group*
 E West Indies
Lesser Caucasus *117 F2 Rus.* Malyy
 Kavkaz. *mountain range* SW Asia
Lesser Khingan Range *see* Xiao Hinggan
 Ling
Lesser Sunda Islands *139 E5 Eng.*
 Lesser Sunda Islands. *island group*
 C Indonesia
Lesser Sunda Islands *see* Nusa Tenggara
Leszno *98 B4 Ger.* Lissa. Wielkopolskie,
 C Poland
Lethbridge *37 E5* Alberta, SW Canada
Lethem *59 F3* S Guyana
Leti, Kepulauan *139 F5 island group*
 E Indonesia
Letpadan *136 B4* Bago, SW Burma
 (Myanmar)
Letsok-aw Kyun *137 B6 var.* Letsutan
 Island; *prev.* Domel Island. *island*
 Mergui Archipelago, S Burma
 (Myanmar)
Letsutan Island *see* Letsôk-aw Kyun
Lettland *see* Latvia
Lëtzebuerg *see* Luxembourg
Leucas *see* Lefkáda
Leuven *87 C6 Fr.* Louvain, *Ger.* Löwen.
 Vlaams Brabant, C Belgium
Leuze *see* Leuze-en-Hainaut
Leuze-en-Hainaut *87 B6 var.* Leuze.
 Hainaut, SW Belgium
Léva *see* Levice
Levanger *84 B4* Nord-Trøndelag,
 C Norway
Levelland *49 E2* Texas, SW USA
Leverkusen *94 A4* Nordrhein-Westfalen,
 W Germany
Levice *99 C6 Ger.* Lewentz, *Hung.* Léva,
 Lewenz. Nitriansky Kraj, SW Slovakia
Levin *150 D4* Manawatu-Wanganui,
 North Island, New Zealand
Levkás *see* Lefkáda
Levkímmi *see* Lefkímmi
Lewentz/Lewenz *see* Levice
Lewis, Isle of *88 B2 island* NW Scotland,
 United Kingdom
Lewis Range *44 B1 mountain range*
 Montana, NW USA
Lewiston *46 C2* Idaho, NW USA
Lewiston *41 G2* Maine, NE USA
Lewistown *44 C1* Montana, NW USA
Lexington *40 C5* Kentucky, S USA
Lexington *45 E4* Nebraska, C USA
Leyden *see* Leiden
Leyte *139 F2 island* C Philippines
Leżajsk *98 E5* Podkarpackie,
 SE Poland
Lezha *see* Lezhë
Lezhë *101 C6 var.* Lezha; *prev.* Lesh,
 Leshi. Lezhë, NW Albania
Lhasa *126 C5 var.* La-sa, Lassa. Xizang
 Zizhiqu, W China
Lhaviyani Atoll *see* Faadhippolhu Atoll
Lhazê *126 C5 var.* Quxar. Xizang
 Zizhiqu, China E Asia
L'Hospitalet de Llobregat *93 G2 var.*
 Hospitalet. Cataluña, NE Spain
Liancourt Rocks *131 A5 island group*
 Japan/South Korea
Lianyungang *128 D4 var.* Xinpu.
 Jiangsu, E China
Liao *see* Liaoning
Liaodong Wan *127 G3 Eng.* Gulf of
 Lantung, Gulf of Liaotung. *gulf*
 NE China
Liao He *125 E1 river* NE China
Liaoning *128 D3 var.* Liao, Liaoning
 Sheng, Shengking, *hist.* Fengtien,
 Shenking. *province* NE China

Liaoning Sheng *see* Liaoning
Liaoyuan *129 E3 var.* Dongliao,
 Shuang-liao, *Jap.* Chengchiatun. Jilin,
 NE China
Liard *see* Fort Liard
Liban *see* Lebanon
Liban, Jebel *118 B4 Ar.* Jabal al Gharbī,
 Jabal Lubnān, *Eng.* Mount Lebanon.
 mountain range C Lebanon
Libau *see* Liepāja
Libby *44 A1* Montana, NW USA
Liberal *45 E5* Kansas, C USA
Liberalitas Julia *see* Évora
Liberec *98 B4 Ger.* Reichenberg.
 Liberecký Kraj, N Czech Republic
Liberia *52 D4* Guanacaste, NW Costa
 Rica
Liberia *74 C5 off.* Republic of Liberia.
 country W Africa

LIBERIA
West Africa

Official name Republic of Liberia
Formation 1847 / 1847
Capital Monrovia
Population 3.5 million / 94 people
per sq mile (36 people per sq km) / 47%
Total area 43,000 sq. miles (111,370 sq. km)
Languages English*, Kpelle, Vai, Bassa, Kru,
Grebo, Kissi, Gola, Loma
Religions Christian 68%, Traditional
beliefs 18%, Muslim 14%
Ethnic mix Indigenous tribes (16 main
groups) 95%, Americo-Liberians 5%
Government Presidential system
Currency Liberian dollar = 100 cents
Literacy rate 58%
Calorie consumption 1900 calories

Liberia, Republic of *see* Liberia
Libian Desert *see* Libyan Desert
Libīyah, Aş Şahrā' al *see* Libyan Desert
Libourne *91 B5* Gironde,
 SW France
Libreville *77 A5 country capital* (Gabon)
 (Gabon) Estuaire, NW Gabon
Libya *71 F3 off.* Great Socialist People's
 Libyan Arab Jamahiriya, *Ar.* Al
 Jamāhīrīyah al 'Arabīyah al Lībīyah ash
 Sha'bīyah al Ishtirākīy; *prev.* Libyan
 Arab Republic. *country* N Africa

LIBYA
North Africa

Official name The Great Socialist
People's Libyan Arab Jamahiriyah
Formation 1951 / 1951
Capital Tripoli
Population 6.1 million / 9 people
per sq mile (3 people per sq km) / 87%
Total area 679,358 sq. miles
(1,759,540 sq. km)
Languages Arabic*, Tuareg
Religions Muslim (mainly Sunni) 97%,
Other 3%
Ethnic mix Arab and Berber 95%,
Other 5%
Government One-party state
Currency Libyan dinar = 1000 dirhams
Literacy rate 82%
Calorie consumption 3320 calories

Libyan Arab Republic *see* Libya
Libyan Desert *71 H4 var.* Libian
 Desert, *Ar.* Aş Şahrā' al Lībīyah. *desert*
 N Africa
Libyan Plateau *103 F4 var.* Aḑ Ḑiffah.
 plateau Egypt/Libya
Lichtenfels *95 C5* Bayern, SE Germany
Lichtenvoorde *86 E4* Gelderland,
 E Netherlands
Lichuan *128 C5* Hubei, C China
Lida *107 B5* Hrodzyenskaya Voblasts',
 W Belarus
Lidhorikón *see* Lidoríki
Lidköping *85 B6* Västra Götaland,
 S Sweden
Lidokhorikion *see* Lidoríki
Lidoríki *105 B5 prev.* Lidhorikón,
 Lidokhorikion. Stereá Ellás,
 C Greece
Lidzbark Warmiński *98 D2 Ger.*
 Heilsberg. Olsztyn, N Poland
Liechtenstein *94 D1 off.* Principality of
 Liechtenstein. *country* C Europe

LIECHTENSTEIN
Central Europe

Official name Principality of
Liechtenstein
Formation 1719 / 1719
Capital Vaduz
Population 34,247 / 552 people
per sq mile (214 people per sq km) / 22%
Total area 62 sq. miles (160 sq. km)
Languages German*, Alemannish
dialect, Italian
Religions Roman Catholic 81%,
Other 12%, Protestant 7%
Ethnic mix Liechtensteiner 66%,
Other 12%, Swiss 10%, Austrian 6%,
German 3%, Italian 3%
Government Parliamentary system
Currency Swiss franc = 100 rappen/
centimes
Literacy rate 99%
Calorie consumption Not available

Liechtenstein, Principality of *see*
 Liechtenstein
Liège *87 D6 Dut.* Luik, *Ger.* Lüttich.
 Liège, E Belgium
Liegnitz *see* Legnica
Lienz *95 D7* Tirol, W Austria
Liepāja *106 B3 Ger.* Libau. Liepāja,
 W Latvia
Lietuva *see* Lithuania
Lievenhof *see* Līvāni
Liezen *95 D7* Steiermark, C Austria
Liffey *89 B6 river* Ireland
Lifou *144 D5 island* Îles Loyauté, E New
 Caledonia
Liger *see* Loire
Ligure, Appennino *96 A2 Eng.* Ligurian
 Mountains. *mountain range* NW Italy
Ligure, Mar *see* Ligurian Sea
Ligurian Mountains *see* Ligure,
 Appennino
Ligurian Sea *96 A3 Fr.* Mer
 Ligurienne, *It.* Mar Ligure. *sea*
 N Mediterranean Sea
Ligurienne, Mer *see* Ligurian Sea
Līhu'e *47 A7 var.* Lihue. Kaua'i,
 Hawaii, USA
Lihue *see* Līhu'e
Lihula *106 D2 Ger.* Leal. Läänemaa,
 W Estonia
Liivi Laht *see* Riga, Gulf of
Likasi *77 D7 prev.* Jadotville. Shaba,
 SE Dem. Rep. Congo
Liknes *85 A6* Vest-Agder, S Norway
Lille *90 C2 var.* l'Isle, *Dut.* Rijssel, *Flem.*
 Ryssel, *prev.* Lisle; *anc.* Insula. Nord,
 N France
Lillehammer *85 B5* Oppland, S Norway
Lillestrøm *85 B6* Akershus, S Norway
Lilongwe *79 E2 country capital* (Malawi)
 (Malawi) Central , W Malawi
Lilybaeum *see* Marsala
Lima *60 C4 country capital* (Peru) (Peru)
 Lima, W Peru
Limanowa *99 D5* Małopolskie, S Poland
Limassol *see* Lemesós
Limerick *89 A6 Ir.* Luimneach. Limerick,
 SW Ireland
Limín Vathéos *see* Sámos
Límnos *103 F3 anc.* Lemnos. *island*
 E Greece
Limoges *91 C5 anc.* Augustoritum
 Lemovicensium, Lemovices. Haute-
 Vienne, C France
Limón *53 E4 var.* Puerto Limón. Limón,
 E Costa Rica
Limón *52 D2* Colón, NE Honduras
Limonum *see* Poitiers
Limousin *91 C5 cultural region* C France
Limoux *91 C6* Aude, S France
Limpopo *78 D3 var.* Crocodile. *river*
 S Africa
Linares *64 B4* Maule, C Chile
Linares *51 E3* Nuevo León, NE Mexico
Linares *92 D4* Andalucía, S Spain
Lincoln *89 D5 anc.* Lindum, Lindum
 Colonia. *hist.* E England, United Kingdom
Lincoln *41 H2* Maine, NE USA
Lincoln *45 F4 state capital* Nebraska,
 C USA
Lincoln Sea *34 C2 sea* Arctic Ocean
Linden *59 F3* E Guyana
Líndhos *see* Líndos
Lindi *73 D8* Lindi, SE Tanzania

Líndos *105 E7 var.* Líndhos. Ródos,
 Dodekánisa, Greece, Aegean Sea
Lindum/Lindum Colonia *see* Lincoln
Line Islands *145 G3 island group*
 E Kiribati
Lingeh *see* Bandar-e Lengeh
Lingen *94 A3 var.* Lingen an der Ems.
 Niedersachsen, NW Germany
Lingen an der Ems *see* Lingen
Lingga, Kepulauan *138 B4 island group*
 W Indonesia
Linköping *85 C6* Östergötland, S Sweden
Linz *95 D6 anc.* Lentia. Oberösterreich,
 N Austria
Lion, Gulf of *91 C7 Eng.* Gulf of Lion,
 Gulf of Lions; *anc.* Sinus Gallicus. *gulf*
 S France
Lion, Gulf of/Lions, Gulf of *see* Lion,
 Golfe du
Liozno *see* Lyozna
Lipari *87 D6 It.* island Isole Eolie, S Italy
Lipari Islands/Lipari, Isole *see* Eolie,
 Isole
Lipetsk *111 B5* Lipetskaya Oblast',
 W Russian Federation
Lipno *98 C3* Kujawsko-pomorskie,
 C Poland
Lipova *108 A4 Hung.* Lippa. Arad,
 W Romania
Lipovets *see* Lypovets'
Lippa *see* Lipova
Lipsia/Lipsk *see* Leipzig
Lira *73 B6* N Uganda
Lisala *77 C5* Equateur, N Dem. Rep.
 Congo
Lisboa *92 B4 Eng.* Lisbon; *anc.*
 Felicitas Julia, Olisipo. *country*
 capital (Portugal) (Portugal) Lisboa,
 W Portugal
Lisbon *see* Lisboa
Lisichansk *see* Lysychans'k
Lisieux *90 B3 anc.* Noviomagus.
 Calvados, N France
Liski *111 B6 prev.* Georgiu-Dezh.
 Voronezhskaya Oblast', W Russian
 Federation
Lisle/l'Isle *see* Lille
Lismore *149 E5* New South Wales,
 SE Australia
Lissa *see* Vis, Croatia
Lissa *see* Leszno, Poland
Lisse *86 C3* Zuid-Holland,
 W Netherlands
Litang *128 A5 var.* Gaocheng. Sichuan,
 C China
Lītāni, Nahr el *119 B5 var.* Nahr el
 Litant. *river* C Lebanon
Litant, Nahr el *see* Litani, Nahr el
Litauen *see* Lithuania
Lithgow *149 D6* New South Wales,
 SE Australia
Lithuania *106 B4 off.* Republic of
 Lithuania, *Ger.* Litauen, *Lith.* Lietuva,
 Pol. Litwa, *Rus.* Litva; *prev.* Lithuanian
 SSR, *Rus.* Litovskaya SSR. *country*
 NE Europe

LITHUANIA
Northeast Europe

Official name Republic of Lithuania
Formation 1991 / 1991
Capital Vilnius
Population 3.4 million / 135 people
per sq mile (52 people per sq km) / 67%
Total area 25,174 sq. miles (65,200 sq. km)
Languages Lithuanian*, Russian
Religions Roman Catholic 83%,
Other 12%, Protestant 5%
Ethnic mix Lithuanian 83%, Polish 7%,
Russian 6%, Other 3%, Belorussian 1%
Government Parliamentary system
Currency Litas = 100 centu
Literacy rate 99%
Calorie consumption 3324 calories

Lithuanian SSR *see* Lithuania
Lithuania, Republic of *see* Lithuania
Litóchoro *104 B4 var.* Litohoro,
 Litókhoron. Kentrikí Makedonía,
 N Greece
Litohoro/Litókhoron *see* Litóchoro
Litovskaya SSR *see* Lithuania
Little Alföld *99 C6 Ger.* Kleines
 Ungarisches Tiefland, *Hung.* Kisalföld,
 Slvk. Podunajská Rovina. *plain*
 Hungary/Slovakia

Little Andaman 133 F2 *island* Andaman Islands, India, NE Indian Ocean
Little Barrier Island 150 D2 *island* N New Zealand
Little Bay 93 H5 *bay* Alboran Sea, Mediterranean Sea
Little Cayman 54 B3 *island* E Cayman Islands
Little Falls 45 F2 Minnesota, N USA
Littlefield 49 E2 Texas, SW USA
Little Inagua 54 D2 *var.* Inagua Islands. *island* S Bahamas
Little Minch, The 88 B3 *strait* NW Scotland, United Kingdom
Little Missouri River 44 D2 *river* NW USA
Little Nicobar 133 G3 *island* Nicobar Islands, India, NE Indian Ocean
Little Rhody *see* Rhode Island
Little Rock 42 B1 *state capital* Arkansas, C USA
Little Saint Bernard Pass 91 D5 *Fr.* Col du Petit St-Bernard, *It.* Colle del Piccolo San Bernardo. *pass* France/Italy
Little Sound 42 A5 *bay* Bermuda, NW Atlantic Ocean
Littleton 44 D4 Colorado, C USA
Littoria *see* Latina
Litva/Litwa *see* Lithuania
Liu-chou/Liuchow *see* Liuzhou
Liuzhou 128 C6 *var.* Liu-chou, Liuchow. Guangxi Zhuangzu Zizhiqu, S China
Livanátai *see* Livanátes
Livanátes 105 B5 *prev.* Livanátai. Stereá Ellás, C Greece
Līvāni 106 D4 *Ger.* Lievenhof. Preiļi, SE Latvia
Liverpool 39 F5 Nova Scotia, SE Canada
Liverpool 89 C5 NW England, United Kingdom
Livingston 44 B2 Montana, NW USA
Livingston 49 H3 Texas, SW USA
Livingstone 49 H3 *var.* Maramba. Southern, S Zambia
Livingstone 78 C3 *var.* Maramba. Southern, S Zambia
Livingstone Mountains 151 A7 *mountain range* South Island, New Zealand
Livno 100 B4 Federicija Bosna I Hercegovina, SW Bosnia and Herzegovina
Livojoki 84 D4 *river* C Finland
Livonia 40 D3 Michigan, N USA
Livorno 96 B3 *Eng.* Leghorn. Toscana, C Italy
Lixian Jiang *see* Black River
Lixoúri 105 A5 *prev.* Lixoúrion. Kefallinía, Iónia Nisiá, Greece, C Mediterranean Sea
Lixoúrion *see* Lixoúri
Lizarra *see* Estella
Ljouwert *see* Leeuwarden
Ljubelj *see* Loibl Pass
Ljubljana 95 D7 *Ger.* Laibach, *It.* Lubiana; *anc.* Aemona, Emona. *country capital* (Slovenia) (Slovenia) C Slovenia
Ljungby 85 B7 Kronoberg, S Sweden
Ljusdal 85 C5 Gävleborg, C Sweden
Ljusnan 85 C5 *river* C Sweden
Llanelli 89 C6 *prev.* Llanelly. SW Wales, United Kingdom
Llanelly *see* Llanelli
Llanes 92 D1 Asturias, N Spain
Llanos 58 D2 *physical region* Colombia/ Venezuela
Lleida 93 F2 *Cast.* Lérida; *anc.* Ilerda. Cataluña, NE Spain
Llucmajor 93 G3 Mallorca, Spain, W Mediterranean Sea
Loaita Island 128 C8 *island* W Spratly Islands
Loanda *see* Luanda
Lobatse 78 C4 *var.* Lobatsi. Kgatleng, SE Botswana
Lobatsi *see* Lobatse
Löbau 94 D4 Sachsen, E Germany
Lobito 78 B2 Benguela, W Angola
Lob Nor *see* Lop Nur
Lobositz *see* Lovosice
Loburi *see* Lop Buri
Locarno 95 B8 *Ger.* Luggarus. Ticino, S Switzerland
Lochem 86 E3 Gelderland, E Netherlands
Lockport 41 E4 New York, NE USA
Lodja 77 D6 Kasai-Oriental, C Dem. Rep. Congo

Lodwar 73 C6 Rift Valley, NW Kenya
Łódź 98 D4 *Rus.* Lodz. Łódź, C Poland
Loei 136 C4 *var.* Loey, Muang Loei. Loei, C Thailand
Loey *see* Loei
Lofoten 84 B3 *var.* Lofoten Islands. *island group* C Norway
Lofoten Islands *see* Lofoten
Logan 44 B3 Utah, W USA
Logan, Mount 36 D3 *mountain* Yukon Territory, W Canada
Logroño 93 E1 *anc.* Vareia, *Lat.* Juliobriga. La Rioja, N Spain
Loibl Pass 95 D7 *Ger.* Loiblpass, *Slvn.* Ljubelj. *pass* Austria/Slovenia
Loiblpass *see* Loibl Pass
Loikaw 136 B4 Kayah State, C Burma (Myanmar)
Loire 90 B4 *var.* Liger. *river* C France
Loja 60 B2 Loja, S Ecuador
Lokitaung 73 C5 Rift Valley, NW Kenya
Lokoja 75 G4 Kogi, C Nigeria
Loksa 106 E2 *Ger.* Loxa. Harjumaa, NW Estonia
Lolland 85 B8 *prev.* Laaland. *island* S Denmark
Lom 104 C1 *prev.* Lom-Palanka. Montana, NW Bulgaria
Lomami 77 D6 *river* C Dem. Rep. Congo
Lomas 60 D4 Arequipa, SW Peru
Lomas de Zamora 64 D4 Buenos Aires, E Argentina
Lombardia 96 B2 *Eng.* Lombardy. *region* N Italy
Lombardy *see* Lombardia
Lombok, Pulau 138 D5 *island* Nusa Tenggara, C Indonesia
Lomé 75 F5 *country capital* (Togo) (Togo) S Togo
Lomela 77 D6 Kasai-Oriental, C Dem. Rep. Congo
Lommel 87 C5 Limburg, N Belgium
Lomond, Loch 88 B4 *lake* C Scotland, United Kingdom
Lomonosov Ridge 155 B3 *var.* Harris Ridge, *Rus.* Khrebet Homonsova. *undersea ridge* Arctic Ocean
Lomonsova, Khrebet *see* Lomonosov Ridge
Lom-Palanka *see* Lom
Lompoc 47 B7 California, W USA
Lom Sak 136 C4 *var.* Muang Lom Sak. Phetchabun, C Thailand
Łomża 98 D3 *Rus.* Lomzha. Podlaskie, NE Poland
Lomzha *see* Łomża
Loncoche 65 B5 Araucanía, C Chile
Londinium *see* London
London 89 A7 *anc.* Augusta, *Lat.* Londinium. *country capital* (United Kingdom) (United Kingdom) SE England, United Kingdom
London 38 C5 Ontario, S Canada
London 40 C5 Kentucky, S USA
Londonderry 88 B4 *var.* Derry, *Ir.* Doire. NW Northern Ireland, United Kingdom
Londonderry, Cape 146 C2 *cape* Western Australia
Londrina 63 E4 Paraná, S Brazil
Lone Star State *see* Texas
Long Bay 43 F2 *bay* W Jamaica
Long Beach 47 C7 California, W USA
Longford 89 B5 *Ir.* An Longfort. Longford, C Ireland
Long Island 54 D2 *island* C Bahamas
Long Island 41 G4 *island* New York, NE USA
Longlac 38 C3 Ontario, S Canada
Longmont 44 D4 Colorado, C USA
Longreach 148 C4 Queensland, E Australia
Long Strait 115 G1 *Eng.* Long Strait. *strait* NE Russian Federation
Long Strait *see* Longa, Proliv
Longview 49 H3 Texas, SW USA
Longview 46 B2 Washington, NW USA
Long Xuyên 137 D6 *var.* Longxuyen. An Giang, S Vietnam
Longxuyen *see* Long Xuyên
Longyan 128 D6 Fujian, SE China
Longyearbyen 83 G2 *dependent territory capital* (Svalbard) Spitsbergen, W Svalbard
Lons-le-Saunier 90 D4 *anc.* Ledo Salinarius. Jura, E France
Lop Buri 137 C5 *var.* Loburi. Lop Buri, C Thailand

Lop Nor *see* Lop Nur
Lop Nur 126 C3 *var.* Lob Nor, Lop Nor, Lo-pu Po. *seasonal lake* NW China
Loppersum 86 E1 Groningen, NE Netherlands
Lo-pu Po *see* Lop Nur
Lorca 93 E4 *Ar.* Lurka; *anc.* Eliocroca, *Lat.* Illurco. Murcia, S Spain
Lord Howe Island 142 C4 *island* E Australia
Lord Howe Rise 142 C4 *undersea rise* SW Pacific Ocean
Loreto 50 B3 Baja California Sur, NW Mexico
Lorient 90 A3 *prev.* l'Orient. Morbihan, NW France
l'Orient *see* Lorient
Lorn, Firth of 88 B4 *inlet* W Scotland, United Kingdom
Loro Sae *see* East Timor
Lörrach 95 A7 Baden-Württemberg, S Germany
Lorraine 90 D3 *cultural region* NE France
Los Alamos 48 C1 New Mexico, SW USA
Los Ángeles 65 B5 Bío Bío, C Chile
Los Angeles 47 C7 California, W USA
Losanna *see* Lausanne
Lošinj 100 A3 *Ger.* Lussin, *It.* Lussino. *island* W Croatia
Loslau *see* Wodzisław Śląski
Los Mochis 50 C3 Sinaloa, C Mexico
Losonc/Losontz *see* Lučenec
Los Roques, Islas 58 D1 *island group* N Venezuela
Lot 91 B5 *cultural region* S France
Lot 91 B5 *river* S France
Lotagipi Swamp 73 C5 *wetland* Kenya/ Sudan
Lötzen *see* Giżycko
Loualaba *see* Lualaba
Louangnamtha 136 C3 *var.* Luong Nam Tha. Louang Namtha, N Laos
Louangphabang 124 D3 *var.* Louangphrabang, Luang Prabang. Louangphabang, N Laos
Louangphrabang *see* Louangphabang
Loubomo *see* Dolisie
Loudéac 90 A3 Côtes d'Armor, NW France
Loudi 128 C5 Hunan, S China
Louga 74 B3 NW Senegal
Louisiade Archipelago 144 B4 *island group* SE Papua New Guinea
Louisiana 42 A2 *off.* State of Louisiana, *also known as* Creole State, Pelican State. *state* S USA
Louisville 40 C5 Kentucky, S USA
Louisville Ridge 143 E4 *undersea ridge* S Pacific Ocean
Loup River 45 E4 *river* Nebraska, C USA
Lourdes 91 B6 Hautes-Pyrénées, S France
Lourenço Marques *see* Maputo
Louth 89 E5 E England, United Kingdom
Loutrá 104 C4 Kentrikí Makedonía, N Greece
Louvain *see* Leuven
Louvain-la-Neuve 87 C6 Walloon Brabant, C Belgium
Louviers 90 C3 Eure, N France
Lovech 104 C2 Lovech, N Bulgaria
Loveland 44 D4 Colorado, C USA
Lovosice 98 A4 *Ger.* Lobositz. Ústecký Kraj, NW Czech Republic
Lóvua 78 C1 Moxico, E Angola
Lowell 41 G3 Massachusetts, NE USA
Löwen *see* Leuven
Lower California 48 A4 *Eng.* Lower California. *peninsula* NW Mexico
Lower California *see* Baja California
Lower Hutt 151 D5 Wellington, North Island, New Zealand
Lower Lough Erne 89 A5 *lake* SW Northern Ireland, United Kingdom
Lower Red Lake 45 F1 *lake* Minnesota, N USA
Lower Rhine *see* Neder Rijn
Lower Tunguska 115 E3 *Eng.* Lower Tunguska. *river* N Russian Federation
Lower Tunguska *see* Nizhnyaya Tunguska
Lowestoft 89 E6 E England, United Kingdom
Loxa *see* Loksa
Lo-yang *see* Luoyang
Loyauté, Îles 144 D5 *island group* S New Caledonia

Loyev *see* Loyew
Loyew 107 D8 *Rus.* Loyev. Homyel'skaya Voblasts', SE Belarus
Loznica 100 C3 Serbia, W Serbia
Lu *see* Shandong, China
Lualaba 77 D6 *Fr.* Loualaba. *river* SE Dem. Rep. Congo
Luanda 78 A1 *var.* Loanda, Port. São Paulo de Loanda. *country capital* (Angola) Luanda, NW Angola
Luang Prabang *see* Louangphabang
Luang, Thale 137 C7 *lagoon* S Thailand
Luangua, Rio *see* Luangwa
Luangwa 73 B8 *var.* Aruângua, Rio Luangua. *river* Mozambique/Zambia
Luanshya 78 D2 Copperbelt, C Zambia
Luarca 92 C1 Asturias, N Spain
Lubaczów 99 E5 *var.* Lúbaczów. Podkarpackie, SE Poland
L'uban' 98 B4 Leningradskaya Oblast', Russian Federation
Lubānas Ezers *see* Lubāns
Lubango 78 B2 *Port.* Sá da Bandeira. Huíla, SW Angola
Lubāns 106 D4 *var.* Lubānas Ezers. *lake* E Latvia
Lubao 77 D6 Kasai-Oriental, C Dem. Rep. Congo
Lübben 94 D4 Brandenburg, E Germany
Lübbenau 94 D4 Brandenburg, E Germany
Lubbock 49 E2 Texas, SW USA
Lübeck 94 C2 Schleswig-Holstein, N Germany
Lubelska, Wyżyna 98 E4 *plateau* SE Poland
Lüben *see* Lubin
Lubiana *see* Ljubljana
Lubin 98 B4 *Ger.* Lüben. Dolnośląskie, SW Poland
Lublin 98 E4 *Rus.* Lyublin. Lubelskie, E Poland
Lubliniec 98 C4 Śląskie, S Poland
Lubnān, Jabal *see* Liban, Jebel
Lubny 109 F2 Poltavs'ka Oblast', NE Ukraine
Lubsko 98 B4 *Ger.* Sommerfeld. Lubuskie, W Poland
Lubumbashi 77 E8 *prev.* Élisabethville. Shaba, SE Dem. Rep. Congo
Lubutu 77 D6 Maniema, E Dem. Rep. Congo
Luca *see* Lucca
Lucan 89 B5 *Ir.* Leamhcán. Dublin, E Ireland
Lucanian Mountains *see* Lucano, Appennino
Lucano, Appennino 97 D5 *Eng.* Lucanian Mountains. *mountain range* S Italy
Lucapa 78 C1 *var.* Lukapa. Lunda Norte, NE Angola
Lucca 96 B3 *anc.* Luca. Toscana, C Italy
Lucea 54 A4 W Jamaica
Lucena 139 E1 *off.* Lucena City. Luzon, N Philippines
Lucena 92 D4 Andalucía, S Spain
Lucena City *see* Lucena
Lučenec 99 D6 *Ger.* Losontz, *Hung.* Losonc. Banskobystrický Kraj, C Slovakia
Lucentum *see* Alicante
Lucerna/Lucerne *see* Luzern
Luchow *see* Hefei
Łuck *see* Luts'k
Lucknow 135 E3 *var.* Lakhnau. *state capital* Uttar Pradesh, N India
Lüda *see* Dalian
Luda Kamchiya 104 D2 *river* E Bulgaria
Lüderitz 78 B4 *prev.* Angra Pequena. Karas, SW Namibia
Ludhiāna 134 D2 Punjab, N India
Ludington 40 C2 Michigan, N USA
Ludsan *see* Ludza
Luduş 108 B4 *Ger.* Ludasch, *Hung.* Maroşludas. Mureş, C Romania
Ludvika 85 C6 Dalarna, C Sweden
Ludwigsburg 95 B6 Baden-Württemberg, SW Germany
Ludwigsfelde 94 D3 Brandenburg, NE Germany
Ludwigshafen 95 B5 *var.* Ludwigshafen am Rhein. Rheinland-Pfalz, W Germany
Ludwigshafen am Rhein *see* Ludwigshafen

Ludwigslust *94 C3* Mecklenburg-Vorpommern, N Germany
Ludza *106 D4* Ger. Ludsan. Ludza, E Latvia
Luebo *77 C6* Kasai-Occidental, SW Dem. Rep. Congo
Luena *78 C2* var. Lwena, Port. Luso. Moxico, E Angola
Lufira *77 E7* river SE Dem. Rep. Congo
Lufkin *49 H3* Texas, SW USA
Luga *110 A4* Leningradskaya Oblast', NW Russian Federation
Lugano *95 B8* Ger. Lauis. Ticino, S Switzerland
Lugansk see Luhans'k
Lugdūnum see Lyon
Lugdunum Batavorum see Leiden
Lugenda, Rio *79 E2* river N Mozambique
Luggarus see Locarno
Lugh Ganana see Luuq
Lugo *92 C1* anc. Lugus Augusti. Galicia, NW Spain
Lugoj *108 A4* Ger. Lugosch, Hung. Lugos. Timiş, W Romania
Lugos/Lugosch see Lugoj
Lugus Augusti see Lugo
Luguvallium/Luguvallum see Carlisle
Luhans'k *109 H3* Rus. Lugansk; prev. Voroshilovgrad. Luhans'ka Oblast', E Ukraine
Luimneach see Limerick
Lukapa see Lucapa
Lukenie *77 C6* river C Dem. Rep. Congo
Lukovit *104 C2* Lovech, N Bulgaria
Łuków *98 E4* Ger. Bogendorf. Lubelskie, E Poland
Łukuga *77 D7* river SE Dem. Rep. Congo
Luleå *84 D4* Norrbotten, N Sweden
Luleälven *84 C3* river N Sweden
Lulonga *77 C5* river NW Dem. Rep. Congo
Lulua *77 D7* river S Dem. Rep. Congo
Luluabourg see Kananga
Lumber State see Maine
Lumbo *79 F2* Nampula, NE Mozambique
Lumsden *151 A7* Southland, South Island, New Zealand
Lund *85 B7* Skåne, S Sweden
Lüneburg *94 C3* Niedersachsen, N Germany
Lunga, Isola see Dugi Otok
Lungkiang see Qiqihar
Lungué-Bungo *78 C2* var. Lungwebungu. river Angola/Zambia
Lungwebungu see Lungué-Bungo
Luninets see Luninyets
Łuniniec see Luninyets
Luninyets *107 B7* Pol. Łuniniec, Rus. Luninets. Brestskaya Voblasts', SW Belarus
Lunteren *86 D4* Gelderland, C Netherlands
Luong Nam Tha see Louangnamtha
Luoyang *128 C4* var. Honan, Lo-yang. Henan, C China
Lupatia see Altamura
Lúrio *79 F2* Nampula, NE Mozambique
Lúrio, Rio *79 E2* river NE Mozambique
Lurka see Lorca
Lusaka *78 D2* country capital (Zambia) (Zambia) Lusaka, SE Zambia
Lushnja see Lushnjë
Lushnjë *101 C6* var. Lushnja. Fier, C Albania
Luso see Luena
Lussin/Lussino see Lošinj
Lūt, Baḥrat/Lut, Bahret see Dead Sea
Lut, Dasht-e *120 D3* var. Kavīr-e Lūt. desert E Iran
Lutetia/Lutetia Parisiorum see Paris
Lūt, Kavīr-e see Lūt, Dasht-e
Luton *89 D6* E England, United Kingdom
Łutselk'e *37 F4* prev. Snowdrift. Northwest Territories, W Canada
Luts'k *108 C1* Pol. Łuck, Rus. Lutsk. Volyns'ka Oblast', NW Ukraine
Lutsk see Luts'k
Lüttich see Liège
Lutzow-Holm Bay *154 C2* var. Lutzow-Holm Bay. bay Antarctica
Lutzow-Holm Bay see Lützow Holmbukta
Luuq *73 D6* It. Lugh Ganana. Gedo, SW Somalia
Luvua *77 D7* river SE Dem. Rep. Congo
Luwego *73 C8* river S Tanzania
Luxembourg *87 D8* country capital (Luxembourg) (Luxembourg) Luxembourg, S Luxembourg

Luxembourg *87 D8* off. Grand Duchy of Luxembourg, var. Lëtzebuerg, Luxemburg. country NW Europe

LUXEMBOURG
Northwest Europe

Official name Grand Duchy of Luxembourg
Formation 1867 / 1867
Capital Luxembourg-Ville
Population 480,222 / 481 people per sq mile (186 people per sq km) / 92%
Total area 998 sq. miles (2586 sq. km)
Languages French*, German*, Luxembourgish*
Religions Roman Catholic 97%, Protestant, Orthodox Christian, and Jewish 3%
Ethnic mix Luxembourger 62%, Foreign residents 38%
Government Parliamentary system
Currency Euro = 100 cents
Literacy rate 99%
Calorie consumption 3701 calories

Luxemburg see Luxembourg
Luxor *72 B2* Ar. Al Uqṣur. E Egypt
Luza *110 C4* Kirovskaya Oblast', NW Russian Federation
Luz, Costa de la *92 C5* coastal region SW Spain
Luzern *95 B7* Fr. Lucerne, It. Lucerna. Luzern, C Switzerland
Luzon *139 E1* island N Philippines
Luzon Strait *125 E3* strait Philippines/Taiwan
L'viv *108 B2* Ger. Lemberg, Pol. Lwów, Rus. L'vov. L'vivs'ka Oblast', W Ukraine
L'vov see L'viv
Lwena see Luena
Lwów see L'viv
Lyakhavichy *107 B6* Rus. Lyakhovichi. Brestskaya Voblasts', SW Belarus
Lyakhovichi see Lyakhavichy
Lyallpur see Faisalābād
Lyangar see Langar
Lyck see Ełk
Lycksele *84 C4* Västerbotten, N Sweden
Lycopolis see Asyūţ
Lyel'chytsy *107 C7* Rus. Lel'chitsy. Homyel'skaya Voblasts', SE Belarus
Lyepyel' *107 D5* Rus. Lepel'. Vitsyebskaya Voblasts', N Belarus
Lyme Bay *89 C7* bay S England, United Kingdom
Lynchburg *41 E5* Virginia, NE USA
Lynn see King's Lynn
Lynn Lake *37 F4* Manitoba, C Canada
Lynn Regis see King's Lynn
Lyon *91 D5* Eng. Lyons; anc. Lugdunum. Rhône, E France
Lyons see Lyon
Lyozna *107 E6* Rus. Liozno. Vitsyebskaya Voblasts', NE Belarus
Lypovets' *108 D2* Rus. Lipovets. Vinnyts'ka Oblast', C Ukraine
Lys see Leie
Lysychans'k *109 H3* Rus. Lisichansk. Luhans'ka Oblast', E Ukraine
Lyttelton *151 C6* South Island, New Zealand
Lyublin see Lublin
Lyubotin see Lyubotyn
Lyubotyn *109 G2* Rus. Lyubotin. Kharkivs'ka Oblast', E Ukraine
Lyulyakovo *104 E2* prev. Keremitlik. Burgas, E Bulgaria
Lyusina *107 B6* Rus. Lyusino. Brestskaya Voblasts', SW Belarus
Lyusino see Lyusina

M

Maale see Male'
Ma'ān *119 B7* Ma'ān, SW Jordan
Maardu *106 D2* Ger. Maart. Harjumaa, NW Estonia
Ma'aret-en-Nu'man see Ma'arrat an Nu'mān
Ma'arrat an Nu'mān *118 B3* var. Ma'aret-en-Nu'man, Fr. Maarret enn Naamâne. Idlib, NW Syria
Maarret enn Naamâne see Ma'arrat an Nu'mān

Maart see Maardu
Maas see Meuse
Maaseik *87 D5* prev. Maeseyck. Limburg, NE Belgium
Maastricht *87 D6* var. Maestricht; anc. Traiectum ad Mosam, Traiectum Tungorum. Limburg, SE Netherlands
Macao *129 C6* Chin. Aomen, Port. Macau. Guangdong, SE China
Macapá *63 E1* state capital Amapá, N Brazil
Macarsca see Makarska
Macassar see Makassar
Macău see Makó, Hungary
Macau see Macao
MacCluer Gulf see Berau, Teluk
Macdonnell Ranges *146 D4* mountain range Northern Territory, C Australia
Macedonia see Macedonia, FYR
Macedonia, FYR *101 D6* off. the Former Yugoslav Republic of Macedonia, Mac. Makedonija, abbrev. FYR Macedonia, FYROM. country SE Europe

MACEDONIA
Southeast Europe

Official name Republic of Macedonia
Formation 1991 / 1991
Capital Skopje
Population 2 million / 201 people per sq mile (78 people per sq km) / 60%
Total area 9781 sq. miles (25,333 sq. km)
Languages Macedonian*, Albanian*, Turkish, Romani, Serbian
Religions Orthodox Christian 59%, Muslim 26%, Other 10%, Roman Catholic 4%, Protestant 1%
Ethnic mix Macedonian 64%, Albanian 25%, Turkish 4%, Roma 3%, Other 2%, Serb 2%
Government Mixed presidential–parliamentary system
Currency Macedonian denar = 100 deni
Literacy rate 96%
Calorie consumption 2655 calories

Macedonia, the Former Yugoslav Republic of see Macedonia, FYR
Maceió *63 G3* state capital Alagoas, E Brazil
Machachi *60 B1* Pichincha, C Ecuador
Machala *60 B2* El Oro, SW Ecuador
Machanga *79 E3* Sofala, E Mozambique
Machilipatnam *132 D1* var. Bandar Masulipatnam. Andhra Pradesh, E India
Machiques *58 C2* Zulia, NW Venezuela
Macías Nguema Biyogo see Bioco, Isla de
Măcin *108 D5* Tulcea, SE Romania
Mackay *148 D4* Queensland, NE Australia
Mackay, Lake *146 C4* salt lake Northern Territory/Western Australia
Mackenzie *37 E3* river Northwest Territories, NW Canada
Mackenzie Bay *154 D3* bay Antarctica
Mackenzie Mountains *36 D3* mountain range Northwest Territories, NW Canada
Macleod, Lake *146 A4* lake Western Australia
Macomb *40 A4* Illinois, N USA
Macomer *97 A5* Sardegna, Italy, C Mediterranean Sea
Mâcon *91 D5* anc. Matisco, Matisco Ædourum. Saône-et-Loire, C France
Macon *42 D2* Georgia, SE USA
Macon *45 G4* Missouri, C USA
Macquarie Ridge *154 C5* undersea ridge SW Pacific Ocean
Macuspana *51 G4* Tabasco, SE Mexico
Ma'dabā *119 B6* var. Mādabā, Madeba; anc. Medeba. Ma'dabā, NW Jordan
Mādabā see Ma'dabā
Madagascar *79 F3* off. Democratic Republic of Madagascar, Malg. Madagasikara; prev. Malagasy Republic. country W Indian Ocean

MADAGASCAR
Indian Ocean

Official name Republic of Madagascar
Formation 1960 / 1960
Capital Antananarivo

MADAGASCAR
(continued)

Population 19.6 million / 87 people per sq mile (34 people per sq km) / 27%
Total area 226,656 sq. miles (587,040 sq. km)
Languages French*, Malagasy*, English*
Religions Traditional beliefs 52%, Christian (mainly Roman Catholic) 41%, Muslim 7%
Ethnic mix Other Malay 46%, Merina 26%, Betsimisaraka 15%, Betsileo 12%, Other 1%
Government Presidential system
Currency Ariary = 5 iraimbilanja
Literacy rate 71%
Calorie consumption 2005 calories

Madagascar *79 F3* island W Indian Ocean
Madagascar Basin *69 E7* undersea basin W Indian Ocean
Madagascar, Democratic Republic of see Madagascar
Madagascar Plateau *69 E7* var. Madagascar Ridge, Madagascar Rise, Rus. Madagaskarskiy Khrebet. undersea plateau W Indian Ocean
Madagascar Rise/Madagascar Ridge see Madagascar Plateau
Madagasikara see Madagascar
Madagaskarskiy Khrebet see Madagascar Plateau
Madang *144 B3* Madang, N Papua New Guinea
Madaniyin see Medenine
Madarska see Hungary
Made *86 C4* Noord-Brabant, S Netherlands
Madeba see Ma'dabā
Madeira *70 A2* var. Ilha de Madeira. island Madeira, Portugal, NE Atlantic Ocean
Madeira Plain *66 C3* abyssal plain E Atlantic Ocean
Madeira, Rio *62 D2* var. Río Madera. river Bolivia/Brazil
Madeleine, Îles de la *39 F4* Eng. Magdalen Islands. island group Québec, E Canada
Madera *47 B6* California, W USA
Madera, Río see Madeira, Rio
Madhya Pradesh *135 E4* prev. Central Provinces and Berar. cultural region C India
Madinat ath Thawrah *118 C2* var. Ath Thawrah. Ar Raqqah, N Syria
Madioen see Madiun
Madison *45 F3* South Dakota, N USA
Madison *40 B3* state capital Wisconsin, N USA
Madiun *138 D5* prev. Madioen. Jawa, C Indonesia
Madoera see Madura, Pulau
Madona *106 D4* Ger. Modohn. Madona, E Latvia
Madras see Chennai
Madras see Tamil Nādu
Madre de Dios, Río *61 E3* river Bolivia/Peru
Madre del Sur, Sierra *51 E5* mountain range S Mexico
Madre, Laguna *51 F3* lagoon NE Mexico
Madre, Laguna *49 G5* lagoon Texas, SW USA
Madre Occidental, Sierra *50 C3* var. Western Sierra Madre. mountain range C Mexico
Madre Oriental, Sierra *51 E3* var. Eastern Sierra Madre. mountain range C Mexico
Madre, Sierra *52 B2* var. Sierra de Soconusco. mountain range Guatemala/Mexico
Madrid *92 D3* country capital (Spain) (Spain) Madrid, C Spain
Madura see Madurai
Madurai *132 C3* prev. Madura, Mathurai. Tamil Nādu, S India
Madura, Pulau *138 D5* prev. Madoera. island C Indonesia
Maebasi *131 D5* var. Maebashi, Mayebashi. Gunma, Honshū, S Japan
Maebasi see Maebashi

Mae Nam Khong see Mekong
Mae Nam Nan 136 C4 river
NW Thailand
Mae Nam Yom 136 C4 river W Thailand
Maeseyck see Maaseik
Maestricht see Maastricht
Maéwo 144 D4 prev. Aurora. island
C Vanuatu
Mafia 73 D7 island E Tanzania
Mafraq/Muḥāfaẓat al Mafraq see Al
Mafraq
Magadan 115 G3 Magadanskaya Oblast',
E Russian Federation
Magallanes see Punta Arenas
Magallanes, Estrecho de see Magellan,
Strait of
Magangué 58 B2 Bolívar, N Colombia
Magdalena 61 F3 Beni, N Bolivia
Magdalena 50 B1 Sonora, NW Mexico
Isla Magdalena 63 B8 island NW Mexico
Magdalena, Río 58 B2 river C Colombia
Magdalen Islands see Madeleine,
Îles de la
Magdeburg 94 C4 Sachsen-Anhalt,
C Germany
Magelang 138 C5 Jawa, C Indonesia
Magellan, Strait of 65 B8 Sp. Estrecho de
Magallanes. strait Argentina/Chile
Magerøy see Magerøya
Magerøya 84 D1 var. Magerøy, Lapp.
Máhkarávju. island N Norway
Maggiore, Lago see Maggiore, Lake
Maggiore, Lake 96 B1 It. Lago Maggiore.
lake Italy/Switzerland
Maglaj 100 C3 Federacija Bosna
I Hercegovina, N Bosnia and
Herzegovina
Maglie 97 E6 Puglia, SE Italy
Magna 44 B4 Utah, W USA
Magnesia see Manisa
Magnitogorsk 114 B4 Chelyabinskaya
Oblast', C Russian Federation
Magnolia State see Mississippi
Magta' Lahjar 74 C3 var. Magta Lahjar,
Magta' Lahjar, Magtá Lahjar. Brakna,
SW Mauritania
Magway 136 A3 var. Magwe. Magway,
W Burma (Myanmar)
Magyar-Becse see Bečej
Magyarkanizsa see Kanjiža
Magyarország see Hungary
Mahajanga 79 F2 var. Majunga.
Mahajanga, NW Madagascar
Mahakam, Sungai 138 D4 var. Koetai,
Kutai. river Borneo, C Indonesia
Mahalapye 78 D3 var. Mahalatswe.
Central, SE Botswana
Mahalatswe see Mahalapye
Māhān 120 D3 Kermān, E Iran
Mahanādi 135 F4 river E India
Mahārāshtra 134 D5 cultural region
W India
Mahbés see El Mahbas
Mahbūbnagar 134 D5 Andhra Pradesh,
C India
Mahdia 71 F2 var. Al Mahdiyah,
Mehdia. NE Tunisia
Mahé 79 H1 island Inner Islands,
NE Seychelles
Mahia Peninsula 150 E4 peninsula
North Island, New Zealand
Mahilyow 107 D6 Rus. Mogilëv.
Mahilyowskaya Voblasts', E Belarus
Máhkarávju see Magerøya
Mahmūd-e 'Erāqī see Maḥmūd-e Rāqī
Maḥmūd-e Rāqī 123 E4 var. Mahmūd-e
'Erāqī. Kāpīsā, NE Afghanistan
Mahón 93 H3 Cat. Maó, Eng. Port
Mahon; anc. Portus Magonis. Menorca,
Spain, W Mediterranean Sea
Mähren see Moravia
Mährisch-Weisskirchen see Hranice
Maicao 58 C1 La Guajira, N Colombia
Mai Ceu/Mai Chio see Maych'ew
Maidstone 89 E7 SE England, United
Kingdom
Maiduguri 75 H4 Borno, NE Nigeria
Mailand see Milano
Maïmäna see Meymaneh
Main 95 B5 river C Germany
Mai-Ndombe, Lac 77 C6 prev. Lac
Léopold II. lake W Dem. Rep. Congo
Maine 41 G2 off. State of Maine, also
known as Lumber State, Pine Tree
State. state NE USA
Maine 90 B3 cultural region NW France
Maine, Gulf of 41 H2 gulf NE USA

Mainland 88 C2 island N Scotland,
United Kingdom
Mainland 88 D1 island NE Scotland,
United Kingdom
Mainz 95 B5 Fr. Mayence. Rheinland-
Pfalz, SW Germany
Maio 74 A3 var. Mayo. island Ilhas de
Sotavento, SE Cape Verde
Maisur see Karnātaka, India
Maisur see Mysore, India
Maizhokunggar 126 C5 Xizang Zizhiqu,
W China
Majorca 93 G3 Eng. Majorca; anc.
Baleares Major. island Islas Baleares,
Spain, W Mediterranean Sea
Majorca see Mallorca
Mājro see Majuro Atoll
Majunga see Mahajanga
Majuro Atoll 144 D2 var. Mājro. atoll
Ratak Chain, SE Marshall Islands
Makale see Mek'elē
Makarov Basin 155 B3 undersea basin
Arctic Ocean
Makarska 100 B4 It. Macarsca. Split-
Dalmacija, SE Croatia
Makasar see Makassar
Makasar, Selat see Makassar Straits
Makassar 139 E4 var. Macassar,
Makasar; prev. Ujungpandang.
Sulawesi, C Indonesia
Makassar Straits 138 D4 Ind. Makasar
Selat. strait C Indonesia
Makay 79 F3 var. Massif du Makay.
mountain range SW Madagascar
Makay, Massif du see Makay
Makedonija see Macedonia, FYR
Makeni 74 C4 C Sierra Leone
Makeyevka see Makiyivka
Makhachkala 114 A4 prev. Petrovsk-
Port. Respublika Dagestan, SW Russian
Federation
Makin 144 D2 prev. Pitt Island. atoll
Tungaru, W Kiribati
Makira see San Cristobal
Makiyivka 109 G3 Rus. Makeyevka;
prev. Dmitriyevsk. Donets'ka Oblast',
E Ukraine
Makkah 121 A5 Eng. Mecca. Makkah,
W Saudi Arabia
Makkovik 39 F2 Newfoundland and
Labrador, NE Canada
Makó 99 D7 Rom. Macău. Csongrád,
SE Hungary
Makoua 77 B5 Cuvette, C Congo
Makran Coast 120 E4 coastal region
SE Iran
Makrany 107 A6 Rus. Mokrany.
Brestskaya Voblasts', SW Belarus
Mākū 120 B2 Āzarbāyjān-e Gharbī,
NW Iran
Makurdi 75 G4 Benue, C Nigeria
Mala see Malaita, Solomon Islands
Malabār Coast 132 B3 coast SW India
Malabo 77 A5 prev. Santa Isabel. country
capital (Equatorial Guinea) (Equatorial
Guinea) Isla de Bioco, NW Equatorial
Guinea
Malaca see Málaga
Malacca, Strait of 138 B3 Ind. Selat
Malaka. strait Indonesia/Malaysia
Malacka see Malacky
Malacky 99 C6 Hung. Malacka.
Bratislavský Kraj, W Slovakia
Maladzyechna 107 C5 Pol. Molodeczno,
Rus. Molodechno. Minskaya Voblasts',
C Belarus
Málaga 92 D5 anc. Malaca. Andalucía,
S Spain
Malagarasi River 73 B7 river
W Tanzania Africa
Malagasy Republic see Madagascar
Malaita 144 C3 var. Mala. island
N Solomon Islands
Malakal 73 B5 Upper Nile, S Sudan
Malakula see Malekula
Malang 138 D5 Jawa, C Indonesia
Malange see Malanje
Malanje 78 B1 var. Malange. Malanje,
NW Angola
Mälaren 85 C6 lake C Sweden
Malatya 117 E4 anc. Melitene. Malatya,
SE Turkey
Mala Vyska 109 E3 Rus. Malaya Viska.
Kirovohrads'ka Oblast', S Ukraine
Malaŵi 79 E1 off. Republic of Malaŵi;
prev. Nyasaland, Nyasaland
Protectorate. country S Africa

MALAWI
Southern Africa

Official name Republic of Malawi
Formation 1964 / 1964
Capital Lilongwe
Population 13.5 million / 372 people
per sq mile (143 people per sq km) / 17%
Total area 45,745 sq. miles (118,480 sq. km)
Languages English*, Chewa, Lomwe,
Yao, Ngoni
Religions Protestant 55%, Roman
Catholic 20%, Muslim 20%, Traditional
beliefs 5%
Ethnic mix Bantu 99%, Other 1%
Government Presidential system
Currency Malawi kwacha = 100 tambala
Literacy rate 64%
Calorie consumption 2155 calories

Malawi, Lake see Nyasa, Lake
Malaŵi, Republic of see Malawi
Malaya Viska see Mala Vyska
Malay Peninsula 124 D4 peninsula
Malaysia/Thailand
Malaysia 138 B3 off. Malaysia, var.
Federation of Malaysia; prev. the
separate territories of Federation of
Malaya, Sarawak and Sabah (North
Borneo) and Singapore. country
SE Asia

MALAYSIA
Southeast Asia

Official name Malaysia
Formation 1963 / 1965
Capital Kuala Lumpur; Putrajaya
(administrative)
Population 26.2 million / 207 people
per sq mile (80 people per sq km) / 64%
Total area 127,316 sq. miles (329,750 sq. km)
Languages Bahasa Malaysia*, Malay,
Chinese, Tamil, English
Religions Muslim (mainly Sunni) 53%,
Buddhist 19%, Chinese faiths 7%,
Other 7%, Christian 7%, Traditional
beliefs 2%
Ethnic mix Malay 50%, Chinese 25%,
Indigenous tribes 11%, Other 7%,
Indian 7%
Government Parliamentary system
Currency Ringgit = 100 sen
Literacy rate 89%
Calorie consumption 2881 calories

Malaysia, Federation of see Malaysia
Malbork 98 C2 Ger. Marienburg,
Marienburg in Westpreussen.
Pomorskie, N Poland
Malchin 94 C3 Mecklenburg-
Vorpommern, N Germany
Malden 45 H5 Missouri, C USA
Malden Island 145 G3 prev.
Independence Island. atoll E Kiribati
Maldives 132 A4 off. Maldivian Divehi,
Republic of Maldives. country N Indian
Ocean

MALDIVES
Indian Ocean

Official name Republic of Maldives
Formation 1965 / 1965
Capital Male'
Population 369,031 / 3181 people
per sq mile (1230 people per sq km) / 29%
Total area 116 sq. miles (300 sq. km)
Languages Dhivehi (Maldivian)*, Sinhala,
Tamil, Arabic
Religions Sunni Muslim 100%
Ethnic mix Arab–Sinhalese–Malay 100%
Government Presidential system
Currency Rufiyaa = 100 laari
Literacy rate 96%
Calorie consumption 2548 calories

Maldives, Republic of see Maldives
Maldivian Divehi see Maldives
Male' 132 B4 Div. Maale. country capital
(Maldives) (Maldives) Male' Atoll,
C Maldives
Male' Atoll 132 B4 var. Kaafu Atoll. atoll
C Maldives
Malekula 144 D4 var. Malakula; prev.
Mallicolo. island W Vanuatu

Malesína 105 C5 Stereá Ellás, E Greece
Malheur Lake 46 C3 lake Oregon,
NW USA
Mali 75 E3 off. Republic of Mali, Fr.
République du Mali; prev. French
Sudan, Sudanese Republic. country
W Africa

MALI
West Africa

Official name Republic of Mali
Formation 1960 / 1960
Capital Bamako
Population 14.3 million / 30 people
per sq mile (12 people per sq km) / 33%
Total area 478,764 sq. miles
(1,240,000 sq. km)
Languages French*, Bambara, Fulani,
Senufo, Soninke
Religions Muslim (mainly Sunni) 80%,
Traditional beliefs 18%, Christian 1%,
Other 1%
Ethnic mix Bambara 32%, Other 26%,
Fulani 14%, Senufu 12%, Soninka 9%,
Tuareg 7%
Government Presidential system
Currency CFA franc = 100 centimes
Literacy rate 19%
Calorie consumption 2174 calories

Malik, Wadi al see Milk, Wadi el
Mali Kyun 137 B5 var. Tavoy Island.
island Mergui Archipelago, S Burma
(Myanmar)
Malin see Malyn
Malindi 73 D7 Coast, SE Kenya
Malines see Mechelen
Mali, Republic of see Mali
Mali, République du see Mali
Malkiye see Al Mālikīyah
Malko Tŭrnovo 104 E3 Burgas,
E Bulgaria
Mallaig 88 B3 N Scotland, United
Kingdom
Mallawī 72 B2 var. Mallawi. C Egypt
Mallawi see Mallawī
Mallicolo see Malekula
Malmberget 84 C3 Lapp. Malmivaara.
Norrbotten, N Sweden
Malmédy 87 D6 Liège, E Belgium
Malmivaara see Malmberget
Malmö 85 B7 Skåne, S Sweden
Maloelap see Maloelap Atoll
Maloelap Atoll 144 D1 var. Maloelap.
atoll E Marshall Islands
Małopolska, Wyżyna 98 D4 plateau
S Poland
Malozemel'skaya Tundra 110 D3
physical region NW Russian Federation
Malta 106 D4 Rēzekne, SE Latvia
Malta 44 C1 Montana, NW USA
Malta 97 C8 off. Republic of Malta.
country C Mediterranean Sea

MALTA
Southern Europe

Official name Republic of Malta
Formation 1964 / 1964
Capital Valletta
Population 401,880 / 3241 people
per sq mile (1256 people per sq km) / 92%
Total area 122 sq. miles (316 sq. km)
Languages Maltese*, English*
Religions Roman Catholic 98%,
Other and nonreligious 2%
Ethnic mix Maltese 96%, Other 4%
Government Parliamentary system
Currency Euro = 100 cents
Literacy rate 88%
Calorie consumption 3587 calories

Malta 97 C8 island Malta,
C Mediterranean Sea
Malta, Canale di see Malta Channel
Malta Channel 97 C8 It. Canale di Malta.
strait Italy/Malta
Malta, Republic of see Malta
Maluku, Laut see Molucca Sea
Malung 85 B6 Dalarna, C Sweden
Malventum see Benevento
Malvina, Isla Gran see West Falkland
Malvinas, Islas see Falkland Islands
Malyn 108 D2 Rus. Malin. Zhytomyrs'ka
Oblast', N Ukraine
Malyy Kavkaz see Lesser Caucasus

Mamberamo, Sungai *139 H4 river* Papua, E Indonesia
Mambij *see* Manbij
Mamonovo *106 A4* Ger. Heiligenbeil. Kaliningradskaya Oblast', W Russian Federation
Mamoré, Rio *61 F3 river* Bolivia/Brazil
Mamou *74 C4* W Guinea
Mamoudzou *79 F2 dependent territory capital* (Mayotte) C Mayotte
Mamuno *78 C3* Ghanzi, W Botswana
Manacor *93 G3* Mallorca, Spain, W Mediterranean Sea
Manado *139 F3 prev.* Menado. Sulawesi, C Indonesia
Managua *34 D4 country capital* (Nicaragua) (Nicaragua) Managua, W Nicaragua
Managua, Lake *52 C3 var.* Xolotlán. *lake* W Nicaragua
Manakara *79 G4* Fianarantsoa, SE Madagascar
Manama *see* Al Manāmah
Mananjary *79 G3* Fianarantsoa, SE Madagascar
Manáos *see* Manaus
Manapouri, Lake *151 A7 lake* South Island, New Zealand
Manar *see* Mannar
Manas, Gora *123 E2 mountain* Kyrgyzstan/Uzbekistan
Manaus *62 D2 prev.* Manáos. *state capital* Amazonas, NW Brazil
Manavgat *116 B4* Antalya, SW Turkey
Manbij *118 C2 var.* Mambij, Fr. Membidj. Ḥalab, N Syria
Manchester *89 D5 Lat* Mancunium. NW England, United Kingdom
Manchester *41 G3* New Hampshire, NE USA
Man-chou-li *see* Manzhouli
Manchurian Plain *125 E1 plain* NE China
Máncio Lima *see* Jaipim
Mancunium *see* Manchester
Mand *see* Mand, Rūd-e
Mandalay *136 B3* Mandalay, C Burma (Myanmar)
Mandan *45 E2* North Dakota, N USA
Mandeville *54 B5* C Jamaica
Mándra *105 C6* Attikí, C Greece
Rud-e Mand *120 D4 var.* Mand. *river* S Iran
Mandurah *147 A6* Western Australia
Manduria *97 E5* Puglia, SE Italy
Mandya *132 C2* Karnātaka, C India
Manfredonia *97 D5* Puglia, SE Italy
Mangai *77 C6* Bandundu, W Dem. Rep. Congo
Mangaia *145 G5 island group* S Cook Islands
Mangalia *108 D5 anc.* Callatis. Constanţa, SE Romania
Mangalmé *76 C3* Guéra, SE Chad
Mangalore *132 B2* Karnātaka, W India
Mangaung *see* Bloemfontein
Mango *see* Sansanné-Mango, Togo
Mangoky *79 F3 river* W Madagascar
Manhattan *45 F4* Kansas, C USA
Manicouagan, Réservoir *38 D3 lake* Québec, E Canada
Manihiki *145 G4 atoll* N Cook Islands
Manihiki Plateau *143 E3 undersea plateau* C Pacific Ocean
Maniitsoq *82 C3 var.* Manîtsoq, *Dan.* Sukkertoppen. Kitaa, S Greenland
Manila *139 E1 off.* City of Manila. *country capital* (Philippines) (Philippines) Luzon, N Philippines
Manila, City of *see* Manila
Manisa *116 A3 var.* Manissa, *prev.* Saruhan; *anc.* Magnesia. Manisa, W Turkey
Manissa *see* Manisa
Manitoba *37 F5 province* S Canada
Manitoba, Lake *37 F5 lake* Manitoba, S Canada
Manitoulin Island *38 C4 island* Ontario, S Canada
Manîtsoq *see* Maniitsoq
Manizales *58 B3* Caldas, W Colombia
Manjimup *147 A7* Western Australia
Mankato *45 F3* Minnesota, N USA
Manlleu *93 G2* Cataluña, NE Spain
Manly *148 E1* Iowa, C USA
Manmād *134 C5* Mahārāshtra, W India
Mannar *132 C3 var.* Manar. Northern Province, NW Sri Lanka

Mannar, Gulf of *132 C3 gulf* India/Sri Lanka
Mannheim *95 B5* Baden-Württemberg, SW Germany
Manono *77 E7* Shaba, SE Dem. Rep. Congo
Manosque *91 D6* Alpes-de-Haute-Provence, SE France
Manra *145 F3 prev.* Sydney Island. *atoll* Phoenix Islands, C Kiribati
Mansa *78 D2 prev.* Fort Rosebery. Luapula, N Zambia
Mansel Island *37 G3 island* Nunavut, NE Canada
Mansfield *40 D4* Ohio, N USA
Manta *60 A2* Manabí, W Ecuador
Manteca *47 B6* California, W USA
Mantoue *see* Mantova
Mantova *96 B2 Eng.* Mantua, *Fr.* Mantoue. Lombardia, NW Italy
Mantua *see* Mantova
Manuae *145 G4 island* S Cook Islands
Manukau *see* Manurewa
Manurewa *150 D3 var.* Manukau. Auckland, North Island, New Zealand
Manzanares *93 E3* Castilla-La Mancha, C Spain
Manzanillo *54 C3* Granma, E Cuba
Manzanillo *50 D4* Colima, SW Mexico
Manzhouli *127 F1 var.* Man-chou-li. Nei Mongol Zizhiqu, N China
Mao *76 B3* Kanem, W Chad
Maó *see* Mahón
Maoke, Pegunungan *139 H4 Dut.* Sneeuw-gebergte, *Eng.* Snow Mountains. *mountain range* Papua, E Indonesia
Maoming *128 C6* Guangdong, C China
Mapmaker Seamounts *125 H2 seamount range* N Pacific Ocean
Maputo *78 D4 prev.* Lourenço Marques. *country capital* (Mozambique) (Mozambique) Maputo, S Mozambique
Marabá *63 F2* Pará, NE Brazil
Maracaibo *58 C1* Zulia, NW Venezuela
Maracaibo, Gulf of *see* Venezuela, Golfo de
Maracaibo, Lake *58 C2 var.* Lake Maracaibo. *inlet* NW Venezuela
Maracaibo, Lake *see* Maracaibo, Lago de
Maracay *58 D2* Aragua, N Venezuela
Marada *see* Marādah
Marādah *71 G3 var.* Marada. N Libya
Maradi *75 G3* Maradi, S Niger
Maragha *see* Marāgheh
Marāgheh *120 C2 var.* Maragha. Āžarbāyjān-e Khāvarī, NW Iran
Marajó, Baía de *63 F1 bay* N Brazil
Marajó, Ilha de *63 E1 island* N Brazil
Marakesh *see* Marrakech
Maramba *see* Livingstone
Maramba *see* Livingstone
Maranhão *63 F2 off.* Estado do Maranhão. *region* E Brazil
Maranhão *63 F2 off.* Estado do Maranhão. *state* E Brazil
Marañón, Río *60 B2 river* N Peru
Marathon *38 C4* Ontario, S Canada
Marathón *see* Marathónas
Marathónas *105 C5 prev.* Marathón. Attikí, C Greece
Mārāzā *117 H2 Rus.* Maraza. E Azerbaijan
Maraza *see* Mārāzā
Marbella *92 D5* Andalucía, S Spain
Marble Bar *146 B4* Western Australia
Marburg *see* Marburg an der Lahn, Germany
Marburg *see* Maribor, Slovenia
Marburg an der Lahn *94 B4 hist.* Marburg. Hessen, W Germany
March *see* Morava
Marche *96 C3 Eng.* Marches. *region* C Italy
Marche *91 C5 cultural region* C France
Marche-en-Famenne *87 C7* Luxembourg, SE Belgium
Marchena, Isla *60 B5 var.* Bindloe Island. *island* Galapagos Islands, Ecuador, E Pacific Ocean
Marches *see* Marche
Mar Chiquita, Laguna *64 C3 lake* C Argentina
Marcounda *see* Markounda
Mardān *134 C1* North-West Frontier Province, N Pakistan

Mar del Plata *65 D5* Buenos Aires, E Argentina
Mardin *117 E4* Mardin, SE Turkey
Maré *144 D5 island* Îles Loyauté, E New Caledonia
Marea Neagră *see* Black Sea
Mareeba *148 D3* Queensland, NE Australia
Marek *see* Dupnitsa
Marganets *see* Marhanets'
Margarita, Isla de *59 E1 island* N Venezuela
Margate *89 E7 prev.* Mergate. SE England, United Kingdom
Margherita *see* Jamaame
Margherita, Lake *73 C5 Eng.* Lake Margherita. *lake* Abbaya Hāyk' SW Ethiopia
Margherita, Lake *see* Abaya Hāyk'
Marghita *108 B3 Hung.* Margitta. Bihor, NW Romania
Margitta *see* Marghita
Marhanets' *109 F3 Rus.* Marganets. Dnipropetrovs'ka Oblast', E Ukraine
María Cleofas, Isla *50 C4 island* C Mexico
Maria Island *149 C8 island* Tasmania, SE Australia
María Madre, Isla *50 C4 island* C Mexico
María Magdalena, Isla *50 C4 island* C Mexico
Mariana Trench *125 G4 var.* Challenger Deep. *trench* W Pacific Ocean
Mariánské Lázně *99 A5* Ger. Marienbad. Karlovarský Kraj, W Czech Republic
Marías, Islas *50 C4 island group* C Mexico
Maria-Theresiopel *see* Subotica
Maribor *95 E7 var.* Marburg. NE Slovenia
Marica *see* Maritsa
Maridi *73 B5* Western Equatoria, SW Sudan
Marie Byrd Land *154 A3 physical region* Antarctica
Marie-Galante *55 G4 var.* Ceyre to the Caribs. *island* SE Guadeloupe
Marienbad *see* Mariánské Lázně
Marienburg *see* Alūksne, Latvia
Marienburg *see* Malbork, Poland
Marienburg in Westpreussen *see* Malbork
Marienhausen *see* Viļaka
Mariental *78 B4* Hardap, SW Namibia
Marienwerder *see* Kwidzyń
Mariestad *85 B6* Västra Götaland, S Sweden
Marietta *42 D2* Georgia, SE USA
Marijampolė *106 B4 prev.* Kapsukas. Marijampolė, S Lithuania
Marília *63 E4* São Paulo, S Brazil
Marín *92 B1* Galicia, NW Spain
Mar"ina Gorka *see* Mar"ina Horka
Mar"ina Horka *107 C6 Rus.* Mar"ina Gorka. Minskaya Voblasts', C Belarus
Maringá *63 F4* Paraná, S Brazil
Marion *45 G3* Iowa, C USA
Marion *40 D4* Ohio, N USA
Marion, Lake *43 E2 reservoir* South Carolina, SE USA
Mariscal Estigarribia *64 D2* Boquerón, NW Paraguay
Maritsa *104 D3 var.* Marica, *Gk.* Évros, *Turk.* Meriç; *anc.* Hebrus. *river* SW Europe
Maritzburg *see* Pietermaritzburg
Mariupol' *109 G4 prev.* Zhdanov. Donets'ka Oblast', SE Ukraine
Marka *73 D6 var.* Merca. Shabeellaha Hoose, S Somalia
Markham, Mount *154 B4 mountain* Antarctica
Markounda *76 C4 var.* Marcounda. Ouham, NW Central African Republic
Marktredwitz *95 C5* Bayern, E Germany
Marlborough *148 D4* Queensland, E Australia
Marmanda *see* Marmande
Marmande *91 B5 anc.* Marmanda. Lot-et-Garonne, SW France
Sea of Marmara *116 A2 Eng.* Sea of Marmara. *sea* NW Turkey
Marmara, Sea of *see* Marmara Denizi
Marmaris *116 A4* Muğla, SW Turkey
Marne *90 D3 cultural region* N France
Marne *90 D3 river* N France
Maro *76 C4* Moyen-Chari, S Chad
Maroantsetra *79 G2* Toamasina, NE Madagascar

Maromokotro *79 G2 mountain* N Madagascar
Maroni *59 G3 Dut.* Marowijne. *river* French Guiana/Suriname
Maroshevíz *see* Toplița
Marosludas *see* Luduş
Marosvásárhely *see* Târgu Mureş
Marotiri *143 F4 var.* Îlots de Bass, Morotiri. *island group* Îles Australes, SW French Polynesia
Maroua *76 B3* Extrême-Nord, N Cameroon
Marowijne *see* Maroni
Marquesas Fracture Zone *153 E3 fracture zone* E Pacific Ocean
Marquette *40 B1* Michigan, N USA
Marrakech *70 C2 var.* Marakesh, *Eng.* Marrakesh; *prev.* Morocco. W Morocco
Marrakesh *see* Marrakech
Marrawah *149 C8* Tasmania, SE Australia
Marree *149 B5* South Australia
Marsá al Burayqah *71 G3 var.* Al Burayqah. N Libya
Marsabit *73 C6* Eastern, N Kenya
Marsala *97 B7 anc.* Lilybaeum. Sicilia, Italy, C Mediterranean Sea
Marsberg *94 B4* Nordrhein-Westfalen, W Germany
Marseille *91 D6 Eng.* Marseilles; *anc.* Massilia. Bouches-du-Rhône, SE France
Marseilles *see* Marseille
Marshall *45 F2* Minnesota, N USA
Marshall *49 H2* Texas, SW USA
Marshall Islands *144 C1 off.* Republic of the Marshall Islands. *country* W Pacific Ocean

Marshall Islands, Republic of the *see* Marshall Islands
Marshall Seamounts *125 H3 seamount range* SW Pacific Ocean
Marsh Harbour *54 C1* Great Abaco, W Bahamas
Martaban *136 B4 var.* Moktama. Mon State, S Burma (Myanmar)
Martha's Vineyard *41 G3 island* Massachusetts, NE USA
Martigues *91 D6* Bouches-du-Rhône, SE France
Martin *99 C5 Ger.* Sankt Martin, *Hung.* Turócszentmárton; *prev.* Turčiansky Svätý Martin. Žilinský Kraj, N Slovakia
Martinique *55 G4 French overseas department* E West Indies
Martinique Channel *see* Martinique Passage
Martinique Passage *55 G4 var.* Dominica Channel, Martinique Channel. *channel* Dominica/Martinique
Marton *150 D4* Manawatu-Wanganui, North Island, New Zealand
Martos *92 D4* Andalucía, S Spain
Marungu *77 E7 mountain range* SE Dem. Rep. Congo
Mary *122 D3 Ger.* Merv. Mary Welaýaty, S Turkmenistan
Maryborough *149 D4* Queensland, E Australia
Maryborough *see* Port Laoise
Mary Island *see* Kanton
Maryland *41 E5 off.* State of Maryland, *also known as* America in Miniature, Cockade State, Free State, Old Line State. *state* NE USA
Maryland, State of *see* Maryland

Maryville *45 F4* Missouri, C USA
Maryville *42 D1* Tennessee, S USA
Masai Steppe *73 C7 grassland*
NW Tanzania
Masaka *73 B6* SW Uganda
Masallı *117 H3 Rus.* Masally.
S Azerbaijan
Masally see Masallı
Masasi *73 C8* Mtwara, SE Tanzania
Masawa/Massawa see Mits'iwa
Masaya *52 D3* Masaya, W Nicaragua
Mascarene Basin *141 B5 undersea basin*
W Indian Ocean
Mascarene Islands *79 H4 island group*
W Indian Ocean
Mascarene Plain *141 B5 abyssal plain*
W Indian Ocean
Mascarene Plateau *141 B5 undersea
plateau* W Indian Ocean
Maseru *78 D4 country capital* (Lesotho)
(Lesotho) W Lesotho
Mas-ḥa *119 D7* W West Bank Asia
Mashhad *120 E2 var.* Meshed.
Khorāsān-Razavī, NE Iran
Masindi *73 B6* W Uganda
Masira see Maşīrah, Jazīrat
Masira, Gulf of *121 E5 var.* Gulf of
Masira. *bay* E Oman
Masira, Gulf of see Maşīrah, Khalīj
Maşīrah, Jazīrat *121 E5 var.* Masira.
island E Oman
Masis see Büyükağrı Dağı
Maskat see Masqaţ
Mason City *45 F3* Iowa, C USA
Masqaţ *121 E5 var.* Maskat, *Eng.* Muscat.
country capital (Oman) (Oman)
NE Oman
Massa *96 B3* Toscana, C Italy
Massachusetts *41 G3 off.*
Commonwealth of Massachusetts, *also
known as* Bay State, Old Bay State, Old
Colony State. *state* NE USA
Massenya *76 B3* Chari-Baguirmi,
SW Chad
Massif Central *91 C5 plateau* C France
Massilia see Marseille
Massoukou see Franceville
Mastanli see Momchilgrad
Masterton *151 D5* Wellington, North
Island, New Zealand
Masty *107 B5 Rus.* Mosty.
Hrodzyenskaya Voblasts', W Belarus
Masuda *131 B6* Shimane, Honshū,
SW Japan
Masuku see Franceville
Masvingo *78 D3 prev.* Fort Victoria,
Nyanda, Victoria. Masvingo,
SE Zimbabwe
Maşyāf *118 B3 Fr.* Misiaf. Ḥamāh,
C Syria
Matadi *77 B6* Bas-Congo, W Dem.
Rep. Congo
Matagalpa *52 D3* Matagalpa,
C Nicaragua
Matale *132 D3* Central Province,
C Sri Lanka
Matam *74 C3* NE Senegal
Matamata *150 D3* Waikato, North
Island, New Zealand
Matamoros *50 D3* Coahuila, NE Mexico
Matamoros *51 E2* Tamaulipas,
C Mexico
Matane *39 E4* Québec, SE Canada
Matanzas *54 B2* Matanzas, NW Cuba
Matara *132 D4* Southern Province,
S Sri Lanka
Mataram *138 D5* Pulau Lombok,
C Indonesia
Mataró *93 G2 anc.* Illuro. Cataluña,
E Spain
Mataura *151 B7* Southland, South Island,
New Zealand
Mataura *151 B7 river* South Island,
New Zealand
Mata Uta see Matā'utu
Matā'utu *145 E4 var.* Mata Uta.
dependent territory capital (Wallis and
Futuna) Île Uvea, Wallis and Futuna
Matera *97 E5* Basilicata, S Italy
Mathurai see Madurai
Matianus see Orūmīyeh, Daryācheh-ye
Matías Romero *51 F5* Oaxaca,
SE Mexico
Matisco/Matisco Ædourum see Mâcon
Mato Grosso *63 E3 off.* Estado de Mato
Grosso; *prev.* Matto Grosso. *state*
W Brazil

Mato Grosso *63 E3 off.* Estado de Mato
Grosso; *prev.* Matto Grosso. *region*
W Brazil
Mato Grosso do Sul *63 E4 off.* Estado de
Mato Grosso do Sul. *state* S Brazil
Mato Grosso do Sul *63 E4 off.* Estado de
Mato Grosso do Sul. *region* S Brazil
Mato Grosso do Sul, Estado de see Mato
Grosso do Sul
Mato Grosso, Estado de see Mato Grosso
Mato Grosso, Planalto de *56 C4 plateau*
C Brazil
Matosinhos *92 B2 prev.* Matozinhos.
Porto, NW Portugal
Matozinhos see Matosinhos
Matsue *131 B6 var.* Matsuye, Matue.
Shimane, Honshū, SW Japan
Matsumoto *131 C5 var.* Matumoto.
Nagano, Honshū, S Japan
Matsuyama *131 B7 var.* Matuyama.
Ehime, Shikoku, SW Japan
Matsuye see Matsue
Matterhorn *95 A8 It.* Monte Cervino.
mountain Italy/Switzerland
Matthews Ridge *59 F2* N Guyana
Matthew Town *54 D2* Great Inagua,
S Bahamas
Matto Grosso see Mato Grosso
Matucana *60 C4* Lima, W Peru
Matue see Matsue
Matumoto see Matsumoto
Maturín *59 E2* Monagas, NE Venezuela
Matuyama see Matsuyama
Mau *135 E3 var.* Maunāth Bhanjan.
Uttar Pradesh, N India
Maui *47 B8 island* Hawai'i, USA,
C Pacific Ocean
Maun *78 C3* North-West, C Botswana
Maunāth Bhanjan see Mau
Mauren *94 E1* NE Liechtenstein Europe
Maurice see Mauritius
Mauritania *74 C2 off.* Islamic Republic of
Mauritania, *Ar.* Mūrītānīyah. *country*
W Africa

MAURITANIA
West Africa

Official name Islamic Republic
of Mauritania
Formation 1960 / 1960
Capital Nouakchott
Population 3.2 million / 8 people
per sq mile (3 people per sq km) / 63%
Total area 397,953 sq. miles
(1,030,700 sq. km)
Languages Hassaniyah Arabic*,
Wolof, French
Religions Sunni Muslim 100%
Ethnic mix Maure 81%, Wolof 7%,
Tukolor 5%, Other 4%, Soninka 3%
Government Presidential system
Currency Ouguiya = 5 khoums
Literacy rate 51%
Calorie consumption 2772 calories

Mauritania, Islamic Republic of see
Mauritania
Mauritius *79 H3 off.* Republic of
Mauritius, *Fr.* Maurice. *country*
W Indian Ocean

MAURITIUS
Indian Ocean

Official name Republic of Mauritius
Formation 1968 / 1968
Capital Port Louis
Population 1.3 million / 1811 people
per sq mile (699 people per sq km) / 44%
Total area 718 sq. miles (1860 sq. km)
Languages English*, French Creole, Hindi,
Urdu, Tamil, Chinese, French
Religions Hindu 52%, Roman
Catholic 26%, Muslim 17%, Other 3%,
Protestant 2%
Ethnic mix Indo-Mauritian 68%,
Creole 27%, Sino-Mauritian 3%,
Franco-Mauritian 2%
Government Parliamentary system
Currency Mauritian rupee = 100 cents
Literacy rate 84%
Calorie consumption 2955 calories

Mauritius *141 B5 island* W Indian Ocean
Mauritius, Republic of see Mauritius
Mawlamyaing see Mawlamyine

Mawlamyine *136 B4 var.* Mawlamyaing,
Moulmein. Mon State, S Burma
(Myanmar)
Mawson *154 D2 Australian research
station* Antarctica
Mayādīn see Al Mayādīn
Mayaguana *54 D2 island* SE Bahamas
Mayaguana Passage *54 D2 passage*
SE Bahamas
Mayagüez *55 F3* W Puerto Rico
Mayamey *120 D2* Semnān, N Iran
Maya Mountains *52 B2 Sp.* Montañas
Mayas. *mountain range* Belize/
Guatemala
Mayas, Montañas see Maya Mountains
Maych'ew *72 C4 var.* Mai Chio, *It.* Mai
Ceu. Tigray, N Ethiopia
Maydān Shahr see Meydān Shahr
Mayebashi see Maebashi
Mayence see Mainz
Mayfield *151 B6* Canterbury, South
Island, New Zealand
Maykop *111 A7* Respublika Adygeya,
SW Russian Federation
Maymana see Meymaneh
Maymyo see Pyin-Oo-Lwin
Mayo see Maio
Mayor Island *150 D3 island* NE New
Zealand
Mayor Pablo Lagerenza see Capitán
Pablo Lagerenza
Mayotte *79 F2 French territorial
collectivity* E Africa
May Pen *54 B5* C Jamaica
Mayyit, Al Bahr al see Dead Sea
Mazabuka *78 D2* Southern, S Zambia
Mazaca see Kayseri
Mazagan see El-Jadida
Mazār-e Sharīf *123 E3 var.* Mazâr-i
Sharīf. Balkh, N Afghanistan
Mazâr-i Sharīf see Mazār-e Sharīf
Mazatlán *50 C3* Sinaloa, C Mexico
Mažeikiai *106 B3* Telšiai, NW Lithuania
Mazirbe *106 C2* Talsi, NW Latvia
Mazra'a see Al Mazra'ah
Mazury *98 D3 physical region* NE Poland
Mazyr *107 C7 Rus.* Mozyr'.
Homyel'skaya Voblasts', SE Belarus
Mbabane *78 D4 country capital*
(Swaziland) (Swaziland) NW Swaziland
Mbacké see Mbaké
Mbaïki *77 C5 var.* M'Baiki. Lobaye,
SW Central African Republic
M'Baiki see Mbaïki
Mbaké *74 B3 var.* Mbacké. W Senegal
Mbala *78 D1 prev.* Abercorn. Northern,
NE Zambia
Mbale *73 C6* E Uganda
Mbandaka *77 C5 prev.* Coquilhatville.
Equateur, NW Dem. Rep. Congo
M'Banza Congo *78 B1 var.* Mbanza
Congo; *prev.* São Salvador, São
Salvador do Congo. Dem. Rep. Congo,
NW Angola
Mbanza-Ngungu *77 B6* Bas-Congo,
W Dem. Rep. Congo
Mbarara *73 B6* SW Uganda
Mbé *76 B4* Nord, N Cameroon
Mbeya *73 C7* Mbeya, SW Tanzania
Mbomou/M'Bomu/Mbomu see Bomu
Mbour *74 B3* W Senegal
Mbuji-Mayi *77 D7 prev.* Bakwanga.
Kasai-Oriental, S Dem. Rep. Congo
McAlester *49 G2* Oklahoma, C USA
McAllen *49 G5* Texas, SW USA
McCamey *49 E3* Texas, SW USA
McClintock Channel *37 F2 channel*
Nunavut, N Canada
McComb *42 B3* Mississippi, S USA
McCook *45 E4* Nebraska, C USA
McKean Island *145 E3 island* Phoenix
Islands, C Kiribati
Mount McKinley *36 C3 var.* Denali.
mountain Alaska, USA
McKinley Park *36 C3* Alaska, USA
McMinnville *46 B3* Oregon, NW USA
McMurdo *154 B4 US research station*
Antarctica
McPherson *45 E5* Kansas, C USA
McPherson see Fort McPherson
Mdantsane *78 D5* Eastern Cape,
SE South Africa
Mead, Lake *47 D6 reservoir* Arizona/
Nevada, W USA
Mecca see Makkah
Mechelen *87 C5 Eng.* Mechlin, *Fr.*
Malines. Antwerpen, C Belgium

Mechlin see Mechelen
Mecklenburger Bucht *94 C2 bay*
N Germany
Mecsek *99 C7 mountain range*
SW Hungary
Medan *138 B3* Sumatera, E Indonesia
Medeba see Ma'dabā
Medellín *58 B3* Antioquia,
NW Colombia
Médenine *71 F2 var.* Madanīyīn.
SE Tunisia
Medeshamstede see Peterborough
Medford *46 B4* Oregon, NW USA
Medgidia *108 D5* Constanța, SE Romania
Medgyes see Mediaș
Mediaș *108 B4 Ger.* Mediasch, *Hung.*
Medgyes. Sibiu, C Romania
Mediasch see Mediaș
Medicine Hat *37 F5* Alberta, SW Canada
Medina see Al Madīnah
Medinaceli *93 E2* Castilla-León, N Spain
Medina del Campo *92 D2* Castilla-León,
N Spain
Medinat Israel see Israel
Mediolanum see Saintes, France
Mediolanum see Milano, Italy
Mediomatrica see Metz
Mediterranean Sea *102 D3 Fr.* Mer
Méditerranée. *sea* Africa/Asia/Europe
Méditerranée, Mer see Mediterranean
Sea
Médoc *91 B5 cultural region* SW France
Medvezh'yegorsk *110 B3* Respublika
Kareliya, NW Russian Federation
Meekatharra *147 B5* Western Australia
Meemu Atoll see Mulakatholhu
Meerssen *87 D6 var.* Mersen. Limburg,
SE Netherlands
Meerut *134 D2* Uttar Pradesh, N India
Megáli Préspa, Límni see Prespa, Lake
Meghālaya *113 G3 cultural region*
NE India
Mehdia see Mahdia
Meheso see Mi'ēso
Me Hka see Nmai Hka
Mehriz *120 D3* Yazd, C Iran
Mehtar Lām *123 F4 var.* Mehtarlām,
Meterlam, Metharlam, Metharlam.
Laghmān, E Afghanistan
Mehtarlām see Mehtar Lām
Meiktila *136 B3* Mandalay, C Burma
(Myanmar)
Méjico see Mexico
Mejillones *64 B2* Antofagasta, N Chile
Mek'elē *72 C4 var.* Makale. Tigray,
N Ethiopia
Mékhé *74 B3* NW Senegal
Mekong *124 D3 var.* Lan-ts'ang Chiang,
Cam. Mékôngk, *Chin.* Lancang Jiang,
Lao. Mènam Khong, *Th.* Mae Nam
Khong, *Tib.* Dza Chu, *Vtn.* Sông Tiên
Giang. *river* SE Asia
Mékôngk see Mekong
Mekong, Mouths of the *137 E6 delta*
S Vietnam
Melaka *138 B3 var.* Malacca. Melaka,
Peninsular Malaysia
Melaka, Selat see Malacca, Strait of
Melanesia *144 D3 island group* W Pacific
Ocean
Melanesian Basin *142 C2 undersea
basin* W Pacific Ocean
Melbourne *149 C7 state capital* Victoria,
SE Australia
Melbourne *43 E4* Florida, SE USA
Meleda see Mljet
Melghir, Chott *71 E2 var.* Chott Melrhir.
salt lake E Algeria
Melilla *80 B5 anc.* Rusaddir, Russadir.
Melilla, Spain, N Africa
Melilla *70 D2 enclave* Spain, N Africa
Melita *37 F5* Manitoba, S Canada
Melita see Mljet
Melitene see Malatya
Melitopol' *109 F4* Zaporiz'ka Oblast',
SE Ukraine
Melle *87 B5* Oost-Vlaanderen,
NW Belgium
Mellerud *85 B6* Västra Götaland,
S Sweden
Mellieha *102 B5* E Malta
Mellizo Sur, Cerro *65 A7 mountain*
S Chile
Melo *64 E4* Cerro Largo, NE Uruguay
Melodunum see Melun
Melrhir, Chott see Melghir, Chott
Melsungen *94 B4* Hessen, C Germany

Melun *90 C3 anc.* Melodunum. Seine-et-Marne, N France
Melville Bay/Melville Bugt *see* Qimusseriarsuaq
Melville Island *146 D2 island* Northern Territory, N Australia
Melville Island *37 E2 island* Parry Islands, Northwest Territories, NW Canada
Melville, Lake *39 F2 lake* Newfoundland and Labrador, E Canada
Melville Peninsula *37 G3 peninsula* Nunavut, NE Canada
Melville Sound *see* Viscount Melville Sound
Membidj *see* Manbij
Memel *see* Neman, NE Europe
Memel *see* Klaipėda, Lithuania
Memmingen *95 B6* Bayern, S Germany
Memphis *42 C1* Tennessee, S USA
Menaam *see* Menaldum
Menado *see* Manado
Ménaka *75 F3* Goa, E Mali
Menaldum *86 D1 Fris.* Menaam. Friesland, N Netherlands
Mènam Sound *see* Mekong
Mendaña Fracture Zone *153 F4 fracture zone* E Pacific Ocean
Mende *91 C5 anc.* Mimatum. Lozère, S France
Mendeleyev Ridge *155 B2 undersea ridge* Arctic Ocean
Mendocino Fracture Zone *152 D2 fracture zone* NE Pacific Ocean
Mendoza *64 B4* Mendoza, W Argentina
Menemen *116 A3* İzmir, W Turkey
Menengiyn Tal *127 F2 plain* E Mongolia
Menongue *78 B2 var.* Vila Serpa Pinto, *Port.* Serpa Pinto. Cuando Cubango, C Angola
Mentawai, Kepulauan *138 A4 island group* W Indonesia
Meppel *86 D2* Drenthe, NE Netherlands
Meran *see* Merano
Merano *96 C1 Ger.* Meran. Trentino-Alto Adige, N Italy
Merca *see* Marka
Mercedes *64 D3* Corrientes, NE Argentina
Mercedes *64 D4* Soriano, SW Uruguay
Meredith, Lake *49 E1 reservoir* Texas, SW USA
Merefa *109 G2* Kharkiv's'ka Oblast', E Ukraine
Mergate *see* Margate
Mergui *see* Myeik
Mergui Archipelago *137 B6 island group* S Burma (Myanmar)
Mérida *51 H3* Yucatán, SW Mexico
Mérida *92 C4 anc.* Augusta Emerita. Extremadura, W Spain
Mérida *58 C2* Mérida, W Venezuela
Meridian *42 C2* Mississippi, S USA
Mérignac *91 B5* Gironde, SW France
Merín, Laguna *see* Mirim Lagoon
Merkulovichi *see* Myerkulavichy
Merowe *72 B3* Northern, N Sudan
Merredin *147 B6* Western Australia
Mersen *see* Meerssen
Mersey *89 D5 river* NW England, United Kingdom
Mersin *116 C4 var.* İçel. İçel, S Turkey
Mērsrags *106 C3* Talsi, NW Latvia
Meru *73 C6* Eastern, C Kenya
Merv *see* Mary
Merzifon *116 D2* Amasya, N Turkey
Merzig *95 A5* Saarland, SW Germany
Mesa *48 B2* Arizona, SW USA
Meseritz *see* Międzyrzecz
Meshed *see* Mashhad
Mesopotamia *57 C5 var.* Mesopotamia Argentina. *physical region* NE Argentina
Mesopotamia Argentina *see* Mesopotamia
Messalo, Rio *79 E2 var.* Mualo. *river* NE Mozambique
Messana/Messene *see* Messina
Messina *97 D7 var.* Messana, Messene; *anc.* Zancle. Sicilia, Italy, C Mediterranean Sea
Messina *see* Musina
Messina, Strait of *97 D7 Eng.* Strait of Messina. *strait* SW Italy
Messina, Strait of *see* Messina, Stretto di
Messíni *105 B6* Pelopónnisos, S Greece
Mesta *see* Néstos
Mestghanem *see* Mostaganem

Mestia *117 F1 var.* Mestiya. N Georgia
Mestiya *see* Mestia
Mestre *96 C2* Veneto, NE Italy
Metairie *42 B3* Louisiana, S USA
Metán *64 C2* Salta, N Argentina
Metapán *52 B2* Santa Ana, NW El Salvador
Meta, Río *58 D3 river* Colombia/Venezuela
Meterlam *see* Mehtar Lām
Methariam/Metharlam *see* Mehtar Lām
Metis *see* Metz
Metković *100 B4* Dubrovnik-Neretva, SE Croatia
Métsovo *104 B4 prev.* Métsovon. Ípeiros, C Greece
Métsovon *see* Métsovo
Metz *90 D3 anc.* Divodurum Mediomatricum, Mediomatrica, Metis. Moselle, NE France
Meulaboh *138 A3* Sumatera, W Indonesia
Meuse *87 C6 Dut.* Maas. *river* W Europe
Mexcala, Río *see* Balsas, Río
Mexicali *50 A1* Baja California Norte, NW Mexico
Mexicanos, Estados Unidos *see* Mexico
México *51 E4 var.* Ciudad de México, *Eng.* Mexico City. *country capital* (Mexico) (Mexico) México, C Mexico
Mexico *45 G4* Missouri, C USA
Mexico *50 C3 off.* United Mexican States, *var.* Méjico, México, *Sp.* Estados Unidos Mexicanos. *country* N Central America

MEXICO
North America

Official name United Mexican States
Formation 1836 / 1848
Capital Mexico City
Population 110 million / 149 people per sq mile (57 people per sq km) / 76%
Total area 761,602 sq. miles (1,972,550 sq. km)
Languages Spanish*, Nahuatl, Mayan, Zapotec, Mixtec, Otomí, Totonac, Tzotzil, Tzeltal
Religions Roman Catholic 88%, Other 7%, Protestant 5%
Ethnic mix Mestizo 60%, Amerindian 30%, European 9%, Other 1%
Government Presidential system
Currency Mexican peso = 100 centavos
Literacy rate 91%
Calorie consumption 3145 calories

México *see* Mexico
Mexico City *see* México
México, Golfo de *see* Mexico, Gulf of
Mexico, Gulf of *51 F2 Sp.* Golfo de México. *gulf* W Atlantic Ocean
Meyadine *see* Al Mayādīn
Meydān Shahr *123 E4 var.* Maydān Shahr. Vardak, E Afghanistan
Meymaneh *122 D3 var.* Maimāna, Maymana. Fāryāb, NW Afghanistan
Mezen' *110 D4 river* NW Russian Federation
Mezőtúr *99 D7* Jász-Nagykun-Szolnok, E Hungary
Mgarr *102 A5* Gozo, N Malta
Miadzioł Nowy *see* Myadzyel
Miahuatlán *51 F5 var.* Miahuatlán de Porfirio Díaz. Oaxaca, SE Mexico
Miahuatlán de Porfirio Díaz *see* Miahuatlán
Miami *43 F5* Florida, SE USA
Miami *49 G1* Oklahoma, C USA
Miami Beach *43 F5* Florida, SE USA
Miāneh *120 C2 var.* Miyāneh. Āzarbāyjān-e Sharqī, NW Iran
Mianyang *128 B5* Sichuan, C China
Miastko *98 C2 Ger.* Rummelsburg in Pommern. Pomorskie, N Poland
Mi Chai *see* Nong Khai
Michalovce *99 E5 Ger.* Grossmichel, *Hung.* Nagymihály. Košický Kraj, E Slovakia
Michigan *40 C1 off.* State of Michigan, *also known as* Great Lakes State, Lake State, Wolverine State. *state* N USA
Michigan, Lake *40 C2 lake* N USA
Michurin *see* Tsarevo
Michurinsk *111 B5* Tambovskaya Oblast', W Russian Federation

Micoud *55 F2* SE Saint Lucia
Micronesia *144 B1 off.* Federated States of Micronesia. *country* W Pacific Ocean

MICRONESIA
Australasia & Oceania

Official name Federated States of Micronesia
Formation 1986 / 1986
Capital Palikir (Pohnpei Island)
Population 107,862 / 398 people per sq mile (154 people per sq km) / 30%
Total area 271 sq. miles (702 sq. km)
Languages English*, Trukese, Pohnpeian, Mortlockese, Kosraean
Religions Roman Catholic 50%, Protestant 48%, Other 2%
Ethnic mix Chuukese 49%, Pohnpeian 24%, Other 14%, Kosraean 6%, Yapese 5%, Asian 2%
Government Nonparty system
Currency US dollar = 100 cents
Literacy rate 81%
Calorie consumption Not available

Micronesia *144 C1 island group* W Pacific Ocean
Micronesia, Federated States of *see* Micronesia
Mid-Atlantic Cordillera *see* Mid-Atlantic Ridge
Mid-Atlantic Ridge *66 C3 var.* Mid-Atlantic Cordillera, Mid-Atlantic Rise, Mid-Atlantic Swell. *undersea ridge* Atlantic Ocean
Mid-Atlantic Rise/Mid-Atlantic Swell *see* Mid-Atlantic Ridge
Middelburg *87 B5* Zeeland, SW Netherlands
Middelharnis *86 B4* Zuid-Holland, SW Netherlands
Middelkerke *87 A5* West-Vlaanderen, W Belgium
Middle America Trench *35 B7 trench* E Pacific Ocean
Middle Andaman *133 F2 island* Andaman Islands, India, NE Indian Ocean
Middle Atlas *70 C2 Eng.* Middle Atlas. *mountain range* N Morocco
Middle Atlas *see* Moyen Atlas
Middle Congo *see* Congo (Republic of)
Middlesboro *40 C5* Kentucky, S USA
Middlesbrough *89 D5* N England, United Kingdom
Middletown *41 F4* New Jersey, NE USA
Middletown *41 F3* New York, NE USA
Mid-Indian Basin *141 C5 undersea basin* N Indian Ocean
Mid-Indian Ridge *141 C5 var.* Central Indian Ridge. *undersea ridge* C Indian Ocean
Midland *38 D5* Ontario, S Canada
Midland *40 C3* Michigan, N USA
Midland *49 E3* Texas, SW USA
Mid-Pacific Mountains *152 C2 var.* Mid-Pacific Seamounts. *seamount range* NW Pacific Ocean
Mid-Pacific Seamounts *see* Mid-Pacific Mountains
Midway Islands *152 D2 US territory* C Pacific Ocean
Miechów *99 D5* Małopolskie, S Poland
Międzyrzec Podlaski *98 E3* Lubelskie, E Poland
Międzyrzecz *98 B3 Ger.* Meseritz. Lubuskie, W Poland
Mielec *99 D5* Podkarpackie, SE Poland
Miercurea-Ciuc *108 C4 Ger.* Szeklerburg, *Hung.* Csíkszereda. Harghita, C Romania
Mieres del Camín *see* Mieres del Camino
Mieres del Camino *92 D1 var.* Mieres del Camín. Asturias, NW Spain
Mi'ēso *73 D5 var.* Meheso, Miesso. Oromīya, C Ethiopia
Miesso *see* Mi'ēso
Mifrats Hefa *119 A5 Eng.* Bay of Haifa; *prev.* MifraẕHefa. *bay* N Israel
Miguel Asua *50 D3 var.* Miguel Auza. Zacatecas, C Mexico
Miguel Auza *see* Miguel Asua

Mikashevichy *107 C7 Pol.* Mikaszewicze, *Rus.* Mikashevichi. Brestskaya Voblasts', SW Belarus
Mikaszewicze *see* Mikashevichy
Mikhaylovgrad *see* Montana
Mikhaylovka *111 B6* Volgogradskaya Oblast', SW Russian Federation
Míkonos *see* Mýkonos
Mikre *104 C2* Lovech, N Bulgaria
Mikun' *110 D4* Respublika Komi, NW Russian Federation
Mikuni-sanmyaku *131 D5 mountain range* Honshū, N Japan Asia
Mikura-jima *131 D6 island* E Japan
Milagro *60 B2* Guayas, SW Ecuador
Milan *see* Milano
Milange *79 E2* Zambézia, NE Mozambique
Milano *96 B2 Eng.* Milan, *Ger.* Mailand; *anc.* Mediolanum. Lombardia, N Italy
Milas *116 A4* Muğla, SW Turkey
Milashavichy *107 C7 Rus.* Milashevichi. Homyel'skaya Voblasts', SE Belarus
Milashevichi *see* Milashavichy
Mildura *149 C6* Victoria, SE Australia
Mile *see* Mili Atoll
Miles *149 D5* Queensland, E Australia
Miles City *44 C2* Montana, NW USA
Milford *see* Milford Haven
Milford Haven *89 C6 prev.* Milford. SW Wales, United Kingdom
Milford Sound *151 A6* Southland, South Island, New Zealand
Milford Sound *151 A6 inlet* South Island, New Zealand
Milh, Bahr al *see* Razāzah, Buhayrat ar
Mili Atoll *144 D2 var.* Mile. *atoll* Ratak Chain, SE Marshall Islands
Mil'kovo *115 H3* Kamchatskaya Oblast', E Russian Federation
Milk River *37 E5* Alberta, SW Canada
Milk River *44 C1 river* Montana, NW USA
Milk, Wadi el *88 B4 var.* Wadi al Malik. *river* C Sudan
Milledgeville *43 E2* Georgia, SE USA
Mille Lacs Lake *45 F2 lake* Minnesota, N USA
Millennium Island *143 F3 prev.* Caroline Island, Thornton Island. *atoll* Line Islands, E Kiribati
Millerovo *111 B6* Rostovskaya Oblast', SW Russian Federation
Mílos *105 C7 island* Kykládes, Greece, Aegean Sea
Mílos *105 C7 island* Kykládes, Greece, Aegean Sea
Mílos *105 C7 island* Kykládes, Greece, Aegean Sea
Milton *151 B7* Otago, South Island, New Zealand
Milton Keynes *89 D6* SE England, United Kingdom
Milwaukee *40 B3* Wisconsin, N USA
Mimatum *see* Mende
Min *see* Fujian
Minā' Qābūs *140 B3* NE Oman
Minas Gerais *63 F3 off.* Estado de Minas Gerais. *state* E Brazil
Minas Gerais *63 F3 off.* Estado de Minas Gerais. *region* E Brazil
Minas Gerais, Estado de *see* Minas Gerais
Minatitlán *51 F4* Veracruz-Llave, E Mexico
Minbu *136 A3* Magway, W Burma (Myanmar)
Minch, The *88 B3 var.* North Minch. *strait* NW Scotland, United Kingdom
Mindanao *139 E2 island* S Philippines
Mindanao Sea *see* Bohol Sea
Mindelheim *95 C6* Bayern, S Germany
Mindello *see* Mindelo
Mindelo *74 A2 var.* Mindello; *prev.* Porto Grande. São Vicente, N Cape Verde
Minden *94 B4 anc.* Minthun. Nordrhein-Westfalen, NW Germany
Mindoro *139 E2 island* N Philippines
Mindoro Strait *139 E2 strait* W Philippines
Mineral Wells *49 F2* Texas, SW USA
Mingäçevir *117 G2 Rus.* Mingechaur, Mingechevir. C Azerbaijan
Mingechaur/Mingechevir *see* Mingäçevir
Mingora *see* Saidu Sharif
Minho *92 B2 former province* N Portugal
Minho *92 B2 Sp.* Miño. *river* Portugal/Spain

Minho, Rio *see* Miño
Minicoy Island *132 B3 island* SW India
Minius *see* Miño
Minna *75 G4* Niger, C Nigeria
Minneapolis *45 F2* Minnesota, N USA
Minnesota *45 F2 off.* State of Minnesota, *also known as* Gopher State, New England of the West, North Star State. *state* N USA
Miño *92 B2 var.* Mino, Minius, *Port.* Rio Minho. *river* Portugal/Spain
Miño *see* Minho, Rio
Minorca *93 H3 Eng.* Minorca; *anc.* Balearis Minor. *island* Islas Baleares, Spain, W Mediterranean Sea
Minorca *see* Menorca
Minot *45 E1* North Dakota, N USA
Minsk *107 C6 country capital* (Belarus) (Belarus) Minskaya Voblasts', C Belarus
Minskaya Wzvyshsha *107 C6 mountain range* C Belarus
Mińsk Mazowiecki *98 D3 var.* Nowo-Minsk. Mazowieckie, C Poland
Minthun *see* Minden
Minto, Lac *38 D2 lake* Québec, C Canada
Minya *see* Al Minyā
Miraflores *50 C3* Baja California Sur, NW Mexico
Miranda de Ebro *93 E1* La Rioja, N Spain
Mirgorod *see* Myrhorod
Miri *138 D3* Sarawak, East Malaysia
Mirim Lagoon *63 E5 var.* Lake Mirim, *Sp.* Laguna Merín. *lagoon* Brazil/Uruguay
Mirim, Lake *see* Mirim Lagoon
Mírina *see* Mýrina
Mírjāveh *120 E4* Sīstān va Balūchestān, SE Iran
Mirny *154 C3 Russian research station* Antarctica
Mirnyy *115 F3* Respublika Sakha (Yakutiya), NE Russian Federation
Mīrpur Khās *134 B3* Sind, SE Pakistan
Mirtoan Sea *105 C6 Eng.* Mirtoan Sea; *anc.* Myrtoum Mare. *sea* S Greece
Mirtoan Sea *see* Mirtóo Pélagos
Misiaf *see* Maşyāf
Miskito Coast *see* La Mosquitia
Miskitos, Cayos *53 E2 island group* NE Nicaragua
Miskolc *99 D6* Borsod-Abaúj-Zemplén, NE Hungary
Misool, Pulau *139 F4 island* Maluku, E Indonesia
Mişrātah *71 F2 var.* Misurata. NW Libya
Mission *49 G5* Texas, SW USA
Mississippi *42 B2 off.* State of Mississippi, *also known as* Bayou State, Magnolia State. *state* SE USA
Mississippi Delta *42 B4 delta* Louisiana, S USA
Mississippi River *35 C6 river* C USA
Missoula *44 B1* Montana, NW USA
Missouri *45 F5 off.* State of Missouri, *also known as* Bullion State, Show Me State. *state* C USA
Missouri River *45 E3 river* C USA
Mistassini, Lac *38 D3 lake* Québec, SE Canada
Mistelbach an der Zaya *95 E6* Niederösterreich, NE Austria
Misti, Volcán *61 E4 volcano* S Peru
Misurata *see* Mişrātah
Mitau *see* Jelgava
Mitchell *149 D5* Queensland, E Australia
Mitchell *45 E3* South Dakota, N USA
Mitchell, Mount *43 E1 mountain* North Carolina, SE USA
Mitchell River *148 C2 river* Queensland, NE Australia
Mi Tho *see* My Tho
Mitilíni *see* Mytilíni
Mito *131 D5* Ibaraki, Honshū, S Japan
Mitrovica/Mitrovicë *see* Kosovska Mitrovica, Serbia
Mitrovica/Mitrowitz *see* Sremska Mitrovica, Serbia
Mitrovicë *101 D5 Serb.* Mitrovica, Kosovska Mitrovica, Titova Mitrovica. N Kosovo
Mits'iwa *72 C4 var.* Masawa, Massawa. E Eritrea
Mitspe Ramon *119 A7 prev.* Mizpe Ramon. Southern, S Israel
Mittelstadt *see* Baia Sprie
Mitú *58 C4* Vaupés, SE Colombia

Mitumba, Chaîne des/Mitumba Range *see* Mitumba, Monts
Mitumba Range *77 E7 var.* Chaîne des Mitumba, Mitumba Range. *mountain range* E Dem. Rep. Congo
Miueru Wantipa, Lake *77 E7 lake* N Zambia
Miyake-jima *131 D6 island* Sakishima-shotō, SW Japan
Miyako *130 D4* Iwate, Honshū, C Japan
Miyakonojō *131 B8 var.* Miyakonzyô. Miyazaki, Kyūshū, SW Japan
Miyakonzyô *see* Miyakonojō
Miyāneh *see* Miâneh
Miyazaki *131 B8* Miyazaki, Kyūshū, SW Japan
Mizil *108 C5* Prahova, SE Romania
Miziya *104 C1* Vratsa, NW Bulgaria
Mizpe Ramon *see* Mitspe Ramon
Mjøsa *85 B6 var.* Mjøsen. *lake* S Norway
Mjøsen *see* Mjøsa
Mladenovac *100 D4* Serbia, C Serbia
Mława *98 D3* Mazowieckie, C Poland
Mljet *101 B5 It.* Meleda; *anc.* Melita. *island* S Croatia
Mmabatho *78 C4* North-West, N South Africa
Moab *44 B5* Utah, W USA
Moa Island *148 C1 island* Queensland, NE Australia
Moanda *77 B6 var.* Mouanda. Haut-Ogooué, SE Gabon
Moba *77 E7* Katanga, E Dem. Rep. Congo
Mobay *see* Montego Bay
Mobaye *77 C5* Basse-Kotto, S Central African Republic
Moberly *45 G4* Missouri, C USA
Mobile *42 C3* Alabama, S USA
Mobutu Sese Seko, Lac *see* Albert, Lake
Moçâmedes *see* Namibe
Mochudi *78 C4* Kgatleng, SE Botswana
Mocímboa da Praia *79 F2 var.* Vila de Mocímboa da Praia. Cabo Delgado, N Mozambique
Môco *78 B2 var.* Morro de Môco. *mountain* W Angola
Mocoa *58 A4* Putumayo, SW Colombia
Môco, Morro de *see* Môco
Mocuba *79 E3* Zambézia, NE Mozambique
Modena *96 B3 anc.* Mutina. Emilia-Romagna, N Italy
Modesto *47 B6* California, W USA
Modica *97 C7 anc.* Motyca. Sicilia, Italy, C Mediterranean Sea
Modimolle *78 D4 prev.* Nylstroom. Limpopo, NE South Africa
Modohn *see* Madona
Modriča *100 C3* Republika Srpska, N Bosnia and Herzegovina
Moe *149 C7* Victoria, SE Australia
Möen *see* Møn, Denmark
Moero, Lac *see* Mweru, Lake
Moeskroen *see* Mouscron
Mogadiscio/Mogadishu *see* Muqdisho
Mogador *see* Essaouira
Mogilëv *see* Mahilyow
Mogilev-Podol'skiy *see* Mohyliv-Podil's'kyy
Mogilno *98 C3* Kujawsko-pomorskie, C Poland
Moḩammadābād-e Rīgān *120 E4* Kermān, SE Iran
Mohammedia *70 C2 prev.* Fédala. NW Morocco
Mohave, Lake *47 D7 reservoir* Arizona/Nevada, W USA
Mohawk River *41 F3 river* New York, NE USA
Mohéli *see* Mwali
Mohns Ridge *83 F3 undersea ridge* Greenland Sea/Norwegian Sea
Moho *61 E4* Puno, SE Peru
Mohoro *73 C7* Pwani, E Tanzania
Mohyliv-Podil's'kyy *108 D3 Rus.* Mogilev-Podol'skiy. Vinnyts'ka Oblast', C Ukraine
Moi *85 A6* Rogaland, S Norway
Moili *see* Mwali
Mo i Rana *84 C3* Nordland, C Norway
Mõisaküla *106 D3 Ger.* Moiseküll. Viljandimaa, S Estonia
Moiseküll *see* Mõisaküla
Moissac *91 B6* Tarn-et-Garonne, S France
Mojácar *93 E5* Andalucía, S Spain

Mojave Desert *47 D7 plain* California, W USA
Mokrany *see* Makrany
Moktama *see* Martaban
Mol *87 C5 prev.* Moll. Antwerpen, N Belgium
Moldavia *see* Moldova
Moldavian SSR/Moldavskaya SSR *see* Moldova
Molde *85 A5* Møre og Romsdal, S Norway
Moldo-Too, Khrebet *see* Moldo-Too, Khrebet
Moldo-Too, Khrebet *123 G2 prev.* Khrebet Moldotau, Moldotau. *mountain range* C Kyrgyzstan
Moldova *108 D3 off.* Republic of Moldova, *var.* Moldavia; *prev.* Moldavian SSR, *Rus.* Moldavskaya SSR. *country* SE Europe

MOLDOVA
Southeast Europe

Official name Republic of Moldova
Formation 1991 / 1991
Capital Chisinau
Population 4.2 million / 323 people per sq mile (125 people per sq km) / 46%
Total area 13,067 sq. miles (33,843 sq. km)
Languages Moldovan*, Ukrainian, Russian
Religions Orthodox Christian 98%, Jewish 2%
Ethnic mix Moldovan 64%, Ukrainian 14%, Russian 13%, Gagauz 4%, Other 3%, Bulgarian 2%
Government Parliamentary system
Currency Moldovan leu = 100 bani
Literacy rate 98%
Calorie consumption 2806 calories

Moldova Nouă *108 A4 Ger.* Neumoldowa, *Hung.* Újmoldova. Caras-Severin, SW Romania
Moldova, Republic of *see* Moldova
Moldoveanu *see* Vârful Moldoveanu
Molfetta *97 E5* Puglia, SE Italy
Moll *see* Mol
Mollendo *61 E4* Arequipa, SW Peru
Mölndal *85 B7* Västra Götaland, S Sweden
Molochans'k *109 G4 Rus.* Molochansk. Zaporiz'ka Oblast', SE Ukraine
Molodechno/Molodeczno *see* Maladzyechna
Molodezhnaya *154 C2 Russian research station* Antarctica
Moloka'i *47 B8 var.* Molokai. *island* Hawaiian Islands, Hawai'i, USA
Molokai Fracture Zone *153 E2 tectonic feature* NE Pacific Ocean
Molopo *78 C4 seasonal river* Botswana/South Africa
Mólos *105 B5* Stereá Ellás, C Greece
Molotov *see* Severodvinsk, Arkhangel'skaya Oblast', Russian Federation
Molotov *see* Perm', Permskaya Oblast', Russian Federation
Moluccas *139 F4 Dut.* Molukken, *Eng.* Moluccas; *prev.* Spice Islands. *island group* E Indonesia
Moluccas *see* Maluku
Molucca Sea *139 F4 Ind.* Laut Maluku. *sea* E Indonesia
Molukken *see* Maluku
Mombasa *73 D7* Coast, SE Kenya
Mombetsu *see* Monbetsu
Momchilgrad *104 D3 prev.* Mastanli. Kŭrdzhali, S Bulgaria
Møn *85 B8 prev.* Möen. *island* SE Denmark
Mona, Canal de la *see* Mona Passage
Monaco *91 C7 var.* Monaco-Ville; *anc.* Monoecus. *country capital* (Monaco) (Monaco) S Monaco
Monaco *91 E6 off.* Principality of Monaco. *country* W Europe

MONACO
Southern Europe

Official name Principality of Monaco
Formation 1861 / 1861
Capital Monaco-Ville
Population 32,671 / 43,561 people per sq mile (16,754 people per sq km) / 100%

MONACO
(continued)

Total area 0.75 sq. miles (1.95 sq. km)
Languages French*, Italian, Monégasque, English
Religions Roman Catholic 89%, Protestant 6%, Other 5%
Ethnic mix French 32%, Other 29%, Italian 20%, Monégasque 19%
Government Mixed monarchical–parliamentary system
Currency Euro = 100 cents
Literacy rate 99%
Calorie consumption Not available

Monaco *see* München
Monaco, Port de *91 C8 bay* S Monaco W Mediterranean Sea
Monaco, Principality of *see* Monaco
Monaco-Ville *see* Monaco
Monahans *49 E3* Texas, SW USA
Mona, Isla *55 E3 island* W Puerto Rico
Mona Passage *55 E3 Sp.* Canal de la Mona. *channel* Dominican Republic/Puerto Rico
Monastir *see* Bitola
Monbetsu *130 D2 var.* Mombetsu, Monbetu. Hokkaidō, NE Japan
Monbetu *see* Monbetsu
Moncalieri *96 A2* Piemonte, NW Italy
Monchegorsk *110 C2* Murmanskaya Oblast', NW Russian Federation
Monclova *50 D2* Coahuila, NE Mexico
Moncton *39 F4* New Brunswick, SE Canada
Mondovì *96 A2* Piemonte, NW Italy
Monfalcone *96 D2* Friuli-Venezia Giulia, NE Italy
Monforte de Lemos *92 C1* Galicia, NW Spain
Mongo *76 C3* Guéra, C Chad
Mongolia *126 C2 Mong.* Mongol Uls. *country* E Asia

MONGOLIA
East Asia

Official name Mongolia
Formation 1924 / 1924
Capital Ulan Bator
Population 2.7 million / 4 people per sq mile (2 people per sq km) / 57%
Total area 604,247 sq. miles (1,565,000 sq. km)
Languages Khalkha Mongolian*, Kazakh, Chinese, Russian
Religions Tibetan Buddhist 96%, Muslim 4%
Ethnic mix Khalkh 82%, Other 9%, Kazakh 4%, Dorvod 3%, Bayad 2%
Government Mixed presidential–parliamentary system
Currency Tugrik (tögrög) = 100 möngö
Literacy rate 98%
Calorie consumption 2249 calories

Mongolia, Plateau of *124 D1 plateau* E Mongolia
Mongol Uls *see* Mongolia
Mongora *see* Saidu Sharif
Mongos, Chaine des *see* Bongo, Massif des
Mongu *78 C2* Western, W Zambia
Monkchester *see* Newcastle upon Tyne
Monkey Bay *79 E2* Southern, SE Malawi
Monkey River *see* Monkey River Town
Monkey River Town *52 C2 var.* Monkey River. Toledo, SE Belize
Monoecus *see* Monaco
Mono Lake *47 C6* lake California, W USA
Monostor *see* Beli Manastir
Monóvar *93 F4 Cat.* Monover. País Valenciano, E Spain
Monover *see* Monóvar
Monroe *42 B2* Louisiana, S USA
Monrovia *74 C5 country capital* (Liberia) (Liberia) W Liberia
Mons *87 B6 Dut.* Bergen. Hainaut, S Belgium
Monselice *96 C2* Veneto, NE Italy
Montana *104 C2 prev.* Ferdinand, Mikhaylovgrad. Montana, NW Bulgaria
Montana *44 B1 off.* State of Montana, *also known as* Mountain State, Treasure State. *state* NW USA

Montargis 90 C4 Loiret, C France
Montauban 91 B6 Tarn-et-Garonne, S France
Montbéliard 90 D4 Doubs, E France
Mont Cenis, Col du 91 D5 pass E France
Mont-de-Marsan 91 B6 Landes, SW France
Monteagudo 61 G4 Chuquisaca, S Bolivia
Montecarlo 91 C8 Misiones, NE Argentina
Monte Caseros 64 D3 Corrientes, NE Argentina
Monte Cristi 54 D3 var. San Fernando de Monte Cristi. NW Dominican Republic
Monte Croce Carnico, Passo di see Plocken Pass
Montegiardino 96 E2 SE San Marino
Montego Bay 54 A4 var. Mobay. W Jamaica
Montélimar 91 D5 anc. Acunum Acusio, Montilium Adhemari. Drôme, E France
Montemorelos 51 E3 Nuevo León, NE Mexico
Montenegro 101 C5 Serb. Crna Gora. country SW Europe

MONTENEGRO
Southeast Europe

Official name Republic of Montenegro
Formation 2006 / 2006
Capital Podgorica
Population 684,736 / 128 people per sq mile (50 people per sq km) / 62%
Total area 5332 sq. miles (13,812 sq. km)
Languages Montenegrin*, Serbian, Albanian, Bosniak, Croatian
Religions Orthodox Christian 74%, Muslim 18%, Other 4%Roman Catholic 4%
Ethnic mix Montenegro 43%, Serb 32%, Other 12%, Bosniak 8%, Albanian 5%
Government Parliamentary system
Currency Euro = 100 cents
Literacy rate 98%
Calorie consumption Not available

Monte Patria 64 B3 Coquimbo, N Chile
Monterey 47 B6 California, W USA
Monterey see Monterrey
Monterey Bay 47 A6 bay California, W USA
Montería 58 B2 Córdoba, NW Colombia
Montero 61 G4 Santa Cruz, C Bolivia
Monterrey 51 E3 var. Monterey. Nuevo León, NE Mexico
Montes Claros 63 F3 Minas Gerais, SE Brazil
Montevideo 64 D4 country capital (Uruguay) (Uruguay) Montevideo, S Uruguay
Montevideo 45 F2 Minnesota, N USA
Montgenèvre, Col de 91 D5 pass France/Italy
Montgomery 42 D2 state capital Alabama, S USA
Montgomery see Sāhiwāl
Monthey 95 A7 Valais, SW Switzerland
Montilium Adhemari see Montélimar
Montluçon 90 C4 Allier, C France
Montoro 92 D4 Andalucía, S Spain
Montpelier 41 G2 state capital Vermont, NE USA
Montpellier 91 C6 Hérault, S France
Montréal 39 E4 Eng. Montreal. Québec, SE Canada
Montrose 88 D3 E Scotland, United Kingdom
Montrose 44 C5 Colorado, C USA
Montserrat 55 G3 var. Emerald Isle. UK dependent territory E West Indies
Monywa 136 B3 Sagaing, C Burma (Myanmar)
Monza 96 B2 Lombardia, N Italy
Monze 78 D2 Southern, S Zambia
Monzón 93 F2 Aragón, NE Spain
Moonie 149 D5 Queensland, E Australia
Moon-Sund see Väinameri
Moora 147 A6 Western Australia
Moore 49 G1 Oklahoma, C USA
Moore, Lake 147 B6 lake Western Australia
Moorhead 45 F2 Minnesota, N USA
Moose 38 C3 river Ontario, S Canada
Moosehead Lake 41 G1 lake Maine, NE USA

Moosonee 38 C3 Ontario, SE Canada
Mopti 75 E3 Mopti, C Mali
Moquegua 61 E4 Moquegua, SE Peru
Mora 85 C5 Dalarna, C Sweden
Morales 52 C2 Izabal, E Guatemala
Morant Bay 54 B5 E Jamaica
Moratalla 93 E4 Murcia, SE Spain
Morava 99 C5 var. March. river C Europe
Morava see Moravia, Czech Republic
Morava see Velika Morava, Serbia
Moravia 99 B5 Cz. Morava, Ger. Mähren. cultural region E Czech Republic
Moray Firth 88 C3 inlet N Scotland, United Kingdom
Morea see Pelopónnisos
Moreau River 44 D2 river South Dakota, N USA
Moree 149 D5 New South Wales, SE Australia
Morelia 51 E4 Michoacán, S Mexico
Morena, Sierra 92 C4 mountain range S Spain
Moreni 108 C5 Dâmbovița, S Romania
Morgan City 42 B3 Louisiana, S USA
Darya-ye Morghab 122 D3 Rus. Murgab, Murghāb, Turkm. Murgap, Murgap Deryasy. river Afghanistan/Turkmenistan
Darya-ye Morghab 122 D3 Rus. Murgab, Murghāb, Turkm. Murgap, Murgap Deryasy. river Afghanistan/Turkmenistan
Morghāb, Daryā-ye see Murgap
Morioka 130 D4 Iwate, Honshū, C Japan
Morlaix 90 A3 Finistère, NW France
Mormon State see Utah
Mornington Abyssal Plain 67 A7 abyssal plain SE Pacific Ocean
Mornington Island 148 B2 island Wellesley Islands, Queensland, N Australia
Morocco 70 B3 off. Kingdom of Morocco, Ar. Al Mamlakah. country N Africa

MOROCCO
North Africa

Official name Kingdom of Morocco
Formation 1956 / 1969
Capital Rabat
Population 32.4 million / 188 people per sq mile (73 people per sq km) / 58%
Total area 172,316 sq. miles (446,300 sq. km)
Languages Arabic*, Tamazight (Berber), French, Spanish
Religions Muslim (mainly Sunni) 99%, Other (mostly Christian) 1%
Ethnic mix Arab 70%, Berber 29%, European 1%
Government Mixed monarchical–parliamentary system
Currency Moroccan dirham = 100 centimes
Literacy rate 52%
Calorie consumption 3052 calories

Morocco see Marrakech
Morocco, Kingdom of see Morocco
Morogoro 73 C7 Morogoro, E Tanzania
Moro Gulf 139 E3 gulf S Philippines
Morón 54 C2 Ciego de Ávila, C Cuba
Mörön 126 D2 Hövsgöl, N Mongolia
Morondava 79 F3 Toliara, W Madagascar
Moroni 79 F2 country capital (Comoros) (Comoros) Grande Comore, NW Comoros
Morotai, Pulau 139 F3 island Maluku, E Indonesia
Morotiri see Marotiri
Morphou see Güzelyurt
Morrinsville 150 D3 Waikato, North Island, New Zealand
Morris 45 F2 Minnesota, N USA
Morris Jesup, Kap 83 E1 headland N Greenland
Morvan 90 D4 physical region C France
Moscow 46 C2 Idaho, NW USA
Moscow see Moskva
Mosel 95 A5 Fr. Moselle. river W Europe
Mosel see Moselle

Moselle 87 E8 Ger. Mosel. river W Europe
Moselle see Mosel
Mosgiel 151 B7 Otago, South Island, New Zealand
Moshi 73 C7 Kilimanjaro, NE Tanzania
Mosjøen 84 B4 Nordland, C Norway
Moskovskiy see Moskva
Moskva 111 B5 Eng. Moscow. country capital (Russian Federation) (Russian Federation) Gorod Moskva, W Russian Federation
Moskva 123 E3 Rus. Moskovskiy; prev. Chubek. SW Tajikistan
Moson and Magyaróvár see Mosonmagyaróvár
Mosonmagyaróvár 99 C6 Ger. Wieselburg-Ungarisch-Altenburg; prev. Moson and Magyaróvár, Ger. Wieselburg and Ungarisch-Altenburg. Győr-Moson-Sopron, NW Hungary
Mosquito Coast 53 E3 var. Miskito Coast, Eng. Mosquito Coast. coastal region E Nicaragua
Mosquito Coast see La Mosquitia
Mosquito Gulf 53 F4 Eng. Mosquito Gulf. gulf N Panama
Mosquito Gulf see Mosquitos, Golfo de los
Moss 85 B6 Østfold, S Norway
Mossâmedes see Namibe
Mosselbaai 78 C5 var. Mosselbai, Eng. Mossel Bay. Western Cape, SW South Africa
Mosselbai/Mossel Bay see Mosselbaai
Mossendjo 77 B6 Niari, SW Congo
Mossoró 63 G2 Rio Grande do Norte, NE Brazil
Most 98 A4 Ger. Brüx. Ústecký Kraj, NW Czech Republic
Mosta 102 B5 var. Musta. C Malta
Mostaganem 70 D2 var. Mestghanem. NW Algeria
Mostar 100 C4 Federacija Bosna I Hercegovina, S Bosnia and Herzegovina
Mosty see Masty
Mosul see Al Mawşil
Mota del Cuervo 93 E3 Castilla-La Mancha, C Spain
Motagua, Río 52 B2 river Guatemala/Honduras
Mother of Presidents/Mother of States see Virginia
Motril 92 D5 Andalucía, S Spain
Motru 108 B4 Gorj, SW Romania
Motueka 151 C5 Tasman, South Island, New Zealand
Motul 51 H3 var. Motul de Felipe Carrillo Puerto. Yucatán, SE Mexico
Motul de Felipe Carrillo Puerto see Motul
Motyca see Modica
Mouanda see Moanda
Mouhoun see Black Volta
Mouila 77 A6 Ngounié, C Gabon
Moukden see Shenyang
Mould Bay 37 E2 Prince Patrick Island, Northwest Territories, N Canada
Moulins 90 C4 Allier, C France
Moulmein see Mawlamyine
Moundou 76 B4 Logone-Occidental, SW Chad
Moŭng Roessei 137 D5 Bătdâmbâng, W Cambodia
Moun Hou see Black Volta
Mountain Home 42 B1 Arkansas, C USA
Mountain State see Montana
Mountain State see West Virginia
Mount Cook 151 B6 Canterbury, South Island, New Zealand
Mount Desert Island 41 H2 island Maine, NE USA
Mount Gambier 149 B7 South Australia
Mount Isa 148 B3 Queensland, C Australia
Mount Magnet 147 B5 Western Australia
Mount Pleasant 45 G4 Iowa, C USA
Mount Pleasant 40 C3 Michigan, N USA
Mount Vernon 40 B5 Illinois, N USA
Mount Vernon 46 B1 Washington, NW USA
Mourdi, Dépression du 76 C2 desert lowland Chad/Sudan
Mouscron 87 A6 Dut. Moeskroen. Hainaut, W Belgium
Mouse River see Souris River
Moussoro 76 B3 Kanem, W Chad

Moyen-Congo see Congo (Republic of)
Mo'ynoq 122 C1 Rus. Muynak. Qoraqalpog'iston Respublikasi, NW Uzbekistan
Moyobamba 60 B2 San Martín, NW Peru
Moyu 126 B3 var. Karakax. Xinjiang Uygur Zizhiqu, NW China
Moynkum, Peski 123 F1 Kaz. Moyynqum. desert S Kazakhstan
Moyynqum see Moynkum, Peski
Mozambika, Lakandranon' i see Mozambique Channel
Mozambique 79 E3 off. Republic of Mozambique; prev. People's Republic of Mozambique, Portuguese East Africa. country S Africa

MOZAMBIQUE
Southern Africa

Official name Republic of Mozambique
Formation 1975 / 1975
Capital Maputo
Population 20.5 million / 68 people per sq mile (26 people per sq km) / 37%
Total area 309,494 sq. miles (801,590 sq. km)
Languages Portuguese*, Makua, Xitsonga, Sena, Lomwe
Religions Traditional beliefs 56%, Christian 30%, Muslim 14%
Ethnic mix Makua Lomwe 47%, Tsonga 23%, Malawi 12%, Shona 11%, Yao 4%, Other 3%
Government Presidential system
Currency New metical = 100 centavos
Literacy rate 46%
Calorie consumption 2079 calories

Mozambique Basin see Natal Basin
Mozambique, Canal de see Mozambique Channel
Mozambique Channel 79 E3 Fr. Canal de Mozambique, Mal. Lakandranon' i Mozambika. strait W Indian Ocean
Mozambique, People's Republic of see Mozambique
Mozambique Plateau 69 D7 var. Mozambique Rise. undersea plateau SW Indian Ocean
Mozambique, Republic of see Mozambique
Mozambique Rise see Mozambique Plateau
Mozyr' see Mazyr
Mpama 77 B6 river C Congo
Mpika 78 D2 Northern, NE Zambia
Mqinvartsveri see Kazbek
Mragowo 98 D2 Ger. Sensburg. Warmińsko-Mazurskie, NE Poland
Mtkvari see Kura
Mtwara 73 D8 Mtwara, SE Tanzania
Mualo see Messalo, Rio
Muang Chiang Rai see Chiang Rai
Muang Kalasin see Kalasin
Muang Khammouan see Thakhèk
Muang Không 137 D5 Champasak, S Laos
Muang Khôngxédôn 137 D5 var. Khong Sedone. Salavan, S Laos
Muang Khon Kaen see Khon Kaen
Muang Lampang see Lampang
Muang Loei see Loei
Muang Lom Sak see Lom Sak
Muang Nakhon Sawan see Nakhon Sawan
Muang Namo 136 C3 Oudômxai, N Laos
Muang Nan see Nan
Muang Phalan 136 D4 var. Muang Phalane. Savannakhét, S Laos
Muang Phalane see Muang Phalan
Muang Phayao see Phayao
Muang Phitsanulok see Phitsanulok
Muang Phrae see Phrae
Muang Roi Et see Roi Et
Muang Sakon Nakhon see Sakon Nakhon
Muang Samut Prakan see Samut Prakan
Muang Sing 136 C3 Louang Namtha, N Laos
Muang Ubon see Ubon Ratchathani
Muang Xaignabouri see Xaignabouri
Muar 138 B3 var. Bandar Maharani. Johor, Peninsular Malaysia
Mucojo 79 F2 Cabo Delgado, N Mozambique
Mudanjiang 129 E3 var. Mu-tan-chiang. Heilongjiang, NE China

Mudon *137 B5* Mon State, S Burma (Myanmar)
Muenchen *see* München
Muenster *see* Münster
Mufulira *78 D2* Copperbelt, C Zambia
Mughla *see* Muğla
Muğla *116 A4 var.* Mughla. Muğla, SW Turkey
Mūḩ, Sabkhat al *118 C3 lake* C Syria
Muhu Väin *see* Väinameri
Muisne *60 A1* Esmeraldas, NW Ecuador
Mukachevo *108 C3 prev.* Munkács, *Rus.* Mukachevo. Zakarpats'ka Oblast', W Ukraine
Mukachevo *see* Mukacheve
Mukalla *see* Al Mukallā
Mukden *see* Shenyang
Mula *93 E4* Murcia, SE Spain
Mulakatholhu *132 B4 var.* Meemu Atoll, Mulaku Atoll. *atoll* C Maldives
Mulaku Atoll *see* Mulakatholhu
Muleshoe *49 E2* Texas, SW USA
Mulhacén *93 E5 var.* Cerro de Mulhacén. *mountain* S Spain
Mulhacén, Cerro de *see* Mulhacén
Mülhausen *see* Mulhouse
Mülheim *95 A6 var.* Mulheim an der Ruhr. Nordrhein-Westfalen, W Germany
Mulheim an der Ruhr *see* Mülheim
Mulhouse *90 E4 Ger.* Mülhausen. Haut-Rhin, NE France
Müller-gerbergte *see* Muller, Pegunungan
Muller, Pegunungan *138 D4 Dut.* Müller-gerbergte. *mountain range* Borneo, C Indonesia
Mull, Isle of *88 B4 island* W Scotland, United Kingdom
Mulongo *77 D7* Katanga, SE Dem. Rep. Congo
Multān *134 C2* Punjab, E Pakistan
Mumbai *134 C5 prev.* Bombay. *state capital* Mahārāshtra, W India
Munamägi *see* Suur Munamägi
Münchberg *95 C5* Bayern, E Germany
München *95 C6 var.* Muenchen, *Eng.* Munich, *It.* Monaco. Bayern, SE Germany
Muncie *40 C4* Indiana, N USA
Mungbere *77 E5* Orientale, NE Dem. Rep. Congo
Mu Nggava *see* Rennell
Munich *see* München
Munkács *see* Mukacheve
Münster *94 A4 var.* Muenster, Münster in Westfalen. Nordrhein-Westfalen, W Germany
Munster *89 A6 Ir.* Cúige Mumhan. *cultural region* S Ireland
Münster in Westfalen *see* Münster
Muong Xiang Ngeun *136 C4 var.* Xieng Ngeun. Louangphabang, N Laos
Muonio *84 D3* Lappi, N Finland
Muonioälv/Muoniojoki *see* Muoniojoki
Muoniojoki *84 D3 var.* Muoniojoki, *Swe.* Muonioälv. *river* Finland/Sweden
Muqāţ *119 C5* Al Mafraq, E Jordan
Muqdisho *73 D6 Eng.* Mogadishu, *It.* Mogadiscio. *country capital* (Somalia) (Somalia) Banaadir, S Somalia
Mur *95 E7 SCr.* Mura. *river* C Europe
Mura *see* Mur
Muradiye *117 F3* Van, E Turkey
Murapara *see* Murupara
Murata *96 E2* S San Marino
Murchison River *147 A5 river* Western Australia
Murcia *93 E4* Murcia, SE Spain
Murcia *93 E4 autonomous community* SE Spain
Mureş *108 A4 river* Hungary/Romania
Murfreesboro *42 D1* Tennessee, S USA
Murgab *see* Morghāb, Daryā-ye/Murgap/ Murghob
Murgab *see* Morghāb, Daryā-ye/Murgap/ Murghob
Murgab *see* Murghob
Murgap *122 D3* Mary Welaýaty, S Turkmenistan
Murgap *122 D3 var.* Deryasy Murgap, Murghāb, *Pash.* Daryā-ye Morghāb, *Rus.* Murgab. *river* Afghanistan/ Turkmenistan
Murgap *see* Morghāb, Daryā-ye
Murgap *see* Morghāb, Daryā-ye

Murgap Deryasy *see* Morghāb, Daryā-ye
Murgap Deryasy *see* Morghāb, Daryā-ye
Murghab *see* Morghāb, Daryā-ye
Murghab *see* Morghāb, Daryā-ye
Murghob *123 F3 Rus.* Murgab. SE Tajikistan
Murgon *149 E5* Queensland, E Australia
Mūrītāniyah *see* Mauritania
Müritz *94 C3 var.* Müritzee. *lake* NE Germany
Müritzee *see* Müritz
Murmansk *110 C2* Murmanskaya Oblast', NW Russian Federation
Murmashi *110 C2* Murmanskaya Oblast', NW Russian Federation
Murom *111 B5* Vladimirskaya Oblast', W Russian Federation
Muroran *130 D3* Hokkaidō, NE Japan
Muros *92 B1* Galicia, NW Spain
Murray Fracture Zone *153 E2 fracture zone* NE Pacific Ocean
Murray Range *see* Murray Ridge
Murray Ridge *112 C5 var.* Murray Range. *undersea ridge* N Arabian Sea
Murray River *149 B6 river* SE Australia
Murrumbidgee River *149 C6 river* New South Wales, SE Australia
Murska Sobota *95 E7 Ger.* Olsnitz. NE Slovenia
Murupara *150 E3 var.* Murapara. Bay of Plenty, North Island, New Zealand
Murviedro *see* Sagunto
Murwāra *135 E4* Madhya Pradesh, N India
Murwillumbah *149 E5* New South Wales, SE Australia
Murzuq, Edeyin *see* Murzuq, Idhān
Murzuq, Idhan *71 F4 var.* Edeyin Murzuq. *desert* SW Libya
Mürzzuschlag *95 E7* Steiermark, E Austria
Muş *117 F3 var.* Mush. Muş, E Turkey
Musa, Gebel *72 C2 var.* Gebel Mûsa. *mountain* NE Egypt
Mûsa, Gebel *see* Mûsá, Jabal
Musala *104 B3 mountain* W Bulgaria
Muscat *see* Masqaţ
Muscat and Oman *see* Oman
Muscatine *45 G3* Iowa, C USA
Musgrave Ranges *147 D5 mountain range* South Australia
Musina *78 D3 prev.* Messina. Limpopo, NE South Africa
Muskegon *40 C3* Michigan, N USA
Muskogean *see* Tallahassee
Muskogee *49 G1* Oklahoma, C USA
Musoma *73 C6* Mara, N Tanzania
Musta *see* Mosta
Mustafa-Pasha *see* Svilengrad
Musters, Lago *65 B6 lake* S Argentina
Muswellbrook *149 D6* New South Wales, SE Australia
Mut *116 C4* İçel, S Turkey
Mu-tan-chiang *see* Mudanjiang
Mutare *78 D3 var.* Mutari; *prev.* Umtali. Manicaland, E Zimbabwe
Mutari *see* Mutare
Mutina *see* Modena
Mutsu-wan *130 D3 bay* N Japan
Muttonbird Islands *151 A8 island group* SW New Zealand
Mu Us Shadi *127 E3 var.* Ordos Desert; *prev.* Mu Us Shamo. *desert* N China
Mu Us Shamo *see* Mu Us Shadi
Muy Muy *52 D3* Matagalpa, C Nicaragua
Muynak *see* Mo'ynoq
Mužlja *100 D3 Hung.* Felsömuzslya; *prev.* Gornja Mužlja. Vojvodina, N Serbia
Mwali *79 F2 var.* Moili, *Fr.* Mohéli. *island* S Comoros
Mwanza *73 B6* Mwanza, NW Tanzania
Mweka *77 C6* Kasai-Occidental, C Dem. Rep. Congo
Mwene-Ditu *77 D7* Kasai-Oriental, S Dem. Rep. Congo
Mweru, Lake *77 D7 var.* Lac Moero. *lake* Dem. Rep. Congo/Zambia
Myadel' *see* Myadzyel
Myadzyel *107 C5 Pol.* Miadziol Nowy, *Rus.* Myadel'. Minskaya Voblasts', N Belarus
Myanaung *136 B4* Ayeyarwady, SW Burma (Myanmar)
Myanmar *136 A3 off.* Union of Myanmar, Myanmar. *country* SE Asia. *See also* Burma

MYANMAR (BURMA)
Southeast Asia

Official name Union of Myanmar
Formation 1948 / 1948
Capital Nay Pyi Taw
Population 51.5 million / 203 people per sq mile (78 people per sq km) / 30%
Total area 261,969 sq. miles (678,500 sq. km)
Languages Burmese*, Shan, Karen, Rakhine, Chin, Yangbye, Kachin, Mon
Religions Buddhist 87%, Christian 6%, Muslim 4%, Other 2%, Hindu 1%
Ethnic mix Burman (Bamah) 68%, Other 13%, Shan 9%, Karen 6%, Rakhine 4%
Government Military-based regime
Currency Kyat = 100 pyas
Literacy rate 90%
Calorie consumption 2937 calories

Myaungmya *136 A4* Ayeyarwady, SW Burma (Myanmar)
Myaydo *see* Aunglan
Myeik *137 B6 var.* Mergui. Tanintharyi, S Burma (Myanmar)
Myerkulavichy *107 D7 Rus.* Merkulovichi. Homyel'skaya Voblasts', SE Belarus
Myingyan *136 B3* Mandalay, C Burma (Myanmar)
Myitkyina *136 B2* Kachin State, N Burma (Myanmar)
Mykolayiv *109 E4 Rus.* Nikolayev. Mykolayiv'ka Oblast', S Ukraine
Mykonos *105 D6 var.* Míkonos. *island* Kykládes, Greece, Aegean Sea
Myrhorod *109 F2 Rus.* Mirgorod. Poltavs'ka Oblast', NE Ukraine
Mýrina *104 D4 var.* Mírina. Límnos, SE Greece
Myrtle Beach *43 F2* South Carolina, SE USA
Mýrtos *105 D8* Kríti, Greece, E Mediterranean Sea
Myrtoum Mare *see* Mirtóo Pélagos
Myślibórz *98 B3* Zachodnio-pomorskie, NW Poland
Mysore *132 C2 var.* Maisur. Karnātaka, W India
Mysore *see* Karnātaka
My Tho *137 E6 var.* Mi Tho. Tiên Giang, S Vietnam
Mytilene *see* Mytilíni
Mytilíni *105 D5 var.* Mitilíni; *anc.* Mytilene. Lésvos, E Greece
Mzuzu *79 E2* Northern, N Malawi

N

Naberezhnyye Chelny *111 D5 prev.* Brezhnev. Respublika Tatarstan, W Russian Federation
Nablus *119 A6 var.* Nābulus, *Heb.* Shekhem; *anc.* Neapolis, *Bibl.* Shechem. N West Bank
Nābulus *see* Nablus
Nacala *79 F2* Nampula, NE Mozambique
Na-Ch'ii *see* Nagqu
Nada *see* Danzhou
Nadi *145 E4 prev.* Nandi. Viti Levu, W Fiji
Nadur *102 A5* Gozo, N Malta
Nadvirna *108 C3 Pol.* Nadwórna, *Rus.* Nadvornaya. Ivano-Frankivs'ka Oblast', W Ukraine
Nadvoitsy *110 B3* Respublika Kareliya, NW Russian Federation
Nadvornaya/Nadwórna *see* Nadvirna
Nadym *114 C3* Yamalo-Nenetskiy Avtonomnyy Okrug, N Russian Federation
Náfpaktos *105 B5 var.* Návpaktos. Dytikí Ellás, C Greece
Náfplio *105 B6 prev.* Návplion. Pelopónnisos, S Greece
Naga *139 E2 off.* Naga City; *prev.* Nueva Caceres. Luzon, N Philippines
Naga City *see* Naga
Nagano *131 C5* Nagano, Honshū, S Japan
Nagaoka *131 C5* Niigata, Honshū, C Japan
Nagara Pathom *see* Nakhon Pathom
Nagara Sridharmaraj *see* Nakhon Si Thammarat
Nagara Svarga *see* Nakhon Sawan
Nagasaki *131 A7* Nagasaki, Kyūshū, SW Japan

Nagato *131 A7* Yamaguchi, Honshū, SW Japan
Nāgercoil *132 C3* Tamil Nādu, SE India
Nagorno-Karabakh *117 G3 var.* Nagorno-Karabakhskaya Avtonomnaya Oblast, *Arm.* Lerrnayin Gharabakh, *Az.* Dağlıq Quarabağ, *Rus.* Nagornyy Karabakh. *former autonomous region* SW Azerbaijan
Nagorno-Karabakhskaya Avtonomnaya Oblast *see* Nagorno-Karabakh
Nagornyy Karabakh *see* Nagorno-Karabakh
Nagoya *131 C6* Aichi, Honshū, SW Japan
Nāgpur *134 D4* Mahārāshtra, C India
Nagqu *126 C5 Chin.* Na-Ch'ii; *prev.* Hei-ho. Xizang Zizhiqu, W China
Nagybánya *see* Baia Mare
Nagybecskerek *see* Zrenjanin
Nagydisznód *see* Cisnădie
Nagyenyed *see* Aiud
Nagykálló *99 E6* Szabolcs-Szatmár-Bereg, E Hungary
Nagykanizsa *99 C7 Ger.* Grosskanizsa. Zala, SW Hungary
Nagykároly *see* Carei
Nagykikinda *see* Kikinda
Nagykőrös *99 D7* Pest, C Hungary
Nagymihály *see* Michalovce
Nagysurány *see* Šurany
Nagyszalonta *see* Salonta
Nagyszeben *see* Sibiu
Nagyszentmiklós *see* Sânnicolau Mare
Nagyszőllős *see* Vynohradiv
Nagyszombat *see* Trnava
Nagytapolcsány *see* Topol'čany
Nagyvárad *see* Oradea
Naha *130 A3* Okinawa, Okinawa, SW Japan
Nahariya *119 A5 prev.* Nahariyya. Northern, N Israel
Nahariyya *see* Nahariya
Nahuel Huapí, Lago *65 B5 lake* W Argentina
Nain *39 F2* Newfoundland and Labrador, NE Canada
Nā'in *120 D3* Eşfahān, C Iran
Nairobi *69 E5 country capital* (Kenya) (Kenya) Nairobi Area, S Kenya
Nairobi *73 C6* Nairobi Area, S Kenya
Naissus *see* Niš
Najaf *see* An Najaf
Najima *see* Fukuoka
Najin *129 E3* NE North Korea
Najrān *121 B6 var.* Abā as Su'ūd. Najrān, S Saudi Arabia
Nakambé *see* White Volta
Nakamura *131 B7 var.* Shimanto. Kōchi, Shikoku, SW Japan
Nakatsugawa *131 C6 var.* Nakatugawa. Gifu, Honshū, SW Japan
Nakatugawa *see* Nakatsugawa
Nakhichevan' *see* Naxçıvan
Nakhodka *115 G5* Primorskiy Kray, SE Russian Federation
Nakhon Pathom *137 C5 var.* Nagara Pathom, Nakorn Pathom. Nakhon Pathom, W Thailand
Nakhon Ratchasima *137 C5 var.* Khorat, Korat. Nakhon Ratchasima, E Thailand
Nakhon Sawan *137 C5 var.* Muang Nakhon Sawan, Nagara Svarga. Nakhon Sawan, W Thailand
Nakhon Si Thammarat *137 C7 var.* Nagara Sridharmaraj, Nakhon Sithamnaraj. Nakhon Si Thammarat, SW Thailand
Nakhon Sithamnaraj *see* Nakhon Si Thammarat
Nakorn Pathom *see* Nakhon Pathom
Nakuru *73 C6* Rift Valley, SW Kenya
Nal'chik *111 B8* Kabardino-Balkarskaya Respublika, SW Russian Federation
Nālūt *71 F2* NW Libya
Namakan Lake *40 A1* lake Canada/USA
Namangan *123 F2* Namangan Viloyati, E Uzbekistan
Nambala *78 D2* Central, C Zambia
Nam Co *126 C5 lake* W China
Nam Đinh *136 D3* Nam Ha, N Vietnam
Namib Desert *78 B3 desert* W Namibia
Namibe *78 A2 Port.* Moçâmedes, Mossâmedes. Namibe, SW Angola

Namibia 78 B3 *off.* Republic of Namibia, *var.* South West Africa, *Afr.* Suidwes-Afrika, *Ger.* Deutsch-Südwestafrika; *prev.* German Southwest Africa, South-West Africa. *country* S Africa

---

NAMIBIA
Southern Africa

Official name Republic of Namibia
Formation 1990 / 1994
Capital Windhoek
Population 2.1 million / 7 people
per sq mile (3 people per sq km) / 33%
Total area 318,694 sq. miles
(825,418 sq. km)
Languages English*, Ovambo, Kavango, Bergdama, German, Afrikaans
Religions Christian 90%, Traditional beliefs 10%
Ethnic mix Ovambo 50%, Other tribes 24%, Kavango 9%, Damara 8%, Herero 8%, Other 1%
Government Presidential system
Currency Namibian dollar = 100 cents
Literacy rate 85%
Calorie consumption 2278 calories

Namibia, Republic of *see* Namibia
Namnetes *see* Nantes
Namo *see* Namu Atoll
Nam Ou 136 C3 *river* N Laos
Nampa 46 D3 Idaho, NW USA
Nampula 79 E2 Nampula, NE Mozambique
Namsos 84 B4 Nord-Trøndelag, C Norway
Nam Tha 136 C4 *river* N Laos
Namu Atoll 144 D2 *var.* Namo. *atoll* Ralik Chain, C Marshall Islands
Namur 87 C6 *Dut.* Namen. Namur, SE Belgium
Namyit Island 128 C8 *island* S Spratly Islands
Nan 136 C4 *var.* Muang Nan. Nan, NW Thailand
Nanaimo 36 D5 Vancouver Island, British Columbia, SW Canada
Nanchang 128 C5 *var.* Nan ch'ang, Nanch'ang-hsien. *province capital* Jiangxi, S China
Nan-ch'ang *see* Nanchang
Nanch'ang-hsien *see* Nanchang
Nan-ching *see* Nanjing
Nancy 90 D3 Meurthe-et-Moselle, NE France
Nandaime 52 D3 Granada, SW Nicaragua
Nānded 134 D5 Mahārāshtra, C India
Nandi *see* Nadi
Nándorhgy *see* Oțelu Roșu
Nandyāl 132 C1 Andhra Pradesh, E India
Nan Hai *see* South China Sea
Naniwa *see* Ōsaka
Nanjing 128 D5 *var.* Nan ching, Nanking; *prev.* Chianning, Chian-ning, Kiang-ning, Jiangsu. *province capital* Jiangsu, E China
Nanking *see* Nanjing
Nanning 128 B6 *var.* Nan-ning; *prev.* Yung-ning. Guangxi Zhuangzu Zizhiqu, S China
Nan-ning *see* Nanning
Nanortalik 82 C5 Kitaa, S Greenland
Nanpan Jiang 136 D2 *river* S China
Nanping 128 D6 *var.* Nan p'ing; *prev.* Yenping. Fujian, SE China
Nan-p'ing *see* Nanping
Nansei Syotō Trench *see* Ryukyu Trench
Nansen Basin 155 C4 *undersea basin* Arctic Ocean
Nansen Cordillera 155 B3 *var.* Arctic Mid Oceanic Ridge, Nansen Ridge. *seamount range* Arctic Ocean
Nansen Ridge *see* Nansen Cordillera
Nansha Qundao *see* Spratly Islands
Nanterre 90 D1 Hauts-de-Seine, N France
Nantes 90 A4 Bret. Naoned; *anc.* Condivincum, Namnetes. Loire-Atlantique, NW France
Nantucket Island 41 G3 *island* Massachusetts, NE USA
Nanumaga 145 E3 *var.* Nanumanga. *atoll* NW Tuvalu
Nanumanga *see* Nanumaga

Nanyang 128 C5 *var.* Nan-yang. Henan, C China
Nan-yang *see* Nanyang
Naoned *see* Nantes
Napa 47 B6 California, W USA
Napier 150 E4 Hawke's Bay, North Island, New Zealand
Naples 43 E5 Florida, SE USA
Naples *see* Napoli
Napo 56 A3 *province* NE Ecuador
Napoléon-Vendée *see* la Roche-sur-Yon
Napoli 97 C5 *Eng.* Naples, *Ger.* Neapel; *anc.* Neapolis. Campania, S Italy
Napo, Río 60 C1 *river* Ecuador/Peru
Naracoorte 149 B7 South Australia
Naradhivas *see* Narathiwat
Narathiwat 137 C7 *var.* Naradhivas. Narathiwat, SW Thailand
Narbada *see* Narmada
Narbo Martius *see* Narbonne
Narbonne 91 C6 *anc.* Narbo Martius. Aude, S France
Narborough Island *see* Fernandina, Isla
Nares Plain 35 E6 *var.* Nares Abyssal Plain. *abyssal plain* NW Atlantic Ocean
Nares Stræde *see* Nares Strait
Nares Strait 82 D1 *Dan.* Nares Stræde. *strait* Canada/Greenland
Narew 98 E3 *river* E Poland
Narmada 124 B3 *var.* Narbada. *river* C India
Narova *see* Narva
Narovlya *see* Narowlya
Narowlya 107 C8 *Rus.* Narovlya. Homyel'skaya Voblasts', SE Belarus
Närpes 85 D5 *Fin.* Närpiö. Länsi-Suomi, W Finland
Närpiö *see* Närpes
Narrabri 149 D6 New South Wales, SE Australia
Narrogin 147 B6 Western Australia
Narva 106 E2 Ida-Virumaa, NE Estonia
Narva 106 E2 *prev.* Narova. *river* Estonia/Russian Federation
Narva Bay 106 E2 *Est.* Narva Laht, *Ger.* Narwa-Bucht, *Rus.* Narvskiy Zaliv. *bay* Estonia/Russian Federation
Narva Laht *see* Narva Bay
Narva Reservoir 106 E2 *Est.* Narva Veehoidla, *Rus.* Narvskoye Vodokhranilishche. *reservoir* Estonia/Russian Federation
Narva Veehoidla *see* Narva Reservoir
Narvik 84 C3 Nordland, C Norway
Narvskiy Zaliv *see* Narva Bay
Narvskoye Vodokhranilishche *see* Narva Reservoir
Narwa-Bucht *see* Narva Bay
Nar'yan-Mar 110 D3 *prev.* Beloshchel'ye, Dzerzhinskiy. Nenetskiy Avtonomnyy Okrug, NW Russian Federation
Naryn 123 G2 Narynskaya Oblast', C Kyrgyzstan
Nassau 54 C1 *country capital* (Bahamas) (Bahamas) New Providence, N Bahamas
Näsäud 108 B3 *Ger.* Nussdorf, *Hung.* Naszód. Bistrița-Năsăud, N Romania
Nase *see* Naze
Näshik 134 C5 *prev.* Nāsik. Mahārāshtra, W India
Nashua 41 G3 New Hampshire, NE USA
Nashville 42 C1 *state capital* Tennessee, S USA
Näsijärvi 85 D5 *lake* SW Finland
Nāsik *see* Näshik
Nasir, Buhayrat/Nâṣir, Buḥeiret *see* Nasser, Lake
Nâsiri *see* Ahvāz
Nasiriya *see* An Nāṣirīyah
Nasser, Lake 72 B3 *var.* Buhayrat Nasir, Buhayrat Nâṣir, Buḥeiret Nâṣir. *lake* Egypt/Sudan
Naszód *see* Näsäud
Nata 78 C3 Central, NE Botswana
Natal 63 G2 *state capital* Rio Grande do Norte, E Brazil
Natal Basin 141 A6 *var.* Mozambique Basin. *undersea basin* W Indian Ocean
Natanya *see* Netanya
Natchez 42 B3 Mississippi, S USA
Natchitoches 42 A2 Louisiana, S USA
Nathanya *see* Netanya
Natitingou 75 F4 NW Benin
Natsrat *see* Natzrat
Natuna Islands *see* Natuna, Kepulauan

Natuna, Kepulauan 124 D4 *var.* Natuna Islands. *island group* W Indonesia
Naturaliste Plateau 141 E6 *undersea plateau* E Indian Ocean
Natzrat 119 A5 *var.* Natsrat, *Ar.* En Nazira, *Eng.* Nazareth; *prev.* Nazerat. Northern, N Israel
Naugard *see* Nowogard
Naujamiestis 106 C4 Panevėžys, C Lithuania
Nauru 144 D2 *off.* Republic of Nauru; *prev.* Pleasant Island. *country* W Pacific Ocean

---

NAURU
Australasia & Oceania

Official name Republic of Nauru
Formation 1968 / 1968
Capital None
Population 13,528 / 1670 people
per sq mile (644 people per sq km) /
Total area 8.1 sq. miles (21 sq. km)
Languages Nauruan*, Kiribati, Chinese, Tuvaluan, English
Religions Nauruan Congregational Church 60%, Roman Catholic 35%, Other 5%
Ethnic mix Nauruan 62%, Other Pacific islanders 27%, Asian 8%, European 3%
Government Nonparty system
Currency Australian dollar = 100 cents
Literacy rate 95%
Calorie consumption Not available

Nauru, Republic of *see* Nauru
Nauta 60 C2 Loreto, N Peru
Navahrudak 107 C6 *Pol.* Nowogródek, *Rus.* Novogrudok. Hrodzyenskaya Voblasts', W Belarus
Navapolatsk 107 D5 *Rus.* Novopolotsk. Vitsyebskaya Voblasts', N Belarus
Navarra 93 E2 *Eng./Fr.* Navarre. *autonomous community* N Spain
Navarre *see* Navarra
Navassa Island 54 C3 *US unincorporated territory* C West Indies
Navoi *see* Navoiy
Navoiy 123 E2 *Rus.* Navoi. Navoiy Viloyati, C Uzbekistan
Navojoa 50 C2 Sonora, NW Mexico
Navolat *see* Navolato
Navolato 50 C3 *var.* Navolat. Sinaloa, C Mexico
Návpaktos *see* Náfpaktos
Návplion *see* Náfplio
Nawabashah *see* Nawābshāh
Nawābshāh 134 B3 *var.* Nawabashah. Sind, S Pakistan
Naxçıvan 117 G3 *Rus.* Nakhichevan'. SW Azerbaijan
Náxos 105 D6 *var.* Naxos. Náxos, Kykládes, Greece, Aegean Sea
Náxos 105 D6 *island* Kykládes, Greece, Aegean Sea
Nayoro 130 D2 Hokkaidō, NE Japan
Nay Pyi Taw 136 B4 *country capital* (Myanmar (Burma)) Mandalay, C Burma (Myanmar)
Nazareth *see* Natzrat
Nazca 60 D4 Ica, S Peru
Nazca Ridge 57 A5 *undersea ridge* E Pacific Ocean
Naze 130 B3 *var.* Nase. Kagoshima, Amami-ōshima, SW Japan
Nazerat *see* Natzrat
Nazilli 116 A4 Aydın, SW Turkey
Nazrēt 73 C5 *var.* Adama. Hadama. Oromīya, C Ethiopia
N'Dalatando 78 B1 *Port.* Salazar, Vila Salazar. Cuanza Norte, NW Angola
Ndélé 76 C4 Bamingui-Bangoran, N Central African Republic
Ndendé 77 B6 Ngounié, S Gabon
Ndindi 77 A6 Nyanga, S Gabon
Ndjamena 76 B3 *var.* N'Djamena; *prev.* Fort-Lamy. *country capital* (Chad) (Chad) Chari-Baguirmi, W Chad
N'Djamena *see* Ndjamena
Ndjolé 77 A5 Moyen-Ogooué, W Gabon
Ndola 78 D2 Copperbelt, C Zambia
Ndzouani *see* Anjouan
Neagh, Lough 89 B5 *lake* E Northern Ireland, United Kingdom
Néa Moudaniá 104 C4 *var.* Néa Moudhaniá. Kentrikí Makedonía, N Greece

---

Néa Moudhaniá *see* Néa Moudaniá
Neapel *see* Napoli
Neápoli 104 B4 *prev.* Neápolis. Dytikí Makedonía, N Greece
Neápoli 105 D8 Kríti, Greece, E Mediterranean Sea
Neápoli 105 C7 Pelopónnisos, S Greece
Neápolis *see* Neápoli, Greece
Neápolis *see* Napoli, Italy
Neapolis *see* Nablus, West Bank
Near Islands 36 A2 *island group* Aleutian Islands, Alaska, USA
Néa Zíchni 104 C3 *var.* Néa Zíkhni; *prev.* Néa Zíkhna. Kentrikí Makedonía, NE Greece
Néa Zíkhna *see* Néa Zíchni
Néa Zíkhna/Néa Zíkhni *see* Néa Zíchni
Nebaj 52 B2 Quiché, W Guatemala
Nebitdag *see* Balkanabat
Neblina, Pico da 62 C1 *mountain* NW Brazil
Nebraska 44 D4 *off.* State of Nebraska, *also known as* Blackwater State, Cornhusker State, Tree Planters State. *state* C USA
Nebraska City 45 F4 Nebraska, C USA
Neches River 49 H3 *river* Texas, SW USA
Neckar 95 B6 *river* SW Germany
Necochea 65 D5 Buenos Aires, E Argentina
Nederland *see* Netherlands
Neder Rijn 86 D4 *Eng.* Lower Rhine. *river* C Netherlands
Neede 86 E3 Gelderland, E Netherlands
Neerpelt 87 D5 Limburg, NE Belgium
Neftekamsk 111 D5 Respublika Bashkortostan, W Russian Federation
Neftezavodsk *see* Seýdi
Negara Brunei Darussalam *see* Brunei
Negēlē 73 D5 *var.* Negelli, *It.* Neghelli. Oromīya, C Ethiopia
Negelli *see* Negēlē
Negev 119 A7 *Eng.* Negev. *desert* S Israel
Negev *see* HaNegev
Neghelli *see* Negēlē
Negomane 79 E2 *var.* Negomano. Cabo Delgado, N Mozambique
Negomano *see* Negomane
Negombo 132 C3 Western Province, SW Sri Lanka
Negotin 100 E4 Serbia, E Serbia
Negra, Punto 60 A3 *headland* NW Peru
Negreşti *see* Negreşti-Oaş
Negreşti-Oaş 108 B3 *Hung.* Avasfelsőfalu; *prev.* Negreşti. Satu Mare, N Romania
Negro, Río 65 C5 *river* E Argentina
Negro, Río 62 D1 *river* N South America
Negro, Río 64 D4 *river* Brazil/Uruguay
Negros 139 E2 *island* C Philippines
Nehbandān 120 E3 Khorāsān, E Iran
Neijiang 120 B5 Sìchuan, C China
Neiva 58 B3 Huila, S Colombia
Nellore 132 D2 Andhra Pradesh, E India
Nelson 151 C5 Nelson, South Island, New Zealand
Nelson 37 G4 *river* Manitoba, C Canada
Néma 74 D3 Hodh ech Chargui, SE Mauritania
Neman 106 B4 *Ger.* Ragnit. Kaliningradskaya Oblast', W Russian Federation
Neman 106 A4 *Bel.* Nyoman, *Ger.* Memel, *Lith.* Nemunas, *Pol.* Niemen. *river* NE Europe
Nemausus *see* Nîmes
Neméa 105 B6 Pelopónnisos, S Greece
Nemetocenna *see* Arras
Nemours 90 C3 Seine-et-Marne, N France
Nemunas *see* Neman
Nemuro 130 E2 Hokkaidō, NE Japan
Neochóri 105 B5 Dytikí Ellás, C Greece
Nepal 135 E3 *off.* Nepal. *country* S Asia

NEPAL
South Asia

Official name Nepal
Formation 1769 / 1769
Capital Kathmandu
Population 28.2 million / 534 people
per sq mile (206 people per sq km) / 15%
Total area 54,363 sq. miles
(140,800 sq. km)

NEPAL
(converted)

Languages Nepali*, Maithili, Bhojpuri
Religions Hindu 90%, Buddhist 5%,
Muslim 3%, Other (including Christian) 2%
Ethnic mix Other 52%, Chhetri 16%,
Hill Brahman 13%, Tharu 7%, Magar 7%,
Tamang 5%
Government Parliamentary system
Currency Nepalese rupee = 100 paisa
Literacy rate 49%
Calorie consumption 2453 calories

Nepal *see* Nepal
Nereta *106 C4* Aizkraukle, S Latvia
Neretva *100 C4 river* Bosnia and
Herzegovina/Croatia
Neris *107 C5 Bel.* Viliya, *Pol.* Wilia; *prev.*
Pol. Wilja. *river* Belarus/Lithuania
Neris *see* Viliya
Nerva *92 C4* Andalucía, S Spain
Neryungri *115 F4* Respublika Sakha
(Yakutiya), NE Russian Federation
Neskaupstadhur *83 E5* Austurland,
E Iceland
Ness, Loch *88 C3 lake* N Scotland,
United Kingdom
Nesterov *see* Zhovkva
Néstos *104 C3 Bul.* Mesta, *Turk.* Kara Su.
river Bulgaria/Greece
Nesvizh *see* Nyasvizh
Netanya *119 A6 var.* Natanya, Nathanya.
Central, C Israel
Netherlands *86 C3 off.* Kingdom
of the Netherlands, *var.* Holland,
Dut. Koninkrijk der Nederlanden,
Nederland. *country* NW Europe

NETHERLANDS
Northwest Europe

Official name Kingdom of the
Netherlands
Formation 1648 / 1839
Capital Amsterdam; The Hague
(administrative)
Population 16.4 million / 1252 people
per sq mile (483 people per sq km) / 66%
Total area 16,033 sq. miles (41,526 sq. km)
Languages Dutch*, Frisian
Religions Roman Catholic 36%,
Other 34%, Protestant 27%, Muslim 3%
Ethnic mix Dutch 82%, Other 12%,
Surinamese 2%, Turkish 2%, Moroccan 2%
Government Parliamentary system
Currency Euro = 100 cents
Literacy rate 99%
Calorie consumption 3362 calories

Netherlands East Indies *see* Indonesia
Netherlands Guiana *see* Suriname
Netherlands, Kingdom of the *see*
Netherlands
Netherlands New Guinea *see* Papua
Nettilling Lake *37 G3 lake* Baffin Island,
Nunavut, N Canada
Netze *see* Noteć
Neu Amerika *see* Puławy
Neubrandenburg *94 D3* Mecklenburg-
Vorpommern, NE Germany
Neuchâtel *95 A7 Ger.* Neuenburg.
Neuchâtel, W Switzerland
Neuchâtel, Lac de *95 A7 Ger.*
Neuenburger See. *lake* W Switzerland
Neuenburger See *see* Neuchâtel, Lac de
Neufchâteau *87 D8* Luxembourg,
SE Belgium
Neugradisk *see* Nova Gradiška
Neuhof *see* Zgierz
Neukuhren *see* Pionerskiy
Neumarkt *see* Târgu Secuiesc, Covasna,
Romania
Neumarkt *see* Târgu Mureş
Neumoldowa *see* Moldova Nouă
Neumünster *94 B2* Schleswig-Holstein,
N Germany
Neunkirchen *95 A5* Saarland,
SW Germany
Neuquén *65 B5* Neuquén, SE Argentina
Neuruppin *94 C3* Brandenburg,
NE Germany
Neusalz an der Oder *see* Nowa Sól
Neu Sandec *see* Nowy Sącz
Neusatz *see* Novi Sad
Neusiedler See *95 E6 Hung.* Fertő. *lake*
Austria/Hungary

Neusohl *see* Banská Bystrica
Neustadt *see* Baia Mare, Maramureş,
Romania
Neustadt an der Haardt *see* Neustadt an
der Weinstrasse
Neustadt an der Weinstrasse *95*
B5 prev. Neustadt an der Haardt,
hist. Niewenstat; *anc.* Nova Civitas.
Rheinland-Pfalz, SW Germany
Neustadtl *see* Novo mesto
Neustettin *see* Szczecinek
Neustrelitz *94 D3* Mecklenburg-
Vorpommern, NE Germany
Neutra *see* Nitra
Neu-Ulm *95 B6* Bayern, S Germany
Neuwied *95 A5* Rheinland-Pfalz,
W Germany
Neuzen *see* Terneuzen
Nevada *47 C5 off.* State of Nevada, *also*
known as Battle Born State, Sagebrush
State, Silver State. *state* W USA
NevadaSierra *92 D5 mountain range*
S Spain
Nevada, Sierra *47 C6 mountain range*
W USA
Nevers *90 C4 anc.* Noviodunum. Nièvre,
C France
Neves *76 E2* São Tomé, S Sao Tome and
Principe, Africa
Nevinnomyssk *111 B7* Stavropol'skiy
Kray, SW Russian Federation
Nevşehir *116 C3 var.* Nevshehr.
Nevşehir, C Turkey
Newala *73 C8* Mtwara, SE Tanzania
New Albany *40 C5* Indiana, N USA
New Amsterdam *59 G3* E Guyana
Newark *41 F4* New Jersey, NE USA
New Bedford *41 G3* Massachusetts,
NE USA
Newberg *46 B3* Oregon, NW USA
New Bern *43 F1* North Carolina,
SE USA
New Braunfels *49 G4* Texas, SW USA
Newbridge *89 B6 Ir.* An Droichead Nua.
Kildare, C Ireland
New Britain *144 B3 island* E Papua
New Guinea
New Brunswick *39 E4 Fr.* Nouveau-
Brunswick. *province* SE Canada
New Caledonia *144 D4 var.* Kanaky, *Fr.*
Nouvelle-Calédonie. *French overseas*
territory SW Pacific Ocean
New Caledonia *144 C5 island* SW Pacific
Ocean
New Caledonia Basin *142 C4 undersea*
basin W Pacific Ocean
Newcastle *149 D6* New South Wales,
SE Australia
Newcastle *see* Newcastle upon Tyne
Newcastle upon Tyne *88 D4 var.*
Newcastle, *hist.* Monkchester, *Lat.* Pons
Aelii. NE England, United Kingdom
New Delhi *134 D3 country capital*
(India) (India) Delhi, N India
New England of the West *see*
Minnesota
Newfoundland *39 G3 Fr.* Terre-Neuve.
island Newfoundland and Labrador,
SE Canada
Newfoundland and Labrador *39 F2 Fr.*
Terre Neuve. *province* E Canada
Newfoundland Basin *66 B3 undersea*
feature NW Atlantic Ocean
New Georgia Islands *144 C3 island*
group NW Solomon Islands
New Glasgow *39 F4* Nova Scotia,
SE Canada
New Goa *see* Panaji
New Guinea *144 A3 Dut.* Nieuw Guinea,
Ind. Irian. *island* Indonesia/Papua
New Guinea
New Hampshire *41 F2 off.* State of New
Hampshire, *also known as* Granite
State. *state* NE USA
New Haven *41 G3* Connecticut,
NE USA
New Hebrides *see* Vanuatu
New Iberia *42 B3* Louisiana, S USA
New Ireland *144 C3 island* NE Papua
New Guinea
New Jersey *41 F4 off.* State of New
Jersey, *also known as* The Garden State.
state NE USA
Newman *147 B4* Western Australia
Newmarket *89 E6* E England, United
Kingdom

New Mexico *48 C2 off.* State of New
Mexico, *also known as* Land of
Enchantment, Sunshine State. *state*
SW USA
New Orleans *42 B3* Louisiana, S USA
New Plymouth *150 C4* Taranaki, North
Island, New Zealand
Newport *89 D7* S England, United
Kingdom
Newport *89 C7* SE Wales, United
Kingdom
Newport *40 C4* Kentucky, S USA
Newport *41 G2* Vermont, NE USA
Newport News *41 F5* Virginia, NE USA
New Providence *54 C1 island*
N Bahamas
Newquay *89 C7* SW England, United
Kingdom
Newry *89 B5 Ir.* An tÚr. SE Northern
Ireland, United Kingdom
New Sarum *see* Salisbury
New Siberian Islands *115 F1 Eng.*
New Siberian Islands. *island group*
N Russian Federation
New Siberian Islands *see* Novosibirskiye
Ostrova
New South Wales *149 C6 state*
SE Australia
Newton *45 G3* Iowa, C USA
Newton *45 F5* Kansas, C USA
Newtownabbey *89 B5 Ir.* Baile na
Mainistreach. E Northern Ireland,
United Kingdom
New Ulm *45 F2* Minnesota, N USA
New York *41 F3* New York, NE USA
New York *41 F3 state* NE USA
New Zealand *150 A4 country* SW Pacific
Ocean

NEW ZEALAND
Australasia & Oceania

Official name New Zealand
Formation 1947 / 1947
Capital Wellington
Population 4.1 million / 40 people
per sq mile (15 people per sq km) / 86%
Total area 103,737 sq. miles
(268,680 sq. km)
Languages English*, Maori*
Religions Anglican 24%, Other 22%,
Presbyterian 18%, Nonreligious 16%,
Roman Catholic 15%, Methodist 5%
Ethnic mix European 75%, Maori 15%,
Other 7%, Samoan 3%
Government Parliamentary system
Currency New Zealand dollar = 100 cents
Literacy rate 99%
Calorie consumption 3219 calories

Neyveli *132 C2* Tamil Nādu, SE India
Nezhin *see* Nizhyn
Ngangze Co *126 B5 lake* W China
Ngaoundéré *76 B4 var.* N'Gaoundéré.
Adamaoua, N Cameroon
N'Gaoundéré *see* Ngaoundéré
Ngazidja *79 F2 Fr.* Grande-Comore.
island NW Comoros
N'Giva *78 B3 var.* Ondjiva, *Port.* Vila
Pereira de Eça. Cunene, S Angola
Ngo *77 B6* Plateaux, SE Congo
Nguko *77 B5 river* Cameroon/Congo
Ngourti *75 H3* Diffa, E Niger
Nguigmi *75 H3 var.* N'Guigmi. Diffa,
SE Niger
N'Guigmi *see* Nguigmi
N'Gunza *see* Sumbe
Nguru *75 G3* Yobe, NE Nigeria
Nha Trang *137 E6* Khanh Hoa,
S Vietnam
Niagara Falls *38 D5* Ontario, S Canada
Niagara Falls *41 E3* New York, NE USA
Niagara Falls *40 D3 waterfall* Canada/
USA
Niamey *75 F3 country capital* (Niger)
(Niger) Niamey, SW Niger
Niangay, Lac *75 E3 lake* E Mali
Nia-Nia *77 E5* Orientale, N Dem.
Rep. Congo
Nias, Pulau *138 A3 island* W Indonesia
Nicaea *see* Nice
Nicaragua *52 D3 off.* Republic of
Nicaragua. *country* Central America

NICARAGUA
Central America

Official name Republic of Nicaragua
Formation 1838 / 1838

NICARAGUA
(continued)

Capital Managua
Population 5.7 million / 124 people
per sq mile (48 people per sq km) / 58%
Total area 49,998 sq. miles (129,494 sq. km)
Languages Spanish*, English
Creole, Miskito
Religions Roman Catholic 80%,
Protestant Evangelical 17%, Other 3%
Ethnic mix Mestizo 69%, White 14%,
Black 8%, Amerindian 5%, Zambo 4%
Government Presidential system
Currency Córdoba oro = 100 centavos
Literacy rate 77%
Calorie consumption 2298 calories

Lake Nicaragua *52 D4 var.* Cocibolca,
Gran Lago, *Eng.* Lake Nicaragua. *lake*
S Nicaragua
Nicaragua, Lake *see* Nicaragua, Lago de
Nicaragua, Republic of *see* Nicaragua
Nicaria *see* Ikaría
Nice *91 D6 It.* Nizza; *anc.* Nicaea. Alpes-
Maritimes, SE France
Nicephorium *see* Ar Raqqah
Nicholas II Land *see* Severnaya Zemlya
Nicholls Town *54 C1* Andros Island,
NW Bahamas
Nicobar Islands *124 B4 island group*
India, E Indian Ocean
Nicosia *102 C5 Gk.* Lefkosía, *Turk.*
Lefkoşa. *country capital* (Cyprus)
(Cyprus) C Cyprus
Nicoya *52 D4* Guanacaste, W Costa Rica
Nicoya, Golfo de *52 D5 gulf* W Costa Rica
Nicoya, Península de *52 D4 peninsula*
NW Costa Rica
Nida *106 A3 Ger.* Nidden. Klaipėda,
SW Lithuania
Nidaros *see* Trondheim
Nidden *see* Nida
Nidzica *98 D3 Ger.* Niedenburg.
Warmińsko-Mazurskie, NE Poland
Niedenburg *see* Nidzica
Niedere Tauern *99 A6 mountain range*
C Austria
Niemen *see* Neman
Nieśwież *see* Nyasvizh
Nieuw Amsterdam *59 G3* Commewijne,
NE Suriname
Nieuw-Bergen *86 D4* Limburg,
SE Netherlands
Nieuwegein *86 C4* Utrecht,
C Netherlands
Nieuw Guinea *see* New Guinea
Nieuw Nickerie *59 G3* Nickerie,
NW Suriname
Niewenstat *see* Neustadt an der
Weinstrasse
Niğde *116 C4* Niğde, C Turkey
Niger *75 F3 off.* Republic of Niger.
country W Africa

NIGER
West Africa

Official name Republic of Niger
Formation 1960 / 1960
Capital Niamey
Population 14.9 million / 30 people
per sq mile (12 people per sq km) / 23%
Total area 489,188 sq. miles
(1,267,000 sq. km)
Languages French*, Hausa, Djerma,
Fulani, Tuareg, Teda
Religions Muslim 85%, Traditional
beliefs 14%, Other (including Christian) 1%
Ethnic mix Hausa 55%, Djerma and
Songhai 21%, Peul 9%, Tuareg 9%,
Other 6%
Government Presidential system
Currency CFA franc = 100 centimes
Literacy rate 29%
Calorie consumption 2130 calories

Niger *75 F4 river* W Africa
Nigeria *75 F4 off.* Federal Republic of
Nigeria. *country* W Africa

NIGERIA
West Africa

Official name Federal Republic of Nigeria
Formation 1960 / 1961
Capital Abuja

NIGERIA
(continued)

Population 137 million / 390 people
per sq mile (151 people per sq km) / 47%
Total area 356,667 sq. miles
(923,768 sq. km)
Languages English*, Hausa, Yoruba, Ibo
Religions Muslim 50%, Christian 40%,
Traditional beliefs 10%
Ethnic mix Other 29%, Hausa 21%,
Yoruba 21%, Ibo 18%, Fulani 11%
Government Presidential system
Currency Naira = 100 kobo
Literacy rate 67%
Calorie consumption 2726 calories

Nigeria, Federal Republic of *see* Nigeria
Niger, Mouths of the *75 F5 delta*
S Nigeria
Niger, Republic of *see* Niger
Nihon *see* Japan
Niigata *131 D5* Niigata, Honshū, C Japan
Niihama *131 B7* Ehime, Shikoku,
SW Japan
Ni'ihau *47 A7 var.* Niihau. *island*
Hawai'i, USA, C Pacific Ocean
Nii-jima *131 D6 island* E Japan
Nijkerk *86 D3* Gelderland, C Netherlands
Nijlen *87 C5* Antwerpen, N Belgium
Nijmegen *86 D4 Ger.* Nimwegen; *anc.*
Noviomagus. Gelderland, SE Netherlands
Nikaria *see* Ikaría
Nikel' *110 C2 Finn.* Kolosjoki.
Murmanskaya Oblast', NW Russian
Federation
Nikíniki *139 E5* Timor, S Indonesia
Niklasmarkt *see* Gheorgheni
Nikolainkaupunki *see* Vaasa
Nikolayev *see* Mykolayiv
Nikol'sk *see* Ussuriysk
Nikol'sk-Ussuriyskiy *see* Ussuriysk
Nikopol' *109 F3* Dnipropetrovs'ka
Oblast', SE Ukraine
Nikšić *101 C5* C Montenegro
Nikumaroro *145 F3 prev.* Gardner
Island. *atoll* Phoenix Islands, C Kiribati
Nikunau *145 E3 var.* Nukunau; *prev.*
Byron Island. *atoll* Tungaru, W Kiribati
Nile *72 B2 former province* NW Uganda
Nile *68 D3 Ar.* Nahr an Nīl. *river* N Africa
Nile Delta *72 B1 delta* N Egypt
Nil, Nahr an *see* Nile
Nîmes *91 C6 anc.* Nemausus, Nismes.
Gard, S France
Nimwegen *see* Nijmegen
Nine Degree Channel *132 B3 channel*
India/Maldives
Ninetyeast Ridge *141 D5 undersea
feature* E Indian Ocean
Ninety Mile Beach *150 C1 beach* North
Island, New Zealand
Ningbo *128 D5 var.* Ningpo, Thsienin,
prev. Ninghsien. Zhejiang, SE China
Ning-hsia *see* Ningxia
Ninghsien *see* Ningbo
Ning-po *see* Ningbo
**Ningsia/Ningsia Hui/Ningsia Hui
Autonomous Region** *see* Ningxia
Ningxia *128 B4 off.* Ningxia Huizu
Zizhiqu, *var.* Ning-hsia, Ningsia, *Eng.*
Ningsia Hui, Ningsia Hui Autonomous
Region. *autonomous region* N China
Ningxia Huizu Zizhiqu *see* Ningxia
Nio *see* Íos
Nio *see* Íos
Niobrara River *45 E3 river* Nebraska/
Wyoming, C USA
Nioro *74 D3 var.* Nioro du Sahel. Kayes,
W Mali
Nioro du Sahel *see* Nioro
Niort *90 B4* Deux-Sèvres, W France
Nipigon *38 B4* Ontario, S Canada
Nipigon, Lake *38 B3 lake* Ontario,
S Canada
Nippon *see* Japan
Niš *101 E5 Eng.* Nish, *Ger.* Nisch; *anc.*
Naissus. Serbia, SE Serbia
Nisab *121 B6 Al Hudud ash Shamālīyah,
N Saudi Arabia
Nisch/Nish *see* Niš
Nisibin *see* Nusaybin
Nísiros *see* Nísyros
Nisko *98 E4* Podkrapackie, SE Poland
Nismes *see* Nîmes

Nistru *see* Dniester
Nísyros *105 E7 var.* Nisiros. *island*
Dodekánisa, Greece, Aegean Sea
Nitra *99 C6 Ger.* Neutra, *Hung.* Nyitra.
Nitriansky Kraj, SW Slovakia
Nitra *99 C6 Ger.* Neutra, *Hung.* Nyitra.
river W Slovakia
Niuatobutabu *see* Niuatoputapu
Niuatoputapu *145 E4 var.*
Niuatobutabu; *prev.* Keppel Island.
island N Tonga
Niue *145 F4 self-governing territory in
free association with New Zealand*
S Pacific Ocean
Niulakita *145 E3 var.* Nurakita. *atoll*
S Tuvalu
Niutao *145 E3 atoll* NW Tuvalu
Nivernais *90 C4 cultural region* C France
Nizāmābād *134 D5* Andhra Pradesh,
C India
Nizhnegorskiy *see* Nyzhn'ohirs'kyy
Nizhnekamsk *111 C5* Respublika
Tatarstan, W Russian Federation
Nizhnevartovsk *114 D3* Khanty-
Mansiyskiy Avtonomnyy Okrug-Yugra,
C Russian Federation
Nizhniy Novgorod *111 C5 prev.* Gor'kiy.
Nizhegorodskaya Oblast', W Russian
Federation
Nizhniy Odes *110 D4* Respublika Komi,
NW Russian Federation
Nizhyn *109 E1 Rus.* Nezhin.
Chernihivs'ka Oblast', NE Ukraine
Nizza *see* Nice
Njombe *73 C8* Iringa, S Tanzania
Nkayi *77 B6 prev.* Jacob. Bouenza,
S Congo
Nkongsamba *76 A4 var.* N'Kongsamba.
Littoral, W Cameroon
N'Kongsamba *see* Nkongsamba
Nmai Hka *136 B2 var.* Me Hka. *river*
N Burma (Myanmar)
Nobeoka *131 B7* Miyazaki, Kyūshū,
SW Japan
Noboribetsu *130 D3 var.* Noboribetu.
Hokkaidō, NE Japan
Noboribetu *see* Noboribetsu
Nogales *50 B1* Sonora, NW Mexico
Nogales *48 B3* Arizona, SW USA
Nogal Valley *see* Dooxo Nugaaleed
Noire, Rivière *see* Black River
Nokia *85 D5* Länsi-Suomi, W Finland
Nokou *76 B3* Kanem, W Chad
Nola *77 B5* Sangha-Mbaéré, SW Central
African Republic
Nolinsk *111 C5* Kirovskaya Oblast',
NW Russian Federation
Nongkaya *see* Nong Khai
Nong Khai *136 C4 var.* Mi Chai,
Nongkaya. Nong Khai, E Thailand
Nonouti *144 D2 prev.* Sydenham Island.
atoll Tungaru, W Kiribati
Noord-Beveland *86 B4 var.* North
Beveland. *island* SW Netherlands
Noordwijk aan Zee *86 C3* Zuid-Holland,
W Netherlands
Noordzee *see* North Sea
Nora *85 C6* Örebro, C Sweden
Norak *123 E3 Rus.* Nurek. W Tajikistan
Nord *83 F1* Avannaarsua, N Greenland
Nordaustlandet *83 G1 island*
NE Svalbard
Norden *94 A3* Niedersachsen,
NW Germany
Norderstedt *94 B3* Schleswig-Holstein,
N Germany
Nordfriesische Inseln *see* North Frisian
Islands
Nordhausen *94 C4* Thüringen,
C Germany
Nordhorn *94 A3* Niedersachsen,
NW Germany
Nord, Mer du *see* North Sea
Nord-Ouest, Territoires du *see*
Northwest Territories
Nordsee/Nordsjøen/Nordsøen *see*
North Sea
Norfolk *45 E3* Nebraska, C USA
Norfolk *41 F5* Virginia, NE USA
Norfolk Island *142 D4 Australian
external territory* SW Pacific Ocean
Norfolk Ridge *142 D4 undersea feature*
W Pacific Ocean
Norge *see* Norway
Norias *49 G5* Texas, SW USA
Noril'sk *114 D3* Taymyrskiy (Dolgano-
Nenetskiy) Avtonomnyy Okrug,
N Russian Federation

Norman *49 G1* Oklahoma, C USA
Normandes, Îles *see* Channel Islands
Normandie *90 B3 Eng.* Normandy.
cultural region N France
Normandy *see* Normandie
Normanton *148 C3* Queensland,
NE Australia
Norrköping *85 C6* Östergötland,
S Sweden
Norrtälje *85 C6* Stockholm, C Sweden
Norseman *147 B6* Western Australia
Norske Havet *see* Norwegian Sea
North Albanian Alps *101 C5 Alb.*
Bjeshkët e Namuna, *SCr.* Prokletije.
mountain range SE Europe
Northallerton *89 D5* N England, United
Kingdom
Northam *147 A6* Western Australia
North America *34 continent*
Northampton *89 D6* C England, United
Kingdom
North Andaman *133 F2 island*
Andaman Islands, India, NE Indian
Ocean
North Australian Basin *141 E5 Fr.*
Bassin Nord de l' Australie. *undersea
feature* E Indian Ocean
North Bay *38 D4* Ontario, S Canada
North Beveland *see* Noord-Beveland
North Borneo *see* Sabah
North Cape *150 C1 headland* North
Island, New Zealand
North Cape *84 D1 Eng.* North Cape.
headland N Norway
North Cape *see* Nordkapp
North Carolina *43 E1 off.* State of North
Carolina, *also known as* Old North
State, Tar Heel State, Turpentine State.
state SE USA
North Channel *40 D2 lake channel*
Canada/USA
North Charleston *43 F2* South Carolina,
SE USA
North Dakota *44 D2 off.* State of North
Dakota, *also known as* Flickertail
State, Peace Garden State, Sioux State.
state N USA
North Devon Island *see* Devon Island
**North East Frontier Agency/North
East Frontier Agency of Assam** *see*
Arunāchal Pradesh
Northeast Providence Channel *54 C1
channel* N Bahamas
Northeim *94 B4* Niedersachsen,
C Germany
Northern Cook Islands *145 F4 island
group* N Cook Islands
Northern Dvina *110 C4 var.* Northern
Dvina. *river* N Russian Federation
Northern Dvina *see* Severnaya Dvina
Northern Ireland *88 B4 var.* The Six
Counties. *cultural region* Northern
Ireland, United Kingdom
Northern Mariana Islands *142 B1 US
commonwealth territory* W Pacific Ocean
Northern Rhodesia *see* Zambia
Northern Sporades *see* Vóreioi
Sporádes, Vórioi Sporádhes, *Eng.*
Northern Sporades. *island group*
E Greece
Northern Sporades *see* Vóries Sporádes
Northern Territory *144 A5 territory*
N Australia
North European Plain *81 E3 plain*
N Europe
Northfield *45 F2* Minnesota, N USA
North Fiji Basin *142 D3 undersea
feature* N Coral Sea
North Frisian Islands *94 B2 var.*
Nordfriesische Inseln. *island group*
N Germany
North Huvadhu Atoll *132 B5 var.* Gaafu
Alifu Atoll. *atoll* S Maldives
North Island *150 B2 island* N New
Zealand
North Korea *129 E3 off.* Democratic
People's Republic of Korea, *Kor.*
Chosŏn-minjujuŭi-inmin-kanghwaguk.
country E Asia

NORTH KOREA
East Asia

Official name Democratic People's
Republic of Korea
Formation 1948 / 1953
Capital Pyongyang

NORTH KOREA
(continued)

Population 22.7 million / 488 people
per sq mile (189 people per sq km) / 61%
Total area 46,540 sq. miles
(120,540 sq. km)
Languages Korean*
Religions Atheist 100%
Ethnic mix Korean 100%
Government One-party state
Currency North Korean won = 100 chon
Literacy rate 98%
Calorie consumption 2142 calories

North Little Rock *42 B1* Arkansas, C USA
North Minch *see* Minch, The
North Mole *93 G4 harbour wall*
NW Gibraltar Europe
North Platte *45 E4* Nebraska, C USA
North Platte River *44 D4 river* C USA
North Pole *155 B3 pole* Arctic Ocean
North Saskatchewan *37 F5 river*
Alberta/Saskatchewan, S Canada
North Sea *80 D3 Dan.* Nordsøen, *Dut.*
Noordzee, *Fr.* Mer du Nord, *Ger.*
Nordsee, *Nor.* Nordsjøen; *prev.* German
Ocean, *Lat.* Mare Germanicum. *sea*
NW Europe
North Siberian Lowland *115 E2 var.*
North Siberian Plain, *Eng.* North
Siberian Lowland. *lowlands* N Russian
Federation
**North Siberian Lowland/North
Siberian Plain** *see* Severo-Sibirskaya
Nizmennost'
North Star State *see* Minnesota
North Taranaki Bight *150 C3 gulf* North
Island, New Zealand
North Uist *88 B3 island* NW Scotland,
United Kingdom
Northwest Atlantic Mid-Ocean Canyon
34 E4 undersea feature N Atlantic Ocean
North West Highlands *88 C3 mountain
range* N Scotland, United Kingdom
Northwest Pacific Basin *113 G4
undersea feature* NW Pacific Ocean
Northwest Territories *37 E3 Fr.*
Territoires du Nord-Ouest. *territory*
NW Canada
Northwind Plain *155 B2 undersea
feature* Arctic Ocean
Norton Sound *36 C2 inlet* Alaska, USA
Norway *85 A5 off.* Kingdom of Norway,
Nor. Norge. *country* N Europe

NORWAY
Northern Europe

Official name Kingdom of Norway
Formation 1905 / 1905
Capital Oslo
Population 4.7 million / 40 people
per sq mile (15 people per sq km) / 80%
Total area 125,181 sq. miles (324,220 sq. km)
Languages Norwegian* (Bokmål
"book language" and Nynorsk
"new Norsk"), Sámi
Religions Evangelical Lutheran 89%,
Other and nonreligious 10%,
Roman Catholic 1%
Ethnic mix Norwegian 93%, Other 6%,
Sámi 1%
Government Parliamentary system
Currency Norwegian krone = 100 øre
Literacy rate 99%
Calorie consumption 3484 calories

Norway, Kingdom of *see* Norway
Norwegian Basin *83 F4 undersea feature*
NW Norwegian Sea
Norwegian Sea *83 F4 var.* Norske Havet.
sea NE Atlantic Ocean
Norwich *89 E6* E England, United
Kingdom
Nösen *see* Bistrița
Noshiro *130 D4 var.* Nosiro; *prev.*
Noshirominato. Akita, Honshū,
C Japan
Noshirominato/Nosiro *see* Noshiro
Nosivka *109 E1 Rus.* Nosovka.
Chernihivs'ka Oblast', NE Ukraine
Nosovka *see* Nosivka
Noşratābād *123 E3* Sīstān va
Balūchestān, E Iran
Nossob *78 C4 river* E Namibia
Noteć *98 C3 Ger.* Netze. *river* NW Poland

Nóties Sporádes see Dodekánisa
Nottingham 89 D6 C England, United
Kingdom
Nouâdhibou 74 B2 prev. Port-Étienne.
Dakhlet Nouâdhibou, W Mauritania
Nouakchott 74 B2 country capital
(Mauritania) (Mauritania) Nouakchott
District, SW Mauritania
Nouméa 144 C5 dependent territory
capital (New Caledonia) Province Sud,
S New Caledonia
Nouveau-Brunswick see New Brunswick
Nouvelle-Calédonie see New Caledonia
Nouvelle Écosse see Nova Scotia
Nova Civitas see Neustadt an der
Weinstrasse
Nova Gorica 95 D8 W Slovenia
Nova Gradiška 100 C3 Ger. Neugradisk,
Hung. Újgradiska. Brod-Posavina,
NE Croatia
Nova Iguaçu 63 F4 Rio de Janeiro,
SE Brazil
Nova Lisboa see Huambo
Novara 96 B2 anc. Novaria. Piemonte,
NW Italy
Novaria see Novara
Nova Scotia 39 F4 Fr. Nouvelle Écosse.
province SE Canada
Nova Scotia 35 E5 physical region
SE Canada
Novaya Sibir', Ostrov 115 F1 island
Novosibirskiye Ostrova, NE Russian
Federation
Novaya Zemlya 110 D1 island group
N Russian Federation
Novaya Zemlya Trough see East Novaya
Zemlya Trough
Novgorod see Velikiy Novgorod
Novi Grad see Bosanski Novi
Novi Iskŭr 104 C2 Sofiya-Grad, W Bulgaria
Noviodunum see Nevers, Nièvre, France
Noviomagus see Lisieux, Calvados, France
Noviomagus see Nijmegen, Netherlands
Novi Pazar 101 D5 Turk. Yenipazar.
Serbia, S Serbia
Novi Sad 100 D3 Ger. Neusatz, Hung.
Újvidék. Vojvodina, N Serbia
Novoazovs'k 109 G4 Rus. Novoazovsk.
Donets'ka Oblast', E Ukraine
Novocheboksarsk 111 C5 Chuvashskaya
Respublika, W Russian Federation
Novocherkassk 111 B7 Rostovskaya
Oblast', SW Russian Federation
Novodvinsk 110 C3 Arkhangel'skaya
Oblast', NW Russian Federation
Novograd-Volynskiy see
Novohrad-Volyns'kyy
Novogrudok see Navahrudak
Novohrad-Volyns'kyy 108 D2 Rus.
Novograd-Volynskiy. Zhytomyrs'ka
Oblast', N Ukraine
Novokazalinsk see Ayteke Bi
Novokuznetsk 114 D4 prev. Stalinsk.
Kemerovskaya Oblast', S Russian
Federation
Novolazarevskaya 154 C2 Russian
research station Antarctica
Novo mesto 95 E8 Ger. Rudolfswert;
prev. Ger. Neustadtl. SE Slovenia
Novomoskovsk 111 B5 Tul'skaya
Oblast', W Russian Federation
Novomoskovs'k 109 F3 Rus.
Novomoskovsk. Dnipropetrovs'ka
Oblast', E Ukraine
Novopolotsk see Navapolatsk
Novoradomsk see Radomsko
Novo Redondo see Sumbe
Novorossiysk 111 A7 Krasnodarskiy
Kray, SW Russian Federation
Novoshakhtinsk 111 B6 Rostovskaya
Oblast', SW Russian Federation
Novosibirsk 114 D4 Novosibirskaya
Oblast', C Russian Federation
Novotroitsk 111 D6 Orenburgskaya
Oblast', W Russian Federation
Novotroitskoye see Novotroyits'ke,
Ukraine
Novotroyits'ke 109 F4 Rus.
Novotroitskoye. Khersons'ka Oblast',
S Ukraine
Novo-Urgench see Urganch
Novovolyns'k 108 C1 Rus. Novovolynsk.
Volyns'ka Oblast', NW Ukraine
Novyy Dvor 107 B6 Rus. Novyy Dvor.
Hrodzyenskaya Voblasts', W Belarus
Novyy Bug see Novyy Buh

Novyy Buh 109 E3 Rus. Novyy Bug.
Mykolayivs'ka Oblast', S Ukraine
Novyy Dvor see Novy Dvor
Novyy Margilan see Farg'ona
Novyy Uzen' see Zhanaozen
Nowa Sól 98 B4 var. Nowasól, Ger.
Neusalz an der Oder. Lubuskie,
W Poland
Nowasól see Nowa Sól
Nowogard 98 B2 var. Nowógard, Ger.
Naugard. Zachodnio-pomorskie,
NW Poland
Nowogródek see Navahrudak
Nowo-Mińsk see Mińsk Mazowiecki
Nowy Dwór Mazowiecki 98 D3
Mazowieckie, C Poland
Nowy Sącz 99 D5 Ger. Neu Sandec.
Małopolskie, S Poland
Nowy Tomyśl 98 B3 var. Nowy Tomysl.
Wielkopolskie, C Poland
Nowy Tomysl see Nowy Tomyśl
Noyon 90 C3 Oise, N France
Nsanje 79 E3 Southern, S Malawi
Nsawam 75 E5 SE Ghana
Ntomba, Lac 77 C6 var. Lac Tumba.
lake NW Dem. Rep. Congo
Nubian Desert 72 B3 desert NE Sudan
Nu Chiang see Salween
Nu'eima 119 E7 E West Bank Asia
Nueva Caceres see Naga
Nueva Gerona 54 B2 Isla de la Juventud,
S Cuba
Nueva Rosita 50 D2 Coahuila,
NE Mexico
Nuevitas 54 C2 Camagüey, E Cuba
Nuevo, Bajo 53 G1 island NW Colombia
South America
Nuevo Casas Grandes 50 C1 Chihuahua,
N Mexico
Nuevo, Golfo 65 C6 gulf S Argentina
Nuevo Laredo 51 E2 Tamaulipas,
NE Mexico
Nui Atoll 145 E3 atoll W Tuvalu
Nu Jiang see Salween
Nûk see Nuuk
Nukha see Şäki
Nuku'alofa 145 E5 country capital
(Tonga) (Tonga) Tongatapu, S Tonga
Nukufetau Atoll 145 E3 atoll C Tuvalu
Nukulaelae Atoll 145 E3 var. Nukulailai.
atoll E Tuvalu
Nukulailai see Nukulaelae Atoll
Nukunau see Nikunau
Nukunonu Atoll 145 E3 island
C Tokelau
Nukus 122 C2 Qoraqalpog'iston
Respublikasi, W Uzbekistan
Nullarbor Plain 147 C6 plateau South
Australia/Western Australia
Nunap Isua 82 C5 var. Uummannarsuaq,
Dan. Kap Farvel, Eng. Cape Farewell.
cape S Greenland
Nunavut 37 F3 territory N Canada
Nuneaton 89 D6 C England, United
Kingdom
Nunivak Island 36 B2 island Alaska,
USA
Nunspeet 86 D3 Gelderland,
E Netherlands
Nuoro 97 A5 Sardegna, Italy,
C Mediterranean Sea
Nuquí 58 A3 Chocó, W Colombia
Nurakita see Niulakita
Nurata see Nurota
Nurek see Norak
Nuremberg see Nürnberg
Nurmes 84 E4 Itä-Suomi, E Finland
Nürnberg 95 C5 Eng. Nuremberg.
Bayern, S Germany
Nurota 123 E2 Rus. Nurata. Navoiy
Viloyati, C Uzbekistan
Nusaybin 117 F4 var. Nisibin. Manisa,
SE Turkey
Nussdorf see Năsăud
Nutmeg State see Connecticut
Nuuk 82 C4 var. Nûk, Dan. Godthaab,
Godthåb. dependent territory capital
(Greenland) Kitaa, SW Greenland
Nyagan' 114 C3 Khanty-Mansiyskiy
Avtonomnyy Okrug-Yugra, N Russian
Federation
Nyainqentanglha Shan 126 C5
mountain range W China
Nyala 72 A4 Southern Darfur,
W Sudan
Nyamapanda 78 D3 Mashonaland East,
NE Zimbabwe

Nyamtumbo 73 C8 Ruvuma, S Tanzania
Nyanda see Masvingo
Nyandoma 110 C4 Arkhangel'skaya
Oblast', NW Russian Federation
Nyantakara 73 B7 Kagera, NW Tanzania
Nyasa, Lake 79 E2 var. Lake Malawi;
prev. Lago Nyassa. lake E Africa
Nyasaland/Nyasaland Protectorate
see Malawi
Nyassa, Lago see Nyasa, Lake
Nyasvizh 107 C6 Pol. Nieśwież, Rus.
Nesvizh. Minskaya Voblasts', C Belarus
Nyaunglebin 136 B4 Bago, SW Burma
(Myanmar)
Nyeri 73 C6 Central, C Kenya
Nyíregyháza 99 D6 Szabolcs-Szatmár-
Bereg, NE Hungary
Nyitra see Nitra
Nykøbing 85 B8 Storstrøm, SE Denmark
Nyköping 85 C6 Södermanland,
S Sweden
Nylstroom see Modimolle
Nyngan 149 D6 New South Wales,
SE Australia
Nyoman see Neman
Nyurba 115 F3 Respublika Sakha
(Yakutiya), NE Russian Federation
Nyzhn'ohirs'kyy 109 F4 Rus.
Nizhnegorskiy. Respublika Krym,
S Ukraine
NZ see New Zealand
Nzega 73 C7 Tabora, C Tanzania
Nzérékoré 74 D4 SE Guinea
Nzwani see Anjouan

O

Oa'hu 47 A7 var. Oahu. island Hawai'ian
Islands, Hawai'i, USA
Oak Harbor 46 B1 Washington,
NW USA
Oakland 47 B6 California, W USA
Oamaru 151 B7 Otago, South Island,
New Zealand
Oaxaca 51 F5 var. Oaxaca de Juárez; prev.
Antequera. Oaxaca, SE Mexico
Oaxaca de Juárez see Oaxaca
Ob' 112 C2 river C Russian Federation
Obal' 107 D5 Rus. Obol'. Vitsyebskaya
Voblasts', N Belarus
Oban 88 C4 W Scotland, United
Kingdom
Oban see Halfmoon Bay
Obando see Puerto Inírida
Obdorsk see Salekhard
Óbecse see Bečej
Obeliai 106 C4 Panevėžys, NE Lithuania
Oberhollabrunn see Tulln
Ob', Gulf of 114 D3 Eng. Gulf of Ob. gulf
N Russian Federation
Ob', Gulf of see Obskaya Guba
Obidovichi see Abidavichy
Obihiro 130 D2 Hokkaidō, NE Japan
Obo 76 D4 Haut-Mbomou, E Central
African Republic
Obock 72 D4 E Djibouti
Obol' see Obal'
Oborniki 98 C3 Wielkopolskie,
W Poland
Obrovo see Abrova
Ob' Tablemount 141 B7 undersea
feature S Indian Ocean
Ocala 43 E4 Florida, SE USA
Ocaña 58 B2 Norte de Santander,
N Colombia
Ocaña 90 D3 Castilla-La Mancha, C Spain
O Carballiño 92 C1 Cast. Carballiño.
Galicia, NW Spain
Occidental, Cordillera 58 B2 mountain
range W South America
Occidental, Cordillera 61 E4 mountain
range Bolivia/Chile
Ocean Falls 36 D5 British Columbia,
SW Canada
Ocean Island see Banaba
Oceanside 47 C8 California, W USA
Ocean State see Rhode Island
Ochakiv 109 E4 Rus. Ochakov.
Mykolayivs'ka Oblast', S Ukraine
Ochakov see Ochakiv
Ochamchira see Och'amch'ire
Och'amch'ire 117 E2 Rus. Ochamchira.
W Georgia
Ocho Rios 54 B4 C Jamaica
Ochrida see Ohrid
Ochrida, Lake see Ohrid, Lake

Ocotal 52 D3 Nueva Segovia,
NW Nicaragua
Ocozocuautla 51 G5 Chiapas, SE Mexico
October Revolution Island 115 E2
Eng. October Revolution Island.
island Severnaya Zemlya, N Russian
Federation
October Revolution Island see
Oktyabr'skoy Revolyutsii, Ostrov
Ocú 53 F5 Herrera, S Panama
Ōdate 130 D3 Akita, Honshū, C Japan
Oddur see Xuddur
Ödemiş 116 A4 İzmir, SW Turkey
Ödenburg see Sopron
Odenpäh see Otepää
Odense 85 B7 Fyn, C Denmark
Oder 98 B3 Cz./Pol. Odra. river
C Europe
Oderhaff see Szczeciński, Zalew
Odesa 109 E4 Rus. Odessa. Odes'ka
Oblast', SW Ukraine
Odessa 49 E3 Texas, SW USA
Odessa see Odesa
Odessus see Varna
Odienné 74 D4 NW Côte d'Ivoire
Ôdôngk 137 D6 Kâmpóng Spoe,
S Cambodia
Odoorn 86 E2 Drenthe, NE Netherlands
Odra see Oder
Oesel see Saaremaa
Of 117 E2 Trabzon, NE Turkey
Ofanto 97 D5 river S Italy
Offenbach 95 B5 var. Offenbach am
Main. Hessen, W Germany
Offenbach am Main see Offenbach
Offenburg 95 B6 Baden-Württemberg,
SW Germany
Ogaadeen see Ogaden
Ogaden 73 D5 Som. Ogaadeen. plateau
Ethiopia/Somalia
Ōgaki 131 C6 Gifu, Honshū, SW Japan
Ogallala 44 D3 Nebraska, C USA
Ogbomosho 75 F4 var. Ogmoboso. Oyo,
W Nigeria
Ogden 44 B4 Utah, W USA
Ogdensburg 41 F2 New York, NE USA
Ogmoboso see Ogbomosho
Ogulin 100 A3 Karlovac, NW Croatia
Ohio 40 C4 off. State of Ohio, also known
as Buckeye State. state N USA
Ohio River 40 C4 river N USA
Ohlau see Oława
Ohri see Ohrid
Ohrid 101 D6 Turk. Ochrida, Ohri.
SW FYR Macedonia
Ohrid, Lake 101 D6 var. Lake Ochrida,
Alb. Liqeni i Ohrit, Mac. Ohridsko
Ezero. lake Albania/FYR Macedonia
Ohridsko Ezero/Ohrit, Liqeni i see
Ohrid, Lake
Ohura 150 D3 Manawatu-Wanganui,
North Island, New Zealand
Oirschot 87 C5 Noord-Brabant,
S Netherlands
Oise 90 C3 river N France
Oistins 55 G2 S Barbados
Ōita 131 B7 Ōita, Kyūshū, SW Japan
Ojinaga 50 D2 Chihuahua, N Mexico
Ojos del Salado, Cerro 64 B3 mountain
W Argentina
Okaihau 150 C2 Northland, North
Island, New Zealand
Okanizsa see Kanjiža
Okāra 134 C2 Punjab, E Pakistan
Okavanggo see Cubango/Okavango
Okavango see Cubango
Okavango Delta 78 C3 wetland
N Botswana
Okayama 131 B6 Okayama, Honshū,
SW Japan
Okazaki 131 C6 Aichi, Honshū, C Japan
Okeechobee, Lake 43 E4 lake Florida,
SE USA
Okefenokee Swamp 43 E3 wetland
Georgia, SE USA
Okhotsk 115 G3 Khabarovskiy Kray,
E Russian Federation
Okhotsk, Sea of 113 F3 sea NW Pacific
Ocean
Okhtyrka 109 F2 Rus. Akhtyrka.
Sums'ka Oblast', NE Ukraine
Oki-guntō see Oki-shotō
Okinawa 130 A3 island SW Japan
Okinawa-shoto 130 A3 island group
Nansei-shotō, SW Japan Asia
Oki-shoto 131 B6 var. Oki-guntō. island
group SW Japan

Oklahoma *49 F2 off.* State of Oklahoma, *also known as* The Sooner State. *state* C USA

Oklahoma City *49 G1 state capital* Oklahoma, C USA

Okmulgee *49 G1* Oklahoma, C USA

Oko, Wadi *72 C3 river* NE Sudan

Oktyabr'skiy *111 D6* Volgogradskaya Oblast', SW Russian Federation

Oktyabr'skiy *see* Aktsyabrski

Okulovka *110 B4 var.* Okulovka. Novgorodskaya Oblast', W Russian Federation

Okulovka *see* Okulovka

Okushiri-to *130 C3 var.* Okusiri Tô. *island* NE Japan

Okusiri Tô *see* Okushiri-tō

Oláh-Toplicza *see* Topliţa

Öland *85 C7 Island* S Sweden

Olavarría *65 D5* Buenos Aires, E Argentina

Oława *98 C4 Ger.* Ohlau. Dolnośląskie, SW Poland

Olbia *97 A5 prev.* Terranova Pausania. Sardegna, Italy, C Mediterranean Sea

Old Bay State/Old Colony State *see* Massachusetts

Old Dominion *see* Virginia

Oldebroek *86 D3* Gelderland, E Netherlands

Oldenburg *94 B3* Niedersachsen, NW Germany

Oldenburg *94 C2 var.* Oldenburg in Holstein. Schleswig-Holstein, N Germany

Oldenburg in Holstein *see* Oldenburg

Oldenzaal *86 E3* Overijssel, E Netherlands

Old Harbour *54 B5* C Jamaica

Old Line State *see* Maryland

Old North State *see* North Carolina

Olëkma *115 F4 river* C Russian Federation

Olëkminsk *115 F3* Respublika Sakha (Yakutiya), NE Russian Federation

Oleksandrivka *109 E3 Rus.* Aleksandrovka. Kirovohrads'ka Oblast', C Ukraine

Oleksandriya *109 F3 Rus.* Aleksandriya. Kirovohrads'ka Oblast', C Ukraine

Olenegorsk *110 C2* Murmanskaya Oblast', NW Russian Federation

Olenëk *115 E3* Respublika Sakha (Yakutiya), NE Russian Federation

Olenëk *115 E3 river* NE Russian Federation

Oléron, Île d' *91 A5 island* W France

Olevs'k *108 D1 Rus.* Olevsk. Zhytomyrs'ka Oblast', N Ukraine

Olevsk *see* Olevs'k

Ölgiy *126 C2* Bayan-Ölgiy, W Mongolia

Olhão *92 B5* Faro, S Portugal

Olifa *78 B3* Kunene, NW Namibia

Ólimbos *see* Olympus

Olimpo *see* Fuerte Olimpo

Olisipo *see* Lisboa

Olita *see* Alytus

Oliva *93 F4* País Valenciano, E Spain

Olivet *90 C4* Loiret, C France

Olmaliq *123 E2 Rus.* Almalyk. Toshkent Viloyati, E Uzbekistan

Olmütz *see* Olomouc

Olomouc *99 C5 Ger.* Olmütz, *Pol.* Ołomuniec. Olomoucký Kraj, E Czech Republic

Ołomuniec *see* Olomouc

Olonets *110 B3* Respublika Kareliya, NW Russian Federation

Olovyannaya *117 F4* Chitinskaya Oblast', S Russian Federation

Olpe *94 B4* Nordrhein-Westfalen, W Germany

Olshanka *see* Vil'shanka

Olsnitz *see* Murska Sobota

Olsztyn *98 D2 Ger.* Allenstein. Warmińsko-Mazurskie, N Poland

Olt *108 B5 var.* Oltul, *Ger.* Alt. *river* S Romania

Olteniţa *108 C5 prev. Eng.* Oltenitsa; *anc.* Constantiola. Călăraşi, SE Romania

Oltenitsa *see* Olteniţa

Oltul *see* Olt

Olvera *92 D5* Andalucía, S Spain

Ol'viopol' *see* Pervomays'k

Olympia *46 B2 state capital* Washington, NW USA

Olympic Mountains *46 A2 mountain range* Washington, NW USA

Olympus, Mount *104 B4 var.* Ólimbos, *Eng.* Mount Olympus. *mountain* N Greece

Omagh *89 B5 Ir.* An Ómaigh. W Northern Ireland, United Kingdom

Omaha *45 F4* Nebraska, C USA

Oman *121 D6 off.* Sultanate of Oman, *Ar.* Salṭanat 'Umān; *prev.* Muscat and Oman. *country* SW Asia

OMAN
Southwest Asia

Official name	Sultanate of Oman
Formation	1951 / 1951
Capital	Muscat
Population	2.7 million / 33 people per sq mile (13 people per sq km) / 78%
Total area	82,031 sq. miles (212,460 sq. km)
Languages	Arabic*, Baluchi, Farsi, Hindi, Punjabi
Religions	Ibadi Muslim 75%, Other Muslim and Hindu 25%
Ethnic mix	Arab 88%, Baluchi 4%, Persian 3%, Indian and Pakistani 3%, African 2%
Government	Monarchy
Currency	Omani rial = 1000 baisa
Literacy rate	81%
Calorie consumption	Not available

Oman, Gulf of *120 E4 Ar.* Khalīj 'Umān. *gulf* N Arabian Sea

Oman, Sultanate of *see* Oman

Omboué *77 A6* Ogooué-Maritime, W Gabon

Omdurman *72 B4 var.* Umm Durmān. Khartoum, C Sudan

Ometepe, Isla de *52 D4 island* S Nicaragua

Ommen *86 E3* Overijssel, E Netherlands

Omsk *114 C4* Omskaya Oblast', C Russian Federation

Ōmuta *131 A7* Fukuoka, Kyūshū, SW Japan

Onda *93 F3* País Valenciano, E Spain

Ondjiva *see* N'Giva

Öndörhaan *127 E2 var.* Undur Khan; *prev.* Tsetsen Khan. Hentiy, E Mongolia

Onega *110 C3* Arkhangel'skaya Oblast', NW Russian Federation

Onega *110 B4 river* NW Russian Federation

Lake Onega *110 B4 Eng.* Lake Onega. *lake* NW Russian Federation

Onega, Lake *see* Onezhskoye Ozero

Onex *95 A7* Genève, SW Switzerland

Ongole *132 D1* Andhra Pradesh, E India

Onitsha *75 G5* Anambra, S Nigeria

Onon Gol *127 E2 river* N Mongolia

Onslow *146 A4 Western Australia*

Onslow Bay *43 F1 bay* North Carolina, E USA

Ontario *38 B3 province* S Canada

Ontario, Lake *41 E3 lake* Canada/USA

Onteniente *see* Ontinyent

Ontinyent *93 F4 var.* Onteniente. País Valenciano, E Spain

Ontong Java Rise *125 H4 undersea feature* W Pacific Ocean

Onuba *see* Huelva

Oodeypore *see* Udaipur

Oos-Londen *see* East London

Oostakker *87 B5* Oost-Vlaanderen, NW Belgium

Oostburg *87 B5* Zeeland, SW Netherlands

Oostende *87 A5 Eng.* Ostend, *Fr.* Ostende. West-Vlaanderen, NW Belgium

Oosterbeek *86 D4* Gelderland, SE Netherlands

Oosterhout *86 C4* Noord-Brabant, S Netherlands

Opatija *100 A2 It.* Abbazia. Primorje-Gorski Kotar, NW Croatia

Opava *99 C5 Ger.* Troppau. Moravskoslezský Kraj, E Czech Republic

Ópazova *see* Stara Pazova

Opelika *42 D2* Alabama, S USA

Opelousas *42 B3* Louisiana, S USA

Ophiusa *see* Formentera

Opmeer *86 C2* Noord-Holland, NW Netherlands

Opochka *110 A4* Pskovskaya Oblast', W Russian Federation

Opole *98 C4 Ger.* Oppeln. Opolskie, S Poland

Oporto *see* Porto

Opotiki *150 E3* Bay of Plenty, North Island, New Zealand

Oppeln *see* Opole

Oqtosh *123 E2 Rus.* Aktash. Samarqand Viloyati, C Uzbekistan

Oradea *108 B3 prev.* Oradea Mare, *Ger.* Grosswardein, *Hung.* Nagyvárad. Bihor, NW Romania

Oradea Mare *see* Oradea

Orahovac *see* Rahovec

Oral *see* Ural'sk

Oran *70 D2 var.* Ouahran, Wahran. NW Algeria

Orange *149 D6* New South Wales, SE Australia

Orange *91 D6 anc.* Arausio. Vaucluse, SE France

Orangeburg *43 E2* South Carolina, SE USA

Orange Cone *see* Orange Fan

Orange Fan *69 C7 var.* Orange Cone. *undersea feature* SW Indian Ocean

Orange Mouth/Orangemund *see* Oranjemund

Orange River *78 B4 Afr.* Oranjerivier. *river* S Africa

Orange Walk *52 C1* Orange Walk, N Belize

Oranienburg *94 D3* Brandenburg, NE Germany

Oranjemund *78 B4 var.* Orangemund; *prev.* Orange Mouth. Karas, SW Namibia

Oranjerivier *see* Orange River

Oranjestad *55 E5 dependent territory capital* (Aruba) W Aruba

Orany *see* Varėna

Oraşul Stalin *see* Braşov

Oravicabánya *see* Oraviţa

Oraviţa *108 A4 Ger.* Orawitza, *Hung.* Oravicabánya. Caraş-Severin, SW Romania

Orawitza *see* Oraviţa

Orbetello *96 B4* Toscana, C Italy

Orcadas *154 A1 Argentinian research station* South Orkney Islands, Antarctica

Orchard Homes *44 B1* Montana, NW USA

Ordino *91 A8* Ordino, NW Andorra Europe

Ordos Desert *see* Mu Us Shadi

Ordu *116 D2 anc.* Cotyora. Ordu, N Turkey

Ordzhonikidze *109 F3* Dnipropetrovs'ka Oblast', E Ukraine

Ordzhonikidze *see* Vladikavkaz, Russian Federation

Ordzhonikidze *see* Yenakiyeve, Ukraine

Orealla *59 F3* E Guyana

Örebro *85 C6* Örebro, C Sweden

Oregon *46 B3 off.* State of Oregon, *also known as* Beaver State, Sunset State, Valentine State, Webfoot State. *state* NW USA

Oregon City *46 B3* Oregon, NW USA

Oregon, State of *see* Oregon

Orekhov *see* Orikhiv

Orël *111 B5* Orlovskaya Oblast', W Russian Federation

Orem *44 B4* Utah, W USA

Ore Mountains *99 C5 Cz.* Krušné Hory, *Eng.* Ore Mountains. *mountain range* Czech Republic/Germany

Ore Mountains *see* Erzgebirge/Krušné Hory

Orenburg *111 D6 prev.* Chkalov. Orenburgskaya Oblast', W Russian Federation

Orense *see* Ourense

Orestiáda *104 D3 prev.* Orestiás. Anatolikí Makedonía kai Thráki, NE Greece

Orestiás *see* Orestiáda

Organ Peak *48 D3 mountain* New Mexico, SW USA

Orgeyev *see* Orhei

Orhei *108 D3 var.* Orheiu, *Rus.* Orgeyev. N Moldova

Orheiu *see* Orhei

Oriental, Cordillera *60 D3 mountain range* Bolivia/Peru

Oriental, Cordillera *58 B3 mountain range* C Colombia

Orihuela *93 F4* País Valenciano, E Spain

Orikhiv *109 G3 Rus.* Orekhov. Zaporiz'ka Oblast', SE Ukraine

Orinoco, Río *59 E2 river* Colombia/Venezuela

Orissa *135 F4 cultural region* NE India

Orissaare *see* Orissaare

Orissaare *106 C2 Ger.* Orissaar. Saaremaa, W Estonia

Oristano *97 A5* Sardegna, Italy, C Mediterranean Sea

Orito *58 A4* Putumayo, SW Colombia

Orizaba, Volcán Pico de *35 C7 var.* Citlaltépetl. *mountain* S Mexico

Orkney *see* Orkney Islands

Orkney Islands *88 C2 var.* Orkney, Orkneys. *island group* N Scotland, United Kingdom

Orkneys *see* Orkney Islands

Orlando *43 E4* Florida, SE USA

Orléanais *90 C4 cultural region* C France

Orléans *90 C4 anc.* Aurelianum. Loiret, C France

Orléansville *see* Chlef

Orly *90 E2* (Paris) Essonne, N France

Orlya *107 B6* Hrodzyenskaya Voblasts', W Belarus

Ormsö *see* Vormsi

Ormuz, Strait of *see* Hormuz, Strait of

Örnsköldsvik *85 C5* Västernorrland, C Sweden

Orolaunum *see* Arlon

Orol Dengizi *see* Aral Sea

Oromocto *39 F4* New Brunswick, SE Canada

Orona *145 F3 prev.* Hull Island. *atoll* Phoenix Islands, C Kiribati

Oropeza *see* Cochabamba

Orosirá Rodhópis *see* Rhodope Mountains

Orpington *89 B8* United Kingdom

Orsha *107 E6* Vitsyebskaya Voblasts', NE Belarus

Orsk *114 B4* Orenburgskaya Oblast', W Russian Federation

Orşova *108 A4 Ger.* Orschowa, *Hung.* Orsova. Mehedinţi, SW Romania

Ortelsburg *see* Szczytno

Orthez *91 B6* Pyrénées-Atlantiques, SW France

Ortona *96 D4* Abruzzo, C Italy

Oruba *see* Aruba

Oruro *61 F4* Oruro, W Bolivia

Oryokko *see* Yalu

Oss *86 D4* Noord-Brabant, S Netherlands

Ōsaka *131 C6 hist.* Naniwa. Ōsaka, Honshū, SW Japan

Ōsaki *see* Furukawa

Osa, Península de *53 E5 peninsula* S Costa Rica

Osborn Plateau *141 D5 undersea feature* E Indian Ocean

Osca *see* Huesca

Ösel *see* Saaremaa

Osh *123 F2* Oshskaya Oblast', SW Kyrgyzstan

Oshawa *38 D5* Ontario, SE Canada

Oshikango *78 B3* Ohangwena, N Namibia

O-shima *131 D6 island* S Japan

Oshkosh *40 B2* Wisconsin, N USA

Oshmyany *see* Ashmyany

Osiek *see* Osijek

Osijek *100 C3 prev.* Osiek, Osjek, *Ger.* Esseg, *Hung.* Eszék. Osijek-Baranja, E Croatia

Osipenko *see* Berdyans'k

Osipovichi *see* Asipovichy

Osjek *see* Osijek

Oskaloosa *45 G4* Iowa, C USA

Oskarshamn *85 C7* Kalmar, S Sweden

Öskemen *see* Ust'-Kamenogorsk

Oskil *109 G2 Rus.* Oskil. *river* Russian Federation/Ukraine

Oskil *see* Oskil

Oslo *85 B6 prev.* Christiania, Kristiania. *country capital* (Norway) (Norway) Oslo, S Norway

Osmaniye *116 D4* Osmaniye, S Turkey

Osnabrück *94 A3* Niedersachsen, NW Germany

Osogov Mountains *104 B3 var.* Osogovske Planine, Osogovski Planina, *Mac.* Osogovski Planini. *mountain range* Bulgaria/FYR Macedonia

Osogovske Planine/Osogovski Planina/ Osogovski Planini *see* Osogov Mountains
Oşorhei *see* Târgu Mureş
Osorno 65 B5 Los Lagos, C Chile
Ossa, Serra d' 92 C4 *mountain range* SE Portugal
Ossora 115 H2 Koryakskiy Avtonomnyy Okrug, E Russian Federation
Ostee *see* Baltic Sea
Ostend/Ostende *see* Oostende
Oster 109 E1 Chernihivs'ka Oblast', N Ukraine
Östermyra *see* Seinäjoki
Osterode/Osterode in Ostpreussen *see* Ostróda
Österreich *see* Austria
Östersund 85 C5 Jämtland, C Sweden
Ostia Aterni *see* Pescara
Ostiglia 96 C2 Lombardia, N Italy
Ostrava 99 C5 Moravskoslezský Kraj, E Czech Republic
Ostróda 98 D3 *Ger.* Osterode, Osterode in Ostpreussen. Warmińsko-Mazurskie, NE Poland
Ostrołęka 98 D3 *Ger.* Wiesenhof, *Rus.* Ostrolenka. Mazowieckie, C Poland
Ostrolenka *see* Ostrołęka
Ostrov 110 A4 *Latv.* Austrava. Pskovskaya Oblast', W Russian Federation
Ostrovets *see* Ostrowiec Świętokrzyski
Ostrovnoy 110 C2 Murmanskaya Oblast', NW Russian Federation
Ostrów *see* Ostrów Wielkopolski
Ostrowiec *see* Ostrowiec Świętokrzyski
Ostrowiec Świętokrzyski 98 D4 *var.* Ostrowiec, *Rus.* Ostrovets. Świętokrzyskie, C Poland
Ostrów Mazowiecka 98 D3 *var.* Ostrów Mazowiecki. Mazowieckie, NE Poland
Ostrów Mazowiecki *see* Ostrów Mazowiecka
Ostrowo *see* Ostrów Wielkopolski
Ostrów Wielkopolski 98 C4 *var.* Ostrów, *Ger.* Ostrowo. Wielkopolskie, C Poland
Ostyako-Voguls'k *see* Khanty-Mansiysk
Osum *see* Osumit, Lumi i
Osumi-shoto 131 B8 *island group* Kagoshima, Nansei-shotō, SW Japan Asia East China Sea Pacific Ocean
Osumit, Lumi i 101 D7 *var.* Osum. *river* SE Albania
Osuna 92 D4 Andalucía, S Spain
Oswego 41 F2 New York, NE USA
Otago Peninsula 151 B7 *peninsula* South Island, New Zealand
Otaki 150 D4 Wellington, North Island, New Zealand
Otaru 130 C2 Hokkaidō, NE Japan
Otavalo 60 B1 Imbabura, N Ecuador
Otavi 78 B3 Otjozondjupa, N Namibia
Oţelu Roşu 108 B4 *Ger.* Ferdinandsberg, *Hung.* Nándorhgy. Caras-Severin, SW Romania
Otepää 106 D3 *Ger.* Odenpäh. Valgamaa, SE Estonia
Oti 75 E4 *river* N Togo
Otira 151 C6 West Coast, South Island, New Zealand
Otjiwarongo 78 B3 Otjozondjupa, N Namibia
Otorohanga 150 D3 Waikato, North Island, New Zealand
Otranto, Canale d' *see* Otranto, Strait of
Otranto, Strait of 101 C6 *It.* Canale d'Otranto. *strait* Albania/Italy
Otrokovice 99 C5 *Ger.* Otrokowitz. Zlínský Kraj, E Czech Republic
Otrokowitz *see* Otrokovice
Ōtsu 131 C6 *var.* Ōtu. Shiga, Honshū, SW Japan
Ottawa 38 D5 *country capital* (Canada) (Canada) Ontario, SE Canada
Ottawa 40 B3 Illinois, N USA
Ottawa 45 F5 Kansas, C USA
Ottawa 41 E2 Fr. Outaouais. *river* Ontario/Québec, SE Canada
Ottawa Islands 38 C1 *island group* Nunavut, C Canada
Ottignies 87 C6 Wallon Brabant, C Belgium
Ottumwa 45 G4 Iowa, C USA
Ōtu *see* Ōtsu
Ouachita Mountains 42 A1 *mountain range* Arkansas/Oklahoma, C USA

Ouachita River 42 B2 *river* Arkansas/ Louisiana, C USA
Ouagadougou 75 E4 *var.* Wagadugu. *country capital* (Burkina Faso) C Burkina Faso
Ouahigouya 75 E3 NW Burkina Faso
Ouahran *see* Oran
Oualâta 74 D3 *var.* Oualata. Hodh ech Chargui, SE Mauritania
Ouanary 59 H3 E French Guiana
Ouanda Djallé 76 D4 Vakaga, NE Central African Republic
Ouarâne 74 D2 *desert* C Mauritania
Ouargla 71 E2 *var.* Wargla. NE Algeria
Ouarzazate 70 C3 S Morocco
Oubangui 77 C5 *Fr.* Oubangui. *river* C Africa
Oubangui *see* Ubangi
Oubangui-Chari *see* Central African Republic
Oubangui-Chari, Territoire de l' *see* Central African Republic
Oudjda *see* Oujda
Ouessant, Île d' 90 A3 *Eng.* Ushant. *island* NW France
Ouésso 77 B5 Sangha, NW Congo
Oujda 70 D2 *Ar.* Oudjda, Ujda. NE Morocco
Oujeft 74 C2 Adrar, C Mauritania
Oulu 84 D4 *Swe.* Uleåborg. Oulu, C Finland
Oulujärvi 84 D4 *Swe.* Uleträsk. *lake* C Finland
Oulujoki 84 D3 *river* N Finland
Ounasjoki 84 D3 *river* N Finland
Ounianga Kébir 76 C2 Borkou-Ennedi-Tibesti, N Chad
Oup *see* Auob
Oupeye 87 D6 Liège, E Belgium
Our 87 D6 *river* NW Europe
Ourense 92 C1 *Cast.* Orense, *Lat.* Aurium. Galicia, NW Spain
Ourique 92 B4 Beja, S Portugal
Ours, Grand Lac de l' *see* Great Bear Lake
Ourthe 87 D7 *river* E Belgium
Ouse 89 D5 *river* N England, United Kingdom
Outaouais *see* Ottawa
Outer Hebrides 88 B3 *var.* Western Isles. *island group* NW Scotland, United Kingdom
Outer Islands 79 G1 *island group* SW Seychelles Africa W Indian Ocean
Outes 92 B1 Galicia, NW Spain
Ouvéa 144 D5 *island* Îles Loyauté, NE New Caledonia
Ouyen 149 C6 Victoria, SE Australia
Ovalle 64 B3 Coquimbo, N Chile
Ovar 92 B2 Aveiro, N Portugal
Overflakkee 86 B4 *island* SW Netherlands
Overijse 87 C6 Vlaams Brabant, C Belgium
Oviedo 92 C1 *anc.* Asturias. Asturias, NW Spain
Ovilava *see* Wels
Ovruch 108 D1 Zhytomyrs'ka Oblast', N Ukraine
Owando 77 B5 *prev.* Fort Rousset. Cuvette, C Congo
Owase 131 C6 Mie, Honshū, SW Japan
Owatonna 45 F3 Minnesota, N USA
Owen Fracture Zone 140 B4 *tectonic feature* W Arabian Sea
Owen, Mount 151 C5 *mountain* South Island, New Zealand
Owensboro 40 B5 Kentucky, S USA
Owen Stanley Range 144 B3 *mountain range* S Papua New Guinea
Owerri 75 G5 Imo, S Nigeria
Owo 75 F5 Ondo, SW Nigeria
Owyhee River 46 C4 *river* Idaho/Oregon, NW USA
Oxford 151 C6 Canterbury, South Island, New Zealand
Oxford 89 D6 *Lat.* Oxonia. S England, United Kingdom
Oxkutzcab 51 H4 Yucatán, SE Mexico
Oxnard 47 B7 California, W USA
Oxonia *see* Oxford
Oxus *see* Amu Darya
Oyama 131 D5 Tochigi, Honshū, S Japan
Oyem 77 B5 Woleu-Ntem, N Gabon
Oyo 77 B6 Cuvette, C Congo
Oyo 75 F4 Oyo, W Nigeria
Ozark 42 D3 Alabama, S USA
Ozark Plateau 45 G5 *plain* Arkansas/ Missouri, C USA
Ozarks, Lake of the 45 F5 *reservoir* Missouri, C USA

Ozbourn Seamount 152 D4 *undersea feature* W Pacific Ocean
Ózd 99 D6 Borsod-Abaúj-Zemplén, NE Hungary
Ozieri 97 A5 Sardegna, Italy, C Mediterranean Sea

P

Paamiut 82 B4 *var.* Pâmiut, *Dan.* Frederikshåb. S Greenland
Pa-an *see* Hpa-an
Pabianice 98 C4 Łódzski, Poland
Pabna 135 G4 Rajshahi, W Bangladesh
Pacaraima, Sierra/Pacaraim, Serra *see* Pakaraima Mountains
Pachuca 51 E4 *var.* Pachuca de Soto. Hidalgo, C Mexico
Pachuca de Soto *see* Pachuca
Pacific-Antarctic Ridge 154 B5 *undersea feature* S Pacific Ocean
Pacific Ocean 152 D3 *ocean*
Padalung *see* Phatthalung
Padang 138 B4 Sumatera, W Indonesia
Paderborn 94 B4 Nordrhein-Westfalen, NW Germany
Padma *see* Brahmaputra
Padma *see* Ganges
Padova 96 C2 *Eng.* Padua; *anc.* Patavium. Veneto, NE Italy
Padre Island 49 G5 *island* Texas, SW USA
Padua *see* Padova
Paducah 40 B5 Kentucky, S USA
Paeroa 150 D3 Waikato, North Island, New Zealand
Páfos 102 C5 *var.* Paphos. W Cyprus
Pag 100 A3 *It.* Pago. *island* Zadar, C Croatia
Page 48 B1 Arizona, SW USA
Pago *see* Pag
Pago Pago 145 F4 *dependent territory capital* (American Samoa) Tutuila, W American Samoa
Pahiatua 150 D4 Manawatu-Wanganui, North Island, New Zealand
Pahsien *see* Chongqing
Paide 106 D2 *Ger.* Weissenstein. Järvamaa, N Estonia
Paihia 150 D2 Northland, North Island, New Zealand
Päijänne 85 D5 *lake* S Finland
Paine, Cerro 65 A7 *mountain* S Chile
Painted Desert 48 B1 *desert* Arizona, SW USA
Paisance *see* Piacenza
Paisley 88 C4 W Scotland, United Kingdom
País Valenciano 93 F3 *var.* Valencia, *Cat.* València; *anc.* Valentia. *autonomous community* NE Spain
País Vasco 93 E1 *cultural region* N Spain
Paita 60 B3 Piura, NW Peru
Pakanbaru *see* Pekanbaru
Pakaraima Mountains 59 E3 *var.* Serra Pacaraim, Sierra Pacaraima. *mountain range* N South America
Pakistan 135 A2 *off.* Islamic Republic of Pakistan, *var.* Islami Jamhuriya e Pakistan. *country* S Asia

PAKISTAN
South Asia

Official name Islamic Republic of Pakistan
Formation 1947 / 1971
Capital Islamabad
Population 165 million / 553 people per sq mile (214 people per sq km) / 34%
Total area 310,401 sq. miles (803,940 sq. km)
Languages Urdu*, Punjabi, Sindhi, Pashtu, Baluchi, Brahui
Religions Sunni Muslim 77%, Shi'a Muslim 20%, Hindu 2%, Christian 1%
Ethnic mix Punjabi 56%, Pashtun (Pashtun) 15%, Sindhi 14%, Mohajir 7%, Other 4%, Baluchi 4%
Government Presidential system
Currency Pakistani rupee = 100 paisa
Literacy rate 50%
Calorie consumption 2419 calories

Pakistan, Islamic Republic of *see* Pakistan

Pakistan, Islami Jamhuriya e *see* Pakistan
Paknam *see* Samut Prakan
Pakokku 136 A3 Magway, C Burma (Myanmar)
Pak Phanang 137 C7 *var.* Ban Pak Phanang. Nakhon Si Thammarat, SW Thailand
Pakruojis 106 C4 Šiaulai, N Lithuania
Paks 99 C7 Tolna, S Hungary
Paksé *see* Pakxé
Pakxé 137 D5 *var.* Paksé. Champasak, S Laos
Palafrugell 93 G2 Cataluña, NE Spain
Palagruža 101 B5 *It.* Pelagosa. *island* SW Croatia
Palaiá Epídavros 105 C6 Pelopónnisos, S Greece
Palaiseau 90 D2 Essonne, N France
Palamós 93 G2 Cataluña, NE Spain
Palamuse 106 E2 *Ger.* Sankt-Bartholomäi. Jõgevamaa, E Estonia
Palanka *see* Bačka Palanka
Pālanpur 134 C4 Gujarāt, W India
Palantia *see* Palencia
Palapye 78 D3 Central, SE Botswana
Palau 144 A2 *var.* Belau. *country* W Pacific Ocean

PALAU
Australasia & Oceania

Official name Republic of Palau
Formation 1994 / 1994
Capital Melekeok
Population 20,842 / 106 people per sq mile (41 people per sq km) /
68%**Total area** 177 sq. miles (458 sq. km)
Languages Palauan*, English*, Japanese, Angaur, Tobi, Sonsorolese
Religions Christian 66%, Modekngei 34%
Ethnic mix Palauan 74%, Filipino 16%, Other 6%, Chinese and other Asian 4%
Government Nonparty system
Currency US dollar = 100 cents
Literacy rate 98%
Calorie consumption Not available

Palawan 139 E2 *island* W Philippines
Palawan Passage 138 D2 *passage* W Philippines
Paldiski 106 D2 *prev.* Baltiski, *Eng.* Baltic Port, *Ger.* Baltischport. Harjumaa, NW Estonia
Palembang 138 B4 Sumatera, W Indonesia
Palencia 92 D2 *anc.* Palantia, Pallantia. Castilla-León, NW Spain
Palerme *see* Palermo
Palermo 97 C7 *Fr.* Palerme; *anc.* Panhormus, Panormus. Sicilia, Italy, C Mediterranean Sea
Pāli 134 C3 Rājasthān, N India
Palikir 144 C2 *country capital* (Micronesia) (Micronesia) Pohnpei, E Micronesia
Palimé *see* Kpalimé
Palioúri, Akrotírio 104 C4 *var.* Akrotírio Kanestron. *headland* N Greece
Palk Strait 132 C3 *strait* India/Sri Lanka
Pallantia *see* Palencia
Palliser, Cape 151 D5 *headland* North Island, New Zealand
Palma 93 G3 *var.* Palma de Mallorca. Mallorca, Spain, W Mediterranean Sea
Palma del Río 92 D4 Andalucía, S Spain
Palma de Mallorca *see* Palma
Palmar Sur 53 E5 Puntarenas, SE Costa Rica
Palma Soriano 54 C3 Santiago de Cuba, E Cuba
Palm Beach 148 E1 New South Wales, E Australia
Palmer 154 A2 *US research station* Antarctica
Palmer Land 154 A3 *physical region* Antarctica
Palmerston 145 F4 *island* S Cook Islands
Palmerston *see* Darwin
Palmerston North 150 D4 Manawatu-Wanganui, North Island, New Zealand
The Palmetto State *see* South Carolina
Palmi 97 D7 Calabria, SW Italy
Palmira 58 B3 Valle del Cauca, W Colombia
Palm Springs 47 D7 California, W USA
Palmyra *see* Tudmur

Palmyra Atoll 145 G2 *US privately owned unincorporated territory* C Pacific Ocean
Palo Alto 47 B6 California, W USA
Paloe *see* Denpasar, Bali, C Indonesia
Paloe *see* Palu
Palu 139 E4 *prev.* Paloe. Sulawesi, C Indonesia
Pamiers 91 B6 Ariège, S France
Pāmīr 123 F3 *var.* Darya-ye Pāmīr, *Taj.* Dar''yoi Pomir. *river* Afghanistan/ Tajikistan
Pāmir, Daryā-ye *see* Pamir
Pamir/Pāmir, Daryā-ye *see* Pamirs
Pamirs 123 F3 *Pash.* Daryā-ye Pāmīr, *Rus.* Pamir. *mountain range* C Asia
Pāmiut *see* Paamiut
Pamlico Sound 43 G1 *sound* North Carolina, SE USA
Pampa 49 E1 Texas, SW USA
Pampa Aullagas, Lago *see* Poopó, Lago
Pampeluna *see* Pamplona
Pamplona 58 C2 Norte de Santander, N Colombia
Pamplona 93 E1 *Basq.* Iruña, *prev.* Pampeluna; *anc.* Pompaelo. Navarra, N Spain
Panaji 132 B1 *var.* Pangim, Panjim, New Goa. *state capital* Goa, W India
Panamá 53 G4 *var.* Ciudad de Panama, *Eng.* Panama City. *country capital* (Panama) (Panama) Panamá, C Panama
Panama 53 G5 *off.* Republic of Panama. *country* Central America

PANAMA
Central America

Official name Republic of Panama
Formation 1903 / 1903
Capital Panama City
Population 3.3 million / 112 people per sq mile (43 people per sq km) / 57%
Total area 30,193 sq. miles (78,200 sq. km)
Languages English Creole, Spanish*, Amerindian languages, Chibchan languages
Religions Roman Catholic 86%, Other 8%, Protestant 6%
Ethnic mix Mestizo 60%, White 14%, Black 12%, Amerindian 8%, Asian 4%, Other 2%
Government Presidential system
Currency Balboa = 100 centésimos
Literacy rate 92%
Calorie consumption 2272 calories

Panama Basin 35 C8 *undersea feature* E Pacific Ocean
Panama Canal 53 F4 *canal* E Panama
Panama City 47 D3 Florida, SE USA
Panama City *see* Panamá
Gulf of Panama 53 G5 *var.* Gulf of Panama. *gulf* S Panama
Panama, Gulf of *see* Panamá, Golfo de
Isthmus of Panama 53 G4 *Eng.* Isthmus of Panama; *prev.* Isthmus of Darien. *isthmus* E Panama
Panama, Isthmus of *see* Panama, Istmo de
Panama, Republic of *see* Panama
Panay Island 139 E2 *island* C Philippines
Pančevo 100 D3 *Ger.* Pantschowa, *Hung.* Pancsova. Vojvodina, N Serbia
Pancsova *see* Pančevo
Paneas *see* Bāniyās
Panevėžys 106 C4 Panevėžys, C Lithuania
Pangim *see* Panaji
Pangkalpinang 138 C4 Pulau Bangka, W Indonesia
Pang-Nga *see* Phang-Nga
Panjim *see* Panaji
Panopolis *see* Akhmīm
Pánormos 105 C7 Kríti, Greece, E Mediterranean Sea
Panormus *see* Palermo
Pantanal 63 E3 *var.* Pantanalmato-Grossense. *swamp* SW Brazil
Pantanalmato-Grossense *see* Pantanal
Pantelleria, Isola di 97 B7 *island* SW Italy

Pantschowa *see* Pančevo
Pánuco 51 E3 Veracruz-Llave, E Mexico
Pao-chi/Paoki *see* Baoji
Paola 102 B5 E Malta
Pao-shan *see* Baoshan
Pao-t'ou/Paotow *see* Baotou
Papagayo, Golfo de 52 C4 *gulf* NW Costa Rica
Papakura 150 D3 Auckland, North Island, New Zealand
Papantla 51 F4 *var.* Papantla de Olarte. Veracruz-Llave, E Mexico
Papantla de Olarte *see* Papantla
Papeete 145 H4 *dependent territory capital* (French Polynesia) Tahiti, W French Polynesia
Paphos *see* Páfos
Papilė 106 B3 Šiauliai, NW Lithuania
Papillion 45 F4 Nebraska, C USA
Papua 139 H4 *var.* Irian Barat, West Irian, West New Guinea, West Papua; *prev.* Dutch New Guinea, Irian Jaya, Netherlands New Guinea. *province* E Indonesia
Papua and New Guinea, Territory of *see* Papua New Guinea
Papua, Gulf of 144 B3 *gulf* S Papua New Guinea
Papua New Guinea 144 B3 *off.* Independent State of Papua New Guinea; *prev.* Territory of Papua and New Guinea. *country* NW Melanesia

PAPUA NEW GUINEA
Australasia & Oceania

Official name Independent State of Papua New Guinea
Formation 1975 / 1975
Capital Port Moresby
Population 6.1 million / 35 people per sq mile (13 people per sq km) / 13%
Total area 178,703 sq. miles (462,840 sq. km)
Languages English*, Pidgin English, Papuan, Motu, 750 (est.) native languages
Religions Protestant 69%, Roman Catholic 37%, Other 3%
Ethnic mix Melanesian and mixed race 100%
Government Parliamentary system
Currency Kina = 100 toea
Literacy rate 57%
Calorie consumption 2193 calories

Papua New Guinea, Independent State of *see* Papua New Guinea
Papuk 100 C3 *mountain range* NE Croatia
Pará 63 E2 *off.* Estado do Pará. *state* NE Brazil
Pará 63 E2 *off.* Estado do Pará. *region* NE Brazil
Pará *see* Belém
Paracel Islands 125 E3 *disputed territory* SE Asia
Paraćin 100 D4 Serbia, C Serbia
Paradise of the Pacific *see* Hawai'i
Pará, Estado do *see* Pará
Paragua, Río 59 E3 *river* SE Venezuela
Paraguay 64 C2 *country* C South America

PARAGUAY
South America

Official name Republic of Paraguay
Formation 1811 / 1938
Capital Asunción
Population 6.4 million / 42 people per sq mile (16 people per sq km) / 58%
Total area 157,046 sq. miles (406,750 sq. km)
Languages Spanish*, Guaraní, German
Religions Roman Catholic 96%, Protestant (including Mennonite) 4%
Ethnic mix Mestizo 91%, Other 7%, Amerindian 2%
Government Presidential system
Currency Guaraní = 100 céntimos
Literacy rate 93%
Calorie consumption 2565 calories

Paraguay 64 D2 *var.* Río Paraguay. *river* C South America

Paraguay, Río *see* Paraguay
Parahiba/Parahyba *see* Paraíba
Paraíba 63 G2 *off.* Estado da Paraíba; *prev.* Parahiba, Parahyba. *region* E Brazil
Paraíba 63 G2 *off.* Estado da Paraíba; *prev.* Parahiba, Parahyba. *state* E Brazil
Paraíba *see* João Pessoa
Paraíba, Estado da *see* Paraíba
Parakou 75 F4 C Benin
Paramaribo 59 G3 *country capital* (Suriname) Paramaribo, N Suriname
Paramushir, Ostrov 115 H3 *island* SE Russian Federation
Paraná 63 E4 Entre Ríos, E Argentina
Paraná 63 E5 *off.* Estado do Paraná. *state* S Brazil
Paraná 63 E5 *off.* Estado do Paraná. *region* S Brazil
Paraná 57 C5 *var.* Alto Paraná. *river* C South America
Paraná, Estado do *see* Paraná
Paranésti 104 C3 *var.* Paranestio. Anatolikí Makedonía kai Thráki, NE Greece
Paranestio *see* Paranésti
Paraparaumu 151 D5 Wellington, North Island, New Zealand
Parchim 94 C3 Mecklenburg-Vorpommern, N Germany
Parczew 98 E4 Lubelskie, E Poland
Pardubice 99 B5 *Ger.* Pardubitz. Pardubický Kraj, C Czech Republic
Pardubitz *see* Pardubice
Parechcha 107 B5 *Pol.* Porzecze, *Rus.* Porech'ye. Hrodzyenskaya Voblasts', W Belarus
Parecis, Chapada dos 62 D3 *var.* Serra dos Parecis. *mountain range* W Brazil
Parecis, Serra dos *see* Parecis, Chapada dos
Parenzo *see* Poreč
Parepare 139 E4 Sulawesi, C Indonesia
Párga 105 A5 Ípeiros, W Greece
Paria, Golfo de *see* Paria, Gulf of
Paria, Gulf of 59 E1 *var.* Golfo de Paria. *gulf* Trinidad and Tobago/Venezuela
Parika 59 F2 NE Guyana
Paris 90 D1 *anc.* Lutetia, Lutetia Parisiorum, Parisii. *country capital* (France) (France) Paris, N France
Paris 49 G2 Texas, SW USA
Parisii *see* Paris
Parkersburg 40 D4 West Virginia, NE USA
Parkes 149 D6 New South Wales, SE Australia
Parkhar *see* Farkhor
Parma 96 B2 Emilia-Romagna, N Italy
Parnahyba *see* Parnaíba
Parnaíba 63 F2 *var.* Parnahyba. Piauí, E Brazil
Parnu 106 D2 *Ger.* Pernau, *Latv.* Pērnava; *prev. Rus.* Pernov. Pärnumaa, SW Estonia
Pärnu 106 D2 *var.* Parnu Jōgi, *Ger.* Pernau. *river* SW Estonia
Pärnu-Jaaguri 106 D2 *Ger.* Sankt-Jakobi. Pärnumaa, SW Estonia
Parnu Jōgi *see* Pärnu
Pärnu Laht 106 C2 *Ger.* Pernauer Bucht. *bay* SW Estonia
Paropamisus Range *see* Sefid Kūh, Selseleh-ye
Páros 105 D6 *island* Kykládes, Greece, Aegean Sea
Páros 105 D6 *island* Kykládes, Greece, Aegean Sea
Páros 105 C6 *island* Kykládes, Greece, Aegean Sea
Parral 64 B4 Maule, C Chile
Parral *see* Hidalgo del Parral
Parramatta 148 D1 New South Wales, SE Australia
Parras 50 D3 *var.* Parras de la Fuente. Coahuila, NE Mexico
Parras de la Fuente *see* Parras
Parsons 45 F5 Kansas, C USA
Pasadena 47 C7 California, W USA
Pasadena 49 H4 Texas, SW USA
Paşcani 108 C3 *Hung.* Páskán. Iaşi, NE Romania
Pasco 46 C2 Washington, NW USA
Pasewalk 94 D3 Mecklenburg-Vorpommern, NE Germany
Pashkeni *see* Bolyarovo
Pasinler 117 F3 Erzurum, NE Turkey

Páskán *see* Paşcani
Paslęk 98 D2 *Ger.* Preußisch Holland. Warmińsko-Mazurskie, NE Poland
Pasni 134 A3 Baluchistān, SW Pakistan
Paso de Indios 65 B6 Chubut, S Argentina
Passarowitz *see* Požarevac
Passau 95 D6 Bayern, SE Germany
Passo Fundo 63 E5 Rio Grande do Sul, S Brazil
Pastavy 107 C5 *Pol.* Postawy, *Rus.* Postavy. Vitsyebskaya Voblasts', NW Belarus
Pastaza, Río 60 B2 *river* Ecuador/Peru
Pasto 58 A4 Nariño, SW Colombia
Pasvalys 106 C4 Panevėžys, N Lithuania
Patagonia 57 B7 *physical region* Argentina/Chile
Patalung *see* Phatthalung
Patani *see* Pattani
Patavium *see* Padova
Patea 150 D4 Taranaki, North Island, New Zealand
Paterson 41 F3 New Jersey, NE USA
Pathein 136 A4 *var.* Bassein. Ayeyarwady, SW Burma (Myanmar)
Pátmos 105 D6 *island* Dodekánisa, Greece, Aegean Sea
Patna 135 F3 *var.* Azimabad. *state capital* Bihār, N India
Patnos 117 F3 Ağrı, E Turkey
Patos, Lagoa dos 63 E5 *lagoon* S Brazil
Pátra 105 B5 *Eng.* Patras; *prev.* Pátrai. Dytikí Ellás, S Greece
Pátrai/Patras *see* Pátra
Pattani 137 C7 *var.* Patani. Pattani, SW Thailand
Pattaya 137 C5 Chon Buri, S Thailand
Patuca, Río 52 D2 *river* E Honduras
Pau 91 B6 Pyrénées-Atlantiques, SW France
Paulatuk 37 E3 Northwest Territories, NW Canada
Paungde 136 B4 Bago, C Burma (Myanmar)
Pautalia *see* Kyustendil
Pavia 96 B2 *anc.* Ticinum. Lombardia, N Italy
Pāvilosta 106 B3 Liepāja, W Latvia
Pavlikeni 104 D2 Veliko Tŭrnovo, N Bulgaria
Pavlodar 114 C4 Pavlodar, NE Kazakhstan
Pavlograd *see* Pavlohrad
Pavlohrad 109 G3 *Rus.* Pavlograd. Dnipropetrovs'ka Oblast', E Ukraine
Pawai, Pulau 138 A2 *island* SW Singapore Asia
Pawn 136 B3 *river* C Burma (Myanmar)
Pax Augusta *see* Badajoz
Pax Julia *see* Beja
Paxoí 105 A5 *island* Iónia Nisiá, Greece, C Mediterranean Sea
Payo Obispo *see* Chetumal
Paysandú 64 D4 Paysandú, W Uruguay
Pazar 117 E2 Rize, NE Turkey
Pazardzhik 104 C3 *prev.* Tatar Pazardzhik. Pazardzhik, SW Bulgaria
Peace Garden State *see* North Dakota
Peach State *see* Georgia
Pearl Islands 53 G5 *Eng.* Pearl Islands. *island group* SE Panama
Pearl Islands *see* Perlas, Archipiélago de las
Pearl Lagoon 53 E3 *Eng.* Pearl Lagoon. *lagoon* E Nicaragua
Pearl Lagoon *see* Perlas, Laguna de
Pearl River 42 B3 *river* Louisiana/ Mississippi, S USA
Pearsall 49 F4 Texas, SW USA
Peawanuk 38 C2 *river* Ontario, S Canada
Peć *see* Pejë
Pechora 110 D3 Respublika Komi, NW Russian Federation
Pechora 110 D3 *river* NW Russian Federation
Pechora Sea 110 D2 *Eng.* Pechora Sea. *sea* NW Russian Federation
Pechora Sea *see* Pechorskoye More
Pecos 49 E3 Texas, SW USA
Pecos River 49 E3 *river* New Mexico/ Texas, SW USA
Pécs 99 C7 *Ger.* Fünfkirchen, *Lat.* Sopianae. Baranya, SW Hungary
Pedra Lume 74 A3 Sal, NE Cape Verde
Pedro Cays 54 C3 *island group* Greater Antilles, S Jamaica North America N Caribbean Sea W Atlantic Ocean

Pedro Juan Caballero *64 D2* Amambay, E Paraguay
Peer *87 D5* Limburg, NE Belgium
Pegasus Bay *151 C6 bay* South Island, New Zealand
Pegu *see* Bago
Pehuajó *64 C4* Buenos Aires, E Argentina
Pei-ching *see* Beijing/Beijing Shi
Peine *94 B3* Niedersachsen, C Germany
Pei-p'ing *see* Beijing/Beijing Shi
Peipsi Järv/Peipus-See *see* Peipus, Lake
Peipus, Lake *106 E3 Est.* Peipsi Järv, *Ger.* Peipus-See, *Rus.* Chudskoye Ozero. *lake* Estonia/Russian Federation
Peiraías *105 C6 prev.* Piraiévs, *Eng.* Piraeus. Attikí, C Greece
Pejë *101 D5 Serb.* Peć. W Kosovo
Pèk *136 D4 var.* Xieng Khouang; *prev.* Xiangkhoang. Xiangkhoang, N Laos
Pekalongan *138 C4* Jawa, C Indonesia
Pekanbaru *138 B3 var.* Pakanbaru. Sumatera, W Indonesia
Pekin *40 B4* Illinois, N USA
Peking *see* Beijing/Beijing Shi
Pelagie *97 B8 island group* SW Italy
Pelagosa *see* Palagruža
Pelican State *see* Louisiana
Pelly Bay *see* Kugaaruk
Pélmonostor *see* Beli Manastir
Peloponnese *105 B6 var.* Morea, *Eng.* Peloponnese; *anc.* Peloponnesus. *peninsula* S Greece
Peloponnese/Peloponnesus *see* Pelopónnisos
Pematangsiantar *138 B3* Sumatera, W Indonesia
Pemba *79 F2 prev.* Port Amelia, Porto Amélia. Cabo Delgado, NE Mozambique
Pemba *73 D7 island* E Tanzania
Pembroke *38 D4* Ontario, SE Canada
Penang *see* Pinang, Pulau, Peninsular Malaysia
Penang *see* George Town
Peñas, Golfo de *65 A7 gulf* S Chile
Penderma *see* Bandırma
Pendleton *46 C3* Oregon, NW USA
Pend Oreille, Lake *46 D2 lake* Idaho, NW USA
Peneius *see* Pineiós
Peng-pu *see* Bengbu
Penibético, Sistema *see* Béticos, Sistemas
Peniche *92 B3* Leiria, W Portugal
Peninsular State *see* Florida
Penninae, Alpes/Pennine, Alpi *see* Pennine Alps
Pennine Alps *95 A8 Fr.* Alpes Pennines, *It.* Alpi Pennine, *Lat.* Alpes Penninae. *mountain range* Italy/Switzerland
Pennine Chain *see* Pennines
Pennines *89 D5 var.* Pennine Chain. *mountain range* N England, United Kingdom
Pennines, Alpes *see* Pennine Alps
Pennsylvania *41 E4 off.* Commonwealth of Pennsylvania, *also known as* Keystone State. *state* NE USA
Penobscot River *41 G2 river* Maine, NE USA
Penong *149 A6 South Australia*
Penonomé *53 F5* Coclé, C Panama
Penrhyn *145 G3 atoll* N Cook Islands
Penrhyn Basin *143 F3 undersea feature* C Pacific Ocean
Penrith *148 D1* New South Wales, SE Australia
Penrith *89 D5* NW England, United Kingdom
Pensacola *42 C3* Florida, SE USA
Pentecost *144 D4 Fr.* Pentecôte. *island* C Vanuatu
Pentecôte *see* Pentecost
Penza *111 C6* Penzenskaya Oblast', W Russian Federation
Penzance *89 C7* SW England, United Kingdom
Peoria *40 B4* Illinois, N USA
Perchtoldsdorf *95 E6* Niederösterreich, NE Austria
Percival Lakes *146 C4 lakes* Western Australia
Perdido, Monte *93 F1 mountain* NE Spain
Perece Vela Basin *see* West Mariana Basin
Pereira *58 B3* Risaralda, W Colombia
Peremyshl *see* Przemyśl

Pergamino *64 C4* Buenos Aires, E Argentina
Périgueux *91 C5 anc.* Vesuna. Dordogne, SW France
Perito Moreno *65 B6* Santa Cruz, S Argentina
Perleberg *94 C3* Brandenburg, N Germany
Perlepe *see* Prilep
Perm' *114 C3 prev.* Molotov. Permskaya Oblast', NW Russian Federation
Pernambuco *63 G2 off.* Estado de Pernambuco. *state* E Brazil
Pernambuco *63 G2 off.* Estado de Pernambuco. *region* E Brazil
Pernambuco *see* Recife
Pernambuco Abyssal Plain *see* Pernambuco Plain
Pernambuco, Estado de *see* Pernambuco
Pernambuco Plain *67 C5 var.* Pernambuco Abyssal Plain. *undersea feature* E Atlantic Ocean
Pernau *see* Pärnu
Pernauer Bucht *see* Pärnu Laht
Pērnava *see* Pärnu
Pernik *104 B2 prev.* Dimitrovo. Pernik, W Bulgaria
Pernov *see* Pärnu
Perote *51 F4* Veracruz-Llave, E Mexico
Pérouse *see* Perugia
Perovsk *see* Kzylorda
Perpignan *91 C6* Pyrénées-Orientales, S France
Perryton *49 F1* Texas, SW USA
Perryville *45 H5* Missouri, C USA
Persia *see* Iran
Persian Gulf *120 C4 var.* The Gulf, *Per.* Khalīj al 'Arabī, *Per.* Khalīj-e Fars. *gulf* SW Asia
Perth *147 A6 state capital* Western Australia
Perth *88 C4* C Scotland, United Kingdom
Perth Basin *141 E6 undersea feature* SE Indian Ocean
Peru *60 C3 off.* Republic of Peru. *country* W South America

PERU
South America

Official name Republic of Peru
Formation 1824 / 1941
Capital Lima
Population 28.8 million / 58 people per sq mile (22 people per sq km) / 74%
Total area 496,223 sq. miles (1,285,200 sq. km)
Languages Spanish*, Quechua*, Aymara
Religions Roman Catholic 95%, Other 5%
Ethnic mix Amerindian 50%, Mestizo 40%, White 7%, Other 3%
Government Presidential system
Currency New sol = 100 céntimos
Literacy rate 88%
Calorie consumption 2571 calories

Peru *see* Beru
Peru Basin *67 A5 undersea feature* E Pacific Ocean
Peru-Chile Trench *56 A1 undersea feature* E Pacific Ocean
Perugia *96 C4 Fr.* Pérouse; *anc.* Perusia. Umbria, C Italy
Perugia, Lake of *see* Trasimeno, Lago
Peru, Republic of *see* Peru
Perusia *see* Perugia
Péruwelz *87 B6* Hainaut, SW Belgium
Pervomays'k *109 E3 prev.* Ol'viopol'. Mykolayivs'ka Oblast', S Ukraine
Pervyy Kuril'skiy Proliv *115 H3 strait* E Russian Federation
Pesaro *96 C3 anc.* Pisaurum. Marche, C Italy
Pescara *96 D4 anc.* Aternum, Ostia Aterni. Abruzzo, C Italy
Peshāwar *134 C1* North-West Frontier Province, N Pakistan
Peshkopi *101 C4 var.* Peshkopia, Peshkopija. Dibër, NE Albania
Peshkopia/Peshkopija *see* Peshkopi
Pessac *91 B5* Gironde, SW France
Petach-Tikva *see* Petah Tikva
Petah Tikva *119 A6 var.* Petach-Tikva, Petah Tiqva, Petakh Tikva; *prev.* Petaḥ Tiqwa. Tel Aviv, C Israel
Petaḥ Tiqwa *see* Petah Tikva

Petakh Tikva/Petah Tiqva *see* Petah Tikva
Pétange *87 D8* Luxembourg, SW Luxembourg
Petchaburi *see* Phetchaburi
Peterborough *149 B6* South Australia
Peterborough *38 D5* Ontario, SE Canada
Peterborough *89 E6 prev.* Medeshamstede. E England, United Kingdom
Peterhead *88 D3* NE Scotland, United Kingdom
Peter I Øy *154 A3 Norwegian dependency* Antarctica
Petermann Bjerg *83 E3 mountain* C Greenland
Petersburg *41 E5* Virginia, NE USA
Peters Mine *59 F3 var.* Peter's Mine. N Guyana
Petit St-Bernard, Col du *see* Little Saint Bernard Pass
Peto *51 H4* Yucatán, SE Mexico
Petoskey *40 C2* Michigan, N USA
Petra *see* Wādī Mūsá
Petrich *104 C3* Blagoevgrad, SW Bulgaria
Petrikau *see* Piotrków Trybunalski
Petrikov *see* Pyetrykaw
Petrinja *100 B3* Sisak-Moslavina, C Croatia
Petroaleksandrovsk *see* To'rtkok'l
Petrodvorets *110 A4 Fin.* Pietarhovi. Leningradskaya Oblast', NW Russian Federation
Petrograd *see* Sankt-Peterburg
Petrokov *see* Piotrków Trybunalski
Petropavl *see* Petropavlovsk
Petropavlovsk *114 C4 Kaz.* Petropavl. Severnyy Kazakhstan, N Kazakhstan
Petropavlovsk-Kamchatskiy *115 H3* Kamchatskaya Oblast', E Russian Federation
Petroşani *108 B4 var.* Petroşeni, *Ger.* Petroschen, *Hung.* Petrozsény. Hunedoara, W Romania
Petroschen/Petroşeni *see* Petroşani
Petroskoi *see* Petrozavodsk
Petrovgrad *see* Zrenjanin
Petrovsk-Port *see* Makhachkala
Petrozavodsk *114 B2 Fin.* Petroskoi. Respublika Kareliya, NW Russian Federation
Petrozsény *see* Petroşani
Pettau *see* Ptuj
Pevek *115 G1* Chukotskiy Avtonomnyy Okrug, NE Russian Federation
Pezinok *99 C6 Ger.* Bösing, *Hung.* Bazin. Bratislavský Kraj, W Slovakia
Pforzheim *95 B6* Baden-Württemberg, SW Germany
Pfungstadt *95 B5* Hessen, W Germany
Phangan, Ko *137 C6 island* SW Thailand
Phang-Nga *137 B7 var.* Pang-Nga, Phangnga. Phangnga, SW Thailand
Phangnga *see* Phang-Nga
Phan Rang/Phanrang *see* Phan Rang-Thap Cham
Phan Rang-Thap Cham *137 E6 var.* Phanrang, Phan Rang, Phan Rang Thap Cham. Ninh Thuân, S Vietnam
Phan Thiêt *137 E6* Binh Thuân, S Vietnam
Pharnacia *see* Giresun
Pharus *see* Hvar
Phatthalung *137 C7 var.* Padalung, Patalung. Phatthalung, SW Thailand
Phayao *136 C4 var.* Muang Phayao. Phayao, NW Thailand
Phenix City *42 D2* Alabama, S USA
Phet Buri *see* Phetchaburi
Phetchaburi *137 C5 var.* Bejraburi, Petchaburi, Phet Buri. Phetchaburi, SW Thailand
Philadelphia *41 F4* Pennsylvania, NE USA
Philadelphia *see* 'Ammān
Philippine Basin *125 F3 undersea feature* W Pacific Ocean
Philippine Islands *139 E1 island group* W Pacific Ocean
Philippines *139 E1 off.* Republic of the Philippines. *country* SE Asia

PHILIPPINES
Southeast Asia

Official name Republic of the Philippines
Formation 1946 / 1946

PHILIPPINES
(continued)

Capital Manila
Population 85.9 million / 746 people per sq mile (288 people per sq km) / 62%
Total area 115,830 sq. miles (300,000 sq. km)
Languages English*, Filipino*, Tagalog, Cebuano, Ilocano, Hiligaynon, many other local languages
Religions Roman Catholic 83%, Protestant 9%, Muslim 5%, Other (including Buddhist) 3%
Ethnic mix Other 34%, Tagalog 28%, Cebuano 13%, Ilocano 9%, Hiligaynon 8%, Bisaya 8%
Government Presidential system
Currency Philippine peso = 100 centavos
Literacy rate 93%
Calorie consumption 2379 calories

Philippine Sea *125 F3 sea* W Pacific Ocean
Philippines, Republic of the *see* Philippines
Philippine Trench *142 A1 undersea feature* W Philippine Sea
Philippopolis *see* Plovdiv
Phitsanulok *136 C4 var.* Bisnulok, Muang Phitsanulok, Pitsanulok. Phitsanulok, C Thailand
Phlórina *see* Flórina
Phnom Penh *see* Phnum Penh
Phnum Penh *137 D6 var.* Phnom Penh. *country capital* (Cambodia) (Cambodia) Phnum Penh, S Cambodia
Phoenix *48 B2 state capital* Arizona, SW USA
Phoenix Islands *145 E3 island group* C Kiribati
Phôngsali *136 C3 var.* Phong Saly. Phôngsali, N Laos
Phong Saly *see* Phôngsali
Phrae *136 C4 var.* Muang Phrae, Prae. Phrae, NW Thailand
Phra Nakhon Si Ayutthaya *see* Ayutthaya
Phra Thong, Ko *137 B6 island* SW Thailand
Phuket *137 B7 var.* Bhuket, Puket, *Mal.* Ujung Salang; *prev.* Junkseylon, Salang. Phuket, SW Thailand
Phuket, Ko *137 B7 island* SW Thailand
Phumì Kâmpóng Trâbêk *137 D5 prev.* Phum Kompong Trabek. Kâmpóng Thum, C Cambodia
Phumì Sâmraông *137 D5 prev.* Phum Samrong. Siêmréab, NW Cambodia
Phum Kompong Trabek *see* Phumì Kâmpóng Trâbêk
Phum Samrong *see* Phumì Sâmraông
Phu Vinh *see* Tra Vinh
Phyu *136 B4 var.* Hpyu, Pyu. Bago, C Burma (Myanmar)
Piacenza *96 B2 Fr.* Paisance; *anc.* Placentia. Emilia-Romagna, N Italy
Piatra-Neamţ *108 C4 Hung.* Karácsonkő. Neamţ, NE Romania
Piauhy *see* Piauí
Piauí *63 F2 off.* Estado do Piauí; *prev.* Piauhy. *state* E Brazil
Piauí *63 F2 off.* Estado do Piauí; *prev.* Piauhy. *region* E Brazil
Piauí, Estado do *see* Piauí
Picardie *90 C3 Eng.* Picardy. *cultural region* N France
Picardy *see* Picardie
Piccolo San Bernardo, Colle di *see* Little Saint Bernard Pass
Pichilemu *64 B4* Libertador, C Chile
Pico *92 A5 var.* Ilha do Pico. *island* Azores, Portugal, NE Atlantic Ocean
Pico, Ilha do *see* Pico
Picos *63 F2* Piauí, E Brazil
Picton *151 C5* Marlborough, South Island, New Zealand
Piedmont *see* Piemonte
Piedras Negras *51 E2 var.* Ciudad Porfirio Díaz. Coahuila, NE Mexico
Pielavesi *84 D4 lake* C Finland
Pielinen *84 E4 var.* Pielisjärvi. *lake* E Finland
Pielisjärvi *see* Pielinen
Piemonte *96 A2 Eng.* Piedmont. *region* NW Italy

Pierre 45 E3 state capital South Dakota, N USA
Piešťany 99 C6 Ger. Pistyan, Hung. Pöstyén. Tranavský Kraj, W Slovakia
Pietarhovi see Petrodvorets
Pietari see Sankt-Peterburg
Pietarsaari see Jakobstad
Pietermaritzburg 78 C5 var. Maritzburg. KwaZulu/Natal, E South Africa
Pietersburg see Polokwane
Bay of Pigs 54 B2 Eng. Bay of Pigs. bay SE Cuba
Pigs, Bay of see Cochinos, Bahía de
Pihkva Järv see Pskov, Lake
Pijijiapán 51 G5 Chiapas, SE Mexico
Pikes Peak 44 C5 mountain Colorado, C USA
Pikeville 40 D5 Kentucky, S USA
Pikinni see Bikini Atoll
Piła 98 B3 Ger. Schneidemühl. Wielkopolskie, C Poland
Pilar 64 D3 var. Villa del Pilar. Ñeembucú, S Paraguay
Pilcomayo, Rio 57 C5 river C South America
Pilos see Pýlos
Pilsen see Plzeň
Pilzno see Plzeň
Pinang see George Town
Pinang see Pinang, Pulau, Peninsular Malaysia
Pinang, Pulau 138 B3 var. Penang, Pinang; prev. Prince of Wales Island. island Peninsular Malaysia
Pinar del Río 54 A2 Pinar del Río, W Cuba
Píndhos/Píndhos Óros see Píndos
Pindus Mountains 104 A4 var. Píndhos Óros, Eng. Pindus Mountains; prev. Píndhos. mountain range C Greece
Pindus Mountains see Píndos
Pine Bluff 42 B2 Arkansas, C USA
Pine Creek 146 D2 Northern Territory, N Australia
Pinega 110 C3 river NW Russian Federation
Pineios 104 B4 var. Piniós; anc. Pencius. river C Greece
Pineland 49 H3 Texas, SW USA
Pínes, Akrotírio 104 C4 var. Akrotírio Pínnes. headland N Greece
Pines, The Isle of the see Juventud, Isla de la
Pine Tree State see Maine
Pingdingshan 128 C4 Henan, C China
Pingkiang see Harbin
Ping, Mae Nam 136 B4 river W Thailand
Piniós see Pineios
Pinkiang see Harbin
Pínnes, Akrotírio see Pínes, Akrotírio
Pínos, Isla de see Juventud, Isla de la
Pinotepa Nacional 51 F5 var. Santiago Pinotepa Nacional. Oaxaca, SE Mexico
Pinsk 107 B7 Pol. Pińsk. Brestskaya Voblasts', SW Belarus
Pinta, Isla 60 A5 var. Abingdon. island Galapagos Islands, Ecuador, E Pacific Ocean
Piombino 96 B3 Toscana, C Italy
Pioneer Mountains 46 D3 mountain range Montana, N USA North America
Pionerskiy 106 A4 Ger. Neukuhren. Kaliningradskaya Oblast', W Russian Federation
Piotrków Trybunalski 98 D4 Ger. Petrikau, Rus. Petrokov. Łódzkie, C Poland
Piraeus/Piraiévs see Peiraiás
Pírgos see Pýrgos
Pirineos see Pyrenees
Piripiri 63 F2 Piauí, E Brazil
Pirna 94 D4 Sachsen, E Germany
Pirot 101 E5 Serbia, SE Serbia
Piryatin see Pyryatyn
Pisa 96 B3 var. Pisae. Toscana, C Italy
Pisae see Pisa
Pisaurum see Pesaro
Pisco 60 D4 Ica, SW Peru
Písek 99 A5 Budějovický Kraj, S Czech Republic
Pishan 126 A3 var. Guma. Xinjiang Uygur Zizhiqu, NW China
Pishpek see Bishkek
Pistoia 96 B3 anc. Pistoria, Pistoriæ. Toscana, C Italy
Pistoria/Pistoriæ see Pistoia

Pistyan see Piešťany
Pisz 98 D3 Ger. Johannisburg. Warmińsko-Mazurskie, NE Poland
Pita 74 C4 NW Guinea
Pitalito 58 B4 Huila, S Colombia
Pitcairn Island 143 G4 island S Pitcairn Islands
Pitcairn Islands 143 G4 UK dependent territory C Pacific Ocean
Piteå 84 D4 Norrbotten, N Sweden
Pitești 108 B5 Argeș, S Romania
Pitsanulok see Phitsanulok
Pitt Island see Makin
Pittsburg 45 F5 Kansas, C USA
Pittsburgh 41 E4 Pennsylvania, NE USA
Pittsfield 41 F3 Massachusetts, NE USA
Piura 60 B2 Piura, NW Peru
Pivdennyy Buh 109 E3 Rus. Yuzhnyy Bug. river S Ukraine
Placentia see Piacenza
Placetas 54 C2 Villa Clara, C Cuba
Plainview 49 E2 Texas, SW USA
Planeta Rica 58 B2 Córdoba, NW Colombia
Planken 94 E1 C Liechtenstein Europe
Plano 49 G2 Texas, SW USA
Plasencia 92 C3 Extremadura, W Spain
Plate, River 64 D4 var. River Plate. estuary Argentina/Uruguay
Plate, River see Plata, Río de la
Platinum 36 C3 Alaska, USA
Plattensee see Balaton
Platte River 45 E4 river Nebraska, C USA
Plattsburgh 41 F2 New York, NE USA
Plauen 95 C5 var. Plauen im Vogtland. Sachsen, E Germany
Plauen im Vogtland see Plauen
Pļaviņas 106 D4 Ger. Stockmannshof. Aizkraukle, S Latvia
Plây Cu 137 E5 var. Pleiku. Gia Lai, C Vietnam
Pleasant Island see Nauru
Pleiku see Plây Cu
Plenty, Bay of 150 E3 bay North Island, New Zealand
Plérin 90 A3 Côtes d'Armor, NW France
Plesetsk 110 C3 Arkhangel'skaya Oblast', NW Russian Federation
Pleshchenitsy see Plyeshchanitsy
Pleskau see Pskov
Pleskauer See see Pskov, Lake
Pleskava see Pskov
Pleszew 98 C4 Wielkopolskie, C Poland
Pleven 104 C2 prev. Plevna. Pleven, N Bulgaria
Plevlja/Plevlje see Pljevlja
Plevna see Pleven
Pljevlja 100 C4 prev. Plevlja, Plevlje. N Montenegro
Plocce see Ploče
Ploče 100 B4 It. Plocce; prev. Kardeljevo. Dubrovnik-Neretva, SE Croatia
Płock 98 D3 Ger. Plozk. Mazowieckie, C Poland
Plöcken Pass 95 C7 Ger. Plöckenpass, It. Passo di Monte Croce Carnico. pass SW Austria
Plöckenpass see Plöcken Pass
Ploeşti see Ploieşti
Ploieşti 108 C5 prev. Ploeşti. Prahova, SE Romania
Plomári 105 D5 prev. Plomárion. Lésvos, E Greece
Plomárion see Plomári
Płońsk 98 D3 Mazowieckie, C Poland
Plovdiv 104 C3 prev. Eumolpias; anc. Evmolpia, Philippopolis, Lat. Trimontium. Plovdiv, C Bulgaria
Plozk see Płock
Plungė 106 B3 Telšiai, W Lithuania
Plyeshchanitsy 107 D5 Rus. Pleshchenitsy. Minskaya Voblasts', N Belarus
Plymouth 55 G3 dependent territory capital (Montserrat) SW Montserrat
Plymouth 89 C7 SW England, United Kingdom
Plzeň 99 A5 Ger. Pilsen, Pol. Pilzno. Plzeňský Kraj, W Czech Republic
Po 80 D4 river N Italy
Pobedy, Pik 126 B3 Chin. Tomür Feng. mountain China/Kyrgyzstan
Po, Bocche del see Po, Foci del
Pocahontas 42 B1 Arkansas, C USA
Pocatello 46 E4 Idaho, NW USA
Pochinok 111 A5 Smolenskaya Oblast', W Russian Federation

Pocking 95 D6 Bayern, SE Germany
Poděbrady 99 B5 Ger. Podiebrad. Středočeský Kraj, C Czech Republic
Podgorica 101 C5 prev. Titograd. country capital (Montenegro) S Montenegro
Podiebrad see Poděbrady
Podil's'ka Vysochina 108 D3 plateau W Ukraine
Podium Anicensis see le Puy
Podol'sk 111 B5 Moskovskaya Oblast', W Russian Federation
Podravska Slatina see Slatina
Podujevë 101 D5 Serb. Podujevo. N Kosovo
Podujevo see Podujevë
Pudunajská Rovina see Little Alföld
Poctovio see Ptuj
Pogradec 101 D6 var. Pogradeci. Korçë, SE Albania
Pogradeci see Pogradec
Pohjanlahti see Bothnia, Gulf of
Pohnpei 144 C2 prev. Ponape Ascension Island. island E Micronesia
Poitiers 90 B4 prev. Poictiers; anc. Limonum. Vienne, W France
Poitou 90 B4 cultural region W France
Pokharā 135 E3 Western, C Nepal
Pokrovka see Kyzyl-Suu
Pokrovs'ke 109 G3 Rus. Pokrovskoye. Dnipropetrovs'ka Oblast', E Ukraine
Pokrovskoye see Pokrovs'ke
Pola see Pula
Pola de Lena 92 D1 Asturias, N Spain
Poland 78 B4 off. Republic of Poland, var. Polish Republic, Pol. Polska, Rzeczpospolita Polska; prev. Pol. Polska Rzeczpospolita Ludowa, The Polish People's Republic. country C Europe

---

POLAND
Northern Europe

Official name Republic of Poland
Formation 1918 / 1945
Capital Warsaw
Population 38.5 million / 328 people per sq mile (126 people per sq km) / 62%
Total area 120,728 sq. miles (312,685 sq. km)
Languages Polish*
Religions Roman Catholic 93%, Other and nonreligious 5%, Orthodox Christian 2%
Ethnic mix Polish 97%, Other 3%
Government Parliamentary system
Currency Złoty = 100 groszy
Literacy rate 99%
Calorie consumption 3374 calories

Poland, Republic of see Poland
Polatlı 116 C3 Ankara, C Turkey
Polatsk 107 D5 Rus. Polotsk. Vitsyebskaya Voblasts', N Belarus
Pol-e Khomrī 123 E4 var. Pul-i-Khumri. Baghlān, NE Afghanistan
Poli see Pólis
Polikastro/Polikastron see Polýkastro
Polikrayshte 104 D2 Veliko Tŭrnovo, N Bulgaria
Pólis 102 C5 var. Poli. W Cyprus
Polish People's Republic, The see Poland
Polish Republic see Poland
Polkowice 98 B4 Ger. Heerwegen. Dolnośląskie, W Poland
Pollença 93 G3 Mallorca, Spain, W Mediterranean Sea
Pologi see Polohy
Polohy 109 G3 Rus. Pologi. Zaporiz'ka Oblast', SE Ukraine
Polokwane 78 D4 prev. Pietersburg. Limpopo, NE South Africa
Polonne 108 D2 Rus. Polonnoye. Khmel'nyts'ka Oblast', NW Ukraine
Polonnoye see Polonne
Polotsk see Polatsk
Polska/Polska, Rzeczpospolita/Polska Rzeczpospolita Ludowa see Poland
Polsko Kosovo 104 D2 Ruse, N Bulgaria

Poltava 109 F2 Poltavs'ka Oblast', NE Ukraine
Poltoratsk see Aşgabat
Põlva 106 E3 Ger. Pölwe. Põlvamaa, SE Estonia
Pölwe see Põlva
Polyarnyy 110 C2 Murmanskaya Oblast', NW Russian Federation
Polýkastro 104 B3 var. Polikastro; prev. Polikastron. Kentrikí Makedonía, N Greece
Polynesia 143 F4 island group C Pacific Ocean
Pomeranian Bay 94 D2 Ger. Pommersche Bucht, Pol. Zatoka Pomorska. bay Germany/Poland
Pomir, Dar''yoi see Pamir/Pāmīr, Daryā-ye
Pommersche Bucht see Pomeranian Bay
Pomorska, Zatoka see Pomeranian Bay
Pomorskiy Proliv 110 D2 strait NW Russian Federation
Po, Mouth of the 96 C2 var. Bocche del Po. river NE Italy
Pompaelo see Pamplona
Pompano Beach 43 F5 Florida, SE USA
Ponape Ascension Island see Pohnpei
Ponca City 49 G1 Oklahoma, C USA
Ponce 55 F3 C Puerto Rico
Pondicherry 132 C2 var. Puduchcheri, Fr. Pondichéry. Pondicherry, SE India
Ponferrada 92 C1 Castilla-León, NW Spain
Poniatowa 98 E4 Lubelskie, E Poland
Pons Aelii see Newcastle upon Tyne
Pons Vetus see Pontevedra
Ponta Delgada 92 B5 São Miguel, Azores, Portugal, NE Atlantic Ocean
Ponta Grossa 63 E4 Paraná, S Brazil
Pontarlier 90 D4 Doubs, E France
Ponteareas 92 B2 Galicia, NW Spain
Ponte da Barca 92 B2 Viana do Castelo, N Portugal
Pontevedra 92 B1 anc. Pons Vetus. Galicia, NW Spain
Pontiac 40 D3 Michigan, N USA
Pontianak 138 C4 Borneo, C Indonesia
Pontisarae see Pontoise
Pontivy 90 A3 Morbihan, NW France
Pontoise 90 C3 anc. Briva Isarae, Cergy-Pontoise, Pontisarae. Val-d'Oise, N France
Ponziane Island 97 C5 island C Italy
Poole 89 D7 S England, United Kingdom
Poona see Pune
Poopó, Lago 61 F4 var. Lago Pampa Aullagas. lake W Bolivia
Popayán 58 B4 Cauca, SW Colombia
Poperinge 87 A6 West-Vlaanderen, W Belgium
Poplar Bluff 45 G5 Missouri, C USA
Popocatépetl 51 E4 volcano S Mexico
Popper see Poprad
Poprad 99 D5 Ger. Deutschendorf, Hung. Poprád. Prešovský Kraj, E Slovakia
Poprád 99 D5 Ger. Popper, Hung. Poprád. river Poland/Slovakia
Porbandar 134 B4 Gujarāt, W India
Porcupine Plain 80 B3 undersea feature E Atlantic Ocean
Pordenone 96 C2 anc. Portenau. Friuli-Venezia Giulia, NE Italy
Poreč 100 A2 It. Parenzo. Istra, NW Croatia
Porech'ye see Parechcha
Pori 85 D5 Swe. Björneborg. Länsi-Suomi, SW Finland
Porirua 151 D5 Wellington, North Island, New Zealand
Porkhov 110 A4 Pskovskaya Oblast', W Russian Federation
Porlamar 59 E1 Nueva Esparta, NE Venezuela
Póros 105 C6 Póros, S Greece
Póros 105 A5 Kefallinía, Iónia Nisiá, Greece, C Mediterranean Sea
Pors see Porsangenfjorden
Porsangenfjorden 84 D2 Lapp. Pors. fjord N Norway
Porsgrunn 85 B6 Telemark, S Norway
Portachuelo 61 G4 Santa Cruz, C Bolivia
Portadown 89 B5 Ir. Port an Dúnáin. S Northern Ireland, United Kingdom
Portalegre 92 C3 anc. Ammaia, Amoea. Portalegre, E Portugal

Port Alexander *36 D4* Baranof Island, Alaska, USA
Port Alfred *78 D5* Eastern Cape, S South Africa
Port Amelia *see* Pemba
Port An Dúnáin *see* Portadown
Port Angeles *46 B1* Washington, NW USA
Port Antonio *54 B5* NE Jamaica
Port Arthur *49 H4* Texas, SW USA
Port Augusta *149 B6* South Australia
Port-au-Prince *54 D3 country capital* (Haiti) (Haiti) C Haiti
Port Blair *133 F2* Andaman and Nicobar Islands, SE India
Port Charlotte *43 E4* Florida, SE USA
Port Darwin *see* Darwin
Port d'Envalira *91 B8* E Andorra Europe
Port Douglas *148 D3* Queensland, NE Australia
Port Elizabeth *78 C5* Eastern Cape, S South Africa
Portenau *see* Pordenone
Porterville *47 C7* California, W USA
Port-Étienne *see* Nouâdhibou
Port Florence *see* Kisumu
Port-Francqui *see* Ilebo
Port-Gentil *77 A6* Ogooué-Maritime, W Gabon
Port Harcourt *75 G5* Rivers, S Nigeria
Port Hardy *36 D5* Vancouver Island, British Columbia, SW Canada
Port Harrison *see* Inukjuak
Port Hedland *146 B4* Western Australia
Port Huron *40 D3* Michigan, N USA
Portimão *92 B4 var.* Vila Nova de Portimão. Faro, S Portugal
Port Jackson *148 E1 harbour* New South Wales, E Australia
Portland *149 B7* Victoria, SE Australia
Portland *41 G2* Maine, NE USA
Portland *46 B3* Oregon, NW USA
Portland *49 G4* Texas, SW USA
Portland Bight *54 B5 bay* S Jamaica
Portlaoighise *see* Port Laoise
Port Laoise *89 B6 var.* Portlaoise, *Ir.* Portlaoighise; *prev.* Maryborough. C Ireland
Portlaoise *see* Port Laoise
Port Lavaca *49 G4* Texas, SW USA
Port Lincoln *149 A6* South Australia
Port Louis *79 H3 country capital* (Mauritius) (Mauritius) NW Mauritius
Port-Lyautey *see* Kénitra
Port Macquarie *149 E6* New South Wales, SE Australia
Port Mahon *see* Mahón
Portmore *54 B5* C Jamaica
Port Moresby *144 B3 country capital* (Papua New Guinea) (Papua New Guinea) Central/National Capital District, SW Papua New Guinea
Port Natal *see* Durban
Porto *92 B2 Eng.* Oporto; *anc.* Portus Cale. Porto, NW Portugal
Porto Alegre *63 E5 var.* Pôrto Alegre. *state capital* Rio Grande do Sul, S Brazil
Porto Alegre *76 E2* São Tomé, S Sao Tome and Principe, Africa
Porto Alegre *76 E2* São Tomé, S Sao Tome and Principe, Africa
Porto Alexandre *see* Tombua
Porto Bello *see* Portobelo
Portobelo *53 G4 var.* Porto Bello, Puerto Bello. Colón, N Panama
Porto O'Connor *49 G4* Texas, SW USA
Porto Edda *see* Sarandë
Portoferraio *96 B4* Toscana, C Italy
Port-of-Spain *55 H5 country capital* (Trinidad and Tobago) (Trinidad and Tobago) Trinidad, Trinidad and Tobago
Porto Grande *see* Mindelo
Portogruaro *96 C2* Veneto, NE Italy
Porto-Novo *75 F5 country capital* (Benin) (Benin) S Benin
Porto Rico *see* Puerto Rico
Porto Santo *70 A2* Ilha do Porto Santo. *island* Madeira, Portugal, NE Atlantic Ocean
Porto Santo, Ilha do *see* Porto Santo
Porto Torres *97 A5* Sardegna, Italy, C Mediterranean Sea
Porto Velho *62 D2 var.* Velho. *state capital* Rondônia, W Brazil

Portoviejo *60 A2 var.* Puertoviejo. Manabí, W Ecuador
Port Pirie *149 B6* South Australia
Port Rex *see* East London
Port Said *see* Bûr Sa'îd
Portsmouth *89 D7* S England, United Kingdom
Portsmouth *41 G3* New Hampshire, NE USA
Portsmouth *40 D4* Ohio, N USA
Portsmouth *41 F5* Virginia, NE USA
Port Stanley *see* Stanley
Port Sudan *72 C3* Red Sea, NE Sudan
Port Swettenham *see* Klang/Pelabuhan Klang
Port Talbot *89 C7* S Wales, United Kingdom
Portugal *92 B3 off.* Portuguese Republic. *country* SW Europe

PORTUGAL
Southwest Europe

Official name	The Portuguese Republic
Formation	1139 / 1640
Capital	Lisbon
Population	10.6 million / 299 people per sq mile (115 people per sq km) / 55%
Total area	35,672 sq. miles (92,391 sq. km)
Languages	Portuguese*
Religions	Roman Catholic 97%, Other 2%, Protestant 1%
Ethnic mix	Portuguese 98%, African and other 2%
Government	Parliamentary system
Currency	Euro = 100 cents
Literacy rate	92%
Calorie consumption	3741 calories

Portuguese East Africa *see* Mozambique
Portuguese Guinea *see* Guinea-Bissau
Portuguese Republic *see* Portugal
Portuguese Timor *see* East Timor
Portuguese West Africa *see* Angola
Portus Cale *see* Porto
Portus Magnus *see* Almería
Portus Magonis *see* Mahón
Port-Vila *144 D4 var.* Vila. *country capital* (Vanuatu) (Vanuatu) Éfaté, C Vanuatu
Porvenir *61 B3* Pando, NW Bolivia
Porvenir *65 B8* Magallanes, S Chile
Porvoo *85 E6 Swe.* Borgå. Etelä-Suomi, S Finland
Porzecze *see* Parechcha
Posadas *64 D3* Misiones, NE Argentina
Poschega *see* Požega
Posen *see* Poznań
Posnania *see* Poznań
Postavy/Postawy *see* Pastavy
Posterholt *87 D5* Limburg, SE Netherlands
Postojna *95 D8 Ger.* Adelsberg, *It.* Postumia. SW Slovenia
Postumia *see* Postojna
Pöstyén *see* Piešťany
Potamós *105 C7* Antikýthira, S Greece
Potentia *see* Potenza
Potenza *97 D5 anc.* Potentia. Basilicata, S Italy
P'ot'i *117 F2* W Georgia
Potiskum *75 G4* Yobe, NE Nigeria
Potomac River *41 E5 river* NE USA
Potosí *61 F4* Potosí, S Bolivia
Potsdam *94 D3* Brandenburg, NE Germany
Potwar Plateau *134 C2 plateau* NE Pakistan
Poŭthisăt *137 D6 prev.* Pursat. Poŭthisăt, W Cambodia
Po, Valle del *see* Po Valley
Po Valley *96 C2 It.* Valle del Po. *valley* N Italy
Považská Bystrica *99 C5 Ger.* Waagbistritz, *Hung.* Vágbeszterce. Trenčiansky Kraj, W Slovakia
Poverty Bay *150 E4 inlet* North Island, New Zealand
Póvoa de Varzim *92 B2* Porto, NW Portugal
Powder River *44 D2 river* Montana/ Wyoming, NW USA
Powell *44 C2* Wyoming, C USA
Powell, Lake *44 B5 lake* Utah, W USA
Požarevac *100 D4 Ger.* Passarowitz. Serbia, NE Serbia
Poza Rica *51 F4 var.* Poza Rica de Hidalgo. Veracruz-Llave, E Mexico

Poza Rica de Hidalgo *see* Poza Rica
Požega *100 D4 prev.* Slavonska Požega, *Ger.* Poschega, *Hung.* Pozsega. Požega-Slavonija, NE Croatia
Požega *100 D4* Serbia
Poznań *98 C3 Ger.* Posen, Posnania. Wielkopolskie, C Poland
Pozoblanco *92 D4* Andalucía, S Spain
Pozsega *see* Požega
Pozsony *see* Bratislava
Pozzallo *97 C8* Sicilia, Italy, C Mediterranean Sea
Prachatice *99 A5 Ger.* Prachatitz. Jihočeský Kraj, S Czech Republic
Prachatitz *see* Prachatice
Prado del Ganso *see* Goose Green
Prae *see* Phrae
Prag/Praga/Prague *see* Praha
Praha *99 A5 Eng.* Prague, *Ger.* Prag, *Pol.* Praga. *country capital* (Czech Republic) (Czech Republic) Středočeský Kraj, NW Czech Republic
Praia *74 A3 country capital* (Cape Verde) (Cape Verde) Santiago, S Cape Verde
Prairie State *see* Illinois
Prathet Thai *see* Thailand
Prato *96 B3* Toscana, C Italy
Pratt *45 E5* Kansas, C USA
Prattville *42 D2* Alabama, S USA
Pravda *104 D1 prev.* Dogrular. Silistra, NE Bulgaria
Pravia *92 C1* Asturias, N Spain
Preny *see* Prienai
Prenzlau *94 D3* Brandenburg, NE Germany
Prerau *see* Přerov
Přerov *99 C5 Ger.* Prerau. Olomoucký Kraj, E Czech Republic
Preschau *see* Prešov
Prescott *48 B2* Arizona, SW USA
Prešov *101 D5* Serbia, SE Serbia
Presidente Epitácio *63 E4* São Paulo, S Brazil
Presidente Stroessner *see* Ciudad del Este
Prešov *99 D5 var.* Preschau, *Ger.* Eperies, *Hung.* Eperjes. Prešovský Kraj, E Slovakia
Prespa, Lake *101 D6 Alb.* Liqen i Prespës, *Gk.* Límni Megáli Préspa, Límni Prespa, *Mac.* Prespansko Ezero, *Serb.* Prespansko Jezero. *lake* SE Europe
Prespa, Limni/Prespansko Ezero/ Prespansko Jezero/Prespës, Liqen i *see* Prespa, Lake
Presque Isle *41 H1* Maine, NE USA
Pressburg *see* Bratislava
Preston *89 D5* NW England, United Kingdom
Prestwick *88 C4* W Scotland, United Kingdom
Preussisch Eylau *see* Bagrationovsk
Preußisch Holland *see* Pasłęk
Preussisch-Stargard *see* Starogard Gdański
Préveza *105 A5* Ípeiros, W Greece
Pribilof Islands *36 A3 island group* Alaska, USA
Priboj *100 C4* Serbia, W Serbia
Price *44 B4* Utah, W USA
Prichard *42 C3* Alabama, S USA
Priekule *106 B3 Ger.* Prökuls. Klaipėda, W Lithuania
Prienai *107 B5 Pol.* Preny. Kaunas, S Lithuania
Prieska *78 C4* Northern Cape, C South Africa
Prijedor *100 B3* Republika Srpska, NW Bosnia and Herzegovina
Prijepolje *100 D4* Serbia, W Serbia
Prikaspiyskaya Nizmennost' *see* Caspian Depression
Prilep *101 D6 Turk.* Perlepe. S FYR Macedonia
Priluki *see* Pryluky
Primorsk *106 A4 Ger.* Fischhausen. Kaliningradskaya Oblast', W Russian Federation
Primorsko *104 E2 prev.* Keupriya. Burgas, E Bulgaria
Primorsk/Primorskoye *see* Prymors'k
Prince Albert *37 F5* Saskatchewan, S Canada
Prince Edward Island *39 F4 Fr.* Île-du Prince-Édouard. *province* SE Canada

Prince Edward Islands *69 E8 island group* S South Africa
Prince George *37 E5* British Columbia, SW Canada
Prince of Wales Island *148 B1 island* Queensland, E Australia
Prince of Wales Island *37 F2 island* Queen Elizabeth Islands, Nunavut, NW Canada
Prince of Wales Island *see* Pinang, Pulau
Prince Patrick Island *37 E2 island* Parry Islands, Northwest Territories, NW Canada
Prince Rupert *36 D4* British Columbia, SW Canada
Prince's Island *see* Príncipe
Princess Charlotte Bay *148 C2 bay* Queensland, NE Australia
Princess Elizabeth Land *154 C3 physical region* Antarctica
Príncipe *77 A5 var.* Príncipe Island, *Eng.* Prince's Island. *island* N Sao Tome and Principe
Príncipe Island *see* Príncipe
Prinzapolka *53 E3* Región Autónoma Atlántico Norte, NE Nicaragua
Pripet *107 C7 Bel.* Prypyats', *Ukr.* Pryp"yat'. *river* Belarus/Ukraine
Pripet Marshes *107 B7 wetland* Belarus/ Ukraine
Prishtinë *101 D5 Eng.* Pristina, *Serb.* Priština. C Kosovo
Priština *see* Prishtinë
Pristina *see* Prishtinë
Privas *91 D5* Ardèche, E France
Prizren *101 D5* S Kosovo
Probolinggo *138 D5* Jawa, C Indonesia
Probstberg *see* Wyszków
Progreso *51 H3* Yucatán, SE Mexico
Prokhladnyy *111 B8* Kabardino-Balkarskaya Respublika, SW Russian Federation
Prokletije *see* North Albanian Alps
Prökuls *see* Priekule
Prokuplje *101 D5* Serbia, SE Serbia
Prome *see* Pyay
Promyshlennyy *110 E3* Respublika Komi, NW Russian Federation
Prościejów *see* Prostějov
Proskurov *see* Khmel'nyts'kyy
Prossnitz *see* Prostějov
Prostějov *99 C5 Ger.* Prossnitz, *Pol.* Prościejów. Olomoucký Kraj, E Czech Republic
Provence *91 D6 cultural region* SE France
Providence *41 G3 state capital* Rhode Island, NE USA
Providence *see* Fort Providence
Providencia, Isla de *53 F3 island* NW Colombia, Caribbean Sea
Provideniya *155 B1* Chukotskiy Avtonomnyy Okrug, NE Russian Federation
Provo *44 B4* Utah, W USA
Prudhoe Bay *36 D2* Alaska, USA
Prusa *see* Bursa
Pruszków *98 D3 Ger.* Kaltdorf. Mazowieckie, C Poland
Prut *108 D4 Ger.* Pruth. *river* E Europe
Pruth *see* Prut
Pružana *see* Pruzhany
Pruzhany *107 B6 Pol.* Pružana. Brestskaya Voblasts', SW Belarus
Prychornomor'ska Nyzovyna *see* Black Sea Lowland
Prydniprovs'ka Nyzovyna/ Prydnyaprowskaya Nizina *see* Dnieper Lowland
Prydz Bay *154 D3 bay* Antarctica
Pryluky *109 E2 Rus.* Priluki. Chernihivs'ka Oblast', NE Ukraine
Prymors'k *109 G4 Rus.* Primorsk; *prev.* Primorskoye. Zaporiz'ka Oblast', SE Ukraine
Pryp"yat'/Prypyats' *see* Pripet
Przemyśl *99 E5 Rus.* Peremyshl. Podkarpackie, C Poland
Przheval'sk *see* Karakol
Psará *105 D5 island* E Greece
Psël *109 F2 Rus.* Psël. *river* Russian Federation/Ukraine
Psël *see* Psel
Pskov *114 B2 Ger.* Pleskau, *Latv.* Pleskava. Pskovskaya Oblast', W Russian Federation
Pskov, Lake *106 E3 Est.* Pihkva Järv, *Ger.* Pleskauer See, *Rus.* Pskovskoye Ozero. *lake* Estonia/Russian Federation

Pskovskoye Ozero see Pskov, Lake
Ptich' see Ptsich
Ptsich 107 C7 *Rus.* Ptich'. Homyel'skaya
Voblasts', SE Belarus
Ptsich 107 C7 *Rus.* Ptich'. *river*
SE Belarus
Ptuj 95 E7 *Ger.* Pettau; *anc.* Poetovio.
NE Slovenia
Pucallpa 60 C3 Ucayali, C Peru
Puck 98 C2 Pomorskie, N Poland
Pudasjärvi 84 D4 Oulu, C Finland
Puebla 51 F4 *var.* Puebla de Zaragoza.
Puebla, S Mexico
Puebla de Zaragoza see Puebla
Pueblo 44 D5 Colorado, C USA
Puerto Acosta 61 E4 La Paz, W Bolivia
Puerto Aisén 65 B6 Aisén, S Chile
Puerto Ángel 51 F5 Oaxaca, SE Mexico
Puerto Argentino see Stanley
Puerto Ayacucho 58 D3 Amazonas,
SW Venezuela
Puerto Baquerizo Moreno 60 B5 *var.*
Baquerizo Moreno. Galapagos Islands,
Ecuador, E Pacific Ocean
Puerto Barrios 52 C2 Izabal,
E Guatemala
Puerto Bello see Portobelo
Puerto Berrío 58 B2 Antioquia,
C Colombia
Puerto Cabello 58 D1 Carabobo,
N Venezuela
Puerto Cabezas 53 E2 *var.* Bilwi.
Región Autónoma Atlántico Norte,
NE Nicaragua
Puerto Carreño 58 D3 Vichada,
E Colombia
Puerto Cortés 52 C2 Cortés,
NW Honduras
Puerto Cumarebo 58 C1 Falcón,
N Venezuela
Puerto Deseado 65 C7 Santa Cruz,
SE Argentina
Puerto Escondido 51 F5 Oaxaca,
SE Mexico
Puerto Gallegos see Río Gallegos
Puerto Inírida 58 D3 *var.* Obando.
Guainía, E Colombia
Puerto La Cruz 59 E1 Anzoátegui,
NE Venezuela
Puerto Lempira 53 E2 Gracias a Dios,
E Honduras
Puerto Limón see Limón
Puertollano 92 D4 Castilla-La Mancha,
C Spain
Puerto López 58 C1 La Guajira,
N Colombia
Puerto Maldonado 61 E3 Madre de
Dios, E Peru
Puerto México see Coatzacoalcos
Puerto Montt 65 B5 Los Lagos, C Chile
Puerto Natales 65 B7 Magallanes, S Chile
Puerto Obaldía 53 H5 Kuna Yala,
NE Panama
Puerto Plata 55 E3 *var.* San Felipe de
Puerto Plata. N Dominican Republic
Puerto Presidente Stroessner see Ciudad
del Este
Puerto Princesa 139 E2 *off.* Puerto
Princesa City. Palawan, W Philippines
Puerto Princesa City see Puerto Princesa
Puerto Príncipe see Camagüey
Puerto Rico 55 F3 *off.* Commonwealth
of Puerto Rico; *prev.* Porto Rico. *US
commonwealth territory* C West Indies
Puerto Rico 56 B1 *island* C West Indies
Puerto Rico, Commonwealth of see
Puerto Rico
Puerto Rico Trench 56 B1 *trench*
NE Caribbean Sea
Puerto San José see San José
Puerto San Julián 65 B7 *var.* San Julián.
Santa Cruz, SE Argentina
Puerto Suárez 61 H4 Santa Cruz,
E Bolivia
Puerto Vallarta 50 D4 Jalisco,
SW Mexico
Puerto Varas 65 B5 Los Lagos, C Chile
Puerto Viejo 53 E4 Heredia, NE Costa
Rica
Puertoviejo see Portoviejo
Puget Sound 46 B1 *sound* Washington,
NW USA
Puglia 97 E5 *var.* Le Puglie, *Eng.* Apulia.
region SE Italy
Pukaki, Lake 151 B6 *lake* South Island,
New Zealand

Pukekohe 150 D3 Auckland, North
Island, New Zealand
Puket see Phuket
Pukhavichy 107 C6 *Rus.* Pukhovichi.
Minskaya Voblasts', C Belarus
Pukhovichi see Pukhavichy
Pula 100 A3 *It.* Pola; *prev.* Pulj. Istra,
NW Croatia
Pulaski 40 D5 Virginia, NE USA
Puławy 98 E4 *Ger.* Neu Amerika.
Lubelskie, E Poland
Pul-i-Khumri see Pol-e Khomrī
Pulj see Pula
Pullman 46 C2 Washington, NW USA
Pułtusk 98 D3 Mazowieckie, C Poland
Puná, Isla 60 A2 *island* SW Ecuador
Pune 134 C5 *prev.* Poona. Mahārāshtra,
W India
Punjab 134 C2 *prev.* West Punjab,
Western Punjab. *province* E Pakistan
Puno 61 E4 Puno, SE Peru
Punta Alta 65 C5 Buenos Aires,
E Argentina
Punta Arenas 65 B8 *prev.* Magallanes.
Magallanes, S Chile
Punta Gorda 52 C2 Toledo, SE Belize
Punta Gorda 53 E4 Región Autónoma
Atlántico Sur, SE Nicaragua
Puntarenas 52 D4 Puntarenas, W Costa
Rica
Punto Fijo 58 C1 Falcón, N Venezuela
Pupuya, Nevado 61 E4 *mountain*
W Bolivia
Puri 135 F5 *var.* Jagannath. Orissa,
E India
Puriramya see Buriram
Purmerend 86 C3 Noord-Holland,
C Netherlands
Pursat see Poŭthĭsăt, Poŭthĭsăt, W
Cambodia
Purus, Rio 62 C2 *var.* Río Purús. *river*
Brazil/Peru
Pusan 129 E4 *off.* Pusan-gwangyŏksi, *var.*
Busan, *Jap.* Fusan. SE South Korea
Pusan-gwangyŏksi see Pusan
Pushkino see Biläsuvar
Püspökladány 99 D6 Hajdú-Bihar,
E Hungary
Putorana, Gory/Putorana Mountains
see Putorana, Plato
Putorana Mountains 115 E3 *var.*
Gory Putorana, *Eng.* Putorana
Mountains. *mountain range* N Russian
Federation
Putrajaya 138 B3 *country capital*
(Malaysia) (Malaysia) Kuala Lumpur,
Peninsular Malaysia
Puttalam 132 C3 North Western
Province, W Sri Lanka
Puttgarden 94 C2 Schleswig-Holstein,
N Germany
Putumayo, Río 58 B5 *var.* Içá, Rio.
river NW South America
Putumayo, Rio see Içá, Rio
Puurmani 106 D2 *Ger.* Talkhof.
Jõgevamaa, E Estonia
Pyatigorsk 111 B7 Stavropol'skiy Kray,
SW Russian Federation
Pyatikhatki see P''yatykhatky
P''yatykhatky 109 F3 *Rus.* Pyatikhatki.
Dnipropetrovs'ka Oblast', E Ukraine
Pyay 136 B4 *var.* Prome, Pye. Bago,
C Burma (Myanmar)
Pye see Pyay
Pyetrykaw 107 C7 *Rus.* Petrikov.
Homyel'skaya Voblasts', SE Belarus
Pyinmana 136 B4 *country capital*
(Myanmar (Burma)) Mandalay,
C Burma (Myanmar)
Pyin-Oo-Lwin 136 B3 *var.* Maymyo.
Mandalay, C Burma (Myanmar)
P'yŏngyang 129 E3 *var.* P'yŏngyang-si,
Eng. Pyongyang. *country capital*
(North Korea) (North Korea) SW North
Korea
P'yŏngyang-si see P'yŏngyang
Pyramid Lake 47 C5 *lake* Nevada,
W USA
Pyrenaei Montes see Pyrenees
Pyrenees 102 B2 *Fr.* Pyrénées, *Sp.*
Pirineos; *anc.* Pyrenaei Montes.
mountain range SW Europe
Pýrgos 105 B6 *var.* Pírgos. Dytikí Ellás,
S Greece
Pyritz see Pyrzyce

Pyryatyn 109 E2 *Rus.* Piryatin.
Poltavs'ka Oblast', NE Ukraine
Pyrzyce 98 B3 *Ger.* Pyritz. Zachodnio-
pomorskie, NW Poland
Pyu see Phyu
Pyuntaza 136 B4 Bago, SW Burma
(Myanmar)

Q

Qā' al Jafr 119 C7 *lake* S Jordan
Qaanaaq 82 D1 *var.* Qânâq, *Dan.* Thule.
Avannaarsua, N Greenland
Qabātiya 119 E6 N West Bank Asia
Qābis see Gabès
Qābis, Khalīj see Gabès, Golfe de
Qacentina see Constantine
Qafşah see Gafsa
Qagan Us see Dulan
Qahremānshahr see Kermānshāh
Qaidam Pendi 126 C4 *basin* C China
Qal'aikhum 123 F3 *Rus.* Kalaikhum.
S Tajikistan
Qalāt 123 E5 *Per.* Kalāt. Zābol,
S Afghanistan
Qal'at Bīshah 121 B5 'Asīr, SW Saudi
Arabia
Qalqīlya see Qalqīlya
Qalqīlya 119 D6 *var.* Qalqiliya. Central,
W West Bank Asia
Qamdo 126 D5 Xizang Zizhiqu, W China
Qamishly see Al Qāmishlī
Qânâq see Qaanaaq
Qaqortoq 82 C4 *Dan.* Julianehåb.
Kitaa, S Greenland
Qaraghandy/Qaraghandy Oblysy see
Karaganda
Qara Qum see Garagum
Qaratau see Karatau, Zhambyl,
Kazakhstan
Qarkilik see Ruoqiang
Qarokŭl 123 F3 *Rus.* Karakul'.
E Tajikistan
Qarqannah, Juzur see Kerkenah, Îles de
Qars see Kars
Qarshi 123 E3 *Rus.* Karshi; *prev.*
Bek-Budi. Qashqadaryo Viloyati,
S Uzbekistan
Qasigianguit see Qasigiannguit
Qasigiannguit 82 C3 *var.* Qasigianguit,
Dan. Christianshåb. Kitaa,
C Greenland
Qaşr al Farāfirah 72 B2 *var.* Qasr
Farāfra. N Egypt
Qasr Farāfra see Qaşr al Farāfirah
Qaţanā 119 B5 *var.* Katana. Dimashq,
S Syria
Qatar 120 C4 *off.* State of Qatar, *Ar.*
Dawlat Qatar. *country* SW Asia

QATAR
Southwest Asia

Official name	State of Qatar
Formation	1971 / 1971
Capital	Doha
Population	907,229 / 214 people per sq mile (82 people per sq km) / 92%
Total area	4416 sq. miles (11,437 sq. km)
Languages	Arabic*
Religions	Muslim (mainly Sunni) 95%, Other 5%
Ethnic mix	Arab 40%, Indian 18%, Pakistani 18%, Other 14%, Iranian 10%
Government	Monarchy
Currency	Qatar riyal = 100 dirhams
Literacy rate	89%
Calorie consumption	Not available

Qatar, State of see Qatar
Qattara Depression 72 A1 *var.*
Munkhafad al Qattārah *var.* Monkhafad
el Qattâra, *Eng.* Qattara Depression.
desert NW Egypt
**Qattara Depression/Qattārah,
Munkhafad al** see Qattara Depression,
Munkhafad al
Qattāra, Monkhafad el see Qattāra,
Munkhafad al
Qausuittuq see Resolute
Qazaqstan/Qazaqstan Respublikasy see
Kazakhstan
Qazimämmäd 117 H3 *Rus.* Kazi
Magomed. SE Azerbaijan
Qazris see Cáceres

Qazvīn 120 C2 *var.* Kazvin. Qazvīn,
N Iran
Qena see Qinā
Qeqertarssuaq see Qeqertarsuaq
Qeqertarsuaq 82 C3 *var.* Qeqertarssuaq,
Dan. Godhavn. Kitaa, S Greenland
Qeqertarsuaq 82 C3 *island* W Greenland
Qeqertsuup Tunua 82 C3 *Dan.* Disko
Bugt. *inlet* W Greenland
Qerveh see Qorveh
Qeshm 120 D4 *var.* Jazireh-ye Qeshm,
Qeshm Island. *island* S Iran
Qeshm Island/Qeshm, Jazīreh-ye
see Qeshm
Qilian Shan 126 D3 *var.* Kilien
Mountains. *mountain range* N China
Qimusseriarsuaq 82 C2 *Dan.*
Melville Bugt, *Eng.* Melville Bay. *bay*
NW Greenland
Qinā 72 B2 *var.* Qena; *anc.* Caene,
Caenepolis. E Egypt
Qing see Qinghai
Qingdao 128 D4 *var.* Ching-Tao,
Ch'ing-tao, Tsingtao, Tsintao, *Ger.*
Tsingtau. Shandong, E China
Qinghai 126 C4 *var.* Chinghai, Koko
Nor, Qing, Qinghai Sheng, Tsinghai.
province C China
Qinghai Hu 126 D4 *var.* Ch'ing Hai,
Tsing Hai, *Mong.* Koko Nor. *lake*
C China
Qinghai Sheng see Qinghai
Qinhuangdao 128 D3 Hebei, E China
Qinzhou 128 B6 Guangxi Zhuangzu
Zizhiqu, S China
Qiong see Hainan
Qiqihar 128 D2 *var.* Ch'i-ch'i-ha-
erh, Tsitsihar; *prev.* Lungkiang.
Heilongjiang, NE China
Qira 126 B4 Xinjiang Uygur Zizhiqu,
NW China
Qita Ghazzah see Gaza Strip
Qitai 126 C3 Xinjiang Uygur Zizhiqu,
NW China
Qīzān see Jīzān
Qizil Orda see Kzylorda
Qizil Qum/Qizilqum see Kyzyl Kum
Qizilrabot 123 G3 *Rus.* Kyzylrabot.
SE Tajikistan
Qogir Feng see K2
Qom 120 C3 *var.* Kum, Qum, Qom,
N Iran
Qomolangma Feng see Everest, Mount
Qomul see Hami
Qo'qon 123 F2 *var.* Khokand,
Rus. Kokand. Farg'ona Viloyati,
E Uzbekistan
Qorveh 120 C3 *var.* Qerveh, Qurveh.
Kordestān, W Iran
Qostanay/Qostanay Oblysy see
Kostanay
Qoubaïyât 118 B4 *var.* Al Qubayyāt.
N Lebanon
Qoussantina see Constantine
Quang Ngai 137 E5 *var.* Quangngai,
Quang Nghia. Quang Ngai, C Vietnam
Quangngai see Quang Ngai
Quang Nghia see Quang Ngai
Quanzhou 128 D6 *var.* Ch'uan-chou,
Tsinkiang; *prev.* Chin-chiang. Fujian,
SE China
Quanzhou 128 C6 Guangxi Zhuangzu
Zizhiqu, S China
Qu'Appelle 37 F5 *river* Saskatchewan,
S Canada
Quarles, Pegunungan 139 E4 *mountain
range* Sulawesi, C Indonesia
Quarnero see Kvarner
Quartu Sant' Elena 97 A6 Sardegna,
Italy, C Mediterranean Sea
Quba 117 H2 *Rus.* Kuba. N Azerbaijan
Qubba see Ba'qūbah
Québec 39 E4 *var.* Quebec. *province
capital* Québec, SE Canada
Québec 38 D3 *var.* Quebec. *province*
SE Canada
Queen Charlotte Islands 36 C5 *Fr.* Îles
de la Reine-Charlotte. *island group*
British Columbia, SW Canada
Queen Charlotte Sound 36 C5 *sea area*
British Columbia, W Canada
Queen Elizabeth Islands 37 E1 *Fr.* Îles
de la Reine-Élisabeth. *island group*
Nunavut, N Canada
Queensland 148 B4 *state* N Australia

231

Queenstown 151 B7 Otago, South Island, New Zealand
Queenstown 78 D5 Eastern Cape, S South Africa
Quelimane 79 E3 var. Kilimane, Kilmain, Quilimane. Zambézia, NE Mozambique
Quelpart see Cheju-do
Quepos 53 E4 Puntarenas, S Costa Rica
Que Que see Kwekwe
Quera see Chur
Querétaro 51 E4 Querétaro de Arteaga, C Mexico
Quesada 53 E4 var. Ciudad Quesada, San Carlos. Alajuela, N Costa Rica
Quetta 134 B2 Baluchistān, SW Pakistan
Quetzalcoalco see Coatzacoalcos
Quezaltenango 52 A2 var. Quetzaltenango. Quezaltenango, W Guatemala
Quibdó 58 A3 Chocó, W Colombia
Quilimane see Quelimane
Quillabamba 60 D3 Cusco, C Peru
Quilon 132 C3 var. Kollam. Kerala, SW India
Quimper 90 A3 anc. Quimper Corentin. Finistère, NW France
Quimper Corentin see Quimper
Quimperlé 90 A3 Finistère, NW France
Quincy 40 A4 Illinois, N USA
Qui Nhon/Quinhon see Quy Nhơn
Quissico 79 E4 Inhambane, S Mozambique
Quito 60 B1 country capital (Ecuador) (Ecuador) Pichincha, N Ecuador
Qulyndy Zhazyghy see Kulunda Steppe
Qum see Qom
Qurein see Al Kuwayt
Qürghonteppa 123 E3 Rus. Kurgan-Tyube. SW Tajikistan
Qurlurtuuq see Kugluktuk
Qurveh see Qorveh
Quşayr see Al Quşayr
Quxar see Lhazê
Quy Nhơn 137 E5 var. Quinhon, Qui Nhon. Binh Dinh, C Vietnam
Qyteti Stalin see Kuçovë
Qyzlorda see Kzylorda

R

Raab 100 B1 Hung. Rába. river Austria/ Hungary
Raab see Rába
Raab see Győr
Raahe 84 D4 Swe. Brahestad. Oulu, W Finland
Raalte 86 D3 Overijssel, E Netherlands
Raamsdonksveer 86 C4 Noord-Brabant, S Netherlands
Raasiku 106 D2 Ger. Rasik. Harjumaa, NW Estonia
Rába 99 B7 Ger. Raab. river Austria/ Hungary
Rába see Raab
Rabat 70 C2 var. al Dar al Baida. country capital (Morocco) (Morocco) NW Morocco
Rabat 102 B5 W Malta
Rabat see Victoria
Rabbah Ammon/Rabbath Ammon see ʿAmmān
Rabinal 52 B2 Baja Verapaz, C Guatemala
Rabka 99 D5 Małopolskie, S Poland
Râbniţa see Rîbniţa
Rabyanah Ramlat 71 G4 var. Rebiana Sand Sea, Şaḩrāʾ Rabyānah. desert SE Libya
Rabyānah, Şaḩrāʾ see Rabyānah, Ramlat
Răcari see Durankulak
Race, Cape 39 H3 headland Newfoundland, Newfoundland and Labrador, E Canada
Rach Gia 137 D6 Kiên Giang, S Vietnam
Rach Gia, Vinh 137 D6 bay S Vietnam
Racine 40 B3 Wisconsin, N USA
Rácz-Becse see Bečej
Rădăuţi 108 C3 Ger. Radautz, Hung. Rádócz. Suceava, N Romania
Radauz see Rădăuţi
Rádeyilíkóé see Fort Good Hope
Rádóc see Rădăuţi
Radom 98 D4 Mazowieckie, C Poland
Radomsko 98 D4 Rus. Novoradomsk. Łódzkie, C Poland

Radomyshl' 108 D2 Zhytomyrs'ka Oblast', N Ukraine
Radoviš 101 E6 prev. Radovište. E Macedonia
Radovište see Radoviš
Radviliškis 106 B4 Šiauliai, N Lithuania
Radzyń Podlaski 98 E4 Lubelskie, E Poland
Rae-Edzo see Edzo
Raetihi 150 D4 Manawatu-Wanganui, North Island, New Zealand
Rafa see Rafah
Rafaela 64 C3 Santa Fe, E Argentina
Rafah 119 A7 var. Rafa, Rafaḩ, Heb. Rafiaḥ, Raphiah. SW Gaza Strip
Rafḩah 120 B4 Al Ḩudūd ash Shamāliyah, N Saudi Arabia
Rafiaḥ see Rafah
Raga 73 A5 Western Bahr el Ghazal, SW Sudan
Ragged Island Range 54 C2 island group S Bahamas
Ragnit see Neman
Ragusa 97 C7 Sicilia, Italy, C Mediterranean Sea
Ragusa see Dubrovnik
Rahachow 107 D7 Rus. Rogachëv. Homyel'skaya Voblasts', SE Belarus
Rahaeng see Tak
Rahaṭ, Ḥarrat 121 B5 lava flow W Saudi Arabia
Rahīmyār Khān 134 C3 Punjab, SE Pakistan
Rahovec 101 D5 Serb. Orahovac. W Kosovo
Raiatea 145 G4 island Îles Sous le Vent, W French Polynesia
Rāichūr 132 C1 Karnātaka, C India
Raidestos see Tekirdağ
Rainier, Mount 34 A4 volcano Washington, NW USA
Rainy Lake 38 A4 lake Canada/USA
Raipur 135 E4 Chhattīsgarh, C India
Rājahmundry 135 E5 Andhra Pradesh, E India
Rajang see Rajang, Batang
Rajang, Batang 138 D3 var. Rajang. river East Malaysia
Rājapālaiyam 132 C3 Tamil Nādu, SE India
Rājasthān 134 C3 cultural region NW India
Rājkot 134 C4 Gujarāt, W India
Rāj Nāndgaon 135 E4 Chhattīsgarh, C India
Rajshahi 135 G3 prev. Rampur Boalia. Rajshahi, W Bangladesh
Rakahanga 145 F3 atoll N Cook Islands
Rakaia 151 B6 river South Island, New Zealand
Rakka see Ar Raqqah
Rakke 106 E2 Lääne-Virumaa, NE Estonia
Rakvere 106 E2 Ger. Wesenberg. Lääne-Virumaa, N Estonia
Raleigh 43 F1 state capital North Carolina, SE USA
Ralik Chain 144 D1 island group Ralik Chain, W Marshall Islands
Ramadi see Ar Ramādī
Râmnicul-Sărat 108 C4 prev. Râmnicul-Sărat, Rîmnicu-Sărat. Buzău, E Romania
Râmnicu Vâlcea 108 B4 prev. Rîmnicu Vîlcea. Vâlcea, C Romania
Rampur Boalia see Rajshahi
Ramree Island 136 A4 island W Burma (Myanmar)
Ramtha see Ar Ramthā
Rancagua 64 B4 Libertador, C Chile
Rānchī 135 F4 Jhārkhand, N India
Randers 85 B7 Århus, C Denmark
Ránes see Ringvassøya
Rangiora 151 C6 Canterbury, South Island, New Zealand
Rangitikei 150 D4 river North Island, New Zealand
Rangoon see Yangon
Rangpur 135 G3 Rajshahi, N Bangladesh
Rankin Inlet 37 G3 Nunavut, C Canada
Rankovićevo see Kraljevo
Ranong 137 B6 Ranong, SW Thailand
Rapa Nui see Pascua, Isla de
Raphiah see Rafah
Rapid City 44 D3 South Dakota, N USA
Räpina 106 E3 Ger. Rappin. Põlvamaa, SE Estonia

Rapla 106 D2 Ger. Rappel. Raplamaa, NW Estonia
Rappel see Rapla
Rappin see Räpina
Rarotonga 145 G5 island S Cook Islands, C Pacific Ocean
Ras al'Ain see Ra's al ʿAyn
Ra's al ʿAyn 118 D1 var. Ras al'Ain. Al Ḩasakah, N Syria
Ra's an Naqb 119 B7 Maʿān, S Jordan
Raseiniai 106 B4 Kaunas, C Lithuania
Rasht 120 C2 var. Resht. Gīlān, NW Iran
Rasik see Raasiku
Râşnov 108 C4 prev. Râșno, Rozsnyó, Hung. Barcarozsnyó. Brașov, C Romania
Rastenburg see Kętrzyn
Ratak Chain 144 D1 island group Ratak Chain, E Marshall Islands
Ratan 85 C5 Jämtland, C Sweden
Rat Buri see Ratchaburi
Ratchaburi 137 C5 var. Rat Buri. Ratchaburi, W Thailand
Ratibor see Racibórz
Ratisbon/Ratisbona/Ratisbonne see Regensburg
Rat Islands 36 A2 island group Aleutian Islands, Alaska, USA
Ratlām 134 D4 prev. Rutlam. Madhya Pradesh, C India
Ratnapura 132 D4 Sabaragamuwa Province, S Sri Lanka
Raton 48 D1 New Mexico, SW USA
Rättvik 85 C5 Dalarna, C Sweden
Raudhatain see Ar Rawḑatayn
Raufarhöfn 83 E4 Nordhurland Eystra, NE Iceland
Raukawa see Cook Strait
Raukumara Range 150 E3 mountain range North Island, New Zealand
Rāulakela 135 F4 var. Raurkela; prev. Rourkela. Orissa, E India
Rauma 85 D5 Swe. Raumo. Länsi-Suomi, SW Finland
Raumo see Rauma
Raurkela see Rāulakela
Ravenna 96 C3 Emilia-Romagna, N Italy
Ravi 134 C2 river India/Pakistan
Rāwalpindi 134 C1 Punjab, NE Pakistan
Rawa Mazowiecka 98 D4 Łódzkie, C Poland
Rawicz 98 C4 Ger. Rawitsch. Wielkopolskie, C Poland
Rawitsch see Rawicz
Rawlins 44 C3 Wyoming, C USA
Rawson 65 C6 Chubut, SE Argentina
Rayak 118 B4 var. Rayaq, Riyāq. E Lebanon
Rayaq see Rayak
Rayong 137 C5 Rayong, S Thailand
Razazah, Buhayrat ar 120 B3 var. Baḩr al Milḩ. lake C Iraq
Razdolnoye see Rozdol'ne
Razelm, Lacul see Razim, Lacul
Razgrad 104 D2 Razgrad, N Bulgaria
Razim, Lacul 108 D5 prev. Lacul Razelm. lagoon NW Black Sea
Reading 89 D7 S England, United Kingdom
Reading 41 F4 Pennsylvania, NE USA
Realicó 64 C4 La Pampa, C Argentina
Reäng Kesei 137 D5 Bătdâmbâng, C Greece
Rebecca, Lake 147 C6 lake Western Australia
Rebiana Sand Sea see Rabyānah, Ramlat
Rebun-to 130 C2 island NE Japan
Rechitsa see Rechytsa
Rechytsa 107 D7 Rus. Rechitsa. Brestskaya Voblasts', SW Belarus
Recife 63 H2 prev. Pernambuco. state capital Pernambuco, E Brazil
Recklinghausen 94 A4 Nordrhein-Westfalen, W Germany
Recogne 87 C7 Luxembourg, SE Belgium
Reconquista 64 D3 Santa Fe, C Argentina
Red Deer 37 E5 Alberta, SW Canada
Redding 47 B5 California, W USA
Redon 90 A4 Ille-et-Vilaine, NW France
Red River 136 C2 var. Yuan, Chin. Yuan Jiang, Vtn. Sông Hông Hà. river China/ Vietnam
Red River 35 C6 river S USA
Red River 42 B3 river Louisiana, S USA

Red Sea 72 C3 var. Sinus Arabicus. sea Africa/Asia
Red Wing 45 G2 Minnesota, N USA
Reefton 151 C5 West Coast, South Island, New Zealand
Reese River 47 C5 river Nevada, W USA
Refahiye 117 E3 Erzincan, C Turkey
Regensburg 95 C6 Eng. Ratisbon, Fr. Ratisbonne, hist. Ratisbona; anc. Castra Regina, Reginum. Bayern, SE Germany
Regenstauf 95 C6 Bayern, SE Germany
Reggane 70 D3 C Algeria
Reggio see Reggio nell'Emilia
Reggio Calabria see Reggio di Calabria
Reggio di Calabria 97 D7 var. Reggio Calabria, Gk. Rhegion; anc. Regium, Rhegium. Calabria, SW Italy
Reggio Emilia see Reggio nell'Emilia
Reggio nell'Emilia 96 B2 var. Reggio Emilia, abbrev. Reggio; anc. Regium Lepidum. Emilia-Romagna, N Italy
Reghin 108 C4 Ger. Sächsisch-Reen, Hung. Szászrégen; prev. Reghinul Săsesc, Ger. Sächsisch-Regen. Mureş, C Romania
Reghinul Săsesc see Reghin
Regina 37 F5 province capital Saskatchewan, S Canada
Reginum see Regensburg
Registan see Rīgestān
Regium see Reggio di Calabria
Regium Lepidum see Reggio nell'Emilia
Rehoboth 78 B3 Hardap, C Namibia
Rehovot 119 A6; prev. Reḥovot. Central, C Israel
Reḥovot see Rehovot
Reichenau see Bogatynia, Poland
Reichenberg see Liberec
Reid 147 D6 Western Australia
Reikjavík see Reykjavík
Ré, Île de 90 A4 island W France
Reims 90 D3 Eng. Rheims; anc. Durocortorum, Remi. Marne, N France
Reindeer Lake 37 F4 lake Manitoba/ Saskatchewan, C Canada
Reine-Charlotte, Îles de la see Queen Charlotte Islands
Reine-Élisabeth, Îles de la see Queen Elizabeth Islands
Reinga, Cape 150 C1 headland North Island, New Zealand
Reinosa 92 D1 Cantabria, N Spain
Reka see Rijeka
Rekhovot see Rehovot
Reliance 37 F4 Northwest Territories, C Canada
Remi see Reims
Rendina see Rentína
Rendsburg 94 B2 Schleswig-Holstein, N Germany
Rengat 138 B4 Sumatera, W Indonesia
Reni 108 D4 Odes'ka Oblast', SW Ukraine
Rennell 144 C4 var. Mu Nggava. island S Solomon Islands
Rennes 90 B3 Bret. Roazon; anc. Condate. Ille-et-Vilaine, NW France
Reno 47 C5 Nevada, W USA
Renqiu 128 C4 Hebei, E China
Rentína 105 B5 var. Rendina. Thessalía, C Greece
Reps see Rupea
Repulse Bay 37 G3 Northwest Terretories, N Canada
Reschitza see Reşiţa
Resht see Rasht
Resicabánya see Reşiţa
Resistencia 64 D3 Chaco, NE Argentina
Reşiţa 108 A4 Ger. Reschitza, Hung. Resicabánya. Caraş-Severin, W Romania
Resolute 37 F2 Inuit Qausuittuq. Cornwallis Island, Nunavut, N Canada
Resolution Island 39 E1 island Nunavut, NE Canada
Resolution Island 151 A7 island SW New Zealand
Réunion 79 H4 off. La Réunion. French overseas department W Indian Ocean
Réunion 141 B5 island W Indian Ocean
Reus 93 F2 Cataluña, E Spain
Reutlingen 95 B6 Baden-Württemberg, S Germany
Reuver 87 D5 Limburg, SE Netherlands
Reval/Revel see Tallinn

Revillagigedo Island *50 B5 island*
Alexander Archipiélago, Alaska, USA
Rexburg *46 E3* Idaho, NW USA
Reyes *61 F3* Beni, NW Bolivia
Rey, Isla del *53 G5 island* Archipiélago
de las Perlas, SE Panama
Reykjanes Basin *82 C5 var.* Irminger
Basin. *undersea basin* N Atlantic Ocean
Reykjanes Ridge *80 A1 undersea ridge*
N Atlantic Ocean
Reykjavík *83 E5 var. Reikjavik.*
country capital (Iceland) (Iceland)
Höfudhborgarsvaedhi, W Iceland
Reynosa *51 E2* Tamaulipas, C Mexico
Reza'iyeh, Daryācheh-ye *see* Orūmīyeh,
Daryācheh-ye
Rezé *90 A4* Loire-Atlantique, NW France
Rēzekne *106 D4* Ger. Rositten; *prev. Rus.*
Rezhitsa. Rēzekne, SE Latvia
Rezhitsa *see* Rēzekne
Rezovo *104 E3* Turk. Rezve Burgas,
E Bulgaria
Rezve *see* Rezovo
Rhaedestus *see* Tekirdağ
Rhegion/Rhegium *see* Reggio di Calabria
Rheims *see* Reims
Rhein *see* Rhine
Rheine *94 A3 var.* Rheine in Westfalen.
Nordrhein-Westfalen, NW Germany
Rheine in Westfalen *see* Rheine
Rheinisches Schiefergebirge *95 A5 var.*
Rhine State Uplands, *Eng.* Rhenish
Slate Mountains. *mountain range*
W Germany
Rhenish Slate Mountains *see* Rheinisches
Schiefergebirge
Rhin *see* Rhine
Rhine *80 D4 Dut.* Rijn, *Fr.* Rhin, *Ger.*
Rhein. *river* W Europe
Rhinelander *40 B2* Wisconsin, N USA
Rhine State Uplands *see* Rheinisches
Schiefergebirge
Rho *96 B2* Lombardia, N Italy
Rhode Island *41 G3 off.* State of Rhode
Island and Providence Plantations, *also
known as* Little Rhody, Ocean State.
state NE USA
Rhodes *105 E7 var.* Ródhos, *Eng.*
Rhodes, *It.* Rodi; *anc.* Rhodus. *island*
Dodekánisa, Greece, Aegean Sea
Rhodes *see* Ródos
Rhodesia *see* Zimbabwe
Rhodope Mountains *104 C3 var.*
Rodhópi Óri, *Bul.* Rhodope Planina,
Rodopi, *Gk.* Orosirá Rodhópis, *Turk.*
Dospad Dagh. *mountain range*
Bulgaria/Greece
Rhodope Planina *see* Rhodope Mountains
Rhône *80 C4 river* France/Switzerland
Rhum *88 B3 var.* Rum. *island*
W Scotland, United Kingdom
Ribble *89 D5 river* NW England, United
Kingdom
Ribeira *92 B1* Galicia, NW Spain
Ribeirão Preto *63 F4* São Paulo, S Brazil
Riberalta *61 F2* Beni, N Bolivia
Rîbniţa *108 D3 var.* Rãbniţã, *Rus.*
Rybnitsa. NE Moldova
Rice Lake *40 A2* Wisconsin, N USA
Richard Toll *74 B3* N Senegal
Richfield *44 B4* Utah, W USA
Richland *46 C2* Washington, NW USA
Richmond *151 C5* Tasman, South Island,
New Zealand
Richmond *40 C5* Kentucky, S USA
Richmond *41 E5 state capital* Virginia,
NE USA
Richmond Range *151 C5 mountain
range* South Island, New Zealand
Ricobayo, Embalse de *92 C2 reservoir*
NW Spain
Ricomagus *see* Riom
Ridder *114 D4 Kaz.* Leninġor.
Vostochnyy Kazakhstan, E Kazakhstan
Ridgecrest *47 C7* California, W USA
Ried *see* Ried im Innkreis
Ried im Innkreis *95 D6 var.* Ried.
Oberösterreich, NW Austria
Riemst *87 D6* Limburg, NE Belgium
Riesa *94 D4* Sachsen, E Germany
Rift Valley *see* Great Rift Valley
Riga *106 C3 Eng.* Riga. *country capital*
(Latvia) (Latvia) Rīga, C Latvia
Rigaer Bucht *see* Riga, Gulf of
Riga, Gulf of *106 C3 Est.* Liivi Laht, *Ger.*
Rigaer Bucht, *Latv.* Rīgas Jūras Līcis,
Rus. Rizhskiy Zaliv; *prev. Est.* Riia Laht.
gulf Estonia/Latvia

Rīgas Jūras Līcis *see* Riga, Gulf of
Rigestan *122 D5 var.* Registan. *desert
region* S Afghanistan
Riia Laht *see* Riga, Gulf of
Riihimäki *85 D5* Etelä-Suomi, S Finland
Rijeka *100 A2 Ger.* Sankt Veit am Flaum,
It. Fiume, *Slvn.* Reka; *anc.* Tarsatica.
Primorje-Gorski Kotar, NW Croatia
Rijn *see* Rhine
Rijssel *see* Lille
Rijssen *86 E3* Overijssel, E Netherlands
Rimah, Wādi ar *120 B4 var.* Wādi ar
Rummah. *dry watercourse* C Saudi
Arabia
Rimini *96 C3 anc.* Ariminum. Emilia-
Romagna, N Italy
Rîmnicu-Sărat *see* Râmnicu Sărat
Rîmnicu Vîlcea *see* Râmnicu Vâlcea
Rimouski *39 F4* Québec, SE Canada
Ringebu *85 B5* Oppland, S Norway
Ringen *see* Rõngu
Ringkøbing Fjord *85 A7 fjord*
W Denmark
Ringvassøya *84 C2 Lapp.* Ráneš. *island*
N Norway
Rio *see* Rio de Janeiro
Riobamba *60 B1* Chimborazo,
C Ecuador
Rio Branco *56 B3 state capital* Acre,
W Brazil
Rio Branco, Território de *see* Roraima
Río Bravo *51 E2* Tamaulipas, C Mexico
Río Cuarto *64 C4* Córdoba, C Argentina
Rio de Janeiro *63 F4 var.* Rio. *state
capital* Rio de Janeiro, SE Brazil
Rio de Janeiro *63 F4 off.* Estado de
Rio de Janeiro, SE Brazil
Río Gallegos *65 B7 var.* Gallegos, Puerto
Gallegos. Santa Cruz, S Argentina
Río Grande *63 E5 var.* São Pedro do
Rio Grande do Sul. Rio Grande do
Sul, S Brazil
Río Grande *50 D3* Zacatecas, C Mexico
Rio Grande do Norte *63 G2 off.* Estado
do Rio Grande do Norte. *region* E Brazil
Rio Grande do Norte *63 G2 off.* Estado
do Rio Grande do Norte. *state* E Brazil
Rio Grande do Norte *63 G2* Estado
Grande do Norte
Rio Grande do Sul *63 E5 off.* Estado do
Rio Grande do Sul. *region* S Brazil
Rio Grande do Sul *63 E5 off.* Estado do
Rio Grande do Sul. *state* S Brazil
Rio Grande do Sul, Estado do *see* Rio
Grande do Sul
Rio Grande Plateau *see* Rio Grande Rise
Rio Grande Rise *57 E6 var.* Rio Grande
Plateau. *undersea plateau* SW Atlantic
Ocean
Ríohacha *58 B1* La Guajira, N Colombia
Río Lagartos *51 H3* Yucatán, SE Mexico
Riom *91 C5 anc.* Ricomagus. Puy-de-
Dôme, C France
Rio Verde *51 E4 var.* Rioverde. San Luis
Potosí, C Mexico
Rioverde *see* Río Verde
Ripoll *93 G2* Cataluña, NE Spain
Rishiri-to *130 C2 var.* Risiri Tō. *island*
NE Japan
Risiri Tō *see* Rishiri-tō
Rişno *see* Râşnov
Risti *106 D2 Ger.* Kreuz. Läänemaa,
W Estonia
Rivas *52 D4* Rivas, SW Nicaragua
Rivera *64 D3* Rivera, NE Uruguay
River Falls *40 A2* Wisconsin, N USA
Riverside *47 C7* California, W USA
Riverton *151 A7* Southland, South
Island, New Zealand
Riverton *44 C3* Wyoming, C USA
Rivière-du-Loup *39 E4* Québec,
SE Canada
Rivne *108 C2 Pol.* Rôwne, *Rus.* Rovno.
Rivnens'ka Oblast', NW Ukraine
Rivoli *96 A2* Piemonte, NW Italy
Riyadh/Riyāḍ, Minṭaqat ar *see* Ar Riyāḍ
Riyāq *see* Rayak
Rize *117 E2* Rize, NE Turkey
Rizhao *128 D4* Shandong, E China
Rizhskiy Zaliv *see* Riga, Gulf of
Rkîz *74 C3* Trarza, W Mauritania
Road Town *55 F3 dependent territory
capital* (British Virgin Islands) Tortola,
C British Virgin Islands
Roanne *91 C5 anc.* Rodunma. Loire,
E France
Roanoke *41 E5* Virginia, NE USA
Roanoke River *43 F1 river* North
Carolina/Virginia, SE USA

Roatán *52 C2 var.* Coxen Hole, Coxin
Hole. Islas de la Bahía, N Honduras
Roat Kampuchea *see* Cambodia
Roazon *see* Rennes
Robbie Ridge *143 E3 undersea ridge*
W Pacific Ocean
Robert Williams *see* Caála
Robinson Range *147 B5 mountain range*
Western Australia
Robson, Mount *37 E5 mountain* British
Columbia, SW Canada
Robstown *49 G4* Texas, SW USA
Roca Partida, Isla *50 B5 island*
W Mexico
Rocas, Atol das *63 G2 island* E Brazil
Rochefort *87 C7* Namur, SE Belgium
Rochefort *90 B4 var.* Rochefort sur Mer.
Charente-Maritime, W France
Rochefort sur Mer *see* Rochefort
Rochester *45 G3* Minnesota, N USA
Rochester *41 G2* New Hampshire,
NE USA
Rocheuses, Montagnes/Rockies *see*
Rocky Mountains
Rockall Bank *80 B2 undersea bank*
N Atlantic Ocean
Rockall Trough *80 B2 trough* N Atlantic
Ocean
Rockdale *148 E2* Texas, SW USA
Rockford *40 B3* Illinois, N USA
Rockhampton *148 D4* Queensland,
E Australia
Rock Hill *43 E1* South Carolina, SE USA
Rockingham *147 A6* Western Australia
Rock Island *40 B3* Illinois, N USA
Rock Sound *54 C1* Eleuthera Island,
C Bahamas
Rock Springs *44 C3* Wyoming, C USA
Rockstone *59 F3* C Guyana
Rocky Mount *43 F1* North Carolina,
SE USA
Rocky Mountains *34 B4 var.* Rockies,
Fr. Montagnes Rocheuses. *mountain
range* Canada/USA
Roden *86 E2* Drenthe, NE Netherlands
Rodez *91 C5 anc.* Segodunum. Aveyron,
S France
Rodhópi Óri *see* Rhodope Mountains
Ródhos/Rodi *see* Ródos
Rodopi *see* Rhodope Mountains
Rodosto *see* Tekirdağ
Rodunma *see* Roanne
Roermond *87 D5* Limburg,
SE Netherlands
Roeselare *87 A6 Fr.* Roulers; *prev.*
Rousselaere. West-Vlaanderen,
W Belgium
Rogachov *see* Rahachow
Rugatica *100 C4* Republika Srpska,
SE Bosnia and Herzegovina
Rogers *42 A1* Arkansas, C USA
Roger Simpson Island *see* Abemama
Roi Ed *see* Roi Et
Roi Et *127 D5 var.* Muang Roi Et, Roi
Ed. Roi Et, E Thailand
Roja *106 C2* Talsi, NW Latvia
Rokiškis *106 C4* Panevėžys,
NE Lithuania
Rokycany *99 A5 Ger.* Rokytzan.
Plzeňský Kraj, W Czech Republic
Rokytzan *see* Rokycany
Rôlas, Ilha das *76 E2 island* S Sao Tome
and Principe, Africa, E Atlantic Ocean
Rolla *45 G5* Missouri, C USA
Rôm *see* Rome
Roma *96 C4 Eng.* Rome. *country capital*
(Italy) (Italy) Lazio, C Italy
Roma *149 D5* Queensland, E Australia
Roman *104 C3* Vratsa, NW Bulgaria
Roman *108 C4 Hung.* Románvásár.
Neamţ, NE Romania
Romania *108 B4 Bul.* Rumŭniya, *Ger.*
Rumänien, *Hung.* Románia, *Rom.*
România, *SCr.* Rumunjska, *Ukr.*
Rumuniya; *prev.* Republica Socialistă
România, Roumania, Rumania,
Socialist Republic of Romania, *prev.*
Rom. Romînia. *country capital* SE Europe

ROMANIA
Southeast Europe

Official name Romania
Formation 1878 / 1947
Capital Bucharest
Population 21.5 million / 242 people
per sq mile (93 people per sq km) / 55%

ROMANIA
(continued)

Total area 91,699 sq. miles (237,500 sq. km)
Languages Romanian*, Hungarian
(Magyar), Romani, German
Religions Romanian Orthodox 87%,
Roman Catholic 5%, Protestant 4%,
Other 2%, Greek Orthodox 1%,
Greek Catholic (Uniate) 1%
Ethnic mix Romanian 89%, Magyar 7%,
Roma 2%, Other 2%
Government Presidential system
Currency New Romanian leu = 100 bani
Literacy rate 97%
Calorie consumption 3455 calories

Románia, Republica Socialistă *see*
Romania
Romania, Socialist Republic of *see*
Romania
Romaniv *109 F3 Rus.* Dneprodzerzhinsk,
prev. Dniprodzerzhyns'k, *prev.*
Kamenskoye. Dnipropetrovs'ka
Oblast', E Ukraine
Románvásár *see* Roman
Rome *42 D2* Georgia, SE USA
Rome *see* Roma
Romînia *see* Romania
Romny *109 F2* Sums'ka Oblast',
NE Ukraine
Rømø *85 A7 Ger.* Röm. *island*
SW Denmark
Roncador, Serra do *56 D4 mountain
range* C Brazil
Ronda *92 D5* Andalucía, S Spain
Rondônia *62 D3 off.* Estado de
Rondônia; *prev.* Território de
Rondônia. *state* W Brazil
Rondônia *62 D3 off.* Estado de
Rondônia; *prev.* Território de
Rondônia. *region* W Brazil
Rondônia, Estado de *see* Rondônia
Rondônia, Território de *see* Rondônia
Rondonópolis *63 E3* Mato Grosso,
W Brazil
Rongelap Atoll *144 D1 var.* Rönlap.
atoll Ralik Chain, NW Marshall Islands
Rõngu *106 D3 Ger.* Ringen. Tartumaa,
SE Estonia
Rönlap *see* Rongelap Atoll
Rønne *85 B8* Bornholm, E Denmark
Ronne Ice Shelf *154 A3 ice shelf*
Antarctica
Roosendaal *87 C5* Noord-Brabant,
S Netherlands
Roosevelt Island *154 B4 island*
Antarctica
Roraima *62 D1 off.* Estado de Roraima;
prev. Território de Rio Branco,
Território de Roraima. *state* N Brazil
Roraima *62 D1 off.* Estado de Roraima;
prev. Território de Rio Branco,
Território de Roraima. *region* N Brazil
Roraima, Estado de *see* Roraima
Roraima, Mount *59 E3 mountain*
N South America
Roraima, Território de *see* Roraima
Røros *85 B5* Sør-Trøndelag, S Norway
Ross *151 B6* West Coast, South Island,
New Zealand
Rosa, Lake *54 D2 lake* Great Inagua,
S Bahamas
Rosario *64 D4* Santa Fe, C Argentina
Rosario *64 D2* San Pedro, C Paraguay
Rosario *see* Rosarito
Rosarito *50 A1 var.* Rosario. Baja
California Norte, NW Mexico
Roscianum *see* Rossano
Roscommon *20 C2* Michigan, N USA
Roseau *55 G4 prev.* Charlotte Town.
country capital (Dominica) (Dominica)
SW Dominica
Roseburg *46 B4* Oregon, NW USA
Rosenau *see* Rožňava
Rosenberg *49 G4* Texas, SW USA
Rosenberg *see* Ružomberok, Slovakia
Rosengarten *94 B3* Niedersachsen,
N Germany
Rosenheim *95 C6* Bayern, S Germany
Rosia *93 H5* W Gibraltar Europe
Rosia Bay *93 H5 bay* SW Gibraltar
Europe W Mediterranean Sea Atlantic
Ocean
Roşiori de Vede *108 B5* Teleorman,
S Romania
Rositten *see* Rēzekne

233

Roslavl' *111 A5* Smolenskaya Oblast', W Russian Federation
Rosmalen *86 C4* Noord-Brabant, S Netherlands
Rossano *97 E6 anc.* Roscianum. Calabria, SW Italy
Ross Ice Shelf *154 B4 ice shelf* Antarctica
Rossiyskaya Federatsiya *see* Russian Federation
Rosso *74 B3* Trarza, SW Mauritania
Rossosh' *111 B6* Voronezhskaya Oblast', W Russian Federation
Ross Sea *154 B4 sea* Antarctica
Rostak *see* Ar Rustāq
Rostock *94 C2* Mecklenburg-Vorpommern, NE Germany
Rostov *see* Rostov-na-Donu
Rostov-na-Donu *111 B7 var.* Rostov, *Eng.* Rostov-on-Don. Rostovskaya Oblast', SW Russian Federation
Rostov-on-Don *see* Rostov-na-Donu
Roswell *48 D2* New Mexico, SW USA
Rota *144 B1 island* S Northern Mariana Islands
Rotcher Island *see* Tamana
Rothera *154 A2 UK research station* Antarctica
Rotomagus *see* Rouen
Rotorua *150 D3* Bay of Plenty, North Island, New Zealand
Rotorua, Lake *150 D3 lake* North Island, New Zealand
Rotterdam *86 C4* Zuid-Holland, SW Netherlands
Rottweil *95 B6* Baden-Württemberg, S Germany
Rotuma *145 E4 island* NW Fiji Oceania S Pacific Ocean
Roubaix *90 C2* Nord, N France
Rouen *90 C3 anc.* Rotomagus. Seine-Maritime, N France
Roulers *see* Roeselare
Roumania *see* Romania
Round Rock *49 G3* Texas, SW USA
Rourkela *see* Rāulakela
Rousselaere *see* Roeselare
Roussillon *91 C6 cultural region* S France
Rouyn-Noranda *38 D4* Québec, SE Canada
Rovaniemi *84 D3* Lappi, N Finland
Rovigno *see* Rovinj
Rovigo *96 C2* Veneto, NE Italy
Rovinj *100 A3 It.* Rovigno. Istra, NW Croatia
Rovno *see* Rivne
Rovuma, Rio *79 F2 var.* Ruvuma. *river* Mozambique/Tanzania
Rovuma, Rio *see* Ruvuma
Równe *see* Rivne
Roxas City *139 E2* Panay Island, C Philippines
Royale, Isle *40 B1 island* Michigan, N USA
Royan *91 B5* Charente-Maritime, W France
Rozdol'ne *109 F4 Rus.* Razdolnoye. Respublika Krym, S Ukraine
Rožňava *99 D6 Ger.* Rosenau, *Hung.* Rozsnyó. Košický Kraj, E Slovakia
Rózsahegy *see* Ružomberok
Rozsnyó *see* Râsnov, Romania
Rozsnyó *see* Rožňava, Slovakia
Ruanda *see* Rwanda
Ruapehu, Mount *150 D4 volcano* North Island, New Zealand
Ruapuke Island *151 B8 island* SW New Zealand
Ruatoria *150 E3* Gisborne, North Island, New Zealand
Ruawai *150 D2* Northland, North Island, New Zealand
Rubezhnoye *see* Rubizhne
Rubizhne *109 H3 Rus.* Rubezhnoye. Luhans'ka Oblast', E Ukraine
Ruby Mountains *47 D5 mountain range* Nevada, W USA
Rucava *106 B3* Liepāja, SW Latvia
Rudensk *see* Rudzyensk
Rūdiškės *107 B5* Vilnius, S Lithuania
Rudnik *104 E2* Varna, E Bulgaria
Rudny *see* Rudnyy
Rudnyy *114 C4 var.* Rudny. Kostanay, N Kazakhstan
Rudolf, Lake *see* Turkana, Lake
Rudolfswert *see* Novo mesto
Rudzyensk *107 C6 Rus.* Rudensk. Minskaya Voblasts', C Belarus

Rufiji *73 C7 river* E Tanzania
Rufino *64 C4* Santa Fe, C Argentina
Rugāji *106 D4* Balvi, E Latvia
Rügen *94 D2 headland* NE Germany
Ruggell *94 E1* N Liechtenstein Europe
Ruhja *see* Rūjiena
Ruhnu *106 C2 var.* Ruhnu Saar, *Swe.* Runö. *island* SW Estonia
Ruhnu Saar *see* Ruhnu
Rujen *see* Rūjiena
Rūjiena *106 D3 Est.* Ruhja, *Ger.* Rujen. Valmiera, N Latvia
Rukwa, Lake *73 B7 lake* SE Tanzania
Rum *see* Rhum
Ruma *100 D3* Vojvodina, N Serbia
Rumadiya *see* Ar Ramādī
Rumania/Rumänien *see* Romania
Rumbek *73 B5* El Buhayrat, S Sudan
Rum Cay *54 D2 island* C Bahamas
Rumia *98 C2* Pomorskie, N Poland
Rummah, Wādī ar *see* Rimah, Wādī ar
Rummelsburg in Pommern *see* Miastko
Rumuniya/Rumŭniya/Rumunjska *see* Romania
Runanga *151 B5* West Coast, South Island, New Zealand
Rundu *78 C3 var.* Runtu. Okavango, NE Namibia
Runö *see* Ruhnu
Runtu *see* Rundu
Ruoqiang *126 C3 var.* Jo-ch'iang, Uigh. Charkhlik, Charkhliq, Qarkilik. Xinjiang Uygur Zizhiqu, NW China
Rupea *108 C4 Ger.* Reps, *Hung.* Kőhalom; *prev.* Cohalm. Brașov, C Romania
Rupel *87 B5 river* N Belgium
Rupella *see* la Rochelle
Rupert, Rivière de *38 D3 river* Québec, C Canada
Rusaddir *see* Melilla
Ruschuk/Rusçuk *see* Ruse
Ruse *104 D1 var.* Ruschuk, Rustchuk, *Turk.* Rusçuk. Ruse, N Bulgaria
Russadir *see* Melilla
Russellville *42 A1* Arkansas, C USA
Russia *see* Russian Federation
Russian America *see* Alaska
Russian Federation *112 D2 off.* Russian Federation, *var.* Russia, *Latv.* Krievija, *Rus.* Rossiyskaya Federatsiya. *country* Asia/Europe

RUSSIAN FEDERATION
Europe / Asia

Official name Russian Federation
Formation 1480 / 1991
Capital Moscow
Population 142 million / 22 people per sq mile (8 people per sq km) / 73%
Total area 6,592,735 sq. miles (17,075,200 sq. km)
Languages Russian*, Tatar, Ukrainian, Chavash, various other national languages
Religions Orthodox Christian 75%, Muslim 14%, Other 11%
Ethnic mix Russian 80%, Other 12%, Tatar 4%, Ukrainian 2%, Bashkir 1%, Chavash 1%
Government Mixed Presidential–Parliamentary system
Currency Russian rouble = 100 kopeks
Literacy rate 99%
Calorie consumption 3072 calories

Rustaq *see* Ar Rustāq
Rust'avi *117 G2* SE Georgia
Rustchuk *see* Ruse
Ruston *42 B2* Louisiana, S USA
Rutanzige, Lake *see* Edward, Lake
Rutba *see* Ar Ruţbah
Rutlam *see* Ratlām
Rutland *41 F2* Vermont, NE USA
Rutog *126 A4 var.* Rutög, Rutok. Xizang Zizhiqu, W China
Rutok *see* Rutog
Ruvuma *69 E5 var.* Rio Rovuma. *river* Mozambique/Tanzania
Ruvuma, Rio *see* Rovuma, Rio
Ruwenzori *77 E5 mountain range* Dem. Rep. Congo/Uganda
Ruzhany *107 B6* Brestskaya Voblasts', SW Belarus

Ružomberok *99 C5 Ger.* Rosenberg, *Hung.* Rózsahegy. Žilinský Kraj, N Slovakia
Rwanda *73 B6 off.* Rwandese Republic; *prev.* Ruanda. *country* C Africa

RWANDA
Central Africa

Official name Republic of Rwanda
Formation 1962 / 1962
Capital Kigali
Population 9.4 million / 976 people per sq mile (377 people per sq km) / 20%
Total area 10,169 sq. miles (26,338 sq. km)
Languages Kinyarwanda*, French*, English*, Kiswahili
Religions Roman Catholic 56%, Traditional beliefs 25%, Muslim 10%, Protestant 9%
Ethnic mix Hutu 90%, Tutsi 9%, Other (including Twa) 1%
Government Presidential system
Currency Rwanda franc = 100 centimes
Literacy rate 65%
Calorie consumption 2084 calories

Rwandese Republic *see* Rwanda
Ryazan' *111 B5* Ryazanskaya Oblast', W Russian Federation
Rybach'ye *see* Balykchy
Rybinsk *110 B4 prev.* Andropov. Yaroslavskaya Oblast', W Russian Federation
Rybnik *99 C5* Śląskie, S Poland
Rybnitsa *see* Rîbniţa
Ryde *89 D7* S United Kingdom
Ryki *98 D4* Lubelskie, E Poland
Rykovo *see* Yenakiyeve
Rypin *98 C3* Kujawsko-pomorskie, C Poland
Ryssel *see* Lille
Rysy *99 C5 mountain* S Poland
Ryukyu Islands *130 A2 Eng.* Ryukyu Islands. *island group* SW Japan
Ryukyu Islands *125 E3 Eng.* Ryukyu Islands. *island group* SW Japan
Ryukyu Islands *see* Nansei-shotō
Ryukyu Islands *see* Nansei-shotō
Ryukyu Trench *125 F3 var.* Nansei Syotō Trench. *trench* S East China Sea
Rzeszów *99 E5* Podkarpackie, SE Poland
Rzhev *110 B4* Tverskaya Oblast', W Russian Federation

S

Saale *94 C4 river* C Germany
Saalfeld *95 C5 var.* Saalfeld an der Saale. Thüringen, C Germany
Saalfeld an der Saale *see* Saalfeld
Saarbrücken *95 A6 Fr.* Sarrebruck. Saarland, SW Germany
Sääre *106 C2 var.* Sjar. Saaremaa, W Estonia
Saare *see* Saaremaa
Saaremaa *106 C2 Ger.* Oesel, Ösel; *prev.* Saare. *island* W Estonia
Saariselkä *84 D2 Lapp.* Suoločielgi. Lappi, N Finland
Sab' Ābār *118 C4 var.* Sab'a Biyar, Sa'b Bi'ār. Ḩimş, C Syria
Sab'a Biyar *see* Sab' Ābār
Šabac *100 D3* Serbia, W Serbia
Sabadell *93 G2* Cataluña, E Spain
Sabah *138 D3 prev.* British North Borneo, North Borneo. *state* East Malaysia
Sabanalarga *58 B1* Atlántico, N Colombia
Sabaneta *58 C1* Falcón, N Venezuela
Sabaria *see* Szombathely
Sab'atayn, Ramlat as *121 C6 desert* C Yemen
Sabaya *61 F4* Oruro, S Bolivia
Sa'b Bi'ār *see* Sab' Ābār
Saberi, Hamun-e *122 C5 var.* Daryācheh-ye Hāmun, Daryācheh-ye Sīstān. *lake* Afghanistan/Iran
Sabhā *71 F3* C Libya
Sabi *see* Save
Sabinas *51 E2* Coahuila, NE Mexico
Sabinas Hidalgo *51 E2* Nuevo León, NE Mexico
Sabine River *49 H3 river* Louisiana/Texas, SW USA

Sabkha *see* As Sabkhah
Sable, Cape *43 E5 headland* Florida, SE USA
Sable Island *39 G4 island* Nova Scotia, SE Canada
Ṣabyā *121 B6 Jīzān*, SW Saudi Arabia
Sabzawar *see* Sabzevār
Sabzevār *120 D2 var.* Sabzawar. Khorāsān-Razavī, NE Iran
Sachsen *94 D4 Eng.* Saxony, *Fr.* Saxe. *state* E Germany
Sachs Harbour *37 E2 var.* Ikaahuk. Banks Island, Northwest Territories, N Canada
Sächsisch-Reen/Sächsisch-Regen *see* Reghin
Sacramento *47 B5 state capital* California, W USA
Sacramento Mountains *48 D2 mountain range* New Mexico, SW USA
Sacramento River *47 B5 river* California, W USA
Sacramento Valley *47 B5 valley* California, W USA
Sá da Bandeira *see* Lubango
Ṣa'dah *121 B6* NW Yemen
Sado *131 C5 var.* Sadoga-shima. *island* C Japan
Sadoga-shima *see* Sado
Saena Julia *see* Siena
Safad *see* Tsefat
Şafāqis *see* Sfax
Şafāshahr *120 D3 var.* Deh Bīd. Fārs, C Iran
Safed *see* Tsefat
Säffle *85 B6* Värmland, C Sweden
Safford *48 C3* Arizona, SW USA
Safi *70 B2* W Morocco
Selseleh-ye Safīd Kuh *122 D4 Eng.* Paropamisus Range. *mountain range* W Afghanistan
Sagaing *136 B3* Sagaing, C Burma (Myanmar)
Sagami-nada *131 D6 inlet* SW Japan
Sagan *see* Żagań
Sāgar *134 D4 prev.* Saugor. Madhya Pradesh, C India
Sagarmāthā *see* Everest, Mount
Sagebrush State *see* Nevada
Saghez *see* Saqqez
Saginaw *40 C3* Michigan, N USA
Saginaw Bay *40 D2 lake bay* Michigan, N USA
Sagua la Grande *54 B2* Villa Clara, C Cuba
Sagunto *93 F3 Cat.* Sagunt, *Ar.* Murviedro; *anc.* Saguntum. País Valenciano, E Spain
Sagunt/Saguntum *see* Sagunto
Sahara *68 B3 desert* Libya/Algeria
Sahara el Gharbîya *see* Şaḥrā' al Gharbiyah
Saharan Atlas *70 D2 var.* Saharan Atlas. *mountain range* Algeria/Morocco
Saharan Atlas *see* Atlas Saharien
Sahel *74 D3 physical region* C Africa
Sāḩiliyah, Jibāl as *118 B3 mountain range* NW Syria
Sāhīwāl *134 C2 prev.* Montgomery. Punjab, E Pakistan
Saïda *119 A5 var.* Şaydā, Sayida; *anc.* Sidon. W Lebanon
Sa'īdābād *see* Sīrjān
Saidpur *135 G3 var.* Syedpur Rajshahi, NW Bangladesh
Saidu Sharif *134 C1 var.* Mingora, Mongora. North-West Frontier Province, N Pakistan
Saigon *see* Hồ Chí Minh
Saimaa *85 E5 lake* SE Finland
St Albans *89 E6 anc.* Verulamium. E England, United Kingdom
Saint Albans *40 D5* West Virginia, NE USA
St Andrews *88 C4* E Scotland, United Kingdom
Saint Anna Trough *see* Svyataya Anna Trough
St. Ann's Bay *54 B4* C Jamaica
St. Anthony *39 G3* Newfoundland and Labrador, SE Canada
Saint Augustine *43 E3* Florida, SE USA
St Austell *89 C7* SW England, United Kingdom
St.Botolph's Town *see* Boston
St-Brieuc *90 A3* Côtes d'Armor, NW France

St. Catharines 38 D5 Ontario, S Canada
St-Chamond 91 D5 Loire, E France
Saint Christopher and Nevis, Federation of see Saint Kitts and Nevis
Saint Christopher-Nevis see Saint Kitts and Nevis
Saint Clair, Lake 40 D3 var. Lac à L'Eau Claire. lake Canada/USA
St-Claude 91 D5 anc. Condate. Jura, E France
Saint Cloud 45 F2 Minnesota, N USA
Saint Croix 55 F3 island S Virgin Islands (US)
Saint Croix River 40 A2 river Minnesota/Wisconsin, N USA
St David's Island 42 B5 island E Bermuda
St-Denis 79 G4 dependent territory capital (Réunion) NW Réunion
St-Dié 90 E4 Vosges, NE France
St-Egrève 91 D5 Isère, E France
Sainte Marie, Cap see Vohimena, Tanjona
Saintes 91 B5 anc. Mediolanum. Charente-Maritime, W France
St-Étienne 91 D5 Loire, E France
St-Flour 91 C5 Cantal, C France
St-Gall/Saint Gall/St. Gallen see Sankt Gallen
St-Gaudens 91 B6 Haute-Garonne, S France
Saint George 149 D5 Queensland, E Australia
St George 42 B4 N Bermuda
Saint George 44 A5 Utah, W USA
St. George's 55 G5 country capital (Grenada) (Grenada) SW Grenada
St-Georges 39 E4 Québec, SE Canada
St-Georges 59 H3 E French Guiana
Saint George's Channel 89 B6 channel Ireland/Wales, United Kingdom
St George's Island 42 B4 island E Bermuda
Saint Helena 69 B6 UK dependent territory C Atlantic Ocean
St Helier 89 D8 dependent territory capital (Jersey) S Jersey, Channel Islands
St.Iago de la Vega see Spanish Town
Saint Ignace 40 C2 Michigan, N USA
St-Jean, Lac 39 E4 lake Québec, SE Canada
Saint Joe River 46 D2 river Idaho, NW USA North America
St. John 39 F4 New Brunswick, SE Canada
Saint-John see Saint John
Saint John River 41 H1 Fr. Saint-John. river Canada/USA
St John's 55 G3 country capital (Antigua and Barbuda) (Antigua and Barbuda) Antigua, Antigua and Barbuda
St. John's 39 H3 province capital Newfoundland and Labrador, E Canada
Saint Joseph 45 F4 Missouri, C USA
St Julian's 102 B5 N Malta
St Kilda 88 A3 island NW Scotland, United Kingdom
Saint Kitts and Nevis 55 F3 off. Federation of Saint Christopher and Nevis, var. Saint Christopher-Nevis. country E West Indies

SAINT KITTS & NEVIS
West Indies

Official name Federation of Saint Christopher and Nevis
Formation 1983 / 1983
Capital Basseterre
Population 39,349 / 283 people per sq mile (109 people per sq km) / 32%
Total area 101 sq. miles (261 sq. km)
Languages English*, English Creole
Religions Anglican 33%, Methodist 29%, Other 22%, Moravian 9%, Roman Catholic 7%
Ethnic mix Black 95%, Mixed race 3%, White 1%, Other and Amerindian 1%
Government Parliamentary system
Currency Eastern Caribbean dollar = 100 cents
Literacy rate 98%
Calorie consumption 2609 calories

St-Laurent see St-Laurent-du-Maroni
St-Laurent-du-Maroni 59 H3 var. St-Laurent. NW French Guiana
St-Laurent, Fleuve see St. Lawrence
St. Lawrence 39 E4 Fr. Fleuve St-Laurent. river Canada/USA
St. Lawrence, Gulf of 39 F3 gulf NW Atlantic Ocean
Saint Lawrence Island 36 B2 island Alaska, USA
St-Lô 90 B3 anc. Briovera, Laudus. Manche, N France
St-Louis 90 E4 Haut-Rhin, NE France
Saint Louis 74 B3 NW Senegal
Saint Louis 45 G4 Missouri, C USA
Saint Lucia 55 F1 country SE West Indies

SAINT LUCIA
West Indies

Official name Saint Lucia
Formation 1979 / 1979
Capital Castries
Population 170,649 / 723 people per sq mile (280 people per sq km) / 31%
Total area 239 sq. miles (620 sq. km)
Languages English*, French Creole
Religions Roman Catholic 90%, Other 10%
Ethnic mix Black 83%, Mulatto (mixed race) 13%, Asian 3%, Other 1%
Government Parliamentary system
Currency Eastern Caribbean dollar = 100 cents
Literacy rate 95%
Calorie consumption 2988 calories

Saint Lucia Channel 55 H4 channel Martinique/Saint Lucia
St-Malo 90 B3 Ille-et-Vilaine, NW France
St-Malo, Golfe de 90 A3 gulf NW France
Saint Matthew's Island see Zadetkyi Kyun
St.Matthias Group 144 B3 island group NE Papua New Guinea
St. Moritz 95 B7 Ger. Sankt Moritz, Rmsch. San Murezzan. Graubünden, SE Switzerland
St-Nazaire 90 A4 Loire-Atlantique, NW France
Saint Nicholas see São Nicolau
Saint-Nicolas see Sint-Niklaas
St-Omer 90 C2 Pas-de-Calais, N France
Saint Paul 45 F2 state capital Minnesota, N USA
St-Paul, Île 141 C6 var. St.Paul Island. island Île St. Paul, NE French Southern and Antarctic Territories Antarctica Indian Ocea
St.Paul Island see St-Paul, Île
St Peter Port 89 D8 dependent territory capital (Guernsey) C Guernsey, Channel Islands
Saint Petersburg 43 E4 Florida, SE USA
Saint Petersburg see Sankt-Peterburg
St-Pierre and Miquelon 39 G4 Fr. Îles St-Pierre and Miquelon. French territorial collectivity NE North America
St-Quentin 90 C3 Aisne, N France
Saint Thomas see São Tomé, Sao Tome and Principe
Saint Thomas see Charlotte Amalie, Virgin Islands (US)
Saint Ubes see Setúbal
Saint Vincent 55 G4 island N Saint Vincent and the Grenadines
Saint Vincent see São Vicente
Saint Vincent and the Grenadines 55 H4 country SE West Indies

SAINT VINCENT & THE GRENADINES
West Indies

Official name Saint Vincent and the Grenadines
Formation 1979 / 1979
Capital Kingstown
Population 118,149 / 902 people per sq mile (347 people per sq km) / 59%
Total area 150 sq. miles (389 sq. km)
Languages English*, English Creole
Religions Anglican 47%, Methodist 28%, Roman Catholic 13%, Other 12%
Ethnic mix Black 77%, Mulatto (mixed race) 16%, Other 3%, Carib 3%, Asian 1%
Government Parliamentary system

SAINT VINCENT & THE GRENADINES
(continued)

Currency Eastern Caribbean dollar = 100 cents
Literacy rate 88%
Calorie consumption 2599 calories

Saint Vincent, Cape see São Vicente, Cabo de
Saint Vincent Passage 55 H4 passage Saint Lucia/Saint Vincent and the Grenadines
Saint Yves see Setúbal
Saipan 142 B1 island/country capital (Northern Mariana Islands) S Northern Mariana Islands
Saishū see Cheju-do
Sajama, Nevado 61 F4 mountain W Bolivia
Sajószentpéter 99 D6 Borsod-Abaúj-Zemplén, NE Hungary
Sakākah 120 B4 Al Jawf, NW Saudi Arabia
Sakakawea, Lake 44 D1 reservoir North Dakota, N USA
Sak'art'velo see Georgia
Sakata 130 D4 Yamagata, Honshū, C Japan
Sakhalin 115 G4 var. Sakhalin. island SE Russian Federation
Sakhalin see Sakhalin, Ostrov
Sakhon Nakhon see Sakon Nakhon
Şäki 117 G2 Rus. Sheki; prev. Nukha. NW Azerbaijan
Saki see Saky
Sakishima-shoto 130 A3 var. Sakisima Syotō. island group SW Japan
Sakisima Syotō see Sakishima-shotō
Sakiz see Saqqez
Sakiz-Adasi see Chíos
Sakon Nakhon 136 D4 var. Muang Sakon Nakhon, Sakhon Nakhon. Sakon Nakhon, E Thailand
Saky 109 F5 Rus. Saki. Respublika Krym, S Ukraine
Sal 74 A3 island Ilhas de Barlavento, NE Cape Verde
Sala 85 C6 Västmanland, C Sweden
Salacgrīva 106 C3 Est. Salatsi. Limbaži, N Latvia
Sala Consilina 97 D5 Campania, S Italy
Salado, Río 62 D5 river E Argentina
Salado, Río 64 C3 river C Argentina
Salamá 52 B2 Baja Verapaz, C Guatemala
Salamanca 64 B4 Coquimbo, C Chile
Salamanca 92 D2 anc. Helmantica, Salmantica. Castilla-León, NW Spain
Salamīyah 118 B3 var, As Salamīyah. Ḥamāh, W Syria
Salang see Phuket
Salantai 106 B3 Klaipėda, NW Lithuania
Salatsi see Salacgrīva
Salavan 137 D5 var. Saravan, Saravane. Salavan, S Laos
Salavat 111 D6 Respublika Bashkortostan, W Russian Federation
Salawati 139 F3 prev. Obdorsk. Yamalo-Nenetskiy Avtonomnyy Okrug, N Russian Federation
Salem 132 C2 Tamil Nādu, SE India
Salem 46 B3 state capital Oregon, NW USA
Salerno 97 D5 anc. Salernum. Campania, S Italy
Salerno, Gulf of 97 C5 Eng. Gulf of Salerno. gulf S Italy
Salerno, Gulf of see Salerno, Golfo di
Salernum see Salerno

Salihorsk 107 C7 Rus. Soligorsk. Minskaya Voblasts', S Belarus
Salima 79 E2 Central, C Malawi
Salina 45 E5 Kansas, C USA
Salina Cruz 51 F5 Oaxaca, SE Mexico
Salinas 60 A2 Guayas, W Ecuador
Salinas 47 B6 California, W USA
Salisbury 89 D7 var. New Sarum. S England, United Kingdom
Salisbury see Harare
Sállan see Sørøya
Sallyana see Şalyān
Salmantica see Salamanca
Salmon River 46 D3 river Idaho, NW USA
Salmon River Mountains 46 D3 mountain range Idaho, NW USA
Salo 85 D6 Länsi-Suomi, SW Finland
Salon-de-Provence 91 D6 Bouches-du-Rhône, SE France
Salonica/Salonika see Thessaloníki
Salonta 108 A3 Hung. Nagyszalonta. Bihor, W Romania
Sal'sk 111 B7 Rostovskaya Oblast', SW Russian Federation
Salt see As Salţ
Salta 64 C2 Salta, NW Argentina
Saltash 89 C7 SW England, United Kingdom
Saltillo 51 E3 Coahuila, NE Mexico
Salt Lake City 44 B4 state capital Utah, W USA
Salto 64 D4 Salto, N Uruguay
Salton Sea 47 D8 lake California, W USA
Salvador 63 G3 prev. São Salvador. state capital Bahia, E Brazil
Salween 124 F2 Bur. Thanlwin, Chin. Nu Chiang, Nu Jiang. river SE Asia
Şalyān 135 E3 var. Sallyana. Mid Western, W Nepal
Salzburg 95 D6 anc. Juvavum. Salzburg, N Austria
Salzgitter 94 C4 prev. Watenstedt-Salzgitter. Niedersachsen, C Germany
Salzwedel 94 C3 Sachsen-Anhalt, N Germany
Šamac see Bosanski Šamac
Samakhixai 137 E5 var. Attapu, Attopeu. Attapu, S Laos
Samalayuca 50 C1 Chihuahua, N Mexico
Samar 139 F2 island C Philippines
Samara 114 B3 prev. Kuybyshev. Samarskaya Oblast', W Russian Federation
Samarang see Semarang
Samarinda 138 D4 Borneo, C Indonesia
Samarkand see Samarqand
Samarkandski/Samarkandskoye see Temirtau
Samarobriva see Amiens
Samarqand 123 E2 Rus. Samarkand. Samarqand Viloyati, C Uzbekistan
Samawa see Samawah
Sambalpur 135 F4 Orissa, E India
Sambava 79 G2 Antsiranana, NE Madagascar
Sambir 108 B2 Rus. Sambor. L'vivs'ka Oblast', NW Ukraine
Sambor see Sambir
Sambre 90 D2 river Belgium/France
Samfya 78 D2 Luapula, N Zambia
Saminatal 94 E2 valley Austria/Liechtenstein Europe
Samnän see Semnän
Sam Neua see Xam Nua
Samoa 145 E4 off. Independent State of Western Samoa, var. Samoa; prev. Western Samoa. country W Polynesia

SAMOA
Australasia & Oceania

Official name Independent State of Samoa
Formation 1962 / 1962
Capital Apia
Population 214,265 / 196 people per sq mile (76 people per sq km) / 22%
Total area 1104 sq. miles (2860 sq. km)
Languages Samoan*, English*
Religions Christian 99%, Other 1%
Ethnic mix Polynesian 90%, Euronesian 9%, Other 1%
Government Parliamentary system
Currency Tala = 100 sene
Literacy rate 99%
Calorie consumption 2945 calories

Sāmoa see Samoa
Samoa Basin *143 E3 undersea basin* W Pacific Ocean
Samobor *100 A2* Zagreb, N Croatia
Sámos *105 E6 prev.* Limín Vathéos.
Sámos, Dodekánisa, Greece, Aegean Sea
Sámos *105 D6 island* Dodekánisa, Greece, Aegean Sea
Samothrace see Samothráki
Samothráki *104 D4* Samothráki, NE Greece
Samothráki *104 C4 anc.* Samothrace. *island* NE Greece
Sampit *138 C4* Borneo, C Indonesia
Samsun *116 D2 anc.* Amisus. Samsun, N Turkey
Samtredia *117 F2* W Georgia
Samui, Ko *137 C6 island* SW Thailand
Samut Prakan *137 C5 var.* Muang Samut Prakan, Paknam. Samut Prakan, C Thailand
San *74 D3* Ségou, C Mali
San *99 E5 river* SE Poland
Şan'ā' *121 B6 Eng.* Sana. *country capital* (Yemen) (Yemen) W Yemen
Sana *100 B3 river* NW Bosnia and Herzegovina
Sanae *154 B2 South African research station* Antarctica
Sanaga *77 B5 river* C Cameroon
San Ambrosio, Isla *57 A5 Eng.* San Ambrosio Island. *island* W Chile
San Ambrosio Island see San Ambrosio, Isla
Sanandaj *120 C3 prev.* Sinneh. Kordestān, W Iran
San Andrés, Isla de *53 F3 island* NW Colombia, Caribbean Sea
San Andrés Tuxtla *51 F4 var.* Tuxtla. Veracruz-Llave, E Mexico
San Angelo *47 B6* California, W USA
San Antonio *52 B2* Toledo, S Belize
San Antonio *64 B4* Valparaíso, C Chile
San Antonio *49 F4* Texas, SW USA
San Antonio Oeste *65 C5* Río Negro, E Argentina
San Antonio River *49 G4 river* Texas, SW USA
Sanāw *121 C6 var.* Sanaw. NE Yemen
San Benedicto, Isla *50 B4 island* W Mexico
San Benito *52 B1* Petén, N Guatemala
San Benito *49 G5* Texas, SW USA
San Bernardino *47 C7* California, W USA
San Blas *50 C3* Sinaloa, C Mexico
San Blas, Cape *42 D3 headland* Florida, SE USA
San Blas, Cordillera de *53 G4 mountain range* NE Panama
San Carlos *52 D4* Río San Juan, S Nicaragua
San Carlos *48 B2* Arizona, SW USA
San Carlos see Quesada, Costa Rica
San Carlos de Ancud see Ancud
San Carlos de Bariloche *65 B5* Río Negro, SW Argentina
San Carlos del Zulia *58 C2* Zulia, W Venezuela
San Clemente Island *47 B8 island* Channel Islands, California, W USA
San Cristóbal *58 C2* Táchira, W Venezuela
San Cristóbal *144 C4 var.* Makira. *island* SE Solomon Islands
San Cristóbal see San Cristóbal de Las Casas
San Cristóbal de Las Casas *51 G5 var.* San Cristóbal. Chiapas, SE Mexico
San Cristóbal, Isla *60 B5 var.* Chatham Island. *island* Galapagos Islands, Ecuador, E Pacific Ocean
Sancti Spíritus *54 B2* Sancti Spíritus, C Cuba
Sandakan *138 D3* Sabah, East Malaysia
Sandalwood Island see Sumba, Pulau
Sandanski *114 C3 prev.* Sveti Vrach. Blagoevgrad, SW Bulgaria
Sanday *88 D2 island* NE Scotland, United Kingdom
Sanders *48 C2* Arizona, SW USA
Sand Hills *44 D3 mountain range* Nebraska, C USA
San Diego *47 C8* California, W USA
Sandnes *85 A6* Rogaland, S Norway
Sandomierz *98 D4 Rus.* Sandomir. Świętokrzyskie, C Poland

Sandomir see Sandomierz
Sandoway see Thandwe
Sandpoint *46 C1* Idaho, NW USA
Sand Springs *49 G1* Oklahoma, C USA
Sandusky *40 D3.* Ohio, N USA
Sandvika *85 A6* Akershus, S Norway
Sandviken *85 C6* Gävleborg, C Sweden
Sandwich Island see Efate
Sandwich Islands see Hawaiian Islands
Sandy Bay *93 H5* Saskatchewan, C Canada
Sandy City *44 B4* Utah, W USA
Sandy Lake *38 B3 lake* Ontario, C Canada
San Esteban *52 D2* Olancho, C Honduras
San Eugenio/San Eugenio del Cuareim see Artigas
San Felipe *58 D1* Yaracuy, NW Venezuela
San Felipe de Puerto Plata see Puerto Plata
San Félix, Isla *57 A5 Eng.* San Felix Island. *island* W Chile
San Felix Island see San Félix, Isla
San Fernando *92 C5 prev.* Isla de León. Andalucía, S Spain
San Fernando *55 H5* Trinidad, Trinidad and Tobago
San Fernando *46 D1* California, W USA
San Fernando *58 D2 var.* San Fernando de Apure. Apure, C Venezuela
San Fernando de Apure see San Fernando
San Fernando del Valle de Catamarca *64 C3 var.* Catamarca. Catamarca, NW Argentina
San Fernando de Monte Cristi see Monte Cristi
San Francisco *47 B6* California, W USA
San Francisco del Oro *50 C2* Chihuahua, N Mexico
San Francisco de Macorís *55 E3* C Dominican Republic
San Fructuoso see Tacuarembó
San Gabriel *60 B1* Carchi, N Ecuador
San Gabriel Mountains *46 E1 mountain range* California, USA
Sangihe, Kepulauan see Sangir, Kepulauan
Sangir, Kepulauan *139 F3 var.* Kepulauan Sangihe. *island group* N Indonesia
Sāngli *132 B1* Mahārāshtra, W India
Sangmélima *77 B5* Sud, S Cameroon
Sangre de Cristo Mountains *48 D1 mountain range* Colorado/New Mexico, C USA
San Ignacio *52 B1 prev.* Cayo, El Cayo. Cayo, W Belize
San Ignacio *61 F3* Beni, N Bolivia
San Ignacio *50 B2* Baja California Sur, NW Mexico
San Joaquin Valley *47 B7 valley* California, W USA
San Jorge, Gulf of *65 C6 var.* Gulf of San Jorge. *gulf* S Argentina
San Jorge, Gulf of see San Jorge, Golfo
San José *53 E4 country capital* (Costa Rica) (Costa Rica) San José, C Costa Rica
San José *61 G3 var.* San José de Chiquitos. Santa Cruz, E Bolivia
San José *52 B3 var.* Puerto San José. Escuintla, S Guatemala
San José *47 B6* California, W USA
San José see San José del Guaviare, Colombia
San José de Chiquitos see San José
San José de Cúcuta see Cúcuta
San José del Guaviare *58 C4 var.* San José. Guaviare, S Colombia
San Juan *64 B3* San Juan, W Argentina
San Juan *55 F3 dependent territory capital* (Puerto Rico) NE Puerto Rico
San Juan see San Juan de los Morros
San Juan Bautista *64 D3* Misiones, S Paraguay
San Juan Bautista see Villahermosa
San Juan Bautista Tuxtepec see Tuxtepec
San Juan de Alicante *93 F4* País Valenciano, E Spain
San Juan del Norte *53 E4 var.* Greytown. Río San Juan, SE Nicaragua
San Juan de los Morros *58 D2 var.* San Juan. Guárico, N Venezuela
San Juanito, Isla *50 C4 island* C Mexico
San Juan Mountains *48 D1 mountain range* Colorado, C USA

San Juan, Río *53 E4 river* Costa Rica/ Nicaragua
San Juan River *48 C1 river* Colorado/ Utah, W USA
San Julián see Puerto San Julián
Sankt-Bartholomäi see Palamuse
Sankt Gallen *95 B7 var.* St. Gallen, *Eng.* Saint Gall, *Fr.* St-Gall. Sankt Gallen, NE Switzerland
Sankt-Georgen see Sfântu Gheorghe
Sankt-Jakobi see Pärnu-Jaagupi, Pärnumaa, Estonia
Sankt Martin see Martin
Sankt Moritz see St. Moritz
Sankt-Peterburg *110 B4 prev.* Leningrad, Petrograd, *Eng.* Saint Petersburg, *Fin.* Pietari. Leningradskaya Oblast', NW Russian Federation
Sankt Pölten *95 E6* Niederösterreich, N Austria
Sankt Veit am Flaum see Rijeka
Sankuru *77 D6 river* C Dem. Rep. Congo
Şanlıurfa *117 E4 prev.* Sanli Urfa, Urfa; *anc.* Edessa. Şanlıurfa, S Turkey
Sanli Urfa see Şanlıurfa
San Lorenzo *61 G5* Tarija, S Bolivia
San Lorenzo *60 A1* Esmeraldas, N Ecuador
San Lorenzo, Isla *60 C4 island* W Peru
Sanlúcar de Barrameda *92 C5* Andalucía, S Spain
San Luis *64 C4* San Luis, C Argentina
San Luis *52 B2* Petén, NE Guatemala
San Luis *50 A1 var.* San Luis Río Colorado. Sonora, NW Mexico
San Luis Obispo *47 B7* California, W USA
San Luis Potosí *51 E3* San Luis Potosí, C Mexico
San Luis Río Colorado see San Luis
San Marcos *52 A2* San Marcos, W Guatemala
San Marcos *49 G4* Texas, SW USA
San Marcos de Arica see Arica
San Marino *96 E1 country capital* (San Marino) (San Marino) C San Marino
San Marino *96 D1 off.* Republic of San Marino. *country* S Europe

SAN MARINO
Southern Europe

Official name Republic of San Marino
Formation 1631 / 1631
Capital San Marino
Population 29,615 / 1234 people per sq mile (485 people per sq km) / 89%
Total area 23.6 sq. miles (61 sq. km)
Languages Italian*
Religions Roman Catholic 93%, Other and nonreligious 7%
Ethnic mix Sammarinese 88%, Italian 10%, Other 2%
Government Parliamentary system
Currency Euro = 100 cents
Literacy rate 99%
Calorie consumption Not available

San Marino, Republic of see San Marino
San Martín *154 A2 Argentinian research station* Antarctica
San Mateo *59 E2* Anzoátegui, NE Venezuela
San Matías *61 H3* Santa Cruz, E Bolivia
San Matías, Gulf of *65 C5 var.* Gulf of San Matías. *gulf* E Argentina
San Matías, Gulf of see San Matías, Golfo
Sanmenxia *128 C4 var.* Shan Xian. Henan, C China
Sânnicolaul Mare see Sânnicolau Mare
San Miguel *52 C3* San Miguel, SE El Salvador
San Miguel *50 D2* Coahuila, N Mexico
San Miguel de Ibarra see Ibarra
San Miguel de Tucumán *64 C3 var.* Tucumán. Tucumán, N Argentina
San Miguelito *53 G4* Panamá, C Panama
San Miguel, Río *61 G3 river* E Bolivia
San Murezzan see St. Moritz
Sannär see Sennar
Sânnicolaul-Mare see Sânnicolau Mare
Sânnicolau Mare *108 A3 var.* Sânnicolaul-Mare, *Hung.* Nagyszentmiklós; *prev.* Sânmiclăuş Mare, Sînnicolau Mare. Timiş, W Romania

Sanok *99 E5* Podkarpackie, SE Poland
San Pablo *61 F5* Potosí, S Bolivia
San Pedro *52 C1* Corozal, NE Belize
San-Pédro *74 D5* S Côte d'Ivoire
San Pedro *50 D3 var.* San Pedro de las Colonias. Coahuila, NE Mexico
San Pedro de la Cueva *50 C2* Sonora, NW Mexico
San Pedro de las Colonias see San Pedro
San Pedro de Lloc *60 B3* La Libertad, NW Peru
San Pedro Mártir, Sierra *50 A1 mountain range* NW Mexico
San Pedro Sula *52 C2* Cortés, NW Honduras
San Rafael *64 B4* Mendoza, W Argentina
San Rafael Mountains *47 C7 mountain range* California, W USA
San Ramón de la Nueva Orán *64 C2* Salta, N Argentina
San Remo *96 A3* Liguria, NW Italy
San Salvador *52 B3 country capital* (El Salvador) (El Salvador) San Salvador, SW El Salvador
San Salvador *54 D2 prev.* Watlings Island. *island* E Bahamas
San Salvador de Jujuy *64 C2 var.* Jujuy. Jujuy, N Argentina
San Salvador, Isla *60 A4 island* Ecuador
Sansanné-Mango *75 E4 var.* Mango. N Togo
Sansepolcro *96 C3* Toscana, C Italy
San Severo *97 D5* Puglia, SE Italy
Santa Ana *61 F3* Beni, N Bolivia
Santa Ana *52 B3* Santa Ana, NW El Salvador
Santa Ana *46 D2* California, W USA
Santa Ana de Coro see Coro
Santa Ana Mountains *46 E2 mountain range* California, W USA
Santa Barbara *50 C2* Chihuahua, N Mexico
Santa Barbara *47 C7* California, W USA
Santa Catalina Island *47 B8 island* Channel Islands, California, W USA
Santa Catarina *63 E5 off.* Estado de Santa Catarina. *region* S Brazil
Santa Catarina *63 E5 off.* Estado de Santa Catarina. *state* S Brazil
Santa Catarina, Estado de see Santa Catarina
Santa Clara *54 B2* Villa Clara, C Cuba
Santa Clarita *46 D1* California, USA
Santa Comba *92 B1* Galicia, NW Spain
Santa Cruz *76 E2* São Tomé, S Sao Tome and Principe, Africa
Santa Cruz *47 B6* California, W USA
Santa Cruz *61 G4 department* E Bolivia
Santa Cruz Barillas see Barillas
Santa Cruz del Quiché *52 B2* Quiché, W Guatemala
Santa Cruz de Tenerife *70 A3* Tenerife, Islas Canarias, Spain, NE Atlantic Ocean
Santa Cruz, Isla *60 B5 var.* Indefatigable Island, Isla Chávez. *island* Galapagos Islands, Ecuador, E Pacific Ocean
Santa Cruz Islands *144 D3 island group* E Solomon Islands
Santa Cruz, Río *65 B7 river* S Argentina
Santa Elena *52 B1* Cayo, W Belize
Santa Fe *64 C4* Santa Fe, C Argentina
Santa Fe *48 D1 state capital* New Mexico, SW USA
Santa Fe see Bogotá
Santa Fe de Bogotá see Bogotá
Santa Genoveva *50 B3* Durango, NW Mexico
Santa Isabel *144 C3 var.* Bughotu. *island* N Solomon Islands
Santa Isabel see Malabo
Santa Lucia Range *47 B7 mountain range* California, W USA
Santa Margarita, Isla *50 B3 island* NW Mexico
Santa Maria *63 E5* Rio Grande do Sul, S Brazil
Santa Maria *47 B7* California, USA
Santa Maria *92 A5 island* Azores, Portugal, NE Atlantic Ocean
Santa Maria del Buen Aire see Buenos Aires
Santa María, Isla *60 A5 var.* Isla Floreana, Charles Island. *island* Galapagos Islands, Ecuador, E Pacific Ocean

Santa Marta *58 B1* Magdalena, N Colombia
Santa Maura *see* Lefkáda
Santa Monica *46 D1* California, W USA
Santana *76 E2* São Tomé, C Sao Tome and Principe, Africa
Santander *92 D1* Cantabria, N Spain
Santarém *63 E2* N Brazil
Santarém *92 B3* anc. Scalabis. Santarém, W Portugal
Santa Rosa *64 C4* La Pampa, C Argentina
Santa Rosa *see* Santa Rosa de Copán
Santa Rosa de Copán *52 C2* var. Santa Rosa. Copán, W Honduras
Santa Rosa Island *47 B8* island California, W USA
Sant Carles de la Rápida *see* Sant Carles de la Ràpita
Sant Carles de la Ràpita *93 F3* var. Sant Carles de la Rápida. Cataluña, NE Spain
Santiago *64 B4* var. Gran Santiago. country capital (Chile) (Chile) Santiago, C Chile
Santiago *55 E3* var. Santiago de los Caballeros. N Dominican Republic
Santiago *53 F5* Veraguas, S Panama
Santiago *92 B1* var. Santiago de Compostela; Eng. Compostella; anc. Campus Stellae. Galicia, NW Spain
Santiago *74 A3* var. São Tiago. island Ilhas de Sotavento, S Cape Verde
Santiago *see* Santiago de Cuba, Cuba
Santiago de Compostela *see* Santiago
Santiago de Cuba *54 C3* var. Santiago. Santiago de Cuba, E Cuba
Santiago de Guayaquil *see* Guayaquil
Santiago del Estero *64 C3* Santiago del Estero, C Argentina
Santiago de los Caballeros *see* Santiago, Dominican Republic
Santiago de los Caballeros *see* Ciudad de Guatemala, Guatemala
Santiago Pinotepa Nacional *see* Pinotepa Nacional
Santiago, Río *60 B2* river N Peru
Santi Quaranta *see* Sarandë
Santissima Trinidad *see* Chilung
Sant Julià de Lòria *91 A8* Sant Julià de Lòria, SW Andorra Europe
Santo *see* Espíritu Santo
Santo Antão *74 A3* island Ilhas de Barlavento, N Cape Verde
Santo António *76 E1* Príncipe, N Sao Tome and Principe, Africa
Santo Domingo *55 D3* prev. Ciudad Trujillo. country capital (Dominican Republic) (Dominican Republic) SE Dominican Republic
Santo Domingo de los Colorados *60 B1* Pichincha, NW Ecuador
Santo Domingo Tehuantepec *see* Tehuantepec
Santo Tomé de Guayana *see* Ciudad Guayana
Santos *63 F4* São Paulo, S Brazil
Santos Plateau *57 D5* undersea plateau SW Atlantic Ocean
Santo Tomé *64 D3* Corrientes, NE Argentina
Santo Tomé de Guayana *see* Ciudad Guayana
San Valentín, Cerro *65 A6* mountain S Chile
San Vicente *52 C3* San Vicente, C El Salvador
São Francisco, Rio *63 F3* river E Brazil
Sao Hill *73 C7* Iringa, S Tanzania
São João da Madeira *92 B2* Aveiro, N Portugal
São Jorge *92 A5* island Azores, Portugal, NE Atlantic Ocean
São Luís *63 F2* state capital Maranhão, NE Brazil
São Mandol *see* São Manuel, Rio
São Manuel, Rio *63 E3* var. São Mandol, Teles Pirés. river C Brazil
São Marcos, Baía de *63 F1* bay N Brazil
São Miguel *92 A5* island Azores, Portugal, NE Atlantic Ocean
Saona, Isla *55 E3* island SE Dominican Republic
Saône *91 D5* river E France
São Nicolau *74 A3* Eng. Saint Nicholas. island Ilhas de Barlavento, N Cape Verde

São Paulo *63 E4* state capital São Paulo, S Brazil
São Paulo *63 E4* off. Estado de São Paulo. state S Brazil
São Paulo *63 E4* off. Estado de São Paulo. region S Brazil
São Paulo de Loanda *see* Luanda
3ão Paulo, Estado de *see* São Paulo
São Pedro do Rio Grande do Sul *see* Rio Grande
São Roque, Cabo de *63 G2* headland E Brazil
São Salvador *see* Salvador, Brazil
São Salvador/São Salvador do Congo *see* M'Banza Congo, Angola
São Tiago *see* Santiago
São Tomé *77 A5* country capital (Sao Tome and Principe) (São Tome and Principe) São Tome and Principe Principe
São Tomé *76 E2* Eng. Saint Thomas. island S Sao Tome and Principe
Sao Tome and Principe *76 D1* off. Democratic Republic of Sao Tome and Principe. country E Atlantic Ocean

SÃO TOMÉ & PRÍNCIPE
West Africa

Official name The Democratic Republic of Sao Tome and Principe
Formation 1975 / 1975
Capital São Tomé
Population 199,579 / 538 people per sq mile (208 people per sq km) / 38%
Total area 386 sq. miles (1001 sq. km)
Languages Portuguese*, Portuguese Creole
Religions Roman Catholic 84%, Other 16%
Ethnic mix Black 90%, Portuguese and Creole 10%
Government Presidential system
Currency Dobra = 100 céntimos
Literacy rate 83%
Calorie consumption 2460 calories

Sao Tome and Principe, Democratic Republic of *see* Sao Tome and Principe
São Tomé, Pico de *76 D2* mountain São Tomé, C Sao Tome and Principe, Africa
São Vicente *74 A3* Eng. Saint Vincent. island Ilhas de Barlavento, N Cape Verde
São Vicente, Cabo de *92 B5* Eng. Cape Saint Vincent, Port. Cabode São Vicente. cape S Portugal
São Vicente, Cabo de *see* São Vicente, Cabo de
Sápai *see* Sápes
Sapele *75 F5* Delta, S Nigeria
Sápes *104 D3* var. Sápai. Anatolikí Makedonía kai Thráki, NE Greece
Sápir *119 B7* prev. Sappir. Southern, S Israel
Sa Pobla *93 G3* Mallorca, Spain, W Mediterranean Sea
Sappir *see* Sapir
Sapporo *130 D2* Hokkaidō, NE Japan
Sapri *97 D6* Campania, S Italy
Sapulpa *49 G1* Oklahoma, C USA
Saqqez *120 C2* var. Saghez, Sakiz, Saqqiz. Kordestān, NW Iran
Saqqiz *see* Saqqez
Sara Buri *137 C5* var. Saraburi. Saraburi, C Thailand
Saraburi *see* Sara Buri
Saragossa *see* Zaragoza
Saragt *see* Sarahs
Saraguro *60 B2* Loja, S Ecuador
Sarahs *122 D3* var. Saragt, Rus. Serakhs. Ahal Welaýaty, S Turkmenistan
Sarajevo *100 C4* country capital (Bosnia and Herzegovina) (Bosnia and Herzegovina) Federacija Bosna I Herzegovina, SE Bosnia and Herzegovina
Sarakhs *120 E2* Khorāsān-Razavī, NE Iran
Saraktash *111 D6* Orenburgskaya Oblast', W Russian Federation
Saran' *114 C4* Kaz. Saran. Karaganda, C Kazakhstan
Saranda *see* Sarandë
Sarandë *101 C7* var. Saranda, It. Porto Edda; prev. Santi Quaranta. Vlorë, S Albania

Saransk *111 C5* Respublika Mordoviya, W Russian Federation
Sarasota *43 E4* Florida, SE USA
Saratov *114 B3* Saratovskaya Oblast', W Russian Federation
Saravan/Saravane *see* Salavan
Sarawak *138 D3* state East Malaysia
Sarawak *see* Kuching
Sarcelles *90 D1* Val-d'Oise, Île-de-France, N France Europe
Sardinia *97 A5* Eng. Sardinia. island Italy, C Mediterranean Sea
Sardinia *see* Sardegna
Sarera, Teluk *see* Cenderawasih, Teluk
Sargasso Sea *66 B4* sea W Atlantic Ocean
Sargodha *134 C2* Punjab, NE Pakistan
Sarh *76 C4* prev. Fort-Archambault. Moyen-Chari, S Chad
Sārī *120 D2* var. Sari, Sāri. Māzandarān, N Iran
Saría *105 E7* island SE Greece
Sarıkamış *117 F3* Kars, NE Turkey
Sarikol Range *123 G3* Rus. Sarykol'skiy Khrebet. mountain range China/Tajikistan
Sark *89 D8* Fr. Sercq. island Channel Islands
Şarkışla *116 D3* Sivas, C Turkey
Sarmiento *65 B6* Chubut, S Argentina
Sarnia *38 C5* Ontario, S Canada
Sarny *108 C1* Rivnens'ka Oblast', NW Ukraine
Sarochyna *107 D5* Rus. Sorochino. Vitsyebskaya Voblasts', N Belarus
Sarov *111 C5* prev. Sarova. Respublika Mordoviya, SW Russian Federation
Sarova *see* Sarov
Sarpsborg *85 B6* Østfold, S Norway
Sarrebruck *see* Saarbrücken
Sartène *91 E7* Corse, France, C Mediterranean Sea
Sarthe *90 B4* river N France
Sárti *104 C4* Kentrikí Makedonía, N Greece
Saruhan *see* Manisa
Saryarqa *see* Kazakhskiy Melkosopochnik
Sarykol'skiy Khrebet *see* Sarikol Range
Sary-Tash *123 F2* Oshskaya Oblast', SW Kyrgyzstan
Saryyesik-Atyrau, Peski *123 G1* desert E Kazakhstan
Sasebo *131 A7* Nagasaki, Kyūshū, SW Japan
Saskatchewan *37 F5* province SW Canada
Saskatchewan *37 F5* river Manitoba/ Saskatchewan, C Canada
Saskatoon *37 F5* Saskatchewan, S Canada
Sasovo *111 B5* Ryazanskaya Oblast', W Russian Federation
Sassandra *74 D5* S Côte d'Ivoire
Sassandra *74 D5* var. Ibo, Sassandra Fleuve. river S Côte d'Ivoire
Sassandra Fleuve *see* Sassandra
Sassari *97 A5* Sardegna, Italy, C Mediterranean Sea
Sassenheim *86 C3* Zuid-Holland, W Netherlands
Sassnitz *94 D2* Mecklenburg-Vorpommern, NE Germany
Sathmar *see* Satu Mare
Sátoraljaújhely *99 D6* Borsod-Abaúj-Zemplén, NE Hungary
Satpura Range *134 D4* mountain range C India
Satsuma-Sendai *see* Sendai
Satsuman-shotō *130 A3* island group Nansei-shotō, SW Japan Asia
Sattanen *84 D3* Lappi, NE Finland
Satu Mare *108 B3* Ger. Sathmar, Hung. Szatmárnémeti. Satu Mare, NW Romania
Sau *see* Sava
Saudi Arabia *121 B5* off. Kingdom of Saudi Arabia, Ar. Al 'Arabīyah as Su'ūdīyah, Ar. Al Mamlakah al 'Arabīyah as Su'ūdīyah. country SW Asia

SAUDI ARABIA
Southwest Asia

Official name Kingdom of Saudi Arabia
Formation 1932 / 1932
Capital Riyadh
Population 25.8 million / 32 people per sq mile (12 people per sq km) / 88%

SAUDI ARABIA
(continued)

Total area 756,981 sq. miles (1,960,582 sq. km)
Languages Arabic*
Religions Sunni Muslim 85%, Shi'a Muslim 15%
Ethnic mix Arab 90%, Afro-Asian 10%
Government Monarchy
Currency Saudi riyal = 100 halalat
Literacy rate 79%
Calorie consumption 2844 calories

Saudi Arabia, Kingdom of *see* Saudi Arabia
Sauer *see* Sûre
Saugor *see* Sāgar
Saulkrasti *106 C3* Rīga, C Latvia
Sault Sainte Marie *40 C1* Michigan, N USA
Sault Sainte Marie *38 C4* Michigan, N USA
Sault Ste. Marie *38 C4* Ontario, S Canada
Saumur *90 B4* Maine-et-Loire, NW France
Saurimo *78 C1* Port. Henrique de Carvalho, Vila Henrique de Carvalho. Lunda Sul, NE Angola
Sava *107 E6* Mahilyowskaya Voblasts', E Belarus
Savá *52 D2* Colón, N Honduras
Savai'i *145 E4* island NW Samoa
Savannah *43 E2* Georgia, SE USA
Savannah River *43 E2* river Georgia/ South Carolina, SE USA
Savannakhét *see* Khanthabouli
Savanna-La-Mar *54 A5* W Jamaica
Savaria *see* Szombathely
Save *100 B3* Eng. Save, Ger. Sau, Hung. Száva. river SE Europe
Save *see* Sava
Save, Rio *79 E3* var. Sabi. river Mozambique/Zimbabwe
Saverne *90 E3* var. Zabern; anc. Tres Tabernae. Bas-Rhin, NE France
Savigliano *96 A2* Piemonte, NW Italy
Savigsivik *see* Savissivik
Savinski *see* Savinskiy
Savinskiy *110 C3* var. Savinski. Arkhangel'skaya Oblast', NW Russian Federation
Savissivik *82 D1* var. Savigsivik. Avannaarsua, N Greenland
Savoie *91 D5* cultural region E France
Savona *96 A2* Liguria, NW Italy
Savu Sea *139 E5* Ind. Laut Sawu. sea S Indonesia
Sawakin *see* Suakin
Sawdiri *see* Sodiri
Sawhāj *72 B2* var. Sohâg var. Sawhāj, Eng. Egypt** C Egypt
Sawhaj *see* Sawhāj
Şawqirah *121 D6* var. Suqrah. S Oman
Sawu, Laut *see* Savu Sea
Saxe *see* Sachsen
Saxony *see* Sachsen
Sayaboury *see* Xaignabouli
Sayanskiy Khrebet *112 D3* mountain range S Russian Federation
Saýat *122 D3* Rus. Sayat. Lebap Welaýaty, E Turkmenistan
Sayaxché *52 B2* Petén, N Guatemala
Şaydā/Sayida *see* Saïda
Sayhūt *121 D6* E Yemen
Saynshand *127 E2* Dornogovi, SE Mongolia
Sayre *41 E3* Pennsylvania, NE USA
Say'ūn *121 C6* var. Saywūn. C Yemen
Saywūn *see* Say'ūn
Scalabis *see* Santarém
Scandinavia *66 D2* geophysical region NW Europe
Scarborough *89 D5* N England, United Kingdom
Scarpanto *see* Kárpathos
Scebeli *see* Shebeli
Schaan *94 E1* W Liechtenstein Europe
Schaerbeek *87 C6* Brussels, C Belgium
Schaffhausen *95 B7* Fr. Schaffhouse. Schaffhausen, N Switzerland
Schaffhouse *see* Schaffhausen
Schagen *86 C2* Noord-Holland, NW Netherlands
Schaulen *see* Šiauliai
Schebschi Mountains *see* Shebshi Mountains

Scheessel *94 B3* Niedersachsen, NW Germany
Schefferville *39 E2* Québec, E Canada
Schelde *see* Scheldt
Scheldt *87 B5* *Dut.* Schelde, *Fr.* Escaut. *river* W Europe
Schell Creek Range *47 D5* *mountain range* Nevada, W USA
Schenectady *41 F3* New York, NE USA
Schertz *49 G4* Texas, SW USA
Schiermonnikoog *86 D1* Fris. Skiermûntseach. *island* Waddeneilanden, N Netherlands
Schijndel *86 D4* Noord-Brabant, S Netherlands
Schil *see* Jiu
Schiltigheim *90 E3* Bas-Rhin, NE France
Schivelbein *see* Świdwin
Schleswig *94 B2* Schleswig-Holstein, N Germany
Schleswig-Holstein *94 B2* *state* N Germany
Schlettstadt *see* Sélestat
Schlochau *see* Człuchów
Schneekoppe *see* Sněžka
Schneidemühl *see* Piła
Schoden *see* Skuodas
Schönebeck *94 C4* Sachsen-Anhalt, C Germany
Schönlanke *see* Trzcianka
Schooten *see* Schoten
Schoten *87 C5* *var.* Schooten. Antwerpen, N Belgium
Schouwen *86 B4* *island* SW Netherlands
Schwabenalb *see* Schwäbische Alb
Schwäbische Alb *95 B6* *var.* Schwabenalb, *Eng.* Swabian Jura. *mountain range* S Germany
Schwandorf *95 C5* Bayern, SE Germany
Schwaz *95 C7* Tirol, W Austria
Schweidnitz *see* Świdnica
Schweinfurt *95 B5* Bayern, SE Germany
Schweiz *see* Switzerland
Schwerin *94 C3* Mecklenburg-Vorpommern, N Germany
Schwertberg *see* Świecie
Schwiebus *see* Świebodzin
Schwyz *95 B7* *var.* Schwiz. Schwyz, C Switzerland
Schyl *see* Jiu
Scio *see* Chíos
Scoresby Sound/Scoresbysund *see* Ittoqqortoormiit
Scoresby Sund *see* Kangertittivaq
Scotia Sea *57 C8* *sea* SW Atlantic Ocean
Scotland *88 C3* *cultural region* Scotland, U K
Scott Base *154 B4* NZ research station Antarctica
Scott Island *154 B5* *island* Antarctica
Scottsbluff *44 D3* Nebraska, C USA
Scottsboro *42 D1* Alabama, S USA
Scottsdale *48 B2* Arizona, SW USA
Scranton *41 F3* Pennsylvania, NE USA
Scrobesbyrig' *see* Shrewsbury
Scupi *see* Skopje
Scutari *see* Shkodër
Scutari, Lake *101 C5* Alb. Liqeni i Shkodrës, SCr. Skadarsko Jezero. *lake* Albania/Montenegro
Scyros *see* Skýros
Searcy *42 B1* Arkansas, C USA
Seattle *46 B2* Washington, NW USA
Sébaco *52 D3* Matagalpa, W Nicaragua
Sebaste/Sebastia *see* Sivas
Sebastián Vizcaíno, Bahía *50 A2* *bay* NW Mexico
Sebastopol *see* Sevastopol'
Sebenico *see* Šibenik
Sechura, Bahía de *60 A3* *bay* NW Peru
Secunderābād *134 D5* *var.* Sikandarabad. Andhra Pradesh, C India
Sedan *90 D3* Ardennes, N France
Seddon *151 D5* Marlborough, South Island, New Zealand
Seddonville *151 C5* West Coast, South Island, New Zealand
Sédhiou *74 B3* SW Senegal
Sedlez *see* Siedlce
Sedona *48 B2* Arizona, SW USA
Sedunum *see* Sion
Seeland *see* Sjælland
Seenu Atoll *see* Addu Atoll
Seesen *94 B4* Niedersachsen, C Germany
Segestica *see* Sisak

Segezha *110 B3* Respublika Kareliya, NW Russian Federation
Seghedin *see* Szeged
Segna *see* Senj
Segodunum *see* Rodez
Ségou *74 D3* *var.* Segu. Ségou, C Mali
Segovia *92 D2* Castilla-León, C Spain
Segoviao Wangkí *see* Coco, Río
Segu *see* Ségou
Séguédine *75 H2* Agadez, NE Niger
Seguin *49 G4* Texas, SW USA
Segura *93 E4* *river* S Spain
Seinäjoki *85 D5* Swe. Östermyra. Länsi-Suomi, W Finland
Seine *90 D1* *river* N France
Seine, Baie de la *90 B3* *bay* N France
Sekondi *see* Sekondi-Takoradi
Sekondi-Takoradi *75 E5* *var.* Sekondi. S Ghana
Selânik *see* Thessaloníki
Selenga *127 E1* Mong. Selenge Mörön. *river* Mongolia/Russian Federation
Selenge Mörön *see* Selenga
Sélestat *90 E4* Ger. Schlettstadt. Bas-Rhin, NE France
Seleucia *see* Silifke
Selfoss *83 E5* Sudhurland, SW Iceland
Sélibabi *74 C3* *var.* Sélibaby. Guidimaka, S Mauritania
Sélibaby *see* Sélibabi
Selma *47 C6* California, W USA
Selway River *46 D2* *river* Idaho, NW USA North America
Selwyn Range *148 B3* *mountain range* Queensland, C Australia
Selzaete *see* Zelzate
Semarang *138 C5* *var.* Samarang. Jawa, C Indonesia
Sembé *77 B5* Sangha, NW Congo
Semendria *see* Smederevo
Semey *see* Semipalatinsk
Semezhevo *see* Syemyezhava
Seminole *49 E3* Texas, SW USA
Seminole, Lake *42 D3* *reservoir* Florida/Georgia, SE USA
Semipalatinsk *114 D4* Kaz. Semey. Vostochnyy Kazakhstan, E Kazakhstan
Semnān *120 D3* *var.* Samnān. Semnān, N Iran
Semois *87 C8* *river* SE Belgium
Sendai *131 A8* *var.* Satsuma-Sendai. Kagoshima, Kyūshū, SW Japan
Sendai *130 D4* Miyagi, Honshū, C Japan
Sendai-wan *130 D4* *bay* E Japan
Senec *99 C6* Ger. Wartberg, Hung. Szenc; *prev.* Szempcz. Bratislavský Kraj, W Slovakia
Senegal *74 B3* *off.* Republic of Senegal, Fr. Sénégal. *country* W Africa

SENEGAL
West Africa

Official name Republic of Senegal
Formation 1960 / 1960
Capital Dakar
Population 12.2 million / 164 people per sq mile (63 people per sq km) / 50%
Total area 75,749 sq. miles (196,190 sq. km)
Languages French*, Wolof, Pulaar, Serer, Diola, Mandinka, Malinke, Soninke
Religions Sunni Muslim 90%, Christian (mainly Roman Catholic) 5%, Traditional beliefs 5%
Ethnic mix Wolof 43%, Serer 15%, Other 14%, Peul 14%, Toucouleur 9%, Diola 5%
Government Presidential system
Currency CFA franc = 100 centimes
Literacy rate 39%
Calorie consumption 2279 calories

Senegal *74 C3* Fr. Sénégal. *river* W Africa
Senegal, Republic of *see* Senegal
Senftenberg *94 D4* Brandenburg, E Germany
Senia *see* Senj
Senica *99 C6* Ger. Senitz, Hung. Szenice. Trnavský Kraj, W Slovakia
Seniça *see* Sjenica
Senitz *see* Senica
Senj *100 A3* Ger. Zengg, It. Segna; *anc.* Senia. Lika-Senj, NW Croatia
Senja *84 C2* *prev.* Senjen. *island* N Norway
Senjen *see* Senja

Senkaku-shoto *130 A3* *island group* SW Japan
Senlis *90 C3* Oise, N France
Sennar *72 C4* *var.* Sannâr. Sinnar, C Sudan
Senones *see* Sens
Sens *90 C3* *anc.* Agendicum, Senones. Yonne, C France
Sensburg *see* Mragowo
Sên, Stœng *137 D5* *river* C Cambodia
Senta *100 D3* Hung. Zenta. Vojvodina, N Serbia
Seo de Urgel *see* La See d'Urgel
Seoul *see* Sŏul
Sępólno *see* Sępólno
Sept-Îles *39 E3* Québec, SE Canada
Seraing *87 D6* Liège, E Belgium
Serakhs *see* Sarahs
Seram, Laut *see* Ceram Sea
Pulau Seram *139 F4* *var.* Serang, Eng. Ceram. *island* Maluku, E Indonesia
Serang *138 C5* Jawa, C Indonesia
Serang *see* Seram, Pulau
Serasan, Selat *138 C3* *strait* Indonesia/Malaysia
Serbia *100 D4* *off.* Federal Republic of Serbia; *prev.* Yugoslavia, SCr. Jugoslavija. *country* SE Europe

SERBIA
Southeast Europe

Official name Republic of Serbia
Formation 2006 / 2008
Capital Belgrade
Population 8.1 million / 271 people per sq mile (105 people per sq km) / 52%
Total area 29,905 sq miles (77,453 sq km)
Languages Serbian*, Hungarian (Magyar)
Religions Orthodox Christian 85%, Other 6%, Roman Catholic 6%, Muslim 3%
Ethnic mix Serb 83%, Other 10%, Magyar 4%, Bosniak 2%, Roma 1%
Government Parliamentary system
Currency Dinar = 100 para
Literacy rate 96%
Calorie consumption 2678 calories

Serbia, Federal Republic of *see* Serbia
Sercq *see* Sark
Serdar *122 C2* *prev.* Rus. Gyzyrlabat, Kizyl-Arvat. Balkan Welaýaty, W Turkmenistan
Serdica *see* Sofiya
Serdobol' *see* Sortavala
Serenje *78 D2* Central, E Zambia
Seres *see* Sérres
Seret/Sereth *see* Siret
Serhetabat *122 D4* *prev.* Rus. Gushgy, Kushka. Mary Welaýaty, S Turkmenistan
Sérifos *105 C6* *anc.* Seriphos. *island* Kykládes, Greece, Aegean Sea
Seriphos *see* Sérifos
Serov *114 C3* Sverdlovskaya Oblast', C Russian Federation
Serowe *78 D3* Central, SE Botswana
Serpa Pinto *see* Menongue
Serpent's Mouth, The *59 F2* Sp. Boca de la Serpiente. *strait* Trinidad and Tobago/Venezuela
Serpiente, Boca de la *see* Serpent's Mouth, The
Serpukhov *111 B5* Moskovskaya Oblast', W Russian Federation
Sérrai *see* Sérres
Serrana, Cayo de *53 F2* *island group* NW Colombia South America
Serranilla, Cayo de *53 F2* *island group* NW Colombia South America Caribbean Sea
Serravalle *96 E1* N San Marino
Sérres *104 C3* *var.* Seres; *prev.* Sérrai. Kentrikí Makedonía, NE Greece
Sesdlets *see* Siedlce
Sesto San Giovanni *96 B2* Lombardia, N Italy
Sesvete *100 B2* Zagreb, N Croatia
Setabis *see* Xàtiva
Sète *91 C6* *prev.* Cette. Hérault, S France
Setesdal *85 A6* *valley* S Norway
Sétif *71 E2* *var.* Stif. N Algeria
Setté Cama *77 A6* Ogooué-Maritime, SW Gabon

Setúbal *92 B4* Eng. Saint Ubes, Saint Yves. Setúbal, W Portugal
Setúbal, Baía de *92 B4* *bay* W Portugal
Seul, Lac *38 B3* *lake* Ontario, S Canada
Sevan *117 G2* C Armenia
Sevan, Lake *117 G3* Eng. Lake Sevan, Rus. Ozero Sevan. *lake* E Armenia
Sevan, Lake/Sevan, Ozero *see* Sevana Lich
Sevastopol' *109 F5* Eng. Sebastopol. Respublika Krym, S Ukraine
Severn *38 B2* *river* Ontario, S Canada
Severn *89 D6* Wel. Hafren. *river* England/Wales, United Kingdom
Severnaya Zemlya *115 E2* *var.* Nicholas II Land. *island group* N Russian Federation
Severnyy *110 E3* Respublika Komi, NW Russian Federation
Severodonetsk *see* Syeverodonets'k
Severodvinsk *110 C3* *prev.* Molotov, Sudostroy. Arkhangel'skaya Oblast', NW Russian Federation
Severomorsk *110 C2* Murmanskaya Oblast', NW Russian Federation
Seversk *114 D4* Tomskaya Oblast', C Russian Federation
Sevier Lake *44 A4* *lake* Utah, W USA
Sevilla *92 C4* Eng. Seville; *anc.* Hispalis. Andalucía, SW Spain
Seville *see* Sevilla
Sevlievo *104 D2* Gabrovo, N Bulgaria
Sevluš/Sevlyush *see* Vynohradiv
Seward's Folly *see* Alaska
Seychelles *79 G1* *off.* Republic of Seychelles. *country* W Indian Ocean

SEYCHELLES
Indian Ocean

Official name Republic of Seychelles
Formation 1976 / 1976
Capital Victoria
Population 81,895 / 787 people per sq mile (303 people per sq km) / 50%
Total area 176 sq. miles (455 sq. km)
Languages French Creole*, English*, French*
Religions Roman Catholic 90%, Anglican 8%, Other (including Muslim) 2%
Ethnic mix Creole 89%, Indian 5%, Other 4%, Chinese 2%
Government Presidential system
Currency Seychelles rupee = 100 cents
Literacy rate 92%
Calorie consumption 2465 calories

Seychelles, Republic of *see* Seychelles
Seydhisfjördhur *83 E5* Austurland, E Iceland
Seydi *122 D2* Rus. Seydi; *prev.* Neftezavodsk. Lebap Welaýaty, E Turkmenistan
Seyhan *see* Adana
Sfákia *see* Chóra Sfakíon
Sfântu Gheorghe *108 C4* Ger. Sankt-Georgen, Hung. Sepsiszentgyörgy; *prev.* Şepşi-Sângeorz, Sfîntu Gheorghe. Covasna, C Romania
Sfax *71 F2* Ar. Şafāqis. E Tunisia
Sfîntu Gheorghe *see* Sfântu Gheorghe
's-Gravenhage *86 B4* var. Den Haag, Eng. The Hague, Fr. La Haye. *country capital* (Netherlands-seat of government) (Netherlands-seat of government) Zuid-Holland, W Netherlands
's-Gravenzande *86 B4* Zuid-Holland, W Netherlands
Shaan/Shaanxi Sheng *see* Shaanxi
Shaanxi *128 B5* *var.* Shaan, Shaanxi Sheng, Shan-hsi, Shenshi, Shensi. *province* C China
Shabani *see* Zvishavane
Shabeelle, Webi *see* Shebeli
Shache *126 A3* *var.* Yarkant. Xinjiang Uygur Zizhiqu, NW China
Shacheng *see* Huailai
Shackleton Ice Shelf *154 D3* *ice shelf* Antarctica
Shaddādī *see* Ash Shadādah
Shagra *see* Eslāmābād
Sha Hī *see* Orūmīyeh, Daryācheh-ye
Shahjahanabad *see* Delhi
Shahr-e Kord *120 C3* *var.* Shahr Kord. Chahār Maḩāll va Bakhtīārī, C Iran

Shahr Kord *see* Shahr-e Kord
Shāhrūd *120 D2 prev.* Emāmrūd,
Emāmshahr. Semnān, N Iran
Shalkar *114 B4 var.* Chelkar.
Aktyubinsk, W Kazakhstan
Shām, Bādiyat ash *see* Syrian Desert
Shana *see* Kuril'sk
Shandī *see* Shendi
Shandong *128 D4 var.* Lu, Shandong
Sheng, Shantung. *province* E China
Shandong Sheng *see* Shandong
Shanghai *128 D5 var.* Shang-hai.
Shanghai Shi, E China
Shangrao *128 D5* Jiangxi, S China
Shan-hsi *see* Shaanxi, China
Shan-hsi *see* Shanxi, China
Shannon *89 A6 Ir.* An tSionainn. *river*
W Ireland
Shan Plateau *136 B3 plateau* E Burma
(Myanmar)
Shansi *see* Shanxi
Shantar Islands *see* Shantarskiye Ostrova
Shantarskiye Ostrova *115 G3 Eng.*
Shantar Islands. *island group* E Russian
Federation
Shantou *128 D6 var.* Shan-t'ou, Swatow.
Guangdong, S China
Shan-t'ou *see* Shantou
Shantung *see* Shandong
Shanxi *128 C4 var.* Jin, Shan-hsi,
Shansi, Shanxi Sheng. *province*
C China
Shan Xian *see* Sanmenxia
Shanxi Sheng *see* Shanxi
Shaoguan *128 C6 var.* Shao-kuan,
Cant. Kukong; *prev.* Ch'u-chiang.
Guangdong, S China
Shao-kuan *see* Shaoguan
Shaqrā' *120 B4 Ar* Riyāḍ, C Saudi Arabia
Shaqrā *see* Shuqrah
Shar *114 D5 var.* Charsk. Vostochnyy
Kazakhstan, E Kazakhstan
Shari *130 D2* Hokkaidō, NE Japan
Shari *see* Chari
Sharjah *see* Ash Shāriqah
Shark Bay *147 A5 bay* Western Australia
Sharqī, Al Jabal ash/Sharqi, Jebel esh
see Anti-Lebanon
Shashe *78 D3 var.* Shashi. *river*
Botswana/Zimbabwe
Shashi *see* Shashe
Shatskiy Rise *125 G1 undersea rise*
N Pacific Ocean
Shawnee *49 G1* Oklahoma, C USA
Shaykh, Jabal ash *see* Hermon, Mount
Shchadryn *107 D7 Rus.* Shchedrin.
Homyel'skaya Voblasts', SE Belarus
Shchedrin *see* Shchadryn
Shcheglovsk *see* Kemerovo
Shchëkino *111 B5* Tul'skaya Oblast',
W Russian Federation
Shchors *109 E1* Chernihivs'ka Oblast',
N Ukraine
Shchuchin *see* Shchuchyn
Shchuchinsk *114 C4 prev.* Shchuchye.
Akmola, N Kazakhstan
Shchuchye *see* Shchuchinsk
Shchuchyn *107 B5 Pol.* Szczuczyn
Nowogródzki, *Rus.* Shchuchin.
Hrodzyenskaya Voblasts', W Belarus
Shebekino *111 A6* Belgorodskaya
Oblast', W Russian Federation
Shebelē Wenz, Wabē *see* Shebeli
Shebeli *73 D5 Amh.* Wabē Shebelē Wenz,
It. Scebeli, *Som.* Webi Shabeelle. *river*
Ethiopia/Somalia
Sheberghān *123 E3 var.* Shibarghān,
Shiberghan, Shibirghān. Jowzjān,
N Afghanistan
Sheboygan *40 B2* Wisconsin, N USA
Shebshi Mountains *76 A4 var.*
Schebschi Mountains. *mountain range*
E Nigeria
Shechem *see* Nablus
Shedadi *see* Ash Shadādah
Sheffield *89 D5* N England, United
Kingdom
Shekhem *see* Nablus
Sheki *see* Şäki
Shelby *44 B1* Montana, NW USA
Sheldon *45 F3* Iowa, C USA
Shelekhov Gulf *115 G2 Eng.* Shelekhov
Gulf. *gulf* E Russian Federation
Shelekhov Gulf *see* Shelikhova, Zaliv
Shendi *72 C4 var.* Shandī. River Nile,
NE Sudan
Shengking *see* Liaoning

Shenking *see* Liaoning
Shenshi/Shensi *see* Shaanxi
Shenyang *128 D3 Chin.* Shen-yang, *Eng.*
Moukden, Mukden; *prev.* Fengtien.
province capital Liaoning, NE China
Shen-yang *see* Shenyang
Shepetivka *108 D2 Rus.* Shepetovka.
Khmel'nyts'ka Oblast', NW Ukraine
Shepetovka *see* Shepetivka
Shepparton *149 C7* Victoria,
SE Australia
Sherbrooke *39 E4* Québec, SE Canada
Shereik *72 C3* River Nile, N Sudan
Sheridan *44 C2* Wyoming, C USA
Sherman *49 G2* Texas, SW USA
's-Hertogenbosch *86 C4 Fr.* Bois-le-
Duc, *Ger.* Herzogenbusch. Noord-
Brabant, S Netherlands
Shetland Islands *88 D1 island group*
NE Scotland, United Kingdom
Shevchenko *see* Aktau
Shibarghān *see* Sheberghān
Shiberghan/Shiberghān *see* Sheberghān
Shibetsu *130 D2 var.* Sibetu. Hokkaidō,
NE Japan
Shibh Jazīrat Sīnā' *see* Sinai
Shibushi-wan *131 B8 bay* SW Japan
Shigatse *see* Xigazē
Shih-chia-chuang/Shihmen *see*
Shijiazhuang
Shihezi *127 C3* Xinjiang Uygur Zizhiqu,
NW China
Shiichi *see* Shyichy
Shijiazhuang *128 C4 var.* Shih-chia-
chuang; *prev.* Shihmen. *province*
capital Hebei, E China
Shikārpur *134 B3* Sind, S Pakistan
Shikoku *131 C7 var.* Sikoku. *island*
SW Japan
Shikoku Basin *125 F2 var.* Sikoku Basin.
undersea basin N Philippine Sea
Shikotan, Ostrov *130 E2 Jap.* Shikotan-
tō. *island* NE Russian Federation
Shikotan-tō *see* Shikotan, Ostrov
Shilabo *73 D5* Sumalē, E Ethiopia
Shiliguri *135 F3 prev.* Siliguri. West
Bengal, NE India
Shiika *115 F4 river* S Russian Federation
Shillong *135 G3 state capital* Meghālaya,
NE India
Shimanto *see* Nakamura
Shimbir Berris *see* Shimbiris
Shimbiris *72 E4 var.* Shimbir Berris.
mountain N Somalia
Shimoga *132 C2* Karnātaka, W India
Shimonoseki *131 A7 var.* Simonoseki,
hist. Akamagaseki, Bakan. Yamaguchi,
Honshū, SW Japan
Shinano-gawa *131 C5 var.* Sinano Gawa.
river Honshū, C Japan
Shīndand *122 D4* Herāt, W Afghanistan
Shingū *131 C6 var.* Singū. Wakayama,
Honshū, SW Japan
Shinjō *130 D4 var.* Sinzyô. Yamagata,
Honshū, C Japan
Shinyanga *73 C7* Shinyanga,
NW Tanzania
Shiprock *48 C1* New Mexico, SW USA
Shīrāz *120 D4 var.* Shīrāz. Fārs, S Iran
Shishchitsy *see* Shyshchytsy
Shivpuri *134 D3* Madhya Pradesh,
C India
Shizugawa *130 D4* Miyagi, Honshū,
NE Japan
Shizuoka *131 D6 var.* Sizuoka. Shizuoka,
Honshū, S Japan
Shklov *see* Shklow
Shklow *107 D6 Rus.* Shklov.
Mahilyowskaya Voblasts', E Belarus
Shkodër *101 C5 var.* Shkodra, *It.* Scutari,
SCr. Skadar. Shkodër, NW Albania
Shkodra *see* Shkodër
Shkodrës, Liqeni i *see* Scutari, Lake
Shkumbinit, Lumi i *101 C6 var.*
Shkumbi, Shkumbin. *river* C Albania
Shkumbî/Shkumbin *see* Shkumbinit,
Lumi i
Sholāpur *see* Solāpur
Shostka *109 F1* Sums'ka Oblast',
NE Ukraine
Show Low *48 B2* Arizona, SW USA
Show Me State *see* Missouri
Shpola *109 E3* Cherkas'ka Oblast',
N Ukraine
Shqipëria/Shqipërisë, Republika e
see Albania

Shreveport *42 A2* Louisiana, S USA
Shrewsbury *89 D6 hist.* Scrobesbyrig'.
W England, United Kingdom
Shu *114 C5 Kaz.* Shū. Zhambyl,
SE Kazakhstan
Shuang-liao *see* Liaoyuan
Shū, Kazakhstan *see* Shu
Shumagin Islands *36 B3 island group*
Alaska, USA
Shumen *104 D2* Shumen, NE Bulgaria
Shumilina *107 E5 Rus.* Shumilino.
Vitsyebskaya Voblasts', NE Belarus
Shumilino *see* Shumilina
Shunsen *see* Ch'unch'ŏn
Shuqrah *121 B7 var.* Shaqrā. SW Yemen
Shwebo *136 B3* Sagaing, C Burma
(Myanmar)
Shyichy *107 C7 Rus.* Shiichi.
Homyel'skaya Voblasts', SE Belarus
Shymkent *114 B5 prev.* Chimkent.
Yuzhnyy Kazakhstan, S Kazakhstan
Shyshchytsy *107 C6 Rus.* Shishchitsy.
Minskaya Voblasts', C Belarus
Siam *see* Thailand
Siam, Gulf of *see* Thailand, Gulf of
Sian *see* Xi'an
Siang *see* Brahmaputra
Siangtan *see* Xiangtan
Šiauliai *106 B4 Ger.* Schaulen. Šiauliai,
N Lithuania
Siazan' *see* Siyäzän
Sibay *111 D6* Respublika Bashkortostan,
W Russian Federation
Siberia *115 E3 var.* Siberia. *physical*
region NE Russian Federation
Siberia *see* Sibir'
Siberoet *see* Siberut, Pulau
Siberut, Pulau *138 A4 prev.* Siberoet.
island Kepulauan Mentawai,
W Indonesia
Sibi *134 B2* Baluchistān, SW Pakistan
Sibiti *77 B6* Lékoumou, S Congo
Sibiu *108 B4 Ger.* Hermannstadt, *Hung.*
Nagyszeben. Sibiu, C Romania
Sibolga *138 B3* Sumatera, W Indonesia
Sibu *138 D3* Sarawak, East Malaysia
Sibut *76 C4 prev.* Fort-Sibut. Kémo,
S Central African Republic
Sibuyan Sea *139 E2 sea* W Pacific Ocean
Sichon *137 C6 var.* Ban Sichon, Si Chon.
Nakhon Si Thammarat, SW Thailand
Si Chon *see* Sichon
Sichuan *128 B5 var.* Chuan, Sichuan
Sheng, Ssu-ch'uan, Szechuan,
Szechwan. *province* C China
Sichuan Pendi *128 B5 basin* C China
Sichuan Sheng *see* Sichuan
Sicilian Channel *see* Sicily, Strait of
Sicily *97 C7 Eng* Sicily; *anc.* Trinacria.
island Italy, C Mediterranean Sea
Sicily, Strait of *97 B7 var.* Sicilian
Channel. *strait* C Mediterranean Sea
Sicuani *61 E4* Cusco, S Peru
Sidári *100 A4* Kérkyra, Iónia Nisiá,
Greece, C Mediterranean Sea
Sidas *138 D4* Borneo, C Indonesia
Siderno *97 D7* Calabria, SW Italy
Sidhirókastron *see* Sidirókastro
Sidi Barrāni *72 A1* NW Egypt
Sidi Bel Abbès *70 D2 var.* Sidi bel Abbès,
Sidi-Bel-Abbès. NW Algeria
Sidirókastro *104 C3 prev.*
Sidhirókastron. Kentrikí Makedonía,
NE Greece
Sidley, Mount *154 B4 mountain*
Antarctica
Sidney *44 D1* Montana, NW USA
Sidney *44 D4* Nebraska, C USA
Sidney *40 C4* Ohio, N USA
Sidon *see* Saïda
Sidra *see* Surt
Sidra/Sidrs, Gulf of *see* Surt, Khalīj,
N Libya
Siebenbürgen *see* Transylvania
Siedlce *98 E3 Ger.* Sedlez, *Rus.* Sesdlets.
Mazowieckie, C Poland
Siegen *94 B4* Nordrhein-Westfalen,
W Germany
Siemiatycze *98 E3* Podlaskie, NE Poland
Siena *96 B3 Fr.* Sienne; *anc.* Saena Julia.
Toscana, C Italy
Sienne *see* Siena
Sieradz *98 C4* Sieradz, C Poland
Sierpc *98 D3* Mazowieckie, C Poland
Sierra Leone *74 A4 off.* Republic of Sierra
Leone. *country* W Africa

SIERRA LEONE
West Africa

Official name Republic of Sierra Leone
Formation 1961 / 1961
Capital Freetown
Population 5.8 million / 210 people
per sq mile (81 people per sq km) / 40%
Total area 27,698 sq. miles (71,740 sq. km)
Languages English*, Mende, Temne, Krio
Religions Muslim 30%, Traditional
beliefs 30%, Other 30%, Christian 10%
Ethnic mix Mende 35%, Temne 32%,
Other 21%, Limba 8%, Kuranko 4%
Government Presidential system
Currency Leone = 100 cents
Literacy rate 35%
Calorie consumption 1936 calories

Sierra Leone Basin *66 C4 undersea basin*
E Atlantic Ocean
Sierra Leone, Republic of *see* Sierra Leone
Sierra Leone Ridge *see* Sierra Leone Rise
Sierra Leone Rise *66 C4 var.* Sierra
Leone Ridge, Sierra Leone Schwelle.
undersea rise E Atlantic Ocean
Sierra Leone Schwelle *see* Sierra
Leone Rise
Sierra Vista *48 B3* Arizona, SW USA
Sífnos *105 C6 anc.* Siphnos. *island*
Kykládes, Greece, Aegean Sea
Sigli *138 A3* Sumatera, W Indonesia
Siglufjördhur *83 E4* Nordhurland
Vestra, N Iceland
Signal Peak *48 A2 mountain* Arizona,
SW USA
Signan *see* Xi'an
Signy *154 A2 UK research station* South
Orkney Islands, Antarctica
Siguatepeque *52 C2* Comayagua,
W Honduras
Siguiri *74 D4* NE Guinea
Sihanoukville *see* Kâmpóng Saôm
Siilinjärvi *84 E4* Itä-Suomi, C Finland
Siirt *117 F4 var.* Sert; *anc.* Tigranocerta.
Siirt, SE Turkey
Sikandarabad *see* Secunderābād
Sikasso *74 D4* Sikasso, S Mali
Sikeston *45 H5* Missouri, C USA
Sikhote-Alin', Khrebet *115 G4*
mountain range SE Russian Federation
Siking *see* Xi'an
Siklós *99 C7* Baranya, SW Hungary
Sikoku *see* Shikoku
Sikoku Basin *see* Shikoku Basin
Silalē *106 B4* Tauragé, W Lithuania
Silchar *135 G3* Assam, NE India
Silesia *98 B4 physical region* SW Poland
Silifke *116 C4 anc.* Seleucia. İçel,
S Turkey
Siliguri *see* Shiliguri
Siling Co *126 C5 lake* W China
Silinhot *see* Xilinhot
Silistra *104 E1 var.* Silistria; *anc.*
Durostorum. Silistra, NE Bulgaria
Silistria *see* Silistra
Sillamäe *106 E2 Ger.* Sillamäggi. Ida-
Virumaa, NE Estonia
Sillamäggi *see* Sillamäe
Sillein *see* Žilina
Šilutė *106 B4 Ger.* Heydekrug. Klaipéda,
W Lithuania
Sılvan *117 F4* Diyarbakır, SE Turkey
Silva Porto *see* Kuito
Silver State *see* Colorado
Silver State *see* Nevada
Simanichi *see* Simonichi
Simanichi *see* Simonichi.
Homyel'skaya Voblasts', SE Belarus
Simav *116 B3* Kütahya, W Turkey
Simav Çayı *116 A3 river* NW Turkey
Simbirsk *see* Ul'yanovsk
Simeto *97 C7 river* Sicily, Italy,
C Mediterranean Sea
Simeulue, Pulau *138 A3 island*
NW Indonesia
Simferopol' *109 F5* Respublika Krym,
S Ukraine
Simitla *104 C3* Blagoevgrad, SW Bulgaria
Şimlăul Silvaniei/Şimleul Silvaniei *see*
Şimleu Silvaniei
Şimleu Silvaniei *108 B3 Hung.*
Szilágysomlyó; *prev.* Şimlăul Silvaniei,
Şimleul Silvaniei. Sălaj, NW Romania
Simonichi *see* Simanichi
Simonoseki *see* Shimonoseki
Simpelveld *87 D6* Limburg,
SE Netherlands

Simplon Pass 95 B8 *pass* S Switzerland
Simpson *see* Fort Simpson
Simpson Desert 148 B4 *desert* Northern Territory/South Australia
Sinai 72 C2 *var.* Sinai Peninsula, Ar. Shibh Jazīrat Sīnā', Sīnā. *physical region* NE Egypt
Sinaia 108 C4 Prahova, SE Romania
Sinano Gawa *see* Shinano-gawa
Sinā/Sinai Peninsula *see* Sinai
Sincelejo 58 B2 Sucre, NW Colombia
Sind 134 B3 *var.* Sindh. *province* SE Pakistan
Sindelfingen 95 B6 Baden-Württemberg, SW Germany
Sindh *see* Sind
Sindi 106 D2 *Ger.* Zintenhof. Pärnumaa, SW Estonia
Sines 92 B4 Setúbal, S Portugal
Singan *see* Xi'an
Singapore 138 B3 *country capital* (Singapore) (Singapore) S Singapore
Singapore 138 A1 *off.* Republic of Singapore. *country* SE Asia

SINGAPORE
Southeast Asia

Official name Republic of Singapore
Formation 1965 / 1965
Capital Singapore
Population 4.4 million / 18644 people per sq mile (7213 people per sq km) / 100%
Total area 250 sq. miles (648 sq. km)
Languages Mandarin*, Malay*, Tamil*, English*
Religions Buddhist 55%, Taoist 22%, Muslim 16%, Hindu, Christian, and Sikh 7%
Ethnic mix Chinese 77%, Malay 14%, Indian 8%, Other 1%
Government Parliamentary system
Currency Singapore dollar = 100 cents
Literacy rate 93%
Calorie consumption Not available

Singapore, Republic of *see* Singapore
Singen 95 B6 Baden-Württemberg, S Germany
Singida 73 C7 Singida, C Tanzania
Singkang 139 E4 Sulawesi, C Indonesia
Singkawang 138 C3 Borneo, C Indonesia
Singora *see* Songkhla
Singū *see* Shingū
Sining *see* Xining
Siniscola 97 A5 Sardegna, Italy, C Mediterranean Sea
Sinj 100 B4 Split-Dalmacija, SE Croatia
Sinkiang/Sinkiang Uighur Autonomous Region *see* Xinjiang Uygur Zizhiqu
Sinnamarie *see* Sinnamary
Sinnamary 59 H3 *var.* Sinnamarie. N French Guiana
Sinneh *see* Sanandaj
Sînnicolau Mare *see* Sânnicolau Mare
Sinoe, Lacul *see* Sinoie, Lacul
Sinoie, Lacul 108 D5 *prev.* Lacul Sinoe. *lagoon* SE Romania
Sinop 116 D2 *anc.* Sinope. Sinop, N Turkey
Sinope *see* Sinop
Sinsheim 95 B6 Baden-Württemberg, SW Germany
Sint Maarten 55 G3 *Eng.* Saint Martin. *Dutch autonomous region* S Caribbean Sea
Sint-Michielsgestel 86 C4 Noord-Brabant, S Netherlands
Sîn-Miclăuş *see* Gheorgheni
Sint-Niklaas 87 B5 *Fr.* Saint-Nicolas. Oost-Vlaanderen, N Belgium
Sint-Pieters-Leeuw 87 B6 Vlaams Brabant, C Belgium
Sintra 92 B3 *prev.* Cintra. Lisboa, W Portugal
Sinujiif 73 E5 Nugaal, NE Somalia
Sinus Aelaniticus *see* Aqaba, Gulf of
Sinus Gallicus *see* Lion, Golfe du
Sinyang *see* Xinyang
Sinzyô *see* Shinjō
Sion 95 A7 *Ger.* Sitten; *anc.* Sedunum. Valais, SW Switzerland
Sioux City 45 F3 Iowa, C USA
Sioux Falls 45 F3 South Dakota, N USA
Sioux State *see* North Dakota
Siphnos *see* Sífnos

Siping 128 D3 *var.* Ssu-p'ing, Szeping; *prev.* Ssu-p'ing-chieh. Jilin, NE China
Siple, Mount 154 A4 *mountain* Siple Island, Antarctica
Siquirres 53 E4 Limón, E Costa Rica
Siracusa 97 D7 *Eng.* Syracuse. Sicilia, Italy, C Mediterranean Sea
Sir Edward Pellew Group 148 B2 *island group* Northern Territory, NE Australia
Siret 108 C3 *var.* Siretul, *Ger.* Sereth, *Rus.* Seret. *river* Romania/Ukraine
Siretul *see* Siret
Siria *see* Syria
Sirikit Reservoir 136 C4 *lake* N Thailand
Sīrjān 120 D4 *prev.* Sa'īdābād. Kermān, S Iran
Sirna *see* Sýrna
Şırnak 117 F4 Şırnak, SE Turkey
Síros *see* Sýros
Sirte *see* Surt
Sirte, Gulf of 71 F2 *Eng.* Gulf of Sidra, Gulf of Sirti, Sidra. *gulf* N Libya
Sirti, Gulf of *see* Surt, Khalīj
Sisak 100 B3 *var.* Siscia, *Ger.* Sissek, *Hung.* Sziszek; *anc.* Segestica. Sisak-Moslavina, C Croatia
Siscia *see* Sisak
Sisimiut 82 C3 *var.* Holsteinborg, Holsteinsborg, Holstenborg, Holstensborg. Kitaa, S Greenland
Sissek *see* Sisak
Sīstān, Daryācheh-ye *see* Şāberī, Hāmūn-e
Sitaş Cristuru *see* Cristuru Secuiesc
Siteía 105 D8 *var.* Sitía. Kriti, Greece, E Mediterranean Sea
Sitges 93 G2 Cataluña, NE Spain
Sitía *see* Siteía
Sittang *see* Sittoung
Sittard 87 D5 Limburg, SE Netherlands
Sitten *see* Sion
Sittoung 136 B4 *var.* Sittang. *river* S Burma (Myanmar)
Sittwe 136 A3 *var.* Akyab. Rakhine State, W Burma (Myanmar)
Siuna 52 D3 Región Autónoma Atlántico Norte, NE Nicaragua
Siut *see* Asyūţ
Sivas 116 D3 *anc.* Sebastia, Sebaste. Sivas, C Turkey
Siverek 117 E4 Şanlıurfa, S Turkey
Siwa *see* Sīwah
Sīwah 72 A2 *var.* Siwa. NW Egypt
Six Counties, The *see* Northern Ireland
Six-Fours-les-Plages 91 D6 Var, SE France
Siyäzän 117 H2 *Rus.* Siazan'. NE Azerbaijan
Sjar *see* Sääre
Sjenica 101 D5 *Turk.* Seniça. Serbia, SW Serbia
Skadar *see* Shkodër
Skadarsko Jezero *see* Scutari, Lake
Skagerak *see* Skagerrak
Skagerrak 85 A6 *var.* Skagerak. *channel* N Europe
Skagit River 46 B1 *river* Washington, NW USA
Skalka 84 C3 *lake* N Sweden
Skarżysko-Kamienna 98 D4 Świętokrzyskie, C Poland
Skaudvile 106 B4 Tauragė, SW Lithuania
Skegness 89 E6 E England, United Kingdom
Skellefteå 84 D4 Västerbotten, N Sweden
Skellefteälven 84 C4 *river* N Sweden
Ski 85 B6 Akershus, S Norway
Skíathos 105 C5 Skíathos, Vóreies Sporádes, Greece, Aegean Sea
Skidal' 107 B5 *Rus.* Skidel'. Hrodzyenskaya Voblasts', W Belarus
Skidel' *see* Skidal'
Skiermûntseach *see* Schiermonnikoog
Skierniewice 98 D3 Łódzkie, C Poland
Skíftet 102 C1 *strait* Finland Atlantic Ocean Baltic Sea Gulf of Bothnia/Gulf of Finland
Skíros *see* Skýros
Skópelos 105 C5 Skópelos, Vóreies Sporádes, Greece, Aegean Sea
Skopje 116 D3 *var.* Üsküb, *Turk.* Üsküp, *prev.* Skoplje; *anc.* Scupi. *country capital* (FYR Macedonia) (FYR Macedonia) N FYR Macedonia
Skoplje *see* Skopje
Skovorodino 115 F4 Amurskaya Oblast', SE Russian Federation

Skuodas 106 B3 *Ger.* Schoden, *Pol.* Szkudy. Klaipėda, NW Lithuania
Skye, Isle of 88 B3 *island* NW Scotland, United Kingdom
Skylge *see* Terschelling
Skýros 105 C5 *var.* Skíros. Skýros, Vóreies Sporádes, Greece, Aegean Sea
Skýros 105 C5 *var.* Skíros; *anc.* Scyros. *island* Vóreies Sporádes, Greece, Aegean Sea
Slagelse 85 B7 Vestsjælland, E Denmark
Slatina 100 C3 *Hung.* Szlatina; *prev.* Podravska Slatina. Virovitica-Podravina, NE Croatia
Slatina 108 B5 Olt, S Romania
Slavgorod *see* Slawharad
Slavonski Brod 100 C3 *Ger.* Brod, *Hung.* Bród; *prev.* Brod, Brod na Savi. Brod-Posavina, NE Croatia
Slavuta 108 C2 Khmel'nyts'ka Oblast', NW Ukraine
Slavyansk *see* Slov"yans'k
Slawharad 107 E7 *Rus.* Slavgorod. Mahilyowskaya Voblasts', E Belarus
Sławno 98 C2 Zachodnio-pomorskie, NW Poland
Slēmānī *see* As Sulaymānīyah
Sliema 102 B5 N Malta
Sligo 89 A5 *Ir.* Sligeach. Sligo, NW Ireland
Sliven 104 D2 *var.* Slivno. Sliven, C Bulgaria
Slivnitsa 104 B2 Sofiya, W Bulgaria
Slivno *see* Sliven
Slobozia 108 C5 Ialomiţa, SE Romania
Slonim 107 B6 *Pol.* Słonim. Hrodzyenskaya Voblasts', W Belarus
Słonim *see* Slonim
Slovakia 99 C6 *off.* Slovenská Republika, *Ger.* Slowakei, *Hung.* Szlovákia, *Slvk.* Slovensko. *country* C Europe

SLOVAKIA
Central Europe

Official name Slovak Republic
Formation 1993 / 1993
Capital Bratislava
Population 5.4 million / 285 people per sq mile (110 people per sq km) / 58%
Total area 18,859 sq. miles (48,845 sq. km)
Languages Slovak*, Hungarian (Magyar), Czech
Religions Roman Catholic 60%, Other 18%, Atheist 10%, Protestant 8%, Orthodox Christian 4%
Ethnic mix Slovak 86%, Magyar 10%, Roma 2%, Other 1%, Czech 1%
Government Parliamentary system
Currency Euro = 100 cents
Literacy rate 99%
Calorie consumption 2889 calories

Slovak Ore Mountains *see* Slovenské rudohorie
Slovenia 95 D8 *off.* Republic of Slovenia, *Ger.* Slowenien, *Slvn.* Slovenija. *country* SE Europe

SLOVENIA
Central Europe

Official name Republic of Slovenia
Formation 1991 / 1991
Capital Ljubljana
Population 2 million / 256 people per sq mile (99 people per sq km) / 51%
Total area 7820 sq. miles (20,253 sq. km)
Languages Slovenian*
Religions Roman Catholic 96%, Other 3%, Muslim 1%
Ethnic mix Slovene 83%, Other 12%, Serb 2%, Croat 2%, Bosniak 1%
Government Parliamentary system
Currency Euro = 100 cents
Literacy rate 99%
Calorie consumption 3001 calories

Slovenia, Republic of *see* Slovenia
Slovenija *see* Slovenia
Slovenké Republika *see* Slovakia
Slovenské rudohorie 99 D6 *Eng.* Slovak Ore Mountains, *Ger.* Slowakisches Erzgebirge, Ungarisches Erzgebirge. *mountain range* C Slovakia
Slovensko *see* Slovakia

Slov"yans'k 109 G3 *Rus.* Slavyansk. Donets'ka Oblast', E Ukraine
Slowakei *see* Slovakia
Slowakisches Erzgebirge *see* Slovenské rudohorie
Slowenien *see* Slovenia
Słubice 98 B3 *Ger.* Frankfurt. Lubuskie, W Poland
Sluch 108 D1 *river* NW Ukraine
Słupsk 98 C2 *Ger.* Stolp. Pomorskie, N Poland
Slutsk 107 C6 Minskaya Voblasts', S Belarus
Smallwood Reservoir 39 F2 *lake* Newfoundland and Labrador, S Canada
Smara 70 B3 *var.* Es Semara. N Western Sahara
Smarhon' 107 C5 *Pol.* Smorgonie, *Rus.* Smorgon'. Hrodzyenskaya Voblasts', W Belarus
Smederevo 100 D4 *Ger.* Semendria. Serbia, N Serbia
Smederevska Palanka 100 D4 Serbia, C Serbia
Smela *see* Smila
Smila 109 E2 *Rus.* Smela. Cherkas'ka Oblast', C Ukraine
Smilten *see* Smiltene
Smiltene 106 D3 *Ger.* Smilten. Valka, N Latvia
Smøla 84 A4 *island* W Norway
Smolensk 111 A5 Smolenskaya Oblast', W Russian Federation
Smorgon'/Smorgonie *see* Smarhon'
Smyrna *see* İzmir
Snake 34 B4 *river* Yukon Territory, NW Canada
Snake River 46 C3 *river* NW USA
Snake River Plain 46 D4 *plain* Idaho, NW USA
Sneek 86 D2 Friesland, N Netherlands
Sneeuw-gebergte *see* Maoke, Pegunungan
Snēžka 98 B4 *Ger.* Schneekoppe, *Pol.* Śnieżka. *mountain* N Czech Republic/Poland
Śniardwy, Jezioro 98 D2 *Ger.* Spirdingsee. *lake* NE Poland
Sniečkus *see* Visaginas
Śnieżka *see* Snēžka
Snina 99 E5 *Hung.* Szinna. Prešovský Kraj, E Slovakia
Snowdonia 89 C6 *mountain range* NW Wales, United Kingdom
Snowdrift *see* Lutselk'e
Snow Mountains *see* Maoke, Pegunungan
Snyder 49 F3 Texas, SW USA
Sobradinho, Barragem de *see* Sobradinho, Represa de
Sobradinho, Represa de 63 F2 *var.* Barragem de Sobradinho. *reservoir* E Brazil
Sochi 111 A7 Krasnodarskiy Kray, SW Russian Federation
Société, Îles de la/Society Islands *see* Société, Archipel de la
Society Islands 145 G4 *var.* Archipel de Tahiti, Îles de la Société, Eng. Society Islands. *island group* W French Polynesia
Soconusco, Sierra de *see* Madre, Sierra
Socorro 48 D2 New Mexico, SW USA
Socorro, Isla 50 B5 *island* W Mexico
Socotra 121 C7 *var.* Sokotra, *Eng.* Socotra. *island* SE Yemen
Socotra *see* Suquţrā
Soc Trăng 137 D6 *var.* Khanh Hung. Soc Trăng, S Vietnam
Socuéllamos 93 E3 Castilla-La Mancha, C Spain
Sodankylä 84 D3 Lappi, N Finland
Sodari *see* Sodiri
Söderhamn 85 C5 Gävleborg, C Sweden
Södertälje 85 C6 Stockholm, C Sweden
Sodiri 72 B4 *var.* Sawdirī, Sodari. Northern Kordofan, C Sudan
Soekaboemi *see* Sukabumi
Soemba *see* Sumba, Pulau
Soengaipenoeh *see* Sungaipenuh
Soerabaja *see* Surabaya
Soerakarta *see* Surakarta
Sofia *see* Sofiya
Sofiya 104 C2 *var.* Sophia, *Eng.* Sofia, *Lat.* Serdica. *country capital* (Bulgaria) (Bulgaria) Sofiya-Grad, W Bulgaria
Sogamoso 58 B3 Boyacá, C Colombia
Sognefjorden 85 A5 *fjord* NE North Sea

Sohâg see Sawhâj
Sohar see Şuḥār
Sohm Plain 66 B3 abyssal plain NW Atlantic Ocean
Sohrau see Żory
Sokal' 108 C2 Rus. Sokal. L'vivs'ka Oblast', NW Ukraine
Söke 116 A4 Aydın, SW Turkey
Sokhumi 117 E1 Rus. Sukhumi. NW Georgia
Sokodé 75 F4 C Togo
Sokol 110 C4 Vologodskaya Oblast', NW Russian Federation
Sokółka 98 E3 Podlaskie, NE Poland
Sokolov 99 A5 Ger. Falkenau an der Eger; prev. Falknov nad Ohří. Karlovarský Kraj, W Czech Republic
Sokone 74 B3 W Senegal
Sokoto 75 F3 Sokoto, NW Nigeria
Sokoto 75 F4 river NW Nigeria
Sokotra see Suquṭrā
Solāpur 124 B1 var. Sholāpur. Mahārāshtra, W India
Solca 108 C3 Ger. Solka. Suceava, N Romania
Sol, Costa del 92 D5 coastal region S Spain
Soldeu 91 B7 NE Andorra Europe
Solec Kujawski 98 C3 Kujawsko-pomorskie, C Poland
Soledad 58 B1 Atlántico, N Colombia
Isla Soledad see East Falkland
Soligorsk see Salihorsk
Solikamsk 114 C3 Permskaya Oblast', NW Russian Federation
Sol'-Iletsk 111 D6 Orenburgskaya Oblast', W Russian Federation
Solingen 94 A4 Nordrhein-Westfalen, W Germany
Solka see Solca
Sollentuna 85 C6 Stockholm, C Sweden
Solo see Surakarta
Solok 138 B4 Sumatera, W Indonesia
Solomon Islands 144 C3 prev. British Solomon Islands Protectorate. country W Solomon Islands N Melanesia W Pacific Ocean

SOLOMON ISLANDS
Australasia & Oceania

Official name Solomon Islands
Formation 1978 / 1978
Capital Honiara
Population 566,842 / 52 people per sq mile (20 people per sq km) / 17%
Total area 10,985 sq. miles (28,450 sq. km)
Languages English*, Pidgin English, Melanesian Pidgin
Religions Church of Melanesia (Anglican) 34%, Roman Catholic 19%, South Seas Evangelical Church 17%, Methodist 11%, Seventh-day Adventist 10%, Other 9%
Ethnic mix Melanesian 94%, Polynesian 4%, Other 2%
Government Parliamentary system
Currency Solomon Islands dollar = 100 cents
Literacy rate 77%
Calorie consumption 2265 calories

Solomon Islands 144 C3 island group Papua New Guinea/Solomon Islands
Solomon Sea 144 B3 sea W Pacific Ocean
Soltau 94 B3 Niedersachsen, NW Germany
Sol'tsy 110 A4 Novgorodskaya Oblast', W Russian Federation
Solun see Thessaloníki
Solwezi 78 D2 North Western, NW Zambia
Sōma 130 D4 Fukushima, Honshū, C Japan
Somalia 73 D5 off. Somali Democratic Republic, Som. Jamuuriyada Demuqraadiga Soomaaliyeed, Soomaaliya; prev. Italian Somaliland, Somaliland Protectorate. country E Africa

SOMALIA
East Africa

Official name The Somali Democratic Republic
Formation 1960 / 1960

SOMALIA
(continued)

Capital Mogadishu
Population 8.8 million / 36 people per sq mile (14 people per sq km) / 35%
Total area 246,199 sq. miles (637,657 sq. km)
Languages Somali*, Arabic*, English, Italian
Religions Sunni Muslim 98%, Christian 2%
Ethnic mix Somali 85%, Other 15%
Government Transitional regime
Currency Somali shilin = 100 senti
Literacy rate 24%
Calorie consumption 1628 calories

Somali Basin 69 E5 undersea basin W Indian Ocean
Somali Democratic Republic see Somalia
Somaliland 73 D5 disputed territory N Somalia
Somaliland Protectorate see Somalia
Sombor 100 C3 Hung. Zombor. Vojvodina, NW Serbia
Someren 87 D5 Noord-Brabant, SE Netherlands
Somerset 44 var. Somerset Village. W Bermuda
Somerset 40 C5 Kentucky, S USA
Somerset Island 42 A5 island W Bermuda
Somerset Island 37 F2 island Queen Elizabeth Islands, Nunavut, NW Canada
Somerset Village see Somerset
Somers Islands see Bermuda
Somerton 48 A2 Arizona, SW USA
Someş 108 B3 river Hungary/Romania Europe
Somme 90 C2 river N France
Sommerfeld see Lubsko
Somotillo 52 C3 Chinandega, NW Nicaragua
Somoto 52 D3 Madriz, NW Nicaragua
Songea 73 C8 Ruvuma, S Tanzania
Sŏngjin see Kimch'aek
Songkhla 137 C7 var. Songkla, Mal. Singora. Songkhla, SW Thailand
Songkla see Songkhla
Sonoran Desert 48 A3 var. Desierto de Altar. desert Mexico/USA
Sonsonate 52 B3 Sonsonate, W El Salvador
Soochow see Suzhou
Soomaaliya/Soomaaliyeed, Jamuuriyada Demuqraadiga see Somalia
Soome Laht see Finland, Gulf of
Sop Hao 136 D3 Houaphan, N Laos
Sophia see Sofiya
Sopianae see Pécs
Sopot 98 C2 Ger. Zoppot. Pomorskie, N Poland
Sopron 99 B6 Ger. Ödenburg. Győr-Moson-Sopron, NW Hungary
Sorau/Sorau in der Niederlausitz see Żary
Sorgues 91 D6 Vaucluse, SE France
Sorgun 116 D3 Yozgat, C Turkey
Soria 93 E2 Castilla-León, N Spain
Soroca 108 D3 Rus. Soroki. N Moldova
Sorochinsk see Sarochyna
Soroki see Soroca
Sorong 139 F4 Papua, E Indonesia
Sørøya see Sørøya
Sørøya 84 C2 var. Sørøy, Lapp. Sállan. island N Norway
Sortavala 110 B3 prev. Serdobol'. Respublika Kareliya, NW Russian Federation
Sotavento, Ilhas de 74 A3 var. Leeward Islands. island group S Cape Verde
Sotkamo 84 E4 Oulu, C Finland
Souanké 77 B5 Sangha, NW Congo
Soueida see As Suwaydā'
Souflí 104 D3 prev. Souflíon. Anatolikí Makedonía kai Thráki, NE Greece
Souflíon see Souflí
Soufrière 55 F2 W Saint Lucia
Soukhné see As Sukhnah
Sŏul 129 E4 off. Sŏul-t'ŭkpyŏlsi, Eng. Seoul, Jap. Keijō; prev. Kyŏngsŏng. country capital (South Korea) (South Korea) NW South Korea
Sŏul-t'ŭkpyŏlsi see Sŏul

Soûr 119 A5 var. Şūr; anc. Tyre. SW Lebanon
Souris River 45 E1 var. Mouse River. river Canada/USA
Soúrpi 105 B5 Thessalía, C Greece
Sousse 71 F2 var. Sūsah. NE Tunisia
South Africa 78 C4 off. Republic of South Africa, Afr. Suid-Afrika. country S Africa

SOUTH AFRICA
Southern Africa

Official name Republic of South Africa
Formation 1934 / 1994
Capital Tshwane / Pretoria; Cape Town; Bloemfontein
Population 47.7 million / 101 people per sq mile (39 people per sq km) / 57%
Total area 471,008 sq. miles (1,219,912 sq. km)
Languages English, isiZulu, isiXhosa, Afrikaans, Sepedi, Setswana, Sesotho, Xitsonga, siSwati, Tshivenda, isiNdebele
Religions Christian 68%, Traditional beliefs and animist 29%, Muslim 2%, Hindu 1%
Ethnic mix Black 79%, Colored 10%, White 9%, Asian 2%
Government Presidential system
Currency Rand = 100 cents
Literacy rate 82%
Calorie consumption 2956 calories

South Africa, Republic of see South Africa
South America 56 continent
Southampton 89 D7 hist. Hamwih, Lat. Clausentum. S England, United Kingdom
Southampton Island 37 G3 island Nunavut, NE Canada
South Andaman 133 F2 island Andaman Islands, India, NE Indian Ocean
South Australia 149 A5 state S Australia
South Australian Basin 142 B5 undersea basin SW Indian Ocean
South Bend 40 C3 Indiana, N USA
South Beveland see Zuid-Beveland
South Bruny Island 149 C8 island Tasmania, SE Australia
South Carolina 43 E2 off. State of South Carolina, also known as The Palmetto State. state SE USA
South Carpathians see Carpaţii Meridionali
South China Basin 125 E4 undersea basin SE South China Sea
South China Sea 125 E4 Chin. Nan Hai, Ind. Laut Cina Selatan, Vtn. Biển Đông. sea SE Asia
South Dakota 44 D2 off. State of South Dakota, also known as The Coyote State, Sunshine State. state N USA
Southeast Indian Ridge 141 D7 undersea ridge Indian Ocean/Pacific Ocean
Southeast Pacific Basin 153 E5 var. Belling Hausen Mulde. undersea basin SE Pacific Ocean
South East Point 149 C7 headland Victoria, S Australia
Southend-on-Sea 89 E6 E England, United Kingdom
Southern Alps 151 B6 mountain range South Island, New Zealand
Southern Cook Islands 145 F4 island group S Cook Islands
Southern Cross 147 B6 Western Australia
Southern Indian Lake 37 F4 lake Manitoba, C Canada
Southern Ocean 67 B7 ocean Atlantic Ocean/Indian Ocean/Pacific Ocean
Southern Uplands 88 C4 mountain range S Scotland, United Kingdom
South Fiji Basin 142 D4 undersea basin S Pacific Ocean
South Geomagnetic Pole 154 B3 pole Antarctica
South Georgia 57 D8 island South Georgia and the South Sandwich Islands, SW Atlantic Ocean
South Goulburn Island 146 E2 island Northern Territory, N Australia
South Huvadhu Atoll 132 A5 atoll S Maldives
South Indian Basin 141 D7 undersea basin Indian Ocean/Pacific Ocean

South Island 151 C6 island S New Zealand
South Korea 129 E4 off. Republic of Korea, Kor. Taehan Min'guk. country E Asia

SOUTH KOREA
East Asia

Official name Republic of Korea
Formation 1948 / 1953
Capital Seoul
Population 48.1 million / 1262 people per sq mile (487 people per sq km) / 81%
Total area 38,023 sq. miles (98,480 sq. km)
Languages Korean*
Religions Mahayana Buddhist 47%, Protestant 38%, Roman Catholic 11%, Confucianist 3%, Other 1%
Ethnic mix Korean 100%
Government Presidential system
Currency South Korean won = 100 chon
Literacy rate 98%
Calorie consumption 3058 calories

South Lake Tahoe 47 C5 California, W USA
South Orkney Islands 154 A2 island group Antarctica
South Ossetia 117 F2 former autonomous region SW Georgia
South Pacific Basin see Southwest Pacific Basin
South Platte River 44 D4 river Colorado/Nebraska, C USA
South Pole 154 B3 pole Antarctica
South Sandwich Islands 57 D8 island group SW Atlantic Ocean
South Sandwich Trench 57 E8 trench SW Atlantic Ocean
South Shetland Islands 154 A2 island group Antarctica
South Shields 88 D4 NE England, United Kingdom
South Sioux City 45 F3 Nebraska, C USA
South Taranaki Bight 150 C4 bight SE Tasman Sea
South Tasmania Plateau see Tasman Plateau
South Uist 88 B3 island NW Scotland, United Kingdom
South-West Africa/South West Africa see Namibia
South West Cape 151 A8 headland Stewart Island, New Zealand
Southwest Indian Ocean Ridge see Southwest Indian Ridge
Southwest Indian Ridge 141 B6 var. Southwest Indian Ocean Ridge. undersea ridge SW Indian Ocean
Southwest Pacific Basin 143 E4 var. South Pacific Basin. undersea basin SE Pacific Ocean
Sovereign Base Area 102 C5 uk military installation S Cyprus
Soweto 78 D4 Gauteng, NE South Africa
Sōya-kaikyō see La Perouse Strait
Spain 92 D3 off. Kingdom of Spain, Sp. España; anc. Hispania, Iberia, Lat. Hispana. country SW Europe

SPAIN
Southwest Europe

Official name Kingdom of Spain
Formation 1492 / 1713
Capital Madrid
Population 43.6 million / 226 people per sq mile (87 people per sq km) / 77%
Total area 194,896 sq. miles (504,782 sq. km)
Languages Spanish*, Catalan*, Galician*, Basque*
Religions Roman Catholic 96%, Other 4%
Ethnic mix Castilian Spanish 72%, Catalan 17%, Galician 6%, Basque 2%, Other 2%, Roma 1%
Government Parliamentary system
Currency Euro = 100 cents
Literacy rate 98%
Calorie consumption 3371 calories

Spain, Kingdom of see Spain
Spalato see Split
Spanish Town 54 B5 hist. St.Iago de la Vega. C Jamaica
Sparks 47 C5 Nevada, W USA

Sparta see Spárti
Spartanburg 43 E1 South Carolina, SE USA
Spárti 105 B6 Eng. Sparta. Pelopónnisos, S Greece
Spearfish 44 D2 South Dakota, N USA
Speightstown 55 G1 NW Barbados
Spencer 45 F3 Iowa, C USA
Spencer Gulf 149 B6 gulf South Australia
Spey 88 C3 river NE Scotland, United Kingdom
Spice Islands see Maluku
Spiess Seamount 67 C7 seamount S Atlantic Ocean
Spijkenisse 86 B4 Zuid-Holland, SW Netherlands
Spíli 105 C8 Kríti, Greece, E Mediterranean Sea
Spīn Būldak 123 E5 Kandahār, S Afghanistan
Spirdingsee see Śniardwy, Jezioro
Spitsbergen 83 F2 island NW Svalbard
Split 100 B4 It. Spalato. Split-Dalmacija, S Croatia
Špoği 106 D4 Daugvapils, SE Latvia
Spokane 46 C2 Washington, NW USA
Spratly Islands 138 B2 Chin. Nansha Qundao. disputed territory SE Asia
Spree 94 D4 river E Germany
Springfield 40 B4 state capital Illinois, N USA
Springfield 41 G3 Massachusetts, NE USA
Springfield 45 G5 Missouri, C USA
Springfield 40 C4 Ohio, N USA
Springfield 46 B3 Oregon, NW USA
Spring Garden 59 F2 NE Guyana
Spring Hill 43 E4 Florida, SE USA
Springs Junction 151 C5 West Coast, South Island, New Zealand
Springsure 148 D4 Queensland, E Australia
Sprottau see Szprotawa
Spruce Knob 41 E4 mountain West Virginia, NE USA
Srbinje see Foča
Srbobran 100 D3 var. Bácsszenttamás, Hung. Szenttamás. Vojvodina, N Serbia
Srebrenica 100 C4 Republika Srpska, E Bosnia and Herzegovina
Sredets 104 D2 prev. Syulemeshlii. Stara Zagora, C Bulgaria
Sredets 104 E2 prev. Grudovo. Burgas, E Bulgaria
Sremska Mitrovica 100 C3 prev. Mitrovica, Ger. Mitrowitz. Vojvodina, NW Serbia
Srepok, Sông see Srêpôk, Tônle
Srêpôk, Tônle 137 E5 var. Sông Srepok. river Cambodia/Vietnam
Sri Aman 138 C3 Sarawak, East Malaysia
Sri Jayawardanapura see Sri Jayewardanapura Kotte
Sri Jayewardanapura Kotte 132 D3 var. Sri Jayawardanapura. Western Province, W Sri Lanka
Srīkākulam 135 F5 Andhra Pradesh, E India
Sri Lanka 132 D3 off. Democratic Socialist Republic of Sri Lanka; prev. Ceylon. country S Asia

SRI LANKA
South Asia

Official name Democratic Socialist Republic of Sri Lanka
Formation 1948 / 1948
Capital Colombo
Population 21.1 million / 844 people per sq mile (326 people per sq km) / 21%
Total area 25,332 sq. miles (65,610 sq. km)
Languages Sinhala*, Tamil*, Sinhala-Tamil, English
Religions Buddhist 69%, Hindu 15%, Muslim 8%, Christian 8%
Ethnic mix Sinhalese 82%, Tamil 9%, Moor 8%, Other 1%
Government Mixed presidential–parliamentary system
Currency Sri Lanka rupee = 100 cents
Literacy rate 91%
Calorie consumption 2385 calories

Sri Lanka, Democratic Socialist Republic of see Sri Lanka

Srinagarind Reservoir 137 C5 lake W Thailand
Srpska, Republika 100 B3 republic Bosnia and Herzegovina
Ssu-ch'uan see Sichuan
Ssu-p'ing/Ssu-p'ing-chieh see Siping
Stabroek 87 B5 Antwerpen, N Belgium
Stade 94 B3 Niedersachsen, NW Germany
Stadskanaal 86 E2 Groningen, NE Netherlands
Stafford 89 D6 C England, United Kingdom
Staicele 106 D3 Limbaži, N Latvia
Ştaierdorf-Anina see Anina
Stájerlakanina see Anina
Stakhanov 109 H3 Luhans'ka Oblast', E Ukraine
Stalin see Varna
Stalinabad see Dushanbe
Stalingrad see Volgograd
Stalino see Donets'k
Stalinobad see Dushanbe
Stalinsk see Novokuznetsk
Stalinski Zaliv see Varnenski Zaliv
Stalin, Yazovir see Iskŭr, Yazovir
Stalowa Wola 98 E4 Podkarpackie, SE Poland
Stamford 41 F3 Connecticut, NE USA
Stampalia see Astypálaia
Stanislau see Ivano-Frankivs'k
Stanislav see Ivano-Frankivs'k
Stanisławów see Ivano-Frankivs'k
Stanke Dimitrov see Dupnitsa
Stanley 65 D7 var. Port Stanley, Puerto Argentino. dependent territory capital (Falkland Islands) East Falkland, Falkland Islands
Stanleyville see Kisangani
Stann Creek see Dangriga
Stanovoy Khrebet 113 E3 mountain range SE Russian Federation
Stanthorpe 149 D5 Queensland, E Australia
Staphorst 86 D2 Overijssel, E Netherlands
Starachowice 98 D4 Świętokrzyskie, C Poland
Stara Kanjiža see Kanjiža
Stara Pazova 100 D3 Ger. Altpasua, Hung. Ópazova. Vojvodina, N Serbia
Stara Planina see Balkan Mountains
Stara Zagora 104 D2 Lat. Augusta Trajana. Stara Zagora, C Bulgaria
Starbuck Island 145 G3 prev. Volunteer Island. island E Kiribati
Stargard in Pommern see Stargard Szczeciński
Stargard Szczeciński 98 B3 Ger. Stargard in Pommern. Zachodnio-pomorskie, NW Poland
Stari Bečej see Bečej
Starobel'sk see Starobil's'k
Starobil's'k 109 H2 Rus. Starobel'sk. Luhans'ka Oblast', E Ukraine
Starobin 107 C7 var. Starobyn. Minskaya Voblasts', S Belarus
Starobyn see Starobin
Starogard Gdański 98 C2 Ger. Preussisch-Stargard. Pomorskie, N Poland
Starokonstantinov see Starokostyantyniv
Starokostyantyniv 108 D2 Rus. Starokonstantinov. Khmel'nyts'ka Oblast', NW Ukraine
Starominskaya 111 A7 Krasnodarskiy Kray, SW Russian Federation
Staryya Darohi 107 C6 Rus. Staryye Dorogi. Minskaya Voblasts', S Belarus
Staryye Dorogi see Staryya Darohi
Staryy Oskol 111 B6 Belgorodskaya Oblast', W Russian Federation
State College 41 E4 Pennsylvania, NE USA
Staten Island see Estados, Isla de los
Statesboro 43 E2 Georgia, SE USA
States, The see United States of America
Staunton 41 E5 Virginia, NE USA
Stavanger 85 A6 Rogaland, S Norway
Stavers Island see Vostok Island
Stavropol' 111 B7 prev. Voroshilovsk. Stavropol'skiy Kray, SW Russian Federation
Stavropol' see Tol'yatti
Steamboat Springs 44 C4 Colorado, C USA
Steenwijk 86 D2 Overijssel, N Netherlands

Steier see Steyr
Steierdorf/Steierdorf-Anina see Anina
Steinamanger see Szombathely
Steinkjer 84 B4 Nord-Trøndelag, C Norway
Stejarul see Karapelit
Stendal 94 C3 Sachsen-Anhalt, C Germany
Stepanakert see Xankändi
Stephenville 49 F3 Texas, SW USA
Sterling 44 D4 Colorado, C USA
Sterling 40 B3 Illinois, N USA
Sterlitamak 114 B3 Respublika Bashkortostan, W Russian Federation
Stettin see Szczecin
Stettiner Haff see Szczeciński, Zalew
Stevenage 89 E6 E England, United Kingdom
Stevens Point 40 B2 Wisconsin, N USA
Stewart Island 151 A8 island S New Zealand
Steyerlak-Anina see Anina
Steyr 95 D6 var. Steier. Oberösterreich, N Austria
St. Helena Bay 78 B5 bay SW South Africa
Stif see Sétif
Stillwater 49 G1 Oklahoma, C USA
Ştip 101 E6 E FYR Macedonia
Stirling 88 C4 C Scotland, United Kingdom
Stjørdalshalsen 84 B4 Nord-Trøndelag, C Norway
St-Maur-des-Fossés 90 E2 Val-de-Marne, Île-de-France, N France Europe
Stockach 95 B6 Baden-Württemberg, S Germany
Stockholm 85 C6 country capital (Sweden) (Sweden) Stockholm, C Sweden
Stockmannshof see Pļaviņas
Stockton 47 B6 California, W USA
Stockton Plateau 49 E4 plain Texas, SW USA
Stœng Trêng 137 D5 prev. Stung Treng. Stœng Trêng, NE Cambodia
Stoke see Stoke-on-Trent
Stoke-on-Trent 89 D6 var. Stoke. C England, United Kingdom
Stolbce see Stowbtsy
Stolbtsy see Stowbtsy
Stolp see Słupsk
Stolpmünde see Ustka
Stómio 104 B4 Thessalía, C Greece
Store Bælt see Storebælt
Storebelt see Storebælt
Støren 85 B5 Sør-Trøndelag, S Norway
Storfjorden 83 G2 fjord S Norway
Storhammer see Hamar
Stornoway 88 B2 NW Scotland, United Kingdom
Storsjön 85 B5 lake C Sweden
Storuman 84 C4 Västerbotten, N Sweden
Storuman 84 C4 lake N Sweden
Stowbtsy 107 C6 Pol. Stolbce, Rus. Stolbtsy. Minskaya Voblasts', C Belarus
Strabane 89 B5 Ir. An Srath Bán. W Northern Ireland, United Kingdom
Strakonice 99 A5 Ger. Strakonitz. Jihočeský Kraj, S Czech Republic
Strakonitz see Strakonice
Stralsund 94 D2 Mecklenburg-Vorpommern, NE Germany
Stranraer 89 C5 S Scotland, United Kingdom
Strasbourg 90 E3 Ger. Strassburg; anc. Argentoratum. Bas-Rhin, NE France
Strășeni 108 D3 var. Strasheny. C Moldova
Strasheny see Strășeni
Strassburg see Strasbourg, France
Strassburg see Aiud, Romania
Stratford 150 D4 Taranaki, North Island, New Zealand
Strathfield 148 E2 New South Wales, E Australia
Straubing 95 C6 Bayern, SE Germany
Strehaia 108 B5 Mehedinți, SW Romania
Strelka 114 D4 Krasnoyarskiy Kray, C Russian Federation
Strigonium see Esztergom
Strofília 105 C5 var. Strofilia. Évvoia, C Greece
Strofilia 105 C5 var. Strofilia. Évvoia, C Greece
Stromboli 97 D6 island Isole Eolie, S Italy

Stromeferry 88 C3 N Scotland, United Kingdom
Strömstad 85 B6 Västra Götaland, S Sweden
Strömsund 84 C4 Jämtland, C Sweden
Struga 101 D6 SW FYR Macedonia
Struma see Strymónas
Strumica 101 E6 E FYR Macedonia
Strumyani 104 C3 Blagoevgrad, SW Bulgaria
Strymónas 104 C3 Bul. Struma. river Bulgaria/Greece
Stryy 108 B2 L'vivs'ka Oblast', NW Ukraine
Studholme 151 B6 Canterbury, South Island, New Zealand
Stuhlweissenberg see Székesfehérvár
Stung Treng see Stœng Trêng
Sturgis 44 D3 South Dakota, N USA
Stuttgart 95 B6 Baden-Württemberg, SW Germany
Stykkishólmur 83 E4 Vesturland, W Iceland
Styr 108 C1 Rus. Styr'. river Belarus/Ukraine
Su see Jiangsu
Suakin 72 C3 var. Sawakin. Red Sea, NE Sudan
Subačius 106 C4 Panevėžys, NE Lithuania
Subaykhān 118 E3 Dayr az Zawr, E Syria
Subotica 100 D2 Ger. Maria-Theresiopel, Hung. Szabadka. Vojvodina, N Serbia
Suceava 108 C3 Ger. Suczawa, Hung. Szucsava. Suceava, NE Romania
Su-chou see Suzhou
Suchow see Suzhou, Jiangsu, China
Suchow see Suzhou, Jiangsu, China
Sucker State see Illinois
Sucre 61 F4 hist. Chuquisaca, La Plata. country capital (Bolivia-legal capital) (Bolivia-legal capital) Chuquisaca, S Bolivia
Suczawa see Suceava
Sudan 72 A4 off. Republic of Sudan, Ar. Jumhuriyat as-Sudan; prev. Anglo-Egyptian Sudan. country N Africa

SUDAN
East Africa

Official name Republic of the Sudan
Formation 1956 / 1956
Capital Khartoum
Population 37.8 million / 39 people per sq mile (15 people per sq km) / 40%
Total area 967,493 sq. miles (2,505,810 sq. km)
Languages Arabic / Arabic, Dinka, Nuer, Nubian, Beja, Zande, Bari, Fur, Shilluk, Lotuko
Religions Muslim (mainly Sunni) 70%, Traditional beliefs 20%, Christian 9%, Other 1%
Ethnic mix Other Black 52%, Arab 40%, Dinka and Beja 7%, Other 1%
Government Presidential system
Currency new Sudanese pound or dinar = 100 piastres
Literacy rate 61%
Calorie consumption 2228 calories

Sudanese Republic see Mali
Sudan, Jumhuriyat as- see Sudan
Sudan, Republic of see Sudan
Sudbury 38 C4 Ontario, S Canada
Sudd 73 B5 swamp region S Sudan
Sudeten 98 B4 var. Sudetes, Sudetic Mountains, Cz./Pol. Sudety. mountain range Czech Republic/Poland
Sudetes/Sudetic Mountains/Sudety see Sudeten
Südkarpaten see Carpații Meridionalii
Südliche Morava see Južna Morava
Sudong, Pulau 138 A2 island SW Singapore Asia
Sudostroy see Severodvinsk
Sue 73 B5 river S Sudan
Sueca 93 F3 País Valenciano, E Spain
Sue Wood Bay 42 B5 bay W Bermuda North America W Atlantic Ocean
Suez 72 B1 Ar. as Suways, El Suweis. NE Egypt
Suez Canal 72 B1 Ar. Qanāt as Suways. canal NE Egypt
Suez, Gulf of see Khalij as Suways

Suğla Gölü 116 C4 *lake* SW Turkey
Şuhār 121 D5 *var.* Sohar. N Oman
Sühbaatar 127 E1 Selenge, N Mongolia
Suhl 95 C5 Thüringen, C Germany
Suicheng *see* Suixi
Suid-Afrika *see* South Africa
Suidwes-Afrika *see* Namibia
Suixi 128 C6 *var.* Suicheng. Guangdong, S China
Sujāwal 134 B3 Sind, SE Pakistan
Sukabumi 138 C5 *prev.* Soekaboemi. Jawa, C Indonesia
Sukagawa 131 D5 Fukushima, Honshū, C Japan
Sukarnapura *see* Jayapura
Sukarno, Puntjak *see* Jaya, Puncak
Sukhne *see* As Sukhnah
Sukhona 110 C4 *var.* Tot'ma. *river* NW Russian Federation
Sukhumi *see* Sokhumi
Sukkertoppen *see* Maniitsoq
Sukkur 134 B3 Sind, SE Pakistan
Sukumo 131 B7 Kōchi, Shikoku, SW Japan
Sulaimaniya *see* As Sulaymānīyah
Sulaiman Range 134 C2 *mountain range* C Pakistan
Sula, Kepulauan 139 E4 *island group* C Indonesia
Sulawesi, Laut *see* Celebes Sea
Sulechów 98 B3 Ger. Züllichau. Lubuskie, W Poland
Suliag *see* Sawhāj
Sullana 60 B2 Piura, NW Peru
Sullivan Island *see* Lanbi Kyun
Sulphur Springs 49 G2 Texas, SW USA
Sultānābād *see* Arāk
Sulu Archipelago 139 E3 *island group* SW Philippines
Sülüktü *see* Sulyukta
Sulu, Laut *see* Sulu Sea
Sulu Sea 139 E2 *var.* Laut Sulu. *sea* SW Philippines
Sulyukta 123 E2 Kir. Sülüktü. Batkenskaya Oblast', SW Kyrgyzstan
Sumatra 137 B8 Eng. Sumatra. *island* W Indonesia
Sumatra *see* Sumatera
Šumava *see* Bohemian Forest
Sumba, Pulau 139 E5 Eng. Sandalwood Island; *prev.* Soemba. *island* Nusa Tenggara, C Indonesia
Sumba, Selat 139 E5 *strait* Nusa Tenggara, S Indonesia
Sumbawanga 73 B7 Rukwa, W Tanzania
Sumbe 78 B2 *var.* N'Gunza, Port. Novo Redondo. Cuanza Sul, W Angola
Sumeih 73 B5 Southern Darfur, S Sudan
Sumgait *see* Sumqayıt, Azerbaijan
Summer Lake 46 B4 *lake* Oregon, NW USA
Summit 93 H5 Alaska, USA
Sumqayıt 117 H2 Rus. Sumgait. E Azerbaijan
Sumy 109 F2 Sums'ka Oblast', NE Ukraine
Sunda Islands *see* Greater Sunda Islands
Sunda, Selat 138 B5 *strait* Jawa/Sumatera, SW Indonesia
Sunda Trench *see* Java Trench
Sunderland 88 D4 *var.* Wearmouth. NE England, United Kingdom
Sundsvall 85 C5 Västernorrland, C Sweden
Sunflower State *see* Kansas
Sungaipenuh 138 B4 *prev.* Soengaipenoeh. Sumatera, W Indonesia
Sunnyvale 47 A6 California, W USA
Sunset State *see* Oregon
Sunshine State *see* Florida
Sunshine State *see* New Mexico
Sunshine State *see* South Dakota
Suntar 115 F3 Respublika Sakha (Yakutiya), NE Russian Federation
Sunyani 75 E5 W Ghana
Suoločielgi *see* Saariselkä
Suomenlahti *see* Finland, Gulf of
Suomen Tasavalta/Suomi *see* Finland
Suomussalmi 84 E4 Oulu, E Finland
Suŏng 137 D6 Kâmpóng Cham, C Cambodia
Suoyarvi 110 B3 Respublika Kareliya, NW Russian Federation
Supe 60 C3 Lima, W Peru
Supérieur, Lac *see* Superior, Lake

Superior 40 A1 Wisconsin, N USA
Superior, Lake 40 B1 Fr. Lac Supérieur. *lake* Canada/USA
Suqrah *see* Şawqirah
Şūr 121 E5 NE Oman
Şūr *see* Soûr
Surabaja *see* Surabaya
Surabaya 138 D5 *prev.* Surabaja, Soerabaja. Jawa, C Indonesia
Surakarta 138 C5 Eng. Solo; *prev.* Soerakarta. Jawa, S Indonesia
Šurany 99 C6 Hung. Nagysurány. Nitriansky Kraj, SW Slovakia
Sūrat 134 C4 Gujarāt, W India
Suratdhani *see* Surat Thani
Surat Thani 137 C6 *var.* Suratdhani, Surat Thani, SW Thailand
Surazh 107 E5 Vitsyebskaya Voblasts', NE Belarus
Surdulica 101 E5 Serbia, SE Serbia
Sûre 87 D7 *var.* Sauer. *river* W Europe
Surendranagar 134 C4 Gujarāt, W India
Surfers Paradise 149 E5 Queensland, E Australia
Surgut 114 D3 Khanty-Mansiyskiy Avtonomnyy Okrug-Yugra, C Russian Federation
Surin 137 D5 Surin, E Thailand
Surinam *see* Suriname
Suriname 59 G3 *off.* Republic of Suriname, *var.* Surinam; *prev.* Dutch Guiana, Netherlands Guiana. *country* N South America

SURINAME
South America

Official name Republic of Suriname
Formation 1975 / 1975
Capital Paramaribo
Population 470,784 / 8 people per sq mile (3 people per sq km) / 77%
Total area 63,039 sq. miles (163,270 sq. km)
Languages Sranan (Creole), Dutch*, Javanese, Sarnami Hindi, Saramaccan, Chinese, Carib
Religions Hindu 27%, Protestant 25%, Roman Catholic 23%, Muslim 20%, Traditional beliefs 5%
Ethnic mix Creole 34%, South Asian 34%, Javanese 18%, Black 9%, Other 5%
Government Parliamentary system
Currency Surinamese dollar = 100 cents
Literacy rate 90%
Calorie consumption 2652 calories

Suriname, Republic of *see* Suriname
Sūrīya/Sūrīyah, Al-Jumhūrīyah al-'Arabīyah as- *see* Syria
Surkhab, Darya-i- *see* Kahmard, Darya-ye
Surkhob 123 F3 *river* C Tajikistan
Surt 71 G2 *var.* Sidra, Sirte. N Libya
Surtsey 83 E5 *island* S Iceland
Suruga-wan 131 D6 *bay* SE Japan
Susa 87 D7 *var.* Piemonte, NE Italy
Sūsah *see* Sousse
Susanville 47 B5 California, W USA
Susitna 36 C3 Alaska, USA
Susteren 87 D5 Limburg, SE Netherlands
Susuman 115 G3 Magadanskaya Oblast', E Russian Federation
Sutlej 134 C2 *river* India/Pakistan
Suur Munamägi 106 D3 *var.* Munamägi, Ger. Eier-Berg. *mountain* SE Estonia
Suur Väin 106 C2 Ger. Grosser Sund. *strait* W Estonia
Suva 145 E4 *country capital* (Fiji) (Fiji) Viti Levu, W Fiji
Suvalkai/Suvalki *see* Suwałki
Suwałki 98 E2 Lith. Suvalkai, Rus. Suvalki. Podlaskie, NE Poland
Şuwār *see* Suwār
Suways, Qanāt as *see* Suez Canal
Suweida *see* As Suwaydā'
Suzhou 128 D5 *var.* Soochow, Su-chou, Suchow; *prev.* Wuhsien. Jiangsu, E China
Svalbard 83 E1 Norwegian dependency Arctic Ocean
Svartisen 84 C3 *glacier* C Norway
Svay Rieng 137 D6 Svay Riĕng, S Cambodia
Sveg 85 B5 Jämtland, C Sweden
Svenstavik 85 C5 Jämtland, C Sweden
Sverdlovsk *see* Yekaterinburg
Sverige *see* Sweden

Sveti Vrach *see* Sandanski
Svetlogorsk *see* Svyetlahorsk
Svetlograd 111 B7 Stavropol'skiy Kray, SW Russian Federation
Svetlovods'k *see* Svitlovods'k
Svetozarevo *see* Jagodina
Svilengrad 104 D3 *prev.* Mustafa-Pasha Khaskovo, S Bulgaria
Svitlovods'k 109 F3 Rus. Svetlovodsk. Kirovohrads'ka Oblast', C Ukraine
Svizzera *see* Switzerland
Svobodnyy 115 G4 Amurskaya Oblast', SE Russian Federation
Svyataya Anna Trough 155 C4 *var.* Saint Anna Trough. *trough* N Kara Sea
Svyetlahorsk 107 D7 Rus. Svetlogorsk. Homyel'skaya Voblasts', SE Belarus
Swabian Jura *see* Schwäbische Alb
Swakopmund 78 B3 Erongo, W Namibia
Swan Islands 53 E1 *island group* NE Honduras North America
Swansea 89 C7 Wel. Abertawe. S Wales, United Kingdom
Swarzędz 98 C3 Poznań, W Poland
Swatow *see* Shantou
Swaziland 78 D4 *off.* Kingdom of Swaziland. *country* S Africa

SWAZILAND
Southern Africa

Official name Kingdom of Swaziland
Formation 1968 / 1968
Capital Mbabane
Population 1 million / 151 people per sq mile (58 people per sq km) / 24%
Total area 6704 sq. miles (17,363 sq. km)
Languages English*, siSwati*, isiZulu, Xitsonga
Religions Christian 60%, Traditional beliefs 40%
Ethnic mix Swazi 97%, Other 3%
Government Monarchy
Currency Lilangeni = 100 cents
Literacy rate 80%
Calorie consumption 2322 calories

Swaziland, Kingdom of *see* Swaziland
Sweden 84 B4 *off.* Kingdom of Sweden, Swe. Sverige. *country* N Europe

SWEDEN
Northern Europe

Official name Kingdom of Sweden
Formation 1523 / 1921
Capital Stockholm
Population 9.1 million / 57 people per sq mile (22 people per sq km) / 83%
Total area 173,731 sq. miles (449,964 sq. km)
Languages Swedish*, Finnish, Sámi
Religions Evangelical Lutheran 82%, Other 13%, Roman Catholic 2%, Muslim 2%, Orthodox Christian 1%
Ethnic mix Swedish 86%, Foreign-born or first-generation immigrant 12%, Finnish and Sámi 2%
Government Parliamentary system
Currency Swedish krona = 100 öre
Literacy rate 99%
Calorie consumption 3185 calories

Sweden, Kingdom of *see* Sweden
Sweetwater 49 F3 Texas, SW USA
Świdnica 98 B4 Ger. Schweidnitz. Wałbrzych, SW Poland
Świdwin 98 B2 Ger. Schivelbein. Zachodnio-pomorskie, NW Poland
Świebodzice 98 B4 Ger. Freiburg in Schlesien, Swiebodzice. Walbrzych, SW Poland
Świebodzin 98 B3 Ger. Schwiebus. Lubuskie, W Poland
Świecie 98 C3 Ger. Schwertberg. Kujawsko-pomorskie, C Poland
Swindon 89 D7 S England, United Kingdom
Swinemünde *see* Świnoujście
Świnoujście 98 B2 Ger. Swinemünde. Zachodnio-pomorskie, NW Poland
Swiss Confederation *see* Switzerland

Switzerland 95 A7 *off.* Swiss Confederation, Fr. La Suisse, Ger. Schweiz, It. Svizzera; *anc.* Helvetia. *country* C Europe

SWITZERLAND
Central Europe

Official name Swiss Confederation
Formation 1291 / 1857
Capital Bern
Population 7.3 million / 475 people per sq mile (184 people per sq km) / 68%
Total area 15,942 sq. miles (41,290 sq. km)
Languages German*, Swiss-German, French*, Italian*, Romansch
Religions Roman Catholic 42%, Protestant 35%, Other and nonreligious 19%, Muslim 4%
Ethnic mix German 64%, French 20%, Other 9%, Italian 6%, Romansch 1%
Government Parliamentary system
Currency Swiss franc = 100 rappen/centimes
Literacy rate 99%
Calorie consumption 3526 calories

Sycaminum *see* Hefa
Sydenham Island *see* Nonouti
Sydney 148 D1 *state capital* New South Wales, SE Australia
Sydney 39 G4 Cape Breton Island, Nova Scotia, SE Canada
Sydney Island *see* Manra
Syedpur *see* Saidpur
Syemyezhava 107 C6 Rus. Semezhevo. Minskaya Voblasts', C Belarus
Syene *see* Aswān
Syeverodonets'k 109 H3 Rus. Severodonetsk. Luhans'ka Oblast', E Ukraine
Syktyvkar 110 D4 *prev.* Ust'-Sysol'sk. Respublika Komi, NW Russian Federation
Sylhet 135 G3 Sylhet, NE Bangladesh
Synel'nykove 109 G3 Dnipropetrovs'ka Oblast', E Ukraine
Syowa 154 C2 Japanese research station Antarctica
Syracuse 41 F3 New York, NE USA
Syracuse *see* Siracusa
Syrdar'ya 114 B4 Sirdaryo Viloyati, E Uzbekistan
Syria 118 B3 *off.* Syrian Arab Republic, *var.* Siria, Syrie, Ar. Al-Jumhūrīyah al-'Arabīyah as-Sūrīyah, Sūrīya. *country* SW Asia

SYRIA
Southwest Asia

Official name Syrian Arab Republic
Formation 1941 / 1967
Capital Damascus
Population 20 million / 281 people per sq mile (109 people per sq km) / 50%
Total area 71,498 sq. miles (184,180 sq. km)
Languages Arabic*, French, Kurdish, Armenian, Circassian, Turkic languages, Assyrian, Aramaic
Religions Sunni Muslim 74%, Other Muslim 16%, Christian 10%
Ethnic mix Arab 89%, Kurdish 6%, Other 3%, Armenian, Turkmen, and Circassian 2%
Government One-party state
Currency Syrian pound = 100 piastres
Literacy rate 80%
Calorie consumption 3038 calories

Syrian Arab Republic *see* Syria
Syrian Desert 119 D5 Ar. Al Hamad, Bādiyat ash Shām. *desert* SW Asia
Syrie *see* Syria
Sýrna 105 E7 *var.* Sirna. *island* Kykládes, Greece, Aegean Sea
Sýros 105 C6 *var.* Síros. *island* Kykládes, Greece, Aegean Sea
Syulemeshlii *see* Sredets
Syvash, Zaliv *see* Syvash, Zatoka
Syvash, Zatoka 109 F4 Rus. Zaliv Syvash. *inlet* S Ukraine
Syzran' 111 C6 Samarskaya Oblast', W Russian Federation
Szabadka *see* Subotica

Szamotuły *98 B3* Poznań, W Poland
Szászrégen *see* Reghin
Szatmárrnémeti *see* Satu Mare
Száva *see* Sava
Szczecin *98 B3 Eng./Ger.* Stettin.
  Zachodnio-pomorskie, NW Poland
Szczecinek *98 B2 Ger.* Neustettin.
  Zachodnio-pomorskie, NW Poland
Szczeciński, Zalew *98 A2 var.* Stettiner
  Haff, *Ger.* Oderhaff. *bay* Germany/
  Poland
Szczuczyn Nowogródzki *see* Shchuchyn
Szczytno *98 D3 Ger.* Ortelsburg.
  Warmińsko-Mazurskie, NE Poland
Szechuan/Szechwan *see* Sichuan
Szeged *99 D7 Ger.* Szegedin, *Rom.*
  Seghedin. Csongrád, SE Hungary
Szegedin *see* Szeged
Székelykeresztúr *see* Cristuru Secuiesc
Székesfehérvár *99 C6 Ger.*
  Stuhlweissenberg; *anc.* Alba Regia.
  Fejér, W Hungary
Szeklerburg *see* Miercurea-Ciuc
Szekler Neumarkt *see* Târgu Secuiesc
Szekszárd *99 C7* Tolna, S Hungary
Szempcz/Szenc *see* Senec
Szenice *see* Senica
Szenttamás *see* Srbobran
Szeping *see* Siping
Szilágysomlyó *see* Şimleu Silvaniei
Szinna *see* Snina
Sziszek *see* Sisak
Szitás-Keresztúr *see* Cristuru Secuiesc
Szkudy *see* Skuodas
Szlatina *see* Slatina
Szlovákia *see* Slovakia
Szolnok *99 D6* Jász-Nagykun-Szolnok,
  C Hungary
Szombathely *99 B6 Ger.* Steinamanger;
  anc. Sabaria, Savaria. Vas, W Hungary
Szprotawa *98 B4 Ger.* Sprottau.
  Lubuskie, W Poland
Sztálinváros *see* Dunaújváros
Szucsava *see* Suceava

T

Tabariya, Bahrat *see* Tiberias, Lake
Table Rock Lake *49 G1 reservoir*
  Arkansas/Missouri, C USA
Tábor *99 B5* Jihočeský Kraj, S Czech
  Republic
Tabora *73 B7* Tabora, W Tanzania
Tabriz *120 C2 var.* Tebriz; *anc.* Tauris.
  Āzarbāyjān-e Sharqī, NW Iran
Tabuaeran *145 G2 prev.* Fanning Island.
  atoll Line Islands, E Kiribati
Tabūk *120 A4* Tabūk, NW Saudi Arabia
Täby *85 C6* Stockholm, C Sweden
Tachau *see* Tachov
Tachov *99 A5 Ger.* Tachau. Plveňský
  Kraj, W Czech Republic
Tacloban *139 F2 off.* Tacloban City.
  Leyte, C Philippines
Tacloban City *see* Tacloban
Tacna *61 E4* Tacna, SE Peru
Tacoma *46 B2* Washington,
  NW USA
Tacuarembó *64 D4 prev.* San Fructuoso.
  Tacuarembó, C Uruguay
Tademaït, Plateau du *70 D3 plateau*
  C Algeria
Tadmor/Tadmur *see* Tudmur
Tādpatri *132 C2* Andhra Pradesh,
  E India
Tadzhikistan *see* Tajikistan
Taegu *129 E4 off.* Taegu-gwangyŏksi,
  var. Daegu, *Jap.* Taikyū. SE South
  Korea
Taegu-gwangyŏksi *see* Taegu
Taehan-haehyŏp *see* Korea Strait
Taehan Min'guk *see* South Korea
Taejŏn *129 E4 off.* Taejŏn-gwangyŏksi,
  Jap. Taiden. C South Korea
Taejŏn-gwangyŏksi *see* Taejŏn
Tafassâsset, Ténéré du *75 G2 desert*
  N Niger

Taganrogskiy Zaliv *see* Taganrog,
  Gulf of
Taguatinga *63 F3* Tocantins, C Brazil
Tagus *92 C3 Port.* Rio Tejo, *Sp.* Río Tajo.
  river Portugal/Spain
Tagus Plain *80 A4 abyssal plain*
  E Atlantic Ocean
Tahanroz'ka Zatoka *see* Taganrog,
  Gulf of
Tahat *71 E4 mountain* SE Algeria
Tahiti *145 H4 island* Îles du Vent,
  W French Polynesia
Tahiti, Archipel de *see* Société, Archipel
  de la
Tahlequah *49 G1* Oklahoma, C USA
Tahoe, Lake *47 B5 lake* California/
  Nevada, W USA
Tahoua *75 F3* Tahoua, W Niger
Taichū *see* T'aichung
T'aichung *128 D6 Jap.* Taichū; *prev.*
  Taiwan. C Taiwan
Taiden *see* Taejŏn
Taieri *151 B7 river* South Island, New
  Zealand
Taihape *150 D4* Manawatu-Wanganui,
  North Island, New Zealand
Taihoku *see* T'aipei
Taikyū *see* Taegu
Tailem Bend *149 B7* South Australia
T'ainan *128 D6 Jap.* Tainan; *prev.*
  Dainan. S Taiwan
T'aipei *128 D6 Jap.* Taihoku; *prev.*
  Daihoku. *country capital* (Taiwan)
  (Taiwan) N Taiwan
Taiping *138 B3* Perak, Peninsular
  Malaysia
Taiwan *128 D6 off.* Republic of China,
  var. Formosa, Formo'sa. *country*
  E Asia

TAIWAN
East Asia

Official name Republic of China (ROC)
Formation 1949 / 1949
Capital Taipei
Population 22.9 million / 1835 people
  per sq mile (709 people per sq km) / 80%
Total area 13,892 sq. miles (35,980 sq. km)
Languages Amoy Chinese, Mandarin
  Chinese*, Hakka Chinese
Religions Buddhist, Confucianist, and
  Taoist 93%, Christian 5%, Other 2%
Ethnic mix Han (pre-20th-century
  migration) 84%, Han (20th-century
  migration) 14%, Aboriginal 2%
Government Presidential system
Currency Taiwan dollar = 100 cents
Literacy rate 97%
Calorie consumption Not available

Taiwan *see* T'aichung
T'aiwan Haihsia/Taiwan Haixia *see*
  Taiwan Strait
Taiwan Strait *128 D6 var.* Formosa
  Strait, *Chin.* T'aiwan Haihsia, Taiwan
  Haixia. *strait* China/Taiwan
Taiyuan *128 C4 var.* T'ai-yuan, T'ai-
  yüan; *prev.* Yangku. *province capital*
  Shanxi, C China
T'ai-yuan/T'ai-yüan *see* Taiyuan
Ta'izz *121 B7* SW Yemen
Tajikistan *123 E3 off.* Republic of
  Tajikistan, *Rus.* Tadzhikistan, *Taj.*
  Jumhurii Tojikiston; *prev.* Tajik S.S.R.
  country C Asia

TAJIKISTAN
Central Asia

Official name Republic of Tajikistan
Formation 1991 / 1991
Capital Dushanbe
Population 6.7 million / 121 people
  per sq mile (47 people per sq km) / 25%
Total area 55,251 sq. miles (143,100 sq. km)
Languages Tajik*, Uzbek, Russian
Religions Sunni Muslim 80%, Other 15%,
  Shi'a Muslim 5%
Ethnic mix Tajik 80%, Uzbek 15%,
  Other 3%, Russian 1%, Kyrgyz 1%
Government Presidential system
Currency Somoni = 100 diram
Literacy rate 99%
Calorie consumption 1828 calories

Tajikistan, Republic of *see* Tajikistan

Tajik S.S.R *see* Tajikistan
Tajo, Río *see* Tagus
Tak *136 C4 var.* Rahaeng. Tak,
  W Thailand
Takao *see* Kaohsiung
Takaoka *131 C5* Toyama, Honshū,
  SW Japan
Takapuna *150 D2* Auckland, North
  Island, New Zealand
Takhiatash *see* Taxiatosh
Takhtakupyr *see* Taxtako'pir
Takikawa *130 D2* Hokkaidō, NE Japan
Takla Makan Desert *126 B3 Eng.* Takla
  Makan Desert. *desert* NW China
Takla Makan Desert *see* Taklimakan
  Shamo
Takow *see* Kaohsiung
Takutea *145 G4 island* S Cook Islands
Talabriga *see* Aveiro, Portugal
Talabriga *see* Talavera de la Reina, Spain
Talachyn *107 D5 Rus.* Tolochin.
  Vitsyebskaya Voblasts', NE Belarus
Talamanca, Cordillera de *53 E5*
  mountain range S Costa Rica
Talara *60 B2* Piura, NW Peru
Talas *123 F2* Talasskaya Oblast',
  NW Kyrgyzstan
Talaud, Kepulauan *139 F3 island group*
  E Indonesia
Talavera de la Reina *92 D3 anc.*
  Caesarobriga, Talabriga. Castilla-La
  Mancha, C Spain
Talca *64 B4* Maule, C Chile
Talcahuano *65 B5* Bío Bío, C Chile
Taldykorgan *114 C5 Kaz.* Taldyqorghan;
  prev. Taldy-Kurgan. Taldykorgan,
  SE Kazakhstan
Taldy-Kurgan/Taldyqorghan *see*
  Taldykorgan
Ta-lien *see* Dalian
Taliq-an *see* Tāloqān
Tal'ka *107 C6* Minskaya Voblasts',
  C Belarus
Talkhof *see* Puurmani
Tallahassee *42 D3 prev.* Muskogean.
  state capital Florida, SE USA
Tall al Abyaḍ *see* At Tall al Abyaḍ
Tallin *see* Tallinn
Tallinn *106 D2 Ger.* Reval, *Rus.* Tallin;
  prev. Revel. *country capital* (Estonia)
  (Estonia) Harjumaa, NW Estonia
Tall Kalakh *118 B4 var.* Tell Kalakh.
  Ḥimṣ, C Syria
Tallulah *42 B2* Louisiana, S USA
Talnakh *114 D3* Taymyrskiy (Dolgano-
  Nenetskiy) Avtonomnyy Okrug,
  N Russian Federation
Tal'ne *109 E3 Rus.* Tal'noye. Cherkas'ka
  Oblast', C Ukraine
Tal'noye *see* Tal'ne
Taloga *49 F1* Oklahoma, C USA
Tāloqān *123 E3 var.* Taliq-an. Takhār,
  NE Afghanistan
Talsen *see* Talsi
Talsi *106 C3 Ger.* Talsen. Talsi,
  NW Latvia
Taltal *64 B2* Antofagasta, N Chile
Talvik *84 D2* Finnmark, N Norway
Tamabo, Banjaran *138 D3 mountain
  range* East Malaysia
Tamale *75 E4* C Ghana
Tamana *145 E3 prev.* Rotcher Island.
  atoll Tungaru, W Kiribati
Tamanrasset *71 E4 var.* Tamenghest.
  S Algeria
Tamar *89 C7 river* SW England, United
  Kingdom
Tamar *see* Tudmur
Tamatave *see* Toamasina
Tamazunchale *51 E4* San Luis Potosí,
  C Mexico
Tambacounda *74 C3* SE Senegal
Tambov *111 B6* Tambovskaya Oblast',
  W Russian Federation
Tambura *73 B5* Western Equatoria,
  SW Sudan
Tamchekket *see* Tâmchekkeṭ
Tâmchekkeṭ *74 C3 var.* Tamchaket.
  Hodh el Gharbi, S Mauritania
Tamenghest *see* Tamanrasset
Tamil Nādu *132 C3 Prev.* Madras.
  cultural region SE India
Tam Ky *137 E5* Quang Nam-fa Năng,
  C Vietnam
Tammerfors *see* Tampere
Tampa *43 E4* Florida, SE USA
Tampa Bay *43 E4 bay* Florida, SE USA

Tampere *85 D5 Swe.* Tammerfors.
  Länsi-Suomi, W Finland
Tampico *51 E3* Tamaulipas, C Mexico
Tamworth *149 D6* New South Wales,
  SE Australia
Tanabe *131 C7* Wakayama, Honshū,
  SW Japan
Tana Bru *84 D2* Finnmark, N Norway
Tanais *see* Don
Lake Tana *72 C4 var.* Lake Tana. *lake*
  NW Ethiopia
Tana, Lake *see* T'ana Hāyk'
Tanami Desert *146 D3 desert* Northern
  Territory, N Australia
Tananarive *see* Antananarivo
Tăndărei *108 D5* Ialomiṭa, SE Romania
Tandil *65 D5* Buenos Aires, E Argentina
Tandjoengkarang *see* Bandar Lampung
Tanega-shima *131 B8 island* Nansei-
  shotō, SW Japan
Tanen Tonggyi *see* Tane Range
Tane Range *136 B4 Bur.* Tanen
  Taunggyi. *mountain range* W Thailand
Tanezrouft *70 D4 desert* Algeria/Mali
Ṭanf, Jabal aṭ *118 D4 mountain* SE Syria
Tanga *73 C7* Tanga, E Tanzania
Tanganyika and Zanzibar *see* Tanzania
Tanganyika, Lake *73 B7 lake* E Africa
Tanger *70 C2 var.* Tangiers, Tangier, *Fr./
  Ger.* Tangerk, *Sp.* Tánger; *anc.* Tingis.
  NW Morocco
Tangerk *see* Tanger
Tanggula Shan *126 C4 mountain* W China
Tangier *see* Tanger
Tangiers *see* Tanger
Tangra Yumco *126 B5 var.* Tangro Tso.
  lake W China
Tangro Tso *see* Tangra Yumco
Tangshan *128 D3 var.* T'ang-shan.
  Hebei, E China
T'ang-shan *see* Tangshan
Tanimbar, Kepulauan *139 F5 island
  group* Maluku, E Indonesia
**Tanjungkarang/Tanjungkarang-
  Telukbetung** *see* Bandar Lampung
Tanna *144 D4 island* S Vanuatu
Tannenhof *see* Krynica
Tan-Tan *70 B3* SW Morocco
Tan-tung *see* Dandong
Tanzania *73 C7 off.* United Republic of
  Tanzania, *Swa.* Jamhuri ya Muungano
  wa Tanzania; *prev.* German East Africa,
  Tanganyika and Zanzibar. *country*
  E Africa

TANZANIA
East Africa

Official name United Republic
  of Tanzania
Formation 1964 / 1964
Capital Dodoma
Population 39.7 million / 116 people
  per sq mile (45 people per sq km) / 36%
Total area 364,898 sq. miles
  (945,087 sq. km)
Languages Kiswahili*, Sukuma, Chagga,
  Nyamwezi, Hehe, Makonde, Yao,
  Sandawe, English*
Religions Muslim 33%, Christian 33%,
  Traditional beliefs 30%, Other 4%
Ethnic mix Native African (over 120
  tribes) 99%, European, Asian, and Arab 1%
Government Presidential system
Currency Tanzanian shilling = 100 cents
Literacy rate 69%
Calorie consumption 1975 calories

Tanzania, Jamhuri ya Muungano wa
  see Tanzania
Tanzania, United Republic of *see*
  Tanzania
Taoudenni *see* Taoudenni
Taoudenni *75 E2 var.* Taoudenit.
  Tombouctou, N Mali
Tapa *106 E2 Ger.* Taps. Lääne-Virumaa,
  N Estonia
Tapachula *51 G5* Chiapas, SE Mexico
Tapaiu *see* Gvardeysk
Tapajós, Rio *63 E2 var.* Tapajóz. *river*
  NW Brazil
Tapajóz *see* Tapajós, Rio
Taps *see* Tapa
Ṭarābulus *71 F2 var.* Ṭarābulus al Gharb,
  Eng. Tripoli. *country capital* (Libya)
  (Libya) NW Libya
Ṭarābulus al Gharb *see* Ṭarābulus

Tarābulus/Ṭarābulus ash Shām *see* Tripoli
Taraclia 108 D4 *Rus.* Tarakilya. S Moldova
Tarakilya *see* Taraclia
Mount Taranaki 150 C4 *var.* Egmont. *volcano* North Island, New Zealand
Tarancón 93 E3 Castilla-La Mancha, C Spain
Taranto 97 E5 *var.* Tarentum. Puglia, SE Italy
Taranto, Gulf of 97 E6 Eng. Gulf of Taranto. *gulf* S Italy
Taranto, Gulf of *see* Taranto, Golfo di
Tarapoto 60 C2 San Martín, N Peru
Tarare 91 D5 Rhône, E France
Tarascon 91 D6 Bouches-du-Rhône, SE France
Tarawa 144 D2 *atoll* Tungaru, W Kiribati
Taraz 114 C5 *prev.* Aulie Ata, Auliye-Ata, Dzhambul, Zhambyl. Zhambyl, S Kazakhstan
Tarazona 93 E2 Aragón, NE Spain
Tarbes 91 B6 *anc.* Bigorra. Hautes-Pyrénées, S France
Tarcoola 149 A6 South Australia
Taree 149 D6 New South Wales, SE Australia
Tarentum *see* Taranto
Târgoviște 108 C5 *prev.* Tîrgoviște. Dâmbovița, S Romania
Targu Jiu 108 B4 *prev.* Tîrgu Jiu. Gorj, W Romania
Târgul-Neamţ *see* Târgu-Neamţ
Târgul-Săcuiesc *see* Târgu Secuiesc
Târgu Mureş 108 B4 *prev.* Oşorhei, Tîrgu Mures, Ger. Neumarkt, *Hung.* Marosvásárhely. Mureş, C Romania
Târgu-Neamţ 108 C3 *var.* Târgul-Neamţ; *prev.* Tîrgu-Neamţ. Neamţ, NE Romania
Târgu Ocna 108 C4 *Hung.* Aknavásár; *prev.* Tîrgu Ocna. Bacău, E Romania
Târgu Secuiesc 108 C4 Ger. Neumarkt, Szekler Neumarkt, *Hung.* Kezdivásárhely; *prev.* Chezdi-Oşorheiu, Târgul-Săcuiesc, Tîrgu Secuiesc. Covasna, E Romania
Tar Heel State *see* North Carolina
Tarija 61 G5 Tarija, S Bolivia
Tarim 121 C6 C Yemen
Tarim Basin 124 C2 *Eng.* Tarim Basin. *basin* NW China
Tarim Basin *see* Tarim Pendi
Tarim He 126 B3 *river* NW China
Tarma 60 C3 Junín, C Peru
Tarn 91 C6 *cultural region* S France
Tarn 91 C6 *river* S France
Tarnobrzeg 98 D4 Podkarpackie, SE Poland
Tarnopol *see* Ternopil'
Tarnów 99 D5 Małopolskie, S Poland
Tarraco *see* Tarragona
Tarragona 93 G2 *anc.* Tarraco. Cataluña, E Spain
Tarrasa *see* Terrassa
Tàrrega 93 F2 *var.* Tarrega. Cataluña, NE Spain
Tarsatica *see* Rijeka
Tarsus 116 C4 İçel, S Turkey
Tartous/Tartus *see* Ṭarṭūs
Tartu 106 D3 *Ger.* Dorpat; *prev. Rus.* Yurev, Yury'ev. Tartumaa, SE Estonia
Ṭarṭūs 118 A3 *off.* Muḥāfaẓat Ṭarṭūs, *var.* Tartous, Tartus. *governorate* W Syria
Ṭarṭūs, Muḥāfaẓat *see* Ṭarṭūs
Ta Ru Tao, Ko 137 B7 *island* S Thailand Asia
Tarvisio 96 D2 Friuli-Venezia Giulia, NE Italy
Tarvisium *see* Treviso
Tashauz *see* Daşoguz
Tashi Chho Dzong *see* Thimphu
Tashkent *see* Toshkent
Tash-Kömür *see* Tash-Kumyr
Tash-Kumyr 123 F2 *Kir.* Tash-Kömür. Dzhalal-Abadskaya Oblast', W Kyrgyzstan
Tashqurghan *see* Kholm
Tasikmalaja *see* Tasikmalaya
Tasikmalaya 138 C5 *prev.* Tasikmalaja. Jawa, C Indonesia
Tasman Basin 142 C5 *var.* East Australian Basin. *undersea basin* S Tasman Sea

Tasman Bay 151 C5 *inlet* South Island, New Zealand
Tasmania 149 B8 *prev.* Van Diemen's Land. *state* SE Australia
Tasmania 152 B4 *island* SE Australia
Tasman Plateau 142 C5 *var.* South Tasmania Plateau. *undersea plateau* SW Tasman Sea
Tasman Sea 142 C5 *sea* SW Pacific Ocean
Tassili-n-Ajjer 71 E4 *plateau* E Algeria
Tatabánya 99 C6 Komárom-Esztergom, NW Hungary
Tatar Pazardzhik *see* Pazardzhik
Tathlith 121 B5 'Asir, S Saudi Arabia
Tatra Mountains 99 D5 *Ger.* Tatra, *Hung.* Tátra, *Pol./Slvk.* Tatry. *mountain range* Poland/Slovakia
Tatra/Tátra *see* Tatra Mountains
Tatry *see* Tatra Mountains
Ta-t'ung/Tatung *see* Datong
Tatvan 117 F3 Bitlis, SE Turkey
Ta'ü 145 F4 *var.* Tau. *island* Manua Islands, E American Samoa
Taukum, Peski 123 G1 *desert* SE Kazakhstan
Taumarunui 150 D4 Manawatu-Wanganui, North Island, New Zealand
Taungdwingyi 136 B3 Magway, C Burma (Myanmar)
Taunggyi 136 B3 Shan State, C Burma (Myanmar)
Taungoo 136 B4 Bago, C Burma (Myanmar)
Taunton 89 C7 SW England, United Kingdom
Taupo 150 D3 Waikato, North Island, New Zealand
Taupo, Lake 150 D3 *lake* North Island, New Zealand
Tauragė 106 B4 *Ger.* Tauroggen. Tauragė, SW Lithuania
Tauranga 150 D3 Bay of Plenty, North Island, New Zealand
Tauris *see* Tabrīz
Tauroggen *see* Tauragė
Taurus Mountains 116 C4 *Eng.* Taurus Mountains. *mountain range* S Turkey
Taurus Mountains *see* Toros Dağları
Tavas 116 B4 Denizli, SW Turkey
Tavastehus *see* Hämeenlinna
Tavira 92 C5 Faro, S Portugal
Tavoy *see* Dawei
Tavoy Island *see* Mali Kyun
Ta Waewae Bay 151 A7 *bay* South Island, New Zealand
Tawakoni, Lake 49 G2 *reservoir* Texas, SW USA
Tawau 138 D3 Sabah, East Malaysia
Ţawkar *see* Tokar
Tawzar *see* Tozeur
Taxco 51 E4 *var.* Taxco de Alarcón. Guerrero, S Mexico
Taxco de Alarcón *see* Taxco
Taxiatosh 122 C2 *Rus.* Takhiatash. Qoraqalpog'iston Respublikasi, W Uzbekistan
Taxtako'pir 122 D1 *Rus.* Takhtakupyr. Qoraqalpog'iston Respublikasi, NW Uzbekistan
Tay 88 C3 *river* C Scotland, United Kingdom
Taylor 49 G3 Texas, SW USA
Taymā' 120 A4 Tabūk, NW Saudi Arabia
Taymyr, Ozero 115 E2 *lake* N Russian Federation
Taymyr, Poluostrov 114 D2 *peninsula* N Russian Federation
Taz 114 D3 *river* N Russian Federation
T'bilisi 117 G2 *Eng.* Tiflis. *country capital* (Georgia) (Georgia) SE Georgia
Tchad *see* Chad
Tchad, Lac *see* Chad, Lake
Tchien *see* Zwedru
Tchongking *see* Chongqing
Tczew 98 C2 *Ger.* Dirschau. Pomorskie, N Poland
Te Anau 151 A7 Southland, South Island, New Zealand
Te Anau, Lake 151 A7 *lake* South Island, New Zealand
Teapa 51 G4 Tabasco, SE Mexico
Teate *see* Chieti
Tebingtinggi 138 B3 Sumatera, N Indonesia
Tebriz *see* Tabrīz

Techirghiol 108 D5 Constanţa, SE Romania
Tecomán 50 D4 Colima, SW Mexico
Tecpan 51 E5 *var.* Tecpan de Galeana. Guerrero, S Mexico
Tecpan de Galeana *see* Tecpan
Tecuci 108 C4 Galaţi, E Romania
Tedzhen *see* Harīrūd/Tejen
Tedzhen *see* Tejen
Tees 89 D5 *river* N England, United Kingdom
Tefé 62 D2 Amazonas, N Brazil
Tegal 138 C4 Jawa, C Indonesia
Tegelen 87 D5 Limburg, SE Netherlands
Tegucigalpa 52 C3 *country capital* (Honduras) (Honduras) Francisco Morazán, SW Honduras
Teheran *see* Tehrān
Tehrān 120 C3 *var.* Teheran. *country capital* (Iran) (Iran) Tehrān, N Iran
Tehuacán 51 F4 Puebla, S Mexico
Tehuantepec 51 F5 *var.* Santo Domingo Tehuantepec. Oaxaca, SE Mexico
Gulf of Tehuantepec 51 F5 *var.* Gulf of Tehuantepec. *gulf* S Mexico
Tehuantepec, Gulf of *see* Tehuantepec, Golfo de
Isthmus of Tehuantepec 51 F5 *var.* Isthmus of Tehuantepec. *isthmus* SE Mexico
Tehuantepec, Isthmus of *see* Tehuantepec, Istmo de
Tejen 122 C3 *Rus.* Tedzhen. Ahal Welaýaty, S Turkmenistan
Tejen *see* Harīrūd
Tejo, Rio *see* Tagus
Te Kao 150 C1 Northland, North Island, New Zealand
Tekax 51 H4 *var.* Tekax de Álvaro Obregón. Yucatán, SE Mexico
Tekax de Álvaro Obregón *see* Tekax
Tekeli 114 C5 Almaty, SE Kazakhstan
Tekirdağ 116 A2 *It.* Rodosto; *anc.* Bisanthe, Raidestos, Rhaedestus. Tekirdağ, NW Turkey
Te Kuiti 150 D3 Waikato, North Island, New Zealand
Tela 52 C2 Atlántida, NW Honduras
Telanaipura *see* Jambi
Tel Aviv-Jaffa *see* Tel Aviv-Yafo
Tel Aviv-Yafo 119 A6 *var.* Tel Aviv-Jaffa. Tel Aviv, C Israel
Teles Pirés *see* São Manuel, Rio
Telish 104 C2 *prev.* Azizie. Pleven, N Bulgaria
Tell Abiad/Tell Abyad *see* At Tall al Abyaḍ
Tell Kalakh *see* Tall Kalakh
Tell Shedadi *see* Ash Shadadah
Tel'man/Tel'mansk *see* Gubadag
Teloekbetoeng *see* Bandar Lampung
Telo Martius *see* Toulon
Telschen *see* Telšiai
Telšiai 106 B3 *Ger.* Telschen. Telšiai, NW Lithuania
Telukbetung *see* Bandar Lampung
Temerin 100 D3 Vojvodina, N Serbia
Temeschburg/Temeschwar *see* Timişoara
Temesvár/Temeswar *see* Timişoara
Temirtau 114 C4 *prev.* Samarkandski, Samarkandskoye. Karaganda, C Kazakhstan
Tempio Pausania 97 A5 Sardegna, Italy, C Mediterranean Sea
Temple 49 G3 Texas, SW USA
Temuco 65 B5 Araucanía, C Chile
Temuka 151 B6 Canterbury, South Island, New Zealand
Tenasserim 137 B6 Tanintharyi, S Burma (Myanmar)
Ténenkou 74 D3 Mopti, C Mali
Ténéré 75 G3 *physical region* C Niger
Tenerife 70 A3 *island* Islas Canarias, Spain, NE Atlantic Ocean
Tengger Shamo 127 E3 *desert* N China
Tengréla 74 D4 *var.* Tingréla. N Côte d'Ivoire
Tenkodogo 75 E4 S Burkina Faso
Tennant Creek 148 A3 Northern Territory, C Australia
Tennessee 42 C1 *off.* State of Tennessee, *also known as* The Volunteer State. *state* SE USA
Tennessee River 42 C1 *river* S USA
Tenos *see* Tínos
Tepelena *see* Tepelenë

Tepelenë 101 C7 *var.* Tepelena, *It.* Tepeleni. Gjirokastër, S Albania
Tepeleni *see* Tepelenë
Tepic 50 D4 Nayarit, C Mexico
Teplice 98 A4 *Ger.* Teplitz; *prev.* Teplice-Sanov, Teplitz-Schönau. Ústecký Kraj, NW Czech Republic
Teplice-Šanov/Teplitz/Teplitz-Schönau *see* Teplice
Tequila 50 D4 Jalisco, SW Mexico
Teraina 145 G2 *prev.* Washington Island. *atoll* Line Islands, E Kiribati
Teramo 96 C4 *anc.* Interamna. Abruzzi, C Italy
Tercan 117 E3 Erzincan, NE Turkey
Terceira 92 A5 *var.* Ilha Terceira. *island* Azores, Portugal, NE Atlantic Ocean
Terceira, Ilha *see* Terceira
Terekhovka *see* Tsyerakhowka
Teresina 63 F2 *var.* Therezina. *state capital* Piauí, NE Brazil
Termez *see* Termiz
Termia *see* Kýthnos
Términos, Laguna de 51 G4 *lagoon* SE Mexico
Termiz 123 E3 *Rus.* Termez. Surkhondaryo Viloyati, S Uzbekistan
Termoli 96 D4 Molise, C Italy
Terneuzen 87 B5 *var.* Neuzen. Zeeland, SW Netherlands
Terni 96 C4 *anc.* Interamna Nahars. Umbria, C Italy
Ternopil' 108 C2 *Pol.* Tarnopol, *Rus.* Ternopol'. Ternopil's'ka Oblast', W Ukraine
Ternopol' *see* Ternopil'
Terracina 97 C5 Lazio, C Italy
Terranova di Sicilia *see* Gela
Terranova Pausania *see* Olbia
Terrassa 93 G2 *Cast.* Tarrasa. Cataluña, E Spain
Terre Adélie 154 C4 *physical region* Antarctica
Terre Haute 40 B4 Indiana, N USA
Terre Neuve *see* Newfoundland and Labrador
Terschelling 86 C1 *Fris.* Skylge. *island* Waddeneilanden, N Netherlands
Teruel 93 F3 *anc.* Turba. Aragón, E Spain
Tervel 104 E1 *prev.* Kurtbunar, *Rom.* Curtbunar. Dobrich, NE Bulgaria
Tervueren *see* Tervuren
Tervuren 87 C6 *var.* Tervueren. Vlaams Brabant, C Belgium
Teseney 72 C4 *var.* Tessenei. W Eritrea
Tessalit 75 E2 Kidal, NE Mali
Tessaoua 75 G3 Maradi, S Niger
Tessenderlo 87 C5 Limburg, NE Belgium
Tessenei *see* Teseney
Testigos, Islas los 59 E1 *island group* N Venezuela
Tete 79 E2 Tête, NW Mozambique
Teterow 94 C3 Mecklenburg-Vorpommern, NE Germany
Tétouan 70 C2 *var.* Tetouan, Tetuán. N Morocco
Tetovo 101 D5 Razgrad, N Bulgaria
Tetschen *see* Děčín
Tetuán *see* Tétouan
Teveryа *see* Tverya
Te Waewae Bay 151 A7 *bay* South Island, New Zealand
Texarkana 42 A2 Arkansas, C USA
Texarkana 49 H2 Texas, SW USA
Texas 49 F3 *off.* State of Texas, *also known as* Lone Star State. *state* S USA
Texas City 49 H4 Texas, SW USA
Texel 86 C2 *island* Waddeneilanden, NW Netherlands
Texoma, Lake 49 G2 *reservoir* Oklahoma/Texas, C USA
Teziutlán 51 F4 Puebla, S Mexico
Thaa Atoll *see* Kolhumadulu
Thai, Ao *see* Thailand, Gulf of
Thai Binh 136 D3 Thai Binh, N Vietnam
Thailand 137 C5 *off.* Kingdom of Thailand, *Th.* Prathet Thai; *prev.* Siam. *country* SE Asia

---

THAILAND
Southeast Asia

Official name Kingdom of Thailand
Formation 1238 / 1907
Capital Bangkok
Population 68.3 million / 346 people

THAILAND
(continued)

per sq mile (134 people per sq km) / 32%
Total area 198,455 sq. miles
(514,000 sq. km)
Languages Thai*, Chinese, Malay, Khmer,
Mon, Karen, Miao
Religions Buddhist 95%, Muslim 4%,
Other (including Christian) 1%
Ethnic mix Thai 83%, Chinese 12%,
Malay 3%, Khmer and Other 2%
Government Parliamentary system
Currency Baht = 100 satang
Literacy rate 93%
Calorie consumption 2467 calories

Thailand, Gulf of 137 C6 *var.* Gulf of
Siam, *Th.* Ao Thai, *Vtn.* Vinh Thai Lan.
gulf SE Asia
Thailand, Kingdom of *see* Thailand
Thai Lan, Vinh *see* Thailand, Gulf of
Thai Nguyên 136 D3 Bâc Thai, N Vietnam
Thakhèk 136 D4 *var.* Muang
Khammouan. Khammouan, C Laos
Thamarīd *see* Thamarīt
Thamarīt 121 D6 *var.* Thamarīd,
Thumrayt. SW Oman
Thames 150 D3 Waikato, North Island,
New Zealand
Thames 89 B8 *river* S England, United
Kingdom
Thandwe 136 A4 *var.* Sandoway.
Rakhine State, W Burma (Myanmar)
Thanh Hoa 136 D3 Thanh Hoa,
N Vietnam
Thanintari Taungdan *see* Bilauktaung
Range
Thanlwin *see* Salween
Thar Desert 134 C3 *var.* Great Indian
Desert, Indian Desert. *desert* India/
Pakistan
Tharthar, Buhayrat ath 120 B3 *lake*
C Iraq
Thásos 104 C4 Thásos, E Greece
Thásos 104 C4 *island* E Greece
Thaton 136 B4 Mon State, S Burma
(Myanmar)
Thayetmyo 136 A4 Magway, C Burma
(Myanmar)
The Crane 55 H2 *var.* Crane. S Barbados
The Dalles 46 B3 Oregon, NW USA
The Flatts Village *see* Flatts Village
The Hague *see* 's-Gravenhage
Theodosia *see* Feodosiya
The Pas 37 F5 Manitoba, C Canada
Therezina *see* Teresina
Thérma 105 D6 Ikaría, Dodekánisa,
Greece, Aegean Sea
Thermaic Gulf 104 B4 *Eng.* Thermaic
Gulf; *anc.* Thermaicus Sinus. *gulf*
N Greece
Thermaic Gulf/Thermaicus Sinus *see*
Thermaïkós Kólpos
Thermiá *see* Kýthnos
Thérmo 105 B5 Dytikí Ellás, C Greece
The Rock 93 H4 New South Wales,
SE Australia
The Sooner State *see* Oklahoma
Thessaloníki 104 C3 *Eng.* Salonica,
Salonika, *SCr.* Solun, *Turk.* Selânik.
Kentrikí Makedonía, N Greece
The Valley 55 G3 *dependent territory
capital* (Anguilla) E Anguilla
The Village 49 G1 Oklahoma, C USA
The Volunteer State *see* Tennessee
Thiamis *see* Kalamás
Thian Shan *see* Tien Shan
Thibet *see* Xizang Zizhiqu
Thief River Falls 45 F1 Minnesota,
N USA
Thienen *see* Tienen
Thiers 91 C5 Puy-de-Dôme, C France
Thiès 74 B3 W Senegal
Thikombia *see* Cikobia
Thimbu *see* Thimphu
Thimphu 135 G3 *var.* Thimbu; *prev.*
Tashi Chho Dzong. *country capital*
(Bhutan) (Bhutan) W Bhutan
Thionville 90 D3 *Ger.* Diedenhofen.
Moselle, NE France
Thíra 105 D7 Santoríni, Kykládes,
Greece, Aegean Sea
Thíra 105 D7 Santoríni, Kykládes,
Greece, Aegean Sea
Thíra 105 D7 Santoríni, Kykládes,
Greece, Aegean Sea

Thitu Island 128 C8 *island* NW Spratly
Islands
Tholen 86 B4 *island* SW Netherlands
Thomasville 42 D3 Georgia, SE USA
Thompson 37 F4 Manitoba, C Canada
Thonon-les-Bains 91 D5 Haute-Savoie,
E France
Thorenburg *see* Turda
Thorlákshöfn 83 E5 Sudhurland,
SW Iceland
Thorn *see* Toruń
Thornton Island *see* Millennium Island
Thorshavn *see* Tórshavn
Thospitis *see* Van Gölü
Thouars 90 B4 Deux-Sèvres, W France
Thoune *see* Thun
Thracian Sea 104 D4 *Gk.* Thrakikó
Pélagos; *anc.* Thracium Mare. *sea*
Greece/Turkey
Thracium Mare/Thrakikó Pélagos *see*
Thracian Sea
Three Kings Islands 150 C1 *island
group* N New Zealand
Thuin 87 B7 Hainaut, S Belgium
Thule *see* Qaanaaq
Thumrayt *see* Thamarīt
Thun 95 A7 *Fr.* Thoune. Bern,
W Switzerland
Thunder Bay 38 B4 Ontario, S Canada
Thuner See 95 A7 *lake* C Switzerland
Thung Song 137 C7 *var.* Cha Mai.
Nakhon Si Thammarat, SW Thailand
Thurso 88 C2 N Scotland, United
Kingdom
Thýamis *see* Kalamás
Tianjin 128 D4 *var.* Tientsin. Tianjin
Shi, E China
Tianjin *see* Tianjin Shi
Tianjin Shi 128 D4 *var.* Jin, Tianjin,
T'ien-ching, Tientsin. *municipality*
E China
Tian Shan *see* Tien Shan
Tianshui 128 B4 Gansu, C China
Tiba *see* Chiba
Tiber 96 C4 *Eng.* Tiber. *river* C Italy
Tiber *see* Tevere, Italy
Tiber *see* Tivoli, Italy
Tiberias *see* Tverya
Tiberias, Lake 119 B5 *var.* Chinnereth,
Sea of Bahr Tabariya, Sea of Galilee, *Ar.*
Bahrat Tabariya, *Heb.* Yam Kinneret.
lake N Israel
Tibesti 76 C2 *var.* Tibesti Massif, *Fr.*
Tibísti. *mountain range* N Africa
Tibesti Massif *see* Tibesti
Tibet *see* Xizang Zizhiqu
Tibetan Autonomous Region *see* Xizang
Zizhiqu
Tibet, Plateau of 126 B4 *var.* Xizang
Gaoyuan, *Eng.* Plateau of Tibet. *plateau*
W China
Tibet, Plateau of *see* Qingzang Gaoyuan
Tibísti *see* Tibesti
Tibní *see* At Tibnī
Tiburón, Isla 50 B2 *var.* Isla del Tiburón.
island NW Mexico
Tiburón, Isla del *see* Tiburón, Isla
Tichau *see* Tychy
Tichît 74 D2 *var.* Tichitt. Tagant,
C Mauritania
Tichitt *see* Tichît
Ticinum *see* Pavia
Ticul 51 H3 Yucatán, SE Mexico
Tidjikdja *see* Tidjikja
Tidjikja 74 C2 *var.* Tidjikdja; *prev.* Fort-
Cappolani. Tagant, C Mauritania
T'ien-ching *see* Tianjin Shi
Tienen 87 C6 *var.* Thienen, *Fr.*
Tirlemont. Vlaams Brabant, C Belgium
Tiên Giang, Sông *see* Mekong
Tien Shan 126 B3 *Chin.* Thian Shan,
Tian Shan, T'ien Shan, *Rus.* Tyan'-
Shan'. *mountain range* C Asia
Tientsin *see* Tianjin
Tierp 85 C6 Uppsala, C Sweden
Tierra del Fuego 65 B8 *island* Argentina/
Chile
Tiflis *see* T'bilisi
Tifton 42 D3 Georgia, SE USA
Tifu 139 F4 Pulau Buru, E Indonesia
Tighina 108 D4 *Rus.* Bendery; *prev.*
Bender. E Moldova
Tigranocerta *see* Siirt
Tigris 120 B2 *Ar.* Dijlah, *Turk.* Dicle.
river Iraq/Turkey
Tiguentourine 71 E3 E Algeria
Ti-hua/Tihwa *see* Ürümqi

Tijuana 50 A1 Baja California Norte,
NW Mexico
Tikhoretsk 111 A7 Krasnodarskiy Kray,
SW Russian Federation
Tikhvin 110 B4 Leningradskaya Oblast',
NW Russian Federation
Tiki Basin 143 G3 *undersea basin*
S Pacific Ocean
Tiksi 115 F2 Respublika Sakha
(Yakutiya), NE Russian Federation
Tilburg 86 C4 Noord-Brabant,
S Netherlands
Tilimsen *see* Tlemcen
Tilio Martius *see* Toulon
Tillabéri 75 F3 *var.* Tillabéry. Tillabéri,
W Niger
Tillabéry *see* Tillabéri
Tílos 105 E7 *island* Dodekánisa, Greece,
Aegean Sea
Timan Ridge 110 D3 *Eng.* Timan Ridge.
ridge NW Russian Federation
Timan Ridge *see* Timanskiy Kryazh
Timaru 151 B6 Canterbury, South Island,
New Zealand
Timbaki/Timbákion *see* Tympáki
Timbedgha 74 D3 *var.* Timbédra. Hodh
ech Chargui, SE Mauritania
Timbédra *see* Timbedgha
Timbuktu *see* Tombouctou
Timiş 108 A4 *county* SW Romania
Timişoara 108 A4 *Ger.* Temeschwar,
Temeswar, *Hung.* Temesvár; *prev.*
Temeschburg. Timiş, W Romania
Timmins 38 C4 Ontario, S Canada
Timor 125 F5 *island* Nusa Tenggara,
C Indonesia
Timor Sea 125 F5 *sea* E Indian Ocean
Timor Timur *see* East Timor
Timor Trench *see* Timor Trough
Timor Trough 125 F5 *var.* Timor
Trench. *trough* NE Indian Ocean
Timrå 85 C5 Västernorrland,
C Sweden
Tindouf 70 C3 W Algeria
Tineo 92 C1 Asturias, N Spain
Tingis *see* Tanger
Tingo María 60 C3 Huánuco, C Peru
Tingréla *see* Tengréla
Tinhosa Grande 76 E2 *island*
N Sao Tome and Principe, Africa,
E Atlantic Ocean
Tinhosa Pequena 76 E1 *island*
N Sao Tome and Principe, Africa,
E Atlantic Ocean
Tinian 144 B1 *island* S Northern Mariana
Islands
Tínos 105 D6 Tínos, Kykládes, Greece,
Aegean Sea
Tínos 105 D6 *anc.* Tenos. *island*
Kykládes, Greece, Aegean Sea
Tip 101 E6 Papua, E Indonesia
Tipitapa 52 D3 Managua, W Nicaragua
Tip Top Mountain 38 C4 *mountain*
Ontario, S Canada
Tirana *see* Tiranë
Tiranë 101 C6 *var.* Tirana. *country
capital* (Albania) (Albania) Tiranë,
C Albania
Tiraspol 108 D4 *Rus.* Tiraspol'.
E Moldova
Tiraspol' *see* Tiraspol
Tiree 88 B3 *island* W Scotland, United
Kingdom
Tirgovişte *see* Târgovişte
Tîrgu Jiu *see* Targu Jiu
Tîrgu Mureş *see* Târgu Mureş
Tîrgu-Neamţ *see* Târgu-Neamţ
Tîrgu Ocna *see* Târgu Ocna
Tîrgu Secuiesc *see* Târgu Secuiesc
Tirlemont *see* Tienen
Tîrnavos *see* Týrnavos
Tirnovo *see* Veliko Tŭrnovo
Tirol 95 C7 *off.* Land Tirol, *var.* Tyrol, *It.*
Tirolo. *state* W Austria
Tirol, Land *see* Tirol
Tirolo *see* Tirol
Tirreno, Mare *see* Tyrrhenian Sea
Tiruchchirāppalli 132 C3 *prev.*
Trichinopoly. Tamil Nādu,
SE India
Tiruppattūr 132 C2 Tamil Nādu,
SE India
Tiruvanantapuram Thiruvananthapuram/
Trivandrum
Tisa 101 F1 *Ger.* Theiss, *Rom./Slvn./
SCr.* Tisa, *Rus.* Tissa, *Ukr.* Tysa. *river*
SE Europe

Tisa *see* Tisza
Tiszakécske 99 D7 Bács-Kiskun,
C Hungary
Titano, Monte 96 E1 *mountain* C San
Marino
Titicaca, Lake 61 E4 *lake* Bolivia/Peru
Titograd *see* Podgorica
Titose *see* Chitose
Titova Mitrovica *see* Mitrovicë
Titovo Užice *see* Užice
Titu 108 C5 Dâmboviţa, S Romania
Titule 77 D5 Orientale, N Dem. Rep.
Congo
Tiverton 89 C7 SW England, United
Kingdom
Tivoli 96 C4 *anc.* Tiber. Lazio, C Italy
Tizimín 51 H3 Yucatán, SE Mexico
Tizi Ouzou 71 E1 *var.* Tizi-Ouzou.
N Algeria
Tizi-Ouzou *see* Tizi Ouzou
Tiznit 70 B3 SW Morocco
Tjilatjap *see* Cilacap
Tjirebon *see* Cirebon
Tlaquepaque 50 D4 Jalisco, C Mexico
Tlascala *see* Tlaxcala
Tlaxcala 51 F4 *var.* Tlascala, Tlaxcala de
Xicohténcatl. Tlaxcala, C Mexico
Tlaxcala de Xicohténcatl *see* Tlaxcala
Tlemcen 70 D2 *var.* Tilimsen, Tlemsen.
NW Algeria
Tlemsen *see* Tlemcen
Toamasina 79 G3 *var.* Tamatave.
Toamasina, E Madagascar
Toamasina *see* Tamatave
Toba, Danau 138 B3 *lake* Sumatera,
W Indonesia
Tobago 55 H5 *island* NE Trinidad and
Tobago
Toba Kakar Range 134 B2 *mountain
range* NW Pakistan
Tobol 114 C4 *Kaz.* Tobyl. *river*
Kazakhstan/Russian Federation
Tobol'sk 114 C3 Tyumenskaya Oblast',
C Russian Federation
Tobruch/Tobruk *see* Ţubruq
Tobyl *see* Tobol
Tocantins 63 E3 *off.* Estado do
Tocantins. *state* C Brazil
Tocantins 63 E3 *off.* Estado do
Tocantins. *region* C Brazil
Tocantins, Estado do *see* Tocantins
Tocantins, Rio 63 F2 *river* N Brazil
Tocoa 52 D2 Colón, N Honduras
Tocopilla 64 B2 Antofagasta, N Chile
Todi 96 C4 Umbria, C Italy
Todos os Santos, Baía de 63 G3 *bay*
E Brazil
Toetoes Bay 151 B8 *bay* South Island,
New Zealand
Tofua 145 E4 *island* Ha'apai Group,
C Tonga
Togo 75 E4 *off.* Togolese Republic; *prev.*
French Togoland. *country* W Africa

TOGO
West Africa

Official name The Togolese Republic
Formation 1960 / 1960
Capital Lomé
Population 6.5 million / 310 people
per sq mile (120 people per sq km) / 36%
Total area 21,924 sq. miles (56,785 sq. km)
Languages French*, Ewe, Kabye, Gurma
Religions Traditional beliefs 50%,
Christian 35%, Muslim 15%
Ethnic mix Ewe 46%, Other African 41%,
Kabye 12%, European 1%
Government Presidential system
Currency CFA franc = 100 centimes
Literacy rate 53%
Calorie consumption 2345 calories

Togolese Republic *see* Togo
Tojikiston, Jumhurii *see* Tajikistan
Tokanui 151 B7 Southland, South Island,
New Zealand
Tokar 72 C3 *var.* Ţawkar. Red Sea,
NE Sudan
Tokat 116 D3 Tokat, N Turkey
Tokelau 145 E3 *NZ overseas territory*
W Polynesia
Tőketerebes *see* Trebišov
Tokio *see* Tōkyō
Tokmak 123 G2 *Kir.* Tokmok.
Chuyskaya Oblast', N Kyrgyzstan
Tokmak 109 G4 *var.* Velykyy Tokmak.
Zaporiz'ka Oblast', SE Ukraine

Tokmok see Tokmak
Tokoroa 150 D3 Waikato, North Island, New Zealand
Tokounou 74 C4 C Guinea
Tokushima 131 C6 var. Tokusima. Tokushima, Shikoku, SW Japan
Tōkyō 130 A1 var. Tokio. country capital (Japan) (Japan) Tōkyō, Honshū, S Japan
Tōkyō-wan 130 A2 bay S Japan
Tolbukhin see Dobrich
Toledo 92 D3 anc. Toletum. Castilla-La Mancha, C Spain
Toledo 40 D3 Ohio, N USA
Toledo Bend Reservoir 49 G3 reservoir Louisiana/Texas, SW USA
Toletum see Toledo
Toliara 79 F4 var. Toliary; prev. Tuléar. Toliara, SW Madagascar
Toliary see Toliara
Tolmein see Tolmin
Tolmin 95 D7 Ger. Tolmein, It. Tolmino. W Slovenia
Tolmino see Tolmin
Tolna 99 C7 Ger. Tolnau. Tolna, S Hungary
Tolnau see Tolna
Tolochin see Talachyn
Tolosa 93 E1 País Vasco, N Spain
Tolosa see Toulouse
Toluca 51 E4 var. Toluca de Lerdo. México, S Mexico
Toluca de Lerdo see Toluca
Tol'yatti 111 C6 prev. Stavropol'. Samarskaya Oblast', W Russian Federation
Tomah 40 B2 Wisconsin, N USA
Tomakomai 130 D2 Hokkaidō, NE Japan
Tomar 92 B3 Santarém, W Portugal
Tomaschow see Tomaszów Mazowiecki
Tomaschow see Tomaszów Lubelski
Tomaszów see Tomaszów Mazowiecki
Tomaszów Lubelski 98 E4 Ger. Tomaschow. Lubelskie, E Poland
Tomaszów Mazowiecka see Tomaszów Mazowiecki
Tomaszów Mazowiecki 98 D4 var. Tomaszów Mazowiecka; prev. Tomaszów, Ger. Tomaschow. Łódzkie, C Poland
Tombigbee River 42 C3 river Alabama/ Mississippi, S USA
Tombouctou 75 E3 Eng. Timbuktu. Tombouctou, N Mali
Tombua 78 A2 Port. Porto Alexandre. Namibe, SW Angola
Tomelloso 93 E3 Castilla-La Mancha, C Spain
Tomini, Gulf of 139 E4 var. Teluk Tomini, prev. Teluk Gorontalo. bay Sulawesi, C Indonesia
Tomini, Teluk see Tomini, Gulf of
Tomsk 114 D4 Tomskaya Oblast', C Russian Federation
Tomür Feng see Pobedy, Pik
Tonezh see Tonyezh
Tonga 145 E4 off. Kingdom of Tonga, var. Friendly Islands. country SW Pacific Ocean

TONGA
Australasia & Oceania

Official name Kingdom of Tonga
Formation 1970 / 1970
Capital Nuku'alofa
Population 116,921 / 421 people per sq mile (162 people per sq km) / 34%
Total area 289 sq. miles (748 sq. km)
Languages English*, Tongan*
Religions Free Wesleyan 41%, Other 17%, Roman Catholic 16%, Church of Jesus Christ of Latter-day Saints 14%, Free Church of Tonga 12%
Ethnic mix Tongan 98%, Other 2%
Government Monarchy
Currency Pa'anga (Tongan dollar) = 100 seniti
Literacy rate 99%
Calorie consumption Not available

Tonga, Kingdom of see Tonga
Tongatapu 145 E5 island Tongatapu Group, S Tonga
Tongatapu Group 145 E5 island group S Tonga

Tonga Trench 143 E3 trench S Pacific Ocean
Tongchuan 128 C4 Shaanxi, C China
Tongeren 87 D6 Fr. Tongres. Limburg, NE Belgium
Tongking, Gulf of 128 B7 Chin. Beibu Wan, Vtn. Vinh Băc Bô. gulf China/ Vietnam
Tongliao 127 G2 Nei Mongol Zizhiqu, N China
Tongres see Tongeren
Tongshan see Xuzhou, Jiangsu, China
Tongtian He 126 C4 river C China
Tonj 73 B5 Warab, SW Sudan
Tônlé Sap 137 D5 Eng. Great Lake. lake W Cambodia
Tonopah 47 C6 Nevada, W USA
Tonyezh 107 C7 Rus. Tonezh. Homyel'skaya Voblasts', SE Belarus
Tooele 44 B4 Utah, W USA
Toowoomba 149 E5 Queensland, E Australia
Topeka 45 F4 state capital Kansas, C USA
Toplița 108 C3 Ger. Töplitz, Hung. Maroshévíz; prev. Toplița Română, Hung. Oláh-Toplicza, Toplicza. Harghita, C Romania
Toplița Română/Töplitz see Toplița
Topol'čany 99 C6 Hung. Nagytapolcsány. Nitriansky Kraj, W Slovakia
Topolovgrad 104 D3 prev. Kavakli. Khaskovo, S Bulgaria
Topolya see Bačka Topola
Top Springs Roadhouse 146 E3 Northern Territory, N Australia
Torda see Turda
Torez 109 H3 Donets'ka Oblast', SE Ukraine
Torgau 94 D4 Sachsen, E Germany
Torhout 87 A5 West-Vlaanderen, W Belgium
Torino 96 A2 Eng. Turin. Piemonte, NW Italy
Tornacum see Tournai
Torneä see Tornio
Torneträsk 84 C3 lake N Sweden
Tornio 84 D4 Swe. Torneä. Lappi, NW Finland
Tornionjoki 84 D3 river Finland/Sweden
Tornionjoki 84 D3 river Finland/Sweden
Toro 92 D2 Castilla-León, N Spain
Toronto 38 D5 province capital Ontario, S Canada
Torquay 89 C7 SW England, United Kingdom
Torrance 46 D2 California, W USA
Torre, Alto da 92 B3 mountain C Portugal
Torre del Greco 97 D5 Campania, S Italy
Torrejón de Ardoz 93 E3 Madrid, C Spain
Torrelavega 92 D1 Cantabria, N Spain
Torrens, Lake 149 A6 salt lake South Australia
Torrent 93 F3 Cas. Torrente, var. Torrent de l'Horta. País Valenciano, E Spain
Torrent de l'Horta/Torrente see Torrent
Torreón 50 D3 Coahuila, NE Mexico
Torres Strait 148 C1 strait Australia/ Papua New Guinea
Torres Vedras 92 B3 Lisboa, C Portugal
Torrington 44 D3 Wyoming, C USA
Tórshavn 83 F5 Dan. Thorshavn. Dependent territory capital Faeroe Islands
To'rtko'l 122 D2 var. Türtkül, Rus. Turtkul'; prev. Petroaleksandrovsk. Qoraqalpog'iston Respublikasi, W Uzbekistan
Tortoise Islands see Colón, Archipiélago de
Tortosa 93 F2 anc. Dertosa. Cataluña, E Spain
Tortue, Montagne 59 H3 mountain range C French Guiana
Tortuga, Isla see La Tortuga, Isla
Toruń 98 C3 Ger. Thorn. Toruń, Kujawsko-pomorskie, C Poland
Tõrva 106 D3 Ger. Tõrwa. Valgamaa, S Estonia
Tõrwa see Tõrva
Torzhok 110 B4 Tverskaya Oblast', W Russian Federation
Tosa-wan 131 B7 bay SW Japan

Toscana 96 B3 Eng. Tuscany. region C Italy
Toscano, Archipelago 96 B4 Eng. Tuscan Archipelago. island group C Italy
Toshkent 123 E2 Eng./Rus. Tashkent. country capital (Uzbekistan) Toshkent Viloyati, E Uzbekistan
Totana 93 E4 Murcia, SE Spain
Tot'ma see Sukhona
Totness 59 G3 Coronie, N Suriname
Tottori 131 B6 Tottori, Honshū, SW Japan
Touâjîl 74 C2 Tiris Zemmour, N Mauritania
Touggourt 71 E2 NE Algeria
Toukoto 74 C3 Kayes, W Mali
Toul 90 D3 Meurthe-et-Moselle, NE France
Toulon 91 D6 anc. Telo Martius, Tilio Martius. Var, SE France
Toulouse 91 B6 anc. Tolosa. Haute-Garonne, S France
Toungoo see Taungoo
Touraine 90 B4 cultural region C France
Tourane see Đà Nẵng
Tourcoing 90 C2 Nord, N France
Tournai 87 A6 var. Tournay, Dut. Doornik; anc. Tornacum. Hainaut, SW Belgium
Tournay see Tournai
Tours 90 B4 anc. Caesarodunum, Turoni. Indre-et-Loire, C France
Tovarkovskiy 111 B5 Tul'skaya Oblast', W Russian Federation
Tower Island see Genovesa, Isla
Townsville 148 D3 Queensland, NE Australia
Towoeti Meer see Towuti, Danau
Towraghoudi 122 D4 Herāt, NW Afghanistan
Towson 41 F4 Maryland, NE USA
Towuti, Danau 139 E4 Dut. Towoeti Meer. lake Sulawesi, C Indonesia
Toyama 131 C5 Toyama, Honshū, SW Japan
Toyama-wan 131 B5 bay W Japan
Toyohara see Yuzhno-Sakhalinsk
Toyota 131 C6 Aichi, Honshū, SW Japan
Tozeur 71 E2 var. Tawzar. W Tunisia
Trâblous see Tripoli
Trabzon 117 E2 Eng. Trebizond; anc. Trapezus. Trabzon, NE Turkey
Traiectum ad Mosam/Traiectum Tungorum see Maastricht
Traiskirchen 95 E6 Niederösterreich, NE Austria
Trajani Portus see Civitavecchia
Trajectum ad Rhenum see Utrecht
Trakai 107 C5 Ger. Traken, Pol. Troki. Vilnius, SE Lithuania
Traken see Trakai
Tralee 89 A6 Ir. Trá Lí. SW Ireland
Trá Lí see Tralee
Tralles Aydin see Aydın
Trang 137 C7 Trang, S Thailand
Transantarctic Mountains 154 B3 mountain range Antarctica
Transilvania see Transylvania
Transilvaniei, Alpi see Carpații Meridionalii
Transjordan see Jordan
Transsylvanische Alpen/Transylvanian Alps see Carpații Meridionalii
Transylvania 108 B4 Eng. Ardeal, Transilvania, Ger. Siebenbürgen, Hung. Erdély. cultural region NW Romania
Transylvanian Alps 108 B4 var. Alpi Transilvaniei, Carpații Sudici, Eng. South Carpathians, Transylvanian Alps, Ger. Südkarpaten, Transsylvanische Alpen, Hung. Déli-Kárpátok, Erdélyi-Havasok. mountain range C Romania
Trapani 97 B7 anc. Drepanum. Sicilia, Italy, C Mediterranean Sea
Trápeăng Vêng 137 D5 Kâmpóng Thum, C Cambodia
Trapezus see Trabzon
Traralgon 149 C7 Victoria, SE Australia
Trasimenischersee see Trasimeno, Lago
Trasimeno, Lago 96 C4 Eng. Lake of Perugia, Ger. Trasimenischersee. lake C Italy
Traù see Trogir
Traverse City 40 C2 Michigan, N USA
Tra Vinh 137 D6 var. Phu Vinh. Tra Vinh, S Vietnam

Travis, Lake 49 F3 reservoir Texas, SW USA
Travnik 100 C4 Federacija Bosna I Hercegovina, C Bosnia and Herzegovina
Trbovlje 95 E7 Ger. Trifail. C Slovenia
Treasure State see Montana
Třebíč 99 B5 Ger. Trebitsch. Vysočina, C Czech Republic
Trebinje 101 C5 Republika Srpska, S Bosnia and Herzegovina
Trebišov 99 D6 Hung. Tőketerebes. Košický Kraj, E Slovakia
Trebitsch see Třebíč
Trebnitz see Trzebnica
Tree Planters State see Nebraska
Trélazé 90 B4 Maine-et-Loire, NW France
Trelew 65 C6 Chubut, SE Argentina
Tremelo 87 C5 Vlaams Brabant, C Belgium
Trenčín 99 C5 Ger. Trentschin, Hung. Trencsén. Trenčiansky Kraj, W Slovakia
Trencsén see Trenčín
Trengganu, Kuala see Kuala Terengganu
Trenque Lauquen 64 C4 Buenos Aires, E Argentina
Trent see Trento
Trento 96 C2 Eng. Trent, Ger. Trient; anc. Tridentum. Trentino-Alto Adige, N Italy
Trenton 41 F4 state capital New Jersey, NE USA
Trentschin see Trenčín
Tres Arroyos 65 D5 Buenos Aires, E Argentina
Treskavica 100 C4 mountain range SE Bosnia and Herzegovina
Tres Tabernae see Saverne
Treves/Trèves see Trier
Treviso 96 C2 anc. Tarvisium. Veneto, NE Italy
Trichinopoly see Tiruchchirāppalli
Trichūr 132 C3 var. Thrissur. Kerala, SW India
Tridentum/Trient see Trento
Trier 95 A5 Eng. Treves, Fr. Trèves; anc. Augusta Treverorum. Rheinland-Pfalz, SW Germany
Triesen 94 E2 SW Liechtenstein Europe
Triesenberg 94 E2 SW Liechtenstein
Trieste 96 D2 Slvn. Trst. Friuli-Venezia Giulia, NE Italy
Trifail see Trbovlje
Tríkala 104 B4 prev. Trikkala. Thessalía, C Greece
Trikkala see Tríkala
Trimontium see Plovdiv
Trinacria see Sicilia
Trincomalee 132 D3 var. Trinkomali. Eastern Province, NE Sri Lanka
Trindade, Ilha da 67 C5 island Brazil, W Atlantic Ocean
Trinidad 61 F3 Beni, N Bolivia
Trinidad 64 D4 Flores, S Uruguay
Trinidad 44 D5 Colorado, C USA
Trinidad 55 H5 island C Trinidad and Tobago
Trinidad and Tobago 55 H5 off. Republic of Trinidad and Tobago. country SE West Indies

TRINIDAD & TOBAGO
West Indies

Official name Republic of Trinidad and Tobago
Formation 1962 / 1962
Capital Port-of-Spain
Population 1.3 million / 656 people per sq mile (253 people per sq km) / 76%
Total area 1980 sq. miles (5128 sq. km)
Languages English Creole, English*, Hindi, French, Spanish
Religions Roman Catholic 32%, Hindu 24%, Protestant 14%, Anglican 14%, Other and nonreligious 9%, Muslim 7%
Ethnic mix East Indian 40%, Black 40%, Mixed race 18%, Other 1%, White and Chinese 1%
Government Parliamentary system
Currency Trinidad and Tobago dollar = 100 cents
Literacy rate 99%
Calorie consumption 2732 calories

Trinidad and Tobago, Republic of *see* Trinidad and Tobago
Trinité, Montagnes de la 59 *H3 mountain range* C French Guiana
Trinity River 49 *G3 river* Texas, SW USA
Trinkomali *see* Trincomalee
Trípoli 105 *B6 prev.* Trípolis. Pelopónnisos, S Greece
Tripoli 118 *B4 var.* Ṭarābulus, Ṭarābulus ash Shām, Trāblous; *anc.* Tripolis. N Lebanon
Tripoli *see* Ṭarābulus
Trípolis *see* Trípoli, Greece
Tripolis *see* Tripoli, Lebanon
Tristan da Cunha 69 *B7 dependency of Saint Helena* SE Atlantic Ocean
Triton Island 128 *B7 island* S Paracel Islands
Trivandrum 132 *C3 var.* Thiruvananthapuram, Tiruvantapuram. *state capital* Kerala, SW India
Trnava 99 *C6 Ger.* Tyrnau, *Hung.* Nagyszombat. Trnavský Kraj, W Slovakia
Trnovo *see* Veliko Tŭrnovo
Trogir 100 *B4 It.* Traù. Split-Dalmacija, S Croatia
Troglav 100 *B4 mountain* Bosnia and Herzegovina/Croatia
Trois-Rivières 39 *E4* Québec, SE Canada
Troki *see* Trakai
Trollhättan 85 *B6* Västra Götaland, S Sweden
Tromsø 84 *C2 Fin.* Tromssa. Troms, N Norway
Tromssa *see* Tromsø
Trondheim 84 *B4 Ger.* Drontheim; *prev.* Nidaros, Trondhjem. Sør-Trøndelag, S Norway
Trondheimsfjorden 84 *B4 fjord* S Norway
Trondhjem *see* Trondheim
Troódos 102 *C5 var.* Troodos Mountains. *mountain range* C Cyprus
Troodos Mountains *see* Troódos
Troppau *see* Opava
Troy 42 *D3* Alabama, S USA
Troy 41 *F3* New York, NE USA
Troyan 104 *C2* Lovech, N Bulgaria
Troyes 90 *D3 anc.* Augustobona Tricassium. Aube, N France
Trst *see* Trieste
Trstenik 100 *E4* Serbia, C Serbia
Trucial States *see* United Arab Emirates
Trujillo 52 *D2* Colón, NE Honduras
Trujillo 60 *B3* La Libertad, NW Peru
Trujillo 92 *C3* Extremadura, W Spain
Truk Islands *see* Chuuk Islands
Trŭn 104 *B2* Pernik, W Bulgaria
Truro 39 *F4* Nova Scotia, SE Canada
Truro 89 *C7* SW England, United Kingdom
Trzcianka 98 *B3 Ger.* Schönlanke. Pila, Wielkopolskie, C Poland
Trzebnica 98 *C4 Ger.* Trebnitz. Dolnośląskie, SW Poland
Tsalka 117 *F2* S Georgia Asia
Tsamkong *see* Zhanjiang
Tsangpo *see* Brahmaputra
Tsarevo 104 *E2 prev.* Michurin. Burgas, E Bulgaria
Tsarigrad *see* İstanbul
Tsaritsyn *see* Volgograd
Tschakathurn *see* Čakovec
Tschaslau *see* Čáslav
Tschenstochau *see* Częstochowa
Tsefat 119 *B5 var.* Safed, *Ar.* Safad; *prev.* Żefat. Northern, N Israel
Tselinograd *see* Astana
Tsetsen Khan *see* Öndörhaan
Tsetserleg 126 *D2* Arhangay, C Mongolia
Tshela 77 *B6* Bas-Congo, W Dem. Rep. Congo
Tshikapa 77 *C7* Kasai-Occidental, SW Dem. Rep. Congo
Tshuapa 77 *D6 river* C Dem. Rep. Congo
Tshwane 78 *D4 var.* Epitoli; *prev.* Pretoria. *country capital* (South Africa-administrative capital) Gauteng, NE South Africa
Tsinan *see* Jinan
Tsing Hai *see* Qinghai Hu, China
Tsinghai *see* Qinghai, China
Tsingtao/Tsingtau *see* Qingdao
Tsinkiang *see* Quanzhou
Tsintao *see* Qingdao
Tsitsihar *see* Qiqihar

Tsu 131 *C6 var.* Tu. Mie, Honshū, SW Japan
Tsugaru-kaikyo 130 *C3 strait* N Japan
Tsumeb 78 *B3* Otjikoto, N Namibia
Tsuruga 131 *C6 var.* Turuga. Fukui, Honshū, SW Japan
Tsuruoka 130 *D4 var.* Turuoka. Yamagata, Honshū, C Japan
Tsushima 131 *A7 var.* Tsushima-tō, Tusima. *island group* SW Japan
Tsushima-tō *see* Tsushima
Tsyerakhowka 107 *D8 Rus.* Terekhovka. Homyel'skaya Voblasts', SE Belarus
Tsyurupinsk *see* Tsyurupyns'k
Tsyurupyns'k 109 *E4 Rus.* Tsyurupinsk. Khersons'ka Oblast', S Ukraine
Tu *see* Tsu
Tuamotu, Archipel des *see* Tuamotu, Îles
Tuamotu Fracture Zone 143 *H3 fracture zone* E Pacific Ocean
Tuamotu Islands 145 *H4 var.* Archipel des Tuamotu, Dangerous Archipelago, Tuamotu Islands. *island group* N French Polynesia
Tuamotu Islands *see* Tuamotu, Îles
Tuapi 53 *E2* Región Autónoma Atlántico Norte, NE Nicaragua
Tuapse 111 *A7* Krasnodarskiy Kray, SW Russian Federation
Tuba City 48 *B1* Arizona, SW USA
Tubbergen 86 *E3* Overijssel, E Netherlands
Tubeke *see* Tubize
Tubize 87 *B6 Dut.* Tubeke. Walloon Brabant, C Belgium
Tubmanburg 74 *C5* NW Liberia
Ṭubruq 71 *H2 Eng.* Tobruk, *It.* Tobruch. NE Libya
Tubuai, Îles/Tubuai Islands *see* Australes, Îles
Tucker's Town 42 *B5* E Bermuda
Tuckum *see* Tukums
Tucson 48 *B3* Arizona, SW USA
Tucumán *see* San Miguel de Tucumán
Tucumcari 49 *E2* New Mexico, SW USA
Tucupita 59 *E2* Delta Amacuro, NE Venezuela
Tucuruí, Represa de 63 *F2 reservoir* NE Brazil
Tudela 93 *E2 Basq.* Tutera; *anc.* Tutela. Navarra, N Spain
Tudmur 118 *C3 var.* Tadmur, Tamar, *Gk.* Palmyra, *Bibl.* Tadmor. Ḥimṣ, C Syria
Tuguegarao 139 *E1* Luzon, N Philippines
Tuktoyaktuk 37 *E3* Northwest Territories, NW Canada
Tukums 106 *C3 Ger.* Tuckum. Tukums, W Latvia
Tula 111 *B5* Tul'skaya Oblast', W Russian Federation
Tulancingo 51 *E4* Hidalgo, C Mexico
Tulare Lake Bed 47 *C7 salt flat* California, W USA
Tulcán 60 *B1* Carchi, N Ecuador
Tulcea 108 *D5* Tulcea, E Romania
Tul'chin *see* Tul'chyn
Tul'chyn 108 *D3 Rus.* Tul'chin. Vinnyts'ka Oblast', C Ukraine
Tuléar *see* Toliara
Tulia 49 *E2* Texas, SW USA
Tülkarm 119 *D7* West Bank, Israel
Tulle 91 *C5 anc.* Tutela. Corrèze, C France
Tulln 95 *E6 var.* Oberhollabrunn. Niederösterreich, NE Austria
Tully 148 *D3* Queensland, NE Australia
Tulsa 49 *G1* Oklahoma, C USA
Tuluá 58 *B3* Valle del Cauca, W Colombia
Tulun 115 *E4* Irkutskaya Oblast', S Russian Federation
Tumaco 58 *A4* Nariño, SW Colombia
Tumba, Lac *see* Ntomba, Lac
Tumbes 60 *A2* Tumbes, NW Peru
Tumkür 132 *C2* Karnātaka, W India
Tumuc-Humac Mountains 63 *E3 var.* Serra Tumucumaque. *mountain range* N South America
Tumucumaque, Serra *see* Tumuc-Humac Mountains
Tunca Nehri *see* Tundzha
Tunduru 73 *C8* Ruvuma, S Tanzania
Tundzha 104 *D3 Turk.* Tunca Nehri. *river* Bulgaria/Turkey
Tungabhadra Reservoir 132 *C2 lake* S India

Tungaru 145 *E2 prev.* Gilbert Islands. *island group* W Kiribati
T'ung-shan *see* Xuzhou
Tungsten 36 *D4* Northwest Territories, W Canada
Tung-t'ing Hu *see* Dongting Hu
Tunis 71 *E1 var.* Tūnis. *country capital* (Tunisia) (Tunisia) NE Tunisia
Tunis, Golfe de 102 *D3 Ar.* Khalīj Tūnis. *gulf* NE Tunisia
Tunisia 71 *F2 off.* Tunisian Republic, *Ar.* Al Jumhūrīyah at Tūnisīyah, *Fr.* République Tunisienne. *country* N Africa

Tunisian Republic *see* Tunisia
Tunisienne, République *see* Tunisia
Tūnisīyah, Al Jumhūrīyah at *see* Tunisia
Tūnis, Khalīj *see* Tunis, Golfe de
Tunja 58 *B3* Boyacá, C Colombia
Tương Buong *see* Tương Đương
Tương Đương 136 *D4 var.* Tuong Buong. Nghệ An, N Vietnam
Tüp *see* Tyup
Tupelo 42 *C2* Mississippi, S USA
Tupiza 61 *G5* Potosí, S Bolivia
Turabah 121 *B5* Makkah, W Saudi Arabia
Turangi 150 *D4* Waikato, North Island, New Zealand
Turan Lowland 122 *C2 var.* Turan Plain, *Kaz.* Turan Oypaty, *Rus.* Turanskaya Nizmennost', *Turk.* Turan Pesligi, *Uzb.* Turan Pasttekisligi. *plain* C Asia
Turan Oypaty/Turan Pesligi/Turan Plain/Turanskaya Nizmennost' *see* Turan Lowland
Turan Pasttekisligi *see* Turan Lowland
Ṭurayf 120 *A3* Al Ḥudūd ash Shamālīyah, NW Saudi Arabia
Turba *see* Teruel
Turbat 134 *A3* Baluchistān, SW Pakistan
Turda 108 *B4 Ger.* Thorenburg, *Hung.* Torda. Cluj, NW Romania
Turek 98 *C3* Wielkopolskie, C Poland
Turfan *see* Turpan
Turin *see* Torino
Turkana, Lake 73 *C6 var.* Lake Rudolf. *lake* N Kenya
Turkestan 114 *B5 Kaz.* Türkistan. Yuzhnyy Kazakhstan, S Kazakhstan
Turkey 116 *B3 off.* Republic of Turkey, *Turk.* Türkiye Cumhuriyeti. *country* SW Asia

Turkey, Republic of *see* Turkey
Turkish Republic of Northern Cyprus 102 *D5 disputed territory* Cyprus
Türkistan *see* Turkestan
Türkiye Cumhuriyeti *see* Turkey
Türkmenabat 122 *D3 prev. Rus.* Chardzhev, Chardzhou, Chardzhui, Lenin-Turkmenski, *Turkm.* Chärjew. Lebap Welaýaty, E Turkmenistan
Türkmen Aylagy 122 *B2 Rus.* Turkmenskiy Zaliv. *lake gulf* W Turkmenistan
Türkmenbashi *see* Türkmenbaşy
Türkmenbaşy 122 *B2 Rus.* Turkmenbashi; *prev.* Krasnovodsk. Balkan Welaýaty, W Turkmenistan
Türkmenbaşy Aýlagy 122 *A2 prev. Rus.* Krasnovodskiy Zaliv, *Turkm.* Krasnowodsk Aylagy. *lake Gulf* W Turkmenistan
Turkmenistan 122 *B2 ; prev.* Turkmenskaya Soviet Socialist Republic. *country* C Asia

Turkmenskaya Soviet Socialist Republic *see* Turkmenistan
Turkmenskiy Zaliv *see* Türkmen Aylagy
Turks and Caicos Islands 55 *E2 UK dependent territory* N West Indies
Turku 85 *D6 Swe.* Åbo. Länsi-Suomi, SW Finland
Turlock 47 *B6* California, W USA
Turnagain, Cape 150 *D4 headland* North Island, New Zealand
Turnau *see* Turnov
Turnhout 87 *C5* Antwerpen, N Belgium
Turnov 98 *B4 Ger.* Turnau. Liberecký Kraj, N Czech Republic
Tŭrnovo *see* Veliko Tŭrnovo
Turnu Măgurele 108 *B5 var.* Turnu-Măgurele. Teleorman, S Romania
Turnu Severin *see* Drobeta-Turnu Severin
Turócszentmárton *see* Martin
Turoni *see* Tours
Turpan 126 *C3 var.* Turfan. Xinjiang Uygur Zizhiqu, NW China
Turpan Depression *see* Turpan Pendi
Turpan Pendi 126 *C3 Eng.* Turpan Depression. *depression* NW China
Turpentine State *see* North Carolina
Türtkül/Turtkul' *see* To'rtkok'l
Turuga *see* Tsuruga
Turuoka *see* Tsuruoka
Tuscaloosa 42 *C2* Alabama, S USA
Tuscan Archipelago *see* Toscano, Archipelago
Tuscany *see* Toscana
Tusima *see* Tsushima
Tutela *see* Tulle, France
Tutela *see* Tudela, Spain
Tutera *see* Tudela
Tuticorin 132 *C3* Tamil Nādu, SE India
Tutrakan 104 *D1* Silistra, NE Bulgaria
Tutuila 145 *F4 island* W American Samoa
Tuvalu 145 *E3 prev.* Ellice Islands. *country* SW Pacific Ocean

TUVALU
(continued)

per sq mile (461 people per sq km) / 57%
Total area 10 sq. miles (26 sq. km)
Languages English*, Tuvaluan, Kiribati
Religions Church of Tuvalu 97%,
Baha'i 1%, Seventh-day Adventist 1%,
Other 1%
Ethnic mix Polynesian 92%, Other 6%,
Kiribati 2%
Government Nonparty system
Currency Australian dollar and Tuvaluan
dollar = 100 cents
Literacy rate 98%
Calorie consumption Not available

Tuwayq, Jabal 121 C5 *mountain range*
C Saudi Arabia
Tuxpan 50 D4 Jalisco, C Mexico
Tuxpan 50 D4 Nayarit, C Mexico
Tuxpán 51 F4 *var.* Tuxpán de Rodríguez
Cano. Veracruz-Llave, E Mexico
Tuxpán de Rodríguez Cano *see* Tuxpán
Tuxtepec 51 F4 *var.* San Juan Bautista
Tuxtepec. Oaxaca, S Mexico
Tuxtla 51 G5 *var.* Tuxtla Gutiérrez.
Chiapas, SE Mexico
Tuxtla *see* San Andrés Tuxtla
Tuxtla Gutiérrez *see* Tuxtla
Tuy Hoa 137 E5 Phu Yên, S Vietnam
Tuz, Lake 116 C3 *lake* C Turkey
Tver' 110 B4 *prev.* Kalinin. Tverskaya
Oblast', W Russian Federation
Tverya 119 B5 *var.* Tiberias; *prev.*
Teverya. Northern, N Israel
Twin Falls 46 D4 Idaho, NW USA
Tyan'-Shan' *see* Tien Shan
Tychy 99 D5 *Ger.* Tichau. Śląskie,
S Poland
Tyler 49 G3 Texas, SW USA
Tylos *see* Bahrain
Tympáki 105 C8 *var.* Timbaki;
prev. Timbákion. Kríti, Greece,
E Mediterranean Sea
Tynda 115 F4 Amurskaya Oblast',
SE Russian Federation
Tyne 88 D4 *river* N England, United
Kingdom
Tyōsi *see* Chōshi
Tyras *see* Dniester
Tyre *see* Soûr
Tyrnau *see* Trnava
Týrnavos 104 B4 *var.* Tírnavos.
Thessalía, C Greece
Tyrol *see* Tirol
Tyros *see* Bahrain
Tyrrhenian Sea 97 B6 *It.* Mare Tirreno.
sea N Mediterranean Sea
Tyumen' 114 C3 Tyumenskaya Oblast',
C Russian Federation
Tyup 123 G2 *Kir.* Tüp. Issyk-Kul'skaya
Oblast', NE Kyrgyzstan
Tywyn 89 C6 W Wales, United Kingdom
Tzekung *see* Zigong
Tziá 105 C6 *prev.* Kéa, Kéos; *anc.* Ceos.
island Kykládes, Greece, Aegean Sea

U

UAE *see* United Arab Emirates
Uanle Uen *see* Wanlaweyn
Uaupés, Rio *see* Vaupés, Río
Ubangi-Shari *see* Central African
Republic
Ube 131 B7 Yamaguchi, Honshū,
SW Japan
Ubeda 63 E4 Andalucía, S Spain
Uberaba 63 F4 Minas Gerais, SE Brazil
Uberlândia 63 F4 Minas Gerais, SE Brazil
Ubol Rajadhani/Ubol Ratchathani *see*
Ubon Ratchathani
Ubon Ratchathani 137 D5 *var.*
Muang Ubon, Ubol Rajadhani, Ubol
Ratchathani, Udon Ratchathani. Ubon
Ratchathani, E Thailand
Ubrique 92 D5 Andalucía, S Spain
Ubsu-Nur, Ozero *see* Uvs Nuur
Ucayali, Río 60 D3 *river* C Peru
Uchiura-wan 130 D3 *bay* NW Pacific
Ocean
Uchkuduk *see* Uchquduq
Uchquduq 122 D2 *Rus.* Uchkuduk.
Navoiy Viloyati, N Uzbekistan
Uchtagan Gumy/Uchtagan, Peski *see*
Uçtagan Gumy

Uçtagan Gumy 122 C2 *var.* Uchtagan
Gumy, *Rus.* Peski Uchtagan. *desert*
NW Turkmenistan
Udaipur 134 C3 *prev.* Oodeypore.
Rājasthān, N India
Uddevalla 85 B6 Västra Götaland,
S Sweden
Udine 96 D2 *anc.* Utina. Friuli-Venezia
Giulia, NE Italy
Udintsev Fracture Zone 154 A5 *tectonic
feature* S Pacific Ocean
Udipi *see* Udupi
Udon Ratchathani *see* Ubon Ratchathani
Udon Thani 136 C4 *var.* Ban Mak
Khaeng, Udorndhani. Udon Thani,
N Thailand
Udorndhani *see* Udon Thani
Udupi 132 B2 *var.* Udipi. Karnātaka,
SW India
Uele 77 D5 *var.* Welle. *river* NE Dem.
Rep. Congo
Uelzen 94 C3 Niedersachsen, N Germany
Ufa 111 D6 Respublika Bashkortostan,
W Russian Federation
Ugāle 106 C2 Ventspils, NW Latvia
Uganda 73 B6 *off.* Republic of Uganda.
country E Africa

UGANDA
East Africa

Official name Republic of Uganda
Formation 1962 / 1962
Capital Kampala
Population 30.9 million / 401 people
per sq mile (155 people per sq km) / 12%
Total area 91,135 sq. miles (236,040 sq. km)
Languages English*, Luganda, Nkole,
Chiga, Lango, Acholi, Teso, Lugbara
Religions Roman Catholic 38%,
Protestant 33%, Traditional beliefs 13%,
Muslim (mainly Sunni) 8%, Other 8%
Ethnic mix Other 50%, Baganda 17%,
Banyakole 10%, Basoga 9%, Iteso 7%,
Bakiga 7%
Government Presidential system
Currency New Uganda shilling = 100 cents
Literacy rate 67%
Calorie consumption 2410 calories

Uganda, Republic of *see* Uganda
Uhorshchyna *see* Hungary
Uhuru Peak *see* Kilimanjaro
Uíge 78 B1 *Port.* Carmona, Vila
Marechal Carmona. Uíge, NW Angola
Uinta Mountains 44 B4 *mountain range*
Utah, W USA
Uitenhage 78 C4 *var.* Uitenhage. Eastern Cape, S South
Africa
Uithoorn 86 C3 Noord-Holland,
C Netherlands
Ujda *see* Oujda
Ujelang Atoll 144 C1 *var.* Wujlān. *atoll*
Ralik Chain, W Marshall Islands
Ujgradiska *see* Nova Gradiška
Ujmoldova *see* Moldova Nouă
Ujungpandang *see* Makassar
Ujung Salang *see* Phuket
UK *see* United Kingdom
Ukhta 114 C3 Respublika Komi,
NW Russian Federation
Ukiah 47 B5 California, W USA
Ukmergė 106 C4 *Pol.* Wiłkomierz.
Vilnius, C Lithuania
Ukraina *see* Ukraine
Ukraine 108 C2 *off.* Ukraine, *Rus.*
Ukraina, *Ukr.* Ukrayina; *prev.*
Ukrainian Soviet Socialist Republic,
Ukrainskay S.S.R. *country* SE Europe

UKRAINE
Eastern Europe

Official name Ukraine
Formation 1991 / 1991
Capital Kiev
Population 45.5 million / 195 people
per sq mile (75 people per sq km) / 67%
Total area 233,089 sq. miles
(603,700 sq. km)
Languages Ukrainian*, Russian, Tatar
Religions Christian (mainly
Orthodox) 95%, Other 5%
Ethnic mix Ukrainian 78%, Russian 17%,
Other 5%
Government Presidential system

UKRAINE
(continued)

Currency Hryvna = 100 kopiykas
Literacy rate 99%
Calorie consumption 3054 calories

Ukraine *see* Ukraine
Ukrainian Soviet Socialist Republic
see Ukraine
Ukrainskay S.S.R/Ukrayina *see* Ukraine
Ulaanbaatar 127 E2 *Eng.* Ulan Bator;
prev. Urga. *country capital* (Mongolia)
(Mongolia) Töv, C Mongolia
Ulaangom 126 C2 Uvs, NW Mongolia
Ulan Bator *see* Ulaanbaatar
Ulanhad *see* Chifeng
Ulan-Ude 115 E4 *prev.* Verkhneudinsk.
Respublika Buryatiya, S Russian
Federation
Uleälv *see* Oulujoki
Uleträsk *see* Oulujärvi
Ulft 86 E4 Gelderland, E Netherlands
Ullapool 88 C3 N Scotland, United
Kingdom
Ulm 95 B6 Baden-Württemberg,
S Germany
Ulsan 129 E4 *Jap.* Urusan. SE South Korea
Ulster 89 B5 *province* Northern Ireland,
United Kingdom/Ireland
Ulungur Hu 126 B2 *lake* NW China
Uluru 147 D5 *var.* Ayers Rock. *monolith*
Northern Territory, C Australia
Ulyanivka 109 E3 *Rus.* Ul'yanovka.
Kirovohrads'ka Oblast', C Ukraine
Ul'yanovka *see* Ulyanivka
Ul'yanovsk 111 C5 *prev.* Simbirsk.
Ul'yanovskaya Oblast', W Russian
Federation
Umán 51 H3 Yucatán, SE Mexico
Uman' 109 E3 *Rus.* Uman. Cherkas'ka
Oblast', C Ukraine
Uman *see* Uman'
Umanak/Umanaq *see* Uummannaq
'Umān, Khalīj *see* Oman, Gulf of
'Umān, Saltanat *see* Oman
Umbrian-Machigian Mountains *see*
Umbro-Marchigiano, Appennino
Umbro-Marchigiano, Appennino
96 C3 *Eng.* Umbrian-Machigian
Mountains. *mountain range* C Italy
Umeå 84 C4 Västerbotten, N Sweden
Umeälven 84 C4 *river* N Sweden
Umiat 36 D2 Alaska, USA
Umm Buru 72 A4 Western Darfur,
W Sudan
Umm Durmān *see* Omdurman
Umm Ruwaba 72 C4 *var.* Umm
Ruwābah, Um Ruwāba. Northern
Kordofan, C Sudan
Umm Ruwābah *see* Umm Ruwaba
Umnak Island 36 A3 *island* Aleutian
Islands, Alaska, USA
Um Ruwāba *see* Umm Ruwaba
Umtali *see* Mutare
Umtata 78 D5 Eastern Cape, SE South
Africa
Una 100 B3 *river* Bosnia and
Herzegovina/Croatia
Unac 100 B3 *river* W Bosnia and
Herzegovina
Unalaska Island 36 A3 *island* Aleutian
Islands, Alaska, USA
'Unayzah 120 B4 *var.* Anaiza. Al Qasīm,
C Saudi Arabia
Unci *see* Almería
Uncía 61 F4 Potosí, C Bolivia
Uncompahgre Peak 44 B5 *mountain*
Colorado, C USA
Undur Khan *see* Öndörhaan
Ungaria *see* Hungary
Ungarisches Erzgebirge *see* Slovenské
rudohorie
Ungarn *see* Hungary
Ungava Bay 39 E1 *bay* Québec, E Canada
Ungava Peninsula 38 D1 *peninsula*
Québec, SE Canada
Ungeny *see* Ungheni
Ungheni 108 D3 *Rus.* Ungeny.
W Moldova
Unguja *see* Zanzibar
Üngüz Angyrsyndaky Garagum 122 C2
Rus. Zaunguzskiye Garagumy. *desert*
N Turkmenistan
Ungvár *see* Uzhhorod
Unimak Island 36 B3 *island* Aleutian
Islands, Alaska, USA

Union 43 E1 South Carolina, SE USA
Union City 42 C1 Tennessee, S USA
Union of Myanmar *see* Burma
United Arab Emirates 121 C5 *Ar.* Al
Imārāt al 'Arabiyah al Muttahidah,
abbrev. UAE; *prev.* Trucial States.
country SW Asia

UNITED ARAB EMIRATES
Southwest Asia

Official name United Arab Emirates
Formation 1971 / 1972
Capital Abu Dhabi
Population 4.8 million / 149 people
per sq mile (57 people per sq km) / 85%
Total area 32,000 sq. miles (82,880 sq. km)
Languages Arabic*, Farsi, Indian and
Pakistani languages, English
Religions Muslim (mainly Sunni) 96%,
Christian, Hindu, and other 4%
Ethnic mix Asian 60%, Emirian 25%,
Other Arab 12%, European 3%
Government Monarchy
Currency UAE dirham = 100 fils
Literacy rate 77%
Calorie consumption 3225 calories

United Arab Republic *see* Egypt
United Kingdom 89 B5 *off.* United
Kingdom of Great Britain and
Northern Ireland, *abbrev.* UK. *country*
NW Europe

UNITED KINGDOM
Northwest Europe

Official name United Kingdom of Great
Britain and Northern Ireland
Formation 1707 / 1922
Capital London
Population 60 million / 643 people
per sq mile (248 people per sq km) / 89%
Total area 94,525 sq. miles
(244,820 sq. km)
Languages English*, Welsh* (in Wales),
Scottish Gaelic, Irish Gaelic
Religions Anglican 45%, Roman
Catholic 9%, Presbyterian 4%, Other 42%
Ethnic mix English 80%, Scottish 9%,
West Indian, Asian, and other 5%,
Northern Irish 3%, Welsh 3%
Government Parliamentary system
Currency Pound sterling = 100 pence
Literacy rate 99%
Calorie consumption 3412 calories

**United Kingdom of Great Britain and
Northern Ireland** *see* United Kingdom
United Mexican States *see* Mexico
United Provinces *see* Uttar Pradesh
United States of America 35 B5 *off.*
United States of America, *var.* America,
The States, *abbrev.* U.S., USA. *country*
North America

UNITED STATES
North America

Official name United States of America
Formation 1776 / 1959
Capital Washington D.C.
Population 304 million / 86 people
per sq mile (33 people per sq km) / 80%
Total area 3,717,792 sq. miles
(9,626,091 sq. km)
Languages English 82%, Spanish 11%,
other 7%
Religions Protestant 52%, Roman Catholic
25%, Muslim 2%, Jewish 2%, Other 19%
Ethnic mix White 62%, Hispanic 13%,
Black American/African 13%, Other 7%,
Asian 4%, Native American 1%
Government Presidential system
Currency US dollar = 100 cents
Literacy rate 99%
Calorie consumption 3774 calories

United States of America *see* United
States of America
Unst 88 D1 *island* NE Scotland, United
Kingdom
Ünye 116 D2 Ordu, W Turkey
Upala 52 D4 Alajuela, NW Costa Rica
Upata 59 E2 Bolívar, E Venezuela
Upemba, Lac 77 D7 *lake* SE Dem.
Rep. Congo

Upernavik 82 C2 var. Upernivik. Kitaa, C Greenland
Upernivik see Upernavik
Upington 78 C4 Northern Cape, W South Africa
'Upolu 145 F4 island SE Samoa
Upper Klamath Lake 46 A4 lake Oregon, NW USA
Upper Lough Erne 89 A5 lake SW Northern Ireland, United Kingdom
Upper Red Lake 45 F1 lake Minnesota, N USA
Upper Volta see Burkina Faso
Uppsala 85 C6 Uppsala, C Sweden
Uqsuqtuuq see Gjoa Haven
Ural 112 B3 Kaz. Zayyq. river Kazakhstan/Russian Federation
Ural Mountains 114 C3 var. Ural'skiy Khrebet, Eng. Ural Mountains. mountain range Kazakhstan/Russian Federation
Ural Mountains see Ural'skiye Gory
Ural'sk 114 B3 Kaz. Oral. Zapadnyy Kazakhstan, NW Kazakhstan
Ural'skiy Khrebet see Ural'skiye Gory
Uraricoera 62 D1 Roraima, N Brazil
Ura-Tyube see Ŭroteppa
Urbandale 45 F3 Iowa, C USA
Urdunn see Jordan
Uren' 111 C5 Nizhegorodskaya Oblast', W Russian Federation
Urga see Ulaanbaatar
Urganch 122 D2 Rus. Urgench; prev. Novo-Urgench. Xorazm Viloyati, W Uzbekistan
Urgench see Urganch
Urgut 123 E3 Samarqand Viloyati, C Uzbekistan
Lake Urmia 121 C2 var. Matianus, Sha Hi, Urumi Yeh, Eng. Lake Urmia; prev. Daryācheh-ye Rezā'īyeh. lake NW Iran
Urmia, Lake see Orūmīyeh, Daryācheh-ye
Uroševac see Ferizaj
Ŭroteppa 123 E2 Rus. Ura-Tyube. NW Tajikistan
Uruapan 51 E4 var. Uruapan del Progreso. Michoacán, SW Mexico
Uruapan del Progreso see Uruapan
Uruguai, Río see Uruguay
Uruguay 64 D4 off. Oriental Republic of Uruguay; prev. La Banda Oriental. country E South America

URUGUAY
South America
Official name The Oriental Republic of Uruguay
Formation 1828 / 1828
Capital Montevideo
Population 3.5 million / 52 people per sq mile (20 people per sq km) / 93%
Total area 68,039 sq. miles (176,220 sq. km)
Languages Spanish*
Religions Roman Catholic 66%, Other and nonreligious 30%, Jewish 2%, Protestant 2%
Ethnic mix White 90%, Mestizo 6%, Black 4%
Government Presidential system
Currency Uruguayan peso = 100 centésimos
Literacy rate 98%
Calorie consumption 2828 calories

Uruguay 64 D3 var. Rio Uruguai, Río Uruguay. river E South America
Uruguay, Oriental Republic of see Uruguay
Uruguay, Río see Uruguay
Urumchi see Ürümqi
Urumi Yeh see Orūmīyeh, Daryācheh-ye
Ürümqi 126 C3 var. Tihwa, Urumchi, Urumqi, Urumtsi, Wu-lu-k'o-mu-shi, Wu-lu-mu-ch'i; prev. Ti-hua. Xinjiang Uygur Zizhiqu, NW China
Urumtsi see Ürümqi
Urundi see Burundi
Urup, Ostrov 115 H4 island Kuril'skiye Ostrova, SE Russian Federation
Urusan see Ulsan
Urziceni 108 C5 Ialomiţa, SE Romania
Usa 110 E3 river NW Russian Federation
Uşak 116 B3 prev. Ushak. Uşak, W Turkey
Ushak see Uşak

Ushuaia 65 B8 Tierra del Fuego, S Argentina
Usinsk 110 E3 Respublika Komi, NW Russian Federation
Üsküb/Üsküp see Skopje
Usmas Ezers 106 B3 lake NW Latvia
Usol'ye-Sibirskoye 115 E4 Irkutskaya Oblast', C Russian Federation
Ussel 91 C5 Corrèze, C France
Ussuriysk 115 G5 prev. Nikol'sk, Nikol'sk-Ussuriyskiy, Voroshilov. Primorskiy Kray, SE Russian Federation
Ustica 97 B6 island S Italy
Ust'-Ilimsk 115 E4 Irkutskaya Oblast', C Russian Federation
Ústí nad Labem 98 A4 Ger. Aussig. Ústecký Kraj, NW Czech Republic
Ustinov see Izhevsk
Ustka 98 C2 Ger. Stolpmünde. Pomorskie, N Poland
Ust'-Kamchatsk 115 H2 Kamchatskaya Oblast', E Russian Federation
Ust'-Kamenogorsk 114 D5 Kaz. Öskemen. Vostochnyy Kazakhstan, E Kazakhstan
Ust'-Kut 115 E4 Irkutskaya Oblast', C Russian Federation
Ust'-Olenëk 115 E3 Respublika Sakha (Yakutiya), NE Russian Federation
Ustrzyki Dolne 99 E5 Podkarpackie, SE Poland
Ust'-Sysol'sk see Syktyvkar
Ust Urt see Ustyurt Plateau
Ustyurt Plateau 122 B1 var. Ust Urt, Uzb. Ustyurt Platosi. plateau Kazakhstan/Uzbekistan
Ustyurt Platosi see Ustyurt Plateau
Usulután 52 C3 Usulután, SE El Salvador
Usumacinta, Río 52 B1 river Guatemala/Mexico
Usumbura see Bujumbura
U.S./USA see United States of America
Utah 44 B4 off. State of Utah, also known as Beehive State, Mormon State. state W USA
Utah Lake 44 B4 lake Utah, W USA
Utena 106 C4 Utena, E Lithuania
Utica 41 F3 New York, NE USA
Utina see Udine
Utrecht 86 C4 Lat. Trajectum ad Rhenum. Utrecht, C Netherlands
Utsunomiya 131 D5 var. Utunomiya. Tochigi, Honshū, S Japan
Uttarakhand 135 E2 cultural region N India
Uttar Pradesh 135 E3 prev. United Provinces, United Provinces of Agra and Oudh. cultural region N India
Utunomiya see Utsunomiya
Uulu 106 D2 Pärnumaa, SW Estonia
Uummannaq 82 C3 var. Umanak, Umanaq. Kitaa, C Greenland
Uummannarsuaq see Nunap Isua
Uvalde 49 F4 Texas, SW USA
Uvarovichi 107 D7 Rus. Uvarovichi. Homyel'skaya Voblasts', SE Belarus
Uvarovichi see Uvarovichi
Uvea, Île 145 E4 island N Wallis and Futuna
Uvs Nuur 126 C1 var. Ozero Ubsu-Nur. lake Mongolia/Russian Federation
'Uwaynāt, Jabal al 88 A3 var. Jebel Uweinat. mountain Libya/Sudan
Uweinat, Jebel see 'Uwaynāt, Jabal al
Uyo 75 G5 Akwa Ibom, S Nigeria
Uyuni 61 F5 Potosí, W Bolivia
Uzbekistan 122 D2 off. Republic of Uzbekistan. country C Asia

UZBEKISTAN
Central Asia
Official name Republic of Uzbekistan
Formation 1991 / 1991
Capital Tashkent
Population 27.4 million / 159 people per sq mile (61 people per sq km) / 37%
Total area 172,741 sq. miles (447,400 sq. km)
Languages Uzbek*, Russian, Tajik, Kazakh
Religions Sunni Muslim 88%, Orthodox Christian 9%, Other 3%
Ethnic mix Uzbek 80%, Other 6%, Russian 6%, Tajik 5%, Kazakh 3%
Government Presidential system
Currency Som = 100 tiyin

UZBEKISTAN
(continued)
Literacy rate 99%
Calorie consumption 2241 calories

Uzbekistan, Republic of see Uzbekistan
Uzhgorod see Uzhhorod
Uzhhorod 108 B2 Rus. Uzhgorod; prev. Ungvár. Zakarpats'ka Oblast', W Ukraine
Užice 100 D4 prev. Titovo Užice. Serbia, W Serbia

V

Vaal 78 D4 river C South Africa
Vaals 87 D6 Limburg, SE Netherlands
Vaasa 85 D5 Swe. Vasa; prev. Nikolainkaupunki. Länsi-Suomi, W Finland
Vaassen 86 D3 Gelderland, E Netherlands
Vác 99 C6 Ger. Waitzen. Pest, N Hungary
Vadodara 134 C4 prev. Baroda. Gujarāt, W India
Vaduz 94 E2 country capital (Liechtenstein) (Liechtenstein) W Liechtenstein
Vág see Váh
Vágbeszterce see Považská Bystrica
Váh 99 C5 Ger. Waag, Hung. Vág. river W Slovakia
Váhtjer see Gällivare
Väinameri 106 C2 prev. Muhu Väin, Ger. Moon-Sund. sea E Baltic Sea
Vajdahunyad see Hunedoara
Valachia see Wallachia
Valday 110 B4 Novgorodskaya Oblast', W Russian Federation
Valdecañas, Embalse de 92 D3 reservoir W Spain
Valdepeñas 93 E4 Castilla-La Mancha, C Spain
Valdés, Península 65 C6 peninsula SE Argentina
Valdez 36 C3 Alaska, USA
Valdia see Weldiya
Valdivia 65 B5 Los Lagos, C Chile
Val-d'Or 38 D4 Québec, SE Canada
Valdosta 43 E3 Georgia, SE USA
Valence 91 D5 anc. Valentia, Valentia Julia, Ventia. Drôme, E France
Valencia 93 F3 País Valenciano, E Spain
Valencia 46 D1 California, USA
Valencia 58 D1 Carabobo, N Venezuela
Valencia, Gulf of 93 F3 var. Gulf of Valencia. gulf E Spain
Valencia, Gulf of see Valencia, Golfo de
Valencia/València see País Valenciano
Valenciennes 90 D2 Nord, N France
Valentia see Valence, France
Valentia see País Valenciano
Valentia Julia see Valence
Valentine State see Oregon
Valera 58 C2 Trujillo, NW Venezuela
Valetta see Valletta
Valga 106 D4 Ger. Walk, Latv. Valka. Valgamaa, S Estonia
Valira 91 A8 river Andorra/Spain Europe
Valjevo 100 C4 Serbia, W Serbia
Valjok see Válljohka
Valka 106 D3 Ger. Walk. Valka, N Latvia
Valka see Valga
Valkenswaard 87 D5 Noord-Brabant, S Netherlands
Valladolid 51 H3 Yucatán, SE Mexico
Valladolid 92 D2 Castilla-León, NW Spain
Vall D'Uxó see La Vall d'Uixó
Valle de la Pascua 58 D2 Guárico, N Venezuela
Valledupar 58 B1 Cesar, N Colombia
Vallejo 47 B6 California, W USA
Vallenar 64 B3 Atacama, N Chile
Valletta 97 C8 prev. Valetta. country capital (Malta) (Malta) E Malta
Valley City 45 E2 North Dakota, N USA
Válljohka 84 D2 var. Valjok. Finnmark, N Norway
Valls 93 G2 Cataluña, NE Spain
Valmiera 106 D3 Est. Volmari, Ger. Wolmar. Valmiera, N Latvia
Valona see Vlorë

Valozhyn 107 C5 Pol. Wołożyn, Rus. Volozhin. Minskaya Voblasts', C Belarus
Valparaíso 64 B4 Valparaíso, C Chile
Valparaiso 40 C3 Indiana, N USA
Valverde del Camino 92 C4 Andalucía, S Spain
Van 117 F3 Van, E Turkey
Vanadzor 117 F2 prev. Kirovakan. N Armenia
Vancouver 36 D5 British Columbia, SW Canada
Vancouver 46 B3 Washington, NW USA
Vancouver Island 36 D5 island British Columbia, SW Canada
Vanda see Vantaa
Van Diemen Gulf 146 D2 gulf Northern Territory, N Australia
Van Diemen's Land see Tasmania
Vaner, Lake see Vänern
Vänern 85 B6 Eng. Lake Vaner; prev. Lake Vener. lake S Sweden
Vangaindrano 79 G4 Fianarantsoa, SE Madagascar
Van Horn 48 D3 Texas, SW USA
Lake Van 117 F3 Eng. Lake Van; anc. Thospitis. salt lake E Turkey
Van, Lake see Van Gölü
Vannes 90 A3 anc. Dariorigum. Morbihan, NW France
Vantaa 85 D6 Swe. Vanda. Etelä-Suomi, S Finland
Vanua Levu 145 E4 island N Fiji
Vanuatu 144 C4 off. Republic of Vanuatu; prev. New Hebrides. country SW Pacific Ocean

VANUATU
Australasia & Oceania
Official name Republic of Vanuatu
Formation 1980 / 1980
Capital Port Vila
Population 211,971 / 45 people per sq mile (17 people per sq km) / 23%
Total area 4710 sq. miles (12,200 sq. km)
Languages Bislama* (Melanesian pidgin), English*, French*, other indigenous languages
Religions Presbyterian 37%, Other 19%, Anglican 15%, Roman Catholic 15%, Traditional beliefs 8%, Seventh-day Adventist 6%
Ethnic mix Melanesian 98%, Other 1%, European 1%
Government Parliamentary system
Currency Vatu = 100 centimes
Literacy rate 74%
Calorie consumption 2587 calories

Vanuatu, Republic of see Vanuatu
Van Wert 40 C4 Ohio, N USA
Vapincum see Gap
Varakļāni 106 D4 Madona, C Latvia
Vāranasi 135 E3 prev. Banaras, Benares, hist. Kasi. Uttar Pradesh, N India
Varangerfjorden 84 E2 Lapp. Várjjatvuotna. fjord N Norway
Varangerhalvøya 84 D2 Lapp. Várnjárga. peninsula N Norway
Varannó see Vranov nad Topl'ou
Varasd see Varaždin
Varaždin 100 B2 Ger. Warasdin, Hung. Varasd. Varaždin, N Croatia
Varberg 85 B7 Halland, S Sweden
Vardar 101 E6 Gk. Axiós. river FYR Macedonia/Greece
Varde 85 A7 Ribe, W Denmark
Vareia see Logroño
Varėna 107 B5 Pol. Orany. Alytus, S Lithuania
Varese 96 B2 Lombardia, N Italy
Vârful Moldoveanu 108 B4 var. Moldoveanul; prev. Vîrful Moldoveanu. mountain C Romania
Várjjatvuotna see Varangerfjorden
Varkaus 85 E5 Itä-Suomi, C Finland
Varna 104 E2 prev. Stalin; anc. Odessus. Varna, E Bulgaria
Varnenski Zaliv 104 E2 prev. Stalinski Zaliv. bay E Bulgaria
Várnjárga see Varangerhalvøya
Varshava see Warszawa
Vasa see Vaasa
Vasilíki 105 A5 Lefkáda, Iónia Nisiá, Greece, C Mediterranean Sea
Vasilishki 107 B5 Pol. Wasiliszki. Hrodzyenskaya Voblasts', W Belarus

Vasil'kov see Vasyl'kiv
Vaslui 108 D4 Vaslui, C Romania
Västerås 85 C6 Västmanland, C Sweden
Vasyl'kiv 109 E2 var. Vasil'kov.
Kyyivs'ka Oblast', N Ukraine
Vaté see Efate
Vatican City 97 A7 off. Vatican City.
country S Europe

VATICAN CITY
Southern Europe

Official name The Vatican City
Formation 1929 / 1929
Capital Vatican City
Population 821 / 4829 people per sq mile
(1866 people per sq km) / 100%
Total area 0.17 sq. miles (0.44 sq. km)
Languages Italian*, Latin*
Religions Roman Catholic 100%
Government Papal state
Currency Euro = 100 cents
Literacy rate 99%
Calorie consumption Not available

Vatican City see Vatican City
Vatnajökull 83 E5 glacier SE Iceland
Vatter, Lake see Vättern
Vättern 85 B6 Eng. Lake Vatter; prev.
Lake Vetter. lake S Sweden
Vaughn 48 D2 New Mexico, SW USA
Vaupés, Río 58 C4 var. Rio Uaupés.
river Brazil/Colombia
Vava'u Group 145 E4 island group
N Tonga
Vavuniya 132 D3 Northern Province,
N Sri Lanka
Vawkavysk 107 B6 Pol. Wołkowysk,
Rus. Volkovysk. Hrodzyenskaya
Voblasts', W Belarus
Växjö 85 C7 var. Vexiö. Kronoberg,
S Sweden
Vaygach, Ostrov 110 E2 island
NW Russian Federation
Veendam 86 E2 Groningen,
NE Netherlands
Veenendaal 86 D4 Utrecht, C Netherlands
Vega 84 B4 island C Norway
Veglia see Krk
Veisiejai 107 B5 Alytus, S Lithuania
Vejer de la Frontera 92 C5 Andalucía,
S Spain
Veldhoven 87 D5 Noord-Brabant,
S Netherlands
Velebit 100 A3 mountain range
C Croatia
Velenje 95 E7 Ger. Wöllan. N Slovenia
Veles 101 E6 Turk. Köprülü. C
FYR Macedonia
Velho see Porto Velho
Velika Kikinda see Kikinda
Velika Morava 100 D4 var. Glavn'a
Morava, Morava, Ger. Grosse Morava.
river C Serbia
Velikaya 113 G2 river NE Russian
Federation
Veliki Bečkerek see Zrenjanin
Velikiye Luki 110 A4 Pskovskaya
Oblast', W Russian Federation
Velikiy Novgorod 110 B4 prev.
Novgorod. Novgorodskaya Oblast',
W Russian Federation
Veliko Túrnovo 104 D2 prev. Tirnovo,
Trnovo, Túrnovo. Veliko Túrnovo,
N Bulgaria
Velingrad 104 C3 Pazardzhik, C Bulgaria
Vel'ký Krtíš 99 D6 Banskobystrický
Kraj, C Slovakia
Vellore 132 C2 Tamil Nādu, SE India
Velobriga see Viana do Castelo
Velsen see Velsen-Noord
Velsen-Noord 86 C3 var. Velsen.
Noord-Holland, W Netherlands
Vel'sk 110 C4 var. Velsk.
Arkhangel'skaya Oblast', NW Russian
Federation
Velykyy Tokmak see Tokmak
Vendôme 90 B4 Loir-et-Cher,
C France
Venedig see Venezia
Vener, Lake see Vänern
Venetia see Venezia
Venezia 96 C2 Eng. Venice, Fr. Venise,
Ger. Venedig; anc. Venetia. Veneto,
NE Italy
Venezia, Golfo di see Venice,
Gulf of

Venezuela 58 D2 off. Republic of
Venezuela; prev. Estados Unidos de
Venezuela, United States of Venezuela.
country N South America

VENEZUELA
South America

Official name Bolivarian Republic of
Venezuela
Formation 1830 / 1830
Capital Caracas
Population 27.7 million / 81 people
per sq mile (31 people per sq km) / 88%
Total area 352,143 sq. miles
(912,050 sq. km)
Languages Spanish*,
Amerindian languages
Religions Roman Catholic 89%,
Protestant and other 11%
Ethnic mix Mestizo 69%, White 20%,
Black 9%, Amerindian 2%
Government Presidential system
Currency Bolívar = 100 céntimos
Literacy rate 93%
Calorie consumption 2336 calories

Venezuela, Estados Unidos de see
Venezuela
Venezuela, Gulf of 58 C1 Eng. Gulf of
Maracaibo, Gulf of Venezuela. gulf
NW Venezuela
Venezuela, Golfo de see Venezuela,
Golfo de
Venezuelan Basin 56 B1 undersea basin
E Caribbean Sea
Venezuela, Republic of see Venezuela
Venezuela, United States of see
Venezuela
Venice 42 C4 Louisiana, S USA
Venice see Venezia
Venice, Gulf of 96 C2 It. Golfo di
Venezia, Slvn. Beneški Zaliv. gulf
N Adriatic Sea
Venise see Venezia
Venlo 87 D5 prev. Venloo. Limburg,
SE Netherlands
Venloo see Venlo
Venta 106 B3 Ger. Windau. river Latvia/
Lithuania
Venta Belgarum see Winchester
Ventia see Valence
Ventimiglia 96 A3 Liguria, NW Italy
Ventspils 106 B2 Ger. Windau.
Ventspils, NW Latvia
Vera 64 D3 Santa Fe, C Argentina
Veracruz 51 F4 var. Veracruz Llave.
Veracruz-Llave, E Mexico
Veracruz Llave see Veracruz
Vercellae see Vercelli
Vercelli 96 A2 anc. Vercellae. Piemonte,
NW Italy
Verdal see Verdalsøra
Verdalsøra 84 B4 var. Verdal. Nord-
Tröndelag, C Norway
Verde, Cabo see Cape Verde
Verde, Costa 92 D1 coastal region
N Spain
Verden 94 B3 Niedersachsen,
NW Germany
Veria see Véroia
Verkhnedvinsk see Vyerkhnyadzvinsk
Verkhneudinsk see Ulan-Ude
Verkhoyanskiy Khrebet 115 F3
mountain range NE Russian Federation
Vermillion 45 F3 South Dakota, N USA
Vermont 41 F2 off. State of Vermont,
also known as Green Mountain State.
state NE USA
Vernal 44 B4 Utah, W USA
Vernon 49 F2 Texas, SW USA
Veröcze see Virovitica
Véroia 104 B4 var. Veria, Vérroia,
Turk. Karaferiye. Kentrikí Makedonía,
N Greece
Verona 96 C2 Veneto, NE Italy
Vérroia see Véroia
Versailles 90 D1 Yvelines, N France
Versecz see Vršac
Verulamium see St Albans
Verviers 87 D6 Liège, E Belgium
Vesdre 87 D6 river E Belgium
Veselinovo 104 D2 Shumen, NE Bulgaria
Vesontio see Besançon
Vesoul 90 D4 anc. Vesulium, Vesulum.
Haute-Saône, E France
Vesterålen 84 B2 island group N Norway

Vestfjorden 84 C3 fjord C Norway
Vestmannaeyjar 83 E5 Sudhurland,
S Iceland
Vesulium/Vesulum see Vesoul
Vesuna see Périgueux
Vesuvius 97 D5 Eng. Vesuvius. volcano
S Italy
Vesuvius see Vesuvio
Veszprém 99 C7 Ger. Veszprim.
Veszprém, W Hungary
Veszprim see Veszprém
Vetrino 104 E2 Varna, E Bulgaria
Vetrino see Vyetryna
Vetter, Lake see Vättern
Veurne 87 A5 var. Furnes. West-
Vlaanderen, W Belgium
Vexiö see Växjö
Viacha 61 F4 La Paz, W Bolivia
Viana de Castelo see Viana do Castelo
Viana do Castelo 92 B2 var. Viana de
Castelo; anc. Velobriga. Viana do
Castelo, NW Portugal
Vianen 86 C4 Utrecht, C Netherlands
Viangchan 136 C4 Eng./Fr. Vientiane.
country capital (Laos) (Laos) C Laos
Viangphoukha 136 C3 var. Vieng Pou
Kha. Louang Namtha, N Laos
Viareggio 96 B3 Toscana, C Italy
Viborg 85 A7 Viborg, NW Denmark
Vic 93 G2 var. Vich; anc. Ausa, Vicus
Ausonensis. Cataluña, NE Spain
Vicentia see Vicenza
Vicenza 96 C2 anc. Vicentia. Veneto,
NE Italy
Vich see Vic
Vichy 91 C5 Allier, C France
Vicksburg 42 B2 Mississippi, S USA
Victoria 79 H1 country capital
(Seychelles) (Seychelles) Mahé,
SW Seychelles
Victoria 36 D5 province capital
Vancouver Island, British Columbia,
SW Canada
Victoria 102 A5 var. Rabat. Gozo,
NW Malta
Victoria 49 G4 Texas,
SW USA
Victoria 149 C7 state
SE Australia
Victoria see Masvingo, Zimbabwe
Victoria Bank see Vitória Seamount
Victoria de Durango see Durango
Victoria de las Tunas see Las Tunas
Victoria Falls 78 C3 Matabeleland
North, W Zimbabwe
Victoria Falls 58 waterfall Zambia/
Zimbabwe
Victoria Island 37 F3 island Northwest
Territories/Nunavut, NW Canada
Victoria, Lake 73 B6 var. Victoria
Nyanza. lake E Africa
Victoria Land 154 C4 physical region
Antarctica
Victoria Nyanza see Victoria, Lake
Victoria River 146 D3 river Northern
Territory, N Australia
Victorville 47 C7 California,
W USA
Vicus Ausonensis see Vic
Vicus Elbii see Viterbo
Vidalia 43 E2 Georgia, SE USA
Videm-Krško see Krško
Víðerð see Vidin
Vidin 104 B1 anc. Bononia. Vidin,
NW Bulgaria
Vidzy 107 C5 Vitsyebskaya Voblasts',
NW Belarus
Viedma 65 C5 Río Negro,
E Argentina
Vieja, Sierra 48 D3 mountain range
Texas, SW USA
Vieng Pou Kha see Viangphoukha
Vienna 43 E1 Georgia, SE USA
Vienna see Wien, Austria
Vienna see Vienne, France
Vienne 91 D5 anc. Vienna. Isère,
E France
Vienne 90 B4 river W France
Vientiane see Viangchan
Vientos, Paso de los see Windward
Passage
Vierzon 90 C4 Cher, C France
Viesīte 106 C4 Ger. Eckengraf. Jēkabpils,
S Latvia
Vietnam 136 D4 off. Socialist Republic of
Vietnam, Vtn. Công Hoa Xa Hôi Chu
Nghia Viêt Nam. country SE Asia

VIETNAM
Southeast Asia

Official name Socialist Republic
of Vietnam
Formation 1976 / 1976
Capital Hanoi
Population 86.4 million / 688 people
per sq mile (266 people per sq km) / 26%
Total area 127,243 sq. miles
(329,560 sq. km)
Languages Vietnamese*, Chinese, Thai,
Khmer, Muong, Nung, Miao, Yao, Jarai
Religions Nonreligious 81%, Buddhist 9%,
Christian 7%, Other 3%
Ethnic mix Vietnamese 86%, Other 10%,
Tay 2%, Thai 2%
Government One-party state
Currency Dông = 10 hao = 100 xu
Literacy rate 90%
Calorie consumption 2566 calories

Vietnam, Socialist Republic of see
Vietnam
Vietri see Viêt Tri
Viêt Tri 136 D3 var. Vietri. Vinh Phu,
N Vietnam
Vieux Fort 55 F2 S Saint Lucia
Vigo 92 B2 Galicia, NW Spain
Viipuri see Vyborg
Vijayawāda 132 D1 prev. Bezwada.
Andhra Pradesh, SE India
Vila see Port-Vila
Vila Artur de Paiva see Cubango
Vila da Ponte see Cubango
Vila de João Belo see Xai-Xai
Vila de Mocímboa da Praia see
Mocímboa da Praia
Vila do Conde 92 B2 Porto,
NW Portugal
Vila do Zumbo 78 D2 prev.
Vila do Zumbo, Zumbo. Tete,
NW Mozambique
Vila do Zumbo see Vila do Zumbo
Vilafranca del Penedès 93 G2 var.
Villafranca del Panadés. Cataluña,
NE Spain
Vila General Machado see Camacupa
Vila Henrique de Carvalho see Saurimo
Vilaka 106 D4 Ger. Marienhausen. Balvi,
NE Latvia
Vilalba 92 C1 Galicia, NW Spain
Vila Marechal Carmona see Uíge
Vila Nova de Gaia 92 B2 Porto,
NW Portugal
Vila Nova de Portimão see Portimão
Vila Pereira de Eça see N'Giva
Vila Real 92 C2 var. Vila Rial. Vila Real,
N Portugal
Vila Rial see Vila Real
Vila Robert Williams see Caála
Vila Salazar see N Dalatando
Vila Serpa Pinto see Menongue
Vileyka see Vilyeyka
Vilhelmina 84 C4 Västerbotten, N Sweden
Vilhena 62 D3 Rondônia, W Brazil
Vília 105 C5 Attikí, C Greece
Viliya 107 C5 Lith. Neris. river
W Belarus
Viliya see Neris
Viljandi 106 D2 Ger. Fellin.
Viljandimaa, S Estonia
Vilkaviškis 106 B4 Pol. Wyłkowyszki.
Marijampolė, SW Lithuania
Villa Acuña 50 D2 var. Ciudad Acuña.
Coahuila, NE Mexico
Villa Bella 61 F2 Beni, N Bolivia
Villacarrillo 93 E4 Andalucía, S Spain
Villa Cecilia see Ciudad Madero
Villach 95 D7 Slvn. Beljak. Kärnten,
S Austria
Villacidro 97 A5 Sardegna, Italy,
C Mediterranean Sea
Villa Concepción see Concepción
Villa del Pilar see Pilar
Villafranca de los Barros 92 C4
Extremadura, W Spain
Villafranca del Panadés see Vilafranca
del Penedès
Villahermosa 51 G4 prev. San Juan
Bautista. Tabasco, SE Mexico
Villajoyosa 93 F4 Cat. La Vila Joíosa.
País Valenciano, E Spain
Villa María 64 C4 Córdoba, C Argentina
Villa Martín 61 F5 Potosí, SW Bolivia
Villa Mercedes 64 C4 San Juan,
Argentina

Villanueva 50 D3 Zacatecas, C Mexico
Villanueva de la Serena 92 C3 Extremadura, W Spain
Villanueva de los Infantes 93 E4 Castilla-La Mancha, C Spain
Villarrica 64 D2 Guairá, SE Paraguay
Villavicencio 58 B3 Meta, C Colombia
Villaviciosa 92 D1 Asturias, N Spain
Villazón 61 G5 Potosí, S Bolivia
Villena 93 F4 País Valenciano, E Spain
Villeurbanne 91 D5 Rhône, E France
Villingen-Schwenningen 95 B6 Baden-Württemberg, S Germany
Villmanstrand see Lappeenranta
Vilna see Vilnius
Vilnius 107 C5 Pol. Wilno, Ger. Wilna; prev. Rus. Vilna. country capital (Lithuania) (Lithuania) Vilnius, SE Lithuania
Vil'shanka 109 E3 Rus. Olshanka. Kirovohrads'ka Oblast', C Ukraine
Vilvoorde 87 C6 Fr. Vilvorde. Vlaams Brabant, C Belgium
Vilvorde see Vilvoorde
Vilyeyka 107 C5 Pol. Wilejka, Rus. Vileyka. Minskaya Voblasts', NW Belarus
Vilyuy 115 F3 river NE Russian Federation
Viña del Mar 64 B4 Valparaíso, C Chile
Vinaròs 93 F3 País Valenciano, E Spain
Vincennes 40 B4 Indiana, N USA
Vindhya Mountains see Vindhya Range
Vindhya Range 134 D4 var. Vindhya Mountains. mountain range N India
Vindobona see Wien
Vineland 41 F4 New Jersey, NE USA
Vinh 136 D4 Nghệ An, N Vietnam
Vinh Loi see Bac Liêu
Vinishte 104 C2 Montana, NW Bulgaria
Vinita 49 G1 Oklahoma, C USA
Vinkovci 100 C3 Ger. Winkowitz, Hung. Vinkovce. Vukovar-Srijem, E Croatia
Vinkovce see Vinkovci
Vinnitsa see Vinnytsya
Vinnytsya 108 D2 Rus. Vinnitsa. Vinnyts'ka Oblast', C Ukraine
Vinogradov see Vynohradiv
Vinson Massif 154 A3 mountain Antarctica
Viranşehir 117 E4 Şanlıurfa, SE Turkey
Vîrful Moldoveanu see Vârful Moldoveanu
Virginia 45 G1 Minnesota, N USA
Virginia 41 E5 off. Commonwealth of Virginia, also known as Mother of Presidents, Mother of States, Old Dominion. state NE USA
Virginia Beach 41 F5 Virginia, NE USA
Virgin Islands see British Virgin Islands
Virgin Islands (US) 55 F3 var. Virgin Islands of the United States; prev. Danish West Indies. US unincorporated territory E West Indies
Virgin Islands of the United States see Virgin Islands (US)
Virôchey 137 E5 Rôtánôkiri, NE Cambodia
Virovitica 100 C2 Ger. Virovititz, Hung. Verőcze; prev. Ger. Werowitz. Virovitica-Podravina, NE Croatia
Virovititz see Virovitica
Virton 87 D8 Luxembourg, SE Belgium
Virtsu 106 D2 Ger. Werder. Läänemaa, W Estonia
Vis 100 B4 It. Lissa; anc. Issa. island S Croatia
Vis see Fish
Visaginas 106 C4 prev. Sniečkus. Utena, E Lithuania
Visākhapatnam 135 E5 var. Vishakhapatnam. Andhra Pradesh, SE India
Visalia 47 C6 California, W USA
Visby 85 C7 Ger. Wisby. Gotland, SE Sweden
Viscount Melville Sound 37 F2 prev. Melville Sound. sound Northwest Territories, N Canada
Visé 87 D6 Liège, E Belgium
Viseu 92 C2 prev. Vizeu. Viseu, N Portugal
Vishakhapatnam see Visākhapatnam
Vislinskiy Zaliv see Vistula Lagoon
Visoko 100 C4 Federacija Bosna I Hercegovina, C Bosnia and Herzegovina
Visttasjohka 84 D3 river N Sweden

Vistula 98 C2 Eng. Vistula, Ger. Weichsel. river C Poland
Vistula see Wisła
Vistula Lagoon 98 C2 Ger. Frisches Haff, Pol. Zalew Wiślany, Rus. Vislinskiy Zaliv. lagoon Poland/Russian Federation
Vitebsk see Vitsyebsk
Viterbo 96 C4 anc. Vicus Elbii. Lazio, C Italy
Viti see Fiji
Viti Levu 145 E4 island W Fiji
Vitim 115 F4 river C Russian Federation
Vitória 63 F4 state capital Espírito Santo, SE Brazil
Vitoria see Vitoria-Gasteiz
Vitoria Bank see Vitória Seamount
Vitória da Conquista 63 F3 Bahia, E Brazil
Vitoria-Gasteiz 93 E1 var. Vitoria, Eng. Vittoria. País Vasco, N Spain
Vitória Seamount 67 B5 var. Victoria Bank, Vitoria Bank. seamount C Atlantic Ocean
Vitré 90 B3 Ille-et-Vilaine, NW France
Vitsyebsk 107 E5 Rus. Vitebsk. Vitsyebskaya Voblasts', NE Belarus
Vittoria 97 C7 Sicilia, Italy, C Mediterranean Sea
Vittoria see Vitoria-Gasteiz
Vizcaya, Golfo de see Biscay, Bay of
Vizianagaram 135 E5 var. Vizianagram. Andhra Pradesh, E India
Vizianagram see Vizianagaram
Vjosës, Lumi i 101 C7 var. Vijosa, Vijosë, Gk. Aóos. river Albania/Greece
Vlaanderen see Flanders
Vlaardingen 86 B4 Zuid-Holland, SW Netherlands
Vladikavkaz 111 B8 prev. Dzaudzhikau, Ordzhonikidze. Respublika Severnaya Osetiya, SW Russian Federation
Vladimir 111 B5 Vladimirskaya Oblast', W Russian Federation
Vladimirovka see Yuzhno-Sakhalinsk
Vladimir-Volynskiy see Volodymyr-Volyns'kyy
Vladivostok 115 G5 Primorskiy Kray, SE Russian Federation
Vlagtwedde 86 E2 Groningen, NE Netherlands
Vlasotince 101 E6 Serbia, SE Serbia
Vlieland 86 C1 Fris. Flylân. island Waddeneilanden, N Netherlands
Vlijmen 86 C4 Noord-Brabant, S Netherlands
Vlissingen 87 B5 Eng. Flushing, Fr. Flessingue. Zeeland, SW Netherlands
Vlodava see Włodawa
Vlonë/Vlora see Vlorë
Vlorë 101 C7 prev. Vlonë, It. Valona, Vlora. Vlorë, SW Albania
Vlotslavsk see Włocławek
Vöcklabruck 95 D6 Oberösterreich, NW Austria
Vogelkop see Doberai, Jazirah
Vohimena, Tanjona 79 F4 Fr. Cap Sainte Marie. headland S Madagascar
Voiron 91 D5 Isère, E France
Vojvodina 100 D3 Ger. Wojwodina. Vojvodina, N Serbia
Volga 111 B7 river NW Russian Federation
Volga Uplands 81 G3 var. Volga Uplands. mountain range W Russian Federation
Volga Uplands see Privolzhskaya Vozvyshennost'
Volgodonsk 111 B7 Rostovskaya Oblast', SW Russian Federation
Volgograd 111 B7 prev. Stalingrad, Tsaritsyn. Volgogradskaya Oblast', SW Russian Federation
Volkhov 110 B4 Leningradskaya Oblast', NW Russian Federation
Volkovysk see Vawkavysk
Volmari see Valmiera
Volnovakha 109 G3 Donets'ka Oblast', SE Ukraine
Volodymyr-Volyns'kyy 108 C1 Pol. Włodzimierz, Rus. Vladimir-Volynskiy. Volyns'ka Oblast', NW Ukraine
Vologda 110 B4 Vologodskaya Oblast', W Russian Federation
Vólos 105 B5 Thessalía, C Greece
Volozhin see Valozhyn

Vol'sk 111 C6 Saratovskaya Oblast', W Russian Federation
Volta 75 E5 river SE Ghana
Volta Blanche see White Volta
Volta, Lake 75 E5 reservoir SE Ghana
Volta Noire see Black Volta
Volturno 97 D5 river S Italy
Volunteer Island see Starbuck Island
Volzhskiy 111 B6 Volgogradskaya Oblast', SW Russian Federation
Võnnu 106 E3 Ger. Wendau. Tartumaa, SE Estonia
Voorst 86 D3 Gelderland, E Netherlands
Voranava 107 C5 Pol. Werenów, Rus. Voronovo. Hrodzyenskaya Voblasts', W Belarus
Vorderrhein 95 B7 river SE Switzerland
Vóreioi Sporádes see Vóreies Sporádes
Vórioi Sporádhes see Vóreies Sporádes
Vorkuta 114 C2 Respublika Komi, NW Russian Federation
Vormsi 106 C2 var. Vormsi Saar, Ger. Worms, Swed. Ormsö. island W Estonia
Vormsi Saar see Vormsi
Voronezh 111 B6 Voronezhskaya Oblast', W Russian Federation
Voronovo see Voranava
Voroshilov see Ussuriysk
Voroshilovgrad see Luhans'k, Ukraine
Voroshilovsk see Stavropol', Russian Federation
Võru 106 E3 Ger. Werro. Võrumaa, SE Estonia
Vosges 90 E4 mountain range NE France
Vostochnyy Sayan see Eastern Sayans
Vostock Island see Vostok Island
Vostok 154 C3 Russian research station Antarctica
Vostok Island 145 G3 var. Vostok Island; prev. Stavers Island. island Line Islands, SE Kiribati
Voznesens'k 109 E3 Rus. Voznesensk. Mykolayivs'ka Oblast', S Ukraine
Vranje 101 E5 Serbia, SE Serbia
Vranov see Vranov nad Topl'ou
Vranov nad Topl'ou 99 D5 var. Vranov, Hung. Varannó. Prešovský Kraj, E Slovakia
Vratsa 104 C2 Vratsa, NW Bulgaria
Vrbas 100 C3 Vojvodina, NW Serbia
Vrbas 100 C3 river N Bosnia and Herzegovina
Vršac 100 E3 Ger. Werschetz, Hung. Versecz. Vojvodina, NE Serbia
Vsetín 99 C5 Ger. Wsetin. Zlínský Kraj, E Czech Republic
Vučitrn see Vushtrri
Vukovar 100 C3 Hung. Vukovár. Vukovar-Srijem, E Croatia
Vulcano, Isola 97 C7 island Isole Eolie, S Italy
Vung Tau 137 E6 prev. Fr. Cape Saint Jacques, Cap Saint-Jacques. Ba Ria-Vung Tau, S Vietnam
Vushtrri 101 D5 Serb. Vučitrn. N Kosovo
Vyatka 111 C5 river NW Russian Federation
Vyatka see Kirov
Vyborg 110 B3 Fin. Viipuri. Leningradskaya Oblast', NW Russian Federation
Vyerkhnyadzvinsk 107 D5 Rus. Verkhnedvinsk. Vitsyebskaya Voblasts', N Belarus
Vyetryna 107 D5 Rus. Vetrino. Vitsyebskaya Voblasts', N Belarus
Vynohradiv 108 B3 Cz. Sevluš, Hung. Nagyszöllös, Rus. Vinogradov; prev. Sevlyush. Zakarpats'ka Oblast', W Ukraine

W

Wa 75 E4 NW Ghana
Waag see Váh
Waagbistritz see Považská Bystrica
Waal 86 C4 river S Netherlands
Wabash 40 C4 Indiana, N USA
Wabash River 40 B5 river N USA
Waco 49 G3 Texas, SW USA
Wad Al-Hajarah see Guadalajara
Waddān 71 F3 NW Libya

Waddenzee 86 C1 var. Wadden Zee. sea SE North Sea
Wadden Zee see Waddenzee
Waddington, Mount 36 D5 mountain British Columbia, SW Canada
Wādī as Sīr 119 B6 var. Wadi es Sir. 'Ammān, NW Jordan
Wadi es Sir see Wādī as Sīr
Wadi Halfa 72 B3 var. Wādī Ḥalfā'. Northern, N Sudan
Wādī Mūsā 119 B7 var. Petra. Ma'ān, S Jordan
Wad Madani see Wad Medani
Wad Medani 72 C4 var. Wad Madanī. Gezira, C Sudan
Waflia 139 F4 Pulau Buru, E Indonesia
Wagadugu see Ouagadougou
Wagga Wagga 149 C7 New South Wales, SE Australia
Wagin 147 B7 Western Australia
Wāh 134 C1 Punjab, NE Pakistan
Wahai 139 F4 Pulau Seram, E Indonesia
Wahaybah, Ramlat Al see Wahibah, Ramlat Āl
Wahiawā 47 A8 var. Wahiawa. O'ahu, Hawaii, USA, C Pacific Ocean
Wahibah, Ramlat Āl see Wahibah, Ramlat Āl
Wahibah Sands 121 E5 var. Ramlat Ahl Wahībah, Ramlat Al Wahaybah, Eng. Wahibah Sands. desert N Oman
Wahibah Sands see Wahibah, Ramlat Āl
Wahpeton 45 F2 North Dakota, N USA
Wahran see Oran
Waiau 151 A7 river South Island, New Zealand
Waigeo, Pulau 139 G4 island Maluku, E Indonesia
Waikaremoana, Lake 150 E4 lake North Island, New Zealand
Wailuku 47 B8 Maui, Hawaii, USA, C Pacific Ocean
Waimate 151 B6 Canterbury, South Island, New Zealand
Waiouru 150 D4 Manawatu-Wanganui, North Island, New Zealand
Waipara 151 C6 Canterbury, South Island, New Zealand
Waipawa 150 E4 Hawke's Bay, North Island, New Zealand
Waipukurau 150 D4 Hawke's Bay, North Island, New Zealand
Wairau 151 C5 river South Island, New Zealand
Wairoa 150 E4 Hawke's Bay, North Island, New Zealand
Wairoa 150 D2 river North Island, New Zealand
Waitaki 151 B6 river South Island, New Zealand
Waitara 150 D4 Taranaki, North Island, New Zealand
Waitzen see Vác
Waiuku 150 D3 Auckland, North Island, New Zealand
Wakasa-wan 131 C6 bay C Japan
Wakatipu, Lake 151 A7 lake South Island, New Zealand
Wakayama 131 C6 Wakayama, Honshū, SW Japan
Wake Island 152 C2 US unincorporated territory NW Pacific Ocean
Wake Island 142 D1 atoll NW Pacific Ocean
Wakkanai 130 C1 Hokkaidō, NE Japan
Walachei/Walachia see Wallachia
Wałbrzych 98 B4 Ger. Waldenburg, Waldenburg in Schlesien. Dolnośląskie, SW Poland
Walcourt 87 C7 Namur, S Belgium
Wałcz 98 B3 Ger. Deutsch Krone. Zachodnio-pomorskie, NW Poland
Waldenburg/Waldenburg in Schlesien see Wałbrzych
Waldia see Weldiya
Wales 36 C2 Alaska, USA
Wales 89 C6 Wel. Cymru. cultural region Wales, United Kingdom
Walgett 149 D5 New South Wales, SE Australia
Walk see Valga, Estonia
Walk see Valka, Latvia
Walker Lake 47 C5 lake Nevada, W USA
Wallachia 108 B5 var. Walachia, Ger. Walachei, Rom. Valachia. cultural region S Romania

Walla Walla *46 C2* Washington,
NW USA
Wallenthal *see* Hațeg
Wallis and Futuna *145 E4 Fr.* Territoire
de Wallis et Futuna. *French overseas
territory* C Pacific Ocean
Wallis et Futuna, Territoire de *see*
Wallis and Futuna
Walnut Ridge *42 B1* Arkansas, C USA
Waltenberg *see* Zalău
Walthamstow *89 B7* Waltham Forest,
SE England, United Kingdom
Walvisbaai *see* Walvis Bay
Walvis Bay *78 A4 Afr.* Walvisbaai.
Erongo, NW Namibia
Walvish Ridge *see* Walvis Ridge
Walvis Ridge *69 B7 var.* Walvish Ridge.
undersea ridge E Atlantic Ocean
Wan *see* Anhui
Wanaka *151 B6* Otago, South Island,
New Zealand
Wanaka, Lake *151 A6 lake* South Island,
New Zealand
Wanchuan *see* Zhangjiakou
Wandel Sea *83 E1 sea* Arctic Ocean
Wandsworth *89 A8* Wandsworth,
SE England, United Kingdom
Wanganui *150 D4* Manawatu-
Wanganui, North Island, New Zealand
Wangaratta *149 C7* Victoria,
SE Australia
Wankie *see* Hwange
Wanki, Río *see* Coco, Río
Wanlaweyn *73 D6 var.* Wanle Weyn,
It. Uanle Uen. Shabeellaha Hoose,
SW Somalia
Wanle Weyn *see* Wanlaweyn
Wanxian *see* Wanzhou
Wanzhou *128 B5 var.* Wanxian.
Chongqing Shi, C China
Warangal *135 E5* Andhra Pradesh,
C India
Warasdin *see* Varaždin
Warburg *94 B4* Nordrhein-Westfalen,
W Germany
Ware *37 E4* British Columbia, W Canada
Waremme *87 C6* Liège, E Belgium
Waren *94 C3* Mecklenburg-
Vorpommern, NE Germany
Wargla *see* Ouargla
Warkworth *150 D2* Auckland, North
Island, New Zealand
Warnemünde *94 C2* Mecklenburg-
Vorpommern, NE Germany
Warner *49 G1* Oklahoma, C USA
Warnes *61 G4* Santa Cruz, C Bolivia
Warrego River *149 C5 seasonal river*
New South Wales/Queensland,
E Australia
Warren *40 D3* Michigan, N USA
Warren *40 D3* Ohio, N USA
Warren *41 E3* Pennsylvania, NE USA
Warri *75 F5* Delta, S Nigeria
Warrnambool *149 B7* Victoria,
SE Australia
Warsaw/Warschau *see* Warszawa
Warszawa *98 D3 Eng.* Warsaw, *Ger.*
Warschau, *Rus.* Varshava. *country
capital* (Poland) (Poland) Mazowieckie,
C Poland
Warta *98 B3 Ger.* Warthe. *river* W Poland
Wartberg *see* Senec
Warthe *see* Warta
Warwick *149 E5* Queensland, E Australia
Washington *44 A2* NE England, United
Kingdom
Washington DC *41 E4 country capital*
(USA) (USA) District of Columbia,
NE USA
Washington Island *see* Teraina
Washington, Mount *41 G2 mountain*
New Hampshire, NE USA
Wash, The *89 E6 inlet* E England, United
Kingdom
Wasiliszki *see* Vasilishki
Waspam *53 E2 var.* Waspán. Región
Autónoma Atlántico Norte,
NE Nicaragua
Waspán *see* Waspam
Watampone *139 D4 var.* Bone. Sulawesi,
C Indonesia
Watenstedt-Salzgitter *see* Salzgitter
Waterbury *41 F3* Connecticut, NE USA
Waterford *89 B6 Ir.* Port Láirge.
Waterford, S Ireland
Waterloo *45 G3* Iowa, C USA
Watertown *41 F2* New York, NE USA

Watertown *45 F2* South Dakota,
N USA
Waterville *41 G2* Maine, NE USA
Watford *89 A7* E England, United
Kingdom
Watlings Island *see* San Salvador
Watsa *77 E5* Orientale, NE Dem. Rep.
Congo
Watts Bar Lake *42 D1 reservoir*
Tennessee, S USA
Wau *73 B5 var.* Wāw. Western Bahr el
Ghazal, S Sudan
Waukegan *40 B3* Illinois, N USA
Waukesha *40 B3* Wisconsin, N USA
Wausau *40 B2* Wisconsin, N USA
Waverly *45 G3* Iowa, C USA
Wavre *87 C6* Walloon Brabant,
C Belgium
Wāw *see* Wau
Wawa *38 C4* Ontario, S Canada
Waycross *43 E3* Georgia, SE USA
Wearmouth *see* Sunderland
Webfoot State *see* Oregon
Webster City *45 F3* Iowa, C USA
Weddell Plain *154 A2 abyssal plain*
SW Atlantic Ocean
Weddell Sea *154 A2 sea* SW Atlantic
Ocean
Weener *94 A3* Niedersachsen,
NW Germany
Weert *87 D5* Limburg, SE Netherlands
Weesp *86 C3* Noord-Holland,
C Netherlands
Węgorzewo *98 D2 Ger.* Angerburg.
Warmińsko-Mazurskie, NE Poland
Weichsel *see* Wisła
Weimar *94 C4* Thüringen, C Germany
Weissenburg *see* Alba Iulia, Romania
Weissenburg in Bayern *95 C6* Bayern,
SE Germany
Weissenstein *see* Paide
Weisskirchen *see* Bela Crkva
Weiswampach *87 D7* Diekirch,
N Luxembourg
Wejherowo *98 C2* Pomorskie,
NW Poland
Welchman Hall *55 G1* C Barbados
Weldiya *72 C4 var.* Waldia, *It.* Valdia.
Āmara, N Ethiopia
Welkom *78 D4* Free State, C South Africa
Welle *see* Uele
Wellesley Islands *148 B2 island group*
Queensland, N Australia
Wellington *151 D5 country capital* (New
Zealand) Wellington, North Island,
New Zealand
Wellington *45 F5* Kansas, C USA
Wellington *see* Wellington, Isla
Wellington, Isla *65 A7 var.* Wellington.
island S Chile
Wells *46 D4* Nevada, W USA
Wellsford *150 D2* Auckland, North
Island, New Zealand
Wells, Lake *147 C5 lake* Western
Australia
Wels *95 D6 anc.* Ovilava. Oberösterreich,
N Austria
Wembley *89 A8* Alberta, W Canada
Wemmel *87 B6* Vlaams Brabant,
C Belgium
Wenatchee *46 B2* Washington, NW USA
Wenchi *75 E4* W Ghana
Wen-chou/Wenchow *see* Wenzhou
Wendau *see* Võnnu
Wenden *see* Cēsis
Wenzhou *128 D5 var.* Wen-chou,
Wenchow. Zhejiang, SE China
Werda *78 C4* Kgalagadi, S Botswana
Werder *see* Virtsu
Werenów *see* Voranava
Werkendam *86 C4* Noord-Brabant,
S Netherlands
Werowitz *see* Virovitica
Werro *see* Võru
Werschetz *see* Vršac
Wesenberg *see* Rakvere
Weser *94 B3 river* NW Germany
Wessel Islands *148 B1 island group*
Northern Territory, N Australia
West Antarctica *154 A3 var.* Lesser
Antarctica. *physical region* Antarctica
West Australian Basin *see* Wharton Basin
West Bank *119 A6 disputed region*
SW Asia
West Bend *40 B3* Wisconsin, N USA
West Bengal *135 F4 cultural region*
NE India

West Cape *151 A7 headland* South
Island, New Zealand
West Des Moines *45 F3* Iowa, C USA
Westerland *94 B2* Schleswig-Holstein,
N Germany
Western Australia *146 B4 state*
W Australia
Western Bug *see* Bug
Western Carpathians *99 E7 mountain
range* W Romania Europe
Western Desert *72 B2 var.* Sahara el
Gharbīya, *Eng.* Western Desert. *desert*
C Egypt
Western Desert *see* Şaḩrā' al Gharbīyah
Western Dvina *85 E7 Bel.* Dzvina, *Ger.*
Düna, *Latv.* Daugava, *Rus.* Zapadnaya
Dvina. *river* W Europe
Western Ghats *134 C5 mountain range*
SW India
Western Isles *see* Outer Hebrides
Western Punjab *see* Punjab
Western Sahara *70 B3 disputed territory*
N Africa
Western Samoa *see* Samoa
**Western Samoa, Independent State
of** *see* Samoa
Western Sayans *114 D4 Eng.* Western
Sayans. *mountain range* S Russian
Federation
Western Sayans *see* Zapadnyy Sayan
Western Scheldt *87 B5 Eng.* Western
Scheldt; *prev.* Honte. *inlet* S North Sea
Western Scheldt *see* Westerschelde
Western Sierra Madre *see* Madre
Occidental, Sierra
West Falkland *65 C7 var.* Gran Malvina,
Isla Gran Malvina. *island* W Falkland
Islands
West Fargo *45 E2* North Dakota, N USA
West Frisian Islands *86 C1 Eng.*
West Frisian Islands. *island group*
N Netherlands
West Frisian Islands *see*
Waddeneilanden
West Irian *see* Papua
Westliche Morava *see* Zapadna Morava
West Mariana Basin *142 B1 var.* Perece
Vela Basin. *undersea feature* W Pacific
Ocean
West Memphis *42 B1* Arkansas, C USA
West New Guinea *see* Papua
Weston-super-Mare *89 D7* SW England,
United Kingdom
West Palm Beach *43 F4* Florida, SE USA
West Papua *see* Papua
Westport *151 C5* West Coast, South
Island, New Zealand
West Punjab *see* Punjab
West River *see* Xi Jiang
West Siberian Plain *114 C3 Eng.*
West Siberian Plain. *plain* C Russian
Federation
West Siberian Plain *see* Zapadno-
Sibirskaya Ravnina
West Virginia *40 D4 off.* State of West
Virginia, *also known as* Mountain State.
state NE USA
Wetar, Pulau *139 F5 island* Kepulauan
Damar, E Indonesia
Wetzlar *95 B5* Hessen, W Germany
Wevok *36 C2 var.* Wewuk. Alaska, USA
Wewuk *see* Wevok
Wexford *89 B6 Ir.* Loch Garman.
SE Ireland
Weyburn *37 F5* Saskatchewan, S Canada
Weymouth *89 D7* S England, United
Kingdom
Wezep *86 D3* Gelderland, E Netherlands
Whakatane *150 E3* Bay of Plenty, North
Island, New Zealand
Whale Cove *37 G3* Nunavut, C Canada
Whangarei *150 D2* Northland, North
Island, New Zealand
Wharton Basin *141 D5 var.* West
Australian Basin. *undersea feature*
E Indian Ocean
Whataroa *151 B6* West Coast, South
Island, New Zealand
Wheatland *44 D3* Wyoming, C USA
Wheeler Peak *48 D1 mountain* New
Mexico, SW USA
Wheeling *40 D4* West Virginia, NE USA
Whitby *89 D5* N England, United
Kingdom
Whitefish *44 B1* Montana, NW USA
Whitehaven *89 C5* NW England, United
Kingdom

Whitehorse *35 D4 territory capital*
Yukon Territory, W Canada
White Nile *72 B4 var.* Bahr el Jebel.
river S Sudan
White Nile *72 B4 Ar.* Al Baḩr al Abyaḍ,
An Nīl al Abyaḍ, Bahr el Jebel. *river*
SE Sudan
White River *44 D3 river* South Dakota,
N USA
White Sea *110 C3 Eng.* White Sea. *sea*
NW Russian Federation
White Sea *see* Beloye More
White Volta *75 E4 var.* Nakambé, *Fr.*
Volta Blanche. *river* Burkina/Ghana
Whitianga *150 D2* Waikato, North
Island, New Zealand
Whitney, Mount *47 C6 mountain*
California, W USA
Whitsunday Group *148 D3 island group*
Queensland, E Australia
Whyalla *149 B6* South Australia
Wichita *45 F5* Kansas, C USA
Wichita Falls *49 F2* Texas, SW USA
Wichita River *49 F2 river* Texas,
SW USA
Wickenburg *48 B2* Arizona, SW USA
Wicklow *89 B6 Ir.* Cill Mhantáin. *county*
E Ireland
Wicklow Mountains *89 B6 Ir.* Sléibhte
Chill Mhantáin. *mountain range*
E Ireland
Wieliczka *99 D5* Małopolskie, S Poland
Wieluń *98 C4* Łódź, C Poland
Wien *95 E6 Eng.* Vienna, *Hung.*
Bécs, *Slvk.* Viedeň, *Slvn.* Dunaj; *anc.*
Vindobona. *country capital* (Austria)
(Austria) Wien, NE Austria
Wiener Neustadt *95 E6*
Niederösterreich, E Austria
Wierden *86 E3* Overijssel, E Netherlands
Wiesbaden *95 B5* Hessen, W Germany
**Wieselburg and Ungarisch-Altenburg/
Wieselburg-Ungarisch-Altenburg**
see Mosonmagyaróvár
Wiesenhof *see* Ostrołęka
Wight, Isle of *89 D7 island* United
Kingdom
Wigorna Ceaster *see* Worcester
Wijchen *86 D4* Gelderland,
SE Netherlands
Wijk bij Duurstede *86 D4* Utrecht,
C Netherlands
Wilcannia *149 C6* New South Wales,
SE Australia
Wilejka *see* Vilyeyka
Wilhelm, Mount *144 B3 mountain*
C Papua New Guinea
Wilhelm-Pieck-Stadt *see* Guben
Wilhelmshaven *94 B3* Niedersachsen,
NW Germany
Wilia/Wilja *see* Neris
Wilkes Barre *41 F3* Pennsylvania,
NE USA
Wilkes Land *154 C4 physical region*
Antarctica
Wiłkomierz *see* Ukmergė
Willard *48 D2* New Mexico, SW USA
Willcox *48 C3* Arizona, SW USA
Willebroek *87 B5* Antwerpen, C Belgium
Willemstad *55 E5 dependent territory
capital* (Netherlands Antilles) Curaçao,
Netherlands Antilles
Williston *44 D1* North Dakota, N USA
Wilmington *41 F4* Delaware, NE USA
Wilmington *43 F2* North Carolina,
SE USA
Wilmington *40 C4* Ohio, N USA
Wilna/Wilno *see* Vilnius
Wilrijk *87 C5* Antwerpen, N Belgium
Winchester *89 D7 hist.* Wintanceaster,
Lat. Venta Belgarum. S England,
United Kingdom
Winchester *41 E4* Virginia, NE USA
Windau *see* Ventspils, Latvia
Windau *see* Venta, Latvia/Lithuania
Windhoek *78 B3 Ger.* Windhuk. *country
capital* (Namibia) (Namibia) Khomas,
C Namibia
Windhuk *see* Windhoek
Windorah *148 C4* Queensland,
C Australia
Windsor *38 C5* Ontario, S Canada
Windsor *89 D7* S England, United
Kingdom
Windsor *41 G3* Connecticut, NE USA
Windward Islands *55 H4 island group*
E West Indies

253

Windward Islands *see* Barlavento, Ilhas de, Cape Verde
Windward Passage 54 D3 *Sp.* Paso de los Vientos. *channel* Cuba/Haiti
Winisk 38 C2 *prev.* Winisk. Ontario, C Canada
Winisk *see* Winisk
Winkowitz *see* Vinkovci
Winnebago, Lake 40 B2 *lake* Wisconsin, N USA
Winnemucca 47 C5 Nevada, W USA
Winnipeg 37 G5 *province capital* Manitoba, S Canada
Winnipeg, Lake 37 G5 *lake* Manitoba, C Canada
Winnipegosis, Lake 38 A3 *lake* Manitoba, C Canada
Winona 45 G3 Minnesota, N USA
Winschoten 86 E2 Groningen, NE Netherlands
Winsen 94 B3 Niedersachsen, N Germany
Winston Salem 43 E1 North Carolina, SE USA
Winsum 86 D1 Groningen, NE Netherlands
Wintanceaster *see* Winchester
Winterswijk 86 E4 Gelderland, E Netherlands
Winterthur 95 B7 Zürich, NE Switzerland
Winton 148 C4 Queensland, E Australia
Winton 151 A7 Southland, South Island, New Zealand
Wisby *see* Visby
Wisconsin 40 A2 *off.* State of Wisconsin, *also known as* Badger State. *state* N USA
Wisconsin Rapids 40 B2 Wisconsin, N USA
Wisconsin River 40 B3 *river* Wisconsin, N USA
Wiślany, Zalew *see* Vistula Lagoon
Wismar 94 C2 Mecklenburg-Vorpommern, N Germany
Wittenberge 94 C3 Brandenburg, N Germany
Wittlich 95 A5 Rheinland-Pfalz, SW Germany
Wittstock 94 C3 Brandenburg, NE Germany
W. J. van Blommesteinmeer 59 G3 *reservoir* E Suriname
Władysławowo 98 C2 Pomorskie, N Poland
Włocławek 98 C3 *Ger./Rus.* Vlotslavsk. Kujawsko-pomorskie, C Poland
Włodawa 98 E4 *Rus.* Vlodava. Lubelskie, SE Poland
Włodzimierz *see* Volodymyr-Volyns'kyy
Wlotzkasbaken 78 B3 Erongo, W Namibia
Wodonga 149 C7 Victoria, SE Australia
Wodzisław Śląski 99 C5 *Ger.* Loslau. Śląskie, S Poland
Wojerecy *see* Hoyerswerda
Wöjjä *see* Wotje Atoll
Wojwodina *see* Vojvodina
Woking 89 D7 SE England, United Kingdom
Wolf, Isla 60 A4 *island* Galápagos, Galapagos Islands, W Ecuador South America
Wolfsberg 95 D7 Kärnten, SE Austria
Wolfsburg 94 C3 Niedersachsen, N Germany
Wolgast 94 D2 Mecklenburg-Vorpommern, NE Germany
Wołkowysk *see* Vawkavysk
Wöllan *see* Velenje
Wollaston Lake 37 F4 Saskatchewan, C Canada
Wollongong 149 D6 New South Wales, SE Australia
Wolmar *see* Valmiera
Wołożyn *see* Valozhyn
Wolvega 86 D2 *Fris.* Wolvegea. Friesland, N Netherlands
Wolvegea *see* Wolvega
Wolverhampton 89 D6 C England, United Kingdom
Wolverine State *see* Michigan
Wŏnsan 129 E3 SE North Korea
Woodburn 46 B3 Oregon, NW USA
Woodland 47 B5 California, W USA
Woodruff 40 B2 Wisconsin, N USA
Woods, Lake of the 38 A3 *Fr.* Lac des Bois. *lake* Canada/USA

Woodville 150 D4 Manawatu-Wanganui, North Island, New Zealand
Woodward 49 F1 Oklahoma, C USA
Worcester 78 C5 Western Cape, SW South Africa
Worcester 89 D6 *hist.* Wigorna Ceaster. W England, United Kingdom
Worcester 41 G3 Massachusetts, NE USA
Workington 89 C5 NW England, United Kingdom
Worland 44 C3 Wyoming, C USA
Wormatia *see* Worms
Worms 95 B5 *anc.* Augusta Vangionum, Borbetomagus, Wormatia. Rheinland-Pfalz, SW Germany
Worms *see* Vormsi
Worthington 45 F3 Minnesota, N USA
Wotje Atoll 144 D1 *var.* Wōjjä. *atoll* Ratak Chain, E Marshall Islands
Woudrichem 86 C4 Noord-Brabant, S Netherlands
Wrangel Island 115 F1 *Eng.* Wrangel Island. *island* NE Russian Federation
Wrangel Island *see* Vrangelya, Ostrov
Wrangel Plain 155 B2 *undersea feature* Arctic Ocean
Wrocław 98 C4 *Eng./Ger.* Breslau. Dolnośląskie, SW Poland
Września 98 C3 Wielkopolskie, C Poland
Wsetin *see* Vsetín
Wuchang *see* Wuhan
Wuday'ah 121 C6 *spring/well* S Saudi Arabia
Wuhai 127 E3 *var.* Haibowan. Nei Mongol Zizhiqu, N China
Wuhan 128 C5 *var.* Han-kou, Han-k'ou, Hanyang, Wuchang, Wu-han; *prev.* Hankow. *province capital* Hubei, C China
Wuhsien *see* Suzhou
Wuhsi/Wu-his *see* Wuxi
Wuhu 128 D5 *var.* Wu-na-mu. Anhui, E China
Wujlân *see* Ujelang Atoll
Wukari 75 G4 Taraba, E Nigeria
Wuliang Shan 128 A6 *mountain range* SW China
Wu-lu-k'o-mu-shi/Wu-lu-mu-ch'i *see* Ürümqi
Wu-na-mu *see* Wuhu
Wuppertal 94 A4 *prev.* Barmen-Elberfeld. Nordrhein-Westfalen, W Germany
Würzburg 95 B5 Bayern, SW Germany
Wusih *see* Wuxi
Wuxi 128 D5 *var.* Wuhsi, Wu-hsi, Wusih. Jiangsu, E China
Wuyi Shan 125 E3 *mountain range* SE China
Wye 89 C6 *Wel.* Gwy. *river* England/Wales, United Kingdom
Wyłkowyszki *see* Vilkaviškis
Wyndham 146 D3 Western Australia
Wyoming 40 C3 Michigan, N USA
Wyoming 44 B3 *off.* State of Wyoming, *also known as* Equality State. *state* C USA
Wyszków 98 D3 *Ger.* Probstberg. Mazowieckie, NE Poland

X

Xaafuun, Raas 72 E4 *var.* Ras Hafun. *cape* NE Somalia
Xaçmaz 117 H2 *Rus.* Khachmas. N Azerbaijan
Xaignabouli 136 C4 *prev.* Muang Xaignabouri, Fr. Sayaboury. Xaignabouli, N Laos
Xai-Xai 79 E4 *prev.* João Belo, Vila de João Belo. Gaza, S Mozambique
Xalapa 51 F4 Veracruz-Llave, Mexico
Xam Nua 136 D3 *var.* Sam Neua. Houaphan, N Laos
Xankändi 117 G3 *Rus.* Khankendi; *prev.* Stepanakert. SW Azerbaijan
Xánthi 104 C3 Anatoliki Makedonía kai Thráki, NE Greece
Xátiva 93 F3 *Cas.* Xàtiva; *anc.* Setabis, *var.* Jativa. País Valenciano, E Spain
Xauen *see* Chefchaouen
Xäzär Dänizi *see* Caspian Sea
Xeres *see* Jeréz de la Frontera
Xiaguan *see* Dali
Xiamen 128 D6 *var.* Hsia-men; *prev.* Amoy. Fujian, SE China

Xi'an 128 C4 *var.* Changan, Sian, Signan, Siking, Singan, Xian. *province capital* Shaanxi, C China
Xiang *see* Hunan
Xianggang *see* Hong Kong
Xiangkhoang *see* Pèk
Xiangtan 128 C5 *var.* Hsiang-t'an, Siangtan. Hunan, S China
Xiao Hinggan Ling 128 D2 *Eng.* Lesser Khingan Range. *mountain range* NE China
Xichang 128 B5 Sichuan, C China
Xieng Khouang *see* Pèk
Xieng Ngeun *see* Muong Xiang Ngeun
Xigazê 126 C5 *var.* Jih-k'a-tse, Shigatse, Xigaze. Xizang Zizhiqu, W China
Xi Jiang 124 D3 *var.* Hsi Chiang, *Eng.* West River. *river* S China
Xilinhot 127 E2 *var.* Silinhot. Nei Mongol Zizhiqu, N China
Xilokastro *see* Xylókastro
Xin *see* Xinjiang Uygur Zizhiqu
Xingkai Hu *see* Khanka, Lake
Xingu, Rio 63 E2 *river* C Brazil
Xingxingxia 126 D3 Xinjiang Uygur Zizhiqu, NW China
Xining 127 E4 *var.* Hsining, Hsi-ning, Sining. *province capital* Qinghai, C China
Xinjiang *see* Xinjiang Uygur Zizhiqu
Xinjiang Uygur Zizhiqu 126 B3 *var.* Sinkiang, Sinkiang Uighur Autonomous Region, Xin, Xinjiang. *autonomous region* NW China
Xinpu *see* Lianyungang
Xinxiang 128 C4 Henan, C China
Xinyang 128 C5 *var.* Hsin-yang, Sinyang. Henan, C China
Xinzo de Limia 92 C2 Galicia, NW Spain
Xiqing Shan 124 D2 *mountain range* C China
Xiva 122 D2 *Rus.* Khiva, Khiwa. Xorazm Viloyati, W Uzbekistan
Xixón *see* Gijón
Xizang *see* Xizang Zizhiqu
Xizang Gaoyuan *see* Qingzang Gaoyuan
Xizang Zizhiqu 126 B4 *var.* Thibet, Tibetan Autonomous Region, Xizang, *Eng.* Tibet. *autonomous region* W China
Xolotlán *see* Managua, Lago de
Xucheng *see* Xuwen
Xuddur 73 D5 *var.* Hudur, *It.* Oddur. Bakool, SW Somalia
Xuwen 128 C7 *var.* Xucheng. Guangdong, S China
Xuzhou 128 D4 *var.* Hsu-chou, Suchow, Tongshan; *prev.* T'ung-shan. Jiangsu, E China
Xylókastro 105 B5 *var.* Xilokastro. Pelopónnisos, S Greece

Y

Ya'an 128 B5 *var.* Yaan. Sichuan, C China
Yabëlo 73 C5 Oromīya, C Ethiopia
Yablis 53 E2 Región Autónoma Atlántico Norte, NE Nicaragua
Yablonovyy Khrebet 115 F4 *mountain range* S Russian Federation
Yabrai Shan 127 E3 *mountain range* NE China
Yafran 71 F2 NW Libya
Yaghan Basin 67 B7 *undersea feature* SE Pacific Ocean
Yagotin *see* Yahotyn
Yahotyn 109 E2 *Rus.* Yagotin. Kyyivs'ka Oblast', N Ukraine
Yahualica 50 D4 Jalisco, SW Mexico
Yakima 46 B2 Washington, NW USA
Yakima River 46 B2 *river* Washington, NW USA
Yakoruda 104 C3 Blagoevgrad, SW Bulgaria
Yaku-shima 131 B8 *island* Nansei-shotō, SW Japan
Yakutat 36 D4 Alaska, USA
Yakutsk 115 F3 Respublika Sakha (Yakutiya), NE Russian Federation
Yala 137 C7 Yala, SW Thailand
Yalizava 107 D6 *Rus.* Yelizovo. Mahilyowskaya Voblasts', E Belarus
Yalong Jiang 128 A5 *river* C China
Yalova 116 B3 Yalova, NW Turkey
Yalpug, Ozero *see* Yalpuh, Ozero

Yalpuh, Ozero 108 D4 *Rus.* Ozero Yalpug. *lake* SW Ukraine
Yalta 109 F5 Respublika Krym, S Ukraine
Yalu 125 E2 Chin. Yalu Jiang, *Jap.* Oryokko, *Kor.* Amnok-kang. *river* China/North Korea
Yalu Jiang *see* Yalu
Yamaguchi 131 B7 *var.* Yamaguti. Yamaguchi, Honshū, SW Japan
Yamal, Poluostrov 114 D2 *peninsula* N Russian Federation
Yamanīyah, Al Jumhūrīyah al *see* Yemen
Yambio 73 B5 *var.* Yambiyo. Western Equatoria, S Sudan
Yambiyo *see* Yambio
Yambol 104 D2 *Turk.* Yanboli. Yambol, E Bulgaria
Yamdena, Pulau 139 G5 *prev.* Jamdena. *island* Kepulauan Tanimbar, E Indonesia
Yamoussoukro 74 D5 *country capital* (Côte d'Ivoire) C Côte d'Ivoire
Yamuna 134 D3 *prev.* Jumna. *river* N India
Yana 115 F2 *river* NE Russian Federation
Yanboli *see* Yambol
Yanbu 'al Baḥr 121 A5 Al Madīnah, W Saudi Arabia
Yangambi 77 D5 Orientale, N Dem. Rep. Congo
Yangchow *see* Yangzhou
Yangiyo'l 123 E2 *Rus.* Yangiyul'. Toshkent Viloyati, E Uzbekistan
Yangiyul' *see* Yangiyo'l
Yangku *see* Taiyuan
Yangon 136 B4 *Eng.* Rangoon. Yangon, S Burma (Myanmar)
Yangtze 128 D5 *var.* Yangtze Kiang, *Eng.* Yangtze. *river* C China
Yangtze *see* Chang Jiang/Jinsha Jiang
Yangtze *see* Jinsha Jiang
Yangtze Kiang *see* Chang Jiang
Yangzhou 128 D5 *var.* Yangchow. Jiangsu, E China
Yankton 45 E3 South Dakota, N USA
Yannina *see* Ioánnina
Yanskiy Zaliv 113 F2 *bay* N Russian Federation
Yantai 128 D4 *var.* Yan-t'ai; *prev.* Chefoo, Chih-fu. Shandong, E China
Yaoundé 77 B5 *var.* Yaunde. *country capital* (Cameroon) Centre, S Cameroon
Yap 144 A1 *island* Caroline Islands, W Micronesia
Yapanskoye More *see* East Sea/Japan, Sea of
Yapen, Pulau 139 G4 *prev.* Japen. *island* E Indonesia
Yap Trench 142 B2 *var.* Yap Trough. *undersea feature* SE Philippine Sea
Yap Trough *see* Yap Trench
Yapurá *see* Caquetá, Río, Brazil/Colombia
Yapurá *see* Japurá, Rio, Brazil/Colombia
Yaqui, Río 50 C2 *river* NW Mexico
Yaransk 111 C5 Kirovskaya Oblast', NW Russian Federation
Yarega 110 D4 Respublika Komi, NW Russian Federation
Yarkant *see* Shache
Yarlung Zangbo Jiang *see* Brahmaputra
Yarmouth 39 F5 Nova Scotia, SE Canada
Yarmouth *see* Great Yarmouth
Yaroslav *see* Jarosław
Yaroslavl' 110 B4 Yaroslavskaya Oblast', W Russian Federation
Yarumal 58 B2 Antioquia, NW Colombia
Yasyel'da 107 B7 *river* Brestskaya Voblasts', SW Belarus Europe
Yatsushiro 131 A7 *var.* Yatusiro. Kumamoto, Kyūshū, SW Japan
Yatusiro *see* Yatsushiro
Yaunde *see* Yaoundé
Yavari *see* Javari, Rio
Yavari Río 62 C2 *var.* Yavarí. *river* Brazil/Peru
Yaviza 53 H5 Darién, SE Panama
Yavoriv 108 B2 *Pol.* Jaworów, *Rus.* Yavorov. L'vivs'ka Oblast', NW Ukraine
Yavorov *see* Yavoriv
Yazd 120 D3 *var.* Yezd. Yazd, C Iran
Yazoo City 42 B2 Mississippi, S USA
Yding Skovhøj 85 A7 *hill* C Denmark
Ýdra 105 C6 *var.* Ídhra. *island* Ýdra, S Greece

Ye *137 B5* Mon State, S Burma (Myanmar)
Yecheng *126 A3* var. Kargilik. Xinjiang Uygur Zizhiqu, NW China
Yefremov *111 B5* Tul'skaya Oblast', W Russian Federation
Yekaterinburg *114 C3* prev. Sverdlovsk. Sverdlovskaya Oblast', C Russian Federation
Yekaterinodar see Krasnodar
Yekaterinoslav see Dnipropetrovs'k
Yelets *111 B5* Lipetskaya Oblast', W Russian Federation
Yelisavetpol see Gäncä
Yelizavetgrad see Kirovohrad
Yelizovo see Yalizava
Yell *88 D1* island NE Scotland, United Kingdom
Yellowhammer State see Alabama
Yellowknife *37 E4* territory capital Northwest Territories, W Canada
Yellow River *128 C4* var. Yellow River. river C China
Yellow River see Huang He
Yellow Sea *128 D4* Chin. Huang Hai, Kor. Hwang-Hae. sea E Asia
Yellowstone River *44 C2* river Montana/Wyoming, NW USA
Yel'sk *107 C7* Homyel'skaya Voblasts', SE Belarus
Yelwa *75 F4* Kebbi, W Nigeria
Yemen *121 C7* off. Republic of Yemen, Ar. Al Jumhuriyah al Yamaniyah, Al Yaman. country SW Asia

YEMEN
Southwest Asia

Official name Republic of Yemen
Formation 1990 / 1990
Capital Sana
Population 22.3 million / 103 people per sq mile (40 people per sq km) / 26%
Total area 203,849 sq. miles (527,970 sq. km)
Languages Arabic.*
Religions Sunni Muslim 55%, Shi'a Muslim 42%, Christian, Hindu, and Jewish 3%
Ethnic mix Arab 99%, Other 1%
Government Presidential system
Currency Yemeni rial = 100 fils
Literacy rate 49%
Calorie consumption 2038 calories

Yemen, Republic of see Yemen
Yemva *110 D4* prev. Zheleznodorozhnyy. Respublika Komi, NW Russian Federation
Yenakiyeve *109 G3* Rus. Yenakiyevo; prev. Ordzhonikidze, Rykovo. Donets'ka Oblast', E Ukraine
Yenakiyevo see Yenakiyeve
Yenangyaung *136 A3* Magway, W Burma (Myanmar)
Yendi *75 E4* N Ghana
Yengisar *126 A3* Xinjiang Uygur Zizhiqu, NW China
Yenierenköy *102 D4* var. Yialousa, Gk. Agialousa. NE Cyprus
Yenipazar see Novi Pazar
Yenisey *114 D3* river Mongolia/Russian Federation
Yenping see Nanping
Yeovil *89 D7* SW England, United Kingdom
Yeppoon *148 D4* Queensland, E Australia
Yerevan *117 F3* Eng. Erivan. country capital (Armenia) (Armenia) C Armenia
Yeriho see Jericho
Yerushalayim see Jerusalem
Yeso see Hokkaidō
Yevpatoriya *109 F5* Respublika Krym, S Ukraine
Yeya *109 H4* river SW Russian Federation
Yezerishche see Yezyaryshcha
Yezo see Hokkaidō
Yezyaryshcha *107 E5* Rus. Yezerishche. Vitsyebskaya Voblasts', NE Belarus
Yialousa see Yenierenköy

Yiannitsá see Giannitsá
Yichang *128 C5* Hubei, C China
Yıldızeli *116 D3* Sivas, N Turkey
Yinchuan *128 B4* var. Yinch'uan, Yinch'uan, Yinchwan. province capital Ningxia, N China
Yinchwan see Yinchuan
Yindu He see Indus
Yin-hsien see Ningbo
Yining *126 B2* var. I-ning, Uigh. Gulja, Kuldja. Xinjiang Uygur Zizhiqu, NW China
Yin-tu Ho see Indus
Yisrael/Yisra'el see Israel
Yíthion see Gýtheio
Yogyakarta *138 C5* prev. Djokjakarta, Jogjakarta, Jokyakarta. Jawa, C Indonesia
Yokohama *131 D5* Aomori, Honshū, C Japan
Yokohama *130 A2* Kanagawa, Honshū, S Japan
Yokote *130 D4* Akita, Honshū, C Japan
Yola *75 H4* Adamawa, E Nigeria
Yonago *131 B6* Tottori, Honshū, SW Japan
Yong'an *128 D6* var. Yongan. Fujian, SE China
Yongzhou *129 C6* var. Lengshuitan. Hunan, S China
Yonkers *41 F3* New York, NE USA
Yonne *90 C4* river C France
Yopal *58 C3* var. El Yopal. Casanare, C Colombia
York *89 D5* anc. Eboracum, Eburacum. N England, United Kingdom
York *45 E4* Nebraska, C USA
York, Cape *148 C1* headland Queensland, NE Australia
York, Kap see Innaanganeq
Yorkton *37 F5* Saskatchewan, S Canada
Yoro *52 C2* Yoro, C Honduras
Yoshkar-Ola *111 C5* Respublika Mariy El, W Russian Federation
Yösönbulag see Altay
Youngstown *40 D4* Ohio, N USA
Youth, Isle of *54 A2* var. Isla de Pinos, Eng. Isle of Youth; prev. The Isle of the Pines. island W Cuba
Youth, Isle of see Juventud, Isla de la
Ypres see Ieper
Yreka *46 B4* California, W USA
Yrendagüé see General Eugenio A. Garay
Yssel see IJssel
Ysyk-Köl see Balykchy
Ysyk-Köl see Issyk-Kul', Ozero
Yu see Henan
Yuan see Red River
Yuan Jiang see Red River
Yuba City *47 B5* California, W USA
Yucatán, Canal de see Yucatan Channel
Yucatan Channel *51 H3* Sp. Canal de Yucatán. channel Cuba/Mexico
Yucatan Peninsula *35 C7* Eng. Yucatan Peninsula. peninsula Guatemala/Mexico
Yucatan Peninsula see Yucatán, Península de
Yuci see Jinzhong
Yue see Guangdong
Yue Shan, Tai see Lantau Island
Yueyang *128 C5* Hunan, S China
Yugoslavia see Serbia
Yukhavichy *107 D5* Rus. Yukhovichi. Vitsyebskaya Voblasts', N Belarus
Yukhovichi see Yukhavichy
Yukon see Yukon Territory
Yukon River *36 C2* river Canada/USA
Yukon, Territoire du see Yukon Territory
Yukon Territory *36 D3* var. Yukon, Fr. Territoire du Yukon. territory NW Canada
Yulin *128 C6* Guangxi Zhuangzu Zizhiqu, S China
Yun see Yunnan
Yungki see Jilin
Yung-ning see Nanning
Yunki see Jilin
Yunnan *128 A6* var. Yun, Yunnan Sheng, Yún, Yunnan, Yun-nan. province SW China
Yunnan see Kunming
Yunnan Sheng see Yunnan
Yünnan/Yun-nan see Yunnan

Yurev see Tartu
Yurihonjō see Honjō
Yuruá, Río see Juruá, Rio
Yury'ev see Tartu
Yushu *126 D4* var. Gyêgu. Qinghai, C China
Yuty *64 D3* Caazapá, S Paraguay
Yuzhno-Sakhalinsk *115 H4* Jap. Toyohara; prev. Vladimirovka. Ostrov Sakhalin, Sakhalinskaya Oblast', SE Russian Federation
Yuzhnyy Bug see Pivdennyy Buh
Yuzhou see Chongqing
Ýylanly see Gurbansoltan Eje

Z

Zaandam see Zaanstad
Zaanstad *86 C3* prev. Zaandam. Noord-Holland, C Netherlands
Zabaykal'sk *115 F5* Chitinskaya Oblast', S Russian Federation
Zabern see Saverne
Zabid *121 B7* W Yemen
Žabinka see Zhabinka
Ząbkowice see Ząbkowice Śląskie
Ząbkowice Śląskie *98 B4* var. Ząbkowice, Ger. Frankenstein, Frankenstein in Schlesien. Dolnośląskie, SW Poland
Zábřeh *99 C5* Ger. Hohenstadt. Olomoucký Kraj, E Czech Republic
Zacapa *52 B7* Zacapa, E Guatemala
Zacatecas *50 D3* Zacatecas, C Mexico
Zacatepec *51 E4* Morelos, S Mexico
Zacháro *105 B6* var. Zaharo, Zakháro. Dytikí Ellás, S Greece
Zadar *100 A3* It. Zara; anc. Iader. Zadar, SW Croatia
Zadetkyi Kyun *137 B6* var. St.Matthew's Island. island Mergui Archipelago, S Burma (Myanmar)
Zafra *92 C4* Extremadura, W Spain
Żagań *98 B4* var. Żagań, Żegań, Ger. Sagan. Lubuskie, W Poland
Zagazig see Az Zaqāziq
Zágráb see Zagreb
Zagreb *100 B2* Ger. Agram, Hung. Zágráb. country capital (Croatia) (Croatia) Zagreb, N Croatia
Zagros Mountains *120 C3* Eng. Zagros Mountains. mountain range W Iran
Zagros Mountains see Zagros, Kūhhā-ye
Zaharo see Zacháro
Zähedän *120 E4* var. Zahidan; prev. Duzdab. Sīstān va Balūchestān, SE Iran
Zahidan see Zähedän
Zahlah see Zahlé
Zahlé *118 B4* var. Zaḥlah. C Lebanon
Záhony *99 E6* Szabolcs-Szatmár-Bereg, NE Hungary
Zaire see Congo (river)
Zaire see Congo (Democratic Republic of)
Zaječar *100 E4* Serbia, E Serbia
Zakataly see Zaqatala
Zakháro see Zacháro
Zakhidnyy Buh/Zakhodni Buh see Bug
Zākhō *120 B2* var. Zākhū. Dahūk, N Iraq
Zākhū see Zākhō
Zakopane *99 D5* Małopolskie, S Poland
Zákynthos *105 A6* var. Zákinthos, It. Zante. island Iónia Nísoi, Greece, C Mediterranean Sea
Zalaegerszeg *99 B7* Zala, W Hungary
Zalău *108 B3* Ger. Waltenberg, Hung. Zilah; prev. Ger. Zillenmarkt. Sălaj, NW Romania
Zalim *121 B5* Makkah, W Saudi Arabia
Zambesi/Zambeze see Zambezi
Zambezi *78 C2* North Western, W Zambia
Zambezi *78 D2* var. Zambesi, Port. Zambeze. river S Africa
Zambia *78 C2* off. Republic of Zambia; prev. Northern Rhodesia. country S Africa

ZAMBIA
Southern Africa

Official name Republic of Zambia
Formation 1964 / 1964
Capital Lusaka
Population 12.1 million / 42 people per sq mile (16 people per sq km) / 36%
Total area 290,584 sq. miles

ZAMBIA
(continued)

(752,614 sq. km)
Languages English*, Bemba, Tonga, Nyanja, Lozi, Lala-Bisa, Nsenga
Religions Christian 63%, Traditional beliefs 36%, Muslim and Hindu 1%
Ethnic mix Bemba 34%, Other African 26%, Tonga 16%, Nyanja 14%, Lozi 9%, European 1%
Government Presidential system
Currency Zambian kwacha = 100 ngwee
Literacy rate 68%
Calorie consumption 1927 calories

Zambia, Republic of see Zambia
Zamboanga *139 E3* off. Zamboanga City. Mindanao, S Philippines
Zamboanga City see Zamboanga
Zambrów *98 E3* Łomża, E Poland
Zamora *92 D2* Castilla-León, NW Spain
Zamora de Hidalgo *50 D4* Michoacán, SW Mexico
Zamość *98 E4* Rus. Zamoste. Lubelskie, E Poland
Zamoste see Zamość
Zancle see Messina
Zanda *126 A4* Xizang Zizhiqu, W China
Zanesville *40 D4* Ohio, N USA
Zanjān *120 C2* var. Zenjan, Zinjan. Zanján, NW Iran
Zante see Zákynthos
Zanthus *147 C6* Western Australia, S Australia Oceania
Zanzibar *73 D7* Zanzibar, E Tanzania
Zanzibar *73 C7* Swa. Unguja. island E Tanzania
Zaozhuang *128 D4* Shandong, E China
Zapadna Morava *100 D4* Ger. Westliche Morava. river C Serbia
Zapadnaya Dvina *110 A4* Tverskaya Oblast', W Russian Federation
Zapadnaya Dvina see Western Dvina
Zapadnyy Bug see Bug
Zapala *65 B5* Neuquén, W Argentina
Zapiola Ridge *67 B6* undersea feature SW Atlantic Ocean
Zapolyarnyy *110 C2* Murmanskaya Oblast', NW Russian Federation
Zaporizhzhya *109 F3* Rus. Zaporozh'ye; prev. Aleksandrovsk. Zaporiz'ka Oblast', SE Ukraine
Zaporozh'ye see Zaporizhzhya
Zapotiltic *50 D4* Jalisco, SW Mexico
Zaqatala *117 G2* Rus. Zakataly. NW Azerbaijan
Zara *116 D3* Sivas, C Turkey
Zara see Zadar
Zarafshan see Zarafshon
Zarafshon *122 D2* Rus. Zarafshan. Navoiy Viloyati, N Uzbekistan
Zarafshon see Panjakent
Zaragoza *93 F2* Eng. Saragossa; anc. Caesaraugusta, Salduba. Aragón, NE Spain
Zarand *120 D3* Kermān, C Iran
Zaranj *122 D5* Nīmrūz, SW Afghanistan
Zarasai *106 C4* Utena, E Lithuania
Zárate *64 D4* prev. General José F.Uriburu. Buenos Aires, E Argentina
Zarautz *93 E1* var. Zarauz. País Vasco, N Spain
Zarauz see Zarautz
Zaraza *59 E2* Guárico, N Venezuela
Zarghün Shahr *123 E4* var. Katawaz. Paktikā, SE Afghanistan
Zaria *75 G4* Kaduna, C Nigeria
Zarós *105 D8* Kríti, Greece, E Mediterranean Sea
Zarqa see Az Zarqā'
Żary *98 B4* Ger. Sorau, Sorau in der Niederlausitz. Lubuskie, W Poland
Zaunguzskiye Garagumy see Üngüz Angyrsyndaky Garagum
Zavertse see Zawiercie
Zavet *104 D1* Razgrad, NE Bulgaria
Zavidovići *100 C3* Federacija Bosna I Hercegovina, N Bosnia and Herzegovina
Zawia see Az Zāwiyah
Zawiercie *98 D4* Rus. Zavertse. Śląskie, S Poland
Zawilah *71 F3* var. Zuwaylah, It. Zueila. C Libya
Zaysan Köl see Zaysan, Ozero

Zaysan, Ozero *114 D5 Kaz.* Zaysan Köl. *lake* E Kazakhstan
Zayyq *see* Ural
Zbarazh *108 C2* Ternopil's'ka Oblast', W Ukraine
Zduńska Wola *98 C4* Sieradz, C Poland
Zealand *85 B8 Eng.* Zealand, *Ger.* Seeland. *island* E Denmark
Zealand *see* Sjælland
Zeebrugge *87 A5* West-Vlaanderen, NW Belgium
Zeewolde *86 D3* Flevoland, C Netherlands
Zefat *see* Tsefat
Żegań *see* Żagań
Zeiden *see* Codlea
Zeist *86 C4* Utrecht, C Netherlands
Zele *87 B5* Oost-Vlaanderen, NW Belgium
Zelenoborskiy *110 B2* Murmanskaya Oblast', NW Russian Federation
Zelenograd *111 B5* Moskovskaya Oblast', W Russian Federation
Zelenogradsk *106 A4 Ger.* Cranz, Kranz. Kaliningradskaya Oblast', W Russian Federation
Zelle *see* Celle
Zel'va *107 B6 Pol.* Zelwa. Hrodzyenskaya Voblasts', W Belarus
Zelwa *see* Zel'va
Zelzate *87 B5 var.* Selzaete. Oost-Vlaanderen, NW Belgium
Zemst *87 C5* Vlaams Brabant, C Belgium
Zemun *100 D3* Serbia, N Serbia
Zengg *see* Senj
Zenica *100 C4* Federacija Bosna I Hercegovina, C Bosnia and Herzegovina
Zenta *see* Senta
Zeravshan *123 E3 Taj./Uzb.* Zarafshon. *river* Tajikistan/Uzbekistan
Zevenaar *86 D4* Gelderland, SE Netherlands
Zevenbergen *86 C4* Noord-Brabant, S Netherlands
Zeya *113 E3 river* SE Russian Federation
Zgerzh *see* Zgierz
Zgierz *98 C4 Ger.* Neuhof, *Rus.* Zgerzh. Łódź, C Poland
Zgorzelec *98 B4 Ger.* Görlitz. Dolnośląskie, SW Poland
Zhabinka *107 A6 Pol.* Żabinka. Brestskaya Voblasts', SW Belarus
Zhambyl *see* Taraz
Zhanaozen *114 A4 Kaz.* Zhangaözen; *prev.* Novyy Uzen'. Mangistau, W Kazakhstan
Zhangaözen *see* Zhanaozen
Zhangaqazaly *see* Ayteke Bi
Zhang-chia-k'ou *see* Zhangjiakou
Zhangdian *see* Zibo
Zhangjiakou *128 C3 var.* Changkiakow, Zhang-chia-k'ou, *Eng.* Kalgan; *prev.* Wanchuan. Hebei, E China
Zhangzhou *128 D6* Fujian, SE China
Zhanjiang *128 C7 var.* Chanchiang, Chan-chiang, *Cant.* Tsamkong, *Fr.* Fort-Bayard. Guangdong, S China

Zhaoqing *128 C6* Guangdong, S China
Zhdanov *see* Mariupol'
Zhe *see* Zhejiang
Zhejiang *128 D5 var.* Che-chiang, Chekiang, Zhe, Zhejiang Sheng. *province* SE China
Zhejiang Sheng *see* Zhejiang
Zheleznodorozhnyy *106 A4* Irkutskaya Oblast', C Russian Federation
Zheleznodorozhnyy *see* Yemva
Zheleznogorsk *111 A5* Kurskaya Oblast', W Russian Federation
Zhëltyye Vody *see* Zhovti Vody
Zhengzhou *128 C4 var.* Ch'eng-chou, Chengchow; *prev.* Chenghsien. *province capital* Henan, C China
Zhezkazgan *114 C4 Kaz.* Zhezqazghan; *prev.* Dzhezkazgan. Karaganda, C Kazakhstan
Zhezqazghan *see* Zhezkazgan
Zhidachov *see* Zhydachiv
Zhitkovichi *see* Zhytkavichy
Zhitomir *see* Zhytomyr
Zhlobin *107 D7* Homyel'skaya Voblasts', SE Belarus
Zhmerinka *see* Zhmerynka
Zhmerynka *108 D2 Rus.* Zhmerinka. Vinnyts'ka Oblast', C Ukraine
Zhodino *see* Zhodzina
Zhodzina *107 D6 Rus.* Zhodino. Minskaya Voblasts', C Belarus
Zholkev/Zholkva *see* Zhovkva
Zhonghua Renmin Gongheguo *see* China
Zhosaly *see* Dzhusaly
Zhovkva *108 B2 Pol.* Żółkiew, *Rus.* Zholkev, Zholkva; *prev.* Nesterov. L'vivs'ka Oblast', NW Ukraine
Zhovti Vody *109 F3 Rus.* Zhëltyye Vody. Dnipropetrovs'ka Oblast', E Ukraine
Zhovtneve *109 E4 Rus.* Zhovtnevoye. Mykolayivs'ka Oblast', S Ukraine
Zhovtnevoye *see* Zhovtneve
Zhydachiv *108 B2 Pol.* Żydaczów, *Rus.* Zhidachov. L'vivs'ka Oblast', NW Ukraine
Zhytkavichy *107 C7 Rus.* Zhitkovichi. Homyel'skaya Voblasts', SE Belarus
Zhytomyr *108 D2 Rus.* Zhitomir. Zhytomyrs'ka Oblast', NW Ukraine
Zibo *128 D4 var.* Zhangdian. Shandong, E China
Zichenau *see* Ciechanów
Zielona Góra *98 B4 Ger.* Grünberg, Grünberg in Schlesien, Grüneberg. Lubuskie, W Poland
Zierikzee *86 B4* Zeeland, SW Netherlands
Zigong *128 B5 var.* Tzekung. Sichuan, C China
Ziguinchor *74 B3* SW Senegal
Zilah *see* Zalău
Žilina *99 C5 Ger.* Sillein, *Hung.* Zsolna. Žilinský Kraj, N Slovakia
Zillenmarkt *see* Zalău
Zimbabwe *78 D3 off.* Republic of Zimbabwe; *prev.* Rhodesia. *country* S Africa

ZIMBABWE
Southern Africa

Official name Republic of Zimbabwe
Formation 1980 / 1980
Capital Harare
Population 13.2 million / 88 people per sq mile (34 people per sq km) / 35%
Total area 150,803 sq. miles (390,580 sq. km)
Languages English*, Shona, isiNdebele
Religions Syncretic (Christian/traditional beliefs) 50%, Christian 25%, Traditional beliefs 24%, Other (including Muslim) 1%
Ethnic mix Shona 71%, Ndebele 16%, Other African 11%, White 1%Asian 1%
Government Presidential system
Currency Zimbabwe dollar = 100 cents
Literacy rate 90%
Calorie consumption 1943 calories

Zimbabwe, Republic of *see* Zimbabwe
Zimnicea *108 C5* Teleorman, S Romania
Zimovniki *111 B7* Rostovskaya Oblast', SW Russian Federation
Zinder *75 G3* Zinder, S Niger
Zinov'yevsk *see* Kirovohrad
Zintenhof *see* Sindi
Zipaquirá *58 B3* Cundinamarca, C Colombia
Zittau *94 D4* Sachsen, E Germany
Zlatni Pyasŭtsi *104 E2* Dobrich, NE Bulgaria
Zlín *99 C5 prev.* Gottwaldov. Zlínský Kraj, E Czech Republic
Złoczów *see* Zolochev
Złotów *98 C3* Wielkopolskie, C Poland
Znamenka *see* Znam"yanka
Znam"yanka *109 F3 Rus.* Znamenka. Kirovohrads'ka Oblast', C Ukraine
Żnin *98 C3* Kujawsko-pomorskie, C Poland
Zoetermeer *86 C4* Zuid-Holland, W Netherlands
Zólkiew *see* Zhovkva
Zolochev *108 C2 Pol.* Złoczów, *Rus.* Zolochiv. L'vivs'ka Oblast', W Ukraine
Zolochiv *109 G2 Rus.* Zolochev. Kharkivs'ka Oblast', E Ukraine
Zolochiv *see* Zolochev
Zolote *109 H3 Rus.* Zolotoye. Luhans'ka Oblast', E Ukraine
Zolotonosha *109 E2* Cherkas'ka Oblast', C Ukraine
Zolotoye *see* Zolote
Zólyom *see* Zvolen
Zomba *79 E2* Southern, S Malawi
Zombor *see* Sombor
Zongo *77 C5* Equateur, N Dem. Rep. Congo
Zonguldak *116 C2* Zonguldak, NW Turkey
Zonhoven *87 D6* Limburg, NE Belgium
Zoppot *see* Sopot
Żory *99 C5 var.* Zory, *Ger.* Sohrau. Śląskie, S Poland

Zouar *76 C2* Borkou-Ennedi-Tibesti, N Chad
Zouérat *74 C2 var.* Zouérate, Zouîrât. Tiris Zemmour, N Mauritania
Zouérate *see* Zouérat
Zouîrât *see* Zouérat
Zrenjanin *100 D3 prev.* Petrovgrad, Veliki Bečkerek, *Ger.* Grossbetschkerek, *Hung.* Nagybecskerek. Vojvodina, N Serbia
Zsil/Zsily *see* Jiu
Zsolna *see* Žilina
Zsombolya *see* Jimbolia
Zsupanya *see* Županja
Zubov Seamount *67 D5 undersea feature* E Atlantic Ocean
Zueila *see* Zawilah
Zug *95 B7 Fr.* Zoug. Zug, C Switzerland
Zugspitze *95 C7 mountain* S Germany
Zuid-Beveland *87 B5 var.* South Beveland. *island* SW Netherlands
Zuider Zee *see* IJsselmeer
Zuidhorn *86 E1* Groningen, NE Netherlands
Zuidlaren *86 E2* Drenthe, NE Netherlands
Zula *72 C4* E Eritrea
Züllichau *see* Sulechów
Zumbo *see* Vila do Zumbo
Zundert *87 C5* Noord-Brabant, S Netherlands
Zunyi *128 B5* Guizhou, S China
Župa *100 C3 Hung.* Zsupanya. Vukovar-Srijem, E Croatia
Zürich *95 B7 Eng./Fr.* Zurich, *It.* Zurigo. Zürich, N Switzerland
Zurich, Lake *95 B7 Eng.* Lake Zurich. *lake* NE Switzerland
Zurich, Lake *see* Zürichsee
Zurigo *see* Zürich
Zutphen *86 D3* Gelderland, E Netherlands
Zuwärah *71 F2* NW Libya
Zuwaylah *see* Zawilah
Zuyevka *111 D5* Kirovskaya Oblast', NW Russian Federation
Zvenigorodka *see* Zvenyhorodka
Zvenyhorodka *109 E2 Rus.* Zvenigorodka. Cherkas'ka Oblast', C Ukraine
Zvishavane *78 D3 prev.* Shabani. Matabeleland South, S Zimbabwe
Zvolen *99 C6 Ger.* Altsohl, *Hung.* Zólyom. Banskobystrický Kraj, C Slovakia
Zvornik *100 C4* E Bosnia and Herzegovina
Zwedru *74 D5 var.* Tchien. E Liberia
Zwettl *95 E6* Wien, NE Austria
Zwevegem *87 A6* West-Vlaanderen, W Belgium
Zwickau *95 C5* Sachsen, E Germany
Zwolle *86 D3* Overijssel, E Netherlands
Żydaczów *see* Zhydachiv
Zyóetu *see* Jōetsu
Żyrardów *98 D3* Mazowieckie, C Poland
Zyryanovsk *114 D5* Vostochnyy Kazakhstan, E Kazakhstan